MW00491461

Real Estate Law

EIGHTH EDITION

ROBERT J. AALBERTS

University of Nevada, Las Vegas

SOUTH-WESTERN
CENGAGE Learning™

Australia • Brazil • Japan • Korea • Mexico • Singapore • Spain • United Kingdom • United States

© MACIEJ NOSKOWSKI/iStockphoto (RF)

Real Estate Law, Eighth Edition
Robert J. Aalberts

Vice President of Editorial, Business: Jack W. Calhoun

Editor-in-Chief: Rob Dewey

Senior Acquisitions Editor: Vicky True-Baker

Senior Developmental Editor: Jan Lamar

Editorial Assistant: Patrick Ian Clark

Marketing Manager: Laura-Aurora Stopa

Marketing Coordinator: Nicole Parsons

Director, Content and Media Production: Barbara Fuller Jacobsen

Content Project Manager: Emily Nesheim

Senior Media Editor: Kristen Meere

Senior Buyer: Kevin Kluck

Production Service: KnowledgeWorks Global Limited

Senior Art Director: Michelle Kunkler

Internal Designer: Juli Cook/Plan-It Publishing, Inc.

Cover Designer: Tin Box Studio

Cover Image: © MACIEJ NOSKOWSKI/iStockphoto

Senior Rights Acquisitions Specialist: Mardell Glinski Schultz

Rights Acquisitions Specialist: John Hill

Text Permissions Research: PreMedia Global

Images Permissions Research: Scott Rosen/Bill Smith Group

© 2012, 2009 South-Western, Cengage Learning

ALL RIGHTS RESERVED. No part of this work covered by the copyright herein may be reproduced, transmitted, stored, or used in any form or by any means graphic, electronic, or mechanical, including but not limited to photocopying, recording, scanning, digitizing, taping, web distribution, information networks, or information storage and retrieval systems, except as permitted under Section 107 or 108 of the 1976 United States Copyright Act, without the prior written permission of the publisher.

For product information and technology assistance, contact us at
Cengage Learning Customer & Sales Support, 1-800-354-9706

For permission to use material from this text or product, submit all requests online at **www.cengage.com/permissions**

Further permissions questions can be emailed to **permissionrequest@cengage.com**

Library of Congress Control Number: 2010935867
ISBN-13: 978-0-8400-5359-6
ISBN-10: 0-8400-5359-2

South-Western Cengage Learning
5191 Natorp Boulevard
Mason, OH 45040
USA

Cengage Learning products are represented in Canada by Nelson Education, Ltd.

For your course and learning solutions, visit www.cengage.com
Purchase any of our products at your local college store or at our preferred online store **www.CengageBrain.com**

Printed in the United States of America
1 2 3 4 5 6 7 14 13 12 11 10

Dedication

To Carrie as you embark on a new and exciting college experience.

R.J.A.

BRIEF CONTENTS

CONTENTS

PART 1 The Legal System and the Nature of Real Property 1

An understanding of real estate law is valuable in one's personal and professional lives. Real estate law is important when a person acquires real estate (through purchase or lease), engages in estate planning, or invests in and develops real estate.

Real estate, from a business perspective, represents an important but frequently undermanaged asset. In the United States alone, land and structures make up about two-thirds of the nation's wealth.[1] Therefore, management of real estate assets has achieved new prominence in the corporate world.

Since the severe recession of 2007–2009, real estate has been at the epicenter of unprecedented economic problems. This has spawned vast changes in public policy pertaining to real estate practices and the introduction of an extensive array of new laws and regulations. Indeed, during that two-year span, the U.S. government has pumped more money into the residential mortgage market than was spent on "Medicare or Social Security or the defense budget, more even than Washington has paid to bail out banks and other struggling industries."[2] For all of these reasons, studying real estate as part of a business related or public policy oriented degree or for just personal reasons is arguably more important than ever.

The law of property has achieved prominence in international business because of its relationship to the success of market economies. As governments in former communist lands have learned, a market system cannot be established "without first creating a legal system that protects the right of all individuals to lend, buy and sell property...."[3] The study of real estate law is especially important for those who want to understand and participate in the free market system.

This book was written in response to a need for a real estate law textbook that combines text, short case summaries, longer teaching cases, and problems. This eighth edition of *Real Estate Law* contains several new features as well as a major change. George J. Seidel III, who originated this textbook and whose personality, intelligence, hard work, and dedication to real estate legal education will always animate its pages, is no longer a participating author. Robert Aalberts will be taking over as sole author and assume all the responsibilities for its content.

The "Ethical and Public Policy Issues," a feature introduced in the last edition, presents the following new topics:

- *Should Lenders Pay Defaulting Parties Not to Steal or Destroy Fixtures?*
- *Is It Ethical Public Policy to Allow Solar Energy Development Even If It Threatens Certain Protected Plant and Animal Species?*
- *Is Outlawing the Harvesting of Rainwater an Ethical Public Policy?*
- *Is a Carbon Tax an Effective and Ethical Public Policy?*

---

1. C. Floyd and M. Allen, *Real Estate Principles* 7 (6th ed. 1999).

2. Z. Goldfarb and D. El Boghdady, *Major government role limits new home loans*, Washington Post (Sept. 7, 2009), http://www.washingtonpost.com/wp-dyn/content/article/2009/09/06/AR2009090602033.html (last accessed August 7, 2010).

3. G. Melloan, *Coase Was Clear: Laws Can Cure or Kill*, Wall Street Journal A21 (Oct. 21, 1991).

- *Is It Ethical for Borrowers to Strategically Default on Their Mortgage Notes?*
- *Should There Be a "Good Faith" Requirement for a Person to Claim Adverse Possession?*
- *Are Rent Control Laws a Fair and Ethical Public Policy?*
- *Are Patdowns to Gain Entrance to Sporting and Other Events an Invasion of Privacy?*
- *Should There Be Limitations to How Abandoned DNA Is Collected by the Police?*
- *Are Conservation Banks an Effective Policy for Preserving Endangered Species?*

Moreover, the features introduced in recent editions have been continued and, in some cases, expanded in this edition. These include (1) revision of the text to reflect changes in the law, particularly in Chapter 9 which is titled "Financing the Real Estate Purchase," (2) references within the text to the end-of-chapter cases, (3) margin definitions for key legal terms appearing in the text, (4) new lists of and references to the real estate laws used by the states, and (5) substantial revisions that bring legal principles to life for students and real estate professionals, with new and added material on commercial real estate practices.

Two fundamental assumptions guided the preparation of this book. The *first* is that legal principles and terms are closely intertwined with business practices in the real estate industry. The broker, the lender, the architect, the planner, the contractor, the appraiser, the developer, and others must understand fundamental legal principles in their professional practices. *Second*, most individuals handle their own real estate transactions without the assistance of an attorney. It is simply too time-consuming and expensive to consult an attorney every time a legal question arises. Yet an individual must have some basis for recognizing when an attorney should be consulted. A person acting without an attorney must pay the financial—or even criminal—consequences of a mistake being made. Ignorance of the law is rarely an excuse. Given these assumptions, all parties in a real estate transaction must recognize when legal problems are significant enough to justify professional legal counsel and to communicate effectively with attorneys whose advice is sought.

This book is not written or intended to provide specific legal advice and should not be used as a substitute for the advice of professional counsel.

Coverage

All major areas of real estate law are covered in this book. Part 1 describes the nature of real property, including fixtures, air rights, water rights, and easements.

Part 2 covers the real estate transaction, including forms of ownership, the role of real estate professionals, real estate contracts, title, financing, the closing, and landlord and tenant law. The real estate transaction—known as the "deal" in everyday parlance—is an area of special concern to real estate professionals, paralegals, homeowners, lenders, and real estate investors.

The chapters in Part 2 have been organized in chronological order, from the initial step of selecting a form of ownership through the closing, to illustrate the relationship between the various topics. The book is meant to tell the "story" of real estate acquisition from start to finish. The same approach is used within certain chapters. For example, Chapter 9, "Financing the Real Estate Purchase," begins with the mortgage application and follows the mortgage process through foreclosure.

Finally, Part 3 covers land use and regulation, including landowner rights and duties, eminent domain, dedication, zoning, land use planning, and environmental law.

Chapter Text Revisions and Case Summaries

Each chapter has been updated to reflect numerous changes in real estate law since publication of the seventh edition. These changes and additions include:

- *A discussion of the* Whitco *factors used by the Internal Revenue Service (IRS) to determine fixtures from personal property*
- *The effect of the Copenhagen Conference on global warming*
- *Legal conflicts between mineral lessees and owners of methane gas producing landfills*
- *Dormant mineral laws*
- *Added material on oil and gas law and practices and alternative energy sources*
- *A discussion of New Mexico's solar energy easement law, which will likely serve as a model for other states*
- *Extensive coverage of trusts and estate planning*
- *The implications of the expiration of the estate tax exemption in 2010*
- *Equitable distribution of property in a divorce under the common law*
- *Expanded discussion of sales and brokerage licensing requirements*
- *Expanded material on the Interstate Land Sales Full Disclosure Act*
- *An introduction to the Housing for Older Persons Act (HOPA)*
- *The National Federation of the Blind's lawsuit against Target to create virtual accessibility to its store and products*
- *An updating of the National Association of Realtors' conflicts with the Department of Justice and Federal Trade Commission over its multiple listing services*
- *Discount brokerage and other new brokerage types*
- *Historical information on livery of seisin*
- *E-mail transmissions and the statute of frauds for land sales*
- *An introduction to lease-to-own contracts*
- *Fraudulent Qualified Intermediaries in §1031 transactions*
- *Legal issues arising from Chinese drywall in new construction*
- *Extensive discussion of legal issues surrounding Leadership in Energy and Environmental Design (LEED) buildings*
- *Alternative dispute resolution applied to real estate contract disputes*
- *Historical discussion of the Statute of Enrollments*
- *An introductory discussion of inquiry notice as it relates to recordation*
- *Problems caused by misfiling and wild deeds*
- *New information about tract indexing and slander of title*
- *Added discussion on the Torrens System*
- *New coverage about all-risk homeowner's insurance*
- *"Hard money" lending*
- *New material on reverse mortgages*
- *Update on the Community Reinvestment Act and its alleged role in the mortgage meltdown*
- *Expansion on predatory lending occurring during the Great Recession of 2007–2009*
- *Significant expansion of the Real Estate Settlement Protection Act (RESPA), including new provisions and forms*
- *Added discussion on real estate mortgage brokers*
- *"Option ARMS," mortgage-backed securities, rating agencies, Fannie Mae and Freddie Mac, the holder-in-due-course law, and how all of these new developments may have contributed to the mortgage meltdown and Great Recession of 2007–2009*
- *An update on prepayment penalty laws and other new provisions under the Dodd-Frank Act of 2010, the Helping Families Save Their Homes Act, the Home Affordable*

Foreclosure Alternatives Act (HAFA), the Home Affordable Modification Program Act (HAMP), The HOPE for Homeowners program, and the Home Affordability Refinance Program and the roles these laws and policies have had in helping mortgagors after foreclosure

- Issues relating to holders of mortgage notes who cannot be identified
- Expanded discussion of antideficiency judgment laws and no-recourse loans
- The effect of bankruptcy and reaffirmation of mortgage notes
- Added material on subprime lending and its effects on foreclosure and deficiency judgments
- The effect of inflated appraisals on the loan process
- New laws affecting appraisers and how they are now selected under the Home Valuation Code of Conduct (HVCC)
- Workouts to avoid foreclosure including expansion of short sales
- An introduction to acquiring land through avulsion, accretion, and reliction
- Historical information on Western-style closings
- An expansion of material regarding tax benefits in real estate investing including how the IRS distinguishes "dealers" from "investors"
- New policy arguments over the Foreign Investment in Real Property Tax Act (FIRPTA)
- New historical discussion of dower and curtesy rights
- Expanded coverage of homestead exemptions
- Added discussion on adverse possession
- New coverage of anti-sexual-orientation discrimination laws among the states and sexual harassment of tenants by landlords
- New discussion on rent control laws
- Development in the law regarding waivers of the implied warranty of habitability
- New laws protecting tenants after the properties they rent go into foreclosure
- Updating laws regarding landlord's tort liability
- The use of the trespass doctrine in Arizona's new laws on illegal aliens
- An update on lead paint liability
- Major revision of section on lost, mislaid, and abandoned property
- Expansion of the firefighter's rule
- Updating law of licensees and invitees
- Introduction to the new Freedom to Display the American Flag Act
- Homeowners Associations (HOAs) and First Amendment rights of expression
- HOAs and new super lien laws
- The possible effect of the Religious Land Use and Institutionalized Persons Act of 2000 (RLUIPA) on the building of a mosque in Ground Zero in New York City
- Effects of the Great Recession of 2007–2009 on the expenses condominium owners must pay to maintain common grounds
- Expansion of the history leading up to federalizing environmental laws
- Updating the Kyoto Protocol and the U.S. involvement
- An update of findings by the Environmental Protection Agency (EPA) concerning greenhouse gases and their health effects
- New discussion on wetlands and their current state
- New material on the Clean Air Act and global warming and climate change, and role of the private sector in preserving endangered species including conservation banks

The text is also filled with short case summaries that provide real-life examples of legal principles. New short case summaries and discussion include "neighbor law" issues relating to trees as a nuisance, slander of title, workers' compensation and home offices, the Mortgage Electronic Registration System (MERS) and identifying holders of mortgage notes, liability of homeowners for dog bites, money from sale of homesteaded property protected from general creditors, liability of a homeowner for allowing bees to nest on his land, beach renourishment and property rights of littoral landowners, local ordinances protecting religious practices and sacrificing animals, and new environmental cases on ripeness, reviewability, and exhaustion of administrative remedies.

1. References to the end-of-chapter cases appear at appropriate points in the text. These references are designed to facilitate integration of the cases with their governing legal principles.
2. Key terms appear in boldfaced type upon first mention in the text, and most of the key terms are defined in the margin. At first exposure, these terms may appear to be foreign and novel; yet they are important to understanding real estate law and practice. Key terms are also listed alphabetically at the end of each chapter.

The eighth edition also includes new tables that explain complex legal concepts: what laws are used when real property is severed, how fixture financing works, how a deed becomes a wild deed, and lost, mislaid, and abandoned property.

Teaching Cases and Problems

Unlike students in many other courses, real estate law students have the opportunity to study primary source material in the form of actual court cases. With the exception of Chapter 1, each chapter is followed by an average of six teaching cases. These cases provide insights into the development of the law and the impact of legal theories on everyday real estate transactions. The eighth edition contains a number of new teaching cases that have been concisely edited so that students can appreciate the flavor of the law without becoming enmeshed in details of legal procedure. Asterisks are used to indicate where sections of the original opinion were deleted, although no asterisks are used to indicate omission of case citations.

Three criteria were used in selecting the teaching cases:

* *Does the case cover fundamental principles of real estate law?*
* *Does the case illustrate the impact of the law on current real estate practices?*
* *Are the facts in the case interesting and likely to generate lively class discussion?*

Using those criteria, teaching classics have been retained, such as the *Katko* case involving the liability of a farmer to a criminal trespasser and the *Fountainebleau* air rights battle between two luxury hotels.

New end-of-chapter cases include *In re Estate of Max Feinberg* (trust provisions which violate public policy), *Antonis v. Liberati* (lawyer liability for negligent filing of a mortgage), *Landmark National Bank v. Kesler* (Mortgage Electronic Registration System [MERS] and identifying holders of mortgage notes), and *City of Platte v. Overweg* (grandfathering nonconforming uses),

The cases are supplemented with numerous end-of-chapter problems. These problems provide additional illustrations of legal principles discussed in the text.

Appendices

Appendices, which are now on the companion web site www.cengagebrain.com, include real estate forms and checklists, including a checklist for use in drafting shopping center leases that illustrates key issues arising in commercial leasing generally. In addition to the forms in the appendices, a complete short abstract of title is reprinted in Chapter 8.

Supplements

Instructor's Manual with Test Bank

The new edition of the Instructor's Manual is available electronically on the text companion web site www.cengagebrain.com. The manual includes (1) a chapter outline that incorporates cases, end-of-chapter problems, and teaching suggestions; (2) the answers to text problems; (3) additional essay, true-false, and multiple-choice questions, with answers; and (4) numerous transparency masters. When combined with problems in the text, the additional questions provide more than 500 problems and questions for use in lectures, examinations, and student research assignments. You also can find additional teaching resources on the companion web site at www.cengagebrain.com.

PowerPoint™ Slides

The text makes available to adopters a set of PowerPoint™ slides for each chapter.

Text Companion Web Site

To access additional course materials, including CourseMate, please visit www.cengagebrain.com. At the CengageBrain.com home page, search for the ISBN of your text (found on the back cover) using the search box at the top of the page. This will take you to the product page where additional resources can be found. To access the free study tools for this text, click on the green Access Now button. Since you might want to access this site again, it is suggested that you bookmark the page for the book companion web site. The book companion site offers links to web sites referenced in the text and links to forms often used in real estate.

Business Law Video Library

Featuring more than 60 segments on the most important topics in business law, the video library helps students make the connection between their textbook and the business world. Four types of clips are represented: (1) **Legal Conflicts in Business** clips feature modern business scenarios; (2) **Ask the Instructor** clips offer concept review; (3) **Drama of the Law** clips present classic legal situations; and (4) **LawFlix** clips feature segments from widely recognized, modern-day movies. Together these clips bring business law to life. Access to the Business Law Video Library is free when bundled with a new text. If Digital Video Library access did not come packaged with the textbook, students can purchase it online at www.cengagebrain.com.

Buy.Rent.Access.

At CengageBrain.com students can buy or rent Real Estate Law, 8e, and instantly access eBooks, eChapters, and digital study tools for 60 percent below retail prices—plus get a free chapter, flashcards, and more.

Acknowledgments

I want to thank the following individuals for their helpful comments and suggestions regarding the current and earlier editions of this text.

Acknowledgments for Previous Editions

Robert H. Abrams
Wayne State University Law School

John Bost
San Diego State University

E. Elizabeth Arnold
University of San Diego

Heidi M. Bulich
Michigan State University

Daniel R. Cahoy
The Pennsylvania State University

Maurice McCann
Southern Illinois University

Corey Ciocchetti
University of Denver

John McGee
Texas State University, San Marcos

Katherine Cobb
Brevard Community College

Donna Wood McQueen
Horry-Georgetown Technical College

Martin Conboy
University of Nebraska at Omaha

D. Geno Menchetti
Western Nevada Community College

James R. Cooper
Georgia State University

Richard Murphey
Hilbert College

Judith Craven
Newbury College

Paula C. Murray
University of Texas, Austin

Thomas Enerva
Lakeland Community College

Ed Norris
Norris School of Real Estate

L. Fallasha Erwin
Commercial Law Corporation

Robert Notestine
Nashville State Technical College

C. Kerry Fields
University of Southern California

Lynda J. Oswald
University of Michigan

Thomas Guild
University of Central Oklahoma

Thomas Rhoads
California State University, Long Beach

James Holloway
East Carolina University

Marty Saradijan
Bentley College

Madeline Huffmire
University of Connecticut

Terry Selles
Grand Valley State University

Hans R. Isakson
University of Northern Iowa

Donald Skadden
Ernst & Young

Jeffrey Keil
J. Sargeant Reynolds Community College

Leo J. Stevenson
Western Michigan University

John Keller
The Paralegal Institute

Virginia K. Tompkins
Volunteer State Community College

Alice Lawson
Mountain Empire Community College

Linda Carnes Wimberly
Eastern Kentucky University

Murray Levin
University of Kansas

Thomas A. Wurtz
University of Nebraska, Omaha

Michael Mass
American University

Bruce Zucker
California State University, Northridge

Acknowledgments for Eighth Edition

Robynn Allveri
San Diego State University

Stephen L. Cleary
Roosevelt University

Mike Chikeleze
Cincinnati State College

Martin Conboy
University of Nebraska, Omaha

Louis Jiannine
Brevard Community College

Sandra Robertson
Thomas Nelson Community College

Charles J. Junek III
Pearl River Community College

Nancy White
Central Michigan University

Ben Marshall, J.D.
Bulldog Title Insurance LLC, Monroe, LA

John Zimmerman
University of Nevada, Las Vegas

Lynda Oswald
University of Michigan

I want to give a special thanks to the following people at Cengage Learning: Vicky True-Baker, Senior Acquisitions Editor; Jan Lamar, Senior Developmental Editor; Laura-Aurora Stopa, Marketing Manager; Kristen Meere, Media Editor; and Emily Nesheim, Content Project Manager. I also want to recognize the production manager, Devanand Srinivasan of Knowledgeworks Global, and the copy editor, Anne Munson.

Chapter 1 of this book has been adapted from Chapter 1 of *The Law of Hospital and Health Care Administration*, which George Siedel jointly authored with principal author Arthur F. Southwick. This chapter is used with permission of The Health Administration Press. Chapter 14 is derived in part from George Siedel's contribution to the *Environmental Law Handbook*, published by the State Bar of Michigan.

Finally, I owe a special debt of gratitude to my students. Their comments and encouragement have made teaching real estate law and preparing this edition both challenging and stimulating. In a landlord and tenant case, a judge once observed that the tenant had made a costly legal mistake, but "such is the tuition in the school of hard knocks where lessons are learned that will be of incalculable value in determining the course of future policies and operations."[4] If the numerous examples and cases in this book serve as vicarious experience for students so that some of the "tuition in the school of hard knocks" can be avoided, my debt to them will be partially repaid.

Robert J. Aalberts,
Las Vegas, Nevada,

August 2010

---

4. *Gullenkian v. Patcraft Mills, Inc.*, 104 Ga. App. 102, 121 S.E. 2d 179 (1961).

TABLE OF CASES

Principal cases are in bold type. Non-principal cases are in roman type. References are to pages.

The Legal System and the Nature of Real Property

© MACIEJ NOSKOWSKI/iStockphoto (RF)

Introduction to the Legal System

© MACIEJ NOSKOWSKI/iStockphoto (RF)

LEARNING OBJECTIVES

After studying Chapter 1, you should:

- Know the sources of law
- Understand the court system and legal procedures
- Comprehend alternative methods for resolving disputes

"How do you like the law, Mr. Micawber?" "My dear Copperfield," he replied, "to a man possessed of the higher imaginative powers, the objection to legal studies is the amount of detail which they involve. Even in our professional correspondence," said Mr. Micawber, glancing at some letters he was writing, "the mind is not at liberty to soar to any exalted form of expression. Still, it is a great pursuit. A great pursuit!"

Charles Dickens, *David Copperfield*

"Law is the embodiment of the moral sentiment of the people."

Sir William Blackstone

The study of law is essential to real estate professionals, including brokers, sales agents, appraisers, surveyors, developers, contractors, and lenders. Social and technological changes, together with government regulations, have caused the law to assume great, even exaggerated, importance in real estate transactions. Real estate professionals are unable to constantly have an attorney at hand to provide guidance about the myriad statutes, administrative regulations, and court decisions that have become so important in real estate transactions. A fundamental understanding of the law assists the real estate professional in recognizing problems that require legal counsel. An understanding of the law also helps make sense of the daily professional requirements in real estate and related fields.

The homebuyer, the landlord, the tenant, and the investor may deal with real estate law less frequently. Knowledge of real estate law, however, is also important to these individuals. Although the purchase of a home is the most important contract most people ever sign, this legal agreement is often made without the assistance of an attorney. It is only after making a large financial commitment that the occasional homebuyer painfully learns the adage: "Ignorance of the law is no excuse." To avoid financial embarrassment, the person who deals with real estate infrequently, as well as the professional, should know when legal counsel is necessary during the course of a real estate transaction. A basic understanding of real estate law makes the real estate transaction more meaningful and less menacing.

This chapter examines some general concepts essential to any study of law and places these concepts in the context of real estate. Four areas are emphasized: the sources of the law, the court system, legal procedure, and alternative dispute resolution. First, however, a student will find a working definition of **law**[1] to be useful. Defined in its simplest and broadest sense, law is a system of principles and rules devised by organized society for the purpose of controlling human conduct. Society must have certain specified standards of behavior and the means to enforce these standards. In the final analysis, the purpose of law is to avoid conflicts between individuals and between government and citizens. Conflicts do inevitably occur, however, and then legal institutions and doctrines supply the means of resolving the disputes in an organized, controlled fashion.

Since law is concerned with human behavior, it falls short of being an exact science. Much of the law is uncertain. Rules of law can be difficult to apply to specific facts, and they often fail to guarantee particular results in individual controversies. Lawyers are unable to predict with precision the outcome of a current conflict. As economic and social conditions change, and as new events lead to different applications of existing rules, laws must be changed. These changes frequently produce legal uncertainties. Yet, in one respect, uncertainty about the law is a virtue and the law's greatest strength. Its opposite—legal rigidity—produces decay by discouraging initiative with respect to economic growth and the development of social institutions. The ability of the courts to adapt the law to social, economic and technological changes has been viewed as one strength of the "common law" tradition discussed later in this chapter.

Sources of Law

Mario Veliz has accepted a job offer from a company in another city, and he needs to sell his house and purchase a home closer to work. He signs a listing agreement with a local broker to sell his home and contacts a broker in his destination city to search for a new home. This example touches on the two basic classifications of the law: **public law** and **private law**. Public law, the law that concerns the government or its relations with individuals, is involved because real estate brokers in every state are required to be licensed. The license is typically issued by the state only after background checks are conducted and the broker meets educational and competency standards. As discussed in Chapter 6, licensing requirements are established under public law to protect citizens like Mario.

The listing agreement between Mario and the broker is a private contract that typically describes the broker's obligations in marketing and selling the home and Mario's obligation to pay a commission to the broker. The listing agreement is interpreted by private law—in this case, the law of contracts. The term *private law* refers to the rules and principles that define and regulate individuals' rights and duties.

Without a doubt, the broad classifications of private law and public law have become intermixed. It is not always possible to assign a given rule of law to one classification or the other. For example, the broker is required by public policy and public law to deal

---

▼ law

A body of rules of action or conduct prescribed by controlling authority and having binding legal force. That which must be obeyed and followed by citizens subject to sanctions is a law.

public law

A law that applies generally to the people of a nation or of a state; the law concerned with the organization of the state, the relations between the state and the people, the responsibilities of public officers, and the relationship between states.

private law

The law governing relations between private individuals.

honestly with Mario and members of the public. No private contract can impair this obligation of honesty, which exists to promote the overall good of society. Yet the public and private law classifications are useful in understanding Anglo-American legal doctrine.

Private law embraces much of the law of property, contracts, and tort. The law of property regulates the ownership, employment, and disposition of property. Property includes real property, such as land, a house, or an apartment; tangible personal property, such as a suitcase; and intangible personal property, such as a promissory note, a trust, or a copyright. The law of contracts is concerned with the sale of goods, the furnishing of services, the employment of others, and the loan of money. Tort law—the law dealing with private wrongs or injuries such as negligence, libel, and battery—defines and enforces the respective duties and rights that exist between the parties. Contract law and tort law are often intertwined with property law and are covered in more depth in later chapters.

In contrast to private law, the purpose of public law is to define, regulate, and enforce rights where any level or agency of government is a party to the subject matter. It includes labor relations, taxation, antitrust, and municipal corporations. Public law also influences private transactions and often sets the boundaries for acceptable private behavior, including nullifying privately executed contracts that violate public policy. In general, the primary sources of public law are the written constitutions and statutory enactments of a legislative body. Legislatures, both state and federal, delegate the responsibility for developing and enforcing regulations to administrative agencies. A third source of law, administrative law, has great impact on the real estate industry. Sources of law are summarized in Table 1.1.

Constitutions

The U.S. Constitution is aptly called the "supreme law of the land" because the Constitution provides a standard against which all other laws are to be judged. In the most basic terms, the Constitution is a grant of power from the states to the federal government. All powers not granted to the federal government by the Constitution are reserved

TABLE 1.1 Sources of Law

SOURCE OF LAW	WHO CREATES LAW?	EXAMPLES OF REAL ESTATE-RELATED LAWS
U.S. Constitution	U.S. Constitution originally ratified by states	Fifth Amendment requires just compensation for land expropriated for public purposes
State Constitutions	Enactment varies by state	Homesteads are exempt from general creditors under some state constitutions
Federal Statutes	U.S. Congress	Fair Housing Act, Real Estate Settlement Procedures Act
State Statutes	State Legislatures	Licensing requirements for real estate salespersons and brokers, probate laws
Common Law	Courts	Trespass and nuisance
Equity	Originally courts of equity, now in courts of general jurisdiction	Injunctions, specific performance
Federal Administrative Regulations	Federal Administrative Agencies	Clean air standards, disclosure requirements in interstate land sales
State Administrative Rules and Regulations	State Administrative Agencies	Regulation of real estate salespersons, brokers, and building contractors
County and City Ordinances	County Commissions, City Councils	Building permits and inspections, fire codes

to the individual states. The grant of power to the federal government is both express and implied. The Constitution, for example, expressly authorizes Congress to levy and collect taxes, to borrow and coin money, to declare war, to raise and support armies, and to regulate interstate commerce. But Congress may also enact laws that are "necessary and proper" for exercising these powers.

The Constitution can be divided into two parts. The main body establishes and defines the power of the three branches of the federal government: (1) the legislative branch makes the laws, (2) the executive arm enforces the laws, and (3) the judicial branch interprets them. As you will see, this simple breakdown is often imprecise.

Following the main body of the Constitution are twenty-seven amendments. The first ten, the Bill of Rights, were ratified shortly after the adoption of the Constitution. According to James Madison, the amendments served to calm the apprehensions of persons who believed that unless a specific declaration was made, the federal government might be considered to possess these rights. The provisions of the Bill of Rights include the well-known individual rights to free speech, to the free exercise of religion, to be secure from unreasonable searches and seizures, to bear arms, to demand a jury trial, to be protected against self-incrimination, to be accorded due process (fundamentally fair procedural and substantive laws), and to be awarded just compensation for land when it is expropriated by the government. Despite the granting of these rights to individuals, however, the scope of the first ten amendments is limited; in and of themselves, the amendments apply only to the federal government. Does this mean that a state government could take away any or all of these rights unless limited by the state's own constitution?

The answer, at least before the ratification of the Fourteenth Amendment in 1870, was yes. However, the concluding phrases of the Fourteenth Amendment provide an important safeguard:

> ... nor shall any State deprive any person of life, liberty, or property, without due process of law, nor deny to any person within its jurisdiction the equal protection of the laws.

The Fourteenth Amendment is especially important for *two* reasons. *First*, the Supreme Court has generally defined due process as specifically including those rights that are fundamental to a free society as set forth in the Bill of Rights. Consequently, neither the state nor the federal government may infringe upon these rights. *Second*, what constitutes the "State" or "state action" for purposes of the first four words in the Fourteenth Amendment has been broadly defined by many courts, as the next landmark U.S. Supreme Court case addressing an important real estate law issue discusses.

A CASE IN POINT

In *Shelley v. Kraemer*,[2] the U.S. Supreme Court held that a private agreement by property owners not to sell or lease to "any person not of the Caucasian race" could not be enforced by a court in equity. Such enforcement by a court, the Supreme Court held, would violate the prohibition established by the Fourteenth Amendment against state action that denies equal protection of the law.

In addition to being bound by the federal Constitution, each state has its own constitution. The supreme court of each state is primarily responsible for interpreting the state constitution, which is the supreme law of that state. The state constitution is subordinate to the federal Constitution and to federal law under the Supremacy Clause of the U.S. Constitution, which states:

This Constitution, and the Laws of the United States which shall be made in Pursuance thereof, and all Treaties made, or which shall be made, under the authority of the United States, shall be the Supreme Law of the Land; and the Judges in every State shall be bound thereby, any Thing in the Constitution or Laws of any State to the Contrary notwithstanding.

The state constitution cannot dilute or impair individual rights granted under the Fourteenth Amendment. State constitutions can, generally, broaden or strengthen these individual rights. For example, under some state constitutions, such as California's, citizens are accorded more rights of privacy than those granted under the U.S. Constitution. Still, the state and federal constitutions are often similar although state constitutions are more detailed and cover such matters as the financing of public works and the organization of local governments.

State and local law also cannot impair rights given under federal statutes. Yet, much like the way the U.S. Constitution and state constitutions are harmonized, state law generally can confer greater rights to its citizens. For instance, although the U.S. Fair Housing Act does not protect people from unfair housing practices based on their sexual orientation, some states (for example, Massachusetts) have laws that do.

Statutes

statutory law

An act of a legislative body declaring, commanding, or prohibiting something.

The second source of law, **statutory law**, is the law enacted by a legislative body, normally the U.S. Congress, a state legislature, or a local governmental unit such as a city council. The statutes passed by each of these bodies often affect real estate transactions. For instance, a person selling real estate must comply with antidiscrimination legislation enacted by federal, state, and local legislative bodies.

As subsequently explained, statutes have priority over judicial decisions, such as those created under the common law. In fact, legislatures often pass statutes in order to modify or even remove existing judicial decisions that have become outdated. Judges are also faced with the task of interpreting statutes. This is especially difficult if the statutory wording is vague or ambiguous. In interpreting statutes, the courts have developed several rules of "construction" or interpretation. In some states, these rules of construction are the subject of a separate statute. Whatever the source, the rules are designed to help clarify the intention of the legislature. The following section from Pennsylvania's Statutory Construction Act illustrates the guidelines a court uses to determine legislative intent:

The object of all interpretation and construction of laws is to ascertain and effectuate the intention of the Legislature. Every law shall be construed, if possible, to give effect to all its provisions.

When the words of a law are clear and free from all ambiguity, the letter of it is not to be disregarded under the pretext of pursuing its spirit.

When the words of a law are not explicit, the intention of the Legislature may be ascertained by considering, among other matters, (1) the occasion and necessity for the law; (2) the circumstances under which it was enacted; (3) the mischief to be remedied; (4) the object to be attained; (5) the former law, if any, including other laws upon the same or similar subject; (6) the consequences of a particular interpretation; (7) the contemporaneous legislative history; and (8) legislative and administrative interpretations of such law.[3]

Administrative Law

administrative law

The body of law created by administrative agencies in the form of rules, regulations, orders, and decisions to carry out regulatory powers and duties of such agencies.

The rules under which a broker can obtain a license or a contractor can obtain a building permit are typically established by administrative agencies such as the board of real estate examiners and the building department. Such rules and regulations fall under the classification of **administrative** law, a third source of law.

The three branches of government—executive, legislative, and judicial—are widely viewed as creating political safeguards through the separation of governmental powers. An administrative agency often wields each type of governmental power.

The significance of administrative law goes far beyond procedural matters. In fact, this division of public law is the source of much law that directly affects the rights and duties of individuals and their relationship to governmental authority. In Anglo-American governments, the phrase *administrative government* embraces all departments of the executive branch and all governmental agencies created by legislation for specific public purposes.

administrative agency

A governmental body charged with administering and implementing particular legislation.

Administrative agencies are created by federal, state, and local legislative bodies to provide assistance and expertise in specific, often highly technical areas. The legislative body creates the administrative agency and then delegates specific authority to it. The term *administrative law* refers to the laws and regulations created by administrative agencies. Administrative law also "determines the organization, powers and duties of administrative authorities."[4] Questions concerning the organization and the power of an administrative authority raise fundamental principles of constitutional law.

Examples of administrative agencies or tribunals abound. In the United States, they exist at all levels of government: local, state, and federal. Well-known federal agencies include the Internal Revenue Service (IRS), the Environmental Protection Agency (EPA), the National Labor Relations Board (NLRB), the Department of the Interior (DOI), the Federal Communications Commission (FCC), the Federal Trade Commission (FTC), and the Food and Drug Administration (FDA). At the state level, there are licensing boards for architects, contractors, real estate brokers, and physicians; there are also workers' compensation commissions, labor relations boards, and numerous other agencies. At the local level, there are planning boards, zoning boards, and boards of adjustment. Such boards are known by different names in different places, but they invariably make major decisions about land use, real estate taxes, and other real property concerns.

The lawmaking and judicial powers of administrative government result from delegated, or subordinate, legislation. The U.S. Congress and state legislatures delegate by statute to various administrative bodies the right to implement statutory law through regulations or rules. Although it is an administrative agency, the federal EPA, for example, creates regulations that establish air quality standards under the Clean Air Act. The Department of Housing and Urban Development (HUD) issues regulations to implement the Interstate Land Sales Full Disclosure Act. Another example is the IRS, which regulates tax administration.

Administrative agencies such as those discussed above issue or promulgate rules and regulations after a sometimes complicated and lengthy process known as *rule making*. If a federal agency such as HUD proposes a regulation, the procedure begins with a notice in the *Federal Register*. Typically, the notice provides the agency's legal or statutory authority for making the regulation; the text of the regulation; a description of the regulation's purpose; and physical and e-mail addresses for submitting comments by a deadline, usually sixty to ninety days. In cases where formal hearings are required, their date, time, and place are provided as well.

A real estate example of this process occurred in 2003 when HUD proposed a rule requiring mortgage lenders to give consumers more categorical estimates for their home loans, a sometimes contentious issue that is discussed at length in Chapter 9. HUD estimated that homebuyers would save $700 per transaction (totaling $8 billion a year) if the regulation were promulgated. The agency collected almost 43,000 comment letters on its proposal, the most it has ever received.[5]

The Internet now facilitates the process of submitting comments on proposed rules and regulations. Anyone (including students!) who wants to do so can access proposed federal rules and regulations on the government's web site. An interactive web site, which can be accessed at http://www.regulations.gov, allows anyone who has a stake or who is simply interested in the proposed regulations listed on the site, to offer opinions directly to the appropriate agency.[6]

The amount of authority delegated to administrative agencies, as well as the scope of administrative regulations, has increased tremendously since World War II. The reasons are clear. Economic and social conditions inevitably change as society becomes increasingly complex. Legislatures cannot directly provide the mass of rules necessary to govern society. Elected representatives lack the time. They also lack sufficient technical information and background to formulate detailed laws Thus, delegating legislative authority makes it possible to put in the hands of experts the responsibility for formulating detailed regulations that implement the social and economic policies expressed in the primary legislation.

All legislation, whether federal or state, must be consistent with the federal Constitution. The Supreme Court of the United States has the power to declare that an act of Congress or the act of a state legislature is unconstitutional.[7] Issues of constitutional law are also raised when Congress delegates legislative authority to administrative government. Congress may not abdicate its responsibility, even in the case of specialized subject matter, by delegating complete authority. Legislation enacted by Congress must generally stipulate which regulations an administrative body is empowered to make. At the level of state government, the legislature's power to delegate authority is similarly limited. Furthermore, the administrative body receives judicial or quasi-judicial power to enforce regulations. This delegation of power again raises a question of American constitutional law because the federal Constitution vests "judicial power" in the Supreme Court.

Judicial Decisions

The last major source of law is the judicial decision. Judicial decisions are subordinate, of course, to the Constitution and to statutes as long as the statute is consistent with the Constitution. Judicial decisions are a primary source for determining how the Constitution is interpreted and applied. The Constitution requires that courts decide actual cases or controversies and not issue opinions that are merely advisory. Although a judicial decision, by definition, resolves a particular conflict, it becomes a precedent that is used as a source of guidance for the courts in resolving similar issues and for society in interpreting the law. Judicial decisions are thereby the primary source of private law, especially real estate law.

Many court decisions are published in bound volumes. As discussed later in this chapter, the opinions of the appellate courts are a principal source of guidance about the law. Cases can be located by reference to their **citation**.

citation
Information that enables researchers to find the volume and pages where cases are published.

In this book, citations are given when cases are mentioned. Citations provide important information about which court decided a case. Clearly, you would have a different view of the importance of an opinion if it was decided by the Supreme Court of the United States rather than a state appellate court. The citation is also important when you want to find the case and read the court's full opinion. The citation "374 Mich. 524, 132 N.W.2d 634 (1965)," for example, shows that the case was a 1965 Michigan case and that the complete opinion can be found in volume 374 on page 524 of the Michigan reports. The case can also be found in volume 132 on page 634 of a regional collection of cases, North Western Reporter, second series. "309 F.Supp. 548 (D.C. Utah 1970)" indicates that the case was decided in 1970 by the U.S. District Court in Utah and can be found in volume 309 on page 548 of the Federal Supplement. "504 F.2d 325 (5th Cir. 1974)" means that the case was decided in 1974 by the U.S. Court of Appeals for the Fifth Circuit and can be found in volume 504 on page 325 of the Federal Reporter, second series, and "118 U.S. 356,

6 S.Ct. 1064, 30 L.Ed. 220 (1886)" shows that the case was decided by the U.S. Supreme Court in 1886 and can be found in three different sets of reports: the U.S. Supreme Court Reports, the Supreme Court Reporter, and Lawyers Edition. In the Supreme Court Reporter, the case would be found in volume 6 on page 1064.

Cases that are published in bound volumes, as well as some that aren't, are available in the legal database Westlaw. The Westlaw citations differ from those previously discussed. For example, the citation "No. CIV.A. 90-1380-T, 1991 WL 55402, (D. Kan. Apr. 10, 1991)" indicates the docket number, then the year the case was decided. WL shows that the case is found in the Westlaw database, and 55402 is a number assigned by Westlaw to identify this document. In parentheses is the court (in this case, the federal district court of Kansas), followed by the full date of the final disposition of the case, April 10, 1991.

Deriving consistent legal principles from case law can be a complex exercise. Legal scholars affiliated with the American Law Institute (ALI) have derived principles of law from these decisions, which are found in a series of "Restatements" published by the ALI. The ALI was established in the 1920s, and its membership includes practicing attorneys, legal scholars, and judges. The Restatement of Property, for instance, summarizes property law as determined by legal scholars after a review of cases decided throughout the United States. The Restatements are often persuasive to the courts and provide a useful synthesis of complex topics. The courts, however, are not required to apply the principles found in the Restatements to the cases they are deciding.

Common Law   Historically, judicial decisions came either from common law courts or from equity courts. The **common law**—that is, the law that is common to England—originally developed after the Norman invasion in 1066.

Two factors especially influenced the development of the common law in England. *First*, the English court system was centralized with the appearance of the royal courts—the Court of Common Pleas, the Court of King's Bench, and the Exchequer. An important procedural device utilized by the courts and developed during the reign of Henry II (1154–1189) was the writ, an order purchased by the plaintiff that directed the defendant to appear before the King's Court. Each writ, or form of action, differed from the others. One of the earliest and most important writs was the Writ of Trespass, which survives in part today as an action in trespass. Separate bodies of substantive law developed from the writs, prompting Maitland to note that although the old forms of action are buried and no longer used, "they still rule us from their graves."[8]

Second, the common law courts developed the principle of **stare decisis**, of abiding by decided cases. Under the doctrine of stare decisis, courts would look to past disputes involving similar facts and determine the outcome of the current case on the basis of earlier decisions. The use of earlier cases as precedent encourages stability, predictability, and fairness in the Anglo-American legal system since a person embarking on a new enterprise may be guided by judicial decisions already rendered in similar circumstances. Today the common law is generally used in the United Kingdom (UK) as well as countries that were formerly English colonies. These countries include the United States; Ireland; Canada; Australia; New Zealand; Hong Kong; Singapore; and some African countries such as Ghana, Kenya, and Nigeria.

While the common law uses earlier decisions to determine the substance of the law, the civil or Roman law system relies principally on a comprehensive code of laws to decide a case currently under consideration. The civil law is widely used throughout the world and is generally the basis, in varying degrees, for the law in Europe, Central and South America, and the Asian countries of Japan, South Korea, and Indonesia. The civil law is also used in many countries in Africa that were formerly colonized by France, Portugal, and Belgium. Louisiana, Scotland, and the Canadian province of Quebec also use the civil law.

common law

The legal system originating in England after 1066. Judge-made law created when there is no controlling constitutional, statutory, or other law.

stare decisis

To abide by or adhere to decided cases. Doctrine holding that when a court has once laid down a principle of law as applicable to a certain state of facts, the court will adhere to that principle and apply it to all future cases where facts are substantially the same, regardless of whether the parties and property are the same.

It is important to understand the authority of different courts in order to understand the concept of stare decisis. In the United States, stare decisis does not apply to decisions of equal courts in the same system or to decisions of courts from other systems. An Ohio trial court would be bound by the decisions of the higher Ohio courts. For example, a trial court would be bound by a decision of the state's appellate courts. The appellate court would be bound by a decision of the supreme court. A trial court would not, however, be bound by decisions of other Ohio trial courts or by the decisions of out-of-state courts. Because the authority of the supreme court is greater than the authority of the appellate court, the supreme court would not be bound by a decision of the lower court. In fact, the supreme court's job is to review these lower court decisions when a party to the litigation appeals the decision of the lower court.

Likewise, the federal trial court (the district court) would be bound by an appellate court decision for its own circuit but not by the federal appellate decisions of other circuits or by decisions of other district courts. But all courts, both state and federal, are bound by the decisions of the U.S. Supreme Court.

Federal courts may decide "diversity of citizenship" cases. Under Article III, section 2 of the Constitution, the **jurisdiction** of the federal courts extends to cases between citizens of different states if the dispute involves damages exceeding $75,000. Federal courts also decide cases that arise under federal statutes and the U.S. Constitution called "federal question" cases.

A federal court that has jurisdiction over the subject matter of a case because of the diversity of citizenship of the plaintiff and defendant must determine which state law applies to the particular controversy and then follow the decisions of the highest state court. Although they are not bound to do so, courts in one system often examine judicial solutions in other systems to decide cases for which there are no precedents. Cases from other jurisdictions that are used for guidance but do not control the outcome are referred to as "persuasive authority."

> *While* stare decisis *provides stability to the Anglo-American judicial system, the doctrine could also lead to stagnation if courts were forced to adhere blindly to precedents. Consequently, courts have some flexibility in modifying the legal rule embodied by prior decisions. One way in which modifications occur is when the facts vary from the precedent. Because of changes in public policy, a court may even completely overturn its own earlier decision if the court feels there are compelling social, economic, or technological reasons for doing so. As Justice Musmanno noted in* Flagiello v. Pennsylvania Hospital, *"Stare decisis channels the law. It erects lighthouses and flys [sic] the signals of safety. The ships of jurisprudence must follow the well-defined channel which, over the years, has been proved to be secure and trustworthy. But it would not comport with wisdom to insist that, should shoals rise in a heretofore safe course and rocks emerge to encumber the passage, the ship should nonetheless pursue the original course, merely because it presented no hazard in the past. The principle of* stare decisis *does not demand that we follow precedents which shipwreck justice."*[9]

Another important common law doctrine sometimes confused with the doctrine of stare decisis is **res judicata**, which literally means "a thing or matter settled by judgment." In practice, this means that once a legal dispute has been decided by a court and all appeals have been exhausted, the parties may not bring suit later regarding the same matters already decided by the court.

Equity   **Equity** developed as a source of law because of deficiencies in the common law. By the Middle Ages, common law procedures had become rigid, and courts could provide no relief to many parties who had just and pressing claims. For instance, the

---

jurisdiction

Defines the powers of courts to inquire into the facts, apply the law, make decisions, and declare judgment. It is the legal right by which judges exercise their authority.

res judicata

A rule that a final judgment rendered by a court of competent jurisdiction on the merits is conclusive as to the rights of the parties and their privies and as to them constitutes an absolute bar to a subsequent action involving the same claim, demand, or cause of action.

equity

Justice administered according to fairness created in order to temper the strictly formulated rules of the English common law.

common law generally acted only after the fact; damages could be awarded to an injured party only after an injury. As a consequence, a wrongdoer would not be ordered to cease illegal behavior before the injury occurred nor could any action be taken to achieve justice.

As a result of such inadequacies, parties began to seek relief from the king when the common law could provide no satisfaction. The king, through his chancellor, who was referred to as the "Keeper of the King's Conscience," often aided these parties and eventually established a separate court, the Court of Chancery, to hear the cases. These courts attempted to "do equity" and to act in good conscience when the common law courts could not provide relief. The law of equity developed by these courts differed from the common law in two major respects: the remedies available and the procedures used to resolve disputes.

The courts of chancery (also called courts of equity) developed their own remedies. *One* example is the **injunction**, under which the courts provide relief before a wrong occurs. A traditional rationale for an injunction is that it is issued to prevent irreparable harm. Today courts often balance the benefits of the injunction against its costs. The injunction can prohibit or restrain someone from performing a specified act or activity. For example, a landowner may ask the court, through issuance of an injunction, to prohibit someone who threatens physical harm to her property from proceeding with the wrongful act. Land is typically regarded by the courts as unique and irreplaceable, and money would be no substitute for these unique characteristics. Therefore, the equitable remedy of the injunction would be appropriate.

A *second* type of equitable remedy, which is particularly important in real estate law, is the remedy of **specific performance**. When a court issues a decree of specific performance, it orders the defendant to perform a specific act. An order of specific performance compels the defendant to perform his contract. The equitable remedy of specific performance contrasts with the "legal" or common law remedy, which would be an order to pay monetary damages.

> *Contracts for the sale of land have traditionally been accorded a special place in the law of specific performance. A specific tract of land has long been regarded as unique and impossible of duplication by the use of any amount of money. Furthermore, the value of land is to some extent speculative. Damages have therefore been regarded as inadequate to enforce a duty to transfer an interest in land, even if it is less than a fee simple.*

> *Restatement (Second) of Contracts section 360 comment e (1981)*

The procedures in the chancery court differed from procedures in the law courts. Most notably, the parties in the Court of Chancery had no right to a jury trial and certain rules or maxims were applied—for example, "He who comes into equity must have clean hands," which means that the plaintiff must have acted fairly and honestly before he could press his claim in a court of equity.

Gradually, with the development of these rules, equity became almost as inflexible as the common law, prompting Charles Dickens to write in *Bleak House:* "Never can there come fog too thick, never can there come mud and mire too deep, to assort with the groping and floundering condition which (the) High Court of Chancery, most pestilent of hoary sinners, holds ... in the sight of heaven and earth."

Although the dual system of law and equity was initially adopted in the United States, in both the United States and England, law and equity eventually came to be administered by the same court. The relevant Michigan statute, for example, provides that the "circuit courts have the power and jurisdiction possessed by courts of record at the common law ... and possessed by courts and judges in Chancery in England."[10] Despite the merger of law and equity into one court, however, distinctions in procedures and

injunction

A court order prohibiting someone from doing some specified act or commanding someone to undo some wrong or injury.

specific performance

A type of injunction ordering the defendant to perform a specific act.

remedies remain. For instance, the parties in an equitable action are still not entitled to a jury trial and the equitable maxims are still applied by the courts.

The Role of Ethics in the Law

The foregoing discussion of the sources of law begs the question of where the concepts and ideas underlying the law originate. The answer to that question involves a discussion of the study of ethics. Ethics, which is a branch of the discipline of philosophy, is the study of how moral decisions are justified in the view of an individual, a group, or a society. Laws that are created on a local, state, and national level often represent the moral consensus of citizens within these jurisdictions and thus contribute to the ongoing building of the legal system.

Real estate law offers numerous examples of the interaction of law and ethics. For example, until the 1990s, few American states legally required sellers to reveal known defects that existed in their homes. A seller who had a leaky roof did not have to reveal this fact to a prospective buyer under the doctrine of *caveat doctrine*. The onus was generally on the buyer to discover these defects (or to pay inspectors to find them). Purchasers of homes that had defects likely wondered why there was no law against an act they undoubtedly believed was unethical. Eventually, these buyers' concerns were addressed, and homebuyers subsequently became better protected legally from unethical sellers. As discussed in more detail in Chapter 7, sellers today must generally disclose known defects in a form prescribed under state statute. Prior to the creation of these statutes, many would argue that the morally correct path for a seller who knew he had a leaky roof would be to disclose that fact despite the absence of any law.

Since laws such as the seller disclosure statutes are often a reflection of what a society considers morally correct, questions continue to arise as to whether an individual's ethical goal in her personal life as well as her business dealings should be simply to act within the law. A very old law routinely applied today in real estate practices (also discussed in Chapter 7) offers another example of how, even with the existence of a law, questions of what is right and wrong continue to be debated. Assume that a prospective buyer offers to pay $100,000 for the seller's home and further states in writing that he will keep the offer open for three days. On the second day, discovering that he can buy virtually the same house for $90,000, he quickly informs the seller that he is revoking his offer to buy. Under the common law still in effect in most states today, the buyer's actions are legal since the offer was not supported by consideration. This begs the question: Was the buyer, by going back on his word, behaving unethically even though he was obeying the law?

The study of ethics enables you to discuss such issues rationally, by creating assumptions, offering factual evidence, and drawing logical conclusions within the parameters of various ethical theories. Some of these theories of ethics, such as utilitarianism (teleology) and duty-based theories (deontology), as well as theories of fairness and justice (such as Rawl's theories on justice), can often provide you with the foundation for reaching moral decisions in a rational manner.

Real estate, of course, is worth untold amounts of wealth. As a result, individuals who own real estate have, throughout human history, been the victims of greedy, unscrupulous, and unethical people. The recent world economic crisis and the so-called Great Recession of 2007–2009 were at least partly caused by the unethical behavior of American lenders, borrowers, investors, and other parties. This recession aptly illustrates the very practical importance of ethics and the critical role it plays in real estate practices. Thus, the author presents in each chapter pertinent ethical issues that you should find of considerable interest as either a present or future real estate consumer or professional.

In addition, engaging in ethical analyses can be very useful in debating proposed legislation designed to promote public policy goals. Many real estate laws are particularly important because they provide a strong public policy aimed at protecting people—ranging from individuals buying their first home to people involved with billion-dollar commercial ventures—from dishonest business practices. These unethical practices may impact thousands of employees, creditors, suppliers, and investors. Applying an ethical analysis to existing and proposed policies enables you to think clearly and determine objectively whether they are morally correct. Accordingly, throughout this book, the relationship between ethics and the public policies underlying real estate law is discussed.

The Court System

The primary method of resolving disputes in the United States is through the court system. In the United States, each state and the District of Columbia have a court system. In addition there is the federal court system. The large number of different courts makes study of the law in the United States extremely complex, especially when courts in different states use divergent approaches in deciding cases.

Although students of the law must often study a "majority" approach and several "minority" approaches to the same legal issue, the complexity also adds a great deal of strength and vitality to the American legal system. A wide number of resolutions to a particular problem may be tested in individual states before a consensus is reached regarding the best solution. As Justice Brandeis noted in his dissenting opinion in *New State Ice Co. v. Liebmann,* the states should serve as "laboratories" to "try novel social and economic experiments without risk to the rest of the country."[11]

State Courts

The federal court system and many state court systems utilize a three-tier structure comprising the trial courts, the intermediate courts of appeal, and a supreme court. (See Figure 1.1.) In the state court system, the lowest tier (the trial courts) is often

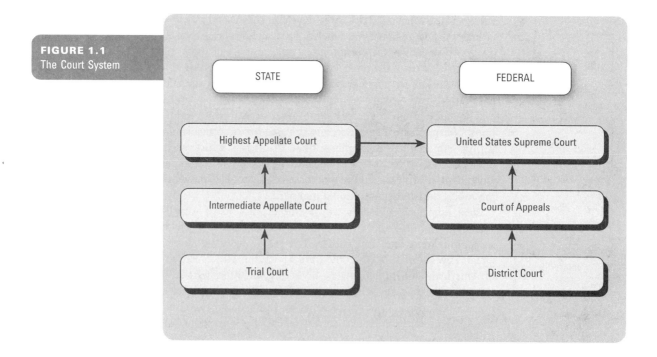

FIGURE 1.1
The Court System

divided into a court of limited jurisdiction (also called courts of limited subject matter jurisdiction) and a court of general jurisdiction (also called courts of general subject matter jurisdiction). Typically, the courts of limited jurisdiction hear criminal trials involving lesser crimes—that is, misdemeanors—and civil cases where the amount in dispute is limited, for example, to less than $10,000. These courts of limited jurisdiction often include a small claims court, in which lawyers are not allowed to practice and legal procedures are less technical.

The state courts of "general jurisdiction" hear all types of controversies except those that are referred to courts of limited jurisdiction that are typically specialized courts. These courts hear the more serious criminal cases involving felonies and civil cases involving larger amounts of money. In some states, only the courts of general jurisdiction may grant equitable relief, such as issuing an injunction. Because of the tremendous volume of cases, the courts of general jurisdiction are often divided into special courts of limited jurisdiction that include a family or domestic relations court, a juvenile court, and a probate court. The role of a probate court in real estate matters can be very important since this court confirms the validity of wills as well as presides over the administration of a decedent's estate. In many cases, title to real estate is transferred to heirs during these proceedings. Often the first appeal from a court of limited jurisdiction is to the trial court, which, in such instances, acts as the first appellate court.

The second tier of most state court systems (the exceptions are those with relatively small populations) is the intermediate appellate court. This court has appellate jurisdiction—that is, the power to hear appeals from final judgments of the trial courts. The court also has limited original jurisdiction with the result that certain cases (for example, a mandamus action to force a government official to perform her duty) may originate in the appellate court. In exercising their appellate jurisdiction, appellate courts generally are limited to the record from the trial court and to questions of law, not of fact.

The highest court in the state court system is usually (but not always) called the supreme court. This court hears appeals from the intermediate appellate court and possesses original jurisdiction similar to that of the lower appellate court. The highest state court is often charged with other duties, such as adopting rules of procedure and supervising the practice of law in the state.

Federal Courts

The bottom tier in the federal court system is the district court, the federal trial court that hears criminal cases involving both felonies and misdemeanors that arise under federal statutes. The district court hears civil cases involving actions arising under either federal statutes, such as federal civil rights actions under the Fair Housing Act, or the Constitution. The district court may also hear suits in which a citizen of one state sues a citizen of another state (that is, where there is **diversity of citizenship**) if the amount in dispute is over $75,000. In such a case, the court usually applies the law of one of the states. Since the district court can only hear diversity and federal question cases, it is considered a court of limited jurisdiction.

Appeals from the district courts go to the U.S. courts of appeals, the second level in the federal system. The United States has thirteen circuits, each of which has a court of appeals functioning in the same manner as the state appellate courts. At the top of the federal court system is the U.S. Supreme Court, which hears appeals from the U.S. courts of appeals and from the highest state courts in cases involving federal statutes, treaties, or the U.S. Constitution. The U.S. Supreme Court is created directly by the Constitution. Article III, section 2 of the Constitution gives the Supreme Court "original jurisdiction," meaning that it is the first court to hear cases "affecting Ambassadors, and other public Ministers and Consuls, and those in which a State shall be Party." The Supreme Court

diversity of citizenship
A phrase used with reference to the jurisdiction of the federal courts, which, under U.S. Constitution Article III, section 2, extends to cases between citizens of different states, when the party on one side of the lawsuit is a citizen of one state and the party on the other side is a citizen of another state or between a citizen of a state and an alien (a citizen of another country).

also exercises appellate jurisdiction over the district courts, the courts of appeals, and the states' highest courts. The Supreme Court has the discretion to decide which of these appellate cases it chooses to hear, and the trend has been for the Court to grant review of a limited number of cases.

Legal Procedure

The law, either public or private, that creates and defines rights and duties is called **substantive law.** Most of this book is devoted to substantive law as it relates to real estate. **Procedural law,** on the other hand, provides the means of enforcing and protecting rights granted by the substantive law. Procedural law, as it relates to the litigation of a case, may be divided into *six* stages, each of which is discussed in the following sections. (See Figure 1.2.) It should be noted, however, that many real estate law disputes are resolved by negotiation or arbitration before the litigation process begins. In fact, because real estate litigation can be very costly and time-consuming—involving extensive negotiations, voluminous amounts of documents, and complicated economic issues, as well as creating the potential for a great deal of animosity between the parties—alternatives to litigation, such as arbitration and mediation, can be very worthwhile options.

Commencement of Legal Action

When claims do go to court, the *first* stage is commencement of the legal action. A claimant who begins a lawsuit or an **action** becomes the plaintiff, and the other party to the action is the defendant. The plaintiff commences the action by filing a **complaint** in court, which states the nature of the claim and the amount of damages sought. The complaint and all papers subsequently filed in court are known as the *pleadings.* A copy of the complaint, along with a summons, is then served on the defendant. The summons advises the defendant that he must answer the complaint or take other action within a limited time (for example, twenty days) and that if the defendant fails to act, the plaintiff will be granted judgment by default.

The Defendant's Response

In the *second* stage of the litigation process, the defendant can pursue several courses of action either successively or simultaneously. At the outset, the defendant generally responds to the plaintiff's complaint by filing an **answer** to the complaint, admitting, denying, or pleading ignorance to each allegation in the complaint. The defendant may also file a complaint against the plaintiff (a countersuit) or against a third party (a third-party action), thus bringing a **third-party defendant** into the litigation.

The defendant in a lawsuit has one other option available at this stage in the proceeding: to ask the court to dismiss the plaintiff's complaint. The defendant may base the motion on a variety of grounds: the court's lack of jurisdiction; a prior judgment on the same matter; or the failure of the opposing party to state a legal claim, assuming that the facts alleged by the plaintiff are true. Although the terminology differs from state to state, the motion to dismiss is usually called a *motion for summary judgment* or a *demurrer.*

When the motion to dismiss is granted by the court, the judgment is final; thus, the losing party can appeal the decision immediately. In many real estate cases, the trial court grants a **summary judgment** in favor of the party seeking to dismiss the case. Often the losing party will appeal; the appellate court then decides whether to uphold the trial court decision or to remand the case, sending it back to the trial court for further action. A motion for summary judgment usually, but not always, is made after discovery, the process discussed next.

---

substantive law
That part of the law that creates, defines, and regulates rights and duties of parties, as opposed to procedural law, which prescribes the method of enforcing the rights or obtaining redress for their invasion.

procedural law
Laws that prescribe processes for enforcing rights or gaining redress for those who have their rights violated.

action
A proceeding in a court of law in which one seeks a remedy for an alleged wrong.

complaint
The original or initial pleading setting forth a plaintiff's claim for relief against the defendant.

answer
A pleading responding to the plaintiff's claim set forth in the complaint.

third-party defendant
A party the original defendant claims is liable for all or part of the damages that the plaintiff may win from the original defendant.

summary judgment
A procedural device available for the prompt disposition of an action without a trial when there is no dispute as to material facts or inferences to be drawn from material facts or when only a question of law is involved.

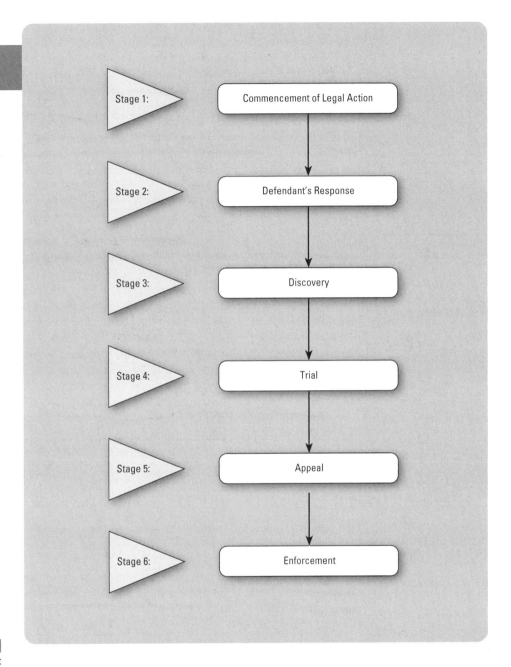

FIGURE 1.2
Stages of Litigation

Stage 1: → Commencement of Legal Action

Stage 2: → Defendant's Response

Stage 3: → Discovery

Stage 4: → Trial

Stage 5: → Appeal

Stage 6: → Enforcement

discovery

The pretrial devices that can be used by one party to obtain facts and information about the case from the other party.

deposition

A pretrial device in which one party orally questions the other party or a witness for the other party.

Discovery—The Deposition

In many cases, especially in urban areas, there is a four- or five-year delay between commencement of the action and the trial. During this time, each party engages in the *third* stage of the litigation process—**discovery**—which is an attempt to "discover" whether the other party has a strong case and, if so, to settle the case as favorably as possible.

Parties use several methods to discover the strength of the other party's case. All methods are limited to matters that are relevant to the subject matter and do not involve privileged information. First, the most common and effective discovery device involves taking a **deposition**, where one party subpoenas a witness whose sworn testimony is taken down in writing by a court reporter. The opposing attorney is also present during the deposition to make appropriate objections and, if desired, to cross-examine the witness. A deposition is generally carried out in one of the attorneys' offices without the presence of the presiding judge. A witness is often required to reveal nearly everything asked of her in discovery, no matter how incriminating or private the question may be. If a witness refuses to answer, a judge may become involved by ruling on whether to compel her to respond to the question.

Besides being useful as a discovery device, the deposition serves at least two other major purposes. First, it may be read into evidence at the trial if the witness is unable to testify. Second, it can be used to impeach the testimony of a witness. For these reasons, especially the second one, people giving a deposition should answer the questions exactly as if they were testifying in court.

Other Methods of Discovery

interrogatories

A discovery device consisting of written questions generally submitted to one side of the lawsuit from the other.

A second method of discovery, written **interrogatories**, is similar to the taking of depositions except that the questions are in writing and presented generally just to the parties to the lawsuit, the plaintiff or defendant. Interrogatories are useful for eliciting categorical kinds of information from the other party, such as whether he signed a lease to an apartment. A third method of discovery allows a party to inspect and copy documents and tangible items in the possession of the opposing party and to inspect and copy items produced by a witness served with a **subpoena *duces tecum***—that is, a subpoena requiring the witness to produce certain books and documents. A request can also be made to inspect certain premises when their condition is important to the litigation. In complex toxic tort cases, a party may even be allowed to enter another's land and test for certain pollutants that allegedly harmed the plaintiffs.

subpoena *duces tecum*

A discovery device in which the court commands the production of specified documents or goods or allows the inspection of real property.

A physical or mental examination, a fourth discovery device, may be used when the physical or mental condition of a person is in dispute and good cause is shown for the examination. When the party being examined demands to see a report of the examination, that party waives any privilege she may have regarding the testimony of other persons who have conducted similar examinations although in some states, the privilege may be waived by bringing a lawsuit.[12]

With still another discovery method, the opposing party is requested to admit certain facts relating to the trial. By using these requests for admission, the parties may save the time and expense involved in unnecessary proof and may substantially limit the factual issues to be decided by the court.

In addition to the methods of discovery already discussed, a *pretrial conference* is held a few months before trial so that the judge and parties can determine what issues are in dispute, discuss settlement, and set a date for trial if settlement is not possible. The pretrial conference also aids discovery because the court requires that parties specify all damage claims in detail; produce all exhibits to be used in the trial; and in some jurisdictions, exchange lists of all witnesses to be called at trial. With all of these discovery devices available—and because the discovery stage often lasts for several years, allowing a lawyer time to assemble the relevant evidence—the calling of an unexpected witness or presentation of other evidence that truly surprises opposing counsel is extremely rare.

The Trial

The great majority of all cases are settled before trial, the *fourth* stage of litigation. For the remaining cases, if either party has requested a jury trial and if the case is one at law rather than equity, a jury is selected. When the jury is seated, each attorney makes an opening statement that explains what the attorney intends to prove during the trial. The plaintiff then calls his witnesses for direct examination and presents other evidence, and the defense attorney is given the opportunity to cross-examine each of the witnesses.

directed verdict

The entry of a verdict by a trial judge, prior to allowing the jury to decide the case, when the party with the burden of proof fails to present a prima facie case.

After the plaintiff has rested his case, the defendant's attorney frequently asks the court to direct a verdict for her client. A **directed verdict** will be granted if the judge, after viewing the facts most favorable to the plaintiff (that is, in a way that gives the plaintiff the benefit of the doubt), believes that the jury could not reasonably return a verdict in the plaintiff's favor that would be in accord with the law. If the directed verdict is denied, the defendant proceeds with her evidence and witnesses, which are subject to cross-examination by the plaintiff.

When all evidence has been presented, either party can move for a directed verdict. If the judge denies the motions, she will instruct the jury as to the law, and the jury will deliberate until reaching a verdict. After the jury has reached its decision, in many cases, the losing party will ask the court for a judgment notwithstanding the verdict (JNOV). The motion will be granted if the judge decides that the jury's verdict is against the weight of the evidence.

The judge and the jury, of course, play key roles in the trial. The judge has the dominant role; she can decide whether evidence is admissible, instruct the jury on the law before deliberation begins, and take the case away from the jury by means of a directed verdict or a JNOV. This power narrows the role of the jury to deciding the facts in the case, ultimately determining whether the plaintiff has proved his case by weight of the evidence.

To illustrate the interplay between judge and jury, assume that Tom sues Dick, the owner of Greenacre, for injuries sustained on Greenacre. The judge must explain to the jury the legal standard of care—that is, that Dick must keep the premises in a reasonably safe condition and must safeguard Tom from dangers of which Dick knew or should have known. It is then the jury's responsibility to determine whether Tom has met the burden of proving that Dick did not meet the standard of care. However, if the judge concludes that reasonable minds could not differ on the facts, she can take the case from the jury and enter a directed verdict.

Concluding Stages

The *fifth* stage in litigation is the appeal. In the appellate court, the party who appeals the case—the losing party in the trial court—is usually referred to as the appellant, while the other party is the appellee. In reading appellate court decisions, one cannot assume that the first name in the case is the plaintiff because many appellate courts reverse the order of the names when the case is appealed. The case of *Smith v. Jones,* for example, where Smith sued Jones in the trial court, might become *Jones v. Smith* on appeal. The appellate court, as previously noted, limits itself to a review of the law applied in the case and normally does not review the facts as determined by the judge or jury. In reviewing the case, the appellate court may affirm the trial court decision, modify or reverse the decision, or reverse and send the case back to the lower court for a new trial.

writ of execution

The process of carrying out a judgment of the court. An officer of the court is ordered to take the losing party's property to satisfy the judgment debt.

The sixth and *final* stage of the litigation process is enforcement of the judgment. The most common methods of enforcement are by **writ of execution** and by **garnishment**. A writ of execution entitles the plaintiff to have a local official seize the defendant's property and have the property sold to satisfy the judgment. A garnishment is an order to a third person who is indebted to the defendant to pay the debt directly to the plaintiff to satisfy the judgment. Often the third party is the employer of the defendant who will be ordered to pay a certain percentage of the defendant's wages directly to the plaintiff.[13]

garnishment

The satisfaction of a debt out of a losing party's property possessed by or owed by another.

Alternative Methods of Resolving Disputes

Settlements

settlement

An agreement to terminate all or part of a lawsuit as a result of the parties' voluntary resolution of the dispute.

One major way in which parties resolve disputes is to reach a **settlement**. The settlement can resolve litigation that has already commenced. A settlement can also be reached to resolve a disagreement before litigation or a more formal dispute resolution procedure such as arbitration commences. Parties often settle disputes through discussion between themselves or with the assistance of their attorneys without using one of the more formalized dispute resolution processes described in the following sections. Although the rate differs from state to state, it is common for over 90 percent of civil cases to be settled before trial.

The Administrative Process

For parties who cannot informally resolve disputes and who do not want to use the court system, two alternative methods of resolving disputes are available: (1) the administrative process and (2) the use of private neutral third parties. With respect to the *first* alternative, adjudication of legal rights as defined by any particular area of administrative law is most often accomplished by an administrative agency or tribunal created by statute or constitution. As a result, many private disputes controlled by administrative law are not resolved by courts at all. For instance, a compensation claim by an injured employee against a private employer for injury suffered in the course of employment is ordinarily adjudicated by a state workers' compensation commission.

Undoubtedly, far more disputes are settled today by administrative adjudicative bodies than by ordinary courts. Moreover, an administrative agency often has the statutory responsibility and power to initiate enforcement of statutes. Frequently, the same agency that brings the initial proceeding also hears the case and decides the dispute. In the United States, for instance, the FTC is empowered by Congress to initiate a proceeding to compel an alleged offender to cease and desist from using unfair methods of competition.

In general, the tasks or goals of procedural administrative law should be the same as those of common law in deciding matters of private law: to provide a "day in court," an independent "judge" or body to decide the dispute, and a rationally justified decision. Statutes, of course, prescribe the powers of administrative authorities. The roles of ordinary courts are most often limited to preventing administrative authorities from exceeding their powers and to hearing appeals from the final decision of the administrative agency.

Neutral Third Party

arbitration
The submission of a dispute to an impartial third party; both parties generally agree in advance to abide by the arbitrator's decision.

The *second* alternative method of resolving disputes involves the use of neutral third parties outside the court and administrative systems. The two most popular third-party processes, also referred to as alternative dispute resolution, or ADR, are **arbitration** and **mediation**. A third party acting as an arbitrator has authority to decide the dispute. Unless it is explicitly stated that the arbitration is non-binding, an arbitrator's decision ends the dispute, and a court can only override if there is evidence of an arbitrator's corruption, fraud or wrongdoing, such as bias exhibited toward one party, or when the arbitrator exceeds the authority conferred on him by the parties or by law. A third-party mediator, on the other hand, attempts to help the disputing parties negotiate a settlement. The mediator, unlike the arbitrator, does not have the authority to bind the parties to a specific outcome.

mediation
The process whereby a neutral third party aids and encourages parties to a dispute to reach a mutually satisfactory outcome.

Alternative dispute resolution for resolving real estate disputes is becoming increasingly common. ADR is often cheaper, quicker and is especially effective for handling smaller disputes that are not economically feasible to litigate. Due to the complexity of how ADR works and its important role in the real estate industry, it is covered in more detail in Chapter 7.

KEY TERMS

action, 16
administrative agency, 8
administrative law, 7
answer, 16
arbitration, 20
citation, 9
common law, 10
complaint, 16
deposition, 17
directed verdict, 19
discovery, 17
diversity of citizenship, 15
equity, 11
garnishment, 19
injunction, 12
interrogatories, 18

jurisdiction, 11
law, 4
mediation, 20
private law, 4
procedural law, 16
public law, 4
res judicata, 11
settlement, 19
specific performance, 12
stare decisis, 10
statutory law, 7
subpoena *duces tecum*, 18
substantive law, 16
summary judgment, 16
third-party defendant, 16
writ of execution, 19

PROBLEMS

1. The end result of litigation, unless it is settled, is a case that may set a precedent and a guiding principle for other courts to follow in the future. An arbitrator's decision does not create a legal precedent. What would happen if suddenly all disputes were solved by arbitration instead of litigation? Could statutes and administrative rules alone be applied to settle all disputes effectively and fairly if no legal precedents were being set?

2. In a dispute between Garcia Construction Company and its subcontractor, Clark Electric, Garcia alleged that Clark failed to wire a section of the house adequately. Clark disputes the allegation, stating that Garcia told its electrician that the particular section in question was supposed to be left alone and that the new owners wanted to wire it themselves to save money. The dispute was submitted to arbitration. After calling several witnesses, the arbitrator, Hames, decided that Garcia was correct and that the section of the house should have been wired and awarded Garcia money damages to finish the job. Clark disputes the testimony, claiming that the witnesses were unreliable. Will Hames's decision stand? What would Clark have to prove to persuade a court to overturn the arbitrator's decision?

3. The American Arbitration Association Demand for Arbitration asks the claimant to describe the "APPROPRIATE QUALIFICATIONS FOR ARBITRATOR(S) TO BE APPOINTED TO HEAR THIS DISPUTE." Unlike judges, arbitrators do not have to be lawyers. What type of qualifications would you expect of an arbitrator in a situation where you just bought a new house with a

construction defect? What kind of arbitrator do you think the contractor respondent would select?

4. In 2009 there were 1,180,386 licensed attorneys in the United States according to the American Bar Association. This represents an all-time high, up from 1,066,328 in 2000. The U.S. has 5% of the world's population and 70% of the lawyers. Despite the numbers and competition, more law schools than ever are opening up with 196 law schools now accredited by the American Bar Association. There are now even some online law schools. Interestingly, in the late 1790s there were only 200 lawyers in the entire country. This begs the question of whether the U.S. has too many lawyers, which may, among other things, have a negative effect on the American economy, including the real estate industry. For example, in recent years, builders and developers have bitterly complained about lawyers who stir up trouble particularly in the area of construction defects in residential housing. Others argue that rapid growth in the real estate industry created conditions for shoddy workmanship as homebuilders raced to build as fast as possible to meet demand and make large profits. Do we have too many lawyers or are lawyers necessary for protecting the rights of those who have been aggrieved? What are your thoughts?

5. It is now possible to settle disputes online. For example, Cybersettle.com (found at http://www.cybersettle.com) allows parties three rounds to settle their dispute. One demand and one offer to settle the demand is made in each round. A settlement occurs when an offer is made within 30 percent or $5,000 (whichever is less) of what the parties are demanding. When this occurs,

a confirmation is sent to the parties. Many real estate disputes involve relatively small amounts of money but create a great deal of ill will between parties such as buyers and sellers, real estate licensees and their clients, and contractors and new homeowners. Would this kind of settlement procedure work well in real estate?

6. California has issued its own emission control standards for cars sold within the state. The EPA also has emission control standards that were created by one of its regulations, but these standards are not as strict as California's standards. If Ford wants to sell cars in California, which emission standards must it abide by? Would Ford's situation be any different if the standards were established by a federal statute instead of by an administrative agency's rule or regulation?

7. Wendell, an African-American male, unsuccessfully attempted to rent an apartment from Mike. Later Pam overheard Mike telling Ken that he would never rent one of his apartments to a minority. Pam relates what she heard to Wendell, who subsequently sues Mike for violating the Fair Housing Act. What tools of discovery should Wendell's attorney use to preserve this testimony for a possible trial? If the testimony is preserved, how might it help Wendell's attorney at trial? What is the likelihood that this case will ever get to trial?

8. Duncan sues Mark for breach of contract when Mark, a general contractor, refuses to finish building Duncan's swimming pool. Duncan is now forced to hire Percy's Pools Inc. to finish the job, which will cost him $15,000. Duncan lives in Kansas City, Kansas; Mark lives in Kansas City, Missouri, where his business also is located. Duncan wants to sue Mark in federal district court in Kansas. Can he succeed in bringing the case to that court? If he cannot sue in federal court, to what court can he bring this action?

9. Whiteside signs a real estate contract to buy Gustafson's house. Pursuant to the agreement, Whiteside gives Gustafson $2,000 in earnest money. After a while, both voluntarily agree not to go through with the sale, and Gustafson returns Whiteside's earnest money. Whiteside, however, later claims that he did not receive the earnest money and sues Gustafson for its return. Gustafson has a receipt in which Whiteside acknowledged receiving the money. What motion would enable Gustafson to dispose of this case quickly without having to go to trial? If Whiteside loses the motion, can he appeal the judge's decision?

10. Following the corporate scandals of the early 2000s involving Enron, WorldCom, Adelphia, and other large companies, the role of ethics in business quickly gained public attention. In the Enron case, some of the top executives argued that they were behaving within the parameters of existing laws when they transferred company debt to hundreds of offshore companies. The absence of the debt on Enron's books, however, created the appearance of a company that was more solvent than many observers actually realized. After the executives' actions were publicized, Enron's stock plummeted. The company eventually applied for Chapter 11 bankruptcy protection, most of its employees lost their jobs and pensions (consisting primarily of Enron stock), and shareholders' investments vanished. Assuming that Enron's executives were correct in their legal argument, is obeying the law the only ethical level that a company needs to strive toward in doing business in today's highly competitive society?

ENDNOTES

1. This definition is from *Black's Law Dictionary*, Abridged 6th ed. (1991). Many other definitions are from or based on this source or *West's Legal Thesaurus/Dictionary* (1985), compiled by William Stasky.
2. 334 U.S. 1, 68 S.Ct. 836, 92 L.Ed. 1161 (1948).
3. 1 Pa.Const.Stat.Ann. §§1501 et seq. (1972).
4. I. Jennings, *The Law and the Constitution* (1959).
5. J. Boyat, *Proposed Rules on Mortgages Draw Criticism,* New York Times, http://www.nytimes.com/2004/01/07/business/07home.html (January 7, 2004).
6. C. Skrzycki, *U.S. Opens Portal to Rulemaking,* Washington Post E1 (January 23, 2003).
7. *Marbury v. Madison,* 5 U.S. (1 Cranch) 137, 2 L.Ed. 60 (1803) established the court's power to declare federal legislation unconstitutional.
8. F. Maitland, *The Forms of Action at Common Law* 2 (1965).
9. 417 Pa. 486, 208 A.2d 193 (1965).
10. Mich.Comp.Laws Ann. §600.601 (1961).
11. 285 U.S. 262, 52 S.Ct. 371, 76 L.Ed. 747 (1932).
12. Cal.Evid.Code §996 (1965).
13. The procedure used in a criminal trial differs in several respects from civil procedure. A detailed discussion of criminal procedure is beyond the scope of this book, it being the premise and hope of the author that readers will minimize their contact with the criminal justice system.

© MACIEJ NOSKOWSKI/iStockphoto (RF)

The Nature of Property

2

LEARNING OBJECTIVES

After studying Chapter 2, you should:

- Understand the concept of property

- Know the distinction between real and personal property, and fixtures

"I know of no country, indeed, where the love of money has taken stronger hold on the affections of men and where a profounder contempt is expressed for the theory of the permanent equality of property."

Alexis de Tocqueville, Democracy in America

"When you got nothin', you got nothin' to lose."

Bob Dylan, from the song "Like a Rolling Stone"

The Concept of Property

The meaning of the term *property* varies depending on the context in which the word is used. In one sense, property means things—real or personal, immovable or movable, corporeal or incorporeal, visible or invisible, and tangible or intangible. But the word is also used to describe characteristics; a desk, for example, has unique properties of color, shape, size, and surface. In a legal sense, property describes the relationship between people and things—that is, the right of a person to possess, use, or own things.

The legal meaning of property was described by the English jurist Sir William Blackstone as "the free use, enjoyment, and disposal of all his acquisitions, without any control or diminution, save only by the laws of the land."[1] The Colorado Supreme Court, in the case of *In re Marriage of Graham* on page 43, finds that such exchange value, or the ability to sell property, is a critical factor in deciding whether an MBA degree is "property."

END OF CHAPTER CASE

Blackstone also observed that "there is nothing which so generally strikes the imagination, and engages the affections of mankind, as the right of property; or that sole and despotic dominion which one man claims and exercises over the external things of the world in total exclusion of the right of any other individual in the universe."[2] In Blackstone's definition, the concept of general property under the common law does not differ substantially from its meaning under Roman law: "Property in its nature is an unrestricted and exclusive right. Hence it comprises in itself the right to dispose of the substance of the thing in every legal way, to possess it, to use it, and to exclude every other person from interfering with it."[3]

ETHICAL AND PUBLIC POLICY ISSUES

Is It Ethical to Sell Organs as Property?

Is it moral that federal law forbids the sale of organs, such as a person's kidney, for transplant purposes? Proponents argue that the public policy underlying the law protects sellers, particularly the poor, from being exploited by the rich. Others argue that since people own their bodies just like a piece of property, they should be able to sell their own organs. For example, although there is a health risk associated with selling a kidney, people take greater risks of incurring injuries and death in jobs that are often government regulated such as fishing, construction, and mining. As such, shouldn't it also be possible to create and regulate a fair and efficient market for buying and selling of organs as private property? Isn't this a more ethical approach than the current policy where only about 14 percent of those who need kidney transplants receive them?

Blackstone, however, raised a general question in his commentary on property. He noted that people are often afraid to look beyond their ownership of property to examine the reason or authority upon which the law is built.

We think it enough that our title is derived by grant of the former proprietor, by descent from our ancestors, or the last will and testament of the dying owner; not caring to reflect that … there is no foundation in nature or in natural law why a set of words upon parchment should convey the dominion of land; why the son should have a right to exclude his fellow-creatures from a determined spot of ground, because his father had done so before him; or why the occupier of a particular field or of a jewel, when lying on his death bed and no longer able to maintain possession, should be entitled to tell the rest of the world which of them should enjoy it after him.[4]

This broader question relating to the natural origins of the concept of property has been the concern of legal philosophers for centuries. Jeremy Bentham, a nineteenth-century British philosopher, viewed property as a "basis of expectation, the expectation of deriving certain advantages from a thing which we are said to possess, in consequence of the relation in which we stand towards it."[5] Viewed in this light, the law of property might be considered one of the keystones of civilized society, for the rights and duties that define the "basis of expectation" distinguish modern humans from the savage who must use force to acquire and retain property. Bentham explained the law of property in this way:

The savage who has killed a deer may hope to keep it for himself, so long as his cave is undiscovered; so long as he watches to defend it, and is stronger than his rivals; but that is all. How miserable and precarious is such a possession! If we suppose the least agreement among savages to respect the acquisitions of each other, we see the introduction of a principle to which no name can be given but that of law. A feeble and momentary expectation may result from time to time from circumstances purely physical but a strong and permanent expectation can result only from law. That which, in the natural state, was an almost invisible thread, in the social state becomes a cable. Property and law are born together, and die together. Before laws were made there was no property; take away laws, and property ceases.[6]

The importance of protecting property rights has gained increasing attention since the fall of the Soviet Union in 1989. The initial failure of Russia and other formerly communist nations to succeed economically was linked, in part, to a culture in which individuals did not understand, value, and obey laws that were aimed at protecting property rights. Many experts, supported by extensive studies, believe that only when countries develop a legal system in which a person's property rights and expectations are respected will a foundation for economic prosperity be established.

For example, a 2004 study found that among 100 nations for which statistics were available, the twenty-four countries with the strongest property rights averaged $25,716 in annual income per capita, while the twenty-one nations with the weakest rights averaged just $3,094. Moreover, a 1988 study showed that nations with stronger property rights grew at three times the rate of countries with weaker rights. A third study demonstrated that respect for private property rights predicts prosperity better than a nation's natural resources, favorable climate, geography, education, or technology.[7]

A success story from Peru illustrates the importance of property rights even for citizens of poor and developing countries. The Peruvian government, acting on the advice of a local economist, Hernando de Soto, issued property titles to 1.2 million urban-squatter households. As a consequence, parents were able to go out into the workplace and find jobs, whereas before, they were forced to stay home and protect their property. Work hours increased 20 percent in that country, while child labor decreased 30 percent.[8] De Soto's ideas are influencing other Third World countries as well. According to de Soto, many individuals live in a system in which "nobody can identify who owns what, addresses cannot be verified and the rules that govern property vary from neighborhood to neighborhood, or even from street to street."[9] Obviously, such a system cannot foster the necessary incentives and protections necessary for a productive economy.

Respect for property rights also can be linked to peace. As one noted property rights commentator observed:

Nations with materially prosperous and diverse economies are more likely to be peaceful than nations lacking such property-based economies because prosperous masses have more to lose from war than do poor people and are generally more reluctant to fight and risk losing what belongs to them.[10]

The concept of property and property rights not only is indispensable for a prosperous economy but also continues to evolve over time. For example, in a regrettable period in American history, people could be owned as slaves. The classification of slaves as property was even sanctioned by the U.S. Supreme Court in the Dred Scott case in 1857, when that Court ruled that slaves were chattel (personal property) and could therefore be owned, bought, sold, and collateralized just like any other personal property. Indeed, under Louisiana law at that time, a slave was deemed to be part of the plantation, much like the way an agricultural fixture, discussed later in this chapter, is treated by the law today. Difficult definitional issues, however, continue to surface in our time as well, often fueled by rapid technological changes.

ETHICAL AND PUBLIC POLICY ISSUES

Are Frozen Embryos People, or Are They Property?

The Tennessee Supreme Court was asked to rule on, among other issues, whether frozen embryos were persons protected by the state or property governed by the wishes of their owners. In the case of *Davis v. Davis*,[11] discussed in Problem 10 at the end of the chapter, the court sought the advice of ethicists in resolving the case.

Real and Personal Property

Property can be classified in a variety of ways. For example, private property belongs to an individual who has the exclusive right of disposition, while public property includes those things owned by the public through a federal, state, or local government body. Literary property is the natural common law right of an author to the profits resulting from her composition, while theatrical property includes everything used in producing a play with the exception of the actors' costumes and painted scenery. The most important classifications in a legal sense are real property and personal property.

real property

Land and anything permanently attached to it.

Real property is property that is fixed, immovable, and permanent. It includes land; structures affixed to the land; property affixed to the structures (fixtures, which are discussed in detail later in this chapter); and in some cases, things growing on the land. Ownership of real property includes the right to the air space above the earth's surface and to the soil and minerals below. To describe these rights, courts often cite this rule: *cujus est solum ejus est usque ad coelum et ad inferos*, or "the owner of the soil owns also to the sky and to the depths." The implications of this rule are examined in Chapter 3.

personal property

All property, with the exception of real property, that can be owned.

Personal property includes everything that is not real property. While real property is fixed and immovable, the basic characteristic of personal property is its movability. In fact, within the civil law legal tradition (see Chapter 1), the word *movable* is the legal term for personal property, while real property is called "immovable" property. The word *chattel*, derived from the same Old French root as *cattle*, is often used as a synonym for personal property.

Personal property is tangible or intangible. Tangible personal property refers to things that can be touched, such as books, automobiles, or chairs. In contrast, intangible property includes property that has little or no value in itself but represents something of value. For instance, if a corporation owns one asset, such as a 100-acre farm, and if Smith owns all of the stock in the corporation, Smith's interest would be classified as intangible personal property. As a separate entity, the corporation owns the tangible real property. Smith's stock certificates, which are intangible personal property, represent evidence only of her interest in the corporation. Intellectual property, which includes patents, copyrights, and trademarks, is also a type of intangible personal property.

Sources of Law

Because real and personal property are governed by different legal rules, it is important to distinguish between them. If someone were selling or leasing tangible personal property, the law would be found in the **Uniform Commercial Code** (UCC). The UCC has been enacted in all states but Louisiana (which has adopted all parts of the UCC except Article 2 on sales). Although the UCC has made the law of commercial transactions more uniform, as its name suggests, variations in the Code exist from state to state. These variations arise because of differences in the provisions of the UCC adopted by a state's legislative body and because of differences in the way that state courts interpret or apply the UCC provisions.

Uniform Commercial Code

A code of law (adopted in its entirety by all states except Louisiana) that governs commercial transactions.

The UCC was the work of the National Conference of Commissioners on Uniform State Laws and the American Law Institute (ALI). Pennsylvania was the first state to adopt the UCC in 1953. The Code has its origins in the "law merchant" (also called the lex mercatoria), a system of laws that merchants and traders developed in eleventh-century Europe for resolving disputes among themselves quickly and fairly. The UCC is widely credited with enhancing and simplifying commercial transactions although, as mentioned, variations in the UCC do exist. The UCC is also revised periodically to reflect business and technological changes that have occurred since the original drafting half a century ago. For example, software licenses and notice by facsimile are new commercial realities since the UCC's inception.

Article 2 of the Code covers the sale of goods. Its definition of goods is identical to the definition of personal property: "all things ... which are movable at the time of identification to the contract for sale" (Section 2-105). This definition becomes critical to identifying the source of law in a property dispute. As noted in Chapter 1, the law relating to real property is derived mainly from common law case decisions rather than from the Code.

The application of real property law and the UCC may lead to different results as illustrated by the following example. Jones enters into contracts with Brown to sell a 1954 Rambler for $400 and a tiny strip of land in Arizona for another $400. Must these contracts be in writing to be enforceable? The answer is determined by the **Statute of Frauds**, which provides that certain contracts must be written to be enforced. Section 2-201 of the UCC provides that only contracts for the sale of goods priced at $500 or more must be in writing.[12] However, the Code contains a number of exceptions to the requirement of a written contract even when the value exceeds $500. For example, when a party admits in court that an oral contract for more than $500 was made, the contract is enforceable. Moreover, only the defendant must sign the written contract since the plaintiff, by bringing the lawsuit, is acknowledging his willingness to be bound by the agreement. But under the Statute of Frauds that is applicable to real property, any contract for the sale of land or for an interest in land must be written. Consequently, Jones's contract for the sale of the car can be oral, but the contract for the sale of the land must be written.

Statute of Frauds

A law that disallows any suit or action involving certain classes of contracts, such as those concerning interests in land, unless the agreement is evidenced by a note or memorandum in writing signed by the party to be charged or his authorized agent.

Form of Transfer

The requirements for transferring real and personal property differ. Ownership of real property is normally transferred by a deed, which must meet certain formal requirements. An interest in personal property may be transferred by a **bill of sale** (a document similar in form to a deed) although a bill of sale is usually neither required nor customary. Certificates of title are also used to transfer certain types of personal property, such as automobiles. Other methods for which both real and personal property can be transferred are discussed in detail in Chapters 10 and 12 respectively.

bill of sale

A written agreement in which one person transfers his interest in personal property to another.

Taxation

There are important tax reasons for distinguishing personal and real property. For instance, personal property is generally not taxed, or if it is taxed, the tax is based on a rate structure different than that used for real property as the next case from New York demonstrates.

A CASE IN POINT

In *Roberts v. Assessment Board of Review of the Town of New Windsor,* there was a dispute over New York's real property tax law which excludes personal property from taxation. A homeowner installed an above-ground swimming pool that cost about $5,000. The pool was not attached to the real estate and could be disassembled in a few hours and reassembled in a new location for less than $450. When the homeowner's real estate taxes were increased because of the pool, he filed suit to cancel the extra assessment. The court agreed with the homeowner that the pool had not become real estate and invalidated the assessment.[13]

TABLE 2.1 Summary of Differences between Real and Personal Property		
	REAL PROPERTY	**PERSONAL PROPERTY**
Source of law	common law	UCC Article 2
Form of transfer	deed	bill of sale
Taxation	real estate tax	none or different rate

The distinction between real and personal property is also important in determining depreciation deductions. Because personal property can be written off over a shorter time period than real property can, the value of the depreciation deduction is substantially greater. For example, for an asset that costs $100,000, the tax savings of classifying the property as personal property rather than real property amounts to approximately $15,000.[14] (See Table 2.1.) The IRS employs its own test for determining whether a property is a fixture or not and therefore how much it can be depreciated. In the case of *Whiteco Industries v. Commissioner*,[15] the so-called six *Whiteco* factors generally reflect the fixture tests discussed in this chapter. The factors are provided in endnote 15.

Although the characterization of property as real estate or personal property can result in different outcomes, in some circumstances, the distinction does not make a difference, as illustrated by the following Illinois case.

A CASE IN POINT

In *U.S. v. One 1989 Stratford Fairmont*,[16] the federal government seized eighteen-year-old drug dealer Mark Stover's mobile home. The government argued that the home was subject to forfeiture under a federal statute that allows the government to obtain title to real property and vehicles that are used to commit or facilitate violations of federal drug laws. One section of this forfeiture statute applies to vehicles and another to real property. The trial court concluded that the mobile home was real property, observing, "It is unrealistic to view the wholly non-peripatetic mobile home as something other than 'real property' simply because the word 'mobile' is tacked on before the word 'home.'" The appellate court disagreed with the trial court's characterization of the mobile home as real estate but agreed that it was nonetheless subject to forfeiture. "Recall that §881(a)(4) covers vehicles used to 'facilitate the … sale, receipt, possession, or concealment' of drugs and not just their 'transportation.' Potential movement is enough. A mobile home is a vehicle; a mobile home is real property; either way, Stover's drug distribution center now belongs to the United States."

fixture

A legal hybrid; a piece of personal property that has become affixed to real property in such a way that it becomes part of the real property. The UCC's definition of a fixture is also instructive: [G]oods are "fixtures" when they become so related to particular real estate that an interest in them arises under real estate law.

Fixtures

Because Sally enjoyed shooting billiards, she installed a $10,000 slate-covered pool table in the basement of her home. The legs of the table were screwed to the floor, and Sally installed basement carpeting to match the felt on the table. Sometime after the table had been installed, Sally signed a contract to sell her house to Slim. Slim now claims that he purchased the pool table when he purchased Sally's real estate. Sally claims that she can take the table with her. Who is correct?

The answer to that question depends on whether the table is considered a **fixture**[17]. But as the court noted in the leading case from Ohio of *Teaff v. Hewitt*:

In the great order of nature, when we compare a thing at the extremity of one class with a thing at the extremity of another, the difference is glaring; but when we approach the connecting link between the two divisions, it is often difficult to discover the precise point where the dividing line is drawn…. [T] he precise point in the connection with the realty, where the article loses the legal qualities of a chattel and acquires those of the realty, often presents a question of great nicety and sometimes difficult determination.[18]

severance
The legal principle that defines the mechanical processes required to convert an item of real property into personal property.

In contrast to the transformation of personal property to fixture status, a **severance** occurs when real property is transformed into personal property. An example of a severance is when timber and valuable minerals are removed from the land.

Variations of the concept of severance have evolved, including rules governing standing crops. These are discussed later in this chapter. The importance of the following tests for determining whether property is a fixture is illustrated in the following Alabama case.

In *Ex parte Brown* on page 44, the court resolved an issue relating to an intentional misclassification of property by a wife attempting to gain an unfair financial advantage over her husband during their divorce proceedings.

END OF CHAPTER CASE

Fixture Tests

annexation test
A key fixture test that is met when personal property is in fact annexed, fixed, or fastened onto the real property.

To determine whether personal property has been transformed into a fixture, most American courts apply three tests: annexation, adaptation, and intention. (See Figure 2.1.)

Annexation   The **annexation test** requires that the property be annexed to the real estate. As the *Teaff* court noted, "If there be any thing well settled in the doctrine of fixtures, it is this, that to constitute a fixture, it is an essential requisite that the article be actually affixed or annexed to the realty. The term itself imports this."[19]

constructive annexation
Personal property that is so closely related to real property that it is considered to be annexed even though it has not actually been annexed, fixed, or fastened to the real property.

Although the rule appears easy to apply, courts do not agree as to what constitutes annexation. For instance, in several cases they have decided that there is **constructive annexation** ("just as if" annexed) because of the relationship between the personal property and real estate, even when the personal property is not actually annexed to the real estate. Property that might be considered constructively annexed includes window solar screens, storm doors and windows that have been fitted for a house but are not yet in place, and devices such as garage door openers and television antenna dials. A court also may determine whether the item in question is of comparable value if it is separated from the land. For example, screens and windows fitted to the unique dimensions of a particular house would have little, if any, value to another dwelling. This would likely influence a court in determining whether these items are fixtures.[20]

assembled industrial plant doctrine
A doctrine that provides that plant machinery, even though not actually annexed, is constructively annexed onto real property.

The doctrine of constructive annexation also applies to cases where machinery is installed in industrial plants in such a way as to be considered a fixture. If the machinery is a fixture, essential parts of the machinery are considered fixtures even though they may not be attached. Some courts have gone a step further in adopting the **assembled industrial plant doctrine**, which provides that even unattached machinery is to be considered a fixture if it is essential to the operation of the plant.[21]

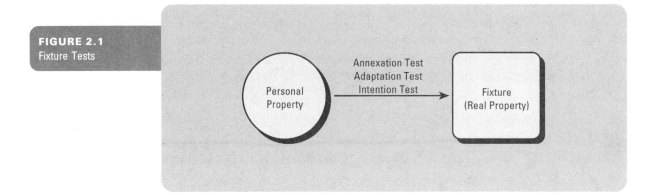

FIGURE 2.1
Fixture Tests

In considering the annexation test, courts also attempt to determine whether removal will damage the real estate although they have not applied this doctrine uniformly. For example, one California court concluded that a Murphy bed was not a fixture because it could be removed without damaging the real estate. But in numerous other cases, items such as millstones, fences, doors, and windows have been considered fixtures even though their removal would not cause injury to the real estate.[22,23]

In some situations, a court will decide that an article is a fixture even though the property is neither constructively annexed nor actually annexed by nails, bolts, screws, or glue. For instance, the weight of an object, such as a large, decorative rock commonly used in desert landscape, might lead a court to conclude that the annexation test has been met. The next classic case from New York drew a similar conclusion.

A CASE IN POINT

In *Snedeker v. Warring*, the court ruled that a three- or four-ton statue that was not cemented or clamped to the floor would be considered a fixture because "a thing may be as firmly affixed to the land by gravitation as by clamps or cement."[24]

One means of conceptualizing whether personal property is constructively annexed to real property is to consider what one would see in a typical moving van. For example, would you expect a couple who had just sold their house to move cross-country to have in their moving van the items discussed previously? Would you likely find a garage door opener or a three-ton statue in most moving vans? Quite likely, a reasonable observer would be very surprised to see those items in the van.

Courts have also decided that a fixture will not become personal property if it was severed from the real estate for purposes of repair or severed by an act of God. In one classic Pennsylvania case, a storm demolished a building, and a dispute arose over the right to the ruins of the building. The court decided that even though the ruins had been detached from the real estate, "the act of God … shall prejudice no one."[25] Consequently, the court decided that the property was still classified as real, not personal, unless the owner had caused the severance.

adaptation test
A test for determining whether personal property has become united with real property by its adaptation to the use and purpose of the real property.

Adaptation   A second test—the **adaptation test**—focuses on the question of whether an article is adapted to the use or purpose of the real estate. Although a few courts have made adaptation the sole test of a fixture, the test is too broad to be applied effectively.

For instance, on this basis alone, fixtures could conceivably include implements on a farm[26] or furniture in an apartment. In applying the test, most courts attempt to determine whether the articles are functionally tied to the real property as well as necessary or beneficial to the enjoyment of the property. Examples of such items include a furnace in a house, power equipment in a mill, and computer systems in bank buildings.[27] The next California case discusses the issue.

A CASE IN POINT

In *Bank of America v. Los Angeles,*[28] the plaintiff bank brought suit seeking a refund of real estate taxes that had been levied on electronic computer systems installed in several buildings. The buildings had been specially designed for use as accounting centers: they had fewer windows than ordinary commercial buildings, they were constructed near a constant electrical power source and away from prime military areas, and they contained an expensive raised floor to support the computer systems. The court decided that the systems were fixtures because they were "necessary or convenient to the use of a building for the purpose for which it is designed" and thus were properly taxed as real property.

Intention   According to modern courts, the controlling test of a fixture is the intention of the party who annexed the article to make it a permanent part of the real estate (the **intention test**). To determine intention, courts examine the actions, purpose, and relationships of the parties. "The intention of the parties is not always governed by what is said by them, but the intention may be determined from the nature of the article, relations, and situation of the parties making the annexation, and the structure, use, and mode of annexation."[29] Even under the modern view, the tests of annexation and adaptation are important in determining intention.

> **intention test**
> A test for determining whether personal property has become united with real property by examining the intent of the annexor.

It is often said that it is not the secret or hidden intention of the parties to the annexation that is important but the intention that can be deduced from the external facts,[30] as illustrated by the following Washington state case.

A CASE IN POINT

In *Strain v. Green*[31] a man installed chandeliers in his house, which had been in the family for many years. When he later sold the house, he took the chandeliers with him even though their removal had never been discussed during negotiations. Deciding that the removal was wrongful because the chandeliers were fixtures, the court stressed its reasons for considering a party's subjective intention to be immaterial: "If a witness testifies that, when he put a chandelier in a house, he intended to take it out if he should ever sell the house, in what possible way can the evidence be disputed? ... If it be held in this case that the secret intention of the defendant is determinative of the question whether or not the articles involved are fixtures, that holding will encourage and invite persons less honest than the respondents to attempt to remove from premises every at-all-movable article that can be disconnected without breakage."

Of the external facts examined by the courts, one of the most important is the relationship between the person who annexed the article and the real estate. For instance, when the owner of real estate annexes personal property such as a heating system that is intended to benefit the general use and occupation of the real estate, the law presumes that the owner intended the property to become a fixture.

Is an airplane hangar, though affixed to the earth, not a fixture if the facts indicate the hangar's owner intended it to be his personal property? In *Adamson v. Sims* on page 45, the court considers which of the various fixture tests would determine the outcome.

END OF CHAPTER CASE

Special Tests Courts often look to a statute to determine whether an article of personal property has become a fixture. The use of statutory guidelines is common when a court must determine whether an article is to be taxed as real property or whether there has been a violation of a zoning ordinance, as illustrated by the following Washington state case.

A CASE IN POINT

In *State v. Work*,[32] a woman was convicted of unlawful habitation of a mobile home in violation of a zoning ordinance. The ordinance did permit buildings but specifically excluded "all forms of vehicles even though immobilized." The tongue, axles, and wheels had been removed from the mobile home in question. Furthermore, the home rested on a foundation of concrete blocks and had been connected with a number of utilities. Guided by the statutory definition and ignoring the three traditional fixture tests, the court concluded that since the structure had always been considered a home, albeit mobile at one time, it could not be an immobilized vehicle. Thus, it did not fall within the plain meaning of the ordinance. The conviction was reversed and remanded with instructions to dismiss.

Special tests have also been developed to determine the status of two types of property vital to agriculture: (1) things growing on land and (2) manure. Growing things commonly have been classified as *fructus naturales* or *fructus industriales*.

fructus naturales
Vegetation that grows naturally on property and not by the efforts of humans.

Fructus naturales—those things produced primarily by the powers of nature, such as trees and perennial bushes—are considered real property. **Fructus industriales**—those things produced primarily by human industry, such as crops or fruits of *fructus naturales* (for example, blueberries)—are considered personal property.

fructus industriales
Vegetation, such as crops, that grows on property by the efforts of humans.

Traditionally, the distinction between *fructus naturales* and *fructus industriales* has been important in resolving two legal issues. The *first* issue is whether the law of real or personal property governs when there is a separate sale of something growing on the land. This issue is now covered by the UCC, an important source of commercial law discussed in this chapter. (However, in interpreting the Code, courts occasionally rely on the traditional distinction in determining whether a contract calls for the sale of growing crops—that is, *fructus industriales*.) The *second* issue involves the question of whether things growing on the land pass with the real estate when it is sold. Most states have adopted a "severance" test: growing things—whether *fructus naturales* or *fructus industriales*—pass to the buyer with the real estate if they have not been severed at the time of sale.

emblements
Crops produced by a tenant's labor to which the tenant is entitled. These crops are grown annually, not spontaneously, by labor and industry.

The term **emblements** is often used as a synonym for *fructus industriales*, but the word is also used to describe the right of a tenant to remove, after the termination of a tenancy, the annual products of the land that have resulted from the tenant's own labor. To claim emblements, the tenant should prove:

1. Existence of a tenancy of uncertain duration.
2. Termination of the tenancy by the act of God or by the act of the lessor.
3. The fact that the crop was planted by the tenant before the tenancy ended.[33]

The doctrine is based on fairness to the tenant who, holding the land for an uncertain time, would be reluctant to use the land productively without such a rule.

Although manure has lost some of its importance in the modern economy, it is now gaining value again as a source of methane gas used as an alternative power source. Disputes regarding the ownership of manure have engaged a surprising number of courts. One of the earliest cases,[34] from sixteenth-century England, involved a defendant who was sued for slander when he exclaimed, "Thou are a thief. Thou has stolen my dung." The defendant contended that the statement could not be slanderous because dung was not personal property and therefore could not be stolen. In discussing this defense, Justice Bacon observed that "dung is a chattel, and may be stolen." However, another justice responded that "dung may be a chattel, and it may not be a chattel; for a heap of dung is a chattel, but if it be spread upon the land it is not." After further discussion, the court concluded that regardless of whether the dung could be stolen, the words of the defendant were still "scandalous."

Most courts have decided that the purchaser of real estate acquires manure that was produced by food grown on the land and fed to farm animals, while manure that is produced by food from outside sources, such as from another farm, belongs to the seller of the real estate. In other words, that which is produced by the land remains with the land.

Fixture Disputes

The law of fixtures becomes especially important when two or more people claim ownership of the same article. There are *four* types of transactions in which ownership disputes are especially common:

1. When a dispute arises in a transfer of real estate over whether certain pieces of property are fixtures.
2. When a dispute arises over whether property that may or may not be a fixture is sold separately from the real estate.
3. When a dispute arises over whether a fixture serves as collateral to secure a loan.
4. When a dispute arises over whether a fixture is wrongfully or mistakenly affixed to another's real estate.

Disputes Arising in the Transfer of Real Estate   A common legal dispute involving fixtures arises when a person agrees to sell real estate without realizing that certain articles in the home might legally be considered fixtures. If the articles are fixtures, the general rule is that they pass to the buyer.[35]

The major problem in these cases is determining whether the article is a fixture. Here, as elsewhere, courts have adopted the three fixture tests, with emphasis on the **intention** of the parties. For example, in one case, a Kentucky court held that an electric stove was not a fixture because the court was "not convinced that the purchaser of a dwelling, knowing there is an electric range in it, thinks for a minute that he is buying the electric range when he buys the dwelling, unless he had some special arrangement whereby the title to the range is to pass with the building."[36]

The "unless" clause of this statement is an important exception to the general rule: the exception applies when the parties include provisions in their contract that determine whether personal property and fixtures remain with the seller or pass to the buyer. For example, a contract could state, "This contract includes the window coverings, built-in wall units in den, and light fixtures except for the dining room chandelier which will

intention
To plan for, design, or expect a certain result.

remain the property of the seller." Although an oral agreement might, in some rare circumstances, be enforceable, a specific statement should be incorporated into the written real estate contract to avoid Statute of Frauds, parol evidence rule, and other legal difficulties and to provide proof of the agreement should a dispute arise. These concepts are discussed in detail in Chapter 7. Such a specific statement is a clear manifestation of the parties' intent.

Disputes Arising in the Transfer of Property Attached to Real Estate Fixtures are frequently sold separately from real estate, and their sale usually follows one of *two fact patterns*. *First*, the fixture may be severed from the real estate and then sold. For instance, a landowner may cut down several walnut trees and sell the logs. Because the trees are personal property at the time of sale, personal property law (UCC Article 2) governs the sale. *Second*, the landowner may sell articles affixed to real estate, such as the walnut trees, before severance; in this case, a determination must be made as to whether real property or personal property rules govern.

The answer to this problem can be found in Section 2-107 of the UCC, which divides items attached to the land into two categories. In the *first* category are those things attached to the real estate that can be severed *without* material harm to the real estate. This category specifically includes timber to be cut and growing crops. In cases where things of this nature are sold while still attached to the land, the contract is considered to be a sale of goods governed by the Code.

In the *second fact pattern* are also issues regarding things attached to the land that cause material harm when removed from the land, such as minerals and structures.[37] When the contract of sale calls for these articles to be *severed by the seller*, the contract is still a sale of goods governed by the Code. When the *buyer is to sever these goods*, however, the contract is treated as a sale of real estate, and real estate principles govern.

The distinction between what laws do and do not apply to the foregoing transactions can be very important. For example, whether the UCC provisions on sales or common law real estate principles apply is an issue that can affect which party bears the risk of loss, how the parties perform their obligations, whether warranties exist, and what potential remedies exist in the event of a breach. Table 2.2 summarizes how the disputes discussed above are legally resolved.

The rules governing the rights of the buyer and seller are also subject to the rights of third parties under real estate law. For instance, the sale of a house to be severed from the real estate and moved by the seller is a contract for the sale of goods. If, however, the seller sold the real estate to an innocent third party before severance, that innocent third

TABLE 2.2 Transfer of Property Attached to Real Estate

TYPE OF DISPUTE	APPLICABLE LAW	EXAMPLE IN BOOK
Property severed and sold by landowner	Considered personal property—UCC Article 2 governs	Owner severs walnut trees and sells as logs
Property sold before severance with no material harm to land	Considered personal property—UCC Article 2 governs	Buyer purchases then severs timber
Property severed by seller that causes material harm to land	Considered personal property—UCC Article 2 governs	Seller removes and sells minerals
Property sold and severed by buyer that causes material harm to land	Real property law	Buyer purchases and severs minerals

party would probably be entitled to the house. The rights of the two buyers (of goods and of real estate) would be influenced by whether either party had *filed* (that is, *recorded*) the contract of sale, which is discussed in Chapter 8.

Tenants' Fixtures   Frequently, a person renting real estate installs fixtures on the property. A farmer renting real estate may install a corn crib on the land; a manufacturer renting a building may purchase and affix to the building thousands of dollars worth of equipment for carrying on his business; a person renting an apartment may attach a bookshelf to a wall or a lamp to the ceiling to make the apartment more comfortable. The legal issue in each instance is whether the tenant may remove the fixture at the termination of the tenancy.[38]

> As noted in the case of *Michigan National Bank v. Lansing* on page 46, the doctrine of tenant fixtures affects the relative rights of the landlord and tenant; the doctrine does not affect the characterization of the fixtures for the purpose of taxation as real estate.

END OF CHAPTER CASE

In earlier cases, courts emphasized the annexation test in deciding that anything the tenant attached to the real estate could not be removed by the tenant at the end of the lease.[39] Today, however, courts in most states allow removal of three types of fixtures—collectively referred to as tenants' fixtures—that a tenant has annexed to the real estate.

trade fixtures
Articles placed in or attached to rented buildings by tenants to carry on the trade or business for which the tenants occupy the premises.

Trade Fixtures   **Trade fixtures** are defined as "those articles placed on the premises by the tenant to carry on the trade or business for which the tenant rents the premises." Courts have decided that trade fixtures include such articles as a kiln, a sawmill, an airplane hangar, a smokehouse, gasoline tanks and pumps, a furnace, machinery, railroad tracks, brass rails, bowling alleys, greenhouses, barber chairs, bars, a pipe organ, and a vault door. The next oft-cited Massachusetts case illustrates the strong public policy existing today for allowing commercial tenants to remove the fixtures that they must initially install to operate their businesses successfully.

A CASE IN POINT

In *Consiglio v. Carey*[40] the operator of a restaurant called Dorsie's Steak House installed a walk-in freezer, a compressor, two air conditioners, and a bar for use in his restaurant business. The air conditioners were so large that the sash from each window casing was removed during their installation. The freezer was too large to be installed in the building, so it was installed on an insulated concrete slab at the back wall of the building with a hole cut in the rear wall of the building to allow for access to the freezer door. Despite the massive nature of this equipment, the court held that the items were removable as tenants' fixtures, "having been installed by the defendant during his tenancy for the purpose to which he was putting the rented premises...." Since removal of the items damaged the premises, "the defendant has an obligation to restore the premises to the condition they were in before the tenancy, reasonable wear and tear excepted...." The court required the restaurateur to restore the window sashing removed to permit installation of the air conditioners and to remove the slab and plywood shell for the freezer unit if desired by the owner of the real estate.

agricultural fixtures
Articles placed in or attached to farm buildings and land for purposes of farming.

domestic fixtures
Articles that tenants attach to a dwelling to render their occupation of the premises more comfortable or convenient.

Agricultural Fixtures   **Agricultural fixtures** are articles annexed by the tenant for the purpose of farming and tilling the soil. Courts have determined that the following articles are agricultural fixtures: a milling plant, a cream separator, an irrigation plant, platform scales, a wooden silo, a brooder house, a hay carrier, a manure carrier, a henhouse, a tool shed, and a maple sugar shed.

Domestic Fixtures   **Domestic fixtures** are articles attached by the tenant to make an apartment more comfortable or convenient. They include carpeting, screens, doors, windows, a toilet, a washing machine, a gas stove, an oil burner, and bookshelves.

In most states, courts allow removal to encourage a tenant to use the property beneficially. Removal is further justified on the grounds that when a tenant makes an improvement to which the landlord has contributed nothing, the tenant intends to retain the improvement as personal property. As one Michigan court stated:

> The right of the tenant to remove the erections made by him in furtherance of the purpose for which the premises were leased is one founded upon public policy and has its foundation in the interest which society has that every person shall be encouraged to make the most beneficial use of his property.... The reason property of this kind is personal, rather than real, is based upon the rule the law implies an agreement that it shall remain personal property from the fact the lessor contributes nothing thereto and should not be enriched at the expense of his tenant....[41]

Nevertheless, the rules governing trade, agricultural, and domestic fixtures have been qualified in a number of ways. (See Figure 2.2.) *First*, the article annexed must fall within one of the tenants' fixture categories. Articles annexed by a tenant may not have been installed for the purposes of carrying on a trade, farming, or making a house more livable. For example, when a court determines that a servant's room, drainage pipe, and cement walk do not fall within the definition of trade or domestic fixtures, the tenant has no right to remove them.[42]

Second, the tenant must be able to remove the fixture without causing substantial injury to the premises, as the following California case illustrates.

A CASE IN POINT

In *Gordon v. Cohn*,[43] the tenant cemented fifty-two square yards of linoleum to the floor of the premises; to remove the linoleum, one-sixteenth of an inch of the floor surface also would have had to be removed. The court held that the tenant had no right to remove the linoleum because the landlord is "not required to sacrifice any part of his building in an effort to restore it to its former use and attractiveness."

Third, the tenant must remove the articles before turning over possession of the premises to the landlord. This rule is designed to protect the landlord, who often will have leased the premises to another tenant, and it is based on the assumption that the tenant has abandoned the articles by failing to remove them before leaving the premises. For example, a radio station that left a radio tower on leased property and claimed a right to the tower more than two years after the lease terminated was held to have lost its right to the tower because of the tardiness of its claim. However, when the landlord has evicted the tenant or the lease is for an indefinite period, the tenant is given a reasonable time after leaving to remove the fixtures.[44,45]

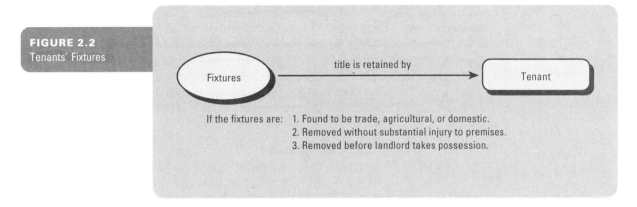

FIGURE 2.2
Tenants' Fixtures

The potential for future tort liability provides another important incentive for a tenant to remove a trade fixture even when the lease is terminated. The following Indiana case discusses this issue.

A CASE IN POINT

In *Dutchman Manufacturing v. Reynolds,*[46] the tenant Dutchman, a manufacturer of recreational trailers, left scaffolding in Chapman's building after the lease termination. Keystone leased Chapman's buildings and acknowledged receipt of the scaffolding from Dutchman. Later Reynolds, a Keystone employee, suffered a broken neck when the scaffolding broke loose from its mountings. The scaffolding was deemed defective because of, among other reasons, Dutchman's "improper welding procedure" during installation of the scaffolding. The Indiana Supreme Court, in denying Dutchman's motion for summary judgment, ruled that the scaffolding was a chattel since Dutchman did not abandon it, nor did Chapman accept it as fixture and therefore part of its realty. Instead, Dutchman conveyed it as a chattel to Keystone. Furthermore, the court stated that Dutchman, as a supplier of a chattel, had a duty of care under tort law to prevent foreseeable risk of harm to subsequent users, including Reynolds.

If there is any doubt about a tenant's right to remove a fixture, the matter should be negotiated, and an appropriate clause should be inserted in the lease. Landlords often include a clause to the effect that "all the improvements, alterations, repairs, and additions" must remain for the benefit of the landlord. However, in a number of decisions, the courts have strictly interpreted those terms.

For instance, in one case in which a lease contained the clause in the previous paragraph, a landlord sued a tenant for damages after the tenant had removed an ornamental mahogany partition and a showcase. The court held for the tenant on the grounds that terms such as *improvements* and *additions* normally refer to changes in the structure of the premises and not to trade fixtures that the tenant has installed.[47]

collateral
Property that is pledged as security for the satisfaction of a debt. Collateral is additional security for performance of principal obligation.

Disputes Arising in Fixture Financing   When fixtures are used as **collateral** to secure a loan, special problems may arise for those involved in the financing arrangements. For example, Dawn obtained a loan to buy a car and pledged the vehicle to the lender as collateral. If Dawn does not make her payments, the lender will have the right to take ownership and possession of its collateral, the car. The lender can sell the car and use the proceeds of the sale to reduce Dawn's debt.

Three basic conflicts frequently occur when fixtures are used as collateral to secure a debt. In the *first* situation, a lender (mortgagee) makes a mortgage loan on a house; the property owner (mortgagor) later installs appliances, air conditioning, and other fixtures on the property. This is called the case of "Mortgagor v. Mortgagee." In the *second* situation, the property owner borrows money to purchase and install kitchen cabinets or other fixtures in her home, and the fixtures are used as collateral. This is called the case of "Owner v. Secured Party." These two situations cause little legal difficulty, as illustrated by the following examples. The *third* situation is more complex. In this situation, both the mortgage lender and the secured party claim an interest in the fixtures. This is called the case of "Secured Party v. Other Creditors."

The Case of Mortgagor v. Mortgagee

When Clyde decided to buy a house, he borrowed $120,000 from a local bank to finance his purchase and gave the bank a mortgage on the house. In legal terms, Clyde became a mortgagor and his lender, First Bank, the mortgagee. Shortly after Clyde moved into the house, he made a number of improvements, including the installation of a built-in oven. Under state law, the oven was considered a fixture. After one year, Clyde defaulted on his mortgage payments. That is, he failed to make his payments as promised in the note and mortgage. The First Bank foreclosed and took title to Clyde's house at the foreclosure sale. Does the mortgage cover not only the real estate as it existed when the mortgage was made but also the fixtures added after execution of the mortgage? As a general rule, the mortgage covers later additions to the real estate.[48] This conclusion is often fortified by language in the mortgage, generally called the *after-acquired title clause*, declaring that all things annexed to the real estate at the time the mortgage is signed or annexed to the property afterward will be security for repayment of the loan.

The Case of Owner v. Secured Party

Mary owned her own home, which was not mortgaged. She decided to improve it by installing new kitchen cabinets, which were considered fixtures under state law. Mary borrowed money from the Friendly Finance Company to finance her purchase. She gave the company a security interest in the cabinets by executing a security agreement and financing statement in favor of Friendly Finance. Later, when she defaulted on her loan payments, Friendly Finance claimed that it had the right to repossess the cabinets. Is repossession of the fixtures allowed? The answer is found in the law of "secured transactions," which is governed by Article 9 of the UCC. Article 9 is used with some variation in all of the states.[49] **Attachment of the security interest** is the process by which a lender such as Friendly Finance acquires a security interest in personal property or in a fixture such as Mary's cabinets.

Attachment of the security interest often occurs when sellers are lenders. For example, retailers such as Sears and Wal-Mart often agree to finance transactions as an incentive for consumers to buy from their stores. The Code defines a **security interest** as "an interest in personal property or fixtures which secures payment or performance of an obligation." The lender's security interest, therefore, gives the lender rights to certain property in the event that the borrower does not make her promised payment. A secured transaction can include the so-called conditional sale, in which the seller delivers goods to a buyer but retains title until payment has been received.

The secured transaction can also result in the seller or lender having a **purchase money security interest** (PMSI) in *two* situations. *First*, a seller, such as Sears, can finance the sale by accepting a deposit from the buyer on the goods being sold and expecting to receive the balance of the purchase price over time. Sears would retain a PMSI in the goods being sold to secure payment of the price. *Second*, when any lender, such as Friendly Finance, takes a security interest in goods that are purchased with the loan, the interest is also a PMSI. In both purchase money situations, the lender or seller *provides the money* to make the purchase.

Two methods are used to create the security interest, both related to who actually possesses the collateral. Using the *first* method, the debtor may sign a written **security agreement**, such

---

attachment of the security interest

The process by which a secured party acquires a security interest in personal property or a fixture.

security interest

An interest in personal property or fixtures that secures payment or performance of an obligation.

purchase money security interest

A security interest taken by a lender or retained by a seller to secure all or part of the price of goods purchased by the borrower.

security agreement

An agreement that creates a security interest.

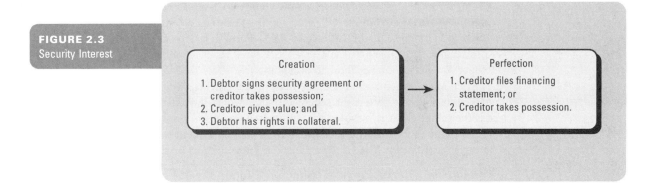

FIGURE 2.3
Security Interest

Creation
1. Debtor signs security agreement or creditor takes possession;
2. Creditor gives value; and
3. Debtor has rights in collateral.

Perfection
1. Creditor files financing statement; or
2. Creditor takes possession.

---

perfection of the security interest
In secured transactions law, the process whereby a security interest is protected, as far as the law permits, against competing claims to the collateral, which usually requires the secured party to give public notice of the interest as by filing in a government office (for example, in the secretary of state's office). Perfection of a security interest deals with those steps legally required to give a secured party a superior interest in subject property against debtor's creditors.

fixture filing
The filing of a financing statement in the real estate public record to perfect the security interest in a fixture.

financing statement
A document filed in the public record to give notice to third parties of the secured party's security interest.

as a PMSI, that contains language indicating that a security interest is being created and a description of the collateral. The debtor can then take possession of the goods he has just financed. If the interest covers crops, oil, gas, minerals to be extracted, or timber to be cut, a description of the real estate is also included.

With the *second* method of creating a security interest, either the creditor lending the money or the seller financing the sale takes or retains possession of the goods. Regardless of which party has actual possession of the goods, three requirements must be met: (1) there must be an agreement between the debtor and the creditor; (2) the creditor must give value (for example, loaning money to the debtor); and (3) the debtor must have rights in the collateral, such as legal title to the goods purchased. (See Figure 2.3.)

In recent years, the law governing how to execute the security agreement has been revised. The change involves the manner in which the security agreement is "authenticated." It can still be accomplished by having the parties sign the agreement, as is done traditionally. However, now a security agreement can be executed by creating an electronic record. In this case, the debtor does not actually sign the security agreement, but authenticates it with a symbol or an encryption that identifies the debtor and indicates that he has accepted the agreement.

Perfection of the security interest is the process whereby a secured party such as Friendly Finance or Sears establishes priority over the potential claims of third parties. While the security interest, created through the process of attachment, gives the creditor rights against the debtor, the creditor should also "perfect" the security interest to gain priority against third parties, such as other creditors, including existing and future mortgagees, or good faith purchasers of the goods. Perfection of the security interest is important, therefore, in the event another creditor or a purchaser also claims a right to the collateral.

Creditors can perfect a security interest in several ways. For example, they can simply take possession of the collateral until the loan is paid off. This is essentially how pawnshops work. In other cases, perfection is automatic when a person buys consumer goods, such as a stereo or television, for personal, family, or household purposes, and a PMSI is created. For fixtures, however, the more common method is a procedure known as **fixture filing**. This involves filing a **financing statement**. The reason for requiring possession or filing is to give public notice to third parties that the creditor is claiming a security interest in the collateral. Generally, all filings to perfect security interests must be made at a central filing location, which is likely to be the secretary of state's office. All real property–related security agreements, such as those pertaining to fixtures, must also be filed in the local real estate records office, which is the register of deeds office in the county in which the real property is located. The financing statement filed in the office of the register of deeds should contain the (1) names of the debtors and secured parties, (2) the debtor's signature, (3) the address of the secured party, (4) the debtor's mailing address, (5) a description of the fixture that serves as the collateral, and (6) a description of the real property. Filing the financing statement provides notice to those claiming an interest in the real estate. UCC Form 1 is a form typically used for filing in the public record. (For UCC Form 1, see www.cengagebrain.com [see page xix in the Preface for instructions on how to access the free study tools for this text].)

After Mary has installed the cabinets in her kitchen, whether or not the security interest has been perfected, the secured creditor would have the right to physically repossess the cabinets if it is assumed that other creditors claim no interest in them. The creditor's right to repossession is established by Mary's agreement to give the security interest. This right exists even though the cabinets are now fixtures firmly attached to her walls.

The Case of Secured Party v. Other Creditors   The first two cases involved competing claims to fixtures by the owner of real estate against either a mortgagee creditor or a secured party creditor. Now you will examine a situation involving a direct conflict between the secured party and the mortgagee. Assume that Sam's Air Conditioning and Repair Co., a dealer, sells an air conditioner to Pete on an installment basis and takes a security interest. The air conditioner, when placed in Pete's home, becomes a fixture. What must Sam, the secured party, do to gain a priority claim to the air conditioner over Pete's bank, the Second National Bank, which holds a mortgage on the property, or to gain priority over a subsequent purchaser of Pete's house who might also claim the air conditioner?

You can begin to solve this problem by looking at Section 9-102(41) of the UCC. This section defines fixtures as goods that have "become so related to particular real estate that an interest in them arises under real estate law." However, this provision does not apply to ordinary building materials that have been incorporated into a structure or into other improvements on land. The following discussion addresses the legal status of a class of personal property, such as Pete's air conditioner, that has become real estate for certain purposes but as to which chattel financing may be preserved.

Under Section 9-334, the secured party, Sam, has priority over mortgagees and other interests in four situations:

1. If Sam has a PMSI and he perfects by a fixture filing within twenty days after the good (in this case, the air conditioner) becomes a fixture, he will prevail over *existing* mortgages.[50] As noted previously, a fixture filing is a filing of the financing statement in the same office in which mortgages are recorded. There is an important exception to this rule, however. Sam does *not* have priority over a prior recorded **construction mortgage** if the good, such as Pete's air conditioner, becomes a fixture before construction is completed. A construction mortgage is given to secure a loan that is used to construct an improvement on the land. The rationale for this exception, sometimes called the *construction mortgage exception*, is that the construction lender is funding the improvements to real estate and expects the construction loan to be secured by those improvements. Fixture lenders who do not want to risk losing their rights to repossess a fixture to construction mortgagees need to obtain an agreement from construction lenders to **subordinate**. Through this agreement, construction lenders allow the fixture lenders to take priority over the construction lenders' rights.

2. A security interest that is perfected by a fixture filing has priority over interests recorded (or acquired by legal proceedings) at a later date.

3. If the fixtures are readily removable factory or office machines or replacements of appliances that are consumer goods, a security interest perfected before the goods become fixtures will prevail over other real estate interests such as mortgages.

4. A secured party will prevail in all cases over other interests if the person owning those interests consents in writing to the security interest.

construction mortgage
A mortgage used to finance the construction or improvement of real property.

subordinate
The process by which one creditor gives up rights to another creditor.

TABLE 2.3 Summary of the Disputes That Arise with Fixture Financing

DISPUTE	FACTS OF DISPUTE	WHO OWNS THE FIXTURE?	APPLICABLE LAW
Case of Mortgagor v. Mortgagee	Clyde finances home with First Bank and buys and installs built-in oven. Defaults on mortgage	Mortgagee—First Bank	State law and After-Acquired Title clause in mortgage
Case of Owner v. Secured Party	Mary owns home, finances purchase of kitchen cabinets with Friendly Finance and defaults	Secured Party—Friendly Finance	UCC Article 9
Case of Secured Party v. Other Creditors	Pete finances home with Second National Bank, then finances air conditioner with Sam's Air Conditioning and Repair	Secured Party—Sam's Air Conditioning and Repair	UCC Article 9*

*If construction mortgage, mortgagee takes priority over secured party of fixture.

If a party pays off the debt owed for the purchase of a fixture that has been perfected, the secured creditor is bound under the UCC to file a statement in the public record. This is done with a standard form used in every state. For fixtures, the form would be filed in the same place where the financing statement was originally filed, such as in the county where the real estate is located. If the lender fails to do so, the debtor may also file a statement. Moreover, the UCC provides that recorded financial statements are effective for only five years. Terminating financing statements can be very important once owners contract to sell their real estate since a financing statement on a fixture that is not terminated would appear as a cloud on the title and may delay the sale.[51] Title issues like this will be discussed in detail in Chapter 8.

Lewiston Bottled Gas sold ninety air conditioning units on credit to Grand Beach Inn. Key Bank had a prior recorded mortgage on the inn's property. The case of *Lewiston Bottled Gas v. Key Bank* on page 47 resolves whether the purchase money seller of the air conditioning units or the bank had first priority in the units.

END OF CHAPTER CASE

ETHICAL AND PUBLIC POLICY ISSUES

Should Lenders Pay Defaulting Parties *Not* to Steal or Destroy Fixtures?

The severe economic recession and housing crisis of 2007–2009 resulted in real property values plummeting, which contributed to mass foreclosures. Some economically strained and resentful property owners, particularly in hard hit states like Arizona, California, Florida and Nevada, reacted by ripping out and taking valuable fixtures including plumbing, cabinets, marble countertops, and light fixtures from their homes before the banks could take ownership. Others even vandalized their homes. To avert these problems, some lenders offered to pay the defaulting parties up to $2,000 to leave their homes intact in a program they called "Cash for Keys." Since destroyed properties can cost much more than $2,000 to restore, the expenditure was viewed as a prudent policy. Should people be paid to *not* commit harmful criminal and civil acts?[52]

wrongful annexation

The illegal attaching or merging of one thing to another.

Disputes Occurring in Wrongful or Mistaken Annexation   The typical **wrongful annexation** case arises when the owner of a fixture wants to recover it because it has been affixed to someone else's real estate without his permission. The following Montana case illustrates the general rule.

A CASE IN POINT

In *Eisenhauer v. Quinn,*[53] Gerarci owned a house that was being moved to a new location. Smith stole the house, placed it on his own lot, and then sold the house and lot to an innocent third party, Eisenhauer. When Gerarci sued to recover the house, now in the custody of Sheriff Quinn, the court ruled that "one of the elementary rules of the law of fixtures is that a chattel, to become an irremovable fixture, must have been annexed to the realty by the owner of the fixture, or with his consent...." The court held that Gerarci did not lose title to his property by Smith's devious actions.

This rule is not followed in cases where personal property has lost its identity by incorporation, such as when stolen brick or timber is used to build a house. In such a case, it would be economically wasteful to allow the owner to destroy the house to recover the brick and timber. Consequently, the better rule would limit the owner to recovery of damages.[54]

A different situation arises when innocent people mistakenly attach their personal property to real estate owned by someone else (**mistaken annexation**). The most expensive of these mistakes occurs when a person builds a house on the wrong lot as the following Florida case demonstrates.

mistaken annexation

The mistaken attachment of personal property to real property owned by someone else.

A CASE IN POINT

In *Brown v. Davis,*[55] the surveyor erroneously subdivided tract 17 instead of tract 16. Due to the surveyor's mistake, Davis, thinking he was building his home on tract 16, mistakenly built his home on tract 17 instead. The Florida Supreme Court ruled that an exchange of deeds was an appropriate remedy to resolve the dispute between Brown and Davis when the owner of one lot mistakenly constructed a dwelling on the adjacent owner's lot.

Courts have adopted a variety of approaches in such situations, but in the absence of a statute, many courts allow the innocent party to recover the value of the improvement to the real estate. In fact, a number of states have enacted statutes that provide relief to the innocent party in certain situations. For instance, in Ohio, a person who purchases property at an execution sale or a tax sale and who makes lasting improvements on the property is entitled to reimbursement from a person who is able to prove better title.[56] As a last resort, where the circumstances permit, a court may order an exchange of the improved property for an undeveloped lot.

CASES

Concept of Property

IN RE MARRIAGE OF GRAHAM
194 Colo. 429, 574 P.2d 75 (1978)

LEE, Justice. This case presents the novel question of whether in a marriage dissolution proceeding a master's degree in business administration (M.B.A.) constitutes marital property which is subject to division by the court. In its opinion in *Graham v. Graham,* the Colorado Court of Appeals held that it was not. We affirm the judgment.

The Uniform Dissolution of Marriage Act requires that a court shall divide marital property, without regard to marital misconduct, in such proportions as the court deems just after considering all relevant factors. The Act defines marital property as follows:

"For purposes of this article only, 'marital property' means all property acquired by either spouse subsequent to the marriage except:

(a) Property acquired by gift, bequest, devise, or descent;

(b) Property acquired in exchange for property acquired prior to the marriage or in exchange for property acquired by gift, bequest, devise, or descent;

(c) Property acquired by a spouse after a decree of legal separation; and

(d) Property excluded by valid agreement of the parties."

The parties to this proceeding were married on August 5, 1968, in Denver, Colorado. Throughout the six-year marriage, Anne P. Graham, wife and petitioner here, was employed full-time as an airline stewardess. She is still so employed. Her husband, Dennis J. Graham, respondent, worked part-time for most of the marriage, although his main pursuit was his education. He attended school for approximately three and one-half years of the marriage, acquiring both a bachelor of science degree in engineering physics and a master's degree in business administration at the University of Colorado. Following graduation, he obtained a job as an executive assistant with a large corporation at a starting salary of $14,000 per year.

The trial court determined that during the marriage petitioner contributed seventy percent of the financial support, which was used both for family expenses and for her husband's education. No marital assets were accumulated during the marriage. In addition, the Grahams together managed an apartment house and petitioner did the majority of housework and cooked most of the meals for the couple. No children were born during the marriage.

The parties jointly filed a petition for dissolution, on February 4, 1974, in the Boulder County District Court. Petitioner did not make a claim for maintenance or for attorney fees.

After a hearing on October 24, 1974, the trial court found, as a matter of law, that an education obtained by one spouse during a marriage is jointly-owned property to which the other spouse has a property right. The future earnings value of the M.B.A. to respondent was evaluated at $82,836 and petitioner was awarded $33,134 of this amount, payable in monthly installments of $100. The court of appeals reversed, holding that an education is not itself "property" subject to division under the Act, although it was one factor to be considered in determining maintenance or in arriving at an equitable property division.

* * *

The legislature intended the term "property" to be broadly inclusive, as indicated by its use of the qualifying adjective "all" in section 14-10-113(2). Previous Colorado cases have given "property" a comprehensive meaning, as typified by the following definition: "In short it embraces anything and everything which may belong to a man and in the ownership of which he has a right to be protected by law."

Nonetheless, there are necessary limits upon what may be considered "property," and we do not find any indication in the Act that the concept as used by the legislature is other than that usually understood to be embodied within the term. One helpful definition is "everything that has an exchangeable value or which goes to make up wealth or estate." *Black's Law Dictionary* 1382 (rev. 4th ed. 1968).

* * *

An educational degree, such as an M.B.A., is simply not encompassed even by the broad views of the concept of "property." It does not have an exchange value or any objective transferable value on an open market. It is personal to the holder. It terminates on death of the holder and is not inheritable. It cannot be assigned, sold, transferred, conveyed, or pledged. An advanced degree is a cumulative product of many years of previous education, combined with diligence and hard work. It may not be acquired by the mere expenditure of money. It is simply an intellectual achievement that may potentially assist in the future acquisition of property. In our view, it has none of the attributes of property in the usual sense of that term.

Our interpretation is in accord with cases in other jurisdictions. We have been unable to find any decision, even in community property states, which appears to have held that an education of one spouse is marital property to be divided on dissolution. This contention was dismissed in *Todd v. Todd,* 78 Cal.Rptr. 131 (Ct.App.), where it was held that a law degree is not a community property asset capable of division, partly because it "cannot have monetary value placed upon it." Similarly, it has been recently held that a person's earning capacity, even where enhanced by a law degree financed by the other spouse, "should not be recognized as a separate, particular item of property." *Stern v. Stern,* 331 A.2d 257.

* * *

A spouse who provides financial support while the other spouse acquires an education is not without a remedy. Where there is marital property to be divided, such contribution to the education of the other spouse may be taken into consideration by the court. Here, we again note that no marital property had been accumulated by the parties. Further, if maintenance is sought and a need is demonstrated, the trial court may make an award based on all relevant factors. Certainly, among the relevant factors to be considered is the contribution of the spouse seeking maintenance to the education of the other spouse from whom the maintenance is sought. Again, we note that in this case petitioner sought no maintenance from respondent.

The judgment is affirmed.

[Author's Note: The ruling of *In re Marriage of Graham* reflects the general rule: courts do not treat degrees as marital property. Still, many states, as in this case, take into account the contributions that one spouse may have made to the education of the other when the marital property is divided upon divorce. The one notable exception is found in the case of *O'Brien v. O'Brien,* 66 N.Y.2d 576, 498 N.Y.S.2d 743, 489 N.E.2d 712 (1985), a New York case in which a husband's medical degree was considered to be marital property.[57]]

Misclassification of Fixtures as Personal Property
EX PARTE BROWN
485 So. 2d 762 (Ala. 1986)

WRIGHT, Judge. Ruby and Louis Brown were divorced by decree of the Lauderdale County Circuit Court in November 1983. As part of this decree, the husband was awarded the family home, "including all fixtures and realty appurtenant thereto." The wife was awarded all furniture in the home with the exception of the master bedroom suite, the dining room furniture, kitchen appliances and one-half of all silver, silverware and other kitchenware, which was awarded to the husband. The wife was to remove all of the furniture and personal property awarded to her prior to relinquishing possession of the home. In February 1984, the husband filed a petition with the circuit court asking that the wife be found to be in contempt for violating the property settlement provisions of the divorce decree. In May 1985, the court issued an order which specifically stated:

> "The evidence shows that under the decree of divorce the Plaintiff [husband] was awarded certain items of personal property which the Defendant [wife] removed from the Plaintiff's home: a microwave of the value of $400.00 and a refrigerator of the value of $500.00. Further, the plaintiff was awarded the family home and there was attached thereto a bookcase and china cabinets of the value of $2,000.00 which the Defendant removed from the home. Therefore, the Plaintiff was deprived of real and personal property of the value of $2,900.00 and the Defendant's action in removing these items is [a] violation of the decree and a contempt of the Court."

For her contempt, the court ordered the wife to serve ten days in the county jail, allowing, however, that she could purge herself of the contempt by making a payment of $2,900.00 to the Clerk of the Circuit Court of Lauderdale County. Thereafter, the wife filed this petition for certiorari asking that we review this finding of contempt.

* * *

We are perplexed by the wife's first argument for reversal. She admits that she acted in contempt of the court's order when she removed the microwave and refrigerator from the home, but argues that the bookcase and china cabinets were not fixtures appurtenant to the home and thus could be removed by her as furniture.

* * *

"A 'fixture' is an article that was once a chattel, but which, by being physically annexed or affixed to realty, has become accessory to it and 'part and parcel' of it. Whether an article is a fixture is a determination that must be made on the particular circumstances of each case. The supreme court has articulated the criteria to be used in making this determination as follows:

"(1) Actual annexation to the realty or to something appurtenant thereto; (2) Appropriateness to the use or purposes of that part of the realty with which it is connected; (3) The intention of the party making the annexation of making permanent attachment to the freehold. This intention of the party making the annexation is inferred; (a) From the nature of the articles annexed; (b) The relation of the party making the annexation; (c) The structure and mode of annexation; (d) The purposes and uses for which the annexation has been made." Id. (quoting Langston v. State, 96 Ala. 44, 11 So. 334 (1891)).

In her own testimony, the wife revealed that the articles had all been custom-built for the express purpose of being used with the family house, not just to be used in any house. All of the articles were anchored to the walls, and the china cabinets were each set into a permanent base. Under our limited scope of review, we cannot say that this testimony does not support a finding that the articles were intended to be fixtures, "part and parcel" of the house.

We are of the opinion that the trial court has not committed error in finding that the wife acted in contempt of the divorce decree. Further, her sentence of ten days in jail, with the opportunity to purge her contempt by paying to the clerk $2,900, is not unconstitutional.

The decision of the trial court is affirmed.

Fixture Tests: Intention of the Parties
ADAMSON V. SIMS
85 Ark. App. 278, 151 S.W.3d 23 (2004)

MAUZEY, Judge. Following a bench trial, appellant Don Adamson was held liable for conversion of an airplane hangar that the Jimmy B. Sims Farm, Inc., Pension Trust claimed to own. The Trust was awarded $10,000 in compensatory damages. On appeal, appellant argues that the trial court erred in finding him liable for conversion. We agree and reverse and remand.

The hangar in question was located on the Cottonwood Plantation in Lonoke County. It was constructed approximately thirty years ago by John McRae for the purpose of housing his personal airplane. In June 2001, McRae decided to sell his airplane. He contacted appellant and orally conveyed the hangar to him in exchange for appellant's repairing and selling the plane. Appellant's plan was to disassemble the hangar, move it to his own airstrip, and erect it there. He expected it to cost him $3,000.

On August 31, 2001, appellee purchased the Cottonwood Plantation from the Mary S. Pemberton Trust for approximately two million dollars. The purchase price included all attached fixtures and equipment. Trustee Jimmy Sims would later testify that he understood the price to include the hangar; he apparently had no knowledge that McRae had sold the hangar to appellant.

In late December 2001, appellant and several other workmen arrived at the Plantation with lifting equipment, a trailer, and other tools and began dismantling the hangar. However, after the structure had been partially disassembled, Jimmy Sims protested, claiming that the hangar was owned by appellee. Appellant eventually left the hangar partially torn down.

On March 27, 2002, appellee sued appellant for trespass and for conversion of the hangar, and appellant counterclaimed for conversion of the hangar. The trial court ruled in appellee's favor on the conversion count and awarded it $10,000 in damages. Appellant appeals from that verdict.

* * *

The key issue on appeal is whether the hangar is a fixture. If it is a fixture, it is owned by appellee by virtue of its purchase of the Cottonwood Plantation; if it is not a fixture, it is owned by appellant as his personal chattel. The trial court determined that the hangar was a fixture based on the following findings: 1) John McRae was a beneficiary of the Pemberton Trust and constructed the hangar for the Trust's benefit; 2) the hangar was affixed and annexed to the Plantation realty; 3) there was no agreement between McRae and the Pemberton Trust as to ownership of the hangar.

Appellant first challenges the trial court's finding that McRae constructed the hangar for the benefit of the Pemberton Trust.

* * *

Appellant argues that the trial court's finding is erroneous on this point, and we agree.

The court's finding was based on testimony by Joe Pennington, the farm manager for the Pemberton Trust, that McRae was a "minority" beneficiary of the Trust and had managed the Plantation sometime before 1998. However, no further evidence was adduced regarding McRae's relationship to the Pemberton Trust or any benefit that the Trust enjoyed in the hangar. By contrast, there was considerable evidence that the hangar had not been constructed for the Trust's benefit. McRae, who did not testify at trial, signed a written memo on March 1, 2002, in which he stated that he had personally paid for the hangar and had built it "over twenty years ago for $9,000." Pennington testified that McRae had constructed the hangar thirty years earlier for storage of McRae's airplane; that it was Pennington's understanding that the hangar was not the Pemberton Trust's property; that McRae had insured and maintained the hangar; that Pennington never expended any Trust money to maintain the hangar and did not insure it, although the Trust insured other buildings on the Plantation; that the Pemberton trustee, Marilyn Houston (McRae's sister), was aware that the Trust was not insuring the hangar; and that the trustee never instructed Pennington to exercise any dominion or control over the hangar. On January 4, 2002, after the controversy in this case began, Pennington wrote a letter to appellee stating that the hangar had been paid for thirty years ago by McRae, was used to shelter McRae's airplane, and that insurance coverage for the hangar was paid for by McRae and "not included under the farm's other insurance coverage."

The evidence points inescapably to the conclusion that McRae, Pennington, and the trustee were all of the opinion that the hangar belonged to McRae and was of no interest to the Trust. The trial court therefore erred in finding that the hangar was built for the Trust's benefit.

* * *

We turn now to appellant's argument that the trial judge erred in characterizing the hangar as a fixture. The question of whether particular property constitutes a fixture is sometimes one of fact only but usually is a mixed question of law and fact. A fixture has been defined by our supreme court as property, originally a personal chattel, that has been affixed to the soil or to a structure legally a part of the soil and, being affixed or attached to the realty, has become a part of the realty. It is annexed to the freehold for use in connection therewith and so arranged that it cannot be removed without injury to the freehold. The courts have devised a three-part test to determine whether an article is a fixture: (1) whether it is annexed to the realty; (2) whether it is appropriate and adapted to the use or purpose of that part of the realty to which it is connected; (3) whether the party making the annexation intended to make it permanent. The third factor—the intention of the party who made the annexation—is considered of primary importance. The courts use an objective test to arrive at the annexer's intention.

On the first factor, there is proof on both sides as to whether the hangar was annexed to the realty. The evidence shows that the hangar was a large building constructed of metal trusses with two-by-four girds and purlins and metal siding attached to the wood with nails. The structure was bolted to a concrete slab, although the slab covered only a part of the surface of the hangar. Jimmy Sims testified that it would be difficult to move the structure without completely damaging it. On the other hand, appellant said that he had no doubt about being able to move the hangar, and he said that he could move it without damaging the real property. He testified that the metal trusses were bolted into concrete footers and that, after removing the outside sheeting, he could remove the trusses by holding them with a cherry picker and unbolting them. At the time he was ordered off the property, he and his crew had worked about nine hours dismantling the building. At that point, he had removed about three-fourths of the sheeting from the roof and half from the walls.

* * *

A structure was also ruled a fixture in *Dobbins v. Lacefield,* 35 Ark.App. 24, 811 S.W.2d 334 (1991), where a canopy was set in concrete with underground cables and gasoline tanks were placed in 20-foot-by-30-foot holes that were 10 feet deep and could be removed only by a backhoe, and in *Barron v. Barron,* 1 Ark.App. 323, 615 S.W.2d 394 (1981), where grain-storage bins and a shop building were set in deep concrete and the cost of moving and reassembling a new bin would cost as much as buying a new one. In contrast, mobile homes were held not to be fixtures even though they had been placed on concrete foundations with extensive modifications and had no tongues, axles, or wheels.

* * *

We distinguish this case from [others] … in which large structures were held to be fixtures. In each of those cases, strong evidence of the annexing party's intention to treat the structure as chattel was lacking. In the case at bar, there was considerable evidence, as set out earlier in this opinion, that McRae, the annexing party, intended to treat the structure as personalty. Further, there was equally strong evidence that the owner of the realty, the Pemberton Trust, shared that intention. Thus, the third factor in the test, which is the factor of primary importance, operates in favor of appellant. As in *Pledger v. Halvorson, supra,* the intention of the parties, being the crucial consideration, should govern.

The second factor in the fixture test also works in favor of appellant. Although the hangar was contiguous to an airstrip that was owned by the Pemberton Trust, there is no evidence that the hangar or airstrip was used in connection with Trust business or that the Trust derived any significant benefit from them. In fact, the airstrip was leased by McRae for the minimal amount of $600 per year.

In light of the foregoing, we reverse the trial court's decision and hold that the hangar was not a fixture. Our decision makes it unnecessary to reach appellant's third argument, that the trial court used an incorrect measure of damages.

Reversed and remanded with directions to enter a finding that the hangar is not a fixture and that it is the property of appellant.

Fixture Tests/Trade Fixtures
MICHIGAN NATIONAL BANK V. LANSING
96 Mich.App. 551, 293 N.W.2d 626 (1980)

J. H. GILLIS, P. J. This is an appeal from a Michigan Tax Tribunal order affirming six real property assessments made by the respondent on certain items of petitioner's property. Five of the assessments concern properties owned by the petitioner and one of the assessments involves property leased by the petitioner. The matter in dispute is whether certain items of bank equipment, specifically, bank vault door, night depository equipment, drive-up teller window equipment and remote transaction systems, are subject to assessment and taxation as real property or whether they are items of personal property which are exempt from taxation under MCL 211.9(m).

In an opinion dated February 14, 1979, the Tax Tribunal affirmed the assessments holding that each of the items was subject to assessment and taxation as real property. The petitioner appeals from that determination as of right.

* * *

For the purpose of taxation, real property includes "all lands within the state, and all buildings and fixtures thereon." Petitioner contends that the Tribunal erred as a matter of law in concluding that the items were fixtures. We disagree.

The test to be applied in order to ascertain whether or not an item is a fixture emphasizes three factors:

1. Annexation to the realty, either actual or constructive;
2. Adaptation or application to the use or purpose of that part of the realty to which it is connected or appropriated; and
3. Intention to make the article a permanent accession to the realty. The intention which controls is that manifested by the objective, visible facts. The permanence required is not equated with perpetuity. It is sufficient if the item is intended to remain where affixed until worn out, until the purpose to which the realty is devoted is accomplished or until the item is superseded by another item more suitable for the purpose.

Applying these factors to the present case necessitates the conclusion that the Tribunal properly found the items in question to be fixtures. All four items are physically annexed to the realty. The night depository equipment, drive-up window equipment, and the vault doors are all cemented into place. Once installed, they are integrated with and become part of the wall in which they are mounted. The remote transaction units are also physically integrated with the land and the buildings. Such a unit consists of a roof-type canopy supported by pillars which extends from the building wall or roof over the customer unit. The customer unit is mounted with steel bolts to a specially constructed concrete island. A pneumatic tube system runs either up into the canopy or down into the ground and then into the building.

Furthermore, each item is adapted to the use of the realty. In fact, not only is the present use of these buildings dependent on the presence of these items, none of these items can be used unless they are affixed to a building or land.

Taken together, these factors establish the petitioner's intent to permanently affix these items to the realty. The Tribunal did not err in classifying them as fixtures. As fixtures they are real property under MCL 211.2.

The petitioner further contends that, even if these items are found to be fixtures, they are trade fixtures and as such are classified as personal property which is exempt from taxation. A trade fixture is merely a fixture which has been annexed to leased realty by a lessee for the purpose of enabling him to engage in a business. The trade fixture doctrine permits the lessee, upon the termination of the lease, to remove such a fixture from the lessor's real property. With respect to the lessee's right of removal, a trade fixture is characterized as personalty. The doctrine by its terms applies only in lessor-lessee situations. Accordingly, the petitioner cannot contend, with respect to the five involved properties which are owned, that the doctrine operates to exempt the items in question from taxation as personalty.

One of the involved properties, however, is leased by the petitioner. With respect to that property, the question remains whether the trade fixture doctrine operates to render the disputed items which are annexed thereto exempt from taxation. The answer is that it does not. The rule regarding trade fixtures which arose out of commercial necessity for the limited purpose of protecting tenants in the ownership of certain kinds of property has no application between other parties in other relationships. Although as between lessor and lessee trade fixtures might be personal property, as to third parties they are properly considered as a part of the realty. Thus, for the purpose of taxation, trade fixtures are properly classified as real property. The petitioner's contention that the Tribunal erred in not applying the trade fixture doctrine to the instant case is, accordingly, without merit.

In summary, the Tax Tribunal neither made an error of law nor applied a wrong principle in concluding that the items in question were properly taxed as realty. Its decision is therefore affirmed.

Fixture Financing
LEWISTON BOTTLED GAS V. KEY BANK
601 A.2d 91 (Me. 1992)

CLIFFORD, Justice. * * * In July 1986, Key Bank loaned $2,580,000 to William J. DiBiase, Jr. The loan was secured by a mortgage on the real estate owned by DiBiase located on East Grand Avenue in Old Orchard Beach. The mortgage, which covered after-acquired fixtures, was properly recorded in the York County Registry of Deeds. On June 10, 1987, DiBiase incorporated Grand Beach Inn, Inc. (Grand Beach) for the purpose of constructing and operating the Grand Beach Inn on DiBiase's East Grand Avenue property. DiBiase was the president and sole shareholder of Grand Beach and at all relevant times was the owner of the property.

On June 15, 1987, Grand Beach contracted to purchase ninety heating and air-conditioning units from LBG [Lewiston Bottled Gas]. The contract provided that the units would remain the personal property of Grand Beach notwithstanding their attachment to the real property. On June 16, Grand Beach granted to LBG a purchase money security interest in the ninety units. Financing statements disclosing the security interest and identifying the debtor as "Grand Beach Inn, Inc., William J. DiBiase, Jr., President" and describing the real estate upon which the units were located as "Grand Beach Inn, East Grand Avenue, Old Orchard Beach, ME 04064" were filed with the Secretary of State and also recorded in the York County Registry of Deeds. In each place, they were indexed under the name "Grand Beach Inn, Inc." Nothing, however, was indexed under DiBiase's name. In September and October 1987, the units were installed in the exterior walls of each room in the Inn.

On June 29, 1987, Key Bank made a second loan to DiBiase secured by a second mortgage on the same property, also covering after-acquired fixtures and also properly recorded. The title search undertaken by Key Bank in the York County Registry of Deeds prior to the execution of the mortgage failed to disclose the financing statement and the existence of LBG's security interest in the units because LBG's financing statement was indexed under the name "Grand Beach" even though DiBiase was the record owner of the property at the time.

In May 1989, Key Bank foreclosed on both its mortgages. LBG was not joined as a party-in-interest because Key Bank was unaware of LBG's interest in the units until after the foreclosure was commenced. The parties agreed to allow the foreclosure to proceed and to litigate the issue of title to the heating and air-conditioning units later. Key Bank was the successful bidder at the foreclosure sale. LBG then filed the present complaint against Key Bank seeking a declaratory judgment that its purchase money security interest in the units had priority over the interest of Key Bank. The Superior Court granted summary judgment to Key Bank concluding that the heating and air-conditioning units were fixtures and that Key Bank's properly recorded mortgages had priority over LBG's unperfected security interest. This appeal followed.

* * *

Section 9-313(1)(a) [Author's Note: Under revised Article 9, Section 9-313(1)(a) is now Section 9-102(41).] provides that "[g]oods are 'fixtures' when they become so related to particular real estate that an interest in them arises under real estate law." That interest arises when the property is (1) physically annexed to the real estate, (2) adapted to the use to which the real estate is put, that is, the personal and real property are united in the carrying out of a common purpose, and (3) annexed with the intent to make it part of the realty.

The evidence compels a conclusion that, under the first prong of the three-part fixture test, the units were physically annexed to the real estate. The heating and air-conditioning units were installed when the Inn was under construction and are part of the walls of the building. The units are attached by bolts and although they could be removed, their removal would create a large hole in the walls of each room.

As to the second prong of the test, it is undisputed that the units, although they are catalogue items and not specially made for the Grand Beach Inn, were adapted to the use of the

real estate as the Grand Beach Inn. The real estate was designed and built as an inn to accommodate overnight guests. The heating and air-conditioning units help create a liveable atmosphere for those guests by providing heat and cooling to the rooms. The personal and real property, therefore, are united in the carrying out of a common enterprise. The fact that the units are catalogue items, and not custom-made, does not preclude them from being fixtures.

The intent of the person annexing the personal property to the real estate is the third and most important of the three prongs of the fixture test. LBG contends that summary judgment was improperly granted to Key Bank because the agreements between DiBiase and LBG granted to LBG a purchase money security interest in the units and expressly stated that the units would remain personal property and therefore demonstrated DiBiase's intent that the units remain personal property. We disagree.

In determining the intent of the parties as to whether a chattel annexed to real estate becomes a fixture, it is not the hidden subjective intent of the person making the annexation that must be considered but rather "the intention which the law deduces from such external facts as the structure and mode of attachment, the purpose and use for which the annexation has been made and the relation and use of the party making it." The agreement DiBiase made with LBG to have the heating and air-conditioning units remain personal property cannot be considered against Key Bank on the fixtures issue because Key Bank was not a party to those agreements and was unaware of them.

The objective manifestation of intent in this case, as evidenced by the physical annexation of the units to the walls of the building and their adaption to the use of the real estate as an inn, leaves no genuine dispute that the units are fixtures and part of the Grand Beach Inn real estate.

Because the heating and air-conditioning units were fixtures and part of the real estate, they became subject to Key Bank's mortgages pursuant to section 9-313. Key Bank's first mortgage takes priority over LBG's security interest in the units unless LBG's security interest falls within one of the exceptions found in section 9-313. The only relevant exception in this case is section 9-313(4)(a), which states:

(4) A perfected security interest in fixtures has priority over the conflicting interest of an encumbrancer or owner of the real estate where:
(a) The security interest is a purchase money security interest, the interest of the encumbrancer or owner arises before the goods become fixtures, the security interest is perfected by a fixture filing before the goods become fixtures or within 10 days thereafter, and the debtor has an interest of record in the real estate or is in possession of the real estate.

[Author's Note: UCC 9-313(4)(a) discussed above is now covered under the revised UCC at Section 9-334(d)(1–3). The major difference between the two provisions is that the security interest can now be perfected if it is done within 20 days instead of 10 days.]

* * *

[The court concluded that LBG's purchase money security interest was not perfected because DiBiase was not identified as the owner of the property. As a result, the court affirmed the lower court's decision that Key Bank's mortgages had priority.]

KEY TERMS

PROBLEMS

1. Clyde lived next door to a funeral parlor. The funeral parlor purchased and installed a large, heavy organ but did not physically attach it to the building in any way. Clyde enjoyed listening to the organ music so much that he purchased and installed an identical organ in his house and bolted the organ to the floor. Are the two organs fixtures? Why or why not?

2. Kloster purchased a piece of real estate. He then moved a barn onto the property and built a house that rested on blocks. Neither the barn nor the house had a foundation, but Kloster never listed the two buildings as personal property for tax purposes. Later the real estate was sold at a tax sale to Nelson. Now Kloster claims that he is entitled to both buildings because he never intended them to become fixtures. Is Kloster or Nelson entitled to the buildings? Why or why not?

3. The Alaska Theater Company leased a movie theater and installed movie projectors, a screen, furnishings for the restrooms, an electric sign, a curtain, and miscellaneous electrical fixtures. May the Alaska Theater Company remove those articles upon termination of the lease? Why or why not?

4. In 1890, Abner leased a country inn for five years. Behind the inn he constructed a brick outhouse on a concrete foundation. He also constructed a wooden storage shed on concrete blocks and nailed one side of the shed to the inn. One week before the lease ended, Abner tore down the outhouse brick by brick and used the brick to build an outhouse at another site. He also removed the storage shed and restored the land under both structures to its original condition. When the landlord learned of Abner's actions, he sued Abner for the value of the buildings. Is Abner liable? Why or why not?

5. Mr. and Mrs. Ott purchased a home in Phoenix that was equipped with a combination heating and cooling system. When they discovered that the system was defective, the Otts sued the builder, claiming a breach of implied warranty that the system was of good, average quality. However, under Arizona law, implied warranties are given by the seller only when personal property is sold. They do not apply to the sale of real estate. Will the Otts win? Why or why not?

6. Smith purchased ranges and refrigerators from Friendly Appliance on a conditional sales contract. Friendly Appliance did everything necessary to create a valid security interest in the appliances but did not perfect its interest. After the appliances were installed, Smith defaulted on his payments. Can Friendly Appliance recover the appliances? Why or why not?

7. Tom built a new house and installed two four-foot by five-foot mirrors on the walls. The mirrors were hung from hooks and were bordered by molding, which was nailed to the wall. When Tom died, he left his real estate to Dick and his personal property to Harry. Who is entitled to the mirrors? Why?

8. A construction company owned a lot on which stood a pile of topsoil twenty feet high and forty feet long. The company sold the lot to Simmons, and the deed made no mention of the topsoil. Simmons spread the topsoil over his lot because the pile constituted a hazard to neighborhood children. The company then sued Simmons for the value of the topsoil, claiming that it had never been purchased by Simmons. Who wins? Why?

9. On January 2, 1998, Juan gave First Bank a mortgage on his twenty-year-old house; and the mortgage was recorded on January 3. On January 5, Juan contracted to buy a new furnace from Fancy Furnace Company for $500 down and $5,000 payable over three years. The $5,000 note was secured by a security interest in the furnace, which was installed on January 7. On January 28, Fancy Furnace made a fixture filing. If the bank forecloses against Juan on January 30, who has prior rights to the furnace? Why?

10. Junior and Mary Sue Davis were married in 1980. After Mrs. Davis had five unsuccessful pregnancies, the couple sought the help of a fertility clinic to conceive through in vitro fertilization (IVF). Nine fertilized embryos were created using IVF, two of which were implanted into Mrs. Davis' womb, while the other seven were frozen so that they could be implanted later if necessary. The two implanted embryos failed to result in pregnancy. The other seven remained frozen in a Knoxville fertility clinic. Later the Davises' marriage failed. Upon dissolution of the marriage, the only issue the couple needed to resolve was who would gain "custody" over the seven frozen embryos. Mrs. Davis sought exclusive control since she saw this as her last chance to become a mother. Mr. Davis argued that the frozen embryos should not be implanted, or he would be forced to be a father against his will. One of the issues that the Tennessee Supreme Court was asked to decide was whether the frozen embryos could be classified as persons or personal property. If the embryos were persons, they would be accorded legal rights and special protections, including the right to continue in existence and to possibly become a fully developed person someday. If the embryos were property, the Davises would own them jointly with Tennessee state law governing personal property and principles of concurrent ownership (discussed in Chapter 5) deciding their fate. Since this was a case of first impression (i.e., a case that is not addressed by any existing constitutional, statutory, or common law in the jurisdiction of Tennessee), using ethical principles to justify a moral decision is a way to resolve this case, as well as to create new law that will have precedent over future similar cases. Are the frozen embryos persons or property? Why?

ENDNOTES

1. W. Blackstone, *Commentaries* 138.
2. W. Blackstone, *Commentaries* 2.
3. Mackeldey, *Roman Law* §265 (1883).
4. W. Blackstone, *Commentaries* 2.
5. J. Bentham, *Theory of Legislation* 111, 112 (1931).
6. *Id.* at 112, 113.
7. O. Lee Reed, *Propositions About Property, Prosperity and Peace*, Presented at the Academy of Legal Studies in Business Annual Convention, Orlando, FL, August, 2006.
8. M. Schroeder and T. Roth, *Heavy Regulation Seen as Obstacle*, Wall Street Journal, A2 (October 7, 2003).
9. M. Miller, *The Poor Man's Capitalist: Hernando de Soto*, New York Times Magazine (July 1, 2001).
10. Reed, supra note 7, at 7.
11. 842 S.W.2d 588 (Tenn. 1992).
12. A revision of the UCC issued in 2003 raises the amount from $500 to $5000. *See* National Conference of Commissioners on Uniform State Laws, *Amendments To Uniform Commercial Code Article 2—Sales*, Section 2-201 (Annual Meeting Draft 2003). As of 2009, no state has adopted the new amount. See: http://www.nccusl.org/Update/uniformact_factsheets/uniformacts-fs-ucc22A03.asp.
13. *Roberts v. Assessment Bd. of Review of the Town of New Windsor*, 84 Misc. 2d 1017, 375 N.Y.S.2d 988 (1975).
14. *How to Maximize Depreciation Deductions*, Mortgage and Real Estate Executives Report 3 (June 15, 1987). This example assumes a 34 percent corporate tax rate and a 12 percent discount rate.
15. *Whiteco Industries v. Commissioner*, 65 TC 664 (1975). These factors are:

    1) Is the property in question capable of being moved and has it been moved?
    2) Is the property designed or constructed to remain permanently in place?
    3) Are there circumstances which tend to show the expected or intended length of time of affixation, i.e., are there circumstances which show that the property may or will have to be moved?
    4) How substantial a job is removal of the property and how time consuming is it?
    5) How much damage will the property sustain upon removal?
    6) What is the manner and extent of affixation of the property?

16. *U.S. v. One 1989 Stratford Fairmont 140 x 700 Mobile Home,* 783 F.Supp. 1154 (N.D. Ill. 1992), aff'd 986 F.2d 177 (7th Cir. 1993).

17. UCC Section 9-313(1)(a).

18. *Teaff v. Hewitt,* 1 Ohio St. 511 (1853).

19. *Id.*

20. *Schwend v. Schwend,* 983 P.2d 988 (Mont. 1999).

21. See W. Burby, *Real Property* 23, 24 (3rd ed. 1965). J. White and R. Summers, *Uniform Commercial Code* 1056 (1980).

22. *Fisher v. Pennington,* 116 Cal.App. 248, 2 P.2d 518 (1931).

23. *Teaff v. Hewitt,* 1 Ohio St. 511 (1853).

24. *Snedeker v. Warring,* 12 N.Y. 170 (1854).

25. *Rogers v. Gilinger,* 30 Pa. 185 (1858).

26. *Teaff v. Hewitt,* 1 Ohio St. 511 (1853).

27. *Zangerle v. Standard Oil Co.,* 144 Ohio St. 506, 60 N.E.2d 52 (1945).

28. 224 Cal.App.2d 108, 36 Cal.Rptr. 413 (1964).

29. *Citizens Bank of Greenfield v. Mergenthaler Linotype Co.,* 216 Ind. 573, 25 N.E.2d 444 (1940).

30. *American Telephone and Telegraph Co. v. Muller,* 299 F.Supp. 157 (D.S.C. 1968).

31. *Strain v. Green,* 25 Wash.2d 692, 172 P.2d 216 (1946).

32. *State v. Work,* 75 Wash.2d 204, 449 P.2d 806 (1969).

33. *Miller v. Wohlford,* 119 Ind. 305, 21 N.E. 894 (1889).

34. *Carver v. Pierce,* 23 Car.Banc.Reg.

35. *Slater v. Dowd,* 79 Ga.App. 272, 53 S.E.2d 598 (1949).

36. *Gas and Electric Shop v. Corey-Scheffel Lumber Co.,* 227 Ky. 657, 13 S.W.2d 1009 (1929).

37. In the 1962 Uniform Commercial Code, timber was included in the second category.

38. A related issue is whether the tenant must remove fixtures that the landlord does not want. The Restatement, Second, Property, Landlord and Tenant Section 11.2 (3) states that the tenant is responsible for removal in such cases.

39. G. Dykstra and L. Dykstra, *The Business Law of Real Estate* 53 (1956).

40. 421 N.E.2d 1257 (Mass. App. Ct. 1981).

41. *Cameron v. Oakland County Gas & Oil Co.,* 277 Mich. 442, 269 N.W. 227 (1936).

42. *Wright v. Du Bignon,* 114 Ga. 765, 40 S.E. 747 (1902).

43. 220 Cal. 193, 30 P.2d 19 (1934).

44. *Southern Massachusetts Broadcasters, Inc. v. Duchaine,* 529 N.E.2d 887 (Mass. App. Ct. 1988).

45. See G. Dykstra and L. Dykstra, *The Business Law of Real Estate,* 58–60 (1956).

46. 849 N.E.2d 516 (Sup. Ct. Ind. 2006).

47. *Smusch v. Kohn,* 22 Misc. 344, 49 N.Y.S. 176 (1898).

48. *Sequist v. Fabian,* 274 Mich. 643, 265 N.W. 488 (1936).

49. J. Blyth, *UCC1 Concerns Under Revised Article 9,* Real Estate Law and Practice Course Handbook Series, 863 (October 2003).

50. In the 1962 Uniform Commercial Code, the secured party was given priority if the security interest attached to the goods before they became fixtures.

51. R. Freyermuth, *Why Mortgagors Can't Get No Satisfaction,* 72 Missouri Law Review 1159 (Fall, 2007).

52. H. Smith, *Anybody Seen the Carpets? Or the Toilets?* Las Vegas Review-Journal E1 (April 19, 2009).

53. 36 Mont. 368, 93 P. 38 (1907).

54. See W. Burby, *Real Property* 29 (3rd ed. 1965).

55. 514 So.2d 54 (Fla. 1987).

56. Ohio Rev.Code §5303.08.

57. See *In re the Marriage of Olar,* 747 P.2d 676, 679 (Colo. Sup. Ct. 1987). B. Grossman, Note, The Evolution of Equitable Distribution in New York, 62 *New York University Annual Survey of American Law* 607 (2007).

The Scope of Real Property

© MACIEJ NOSKOWSKI/iStockphoto (RF)

LEARNING OBJECTIVES

After studying Chapter 3, you should:

- Know about rights to the sky and the depths

- Be familiar with water rights

- Comprehend the law of lateral support

"Whiskey is for drinkin' and Water is for fightin' ..."

Mark Twain

"The diversity in the faculties of men, from which the rights of property originate, is not less an insuperable obstacle to an uniformity of interests. The protection of these faculties is the first object of government."

James Madison, Federalist Papers, no. 39

The owner of the surface of real estate has property rights in the air above the surface and in the soil below. In the words of Lord Coke, "*cujus est solum ejus est usque ad coelum et ad inferos,*" a dictum still cited by modern courts. In the classic Iowa case of *Hannabalson v. Sessions,* for example, the court noted that "the title of the owner of the soil extends not only downward to the centre of the earth, but upward *usque ad coelum,* although it is, perhaps, doubtful whether owners as quarrelsome as the parties in this case will ever enjoy ... their property in the latter direction."[1]

Moreover, the common law has long recognized that property rights, including air and subsurface rights, could be divided and sold. Changes in technology and travel, however, have raised a number of legal questions concerning the scope of real estate ownership, rendering the ancient concept of unrestricted ownership to the heavens and depths unduly simplistic. For example, should limits be placed on the ownership of the air in order to accommodate air travel? Who owns minerals such as gas and oil that are capable of movement beneath the surface? What right does a landowner have to a body of water that adjoins the owner's land? And may one person excavate his land when the excavation will cause a neighbor's property to subside? The focus of this chapter is on these and related questions. (See Figure 3.1.)

FIGURE 3.1
Scope of Real Property

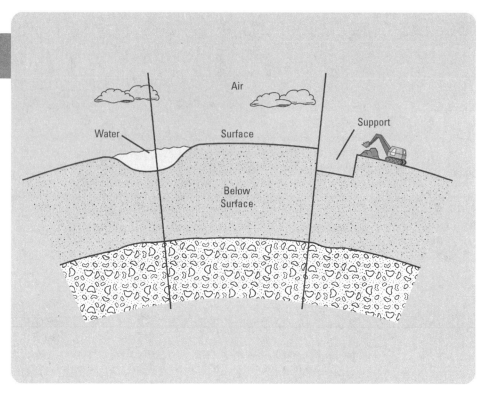

Rights to the Sky
Traditional Approach

ad coelum

A person owns the space above her real estate to the extent that no one may acquire a right to such airspace that will limit the owner's enjoyment of it. This doctrine has been rejected by most courts.

The ancient dictum of Lord Coke, which gave the owner of the surface the rights *ad coelum*[2] (literally, to heaven), was uttered long before the development of air travel. Even today there is little difficulty in applying the rule in cases that do not involve an airplane.

A person who invades the airspace of another individual without permission has committed a trespass. Under the common law, the trespasser would be liable for at least nominal damages even if no actual damages were proven. Invasion of airspace can also involve more mundane disputes between neighbors as the next classic Minnesota case points out.

A CASE IN POINT

In *Whittaker v. Stangvick*,[3] the plaintiff owned a strip of land that formed a "duck pass" between two lakes. He alleged that the defendants were constructing duck blinds on one of the lakes and intended to shoot ducks and other waterfowl that would be flying over the plaintiff's land. According to the testimony, a shotgun's range is 400 feet and about half the shot from the blinds would drop on the plaintiff's land and half would carry over the land. Although the appellate court sent the case back to the trial court for further hearings, it noted that on the basis of the facts presented, there was a trespass and "it is immaterial whether the quantum of harm suffered be great, little, or unappreciable."

For example, a property owner whose tree branches or building eaves hang over another's property is invading his neighbor's airspace. A typical remedy is for a court to order removal of the overhang, a process that can be costly to a homeowner.

Air Travel

In cases involving air travel, courts have had considerable difficulty applying the *ad coelum* principle because the rights of the surface owner must be balanced by the public necessity for air travel. State courts have developed various theories that give landowners ownership rights in the air, including the ancient theory of trespass.[4] Increasingly, however, they use nuisance theory to determine the owner's rights.[5] A **nuisance** results when a flight interferes with the use and enjoyment of one's land. (Nuisance law is discussed further in Chapter 12.)

In determining whether military flights over private land were "so direct and so frequent as to be a direct and immediate interference with the enjoyment and use of the land," the Supreme Court's test in a leading federal case, *United States v. Causby*,[6] was similar to nuisance theory. The Causbys owned a 2.8-acre chicken farm near an airport outside Greensboro, North Carolina, which was used by military aircraft. One of the airport's runways ended approximately 2,200 feet from the farm's outbuildings, while the glide path for the aircraft passed 67 feet above the farmhouse and 63 feet above the outbuildings.

Planes flying over the farm included U.S. bombers, transports, and fighters. According to the Court, these planes

> come close enough at times to appear barely to miss the tops of the trees and at times so close to the tops of the trees as to blow the old leaves off. The noise is startling. And at night the glare from the planes brightly lights up the place. As a result of the noise, respondents had to give up their chicken business. As many as six to ten of their chickens were killed in one day by flying into the walls from fright. The total chickens lost in that manner was about 150. Production also fell off.... Respondents are frequently deprived of their sleep and the family has become nervous and frightened.

As a result, the Causbys sued the government, claiming that there had been a "taking" of their property and that they should receive compensation for the "taking." The law of "takings," a topic discussed in detail in Chapter 13, occurs when a law, regulation, or other actions of a local, state, or federal governmental entity go so far that they greatly diminish or take away the value of a person's property, even though the title is not actually transferred to the government as in a typical taking.

In its decision, the Supreme Court initially noted that under the Air Commerce Act, the United States has exclusive national sovereignty in the airspace over the country, and any citizen has a public right to freedom of transit through the navigable airspace—that is, the airspace above the minimum safe altitudes prescribed by the Civil Aeronautics Authority. And, of course, federal law such as the Air Commerce Act is supreme over state law that contradicts it. Thus, the Court concluded:

> It is ancient doctrine that at common law ownership of the land extended to the periphery of the universe.... But that doctrine has no place in the modern world. The air is a public highway, as Congress has declared. Were that not true, every transcontinental flight would subject the operator to countless trespass claims. Common sense revolts at the idea. To recognize such private claims to the airspace would clog these highways, seriously interfere with their control and development in the public interest, and transfer into private ownership that to which only the public has a just claim.

The Court also noted, however, that the minimum safe altitudes prescribed by the Civil Aeronautics Authority for flight ranged from 300 to 1,000 feet depending on the type of aircraft, the time of day, and the terrain. In the Causby case, military planes

nuisance
An unreasonable interference with the use and enjoyment of land.

flew below the prescribed navigable airspace when they took off and landed. Therefore, the Court was faced with determining the landowner's rights to the air below the navigable airspace. The Court decided:

> *the landowner owns at least as much of the space above the ground as he can occupy or use in connection with the land.... The fact that he does not occupy it in a physical sense—by the erection of buildings and the like—is not material.... Flights over private land are not a taking, unless they are so low and frequent as to be a direct and immediate interference with the enjoyment and use of the land. The flight of airplanes, which skim the surface but do not touch it, is as much an appropriation of the use of the land as a more conventional entry upon it.*

The Supreme Court remanded the case to the Court of Claims for further hearings as to the nature of the taking and its appropriate valuation.

The issues presented by the *Causby* case are still alive today. In *Brown v. U.S.*,[7] frequent low-level overflights by military aircraft did not affect the property's existing use for cattle grazing, but they did cause a "[s]ignificant and immediate decline in market price for that part of the property" most affected by the overflights. Relying on Causby, the court held that the impairment of market value was a compensable taking.

A question left unanswered by the Supreme Court in *Causby* was whether there can be liability for flights within the navigable airspace that interfere with the use of the land. In *Griggs v. County of Allegheny*,[8] the Court decided that there could be liability for such flights and that the county, as the owner and lessor of the airport, should bear this liability. More recently, an owner of valuable land on the famed Las Vegas Strip received $6.5 million as compensation from Clark County and McCarran International Airport due to legal height restrictions placed on his property. The restrictions, which the airport argued existed for important safety reasons, prevented the owner from constructing more floors and potentially cost him millions of dollars in lost revenue.[9]

One means routinely used by airports to prevent such legal problems is to buy "navigation easements." As you will learn in the next chapter, an easement gives someone the right to use the land owned by another. With a navigation easement, landowners grant to the airport the right to fly aircraft over their airspace.

Since airports are hubs for the movement of goods as well as people, many businesses find it profitable to congregate close to them. As a result, airports, which are often owned by municipalities, possess the right of eminent domain. Often they condemn nearby residential property and convert the land to commercial purposes, particularly for warehousing and retailing. Businesses, unlike residential property owners, generally do not view the noise and congestion generated by airports as a nuisance, but rather as the welcome hum of commercial activity. The topics of condemnation and eminent domain are further discussed in Chapter 13.

ETHICAL AND PUBLIC POLICY ISSUES

Is It Right to Condemn Private Property for Business Purposes?

Although generally legal, is it an ethical and fair public policy for governments and their entities to condemn homes near an airport and sell or lease the land to commercial interests? Often the airports make a great deal of money leasing the land for use as stores and warehouses. The profits are then used to support and finance airport activities. Property owners must be given just compensation for their property. However, many people incur inconveniences and some, particularly the elderly, suffer psychologically when they are displaced.

Cloud Seeding

The ancient *ad coelum* doctrine is also being reexamined in an attempt to resolve another modern issue: the practice of cloud seeding. Cloud seeding, which has been used since the 1940s, is a process in which a chemical mixture is sprayed over a propane flame. The mixture then floats up to the clouds, attracting moisture and, according to its proponents, causing precipitation. Although there is no conclusive scientific proof that it actually works, cloud seeding is routinely used in drier parts of the United States, often by irrigation districts and hydroelectric utilities in states such as Nevada, Utah, and California and even by private businesses such as the Vail Ski Resort to enhance its snowpack.[10]

Cloud seeding brings up an intriguing issue: does the owner of the surface have a property right in the clouds? There are several aspects to this issue. For instance, may landowners seed clouds over their land to secure rain for themselves if, by doing so, they deprive their neighbors of rain? This question often carries national and international implications. Israel, for example, has been accused of "rain rustling" by its neighbors; and the state of Washington was threatened with legal action by Idaho because of its cloud-seeding program to alleviate the effects of a prolonged drought. In the next case, landowners attempted to prevent cloud seeding over their properties.

A CASE IN POINT

In *Southwest Weather Research, Inc. v. Rounsaville*[11] a group of Texas ranchers sued participants in a cloud-seeding program to enjoin them from flying over the ranchers' properties in an attempt to seed the clouds and prevent hail. The court held that the defendants could properly be restrained from modifying clouds or weather over the plaintiffs' properties, noting that the landowner "is entitled to such rainfall as may come from the clouds over his own Property that Nature, in her caprice, may provide."

A final question is whether cloud seeders are liable when the seeding results in flooding of a neighbor's land. For example, the case of *Lunsford v. U.S.*[12] was brought to court after a 1972 flood in Rapid City, South Dakota, caused substantial property damage and resulted in 283 deaths. The plaintiffs claimed that the flood was the result of a cloud-seeding program conducted under contract with the federal government. The court noted the difficulty the plaintiffs faced "in proving that cloud seeding caused the alleged flooding or drought."[13]

Sale of Air Rights

While real property owners often think of their interest in two dimensions (marked by four directional corners), the real property interest is more accurately described in three dimensions.[14] The third dimension, airspace, is defined by an Oklahoma statute[15] as:

> *that space which extends from the surface of the earth upward and which is either occupied or subject to being occupied for the reasonable enjoyment and use of the land surface and any structures thereon by the surface owner or owners, his or their heirs, successors or assigns. The airspace owned by a surface owner or owners is that which lies within the vertical upward extension of his or their surface boundaries.*

air rights
The legal interest in the vertical dimension of property.

The owner of **air rights** may sever and sell the rights separately from the surface of the real estate. Some of these sales have created a unique and creative use of space.

For example, in New York, developers constructed the Pan-Am Building (now the MetLife Building) in the airspace over the northern section of the Grand Central railway station. Similarly, the sale of a high-rise condominium usually involves the transfer of a unit of airspace. That unit may be described by any one of the following means:

- *A subdivision plat of air lots, each of which is numbered*
- *A survey that shows the dimensions of each unit with reference to the boundaries of the land*
- *A survey that utilizes a floor plan showing the location of each unit*

Vertical ownership raises a number of interesting issues relating to each owner's rights. For example, what rights does one property owner have when his neighbor's building blocks light and air? Typically, the common law allows a neighbor to build, but many new exceptions are being created by statute, particularly to protect solar energy devices. This issue is addressed in Chapter 4. In a similar vein, what happens if a building settles and an air lot tilts into a neighbor's airspace?[16] The vertical ownership issue of who owns the airspace above a condominium is resolved in the following Connecticut case.

A CASE IN POINT

Condominiums can be high-rise projects; they can also involve adjoining structures rising from the ground to the roofline. *Grey v. Coastal States Holding Co.*[17] involved such a structure. The defendants constructed an additional story on a condominium unit, and the other unit owners objected to the addition. The court determined that the airspace occupied by the addition was a "common element," defined as "all portions of the common interest community other than the units." Because the airspace was a common element, the defendants "essentially appropriated airspace ... that did not belong to them individually, but belonged to them in common with the other unit owners." Damages were awarded to the plaintiff unit owners.

Governmental regulation of real estate typically imposes restrictions on permissible development. Some governmental units allow air rights tied to one parcel to be sold or transferred to another parcel. Such a sale of air rights is typically referred to as **transferable development rights** (TDRs). For instance, one type of development plan allows a person who owns undeveloped air rights to sell those rights to a property owner who has used the maximum airspace allowed by the plan. Thus, if a city's zoning and development plan places a twenty-story limit on a building being developed by Whiteside Development Company, then Gustafson, an owner of a fifteen-story building, could sell the unused five-story air rights he owns to Whiteside, whose building has already reached the limit. Whiteside could then use these rights to legally build five more stories. TDRs are discussed in detail in Chapter 13.

transferable development rights

A market-based system designed to preserve land. Property owners are given financial incentives to grant their rights to develop to others.

In *Wing Ming Properties (U.S.A.) v. Mott Operating Ltd.* on page 82, air rights over a building were transferred to an adjacent parcel. The court resolves the issue of whether the construction of air-conditioning units and a parapet wall by the building owner is a trespass on the interest of the transferee of the air rights.

END OF CHAPTER CASE

TDRs have been used in a number of creative ways for furthering public policy goals affecting real estate. For example, TDRs have been used to preserve historic landmarks, to encourage low-income housing, and to create conservation easements, a topic in Chapter 4.

Environmental legislation includes the concept of transferable rights relating to use of the air. The Clean Air Act, for example, limits the amount of sulfur dioxide that power plants can emit. A 1990 amendment to the Act allows plants that emit less than their limit to bank their excess rights or sell them to other companies that exceed their allowance. A 1992 United Nations (UN) study proposed a similar system to limit pollution on a global basis. In the words of economist Richard Sandor, one of the authors of the study, "Air and water are no longer the 'free goods' that economists once assumed. They must be redefined as property rights so that they can be efficiently allocated."[18]

Sandor's vision of creating a mechanism for efficiently allocating air rights began in 2003 with the creation of the Chicago Climate Exchange (CCX). CCX members, including Ford Motor Company, DuPont, and Motorola, have voluntarily agreed to use the CCX as a means of reducing carbon dioxide—the pollutant that many scientists argue causes global warming. For example, a company such as Motorola can voluntarily buy the right to exceed its voluntary cap on emissions from Ford if Ford has allowances left over due to greater efficiencies in the way it runs its plants. Although the agreements to reduce carbon emissions are voluntary, some corporations have been pressured by their large institutional shareholders, as well as by environmental groups, to become more environmentally sensitive. This happened to the American Electric Power Company, one of the largest users of coal, which is now an active member of the CCX.[19]

While the CCX is voluntary, ten northeastern states, including populous Massachusetts, New York and New Jersey, entered into the nation's first mandatory cap and trade agreement in 2008. Under the Regional Greenhouse Gas Initiative, or RGGI, all fossil fuel-burning power plants must buy credits corresponding to the amount of carbon they emit. The money goes to cash-strapped state governments. Two other state regional groups are being planned in the Midwest and West based on the RGGI model. California is developing a cap-and-trade system as well, which will go into effect in 2012. Under its plan, polluters would have a cap imposed on how much in greenhouse gases they emit every year; a company which continues to emit more than its limit would have to purchase an additional amount at an auction with the proceeds going to California state coffers.

The Obama administration proposed a national plan in 2009 based on much the same principles as RGGI. The bill passed the House of Representatives and at the time of this writing is in the Senate. The legislation has been met with fierce partisan debate, particularly over how much it will raise the price of energy. Both the Senate and House versions call for a long-term 83 percent reduction of greenhouse gases by 2050.[20]

Transactions similar to those within the CCX are also occurring among nations who are signatories to the Kyoto Treaty. Those nations have pledged to reduce carbon emissions by 2012. Currently, most industrialized nations have signed the Treaty.[21] In December 2009, another international conference convened in Copenhagen, Denmark, designed to further the goals set in Kyoto. Although there was a system set up to monitor and report on progress, environmentalists and many European countries that have already set binding limits on greenhouse gas emissions were disappointed that the conference did not result in a global agreement and that no firm goals were established. Critics were also frustrated that only the U.S. and four other countries—China, India, Brazil and South Africa—negotiated the agreement. Still, supporters of the conference contend that an important positive step was taken in combating global warming.[22]

Outer Space

It has long been anticipated that the number of companies preparing commercial ventures for outer space and the associated number of jobs created and revenues generated[23]

> *virtually guarantees that there will be extraterrestrial breaches of contract, that people will be negligent or uncivil toward each other or will act criminally. Spaceships, so to speak, dent each other's fenders, or bend the antennas of satellites. Space churches may want constitutional protection and tax breaks. Space people will marry, then want divorces, have children in and out of wedlock, seek abortions, commit crimes of passion. Injured space workers will sue for damages and compensation. Refugees will seek asylum. There may be piracy, brawls, and hijacks.*[24]

Given those potential problems, countries have been working together to develop a law of outer space. The United States and the former Soviet Union signed several treaties that, among other things, provide that space is owned by no one country.[25] Although there is no agreement to date on where a country's airspace ends and outer space begins,[26] there have been agreements on the use of orbits and spectrums for telecommunications satellites.[27]

Continuing exploration of outer space begs the question of who would have property rights on the moons and planets of the solar system should people ever live, do business, and exploit resources in those extraterrestrial places. A start in addressing these unique issues is the Moon Treaty, signed initially by five nations in 1984. No nation with a serious space program, such as the United States, has yet accepted the treaty, however. The Moon Treaty provides that "the moon and its natural resources are the common heritage of mankind." If the treaty were ratified by the nations of the world, all mankind would share the moon's resources. According to one commentator, the Moon Treaty will never be taken seriously unless a free-market approach, together with international regulatory oversight, exists to create the economic incentives any nation or company would need to develop extraterrestrial resources.[28]

The next case from Nevada discusses the unique property interests that some people claim exist in outer space.

A CASE IN POINT

In *Nemitz v. U.S.*, the plaintiff sought a declaratory judgment after alleging that he owned property rights to asteroid 433, also called Eros. Nemitz based his assertion by registering on the Archimedes Institute web site and filing his property interest in the public records of California. The Archimedes web site was started in the 1990s as an online registry of celestial land claims. Nemitz also alleged that the United States had infringed on his constitutionally protected property rights to Eros when NASA landed an unmanned spacecraft on the asteroid. Accordingly, he sought compensation for "parking" and "storage" fees. The court dismissed the case, stating that the U.S. Constitution does not recognize "a cause of action for the denial of a property interest in outer space."[29]

Rights to the Depths

The corollary of the *ad coelum* doctrine is that the owner of real estate also has the right *ad inferos*, that is, to the depths. Legal controversies involving the depths arise in several contexts. Issues can relate to subsurface improvements. Rights to subsurface assets such as gas, oil, and minerals can have great economic significance. Environmental laws and regulations, discussed in Chapter 14, impose liabilities for subsurface contamination by way of underground storage tanks and improper disposal of contaminants through the ground or water. Should there be more underground developments, some of which may grow to the size of SubTropolis—a former limestone quarry in Kansas City with space for numerous corporate offices, warehouses, and factories—the law relating to subsurface improvements will have yet another reason to further develop.[30]

Courts generally agree that it is a trespass to enter another person's property beneath the surface—for example, to dig a mine under a neighbor's property—yet some courts have modified this approach, as the following New York case illustrates, when a trespass takes place at a great depth.

A CASE IN POINT

In *Boehringer v. Montalto*,[31] the purchaser of real estate in Yonkers sued the vendor, claiming that the vendor had warranted that the property was free from encumbrances when in fact there was a sewer running underneath it at a depth of over 150 feet. But the court decided that because of its depth, the sewer was not an encumbrance: "Title above the surface of the ground is now limited to the extent to which the owner of the soil may reasonably make use thereof. By analogy, the title of an owner of the soil will not be extended to a depth below ground beyond which the owner may not reasonably make use thereof."

Mineral Rights

As with air rights, the rights to the depths may be severed and sold apart from the surface of the real estate. A typical reason to separate subsurface and surface ownership is to convey rights to minerals, oil, and natural gas. Severance of mineral rights from the surface rights, creating what are called "split estates," commonly occurs when a seller conveys ownership to her property to another but reserves the mineral rights or simply conveys the mineral interest to another. When a sale of mineral rights takes place, the purchaser has the right to use, in a reasonable manner, the surface of the real estate for the purpose of tunneling or drilling below it to extract the minerals.

The separate sale of oil and gas rights has created a number of unique legal problems. In some states, such as Texas and Mississippi, oil and gas are considered the property of the surface owner and can be sold as real property to third parties in the same manner as hard minerals such as coal. Under this theory, called the **ownership principle**, the mineral owner actually owns them in their place as a mineral interest or estate under the surface of the earth (see endnote 32 for a list of states applying the ownership principle).[32]

However, other states, including California, Louisiana, and Oklahoma, reject this principle and subscribe to the **exclusive right** principle (see endnote 33 for a list of states applying the exclusive right principle). These laws are based on a line of reasoning that oil, which generally exists in highly porous sandstone, or natural gas, often derived from organic shale fractured for extraction purposes, are "fugitive" minerals. Courts in these states reason that oil and gas, like wild animals and other migratory things, are not owned in place and therefore cannot be owned until captured although the owner of the surface can sell the exclusive right to enter the surface owner's land and extract the minerals.[33] This right can also be sold separately from the surface estate. Under the ownership principle, once the minerals are captured in the production process, the minerals become tangible personal property. Thus, the main difference between the two theories is the property status prior to capture.

ownership principle
A theory under which oil and gas are owned in place and can be severed and sold the same as a solid mineral.

exclusive right
A personal property right to enter, explore for, and extract oil and gas from another's property.

Conveying oil and gas rights as well as rights to other minerals also raises issues relating to the interpretation of language contained in the habendum clauses (clauses which define the extent of the interest conveyed) contained in deeds and leases. For example, a number of older mineral deeds, written when coal was the primary concern, deed the coal "and other minerals" to the purchaser, thereby raising the question of whether oil, gas, and other minerals have also been conveyed. In the leading case from Texas, *Acker v. Guinn,*[34] there had been a conveyance of rights to "oil, gas, and other minerals, in and under, and that may be produced from" a tract of land. The court decided that the term *other minerals* was not specific enough to include iron ore, especially since open pit or strip mining of the ore virtually destroys the surface estate.

In another case, a deed conveyed all coal and gas rights; however, the grantee claimed that coal seam methane gas, a valuable, low-cost, and relatively clean burning fuel that is being increasingly extracted, was included in the coal estate. Since coal seam methane gas is contained within the coal itself, but released by injecting depressurizing processes during mining, a good argument was made that it should be included. Still, the Montana Supreme Court held[35] that the gas was not a chemical component of the coal estate itself and so therefore not part of the estate. In yet another case,[36] the Alabama Supreme Court ruled in an opposite manner and interpreted a lease for coal *and other minerals* to include coal bed methane gas. The *Geothermal Kinetics, Inc.* case covered later in this chapter discusses this issue with respect to geothermal resources. The above cases make it obvious that careful drafting of the mineral deed is necessary to forestall litigation.

One recent problem arising over ambiguous language in mineral leases concerns biomass, which consists of bulk plant and organic material. Methane gas is produced as a by-product of biomass found in landfills and is becoming an increasingly important and cheap alternative energy source. What happens, however, when the landfill area is also leased to a production company and the habendum clause in the lease states "oil, gas and minerals in, on and under, or that may be produced from the land"? Although there is scant legal authority available, commentators believe that the methane gas would be owned by the landfill since the methane gas was never part of the geological reservoir. Moreover, public policy would likely favor those who exploit landfills for capturing a fuel source (and source of greenhouse gas) that would otherwise be lost to the atmosphere through vents.[37]

The owner of a mineral interest can also lease mineral rights. The owner's interest is conveyed with a **mineral lease**, in which the lessor (the owner of the mineral estate or right) grants to the lessee (usually an oil company or a group of investors) many of the same rights as those given the purchaser of a mineral interest discussed previously. (To view a mineral lease, see www.cengagebrain.com [see page xix in the Preface for instructions on how to access the free study tools for this text].) A mineral lease is commonly required because the cost for the normal mineral interest owner, often the landowner, to extract the minerals is prohibitively expensive. In the case of oil and gas drilling, it is also a high risk economically for the investors or the oil company that pays for the pre-drilling activities (such as the geological and geophysical analysis of the prospect) and the production costs for the drilling.

Under an oil and gas lease, the lessee conducts and pays for the exploration and production activities and thus has the exclusive right to explore for and remove the oil and gas. In return for granting this right to the lessee, the lessor normally receives **bonus money** for signing the lease in addition to **delay rentals** and a **royalty interest**. A delay rental is paid to the lessor for the privilege of deferring the drilling activities. The lessor normally receives this payment on the first-year anniversary of the lease's date of execution. It is not uncommon, for example, for oil companies to defer their activities due to adverse market prices, which can fluctuate greatly in this unpredictable industry. When

mineral lease
A lease that grants to a lessee the exclusive right to enter the lessor's premises to explore, drill, produce, store, and remove minerals specified in the lease.

bonus money
Cash paid to the lessor as consideration for the execution of an oil and gas lease.

delay rentals
Consideration paid to the lessor for the privilege of deferring commencement of drilling activities during the primary term of the lease. In the absence of drilling activity or production, failure to pay delay rentals results in termination of the lease.

royalty interest
A lessor's right to share in the oil, gas, or other minerals produced under the lease, generally free of production costs.

oil and gas are found in marketable quantities, the lessor begins to receive a royalty interest, which is a percentage share of the production that is stated as a fraction, such as 1/8.[38]

ETHICAL AND PUBLIC POLICY ISSUES

Should Owners of Mineral Rights Be Able to Retain Their Interests Forever?

With the rapid rise in oil prices in recent years, landowners have discovered, often to their dismay, that they do not own their subsurface mineral rights. Until recently in Pennsylvania, for example, there has been little oil and gas production because prices for the commodities were too low to justify the expense of exploration and production. Now landowners are finding that most of the mineral rights in that state, including oil and natural gas, were conveyed to coal mining companies over 100 years ago. Many of those rights were subsequently sold to others. In general, the mineral owner or lessee must act reasonably under the law when extracting the minerals. However, laws differ across the country. Some states, for example, by law, give the surface owner a voice in the location of the oil rigs and access roads. Even so, many landowners cannot stop the mineral owners or lessees from cutting down trees, impacting animal habitats, creating a great deal of noise, and polluting the local water supply. At the same time, the surface owners receive no royalties from production. When they buy their property, many landowners are not aware of the implications of exploration and production activities on their land even when they know or should know that they do not own the mineral rights.[39]

Since many surface owners are impacted by drilling activities, should owners of minerals rights and estates be able to own their interests forever? Many states have been debating this issue. In Louisiana, a civil law jurisdiction, the public policy is different from the approach used in other states. There the mineral interest is called a *mineral servitude*. Under the civil law, if the mineral servitude owner does not explore and produce minerals within ten years of the mineral servitude's creation, the servitude automatically terminates, and the surface owner is no longer subject to it. The law not only helps keep land ownership whole but also encourages exploration and production by those who own the servitude or their lessees. Therefore, in Louisiana, a state that is a major oil and gas producer, landowners are less likely to be subject to another person's mineral interest than landowners in the rest of the country, which applies the common law. Yet, about 21 states have so-called dormant minerals laws, also referred to as Surface Owner Protection Acts, which allow surface owners to regain mineral rights in split estates (see endnote 40 listing the states). In North Dakota, for example, if the surface owner gives notice of nonuse, after which 20 years passes, the mineral estate is lost.[40] This approach is contained in the Model Dormant Minerals Act issued by the prestigious National Conference of Commissioners on Uniform State Laws. Is the dormant mineral/mineral servitude approach a better and more ethical public policy?

capture doctrine
A doctrine that states that property owners have the right to appropriate all oil and gas from their land, including oil and gas that has migrated from neighboring properties.

conversion
The intentional and unauthorized possession and control over another's personal property.

Both ownership and exclusive right states recognize the migratory character of oil and gas as embodied in the **capture doctrine**. Under this doctrine, derived from the English common law, a person can cause oil and gas to migrate across property lines by drilling a well and creating a low-pressure area. The driller thus acquires title to all oil and gas produced on the driller's land even though the oil or gas migrated from a neighbor's property because of the drilling activity.[41] The policy underlying the capture doctrine is to encourage landowners to explore for oil and gas without having to worry about suits for trespass because the driller, in essence, invades and is possessing portions of what was a component of the neighbor's estate. Suits for **conversion**, which is the intentional and unauthorized possession of another's personal property, are also a concern.

Still, the potentially harsh effects that can occur due to the capture doctrine are limited. Adjoining landowners must deal with each other in good faith. This means that landowner A could not, for example, allow a well fire to burn on his property so that adjoining landowner B could not recover oil or gas from her own property. Moreover, landowners would still be liable for trespass and conversion if they *directionally* drilled underground onto an adjoining property in order to capture that landowner's oil and gas.[42] In the following Texas case, the court decides whether hydraulic fracturing, or "fracing," a common practice in the recovery of oil and gas, might also be a trespass.

In *Coastal Oil and Gas Corp. v. Garza Energy Trust* on page 83, the court discusses whether fracturing or "fracing" can create a subsurface trespass if "the invasion alleged is direct and the action taken is intentional."

END OF CHAPTER CASE

The capture doctrine has lost much of its significance because many states now require that oil and gas be divided among the mineral owners to discourage wasteful drilling practices. An entire reservoir is developed as a single productive unit, generally with one operating well, under a plan known as *unitization* or *pooling*. Under such a plan, owners of the oil or gas reserves receive a designated fraction of the reserve's production based upon their prorated portion of the land or interest. Many states have passed unitization statutes, which are triggered when owners of a designated percentage of mineral rights, typically two-thirds to three-fourths, have voluntarily agreed to a plan. Once a state agency finds that a unitization plan is in the public interest or prevents waste, the agency can order the remaining owners to participate in the plan. State agencies, like the Texas Railroad Commission, can also force mineral owners to pool when not enough owners volunteer.[43] The effects of unitization in the oil industry have been positive for producers and consumers. Having too many oil rigs simultaneously draining the same pool of oil and natural gas not only compromises the reservoir's value by dissipating the pressure in the reservoir resulting in less mineral extraction, but also adds greatly to production costs. One only needs to look at pictures of the veritable forest of drilling rigs vigorously pumping the great oil-rich Spindletop prospect in East Texas in the early 1900s to see the effects of unregulated oil production.

As discussed earlier, oil and gas exploration is a very risky business. It is not uncommon for companies to invest millions of dollars only to find their prospects dry. They also must cope with volatility in oil prices that is often caused by uncontrollable global events, such as price pressure exerted by the Organization of Petroleum Exporting Countries (OPEC), geopolitical events in the oil-rich Middle East (most recently the ongoing war in Iraq beginning in 2003), and heavy demand from newly burgeoning economies such as India and China.

To minimize the risks inherent in exploring for oil and gas, energy support companies have developed more reliable and sophisticated geophysical tools, most notably three-dimensional (3-D) seismic technology, to explore the subsurface. This technology can test for minerals under the ground without actually being present on the land that is being explored. This raises the question of whether exploring property owners' subsurface property without their permission constitutes a trespass. The issue is important because mineral owners often receive significant compensation for granting geophysical companies permits to explore their land. Moreover, if unfavorable geological conditions are revealed, the mineral owner will likely be disadvantaged in bargaining for bonus money, delay rentals, and royalties if oil companies decide to lease in the area. The common law rule, established in 1948 in the landmark case of *Kennedy v. General Geophysical Co.*[44] stated that there must be an actual physical presence on the surface to invoke a geophysical trespass. Various commentators have argued that the common law has not kept up with changes in technology and must be changed to protect owners of mineral rights.[45] At least one state, Colorado, has adopted the doctrine of geophysical trespass without actual physical activity on the land.[46]

Alternative Energy Sources

In the early 1970s, two developments in particular sparked a movement away from traditional reliance on fossil fuels such as oil, natural gas, and coal. One was the burgeoning environmental movement that blamed these energy sources for polluting the air; creating acid rain; and, more recently, possibly creating climate change and global warming. The other, as mentioned, was geopolitical events beginning with the Arab oil embargo of 1973. Nontraditional, renewable energy sources such as solar, wind, and geothermal power were seen as potentially viable, clean, and reliable alternatives—a trend recently ratcheted up since the 2008 election of President Obama, an advocate for alternative energy use. Moreover, in recent years, unprecedented demand has caused an upward spiral in the price of most fossil fuels. The 2010 massive oil spill in the Gulf of Mexico caused by the explosion of BP's Deepwater Horizon rig also places doubts whether the expansion of future offshore production is a prudent policy.

One of the first legal responses was the passage of the federal Public Utility Regulatory Policy Act of 1978 (PURPA). PURPA requires utilities to buy all of the electricity generated by Qualifying Facilities, including that produced by nontraditional sources. In 1992, Congress passed the Energy Policy Act to begin deregulating the utilities industry. The Act opens up power grids to nonutilities, including nontraditional power generators, allowing them to sell electricity to consumers. Indeed, in many states today, windmills and solar panels are becoming a common feature across both the rural and urban landscape although their ability to compete economically against traditional sources is still a problem.[47]

Alternative energy sources give rise to a number of legal issues. Wind power, in particular, requires relatively large, unobstructed expanses of land to capture the wind necessary to generate the windmills. Negative easements (discussed in Chapter 4), which can forbid landowners from building certain kinds of structures on their land, are sometimes required so that future development does not interfere with their operation.

Solar power is also an important alternative energy source. Solar easements, a type of negative easement, are one way to ensure continuous access to the sun. A number of states, such as New Mexico and Wyoming,[48] have passed statutes giving landowners rights to receive sunlight for their solar panels.

Due to high costs of solar and wind power relative to fossil fuels, tax benefits are available to encourage a shift to these alternative sources. In 2008 a federal law was passed providing a 30 percent tax credit for both residential and commercial solar installations from 2006 to 2016. In 2009 an additional personal tax credit for the purchase of solar and wind energy systems for dwellings was passed. Many states provide similar incentives.[49]

**ETHICAL AND
PUBLIC POLICY
ISSUES**

Is It Ethical Public Policy to Allow Solar Energy Development Even If It Threatens Certain Protected Plant and Animal Species?

Despite its current reputation as one of the key sources of alternative, clean energy for the future, solar power is not without its critics, even among environmentalists. One problem in particular arises around the mass generation of solar power, even in sparsely populated areas. In the Mohave Desert in Southern California and Nevada, thousands of acres are being developed and energy generated through a collection of photovoltaic panels, or sun-focusing mirrors, and solar collectors residing atop 70-foot poles. Developing land for solar panels, however, can affect natural habitats, including threatened species such as the desert tortoise and drain a great deal of scarce water necessary for the generation of steam for power. Since the sun is clearly renewable, this timeless commitment to land usage can be a daunting challenge to policy makers who seek to reduce our dependence on foreign oil and reduce carbon dioxide levels but must now contend with those environmentalists who argue that protecting the natural habitat should be our first priority. Is it ethical to prioritize solar energy development over the continued viability of threatened plant and animal species?

Windpower systems, now becoming common across the American landscape, have spawned a number of legal issues. Especially important is the question of who owns the wind. California, with the longest history of using wind energy, was the first state to address the issue.

A CASE IN POINT

In *Contra Costa Water District v. Vaquero Farms,* the Contra Costa Water District condemned the Vaquero Farms under its powers of eminent domain, but severed the wind rights on a portion of its acreage and reserved them for Vaquero. Vaquero argued that the wind rights could not be severed and that it should be compensated for the loss of the wind rights too. The court sided with Contra Costa, stating that "one may have a right to use windpower rights without owning any interest in the land." The court further stated that "windpower rights are 'substantial rights' capable of being bought and sold in the market place."[50]

Windpower, despite its great potential as an alternative energy source, has many critics, including cities, HOAs, and even environmental groups. Some environmental groups wish to exclude windmills for reasons ranging from aesthetics to the threats they pose to birds and bats that are sometimes killed or injured in the windmills' blades. Property owners dislike windmills, citing despoiling of neighborhood views, the loud "whooshing" noises they make, and their "shadow flicker," a strobe-like effect produced by sunlight shining through the blades. Some also complain of a health hazard from flying ice hurled off the blades. These problems, they argue, also reduce property values. In the next case, a citizens' group opposed to a future wind farm attempted to use litigation to slow down the erection of an offshore tower that it argued would become an eyesore in a well-known vacation spot.

A CASE IN POINT

In *Ten Taxpayers Citizen Group v. Cape Wind Associates,*[51] a citizens' group sued Cape Wind Associates, a company seeking to erect a scientific measurement tower. The tower was to be used to collect data to determine the feasibility of a wind farm in an area of Nantucket Sound called Horseshoe Shoals. The tower was located offshore, more than three miles from either Nantucket or Cape Cod. The wind farm would include 170 windmills and be visible from shore. After Cape Wind received a permit from the U.S. Army Corps of Engineers to build the tower, the plaintiffs argued that the defendants also must apply for a Massachusetts license. The court dismissed the case, ruling that the seabed three miles off the coast is the exclusive jurisdiction of the federal government.

The Cape Cod wind power controversy, which has raged since 2002, will finally be decided in 2010 when the Secretary of Interior will make his final ruling. It aptly illustrates the political contentiousness that can arise when energy needs conflict with opposing economic and social interests.

Geothermal energy is heat derived from the earth in which water serves as the medium.[52] Like oil and gas, hot geothermal water is generally treated under state laws as a mineral. In some states, water law (a topic covered in the next section) governs geothermal water, particularly if the geothermal steam is integrated with the regular surface and subsurface water system.[53] Most geothermal energy is located in the western United States. Experts predict that California could derive up to 30 percent of its energy needs from it. Moreover, much of the West's geothermal resources are found on public domain land owned by the federal government. Currently, the federal government is actively encouraging geothermal power as an alternative energy source through the Geothermal Energy Research, Development, and Demonstration Act.[54] Geothermal power not only is carbon free and reliable as a renewable energy source, but also is predicted to be the cheapest future form of energy. Its downside is that geothermal plants can take from six to ten years to become operational.[55]

Private parties also own geothermal power and see it as an important moneymaking resource worth protecting, as the next case demonstrates.

A CASE IN POINT

In *Geothermal Kinetics, Inc. v. Union Company of California,* the surface owners, Union Company, appealed a judgment against it in which the mineral estate holder, Geothermal Kinetics, was awarded title to the minerals, including geothermal steam and energy. Geothermal Kinetics derived its claim from its predecessor in title that conveyed "all minerals in, on or under" the property. Union Company claimed that geothermal energy is not a mineral since the energy is steam heat transported to the surface from molten magma far below the earth's surface. Minerals, it argued, must be a physical substance. The appeals court disagreed and upheld the judgment in favor of Geothermal, ruling that "absent any expressed specific intent to the contrary, the general grant of minerals in, on or under the property included a grant of geothermal resources, including steam therefrom...." The court further stated that "A principal purpose of this [mineral] conveyance was to transfer those underground physical resources which have commercial value and are not necessary for the enjoyment of the surface estate."[56]

Biomass is a more recent alternative energy source, still in the experimental stages. Biomass, which is bulk plant and organic material, can be derived from food crops such as corn and sugar cane used in ethanol or from agricultural residues, wood, and even grasses. Switch grass, which grows naturally in rural areas of the United States, could someday be an important source of energy once scientists are able to produce enzymes that can easily "digest" the grass and convert it into energy uses. When this occurs, millions of relatively unproductive acres of land are likely to become more valuable as a source of energy.[57] Biomass deposited in landfills can also be a source of methane gas.

ETHICAL AND PUBLIC POLICY ISSUES

Is a Carbon Tax on Fossil Fuels an Effective and Ethical Public Policy?

Despite the increased emphasis on alternative energy sources, fossil fuels will almost certainly continue to play a very important role. For example, 70 percent of oil is still used for transportation and will not be easily displaced until electric cars become more common. Even so, the electricity plants that power car batteries will still likely be generated primarily by coal although natural gas, a much cleaner burning fossil fuel, is gaining in importance. The amount of electricity produced by solar or wind is still relatively miniscule and will require the construction of a greatly expanded electric grid system to extend to where these energy sources are, such as the Great Plains and the desert Southwest. Price competition will also pose problems as new domestic fossil fuel discoveries, in particular new and sizeable natural gas discoveries, and ongoing technological improvements for extracting fossil fuels, such as deep water drilling, horizontal drilling, and hydraulic fracturing, continue to reduce production costs, although offshore drilling is now under attack after the oil spill caused by the explosion of the Deepwater Horizon in the Gulf of Mexico. For these reasons, many alternative energy advocates are calling for a "carbon tax" on fossil fuels to discourage their use and to make alternative sources more affordable—a political initiative laden with controversy. Is a carbon tax, which will likely increase energy costs for consumers in the short run, but will likely eventually help the development of alternative energy sources, create a cleaner environment, and possibly reverse climate change, an ethical public policy?[58]

Water Rights

Importance of Water Rights

In recent years, the right to use water has become a valuable part of real estate ownership for several reasons. Water has become increasingly important as a recreational resource, as evidenced by the popularity of vacation homes on seashores, lakefronts, and riverfronts, not to mention as a necessity for fulfilling the needs posed by enormous increases in population in cities such as Las Vegas and Phoenix in the arid Southwest. But more important is the widespread awareness that the future supply of water required for people's basic needs will be limited. These limitations were recognized in the 1950s:

> To most Americans today, pure palatable water in unlimited quantities is a kind of birthright, like citizenship, and not even the Supreme Court can ever take it away. No following generation of Americans is ever likely to share this luxurious attitude. We are rapidly running out of good water. More than a thousand cities and towns already have been forced to curtail their water service. Near Chicago, where artesian wells flowed under their own pressure a hundred years ago, new wells must go down 2,000 feet to reach the water table. Dallas is already pumping the salt-tainted Red River into its mains, and New York faces the likelihood that eventually it will have to purify the polluted Hudson to slake its growing thirst. In Mississippi, wells are now 400 feet deeper,

on the average, than they were only ten years ago. Denver, eager for new industry, has been turning away manufacturers whose production processes involve a heavy use of water.[59]

As a water shortage approaches, Americans who have grown used to considering a product's energy costs will also consider water costs. "Beginning with the water that irrigated the corn that was fed to the steer, [a] steak may have accounted for 3,500 gallons. The water that goes into a 1,000-pound steer would float a destroyer. It takes 14,935 gallons of water to grow a bushel of wheat, 60,000 gallons to produce a ton of steel, 120 gallons to put a single egg on the breakfast table."[60] Moreover, "only 1% of the world's water is fresh and unfrozen—and most of that is found in underground aquifers. Only 0.3% of the world's water is fresh surface water, including huge concentrations like the Great Lakes, the Amazon and Lake Baikal. That's one reason scientists, environmentalists, ecologists and military planners all worry that water shortages could become a source of conflict in coming decades."[61]

The water shortage will also lead to states battling over water, especially the Sunbelt states, where water is in especially short supply, and the Great Lakes states, which have access to 90 percent of the freshwater in the United States.[62] In the desert Southwest, states like Arizona and Nevada are also witnessing battles. Lightly populated, rural counties with ample water aquifers are fighting to preserve their water rights against growing, politically powerful cities searching for new sources. UN officials have expressed concern that water, like oil in the past, may become a trigger for international conflict. The number of people without access to clean, safe water is expected to increase by over a billion in the first quarter of the twenty-first century.

ETHICAL AND PUBLIC POLICY ISSUES

Who Should Own Water?

Due to its indispensability for human survival combined with its threatened supply from pollution, drought, and possibly climate change, fresh water is seen by many as a prime investment. For example, oil man and corporate raider T. Boone Pickens is buying up land overlying the Ogallala Aquifer in West Texas, capturing it (Texas still uses the rule of capture for water) and is planning to sell it to growing urban areas such as Dallas and El Paso. By virtue of his land ownership, Pickens expects to have water rights to 65 billion gallons of water.[63] Is water too important a resource for it to be bought and sold on the free market as a commodity? Should water be closely regulated by the government to prevent abuse and to ensure that individuals get what they need to live on?

In addition to providing vacation pleasures and daily needs, water has gained international prominence because of the mineral and edible resources it contains. Under a 1982 United Nations Convention on the Law of the Sea (UNCLOS) (an agreement that serves as the basis for a treaty) adopted by over 158 countries, nations are given territorial rights twelve nautical miles (22 km) out from an established baseline on shore. Within these waters the coastal country can create and enforce laws although foreign vessels are allowed "innocent passage." Such activities as fishing, polluting, weapons practice, and spying are not considered to be innocent. This treaty also allows a nation to pass laws for regulating customs, immigration or sanitation in an additional 12 nautical mile (27.3 miles or 44 km from the baseline) contiguous zone. Lastly, countries control an exclusive economic zone (EEZ) that provides fishing and drilling rights 200 miles (370.4 km) out from shore. It is beyond this last zone where there are still unanswered questions so that is where much of the contentiousness has arisen.

The convention did not enter into force until 1994. This came about largely because the United States and a few other industrialized nations would not approve it until a prior requirement that forced mining companies to share deep-sea mining technology with developing countries was abandoned. The U.S. argued that it should be replaced with a commercial open market and a first-come, first-served selection process for qualified mining applicants.[64] The 1994 amended version provided that deep-sea mining resources would be owned by all nations as a "Common Heritage of Mankind." This was tempered, however, by provisions to provide workable and reasonable rules for exploitation under the regulatory authority of the International Seabed Authority (ISA).

The 1994 version has not yet been ratified by the U.S. Congress. According to business interests, including those in shipping, fishing, and oil, as well as ocean conservationists, international law enforcement groups, and others who support ratification, the main objection comes from a perception that ratifying the treaty would compromise the nation's sovereignty to an international organization, the UN. There are also doubts about whether the ISA can fairly administer the revenues from the potentially huge amounts of resources that exist on the ocean floor.[65] In her confirmation hearings in 2009, Secretary of State Hillary Clinton stated that ratification of the UNCLOS Treaty would be a priority for the Obama Administration.

Navigable Water

It is sometimes difficult to perceive water as real estate. Yet water, "like air, in its natural state is not a chattel. It is, for legal purposes, a part of the land over which it flows, and the rights, duties and privileges with respect to its use are those which pertain to property in land."[66] Among the important legal questions in a discussion of water rights are the following: Who owns the land under the water? Who has the right to use the surface of water? What use may be made of water for business or domestic purposes? What are the limitations in removing water beneath the surface of real estate?

> **navigable water**
> Any body of water that, by itself or by uniting with other waters, forms a continuous highway over which commerce can be carried on with other states or countries.

The answers to those questions often depend on whether the water is navigable. Although the courts have not adopted any single precise definition of **navigable water**, there is general agreement that for water to be deemed navigable, the water must be navigable in fact. When is water navigable? As the U.S. Supreme Court stated in a legal conflict between Texas and Oklahoma, "Those rivers must be regarded as public navigable rivers in law which are navigable in fact. And they are navigable in fact when they are used, or are susceptible of being used, in their ordinary condition, as highways for commerce, over which trade and travel are or may be conducted in the customary modes of trade and travel on water."[67] When such a body of water, alone or together with other bodies of water, forms a highway that may be used for commerce between or among states, it is said to be navigable water of the United States.[68]

State courts also require navigability in fact. In one case, a Florida court determined that a body of water was *not* navigable in fact because "one witness testified that it was so difficult to get a row boat over it that one had to 'push, cuss, and holler' at the same time to make it go.... From the pictures introduced in evidence one would designate it a cow pasture. Two or three small alligator lairs in the lap of a cow pasture could under no stretch of the imagination meet the test of navigability for useful public purposes."[69]

Once the water has been found to be navigable in fact, however, states have used one of two basic approaches. Most states have adopted the Supreme Court's "highway of commerce" rule referred to previously. The approach used in a minority of states is to determine whether the water may be put to public use regardless of whether it can be used commercially. As the Ohio Supreme Court pointed out, the "increased recreational use of our waters has been accompanied by a corresponding lessening of their use for commerce. We are in accord with the modern view that navigation for pleasure and recreation is as important in the eyes of the law as navigation for a commercial purpose."[70]

Ownership of Land Under Water

Reise has just purchased a cabin on a small tract of riverfront land in northern Minnesota. Reise would be classified as a **riparian owner**; that is, he owns land on a stream or watercourse. Does his real estate extend to the edge of the river, or does Reise also own part of the riverbed? The answer depends on whether the water is considered navigable. If the water is not navigable, the owner of the adjoining land usually owns the riverbed to the center of the river. But if the water is navigable, the general rule is that the state owns the bed to the average or mean high-water mark.[71] Under the public trust doctrine, discussed below, this land cannot be sold by the state unless the sale promotes a public purpose. In some states, such as Louisiana, the distinction between navigable and nonnavigable waters can affect the payment of millions of dollars in royalties for oil and gas production. If the water is navigable, the state receives the royalties since it owns the land under the water; if the water is not navigable, the riparian owner receives the royalties.[72]

Property adjacent to oceans and lakes is sometimes called **littoral** land. Assume that Reise owns littoral land on a navigable inland lake. As it is with riparian owners, he would own his land up to the lake's mean or average high-water mark. If Reise had purchased an oceanfront lot, his ownership would have extended to the mean or average high-tide mark, measured by averaging the tides over a period of eighteen years, although a few states, such as Maine and Massachusetts, extend ownership to the low-water mark. An ocean's mean high-water mark is roughly equivalent to and often discernible by the existence of the so-called "debris" or "wrack" line. Generally, states own the shore, defined as the area between the average high tide and the average low tide, but allow the private owner to use the shore for access to the water. The area beyond the shore comes within state or U.S. jurisdiction.[73] Under the Submerged Lands Act passed by Congress in 1953, the United States relinquished to coastal states all jurisdictional and economic rights to submerged lands within geographic limits not to exceed three marine leagues (nine nautical miles) into the Gulf of Mexico off the shores of Texas and Florida or three nautical miles into the Atlantic and the Pacific oceans and off the coasts of Louisiana, Mississippi, and Alabama. Texas has a broader jurisdiction (and therefore added oil and gas revenues) because it asserted control over a three marine league limit when it broke away from Mexico in 1836. When Texas entered the Union in 1845, the limit remained intact. Florida enjoys its larger offshore jurisdiction due to its 1868 state constitution which was approved by Congress as a condition for its admittance into the Union after the Civil War. After the state limits, the federal government owns all rights out to the 200 mile mark, a mark that roughly corresponds to the continental shelf in many areas.[74]

Although owners typically own their littoral lands on oceans and seas up to the mean or average high-tide mark, use of the beach is generally open to the public under the **Public Trust Doctrine**. This venerable doctrine traces its origins to both Roman law and common law. States apply the doctrine in different ways, however. Most states provide that no trespass occurs when a person is below the average high-tide mark although Massachusetts and Maine consider a person a trespasser between the average high- and low-tide mark. New York and the New England states allow private beaches.[75]

Even if people have a right to use a beach, do they have the right to cross over private property to get to the beach? In certain popular beachfront areas such as Malibu Beach in Southern California, access to the beach is greatly restricted by beach homes that have virtually no space between them. This problem has prompted action by citizens' groups demanding access to the beaches in the form of public easements. Plaintiffs have sometimes successfully based their claims on the public trust doctrine or on old goat paths

riparian owner

The owner of land contiguous to flowing navigable water such as streams and rivers.

littoral

Concerning or belonging to the shore (littoral rights) of coasts and waterfronts.

Public Trust Doctrine

Land held in trust by government for the people to enjoy for purposes of navigation, commerce, and recreation.

and railroad easements under the theory of prescriptive easements, which is discussed in the next chapter. Reaction by littoral landowners has been predictably negative. They complain that their privacy is compromised when the beach lovers walk next to their homes while on their way to enjoy the beach.[76]

ETHICAL AND PUBLIC POLICY ISSUES

Should the Public Have Free Access to Beaches?

Is it an ethically sound public policy that a few private landowners be able to exclude members of the public who want to gain access to the ocean? Should property owners be forced to give up their land and possibly their privacy? Should property rights include, among other things, the ability to exclude others from certain property that also advances the interests of many others?

In recent years, due to severe beach erosion caused particularly by hurricanes, beach homes that were formerly above the mean high-water mark are now on state owned beaches. In Texas, government officials have ordered homes on state land to be removed or demolished as a nuisance and hindrance to the public use of the beaches, often without compensation. Similar problems with shifting beach boundaries have occurred in California, Florida, Hawaii, and New Jersey.[77]

Use and Control of Water

Commerce Clause

A provision in Article I, Section 8 of the U.S. Constitution giving Congress the power to regulate interstate commerce.

Determining rights to use and control water is complicated by Article I, Section 8 of the U.S. Constitution, which gives Congress the power "to regulate commerce ... among the several states." This clause, known as the **Commerce Clause**, has been interpreted to mean that the United States has the right to control navigable waters that affect interstate commerce even when the body of water lies within the boundaries of one state. If the waters are navigable but do not affect interstate commerce, the individual state has the right to their control. Nonnavigable waters are controlled by riparian owners[78] and, unlike navigable waters, may not be used by the general public. In recent years, certain federal government agencies began to assert jurisdiction over isolated waters under certain federal statutes and rules. The following U.S. Supreme Court case illustrates one such attempt.

A CASE IN POINT

In *Solid Waste Agency of Northern Cook County (SWANCC) v. U.S. Army Corps of Engineers*,[79] the plaintiff sought a permit to build a regional nonhazardous landfill in an abandoned sand and gravel strip mine. Within the strip mine were seasonal and permanent ponds, none of which were connected to navigable or interstate bodies of water. The U.S. Army Corps of Engineers, which has the authority to grant permits for dredging and filling operations of navigable waters under the Clean Water Act (CWA), refused to grant the permit.

The Army Corp[s] contended that even though the water was not in interstate commerce, it possessed jurisdiction to control the water under the federal Migratory Bird Rule because birds visited the ponds in interstate flight. The Solid Waste Agency challenged the Army Corps, arguing, among other things, that the Army Corps lacked jurisdiction because these were nonnavigable intrastate waters that were not subject to federal control simply because of the Migratory Bird Rule. The U.S. Supreme Court sided with the Solid Waste Agency and ruled that "[p]ermitting respondents to claim federal jurisdiction over ponds and mudflats falling within the Migratory Bird Rule would result in significant impingement of the state's traditional and primary power over land and water use."

The 2001 ruling in the SWANCC case has had a significant impact on wetlands and land development. Now that "isolated" wetlands are no longer regulated by the U.S. Army Corps of Engineers, land development that was once prohibited or closely regulated has noticeably increased in certain areas. This has been the case particularly in states with weaker environmental laws and enforcement. South Carolina, for example, in the year-and-a-half period after the SWANCC decision, declared 237 wetlands as isolated and therefore unprotected under federal law. Some of those wetlands were subsequently destroyed. Environmentalists argue that wetlands are essential for preventing floods and cleansing water of pollutants and as sanctuaries for wildlife and fish. Developers, on the other hand, maintain that in the past, the U.S. Corps was, at times, overly zealous in classifying small areas (even ditches) as wetlands. These environmentally unimportant areas never constituted a valuable niche in the ecosystem, the developers claim, but now provide land for homes and income-producing commercial developments.[80]

Jurisdiction also has become an important issue regarding wetlands that are not isolated as they were in the SWANCC case but instead exist in close proximity to navigable waters. In 2006, the U.S. Supreme Court decided companion cases *Rapanos v. U.S.* and *Carabel v. U.S.*[81] on what constitutes navigable waters under the CWA (See Chapter 14 for End of Chapter case). The Corps of Engineers, which regulates the CWA, has generally defined navigable waters very broadly, as it did in the SWANCC case. Its definition includes not only waters that are navigable in fact but also land adjacent to those waters that may sometimes appear to be dry but may be part of an integrated watershed. Due to this broad definition, the Corps often denied permits to developers seeking to build in these questionable areas.

In reaction, the conservative plurality in *Rapanos/Carabel* complained that the Corps sometimes excluded land from development that was merely "storm ditches, ripples of sand in the desert that might contain water once a year, and lands that are covered by floodwaters once every 100 years."[82] Due to a 4-4 split, Justice Kennedy's centrist concurring opinion will be, in the view of several experts, the direction that courts are likely to follow. Kennedy stated that navigable waters are bodies of water that include "relatively permanent, standing or continuously flowing bodies of water" as well as water that has a functional tie-in, or nexus, to the water bodies. While it is likely that water with the nexus will cover some wetlands, developers, planners, and others affected by the decision are concerned about the current lack of guidance. It is quite likely that it will take many years of lower court decisions to clarify what constitutes navigable waters under the CWA.[83]

Use of Surface   Even in cases involving nonnavigable water, questions often arise regarding the owner's use of the water's surface and regarding the use of the water itself for business or industrial purposes as this case from Florida demonstrates.

A CASE IN POINT

In *Florio v. State,*[84] the plaintiffs, riparian landowners, sought an injunction to stop the defendants from running a water skiing school and club on nonnavigable Egypt Lake. The complaint stated that defendants' activities made it dangerous and unsafe for those who wanted to fish, swim, and ski. The Chancellor issued an injunction prohibiting defendants' water skiing activities on Egypt Lake. A Florida appeals court, however, ruled that the Chancellor's injunction was overly broad and discriminatory and remanded the case to determine reasonable use for riparian landowners using the lake.

Use of the water's surface may be approached in one of two ways. In most cases, the owners, as in the *Florio* case, can use the full surface, subject to reasonable restrictions. However, in some cases, courts have concluded that the riparian owners intended by implication to divide their surface use rights.[85] A related question is whether one party who owns the underlying land can exclude other riparian landowners from using the water's surface.

> In *Ace Equipment Sales, Inc. v. Buccino* on page 85, the Connecticut supreme court decides whether the owner of land underlying a nonnavigable man-made pond has exclusive control of the water.

END OF CHAPTER CASE

Use of Water   More important than use of the water surface, especially in light of present and future water shortages, are questions relating to the use of water for domestic and commercial purposes. In the United States, a basic east-west dichotomy has developed over the right to use water. The eastern states, which have humid climates and receive precipitation consistently throughout the year, have generally adopted the riparian rights theory. In that part of the country, water is generally not scarce and watercourses run constantly. Western states, which often have semiarid and arid climates, have usually employed the prior appropriation theory, whereby water is allocated very carefully. Many of the states in the Great Plains and far West that straddle humid and dry climates use a hybrid approach, often forced to adjust their laws to a more diverse physical geography as well as to demands caused by subsequent population increases. Texas's geography, for example, ranges from a very wet Gulf Coast in the East to a desert in the Southwest. Similarly, California, Oregon, and Washington have high mountain ranges that block moisture from the Pacific Ocean, creating a wet, humid coast. In the eastern parts of these states, the same mountains produce a rain shadow effect that creates deserts and semiarid regions. In many of these states, when populations increased and moved into the drier areas, the riparian rights theory, which allows all riparian landowners access to water, was no longer practical, resulting in the need to adopt the prior appropriation theory.

Riparian Rights Theory   The use of water becomes controversial when two or more riparian owners attempt to use the same limited supply of water. For instance, if Smith is the riparian owner of land on the Calahootchee River and Jones is a riparian owner downstream from Smith, the issue is whether Smith can use water from the Calahootchee in a way detrimental to Jones. This question was rarely subjected to litigation until the industrial revolution led to increased demands for water. The industrial revolution also led to widespread water pollution, which ultimately resulted in the CWA's extensive regulation of water discharges, as discussed in Chapter 14.

Two theories of **riparian rights** have been developed by eastern states in determining Smith's rights. Although the theory is out of favor today, at one time, some states used the English common law **natural flow theory**, which provides that each riparian owner is entitled to have the water maintained in its natural state. While each riparian owner may use the water for "natural" wants, such as drinking, washing, and cleaning, "artificial" wants, which include agricultural and industrial purposes, are allowable only when

riparian rights
The rights of an owner of land that touches a watercourse to use the water.

natural flow theory
A riparian rights doctrine, originated in England, that confers to riparian owners the right to the ordinary flow of water along their land, but undiminished in quantity and quality.

they do not materially change the quality or quantity of the water. As a result, those industries that polluted the water or used too much of it in their manufacturing processes were subject to injunctions and damages. Under traditional natural flow theory, if the water is used continuously on nonriparian land, such use may be enjoined by a riparian owner even if the owner is not directly harmed.[86] The natural flow theory has functioned well in England, which has a mild, temperate climate characterized by plentiful year-round precipitation. This theory allows substantial use of water without impinging on the rights of other riparian owners.

reasonable use theory
A riparian rights doctrine that confers to riparian owners the reasonable use of the water that flows along their land.

Today the **reasonable use theory** is dominant. The reasonable use theory is a flexible theory that adapts well to the humid climates of the eastern United States, where seasonal drought and water shortages are not uncommon. This theory allows each riparian owner to use and share the water beneficially so long as the use does not interfere unreasonably with the beneficial uses of other riparian owners. In determining whether a particular use of water is reasonable, courts consider the following factors, among others:

- *Economic and social value of the use*
- *Suitability of the use to the watercourse*
- *Practicality of avoiding or preventing harm*
- *Extent of the harm*

Courts also examine whether the uses are natural, such as drinking water and domestic uses, garden irrigation, and watering of animals, or artificial uses, including manufacturing, crop irrigation, and mining. When the two uses clash, courts, as this Missouri case reveals, generally give priority to the natural uses.

A CASE IN POINT

In *Edmondson v. Edwards*,[87] Edmondson was deprived of water from a stream adjacent to his land that he had long used for watering his livestock. The deprivation occurred after Edwards, a riparian landowner upstream from Edmondson, diverted the water for recreational purposes. The appeals court stated that reasonable use of water is a question of fact that includes looking at the "volume of water in the stream, the seasons and climatic condition and the needs of other riparian proprietors." The court further stated that the "needs" of the riparian owners must be considered, especially "'natural wants,' which include drinking water for family and for livestock." The court upheld the lower court's decision in Edmondson's favor, ruling that Edwards' diversion of the stream was not reasonable and that a permanent injunction was the proper remedy since his actions created irreparable harm.

Several states control water use by permit systems in which administrative agencies take into account similar factors in deciding whether to issue permits.[88] The American Society of Civil Engineers (ASCE) has developed a Model State Riparian Water Rights Code, in which "regulated riparian rights"[89] would be quantified by a permit designating the amount and source of water that can be withdrawn, together with the time and means of diversion.

prior appropriation theory
A water rights doctrine that confers the primary rights to the first users of water.

Prior Appropriation Theory   The **prior appropriation theory** has been adopted in one form or another in western states, where water is scarcer than in the East. (See Table 3.1.) Mississippi is also a prior appropriation state. Unlike the riparian rights theory, prior appropriation is based not on equality of rights, but on the principle of "first in

TABLE 3.1 Prior Appropriation States*

PURE PRIOR APPROPRIATION STATES

Alaska	Idaho	New Mexico
Arizona	Montana	Utah
Colorado	Nevada	Wyoming

HYBRID SYSTEMS (PRIOR APPROPRIATION STATES WITH SOME RIPARIAN RIGHTS)

California	North Dakota	South Dakota
Kansas	Oklahoma	Texas
Mississippi	Oregon	Washington
Nebraska		

*All other states follow riparian rights theory except Hawaii (where water rights are based in part on ancient Hawaiian laws) and Louisiana (where water rights are derived from French law).

Source: D. Getches, *Water Law in a Nutshell* 5–8 (3rd ed. 1997).

time, first in right." That is, the first person to appropriate the water, whether or not the person owns land on the water, has priority over later users.

For example, assume that Green owns a farm on a river in a state whose laws are based on prior appropriation; Blue owns a farm twenty miles from the river. There is enough water in the river to irrigate only one of the farms. If Blue was the first person to use the water for irrigation, she becomes the prior appropriator and is entitled to a permit enabling her to use all of the water in the river. Green could use none of it even though he is a riparian owner. However, if Blue, as the senior water rights holder, cannot use all of the water allotted to her farms, she must allocate to Green what water remains. To ensure that Green, the junior water rights holder, does not use more than he is supposed to under the allotment set in the permitting process, a "watermaster" is authorized under state law to oversee that water distribution is done properly.[90]

To establish priority rights, a person must use the water on a regular basis for domestic, industrial, agricultural, mining, power, or other beneficial uses. Unlike the reasonable use theory, the law of prior appropriation does not establish priorities in how the water is used as long as the use is beneficial. How to define what is a beneficial use, however, can be controversial. In recent years, some states, such as Colorado, have expanded their definition to include recreation. The result is that owners of the rights are now preserving the water for sporting activities such as white-water rafting instead of appropriating it for agricultural or urban uses. This legal development pleases environmentalists but has pitted them against the strong interests of other users, particularly farmers and homebuilders.

In prior appropriation states, a prior appropriator must obtain a permit from an agency, which will determine whether the use is beneficial. Generally, if the owners of the rights fail to use the water for beneficial purposes for a statutory period of time, such as five years in Nevada, they must forfeit their rights back to the state.[91] In general, if a person abandons water rights, the rights revert back to the state, and no one, including the former owner, can later gain rights to the water through adverse possession. Adverse possession, discussed in Chapter 10, occurs when a person acquires title to another's property rights by continuously possessing the property in an open and hostile manner for a prescribed period of time. In the New Mexico case of *Turner v. Bassett*[92] the court ruled that public water is exclusively governed by the permit process and, therefore, is not subject to adverse possession.

Moreover, the owner of these rights generally does not have to be a riparian owner.[93] While the prior appropriator's rights can exclude other uses, as in the example of Green and Blue, a water permit often imposes conditions to preserve water quality, navigability, and the preservation of fish and wildlife. For example, when the Alaska Department of Natural Resources issued permits for gold mining on the Tuliksak River and its tributaries, the Department was obligated to impose permit conditions to ensure adequate stream flow for a valuable salmon habitat.[94]

ETHICAL AND PUBLIC POLICY ISSUES

Is Outlawing the Harvesting of Rainwater an Ethical Public Policy?

In at least two prior appropriation states, Colorado and Utah, it is illegal for private citizens to harvest rainwater in barrels, cisterns, and other catchment systems. The law exists because in the aggregate, rainwater that would otherwise go into rivers may significantly deprive the owners of water rights under prior appropriate laws, the rights to the water necessary to sustain farms, cities, and governments. Should owners of water rights be protected to this degree or is rainwater a resource that everyone should be able to use?[95]

Thirsty western states are continually searching for solutions to water shortages. Rainwater, as discussed above, is one important source. In contrast to Colorado and Utah's approach, Tucson, Arizona recently passed the nation's first municipal rainwater harvesting ordinance for commercial projects. Under this law, new corporate and commercial structures will be required to use rainwater for half of the water needed for landscaping.[96]

Hybrid Approach   A number of states, as previously mentioned, have developed a *hybrid system* in which both riparian and appropriative rights are coordinated, typically by statute, to confine riparian uses to actual uses undertaken prior to a specific date. That date is usually when the state converted from a riparian approach to a system of prior appropriation. As mentioned earlier, these are generally states which are subject to both wet and dry climates which have found it impractical to continue the reasonable use theory due to increasing population and therefore greater demands for water, particularly in their drier areas. While such legislation has been upheld in many states,[97] an Oklahoma court has declared that abolishing future reasonable uses of riparian owners is a "taking" under the Oklahoma Constitution.[98]

The Colorado River, the most important river in the dry western United States, has been the subject of extensive legislation and legal action at the state and federal levels for decades. Before the tremendous urban growth in the West during the twentieth century, farmers were the first to assert their rights to the water as the prior appropriators. Conflict, however, was inevitable as farmers and urban consumers fought for the rights to use the river's precious life-sustaining water. A fierce clash between the two was precipitated in 2003 by a U.S. Department of Interior announcement that California's Colorado River allotment would be slashed 800,000 acres feet (an acres foot = 325,851 gallons), enough water to supply 2 million urban households a year. To comply with the federal guidelines, California was forced to make a critical decision. In late 2003, the state cut the allotment of its largest users of Colorado River water, primarily the farmers in the Imperial Valley Irrigation District. In recent years, many western farmers have seen the "writing on the wall." Increasingly, they are selling their rights to water districts and downsizing their activities or leaving the business completely.[99]

TABLE 3.2 A Comparison of Water Rights Theories: Reasonable Use Theory Versus Prior Appropriation Theory

REASONABLE USE THEORY (RIPARIAN RIGHTS)	PRIOR APPROPRIATION THEORY
1. All riparian owners share equally the rights to use the water as long as they do not unreasonably interfere with the beneficial uses of the water by other riparian owners.	1. Water rights are owned by the first party to claim the rights as prior appropriator.
2. Riparian owners generally gain rights to the water simply by owning land adjacent to the water. Some states require permits for water use.	2. Prior appropriators gain rights by intentionally diverting and/or using the water on a regular basis for beneficial purposes, Continued use is subject to securing a permit from an administrative agency.
3. Only riparian owners can own water rights.	3. The prior appropriator does not have to be the riparian owner or generally even own land to have water rights.
4. Riparian owners must use the water on lands contiguous to the water and within the watershed.	4. Prior appropriators may use water anywhere.
5. Riparian owners must use the water for natural and artificial uses. Water for natural uses generally has priority over artificial uses in determining reasonable use.	5. Prior appropriation theory does not create priorities for water use.

Sources: Adapted from R. Boyer, *Survey of the Law of Real Property* (3rd ed. 1981) and O. Matthews, *Water Resources, Geography and Law* (1984).

Colorado River water issues continue to vex the Southwestern states which are so dependent on its steady flow. In the 2000s extensive droughts greatly diminished snowmelt in the western Rocky Mountains, the main source of the river's water. This intensified the battles among states, farmers, and urban areas and even between the U.S. and Mexico, which is entitled by treaty to some of the Colorado River's water before it empties into the Gulf of California.

ETHICAL AND PUBLIC POLICY ISSUES

Is Prior Appropriation a Moral System for Distributing Water?

In Problem 10 on page 91, a discussion of the events presented in the movie *The Milagro Beanfield War* underscores the ethical problems and class struggles that can arise from this legal doctrine.

groundwater

Water beneath the earth's surface fed by rainfall or surface streams. Water that is not part of a defined underground stream.

diffused surface water

Water on the earth's surface that does not flow in a defined channel or stream. Water fed generally by rainfall or melting snow.

Table 3.2 compares and contrasts the two theories of water use.

Groundwater and Surface Water

While the preceding summary of water law focused on water that flows or lies in a defined course, channel, or bed, water often flows outside established channels. Two such forms of water are pertinent here. **Groundwater** (also known as *percolating water*) passes beneath the surface and apart from a definite underground channel fed by rainwater infiltrating the soil profile or stream water that no longer is part of a surface flow. Examples include artesian basins and underground lakes. **Diffused surface water** runs over the earth's surface apart from a watercourse and is usually produced by heavy rains or melting snows. Landowners often must build dams or levees to contain and protect their land or ditches, culverts, and drains to divert the water from its destructive path. In considering the right to use groundwater, most states in the West have adopted the prior

common enemy rule

Rule from the common law allowing landowners the right to take whatever measures necessary to protect and divert diffused surface water from their property.

civil law rule

A water law rule prohibiting landowners from altering or diverting the natural flow of diffused surface water.

reasonable conduct doctrine

Doctrine in water law allowing landowners to divert diffused surface water if their efforts do not unreasonably harm other landowners.

appropriation theory discussed previously. In the East, states use variations of the reasonable use theory or an older common law absolute ownership rule[100] that declares the owner of the surface to be the absolute owner of the water beneath, which may be used as the owner pleases. The reasonable use approach can resolve groundwater conflicts caused, for example, by one neighbor whose excessive use of water causes depletion of an entire reservoir or even subsidence of the adjacent owner's property.

Diffuse surface water has been the subject of considerable litigation, as illustrated by the following example.[101] Assume that three lot owners, Able, Baker, and Chance, own homes on lots situated next to each other in a north-south direction on a hill. The highest and northernmost lot on the hill belongs to Able, the lot below is Baker's, and the lot farthest down the hill belongs to Chance. Each spring melting snow causes a considerable amount of surface water to pass over the three lots.

This diffused surface water could raise *three* legal issues. *First,* may Baker build a wall on the north edge of his property to block the surface water and prevent it from passing over his property even if by doing this, he causes Able's property to be flooded? Under the common law approach, which is called the **common enemy rule**, the surface water is an enemy to every landowner and each landowner is free to deal with it as she sees fit. In such a case, Baker can use defensive measures against this watery enemy by building a wall. Under another approach—the so-called **civil law rule**—a landowner such as Baker cannot interfere with the natural flow of water over his land. A third view—the **reasonable conduct doctrine**—offers a compromise between the common law and the civil law rules and represents the view of most states.[102] To determine reasonable conduct, courts look at all factors, especially the nature of the benefit to Baker and the harm to Able.

In *Heins Implement Company v. Missouri Highway & Transportation Commission* on page 87, the court resolves whether Missouri should reject the common enemy rule in favor of the majority reasonable conduct doctrine.

END OF CHAPTER CASE

Second, may Baker build a dam on the southern edge of his property to create a lake, the result being that Chance has no opportunity to use the water? Under the common enemy rule, the owners may use the surface water as they see fit. However, under the reasonable conduct doctrine, the owners would be required to act reasonably by considering such factors as the purpose for Baker's dam and the way it affects Chance and his property.

Finally, assume that Baker, instead of damming the water, constructs drains or ditches that cause the surface water to flow onto Chance's property and damage it. Under the common enemy rule, Baker could discharge the waters as a means of protecting himself; but under an important exception, he could not accumulate the water and then purposely discharge it onto Chance's land. Likewise, under the reasonable conduct rule, since Chance's property would be damaged, Baker's offensive actions might be deemed as an unreasonable interference. The following Delaware case discusses this important modification of the common enemy rule.

A CASE IN POINT

In *E. J. Hollingsworth Co. v. Jardel Co.,*[103] the plaintiff sought to enjoin the defendant from collecting and dumping surface waters onto his property by means of a storm sewer. The court determined that as a result of the defendant's development of his property, nine-tenths of the water falling on his land during a storm would reach the plaintiff's property, whereas in the past, only two-tenths would flow off the defendant's property. The court issued a permanent injunction concluding that "one may not in effect substantially enlarge or change a natural drainage easement by artificially collecting and casting the surface water on the lower owner to his substantial damage."

ETHICAL AND PUBLIC POLICY ISSUES

Which Public Policy Governing Diffused Surface Water Is Most Ethical?

The three theories governing diffused water are still used in various states. At one time, the common enemy theory was dominant; but now it is used in only a few states. Over a long period of time, many of the common enemy states changed their law to the reasonable conduct theory. Law often lags behind ethics. Do you believe the states that changed their laws did so because it was a more ethical public policy approach to handling the problems created by diffused water? For example, is it ethical for landowners, in order to protect themselves, to discharge excess water onto their neighbors' property? On the other hand, is it ethically correct, as it is under the civil law rule, for landowners to be prohibited from protecting their own lands since landowners cannot interfere with the natural flow? The civil law rule has also been criticized for inhibiting land development. Assuming that is true, what are the ethical implications of that?

Lateral Support

Increased demand for construction, coupled with a limited supply of land, has resulted in more concentrated land development than in the past. Thus, the rights of landowners to support of their soil by their neighbors' land—that is, **lateral support**—have become more important.

lateral support

The right of lateral and subjacent support is the right to have land supported by the adjoining land or the soil beneath.

If Able and Baker own adjoining parcels of real estate, the law is clear that Baker may not excavate and develop his property so as to cause Able's soil to subside. However, the extent of Able's right to support will depend on the nature of the land and the nature of Baker's excavation.

Common Law

A lateral support case usually arises from one of *four* possible situations. *First*, assume that Baker was negligent in developing his property and that Able's soil subsided as a result. Under traditional negligence principles, Baker would be liable for damage to the soil and for damage to any buildings on the soil. Moreover, Baker must pay for the depreciated value of Able's property caused by Baker's negligence. This can include the effects of cracks in sidewalks and in the structure itself and the perception they may give to a potential buyer.[104] As the next case from North Carolina points out, a developer who does not properly gauge the risk of injury to adjacent landowners' property, will face consequences.

A CASE IN POINT

In *S. H. Kress & Co. v. Reaves*,[105] the court held that the failure of a developer to sample soil or to notify the adjoining owners before beginning to excavate was negligence: "One contemplating a project of this character owes the duty to an adjoining property owner of exercising at least ordinary care to ascertain the conditions under which the work would progress, and this includes some reasonable investigation as to the character of the soil to be excavated in making the proposed excavation. Failure to make such an investigation amounts to negligence and renders the one negligent in this respect liable for resulting damages."

Second, assume that Baker was not negligent and that Able's land was in its "natural state"; that is, there were no buildings on it. Able's land still subsided as a result of Baker's excavations. Able would be allowed to recover because Baker has **an absolute duty to support his neighbor's property in its natural state.**

Third, assume that Baker was not negligent but that Able's land contained improvements, the land and buildings were damaged by Baker's excavation, and the land subsided because of the additional weight of the buildings. Courts generally agree that Able cannot recover damages for the land or the buildings.

Fourth, as in the third instance, assume that Baker was not negligent, that Able improved his land, and that the land and buildings were damaged by the excavation. But in this case, the land would have subsided *even without* the additional weight of the buildings. This is the most difficult of the four situations to resolve, and two divergent views have developed in the courts. Some courts allow damages for both the land and the buildings. In most courts, however, Baker would be liable only for damages to the land.

Was a contractor retained by the city liable to a homeowner for cracking of the basement walls and floor, doors that would not shut, and the development of a tilting effect? The court in *Simons v. Tri-State Const. Co.*, on page 89, discusses the contractor's liability of loss of lateral support to the Simons' home.

END OF CHAPTER CASE

Statutory Approach

In several states, the preceding common law rules have been modified by statutes that apply to certain types of excavations. If the statute refers to a particular excavation, the common law rules would not be applied and the rights and duties of the parties would be defined in the statute. In California, for example, the statute requires the person making the excavation to perform the following three elements:

1. Give reasonable notice to adjoining owners, stating how deep the excavation will be when excavation begins
2. Use ordinary care and skill and take reasonable precautions to sustain the adjoining land
3. Allow adjoining owners thirty days to protect their structures if the excavation is to be deeper than the foundations of the adjoining buildings

California courts have also held that an excavator must give notice if the stability of non-contiguous land is threatened by the impending excavation.[106] Furthermore, if the excavation is to be nine feet or more and the foundations of adjoining buildings are at least nine feet, the person making the excavation must protect adjoining lands and buildings from damage at no cost to adjoining owners. If there is damage in such circumstances, the excavator will be liable.[107]

CASES

Air Rights

WING MING PROPERTIES (U.S.A.) v. MOTT OPERATING LTD.
148 Misc.2d 680, 561 N.Y.S.2d 337 (NY. Sup 1990)

SAXE, Justice. Exactly what rights are conveyed when the air rights over a building are transferred to an adjacent parcel of land so that the height of a building constructed on the neighboring property exceeds the limitations set by applicable zoning law height restrictions?

* * *

The events leading to the current dispute began in the early 1970s. Plaintiff's [Wing Ming's] predecessor in interest, Hon Yip, planned to construct a building upon the land he owned adjacent to 5 Chatham Square. He envisioned a structure which would exceed the maximum height permitted under the city zoning regulations. The zoning resolution imposes height restrictions based upon a ratio calculated by dividing the total floor area on a lot ("the sum of the gross areas of the several floors of a building") by the area of the lot upon which a building is to be constructed; the builder is limited to a specified floor area ratio (F.A.R.). Recognizing the hardship imposed upon City builders who have access to finite amounts of landspace but must accommodate large numbers of people in proportion, the Resolution provides a loophole. If two adjacent lots are under "single ownership," the unused floor area ratio may be transferred from one lot to another. Thus, if one lot has a two-story building, but based upon the area of the lot upon which it rests maximum height allocable to it would be ten stories, it may transfer the right to build another eight stories to a contiguous lot under the same ownership. The transaction technically involves the conveyance of airspace from one plot to the next and the rights in the airspace exchanged are probably best viewed as "air development rights."

A two-story theatre, owned by [defendant] Mott, leased by [defendant] Kaplan, and subleased at the time by [defendants] Chu and Tam, was situated upon the lot contiguous to Hon Yip's property. The height of this building was substantially lower than the F.A.R. allocable to it under the zoning resolution. Since the acquisition of a sufficient ownership interest in the adjacent plot of land at 5 Chatham Square could facilitate a transfer of air development rights and enable him to construct the "oversized" building on his Mott Street property, Hon Yip arranged to acquire the status of "single ownership" mandated by the zoning resolution. [Mott and Kaplan conveyed their air rights to Hon Yip in a document entitled "1973 Conveyance of Air Rights" ("Conveyance") and Kaplan temporarily assigned her lease to Hon Yip to meet the "single ownership" requirement.]

* * *

In 1985, defendant Kaplan subleased her retained interest in 5 Chatham Square to defendant Bank of Central Asia (BCA). The agreement between Kaplan and the BCA permitted the installation of new air-conditioning units on BCA's roof and construction of a parapet to conceal these units from view. Both additions were allegedly completed by 1986.

This action in trespass was brought by plaintiff because of its concern that the newly installed air-conditioning units and parapets have increased the utilized floor area space on 5 Chatham Square. If this is so, it fears that the air development rights transferred to Wing Ming's property would be deemed illegal since the rights contained in the airspace are being simultaneously used by both properties. Wing Ming fears that the Building Department will be alerted to the contemporaneous use of air development rights, will confiscate the excess floor area space of the Citibank building, and force it to reduce its multi-story office building to legal size.

Wing Ming asserts that even if as a matter of law the floor area space at 5 Chatham Square has not been increased, the construction of air-conditioning units and parapets on the roof still constitutes a trespass by BCA. He claims that a conveyance of air rights encompasses a transfer of both development rights encapsulated in the exchanged volume of airspace and the right to its exclusive physical occupation and control. Defendant BCA contends that these rights are separate and distinct and that the sole right acquired by Wing Ming was the regulatory development right allowed under the zoning resolution. BCA further defends itself against Wing Ming's allegations by asserting as a matter of law that no trespass to plaintiff's development rights exists.

At issue is the scope of the rights encompassed in the term "air rights" used in the 1973 Conveyance of Air Rights.

* * *

Defendants offer sufficient evidence of the history surrounding both the execution and performance of the provisions contained within the 1973 Conveyance of Air Rights to convince this court that summary judgment is warranted as to interpretation of the term "air rights" as contained in the agreement. Hon Yip's actions prior and subsequent to the execution of the agreement, and the prevalent custom and usage of the term "air rights" clearly manifest the acquisition of air development rights, and not rights to exclusively occupy and control the physical airspace over 5 Chatham Square.

A primary factor to be considered in any attempt to interpret a contract is the purpose of the parties in making the contract. Hon Yip's actions substantiate the fact that he entered into the series of agreements with the defendants for the sole purpose of acquiring the development rights unused by the occupiers of 5 Chatham Square. Hon Yip knew that New York City zoning laws prohibited the building of a 12-story building on his property. He therefore sought to legally "borrow" the unused air development rights of the two-story building situated on the property adjacent to his own.

* * *

BCA's rooftop installations could have potentially constituted a trespass only if it had been proven that construction actually increased the floor area of its building encroaching on the development rights obtained by Wing Ming. The language of Zoning Resolution 12–10 as applied to the present facts, however, clearly indicates the absence of a trespass. Floor area is defined by the Zoning Resolution as:

> "[t]he sum of the gross areas of the several floors of a building ... measured from the exterior faces of exterior walls or from the center lines of walls separating two buildings."

Specifically excluded from this definition of floor area is "floor space used for mechanical equipment and open terraces provided no more than 50% of it is enclosed by a parapet not higher than three feet eight inches." The new air-conditioning equipment falls under the statutory exception of "mechanical equipment" placed in "open (roof) space." The parapets are similarly excepted since they are less than 3 feet 8 inches high. BCA's construction technically did not increase the floor area space of its building. Therefore, as a matter of law, there has been no trespass on the air development rights acquired by plaintiff to build the twelve-story structure presently housing a Citibank facility. [The Court entered judgment for the defendants.]

Trespass: Mineral Estate
COASTAL OIL & GAS CORP. v. GARZA ENERGY TRUST
51 Tex. Sup. Ct. J. 55, 268 S.W. 3d 1 (Tex. 2008)

HECHT, Justice. Royalty interest owners of natural gas lease brought action against gas well operator for subsurface trespass, breach of duty of good faith pooling, and breach of implied covenants to develop, market, and protect against drainage. The 332nd District Court of Hidalgo County, Mario Efrain Ramirez, Jr., J., entered judgment on a jury verdict for royalty interest owners, and well operator appealed. The Court of Appeals, affirmed in part, reversed in part, and remanded. Well operator petitioned for review.

Holdings: Upon grant of review, the Supreme Court held that:

(1) rule of capture prevented royalty interest owners of natural gas lease from recovering damages against well operator on trespass claim;

(2) correct measure of damages for breach of the implied covenant to protect against drainage is value of royalty lost to lessor because of lessee's failure to act as reasonably prudent operator ...

(3) royalty interest owners could not recover on claim for breach of implied covenant to protect against drainage in absence of evidence that reasonably prudent operator should have prevented drainage;

* * *

The primary issue in this appeal is whether subsurface hydraulic fracturing of a natural gas well that extends into another's property is a trespass for which the value of gas drained as a result may be recovered as damages. We hold that the rule of capture bars recovery of such damages.

* * *

Respondents to whom we shall refer collectively as Salinas, own the minerals in a 748-acre tract of land in Hidalgo County called Share 13, which they and their ancestors have occupied for over a century. At all times material to this case, petitioner Coastal Oil & Gas Corp. has been the lessee of the minerals in Share 13 and an adjacent tract, Share 15. Coastal was also the lessee of the minerals in Share 12 until it acquired the mineral estate in that 163-acre tract in 1995. A natural gas reservoir, the Vicksburg T formation, lies between 11,688 and 12,610 feet below these tracts.

* * *

In March, Salinas sued Coastal for breach of its implied covenants to develop Share 13 and prevent drainage. Salinas was concerned that Coastal was allowing Share 13 gas, on which Coastal owed Salinas a royalty, to drain to Share 12, where Coastal, as both owner and operator, was entitled to the gas unburdened by a royalty obligation. Salinas's suit prompted a flurry of drilling by Coastal on Share 13—eight wells in fourteen months. Not until late 1999 did Coastal drill again on Share 12.

The Vicksburg T is a "tight" sandstone formation, relatively imporous and impermeable, from which natural gas cannot be commercially produced without hydraulic fracturing stimulation, or "fracing", as the process is known in the industry. This is done by pumping fluid down a well at high pressure so that it is forced out into the formation. The pressure creates cracks in the rock that propagate along the azimuth of natural fault lines in an elongated elliptical pattern in opposite directions from the well. Behind the fluid comes a slurry containing small granules called proppants—sand, ceramic beads, or bauxite are used—that lodge themselves in the cracks, propping them open against the enormous subsurface pressure that would force them shut as soon as the fluid was gone. The fluid is then drained, leaving the cracks open for gas or oil to flow to the wellbore. Fracing in effect increases the well's exposure to the formation, allowing greater production. First used commercially in 1949, fracing is now essential to economic production of oil and gas and commonly used throughout Texas, the United States, and the world.

* * *

All the wells on Share 12 and Share 13 were fraced. As measured by the amount of proppant injected into the well, the fracing of the Coastal Fee No. 1 and No. 2 wells was, as Economides testified, "massive", much larger than any fracing operation on a well on Share 13.

* * *

Regarding drainage, Salinas's expert, Economides, testified that because of the fracing operation on the Coastal No. 1 well, 25-35% of the gas it produced drained from Share 13. The jury found:

- Coastal failed to reasonably develop Share 13 after 1993, causing Salinas $1.75 million damages for interest on lost royalties;
- Coastal breached its duty to pool in good faith, causing Salinas $1 million damages in lost royalties;
- Coastal's fracing of the Coastal Fee No. 1 well trespassed on Share 13, causing substantial drainage, which a reasonably prudent operator would have prevented, and $1 million damages in lost royalties;
- Coastal acted with malice and appropriated Salinas's property unlawfully, and should be assessed $10 million punitive damages;
- Salinas's reasonable attorney fees for trial were $1.4 million.

* * *

B

Had Coastal caused something like proppants to be deposited on the surface of Share 13, it would be liable for trespass, and from the ancient common law maxim that land ownership extends to the sky above and the earth's center below, one might extrapolate that the same rule should apply two miles

below the surface. But that maxim—*cujus est solum ejus est usque ad coelum et ad inferos*—"has no place in the modern world." Wheeling an airplane across the surface of one's property without permission is a trespass; flying the plane through the airspace two miles above the property is not. Lord Coke, who pronounced the maxim, did not consider the possibility of airplanes. But neither did he imagine oil wells. The law of trespass need no more be the same two miles below the surface than two miles above.

* * *

We have not previously decided whether subsurface fracing can give rise to an action for trespass. That issue, we held in *Gregg v. Delhi-Taylor Oil Corp.,* is one for the courts to decide, not the Railroad Commission. In 1961, when we decided *Gregg,* the Commission had never addressed the subject, and we specifically indicated no view on whether Commission rules could authorize secondary recovery operations that crossed property lines. The next Term, in *Railroad Commission of Texas v. Manziel,* we held that a salt water injection secondary recovery operation did not cause a trespass when the water migrated across property lines, but we relied heavily on the fact that the Commission had approved the operation. Thirty years later, in *Geo Viking, Inc. v. Tex-Lee Operating Company,* we issued a per curiam opinion holding that fracing beneath another's land was a trespass, but on rehearing we withdrew the opinion and expressly did not decide the issue.

* * *

We need not decide the broader issue here. In this case, actionable trespass requires injury, and Salinas's only claim of injury—that Coastal's fracing operation made it possible for gas to flow from beneath Share 13 to the Share 12 wells—is precluded by the rule of capture. That rule gives a mineral rights owner title to the oil and gas produced from a lawful well bottomed on the property, even if the oil and gas flowed to the well from beneath another owner's tract. The rule of capture is a cornerstone of the oil and gas industry and is fundamental both to property rights and to state regulation. Salinas does not claim that the Coastal Fee No. 1 violates any statute or regulation. Thus, the gas he claims to have lost simply does not belong to him. He does not claim that the hydraulic fracturing operation damaged his wells or the Vicksburg T formation beneath his property. In sum, Salinas does not claim damages that are recoverable.

* * *

We are not persuaded by Salinas's arguments. Rather, we find four reasons not to change the rule of capture to allow one property owner to sue another for oil and gas drained by hydraulic fracturing that extends beyond lease lines.

First, the law already affords the owner who claims drainage full recourse. This is the justification for the rule of capture, and it applies regardless of whether the drainage is due to fracing.

* * *

Second, allowing recovery for the value of gas drained by hydraulic fracturing usurps to courts and juries the lawful and preferable authority of the Railroad Commission to regulate oil and gas production.

* * *

Third, determining the value of oil and gas drained by hydraulic fracturing is the kind of issue the litigation process is least equipped to handle. One difficulty is that the material facts are hidden below miles of rock, making it difficult to ascertain what might have happened. Such difficulty in proof is one of the justifications for the rule of capture.

* * *

Fourth, the law of capture should not be changed to apply differently to hydraulic fracturing because no one in the industry appears to want or need the change.

* * *

Accordingly, we hold that damages for drainage by hydraulic fracturing are precluded by the rule of capture. It should go without saying that the rule of capture cannot be used to shield misconduct that is illegal, malicious, reckless, or intended to harm another without commercial justification, should such a case ever arise. But that certainly did not occur in this case, and no instance of it has been cited to us.

* * *

We reverse the court of appeals' judgment, render judgment that Salinas take nothing on his claims for trespass and breach of the implied covenant to protect against drainage, and remand the remainder of the case for a new trial.

Nonnavigable Waters—Surface Use
ACE EQUIPMENT SALES, INC. v. BUCCINO
869 A.2d 626 (Conn. Sup. Ct. 2005)

KATZ, Judge. The principal issue in this certified appeal is whether the owners of property abutting a man-made, nonnavigable pond have the right to use the pond for recreational purposes when the majority of the land beneath the pond is privately owned by another party. The plaintiffs, Ace Equipment Sales, Inc. (Ace), Willington Fish and Game Club, LLC (Willington, LLC), and Willington Fish and Game Club, Inc. (Willington, Inc.), appeal from the judgment of the Appellate Court that affirmed the judgment of the trial court rendering summary judgment in favor of the defendants. The plaintiffs claim that the Appellate Court improperly concluded that the defendants, Thomas Buccino and Irma Buccino, have a riparian right to use the pond for recreational purposes as abutting landowners. They further claim that, irrespective of a riparian right, the Buccinos' deed prohibits them from entering and using the pond for recreational purposes because its language restricts their use of the pond to industrial purposes. We agree with the plaintiffs and, accordingly, we reverse the judgment of the Appellate Court.

The record reveals the following facts and procedural history relevant to our disposition of this appeal. Hall's Pond (pond) is a twenty acre body of water in the town of Willington that was formed by the erection of a dam and spillway at its southwesterly end, thereby impounding the waters of a nonnavigable brook flowing from the Willimantic River. Until the 1950s, Gardiner Hall, Jr., Company (Hall), owned all of the property under and abutting the pond. In December, 1955, Hall conveyed the dam and mill property downstream of the pond to the Buccinos' predecessors in title, and the Buccinos thereafter acquired the dam and mill property in February, 1967. The deed by which the Buccinos acquired the dam and mill property conveyed easement flowage rights to use pond water for industrial purposes and for the needs of the mill and factory on the property, along with the obligation to maintain the dam and the water level of the pond.

The deed also conveyed a twenty-five foot wide right-of-way over Hall's property to the mill.

Hall retained the land upstream from the dam, which included all or most of the pond bed, until July, 1987, when Hall conveyed it to the plaintiffs' predecessors in title. In July, 1996, that parcel subsequently was conveyed to Willington, LLC, which then conveyed all but one-half acre of the pond bed to Ace in September, 1996. Each of the relevant deeds describes the pond bed in metes and bounds, and it is undisputed that the plaintiffs obtained, pursuant to the deeds, at least 99 percent of the land beneath the pond. Ace licenses the pond for recreational fishing to Willington, Inc., for its members only, of which there are no more than thirty-five, and Willington, Inc., in turn stocks the pond with fish. Ace and Willington, Inc., never have opened the pond to the public, and the plaintiffs never have given the Buccinos permission to use the pond for recreational purposes.

Although the extent of the Buccinos' industrial use of the pond is unclear from the record, it reflects that their recreational use amounted to fishing in the pond twice—both times from the land—and swimming in the pond once. In 1999, the Buccinos began leasing the rights to use the pond for recreational purposes to the licensees; and their tenants and guests. Although the Buccinos have no further intention of using the pond themselves for recreational purposes, they have indicated that they would be willing to license as many as 200 people to use the pond for such purposes. Consistent with their intended recreational use, either the Buccinos or the licensees placed a boat dock on the pond, from which they have launched boats and fished in the pond.

In January, 2000, the plaintiffs commenced this action, seeking, inter alia, injunctive relief from the defendants from entering onto or using the pond for recreational purposes, a declaratory judgment prohibiting the defendants from trespassing on the plaintiffs' property, a declaratory judgment that the Buccinos own no part of the pond bed, and damages. In the spring of 2000, the plaintiffs erected a twelve-foot-wide fence along the edge of the pond, located approximately twenty-two feet from the pond's edge, and have since taken similar steps leading to the obstruction of the defendants' access to their right-of-way and the pond. The defendants denied the plaintiffs' allegation that the Buccinos owned no part of the pond bed, and filed a counterclaim seeking injunctive relief to bar the plaintiffs from interfering with the defendants' recreational use of the pond, and access to the pond generally, a declaratory judgment as to their right to use the pond for recreational purposes, and damages. Thereafter, the plaintiffs moved for summary judgment on their complaint, and the defendants moved for summary judgment on their counterclaim. The trial court denied the plaintiffs' motion for summary judgment and granted the defendants' motion as to liability only, declaring that the defendants had the right to use the pond for recreational purposes and prohibiting the plaintiffs from interfering with such use. The court then ordered a hearing to determine the scope of injunctive relief and damages. After the hearing, the trial court, *Levine, J.,* awarded the defendants common-law damages of $2, and ordered the plaintiffs to remove any obstructions interfering with the defendants' access to the pond and mill.

The plaintiffs subsequently appealed to the Appellate Court, which affirmed the trial court's judgment. The Appellate Court, relying on the Restatement (Second) of Torts, Riparian Rights §843 and case law on riparian rights from Minnesota and Michigan, concluded that the trial court properly had determined that ownership of property abutting the pond is sufficient to establish a riparian right to use the pond for reasonable recreational purposes. The court noted that the right to use the pond for such purposes also could stem from the Buccinos' ownership and maintenance of the dam that controls the pond's existence. The court further concluded that there is no distinction between the riparian rights afforded to a landowner whose property abuts a natural body of water and the rights afforded to a landowner whose property abuts a man-made body of water, at least to the extent that the man-made body has existed for a long period of time. The Appellate Court held that, because the pond had existed for nearly one-half century, it had become a natural waterway. Thus, the court reasoned that the Buccinos' riparian rights were not limited based on whether the pond was man-made when it was created. Finally, the Appellate Court rejected the plaintiffs' claim that the defendants' deed prohibited their use of the pond for recreational purposes. This certified appeal followed.

The plaintiffs claim that the defendants do not have a riparian right to use the pond for recreational purposes solely by virtue of the Buccinos' ownership of abutting property because the plaintiffs' ownership of the entire pond bed grants them exclusive riparian rights under our case law applying to a body of water that is nonnavigable. The plaintiffs further claim that, irrespective of a riparian right, the

Buccinos' deed prohibits them from entering and using the pond for recreational purposes because its language restricts their use of the pond to industrial purposes. In response, the defendants contend that: (1) the pond has become a natural body of water because it has existed for a long period of time, thus our case law applying to manmade bodies of water does not apply; (2) the pond's navigability or lack thereof is irrelevant; and (3) the Buccinos' easement flowage rights and duties as owners of the dam that enables the pond's existence afford the defendants the right to use the pond for recreational purposes. We agree with the plaintiffs.

* * *

Turning to the merits of the present case, we begin with an undisputed and essential fact. Because the plaintiffs obtained their ownership of the pond and the underlying pond bed by way of a deed describing their property in terms of metes and bounds, they have ownership in severalty for whatever portion they own, as opposed to littoral ownership. Thus, we start with a well settled common-law principle. With respect to man-made, nonnavigable bodies of water, the prevailing view is the common-law rule that when a party owns a portion of the land beneath the water in severalty, that party has exclusive rights over that portion, and riparian rights with respect to that portion do not attach to other properties abutting the water.

* * *

Connecticut consistently has followed the common law rule. See, e.g., *Adams v. Pease,* 2 Conn. 481, 483 (1818) (holding, with respect to littoral ownership, adjoining property owners have exclusive rights in nonnavigable bodies); *Chapman v. Kimball,* 9 Conn. 37, 40 (1831) (holding, with respect to nonnavigable bodies, owners have same exclusive property rights as over other real estate).

* * *

Similarly, the majority of states that have considered this question also follow the common-law rule.

We acknowledge that there is a minority civil law rule, which provides that owners of land beneath a body of water have the right to reasonable use and enjoyment of the entire body and that this ownership does not include the right to exclude abutting owners. We also recognize, however, that the few states to have followed this rule have an extensive number of natural lakes, and therefore understandably have adopted a policy favoring maximum recreational use.

* * *

Although we similarly appreciate the value of recreational and commercial water use, "there is nothing in [Connecticut's] topography or location that requires a departure from the rules of the common law. Unlike some of our sister States, we have no large inland lakes, which are, in fact, inland seas, upon which an extensive commerce is carried on, or which are the boundaries with a foreign nation." Accordingly, we conclude that the common-law rule should be applied in the present case.

With these principles in mind, we turn to the present case. It is undisputed that the plaintiffs own 99 percent of the pond bed in severalty. In accordance with the common-law principles previously outlined, therefore, the plaintiffs have exclusive control over this portion of the pond bed and the waters above it. This right permits the plaintiffs to exclude others, including the Buccinos, as abutting owners of the lake bed, by erecting a fence or other barrier to prevent others from utilizing the water which overlies the plaintiffs' property. Accordingly, the Appellate Court improperly determined that the Buccinos had a riparian right to use

the entire pond by virtue of their status as abutting landowners.

The judgment of the Appellate Court is reversed and the case is remanded to that court with direction (1) to reverse the judgment of the trial court and (2) to remand the case to the trial court with direction to deny the defendants' motion for summary judgment and for further proceedings according to law.

Reasonable Use Doctrine
HEINS IMPLEMENT COMPANY v. MISSOURI HIGHWAY & TRANSPORTATION COMMISSION
859 S.W.2d 681 (Mo. 1993)

WILLIAM RAY PRICE, JR, Judge. The principal issue raised by this appeal is whether the modified common enemy doctrine should be applied to bar recovery by landowners and tenants whose property was flooded because a culvert under a highway bypass was not designed to handle the normal overflows from a nearby creek. We conclude that the common enemy doctrine no longer reflects the appropriate rule in situations involving surface water runoff and adopt a doctrine of reasonable use in its stead. We reverse the trial court's grant of judgment notwithstanding the verdict and remand.

* * *

Appellants own or rent commercial and agricultural property along the bottomlands of Wakenda Creek, near the intersection of State Route 10 and U.S. Route 65 south of Carrollton. At this location, Route 10 runs east-west and Route 65 runs north-south. Before the obstructing bypass was built, Wakenda Creek regularly escaped its banks after heavy rainfalls. The floodwaters ran south over Route 10 and collected in a small artificial lake. When the lake's capacity was exceeded, the waters headed east over portions of appellants' lands before crossing Route 65 and returning to the creek farther downstream. These floods were always brief and had never reached any of appellants' buildings.

The Missouri Highway & Transportation Commission (MHTC) condemned some of the property owned by each of the appellants, or their predecessors in title, to build a bypass for Route 65. Mel Downs was the chief design engineer for this project. Downs testified that, although he knew Wakenda Creek was prone to flooding toward the north, he did not know that it also commonly overflowed to the south across Routes 10 and 65. Consequently, he designed a five-foot culvert under the bypass to handle normal rainfall drainage from the area west of the bypass. Downs admitted that this culvert was inadequate to drain the creek's other normal overflows.

Work on the bypass project began in 1975 and ended in 1977. The late 1970s happened to be a period of severe drought in the area. But in July 1981, heavy rains swelled Wakenda Creek once more. The errant waters coursed south and east over appellants' lands as they had done before.

However, when they reached Route 65 they met the new bypass arching above Route 10. The raised bypass with its inadequate drainage culvert acted as a dam, pooling the water on appellants' lands, where it remained for seven days. Commercial buildings were invaded by up to thirty inches of water. Numerous items of business and farm equipment and hundreds of acres of crops were destroyed. Similar floods recurred in June 1982, April 1983, February 1985, October 1985, and June 1990.

Appellants filed suit in 1985 against MHTC; Mel Downs; Frank Trager & Sons, the general contractor for the bypass project; and Carroll County Recreation Club, owner of the lake through which the floodwaters passed on their way to appellants' lands. The trial court granted summary judgment on all claims against the contractor, the engineer, and the club, and on the claims of negligence and nuisance against MHTC. The two remaining counts alleging inverse condemnation against MHTC were tried to a jury.

The jury returned verdicts in favor of appellants and assessed their damages at $298,175. Appellants filed motions to increase the jury's award or for a new trial on the issue of damages only. MHTC filed a motion for judgment n.o.v. [Author's Note: judgment notwithstanding the verdict], arguing that appellants' action was barred by the original condemnation proceedings and by the common enemy doctrine. The trial court sustained MHTC's motion and entered judgment in its favor.

* * *

III. The Common Enemy Doctrine/Natural Flow (Civil Law) Rule/Reasonable Use Rule

A.

At the heart of this appeal lies the parties' dispute over the applicability of the modified common enemy doctrine, which has directed the law of surface waters in our state since 1884.

* * *

As the doctrine stands today, upper landowners may be required to act with some degree of care when discharging surface water onto lower-lying lands. On the other hand, lower owners have retained considerable freedom in blocking the flow of surface water onto their lands, subject only to the proviso that they may not dam a natural drainway. Moreover, it has been recently stated that abstract reasonableness is not an issue when a lower owner obstructs the flow of diffuse surface water, and that the lower owner need not establish a good motive or good faith for blocking the water.

* * *

B.

American courts have developed three distinct approaches to controversies involving the diversion or impoundment of diffuse surface waters: the civil law or natural flow rule, the common enemy doctrine, and the reasonable use rule. With the exception of a few Louisiana cases, which had applied the civil law rule as early as 1812, the earliest cases espousing each of the three doctrines appeared independently of one another during the middle years of the last century.

* * *

Extensive analyses of these doctrines have been undertaken by several courts; they need not be repeated here. Briefly, the civil law rule appears to be derived from the French and Spanish civil codes, which in turn have their roots in Roman law. It imposes liability for any interference with the natural surface drainage pattern that causes injury to another's land. Each parcel of land is said to be subject to a natural servitude or easement for the flow of surface water, so that the lower or servient estate is obliged to accept the water that would naturally drain into it, and the higher or dominant estate is precluded from retaining the water that would naturally drain out of it.

The civil law doctrine, with its comforting allusions to the "natural" law, was sometimes adopted or retained as a gentler alternative to the perceived crudity of the common enemy doctrine. Many courts rejected it, however, out of concern that it would impede the development of land and thus would retard the march of progress that was so dear to the nineteenth century. Courts also encountered difficulties in determining "what was the exact course of the 'natural flow' of the surface water before the bulldozers arrived on the scene."

The common enemy doctrine, in contrast, was once believed to derive from the English common law, but it is now accepted that the English law of surface waters was unsettled when the doctrine first appeared in Massachusetts. It is based on an exaggerated view of the notion of absolute ownership of land, as reflected by the rather primitive analysis that justified its original formulation:

The right of a party to the free and unfettered control of his own land above, upon and beneath the surface cannot be interfered with or restrained by any considerations of injury to others which may be occasioned by the flow of mere surface water in consequence of the lawful appropriation of land by its owner to a particular use or mode of enjoyment.

As a consequence of this short-sighted focus on "the due exercise of dominion over [one's] own soil," the doctrine completely ignores the fact that invasion by an unwanted and destructive volume of water might otherwise have been viewed as a classic trespass.

At one time, the common enemy doctrine held sway over most of the United States. Many courts were persuaded that it would best promote land development and economic growth, particularly as compared to the civil law rule. On the other hand, the practical consequence of adherence to this rule has been described as "a neighborhood contest between pipes and dikes from which 'breach of the peace is often inevitable.'" The enduring objection to the common enemy doctrine was aptly put by a member of this Court: "This is a mere reiteration of the doctrine of 'sauve qui peut,' or as popularly translated into our vernacular 'the devil take the hindmost.'"

* * *

The rule of reasonable use differs from the other two rules in that it does not purport to lay down any specific rights or privileges with respect to surface waters, but leaves each case to be determined on its own facts, in accordance with general principles of fairness and common sense. Under the common enemy and civil law regimes, the law of surface waters is treated as a branch of property law. The reasonable use doctrine has a dual nature. While it has been recognized as a distinct property law concept, it also declares that "an invasion of one's interest in the use and enjoyment of land resulting from another's interference with the flow of surface water" is to be analyzed as a form of nuisance.

Under either theory, the thrust and elements of the rule of reasonableness are the same: "each possessor is legally privileged to make a reasonable use of his land, even though the flow of surface waters is altered thereby and causes some harm to others, but incurs liability when his harmful interference with the flow of surface waters is unreasonable." Reasonableness is a question of fact, to be determined in each case by weighing the gravity of the harm to the plaintiff against the utility of the defendant's conduct. Liability arises when the defendant's conduct is either (1) intentional and unreasonable; or (2) negligent, reckless, or in the course of an abnormally dangerous activity. The Restatement (Second) of Torts @ 822 (1977). Perhaps the rule can be stated most simply to impose a duty upon any landowner in the use of his or her land not to needlessly or negligently injure by surface water adjoining lands owned by others, or in the breach thereof to pay for the resulting damages. The greatest virtue of the reasonable use standard is its ability to adapt to any set of circumstances while remaining firmly focused on the equities of the situation.

Some have suggested that the reasonable use rule might be too unpredictable for users of land to follow, or for courts to administer. However, those fears have not materialized. Today, the overwhelming majority of American jurisdictions have either adopted the reasonable use rule outright, or have overlaid a reasonableness requirement upon the existing civil law or common enemy jurisprudence—which, in practical effect, may be a distinction without a difference. Only a handful of courts cling to the common enemy or civil law rule and a few employ different rules in different situations.

* * *

C.

Upon consideration, we are persuaded that the common enemy doctrine, even as modified, has outlived its usefulness in our state. The rule's harsh origins and labyrinth of exceptions are unduly complicated and confusing and threaten arbitrary and unjust results. In its stead, we adopt the rule of reasonable use as the one most likely to promote the optimum development and enjoyment of land, while ensuring that their true costs are equitably distributed among the competing interests at hand. Moreover, its simplicity of concept will allow for a more flexible and sure application to the many factual situations that inevitably will arise.

* * *

VI. Conclusion

The trial court's grant of judgment notwithstanding the verdict in favor of MHTC is reversed and remanded. The denial of appellants' motion for new trial also is reversed and the cause is remanded for reconsideration of this motion. In all other respects, the trial court's judgment is affirmed.

Lateral Support
SIMONS v. TRI-STATE CONST. CO.
33 Wash.App. 315, 655 P.2d 703 (1982)

PETRICH, Acting Chief Judge. Tri-State Construction Co. (Tri-State), which had installed certain sewer pipes for the city of Hoquiam pursuant to a contract with the City, appeals from a partial summary judgment adjudging it liable for damage to Simons' house and property based on the removal of lateral support and from a denial of its motion for summary judgment of dismissal.

For the purposes of the summary judgment motion Simons' claim was predicated upon article 1, §16 of the state constitution.

* * *

Work began in front of Simons' house in November 1977. In January 1978, Simons noticed structural problems with his house: doors on the main floor would not shut; the cement walls and floor in the basement cracked and flooding occurred; the house developed a tilt; and pot holes developed in the front yard. Simons admits there was minor cracking in the basement before the sewer project, but contends the project caused substantial settling, cracking of the basement, and distortion of the house.

Simons brought suit against Tri-State alleging the removal of lateral support damaged the property and that Tri-State negligently performed the work. The City was later joined as a defendant. Simons moved for summary judgment against Tri-State on the theory of loss of lateral support; negligence was not an issue. Tri-State moved for summary judgment of dismissal on the theory that a contractor performing work for a city in accordance with the terms and specifications of the contract is free from any liability for damages resulting from such work absent negligence on his part. The trial court denied Tri-State's motion and granted Simons' motion.

* * *

We turn first to the grant of partial summary judgment in favor of Simons. An adjoining owner who causes his neighbor's property to slide and slip because of loss of lateral support is liable in damages resulting therefrom under the constitution and law of the state regardless of negligence.

However, the sliding and slipping of the soil must occur because of its own weight and not because of the superimposed weight of the buildings or improvements placed thereon. * * * At common law, the right of owner [sic] to damages for loss of lateral support in the absence of negligence extended only to the land in its natural state. However, under the constitution, the owner is entitled to damages not only to the land in its natural state but also to the buildings and improvements on the property once it is demonstrated that additional lateral thrust from the weight of the improvements has not precipitated or caused the damages.

Simons' evidence, as set forth in various affidavits and interrogatories in support of his motion for summary judgment, tends to establish that before November of 1977, when the sewer project was commenced along the street fronting his home, Simons' home was sound with only minor cracks in parts of the concrete and masonry work; that the following

January, after completion of the sewer project, there was a noticeable settling of the home resulting in substantial cracks in the concrete basement floor and masonry walls, and a definite tilt to the floors and walls causing doors to misalign and requiring substantial shimming and jacking of the foundation to help alleviate the problem; that a pot hole developed in the yard; and that the settling and damage to the home was the direct result of the sewer project.

Tri-State's evidence in opposition to Simons and in support of its own motion for summary judgment of dismissal consisted of the affidavit of James Hargett, a civil engineer of the firm engaged by the City, who acted as resident engineer of the project and that of William O'Brien, project manager of the sewer project for Tri-State. This evidence supports the proposition that Tri-State's work on the project was done in strict compliance with the plans and specifications of the City of Hoquiam; that some time after the completion of the project the Simons house was personally examined by them and that the "footings, concrete block wall, basement floor, driveway, walls and partitions alleged to have been damaged ..." were inspected; and that numerous cracks with old paint and mortar were observed. The professional opinion of Jim Hargett based on his experience, inspection, and observation, was that the settlement and cracking conditions then present existed before the start of the sewer project.

Mr. O'Brien made his own observations, considered the statement of Simons that the portions observed were last painted prior to the sewer project, and stated, "it is clear that the evidence of settlement and cracking existed prior to the sewer relocation project."

* * *

Viewing the inferences created by the affidavit of Mr. Hargett in a light most favorable to Tri-State as the nonmoving party, we are satisfied that the opinion expressed therein created an issue of material fact as to whether the claimed damages resulted from Tri-State's sewer project. This necessitates reversal of the partial summary judgment.

We believe there is an additional reason why summary judgment on liability should have been denied. We do not believe that Simons has established that his soil settled by its own weight as a result of loss of lateral support and not because of the superimposed weight of the buildings.

There is only an inference that this may have occurred because of the pot hole in the yard, and this inference is to be resolved against him and in favor of Tri-State. On the basis of this single pot hole, whose dimensions and location in reference to the lot and sewer line are unknown, we can hardly hold that the only reasonable conclusion is that the soil settled by its own weight unaffected by the superimposed weight of the building.

We now turn to Tri-State's motion for summary judgment of dismissal. Tri-State has established that its work on the sewer project was performed pursuant to a contract with the City. Tri-State contends that it strictly complied with the terms and specifications of the contract. Simons does not in his brief challenge this contention nor does Simons contend that Tri-State was in anywise negligent in performance of its work.

The rule in Washington is that where a city contracts for improvement upon a street, and the contractor performs in accordance with the plans and specifications furnished by the city and under the city's supervision, the contractor is the agent of the city and is not liable for damages where he is not otherwise negligent.

* * *

Summary judgment imposing liability on Tri-State is reversed and the matter is remanded with directions to enter a summary judgment of dismissal of the Simons' claim against Tri-State.

KEY TERMS

PROBLEMS

1. In 1958, Congress expressly provided that navigable airspace includes "airspace needed to insure safety in takeoff and landing of aircraft." (Federal Aviation Act of 1958, Section 101(24).) What effect would this provision have on the *Causby* decision discussed in the text. Why?

2. "Red" Baron is planning to build a large airport near Ann Arbor. Five miles from the airport is a mink ranch. Minks are especially sensitive to noise—when they are caged in a noisy area, the production of baby minks drops tremendously. Red now comes to Rocky Feller, his investment consultant, and asks whether he might be liable for damages by operating the airport near the mink ranch. Rocky tells Red that if he designs the airport in such a way that the planes never fly over the mink ranch, he will not be liable to the mink rancher. Is this good advice? Why or why not?

3. Harold owns a piece of real estate. Underlying the surface of the real estate is a coal bed and a large pool of oil. Harold deeds the coal and oil to Maude, giving Maude a deed to the subsurface minerals. The state now sends Maude a real property tax bill claiming that she is the owner of the oil and coal. Maude claims that she owns neither the oil nor the coal until she removes them from the earth. Is Maude correct? Why or why not?

4. Bonnie owns a recreational campsite, Brownacre. Clyde owns Greenacre, a crop farm that lies south of Brownacre in a valley. Bonnie recently constructed a large dam along the southern border of her property to create a reservoir for use by visiting campers. The dam deprives Clyde of water that had previously flowed from Brownacre to Greenacre, and Clyde's crops die. Clyde sues Bonnie, asking the court to order Bonnie to destroy the dam. Who wins? Why?

5. The city of Medina, in need of additional water, purchased 130 acres of land three miles south of the city. The city hopes to use this land to build a large pumping station and to remove four million gallons of groundwater daily. Rufus, a farmer who lives near the pumping station site, claims that the pumping operation will cause his well to go dry. Without water, he would not be able to farm his 400-acre tract. If Rufus sues the city to restrain it from removing water, who will prevail? Why?

6. Green and Blue both own homes and real estate on the Fox River. Green, whose property is upstream from Blue's, has used river water for several years for household purposes. He also transports a large quantity of water to his farm, which is five miles from the river. Green's use of the water lowers the water level significantly. Blue now wants to use the water for farming his riverfront property, but there is only enough water to service one farm. Which farm is entitled to the water? Why?

7. Walter owned a house and lot in the city of Oakdale. The city excavated a ditch forty feet deep near the sidewalk on Walter's lot. When the ditch was near completion, the city encountered a pocket of quicksand extending from the ditch beneath Walter's lot. When the city removed the quicksand, including quicksand that flowed from beneath Walter's lot, his front yard began to sink. As a result, Walter lost support for the front of his house, the plaster and ceiling in the house cracked, and the door and windows could not be opened. Assuming that the city was not negligent and that no statute governs the situation, is the city liable? Why or why not?

8. Butch and Sundance owned adjoining property on Long Island Sound. During a hurricane, the tidewaters washed away part of Butch's seawall and the land in back of it—to within three feet of Sundance's property. Sundance demanded that Butch rebuild the seawall and take other measures to prevent Sundance's soil from subsiding. Butch ignored Sundance's request, and Sundance's land began to wash away. Is Butch liable to Sundance for failing to provide lateral support? Why or why not?

9. In the *Causby* decision (summarized in the text), why did the Causbys sue the government on the theory that there had been a taking of their land by the government? Since the Supreme Court analyzed the case in terms of the tort concepts of trespass and nuisance, why didn't the Causbys assert that the government was liable for committing a tort? Was the Causbys' claim also questionable because the government never commenced condemnation proceedings, which is the usual procedure when private property is taken? Explain your answer.

10. In the 1988 movie *The Milagro Beanfield War*, based on the book by John Nichols, the small village of Milagro, New Mexico, explodes into violence and bloodshed caused in part by the perceived inequities of the prior appropriation theory. Milagro is dirt poor and has seen virtually no change in its standard of living for more than 100 years. An unscrupulous developer owns the water rights to a ditch of water that flows through the village. By the law of prior appropriation, he is the only person entitled to use the water, in this case for golf courses, swimming pools, and spas in a resort at the edge of the village. One of the poor locals, in a drunken stupor, kicks a hole in the small levee next to the ditch and diverts the water to irrigate his field, where he subsequently plants beans. Political struggles and violence ensue between the locals and the developer, who seeks to protect his water rights. The movie raises the ethical issue of whether prior appropriation is a fair and moral system for distributing resources. Should one person be able to own the only right to water when this essential resource is so scarce? Explain your answer.

1. 116 Iowa 457, 90 N.W. 93 (1902).

2. *U.S. v. Causby,* 328 U.S. 256, 66 S.Ct. 1062, 90 L.Ed. 1206.

3. 100 Minn. 386, 111 N.W. 295 (1907).

4. For example, the "technical trespass" theory adopted in *Smith v. New England Aircraft Co.,* 270 Mass. 511, 170 N.E. 385 (1930), divides airspace into two zones. The landowner owns the lower zone, whose boundary is determined by the air that the owner "may reasonably expect to use or occupy" *(Hinman v. Pacific Air Lines Transport Corp.,* 84 F.2d 755 [9th Cir. 1936]); and he may recover at least nominal damages for flights through this "zone of expected use."

5. W. Keeton et al., *Prosser and Keeton on Torts* 80 (5th ed. 1984).

6. 328 U.S. 256, 66 S.Ct. 1062, 90 L.Ed. 1206 (1946).

7. 73 F.3d 1100 (Ct. App. Fed. Cir. 1996).

8. 369 U.S. 84, 82 S.Ct. 531, 7 L.Ed.2d 585 (1962).

9. C. Thevenot, *Regent Sisolak Awarded $5.4 Million in Case Against County, Airport,* Las Vegas Review-Journal B1 (March 8, 2003).

10. P. O'Driscoll, *West Seeks Help in Cloud Seeding,* USA Today 3A (December 2, 2003).

11. *Southwest Weather Research, Inc. v. Rounsaville,* 319 S.W.2d 940 (Tex. Civ. App. 1958), *aff.d,* 320 S.W.2d 417 (Tex. 1959).

12. 570 F.2d 221 (8th Cir. 1977).

13. The court's holding did not reach the factual issue of the effect of cloud seeding, as the sovereign immunity of the federal government for any liability was a threshold issue to be resolved.

14. See S. Galowitz, *The Use and Abuse of the Term "Air Rights,"* Real Estate Review (Spring 1996).

15. 60 Okl. St. Ann. §802 (1994) (Oklahoma Airspace Act).

16. R. Kratovil, *Real Estate Law* 385, 386 (6th ed. 1974).

17. 578 A.2d 1080 (Conn. App. 1990).

18. J. Taylor, *Global Market in Pollution Rights Proposed by U.N.,* Wall Street Journal C1 (January 31, 1992).

19. See *Trading in Carbon Futures,* Public Policy Institute, at http://www.ppionline.org/ndol/print.cfm?contentid=252027, September 5, 2003 (last visited January 21, 2010). See also *Clean Coal,* Public Policy Institute, at http://www.ppionline.org/ppi_ci.cfm?contentid=253047&knlgAreaID=116&subse-cid=900039, December 2, 2004 (last visited January 21, 2010).

20. For more information on the RGGI see: http://www.rggi.org. (last visited on January 21, 2010). See also *Cap and Trade,* New York Times at http://topics.nytimes.com/topics/reference/timestopics/subjects/g/greenhouse_gas_emissions/cap_and_trade/index.html (last visited January 21, 2010).

21. J. Broder, *Many Goals Remain Unmet in 5 Nations Climate Deal,* New York Times at http://www.nytimes.com/2009/12/19/science/earth/19climate.html?pagewanted=1&_r=1 (last visited January 21, 2010).

22. *Id.*

23. M. Zieman, *Lack of Law May Slow the Use of Outer Space by Private Enterprise,* Wall Street Journal 1 (August 20, 1985).

24. R. Lipkin, *Earth-Man Needs Law in Space,* Insight 48 (December 28, 1987).

25. *Id.*

26. B. Appelson, *How Far Up Is Space?* 68 ABA Journal 906 (1982).

27. See J. Thompson, *Space for Rent: The International Telecommunications Union, Space Law, and Orbit/Spectrum Leasing,* 62 Journal of Air Law and Commerce 279 (1996).

28. L. Fountain, *Creating Momentum in Space: Ending the Paralysis Produced by the "Common Heritage of Mankind" Doctrine,* 35 Connecticut Law Review 1753 (Summer 2003).

29. 2004 WL 3167042 (D. Nev. 2004). Case dismissal was upheld on appeal in 126 Fed. Appx. 343 (9th Cir. 2005).

30. *Business Goes Underground in Kansas City,* Guarantor 2, 3 (September/October 1982).

31. 142 Misc. 560, 254 N.Y.S. 276 (1931).

32. See R. Hemingway, *The Law of Oil and Gas,* 27 (3rd ed. 1991) States that apply the ownership principle are Alabama, Alaska, Arkansas, Colorado, Kansas, Maryland, Michigan, Mississippi, Montana, New Mexico, Ohio, Pennsylvania, Tennessee, Texas, Utah, and West Virginia.

33. *Id.* States that apply the exclusive right principle are California, Indiana, Kentucky, Louisiana, New York, Oklahoma, and Wyoming.

34. 464 S.W.2d 348 (Tex. 1971).

35. *Carbon County v. Union Reserve Coal Co., Inc.,* 898 P.2d 680 (Mont. 1995).

36. *Vines v. McKenzie Methane Corp.,* 619 So.2d 1305 (Ala. 1993).

37. J. Goddard and P. Beaton, *Determining the Ownership of Landfill Gas,* Biomass Magazine (June 2008) at http://www.biomassmagazine.com/article-print.jsp?article_id=2068 (last accessed on August 17, 2009).

38. V. Myers, *Interests in Oil and Gas: Creation and Transfer,* 54 Michigan Bar Journal 29 (1975).

39. J. Thomas, *Gas Drilling—Most Mineral Rights Sold Long Ago,* Centre (Pa.) Daily Times 1 (October 22, 2006). See also A. Brown, *Gas Wells Cause Friction Between Neighbors in Texas,* USA Today 8A (June 6, 2007).

40. States that have some type of dormant minerals law are California, Connecticut, Florida, Georgia, Illinois, Indiana, Kansas, Kentucky, Louisiana, Michigan, North Carolina, North Dakota, Ohio, Oregon, Pennsylvania, South Dakota, Tennessee, Virginia, Washington, West Virginia, and Wisconsin. To see the Model Dormant Minerals Act access http://www.law.upenn.edu/bll/archives/ulc/fnact99/1980s/udmia86.pdf (last visited on January 25, 2010).

41. *Elliff v. Texon Drilling Co.,* 146 Tex. 575, 210 S.W.2d 558 (1948); E. Mitchell, *U.S. Energy Policy: A Primer* 29, 30 (1974).

42. *Edwards v. Lachman,* 534 P.2d 670 (Okla. Sup. Ct. 1975).

43. See B. Kramer and P. Martin, *The Law of Pooling and Unitization,* 3rd ed. (1989, 1995 Supp.).

44. 213 S.W.2d 707 (Tex. Ct. App. 1948).

45. H. Blomquist III, *Geophysical Trespass? The Guessing Game Created by the Awkward Combination of Outmoded Laws and Soaring Technology*, 48 Baylor Law Review 21 (1996).

46. *Mallon Oil Company v. Bowen/Edwards Associates, Inc.*, 965 P.2d 105 (Colo. 1998).

47. K. Golden, *Senate Bill 1078: The Renewable Portfolio Standard—California Asserts Its Renewable Energy Leadership*, 30 Ecology Law Quarterly 693 (2003).

48. See, e.g., "Solar Recordation Act," N.M. Stat. Ann. §§47-3-6 et. seq. (1978). The pertinent language of this statute appears in Chapter 4.

49. G. White and J. Driggs, *The Real Estate Law Issues of Solar Energy*, http://www.consilienceblog.org/consilience-the-blog/2009/8/18/solar-energy-law-incentives-caution.html (last visited on January 18, 2010).

50. 68 Cal. Rptr.2d 272, 277 (Cal.Ct.App. 1997).

51. 278 F.Supp.2d 98 (D.Mass. 2003).

52. K. Badiei, *Geothermal Energy: Is It Attractive Enough to Draw Investors for Construction of Geothermal Electric Plants?* 7 Hastings West-Northwest Journal of Environmental Law and Policy 109 (Winter 2001).

53. *Geothermal Kinetics v. Union Oil Company*, 75 Cal.App.3d 56, 63 141 Cal.Rptr. 879 (Cal. App. 1978).

54. 30 U.S.C. §122 (2002).

55. S. Taveres, *Nevada to take lead in geothermal*, Las Vegas Sun 10 (April 19, 2009).

56. *Geothermal Kinetics, supra* note 53 at 83.

57. J. Deutch, *Biomass Movement*, Wall Street Journal A18 (May 10, 2006).

58. R. Samuelson, *The Bias Against Oil and Gas*, Newsweek 46 (May 11/18, 2009).

59. R. Rienow and A. Rienow, *The Day the Taps Run Dry*, Harper's Magazine 72 (October 1958).

60. J. Adler, *The Browning of America*, Newsweek 26, 27 (February 23, 1981).

61. K. Johnson, *How Green is your IQ?* Wall Street Journal Online, http://online.wsj.com/article/SB10001424052748703683804574533633426036464.html (last visited on January 21, 2010).

62. D. Quade, *Water Wars Predicted for a Thirsty Nation*, 68 ABA Journal 1066 (1982).

63. *Update: Boone Pickens*, U.S. News and World Report, EE10 (March 15, 2005).

64. B. Oxman, *The 1994 Agreement and the Convention*, 88 American Journal of International Law 687 (1994); Juda, *International Law and Ocean Use Management* 256–58 (1996).

65. D. Sandalow, *Law of the Sea Convention: Should the U.S. Join?* Brookings Institute Policy Brief #137 (August 2004).

66. Restatement of Torts, Scope Note §§850–57, at 348 (1939).

67. *State of Oklahoma v. State of Texas*, 258 U.S. 574, 42 S.Ct. 406, 66 L.Ed. 771 (1922).

68. *The Daniel Ball*, 77 U.S. (10 Wall.) 557, 19 L.Ed. 999 (1871). For certain federal regulatory purposes, a different test of navigability may apply. Under the Clean Water Act, for example, wetlands are included within the navigable waters that are subject to federal regulation. See *Rapanos v. U.S.*, 126 S.Ct. 2208 (2006).

69. *Baker v. State*, 87 So.2d 497 (Fla. 1956).

70. *Mentor Harbor Yachting Club v. Mentor Lagoons, Inc.*, 170 Ohio St. 193, 163 N.E.2d 373, 10 O.O.2d 131 (1959).

71. 78 Am. Jur. 2d, Waters §44 (1975).

72. D. Getches, *Water Law* 41 (1984).

73. W. Burby, *Real Property* 46, 47 (3rd ed. 1965).

74. *United States v. Louisiana*, 363 U.S. 1, 80 S.Ct. 961, 4 L.Ed.2d 1025 (1960).

75. M. Kasindorf, *Malibu's Rich and Famous Fight to Keep Beach Private*, USA Today 1A (May 3–5, 2002).

76. *Freedom of Beach*, Wall Street Journal W1 (June 28, 2002).

77. K. Hudson, *Whose Beach Is This Anyway? As Shorelines Shift, Owners of Waterfront Homes Fight States Over Property Lines*, Wall Street Journal Online (December 12, 2007) http://online.wsj.com/article/SB119741959764822149.html (last visited on September 8, 2009).

78. 78 Am. Jur. 2d, Waters §§61, 75, 76, 230.

79. 121 S.Ct. 675, 148 L.Ed.2d 576 (2001).

80. T. Watson, *Developers Rush to Build in Wetland after Ruling*, USA Today 15A (December 6, 2002).

81. 126 S. Ct. 2208 (2006).

82. *Id.* at 2215.

83. R. Aalberts, *The Fate of Wetlands After Rapanos/Carabel: Fortuitous or Folly?* 35 Real Estate Law Journal 1 (2006).

84. 119 So.2d 305 (Fla.App. 1960).

85. 203 Va. 467, 124 S.E.2d 892 (1962).

86. D. Getches, *Water Law* 14 (2nd ed. 1990).

87. 111 S.W.3d 906 (Mo. App. Ct. 2003).

88. D. Getches, *Water Law* 4–5, 19, 48–49, 57–58; Restatement (Second) of Torts §§850, 850A (1979); C. Abrams, *Water Allocation by Comprehensive Permit Systems in the East: Considering a Move Away from Orthodoxy*, 9 Va. Environmental Law Journal 255 (1990).

89. R. Davis, *Water, Water Everywhere: Two New Model Water Codes*, Probate & Property (September/October 1995).

90. C. Smith and R. Boyer, *Survey of the Law of Property* 188 (2nd ed. 1971).

91. Nevada Revised Statutes §534.090 (2001).

92. 81 P.3d 564 (N.M. App. 2003).

93. D. Getches, *Water Law* 6, 97–100.

94. *Tulkisarmute Native Community Council v. Heinze*, 898 P.2d 935 (Alaska 1995).

95. S. Simon, *Out West, Catching Raindrops Can Make You an Outlaw*, Wall Street Journal A14 (March 25, 2009).

96. A. Rotstein, *Tucson ordinance requiring rainwater harvesting on commercial building drawing interest*, Los Angeles Times (July 5, 2009) http://www.latimes.com/news/nationworld/nation/wire/sns-ap-us-rainwater-harvesting,1,2752964.story (last visited January 25, 2010).

97. See, for example, *In Re Waters of Long Valley Creek System*, 599 P.2d 656 (Calif. 1979).

98. *Franco-American Charolaise v. Oklahoma Water Resources Board*, 855 P.2d 568 (Okla. 1990). This view was the subject of a vigorous dissent and criticism by commentators.

99. M. Kasindorf, *War Over Water Splits California Cities, Farms*, USA Today 1A (October 1, 2002). G. Martin, *Peace at Last in Key Water Battle: Cities, Salton Sea Win in Colorado River Fight*, San Francisco Examiner, September 30, 2003.

100. J. Sax and R. Abrams, *Legal Control of Water Resources* 787, 792–93 (1986).

101. *Id.* at 201.

102. P. N. Davis, *Law of Repelling Floods in Missouri,* 2 Missouri Environmental Law and Policy Reporter 127 (1995).

103. 40 Del. Ch. 196, 178 A.2d 307 (1962).

104. *Pugel v. Monheimer,* 922 P.2d 1377 (Wash.App.Div. 1996).

105. 85 F.2d 915 (4th Cir. 1936).

106. *Puckett v. Sullivan,* 12 Cal. Rptr. 55 (1961).

107. West's Ann. Cal. Civ. Code §832.

© MACIEJ NOSKOWSKI/iStockphoto (RF)

Rights in Land of Others

LEARNING OBJECTIVES

After studying Chapter 4, you should:

- Categorize and understand the law of easements

- Recognize the role of profits

- Be familiar with licenses and how they differ from easements

easement
An interest in land that gives the owner the right to use real estate owned by another for a specified purpose.

license
A privilege to enter the premises for a certain purpose, which does not operate to confer on, or vest in, the licensee any title, interest, or estate in such property.

profit *a prendre*
An interest in the land of another that confers rights of use and removal of the profits of the soil.

"Persuade your neighbors to compromise whenever you can. Point out to them how the nominal winner is often a real loser—in fees, expenses, and waste of time."

Abraham Lincoln

A power company's ability to supply electricity to your classroom depends on its legal right to place lines across land that it does not own.[1] This legal interest is called an **easement**. Floyd's tickets to the Buffalo Bills home games give him a legal right known as a **license**[2] to enter the stadium to watch the games. Grady's right to hunt deer on a 200-acre tract of land depends on whether he has a legal interest known as a **profit *a prendre***.[3] These rights to enter, use, or remove property from another person's real estate are the subject of this chapter.

Easements
Definitions and Classifications

According to one court, an easement is "an interest in land created by grant or agreement, express or implied, which confers a right upon the owner thereof to some profit, benefit, dominion or lawful use out of or over the estate of another."[4] The person who has the right to use the land of another is referred to as the "owner" of the easement. Since the owner of an easement does not actually own the land, an easement is often referred to as a nonpossessory interest in land.

The **Restatement of the Law of Property** defines an easement as an interest in land in the possession of another that has the following specific characteristics:

1. The owner of the easement is entitled to use and enjoy the land on a limited basis.
2. The easement owner is entitled to protection from third parties in the use and enjoyment of the land.
3. The easement owner is not subject to the will of the possessor of the land, as would be the case with a license.
4. An easement arises from facts other than possession of land by its owner.
5. The easement is capable of conveyance.[5]

Restatement of the Law of Property

A series of volumes published by the American Law Institute (ALI) on various areas of the law, such as property, torts, and contracts. The Restatements state the law; note emerging trends; and, at times, suggest changes in the law. Courts and legislatures may follow the Restatements in making or interpreting law.

affirmative easement

An easement that confers rights to use land burdened by the easement when the use would otherwise be illegal.

Unlike the water rights and right to support discussed in Chapter 3, an easement is not an inherent *natural* attribute of ownership. Instead, it is an acquired, created interest.[6] Easements also have characteristics that are important not only in understanding and classifying them but also in settling legal disputes.

All easements are affirmative or negative, appurtenant or in gross, apparent or nonapparent, continuous or noncontinuous, and exclusive or nonexclusive.[7] Table 4.1 illustrates the various characteristics that easements possess.

Affirmative and Negative Easements   Easements can be either affirmative or negative. The owner of an **affirmative easement** has the right to actively use the land that is subject to the easement. For example, the owner of an easement of access and egress has the right to enter and leave the property by way of the easement. The easement owner might also be allowed to perform acts on her own land that affect the land subject to the easement. Assume that Thorson Trucking Company owns a large fleet of trucks parked on land surrounded by Herington's property. Thorson Trucking also owns an affirmative easement that allows its trucks to cross Herington's land to gain access to Highway 71. It is quite likely that Thorson's fleet of trucks will pollute the air with diesel fumes and generate noise that affects Herington's enjoyment of his land.

TABLE 4.1   Characteristics of Easements*

CHARACTERISTICS	KEY ATTRIBUTES	INTEREST IN LAND OR PERSONAL RIGHT	EXAMPLES
Affirmative	Allows easement owner to do certain acts on the land of another.	Can be both	Private right-of-way, water flowage on adjacent land, right to draw water from a well
Negative	Allows easement owner to prevent another landowner from doing certain acts on his land.	Can be both	Land preservation, rights to receive air, wind, and sun
Appurtenant	Allows the dominant owner to use easement on adjacent land owned by servient owner.	Attaches only to an interest in land	Private right-of-way, water flowage on adjacent land
In Gross	Allows owner to use land of servient landowner. No dominant landowner.	Can only be a personal right	Utilities (e.g., cable TV, electricity, gas lines)
Apparent	Easement is open and visible or understood to be so.	Can be both	Private right-of-way, sewage and utility lines
Nonapparent	Easement is not obvious or ordinarily understood to exist.	Can be both	Land preservation, rights to receive air, wind, or sun
Continuous	Enjoyment of easement can be continuous without interference by man or can be a permanent structure on servient owner's land.	Can be both	Tree overhang, overhanging roof, sewer and utility lines
Noncontinuous	Enjoyment of easement is in intervals. A noncontinuous easement can be considered continuous for creating an easement by prescription.	Can be both	Private right-of-way, right to draw well water from another's land
Exclusive	Right to use easement granted to definable owner.	Can be both	Private right-of-way, sewer and utility lines
Nonexclusive	Right to use easement not granted to definable owners (e.g., the public).	Can be both	Public right-of-way

*Adapted from D. Wilson, *Easements and Reversions* (1991).

negative easement

An easement that prevents landowners from making certain uses of their land that would otherwise be legal.

By contrast, a **negative easement** enables the owner to prevent the person owning the subject real estate from performing certain acts on it. For example, if Hercules buys a lot high on a hill overlooking San Francisco Bay, he would be wise to obtain a negative easement from lot owners lower on the hill to prevent them from building high-rise structures on their lots that would obstruct his view of the bay.

Sunlight to the swimming pool, cabanas, and sunbathing areas of a neighboring hotel would be blocked by an addition to the Fontainebleau Hotel. In *Fontainebleau Hotel Corp. v. Forty-Five Twenty-Five, Inc.,* on page 121, the court decides whether the owner of the neighboring hotel had a negative easement that should bar the Fontainebleau's addition.

END OF CHAPTER CASE

Negative easements have become increasingly important in recent years with the development of technology for heating and cooling buildings with solar energy. Still, most states, as articulated in the following quote from an Alabama Supreme Court decision as well as in the discussion found in the *Hefazi v. Stiglitz* case later in this chapter, still do *not* recognize the right of a property owner to the unobstructed flow of air and sunlight.

One who erects a house in a city or town, on the margin of his lot, with a window opening upon the lot of an adjoining proprietor, does not thereby acquire such a right to use of his window, as to deprive the adjoining proprietor of the right to build on his lot, in any manner his judgment, or fancy may dictate....[8]

Even so, a minority of states have ruled that blocking someone's air and light is a private nuisance. The following Wisconsin case discusses this issue.

A CASE IN POINT

The first homeowner in a new subdivision constructed a solar energy system to provide heat and hot water. The system was dependent on rooftop collectors to capture sunlight. The grading of the neighbor's lot and the distance of the neighbor's proposed residence from the solar collectors would shadow the solar collectors and possibly damage the system. In *Prah v. Maretti,*[9] a Wisconsin court resolved the first homeowner's rights by considering whether the owner had a negative prescriptive easement and whether the law of private nuisance would recognize a claim for the unreasonable obstruction of access to sunlight. The court concluded that the law of private nuisance protects a landowner from unreasonable obstruction of access to sunlight.

It is noteworthy that the *Prah* court's overall policy of allowing landowners the right to receive air and light has been gaining acceptance due mostly to the growing importance of solar and wind energy. For example, some states, such as New Mexico[10] and

Wyoming,[11] allow landowners the right to receive light by statute. New Mexico's statute provides:

> *A solar right may be claimed by an owner of real property upon which a solar collector has been placed. Once vested, the right shall be enforceable against any person who constructs or plans to construct any structure, in violation of the terms of the Solar Rights Act or the Solar Recordation Act. A solar right shall be considered an easement appurtenant, and a suit to enforce a solar right may be brought at law or in equity.*

Other states have ruled that a homeowner's right to receive solar energy can be obtained as an easement by necessity, a topic discussed later in this chapter. Finally, a neighbor could also be enjoined if he purposely and maliciously blocks another's access to the sun, a law developed as an analogy to spite fences.[12]

The benefits of solar energy and, thus, policies to encourage its use are difficult to ignore. In southern Nevada, an area with abundant year-round sunshine, a $15,000 investment (with state and federal tax incentives and rebates) in solar panels cuts electricity bills to the price of a hookup to the power grid—$6.30 a month![13]

Yet, in most states, it is advisable that before installing solar heating and cooling devices, a landowner should obtain a negative easement from the neighbors guaranteeing that they will not erect buildings that block the sunshine. (For the form used to create an "easment for light, air and an unobstructed view," see www.cengagebrain.com [see page xix in the Preface for instructions on how to access the free study tools for this text].) Residents in Homeowners Associations (HOAs) should look to their Declaration of Covenants, Conditions, & Restrictions (CC&Rs) and bylaws (discussed in Chapter 13) to ensure that their solar rights will be protected.

conservation easement

A negative easement that limits potential development or other property uses in order to preserve open space, natural resources, wildlife, and similar land uses.

Landowners also can create easements to preserve certain features or characteristics of their property. Known as **conservation easement**, these are negative easements that limit uses and development of a property that would be inconsistent with its agricultural, scenic, natural, or open character.[14] For example, when the property owner conveys a conservation easement to a qualified organization, such as a charitable conservancy, the property owner receives a charitable deduction equivalent to the value of the easement. The value of the easement is equal to the amount that the land has been devalued by the restrictions the easement imposes on the land. A conservation easement on undeveloped land near an urban area typically reduces the land's value by 50 to 90 percent since it can no longer be used for commercial or residential uses. In essence, a conservation easement permits landowners to give away the unused value of their property in exchange for tax savings.[15] It is noteworthy that during the severe recession of 2007-2009, many land speculators donated their undeveloped land for the creation of conservation easements since the prospects of their investment's value recovering sufficiently to make a profit in the near term appeared to be unachievable.[16]

purchase of development rights

A type of conservation easement conveyed to a local governmental entity in which landowners agree to restrict the use of their land in exchange for a reduction in taxes.

One innovative and increasingly popular type of conservation easement, pioneered in Suffolk County, New York, in the 1970s, occurs when there is a **purchase of development rights (PDR)**, a concept which is related to transferred development rights (TDRs) discussed in Chapter 3. For example, a landowner, usually a farmer, grants an easement to an adjacent community, as opposed to a charity, in which he agrees to use the land only for agricultural purposes. In exchange, he receives a reduced property tax obligation. This policy is designed to create "green belts" around an urban area that might otherwise experience uncontrolled sprawl. Since their inception, PDRs have preserved an estimated 400,000 acres of farmland. Easements can be used to advance a variety of unique and innovative public policy goals, as the following discussion reveals.

ETHICAL AND
PUBLIC POLICY
ISSUES

Are Primary Residence Easements Ethical as Well as Good Public Policy?

Charleston, South Carolina, is an old city with neighborhoods containing beautiful historic antebellum mansions. In recent years, wealthy outsiders have purchased these stately mansions, particularly in the Old and Historic District, and restored them, but have resided in them only while vacationing in the area. Charleston's mayor and other city leaders became alarmed about the effect these property owners were having on the city. The neighborhoods remained virtually empty and the willingness of the owners to pay top price for the mansions was causing land values to rise to the point that locals were relocating to the less expensive suburbs. In response, the mayor promoted a policy introducing a "primary residence easement" on these homes. The homeowner would voluntarily donate the easement to the Historic Charleston Foundation (HCF), which would legally oblige property owners to make these mansions their primary residence. Homeowners who donate these easements see a decrease in the value of their property (although they do get a tax write-off), but many believe that the easements are important to preserve these unique historic neighborhoods. This policy is a new extension of another controversial practice of donating the façade and interior of these mansions as easements to the HCF. Is the development of primary residence easements an ethical public policy? Would your answer be different if the city used its eminent domain powers to create these easements?[17]

easement appurtenant

An easement that benefits a particular tract of land. It is incapable of existence separate and apart from the particular land to which it is annexed.

dominant estate (dominant tenement)

The land that benefits from the easement on another property. The possessor of the dominant estate is entitled to the benefits of uses authorized by the easement.

servient estate (servient tenement)

The land that is burdened by an easement appurtenant or an easement in gross.

easement in gross

An easement that grants a personal right to use the property of another.

Easements Appurtenant and in Gross   Easements also may be classified as "appurtenant" or "in gross." An **easement appurtenant** benefits the easement owner's land; that is, the easement is appurtenant to the land owned. The land that is benefited is called the **dominant estate** (or **dominant tenement**), while the land subject to the easement is the **servient estate** (or **servient tenement**). For example, assume that Squire owns Greenacre and Western owns neighboring Whiteacre. Squire grants to Western and his heirs "the privilege of laying a sewer line from Western's house across Greenacre to the main sewer line." Squire has granted Western an easement appurtenant to Whiteacre, with Whiteacre as the dominant estate and Greenacre as the servient estate. Greenacre serves Whiteacre by providing an easement of access to the sewer line. (See Figure 4.1.)

An **easement in gross** is granted to the owner independent of ownership or possession of real estate. There is a servient estate, but no dominant one.[18] For example, if Farmer MacDonald grants to his neighbor Brown the right to use certain trails on MacDonald's property for riding snowmobiles but stipulates that the right is to be "personal to Brown and in no event is to be considered appurtenant to Brown's real estate," Brown owns an easement in gross and MacDonald's property is the servient estate. When an easement was granted "to be used only as a family right of way" and a subsequent purchaser who was not a member of the original grantee's family sought access to the easement, the court held that the easement was in gross.[19] The subsequent purchaser had no right to use the easement, as it was personal and not an attribute of the real estate.

Many easements in gross are created to provide electric, telephone, cable television, and other utility services. For example, a railroad can grant an electric utility company an easement in gross to lay electric lines in the railroad's property and to enter railroad property to maintain the lines. Utility companies also need easements in gross to provide power to homes, schools, and businesses.[20,21]

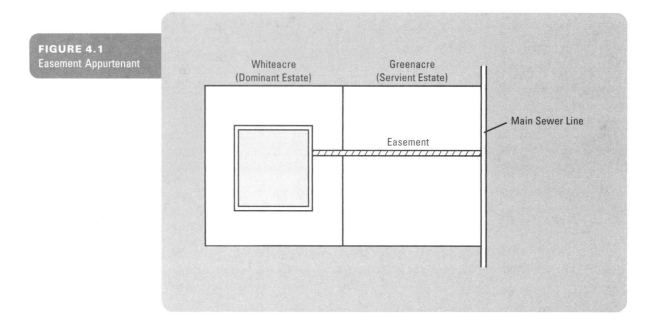

FIGURE 4.1
Easement Appurtenant

Alienability and Apportionment   Easements appurtenant and easements in gross also are distinguished from each other on the basis of whether they can be **alienated** and **apportioned**. Unless expressly limited, an easement appurtenant is alienable; that is, when the dominant estate is transferred, the buyer automatically becomes the owner of the easement. As discussed in the *Sandy Island Corp.* case that follows, when the dominant estate is subdivided, the easement may be apportioned between the purchasers of each of the lots. But an easement appurtenant *cannot* be transferred separately from the dominant estate.

The easement owner's right to sell an easement in gross depends on whether the easement is classified as commercial or noncommercial. A commercial easement in gross, one that provides economic benefit rather than personal satisfaction, is alienable. Although many courts have decided that noncommercial easements in gross—such as the right to use property for snowmobiling or waterskiing—may not be transferred, the majority view considers several factors to determine assignability. These factors include:

1. The personal relationship between the easement owner and the owner of the servient estate when the easement was created.
2. The probable increased burden on the servient estate that would result from allowing transfer.
3. The consideration paid for the easement.

For example, if Guillermo grants his brother Roberto the lifetime right to fish in Guillermo's lake for $1 when the right could be worth $500 in other circumstances, a court would be likely to decide that Roberto could not sell the right because of Factors 1 and 3.

alienated
An easement is "alienated" when it is transferred from one person to another.

apportioned
An easement is "apportioned" when its use is divided or distributed consistent with the subdivision of the dominant tenement.

A CASE IN POINT

In *Sandy Island Corp. v. T. S. Ragsdale*,[22] the Williams Furniture Corporation, which owned extensive acreage on Sandy Island, deeded a 185-acre tract to T. S. Ragsdale but reserved for itself an easement over a road leading from a public road to the Great Pee Dee River. The easement was to "be for purposes of ingress and egress to said Great Pee Dee River ... the said road to be used for transporting logs, forest products, etc., from the river bank out to the old 'River Road.'" Later Williams sold about 8,000 acres on the island to the Sandy Island Corporation, along with the easement. But Ragsdale then built a gate across the easement, which he locked, and refused to allow Sandy Island's employees access to the easement on the grounds that it was an easement in gross.

In its decision, the court made the following distinction: "An easement is either appurtenant or in gross. An appendant or appurtenant easement must inhere in the land, concern the premises, have one terminus on the land of the party claiming it, and be essentially necessary to the enjoyment thereof. It attaches to, and passes with, the dominant tenement as an appurtenance thereof. An easement, or right-of-way, in gross is a mere personal privilege to the owner of the land and incapable of transfer by him, and is not therefore assignable or inheritable."

Although the court agreed with Ragsdale's contention that this easement was an easement in gross, it also noted: "An easement in gross is a right personal to the one to whom it is granted and ordinarily cannot be assigned by him to another. However, there is authority to the effect that the parties may make an easement in gross assignable by the terms of the instrument, particularly where the easement in gross is of a commercial character. Easements for pipe lines, telegraph and telephone lines, and railroad rights of way have been held assignable, although in gross.... An easement in gross is of a commercial character when the use authorized by it results primarily in economic benefit rather than personal satisfaction. Easements, if of a commercial character, are alienable."

The court concluded that in this case, Williams had reserved a commercial easement in gross that could be assigned validly to the Sandy Island Corporation.

If an easement in gross is transferable, can it also be apportioned, that is, sold to more than one buyer? That depends mainly on the intention of the parties as inferred from the terms of the easement. For example, if Jill grants to Vulcan Enterprises the *exclusive* right to mine copper on her farm (an **exclusive easement in gross**), Vulcan would be allowed to apportion the easement by selling the right to mine one-half to Venus, Inc., and the other half to Diana, Ltd. Vulcan can divide the easement in this way because Jill, the owner of the servient estate, granted exclusive mining rights. This means that Vulcan, now the exclusive owner of the easement, possesses all the rights to do what it chooses with the easement, including the right to apportion it. However, had the grant been nonexclusive (a **nonexclusive easement in gross**), Vulcan's apportionment of the easement would not be allowed, since to allow multiple miners would be inconsistent with and tend to deplete Jill's right to grant easements in gross to others to mine copper on her farm. Vulcan cannot grant these rights to someone else since Jill, the owner of the easement, has retained the right to further apportion her easement in gross in the future. Jill's easement in gross could also be characterized as a profit *a prendre*, a topic discussed later in this chapter. Still, as in this example, modern courts typically treat it as an easement in gross.

A related factor in determining whether an exclusive easement in gross can be apportioned is whether apportionment would increase the burden to the servient estate, an issue an Alabama court discussed in the following case.

exclusive easement in gross

A transferable easement in gross in which the grantor conveys personal rights exclusively to the grantee.

nonexclusive easement in gross

A transferable easement in gross in which the grantor does not convey personal rights exclusively to the grantee, but instead retains rights to the easement in gross.

A CASE IN POINT

In *Cousins v. Alabama Power Company*,[23] an electric utility sought to "replace the existing 'ground' wire on the subject transmission line with a different ground wire cable, visually indistinguishable from the former, which also contains a small bundle of hair-sized optical communication fibers." In concluding that the electric utility could share its easement with AT&T without compensating or obtaining permission of the owner of the servient estate, the court found that since there would be no additional burden on the servient estate, the power company had the right under the easement to replace the ground wire with new wire that included fiber optics.

Because of the restrictions on assignability and apportionment of easements in gross, courts attempt whenever possible to construe an easement as appurtenant instead. As noted by an Ohio court in *DeShon v. Parker*,[24] "an easement is never presumed to attach to the person of the grantee where it can fairly be construed as appurtenant to some other estate."

J. A. Shingleton owned an easement of ingress and egress across the Holly Shelter Wildlife Area. In *Shingleton v. State* on page 121, the court determines whether the easement was personal to Mr. Shingleton, which would allow the state of North Carolina to place a locked gate and armed guards at the entrance to the easement and allow only Mr. Shingleton access.

END OF CHAPTER CASE

Creation of Easements

An easement may be created by agreement of the parties or by operation of law. In most cases, its creation falls within one of four categories. (See Figure 4.2.)

Express Conveyance   Easements, both appurtenant and in gross, may be created by an **express conveyance** that meets the formal requirements of a deed, as discussed in Chapter 10. The instrument must describe the real estate sufficiently so that the land can be identified although language such as "the private driveway as presently located" has been held to be sufficient.[25] An easement, like a deed, should be recorded under statutes that require recording of all interests in land. For example, in a case in which the state of Indiana acquired easements for widening a highway but failed to record them, a subsequent purchaser acquired the servient real estate free and clear of the easement.[26] An easement appurtenant is also commonly created by an **express reservation**, typically contained in the deed of conveyance. For example, assume that Clauretie owns a home on a large lot. Every day he drives from his home to a public road and back on a paved driveway he has built on his land. Later Clauretie decides to subdivide his lot and sells to Poon the portion of it nearest the public road. Since Clauretie would still need to cross over Poon's portion of the lot to gain access to the public road, Clauretie must expressly reserve an easement appurtenant. If he does not reserve the easement prior to the sale to Poon, his best recourse would be to create an implied easement from prior use or necessity, as discussed next.

express conveyance
A written instrument in which the grantor transfers an interest in land.

express reservation
A right created and retained by the grantor.

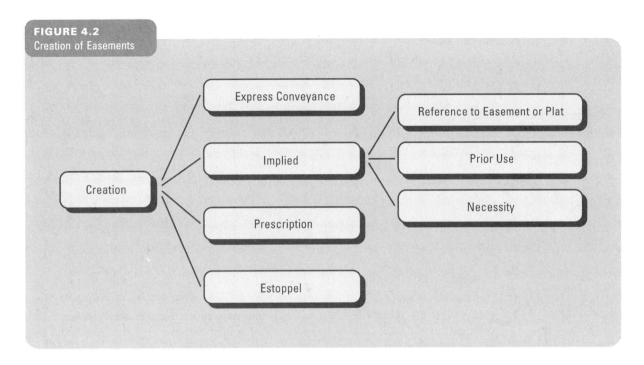

FIGURE 4.2
Creation of Easements

Implied Easements   Although careful legal planning would require that easements be expressly granted or reserved, hasty or uninformed parties sometimes do not pay attention to legal details. This may require the creation of easements after the fact to protect the utility and value of a party's property. As some of the following cases reveal, a property with no appurtenant easement can essentially become landlocked, causing it to greatly diminish in value or become virtually worthless. There are several possible ways to create an **implied easement**:

implied easement
An easement arising impliedly by reference to a plat or map, from prior use, or from necessity of use.

1. From a conveyance describing the premises as bounded by the easement or referring to a plat or map
2. From prior use at the time ownership of land is transferred
3. From strict necessity of use.[27]

Reference to Easement or to Plat   An easement can be created by reference to a road or right-of-way, as the next case illustrates.

A CASE IN POINT

In *Hughes vs. Lippincott,*[28] the defendant claimed an easement in a private way known as Plaza Balentin; the claim was based on this description in her deed: "Beginning at an iron pipe set for the Southeast corner ... thence S. 08A1 38′ W. along the west side of Plaza Balentin 107.75 feet to the Southeast corner, the place and point of beginning. Bounded North by property of Mrs. K. M. Chapman; East by Plaza Balentin...." The court decided that this description was sufficient to create an easement in Plaza Balentin because "it is the general rule and the rule followed in this state [New Mexico] that where the description of property conveyed calls for a road or way as a boundary and the grantor owns the fee in said way, an easement in the way passes to the grantee and his heirs and assigns by implication of law." The court also noted that this rule applies whether or not the easement is necessary.

A Florida case, *Hirlinger v. Stelzer,*[29] illustrates the creation of an easement by reference to a plat.

A CASE IN POINT

The plaintiffs signed a lease for a cooperative apartment that referred to "appurtenances" and a "master plat of the entire project." The plaintiffs claimed that this language gave them the right to a recreation area that was part of the plat; the court decided in their favor, noting that "an easement by implication … can be inferred from a construction of the terms and effect of the instrument involved."[30]

Disputes over right-of-way easements created by reference to maps and plats have become less common because many states now automatically dedicate the roads in new subdivisions for public use. As a result, landowners and the public are able to use the dedicated roads, and access to the property no longer becomes an issue. Sometimes the government abandons dedicated roads, and the roads return to the private owners. Generally, courts have ruled that those who had once used the streets to gain access to their land can continue to use them as easements.[31]

implied easement from prior use

An easement that was apparent at the time an estate was divided and that is reasonably necessary for the use of the quasi-dominant estate.

Implied Easement from Prior Use   The second type of implied easement—an **implied easement from prior use**—can be illustrated with the following example. Lum owned a forty-acre estate on Tobacco Road. A farmhouse was located on the back twenty acres, with a driveway connecting the house to the main road. Lum sold the house and back lot to Abner, but the deed did not mention an easement to use the driveway. Does Abner, who would otherwise be without access to the road, have an easement to cross Lum's property? In deciding whether Abner has an implied easement by prior use, courts refer to the driveway—before the sale to Abner—as a quasi-easement. The front twenty acres would be the quasi-servient estate; the back twenty acres, the quasi-dominant estate. They are *quasi* (a word synonymous with *resembling, almost,* or *as if*) because the definition of easements provides that an owner cannot have an easement in his own land.

Four requirements must be met if the quasi-easement is to be considered an actual easement upon the sale of Lum's property to Abner:

1. The prior use must be *apparent* at the time of the conveyance to Abner.
2. Lum's prior use must be *continuous,* thus indicating that it was permanent, not temporary.
3. Lum's prior use must have been *reasonably necessary* for the enjoyment of the quasi-dominant estate, a requirement that is met by showing that other means of access would be unreasonably expensive.[32]
4. The owner of both the quasi-dominant and the quasi-servient estates must, before the severance, originally have been one person—in this case, Lum.

Of the four elements, the first requirement has been the most troublesome to courts, as illustrated by the following Kansas case.

A CASE IN POINT

In *Van Sandt v. Royster*,[33] the court held that an easement for a sewer line had been created even though the sewer was not visible. After noting that there is a split of authority over whether drainpipes and sewers fit the rule for apparent or visible easements, the court nevertheless took the position that "appearance and visibility are not synonymous, and that the fact that the pipe, sewer, or drain may be hidden underground does not negative its character as an apparent condition, at least where the appliances connected with and leading to it are obvious."

The Nebraska Supreme Court interpreted the second, third, and fourth requirements in *The Hillary Corporation v. U.S. Cold Storage, Inc.*[34] The case involved the parcels described in Figure 4.3.

FIGURE 4.3
Implied Easement from Prior Use

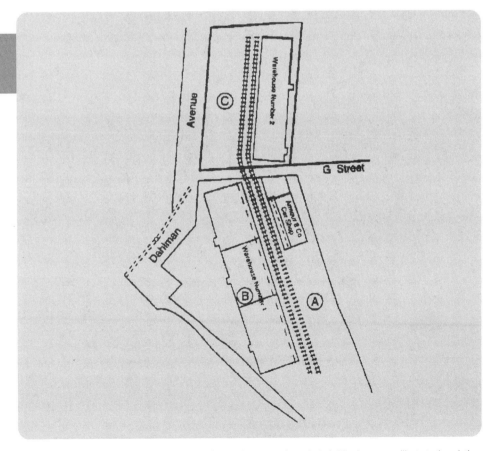

Source: This illustration is taken from the *Hillary Corporation* case and was included by the court to illustrate the relationship of the parcels at issue.

A CASE IN POINT

At issue was whether the Hillary Corporation, the purchaser of tract C, had an implied easement of prior use across a twenty-foot-wide strip along the southern boundary of parcel A. The court relied on testimony that the tracts had been in use for over twenty years at the time the property was subdivided. The court concluded that "the use giving rise to the easement ... had been so long continued and so obvious as to show that it was meant to be permanent," thereby satisfying the requirement of permanent use. The owner of the servient estate argued that the use of the railroad tracks was not necessary because parcel C was accessible by truck on public streets. The court declined to require a showing that the tracks provided the only method of transportation, a showing of "strict necessity." Instead, the court concluded that the easement was "reasonably necessary" as it was the only available access to the tracks. Thus, the third requirement was satisfied. The court also determined that "the elements required for the creation of an implied easement existed at the time of the conveyance subdividing the property," satisfying the fourth test. The court rejected the trial court's requirement that the elements for the implied easement must exist at the time of conveyance to the present owner. Since the easement had become appurtenant to the property, the elements necessary for its creation need not be met at the time of each conveyance.

Can an implied easement from prior use be used to preserve access to air and light? A District of Columbia appellate court addresses the issue as follows.

A CASE IN POINT

In *Hefazi v. Stiglitz*, a common grantor subdivided his property into two units and sold them to two owners. Prior to the subdivision, the common grantor had installed windows in one of the units. One of the grantees, Stiglitz, subsequently blocked the other grantee's (the Hefazis') window. The Hefazis sued, claiming that the light streaming into their window "has been in continuous and uninterrupted use for more than 26 years" and "has provided air, light and ambiance to a first floor/sub-basement tenant apartment continuously since on or before February 20, 1976." The court stated that for an implied easement from prior use to exist, the light must be "reasonably necessary to the enjoyment of the estate and ... retained by the grantor, at the time of the grant, and is, as well, open, apparent and continuous." In this case, the court concluded that "as a matter of law, there is no showing on this record that the burdening of the 2803 Que Street [Stiglitz] property with an implied reservation of light and air with respect to the west wall window was reasonably necessary to the Hefazis' enjoyment of their 28th Street property.[35]

implied easement of necessity

An easement that arises by operation of law after land is divided if one of the parcels is inaccessible.

Implied Easement of Necessity   The third type of implied easement—an **implied easement of necessity**—differs from an implied easement from prior use because necessity may exist even when there has been no prior use. Assume, for example, that Lum had sold Abner a five-acre parcel in the center of his estate and that there was no *existing* right-of-way to the parcel, thus making the parcel inaccessible for Abner from the main road. Obviously, the implied easement from prior use theory cannot be applied here since there was no apparent prior use.[36] However, the law *presumes* that Lum and Abner intended that Abner should have an easement of access over Lum's property and will grant Abner an implied easement of necessity if the following *three* requirements are met:

1. As with the implied easement from prior use, there must be original common ownership in one person—in this case, Lum.

2. The necessity for an easement must exist at the time the common ownership is severed—that is, when Lum sold the parcel to Abner.
3. The necessity must be strictly necessary.

> Could Paul MacCaskill have an easement by necessity across the Ebbert property when, due to the steep terrain in Sun Valley, other access to the public road was expensive and difficult? In *MacCaskill v. Ebbert* on page 123, the court applies the three requirements for an easement by necessity.

END OF CHAPTER CASE

Some courts have determined that the necessity requirement has been met when it is impractical to use another means of ingress and egress; other courts, however, have required proof of actual necessity.[37] In one case, the court refused to declare an implied easement because the plaintiff's property was accessible by water.[38] Many cases, such as the following, address the question of whether an owner has the right to gain access to her property from a public road.

A CASE IN POINT

In *Benedictine Sisters of the Good Shepherd v. Ellison*,[39] Texaco Oil Company and Ellison owned adjacent tracts purchased from a common grantor. Texaco's tract was landlocked and could be accessed only through Ellison's property. Texaco never secured an appurtenant easement across Ellison's land, although it had unwritten permission to cross his land. Texaco subsequently donated its tract to the Benedictine Sisters. Ellison, however, would not allow the Sisters access to the tract. The court ruled that the Sisters proved the three elements of an implied easement of necessity. There was once common ownership of the two tracts, there was necessity at the time of severance exemplified by Texaco's unwritten permission of ingress to and egress from its land, and the creation of an easement over Ellison's land was strictly necessary since it was the only means for the Sisters to gain access to a public road. To deprive the Sisters of the easement, the court decided, would deprive them of the "use, benefit and enjoyment of their land."[40]

Even when these requirements have not been met, owners of landlocked property are allowed an easement over neighboring property under statutes that have been adopted in several states. However, unlike in the creation of easements of necessity, which courts have stated were implicitly paid for in the transfer of ownership since the access was presumed, these statutes usually provide for compensation to the servient owner whose property is being burdened by the new easement.[41]

ETHICAL AND PUBLIC POLICY ISSUES	**Is Imposing an Easement on an Innocent Landowner Ethical?**

In the case of *Schwab v. Timmons*,[42] the landowners subdivided and sold their property, leaving the land they retained inaccessible to a public road. In Problem 10 at the end of the chapter, an ethical issue arises: Should landowners who landlock themselves be able to legally impose the burden of an easement over other landowners?

Prescription   It is possible to acquire title to another's land without paying for it under the law of adverse possession discussed in Chapter 10. Adverse possession requires the possession of land in a certain manner for a minimum period of time. It is also possible for one person to acquire without charge an easement to use another person's property by **prescriptive easement**.

There is a great deal of overlap between the law of adverse possession and prescription. For instance, government-owned property cannot be acquired for free either by prescription or adverse possession, as the following Wisconsin case illustrates.

A CASE IN POINT

In *Portland Water District v. Town of Standish*,[43] the local citizens had for years parked their cars on the side of a road that provided access to Sebago Lake. The Town of Standish sought to claim the public's right to park their cars there, but the Portland Water District argued that the public cannot claim a prescriptive easement against a governmental entity. The appeals court upheld the decision of the trial court and ruled that the "common law rule that a party cannot assert a claim of title by adverse possession or prescriptive easement against a governmental entity" controls under the ancient doctrine that "time does not run against the king (*nullum tempus occurrit regi*)…" The court furthermore stated that "a prescriptive easement against a municipality is prohibited in great part because the acts of possession that establish prescriptive easements are generally even less obvious than those that establish adverse possession and it would be difficult to monitor publicly held lands, many of which are extensive, to interrupt adverse uses."

| **prescriptive easement** |
| A right to use another's property that is inconsistent with the owner's rights and that is acquired by a use—open and notorious, adverse and continuous—for the statutory period. To a certain extent, it resembles title by adverse possession but differs to the extent that the adverse user acquires only an easement and not title. |

The Restatement of the Law of Property, §457, declares that an easement is created by prescription when the following two requirements are met:

1. The use must be adverse.
2. The use must be continuous and uninterrupted for the period of prescription.

Courts originally decided that the time period required to establish prescriptive rights was a period that extended longer than a person could remember; it was based on the fiction that the person claiming the easement must have received a grant that had been lost or forgotten. However, the presumption of a "lost grant" is no longer followed. The period of prescription, which usually runs from ten to twenty years depending on the state (and often is the same time period as the number of years required for adverse possession, discussed in Chapter 10) is now determined by statute.

Adverse Use—Hostile   The first requirement for prescription—that is, adverse use—is actually a combination of separate requirements: the use must be *hostile*, and the use must be *open and notorious.* "Hostility" does not refer to ill will or evil intent, but rather to a claim of right hostile to the property owner's exclusive possession. For example, Nancy crosses Rayna's yard on her way to work every day; and when Rayna asks her to stop using the yard, Nancy retorts, "Try to stop me." Nancy's use would satisfy the requirement for **hostile use**.[44]

| **hostile use** |
| The user must not recognize that the owner of the land has authority to prevent her use. |

If the use is not wrongful, it cannot be considered hostile. For instance, Abbott builds a home that utilizes solar energy for its heating and cooling system; he lives in it for fifteen years, the time required by statute in his state to create an easement by prescription. During the sixteenth year, his neighbor Costello begins to build a high-rise apartment that, when completed, will prevent sunshine from reaching Abbott's property.

Abbott claims that Costello cannot finish his apartment building because he, Abbott, has a negative easement by prescription. Abbott's argument fails because his use of the sunshine was never wrongful to Costello.[45] In a few states, such as New Mexico and Wyoming, discussed earlier in the chapter, Abbott could prevent Costello from finishing his building since the first party to receive light for solar energy, but not sunshine in general, has statutory rights to the light.

It is sometimes stated that if the use is to be considered adverse, the person claiming the easement must use the property under a claim of right. But this is simply another way of saying that the user is acting in a hostile manner by not recognizing the authority of the owner; it does not necessarily mean that the user believes his use of the property is legally justified.[46]

The hostile use requirement is illustrated by the New Jersey case of *Plaza v. Flak*.[47]

A CASE IN POINT

The plaintiff, Plaza, and the defendants, the Flaks, owned houses on adjoining lots in Passaic, New Jersey. Between the adjoining lots was a five-foot-wide alleyway that was bisected by the lot line. The owners had used the alley for several years when the Flaks erected a fence on the boundary line in the center of the alley. Plaza brought a suit to force the Flaks to remove the fence on the grounds that he had acquired an easement by prescription. The Flaks, while admitting that other requirements for prescription had been met, claimed that Plaza's use of the property was not hostile.

The court decided that Plaza had an easement by prescription: "There was never any objection to the use, although it was not concealed; there was no reason to conceal it; there were no agreements concerning the use of the alleyway. 'There was no permission; we just used it.' It is inescapable from a reading of the entire testimony before us that plaintiff's and his predecessor's use was under claim of right and with the intent to claim that right against the true owner, and that it was such use as should have warned defendants that plaintiff might acquire a prescriptive easement. On the other hand, defendants make no proof concerning permissive use. On the contrary, they show no permission was asked or given. It is suggested that their proofs tend to show permissive use in that the alleyway was paved by the joint owners at or near the time the dwellings were erected. If a license to the occupants of either dwelling had been given by the former owners, such would have been revoked by the conveyance of the title to others and the continued use by the occupants of either dwelling would thereafter have been adverse to the owner of the fee of the other lands...."[48]

Adverse Use—Open and Notorious   The second element of adverse use is that it must be *open and notorious*. The reasoning here is that unless the use is open, the owner of the servient estate will have no notice of the adverse use and, without notice, will be unable to take action to prevent it. Under this rationale, a use might be open and notorious even when the user consciously attempts to conceal his use. If, for instance, Hitchcock crosses Christie's land to visit a hidden cave and tries to keep his actions secret by crossing only after midnight, the use is considered open and notorious if Christie discovers it and thus has actual knowledge. On the other hand, Christie's actual knowledge is not necessary if the use is so open that it would be apparent from an ordinary inspection of the property. If Hitchcock had openly crossed Christie's land on a path to the cave that was clearly marked, the use would be open and notorious even if Christie lived in a foreign country and had no actual knowledge of Hitchcock's use.[49] A Washington state court elaborates on this issue next.

The case of *Downie v. City of Renton*[50] illustrates the open and notorious requirement of adverse use. Once a year the city of Renton used an eighteen-foot natural gully on Downie's land to discharge 40,000 gallons of water in a 2 1/2-hour operation. For the first twenty-one years, however, Downie was not aware of how the city was using his land. In its decision, the court held that the city had not acquired an easement on Downie's land because its use was not open enough for Downie to know about it. Even if he had been present during the discharge each year, Downie would have had difficulty discovering the use because the gully was so deep and overgrown.

Continuous Use   The use, in addition to being adverse—that is, hostile, open, and notorious—must be continuous and uninterrupted to establish an easement by prescription. The continuity requirement does not mean that the use must be constant; instead, it refers to the intention of the user. For example, Orville flies model airplanes at low altitudes over his neighbor's property on irregular occasions, but never more than twice a month. His use, although not constant, is continuous and will remain so until he indicates—through his actions or statements—an intent that his use is no longer adverse. The main thing to consider is that Orville is using his neighbor's airspace for flying his airplanes on the occasions he chooses to do so.[51]

The Zuni Indians make a regular pilgrimage on foot or horseback at the time of the summer solstice from their reservation in northwest New Mexico to the mountain area the tribe calls *Kohlu/wala:wa,* which is located in northeast Arizona. Whether the Zunis' use of this land for a short period every four years was sufficient to satisfy the requirement of continuous use is resolved by the court in *United States on Behalf of the Zuni Tribe of New Mexico v. Platt* on page 124.

Uninterrupted Use   In contrast to the continuous use requirement, which relates to the attitude of the user, the requirement that the use be *uninterrupted* relates to activities of owners in obtaining a legal judgment or in taking action on their own to stop the use, such as by placing a fence across a pathway.[52] For example, if Orville's neighbor sues him for trespassing through the neighbor's airspace, Orville could no longer claim he was using the land in an uninterrupted manner.

Exclusive Use   In addition to the Restatement requirements that the use be adverse (hostile, open, and notorious), continuous, and uninterrupted, some courts also require that the use must be *exclusive;* in other words, the person making the claim must make a claim on her own that is not derived from the adverse use of another party.

tacking
The process of gaining a prescriptive easement by adding the user's period of possession to that of a prior adverse user in order to establish a continuous period of use for the statutory period.

   Tacking is an exception to the exclusive use requirement. Assume that Baker, who bought his land from Able, lives in a state that requires ten years to gain an easement by prescription. Baker now seeks to prove that he owns a prescriptive easement on a driveway over Chance's property by showing that he has used the driveway for five years. If Able also used it for five years, Baker can tack Able's years to his to acquire the easement by prescription. This, of course, assumes that both Able and Baker satisfy all of the other elements necessary for establishing the easement. A Montana court illustrates how tacking works as follows.

A CASE IN POINT

In *Westfall v. Motors Ins. Corp.*,[53] the defendants claimed that the plaintiffs did not establish an exclusive use of a road on the defendants' property since the road also was used by the "defendants and their predecessors in interest, and by persons owning irrigation ditches across the road in question, and also to some extent by persons going to and from pasture lands lying south of the plaintiff's land." The court rejected this defense on these grounds: "The rule that the use must be exclusive means no more, in the case of easement for a right of way, than that the right of the claimant must rest upon its own foundations and not depend upon a like right in any other person. It is not necessary under this rule that the person asserting a right of way by prescription should have been the only one who used the way, so long as he has exercised his right under a claim of right independently of others."

estoppel

A party is prevented by his own acts from claiming a right to the detriment of another party who was entitled to rely on such conduct and has acted accordingly.

Easement by Estoppel   An easement may be created by **estoppel** when the owner of the servient estate allows the user to make improvements or expenditures in connection with the use; in such cases, the servient owner is estopped from denying the existence of the easement. An easement by estoppel is sometimes referred to as an "irrevocable license." For example, if the "licensor," or servient owner, gives permission to the "licensee" to use her land but then revokes the license, causing the licensee to suffer an economic loss, the licensee gains an easement by estoppel. Licenses, as discussed later in this chapter, are personal rights and are generally revocable.[54]

A CASE IN POINT

In *Monroe Bowling Lanes v. Woodsfield Livestock Sales*,[55] the plaintiff Monroe had obtained permission from Woodsfield to use the latter's water line. Relying on this permission, Monroe constructed costly bowling lanes and tapped into the water line. A controversy later ensued when Woodsfield used the bowling alley parking lot during its weekly livestock auction. Woodsfield later removed a section of the water line to stop water service to Monroe.

Monroe sought an injunction to prevent the stoppage of water service. The court initially determined that Woodsfield would prevail if the use was a mere license because "a parol license to use real estate is revocable at the will of the licensor." Furthermore, the court noted that Monroe could not prevail on a theory of prescription because "permissive use by plaintiff, as in the instant case, cannot ripen into an easement by prescription no matter how long contained."

Although prescription theory was inappropriate, the court decided that the injunction should be issued because of the estoppel doctrine. "Where an owner of land, without objection, permits another to expend money in reliance upon a supposed easement, when in justice and equity the former ought to have disclaimed his conflicting rights, he is estopped to deny the easement."

Does an easement by estoppel extend to the owner's heirs and assigns? In the 1930s, O. J. Granbury allowed A. H. Richardson to use a lane for better access to his property. No agreement was written or recorded. A. J. Shipp purchased the Granbury property in 1982. The Stokers purchased the Richardson property in 1993. Shipp objected to the Stokers' use of the easement. A Texas court[56] determined that an easement by estoppel had been created. The easement was necessary to the enjoyment of the dominant estate and was assignable under the rules applicable to easements appurtenant.

Extent of the Easement

Once an easement has been created, a number of legal questions arise concerning the scope of its use. The scope is generally determined by the easement's manner of creation. According to one court, "It is also established in the law that the process which creates an easement also fixes its extent. The extent of an easement created by prescription, for instance, is fixed by the use which created it. Likewise, the extent of an easement created by conveyance … is fixed by the conveyance itself."[57] The next case from Ohio illustrates the serious consequences that can befall the dominant estate owner who clearly exceeds the scope of his easement as created in a deed.

A CASE IN POINT

In *Apel v. Katz*,[58] Apel was the owner of the dominant estate with an easement appurtenant described in the deed as a "roadway provision." The roadway gave him ingress to and egress from his property on a thirty-foot-wide strip crossing Katz's land. Apel, however, also used a rough gravel roadway, which was located outside the thirty-foot strip, to cross Katz's land. The court ruled that Apel had to pay compensatory and punitive damages for trespass, as well as all of Katz's attorney's fees.

In another example, Idaho Power Company[59] entered into an agreement with a condominium developer to provide electrical service using underground vaulted transformers. The agreement included an easement. When the Idaho Power Company later removed the underground transformers and relocated them aboveground on concrete pads, the court held that this was an "unauthorized expansion of an underground easement into an above ground easement."

To illustrate the extent of an easement by prescription, assume that Demi walked to a store by crossing her neighbor Ashton's property for ten years, half the period required to establish prescriptive rights. For the following ten-year period, Demi continued to walk across Ashton's land but also used the same path for riding her motorcycle early each morning. The extent of Demi's rights is determined by her use during creation. Since she created the right to use the property only for walking to the store, she has no right to continue riding her motorcycle on her neighbor's property.[60] Once a prescriptive right has been established, some variations in use are allowed if they are close to the original use. In the example, if Demi walked across Ashton's property only in the evening during the twenty-year period, she would later be allowed to change the time of her walk to the morning. Additionally, as discussed shortly, if the easement is appurtenant to a dominant estate, its use may change to meet the needs that arise from the normal development of the dominant estate. However, the changed use must not create an unreasonable burden on the servient estate.[61]

The extent of an easement by implication depends on the nature of the prior use or, if there was no prior use (such as with a reference to a plat or map), on what is reasonably necessary to use the dominant estate.[62]

The owners of an easement appurtenant created by prescription wanted to grade and pave the right-of-way, construct a bridge over a stream they now "ford," and install underground utility lines for electricity and telephones. In *Kuras v. Kope* on page 125, the court determines whether the improvements were permissible.

END OF CHAPTER CASE

Development of the Dominant Estate   In determining the extent of an easement appurtenant, courts assume "that the parties to the conveyance contemplated a normal development" of the dominant estate.[63] What is normal development depends on the facts in each case as this Iowa case illustrates.

A CASE IN POINT

In *McDonnell v. Sheets*,[64] the grant guaranteed to the owners of the dominant estate the right to cross the defendants' land with "team and wagon." The court, in deciding that the grant did not amount to a restriction on the type of vehicle that could use the easement, stated the general rule that "where a right-of-way is granted it may be used for any purpose to which the land accommodated thereby may reasonably be devoted unless the grant contains specific limitations and the grantee can avail himself of modern inventions, if by so doing he can more fully exercise and enjoy or carry out the object for which the easement was granted." The court also emphasized the interpretation of the agreement by the parties, for the right-of-way had been used for over thirty years by all types of vehicles.

Questions about the use of an easement appurtenant frequently arise when the dominant estate is subdivided, with a resulting increase in the number of easement owners. A Rhode Island court addressed that issue as follows.

A CASE IN POINT

In *Crawford Realty Co. v. Ostrow*,[65] complainant Crawford Realty purchased part of a large estate that had been owned originally by William Richmond and claimed the right to use an easement that was appurtenant to the Richmond estate. The court, in deciding for the complainant, cited the following principles: "It is well settled that an easement appurtenant to land exists for the benefit of the dominant tenement as an entirety and not solely for any particular part thereof. The easement that was appurtenant to the land of William Richmond in 1795 clearly accrued to the benefit of that part of his land, which is now owned by Crawford Realty Company. Once an easement appurtenant has been established it becomes an incident of possession of the dominant tenement and it passes automatically with any effective transfer of the land." The court emphasized that "if a dominant tenement is subdivided between two or more owners, the easements appurtenant to it become subdivided and attach to each separate part of the subdivided dominant tenement unless this result is prohibited by the terms of its conveyance."

Easements appurtenant are considered apportionable for *two* major reasons. *First*, because subdivision is so common, it is assumed that the parties consider it a part of normal real estate development. *Second*, the benefits to the dominant tenement generally outweigh the burden to the servient tenement.[66]

The following California case contrasts with the *McDonnell* and *Crawford* decisions.

A CASE IN POINT

In *Wall v. Rudolph*,[67] the dominant estates were originally used for growing citrus fruit, for grazing cattle, and for doing other rural activities; the easements appurtenant were used for the transportation of ranch supplies, produce, and cattle as well as for business and social visits. However, with the development of the dominant estates into dumping grounds for oil field wastes, the traffic became "terrific" in what had been a quiet rural area; 150 to 200 trucks used the easement each day, each one capable of carrying 125 barrels of sludge.

The court, which had to determine whether the use of the easement had become excessive, was guided by the following principles: "The grants here under consideration were made for road purposes in broad terms. It has been held that such phrasing creates 'a general right of way capable of use in connection with the dominant tenement for all reasonable purposes … limited only by the requirement that it be reasonably necessary and consistent with the purposes for which the easement was granted.' This reasonable contemplation presumptively includes normal future development within the scope of the basic purposes but not an abnormal development, one which actually increases the burden upon the servient tenement."

Applying those principles to the facts of the case, the court concluded that the use of the easements was unreasonable: "We are unable to endorse respondents' doctrine that development of an oil field is a reasonable use of a private road over a neighbor's property. It is not permissible to slant drill into his oil pools and we see no reason why one who drills for oil may convert his surface easement for ordinary rural purposes into a heavy traffic which is virtually a public use…. Not only do the trucks interfere with cultivation of plaintiff Wall's property but they also, as they pass each other on these narrow roads, pack down the soil; considerable dust is raised which settles on the citrus trees and damages them."

Courts agree that an easement appurtenant to one tract of land cannot be used to serve another tract even if the tract adjoins the dominant estate and is owned by the same person, as the following Illinois case illustrates.

A CASE IN POINT

In *Miller v. Weingart*,[68] the plaintiff established a subdivision of twenty-four lots and granted the purchasers of the lots an easement to use a driveway that connected with a public highway. The defendant, who owned a farm that adjoined the subdivision, purchased one of the lots next to his farm and proceeded to use the easement to travel to and from the farm, to drive cattle, and to transport a concrete mixer to the farm. The court decided that the easement could not be used for those purposes: "The law is well settled that an easement that is appurtenant to one lot or tract cannot be used in connection with another lot or tract, although the other lot or tract belongs to the owner of the dominant estate to which the easement is appurtenant, and although the two tracts or lots join. The owner of the dominant estate cannot increase the burden imposed on the servient estate by the grant of the easement. This rule is applicable, whether the way was created by grant, reservation, prescription, or as a way of necessity. 'One having a right of way to his land, Blackacre, over the land of another, has no right to drive his cattle to Blackacre, and then to other land beyond it.'"

Repair of Easement; Use by Servient Owner   *Two* final issues conclude the review of the law governing the extent of an easement. *First*, who has the duty to repair the easement? And *second*, may the servient owner use the easement? The majority approach to both of these questions was taken in the century-old California case of *Durfee v. Garvey.*[69]

A CASE IN POINT

Plaintiff Durfee and defendant Garvey owned adjoining land in Los Angeles. Because Durfee's land was swampy, it had to be drained before Durfee could farm it; and for that purpose, as the dominant estate holder, Durfee acquired an easement across Garvey's land to a channel called the Arroyo Honda. In 1870, Durfee constructed a ditch on Garvey's property that was three feet deep and three feet wide. Until 1882, Durfee had entered the property at least twice a year to clean the ditch. At that time, Garvey began to use his land for pasturing horses, mules, and cattle. In feeding along the ditch, these animals filled the ditch and obstructed the flow of water. The court, in awarding damages to Durfee, stated two general rules: (1) the owner of the easement (Durfee) normally has the duty to keep the easement in repair and (2) the owner of the land subject to the easement (Garvey) may use the easement but may "not use it negligently, so as to injure" the easement owner.

Under some circumstances, use of the easement may be critical to accessing the servient estate as a Wyoming court determined.

A CASE IN POINT

In *Wilkoske v. Warren*, an easement cut a servient estate in two, making access to the north and south portions possible only by crossing over the easement.[70] Although the final judgment describing the scope of the easement granted a "perpetual and assignable exclusive easement and right of way," the Wyoming Supreme Court held that the owner of the servient tenement was not excluded from the easement provided that his use did not interfere with the owner of the dominant estate's rights in the easement. The diagram in Figure 4.4 illustrates the easement's location.

Easements also raise difficult liability questions that may be caused by a failure to repair or maintain an easement as discussed in the following case.

A three-year-old girl was severely burned when she wandered into an open electrical switching cabinet in her apartment complex. Who was responsible for maintaining the cabinet? In *Reyna v. Ayco Development Corp.* on page 127, the court resolves whether the easement owner or apartment owner was responsible.

END OF CHAPTER CASE

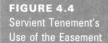
FIGURE 4.4
Servient Tenement's
Use of the Easement

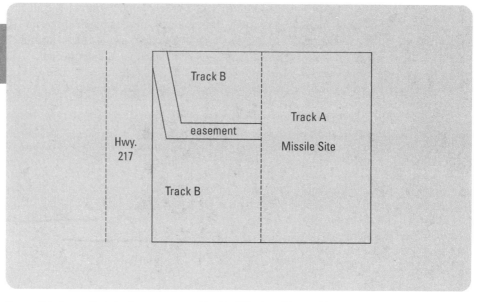

Source: This diagram illustrates the easement considered in *Wilkoske v. Warren,* which cut the servient tenement in two.

Termination of Easements

An easement may be terminated by the following common methods, among others.

Cessation of Purpose   When an easement is created for a particular purpose (for example, an easement used by a carting business),[71] it terminates when that purpose no longer exists.

Expiration of Period   An easement granted for a specific period of time will, of course, terminate at the end of that period.

Merger   As noted earlier, an easement is an interest in land owned by another. If the owner of the easement acquires the servient estate, the easement is terminated (termination by merger) because, as a Michigan court ruled, the land is no longer in another's possession.[72]

A CASE IN POINT

In *Dimoff v. Laboroff,* a six-foot strip of land between two lots was used by the owners for a number of years.[73] The Daskells eventually acquired both lots, but later the lots came into the hands of Laboroff and Dimoff. Laboroff constructed a fence on the strip. Since Dimoff could no longer use the strip because of the fence, he started an action against Laboroff to have the fence removed. The court determined that the easement had been terminated when the Daskells acquired both lots because "the union of dominant and servient estates in the same owner extinguishes prior easements. One cannot have an easement in one's own land."

Abandonment   An easement can be terminated if the owner relinquishes it intentionally, as indicated by her conduct.[74] The main issue is the owner's intent as determined by the facts in each case, including nonuse of the easement and her other activities.[75] A Connecticut court looked at that issue in the following case.

A CASE IN POINT

In *Richardson v. Tumbridge*,[76] although the defendant had an easement to construct a drain over the plaintiffs' property, he had never done so; instead, he excavated a streambed to drain his land. After thirty-nine years, the plaintiffs sought a judgment that their land was no longer subject to the easement. The court applied the following rule: "Whether there has been an abandonment is a question of intention to be determined from all the surrounding circumstances, and is a question of fact and not of law. The proof must clearly indicate that it was the intention of the owner of the dominant estate to abandon the easement. Mere nonuse of an easement created by deed, however long continued, is insufficient to establish abandonment.... A right of way is not extinguished by the habitual use by its owner of another way, equally convenient, unless there has been an intentional abandonment of the former way. Such use of a different way, or as here, of a different method of drainage, may be under such circumstances as clearly to indicate an intention to abandon the right obtained by deed. An abandonment of an easement will be presumed when the owner of the right does or permits to be done some act inconsistent with its future enjoyment, or some other unequivocal act showing the intention permanently to abandon it." In applying those principles, the court decided that the defendant's act did not indicate an intention to abandon the property because even though he had dug out a streambed to use as a drain, this "was not inconsistent with an intention, when occasion required, to exercise his right to build either a tile or stone drain, either in the bed of the stream or elsewhere. The clearing out of the bed of the stream in no way interfered with the building of a drain utilizing the flow of the stream."

As the *Richardson* case illustrates, an expression of intent to abandon, while relevant in determining intent, does not itself result in abandonment unless it complies with the requirements for a release, discussed later.

Destruction of the Servient Estate   If the servient estate is destroyed through no fault of the servient owner, the easement is terminated even though the servient estate is later rebuilt as was ruled in the California case that follows.

A CASE IN POINT

In *Muzio v. Erickson*, an easement owner used a stairway inside a building for access to his own building. When the adjoining building, the servient estate, was destroyed by fire through no fault of the servient owner, the easement was terminated. "It is the established doctrine that where a mere right to use a part of a building is granted, no proprietary interest in the land is conveyed. Upon this principle it has been held that a grant of the right to use the stairway of a building gives no interest in the soil which will survive the destruction of the building, and the right ceases whenever the building is destroyed without the fault of the owner of the servient tenement, and the owner of the right to use the stairway will not acquire any right in any new building which may be erected in the place of the one destroyed."[77]

Estoppel   When the servient owner takes action inconsistent with the rights of the easement owner, the easement is terminated if the following conditions are met:

1. The servient owner acts in reasonable reliance upon the conduct of the easement owner.
2. The servient owner's reliance was foreseeable by the easement owner.
3. Unreasonable harm would be caused to the servient owner by allowing the easement to continue.[78]

A Kentucky case illustrates the point.

A CASE IN POINT

In *Trimble v. King*, a servient owner fenced in the land that had been used as a pathway; constructed a large, valuable pond on it; and made other improvements in the area of the pathway. The court determined that the easement had been terminated because its owner seldom used the easement before the improvement, the owner lived near the easement and knew that improvements were being made but waited three years to advise the servient owner that he wanted to continue using it, and the reopening of the pathway would result in a $1,000 loss to the servient owner.[79]

Prescription   Just as an easement can be created by prescription, it can be terminated by the servient owner's adverse, continuous, and uninterrupted use for the prescriptive period.

Cessation of Necessity   An easement implied by necessity is terminated when the necessity ends. For example, when a previously landlocked dominant estate became accessible because a highway was relocated, an easement that had been implied from necessity was terminated.[80]

Condemnation   When the state, in exercising its sovereignty, acquires a servient estate or an interest in it that is inconsistent with the continuance of an easement, the easement is terminated.[81]

Release   Just as the easement can be created by a deed or a will, it can be terminated by a deed or a will as well. In either case, the instruments must be in a form required by law.[82]

Profits

A profit *a prendre*, literally a profit "to take" but commonly called simply a *profit*, is a special type of easement that gives its owner the right to enter someone else's property to remove part of the land or a product of the land and the right to participate in the profits of the soil. A profit might include the right to take soil, gravel, seaweed, timber, wild animals, crops, or minerals. However, where there is an exclusive, unrestricted right to remove minerals, the person who acquires this right owns the minerals, a topic discussed in Chapter 3, rather than a profit. Although older cases distinguished between easements and profits (the owners of easements, for example, did not participate in the profits of the soil), the widely accepted modern view treats the profit as an easement.[83]

Like any other easement, it may be appurtenant or in gross. In most cases, the rules previously discussed for easements also apply to the profit. For example, a profit appurtenant is automatically transferred with the dominant estate. The right to "hunt and fish on all parts of said 900 acre tract not heretofore or hereafter conveyed as lots similar to the lot hereby conveyed" established a profit appurtenant on the Merriams' property. The court held that absent contrary language in a subsequent deed, the profit appurtenant would pass to a subsequent grantee of the dominant estate.[84]

Most litigation involving profits arises when the owner of the profit attempts to sell the profit to a third party. The general rule—in the absence of an agreement to the contrary—is that profits may be sold. Whether they may be sold to more than one person depends on whether the profit is appurtenant or in gross. A profit appurtenant may be sold to two or more parties if the sale will not increase the burden on the servient estate. The divisibility of a profit in gross depends on the intention of the parties, which is often determined by whether the profit is exclusive or nonexclusive. The hypothetical on page 101 involving Jill's grant to Vulcan Company of an exclusive or nonexclusive easement in gross illustrates this issue. The following case from Tennessee also discusses the same issue.

A CASE IN POINT

In *Stanton v. T. L. Herbert & Sons*,[85] the plaintiffs owned Hill's Island in the Cumberland River, about twenty miles from Nashville. At the time the plaintiffs purchased the property, the grantors reserved "an easement, right, or privilege, to remove sand from said property for a period of ten years from the date of this conveyance." The grantors proceeded to sell their right to three separate building contractors in Nashville.

The court determined that the sale should not be allowed because of the following principle: "If all the minerals are conveyed, or an exclusive right thereto, an interest in the land passes. This is a corporeal interest, which may be assigned, divided or dealt with as any other interest in land. If, under the grant, there passes only a right to remove minerals in common with the grantor, [it] … is assignable, it is not divisible." In this case, the reservation was determined to be nonexclusive because "there is nothing in the language used in the deed to indicate that such right was intended to be exclusive. The right was described 'as an easement, right, or privilege.' The indefinite article 'an' was used, not 'the.' In addition to the right to remove sand, only such other rights and privileges were reserved as were necessary to effectuate the principal right. There is nothing to show an intention to deprive [the plaintiffs] of the right to remove sand themselves. Under the authorities, the presumption is against an exclusive grant or reservation of this nature."

Finally, the court explained the reason for limiting apportionment of profits: "The justice of the rule against the apportionment or division of an incorporeal hereditament, such as this, is strikingly illustrated in the case before us. The complainants here might very well have agreed that their immediate grantors, one of whom was a contractor, should reserve enough sand for use in their own business. The grantors, however, undertook to assign this right to three of the largest contractors in Nashville, who were engaged in the building of the largest plant in the United States—a plant demanded by the exigencies of the great war, and designed by the government to manufacture enough powder to supply the need of the United States and its Allies. To permit the grantor to apportion his right to sand among three such contractors engaged in such an enterprise would have required quantities of sand never dreamed of by the parties at the time this deed was made."

Licenses

Licenses accomplish many mundane as well as important functions today. They range from buying a seat at an NFL football game to staying overnight in a hotel room. A license also can be as commonplace as a homeowner inviting a friend to swim in his pool anytime she wants. A person with a license generally has personal, revocable, non-assignable permission to do one or more acts on another person's land. A license differs from an easement in that the easement is an interest in land and normally must be created by a written instrument. A license, which is not an interest in land, but instead a *privilege*, may be created by any method that shows the landowner's assent.[86]

A license differs from a lease because a licensee does not have exclusive possession of the land. And a license differs from a contract in that a contract requires consideration (that is, must be bargained for and each side must give up something of value), whereas a license may or may not be based on consideration.[87] Sometimes a party also will claim that it has a contract, not just a license. In the next case, a licensee tried to argue that point.

In *Yarde Metals, Inc. v. New England Patriots Limited Partnership* on page 128, a company's season ticket privileges were revoked after the unruly conduct of one of its employees. The court rules on whether the plaintiff possessed a contract or a license.

END OF CHAPTER CASE

Revocation of a license occurs when the licensor transfers the real estate, dies, or decides to exercise her right to revoke as the following Minnesota case demontrates.[88]

A CASE IN POINT

In *Shubert v. Nixon Amusement Co.,*[89] the plaintiff purchased four tickets to a play; but after he and his friends had entered the theater and were seated, they were thrown out. Shubert sued the theater, claiming that the theater "wrongfully and maliciously did … compel plaintiff and his guests to leave the theatre … [and that he] was also injured in his good name and credit, and did suffer great mortification and embarrassment of mind and feelings, and was subjected to the disdain and contempt of people." The court, in citing an earlier decision, held that a plaintiff ejected from a theater might recover damages for breach of contract but could not recover in tort, because "a ticket confers a license essentially revocable; that the fact that a valuable consideration was paid makes no difference; for, if any action would lie, it would have to be founded on a breach of contract."

There are, however, at least *three* well-recognized situations when a license is considered irrevocable. Although courts refer to the right created in these situations as an irrevocable license, it is in fact an easement. *First*, a license is said to be irrevocable when the licensee has exercised the license by expending capital and labor in reliance on the licensor's promise. For instance, in *Monroe Bowling Lanes v. Woodsfield Livestock Sales* (see page 111), the court held that an easement had been created by the defendant's oral promise that the plaintiff could use a water line because the plaintiff relied on the promise when he built a bowling alley.

license coupled with an interest

An irrevocable license granted to a licensee to enter the licensor's property and exercise the legal rights he possesses in the licensor's property.

Second, a **license coupled with an interest** is often irrevocable. The "interest" referred to is an interest, typically a security interest, in personal property located on the land of another. For instance, assume that Best Buy sells a stereo to Marline who signs a purchase money security interest (PMSI) (a topic discussed in Chapter 2) in order to finance it. Best Buy, as the licensee, receives not only a security interest in the stereo, but also an irrevocable license to enter the apartment of the licensor, Marline, if Best Buy needs to repossess the stereo, although Marline can limit the license to a reasonable time.[90] Obviously, if Marline, the debtor-licensor, could revoke the license, Best Buy, the creditor-licensee, could not exercise its rights under the contract.

Third, some states have enacted statutes specifying that certain licenses are irrevocable. For example, under some statutes, it is unlawful for a proprietor to refuse to admit a ticket holder unless the person is "under the influence of liquor … guilty of boisterous conduct or … of lewd or immoral character."[91]

CASES

Easement of Light and Air

FONTAINEBLEAU HOTEL CORP. v. FORTY-FIVE TWENTY-FIVE, INC.

114 So.2d 357 (Fla.App. 1959)

PER CURIAM. This is an interlocutory appeal from an order temporarily enjoining the appellants from continuing with the construction of a 14-story addition to the Fontainebleau Hotel, owned and operated by the appellants. Appellee, plaintiff below, owns the Eden Roc Hotel, which was constructed in 1955, about a year after the Fontainebleau, and adjoins the Fontainebleau on the north. Both are luxury hotels, facing the Atlantic Ocean. The proposed addition to the Fontainebleau is being constructed twenty feet from its north property line, 130 feet from the mean high water mark of the Atlantic Ocean, and 76 feet 8 inches from the ocean bulkhead line. The 14-story tower will extend 160 feet above grade in height and is 416 feet long from east to west. During the winter months, from around two o'clock in the afternoon for the remainder of the day, the shadow of the addition will extend over the cabana, swimming pool, and sunbathing areas of the Eden Roc, which are located in the southern portion of its property.

In this action, plaintiff-appellee sought to enjoin the defendants-appellants from proceeding with the construction of the addition to the Fontainebleau (it appears to have been roughly eight stories high at the time suit was filed), alleging that the construction would interfere with the light and air on the beach in front of the Eden Roc and cast a shadow of such size as to render the beach wholly unfitted for the use and enjoyment of its guests, to the irreparable injury of the plaintiff; further, that the construction of such addition on the north side of defendants' property, rather than the south side, was actuated by malice and ill will on the part of the defendants' president toward the plaintiff's president; and that the construction was in violation of a building ordinance requiring a 100-foot setback from the ocean. It was also alleged that the construction would interfere with the easements of light and air enjoyed by plaintiff and its predecessors in title for more than twenty years and "impliedly granted by virtue of the acts of the plaintiff's predecessors in title, as well as under the common law and the express recognition of such rights by virtue of Chapter 9837, Laws of Florida 1923 * * *." Some attempt was also made to allege an easement by implication in favor of the plaintiff's property, as the dominant, and against the defendants' property, as the servient, tenement.

* * *

This is indeed a novel application of the maxim *sic utere tuo ut alienum non laedas.* This maxim does not mean that one must never use his own property in such a way as to do any injury to his neighbor. It means only that one must use his property so as not to injure the lawful rights of another. In *Reaver v. Martin Theatres,* Fla. 1951, 52 So.2d 682, under this maxim, it was stated that "it is well settled that a property owner may put his own property to any reasonable and lawful use, so long as he does not thereby deprive the adjoining landowner of any right of enjoyment of his property *which is recognized and protected by law, and so long as his use is not such a one as the law will pronounce a nuisance.*" [Emphasis supplied.]

No American decision has been cited, and independent research has revealed none, in which it has been held that—in the absence of some contractual or statutory obligation—a landowner has a legal right to the free flow of light and air across the adjoining land of his neighbor. Even at common law, the landowner had no legal right, in the absence of an easement or uninterrupted use and enjoyment for a period of 20 years, to unobstructed light and air from the adjoining land. And the English doctrine of "ancient lights" has been unanimously repudiated in this country.

There being, then, no legal right to the free flow of light and air from the adjoining land, it is universally held that where a structure serves a useful and beneficial purpose, it does not give rise to a cause of action, either for damages or for an injunction under the maxim *sic utere tuo ut alienum non laedas,* even though it causes injury to another by cutting off the light and air and interfering with the view that would otherwise be available over adjoining land in its natural state, regardless of the fact that the structure may have been erected partly for spite. * * *

Reversed with directions.

Presumption Favoring Easements Appurtenant

SHINGLETON v. STATE

260 N.C. 451, 133 S.E.2d 183 (1963)

MOORE, Justice. The State of North Carolina owns a large body of land in Pender County, known as the Holly Shelter Wildlife Area. It is managed by the North Carolina Wildlife Resources Commission. No public roads or highways adjoin or cross any portion of the Wildlife Area involved in this action. The roads within the area are owned by defendants and used in connection with wildlife management.

There was a dispute between defendants and plaintiff Shingleton with respect to the ownership and location of certain lands within the boundaries of the Area. A suit was instituted, but before trial a compromise settlement was reached. Pursuant to the compromise agreement, plaintiff herein conveyed to the State a portion of the land in dispute and the State deeded to Shingleton a portion. * * *

The said conveyance by the State to plaintiff herein was by quitclaim deed. It conveyed to J. A. Shingleton and "his heirs and assigns" 110 acres situate in Topsail Township, Pender County. This land is described by metes and bounds, and lies entirely within, and a considerable distance from, the boundaries of the Wildlife Area. Immediately below the description are the following easement provisions:

"The party of the first part reserves from this conveyance the right to maintain and use the roads existing on the above described lands; and the said J. A. Shingleton is hereby granted the right to use the roads existing on the other lands of the Wildlife Resources Commission for the purpose of ingress and egress to and from the above described lands by the most direct route."

The present controversy "arose when the plaintiff's (J. A. Shingleton's) brother and other kinsmen were attempting to go over (the) road in question which leads from the public road through the Wildlife Refuge of the defendants by the most direct route to the plaintiff's land and * * * defendants placed a locked gate at the entrance to the road in question and mounted armed guards to keep out all persons except plaintiff."

Plaintiff contends the right-of-way granted him by the State is an easement appurtenant. Defendants contend it is an easement in gross and may be used and enjoyed only by J. A. Shingleton personally. J. A. Shingleton instituted the present action to have determined his rights under the grant of easement, and makes allegations which, he contends, entitle him to injunctive relief.

Trial by jury was waived and the judge made findings of fact and conclusions of law and entered judgment. It was adjudged that the easement granted by the State to the plaintiff "is an unlimited easement appurtenant to plaintiff's land, given to plaintiff for his use and the use of his agents, servants, employees, licensees, and the public generally who have not been refused permission to use the easement by the plaintiff," and "that the defendants, their agents, servants and employees * * * are enjoined from interfering by gate or otherwise with the use of said easement or road as herein provided."

An appurtenant easement is one which is attached to and passes with the dominant tenement as an appurtenance thereof; it is owned in connection with other real estate and as an incident to such ownership. An easement in gross is not appurtenant to any estate in land or not belonging to any person by virtue of his ownership of an estate in other land, but is a mere personal interest in or right to use the land of another; it is purely personal and usually ends with the death of the grantee. An easement appurtenant is incapable of existence apart from the particular land to which it is annexed, it exists only if the same person has title to the easement and the dominant estate; it must bear some relation to the use of the dominant estate, and it must agree in nature and quality to the thing to which it is claimed to be appurtenant. An easement appurtenant is incident to an estate, and inheres in the land, concerns the premises, pertains to its enjoyment, and passes with the transfer of the title to the land, including transfer by descent. If an easement is in gross there is no dominant tenement; an easement is in gross and personal to the grantee because it is not appurtenant to other premises. An easement in gross attaches to the person and not to land.

* * *

In the absence of express provision in the grant restricting the easement to the personal use of plaintiff, the presumption is that it is an easement appurtenant to plaintiff's 110-acre tract. Moreover, the situation of the property and the surrounding circumstances indicate beyond question that an easement appurtenant was intended. The original controversy, in the settlement of which the deed was given, arose from conflicting claims of rights and title to lands. The record does not disclose that plaintiff has ever claimed any personal rights, apart from land ownership, in the Wildlife Area. The deed conveys to plaintiff a tract of land which, without some adequate access over defendants' lands, would be completely cut off from any public or private road.

The grant of easement was so clearly connected with the conveyance of the 110-acre tract that in the deed it follows immediately the description of the land. The words "ingress" and "egress" as used in the grant of easement show clearly it was intended that the easement is connected with and is to be used for the benefit of the land. The road in question is appurtenant to the land in fact, and leads from the land across the Wildlife Area to the public road beyond. Apart from the ownership of the 110-acre tract, the easement is worthless. If plaintiff did not own this land he would have no business or interest of any kind within the Wildlife Area. The land was conveyed to plaintiff in fee. It is not reasonable to conclude that the State would undertake to grant and plaintiff to accept a right of access to land which would end at the death of plaintiff and render the land hereafter inaccessible and worthless. Furthermore, it is not reasonable to suppose that plaintiff could, acting alone, cut and remove timber from his land or cultivate, harvest and remove crops, or make other beneficial use of the land. Certainly the parties did not intend that plaintiff's heirs, devisees or assigns should have no access to the property. We hold that the easement granted by the State to plaintiff is appurtenant to plaintiff's land described in the deed.

Modified and affirmed.

Easement by Necessity
MACCASKILL v. EBBERT
112 Idaho 1115, 739 P.2d 414 (1987)

BURNETT, Judge. This is an appeal from a summary judgment rejecting a claim of easement by necessity to "landlocked" property. Such an easement customarily arises where part of a tract is conveyed and, as a result of the severance, the part conveyed or the part retained is deprived of legal access to a public road. The question presented in this case is whether an easement by necessity might also arise where the severed property has legal access but the access is physically impassable. The district court said no. We reverse.

The following facts are not in dispute. Paul MacCaskill owns property known as tax lot 2742 in the Sun Valley Subdivision near Ketchum, Idaho. At one time the lot was part of a large unified tract owned by Earl and Ethel Weatherhead. [Other lots in the Weatherhead tract, lying directly between MacCaskill's lot and a road, were acquired by the Ebberts.]

* * *

MacCaskill sued the Ebberts, seeking an easement across the Ebbert property for access to lot 2742. MacCaskill asserted that due to steep terrain, no access route [across other property in the Weatherhead tract] to the public road was feasible. His complaint was grounded in two alternative theories—private condemnation under I.C. A4 7-701, and recognition of an easement by necessity. MacCaskill moved for summary judgment on both theories. The district judge denied the motion as it related to condemnation, holding that a genuine issue of fact existed as to whether it was actually necessary to cross the Ebbert property rather than to reach the public road by a different route. However, the judge entered partial summary judgment in favor of the Ebberts on the question of easement by necessity.

* * *

The easement by necessity has evolved into a hybrid reflection of presumed intent and public policy. It is the intent component which distinguishes such an easement from a statutorily condemned easement. Condemnation is an act of public power vested by statute in a private plaintiff who may never have engaged—and whose predecessors may never have engaged—in any previous transaction with the current or prior owners of land across which an easement is sought. Such a taking must be accompanied by just compensation. The common law easement, in contrast, rests on a presumption that when a severance occurs, the parties recognize the necessity, if any exists, for providing a means of access. They strike their bargain accordingly.

Therefore, an easement can be recognized, consistent with public policy, without requiring additional compensation to be paid. The easement endures while the necessity exists, unless by express agreement the easement is negated or extinguished. If the easement has been negated or extin-

guished, another easement may be created only by voluntary negotiations or by an involuntary taking through the power of eminent domain, upon a showing of reasonable necessity. In either of those events, compensation must be paid.

We now consider whether an easement by necessity may arise where the property is landlocked, not because a legal access is nonexistent but because topographical characteristics of the land make the legal access impassable. One who claims an easement by necessity across another's land may establish a prima facie case through proof (1) that the two parcels once were part of a larger tract under common ownership; (2) that a necessity for the easement existed when the parcels were severed; and (3) that the present necessity for the easement is great. When each element is proven, an easement by necessity will be recognized unless a countershowing is made that such an easement has been explicitly bargained away by the parties or their predecessors.

Nothing in these elements, or in the underlying public policy against landlocked properties, explicitly requires that a landlocked condition be caused solely by legal impediments to access. There are cases where a tract of land, though not totally landlocked in a legal sense, cannot yield a beneficial use because the sole legal access is inadequate for the purposes to which the property naturally might be put.

* * *

In the present case, as we have seen, the MacCaskill property and the Ebbert property originally were part of the unified Weatherhead tract. They were severed when the Ebbert property and other roadside lots were sold in 1948. Consequently, the first requirement for establishing an easement by necessity—common ownership followed by severance—has been satisfied. The other requirements—necessity for an easement at the time of severance, and great present necessity—pose nettlesome factual problems.

* * *

If MacCaskill can show that an easement was necessary in 1948 because any other access through the remainder of the Weatherhead tract was not feasible, and if MacCaskill can further show great present necessity for such an easement, he will have established a prima facie case for the easement.

The questions of past and present necessity are factual, and the facts are in sharp dispute. MacCaskill has submitted an affidavit from a civil engineer, stating that construction of an alternate access across [other] property would cost more than $500,000. He also has submitted the minutes of a Ketchum City Council meeting, at which a proposed roadway across [other] property was disapproved because the grade would be too steep to meet city specifications. The Ebberts, though not providing specific cost figures, argue that several alternative routes are feasible. They further contend that the City Council denied permission for the proposed roadway not because the route was unfeasible, but because of other defects in the application. In addition, the parties also have debated what damage an easement might cause to the Ebbert property. MacCaskill's engineer has averred that a roadway using the proposed route could be constructed within a thirty-foot easement in compliance with city regulations. Opposing affidavits indicate that the roadway could not be contained within a thirty-foot easement, that it would occupy a substantial portion of the servient property, and that it could interfere with the Ebberts' access to their home.

Upon this record, we are constrained to hold—as did the district judge when he studied the condemnation issue—that genuine issues of material fact exist. Summary judgment is inappropriate. Neither party has demonstrated as a matter of law that an easement by necessity should or should not be recognized. The case must be remanded for findings as to necessity at the time of severance and great present necessity, in conformity with this opinion. * * *

Easement by Prescription
UNITED STATES ON BEHALF OF THE ZUNI TRIBE OF NEW MEXICO v. PLATT
730 F.Supp. 318 (D.Ariz. 1990)

The Zuni Indians, as a part of their religion, make a regular periodic pilgrimage at the time of the summer solstice, on foot or horseback, from their reservation in northwest New Mexico to the mountain area the tribe calls Kohlu/wala:wa which is located in northeast Arizona. It is believed by the Zuni Indians that Kohlu/wala:wa is their place of origin, the basis for their religious life, and the home of their dead.

* * *

The pilgrimage has been largely uncontested until recent times.

In 1985 defendant, Earl Platt, declared his intention of preventing the Zuni Indians from crossing his land on their pilgrimage. Earl Platt and the estate of Buena Platt (defendant) own or lease from the United States or the state of Arizona land in Apache County over which the Zuni Indians cross on their pilgrimage to Kohlu/wala:wa. On June 12, 1985 the United States on behalf of the Zuni Tribe instituted this action claiming a prescriptive easement by adverse possession across the Platt land.

* * *

The evidence presented at trial shows that the Zuni Indians have gone on their quadrennial pilgrimage, approximately every four years since, at least, the early twentieth century. There was direct evidence presented at trial, in the form of motion picture documentation, of the pilgrimage occurring in 1924.* * *

* * *

The total trek is 110 miles in length. It takes four days for the pilgrims to travel to Kohlu/wala:wa and return back to the reservation. The pilgrimage crosses approximately 18–20 miles of land owned or leased by the defendant Earl Platt.

The path or route used by the Zuni Indians on their religious pilgrimage has been consistent and relatively unchanged. The plaintiffs concede that topographical changes may necessarily alter the route. However, manmade obstacles will not cause the Zuni pilgrims to deviate from their customary path. This is evidenced by the fact the pilgrims cut or take down fences in their way.

The pathway used by the pilgrims is approximately fifty feet wide. The Zuni Indians' use of the route in question is limited to a path or a place crossed enroute to Kohlu/wala:wa. Other than the path itself there are no points or landmarks of religious significance to the Zuni Indians on the defendant's land and the pilgrims do not camp on the defendant's land but they do stop for lunch on Platt land.

The use of the property, by the Zuni Indians, along the pilgrimage route has been open, visible and known to the community. Several witnesses who have been longtime residents of the St. John's area, which is in close proximity to the land in question, testified that they knew of the Zuni pilgrimage and that it was generally known throughout the community.

The Zuni Tribe, and the people going on the pilgrimage, believed that they had a right to cross the lands traversed by their established route. There has been no showing that they sought to cross lands under permission or by authority of other persons.

The Arizona statute defining adverse possession provides:

"Adverse possession" means an actual and visible appropriation of the land, commenced and continued under a claim of right inconsistent with and hostile to the claim of another.

A.R.S. §12-521. The Arizona statutes further provide that:

A. A person who has a cause of action for recovery of any lands, tenements or hereditaments from a person having peaceable and adverse possession thereof, cultivating, using and enjoying such property, shall commence an action therefor[e] within ten years after the cause of action accrues, and not afterward

A.R.S. §12-526.   * * *

The Zuni Tribe has had actual possession of the route used for the religious pilgrimage for a short period of time every four years. They have had actual possession of the land in the sense that they have not recognized any other claim to the land at the time of the pilgrimage, as evidenced by their lack of deviation from the established route and disregard for fences or any other man-made obstacle that blocks their course of travel. This Court also finds that the Zuni Tribe continually used a portion of the defendant's land for a short period of time every four years at least since 1924 and very probably for a period of time spanning many hundreds of years prior to that year.

Therefore, the plaintiffs have established the "actual" and "continuous" possession elements of their claim for adverse possession. Furthermore this "actual" possession has been continuous for over ten years which is required for a claim of a prescriptive right.

* * *

The Zuni Tribe has not attempted to hide their pilgrimage or the route they were taking, although they do regard it as a personal and private activity. It was known generally throughout the community that the Zuni Indians took a pilgrimage every few years. It was also common knowledge in the community, generally, what route or over which lands the pilgrimage took place. Mrs. Hinkson, a resident of the St. John's area since 1938 and an owner of a ranch which the Zuni Indians cross on their pilgrimage, testified it was generally understood that the Zuni Tribe had set a precedent of crossing the land of ranchers that could not be changed even if owners of the land objected to such crossings or use of their property. The Zuni Tribe also cut, tore down or placed gates in fences on the property owned or leased by defendant and others.

This Court draws the reasonable inference, from all the facts and circumstances, that Earl Platt, the defendant in this case, was aware that a pilgrimage occurred, that it occurred approximately every four years and that the pilgrimage went across his property.

Consequently, the Zuni Tribe's open and notorious use of Platt land and the inference that Earl Platt knew of such use satisfies and/or obviates the "open and notorious" element of an adverse possession.

* * *

The record reflects, as discussed earlier, the Zuni pilgrims, at the time of their pilgrimage, claim exclusive right to the path they cross to Kohlu/wala:wa. The claim of right to temporary and periodic use of the defendant's land is evidenced by the cutting or pulling down of fences and the lack of deviation from the route. In recent years the Zuni Indians, with the aid of the Bureau of Land Management, placed gates in fences which impeded the pilgrimage route of the Zuni Indians. The use, by the pilgrims, of the defendant's land is "hostile" to Earl Platt's title. Also there was no evidence presented at trial which would indicate that the Zuni Tribe sought permission to cross the land of Earl Platt. The evidence clearly illustrated that the Zuni Indians never sought permission to cross lands on their pilgrimage but rather it was believed said crossing was a matter of right.

The record leaves no doubt that the "hostile" and "claim of right" elements of adverse possession has been satisfied by the plaintiffs.

Insofar as the exclusivity of possession is required, in the context of the claim asserted here, it is reasonable to conclude that if people are occupying a tract of land at a particular time, another person or other people cannot simultaneously occupy the same space. Therefore, the Zunis participating in the quadrennial pilgrimage have exclusive possession of the land upon which they cross enroute to Kohlu/wala:wa when they are crossing that land.

The Zuni Indians' use and possession of the Platt land has been actual, open and notorious, continuous and uninterrupted for at least 65 years and under a claim of right. Such use was known by the surrounding community.

It is clear from the record that the plaintiffs have established that the Zuni Indians meet the standards of adverse possession, set forth in A.R.S. §12-521 and the applicable case law for purposes of the limited use sought. The Zuni Tribe is entitled to a prescriptive easement over the land of the defendant for the purposes of their quadrennial pilgrimage. The defendant presented no evidence and has not otherwise proven that the Zuni Indians' use of the land in question was permissive or otherwise.

* * *

Extent of Easement
KURAS v. KOPE
205 Conn. 332, 533 A.2d 1202 (1987)

HEALEY, Associate Justice. [The Kopes held an easement by prescription over a dirt road on land owned by the Kurases, who brought suit to prevent the Kopes from improving the easement. The trial court restricted the improvements that the Kopes could make and they appealed the decision.]

* * *

The Kuras parcel is farm property located on the southerly side of Mountain Road, a town highway, in Suffield. The Kope parcel, which is 30.53 acres, abuts the southerly side of the Kuras parcel. The Kope parcel has no frontage on any highway but it does have access to Mountain Road by virtue of the right-of-way in dispute.

* * *

There is a stream that runs roughly east and west across the right-of-way a few hundred feet south of the northerly terminus of the right-of-way. The northerly terminus is the terminus nearest Mountain Road. In order to cross this stream, a person, animal or vehicle must "ford" it and the drop from the bank to the low point in that ford is not less than two feet.

* * *

Even though the common and ordinary use which establishes the prescriptive right also limits and qualifies it, as one court aptly observed, "the use made during the prescriptive period does not fix the scope of the easement *eternally*." [Emphasis added.] *Glenn v. Poole*, 423 N.E.2d 1030 (1981). One commentator in this field states that "[i]f it [the above announced rule] were applied with absolute strictness, the right acquired would frequently be of no utility whatsoever. A right-of-way, for instance, would, as has been judicially remarked … be available for use only by the people and the vehicles which have passed during the prescriptive period. But the rule is not applied with absolute strictness." 4 H. Tiffany, *Real Property* (3d Ed.) §1208, p. 1039.

* * *

The right-of-way in the case before us is an easement appurtenant, which, by definition is one created to serve a dominant parcel of land. Because the owner of a prescriptive easement may repair it and do whatever is reasonably necessary to make it suitable and convenient for his use, it is reasonable to assume that both dominant and servient owners would anticipate, as in this case, that an established right-of-way for ingress and egress to a single-family residence may give rise to the necessity of improvements in that easement to render it of genuine benefit to the owner of the dominant tenement.

* * *

The desire and need for improvements in such a prescriptive easement for ingress and egress emerges from the evolution of the dominant parcel. The nature and scope of such improvements, however, cannot be fully foretold. Acknowledging that the interests and rights of both the dominant and servient tenements often conflict, the problem arises of how present needs may be justified under a prescriptive right that apparently met the needs of another day. This brings into focus the proposition that the use and improvement of this prescriptive easement must not unreasonably burden the servient tenement that is already burdened with the easement.

* * *

We take up first the Kopes' request to grade the right-of-way. The trial court decreed that the Kopes "may not grade the present crown [of the right-of-way] nor raise the tracks." * * * We will not reiterate all the evidence on this branch of the matter. We do, nevertheless, note that the trial court found that the right-of-way is "but 10 feet wide as shown on the Davis survey," that there are tracks that are 5 to 5 1/2 feet apart within the right-of-way and that there are many potholes with some being 12 to 15 inches deep. Significantly, it found that the right-of-way is "crowned in the middle in large part" and that there are "certain stretches where the tracks are as much as 10 to 15 inches lower than the crown of the right-of-way." The mere recital of these findings serves to make evident the need to permit this easement to be graded under all the circumstances of this case. The trial court's refusal to permit grading was clearly erroneous. Because, however, permitting this improvement requires additional factual determinations to be made before entering specific orders concerning such factors as the nature and extent of grading, we remand this issue to the trial court to conduct an evidentiary hearing for that purpose.

We next examine the request to lay asphalt or gravel on the right-of-way. The laying of asphalt or gravel on the right-of-way raises questions that are factual. The trial court's order that prohibited the use of any gravel was clearly erroneous. Whether laying asphalt or gravel, while facilitating the Kopes' use of the right-of-way, also will unreasonably increase the burden on the servient tenement is for the trial court to determine. Here, too, therefore, we remand for an evidentiary hearing for necessary orders on the issue of placing gravel on this easement.

* * *

We come now to the trial court's order that the Kopes "have no right to construct a bridge on the northerly portion of the right-of-way to cross the stream they now 'ford.'" In order to cross this stream, the trial court found that a person, animal or vehicle must "ford" it and that the drop from its bank to the lowest point in the ford "is not less than 2 feet." According to the evidence at trial, there has never been a bridge over this stream. The Kopes argue that they be permitted to build a bridge over this "north ford." Based on the law and the evidence, this finding that the Kopes had no such right is clearly erroneous. The Kopes have the right to a reasonable enjoyment of their right-of-way without increasing the burden on the servient tenement; their request for bridging this stream merits serious consideration in the trial court. Consequently, because this matter also involves factual determinations, we remand this branch of the matter to the trial court for an evidentiary hearing upon which to base factual findings necessary for it to make appropriate orders to effectuate this right.

Finally, the Kopes claim that the trial court erred in not permitting them to install underground utility lines for electric and telephone service. We do not agree. The rule is generally well established that the owner of an easement is entitled to relief upon a showing that he will be disturbed or obstructed in the exercise of his right. Again, however, this right must be balanced against the right of the servient owner not to have the existing servitude unreasonably increased.

Counsel has not cited nor have we been able to discover any decision permitting underground utilities to be installed in a private right-of-way created by prescription for the purpose of access. * * *

In any event, we believe that in the circumstances of this case, the request for this "improvement" at this time exceeds, as a matter of law, the scope of the prescriptive easement * * *. The Kopes argue that such a request takes into consideration needs that result from a normal evolution in the use of its land and that all land is subject to constant changes in its condition. They argue that the result of this changing nature of things means that these emerging "requirements" of dominant tenements must benefit them in their changed condition. Therefore, because the construction of a residence on the dominant tenement is a normal evolu-

tion in its use, the Kopes assert that such underground utility installation should be permitted as it would not "adversely affect" the use by the Kurases of the servient tenement.

Initially, this claim has some appeal, but, on more penetrating consideration, it is not persuasive in this case. A normal development is one that accords with common experience and, therefore, one that might reasonably have been foretold. 5 Restatement, Property §479, comment (a).

Such uses, however, must be consistent with the pattern formed by the adverse use by which the prescriptive easement was created. * * *

There is error, the case is remanded to the trial court for further proceedings not inconsistent with this opinion.

Duty to Maintain Easement
REYNA v. AYCO DEVELOPMENT CORP.
788 S.W.2d 722 (Tex. App.—Austin 1990)

SHANNON, Chief Justice. Appellants Guadencio and Sofia Reyna, individually and as next friends for their minor daughter Patricia, sued appellee Ayco Development Corp., the City of Austin, and others for injuries suffered by their daughter. Upon motion, the district court of Travis County rendered summary judgment that appellants take nothing. This Court will affirm the judgment.

In August 1986, appellants were tenants of the Coronado Apartments located in Austin. Appellee Ayco owned and operated the apartment complex. The City of Austin supplied electrical power to Ayco's rental property.

On August 26, 1986, three-year-old Patricia was severely burned when she wandered into an open electrical switching cabinet located within the City of Austin's easement in Ayco's apartment complex. The switching cabinet was a part of the electrical distribution system owned and operated by the City of Austin. The City of Austin settled with appellants.

Appellants pleaded that Ayco was negligent in the following respects:

1. In failing to inspect the safety and security of the electrical switching cabinet;
2. In failing to lock the switching cabinet;
3. In failing to exercise reasonable care for the protection of children who are foreseeable users of the land from the dangerous conditions;
4. In failing to warn appellants and other tenants that the cabinet contained dangerous and high electrical voltage;
5. In failing to maintain protected access to the switching cabinet;
6. In failing to erect fences or barriers to prevent children from coming into contact with the switching cabinet;
7. In failing to post "danger" and/or other warning signs on the switching cabinet.

Upon hearing, the district court rendered summary judgment that appellants take nothing.

* * *

Ayco asserted by its motion for summary judgment that because it neither owned, nor controlled, nor had the right to control the offending switching cabinet, it owed appellants no duty to exercise ordinary care. In support of its motion, Ayco marshaled summary judgment proof establishing that the City of Austin owned the switching cabinet and such proof showed further that the cabinet was located within the confines of an easement conveyed to the City. By its terms, the easement conferred upon the City "the right to enter and place, construct, operate, repair, maintain and replace electric lines and systems...." The easement further provided that:

> Austin shall have the right to ingress and egress for the purpose of construction [sic], improving, repairing, replacing, inspecting, maintaining, operating and removing said lines and appurtenances; and the right at all times to cut away and keep clear of said lines and appurtenances all trees and *other obstructions, which in the sole judgment of Austin,* may endanger or interfere with the proper maintenance and operation of said lines. [Emphasis supplied.]

In general, an owner or occupier of premises owes a duty of ordinary care to persons entering onto those premises. When, however, an owner has transferred possession or control of the premises to another, the owner owes no duty to those persons coming onto the premises.

The summary judgment proof establishes that by the express terms of the easement Ayco surrendered exclusive use and control of the easement property to the City of Austin. Under the terms of the easement the City had the perpetual right to enter onto the premises to "place, construct, operate, repair, maintain and replace electric lines and systems …" and also to inspect, relocate and remove the lines and systems whenever necessary. Ayco had no right to deny access to the cabinet or to remedy any condition in the cabinet. Any interference or tampering with the City's cabinet would plainly encroach upon the rights conferred upon the City by the easement. Likewise, locking or fencing the cabinet would be inconsistent with the terms of the easement.

Moreover, under general easement law, the owner of the dominant estate (the City of Austin) has a duty to maintain the easement and the owner of the servient estate (Ayco) has no right to interfere with the dominant estate. The servient estate has no duty to repair in the absence of an express agreement.

* * *

The summary judgment is affirmed.

Licensee

YARDE METALS, INC. v. NEW ENGLAND PATRIOTS LIMITED PARTNERSHIP
64 Mass. App. Ct. 656, 834 N.E. 2d 1233 (2005)

GREENBERG, Judge. After twenty years as a season ticket holder of the defendant, New England Patriots Limited Partnership (Patriots), the plaintiff, Yarde Metals, Inc. (Yarde), received a letter from the Patriots' front office advising that Yarde's season ticket privileges had been terminated, "effective immediately." As the reason, the Patriots stated that on October 13, 2002, an individual named Mike LaCroix, using a ticket from Yarde's account, was "ejected from Gillette Stadium for throwing bottles in the seating section." The letter, dated October 17, 2002, requested return of Yarde's remaining season tickets and offered a refund of their value.

Yarde's explanation, which it conveyed to the Patriots through multiple written communications and which is included in the complaint it eventually filed on August 8, 2003, differed. Yarde admitted that LaCroix, a business associate, had been given a ticket for the October 13, 2002, game. Yarde denied that LaCroix had thrown any bottles and offered the following account. Prior to October 13, 2002, and on that date, Gillette Stadium had an insufficient number of men's restrooms in use for football games; the Patriots were aware of the shortage, and it had become the subject of numerous newspaper columns. On the date in question, LaCroix, along with others, used available women's restrooms to answer the call of nature. These patrons were unimpeded by security guards, but for some unexplained reason, as he left the women's restroom, LaCroix was arrested, removed from the stadium, and charged with the crime of disorderly conduct. He subsequently admitted to sufficient facts for a finding of guilt and received a continuance without a finding. The Patriots acknowledged receipt of Yarde's written request to review the season ticket revocation and, in a terse letter dated March 5, 2003, confirmed its decision to terminate Yarde's season ticket account.

Out of options for restoring its season ticket account through dialogue with the Patriots, Yarde filed the complaint in this case. The legal theories in support of the complaint were set forth in two counts. Count I sought to impose liability on the Patriots for breach of its "contractual right to season tickets [that included] a contractual right to renew its

season tickets annually." Count II sought to impose liability on the Patriots based on the "doctrine of equitable estoppel [which] prohibits the Patriots from contradicting the expectation of the plaintiff Yarde which the Patriots have created." For relief, Yarde requested a preliminary and permanent injunction against the Patriots, enjoining them from refusing to sell Yarde six season tickets "of the same or higher quality than the tickets Yarde held in 2002." Yarde's motion for a preliminary injunction was denied, and the Patriots' subsequent motion to dismiss pursuant to Mass.R.Civ.P. 12(b)(6), 365 Mass. 755 (1974), was allowed, precipitating this appeal. We affirm.

1. *Contract claim.* Yarde argues that its twenty-year relationship with the Patriots created a contractual right to renew its season tickets annually. That such a right was part of the bargain between it and the Patriots, Yarde maintains, is evidenced by the Patriots' annual offer of the opportunity to purchase season tickets for the upcoming football season to Yarde because of Yarde's status as a season ticket holder. Yarde claims that by revoking its tickets for the actions of its guest, a course the Patriots originally took believing he had been ejected for throwing bottles rather than for using the women's room, the Patriots breached that contractual obligation. Specifically, Yarde argues that the process the Patriots followed in terminating Yarde's season tickets constituted a violation of the covenant of good faith and fair dealing that would be implied in any contractual right to renew annually. We disagree.

* * *

The purchase of a ticket to a sports or entertainment event typically creates nothing more than a revocable license. No Massachusetts cases, however, address the nature of the relationship between season ticket holders and ticket issuers, and the cases do not preclude parties from contracting for such things as renewal or transfer rights. Picking up on that fact, Yarde suggests we should follow cases from other jurisdictions where it has been concluded that season ticket holders have some protected expectations regarding their season ticket accounts.

* * *

In particular, Yarde urges us to extrapolate from two bankruptcy court decisions that ruled that the opportunity to transfer renewal rights to season tickets was an asset of the bankrupt season ticket holder's estate.

Other cases have concluded that season ticket subscriptions do not include any protected, implied right to renew annually.

The contractual right Yarde asks this court to imply here would substantially expand the reasoning of the decisions that it cites for support. The bankruptcy decisions focus on the nature of the season ticket as an asset of the bankrupt ticket holder's estate. In those cases the teams did not attempt to revoke season tickets, but rather intervened only when the estate tried to transfer season ticket accounts, a practice both teams typically allowed. Therefore, they provide little support for the proposition that a court can enforce a contractual right to renew that trumps a ticket issuer's decision to cancel a specific season ticket on account of the behavior of the ticket holder.

Despite the fact that the parties themselves are not precluded from contracting for renewal rights, Yarde's allegations (which, for purposes of the motion, we assume it would be able to prove) would not justify implying a contractual right that goes beyond any previously recognized in other jurisdictions and that would contradict the explicit language on the ticket. The annual "automatic and unsolicited" offer from the Patriots to purchase season tickets may not thwart the Patriots' right to revoke ticket privileges for cause that the ticket holder agreed to as part of the season ticket package. Where there is a seemingly clear transaction—Yarde purchased six tickets to ten games at $100 each—we cannot infer an annual renewal right, the value of which would dwarf the value of the otherwise clear commercial exchange. More importantly, such a theory would disregard the Patriots' express disclaimers of any right of the purchaser to renew in subsequent years printed on game tickets and informational material provided to season ticket holders. The ticket specifically stated that "[p]urchase of season tickets does not entitle purchaser to renewal in a subsequent

year." See *Vakil v. Anesthesiology Assocs. of Taunton*, 51 Mass.App.Ct. 114, 119-120, 744 N.E.2d 651 (2001), citing *Robert Indus., Inc. v. Spence*, 362 Mass. 751, 753-754, 291 N.E.2d 407 (1973), setting forth the well-settled rule of contract interpretation that "[p]arol evidence is not generally admissible to vary the unambiguous terms of the contract." Yarde has articulated no basis on which we can ignore the language on the ticket.

* * *

2. *Estoppel.* As an alternate theory of recovery, Yarde has alleged entitlement to its season tickets on the basis of estoppel. The point Yarde generally urges is that insofar as season tickets are concerned (as distinct from tickets to a single game), automatic and routine renewals amounted to a representation that it possessed a renewal right. It avers that in purchasing its season tickets it relied to its detriment on this understanding.

For Yarde to prevail on any estoppel claim, it must show, amongst other things, that its reliance on any alleged representation was reasonable. *Turnpike Motors, Inc. v. Newbury Group, Inc.*, 413 Mass. 119, 125, 596 N.E.2d 989 (1992). Given the explicit language printed on the back of the ticket and included on the promotional materials, Yarde's reliance on any purported conflicting representation was unwarranted. See *Kuwaiti Danish Computer Co. v. Digital Equip. Corp.*, 438 Mass. 459, 468, 781 N.E.2d 787 (2003) ("Reliance on any statement or conduct was unreasonable as a matter of law because it conflicted with the qualifying language [in a written document]"). In addition, we cannot agree that it would be reasonable for Yarde, without having any previous experiences with ejection from Patriots' games, to have understood that it had an enforceable right to renew tickets even in the face of a decision by the Patriots to revoke tickets as a disciplinary measure when a fan was arrested in the stadium.

In sum, Yarde's complaint did not plead a justiciable cause of action under either count. The judge did not err in dismissing the complaint.

Judgment affirmed.

KEY TERMS

affirmative easement, 96
alienated, 100
apportioned, 100
conservation easement, 98
dominant estate (dominant tenement), 99
easement, 95
easement appurtenant, 99
easement in gross, 99
estoppel, 111
exclusive easement in gross, 101
express conveyance, 102
express reservation, 102
hostile use, 108

implied easement, 103
implied easement from prior use, 104
implied easement of necessity, 106
license, 95
license coupled with an interest, 120
negative easement, 97
nonexclusive easement in gross, 101
prescriptive easement, 108
profit a *prendre*, 95
purchase of development rights, 98
Restatement of the Law of Property, 95, 96
servient estate (or servient tenement), 99
tacking, 110

1. Petruchio and Katherina owned adjoining tracts of real estate in a residential area. There was no water on Katherina's property. There was, however, a deep well on Petruchio's lot; and Petruchio gave Katherina written permission, creating an easement appurtenant, to enter his property and remove water for use on her lot. After the agreement was signed, Katherina converted her house into a thirty-room hotel. Petruchio claims that she cannot use the water for hotel purposes. Is he correct? Why or why not?

2. Toby works for Olivia Enterprises. He has decided to purchase the back 100 acres of Sebastian's 200-acre farm for his company, which plans to construct a large warehouse on the property. The front parcel, which Sebastian will retain, lies along a major highway; but the back parcel is landlocked. What legal issues relating to easements should be resolved by Toby and Sebastian before the purchase is completed? Why?

3. Constance purchased a general admission football ticket to the Soup Bowl. Halfway through the game, an usher, for no reason, told Constance to "get out of here before I throw you out." Constance left the stadium and later sued the organization that runs the Soup Bowl for damages, alleging that she had (1) an easement, (2) a lease, (3) a contract, and (4) a license. Will Constance prevail on those theories? Why or why not?

4. Anne and Roger owned neighboring estates. In 1984, Roger began to mine and remove coal openly and continuously from Anne's property without her permission. From 1984 until 1995, Roger removed fifteen million tons per year. From 1995 until 2001, he removed twenty million tons per year, five tons more a year from when he initially began to mine Anne's coal. In 2001, Anne sued Roger, asking the court (1) to enjoin further removal of coal and (2) to provide damages for the coal already removed. The period of time necessary to establish an easement by prescription is fifteen years, while the statute of limitations for tort actions, such as trespass, is two years. Decide the case.

5. Helen and Alexander owned adjoining lots. In 1915, Helen granted to Alexander "the right to pass through my land." Alexander drove his horse-drawn wagon over the right-of-way for the next ten years. In 1925, however, Alexander purchased an automobile and now wants to use it on the right-of-way. May he? Why or why not?

6. Duncan and Malcolm own adjoining lots. In 1953, Malcolm began using a common driveway that was bisected by the lot lines. In 1975, Malcolm sold his lot to Angus, who continued to use the driveway. In 1981, Angus and Duncan blacktopped the driveway, each paying one-half of the cost. In 1990, Duncan decided to build a carport on his half of the driveway. Angus sued Duncan, asking the court to enjoin the construction of the carport. At the trial, Malcolm was called to testify. The following exchange was reported: "Q. So I understand you never at any time were using it contrary to the wishes of Duncan? A. Absolutely not. Everything was all right." If you assume that the time period for prescription is twenty-one years, will Angus win? Why or why not?

7. In 1983, L.B.D. Corporation requested permission to erect a billboard on Suzanne and Pat's property, advertising a subdivision. Despite their refusal to grant permission, L.B.D. erected the billboard in early 1984. In 1986, Suzanne and Pat demanded that L.B.D. either pay rent or remove the billboard; they filed suit against L.B.D. in 1987. Weather caused the removal of the sign in 1988. Under applicable Missouri law, the period of time needed to establish a prescriptive easement is ten years. Did L.B.D. acquire a prescriptive easement? For what period of time would Suzanne and Pat claim damages for the billboard's presence?

8. Oswald owned a large apartment building. He leased an apartment on the tenth floor to Lear under a two-year written lease. Lear can reach his apartment by using a stairway or an elevator. The elevator was not mentioned in the lease, although it was used by prior tenants. When Lear used the elevator for the first time, Oswald told him that if he continued to use it, his rent would be raised $600 per month. May Lear use the elevator without paying additional rent? Why or why not?

9. Henry and Isabel owned adjoining farms. Henry ran a lumber mill on his farm, while Isabel's farm was heavily forested. Isabel sold Henry the right to enter her farm for the purpose of cutting down and removing timber. Henry later sold the north half of this farm to York, along with a nonexclusive right to remove timber from Isabel's farm. Henry retained the south half of his farm. When both Henry and York attempted to remove timber, Isabel refused to allow them onto her property. May Isabel refuse them entry to her property? Why or why not?

10. The petitioners, the Schwabs, and a neighbor, McCormick, owned potentially valuable property on the shores of Green Bay, Wisconsin. Their properties extended from the shoreline to above a bluff overlooking the bay. A public highway linked their properties above the bluff. Both owners subdivided their properties above the bluff lines and sold parcels to third parties. The sales of their land effectively landlocked the Schwabs and McCormick. Their only reasonable means of ingress or egress to the public road would now be over the properties of five other landowners. They sued their

neighbors, requesting, among other things, that they should be awarded an easement by necessity. Wisconsin common law, however, is clear on this issue—grantors who landlock themselves cannot later impose an easement of necessity over another's land. Only grantees may gain an easement by necessity over the grantor on land retained by the grantor and third parties. In reaction, the Schwabs and McCormick argued that Wisconsin common law should be expanded by using a

"reasonable use" test based on a utilitarian argument. The court, they maintained, should adopt a test in which it weighs the benefits of allowing access to otherwise worthless land versus the detriment a lack of access may place on landowners. The petitioners further argued that the development of "virtually useless" land far outweighs the costs incurred on the burdened properties. Do you agree with their argument? Why or why not?

ENDNOTES

1. See, for example, *Champaign Nat'l Bank v. Illinois Power Co.*, 125 Ill. App. 3d 424, 465 N.E.2d 1016 (1984).
2. *Bickett v. Buffalo Bills Inc.*, 122 Misc.2d 880, 472 N.Y.S.2d 245 (Sup. Ct. 1983).
3. *Reeves v. Alabama Land Locators, Inc.*, 514 So.2d 917 (Alabama 1994).
4. *Mosier v. Mead*, 45 Cal.2d 629, 290 P.2d 495 (1955).
5. Restatement of Property §450 (1944). The discussion of easement definitions and classifications is drawn generally from the Restatement. See §§451–56, 487–93.
6. J. Bruce and J. Ely, *The Law of Easements and Licenses in Land* 1–2 (1988, 1994 Supp.).
7. D. Wilson, *Easements and Reversions* 7 (1991).
8. *Stewart v. Secor Realty & Investment Corp.*, 667 So.2d 52 (Ala. 1995).
9. 108 Wis.2d 223, 321 N.W.2d 182 (1992).
10. N.M.S.A. §§47-3-1 W *et seq.* (2000). See also http://www .dsireusa.org/solar/solarpolicyguide/?id=19 (last visited February 4, 2010) for a list of states which also regulate solar and wind energy systems.
11. W.S.A. §§34-22-101 *et seq.* (2001).
12. J. Zitter, *Solar energy: landowner's rights against interference with sunlight desired for purposes of solar energy,* 29 American Law Review 349 (1984, Cumulated Supp. 2009).
13. J. Whitely, *Valley Residents Turning to Solar Power to Dramatically Reduce Their Energy Bills,* Las Vegas Review Journal 1 (October 9, 2005).
14. E. Thompson, Jr., *Conservation Easements: Preserving American Farmland,* Probate & Property 13 (Nov./Dec. 1992); J. Rohe, *Conservation Easements and Plain English,* 74 Michigan Bar Journal 402 (May 1995).
15. D. Braun, *Strategies for Using Conservation Easements in Tax and Estate,* Probate & Property 15 (November/December 2002).
16. *The Recession's Green Lining: Conservations Groups Buy Up Dead Development Projects,* Take Part, http://www.takepart .com/news/2010/01/14/the-recessions-green-lining-conservation-groups-buy-up-dead-development-projects (last visited on January 26, 2010).
17. F. Bernstein, *Charleston Battling 'Drive-by Neighbors,'* The Charlotte Observer 6H (November 4, 2004). See also *Primary Historic Easements,* Historic Charleston Foundation, http://www.historiccharleston.org/preservation/how_cov_primary _res.html (last visited February 3, 2010).
18. R. Boyer, H. Hovencamp, and S. Kurtz, *The Law of Property* 310 (4th ed. 1991).
19. *Ratino v. Hart*, 424 S.E.2d 753 (W.Va. 1992).
20. *Trust #030-626-089 v. Illinois Power Co.*, 465 N.E.2d 1016 (Ill.App. Ct. 1984).
21. See, for example, *Village of Lyndonville v. Town of Burke*, 146 Vt. 435, 505 A.2d 1207 (Vt. 1985).
22. 246 S.C. 414, 143 S.E.2d 803 (1965).
23. 597 So.2d 683 (Ala. Sup. Ct. 1992).
24. 49 Ohio App.2d 366, 361 N.E.2d 457, 3 O.O.3d 430 (1974).
25. *Champion v. Neason*, 220 Ga. 15, 136 S.E.2d 718 (1964).
26. *State v. Anderson*, 241 Ind. 184, 170 N.E.2d 812 (1960).
27. *Trattar v. Rausch*, 154 Ohio St. 286, 95 N.E.2d 685, 43 O.O. 186 (1950).
28. 56 N.M. 473, 245 P.2d 390 (1952).
29. 222 So.2d 237 (Fla.App. 1969).
30. *Id.*
31. R. Cunningham et al., *Law of Property* 450 (2nd ed. 1993).
32. W. Burby, *Real Property* 73–74 (3rd ed. 1965).
33. 148 Kan. 495, 83 P.2d 698 (1938).
34. 250 Neb. 397, 550 N.W.2d 889 (1996).
35. 862 A.2d 901 (D.C.Cir. 2004).
36. See also *Broadhead v. Terpening*, 611 So.2d 949 (Miss. 1992).
37. W. Burby, *Real Property* 75 (3rd ed. 1965).
38. *Hildreth v. Googins*, 91 Me. 227, 39 A. 550 (1898).
39. 956 S.W.2d 629 (Tex. App. 1997).
40. *Id.* at 632.
41. *How Easements of Necessity Are Created*, The Mortgage and Real Estate Executives Report 6–7 (July 15, 1991).
42. 224 Wis.2d 27, 389 S.W.2d 1 (1999).
43. 234 Va. 407, 362 S.E.2d 696 (1987).
44. Restatement of Property §458, Comment d (1944).
45. Restatement of Property §458, Comment e (1944).
46. Restatement of Property §458, Comment d (1944).
47. 7 N.J. 215, 81 A.2d 137 (1951).
48. Some courts treat the driveway easement as a special situation and allow a prescriptive easement even when the use is permissive. See 27 A.L.R.2d 332 (1953).
49. Restatement of Property §458, Comment g, Illustration 9 (1944).
50. 167 Wash. 374, 9 P.2d 372 (1932).
51. Restatement of Property §459 (1944).
52. Restatement of Property §459, Comment c (1944).
53. 140 Mont. 564, 374 P.2d 96 (1962).
54. R. Cunningham, et al., *The Law of Property* 456 (1993).
55. 17 Ohio App.2d 146, 244 N.E.2d 762, 46 O.O.2d 208 (1969).
56. *Shipp. v. Stoker*, 923 S.W.2d 100 (Tex. App. 1996).

57. *Hollosy v. Gershkowitz*, 88 Ohio App. 198, 98 N.E.2d 314, 44 O.O. 221 (1950).

58. *Apel v. Katz*, 83 Ohio St. 3d 11, 697 N.E.2d 600 (Ohio 1998).

59. *Villager Condominium Assoc., Inc. v. Idaho Power Co.*, 121 Idaho 986, 829 P.2d 1335 (Idaho 1992).

60. Restatement of Property §477, Comment e (1944).

61. Restatement of Property §478, Comment d, Illustrations (1944).

62. See G. Dykstra and L. Dykstra, *The Business Law of Real Estate* 541 (1956).

63. Restatement of Property §484 (1944).

64. 234 Iowa 1148, 15 N.W.2d 252 (1944).

65. 89 R.I. 12, 150 A.2d 5 (1959).

66. R. Boyer, H. Hovencamp, and S. Kurtz, *The Law of Property* 311 (4th ed. 1991).

67. 198 Cal.App.2d 684, 18 Cal.Rptr. 123 (1961).

68. 317 Ill. 179, 147 N.E. 804 (1925).

69. 78 Cal. 546, 21 P. 302 (1889).

70. 875 P.2d 1256 (Wyoming 1994).

71. *Hohman v. Rochester Swiss Laundry Co.*, 125 Misc. 584, 211 N.Y.S. 217 (1925).

72. Restatement of Property §§497–99 (1944).

73. 296 Mich. 325, 296 N.W. 275 (1941).

74. Restatement of Property §504 (1944).

75. *Charles C. Gardiner Lumber Co. v. Graves*, 63 R.I. 345, 8 A.2d 862 (1939).

76. 111 Conn. 90, 149 A. 241 (1930).

77. 41 Cal.App. 413, 182 P. 974 (1919).

78. Restatement of Property §505 (1944).

79. *Trimble v. King*, 131 Ky. 1, 114 S.W. 317 (1908).

80. *Kux v. Chandler*, 112 N.Y.S.2d 141 (1952).

81. Restatement of Property §507 (1944).

82. See Restatement of Property §§500–03 (1944).

83. D. Wilson, *Easements and Reversions* 3 (1991).

84. *Merriam v. First National Bank of Akron*, 587 So.2d 584 (Fla. 1st DCA 1991).

85. 141 Tenn. 440, 211 S.W. 353 (1918).

86. *Eastman v. Piper*, 68 Cal.App. 554, 229 P. 1002 (1924).

87. R. Boyer, H. Hovencamp, and S. Kurtz, *The Law of Property* 318 (4th ed. 1991).

88. *Minnesota Valley Gun Club v. Northline Corp.*, 207 Minn. 126, 290 N. W. 222 (1940).

89. 83 N.J.L. 101, 83 A. 369 (1912).

90. Restatement of Property §§513, 519 (1944).

91. For a discussion by the U.S. Supreme Court of one such statute, see *Western Turf Ass'n v. Greenburg*, 204 U.S. 359, 27 S.Ct. 384, 51 L.Ed. 520 (1907).

The Real Estate Transaction

2

© MACIEJ NOSKOWSKI/iStockphoto (RF)

© MACIEJ NOSKOWSKI/iStockphoto (RF)

Types of Ownership

LEARNING
OBJECTIVES

After studying Chapter 5,
you should:

- Define, differentiate, and understand estates in land

- Classify and distinguish concurrent ownership

- Recognize and apply forms of ownership for investment purposes

"It's far better to own a portion of the Hope diamond than 100 percent of a rhinestone."

Warren Buffett

Part 1 examined the nature and scope of interests in real property, including fixture law, the implications of the *ad coelum* doctrine, water rights, and rights in real estate owned by others. Part 2 focuses on legal problems that arise when a person attempts to buy or sell the bundle of rights reviewed in Part 1. The chapters in Part 2 cover each step in a typical real estate transaction.

The real estate transaction usually begins with the search for the real estate (Chapter 6), and the search culminates in the signing of a real estate contract (Chapter 7). After the contract is signed, the vendor's title must be examined (Chapter 8); and in most cases, the buyer must arrange for financing (Chapter 9). When these matters have been completed, the contract is performed at the closing (Chapter 10). Alternative methods of real estate transfer or acquisition also are examined in Chapter 10, including adverse possession and transfer at death. Chapter 11 discusses landlord and tenant law.

Two preliminary questions must be resolved before the real estate transaction commences. Are limitations attached to the existing ownership of the land? What type of estate should be bought or sold? This chapter examines those questions.

Estates in Land

A large, grand residential property is typically referred to as an estate. For example, "After attending two fund-raisers in Florida on Thursday night, the President traveled by helicopter and then motorcade to Mr. Norman's Hobe Sound estate."[1] The word *estate*, however, is a word of many meanings. In medieval Europe, a person was classified by his estate, the customary estates being the clergy, nobility, and commoners. The word *estate* described class or status. For example, after William the Conqueror successfully invaded England after the Battle of Hastings in 1066 AD, he established the highest noble class or estate called the chief tenants, or "tenants in capite." Tenants in capite, in turn, possessed the greatest interest or estate in property after the king. Occupying the lowest class or estate were the serfs, or "tenants paravail," who possessed and worked the land only at the will of the noble classes.[2] The property system that the Norman invaders established in England, with its many estates and other complicated features, spawned a very intricate body of law that is still relevant today, as noted by the following:

> *Property students in the United States are likely to have ambivalent feelings about Hastings. As pure history, the story of the Norman Conquest of England is delightful literature, redolent of knights in armor and kingly combat. But for the student of American property law, the pleasure of reading Duke William's glorious expedition against King Harold is likely to be tinctured by the memory that was the same William the Bastard who set in motion the forces that would make American property the monstrously complex and mysterious body of law that it is.*[3]

In modern times, all real and personal property that a person accumulates during her lifetime is also referred to as her estate. The estate is an accumulation of property that a person owns at the time of death. For instance, a person might develop an estate plan, serve as the executor in the probate of a deceased relative's estate, or attempt to minimize the estate tax that will be paid at death.

In legal terms, estate also describes the *nature, quality, and quantity* of a person's interest in real property—an interest that might vary from absolute ownership to naked possession.[4] Legally, estates fall into one of two categories:

freehold estate

An indefinite estate for life or in fee.

nonfreehold or leasehold estate

An ownership interest in land generally of a fixed or determinable duration.

- **Freehold estates**, *estates in fee or for life characterized by their uncertain duration*
- **Nonfreehold or leasehold estates**, *considered to be personal property and that may be of a definite duration*

Leasehold estates are covered in Chapter 11 on landlord and tenant law. This chapter examines four types of freehold estates: the fee simple absolute, the fee simple defeasible, the fee tail, and the life estate. (See Figure 5.1.)

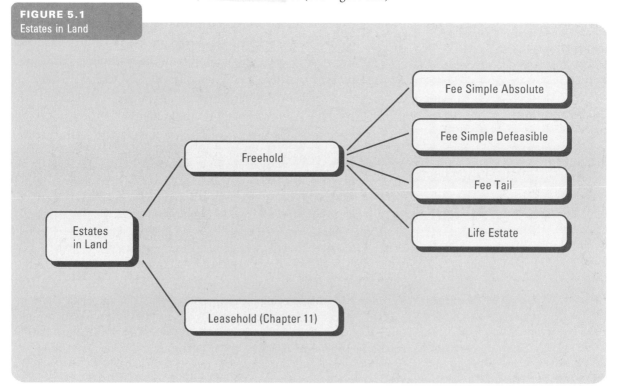

FIGURE 5.1
Estates in Land

Fee Simple Absolute

fee simple absolute
An estate limited absolutely to its owners and their heirs that assigns forever without limitation or condition.

The **fee simple absolute**—often called the *fee simple* or the *fee*—is the greatest estate possible; it corresponds to what the average person thinks of as ownership. A fee simple estate is not subject to special limitations and is controlled absolutely by its owner, subject to governmental regulations such as zoning, discussed in Chapter 13, and duties that arise under tort law, which are addressed in Chapter 12. "The grant of a fee in land conveys to the grantee complete ownership, immediately and forever, with the right of possession from boundary to boundary and from the center of the earth to the sky, together with all the lawful uses thereof."[5] Statutory law is often important in determining the scope of fee simple ownership. A Georgia statute provides the following definition: "An absolute or fee simple estate is one in which the owner is entitled to the entire property, with unconditional powers of disposition during his life, and which descends to his heirs and legal representatives upon his death intestate."[6] In nearly all the states,[7] statutes provide that unless a conveyance expressly states an intent to create another type of estate, a fee simple absolute is created. For instance, a will that grants a farm "to Jones" gives Jones a fee simple absolute.

Fee Simple Defeasible

fee simple defeasible
A fee estate that may end upon the happening of a specified event.

fee simple determinable
A type of defeasible fee that ends automatically when land is used in a manner forbidden in the grant of ownership.

possibility of reverter
Future interest associated with the fee simple determinable estate wherein the interest may return to the grantor when there is a breach of a condition to which it was granted.

In many cases, a fee simple is qualified by language that will cause the fee simple to end when a certain event occurs. In such cases, a **fee simple defeasible** is created. There are *three* common types of such defeasible fees. *First,* a conveyance of a tract of land might read as follows: "To Mehta for the purpose of operating a school and for no other purpose. This conveyance shall be good so long as there is a schoolhouse kept on the property." This is called a **fee simple determinable** because while it may last forever, the estate may also end if the special limitation is not followed. If at a future date a schoolhouse is not kept on the property, Mehta's interest would cease immediately, without action by the grantor. The grantor's interest is called a **possibility of reverter** and is a type of future interest.[8] Various kinds of future interests, presented in Figure 5.2, are discussed throughout this chapter. The following Maryland case demonstrates how a fee simple determinable can be used to care for a disabled relative.

A CASE IN POINT

In *Ringgold v. Queen Anne's County Association for Handicapped Citizens, Inc.,*[9] Roland deeded the family home as a fee simple determinable estate to an association for mentally disabled citizens. The deed provided that: "In the event the said Queen Anne's Chapter, Maryland Association for Retarded Citizens, Incorporated, or its duly and lawfully designated successor, *shall fail, during the lifetime of William Robert Ringgold, properly to provide maintenance and care for said William Robert Ringgold, then, and in that event, title to the real estate conveyed herein shall revert to Roland C. Ringgold, Grantor herein. Grantee shall, however, be compensated at its regular rates for providing such maintenance and care."*[Emphasis added.]

Subsequently, Robert was killed in a car that was negligently driven by his former caregiver and employee of the home. Roland sued to enforce the reverter, arguing that Robert's accidental death was evidence that he was not receiving adequate care. The court dismissed Roland's complaint stating that "a reasonable interpretation of the reversion clause is that it was intended to refer to Robert's general care, particularly while on the premises of the former Ringgold home. It was meant to ensure that Robert's daily needs, such as food, clothing and shelter would be taken care of. Roland has failed to meet his burden to demonstrate that the care provisions in the deed were not satisfied."

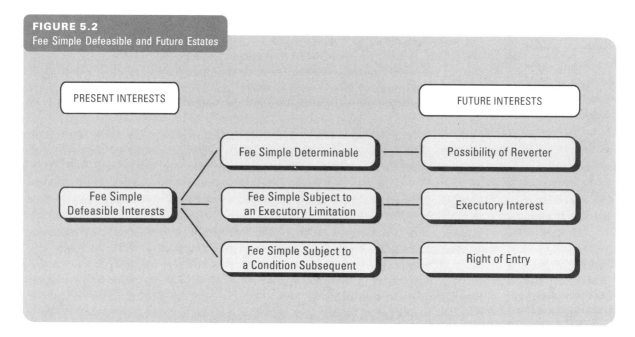

FIGURE 5.2
Fee Simple Defeasible and Future Estates

fee simple subject to an executory limitation or interest

A type of defeasible fee that ends automatically when land is used in a manner forbidden in the grant of ownership, but vests in someone other than the grantor.

executory interest

A future interest associated with the fee simple subject to an executory condition wherein the interest may return to a party other than the grantor when there is a breach of a condition to which it was granted.

fee simple subject to a condition subsequent

A type of defeasible fee that entitles the grantor to end the interest by exercising the right of entry after the grantee breaches a condition under which it was granted.

In creating the *second* type of fee simple defeasible, the grantor might provide as follows: "To Mehta provided that a schoolhouse is kept on the premises; if one is not, then to Chang." This is called a **fee simple subject to an executory limitation or interest**. An **executory interest** also is a type of future interest; but unlike the possibility of reverter, it must vest in a person other than the grantor. In this case, if a schoolhouse was not kept on the premises, the land would go to Chang instead of the grantor. The *third* type of fee simple defeasible might read as follows: "To Mehta provided that if the property is used for purposes other than a schoolhouse, Grantor shall have the right to reenter the property and cause Mehta to forfeit the estate." The grantor in this case must take action by physically retaking the property or by going to court. The technical name for Mehta's estate is a **fee simple subject to a condition subsequent**, and the grantor has a **right of entry**. This future interest, in contrast to the first two that vest automatically when the condition is violated, requires the grantor or his heirs to exercise the right to own the property should Mehta use it for anything other than a schoolhouse.

Although common in commercial transactions in the past, defeasible estates are rare today. The benefits that these estates can provide are accomplished more often today through the creation of trusts, discussed later in this chapter. Even so, defeasible estates are still used usually to advance charitable, educational, and religious purposes by nonprofit groups, such as in the *Ringgold* case above. Yet, although the legal concept of the fee simple defeasible is based on ancient property rules, it is subject to many modern applications.

A family wanted to convey a prime tract of property to the local government, but only if the local government used the land for public purposes. The legal mechanism employed to condition the grant was the fee simple defeasible. When the local government later used the property to host the Lipton tennis tournament, the family argued that this use was not a public purpose. In *White v. Metropolitan Dade County* on page 163, the court determines whether the tennis tournament triggered the grantor's deed restriction.

END OF CHAPTER CASE

right of entry

A future interest associated with the fee simple subject to a condition subsequent in which the grantor may elect to end the interest after the grantee breaches a condition under which it was granted.

restraint on alienation

A provision in an instrument of conveyance that prohibits the grantee from transferring the property that is the subject of the restraint.

The enforcement of fee simple defeasible restrictions or any other limited property interest is tempered by policy disfavoring **restraints on alienation**. Such a restraint attempts to limit or prohibit the buyer's subsequent rights to convey property. The policy against restraints on alienation on property places limits on the grantor's unreasonable restriction of the grantee's ability to transfer the real estate. Limitations on restraints on alienation are the oldest of social restrictions, restrictions that limit the individual liberty for the general benefit.[10] The rationale for restricting the grantor's power to place restraints on alienation by the grantee has been stated as follows:

> *The underlying principle which operates throughout the field of property law is that freedom to alienate property interests which one may own is essential to the welfare of society.... [This is a freedom] found to rest in part upon the necessity of maintaining a society controlled primarily by its living members, in part upon the social desirability of facilitating the utilization of wealth, and in part upon the social desirability of keeping property responsive to the current exigencies of its current beneficial owners.*[11]

A restraint on alienation is in direct conflict with these socially desirable policies and may be invalid depending on the extent of the restriction. In determining whether the restraint is valid, courts consider whether the grantee is permitted to sell the property and whether the restraint is generally reasonable.[12] For instance, assume that Able conveys her real estate, which is suitable only for coal-mining purposes, "to Baker and her heirs, but if Baker or her heirs ever convey said real estate to Chance (Able's brother), Able and her heirs have the right to reenter and terminate the estate." This restraint is reasonable because only one person—Chance—is excluded. However, consider the effect of a conveyance made "to Baker and her heirs, but if Baker or her heirs ever convey said real estate to any coal company, Able or her heirs shall have a right to reenter and terminate the estate." A later conveyance to a coal company would be valid because the restraint unreasonably includes the only parties that would be interested in the land. Restraints on the alienation of property can affect other estates in land besides defeasible estates, including the very common and important fee simple absolute and life estate. A notable example of a restraint that greatly influences how fee simple property is sold is the due on sale clause contained in mortgages. These clauses, for all practical purposes, prevent a seller from conveying title to a buyer until the mortgage is paid off, thus preventing the mortgage debt from being assumed. This restraint, discussed in Chapter 9, was once vigorously challenged as an illegal restraint on the alienation of property, but today is considered legal. On the other hand, a restraint that is not legal (e.g., one forbidding some co-owners from partitioning their real property) is discussed in the *Vinson v. Johnson* case later in this chapter.

Fee Tail

fee tail

An estate in fee that descends to the grantee's direct lineal heirs and through them to the direct lineal heirs of the next generation.

A **fee tail** estate is created when the grantor conveys real estate "to Whitefeather and the heirs of his body." Historically, such a conveyance limited Whitefeather's use of the land to his lifetime. Whitefeather could not convey the real estate outside the family since the property had to pass to his children and grandchildren. If Whitefeather died without heirs, the property would revert to the grantor and his heirs. In modern times, this severe restraint on Whitefeather's ability to alienate his property has been prohibited by most states; in other states, it is legal, but the effect of the fee tail is very limited.[13] For example, a testator left a life estate to his wife and a fee tail to his son. Under Arkansas law, the fee tail is converted into a life estate to the son and a remainder to the son's heirs.[14]

Conventional Life Estates

life estate

An estate in which duration is measured by the life of a person.

A **life estate** is an estate with a duration measured by the life of a person. A conventional life estate is created by deed or will. Life estates such as dower, curtesy, and homestead, which apply to marital property, can be created by operation of law and are discussed in Chapter 10. A life estate may be measured by the life of the grantee or by the life of a third party, in which case it is an estate *pur autre vie*. For example, Van Duren conveys her property "to Opel for life" or "to Opel for the life of Donny." Van Duren may also create a life estate measured by more than one life: "to Opel for the life of the survivor of Bobby and Linda."

reversion

A future interest left in the grantor after the grantor conveys an estate smaller than her own. "It arises merely as a matter of simple subtraction."

Since a life estate must end at someone's death and so is not inheritable, someone must receive title to the property once the life estate ends. These parties will own either a **reversion**[15] or a type of **remainder** interest. Reversions and remainders are also *future interests,* like the possibilities of reverter, rights of entry, and executory interests that were discussed earlier with defeasible estates. For example, in the previous illustrations, the property reverts or returns to Van Duren or her heirs as a fee simple absolute interest once the life estate terminates, thereby giving her a reversion. Another way to view it is that once the life tenant dies and the reversion occurs, Van Duren or her heirs are no longer burdened or subject to the life estate and so now own a fee simple absolute interest.

remainder

A future interest created in favor of a party other than the grantor that generally follows a life estate. A remainder interest can be vested or contingent.

Van Duren might also provide that the property will not revert back to her, but instead pass to a third party. Before the life tenant dies, the third party owns a **vested remainder** interest. Such a provision in the deed would state "to Opel for life and then to Donny." Donny's remainder interest is said to be vested because it is certain that the property will pass to Donny upon Opel's death. Remainders are classified as a **contingent remainder** when they depend upon the occurrence of an uncertain event. Donny's remainder would be contingent if the grant from Van Duren read "to Opel for life and then to Donny if Donny marries before Opel's death."[16] If Donny did not marry before Opel's death, the property would revert back to Van Duren or her heirs. Various kinds of conditions, such as making marriage a contingency for receiving the property, are found in trusts as well. Trusts are discussed later in this chapter. The owner of a vested or contingent remainder interest, such as Donny's, is called a **remainderman**.

vested remainder

A future interest in which the remainderman has an absolute right to a possessory interest at the end of a prior interest.

The life estate—like the fee simple absolute, the fee simple defeasible, and the fee tail—is considered to be a present estate. The owner has an immediate right to possess, enjoy, and sell the property. The owner of a life estate, however, can sell only an interest in property measured by his lifetime. If there is a sale, the purchaser's interest ends upon the death of the person whose life measures the life estate. Thus, if Opel sold her life estate to Donny and Opel dies in just two months, Donny would also lose his life estate at that time. This limitation on the duration of ownership is one reason for scrutinizing titles closely and securing title insurance, which is discussed further in Chapter 8.

contingent remainder

A future interest that depends on the occurrence of an uncertain event.

remainderman

The holder of a remainder interest.

As previously discussed, reversions and remainders as well as possibilities of reverter, rights of reentry, and executory interests are future interests because enjoyment or possession must be postponed until a future date. After the creation of a life estate, disputes often arise between the owners of the present and future interests, as the following example illustrates. Peter owns a large wheat farm, part of which is used as a coal mine. He deeds the farm "to Jim for life" but keeps a reversionary interest. Shortly after Jim moves to the farm, a conflict arises between Jim and Peter over Jim's duties to make insurance, tax, and mortgage payments; his duty to make repairs; and his right to use the property for farming and mining purposes. Of course, these kinds of issues can always be worked out in advance if the parties agree as to how these rights and duties should be allocated. But in the absence of such planning, the following rules have been developed by the courts to resolve such disputes.

Taxes and Interest   The well-established rule states that the life tenant must pay all annual taxes and interest on debts on the land to the extent that the tenant has received profits, rents, or income from the property. For instance, assume that Jim, the life tenant, earns $50,000 per year from the farm for three years and pays taxes and interest of $30,000 each year. During the fourth year, even if Jim has no earnings from the farm, he must still pay the interest and taxes because of his earnings in prior years.[17]

However, the foregoing rule does not apply to special taxes or assessments. Assume that the county installs a new sewer that passes through the owner's farm and that Peter, who owns the reversion, receives a sewer assessment for $10,000, with $1,000 to be paid each year for ten years. Since the sewer is a permanent public improvement that increases the value of Peter's reversion, most courts prorate the assessment in proportion to the benefits that Peter and Jim receive from the sewer. A court might conclude that Jim must pay interest on the assessment and that the owner is liable for the principal.[18] Or a court might calculate the life tenant's share of a special tax by dividing the present value of the life estate by the present value of a life estate that would last as long as the improvement. For instance, you might assume that Jim is sixty-three years old and that his life estate is valued at $50,000. If the present value of a life estate lasting fifty years (the life of the sewer system) is $200,000, Jim might be asked to pay $50,000/$200,000, or 25 percent of the $10,000 assessment. If the special tax is for an improvement that will not last beyond the life estate, the life tenant is responsible for the full amount of the special tax.[19]

Insurance   If the owner's farm included a farmhouse and a number of buildings, two major questions would arise: Who has the duty to insure these buildings? Who is entitled to the insurance proceeds if the buildings are destroyed? The general rule is that neither the life tenant nor the future interest owner, such as the remainderman or the owner of the reversion, has a duty to insure the buildings; if either does insure them, the distribution of the proceeds will depend on the facts of each case. For example, if the owner purchased insurance *before* the life estate was created and the property was destroyed thereafter, the life tenant would be given part of the proceeds of the policy. If an insurance policy is taken out solely by the life tenant or by the remainderman *after* creation of the life estate, as a general rule, the party that purchases the insurance is entitled to the full proceeds of the policy.[20] Even if the value of the proceeds exceeds the insured's interest in the property, the insured will receive the full amount on the theory that an insurance policy is a personal contract between the insured and the company. Whenever possible, however, courts attempt to find an intention that the policy was taken out for the benefit of both the life tenant and the owner of the future interest, often determined by whose name appears on the policy, as this Oregon case points out.[21]

A CASE IN POINT

In *Morris v. Morris,*[22] a woman held a life estate in a farm and her son was the remainderman. The mother purchased a fire policy insuring the farmhouse, and later the farmhouse was totally destroyed by fire. The son sued his mother after the insurance company paid her; the son claimed that he was entitled to part of the proceeds. The court, deciding that the son had no right to the proceeds, noted the general rule that "a life tenant is entitled to all the proceeds for a loss if the life tenant has procured the insurance policy in his own name and for his own benefit and has paid the premium from his own funds. The general rule is not changed by the fact that the insurance is for the full value of the property rather than only for the value of the life tenant's interest in the property."

Repairs   What is a life tenant's duty to keep the property in repair? There is considerable room for controversy over the answer. If a farmhouse needs painting, the roof needs repair, the windows must be replaced, or the farmhouse is totally destroyed, must the life tenant repair or rebuild the house? The answer depends on whether the repairs are considered to be ordinary or extraordinary. The life tenant who receives income, rents, or profits from the real estate has a duty to make ordinary repairs—for example, painting, replacing windows, and making roof repairs. If the repairs are extraordinary, the life tenant will not be responsible. In one case, a court held that a life tenant was not responsible for installing a new furnace because the old furnace was already old and rusted when the tenant took possession. The tenant also was not responsible for replacing gutters that had reached a stage at which patching was not beneficial.[23]

A life tenant may voluntarily go beyond making ordinary repairs and make improvements on the property. For example, Jim, the life tenant, might decide to add a new room to the farmhouse. If the improvements are considered to be fixtures, they may be removed within a reasonable time after the termination of the life estate. However, an improvement that is considered an integral part of the premises cannot be removed at the termination of the life estate; and Peter, the owner of the reversion, is not liable to Jim's estate for its value.

Tenant's Use of Property   A life tenant's use of the property often leads to thorny legal questions. For example, may Jim farm and mine the land and keep all of the profits from those activities? May he cut down timber from the farm and sell it? May he tear down the farmhouse and other buildings? As a general rule, a life tenant may act as the fee simple owner would if she were on the land; but she is limited in her ability to diminish the market value of the remainder or reversion.[24,25]

In applying this test, courts have decided that the life tenant may keep all of the rents and profits that she produces. As noted by one court: "It is a general rule, well established in this and other jurisdictions of this country that … a life tenant is entitled to revenue or income produced by the property during his tenancy."[26] However, as this Oregon case demonstrates, only a living life tenant, not a purported heir, can claim rent when it is due.

A CASE IN POINT

In *Simpson v. McCormmach,* a life tenant was to receive as rent 40 percent of the crops after they were harvested. After the life tenant's death, the remaindermen claimed that they, not the life tenant's estate, were entitled to the crops.[27] The court noted that the dispute did not center on the crops; rather, it was about rent: the crops were the rent. The court held that the remaindermen were entitled to the crops, noting that the rental payment was due after harvest of the crops, which was after the death of the life tenant and that a life estate or the revenue from it is not inheritable.

A life tenant may also sell to a third party whatever interest she has in the land although if the tenant attempts to sell more than the life estate, such as by representing that she owns a fee simple absolute estate, the purchaser obtains only the life tenant's rights. For reasons such as these, title examinations and title insurance are vital, a topic discussed in Chapter 10.[28]

The life tenant may not diminish the market value of the remainder interest. Yet, she is generally entitled to cut timber as needed for repair of structures and fences or for fuel under what is called the "right of estovers."

In addition to having the right of estovers, the tenant may *continue* profitable operations. For example, she can carry on such activities as mining, drilling, or removing timber for sale if the land was used for such operations before the life estate was created. As a Pennsylvania court observed, "The most obvious inference would seem to be that when a man devises land with an open mine upon it, to a person for life, he intended the devisee to derive profit from the mine, as well as from the surface of the land."[29]

In using the land, the life tenant is limited by the general rule that she is not allowed to commit waste. **Waste** is generally defined as "destruction of property by the life tenant, or other lawful possessors of the land, such as a tenant for years, to the harm of the reversion or remainder." A Minnesota court discusses waste in the next case.

waste
A destructive use of real property by one in rightful possession.

A CASE IN POINT

In *Beliveau v. Beliveau,*[30] the defendant, sixty-six years old at the time of trial, was the life tenant on a 320-acre farm. She failed to repair buildings and fences on the farm, allowed "foul weeds" to infest and depreciate the farm, failed to pay taxes, and became involved in serious lawsuits relating to management of the farm. The court, in deciding to appoint a receiver to manage the farm, made this observation: "It was the duty of appellant as a life tenant not to permit waste, to make necessary and reasonable repairs, to pay current taxes, to pay the interest on the mortgage, and not to permit noxious weeds to infest the lands to the injury of the freehold.... Her failure to pay the taxes and make necessary and reasonable repairs of the building and fences constituted waste. While there is some conflict among the authorities we think the better rule is that a life tenant commits waste by permitting farm lands to become infested with noxious weeds which do injury to the freehold. Such acts not only constitute ill husbandry but also injury to the land itself."

A difficult question arises when the life tenant decides to commit waste but, in so doing, actually increases the value of the real estate. The old English rule provided that anything that changed the nature of the real estate, even if it were an improvement, would be considered waste. Modern courts, however, typically allow changes in the property and therefore do not consider it waste if the changes reflect a general change in the neighborhood or in society in general. The following Wisconsin case illustrates the point.

A CASE IN POINT

In *Melms v. Pabst Brewing Co.,*[31] a brewery acquired a life estate to a large brick home on a quarter-acre tract in the city of Milwaukee. The neighborhood changed over the ensuing twenty years, and the home "became wholly undesirable and unprofitable as residential property. Factories and railway tracts increased in the vicinity." The home was left isolated and at a grade substantially above street level. The level of the surrounding property had been substantially graded down in the course of its conversion to business use. The life tenant brewery destroyed the home and graded down the property. The owners of the reversion sued the brewery for waste. The court concluded that "the residence, which at one time was a handsome and desirable one, became of no practical value, and would not rent for enough to pay taxes and insurance thereon; whereas, were the property cut down to the level of the street, so that it was capable of being used as a business property, it would again be useful, and its value would be largely enhanced." The court held that "[u]nder all ordinary circumstances the landlord or reversioner, even in the absence of any contract, is entitled to receive the property at the close of the tenancy substantially in the condition in which it was when the tenant received it; but when, as here, there has occurred a complete and permanent change of surrounding conditions, which has deprived the property of its value and usefulness as previously used," the finder of fact may determine that the change was not waste.

Estate Planning   The creation of a life estate as an estate planning device often creates unforeseen complications. For example, assume that an elderly widow, Clarissa, hopes to avoid the expense of probate court by deeding her house to "my son Jim, a married man, and my daughter Bonnie, excepting and reserving a life estate in Clarissa." Before deciding to use a life estate, Clarissa and the children should decide who will make insurance, mortgage, and tax payments. They also should agree about how the brother and sister will share the use of the property after their mother's death. Furthermore, Clarissa must remember that her ability to sell or mortgage the property is greatly complicated by this device. Selling or mortgaging a mere life estate is difficult; if her plans change and she wants to sell or mortgage more than her life estate, she will need the permission of Jim, Bonnie, and Jim's wife if Jim's wife has a dower interest. And if one of the parties should become incapacitated, a legal proceeding would probably be necessary to complete the sale.

Trusts and Estate Planning   Many of the pitfalls discussed above can be avoided with a carefully drafted **trust**. Trust law originated centuries ago in the English common law. Today trusts are created for many purposes, including estate and tax planning, caring for family members, and charitable reasons. For example, in the *Ringgold* case on page 138, a trust could likely have been used more effectively instead of the fee simple determinable estate for caring for the grantor's mentally disabled relative.

trust
An arrangement in which one party, the trustee, holds and manages property for the benefit of another, the beneficiary.

In a trust, the "settlor" or "trustor" conveys legal title to property to the "trustee" who holds it for the "beneficiary" to whom he owes fiduciary duties. The "beneficiary" owns equitable title to the trust property. A trust instrument must show a clear intention to create a trust; must identify the property, such as real estate, stocks, or bonds; and must name the beneficiary or beneficiaries. Beneficiaries can include future generations not yet born with limitations, in some states, as to how many future generations. A settlor can also confer upon the trustee broad discretionary powers. For instance, a trustee may be instructed to use the income from the trust's property to support the beneficiary as the trustee sees fit and then to dissolve the trust and transfer the principal to a remainderman when the income beneficiary reaches a certain age or dies.

A trustee can be a person or a company. For example, many banks own trust departments or companies comprised of professionals with expertise in investing trust assets, ensuring that they are preserved and accounted for and making periodic reports to the beneficiary. If a trustee fails in its fiduciary duties, such as by investing the assets imprudently, it is personally liable.[32] Trusts are often created in wills, called testamentary trusts, in which property is "poured over" into a trust after the testator dies.

Trusts, like provisions in future estates, are sometimes attacked for violating public policy as in the following case.

> Is it a violation of public policy if a trust contains a provision in which the beneficiaries can only receive their share of the trust property if they first marry a person within the Jewish faith? In *In re Estate of Max Feinberg* on page 164, the Supreme Court of Illinois resolves the issue.

END OF CHAPTER CASE

Concurrent Ownership

The first part of this chapter examined four types of freehold estates—those interests in land measured in terms of duration. Interests in land also are classified by the form of

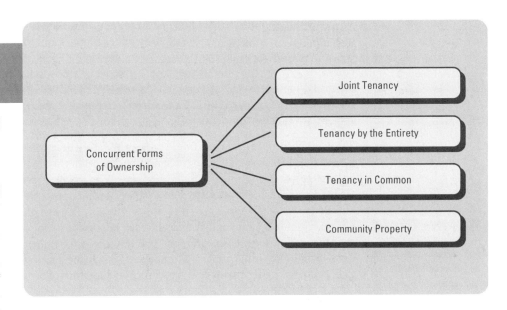

FIGURE 5.3
Concurrent Forms of Ownership

concurrent estate
Ownership or possession of property by two or more people at the same time.

joint tenancy
Ownership of real or personal property by two or more people in which each owns an undivided interest in the whole and each has the right of survivorship.

four unities
The four characteristics of an interest held in joint tenancy: unity of time, unity of title, unity of interest, and unity of possession.

unity of time
The requirement that the interests of joint tenants must vest at the same time. One of four unities needed to create a joint tenancy.

unity of title
The requirement that joint tenants must acquire their interests in the same conveyance. One of four unities needed to create a joint tenancy.

unity of interest
The requirement that joint owners must have equal interests in the land. One of four unities needed to create a joint tenancy.

unity of possession
The requirement that joint tenants must have equal, undivided interests in the possession of the land. One of four unities needed to create a joint tenancy.

ownership. It is common for two or more people to own real estate together (**concurrent estate**). This section examines several forms of concurrent ownership that can be used in purchasing real estate for personal or investment purposes. (See Figure 5.3.)

Joint Tenancy

The most important characteristic of the **joint tenancy** is the right of survivorship. If Jamal sells real estate "to Shaakirrah and Odartey as joint tenants with the right of survivorship and not as tenants in common," upon the death of either Shaakirrah or Odartey, the survivor becomes the sole owner of the real estate. If Shaakirrah and Odartey die under circumstances in which it cannot be determined who died first, the Uniform Simultaneous Death Act states that each estate receives one-half of the property.

A joint tenancy is created by use of a deed or a will. Regardless of the method, however, the common law requires **four unities**—time, title, interest, and possession—to create a valid joint tenancy. According to English jurist Sir William Blackstone, joint tenants must "have one and the same interest, accruing by one and the same conveyance, commencing at one and the same time, and held by one and the same possession."[33]

1. **Unity of time** requires that the interests of the joint owners begin (vest) at the same time. For example, Anne deeded her summer cottage to Jim and Peggy as joint tenants with the right of survivorship. Jim then deeded his interest in the summer cottage to Joe as a joint tenant with the right of survivorship. However, Joe and Peggy are not joint tenants; they did not acquire their interest in the summer cottage at the same time.
2. **Unity of title** means that the parties must acquire their interest in the same conveyance, such as a deed or will.
3. **Unity of interest** requires that each tenant have an equal interest; for instance, one cannot have a life estate and the other a fee simple estate; one owner cannot possess an 80% undivided interest while the other has only 20%.
4. **Unity of possession** has been interpreted to mean that all parties have an undivided interest entitling them to an equal right to take possession of the entire real estate.

At one time, courts strictly adhered to the four unities. For example, a conveyance by an owner to herself and her husband as joint tenants would not create a joint tenancy because two unities—title and time—were missing.[34] This made it necessary for the grantor to convey the interest first to a "strawman," who would then reconvey the interest to the joint tenants. However, the modern view adopted in a majority of states by statute or by court decision is that a direct conveyance from the owner to herself and the joint tenant is valid despite the technical failure of the four unities.[35]

Terminating a Joint Tenancy   A joint tenancy is terminated whenever one of the four unities is destroyed, such as when there has been a voluntary or involuntary conveyance of the owner's interest in the property. The property's ownership, once the joint tenancy is terminated, converts into a tenancy in common (TIC). This conversion of a joint tenancy to a TIC is referred to as a **severance**. For instance, if Brad and Angie own a farm as joint tenants and Angie sells her interest to Jennifer, Brad and Jennifer now own the land as tenants in common. The result would be identical if Angie's conveyance were involuntary—that is, if a sheriff were to sell the real estate to satisfy a judgment against Angie. Other methods of severance include the following:

severance
A joint tenant's transfer of her interest that terminates the joint tenancy and converts it into a tenancy in common.

- *Partition (a voluntary or court-ordered division of the real estate among the joint tenants). This can be a geographic division of the land, called a* partition in kind *(if the land is susceptible to such a division) or a* partition by sale, *in which the proceeds are divided between the joint tenants.*
- *A divorce decree. In some states, a divorce decree severs a joint tenancy. In other states, the decree must refer specifically to the joint tenancy if it is to be severed.[36]*
- *A mortgage. A mortgage taken out by only one of two joint tenants severs the joint tenancy, at least under the title theory to be discussed in Chapter 9.[37]*

If one joint tenant murders the other, should the murderer take title to the entire property under the right of survivorship? A California court ruled on that issue as follows.

A CASE IN POINT

In *Abbey v. Lord*[38] Mr. and Mrs. Lord owned 500 shares of telephone stock as joint tenants. After an argument over his wife's refusal to sign a check, Mr. Lord killed his wife with a butcher knife. He was charged with murder, but later entered a plea of guilty to manslaughter and was ordered to serve one year in the county jail. When a dispute arose concerning ownership of the telephone stock, the court decided that the husband's act of killing his wife terminated the joint tenancy and converted it into a TIC. The heirs of the victim took one-half of the property.

While most states follow the *Abbey* approach, a minority of courts have held that the murderer is entitled to the entire property as a surviving joint tenant. Other courts take the opposite extreme and completely divest the killers of the estate so that even a killer's heirs cannot inherit the killer's property.[39] Generally, the plaintiff must prove the murder was intentional and felonious, but because it is a civil case, the burden of proof is a preponderance of the evidence instead of beyond a reasonable doubt.

Presumption Against Joint Tenancy   In most cases, courts attempt to find severance whenever possible because of judicial bias against joint tenancy. As a Delaware court stated: "[J]oint tenancies are not favored and can only be created by clear and definite language not reasonably capable of a different construction."[40] However, when individuals attempt to devise their interests in a joint tenancy by will, courts uniformly deny claims of severance. To overcome the presumption against a joint tenancy, deeds should emphasize that a joint tenancy is being conveyed with insertion of the words *rights of survivorship* and *joint tenancy*." For example, assume that two bachelors, Jagdesh and Ravi, purchase real estate as joint tenants, the deed stating that there is a right of survivorship. Ravi later marries Ninfa. Ravi then executes a will leaving his interest in the real estate to her. Ninfa inherits none of the real estate on Ravi's death. In the words of the Oklahoma Supreme Court, "As to property held in joint tenancy, there is nothing to inherit from the one dying first."[41]

Tenancy by the Entirety

tenancy by the entirety
A tenancy created between a husband and wife under which they hold title to the whole property with the right of survivorship.

In half the states, it is possible for two people to hold real estate as tenants by the entirety. A **tenancy by the entirety** (also called a tenancy by the entireties) is identical to a joint tenancy, with *two* major qualifications. *First*, a tenancy by the entirety can be created only between husband and wife. Thus, a fifth unity, unity of person (husband and wife), is added to the four unities of joint tenancy. (See Table 5.1.) Courts generally presume that a tenancy by the entirety is created when a husband and wife purchase property jointly and the words of conveyance do not indicate otherwise.[42] If two unmarried parties attempt to purchase property as tenants by the entirety, their ownership will, as a Maryland court ruled, be considered either a joint tenancy or a TIC.

A CASE IN POINT

In *Lopez v. Lopez*,[43] Alejo, while already married to Soledad, married Helen. Alejo and Helen purchased real estate as tenants by the entirety. Later Alejo and Soledad were divorced, and Alejo married Helen again. When Alejo was killed in an accident, the court resolved the nature of Helen's interest in the real estate. The court concluded as follows: "Helen, while admitting that tenancies by the entirety were not created, contends that an intent to create rights of survivorship has been shown, sufficient to vest title in Helen, as the survivor of Alejo. In our view, Helen must prevail. We are here dealing with deeds which convey property to the grantees as husband and wife. Had they been validly married, a tenancy by the entirety would have been created.... However, a tenancy by the entirety can only be created when the parties stand in relationship of husband and wife at the time of the grant to them.... Absent such a relationship, the attempt to create a tenancy by the entirety fails. Generally, in the case of a deed conveying property to grantees as husband and wife who are in fact not married, there is a presumption favoring tenancies in common, but this presumption will yield to the showing of a contrary intent.... In the instant case, we regard Alejo's attempt to take title as tenants by the entirety as a sufficient showing of his intention to create a right of survivorship, and the presumption favoring a TIC must yield to a joint tenancy."

TABLE 5.1 Unities

	TIME	TITLE	INTEREST	POSSESSION	PERSON
Joint Tenancy	✓	✓	✓	✓	
Tenancy by the Entirety	✓	✓	✓	✓	✓
Tenancy in Common				✓	

The *second* and most important distinction between a joint tenancy and a tenancy by the entirety is that the latter can be terminated only by joint action, such as by divorce or contract, of the husband and wife. However, a joint tenancy can be terminated by the action of one joint tenant.

In the following case, a federal district court in Florida looks at whether actions by both spouses are necessary in a drug forfeiture of their property initiated by the federal government.

A CASE IN POINT

In *United States v. One Single Family Residence*,[44] the Aguileras, a married couple, owned a home as tenants by the entirety. Carlomilton Aguilera, the husband, sold cocaine to an undercover DEA agent in his and his wife's home. He was arrested and later convicted for trafficking in cocaine. The U.S. government subsequently filed a complaint for forfeiture of the Aguilera property. The court determined that Ibel Aguilera, the wife, had no knowledge or suspicion of her husband's drug trafficking. The court ruled "because under Florida law, an entireties estate cannot be forfeited due to the independent criminal conduct of one spouse when the other spouse has not participated in and has no knowledge of the crime … that the property was not subject to forfeiture."

Another situation requiring joint action occurs when a husband and wife own property as tenants by the entirety, and the husband attempts to sell or lease his estate without the consent of his wife. The lease would not be valid if she does not consent. Furthermore, generally a creditor of the husband alone may not take or sell the husband's interest in the property although the property could be taken by creditors if the debt were owed by both the husband and wife.

The Pennsylvania Supreme Court, in deciding that a wife who was separated from her husband could not lease the property, defined the situation in these terms:

Neither spouse may separately dispose of any part so as to work a severance of the estate, nor encumber the property in any way. Neither spouse may convey an interest in the estate without the other's authority or consent, nor perform any act or make any contract respecting the property which would prejudicially affect the other, for it belongs to both, and each has a joint right with the other to its possession, use and enjoyment during the existence of the marriage. As a corollary of these principles it follows that a lease of the property can be made only by the act of both parties joining therein, and this, of course, is especially true if it purports to be for a term extending beyond the lifetime of the spouse who executes it. Since a judgment creditor of either spouse cannot sell or execute on his debtor's interest in an estate by the entireties, and a purchaser at a sheriff's sale thereunder would not acquire any right to possession, it is obvious that neither husband nor wife can voluntarily put a stranger, even though a creditor, into possession, and thereby infringe the co-tenant's rights.[45]

ETHICAL AND PUBLIC POLICY ISSUES

Should the Tenancy by the Entirety Be Abolished?

The tenancy by the entirety was created historically under English common law because, once married, a husband and wife were considered to be one person or entity, known as the unity of person. Therefore, third parties, such as creditors, could not sever this concurrent interest. The idea of married

continues

continued couples as one entity is now an archaic doctrine, yet half the states still recognize it in some form. Thus, spousal property owned under the tenancy by the entirety is protected from the creditors of one of the spouses, thereby preventing creditors from seizing the property to satisfy a legitimate debt of one of the spouses. When creditors are forced to write off bad debts, it can drive up the price of borrowing money and adversely affect others seeking loans and possibly the economy. For this and other reasons, England abolished tenancies by the entirety in 1925. Of the twenty-two states that still recognize tenancy by the entirety, nine have modified the concept by allowing the creditor a claim to seize the debtor spouse's one-half share when the tenancy ends due to death or divorce.[46] Since the original purpose of tenancy by the entirety ownership has long passed and it does affect creditor rights and perhaps the price of capital, is it still a morally correct public policy to allow this type of concurrent interest?

When a husband and wife sell their home, which they hold as tenants by the entirety, can the creditor of just the husband reach the proceeds of the sale? A District of Columbia court ruled[47] that the couple held the proceeds of the sale (in this case, payments on a promissory note and mortgage made by the buyer) in the same form as the home they conveyed. Thus, the judgment creditor of the husband could not attach the monthly payment on the purchase money note to the husband and wife.

The tenancy by the entirety provides a strong shield for protecting spousal property, but does it protect the property from back taxes that one of the spouses may owe the federal government? On page 166 in the case of *Hatchett v. United States*, the court answers that question.

END OF CHAPTER CASE

Tenancy in Common (TIC)

tenancy in common
Concurrent tenancy in which there is a unity of possession but unities of time, title, and interest are not required.

A **tenancy in common** (TIC) results when the tenants have unity of possession, with each entitled to occupy the property. Although the unities of time, title, or interest may be present, they are not required to establish a TIC.

Unlike the joint tenancy or the tenancy by the entirety, a TIC need not be created only through a deed or will. The TIC also can be created when a property owner dies without leaving a will and her property passes by operation of law to more than one person. Such an event would occur, for example, if the decedent were survived only by three children. Also, under the common law or under many state statutes, courts generally presume that a TIC has been created when the intention of the parties is not clear. For instance, if real estate is conveyed "to Smith and Wesson," in most states, it is presumed that a TIC has been created. When Smith dies, her undivided one-half interest passes to her heirs rather than to the survivor, Wesson. Thus, if Smith died without a will and left two children, each child would receive one-half of Smith's interest in common.

A tenant in common, like a joint tenant, may sell, lease, or mortgage her undivided interest as she pleases.[48] In addition, the tenant, or a purchaser of the tenant's interest, may seek a partition either by agreement with the other joint tenants or by judicial proceedings. The partition has the effect of severing the unity of possession, thereby terminating the TIC.

Rights of Concurrent Owners

The rights of a cotenant stem from the one unity common to the three types of concurrent ownership—the unity of possession. This means that each tenant has the right to use the real estate as if he were the sole owner, except that "he has no right to exclude his co-owners, or to appropriate to his sole use any particular portion thereof. The tenants out of possession may at any time assert their right to share in the possession, or they may have the property partitioned by a division, each taking a distinct part according to the extent of his interest."[49]

One frequently asked question is whether adjacent landowners are concurrent owners of trees and other vegetation directly on a boundary line. The next case from Washington state resolves the issue with Solomonic precision.

A CASE IN POINT

In *Happy Bunch, LLC v. Grandview North LLC*,[50] Grandview purchased land next to the Happy Bunch property to construct a Wienerschnitzel drive-through restaurant. Twelve mature trees stood either on or near the boundary line between the Happy Bunch and Grandview properties. Grandview, however, felt it could not meet the city's fill requirement unless it removed the trees. Grandview's request to Happy Bunch to have the trees removed was refused, but Grandview chopped them down anyway over Happy Bunch's vehement protests. Happy Bunch sued Grandview for trespass. The court ruled that trees that straddle boundary lines are owned by the adjacent property owners as tenants in common and that "trespass will lie if one cuts and destroys it without the consent of the other." In computing damages, the court further stated that "Grandview had an interest in the trees proportionate to the percentage of their trunks growing on Grandview's property Thus, Happy Bunch [could only receive] that portion of the trees' value reflecting Happy Bunch's property interest in them."

undivided interest

The interest of a concurrent owner entitling her to a share of the whole property but not to a specific part of it.

Concurrent owners, due to the unity of possession, possess an **undivided interest** in their property. The word *undivided* refers to an interest in the real property as a whole, not in any divisible or distinguishable portion. Thus, if Anne, Matthew, and Alexander own a three-bedroom house as joint tenants, each owner has an equal right to use each portion of the house. They can, of course, decide among themselves that a full right to use one bedroom is more appropriate than the right to share three bedrooms with two other people (a right that reflects their undivided interest).

Although the tenants usually share profits from the land, a tenant in sole possession is entitled to keep the profits resulting from his own use and is not required to pay rent to the other tenants as the court in the following California case points out.

A CASE IN POINT

In *Black v. Black*,[51] a father and three sons owned a citrus grove as joint tenants and the father operated the grove. After the father's death, the sons sued their stepmother, claiming that she had to turn over the revenues she had received from her deceased husband. The court decided that she could keep the revenues for the following reasons: "A joint tenant in the sole and exclusive occupancy of the land is not required to account to his cotenant for any portion of the revenues derived therefrom so long as they are the fruitage of his own capital, labor and skill. The risks incurred by the occupier of the land (held jointly) in the cultivation of crops are his as are also the profits he may enjoy or the losses he may sustain in producing crops by his industry. In taking all the fruits grown upon the land, decedent herein received no more than his just share inasmuch as it is no more than the reward for his own labor and capital to no part of which is cotenant entitled."

Duties of Concurrent Tenants   In certain circumstances, the tenant in sole possession will owe duties to cotenants. For instance, he must make tax and mortgage payments and keep the property in repair—expenses that would normally be shared by all tenants. Furthermore, the tenant in possession must account to cotenants for all monies, including access to financial books and records, when refusing to allow them onto the property or when renting the property to a third party.[52]

A difficult situation arises when one tenant decides to expend money to repair or improve the property. Assume that Gert and Amos jointly own a vacant lot worth $50,000. Amos decides to build a large apartment house on the lot and asks Gert to contribute half the cost. When Gert refuses, Amos proceeds to build the structure at a cost of $150,000. In such a case, the law is clear: Amos cannot force Gert to contribute for repairs or improvements. However, Amos could seek an equitable remedy in the form of a partition action. In this case, however, the court probably would not physically divide the property (a partition in kind) even though such partitions are favored in the law[53] because of the nature of the property. Generally, only certain kinds of land, such as farmland, can be fairly divided in this manner. Consequently, the court would order a partition by sale. If the property were sold for $200,000, Amos would receive $175,000, which is the cost of his improvement ($150,000) plus half the remaining proceeds ($25,000), while Gert would receive the other half ($25,000).[54] However, courts are split when the value of the property increases by more than the improvement cost. Some courts would limit Amos to recovery of the cost of the improvement, with the remaining proceeds to be split evenly. Other courts would also allow him to recover the amount of the increase in the value of the land because of his improvements[55] before dividing the remaining proceeds of the sale.

A partition often results when owners have serious disagreements regarding their land. In the next case from Florida, a father's intent was to prevent the partition of his land among his children upon his death.

A CASE IN POINT

In *Vinson v. Johnson*[56], a father left his farm and home to his nine children as tenants in common. A clause in his will stated that there would be no partition of the real property except upon the agreement of all of the children. A subsequent dispute arose among the children resulting in five of the children seeking a partition of the property, suing the other four. The court ruled that the father's clause violated public policy since it constituted a restraint on the alienation of real property. The court ruled that "[T]he right to seek partition of property owned jointly in a TIC is an incident to the right of individual ownership."

Joint Ownership and Estate Planning

probate

The court procedure by which a will is proved to be valid or invalid. In current usage, this term has been expanded to refer generally to the legal procedure wherein the estate of the decedent is administered.

In an attempt to avoid the expense and delay inherent in **probate** proceedings, married couples frequently place all of their property in joint ownership. While joint ownership is useful in estate planning, the dangers of relying solely on joint ownership to transfer an estate are illustrated by the following two examples.

Assume that a young married couple, Tom and Mary, have two young children. Tom and Mary own as tenants by the entirety a house in which their equity interest is worth $50,000, jointly own two automobiles worth a total of $20,000, and have $10,000 in a joint bank account. If their goal is to avoid probate, Tom and Mary have succeeded admirably, for upon the death of one spouse, the survivor automatically becomes the sole owner of the property. Furthermore, the estate is not large enough for federal estate tax to be a concern.

However, what will happen to the estate if Tom and Mary die together in an automobile accident or if Mary dies a few years after Tom? If their death was by a common catastrophe or if the surviving spouse did not prepare a will after the death of the spouse, probate proceedings would be necessary. The property would pass under the state laws of intestacy. These state laws (discussed in Chapter 10) determine who receives the assets of a person who dies without a will.

Also, in the absence of a will, the probate judge would appoint an administrator to supervise the probate proceedings and a guardian. The guardian would control the assets for the children until they reached the age of majority and would have physical custody of the children. Acrimonious disputes often arise among relatives who want to be named guardian.

To avoid potential problems, Tom and Mary should execute wills specifying the people who are to receive the property at their deaths, naming an executor to handle probate of the estate, and naming a guardian for the children and their estate. In addition, Tom and Mary might consider a trust agreement, possibly with a local bank, providing that if they both die, the property will pass to the trustee, who will distribute it to the children when they reach the ages that the parents specified in the agreement.

Now assume that Tom and Mary are elderly and that their children are grown. Tom and Mary have accumulated assets worth well over $1 million in the form of jointly owned real estate, bank accounts, and securities. Once more, they have succeeded in avoiding probate, for upon the death of either Tom or Mary, the survivor becomes sole owner of the property. And with grown children, Tom and Mary are no longer concerned with the appointment of a guardian.

However, even in this situation, Tom and Mary need to establish a more detailed estate plan. If they should die in a common accident, probate proceedings would again be necessary and the property would pass by the laws of intestacy in the absence of a will.

More importantly, federal estate tax has now become a consideration with the increased size of their estate. For example, if Tom dies first, no estate taxes will be due at his death because federal tax law provides that property passes to a surviving spouse tax free. However, Mary will own the entire estate. If she remains single, the property at her death will obviously not pass to a surviving spouse, and so her estate might have to pay hundreds of thousands of dollars in tax. The tax liability would be reduced if Tom and Mary established an estate plan dividing their property between the survivor and a trust, topic explored previously. The property in the trust could be used for the benefit of the survivor but would not be subject to estate tax on the survivor's death. For this plan to work, however, Tom and Mary must sever their ownership of the jointly held property to prevent the entire estate from passing automatically to Mary.

Much of the tax strategy surrounding estate planning is being reexamined due to the passage of the Economic Growth and Tax Relief Reconciliation Act of 2001. Under this Act, the amount of property exempt from estate taxes has gradually increased until 2010, when a total exemption of property subject to the estate tax came into effect. As a result, depending on the value of Tom and Mary's estate, they may not have to sever their estate and put it in trust since the exemption on estate taxes may exceed the value of their estate. However, they must keep in mind that in 2011, estate tax exemptions will be reintroduced at the levels they were at before the passage of this Act unless Congress votes to continue the total or partial exemption of estate property from taxes, perhaps an unlikely prospect due to ballooning federal deficits and the Obama administration's opposition to a total exemption. So does Tom or Mary have to worry about dying prior to December 31, 2010? Although this may sound like a strange, even morbid question, a 2001 article titled

"Dying to Save Taxes" written by University of Michigan economists demonstrated that under 13 changes in U.S. tax laws since 1917, benefactors actually died in greater numbers before tax hikes and right after tax cuts presumably from suicide or even murder![57]

<table>
<tr>
<td>

ETHICAL AND PUBLIC POLICY ISSUES

</td>
<td>

Should Parents Be Required to Leave Their Children Property in a Will?

Under the common law, joint tenancy allows a spouse the right of survivorship of the property of the deceased's spouse. Thus, it is possible that the children of the marriage may not receive property upon the parent's death. Moreover, under the common law, parents do not have to will any property to their children. In civil law jurisdictions such as Louisiana, as well as in France and other countries in Europe and Latin America, a "forced portion" must be given to the children. Thus, under the civil law, ownership of most property in joint tenancy is not allowed. Children who do not receive property under a will can attack the will upon a parent's death and take a legally prescribed portion of the estate. A discussion of the ethics and public policy of these two approaches is found in Problem 10 at the end of the chapter.

</td>
</tr>
</table>

Community Property

community property

Property acquired during a marriage through the efforts of either the husband or wife or both, with each having an undivided one-half interest in the property.

In Wisconsin and eight states in the South and West—Arizona, California, Idaho, Louisiana, Nevada, New Mexico, Texas, and Washington—certain property owned by husband and wife is designated as **community property**. The concept of community property is derived mainly from French and Spanish law, although community property was first used by Germanic tribes in the seventh century.[58] In Wisconsin, community property was created by statute primarily for tax reasons (see endnote 60 for tax discussion) but is still referred to as marital property in that state even though its conceptual basis is rooted in the community property system.[59] In all of these states, the community property regime governs marital property by operation of law. In an interesting variation, Alaska, although not a community property state, passed a law in which married couples can voluntarily agree to a community property regime. Its adoption, as in Wisconsin, was viewed as an attractive alternative for some—due at least in part to certain tax advantages.[60]

separate property

Property acquired before the marriage or acquired by the husband or wife through gift or inheritance during the marriage that is owned by a married person in his or her own right.

Community property is property acquired during a marriage through the efforts of either the husband or wife or both. It is irrelevant which spouse is the most overtly productive in acquiring property as each spouse generally owns an undivided one-half interest, subject to certain exceptions discussed below. Property acquired before the marriage or acquired by the husband or wife through gift or inheritance during the marriage is **separate property**. States disagree about the treatment of rents and profits from property such as real estate, stocks, and bonds, which are derived from separate property. Some states, such as Louisiana, Texas, and Idaho, follow the old Civil Law rule that such rents and profits are considered to be community property; other states, such as Nevada, California, and Washington, follow the so-called American rule classifying them as separate property. For example, if Russell buys a house in Louisiana before he is married and rents it to Ray, and then later he marries Joyce, the rents that Ray pays would be community property. However, if Russell lived in Nevada and bought and rented a house before marriage, the rents would remain his separate property. When earnings from separate property, such as from a separate business, result from the labor and industry of one or both spouses, the earnings are treated as community property even in states that otherwise classify them as separate property.

This is because all earnings (as well as all property acquired) are *presumed* under the law to be community property during marriage. In one case, a husband owned two restaurants as separate property. At the husband's death, the court held that income from the restaurants would be considered community property because it resulted mainly from the husband's efforts in managing the restaurants.[61]

Earnings from separate property, however, must be distinguished from increases in the value of separate property during marriage. In the event that community property is severed because of divorce or death, courts generally will allocate the property to both the community and separate property regimes depending on how much of the increase was through the efforts of both spouses and how much of the increase was due to the natural growth in the separate property's value during marriage. The foregoing issues regarding separate property have become very important in recent years due to the fact that many couples now postpone marriage. This sometimes results in productive businesses owned as separate property by one of the spouses, being brought into a marriage. If the marriage results in a divorce, a somewhat predictable outcome today due to relatively high rates of divorce, the issue becomes crucial to the former couple's future.[62]

Must an Arizona husband who wins a $2.2 million lottery jackpot share the winnings with his estranged wife? In *Lynch v. Lynch* on page 167, the court applies Arizona community property law to resolve that question.

END OF CHAPTER CASE

In most community property states, the husband and wife may change the status of their community property by an agreement before marriage called a prenuptial agreement. Community property regimes can be contractually changed during marriage, too. For instance, spouses may agree to purchase real estate with community property in a joint tenancy form of ownership. Or the parties may partition community property by entering into a property settlement agreement in divorce proceedings. In both situations, both spouses should be represented by their own legal counsel or risk having the agreements vitiated should agreements be contested in a future divorce.

In the absence of a property settlement, some states equally divide community property in a divorce action. Other states allow the court to exercise its discretion in dividing property, looking at such factors as how many years the couple was married; their ages, health, income sources, and employability; whether they have minor children; and whether one of the spouses stayed at home to raise the children. The latter is an approach embraced in common law states.

In contrast to community property states, the division of property upon divorce in common law states is often determined by whether the title to the property was held in joint tenancy, tenancy by the entirety, or TIC because equally owned property acquired during marriage is not presumed to be owned equally. Common law states also employ an "equitable distribution" in divorce proceedings by applying the factors discussed in the previous paragraph. Finally, most common law states now also recognize separate property that is not divisible between the spouses in a divorce.

In community property states, upon the death of the husband or wife, the surviving spouse retains an interest in one-half of the property, while the other half passes according to the will of the deceased person. If there is no will, the one-half interest will pass according to the laws of intestate succession dictated by descent and distribution statutes, a topic discussed in Chapter 10.

Some community property states, such as Nevada and California, now allow married couples to create a hybrid form of a joint tenancy and community property called **community property with the right of survivorship**. This is commonly used when a couple buys a family home. It allows the surviving spouse to avoid probate, as in the case of a joint tenancy, and provides tax benefits by stepping up the basis (property value) on the date the joint tenant dies. This can significantly lower capital gains taxes when the property is subsequently sold.

In states that use the common law system, the laws that govern the decedent spouse's distribution of property in the absence of a will include the state's descent and distribution statutes, rights of dower, curtesy, and homestead, or an elective share if the surviving spouse receives no property or less than a certain amount in the will. These topics are discussed in Chapter 10. Of course, if the spouses owned the property in joint tenancy or tenancy by the entirety, the property will bypass probate and be owned by the surviving spouse.

Community property and common law systems have been contrasted as follows:

> *Categorizing broadly, the marital property systems of the Western nations today are divided into two types: those in which husband and wife own all property separately except those items that they have expressly agreed to hold jointly … and those in which husband and wife own a substantial portion or even all of their property jointly unless they have expressly agreed to hold it separately. The system of separate property is the "common law" system, in force in most jurisdictions where the Anglo-American common law is in force. The system of joint property is the community property system, in force in [some] American states and many of the countries of Western Europe.*[63]

The common law system has been criticized because of concerns that a spouse who does not own property often fails to receive a fair share of the other spouse's property after a divorce or death. As a result, the Uniform Marital Property Act (UMPA) was developed. This Act, which formed the basis for Wisconsin's marital statutes in 1986, essentially adopts, as stated earlier, the community property system. While other states have not yet enacted UMPA, they are gradually moving toward a community property system. This "creeping community property" is illustrated by laws that require equitable distribution of marital property upon divorce and protection from disinheritance at death.[64]

Forms of Ownership for Investment Purposes

The forms of ownership discussed previously may be used in purchasing real estate for personal or business reasons. These forms of ownership, especially the joint tenancy and the tenancy by the entirety, are often inadequate for business and investment purposes for several reasons. Most investors do not want their interest to pass to surviving investors at death. Investors also want to establish procedures to manage the real estate. Tax law affects the form of ownership. Investors may have concerns about limiting their personal liability. They also may need to select an ownership structure that will allow them to attract equity investments in the proposed real estate venture. Investor ownership of real estate, as well as ownership of other investments, is sometimes referred to as **syndication**. The syndication process involves a group of investors who combine their funds and managerial resources, frequently using partnerships, limited partnerships, corporations, limited liability companies, or real estate investment trusts (REITs) to accomplish their goals. While a detailed treatment of these forms of ownership is beyond the scope of this text, a brief overview is provided after the summary in Table 5.2.

community property with the right of survivorship
A hybrid form of concurrent ownership in which property is owned by the spouses as community property but that also provides a right of survivorship.

syndication
A group of investors who combine their funds and managerial resources to acquire real estate and other assets.

TABLE 5.2 Characteristics of Syndications in Real Estate

TYPE OF SYNDICATION	OWNERSHIP INTERESTS	HOW CREATED	LIABILITY	TRANSFERABILITY	INHERITANCE	TAXES
Tenancy in Common	Undivided interests	By deed, will, or intestacy	Unlimited	Yes	By will or intestacy	Gains and losses incurred directly by tenants in common
General Partnership	Tenancy in partnership	By carrying on an informal business or by filing Articles of Partnership	Unlimited	Transfer or assignability allowed, but assignee does not have full rights as the assignor-partner	Partnership interest received by will or intestacy; title in property goes to surviving partners	Gains and losses incurred directly by partners
Limited Partnership	General partner has a tenancy in partnership; limited partner has limited partnership interest	By filing Articles of Limited Partnership	Unlimited for general partner; limited to investment for limited partner	General partner may generally assign interest upon giving notice to other partner; limited partner may assign interest if allowed under Articles	Full partner same as general partnership; limited partner interest is inheritable by will or intestacy	Gains and losses incurred directly by general and limited partners
Corporation	Shareholder	By filing Articles of Incorporation	Limited to investment	Freely transferable	By will or intestacy	Gains and losses incurred by both corporate entity and shareholders
Limited Liability Company (LLC)	Membership	By filing Articles of Organization	Limited to investment	Generally need permission from other members	By will or intestacy; operating agreement often provides LLC with right of first refusal to buy membership	Gains and losses incurred directly by members
Real Estate Investment Trust	Shareholders or beneficiaries of a trust	By filing Articles of Incorporation or by a creation of a business trust	Limited to investment	Freely transferable	By will or intestacy	Gains and losses incurred directly by shareholders or beneficiaries

Tenancy in Common (TIC)

The TIC was discussed earlier as a type of co-ownership that typically exists among a few individual landowners. However, since 2002, when the IRS clarified the use of TICs in Section 1031 exchanges (discussed in Chapter 7), there has been a surge in their use as investment vehicles. For example, as tenants in common, owners invest directly in commercial real estate such as apartments, shopping centers, and factories. Each investor owns an undivided interest that she probably would not be able to finance on her own, allowing her to reap a pro rata share of income through cash flows from tenants. Due to the inherent risks in owning property as tenants in common, such as unlimited personal liability, brokers and sponsors require those wanting to buy these TICs to qualify as "accredited" investors—those who earn a stated high annual income. It is presumed that the investors have the necessary business savvy to engage in these complicated and risky investments, including understanding how to protect their personal assets. Moreover, since some TICs operate as private real estate transactions rather than as securities, they are not subject to the Securities and Exchange Commission (SEC) disclosure and enforcement requirements, which are discussed later in this chapter. For many investors, not being subject to SEC laws and oversight is a welcome advantage for investing in TICs.[65]

Partnerships

partnership

Section 6 of the Uniform Partnership Act defines a partnership as "an association of two or more persons to carry on as co-owners of a business for profit."

joint and several liability

A liability is joint and several when the creditor may demand payment or sue one or more of the parties to such liability separately or all of them together at the creditor's option.

The source of **partnership** law in the United States is the Uniform Partnership Act (UPA), which has been adopted in every state except Louisiana. A person who shares in the profits of a business is usually considered a partner because the receipt of profits is prima facie evidence that a partnership exists.[66] Partners have unlimited **joint and several liability** for partnership obligations and participate in the management and control of the business. Although not technically required, a well-run partnership should have an agreement, called *Articles of Partnership*, that describes the partners' obligations and the extent of their control over partnership matters. (For an Articles of Partnership form, see www.cengagebrain.com [see page xix in the Preface for instructions on how to access the free study tools for this text].)

Partners have mutual agency relationships among themselves. For example, a partner cannot personally appropriate an opportunity that properly belongs to the partnership. As a Wyoming court noted, "[w]hen a partner obtains financing for the development of real property in the course of a plan which had been originally pursued by the partnership for the same purpose, excluding other partners from participating further in the originally intended project, the partner has intercepted a partnership opportunity in breach of his fiduciary duty to the partnership."[67]

Since co-ownership is included in the definition of a partnership, are people who purchase property in one of the previously discussed forms of joint ownership considered to be partners? Assume that two friends, Percy and Dick, purchase a cottage as tenants in common and are co-owners. Does this make them partners? The answer can be found in Section 7 of the Act: "Joint tenancy, TIC, tenancy by the entireties, joint property, common property, or part ownership does not of itself establish a partnership, whether such owners do or do not share profits made by use of the property." The key factor necessary to establish a partnership is co-ownership of a business, defined in the act as "every trade, occupation or profession."[68] For example, assume that Percy and Dick decide to renovate their cottage, rent it, and then leverage the equity to buy another piece of rental property. Their relationship as tenants in common would ripen into an ongoing real estate business partnership, especially if they were sharing profits from their endeavor.

Two partnership rules relate specifically to real estate ownership. *First,* under the common law, a partnership could not buy or sell real estate because it was not a legal entity. However, the modern rule adopted by the UPA validates a conveyance to the partnership in the partnership name. Furthermore, real estate may be conveyed by the partnership in either the name of the partnership or the name of a partner.[69]

Second, the classifications of partnership real estate and other specific property have been a longstanding problem in several jurisdictions. The modern approach, in Section 25 of the UPA, is that each partner is a co-owner with his partners of specific partnership property and holds such property as a tenant in partnership. The incidents of a **tenancy in partnership** are as follows:

tenancy in partnership
The manner in which partners co-own partnership property.

- *Subject to an agreement to the contrary, each partner has an equal right to possession of partnership property.*
- *The interest in specific partnership property is not assignable by an individual partner.*
- *A partner's right in specific property is not subject to attachment or execution for personal debts.*
- *Partners cannot claim a homestead or another exemption when partnership property is attached for partnership debts.*
- *Upon the death of a partner, her interest in specific partnership property passes to the surviving partner.*
- *A partner's right in specific property is* not *subject to dower, curtesy, or allowance provided by law to widows, heirs, or next of kin.*

Having a tenancy in partnership in specific property, such as land, structures, equipment, and inventory, allows the partnership to continue business when one partner goes into debt or dies. However, despite the tenancy in partnership, each partner retains an *interest* in the partnership, defined as a share of profits and surplus. This interest passes to heirs as personal property and is subject to individual creditors' claims. It is for this reason that smart business planning requires that each partner purchase life insurance naming the partnership as beneficiary. Then the partnership can use the proceeds to pay off the heirs' interests without requiring the company to liquidate its property. This allows the surviving partner to continue business operations.[70] The partnership, as a real estate investment vehicle, carries a number of benefits and burdens. For example, as a benefit, the partnership is easy to form; it is even possible for two parties to form a partnership unknowingly by sharing profits from a business enterprise. There are tax benefits from the partnership form; the partnership is a "pass-through" entity for tax purposes, meaning that partnership income, loss, deductions, and other financial results are passed along to the individual partners. The right to share control is an important factor, for each partner has an equal right to manage the partnership business unless the partnership agreement provides otherwise. On the other hand, the major drawback to the partnership form is potential unlimited personal liability for each partner. This includes liability for contracts made by other partners who had been authorized to do so or who appeared to have that authority and for any wrongful act, such as under tort law, of other partners acting within the ordinary course of business.

Limited Partnerships

limited partnership
A type of partnership comprised of one or more general partners who manage the business and who are personally liable for partnership debts and one or more limited partners who contribute capital and share in profits but take no part in running the business and incur no liability with respect to partnership obligations beyond their contribution.

Limited partnerships have been attractive vehicles for real property investments. Like a corporation, they offer centralized management and limited liability. Like a general partnership, there is no taxation at the entity level. (For a limited partnership form, see www.cengagebrain.com [see page xix in the Preface for instructions on how to access the free study tools for this text].)

A limited partnership differs from a partnership in two major respects:

- *To form a limited partnership, two or more people must execute a certificate of limited partnership and file the certificate in the appropriate office.[71]*
- *The limited partnership includes one or more general partners and one or more limited partners.*

The general partner has unlimited personal liability, as in a partnership. This problem can be mitigated by creating a corporation to act as the general partner, since only the corporate entity, not the shareholders, are personally liable. In states that allow this, the corporate entity must be adequately capitalized. The liability of the limited partners is limited to the partners' capital contributions; limited partners are not personally liable for partnership contracts or torts. Despite the general rule of nonliability, a limited partner who takes part in the control of the business may be liable as a general partner. Yet, a limited partner may be able to give advice without incurring liability, as illustrated in the following case from Georgia.

A CASE IN POINT

In *Trans-Am Builders, Inc. v. Woods Mill, Ltd.,*[72] when a limited partnership encountered financial difficulties, the limited partners visited a construction site and made suggestions as to possible courses of action. The court held that the advice did not make them liable as general partners because it is unreasonable that a "limited partner may not advise the general partnership and visit the partnership business, particularly when the project is confronted with severe financial crisis."

Historically, the limited partnership served as an important real estate investment ownership vehicle because it combined the tax advantages of a partnership with the limited liability of a corporation.

Although real estate limited partnerships remain a primary investment vehicle, the Tax Reform Act of 1986 reduced the tax advantages of certain aspects of the real estate limited partnership as follows:

1. Because tax rates were lowered, the value of deductions was lowered.
2. The allowable annual depreciation deduction was reduced.
3. Current deductions can be used only to offset income from the limited partnership and other passive income. *Passive income* is defined as "income from an activity in which the taxpayer does not materially participate," such as a limited partner's income from a limited partnership.
4. The amount that an investor can claim as a loss is generally limited to the investment, that is, the amount the investor has at risk.

Corporations

corporation
A type of business organization that is owned by shareholders but managed by a board of directors who elect the executive officers.

Corporations centralize management in a board of directors elected by the shareholders. The directors, in turn, elect the executive officers of the corporation. Corporate earnings are subject to double taxation.

Forming a corporation involves filing articles of incorporation with the secretary of state and obtaining a corporate charter. (For an Articles of Incorporation form, see www.cengagebrain.com [see page xix in the Preface for instructions on how to access the free study tools for this text].) After the charter is issued, the business must follow corporate procedures: the shareholders and directors must hold annual meetings, financial reports must be filed with the state, personal assets and corporate assets must not be commingled, and the corporation should have adequate capital.

The corporation is first taxed on its earnings, and shareholders are then taxed individually on corporate distributions. This is referred to as "double taxation." Furthermore, shareholders may not deduct corporate expenses and losses from their individual taxable income. These disadvantages are often balanced by the major advantage of the corporation form: the limited liability of the shareholders.

This limitation of liability can, however, be ineffective in several instances. Success in accessing the assets of shareholders, instead of limiting liability to corporate assets, is referred to as "piercing the corporate veil." For example, if business is not conducted according to normal corporate procedures, such as being too thinly capitalized, a court might pierce the corporate veil and hold the shareholders liable as individuals.

In some states, the corporation's liability for employee wages is also a shareholder liability. Moreover, certain shareholders, particularly in smaller start-up corporations commonly seen in real estate, are often required to become personally liable for loans made to the corporation. This means that they agree to act as a surety or guarantor to pay for the corporation's debt should the latter default on the loan.[73] In addition, certain environmental statutes place liability on corporate officers and employees. For example, a corporate principal in New York who knew that hazardous waste was stored on site, although he did not participate in its generation or transportation, was held jointly liable with the corporation under the Comprehensive Environmental Response, Compensation, and Liability Act of 1980 (CERCLA).[74]

Another key corporate characteristic is the perpetual life of the corporation. The corporation's existence is not impaired by the death, bankruptcy, or incompetency of one of its shareholders.

It is possible to combine the liability advantages of the corporation with the tax advantages of the partnership by creating an **S corporation**. To qualify as an S corporation, a corporation must comply with the following requirements:

S corporation	
A closely held corporation with no more than one hundred shareholders who elect to be taxed like partners.	

- *It may have no more than 100 shareholders.*
- *The stock must be owned by individuals (husband and wife and their estates are considered to be one person) who are citizens or residents of the United States, as well as estates, certain trusts, or certain exempt organizations.*
- *The corporation must be a domestic corporation.*
- *The corporation may have only one class of stock issued and outstanding.*

A limited liability company, discussed next, also affords owners liability and tax advantages.

Limited Liability Companies (LLCs)

limited liability company

A hybrid form of business organization that provides the limited liability of a corporation and the tax advantages of a partnership.

A **limited liability company** (LLC) is similar to a corporation in that investors, called "members," are not personally liable for company debts and can elect management to run the business pursuant to an operating agreement. LLCs, which are formed by filing Articles of Organization with the secretary of state in the state in which they are formed, are a recognized business entity in every state and the District of Columbia.[75] (For an Articles of Organization form, see www.cengagebrain.com [see page xix in the Preface for instructions on how to access the free study tools for this text].) Unlike corporate shareholders, however, LLC members cannot generally transfer their interests without the consent of other members. LLCs originated in Wyoming in 1977, and many other states authorized them following a 1988 IRS ruling that a Wyoming real estate LLC was to be treated as a partnership for tax purposes.

An attractive feature of LLCs is that such companies do not have the shareholder requirements, such as the 100 shareholder restriction of S corporations, are easier to form, and do not have as many formalities as S corporations. Members can be individuals, estates, or trusts, as well as corporations or other entities.[76] Unlike limited partnerships, limited liability companies protect all members, not just limited partners, from personal liability and allow members to actively participate in LLC business without incurring personal liability.[77] A member of the LLC has equal status with the other members—there is no distinction, unlike in a limited partnership, between the general partner and the limited partner.[78]

The real estate industry has enthusiastically embraced the LLC concept since it permits members a great deal of flexibility in how they tailor their management arrangements to a specific transaction.[79] As the following Wyoming case demonstrates, one issue that has arisen is whether a plaintiff suing an LLC can pierce the entity veil and impose personal liability on the LLC members.

A CASE IN POINT

In *Kaycee Land and Livestock v. Flahive*,[80] Roger Flahive, the managing member of Flahive Oil and Gas LLC, entered into a contract with Kaycee Land and Livestock that allowed his company to enter Kaycee's land to drill for minerals. When Kaycee sued the company for environmentally contaminating its property, it learned that the LLC had no assets at the time of the lawsuit and that Flahive may have commingled LLC funds with his own. Kaycee sued Flahive personally, claiming that the LLC shield should be pierced. Wyoming's LLC statute did not directly address the issue. The Wyoming Supreme Court ruled that "[w]e can discern no reason, either in law or policy, to treat LLCs differently than we treat a corporation. If the members and officers of an LLC fail to treat it as a separate entity as contemplated by statute, they should not enjoy immunity from individual liability for the LLC's acts that cause damage to third parties."

Real Estate Investment Trusts (REITs)

Business trusts were originally developed to avoid state regulations imposed on corporations. They also enable a small investor to invest in a diversified portfolio of real estate, greatly reducing the risk that would arise with a single piece or several pieces of property. In establishing a business trust, the trust investors (beneficiaries) transfer cash or property to trustees, who hold legal title. The trustees then issue transferable trust certificates to the investors, for whose benefit the trustees hold and manage the trust property.

Real Estate Investment Trusts (REITs) became popular with the 1960 passage of the Real Estate Investment Trust Act. The Act provides that a REIT will not be taxed on the portion of ordinary income and capital gains that are distributed to shareholders. The REIT must meet certain requirements, however, to obtain the tax exemption.

> **Real Estate Investment Trusts (REITs)**
> An entity that invests in real estate ventures and must distribute at least 90 percent of its net income to investors.

- *The interest of the investors must be evidenced by transferable shares or certificates.*
- *There must be 100 or more shareholders or beneficiaries.*
- *Five or fewer individuals may not own over 50 percent of the value of the trust stock.*
- *At least 75 percent of the trust's income must come from real estate sources such as rents, mortgage interest, and gains from the sale of real estate.*
- *At least 90 percent of the net income must be distributed to the investors.[81]*

REITs are a vehicle for allowing the "average investor to participate in real estate investments in a manner similar to the investment in stocks and bonds through mutual funds."[82] REITs, despite their name, can be organized as corporations as well as trusts.[83]

There are *three* basic types of REITs—mortgage, equity, and hybrid—and each must meet the preceding requirements. Mortgage REITs are engaged in financing real estate developments. Mortgage REITs usually borrow money from lenders and then loan this money, along with investors' capital, to builders and developers, some of whom are unable to obtain other financing. With equity REITs, the investors' capital is used to purchase real estate. Although equity REITs often borrow money to finance real estate purchases, the loans are secured by long-term mortgages and are paid with income derived from the real estate. A hybrid REIT's investments include both real estate and real estate mortgages.

> **Umbrella Partnership Real Estate Investment Trust (UPREIT)**
> A type of real estate investment trust in which an umbrella partnership rather than the REIT owns a direct interest in the properties.

The **Umbrella Partnership Real Estate Investment Trust (UPREIT)** is a structure introduced in the early 1990s that avoids the immediate tax recognition of the transfer

securities

The securities law definition of a security is extremely broad. The term *security* means "any note, stock, treasury stock, bond, debenture, evidence of indebtedness, certificate of interest or participation in any profit-sharing agreement, collateral trust certificate, preorganization certificate or subscription, transferable share, investment contract, voting-trust certificate, certificate of deposit for a security, fractional undivided interest in oil, gas, or other mineral rights, any put, call, straddle, option, or privilege entered into on a national securities exchange relating to a foreign currency, or, in general, any interest or instrument commonly known as a 'security,' or any certificate of interest or participation in, temporary or interim certificate for, receipt for, guarantee of, or warrant or right to subscribe to or purchase, any of the foregoing."

of partnership property to a REIT. Some analysts estimate that since its inception, as many as two-thirds of all REITS have been UPREITs.[84] The UPREIT involves the transfer of real estate assets originally owned by separate partnerships to a newly formed "Operating Partnership" in exchange for operating partnership units. The REIT, in turn, contributes the cash proceeds of its stock offering to the Operating Partnership and acts as its managing general partner.

Federal Securities Regulation

The use of real estate investment vehicles under which the investor relies on another's efforts to manage the property frequently causes the transaction to be characterized as a **securities**[85] investment instead of a mere purchase of real estate. Thus, federal securities regulation, under the Securities Act of 1933 and the Securities Exchange Act of 1934, plays an increasingly important role in real estate transactions. In addition to federal securities regulation, states have adopted **Blue Sky Laws** to regulate the sale of securities within their borders.[86]

A person selling securities is subject to a complicated and expensive registration process unless the transaction is exempt from the registration requirement. Failure to register securities can result in liability under securities law provisions designed to prevent fraud. Even if registration of the security with the SEC is not required, the antifraud provisions of securities laws require the disclosure of material information that would influence the investment decision. Therefore, understanding the definition of a security is critical in selecting and managing forms of real estate ownership for investment purposes.

One manner in which real estate investments can be viewed as securities is when they qualify as "investment contracts." A famous case involving Florida orange groves defines these contracts.

A CASE IN POINT

As described in the United States Supreme Court case of *Securities and Exchange Commission v. W. J. Howey Co.*,[87] purchasers would buy narrow strips of land arranged so that an acre was a row of forty-eight trees. Once the land was purchased, the buyer entered into a noncancellable service contract for the grove's cultivation, harvest, management, and marketing. The court concluded that it would be infeasible for each purchaser to economically manage his or her own narrow tract; in fact, the management agreement prohibited the purchaser from entering the grove without the company's consent. The management company pooled all of the oranges and allocated net profits to the purchasers. The court concluded that the purchasers had entered into an investment contract, which it defined as "a contract, transaction or scheme whereby a person invests his money in a common enterprise and is led to expect profits solely from the efforts of a promoter or third party."

Blue Sky Laws

State laws that regulate the offer and sale of securities.

The substance of the transaction rather than the name of the investment determines whether securities law applies. For instance, stock in a corporation does not automatically meet this test,[88] while the sale of a condominium unit combined with an agreement by the developer to perform certain rental services might be an investment contract.[89]

When a Las Vegas resident's rental income from a Hawaii condominium was insufficient to cover his mortgage payment, he sued his real estate agent, claiming that she had violated the antifraud provisions of the Securities Exchange Act of 1934. In *Hocking v. Dubois* on page 168, the court applies the Howey test to this transaction and resolves whether it was an "investment contract."

END OF CHAPTER CASE

Disappointed real estate investors continue to turn to the stringent disclosure requirements of securities laws. In a case involving the purchase of Chattanooga, Tennessee, condominium units by New York investors, the court considered whether the sales promotions emphasized the rental arrangement, whether the rental pool was designated by or tied to the developer, and whether the owner's personal use of the unit was restricted.[90] The court concluded that the condominiums were not investment contracts. Some courts find that the investment contract requirement is satisfied only when the buyer and developer are coventurers in the rental of the unit and income is pooled among the investors.[91]

CASES

Fee Simple Defeasible
WHITE v. METROPOLITAN DADE COUNTY
563 So.2d 117 (Fla.Dist.Ct.App. 1990)

GERSTEN, Judge. Amid the turmoil attendant to living in an urban environment, on an island off an island, called Key Biscayne, there exists a sylvan spot of tranquility—Crandon Park. Key Biscayne, which is actually a barrier island protecting Biscayne Bay from the Atlantic Ocean, was originally owned by a Dade County pioneer family surnamed Matheson. In 1940, the Mathesons gave the people of Dade County, Florida, access to and enjoyment of that portion of Key Biscayne which came to be known as Crandon Park.

* * *

* * * In the recorded deeds, the grantors expressly provided:

This conveyance is made upon the express condition that the lands hereby conveyed shall be perpetually used and maintained for public park purposes only; and in case the use of said land for park purposes shall be abandoned, then and in that event the said [grantor], his heirs, grantees or assigns, shall be entitled upon their request to have the said lands reconveyed to them.

* * *

In 1986, the Dade County Board of County Commissioners passed Resolution R-891-86, which authorized the execution of an agreement with Arvida International Championships, Inc., (Arvida), and the International Players Championship, Inc., (IPC), to construct a permanent tennis complex. The

construction of the court facilities and infrastructure began in the summer of 1986, and terminated in 1987. Initially, the tennis complex consisted of fifteen tennis courts, service roads, utilities, and landscaping, all located on 28 acres.

The agreement provided that for two weeks each year, subject to a renewal provision, the tennis complex would become the site of the Lipton International Players Championship Tennis Tournament (Lipton tournament). This renowned tournament is only open to world class players who compete for two weeks.

* * *

Dade County offered testimony at trial that the public was only excluded from using the facilities for some three to four weeks. However, under the clear wording of the agreement, relative to the 1987 tournament, Arvida had the right to exclude the public from the tennis complex for as long as five months.

* * *

In 1987 and again in 1988, Dade County attempted to obtain the consent of one of the heirs, Hardy Matheson, for the operation of the Lipton tournament. Hardy Matheson refused to give his consent, and informed the County that the tennis complex and the operation of the Lipton tournament was contrary to the deed restriction.

* * *

... [A]ppellant/heirs contend that the operation of the Lipton tournament violates the deed restriction because it deprives the public of the use and enjoyment of Crandon Park, including the use and enjoyment of the tennis facilities. We are persuaded by this argument and rule that the holding of the Lipton tournament violates the deed restriction because it virtually bars the public use of Crandon Park during the tournament, and does bar public use of the tennis complex, for extended periods of time.

* * *

Here, the operation of the Lipton tournament, for all practical purposes, does amount to the virtual ouster of the public from the park for periods of time during the two-week tournament. The contract gives the sponsors "Priority Use" of the parking areas of Crandon Park during the tournament. The contract estimated that the tournament needs "would not exceed 4,000 spaces per day." The amount of parking spaces was not adequate to meet the needs of tournament spectators and other park visitors as the testimony was uncontroverted that people were turned away from parking lots at the park. There was also uncontroverted testimony that some people found it necessary to park at the Marine Stadium.

We recognize that many legitimate park events, such as softball or golf tournaments, might fill up lots and make it difficult for latecomers to find a parking space at a certain area within the park. This, however, is not simply a case of a filled parking lot within a certain area of the park. The testimony demonstrates that the tournament apparently takes up all the available public parking spaces at Crandon Park for periods of time during the tournament. This is a public park parking nightmare.

* * *

Finally, Dade County argues, and we agree, that it is well settled that "equity abhors a forfeiture," that "such restrictions are not favored in law if they have the effect of destroying an estate," and that they "will be construed strictly and will be most strongly construed against the grantor."

Appellant/heirs, however, clearly represented to this court and the trial court that they were not seeking a reversion. What appellant/heirs want is a declaratory judgment that the present use of the park is in violation of the deed restriction and an injunction to prevent any further erosion of the "public park purposes only" deed restriction.

* * *

We therefore declare Dade County to be in violation of the deed restriction. We reverse the trial court order as to the deed restriction, and remand for entry of an order enjoining Dade County from permitting the Lipton tournament to proceed as it is presently held. Our ruling does not prevent Dade County from using the tennis complex for tennis tournaments. It merely seeks to insure that in holding such tournaments, public access to the rest of Crandon Park is not infringed; and use of the tennis complex is not denied to the public for unreasonable periods of time.

We rule that the holding of the Lipton tournament in Crandon Park violates the deed restriction. * * *

Trusts and Public Policy
IN RE ESTATE OF MAX FEINBERG
235 Ill. 2d 256, 919 N.E. 2d 888 (2009)

Justice GARMAN. This case involves a dispute among the surviving children and grandchildren of Max and Erla Feinberg regarding the validity of a trust provision. The circuit court of Cook County found the trust provision unenforceable on the basis that it is contrary to the public policy of the state of Illinois. The appellate court affirmed. Michael Feinberg, the Feinbergs' son and coexecutor of their estates, filed a petition for leave to appeal pursuant to, which we allowed. We also allowed Agudath Israel of America, the National Council of Young Israel, and the Union of Orthodox Jewish Congregations of America to file a brief amici curiae pursuant to Supreme Court Rule 345.

For the reasons that follow, we reverse.

Background

Max Feinberg died in 1986. He was survived by his wife, Erla, their adult children, Michael and Leila, and five grandchildren.

Prior to his death, Max executed a will and created a trust. Max's will provided that upon his death, all of his assets were to "pour over" into the trust, which was to be further divided for tax reasons into two trusts, "Trust A" and "Trust B." If she survived him, Erla was to be the lifetime beneficiary of both trusts, first receiving income from Trust A, with a limited right to withdraw principal. If Trust A were exhausted, Erla would then receive income from Trust B, again with a limited right to withdraw principal.

Upon Erla's death, any assets remaining in Trust A after the payment of estate taxes were to be combined with the assets of Trust B. The assets of Trust B were then to be distributed to Max's descendants in accordance with a provision we shall call the "beneficiary restriction clause." This clause directed that 50% of the assets be held in trust for the benefit of the then-living descendants of Michael and Leila during their lifetimes. The division was to be on a per stirpes basis, with Michael's two children as lifetime beneficiaries of one quarter of the trust and Leila's three children as lifetime beneficiaries of the other one quarter of the trust. However, any such descendant who married outside the Jewish faith or whose non-Jewish spouse did not convert to Judaism within one year of marriage would be "deemed deceased for all purposes of this instrument as of the date of such marriage" and that descendant's share of the trust would revert to Michael or Leila.

In addition, the trust instrument gave Erla a limited testamentary power of appointment over the distribution of the assets of both trusts and a limited lifetime power of appointment over the assets of Trust B. Under the limiting provision, Erla was allowed to exercise her power of appointment only in favor of Max's descendants. Thus, she could not name as remaindermen individuals who were not Max's descendants or appoint to a charity. The parties dispute whether Erla's power of appointment was limited to those descendants not deemed deceased under the beneficiary restriction clause. The trial court did not make a finding on this question and the appellate court did not discuss it.

Erla exercised her lifetime power of appointment over Trust B in 1997, directing that, upon her death, each of her two children and any of her grandchildren who were not deemed deceased under Max's beneficiary restriction clause receive $250,000. In keeping with Max's original plan, if any grandchild was deemed deceased under the beneficiary restriction clause, Erla directed that his or her share be paid to Michael or Leila.

By exercising her power of appointment in this manner, Erla revoked the original distribution provision and replaced it with a plan that differs from Max's plan in two significant respects. First, Erla altered the distribution scheme from *per stirpes* to *per capita,* permitting each of the grandchildren to take an equal share, rather than favoring Michael's two children over Leila's three children. Second, Erla designated a fixed sum to be distributed to each eligible descendant at the time of her death, replacing Max's plan for a lifetime trust for such descendants. The record suggests that Erla's gifts will deplete the corpus of the trust, leaving no trust assets subject to distribution under Max's original plan. Thus, while Erla retained Max's beneficiary restriction clause, his distribution provision never became operative.

All five grandchildren married between 1990 and 2001. By the time of Erla's death in 2003, all five grandchildren had been married for more than one year. Only Leila's son, Jon, met the conditions of the beneficiary restriction clause and was entitled to receive $250,000 of the trust assets as directed by Erla.

This litigation followed, pitting Michael's daughter, Michele, against Michael, coexecutor of the estates of both Max and Erla.

The trial court invalidated the beneficiary restriction clause on public policy grounds. A divided appellate court affirmed, holding that "under Illinois law and under the Restatement (Third) of Trusts, the provision in the case before us is invalid because it seriously interferes with and limits the right of individuals to marry a person of their own choosing." In reaching this conclusion, the appellate court relied on decisions of this court dating back as far as 1898 and, as noted, on the Restatement (Third) of Trusts.

* * *

Public Policy Regarding Terms Affecting Marriage or Divorce

The contrary law relied upon by the appellate court to invalidate Max's beneficiary restriction clause is found in three decisions of this court: *Ransdell,* 172 Ill. 439, 50 N.E. 111 (1898), *Winterland v. Winterland,* 389 Ill. 384, 59 N.E.2d 661 (1945), and *Estate of Gerbing,* 61 Ill.2d 503, 337 N.E.2d 29 (1975). The appellate court concluded that the "language and circumstances" of the testamentary provisions in these cases, "which Illinois courts have found to be against public policy, are strikingly similar to the instant case." Specifically, the appellate court invoked the "principle that testamentary provisions are invalid if they discourage marriage or encourage divorce."

* * *

This court acknowledged the long-standing rule that conditions annexed to a gift that have the tendency to induce spouses to divorce or to live separately are void on grounds of public policy. However, the testator's purpose in this case "was simply to secure the gift to his son in the manner which, in his judgment, would render it of the greatest benefit to him in view of the relations then existing between him and his wife" (*Ransdell,* 172 Ill. at 445, 50 N.E. 111), which were strained, to say the least. "Certainly," this court noted, "it cannot be said that the condition tended to encourage either the separation or the bringing of a divorce suit, both having taken place long prior to the execution of the will." *Ransdell,* 172 Ill. at 446, 50 N.E. 111.

This court weighed two potentially competing public policies, stating that it was "of the first importance to society that contract and testamentary gifts which are calculated to prevent lawful marriages or to bring about the separation or divorcement of husbands and wives should not be upheld." *Ransdell,* 172 Ill. at 446, 50 N.E. 111. On the other hand, "it is no less important that persons of sound mind and memory, free from restraint and undue influence, should be allowed to dispose of their property by will, with such limitations and conditions as they believe for the best interest of their donees." *Ransdell,* 172 Ill. at 446, 50 N.E. 111. Because the testator had not disinherited his son if he remained married, but made one provision for him in case he remained married (a life estate) and a different provision if he divorced (taking title in fee simple), the condition was not contrary to public policy.

Finally, this court distinguished between a condition subsequent (for example, if the will devised property to the beneficiary in trust for life, subject to divestment if he married), and a condition precedent, which directs that upon the fulfillment of the condition, ownership of the property is to vest in the beneficiary. The condition subsequent, such as one that would prohibit marriage generally, would be void and the donee would retain the property, unaffected by the violation of the condition. A condition precedent would be given effect, because until the condition was met, the beneficiary's interest was a mere expectancy.

[Author's Note: *Winterland v. Winterland*, and *Estate of Gerbing* cases were deleted due to space restrictions, but were similar to *Ransdell*.]

* * *

We conclude, * * * that no interest vested in the Feinbergs' grandchildren at the time of Max's death because the terms of his testamentary trust were subject to change until Erla's death. Because they had no vested interest that could be divested by their noncompliance with the condition precedent, they were not entitled to notice of the existence of the beneficiary restriction clause. Further, because they were not the Feinbergs' heirs at law, the grandchildren had, at most, a mere expectancy that failed to materialize for four of them when, at the time of Erla's death, they did not meet the condition established by Max.

* * *

Conclusion

It is impossible to determine whether Erla's distribution plan was the product of her own wisdom, good legal advice, or mere fortuity. In any case, her direction that $250,000 of the assets of Trust B be distributed upon her death to each of the then-living grandchildren of Max who were not "deemed deceased" under the beneficiary restriction clause of Max's trust revoked his plan for prospective application of the clause via a lifetime trust. Because no grandchild had a vested interest in the trust assets and because the distribution plan adopted by Erla has no prospective application, we hold that the beneficiary restriction clause does not violate public policy.

Therefore, we reverse the judgment of the appellate court and remand to the circuit court for further proceedings.

Tenancy by the Entirety
HATCHETT v. UNITED STATES
330 F.3d 875 (6th Cir. 2003)

COLE, Circuit Judge. This case began more than twenty-five years ago when Elbert [Hatchett], a prominent Detroit trial attorney, decided to forego payment of federal and state income taxes. In 1989, Elbert was convicted by a jury of four misdemeanor counts of willful failure to pay federal income taxes. *United States v. Hatchett*, 918 F.2d 631, 633 (6th Cir. 1990). He was sentenced to three consecutive one-year sentences, placed on five years' probation, fined $100,000 and ordered to pay "all back taxes" as a condition of probation. We affirmed that sentence, and Elbert spent three years in prison.

The Internal Revenue Service ("IRS") made an assessment on October 24, 1994 that Hatchett owed more than $6.6 million in federal income taxes and penalties for the tax years 1975 to 1991. As of March 25, 1998, Elbert's tax liabilities totaled more than $8.6 million.

In an attempt to collect the delinquent taxes, the IRS levied against four parcels of real estate owned by the Hatchetts and one series of mortgage payments owed to the Hatchetts on a fifth parcel pursuant to 26 U.S.C. §6331 (2002). The Hatchetts received a Tax Levy, dated October 24, 1994, and four Notices of Seizure, dated October 25, 1994. Two of the properties are owned jointly by the Hatchetts as tenants by the entirety: (1) their primary residence ("West Hickory"), and (2) a property operated as a car wash ("South Saginaw").

* * *

On January 24, 1995, the IRS levied mortgage payments due to the Hatchetts from a property previously owned by the Hatchetts and used for horse breeding and entertaining clients ("Cyclone"). The Cyclone property was sold to a husband and wife, Ernest and Hermetha Blythe Ann Jarrett, in 1991. The Hatchetts took back a mortgage of $80,000 on the Cyclone property, to be paid in semiannual installments of $6,000 on interest and principal, beginning February 19, 1992 and continuing until August 19, 2001.

At the time the IRS issued the four levies in 1994, the Hatchetts held title to the West Hickory and South Saginaw properties as tenants by the entirety. Laurestine [Elbert's wife] has held individual title to the Franklin Boulevard property since 1994, but it was held by the Hatchetts as tenants by the entirety when the federal tax lien first attached in 1978. The Hatchetts held the Cyclone property as tenants by the entirety until it was conveyed by warranty deed to the Jarretts on August 19, 1991.

On November 21, 1994, the Hatchetts commenced a wrongful levy action in the district court pursuant to 26 U.S.C. §7426 (2002) to enjoin the tax sale of the four parcels of real estate and the seizure of the mortgage payments due. The district court entered two stipulated orders, on December 7, 1994 and June 23, 1995, enjoining the IRS from conducting the public auction or levying on the pending mortgage payments until the propriety of the levies was determined.

* * *

On March 31, 2000, the district court entered a judgment deciding the cross-motions for summary judgment filed by the Hatchetts and the Government. The court granted the Hatchetts' summary judgment motion and denied the Government's motion with respect to the West Hickory, Franklin Boulevard, South Saginaw, and Cyclone properties;

* * * [A]pplying *Craft* to this case leads to the rule that, pursuant to §6331, the Government may levy upon property held by a delinquent taxpayer as a tenancy by the entirety. Section 6331(b) specifically states that:

(b) Seizure and sale of property.—The term "levy" as used in this title includes the power of distraint and seizure by any means. Except as otherwise provided in subsection (e), a levy shall extend only to property possessed and obligations existing at the time thereof. *In any case in which the Secretary may levy upon property or rights to property, he may seize and sell such property or rights to property (whether real or personal, tangible or intangible).* (emphasis added). Furthermore, §6331(l) states that "[f]or proceedings applicable to sale of seized property, see section 6335." Title 26 U.S.C. §6335(c) (2002) states that "[i]f any property liable to levy is not divisible, so as to enable the Secretary by sale of a part thereof to raise the whole amount of tax and expenses, the whole of such property *shall* be sold." (emphasis added).

The language of the statutes is clear. The power to levy includes the power to seize and sell these properties as prescribed by §6335; property that cannot be divided in order to satisfy the whole of taxes and expenses shall be sold in its entirety. *Craft* allows the Government to levy upon the West Hickory, Franklin Boulevard, and South Saginaw properties held by the Hatchetts as tenants by the entirety. In 1998, the taxable value of these properties was estimated as follows: (1) West Hickory at $544,400, (2) Franklin Boulevard at $19,720; and (3) South Saginaw at $60,480. Elbert's outstanding tax indebtedness in excess of $8,000,000 far exceeds the value of his interests in the entireties properties.

* * *

For the reasons stated, we **REVERSE** the decision of the district court granting Appellees' motion for summary judgment, and **REMAND** to the district court for further proceedings in accordance with this opinion.

Community Property
LYNCH v. LYNCH
164 Ariz. 127, 791 P.2d 653 (1990)

FIDEL, Judge. * * * Michael Lynch (husband) and Bonnie Lynch (wife) were married in 1968. Their only child was born in 1971. The couple separated in 1985, and within a year husband began living with a woman named Donna Williams. Wife filed for dissolution shortly after.

Wife's petition was uncontested, and at a default hearing on February 10, 1987, wife testified that the marriage was irretrievably broken. A decree of dissolution is ordinarily entered at the conclusion of a default hearing. However, on February 10, the trial court took the matter under advisement and, on February 19, vacated the hearing because husband had received untimely notice.

On February 21, husband and Donna Williams won a $2.2 million jackpot in the Arizona State Lottery. Each owned half a share of the winning ticket. Wife then filed an amended petition in the unconcluded dissolution seeking half of husband's share. This time husband answered, the case went on to trial, and in the ultimate decree of dissolution the trial court awarded wife half of husband's lottery share.

* * *

When an Arizona spouse acquires an asset before marital dissolution, Arizona law treats the asset as community property unless it falls within one of several statutory exceptions: This "bright line" rule is established by A.R.S. §25-211, which provides: "All property acquired by either husband or wife *during the marriage*, except that which is acquired by gift, devise or descent, is the community property of the husband and wife." [Emphasis added.] A marriage endures in Arizona—and thus the acquisition of community property continues—"until the final dissolution is ordered by the court." *Flowers v. Flowers,* 578 P.2d 1006, 1009 (App. 1978).

In some jurisdictions, acquisition of community property ceases when spouses begin to live "separate and apart." In Arizona, however, demarcation by decree "avoids the factual issue of when the couple began living apart, and provides appropriate treatment for the on-again-off-again manner in which some couples try to resolve their differences and patch up their marriages." *Effland, Arizona Community Property Law: Time for Review and Revision,* 1982 Ariz.St.L.J. 1, 10–11.

An Arizona couple that wishes to end the acquisition of community property before (or without) dissolution has a statutory means to do so. A.R.S. §25-313(B) provides for entry of a decree of legal separation that terminates "community property rights and liabilities … as to all property, income and liabilities received or incurred after [its] entry." In the absence of a decree of legal separation, however, acquisition of community property continues in Arizona until the decree of dissolution is filed.

No legal separation decree was entered in this case, and the parties' marriage had not ended when husband won the lottery. Husband's lottery share was not "acquired by gift, devise or descent"; thus, it qualifies as a marital community asset pursuant to A.R.S. §25-211.

* * *

This case displays the hand of chance. Fortune favored husband with a jackpot, but, because his marriage had not ended, fortune dealt his wife a share. Though the lottery was a windfall, spouses marry for better or for worse and share no less in windfalls than in labor's wages. Husband claims that his marriage ended equitably, though not formally, before the winning ticket was acquired. We have given our reasons for rejecting his arguments. The judgment of the trial court is affirmed.

Definition of Security
HOCKING v. DUBOIS
885 F.2d 1449 (9th Cir. 1989)

GOODWIN, Chief Judge. Gerald M. Hocking, a disappointed purchaser of a unit in a condominium complex in Hawaii, sued the brokers who sold the unit, claiming violations of the antifraud provisions of the Securities Exchange Act of 1934. He appeals a summary judgment in favor of the brokers.

* * *

As best we can ascertain from the present record, and reading it in the light most favorable to Hocking, the facts are as follows:

Hocking was a resident of Las Vegas, Nevada. Following a visit to Hawaii, Hocking became interested in purchasing a condominium there as an investment. Dubois was a real estate agent licensed in Hawaii, employed by defendant Vitousek & Dick Realtors, Inc. Dubois met Hocking through her husband, one of Hocking's co-workers.

Dubois agreed to search for a condominium for Hocking, and in the spring of 1979 proposed that Hocking purchase a condominium in the resort complex at 2121 Ala Wai, Honolulu, which had been listed with Vitousek & Dick. The resort complex was developed by Aetna Life Insurance Company, and was still under construction at that time. Hocking had told Dubois that he wanted to buy a condominium directly from the developer, to be a "first person buyer." In fact, the condominium unit sold to Hocking was owned by Tovik and Yaacov Liberman, who had purchased from the developer. Hocking did not independently inquire into who was developing the complex at 2121 Ala Wai, but relied on Dubois' assurances that he would be purchasing directly from the developer. Hocking had no contact with Aetna, and he knew of no connection between defendants and the builders of the condominium complex.

Dubois told Hocking, according to his deposition, that "the investment would be handled [for him] by a local company, or her company or someone that she would help [him] get in touch with." She informed Hocking that a rental pool arrangement (RPA) would be available to Hocking if he were to purchase the condominium. She also told him that the condominiums were renting for an average of $100 a day, from which he calculated the monthly income would be $2,000 to $3,000 per month. He relied on the expected rental income to cover his monthly payments and provide additional income. While Dubois expressed no requirement that Hocking participate in the rental pool arrangement, Hocking testified that but for the availability of the rental pool arrangement he would not have purchased the condominium.

Hocking entered into an agreement to purchase the condominium from the Libermans. He signed the agreement on June 23, 1979 in Nevada, and Tovik Liberman signed on July 2, 1979 in Hawaii. Hocking also entered into several agreements with Hotel Corporation of the Pacific (HCP) concerning rental of the condominium.

On June 29, 1979 he signed a rental management agreement (RMA) appointing HCP exclusive agent to manage his condominium. He also entered into an Individual Agency Rental Agreement for Pooled Operation, the RPA, executed on July 5, 1979, to become effective on December 20, 1979. This agreement placed Hocking's condominium in HCP's rental pool.

* * *

Hocking alleges that his investment was entirely passive, and that he relied on Dubois to select, manage, and protect his investment. He relinquished control of his investment at the time he purchased it and had access to his unit for only two weeks each year. He knew that approximately fifty other condominium owners participated in the rental pooling arrangement. When he visited the building in Hawaii, he observed that it was operated like a hotel, and he received copies of brochures and advertisements which HCP distributed on the mainland.

Hocking purchased the condominium for $115,000, with a down payment of $24,000 and installment payments on the remaining portion of the purchase price through June 1982, at which time all unpaid amounts were to become due. Hocking's complaint states that he "cancelled" his investment when this balloon payment came due. The failure to make the payment apparently caused the forfeiture of his prior payments. He claims the loss of his investment was caused by the failure to receive the expected rental income, and by further misrepresentations of Dubois concerning appreciation in the value of the condominium and her efforts to resell the condominium in 1981 and 1982.

* * *

In order for Hocking to make a claim under the securities laws, he must show that Dubois' alleged misrepresentations were made in connection with the purchase or sale of a security. Both section 2 of the Securities Act of 1933 and section 3 of the Securities Exchange Act of 1934 define the term "security" to include any "investment contract."

* * *

In *Howey*, [*SEC v. W. J. Howey Co.*, 328 U.S. 293 (1946)] the Supreme Court found that the combined sale of land and a land service contract, under which the purchaser relinquished all control over the land for a 10-year period, was an investment contract. The Court there put forward the definition of an investment contract:

> [A]n investment contract for purposes of the Securities Act means a contract, transaction or scheme whereby a person invests his money in a common enterprise and is led to expect profits solely from the efforts of the promoter or a third party, it being immaterial whether the shares in the enterprise are evidenced by formal certificates or by nominal interests in the physical assets employed in the enterprise.

* * *

We must therefore determine whether Hocking's purchase of a condominium and rental pool was (1) an investment of money, (2) in a common enterprise, (3) with an expectation of profits produced by the efforts of others.

In *Howey*, as here, the investors purchased real estate and at the same time relinquished much of the right to use or enter the property. In *Howey*, as here, the investors were not obligated to purchase the service contracts, and in fact some decided to purchase the land without a service contract. In *Howey*, as here, the investors were generally nonresidents who lacked the skill, knowledge and equipment necessary to manage the investment.

There is no doubt that, had Hocking purchased the condominium and the rental pool directly from the developer and an affiliated rental pool operator, and had the rental pool been for a long term without any provision for early termination, Hocking would have purchased a security. If that were the case, we would merely substitute Hocking's Hawaiian condominium for *Howey's* Floridian citrus grove.

Hocking, however, did not purchase the condominium in the initial offering from the developer. He purchased in the secondary market from the Libermans. Further, Hocking entered into the rental pool agreement with HCP, and has, defendants argue, failed to demonstrate any link between HCP and the developer. Finally, unlike the investors in *Howey*, Hocking could legally terminate the RPA according to its terms and regain control over the condominium. We must determine therefore whether these differences from *Howey* make Hocking's alleged transaction into an ordinary real estate purchase or whether it nevertheless could prove to be the purchase of a security.

* * *

The Howey Test

A. Investment of Money

Defendants attempt to pull apart the package into two separate transactions. They argue that even if Hocking did invest money in the condominium, he did not invest money in the RPA, and it is the RPA which provides the elements necessary to satisfy the *Howey* test's other requirements. Therefore, they claim, Hocking did not satisfy this first requirement.

Admittedly, there would be an argument as to whether the "investment of money" requirement had been met if someone who already owned a condominium decided to place the condominium into a rental arrangement, independent of the decision to purchase the condominium. If, however, the condominium and rental agreements were offered as a package, there can be no serious argument that Hocking did not invest money in the package. Since Hocking has created an issue of fact over whether the condominium and RPA were sold as a package, he has met this first requirement of *Howey* for purposes of summary judgment.

B. Common Enterprise

* * *

The participants [in the RPA] pool their assets; they give up any claim to profits or losses attributable to their particular investments in return for a pro rata share of the profits of the enterprise; and they make their collective fortunes dependent on the success of a single common enterprise.

* * *

Of course, whether Hocking can prove [his case] at trial will depend on whether he can show that Dubois offered a package which included the RPA. As discussed above, Hocking has raised a genuine issue of fact as to that question.

C. Expectation of Profits Produced by the Efforts of Others

This third prong of *Howey* forms the greatest hurdle for Hocking, assuming he can prove at trial that the condominium and rental agreements were part of one package. He must show an expectation of profits produced by the efforts of others, that the efforts of others are "those essential managerial efforts which affect the failure or success of the enterprise." *Glenn W. Turner Enters.*, 474 F.2d at 482.

The crux of defendants' argument on this point is that the rental agreements allowed Hocking to maintain a high degree of control over his condominium, thus making any managerial efforts of Dubois or HCP non-essential to the success of Hocking's investment.

* * *

[Because Hocking raised issues of fact with regard to this prong, as well as the "investment of money" and "common enterprise" factors, the court reversed the summary judgment for the brokers and remanded the case.]

PROBLEMS

1. Cicero grants Homer a life estate in Cicero's farm, and the property is to return to Cicero at Homer's death. Which of the following acts is considered waste? Why?

    a. Homer removed timber from the property for the purpose of using the land to grow crops. He sells the timber for $50,000.
    b. Homer tears down the house on the farm.
    c. Homer drills a new oil well and removes oil from the land.
    d. Homer removes timber from a part of the farm that is unfit for agricultural purposes and uses the timber to repair a fence on the farm.

2. Bob and Carol, husband and wife, owned a farm as joint tenants, not as tenants by the entirety. Marital problems developed, and Bob and Carol separated. While they were separated, Bob deeded his interest in the farm to a friend, Alice. Later Bob and Carol were reconciled, and Bob signed a will leaving the farm to Carol. At Bob's death, who owns the farm? Why?

3. Adam had two sons, Cain and Abel. Adam wanted to deed a valuable farm to his sons as joint tenants, but he liked Abel nine times more than he liked Cain. Consequently, Adam worded the deed as follows: "To Cain, a one-tenth interest, and to Abel, a nine-tenths interest, as joint tenants with rights of survivorship." Abel later died of natural causes. Who owns the real estate now? Why?

4. Harry and Wilda, husband and wife, owned a car and a house. The title to the car was in Wilda's name, and the house was owned by Harry and Wilda as tenants by the entirety. One day while driving to the grocery store, Harry caused an automobile accident and seriously injured Macbeth. Macbeth sued Harry and Wilda for $800,000 and claimed that he could take their house if their insurance failed to cover the damage award. Is Macbeth correct? Why or why not?

5. Two brothers, Barry and Harry, owned a farm as joint tenants. They farmed the land together for thirty years. On Barry's death, Harry took his deed to an attorney to have the title changed to his name only. The attorney advised Harry that there had been a mistake in the original deed and that Barry and Harry had owned the land as tenants in common rather than as joint tenants. Barry left no will; and his only heirs were Harry and two sisters, Lettie and Betty.

There was a long-standing feud between the brothers and sisters, who had not spoken to each other for years. Who owns the farm now?

6. Tex owned an apartment building and a blueberry farm. At Tex's death, the apartment and farm passed to Sheryl and Kim as tenants in common. Sheryl and Kim shared the rent from the apartment and the profits from the blueberry farm equally. One evening while driving to the farm to water the blueberries, Kim negligently struck Denny with her car. Is Sheryl liable for Denny's injuries? Why or why not?

7. Hilda, a widow, lives on a 500-acre farm worth $500,000. She has one son, Jim. To avoid probate, Hilda has decided to deed the farm "to Hilda and Jim, as joint tenants with rights of survivorship and not as tenants in common." What potential problems might arise from this arrangement? Why?

8. Taylor and Marty, roommates at Big U, decide to build and run a large racquetball club after graduation. In starting this business, they consider the following forms: (1) corporation, (2) S corporation, (3) partnership, (4) limited partnership, (5) real estate investment trust, and (6) limited liability company. Which form would you recommend? What are the major problems with each form in this situation?

9. George Babbitt was a real estate developer. Whenever George started a new project, he formed one corporation to handle construction and another corporation to own the project. Beyond the development, each corporation had little or no assets. A creditor who is owed $100,000 by one of George's corporations now sues George as an individual for the debt. On what theory would the suit be brought? How can George best defend the suit?

10. Should property owners be required to provide for their children after the owners die? In the states that apply the common law marital property rules and in all states using the community property system except Louisiana, there is freedom to will your property to virtually anyone, subject to possible claims by the surviving spouse. Moreover, joint tenancy held by husband and wife allows the surviving spouse to gain ownership of the decedent's share to the exclusion of the children. Under Louisiana law, due to its civil law roots in French and Spanish law, the inheritance laws are governed by a doctrine called "forced heirship." If the parents write wills, they must give their child(ren) a "forced portion" or "legitime." If a parent does not provide the forced portion in the will, children aged twenty-three and under as well as mentally and/or physically disabled children at any age can take one-fourth of the estate when there is one surviving child or one-half when there are two or more surviving children. The forced heirship doctrine provides that parents have a legal and moral responsibility to support and enrich their children. The age of twenty-three was selected primarily so that a child would have the resources to complete college. The disabled child exception was created so that parents would support the child, thereby relieving society of the burden. Parents in all states (including Louisiana) typically leave much of their property to their children anyway, but Louisiana is the only state in which parents are forced to do so. Which system do you believe is more ethical? Should you be free to use your own judgment about who receives your property, or should the law dictate who is to receive it? Are there circumstances in which either system would have unethical outcomes? For example, what happens when a wealthy parent refuses to support a mentally disabled adult child, leaving it up to the taxpayers to pay the bills? Do all children deserve to inherit property? Louisiana law does provide that a parent can disinherit a child but generally only for extreme behavior such as attempted murder or physical attacks. Moreover, if the child and parent later reconcile, the grounds for the disinheritance are no longer applicable. Isn't a parent in the best position to decide whether the child deserves an inheritance without having to be victimized first by such behavior?

ENDNOTES

1. J. Bennet, *Clinton Has Surgery to Reattach Tendon Torn in a Fall*, New York Times A–9 (March 15, 1997). Former President Clinton was a house guest at golf champion Greg Norman's Florida estate in Hobe Sound.
2. C. Moynihan, *Introduction to the Law of Real Property* 1–24 (2nd ed. 1988).
3. T. Bergin and P. Haskell, *Preface to Estates in Land and Future Interests* 2 (1966).
4. *Black's Law Dictionary* 643 (4th ed.).
5. *Magnolia Petroleum Co. v. Thompson*, 106 F.2d 217 (8th Cir. 1939).
6. Ga.Code Ann. §85-501.
7. See R. Cunningham, et al., *The Law of Property* 30 (2nd ed. 1993).
8. *Lynch v. Bunting*, 42 Del. 171, 29 A.2d 155 (1942).
9. 318 Md. 47, 566 A.2d 777 (1989).
10. Restatement of Property, Introductory Note 2119 (1944).
11. Restatement of Property, Introductory Note 2379 (1944).
12. Restatement of Property §406 (1944).
13. R. Boyer, et al., *The Law of Property* 89, 91 (4th ed. 1991).
14. *Pickens v. Black*, 885 S.W.2d 872 (Ark. 1994).
15. R. Boyer, et al., *The Law of Property* 105 (4th ed. 1991).
16. *Id.* at 169.
17. Restatement of Property §§129, 130 (1944).

18. *Cooper v. Barton,* 208 Iowa 447, 226 N.W. 70 (1929).

19. Restatement of Property §133 (1944).

20. R. Keeton, *Insurance Law—Basic Text* 210 (1971).

21. W. Vance, *Insurance* 783, 784 (1951).

22. 274 Or. 127, 544 P.2d 1034 (1976).

23. *Savings Investment & Trust Co. v. Little,* 135 N.J.Eq. 546, 39 A.2d 392 (1944).

24. R. Boyer, et al., *The Law of Property* 92 (4th ed. 1991).

25. Restatement of Property §§19, 138 (1944).

26. *Medlin v. Medlin,* 203 S.W.2d 635 (Tex.Civ.App. 1947).

27. 866 P.2d 489 (Or.App. 1994).

28. Restatement of Property §124 (1944).

29. *Neel v. Neel,* 19 Pa. 323 (1852).

30. 217 Minn. 235, 14 N.W.2d 360 (1944).

31. 79 N.W. 738 (Wisc. 1899).

32. R. Aalberts and P. Poon, *Derivatives and the Modern Prudent Investor Rule: Too Risky or Too Necessary?* 67 Ohio State Law Review 525 (2006).

33. *Cleaver v. Long,* 69 Ohio L.Abs. 488, 126 N.E.2d 479 (1955).

34. *Deslauriers v. Senesac,* 331 Ill. 437, 163 N.E. 327 (1928).

35. *Cleaver v. Long,* 69 Ohio L.Abs. 488, 126 N.E.2d 479 (1955).

36. See R. Kratovil, *Real Estate Law* 194 (6th ed. 1974).

37. *Van Antwerp v. Horan,* 390 Ill. 449, 61 N.E.2d 358 (1945).

38. 168 Cal.App.2d 499, 336 P.2d 226 (1959).

39. *Cook v. Grierson,* 845 A.2d 1231 (Ct. App. Md. 2004).

40. *Short v. Milby,* 31 Del.Ch. 49, 64 A.2d 36 (1949).

41. *Draughon v. Wright,* 200 Okl. 198, 191 P.2d 921 (1948).

42. *Hardin v. Chapman,* 36 Tenn.App. 343, 255 S.W.2d 707 (1952).

43. 250 Md. 491, 243 A.2d 588 (1968).

44. 894 F.2d 1511 (11th Cir. 1990).

45. *Schweitzer v. Evans,* 360 Pa. 552, 63 A.2d 39 (1949).

46. S. Johnson, *After Drye: The Likely Attachment of the Federal Tax Lien to Tenancy-by-the-Entireties Interests,* 75 Indiana Law Journal 1163 (Fall 2000).

47. *Finley v. Thomas,* 691 A.2d 1163 (D.C. 1997).

48. *Stevahn v. Meidinger,* 79 N.D. 323, 57 N.W.2d 1 (1952).

49. *Massman v. Duffy,* 333 Ill.App. 30, 76 N.E.2d 547 (1947).

50. 142 Wash.App. 81, 173 P.3d 959 (2007).

51. 91 Cal.App.2d 328, 204 P.2d 950 (1949).

52. *Murphy v. Regan,* 8 N.J. Super. 44, 73 A.2d 191 (1950).

53. *Formosa Corp. v. Rogers,* 108 Cal.App.2d 397, 239 P.2d 88 (1951).

54. R. Boyer, et al., *The Law of Property* 104 (4th ed. 1991).

55. *Buschmeyer v. Eikermann,* 378 S.W.2d 468 (Mo. 1964).

56. W. Kopczuk and J. Slemrod, *Dying to Save Taxes: Evidence from Estate Tax Returns on the Death Elasticity,* NBER Working Paper No. W8158 (March 2001).

57. 931 So.2d 245 (Fla. App. Ct. 2006).

58. W. Burby, *Real Property* 236, 237 (3rd ed. 1965).

59. Wis. Stat. Ann. §§766.001–766.97 (Supp. 1991). Community property laws may generally lower federal capital gain taxes after the death of one spouse when the surviving spouse then sells the property. See http://www.irs.gov/pub/irs-pdf/p555.pdf (last visited February 14, 2010) for IRS pamphlet on community property and taxes.

60. J. Blattmachr, H. Zaritsky, and M. Asher, *Tax Planning With Consensual Community: Alaska's New Community Property Law,* 33 Real Property, Probate and Trust Journal 615 (1999).

61. *Steward v. Torrey,* 54 Ariz. 369, 95 P.2d 990 (1939).

62. N. Long, *Community Characterization of the Increased Value of Separately Owned Businesses,* 32 Idaho Law Review 731 (1996).

63. C. Donahue, *What Causes Fundamental Legal Ideas? Marital Property in the Thirteenth Century,* 78 Michigan Law Review 59 (1979).

64. M. Wenig, *UMPA: "A Reform of Historic Proportions,"* Estate Planning Studies 4 (April 1986).

65. V. Marino, *Buying a Small Part of Something Big,* New York Times 22 (October 15, 2006).

66. Uniform Partnership Act §7(4).

67. *Lutz v. Schmillen,* 899 P.2d 861 (Wyoming 1995).

68. Uniform Partnership Act §2.

69. *Id.* §§8(4), 10.

70. *Id.* §§26, 28.

71. Uniform Limited Partnership Act §2.

72. 133 Ga.App. 411, 210 S.E.2d 866 (1974).

73. N.Y. Bus. Corp. Law §630; Wis. Stat. Ann. §180.0622(13).

74. *New York v. Shore Realty Corp.,* 759 F.2d 1032 (2nd Cir. 1985).

75. J. Murray, *Legal and Title Insurance Issues in Limited Liability Company Real Estate Transactions,* Real Estate Law and Practice Course Handbook Series 525 (November 2002).

76. G. Madek, *The Limited Liability Company,* North Atlantic Regional Business Law Review 85 (1989); *Using Limited Liability Companies for Real Estate,* 24 The Mortgage and Real Estate Executives Report 3 (August 1, 1991); *New Partnership-Type Entity OK'd by IRS,* 22 The Mortgage and Real Estate Executives Report 1 (March 1, 1989).

77. See G. Poindexter, *The Limitations of Limited Liability Companies,* Real Estate Review 82 (Winter 1994).

78. L. Witner and D. Rosenberg, *Limited Liability Companies in Real Estate Ventures,* 22 Real Estate Law Journal 55 (1993).

79. C. Banas and J. Block, *Caveat Member: Courts Begin to "Pierce the Entity Veil," Imposing Personal Liability on LLC Members,* 29 Michigan Real Property Review 15 (2002).

80. 46 P.3d 323 (Wyo. 2002).

81. L. Witner, *Tax Ideas,* 22 Real Estate Law Journal 248 (1994). For general information on REITs, visit http://www.reit.com, the official website of the National Association of Real Estate Investment Trusts®.

82. T. Preble, *The Recapitalization of Real Estate,* Probate & Property (March/April 1994).

83. L. Witner, *Tax Ideas,* 22 Real Estate Law Journal 248 (1994).

84. T. Clauretie, *Commercial Real Estate Finance* 33 (2003).

85. Section 2(1), Securities Act of 1933.

86. Sowards and Hirsch, *Blue Sky Regulation* (1994).

87. 328 U.S. 293, 66 S.Ct. 1100, 90 L.Ed. 1244 (1946).

88. *United Housing Foundation, Inc. v. Forman,* 421 U.S. 837, 95 S.Ct. 2051, 44 L.Ed.2d 621 (1975).

89. Price Waterhouse, *Accounting for Condominium Sales* 57 (1981).

90. *Revak v. SEC Realty Corp.,* 18 F.3d 81 (2d Cir. 1994).

91. *Wals v. Fox Hills Development Corporation,* 24 F.3d 1016 (7th Cir. 1994).

The Search for Real Estate

© MACIEJ NOSKOWSKI/iStockphoto (RF)

LEARNING OBJECTIVES

After studying Chapter 6, you should:

- Be able to classify and understand the law regarding real estate agents

- Distinguish among the various listing agreements

- Recognize the duties of the broker

- Know and apply the Interstate Land Full Disclosure Act to real estate practices

- Identify what is discrimination in the selling and leasing of real estate.

"In a real estate man's eye, the most expensive part of the city is where he has a house to sell."

Will Rogers, Humorist

"I think selling techniques are basically the same in every country, except there are different cultures that have different methods of negotiating. But real estate is the same, whether it happens to be in Australia or if it happens to be in New York."

George Ross, Senior Executive—Trump Organization

The typical real estate transaction involves a series of five major contracts:

1. The seller's contract with the broker
2. The purchase agreement between seller and buyer
3. A contract with the party who provides evidence of title
4. The buyer's contract for property insurance
5. The buyer's contract with a lender for financing

In the following chapters, these five contracts are considered in chronological order. When studying these contracts, keep in mind that while the purchase and sale of real estate are typically the most important financial transactions in a person's lifetime, real estate contracts are usually negotiated without the assistance of an attorney. According to an American Bar Association report,

> ... it is probably safe to say that in a high percentage of cases the seller is unrepresented and signs the contracts of brokerage and sale on the basis of his faith in the broker. The buyer does not employ a lawyer. He signs the contract of sale without reading it and, once financing has been obtained, leaves all the details of title search and closing to the lender or broker. The lender or broker may employ an attorney but, where title insurance is furnished by a company maintaining its own title plant, it is possible that no lawyer, not even house counsel will appear.[1]

Consequently, the discussions in the following chapters are especially important for the average person.

The major emphasis in this chapter is on relationships with brokers and on the problems that occur in the search for real estate. The chapter includes an examination of the licensing requirements for brokers, types of listing agreements, and the duties of the broker as an agent once the contract is made. Beyond the contract with the broker, the search for real estate raises special issues regarding interstate land sales and discrimination in selling real estate, issues that are considered near the end of this chapter.

The Real Estate Agent
Licensing Requirements

real estate broker

An agent authorized under state real estate licensing laws to operate independently in a real estate brokerage business.

commission

Payment by a seller of real estate to a real estate broker for finding a buyer.

real estate salesperson

An agent authorized under state real estate licensing laws to act in real estate brokerage transactions only under the control and direction of a licensed real estate broker.

A **real estate broker** is a person hired to negotiate the sale or purchase of real estate for a **commission**. The broker typically acts as an agent for the seller of real estate, although he also can act on behalf of a buyer or even a buyer and a seller at the same time if the parties so agree. This agency relationship imposes certain duties on the broker, which are discussed later in this chapter. All states require the licensing of real estate brokers. State licensing laws normally require that the broker pass an examination. The examination generally covers the principles of real estate practice (including a knowledge of the broker's duties), real estate law and transactions, instruments used in the transactions, and the canons of ethics relating to brokers. In addition, most states require a real estate brokerage applicant to have been associated with a real estate broker as a **real estate salesperson** for one or two years and to have completed a specified number of courses in real estate practice, law, appraisal, and finance.[2] Salespersons who do not choose to become brokers generally cannot own and manage their own real estate companies, but instead must be associated with a licensed broker who does. For example, Virginia requires that salespersons must complete 60 hours of approved classes and pass both a state and national exam to receive a license. A salesperson who aspires to be a broker must complete an additional 180 hours of classes and must work with a licensed broker for 36 of the 48 months before taking the broker's license exam.[3] (For information on all states' requirements for sales and brokerage licenses, see endnote 3).

Licensing requirements are established by statute, and the statutes usually give a state real estate commission the duty of establishing rules or regulations to carry out the statutory requirements. These rules often cover details about applications required to take the examinations, continuing education requirements, and ethical standards governing real estate practice.[4] If brokers or salespeople violate the ethical rules governing the industry, such as commingling a client's money with their own, their licenses may be suspended or revoked. But can brokers and salespeople be suspended for illegal activities not directly related to the real estate industry? The following Oregon case discusses this issue.

A CASE IN POINT

In *Dearborn v. Real Estate Agency,*[5] Dearborn, a licensed real estate broker, was arrested at his home for allegedly engaging in sex with transients, including minors, in exchange for drugs. In a search of his home after his arrest, police found cocaine and methamphetamine. The Oregon State Real Estate Commission suspended his license, placed him on probation, and told him that he could resume work in two years only as a real estate salesperson. Dearborn appealed to the state court. The state court reversed the decision stating that "[a]lthough a conviction for possession of a controlled substance may possibly be linked to a licensee's trustworthiness or competence to engage in professional real estate activity, here the facts simply do not support the nexus between past

continues

continued

criminal conduct and future risks that are cited by the Commissioner.... [N]othing in the record suggest that petitioner ever used his position as a real estate licensee as a basis for soliciting sexual partners. Nothing suggests that he ever approached any client or any member of any client's family for an illicit purpose." The court further noted that Dearborn's choice of sexual partner was "indiscriminate" and therefore not linked to any real estate activity.

REALTORS®

Licensed real estate brokers and salespersons who are members of the National Association of Realtors.

Both real estate brokers and their associated salespeople must be licensed by the state, but they are not legally required to be **REALTORS®**. REALTORS® are members of the National Association of Realtors (NAR), the real estate industry's largest professional association. Only members can use the designation "REALTORS®" since it is a registered trade name. NAR provides its membership with, among other things, educational opportunities and access to a multiple listing service (MLS), which is discussed later in this chapter. NAR also is a large and active advocate and lobbyist in state legislatures and Congress on issues related to the real estate industry.

As noted in Chapter 5, certain interests in real estate can be classified as securities. In addition to meeting state real estate licensing requirements, real estate brokers must register as investment advisers with the Securities and Exchange Commission if they sell investment contracts, mortgage notes, real estate limited partnership interests, or other forms of securities.

Penalties for Acting Without a License

In many states, a person who violates the brokers' licensing statutes faces criminal penalties in the form of a possible fine and imprisonment. Under many statutes, a person acting as a real estate broker without a license faces the added penalty of not being allowed to collect a commission from a client. Even where a statute is silent with regard to civil penalties, courts have decided that to allow an unlicensed broker to collect a commission violates public policy. The broker's license is considered to be a regulatory license; that is, the statute regulates licensing of brokers to protect the public from unscrupulous brokers who lack knowledge of real estate transactions or who fail to meet the ethical requirements of the profession. Denying the unlicensed broker a commission helps serve the public purpose of protecting consumers. Of course, a person can sell her own property without a real estate license since she is not acting in the capacity of an agent.

The same public policy applies in cases where a licensed broker deals in real estate transactions outside the state in which she is licensed, as illustrated by the following Illinois case.

A CASE IN POINT

In *Frankel v. Allied Mills, Inc.,*[6] a broker licensed in Illinois was promised a fee of $17,000 for selling a parcel of Illinois real estate; but the listing agreement was signed in New York, where he was not licensed. The court decided that he could not collect the fee. "The rule is that when a statute declares that it shall be unlawful to perform an act, and imposes a penalty for its violation, contracts for the performance of such acts are void and incapable of enforcement.... The object of the statute is to promote the public welfare by permitting only persons with the necessary qualifications to act as real estate brokers and salesmen. The location of land outside the State of New York does not affect the policy of the statute, since it is the vendor and the purchaser who are sought to be protected. The statute does not in any way seek to regulate the sale of Illinois real estate, but operates only on the brokerage contract."

Enforcing the law against agents licensed in one state but selling real estate in another has become more complex due to the Internet. For example, consider what would happen if a prospective buyer from Kentucky saw a Florida listing that had been placed on the web by a broker in North Dakota. Could the Florida Real Estate Commission exert jurisdiction over an unscrupulous listing broker in North Dakota to protect the citizens of Florida? Since none of the broker's activities were in Florida, some commentators acknowledge that in such situations there may be nothing authorities in Florida could do.[7] This problem brings into play complicated procedural and constitutional issues surrounding whether the broker's activities have sufficient "minimum contacts" or links in Florida so that the state's real estate commission can exert personal jurisdiction and enforce Florida law over the North Dakota broker.[8]

Listing Agreements

Whenever a broker is hired, the broker and client should enter into an agreement covering such matters as the term of the employment, the amount of the commission, and the duties of the broker. Most states require that the broker and client enter into a written agreement before the broker can collect a commission, place advertisements, or display the broker's sign on the property to indicate that it is for sale. The seller of real estate traditionally hires the broker, although there has been a trend toward the buyer retaining a broker, a topic discussed later in this chapter. The written contract between the client and the broker is called a **listing agreement**.

listing agreement
A contract between a seller of real estate and a real estate broker in which the broker is authorized to serve as the seller's agent.

Statute of Frauds

As further discussed in Chapter 7, contracts for the purchase and sale of real estate, as well as certain leases, deeds, mortgages, and generally any other legal instrument pertaining to land, must be in writing to be enforceable under the Statute of Frauds. In many states, the listing agreement is included within the Statute of Frauds and therefore must be in writing. In states where the agreement must be in writing, most courts require that the names of the parties, the percentage of commission, and an exact description of the real estate be included in the listing agreement. Because of the different types of arrangements between brokers and clients, it also is advisable for the listing agreement to specify the beginning and ending date of the broker's listing, the broker's duties, and the desired sales price.[9]

Types of Listing Agreements

Lynn listed her house with a broker, Marilyn, and signed a listing agreement. Lynn later found a buyer without Marilyn's assistance. Then another broker, Adam, brought a second buyer to Lynn. Now Lynn questions whether she will be liable for a commission to Marilyn if she sells the house to either buyer. The answer depends on the type of listing agreement (see Table 6.1) that Lynn signed with Marilyn.

exclusive right to sell
A listing agreement between a seller of real estate and a real estate broker that gives the broker the sole right to sell the property and to receive a commission on the sale regardless of whether the broker is responsible for the sale.

Exclusive Right to Sell   If the broker has an **exclusive right to sell**, she is entitled to a commission even when the owner or another broker locates a buyer. (For an exclusive right to sell agreement, see www.cengagebrain.com [see page xix in the Preface for instructions on how to access the free study tools for this text].) The following language in a listing agreement used in Texas gives a broker the exclusive right to sell the real estate: "Should I [the seller], or anyone acting for me, including my heirs, sell, lease, transfer or otherwise dispose of said property within the time herein fixed for the continuance of the agency, you [the broker] shall be entitled nevertheless to your commission as herein set out."[10]

TABLE 6.1 Seller's Liability for Commission to Broker A

LISTING AGREEMENT	SELLER LOCATES BUYER	BROKER B LOCATES BUYER
Exclusive Right to Sell	Seller Liable	Seller Liable
Exclusive Agency	Not Liable	Seller Liable
Open Listing	Not Liable	Not Liable

The standard form listing agreement that a broker presents to a seller is usually an exclusive right to sell agreement. What is more, since many real estate sellers, particularly residential homeowners, know little about alternative brokerage arrangements, this agreement is the one sellers usually sign as well. Even so, sellers who do sign an exclusive right to sell agreement can still sell their real estate without paying a commission if they exclude names of specific parties in the agreement who formerly expressed an interest in buying the property. Still, it is in a prospective seller's best interests to become better versed in the use of alternative agreements such as the two discussed next.

exclusive agency
A listing agreement between the seller of real estate and a real estate broker that gives the broker the exclusive right to sell the property and a commission on the sale, but the seller may, without owing a commission, use her own efforts to sell the property.

Exclusive Agency   Under an **exclusive agency**, the broker is named as exclusive agent, but the principal (owner) can find his own buyer without incurring liability for the commission. (For an exclusive agency agreement, see www.cengagebrain.com [see page xix in the Preface for instructions on how to access the free study tools for this text].) An exclusive agency is created when the listing agreement uses language similar to the following: "A commission is to be paid the broker whether the purchaser is secured by the broker or by any person other than the seller."

Many listing agreements use language such as this: "The broker has the exclusive right to sell said property." Does that mean that the broker has the exclusive right to sell in the legal sense, or does the language designate the broker as the exclusive agent? The courts are split on that question; but the usual rule is that where a contract is ambiguous, the ambiguity is interpreted against the person who drafted the agreement—in this case, the broker. If this rule of interpretation is used, the broker will become the exclusive agent; but it would still allow the seller, who is the principal, the right to sell and not pay a commission. To avoid this result, the broker should use language similar to the listing agreement previously discussed that created an exclusive right to sell. The owner, on the other hand, will want to add language clarifying the owner's personal right to sell the property without paying a commission to the broker. An example of an exclusive agency agreement is found in a New York case, *Century 21 A.L.P. Realty v. Dolle*.[11] A property owner was liable for a commission of $17,500 plus interest to a broker under an exclusive agency agreement when, during the term of the exclusive agency, the owner accepted an offer from purchasers who were procured by another broker.

open listing agreement
A contract between a seller of real estate and a real estate broker in which the broker has a nonexclusive right to sell the property.

Open Listing   Occasionally, a listing agreement is signed that merely authorizes "the broker to act as agent in securing a purchaser for my property." This language creates an **open listing agreement**. (For an open listing agreement, see www.cengagebrain.com [see page xix in the Preface for instructions on how to access the free study tools for this text].) The broker is not entitled to a commission if a ready, willing, and able purchaser is secured by another broker or by the seller. Open listing agreements are rare in sales of residential properties; they are more commonly used to sell commercial properties.

Procuring Cause of Sale

In certain cases, particularly where an exclusive agency or open listing agreement is used, a dispute occasionally arises between two or more brokers or between the broker and

procuring
cause of sale

The actions of a real estate broker that are the direct and primary cause of a real estate sale.

seller, each of whom claims that the buyer was procured through his efforts. In this instance, the broker who "brings the buyer and seller together, they negotiate, without abandonment, and ultimately agree upon a sale"[12] is generally considered the **procuring cause of sale**. For example, assume that Lynn signed open listing agreements with two brokers, Adam and Corey. Adam finds a prospective buyer, Graham, who wants to buy the property if the closing date can be worked out. Without Adam's knowledge, Corey then negotiates the closing date with Graham and persuades Graham to sign the contract. In this case, the general rule would entitle only Adam to a commission. As stated in a West Virginia case, "If a broker sets in motion machinery by which a sale is made, which without break in its continuity was procuring cause of sale, he is entitled to commission although he does not conduct all negotiations."[13] Or as a Missouri court expressed more eloquently, "he who sows the seed and tills the crop is entitled to reap the harvest—rather than one who volunteers to assist in tilling a crop, the seed for which he has not sown."[14]

Sellers sometimes take elaborate measures in attempting to avoid paying commissions to brokers who have procured buyers. For instance, in *Flamingo Realty, Inc., v. Midwest Development, Inc.,*[15] a seller subject to an open listing agreement sold a Nevada property to a company named Toroscan, Inc., for $5,325,000, which Toroscan immediately resold for $5,900,000 to the company that the broker had procured. Toroscan turned out to be a newly formed Nevada corporation owned by the daughter and two sons of a principal shareholder of the seller. Under these circumstances, the court held that the corporation was set up as a scam to avoid paying a commission and so the real estate agent was due a commission.

One of the hard lessons many new salesperson learn is that buyers are not always loyal, even after the salesperson has spent hours of time together with the buyer incurring expenses trying to find the right property. Thus, if a salesperson finds a potential buyer who then ceases negotiations and leaves her for a second broker, she generally does not earn a commission; however, the second broker, if challenged by the first one, might still have to prove he was the procuring cause of the sale. As the following classic case from New Jersey demonstrates, this practice has been plaguing brokers for a long time.

A CASE IN POINT

In *Vreeland v. Vetterlein,*[16] the plaintiff broker opened negotiations with a prospective buyer, Henderson, but could not persuade Henderson to buy the property for a specified price. Later Henderson learned that a public sewer was being constructed near the property. He then went to another broker, Garrabrants, and agreed to buy the property for a higher price. The court decided that the plaintiff broker was not entitled to a commission because "where the property is openly put in the hands of more than one broker, each of such agents is aware that he is subject to the arts and chances of competition. If he finds a person who is likely to buy, and quits him without having effected a sale, he is aware that he runs the risk of such person falling under the influence of his competitor—and in such case, he may lose his labor. This is a part of the inevitable risk of the business he has undertaken."

An owner who negotiates and signs a contract with a buyer who has been sent by a broker must pay a commission. This rule applies even though the owner was not aware that the buyer had been procured by the broker's efforts. This is one reason why prospective buyers visiting a listed property at an "open house"—a widespread marketing technique brokers employ to sell homes—are asked to sign a sheet. If the seller later tries to consummate a sale to a person who had toured the house, the broker can prove that he was the procuring cause of the sale. Likewise, in recent years, brokers who have sent e-mails or had their web sites accessed by prospective buyers can also make an effective argument that they were the procuring cause of the sale.

Yet, if the seller reduces the sales price on the belief that the buyer was not procured through the broker's efforts and if the broker did not disclose its role, courts have held that no commission is due to the broker.[17] With this in mind, a sophisticated seller who has not entered into an exclusive right to sell agreement with a broker, should ask an apparently independent buyer to represent that no broker made the referral.

ETHICAL AND PUBLIC POLICY ISSUES

Do Buyers and Sellers Owe Brokers Ethical Duties?

The real estate brokerage business is regulated under state and federal law. It is not uncommon to hear of legal and ethical violations by brokers and salespersons. It is unusual, however, to hear about the ethics of sellers and buyers in the treatment of their agents. In both open and exclusive agency listing agreements, a buyer who has engaged a broker who later learns about a listed property from a sign, newspaper ad, etc., paid for by the broker might directly contact the seller instead of the broker to negotiate a lower price. By not having to pay the broker a commission, both the buyer and the seller may benefit at the expense of the broker by saving the cost of the commission. Although it may be true that the broker did not actually deal with the buyer, in all likelihood, her efforts (at least indirectly) put the two parties together. Of course, the broker could sue for her commission, claiming that she was the procuring cause of the sale; but this is often difficult for the broker to prove, and the economics of litigation often preclude pursuing the former client. Partially because of this kind of unethical activity, among other reasons, it is rare for brokers to trust their principals enough to use open or exclusive agency agreements. Do the consequences of this kind of unethical behavior by sellers and buyers affect the real estate industry as a whole? For example, if sellers were more ethical, wouldn't a more fair and efficient real estate sales environment be created? If brokers could trust the sellers, wouldn't more sellers be motivated to list their properties in exclusive or open agency agreements if they knew they could participate in the sale and not have to pay a commission? Sometimes brokers do not market a property to the seller's satisfaction and the seller must then wait until the exclusive listing agreement expires before hiring another broker. If there were more open or exclusive agency listing agreements, would sellers be able to avoid this wait by marketing the property themselves?

Broker's Commission

Many disputes between a seller and a broker relate to the amount of commission due the broker. The commission should be agreed upon when the broker is hired. Most state laws require the commission to be in writing. Still, in those states that do not, if the broker's commission is not agreed upon in advance, courts will allow the broker a reasonable commission based on the fees charged by other brokers in the area unless state law requires the commission to be stated in writing, in which case the broker will recover nothing.

net listing agreement
A contract between a seller of real estate and a real estate broker in which the broker is paid as a commission the amount the sale price exceeds the price set by the seller.

The broker's commission is based on the gross sales price unless the listing agreement states otherwise. For example, if an owner lists her $400,000 home with a broker who charges a 7 percent commission and the house is subject to a $350,000 mortgage, at the closing, the bank obtains $350,000, the broker collects $28,000, and the owner receives $22,000. As an alternative to using a percentage of the gross price, the broker might use a **net listing agreement**, where the owner receives a certain amount (for example, $400,000) and the broker keeps everything above that amount as commission. In several states, net listing agreements are illegal.

Performance of the Listing Agreement

Under the traditional rule, brokers earn the agreed-upon commission whenever they procure a buyer who is "ready, willing, and financially able" to purchase the real estate under the terms and at the price stated in the listing agreement. This is true even when the owner refuses to sign a contract with the buyer. When the purchase agreement is signed by the buyer and the seller, the buyer has shown that she is ready and willing and the seller has indicated that he thinks the buyer is able.

> A buyer failed to close because of a mental condition that prevented her from moving out of her existing home. In *Blackman DeStefano Real Estate v. Smith* on page 202, the court resolves the question of whether the broker who procured this buyer was due a commission.

END OF CHAPTER CASE

The traditional view, discussed in the following Wisconsin case, holds that even if the contract is never performed, the broker is entitled to a commission.

A CASE IN POINT

In *Kruger v. Wesner,*[18] the defendants hired a real estate broker to sell their property for at least $30,000 and promised him a commission of 10 percent. The broker found a buyer who signed an offer to purchase the real estate for $40,000, which was accepted by the defendants. When the buyer later refused to perform the contract, the broker claimed a commission of $4,000. The court decided that the broker should receive the fee: "It may be generally stated that when a real estate broker procures a purchaser who is accepted by the owner, and a valid contract is drawn up between them, the commission for finding such purchaser is earned, although the purchaser later defaults for no known reason, or because the purchaser deliberately refuses to consummate the contract, or because of financial inability of purchaser to comply with the contract. The courts are practically unanimous in holding that a broker employed to sell or exchange lands earns his commission, unless the contract of employment contains a stipulation to the contrary, when a customer and the employer enter into a valid and binding contract for the sale or exchange of lands."

Courts have also reached the same result in cases, such as the following case from Ohio, where the buyer signs a contract but is unable to obtain financing to complete the purchase.

A CASE IN POINT

In *Retterer v. Bender,*[19] a broker located buyers who signed a purchase agreement for the owners' real estate; but the sale was not consummated, apparently because the buyers could not obtain financing. The court decided that the broker is entitled to a commission when he "makes a contract with the owner to find a purchaser for his real estate at a commission for his services and pursuant thereto performs such services by producing a purchaser, and the owner enters into a written contract of sale with such purchaser.... In such case, the broker is not required to prove that the buyer was ready, willing and able to consummate the transaction."

Yet the foregoing *Retterer* decision has been considered too favorable for the broker by some courts, which have held that brokers cannot recover from sellers following a buyer's breach of contract.

How can the seller avoid liability for a commission when the transaction fails to close through no fault of the seller? The seller can include a "no deal, no commission" clause in the listing agreement. This clause provides that if the deal is not closed, the broker is not entitled to a commission. Using another approach, the owner might require the buyer to make a down payment of earnest money, as discussed in Chapter 7, large enough to cover the broker's commission. The specific problem in the *Retterer* case might also be avoided by including in the purchase agreement, the topic of the next chapter, a clause that makes the agreement—and therefore the broker's commission—contingent on the buyer's ability to obtain financing. Indeed, most modern purchase agreements contain this boilerplate (standard, uniform) language. Also, brokers are increasingly requiring buyers to be preapproved for mortgage loans before they will begin serious negotiations on their behalf.

A growing number of jurisdictions recognize that the broker, not the seller, is in a better position to gauge whether the buyer is financially able to close. These states hold that unless the closing is avoided by the seller's willful conduct, the seller's liability for the commission is contingent upon the buyer's actual ability to close.

Joseph Iarussi was unable to obtain necessary financing; thus, he failed to close on the purchase of acreage from the Johnsons. The broker sued both Iarussi and the Johnsons for the commission. In *Ellsworth Dobbs, Inc. v. Johnson* on page 203, the court resolves the issue of whether the seller was liable for the commission.

END OF CHAPTER CASE

Cancellation of the Listing Agreement

Harry has listed his house with a broker. Shortly after signing the listing agreement, Harry decides that he wants to revoke the agreement. May he? The answer often depends on whether the listing agreement is in a form that satisfies legal requirements. For instance, if state law requires the form to include an expiration date and the date is missing, Harry can revoke the agreement. However, even if formal requirements are not met, Harry cannot cancel the agreement unless he acts in good faith. Thus, if Harry knows that the broker is negotiating with a buyer, he cannot cancel the agreement and conclude negotiations with the buyer on his own.[20]

Did sellers owe the broker a commission when they revoked their counteroffer prior to the buyer's acceptance? The good faith requirement is discussed in *Rellinger v. Bremmeyr* on page 204.

END OF CHAPTER CASE

Multiple Listing

As stated earlier, it is common, although not required, for real estate brokers to join private associations or boards at the local, state, and/or national level, including NAR. Many local boards operate **multiple listing services** MLSs that permit properties listed with one board member, traditionally in catalogs, but now also on the Internet, to be sold by any member of the board. As a Colorado court described the functioning of a county MLS:

> *The MLS provides a medium for exchange of information about property for sale in El Paso County, including improved residential real estate. It publishes weekly catalogs containing descriptive listings of such real estate, as well as quarterly "sold properties" catalogs which state the sale price, days on the market and other information about listed properties that have been sold. MLS publications are available to all member brokers and to all salespersons employed in a member broker's office.*[21]

Use of the MLS usually leads to the involvement of two brokers in the transaction. One broker has a listing agreement with the seller; and when the listing broker sells the property without another broker's involvement, she receives the full commission. Typically, however, another board member, the "selling broker," procures the buyer. In this event, the commission is normally split 50/50 between the listing broker and the selling broker. Under the traditional approach, the listing broker is the seller's agent to procure a buyer and the selling broker, also called the *cooperating broker*, is a **subagent** of the *seller*. Under a subagency scenario, the home seller often did not meet his own subagent until the end of negotiations or until the closing. Moreover, many buyers often did not even realize the selling broker he had been engaged with, sometimes for months, was really *not* his agent. Today disclosure of subagency as well as other agency statuses discussed later in this chapter is generally required by law.

Real estate boards have occasionally engaged in practices such as suggesting the rate of commission that each member should charge. The typical MLS system limits use and access of the system to members of the local real estate board, which is often associated with NAR, which sponsors the system. These practices raise antitrust questions under Section 1 of the **Sherman Antitrust Act**, which provides that "[e]very contract, combination in the form of trust or otherwise or conspiracy, in restraint of trade or commerce among the several states, or with foreign nations, is declared to be illegal."

Brokers who are not members of the local board have challenged the restrictions by claiming that it is illegal to tie membership with the local board to the right to access the often valuable MLS system.[22] Limitations on MLS access would be considered under a "rule of reason" approach where proof of economic harm is required to prove a violation of the Act. Some activities, such as price fixing, which can include collusively setting commission rates between and among competing brokers, are considered to be per se violations of the Sherman Act. As the U.S. Supreme Court explains in a case from Virginia, this means that there does not need to be any proof of economic harm since the harm is presumed to exist.

multiple listing service
A service that provides a listing of real estate for sale by competing brokers.

subagent
An agent who represents the interests of another agent. In real estate brokerage law, a broker who assists the listing broker and acts as an agent on behalf of the seller to find a buyer.

Sherman Antitrust Act
An 1890 federal statute that regulates anticompetitive behavior in interstate commerce.

A CASE IN POINT

In *Goldfarb v. Virginia State Bar,*[23] the Goldfarbs needed a title examination before they could purchase a house in Virginia. They contacted nineteen attorneys; and each attorney stated the same fee, which was prescribed by the bar association's minimum fee schedule. When the Goldfarbs brought suit claiming a violation of the Sherman Act, the Supreme Court decided that the fee schedule amounted to price fixing because the schedule was not merely advisory, but amounted to a "fixed, rigid price floor" that was enforced through the possibility of professional discipline by the state bar association.

In a case arising out of Washington D.C. directly relevant to real estate sales agents, the United States Supreme Court in *United States v. National Association of Real Estate Boards*[24] held that the National Association of Real Estate Boards' provision instructing brokers not to use rates lower than those adopted by the boards constituted illegal price fixing. In reaching this decision, the Supreme Court decided that real estate brokers are engaged in a trade rather than a profession, the latter of which might be exempted from the Act.

The Sherman Antitrust Act requires that for such real estate activity to be deemed illegal, it must affect interstate commerce. Whether real estate brokerage involves interstate commerce was addressed in a Louisiana case by the Supreme Court in *McLain v. Real Estate Board of New Orleans, Inc.*[25] The complaint in *McLain* alleged that the defendants—real estate brokers in the Greater New Orleans area—engaged in anticompetitive practices such as the use of fixed commission rates and fee splitting. The Court determined that interstate commerce was involved in the form of loans obtained through interstate channels and title insurance furnished by interstate corporations. The Court concluded that Sherman Act jurisdiction would be established where the brokers' activities "have a not insubstantial effect on interstate commerce."

little Sherman acts
State antitrust laws designed to regulate anticompetitive behavior within the state.

Many states have enacted their own antitrust legislation, known as **little Sherman acts**, which cover many activities beyond price fixing. For instance, when the State of Ohio sued the Cleveland area Board of Realtors, alleging violations of the Ohio antitrust law, the Board agreed to a consent judgment under which it was enjoined from "(1) restricting the offering of real estate training services by members; (2) restricting broker-members as to their recommendations of applicants for salesmen's licenses; (3) restricting broker-members in their selection of salesmen; (4) requiring licensed salesmen working with broker-members to join the Board; and (5) restricting or attempting to restrict salesmen working with broker-members in selecting educational services, materials, or facilities."[26]

The Federal Trade Commission (FTC) released a study that indicated that commission rates charged by brokers are noncompetitively high because, among other reasons, many sellers are unaware that commissions are negotiable. The study also noted that MLSs, while they result in commission uniformity, provide consumers with an efficient arrangement to sell real estate. Overall, the study concluded that sellers are satisfied with services provided by brokers. And competitive pricing of commissions could become more common with the advent of the Internet, a topic discussed later in the chapter.[27]

Recent Developments in Antitrust and Other Anticompetition Issues

More recently, NAR, apparently fearful of the competition created by discount brokerage and the Internet, has been criticized for thwarting competition in the real estate brokerage industry. Its dealings have resulted in regulatory actions and lawsuits from the FTC, the Department of Justice (DOJ), and other governmental bodies, as well as from private parties, to enforce antitrust laws.

Possibly NAR's most controversial actions have been its ongoing battles with brokers who maintain a virtual office web site (VOW). Under this business model, a broker places all of his listings on a web site and often does not maintain a physical office. This often results in buyers circumventing those brokers who maintain the full array of traditional brokerage services. In addition, virtual brokers also offer buyers who want more services than they can provide—such as visiting homes listed for sale—the opportunity to consult with a traditional broker with whom they split a fee. These less expensive and more efficient services have resulted in lower transaction costs for sellers.

However, the lower commissions have, not surprisingly, aroused the ire of many of NAR's membership who do not choose to maintain a VOW. In response, many of the traditional members, who control the practices of the local NAR offices, have reacted by withholding MLS listings from the discount brokers.

In 2008 the DOJ and NAR formally resolved the issue. The settlement provides that NAR cannot "directly or indirectly … prohibit a Broker … from providing to Customers on its VOW all of the Listing Information that a Broker is permitted to Provide to Customers by hand … or any other methods of delivery."[28] In the opinion of Professor Norman Hawker, "the settlement sets the stage for a burst of entrepreneurial activity in the market for brokers' services. This promises to bring about new and potentially better business models that will increase the choices and lower costs faced by home sellers and buyers."[29]

Commercial Listing Services

The manner in which buyers search for commercial properties is different from the way the search is conducted in the residential market. The commercial market does not have the extensive services, such as the MLS, that are available in the residential market. Instead, certain firms actively collect commercial property information from third parties and sell it to brokerage firms, investors, and other interested parties. One of the leading national firms, CoStar Group, has thousands of paid subscribers who access its web site for information on properties. CoStar's competitors rely more on brokers who pay to post their listings on the companies' web sites.[30]

The Duties of the Broker
Authority of the Broker

It is common to speak of a broker as a real estate agent.

> *In the most general terms, an agent is anyone who represents the interests of one person (the principal or client) in dealings with others.… Two ideas are essential to virtually all agency relationships. First, the agent is regarded as an expert on whom the principal relies for specialized professional advice. Second, an agency relationship invariably involves money or property, and the agent has a fiduciary responsibility to the principal (or client); that is, the agent must work in the client's best financial interests at all times.*[31]

general agent
An agent with broad authority to act on behalf of the principal.

special agent
An agent with authority to conduct a single transaction or a limited series of transactions.

express authority
The authority a principal specifically grants an agent.

implied authority
Implementation authority; that authority necessary to carry out the express authority that the principal grants the agent.

Certain agents, called **general agents**, have broad authority to act in place of the principal. The real estate broker's authority, unlike that of the general agent, is limited to the instructions and subject matter described by the principal. Therefore, the broker is considered a **special agent**.

The authority of the broker might be express, implied, or apparent. For example, Claudine, an owner, expressly hires Demitri, a broker, to sell her real estate. Demitri finds a buyer, Marcus, who signs a purchase agreement and gives Demitri a down payment of $30,000. If Demitri absconds with the $30,000, does the loss fall on Claudine because Demitri was her agent or on Marcus, the buyer?

If Claudine gave the broker **express authority** to accept the down payment for her, Claudine, as the principal, would bear the responsibility for the acts of Demitri, her agent, and consequently would bear the loss. Such express authority would typically be explicitly granted in the listing agreement, which could include a statement authorizing Demitri to hold purchaser deposits in escrow. If Claudine did not give Demitri express authority to accept the down payment, Marcus still might argue that authority would be implied by the fact that Claudine hired Demitri as her agent. **Implied authority** means that Demitri can do whatever is necessary and proper, such as advertising and conducting open houses, in carrying out his express authority to sell the home. Still, because Demitri is a special agent, his implied authority is narrowly defined. Thus, a broker hired merely to find a buyer has no implied authority to accept money from a buyer: "Unless specially authorized the broker has no authority other than to state the asking price and to point out the land as described by the owner.... He has no authority to receive all or part of the purchase price or to represent to a buyer who makes a deposit that the deposit will be returned if the buyer cannot obtain a mortgage. He is an agent, but with an authority to speak for the principal almost at the vanishing point."[32]

However, a broker who is expressly authorized to sign a real estate contract has the implied authority to make representations concerning the property, to give the usual warranties of title, and to receive the down payment. And a broker who is expressly authorized to sign a deed has the implied authority to receive the full purchase price for the seller since receiving the money in exchange for the deed is customary as well as necessary and proper in that particular circumstance. Even in the absence of express or implied authority, the owner, Claudine, might still be liable if Demitri had **apparent** (or **ostensible**) **authority**. This would occur if Claudine gave the impression to Marcus that Demitri had the express authority to perform certain acts on her behalf. The principal's apparent authority also creates an *agency by estoppel*. In such a case, Claudine is estopped from denying that she was Demitri's principal since she was holding herself out as such. But as the following Florida case points out, a third party such as Marcus must reasonably rely on the principal's actions and be induced into a situation in which he incurs a loss.

apparent (or ostensible) authority

Authority that a person appears to have to act as an agent of another if the other party's actions led a third party to reasonably believe the agency relationship existed, when, in fact, it did not.

A CASE IN POINT

In *Parsley Brothers Constr. Co. v. Humphrey*,[33] the plaintiff buyer, after initially making a down payment, paid the balance of the purchase price to a broker. When the broker absconded with the money, the court determined that the loss must fall on the seller. The court initially determined that real estate brokers usually have no authority to receive payments on behalf of the principal. However, in this case, the agent (Roberts) had apparent authority, which was defined by the court: "Apparent authority is that which the principal knowingly permits his agent to assume, or which a principal by his actions or words holds the agent out as possessing. Apparent authority is grounded on the estoppel doctrine which embraces generally the elements of (1) a representation by the principal, (2) reliance on that representation by a third party, and, (3) a change of position by the third party in reliance upon such representation.... It is readily discernible that Roberts had operated on a former occasion in the same manner as he had done in the present case.... The record bears out the conclusion that the agent, Roberts, was permitted to act on behalf of the owners over and above his otherwise limited authority. When one of two innocent persons must suffer for the wrongful act of a third person, the loss should fall upon the one who by reasonable diligence or care could have protected himself."

undisclosed principal

A principal whose existence and identity are unknown to the third party with whom its agent is dealing.

partially disclosed principal

A principal whose existence is known but whose identity to the third party with whom its agent is dealing is not known.

The Undisclosed and Partially Disclosed Principal and the Secret Agent

As a general rule, an agent will *not* be held personally liable for contracts negotiated on behalf of a disclosed principal. A major exception to this rule may arise in real estate transactions when there is a **partially disclosed** or an **undisclosed principal**. The primary difference between these two principals is that a partially disclosed principal's existence is known to the third party, such as a seller of land, but *not* its identity.

secret agent

An agent who represents
a principal whose
existence and identity are
unknown to the third party
with whom the agent is
dealing.

An undisclosed principal's existence and identity, on the other hand, are both unknown to the third party. The agents working for undisclosed principals are called **secret agents** because their agency status is kept secret.

Often major developers attempt to acquire large tracts of real estate by using secret agents because if the existence, and particularly, the identity of the principal were discovered before acquisition, the price of the real estate would escalate. For example, the Walt Disney Company used secret agents to assemble the property that is now Disney World in Orlando, Florida, under the pseudonym Real Estate Development Company, doing business out of Kansas City, Missouri. Roy Disney and others who supervised the land purchases also used pseudonyms when visiting properties and in their dealings with the Disney Company's secret agents so that even the agents would not know with whom they were dealing. Today the "fantasy company" is memorialized on windows on Main Street U.S.A.[R] in Disney World's Magic Kingdom.[34] Likewise, oil companies commonly use a secret agent called a "landman" to negotiate oil and gas leases on their behalf to avoid the same risk.

Once a contract with a secret agent is signed, the third party seller is bound to the contract unless the agent falsely represents that she is acting for herself and not for the principal. The buyer, as the undisclosed principal, is also bound to the contract; and after the principal's disclosure has been made, the seller may elect to hold the agent or the principal, but not both, to the contract. The same rule applies to agents working for partially disclosed principals. In order to minimize the risks of being contractually liable to third parties should they elect to go after the agent for a breach of contract, secret agents typically have indemnification clauses contained within the contracts they enter into with their principals. In the following case from Hawaii, the risks inherent in being a secret agent are demonstrated. (See Figure 6.1.)

A CASE IN POINT

In *Southwest Slopes Inc. v. Lum*, Lum contracted, as agent, to purchase 265.84 acres of vacant land in South Kona, Hawaii, for $2.65 million. Lum did not disclose the identity of his principal until eleven days after the date of contract. Although the buyer's obligation to purchase was later voided because of a material nondisclosure of the seller, the court found that Lum would have been personally liable to the seller. "The fact that the principal's identity was disclosed before the closing date of the Contract and before the end of the due diligence period is inconsequential. To avoid personal liability, Lum had to have disclosed his principal's identity on or before entering into the Contract."[35]

FIGURE 6.1
Secret Agency and the
Undisclosed Principal

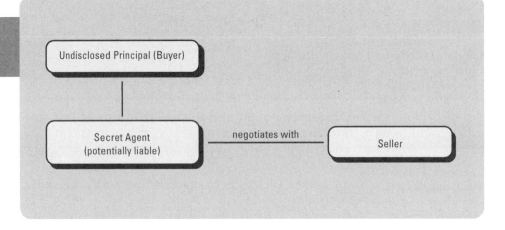

The Broker's Fiduciary Duty

fiduciary duty

A duty to act for someone else's benefit while subordinating one's personal interests to that of another person. It is the highest standard of duty imposed by law.

The real estate broker owes a **fiduciary duty**, a duty of the highest loyalty and trust, to the principal who engaged the broker. If a broker has a personal interest in a transaction, she has divided loyalties. Brokers, because of their fiduciary duty, cannot purchase the principal's real estate for themselves or for their associates without full disclosure to the principal. As a New Jersey court declared, "The broker was and is looked upon as a fiduciary and is required to exercise fidelity, good faith, and primary devotion to the interests of his principal.... [T]he failure of the broker to inform the principal that the purchaser is an *alter ego* of the broker or a relative or partner renders the transaction voidable at the option of the principal."[36]

Furthermore, even when the purchaser is not associated with the broker, the broker must put the interest of the principal first. In a quote from the Arizona Supreme Court in *Haymes v. Rogers:*[37]

> A real estate agent owes the duty of utmost good faith and loyalty to his principal. The immediate problem here is whether the above proposition is applicable to the facts in this instance. The question is, is it a breach of a fiduciary duty and a betrayal of loyalty for a real estate broker to inform a prospective purchaser that a piece of realty may be purchased for less than the list price? We believe that such conduct is a breach of faith and contrary to the interest of his principal, and therefore, is a violation of the fiduciary relationship existing between agent and principal which will preclude the agent from recovering a commission therefrom.

Agents breach their fiduciary duty when they secretly receive a commission from the prospective buyer even though they have performed the contract as promised for the principal, as occurred in the following Georgia case.

A CASE IN POINT

In *Spratlin, Harrington & Thomas, Inc. v. Hawn,*[38] the agent, a mortgage banking firm, was engaged by the principal for a promised $50,000 commission to obtain a $10,000,000 loan commitment. After the agent obtained a commitment from the American National Insurance Company, the principal refused to pay the commission on the grounds that the agent received a finder's fee and a servicing fee from the insurance company without telling the principal. The court, in relying on earlier cases, decided that the principal did not have to pay the commission: "The first duty of an agent is that of loyalty to his trust. He must not put himself in relations which are antagonistic to that of his principal. His duty and interest must not be allowed to conflict. He cannot deal in the business within the scope of his own benefit ... nor is he permitted to compromise himself by attempting to serve two masters having a contrary interest unless it be that such contracts of dual agency are known to each of the principals. ... Simply stated, the Biblical expression ... is apt: 'No man can serve two masters; for either he will hate the one and love the other, or else he will hold to the one and despise the other.'"

MLSs raise complex fiduciary duty issues. Clearly, the broker hired by the seller (the listing broker) owes a fiduciary duty to the seller. But the agent who locates the buyer (the selling broker)—who is legally considered a "subagent"—also owes the seller a fiduciary duty. (See Figure 6.2.) Buyers who consider the subagent to be their agent frequently misunderstand this point. Since these subagents generally deal with the buyers only, they often do not even meet the sellers—the parties to whom they owe their

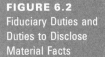

FIGURE 6.2
Fiduciary Duties and
Duties to Disclose
Material Facts

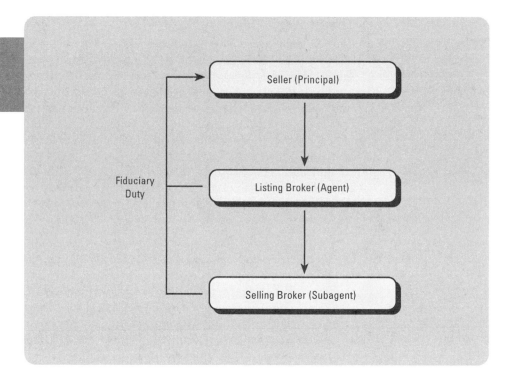

fiduciary duties. This can have negative consequences for buyers who freely give the sub-agent important confidential information, such as what they are willing to pay the seller, thereby compromising their own interests.

ETHICAL AND PUBLIC POLICY ISSUES

Can an Agent Serve "Two Masters"?

That becomes the issue in a dual agency situation in which an agent represents both seller and buyer. This issue is discussed in Problem 10 at the end of the chapter.

However, there are *five* types of protection for buyers, particularly those pertaining to the problems with subagency:

1. The laws in most states require brokers to disclose to their clients, as well as all others involved in the transaction, whether they are representing their principal as a seller, buyer, or dual agent, as well as the duties owed to the party or parties. This important policy development, which resulted in new statutes being passed throughout the 1990s called **mandatory agency disclosure laws** (see www.cengagebrain.com [see page xix in the Preface for instructions on how to access the free study tools for this text] to view Massachusetts' form for disclosing agency status), has lessened the problems associated with subagency in which buyers thought a broker was representing them when, in fact, the agent was a subagent of the seller.[39] Although the requirements differ among the states, in general, agents must inform their client in writing as to the party (buyer, seller, or both) they represent as soon as the principal/ agency relationship begins to take shape. (See endnote 39 to read Nevada's mandatory agency disclosure statute).

mandatory agency disclosure laws

State laws requiring agents to disclose to consumers the type of agents they are and the rights and duties that exist in their relationships with the consumers.

Sellers and buyers can, after disclosure of the risks, agree to a dual agency arrangement. Dual agency, however, is fraught with problems, including the likelihood of mistrust, as the parties in *Bazal v. Rhines, Palma and Skogman Realty Co.* on page 205 discovered.

END OF CHAPTER CASE

dual agency

A relationship created when an agent simultaneously represents opposite sides in a transaction.

2. Brokers have, on occasion, accidentally created a **dual agency** in which they owe a fiduciary duty to both a buyer and a seller. A court, for example, might imply a buyer-broker agency relationship when a broker tells a buyer that a seller's house is overpriced, thus breaching the fiduciary duties he owes the seller. Such situations are costly to brokers, who will lose commissions and may even be disciplined by their state's real estate commission under mandatory agency disclosure laws if the dual agency is not disclosed.[40]

3. Courts in several states have concluded that selling brokers, including subagents, owe a duty of disclosure to buyers even though a fiduciary duty does not exist where the selling agent fails to disclose facts "materially affecting the value or desirability of the property offered for sale." (See discussion on page 191.)

4. It is increasingly common, in the wake of both mandatory agency disclosure statutes and legal/ethical problems associated with subagency, for buyers to hire their own brokers. The agents, called **buyer brokers**, owe only the buyer fiduciary duties.

buyer broker

A real estate agent who acts on behalf of the buyer.

5. States are experimenting with more new models to further improve the quality and choice of service for both sellers and buyers. These models include the following:

   a. *Designated agency*: Under this model, a disclosed dual agent cannot legally represent both buyers and sellers. Instead, the broker must provide for two agents within the company, called *in-house agents* or *split agents*, to represent the buyer and seller independently. Both agents would owe their respective parties fiduciary duties.

   b. *Two-tiered service*: Under this model, buyers and sellers are classified as either customers or clients. An agent owes traditional fiduciary duties to clients, but not to customers for whom they perform only "ministerial acts." These include answering questions and attending open houses. As long as licensees engage in only these acts for their customers, they are provided with a "safe harbor" under the law and cannot be held liable for a breach of fiduciary duties.

   c. *Transactional broker*: In this business model, a broker performs only transactional duties but does not represent either party as an agent. A transactional broker is defined under Colorado law, the first state to create this model, as "[a] broker who assists one or more parties throughout a contemplated real estate transaction with communication, interposition, advisement, negotiation, contract terms, and the closing of such real estate transaction without being an agent or advocate for the interests of any party to such transaction...."[41]

The states that have adopted some or all of these models also retain the traditional model of exclusive agency and subagency and generally permit dual agency as long as it is disclosed. Still, in most states, buyers and sellers, as stated previously, must be informed under mandatory agency disclosure laws about the characteristics of these various kinds of agency models and what the laws mean to real estate consumers.

Buyer Brokering

Due in part to the preceding problems, buyer brokering is becoming increasingly common. (See a buyer broker form at www.cengagebrain.com [see page xix in the Preface for instructions on how to access the free study tools for this text].) As mentioned, many of the legal and ethical problems associated with subagency are avoided when both parties have their own broker. Buying property is complicated, and both sellers and buyers often prefer someone who gives them their undivided loyalty.

The concept of buyer brokering, however, is still encountering problems in an industry that is sometimes slow to change. For example, many buyer brokers are reluctant to obtain written contracts from their clients, at least at the inception of the relationship. Since there never was a contract between the subagent and the buyer, this appears to be an old habit that is difficult to break. However, the problem is lessening as buyer brokering becomes more common.

There also are problems relating to the relationship between the broker and the seller. Because brokers have traditionally acted as the seller's agent, it has been recommended (and is legally required in most states) that "the existence of the buyer brokering arrangement should be made known to the seller or the seller's agent, and [the buyer's broker] should take care that an inadvertent dual agency is not created by a buyer's broker leading a seller to believe that the broker is the listing broker's subagent."[42] With mandatory agency disclosure laws requiring agents to disclose whom they are representing, this problem also is being managed better.

A further problem is that subagents often ask the prospective buyers with whom they are dealing to submit earnest money deposits, sometimes significant amounts, to protect the seller to whom they owe fiduciary duties. Buyer brokers, on the other hand, must negotiate for an amount that is most beneficial for the buyer. According to one commentator, many agents must now be trained to think more in the interests of buyers, when before the emphasis was to represent only the seller's interests.[43]

While buyer brokering arrangements should clarify fiduciary responsibilities owed to the buyer, potential conflicts still exist. For instance, a broker whose fee is a percentage of the purchase price may lack the incentive to negotiate a lower price on behalf of the buyer since that would cause the buyer's broker to lose money.[44] Moreover, while most people think that buyers would automatically want to have their own broker representing only their interests, a broker-client relationship is a two-way street. Since buyer brokers have a heightened responsibility that requires more time and money devoted to their clients, many buyer brokers now require their principal, the prospective buyer, to sign an exclusive agency agreement. This means that if the buyer leaves for another broker or finds his own property to buy, the buyer may owe his own broker a commission since that term is typically agreed to in the contract. Despite these concerns, buyer brokers afford more protection for their clients than a subagent would because of the fiduciary duties they owe, as the next California case demonstrates.

Does a buyer's agent have a fiduciary duty to disclose the statutorily required information supplied by the seller regarding the quality of the house? In *Saiz v. Horn* on page 207, the court answers that question.

END OF CHAPTER CASE

The Selling Broker's Duty of Disclosure to Buyers

Although the listing broker (as well as the subagent) typically owes a fiduciary duty to the seller, courts have increasingly imposed upon the broker the duty to disclose to the *buyer* facts "materially affecting the value or desirability of the property offered for sale"[45] that would not be readily ascertainable by the buyer. With the increasing use of buyer brokers, this problem should lessen since a buyer broker, in contrast to the seller's broker or the subagent, clearly owes a fiduciary duty to her principal to exercise reasonable care in discovering and revealing such material facts about the property. Yet, in the next two cases, from California and New Jersey respectively, the courts ruled that the sellers' brokers also owed duties to disclose certain material facts to the buyers.

A CASE IN POINT

In *Easton v. Strassburger*,[46] the purchasers of a residence that suffered major landslide damage sued the seller's broker, claiming that because the broker knew that the property had earth movement problems in the past, a soil stability test should have been performed. The court concluded that, at least in the sale of residential property, a broker has a duty to disclose not only known facts but also facts that should have been discovered through reasonable diligence.

A CASE IN POINT

In *Strawn v. Canuso*,[47] more than 150 families purchased homes near a closed hazardous waste dump. The New Jersey court held that not only the developers but also their brokers had a "duty to disclose off-site conditions that materially affect the value or desirability of the property."

To protect themselves from such lawsuits, brokers typically require the seller to sign a written disclosure statement describing the condition of the property. Moreover, a majority of states now require that such a disclosure be made prior to closing, while other states require delivery of such a disclosure to the buyer at the time of contracting.[48] Seller disclosure laws are discussed in Chapter 7.

Selling brokers and subagents may also owe certain duties not just to actual buyers but to potential buyers as well. A broker, for example, held an open house at a listed property to attract potential buyers. One visitor slipped and fell. The New Jersey courts supported the visitor's claim that the broker had the duty of making a reasonable inspection of the property and warning her of reasonably discoverable dangerous conditions. Here, the claim was that patterned vinyl flooring concealed a step that led to the fall.[49] A Tennessee court also has held that a broker showing a partially completed home was liable for injuries a prospective purchaser suffered when the broker was showing the property.[50]

ETHICAL AND PUBLIC POLICY ISSUES

Do Real Estate Agents Have a Duty to Inform Buyers about Neighborhood Sex Offenders?

Since New Jersey's passage of "Megan's Law" in 1994, most states now post information in some manner about convicted sex offenders living in certain neighborhoods. The object is to disclose to

continues

continued

parents of young children where these offenders live so the parents can take protective measures. Real estate agents are in a quandary over how to comply with the law. A seller's agent (and subagent) has a fiduciary duty to negotiate for the best price on behalf of her client. Quite possibly, information about convicted child molesters in the vicinity would scare off prospective buyers and even stigmatize and depress overall prices in the neighborhood. On the other hand, the seller's agent must report to buyers material information that may affect the property's value. Since this is not the traditional kind of information divulged to buyers—as opposed to the physical condition of the property and surrounding environs—should sellers' agents and subagents be morally or legally required to make this kind of disclosure?

The Broker's Unauthorized Practice of Law

Every state limits the practice of law within its borders to attorneys who have complied with a regulatory process imposing educational, competency, and character requirements. Thus, just as a broker needs a license, so does a lawyer. A broker's license is not an authorization to practice law, although often a broker's work borders on such practice.

Were real estate sales agents responsible for not correctly explaining a "nonrecourse clause" or for failing to recommend legal counsel to their client sellers? In *Crutchley v. First Trust and Savings Bank* on page 208, the court considers that question.

END OF CHAPTER CASE

The courts are generally divided on the question of what constitutes unauthorized practice of law. Most courts have decided that a broker's law-related activities are limited to filling in blanks on standard printed forms if this service is incidental to the real estate transaction and if the broker makes no separate charge for the service. As a general rule, the broker may not draft the forms and may not give legal advice.

A broker might be reluctant to recommend that buyers or sellers seek legal counsel for fear that doubts raised by attorneys could result in termination of negotiations. Attorneys, however, believe that without sound legal advice, the parties might be pushed into an unfair deal. One solution, adopted as a result of a statewide agreement between lawyers and brokers in New Jersey, is the attorney review clause:

ATTORNEY REVIEW: IF BUYER or SELLER elects to consult an attorney, this contract shall be subject to such attorney's review of all of its terms and conditions within three (3) business days (exclusive of Saturdays, Sundays and legal holidays) from the date of the delivery of the signed contract to the BUYER and SELLER…. An attorney's notice of disapproval shall be served upon the Broker(s) either by certified mail or telegram, effective upon sending, or by personal delivery, effective upon receipt.

Under this clause, an attorney can disapprove the contract for any reason and has no duty to state a reason.[51]

The Internet and the Future of the Real Estate Broker

With the advent of the Internet, an increasing number of real estate commentators believe that the traditional relationships between brokers, sellers, and buyers will change profoundly. Indeed, the success of sellers and buyers using the Internet to facilitate real estate transactions is undeniable. One study suggests that about 70 percent of home-buyers now use the Internet when looking for a house.[52]

Possibly the biggest threat the Internet poses is to the traditional MLS system that, as discussed earlier, created a cartel-like role by the NAR in controlling real estate listings. Information posted on the web bypasses the MLS, offering free information to prospective buyers, often from the property owners themselves. Recognizing the power of the Internet as well as the futility of containing this information, large national real estate brokerage firms such as Coldwell Banker and Prudential now feature their listings on their own web sites and tie these listings to their affiliated brokers. Indeed, there are web sites that not only show buyers prospective homes but also offer virtual "walk-throughs," financing, title and homeowner's insurance, and attorneys. All of these features might reduce the need for a broker, who traditionally contacted and worked with these parties on behalf of the client.[53]

Despite these adaptations to the Internet, the traditional broker must still contend with discount and network brokers, some of whom also maintain a VOW. Moreover, sites directly competing against the MLS, such as Craigslist, Google, and Zillow, which post listings by nontraditional brokers as well as by owners, also challenge the traditional broker for customers.[54]

In the future, the real estate brokerage business will confront new and untested relationships that develop between brokers and the many parties with whom they deal, including those parties who are increasingly bypassing the traditional broker. This development, in turn, will give rise to new cyberlaw issues, including the use of electronic contracts, jurisdictional issues, fraud, computer crimes, and trademark infringement.[55]

Interstate Land Sales Full Disclosure Act

Interstate Land Sales Full Disclosure Act

A 1968 federal statute that regulates the sale of property across state lines by requiring certain advance filings and disclosures to prospective buyers.

Elmer had worked his entire life in a factory in a midwestern state. As he approached retirement, he considered purchasing real estate in a warm climate, where he hoped to relocate after retirement. One day Elmer was contacted by Slick Development Corporation. A representative of Slick invited Elmer to a local restaurant for a free steak dinner and a slide show describing real estate investments in Arizona. Elmer accepted the invitation; and at the restaurant, the representative used a combination of cajolery and threats to persuade Elmer to use his life's savings to purchase a lot in a new development. A few years later Elmer retired and traveled to Arizona to inspect his lot for the first time. After much searching, he found the lot—in the middle of a desert, miles away from utilities, roads, and civilization.

Cases such as Elmer's led Congress to enact legislation in 1968 to protect buyers in interstate land sales or leases. The **Interstate Land Sales Full Disclosure Act**,[56] as amended in 1979, imposes *two* major requirements on developers who offer for sale or lease unimproved lots in interstate commerce. *First*, developers must file a statement of record with the Department of Housing and Urban Development (HUD) before offering unimproved lots for sale or lease. *Second*, a property report must be given to buyers before a contract is signed. This report is a summary of the statement of record and includes such information as the existence of liens on the property, the availability of sewer and water service, the type of title the buyer will receive, and the distance by road to nearby communities. The use of the U.S. Postal Service is sufficient to satisfy the Act's broad definition of interstate commerce as pointed out in the following South Carolina case.

A CASE IN POINT

In *Gibbes v. Rose Hill Plantation Development Co.,*[57] Termotto and Gibbes purchased properties at Rose Hill Plantation. Later, they argued that the property report and oral representations were materially inaccurate. Termotto, who was a serious polo player, purchased his property from the developer. Gibbes purchased his property from the Blizzaris because, as a polo player, he was interested in planned stables in the development. The court held that Gibbes had no cause of action under the Interstate Land Sales Full Disclosure Act because he did not purchase from the developer or the developer's agent. Termotto had a cause of action against only the developer, as the sales agent had not commenced its representation of the developer at the time of Termotto's purchase. Yet, the court held that if Termotto could prove that he relied on the developer's oral misrepresentations of the size of the proposed equestrian center, it would be a valid cause of action under the Act.

The Act includes a number of important *exemptions* in the sale or leasing of land as follows:

1. Lots in a subdivision with fewer than 25 lots if they are part of a common promotional plan
2. Lots in subdivisions containing at least 25 but fewer than 100 lots so long as the Act's antifraud provisions are not violated
3. Lots in a subdivision of 20 acres or more in size
4. Sales of securities by a real estate investment trust
5. Land improved by a completed residential, commercial, condominium, or industrial building
6. Land in which the seller is explicitly obligated under the contract to complete the improvement within two years from the date of contract
7. Lots sold to a builder who is in the business of constructing improvements and who intends to resell the lot to the ultimate consumer
8. Land zoned for industrial or commercial use and other land subject to certain land use restrictions
9. Land purchased or leased by a real estate corporation, partnership, trust, or business entity engaged in commercial or industrial business
10. Land owned by the government or its agencies
11. Cemetery lots

With the growth of time-shares and similar types of developments, courts, as in the Michigan case that follows, have been asked to address the issue of whether interests in hotel units fall under the Act.

A CASE IN POINT

In *Becherer v. Merrill Lynch Fenner & Smith,*[58] 298 investors suffered financial losses associated with purchases of unit interests in a proposed 474-room resort hotel. The issue was whether a unit interest is a "lot" under the Interstate Land Sales Full Disclosure Act's definition. A lot is defined as "any portion, piece, division, unit, or undivided interest in land located in any state or foreign country if the interest includes the right to the exclusive use of a specific portion of the land." The court ruled that the investors were not protected under the Interstate Land Sales Full Disclosure Act because the hotel units were to be used for hotel accommodations, not for the exclusive use of the investor. The court explained that under the scheme, "the investors' financing and ownership of the units is in condominium form, but in reality the units are hotel rooms, designed only for use as hotel rooms, may not be used for residential purposes, and were clearly sold as business investments in a hotel."

A seller who fails to comply with the Act is subject to both civil and criminal penalties. The civil penalties can range from $1,000 to $1,000,000. In addition, a plaintiff can sue and recover civil damages, such as the costs of attorneys' fees, travel costs, and appraisals, as well as remedies the court decides are fair and just, such as the right of the buyer to cancel the contract and obtain a refund of payment if a property report was not furnished. The maximum criminal penalty for violation of the Act is a fine of $10,000, five years' imprisonment, or both. The Act applies to developers and "agents." An agent is defined as a person who "represents, or acts for or on behalf of, a developer."[59]

In the wake of the Great Recession of 2007-2009 and real estate crisis, the Act has been increasingly used to nullify real estate contracts for projects that have gone bust. In particular, out-of-state buyers of condominiums have argued that developers failed to complete their projects within two years (see #6 above) and so lost their exemption from the Act's filing and reporting requirements. For example, large condominium projects in West Palm Beach, Florida; Las Vegas; and Orange Beach, Alabama were not completed within two years due to economic and other setbacks suffered by the developers. The Orange Beach developers countered that they were unable to finish construction due to hurricane Katrina and so are attempting to quash the lawsuits under the defense of Force Majeure (act of God).[60]

Discrimination in Selling or Leasing Real Estate

The United States has a long history of segregation in housing. For example, in 1923, the National Association of Real Estate Boards (NAREB) published textbooks that stated that African-American families were a threat to property values and "foreigners" were undesirable residents. As late as 1950, the NAREB code of ethics in many cities directed that:

> [t]he realtor should not be instrumental in introducing into a neighborhood ... members of any race or nationality or any individual whose presence will clearly be detrimental to property values in the neighborhood[61]

Two civil rights acts have been especially important in the battle against discrimination: the Civil Rights Act of 1866 and Title VIII (the Fair Housing Act, FHA) of the Civil Rights Act of 1968.

Civil Rights Act of 1866

1866 Civil Rights Act
A post–Civil War federal statute prohibiting race discrimination in connection with real and personal property transactions.

The **1866 Civil Rights Act** (42 U.S.C.A. §1982) states that "all citizens of the United States shall have the same right in every State and Territory, as is enjoyed by white citizens thereof to inherit, purchase, lease, sell, hold and convey real and personal property." In the leading decision of *Jones v. Alfred H. Mayer Co.*,[62] the Supreme Court held that this statute was valid under the Thirteenth Amendment, which prohibits slavery and involuntary servitude. In the words of the Court, the Act prohibits "all racial discrimination, private as well as public, in the sale or rental of property." A victim of discrimination on racial grounds may take the case to federal court; and the court may award damages, prevent the sale of the house to someone else, or force the seller to transfer the property to the plaintiff.

Fair Housing Legislation

1968 Fair Housing Act
Title VIII of the Civil Rights Act of 1968 that prohibits discrimination in housing based on race, color, religion, sex, and national origin.

Fair Housing Amendments Act of 1988
The Act incorporated into the Fair Housing Act of 1968 that added familial status and handicap as protected classifications and strengthened enforcement procedures.

The **1968 Fair Housing Act** (FHA) extends the 1866 Act's prohibition of discrimination to additional categories. The FHA prohibits discrimination on the grounds of race, color, religion, sex, and national origin. Disability and familial status were added by the **Fair Housing Amendments Act of 1988** (FHAA).

The FHA prohibits the following actions against members of the protected groups:

1. Refusing to sell to, rent to, deal, or negotiate with any person—that is, denying housing because of membership in a protected category
2. Manifesting discrimination in the terms or conditions for buying or renting housing
3. Discriminating by advertising that housing is available only to persons of a certain race, color, religion, or national origin or indicating a discriminatory preference through the use of human models[63]
4. Denying that housing is available for inspection, sale, or rent when it really is available
5. **Steering** and **blockbusting**—for example, persuading owners to sell or rent housing by telling them that minority groups are moving into the neighborhood
6. Denying or establishing different terms for home loans by commercial lenders
7. Denying someone the use of real estate services
8. Using interference, coercion, or intimidation to chill the exercise of fair housing rights
9. Discriminating in financing and insurance[64]

> **steering**
>
> The practice of showing different properties to people of different races or ethnic backgrounds in an attempt to "steer" them to neighborhoods of like composition.

> **blockbusting**
>
> The attempt to promote sales in a racially transitional neighborhood by encouraging the idea that the transition is harmful.

Discriminatory advertisements have long been a contentious issue under the FHA since people often look for a certain kind of person to rent to or live with but cannot, at the same time, discriminate against protected groups. The next case discusses this issue.

> In *Fair Housing Council of San Fernando Valley v. Roommates.com, LLC* on page 210, the court ruled whether an Internet service provider that published advertisements for people seeking roommates may have violated the FHA by allowing specific information about a person's gender, race, family status, and other characteristics on its web site.

END OF CHAPTER CASE

Courts have widely found that principals such as landlords are responsible for the discriminatory conduct of their agents, even when the principal makes serious attempts to avoid discriminatory conduct.[65] Therefore, the owner cannot rely on a management company, but must enforce strict compliance herself.[66]

> Is the owner-broker of a real estate brokerage firm personally liable if one of his agents violates the FHA by engaging in racial discrimination? In *Meyer v. Holley* on page 212, the U.S Supreme Court discusses the issue.

END OF CHAPTER CASE

The FHA is often enforced by using "testers" sent out by the government or private civil rights groups. Testing usually involves using both a black and white tester who individually attempts to buy or lease a particular home or apartment. If the agent, seller, or lessor agrees to deal with the white but not the black tester, or vice versa, he may be subject to a lawsuit, an administrative hearing, and sometimes substantial damages and civil penalties, as discussed shortly.

**ETHICAL AND
PUBLIC POLICY
ISSUES**

Is It Ethical to Lie to Avoid Blockbusting?

Bob is a salesperson prospecting for potential listings in a predominantly white neighborhood in suburban New Orleans. The neighborhood has recently become more racially mixed with the arrival of a few African-American families. Bob works for a real estate company that has been enjoying great success in listing and selling houses in this particular neighborhood for over a year. Bob's marketing efforts involve knocking on doors and asking the homeowners if they would like to list their property for sale. To enhance his chances of securing a listing, Bob adds that the agents in his company are experts on the neighborhood and that they have recently sold a number of homes in the vicinity. Bob also emphasizes that he and his company would work hard to do the same for the homeowners if they decided to list with his company. Bob's managing broker, George, was concerned about the possibility that Bob may appear, albeit unintentionally, to be violating the FHA by blockbusting. Often the homeowners, if they were white, would ask if the new buyer down the street was African American, which, in many cases, they were. If Bob answered yes, it might look as though he was attempting to frighten the seller into listing his home for sale. However, if Bob answered no, he would be lying, which could later taint his relationship with any homeowners who might list their homes with him and affect his professional reputation in general. To solve the dilemma, George advised Bob to simply say that he did not know the race of the buyers since other agents, not he, had dealt with them. However, Bob often *did* know the race of the buyer. Is George's advice ethical? Indeed, blockbusting can often cause "white flight" as sellers drop their prices for fear the prices will go even lower due to the change in racial makeup. However, by being honest and answering yes, Bob could benefit himself since he may get multiple listings and sales as well as attractive investments for himself after the prices reach very low levels. Still, is it ever ethical to lie even if it avoids a legal problem?

In an interesting new twist to housing discrimination practices, African-American real estate agents hired by an Atlanta-based builder, John Weiland Homes and Neighborhoods, sued for employment discrimination under the Civil Rights Act of 1964. The agents are alleging that they are employees who were assigned to sell homes in black neighborhoods only and that as a result, they earned lower commissions than white agents who were sent to sell houses in wealthier white neighborhoods.[67]

Although the 1968 Act prohibits several types of discrimination, it does not cover all types of housing. The Act's exemptions are narrowly interpreted, while the prohibitions against discrimination tend to be broadly interpreted.

The Act does not cover the sale or rental of a single-family house owned by a private individual who owns fewer than four such houses if (1) a broker is not used, (2) discriminatory advertising is not used, and (3) no more than one house in which the owner was not the most recent resident is sold within a two-year period.

The 1968 Act also does not apply to:

1. Rentals in owner-occupied apartment buildings that house fewer than five families as long as discriminatory advertising is not used.
2. Religious organizations that limit the sale or rental of noncommercial dwellings to people of the same religion if the religion is not restricted on the basis of race, color, or national origin.
3. A private club that limits rental of its noncommercial property to its members.[68]

The FHAA added two new protected classifications: familial status and handicap. Handicap includes "a physical or mental disability (including hearing, mobility and visual impairments, chronic alcoholism, chronic mental illness, AIDS, AIDS related complex and mental retardation) that substantially limits one or more major life activities" as well as those who "have a record of such a disability or are regarded as having such a disability."[69] Familial status is meant to protect young families with children who are often raised by a single mother, a grandparent, or a foster parent. Often these families are considered by landlords to be less creditworthy than families headed by a father or two parents.[70] The Act defines familial status as "one or more individuals (who have not attained the age of 18 years) being domiciled with (1) a parent or another person having legal custody of such individual or individuals; or (2) the designee of such parent or other person having such custody...."[71]

However, the Act does exempt certain planned unit developments that adopt a policy specifying that 80 percent of the occupied units must have at least one person who is fifty-five or over living in them. If a development qualifies for the exemption, anyone under nineteen can be legally excluded.[72] The exemption was expanded in 1995 under the Housing for Older Persons Act (HOPA) by eliminating the requirement that a planned unit development provide "significant facilities and services" for the elderly as well as including a safe harbor for those who, in good faith, believed the development was in compliance even when it was not.[73]

The FHAA also strengthened the FHA by adding three new enforcement methods, as follows:

1. HUD may initiate cases that will be heard in a federal court or (if all parties agree) by an administrative law judge. The penalties for violating the law might include (depending on whether an administrative or court proceeding is used) actual and punitive damages; a civil penalty of up to $50,000; and equitable relief, such as issuance of an injunction. The U.S. Attorney General and equivalent state agencies also may enforce the FHA.
2. A person who has been subjected to discrimination may file a private suit in a federal or state court, which is authorized to award actual damages, punitive damages, and equitable relief. Moreover, plaintiffs may file the suit in a federal court even if an administrative complaint had been filed previously in a state administrative proceeding.
3. If a pattern or practice of discrimination is alleged, the attorney general may commence a civil action to enforce the Act. In such cases, a court may award damages and equitable relief and may assess a civil penalty of up to $100,000.

The FHA and its amendments are relevant not only to sellers and landlords but also to real estate brokers. For example, real estate brokers who have disabled clients should be aware of the pertinent FHA laws to ensure that their clients are not the victims of illegal and unethical discrimination with regard to the physical aspects as well as the policies that exist in the apartments and condominiums their clients may want to lease or buy.

The FHAA requires that new multifamily dwellings, defined as those buildings with four or more units in which first occupancy was on or after March 13, 1991, must be made accessible to the disabled. The Act is aimed particularly at helping wheelchair users who may want to buy or lease property. These dwellings, which include most apartments and condominiums, must have the following seven modifications in place:

1. Accessible building entrance on accessible routes
2. Accessible and usable public and common use areas, such as swimming pools and laundry rooms
3. Usable doors within the entire premises, with clear passage of thirty-two inches opening to ninety degrees
4. Routes into and through the dwelling unit, including only a half-inch to three-quarter-inch threshold

5. Light switches, electrical outlets, thermostats, and other environmental controls in accessible locations
6. Reinforced walls for grab bars
7. Usable kitchens and bathrooms for wheelchair maneuverability

In recent years, many developers have been sued for not complying with these modifications, forcing the developers to incur expensive retrofitting costs—costs that would have been negligible had they built their dwellings correctly.[74] If a covered dwelling was occupied before 1991 or is a newer dwelling but a necessary modification, such as a wheelchair ramp, is not one of the seven items listed, a landlord cannot prevent a disabled tenant from modifying his dwelling at the tenant's own expense. But the landlord can require the tenant, upon leaving, to restore the apartment to the condition it was before the modification.

Landlords in dwellings covered under the FHAA also have a duty to accommodate their disabled tenants if their rules or policies might impair the tenants' ability to lease and use the dwelling. In a series of cases, this duty has been construed as accommodating disabled tenants who were late in paying their rent due to a sickness or disability, permitting disabled people with certain kinds of pets—such as hearing dogs—to lease even though the apartment's policy did not allow pets, and even requiring (as the next case from Colorado demonstrates) a landlord to prove why he should not accommodate a mentally disabled and dangerous tenant.[75]

A CASE IN POINT

In *Roe v. City of Boulder*,[76] the tenant Roe was a seventy-nine-year-old manic depressive living in a low-income home for the elderly and disabled. Roe engaged in threatening behavior, including striking other elderly tenants, screaming in loud and obscene outbursts, and causing the discontinuance of Meals on Wheels service due to his hostile conduct. The landlord argued that Roe was a threat to other tenants and sought to evict him. The eviction was stayed until the landlord could prove that no reasonable accommodation was available that might eliminate or acceptably minimize the risks Roe imposed on the other tenants.

The *Roe* case begs the questions of how far the landlord must go in accommodating both new and existing tenants. Although the case law is still developing, the FHAA will not require landlords to accommodate disabled tenants if it imposes an undue financial or administrative burden or fundamentally alters the nature of the premises. Of course, the landlord in *Roe* could argue that forcing an accommodation of a tenant such as Roe would essentially convert the apartment complex into a nursing home, thus altering its primary functions as well as incurring added costs to monitor Roe's behavior and perhaps even his medication. Landlords may face similar problems when leasing to chronic alcoholics, who are considered disabled under the Act and so may also have to be accommodated in some manner.

The net result of the two civil rights acts, just discussed, is that discrimination on the basis of race or color is never allowed, while other types of discrimination covered in the 1968 Act are not allowed unless one of the exemptions applies. As the Supreme Court noted in comparing the 1866 Act (42 U.S.C.A. §1982) with the 1968 Act:

Whatever else it may be, 42 U.S.C.A. §1982 is not a comprehensive open housing law. In sharp contrast to the Fair Housing Title (Title VIII) of the Civil Rights Act of 1968, … the statute in this case deals only with racial discrimination and does not address itself to discrimination on grounds of religion or national origin. It does not deal specifically with discrimination in the provision of services or facilities in connection with the sale or rental of a dwelling. It does not prohibit advertising or other representations that indicate discriminatory preferences. It does not refer explicitly to discrimination in financing arrangements or in the provision of brokerage services. It does not empower a federal administrative agency to assist aggrieved persons. It makes no provision for interventions by the Attorney General. And, although it can be enforced by injunction, it contains no provision expressly authorizing a federal court to order the payment of damages.... [There are] vast differences between, on the one hand, a general statute applicable only to racial discrimination in the rental and sale of property and enforceable only by private parties acting on their own initiative, and, on the other hand, a detailed housing law, applicable to a broad range of discriminatory practices and enforceable by a complete arsenal of federal authority.[77]

Americans with Disabilities Act of 1990

A federal statute that prohibits discrimination based on disability and requires reasonable accommodation by employers and landowners.

The **Americans with Disabilities Act of 1990** (ADA) has also significantly impacted real estate construction and the renovation of existing facilities. For brokers representing buyers and sellers of commercial properties, this can become very important. Such brokers may be breaching their fiduciary duties of care since they are professionals who should be knowledgeable about the ADA and other laws that can greatly impact their principals. For example, Title III of the ADA prohibits hotels, motels, and other places of public accommodation from discriminating against disabled individuals. The Act requires the removal of existing architectural barriers by installing ramps and curb cuts, widening doors, and adding accessible parking if these and other measures are "readily achievable" (that is, able to be accomplished with little difficulty or expense). The Act also provides that places of public accommodation and commercial facilities must make new buildings and areas that are undergoing alterations in existing buildings "readily accessible" to the disabled.[78] For example, Radio Shack agreed to settle a lawsuit in which it must eventually make all of its 5,000 stores more accessible to the handicapped. This includes widening the store aisles to thirty-six inches, clearing them of merchandise, having credit and debit card readers that are accessible to those who cannot reach the counter, and adopting programs to make managers and sales associates more sensitive to issues that impact the disabled.[79] In an interesting variation on this issue, the National Federation of the Blind sued Target arguing that under the ADA, the chain should be made *virtually* accessible through its web site. Target later settled and agreed to add code to permit screen-reader software that vocalizes text and describes the store's products on its web site.[80]

State and Local Laws

In addition to federal law, a number of state and local open housing or fair housing laws are directed at private discrimination in housing. These laws often go further than federal law in prohibiting discrimination on other grounds. Massachusetts, for instance, outlaws housing discrimination based on all of the same protections afforded by the FHA, in addition to sexual orientation, genetic information, ancestry, and status as a military veteran.[81] Local laws also are subject to scrutiny by the federal courts to ensure that they do not compromise the protections offered by the FHA. For example, the Supreme Court has held that a municipality's limit on the number of unrelated people who can live together in a single-family residence is subject to scrutiny under the FHA, a topic discussed in Chapter 13.[82]

Often these zoning ordinances are used to keep out people who are perceived as harming the home value and image of certain neighborhoods. These laws, resulting from an attitude that is sometimes called *NIMBY* (Not In My Backyard), affects the living conditions for many disabled individuals by forcing group homes for the mentally disabled, recovering drug users and alcoholics, AIDS victims, and those suffering from psychological problems to be built in less desirable or accessible parts of the city. Generally, the ordinances violate the FHA's 1988 Amendments as well as Title II of the ADA. However, a recently revitalized Eleventh Amendment to the U.S. Constitution, which now has been construed to prevent citizens, under certain federal laws, from suing their own state and local governments in federal courts, may be interpreted to preempt both the FHA and ADA Title II. Should this occur, aggrieved citizens such as the disabled will have to rely more on state and local antidiscrimination laws.[83]

An intriguing NIMBY issue arose among the over 100,000 people forced to live in Federal Emergency Management Agency (FEMA) trailers in the wake of Hurricane Katrina in 2005. Concerned that these trailer communities, derisively called "FEMA-villes," would depress real estate values and breed crime and blight, local governments in Louisiana and Mississippi attempted to relocate them away from towns and schools to more remote areas or even out of their jurisdictions. This controversy is still ongoing due to a slow economy and bureaucratic inefficiencies.[84]

ETHICAL AND PUBLIC POLICY ISSUES

Should Cities Outlaw Feeding the Homeless in Public Places to Protect Parks and Neighborhoods?

Cities across the United States are wrestling with how to handle the millions of homeless people who frequent public areas, including parks within residential neighborhoods. Homeless people, many of whom have serious mental problems, often refuse to live in government-provided housing and do not want to eat at government food banks to avoid being controlled by social services. As a result, many homeless people congregate in public parks and other areas, begging for food and money. Moreover, some charitable groups hand out meals in these parks. Many people complain that the homeless ruin the parks by littering, including leaving drug needles, garbage, and beer bottles, causing home values in the area to drop and people to use the parks less frequently. In an effort to remove the homeless from the parks, some cities fine those who feed them to discourage the homeless from coming to the parks. Civil liberty groups argue that these laws target the poor, not just those who cause problems, because many people consider the poor to be "unsightly and don't want to have them around."[85] Is this policy ethical? Although it may be unfair to exclude the homeless, shouldn't neighborhoods be protected from an influx of homeless that may cause the desirability and therefore values of their homes to decline? Shouldn't citizens have the right to enjoy the parks free from the litter and other problems that the homeless create? On the other hand, don't the homeless and poor have the right to go to public places like anyone else as well as to be given food by those who wish to feed them? Are there better ways of handling this issue?

Another question that the U.S. Supreme Court considered in a case from New Jersey is whether a township may attempt to stem the flight of white property owners from a racially integrated community by enacting an ordinance prohibiting the posting of "For Sale" and "Sold" signs.

A CASE IN POINT

In *Linmark Associates, Inc. v. Township of Willingboro*,[86] the population growth of Willingboro, New Jersey, located near two military bases and several national corporation offices, had slowed to 3 percent between 1970 and 1973 after a decade of rapid growth. During these three years, the white population declined by 5 percent while the nonwhite population increased by 60 percent. To reduce panic selling, the town council passed an ordinance prohibiting "For Sale" and "Sold" signs except on model homes. When this ordinance was challenged by a property owner and a REALTOR®, the Supreme Court unanimously decided that the ordinance was unconstitutional because it violated the First Amendment.

The court noted that alternative methods of communications, such as newspaper advertising, are often more costly and less effective than the use of signs. Furthermore, the Court believed that the ordinance was not needed to promote the government's objective of stable, integrated housing and that in any event, this objective could not be achieved in a manner that impaired the flow of legitimate commercial information. "If dissemination of this information can be restricted, then every locality in the country can suppress any facts that reflect poorly on the locality, so long as a plausible claim can be made that disclosure would cause the recipient of the information to act 'irrationally.'"[87]

CASES

Performance of Listing Agreement: Majority Approach
BLACKMAN DESTEFANO REAL ESTATE v. SMITH
157 A.D.2d 932, 550 N.Y.S.2d 443 (3 Dept. 1990)

MERCURE, Justice. * * * Defendants David A. Smith and Ann Smith entered into a written listing agreement with plaintiff, a real estate broker, in which they engaged plaintiff to secure a purchaser of their home and agreed to pay plaintiff a commission of 6%, later reduced to 5%, of the purchase price. During the period of the listing agreement, plaintiff did obtain prospective purchasers, defendants James F. Lennon and Adeline Lennon, who entered into a written contract to purchase the Smiths' home for $100,000. Just prior to closing and at a time when all contract contingencies had been satisfied, the Lennons withdrew from the contract, advising that Adeline Lennon suffered from agoraphobia, a mental condition which prevented her from moving out of her existing home. In July 1987, Mina Boilard, an associate real estate broker employed by plaintiff, wrote a letter to David Smith in response to complaints which he had made and stated, in part, that "[n]ot placing business first * * * I decided not to pursue a commission in deference to the great amount of empathy I felt for you and the Lennons" and "the absence of [a commission statement] was simply because of compassion—not because I didn't feel I had earned it."

Plaintiff commenced this action against defendants to recover the $5,000 commission which it alleged was due under the listing agreement. In their answer, the Smiths asserted a cross claim against the Lennons, seeking, *inter alia*, indemnification upon the ground that "any damages which may be adjudged against [the Smiths] were caused in whole or in part by the wrongful actions of [the Lennons]." After successfully moving to have the complaint dismissed as to them, the Lennons moved for an order dismissing the indemnity cross claim and the Smiths cross-moved for an order granting summary judgment thereon. Supreme Court denied the motion and granted the cross motion; the Lennons appeal. In addition, the Smiths moved for summary judgment dismissing the complaint and Supreme Court, exercising its authority under CPLR 3212(b), granted summary judgment in favor of plaintiff; the Smiths appeal.

Initially, we agree with Supreme Court that Adeline Lennon's emotional condition did not render performance of the Lennons' contract with the Smiths impossible as a matter of law. "Impossibility excuses a party's performance only when the destruction of the subject matter of the contract or the means of performance makes performance objectively impossible" (*Kel Kim Corp. v. Central Mkts.,* 519 N.E.2d 295). Although Adeline Lennon's inability to move out of her existing home had the likely effect of making performance under the contract burdensome, it did not render it impossible. Since financing had been arranged, the Lennons were not precluded from purchasing and then reselling the Smiths' home.

We also agree with Supreme Court's grant of summary judgment in favor of plaintiff against the Smiths. It is fundamental that a real estate broker earns its commission when it produces a buyer who is ready, willing and able to purchase the subject property under the terms offered by the seller. In the absence of an agreement providing to the contrary, the broker's right to compensation is not dependent upon the performance of the realty contract or the receipt by the seller of the selling price. It is undisputed that, at the time they entered into the contract with the Smiths, the Lennons were ready, willing and able to purchase the property. Nor did the claim of waiver bar a grant of summary judgment in favor of plaintiff. A finding of waiver will not be made absent a "clear manifestation of intent" to relinquish a known right. We find no such intent. Rather, Boilard's letter represents, at best, an expression of current intent on the part of a real estate salesperson not to pursue a commission.

Significantly, Boilard did not have authority to seek a commission or to release a claim of her corporate principal. In any event, where, as here, the waiver is executory, it may be withdrawn.

Finally, we turn to the issues surrounding the Smiths' cross claim. Although notions of fairness and equity concededly favor a resolution which casts ultimate responsibility for plaintiff's commission upon the Lennons, a defaulting purchaser may not be compelled to indemnify the seller for payment of a realtor's commission in the absence of an express agreement.

Moreover, since, as already determined, the $5,000 commission was earned at the time the Smiths and the Lennons entered into the contract of sale, the Smiths' liability for payment of the commission predated and, thus, could not have been caused by the Lennons' failure to complete the purchase. [The Smiths' cross claim is dismissed.]

Performance of Listing Agreement: Minority Approach
ELLSWORTH DOBBS, INC. v. JOHNSON
50 N.J. 528, 236 A.2d 843 (1967)

FRANCIS, J., Judge. [The] plaintiff Ellsworth Dobbs, Inc., a real estate broker, sued John R. Johnson and Adelaide P. Johnson, his wife, and Joseph Iarussi for commissions allegedly earned in a real estate transaction. The Johnsons, as owners of certain acreage in Bernards Township, New Jersey, and Iarussi as purchaser, entered into a written agreement, the former to sell and the latter to buy the property. There is no doubt that Dobbs brought the parties together, and into the signed contract of sale. Title did not close, however, because of Iarussi's inability to obtain financial backing for his intended development of the property. * * * Dobbs then brought this action charging the Johnsons with breach of an express agreement to pay a commission due for bringing about the contract of sale, and charging Iarussi with breach of an implied agreement to pay the commission if he failed to complete the purchase and thus deprived the broker of commission from the seller. [The trial judge held both the owners (the Johnsons) and the buyer (Iarussi) liable for $15,000, the broker's commission. The intermediate appellate court reversed the trial court judgment. The discussion below is from the decision of the New Jersey Supreme Court.]

* * *

There can be no doubt that ordinarily when an owner of property lists it with a broker for sale, his expectation is that the money for the payment of commission will come out of the proceeds of the sale. He expects that if the broker produces a buyer to whom the owner's terms of sale are satisfactory, and a contract embodying those terms is executed, the buyer will perform, i.e., he will pay the consideration and

accept the deed at the time agreed upon. Considering the realities of the relationship created between owner and broker, that expectation of the owner is a reasonable one, and, in our view, entirely consistent with what should be the expectation of a conscientious broker as to the kind of ready, willing and able purchaser his engagement calls upon him to tender to the owner.

* * *

The principle that binds the seller to pay commission if he signs a contract of sale with the broker's customer, regardless of the customer's financial ability, puts the burden on the wrong shoulders. Since the broker's duty to the owner is to produce a prospective buyer who is financially able to pay the purchase price and take title, a right in the owner to assume such capacity when the broker presents his purchaser ought to be recognized. It follows that the obligation to inquire into the prospect's financial status and to establish his adequacy to fulfill the monetary conditions of the purchase must be regarded logically and sensibly as resting with the broker. Thus when the broker produces his customer, it is only reasonable to hold that the owner may accept him without being obliged to make an independent inquiry into his financial capacity. That right ought not to be taken away from him, nor should he be estopped to assert it, simply because he "accepted" the buyer, i.e., agreed to convey to him if and when he paid the purchase price according to the terms of the contract. In reason and in justice it must be said that the duty to produce a purchaser able in the financial sense to complete the purchase at the time fixed is an incident of the broker's business;

so too, with regard to any other material condition of the agreement to purchase which is to be performed at the closing. In a practical world, the true test of a willing buyer is not met when he signs an agreement to purchase; it is demonstrated at the time of closing of title, and if he unjustifiably refuses or is unable financially to perform then, the broker has not produced a willing buyer.

* * *

We come now to another aspect of the over-all problem. To what extent may the broker, by special contract, thwart the general rules now declared to control the usual relationship between him and an owner who engages him to find a purchaser?

* * *

The record in the present case contains samples of standardized printed forms of special agreements, used by brokers and real estate boards, which are presented to intending sellers for signature when a broker is retained. They are designed to impose on the owner liability for commissions immediately upon execution of a contract to sell to a customer produced by the broker, irrespective of whether the buyer proves unable financially or unwilling for some other unjustifiable reason to complete the sale. Two examples of such agreements are as follows:

"Commission or commissions shall be earned when the agreement of sale is executed by the buyer and seller, and both the agent and his cooperating broker are authorized to deduct all or part of their commissions from the initial deposit at the time of signing of the sales agreement, provided however, that the initial deposit shall be at least double the amount of the commissions deducted."

"The owner or owners of property or properties to be sold or exchanged hereunder hereby recognize(s) _____ as the broker negotiating this agreement of sale and hereby agree(s) to pay said broker, for services rendered, a commission as now established by the real estate board in whose territory the above property is situated, namely _____% of the within-mentioned selling price; same to be paid upon the execution of this agreement. It is the intention of the parties hereto that this provision of this agreement is made for the benefit of said broker."

The rules which we have set down above to govern dealings, rights, and duties between brokers and owners are necessary for the protection of property owners, and constitute the public policy of our State. Whenever there is substantial inequality of bargaining power, position or advantage between the broker and the other party involved, any form of agreement designed to create liability on the part of the owner for commission upon the signing of a contract to sell to a prospective buyer, brought forward by the broker, even though consummation of the sale is frustrated by the inability or the unwillingness of the buyer to pay the purchase money and close the title, we regard as so contrary to the common understanding of men, and also so contrary to common fairness, as to require a court to condemn it as unconscionable.

* * *

[The court held that the owners were not liable for the commission and remanded the case for a new trial to determine whether the buyer was liable to the broker on the basis of an implied promise to complete the transaction.]

Offer and Acceptance; Listing Cancellation
RELLINGER v. BREMMEYR
180 Mich.App. 661, 448 N.W.2d 49 (1989)

PER CURIAM. Plaintiff [Rellinger] appeals as of right from a judgment of no cause of action following a bench trial in Emmet Circuit Court. We affirm.

* * *

Defendants [the Bremmeyrs] were the owners of business property located in Petoskey, Michigan. In September, 1986, defendants entered into a listing agreement with Petoskey Properties, Inc. Patricia McFall was named as the listing agent, however, the agreement provided that the property would be entered on a multiple listing service. Plaintiff, a self-employed real estate broker, was not a member of the multiple listing service at that time.

Defendants received numerous offers from various individuals which were rejected outright or rejected by counteroffers. On Saturday, December 20, 1986, plaintiff submitted an offer on behalf of Thomas Fanning, representing a partnership to be formed, in the amount of $510,000.

McFall immediately contacted defendants who rejected Fanning's offer but presented a counteroffer, requiring Fanning's consent to additional provisions. The counteroffer provided:

RECEIPT IS ACKNOWLEDGED BY SELLER of a copy of this Agreement. "Seller gives Realtor/Broker above named 3 days to obtain written acceptance of this offer/counteroffer."

Plaintiff contacted Fanning later that evening by telephone and obtained Fanning's verbal consent to the additional terms. Plaintiff instructed Fanning to send a letter of acknowledgment.

On Sunday afternoon, December 21, 1986, another realtor presented a new offer to defendants from Rodney Phillips. Defendants were desirous of accepting Phillips' offer and were advised by McFall that they could rescind their outstanding counteroffer anytime prior to acceptance. McFall then prepared a letter that day rescinding the counteroffer to Fanning. Phillips' offer was thereafter accepted and the next morning, December 22, the rescission letter was personally delivered to plaintiff's secretary. Plaintiff thereafter received from Fanning the previously requested letter of acknowledgment, which was dated December 22, 1986. The sale of the property was ultimately consummated with Rodney Phillips on December 31, 1986.

On appeal, plaintiff argues that when defendants extended him a three-day period in which to secure acceptance of their counteroffer they could not legally revoke the counteroffer during this period and sell to another party so as to defeat his right to a commission. We disagree.

* * *

Initially, we note that it is important to distinguish between two related but separate matters, those being revocation of authority to secure acceptance and revocation of potential liability for a commission.

* * *

Thus, although defendants may have had the power to revoke plaintiff's authority to secure a binding purchase agreement, such power does not necessarily absolve them from their separate contractual liability to pay a commission.

* * *

In this case, the record does not indicate that plaintiff promised to make any specific efforts to sell the property or otherwise furnished any consideration in exchange for defendants' promise to pay a commission upon securance of an acceptance of the counteroffer. Plaintiff did not have a listing agreement with defendants, nor was there any personal contact between the parties. Plaintiff was not acting pursuant to an exclusive listing agreement, but instead was merely one of numerous other realtors soliciting offers on behalf of defendants.

Language in the purchase agreement with respect to the relationship between plaintiff and defendants provided that seller would pay to realtor/broker a commission equal to a certain percentage of the sale price for negotiating the sale. Because the counteroffer was withdrawn prior to acceptance, no sale was ever negotiated. The trial court found that * * * the agreement does not recite that plaintiff furnished any consideration in exchange for defendants' promise.

Further, the agreement does not impose any duties or obligations upon plaintiff to present the offer to the intended purchaser or to exert any other specific efforts related thereto. The testimony also indicated that the three-day period to obtain acceptance was not bargained for by plaintiff, but was instead an arbitrary figure arrived at between the listing realtor and defendants.

The agreement appears to reflect nothing more than a unilateral offer granting plaintiff three days to secure acceptance. Such an offer would become binding only upon plaintiff's performance of a task of securing a written acceptance upon the terms provided by defendants. This event did not occur prior to revocation, and the counteroffer was therefore properly revokable.

Having resolved the first part of the issue, the inquiry then becomes whether defendants acted in good faith. In order that a revocation of a broker's authority may defeat his right to commissions or other compensation it must be made in good faith and not as a mere device to appropriate the benefit of his service and efforts and at the same time escape the payment of commissions earned or about to be earned. The trial court found that the evidence did not support a finding of bad faith, and a review of the record indicates such a conclusion was not clearly erroneous.

Although defendants were able to obtain an additional $16,000 by not having to pay a commission to plaintiff, testimony reflected that this was not a motivating factor in their decision to revoke the counteroffer to Fanning. Defendants testified that it was their understanding that, because of changes in the tax laws, savings of approximately $100,000 could be realized if they closed prior to January 1, 1987. Defendants were uneasy about the fact that Fanning's offer was made for a partnership to be formed. Defendants indicated that Phillips was an established person in the community and they were more familiar with him and felt much more confident that he would be able to close by the end of the year. Finally, plaintiff himself stated that he did not believe defendants' actions were the result of any bad motives against him. From this testimony, the trial court's conclusion that defendants' revocation of their counteroffer was not made in bad faith and with an intent to deprive plaintiff of a commission was not clearly erroneous.

* * *

Dual Agency
BAZAL v. RHINES, PALMA AND SKOGMAN REALTY CO.
600 N.W.2d 327 (Iowa App. 1999)

JUDGE S. J. SCHLEGEL. Defendants Marilyn Palma and Skogman Realty Company appeal a district court judgment entered against them on Lonnie and Kathy Bazal's claim for breach of fiduciary duty in connection with a failed real estate transaction. We affirm.

The Bazals decided to sell their home in Bowman Woods in June 1995. They listed their home with Dick Brown, a realtor with Skogman Realty Company. He had been involved when the Bazals purchased the home and they believed Skogman had expertise in selling homes in Bowman Woods.

Skogman and its affiliated companies developed Bowman Woods; Skogman was the exclusive listing agent for all new homes in Bowman Woods. The Bazals signed a Listing Agreement with Skogman on June 20, 1995, and received Skogman's Agency Policy Disclosure and Acknowledgment Form which provided that Skogman must disclose matters reasonably discoverable affecting the property value or desirability.

In mid-July 1995, Paul and Karen Rhines asked their realtor, Marilyn Palma, whether she knew of a home for sale in Bowman Woods which would meet their needs, including space for four dogs. Palma, also a realtor at Skogman, informed the Rhineses she believed the Bazals' home would meet their needs. The Bazals were never informed that the Rhineses required space for four dogs.

On July 22, 1995, the Bazals and the Rhineses agreed upon a cash price of $211,000 with a closing date of September 30, 1995. The Rhineses and the Bazals each signed a Consensual Dual Agency Agreement prepared by Skogman acknowledging that one Skogman realtor (Palma) was representing the Rhineses as buyers and a second Skogman realtor (Brown) was representing the Bazals as sellers in the transaction. The agreement further provided that Skogman would disclose all material defects in the property. Shortly thereafter, the Bazals made a commitment to purchase another home and immediately began making preparations to be out of their home by the closing date.

On September 10, 1995, the Rhineses' attorney, Michael Donohue, prepared a title opinion which disclosed a restrictive covenant on the property limiting dog ownership to one per dwelling unit. Donohue wrote to Palma on September 20, 1995, noting the "dog clause" problem and suggested that waivers be obtained or other solutions be considered. Skogman's response, dated October 2, 1995, suggested the Rhineses had ulterior motives for raising the "dog clause" issue and they had simply changed their minds about purchasing the Bazals' home. None of Skogman's agents or employees took any further action to try to resolve the problem with the "dog clause;" Palma simply repeatedly told the Rhineses the "dog clause" was not a problem. The closing did not take place.

After their sale failed to close, the Bazals re-listed their home with Skogman for $216,000. The property ultimately sold for $201,000 on March 18, 1996. The Bazals had reduced the asking price on the home on Brown's advice and due to the financial pressure of owning two homes and paying two mortgages. The home proved difficult to sell due to the time of year and because it was empty.

The district court concluded the Bazals were entitled to recover damages from Palma and Skogman. The Bazals were awarded damages in the amount of $19,933.16 representing primarily a reduction in the sale price, additional property taxes, and interest. Palma and Skogman appeal.

* * *

II. FIDUCIARY DUTIES. Palma contends she owed no fiduciary duties to the Bazals to disclose the "dog clause." Palma and Skogman maintain they did not have a fiduciary duty to close the transaction. We disagree.

Real estate brokers assume a fiduciary relationship with their principals which creates a duty of fidelity and good faith. By virtue of the Listing Agreement, the Agency Policy Disclosure and Acknowledgment Form, and the Consensual Dual Agency Agreement, Skogman and Palma had a fiduciary duty and a duty of good faith to the Bazals. Skogman and Palma had a duty to discover material facts regarding the property which were reasonably discoverable. Palma was aware of the "dog clause" but never informed the Rhineses about it, but should have.

In addition to the Consensual Dual Agency Agreement and the Agency Policy Disclosure and Acknowledgment Form, the National Association of Realtors Code of Ethics requires realtors to disclose material facts to the buyers and the sellers. Under the facts in this case, the existence of the "dog clause" and the Rhineses' plan to bring four dogs to the property were material facts which should have, if known, been disclosed to all parties. There is substantial evidence to support the district court's finding that Palma failed to disclose these material facts.

Skogman and Palma also had a duty to use their best efforts to resolve any problems which arose and close the transaction. There is substantial evidence to support the district court's finding that Skogman and Palma did not use their best efforts to close the transaction.

III. PROXIMATE CAUSE. Palma and Skogman contend a breach of fiduciary duty, if any, was not the proximate cause of the Bazals' damages. We disagree.

Palma argues that even if the failure to disclose the "dog clause" problem was a breach, it was not the proximate cause of damages because the Rhineses would never have made an offer. However, the evidence shows the Bazals could have sold the property to other interested parties under more favorable sale conditions if the property had not been off the market for two-and-one-half months in reliance upon the contract to sell their home to the Rhineses.

Palma also argues that even if the failure to close the transaction was a breach, it was not the proximate cause of damages because there was no evidence the suggested solution would have cured the "dog clause" problem. However, the evidence shows the Rhineses were willing to close the transaction if a solution to the "dog clause" problem could be found. Palma informed the Rhineses the "dog clause" was not a problem; no further action was taken to resolve the problem. Skogman's letter dated October 2, 1995, was counterproductive. Palma's and Skogman's failure to inform the Bazals about the "dog clause" problem prevented the Bazals from pursuing solutions themselves.

There is substantial evidence to support the district court's findings that defendants' breaches of duties owed to the Bazals were proximate causes of the Bazals' damages. We conclude the district court did not err in entering judgment against Palma and Skogman.

For these reasons, we affirm.

AFFIRMED.

Broker's Duties—Buyer's Broker
SAIZ v. HORN
668 N.W.2d 332 (Sup. Ct. S. D. 2003)

KONENKAMP, Justice. This is an action brought by home-buyers against their realtor. After their purchase, the buyers found that the home they bought had substantial defects. They also learned that the seller had previously given other potential buyers a disclosure statement revealing these defects. The buyers sued their realtor for breach of agency and breach of fiduciary duty in failing to inform them that the seller had a statutory duty to provide them with a disclosure statement. The trial court granted summary judgment for the realtor, finding no duty on the part of the buyers' agent. The court also ruled that the claim was barred by the six-year statute of limitations. Because realtors representing buyers have a duty of ordinary care toward their clients, which includes the duty to disclose statutorily mandated procedures for home sales, we conclude that the realtor here had an obligation to inform his clients of the seller's responsibility to provide a disclosure statement. We also hold that the six-year statute of limitations had not expired. Summary judgment for the realtor is reversed, and the case is remanded for trial.

Background

In 1995, plaintiffs Craig and Patricia Saiz were looking to rent a home in Belle Fourche, South Dakota. Patricia contacted Rod Horn, a real estate broker. Horn suggested that they purchase a home located at 505 Kingsbury Street. Advising them that the price was very low, Horn stated that he would consider buying it himself as an investment property if they chose not to purchase it.

Plaintiffs had no previous experience in buying a house. They agreed that Horn would represent them as their agent. The home was owned by Marjorie Dailey, who was represented by Lookout Mountain Realty of Spearfish. Unknown to plaintiffs, Dailey had previously completed a seller's property condition disclosure statement on February 13, 1995. The statement had been given to earlier potential buyers. The disclosure statement revealed a history of water penetration problems and cracking. Horn never advised plaintiffs of the seller's statutory duty to provide a disclosure statement.

On June 12, 1995, plaintiffs executed an offer and agreement to purchase the home for $39,500. Horn was listed as the selling salesperson for the purpose of a commission split with the seller's broker. Horn continued to represent plaintiffs until the sale closed on August 25, 1995. Plaintiffs were never offered and did not receive a seller's property condition disclosure statement before making their written offer. However, plaintiffs' lender obtained a home inspection report, which stated that the dwelling was structurally

sound and in a state of good repair, with only trim and stain around windows, cellar door repair, and foundation fill necessary.

For a period after closing, the condition of the residence was unremarkable. In 1999, plaintiffs installed seven new windows and replaced two front doors. In 2000, they began to notice cracks in most rooms that successive repainting would not thwart. They also discovered that the walls and insulation contained significant moisture from water penetration occurring over a number of years. They spent thousands of dollars improving the home. Eventually, after consulting with a contractor in 2001, plaintiffs discovered that the house did not have a concrete foundation to stabilize the walls. In actuality, the foundation area was comprised of either cinder blocks or wood posts set into the soil.

On one side of the house, a large expanding sink hole caused a part of the house to pull to the west, gradually tearing the west side away from the rest of the structure. The lack of a concrete foundation and water intrusion caused various problems within the house, including shifting of walls, drywall cracks, peeling of paint, warping of the stairway railing and stairs, and gaps at wall joints. To avoid ground contraction or further erosion of ground support, contractors recommended a concrete foundation structure on part of the house, costing $15,000 to $20,000. Plaintiffs claim that had they been presented with a disclosure statement, they would have renegotiated the terms and conditions of sale or may have decided not to purchase the property.

On August 6, 2001, plaintiffs brought suit. The complaint alleged breach of agency contract and breach of fiduciary duty. The trial court granted summary judgment for Horn, concluding that SDCL 43-4-38 placed the duty to provide a disclosure statement on the seller and that the statute does not impose such a duty on the buyer's agent. The court also ruled that plaintiffs' claim is barred by the six-year statute of limitations in SDCL 15-2-13(1). The court reasoned that because the disclosure statement must be provided "before the buyer makes a written offer," the fact that the agent continued to represent plaintiffs beyond that time was of no consequence. To the court, the cutoff date was June 12, 1995, when the purchase agreement was offered and accepted the next day. Plaintiffs appeal on the following issues: (1) "Whether the trial court erred by granting Horn's motion for judgment on the pleadings and summary judgment by finding no breach of agency duty owed by Horn to Saiz." (2) "Whether the trial court erred by granting Horn's motion for judgment on the pleadings and summary judgment by finding the statute of limitations barred Saiz' claim."

* * *

Analysis and Decision

1. Agency and Fiduciary Duties

This is an action against the buyers' agent for breach of agency and fiduciary duties in failing to inform the buyers that a home seller must provide a disclosure statement. The trial court granted summary judgment for Horn, concluding that SDCL 43-4-38 imposes the duty only on the seller to provide a disclosure statement. SDCL 43-4-38 provides:

The seller of residential real property shall furnish to a buyer a completed copy of the disclosure statement before the buyer makes a written offer. If after delivering the disclosure statement to the buyer or the buyer's agent and prior to the date of closing for the property or the date of possession of the property, whichever comes first, the seller becomes aware of any change of material fact which would affect the disclosure statement, the seller shall furnish a written amendment disclosing the change of material fact.

This statute, of course, imposes no duty on the buyers' agent. Horn had no duty to uncover and disclose defects in the seller's property. At issue in this case, however, is whether Horn, as the buyers' agent, owed a duty to the buyers to inform them that, by law, the seller must give them a disclosure statement. We have previously recognized a fiduciary duty between a real estate agent and a principal. Here, Horn acted as the buyers' agent, and thus he owed a fiduciary duty to them.

Not unlike the requirement of other professionals to inform their clients, real estate agents are expected to advise their principals on the rules and procedures involved in a real estate transaction. Why have realty agents for buyers, if agents, supposedly knowledgeable in real estate transactions, have no obligation to tell clients that sellers are required by law to give a disclosure statement? Such disclosure is legally mandated for the protection of buyers. It can reveal matters that may materially influence a decision whether to purchase a home.

The applicable principles in any agency contract of this kind are well established. As we said in *Hurney*: Unless otherwise agreed, [real estate agents] owe their principals ... a duty to use reasonable efforts to fully, fairly and timely disclose information to their principals within their knowledge, which is or may be material to the subject matter of their agency. Material information depends on the facts and circumstances of each case.

Real estate agents are bound to exercise reasonable care, skill, and diligence in performing the transactions entrusted to them and are responsible for loss proximately resulting from their failure to do so. Any actions or omissions by agents in violation of the duties imposed upon them by their agency contract render them responsible to their principals for loss or damages.

Here, plaintiffs stated that they would not have proceeded with the purchase of the house on the negotiated terms had they known about the revelations in the disclosure statement. The circuit court erred in ruling that Horn had no duty as the buyers' agent to inform them that the seller was legally required to provide a disclosure statement.

* * *

Reversed and remanded for trial.

Brokers' Duties
CRUTCHLEY v. FIRST TRUST AND SAVINGS BANK
450 N.W.2d 877 (Iowa 1990)

CARTER, Justice. The estate of Don Fishel, a deceased real estate salesperson, appeals from a judgment awarding damages to plaintiffs, Harold E. Crutchley and Anita S. Crutchley.

Plaintiffs' action sought to recover for the alleged negligence and breach of contract of Fishel and Jim Short, two licensed real estate agents who represented them in the sale of 600 acres of land in Linn County. Short, who is also a defendant against whom judgment was entered, has not appealed.

In 1980, the plaintiffs listed 600 acres of land for sale through the Mundel, Long & Luce real estate office in Cedar Rapids. Fishel and Short were salespersons associated with that firm. Plaintiffs were well acquainted with Fishel, who had previously represented them in selling other property. Short assisted Fishel on some of the prior sales as well as the transaction giving rise to the present controversy. After advertisement of the 600-acre tract in publications of general circulation in the Midwest, Carl Esker and two medical doctors participating with him agreed to pay a total consideration of $1,650,000 for the property pursuant to an installment contract.

The contract called for a $300,000 down payment with the remaining balance to be paid over a twenty-year period.

The contract of sale came into being as a result of the plaintiffs' acceptance of an offer to purchase which contained the following language:

In the event of default on this contract, the sellers shall only be entitled to possession of the real estate as of the date of said default. Buyers will only lose their interest in said property and any payments made to date of default.

The parties to this litigation have referred to this provision as a nonrecourse clause. Although the price and payment terms of the installment contract evolved from a series of offers and counteroffers, the nonrecourse clause had been included in the original offer and was not altered or amended in any way in the subsequent negotiations between buyers and sellers.

In 1985 the buyers defaulted on the contract. As a result, plaintiffs regained possession of the farmland by forfeiture proceedings. Plaintiffs retained the down payment and annual interest payments received on March 1 of 1982, 1983, and 1984. The parties to this action are in agreement that, as a result of the nonrecourse clause, plaintiffs were entitled to no further relief against the buyers.

Due to a plummeting decline in the value of farm real estate between 1980 and 1985, the value of the 600-acre tract plus the payments which plaintiffs received prior to default did not equal the contract price to be paid by the defaulting parties. Prior to bringing the present action, the plaintiffs sought federal bankruptcy protection. As a part of those proceedings, the 600-acre tract was liquidated in 1986 for $576,465.

On June 9, 1986, plaintiffs commenced the present action against Jim Short and the estate of Fishel, who by that time was deceased, seeking recovery of money damages on theories of negligence and breach of contract. They contended that Short and Fishel misadvised them concerning the legal significance of the nonrecourse clause and failed to observe the provisions of article 17 of the National Association of Realtors' Code of Ethics by not recommending that plaintiffs consult legal counsel on a matter in which their interests required it.

At the trial, plaintiff Harold Crutchley testified that, when the property was sold to Carl Esker and his associates, the sellers did not understand that the nonrecourse clause in the contract left them without any recourse other than to regain the property. Crutchley testified that Short had advised the sellers that this clause only protected certain of the buyers' assets from execution sale and protected the buyers' spouses from personal liability. Crutchley testified that he would not have accepted the offer to buy the land had he realized the legal import of the nonrecourse clause. He stated that neither Fishel nor Short recommended that plaintiffs seek legal counsel in culminating this transaction and that Short had affirmatively dissuaded them from so doing.

Fishel was deceased at the time of trial, but Short was called as a witness. Short conceded the applicability of article 17 of the National Association of Realtors' Code of Ethics for purposes of determining his and Fishel's responsibilities to their clients. He denied that either he or Fishel had dissuaded plaintiffs from seeking the advice of legal counsel on this transaction. He testified that plaintiffs were sophisticated in real estate transactions and that on other land sales in which Short had assisted them they had freely consulted attorneys concerning questions over legal matters.

He testified that both he and Fishel had fully explained the legal significance of the nonrecourse clause to the plaintiffs and that he was satisfied they understood it and accepted it as a means of obtaining a favorable sale.

The case was submitted to the jury under the comparative fault provisions of Iowa Code chapter 668 (1987). The jury found that defendants were at fault under plaintiffs' breach-of-contract and negligence claims and that plaintiffs themselves were also at fault. Fault was apportioned twenty-five percent to plaintiffs and seventy-five percent to Short and the Fishel estate collectively. In response to a special interrogatory, the jury determined that the total amount of damages sustained by plaintiffs was $715,000. After a reduction of damages for plaintiffs' percentage of fault, judgment was entered against the two defendants jointly and severally for the sum of $536,250.

* * *

The district court permitted the jury to find that the defendants were negligent or had breached their duties under the listing agreement in the following particulars: (1) by giving an inadequate and incorrect explanation of the nonrecourse provision, (2) by not affirmatively recommending that plaintiffs obtain legal counsel in a matter in which their interests required it, and (3) in discouraging plaintiffs from seeking legal counsel. Although the Fishel estate strenuously argues that the evidence fails to support any of these theories of negligence or breach of contract, we believe that based on the evidence presented a jury might have found adversely to defendants as to any or all of the three specifications we have listed.

Plaintiffs offered evidence, including the testimony of Short himself, that both Short and Fishel were required to maintain the standards articulated in article 17 of the National Association of Realtors' Code of Ethics in representing their clients. That standard reads as follows:

> The Realtor shall not engage in activities that constitute the unauthorized practice of law and shall recommend that legal counsel be obtained when the interest of any party to the transaction requires it.

We recognized in *Menzel v. Morse,* 362 N.W.2d 465, 473 (Iowa 1985), that proof of a violation of this standard is evidence upon which a trier of fact may find negligence.

The evidence concerning that which was said or not said by the parties to the litigation concerning the legal effect of the nonrecourse clause or the desirability of plaintiffs seeking legal counsel was in sharp dispute. If, however, the evidence presented is viewed in the light most favorable to the plaintiffs, it will support a finding by the jury that defendants failed to exercise the standard of care required of persons engaged in their business or profession.

Because of the interrelationship between the negligence and breach-of-contract issues in the present case, we conclude that proof of a breach of this standard of professional conduct would also establish a violation of the agent's duties under the listing agreement with the broker. The district court did not err in accepting the jury's findings on the negligence and breach-of-contract issues. * * * [The trial court judgment is affirmed.]

KOZINSKI, Judge.

* * *

The Internet has opened new channels of communication and self-expression. Countless individuals use message boards, date matching sites, interactive social networks, blog hosting services and video sharing web sites to make themselves and their ideas visible to the world. While such intermediaries enable the user-driven digital age, they also create new legal problems.

This case involves one such intermediary, Roommates.com, LLC ("Roommate"), which operates an online roommate matching web site at www.roommates.com. This web site helps individuals find roommates based on their descriptions of themselves and their roommate preferences. Roommates.com has approximately 150,000 active listings and receives about a million page views per day.

To become members of Roommate, users respond to a series of online questionnaires by choosing from answers in drop-down and select-a-box menus. Users must disclose information about themselves and their roommate preferences based on such characteristics as age, sex and whether children will live in the household. They can then provide "Additional Comments" through an open-ended essay prompt.

Roommate's free membership allows users to create personal profiles, search lists of compatible roommates and send "roommail" messages to other members. Roommate also sends e-mail newsletters to members seeking housing, listing compatible members who have places to rent out. Roommate's fee-based membership allows users to read their "roommail" and view the "Additional Comments" essays of other members.

The Fair Housing Councils of San Fernando Valley and San Diego ("the Councils") filed suit in federal district court, claiming that Roommate violated the Fair Housing Act ("FHA") and various state laws. The district court held that the Communications Decency Act barred the Councils' FHA claim. As a result, the court granted, in part, Roommate's summary judgment motion and entered judgment in Roommate's favor on the FHA claim. The district court then declined to exercise supplemental jurisdiction over the state-law claims and dismissed them. It also denied Roommate's motion for attorneys' fees and costs. The Councils now appeal the dismissal of their FHA claim and Roommate cross-appeals the denial of fees and costs.

Analysis

According to the CDA, "[n]o provider ... of an interactive computer service shall be treated as the publisher or speaker of any information provided by another information content provider." One of Congress's goals in adopting this provision

was to encourage "the unfettered and unregulated development of free speech on the Internet."

The touchstone of section 230(c) is that providers of interactive computer services are immune from liability for content created by third parties. The immunity applies to a defendant who is the "provider ... of an interactive computer service" and is being sued "as the publisher or speaker of any information provided by" someone else. "[R]eviewing courts have treated §230(c) immunity as quite robust."

The Councils do not dispute that Roommate is a provider of an interactive computer service. As such, Roommate is immune so long as it merely publishes information provided by its members. However, Roommate is not immune for publishing materials as to which it is an "information content provider." A content provider is "any person or entity that is responsible, *in whole or in part*, for the creation or development of information provided through the Internet." In other words, if Roommate passively publishes information provided by others, the CDA protects it from liability that would otherwise attach under state or federal law as a result of such publication. But if it is responsible, in whole or in part, for creating or developing the information, it becomes a content provider and is not entitled to CDA immunity.

* * *

The Councils claim Roommate violates the FHA in three ways: (1) it posts the questionnaires on its web site and requires individuals who want to take advantage of its services to complete them; (2) it posts and distributes by e-mail its members' profiles; and (3) it posts the information its members provide on the "Additional Comments" form. For all three categories, the question is whether Roommate is "responsible, in whole or in part, for the creation or development of [the] information."

1. As previously explained, in order to become members of Roommate and take advantage of the services it offers, individuals must complete a series of questionnaires. Individuals looking for a room must first complete a form about themselves. They must use a drop-down menu to identify themselves as either "Male" or "Female" and to disclose whether "Children will be present" or "Children will not be present." Individuals looking to rent out a room must complete a similar form. They must use a check-box menu to indicate whether "Straight male(s)," "Gay male(s)," "Straight female(s)," and/or "Lesbian(s)" now live in the household, and a drop-down menu to disclose if there are "Children present" or "Children not present." If users fail to provide answers to any of these questions, they cannot complete the membership registration process.

In addition to completing one of the two forms described above, all prospective members must fill out the "My

Roommate Preferences" form. They must use a drop-down menu to indicate whether they are willing to live with "Straight or gay" males, only "Straight" males, only "Gay" males, or "No males," or may choose to select a blank response. Users must make comparable selections for females. They must also declare "I will live with children," "I will not live with children" or change the field to a blank.

As we previously explained, an entity cannot qualify for CDA immunity when it is "responsible, in whole or in part, for the creation or development of [the] information" at issue. Roommate is "responsible" for these questionnaires because it "creat[ed] or develop[ed]" the forms and answer choices. As a result, Roommate is a content provider of these questionnaires and does not qualify for CDA immunity for their publication.

Roommate objects that simply asking questions cannot violate the FHA. Yet the Councils advance two theories under which publication of these forms arguably does violate the FHA. First, the Councils argue that asking users to provide information about themselves and their roommate preferences is a "statement … with respect to the sale or rental of a dwelling that *indicates … an intention* to make [a] preference, limitation or discrimination." Second, the Councils claim that requiring members to answer questions that enable other members to discriminate for or against them violates the FHA by "*caus[ing]*" users "to [make] … any … *statement* … with respect to the sale or rental of a dwelling that indicates any preference, limitation, or discrimination."

At this stage, we are only concerned with whether Roommate is immune from liability under the CDA, not whether it actually violated the FHA. We describe the Councils' FHA theories only to show that the mere asking of questions might, indeed, violate the FHA. It will be up to the district court on remand to decide initially whether Roommate violated the FHA by publishing its form questionnaires.

2. We now turn to the more difficult question of whether the CDA exempts Roommate from liability for publishing and distributing its members' profiles, which it generates from their answers to the form questionnaires.

Roommate strongly urges that *Carafano* settles the issue. In *Carafano*, an unidentified prankster placed a fraudulent personal ad on a date matching web site. This imposter created a profile for Carafano, an actress, listing her real phone number and address. The ad claimed that Carafano was looking for "a one-night stand" with a controlling man. We held that the CDA exempted the service from liability for two reasons.

First, the dating service was not an "information content provider" for the profiles on its web site. Although the web site required users to complete detailed questionnaires consisting of both multiple choice and essay questions that provided "structure and content" and a "menu of 'pre-prepared responses,'" these forms merely "facilitated the expression of information by individual users." We concluded that the service could not "be considered an 'information content

provider' under the [CDA] because no profile ha[d] any content until a user actively create[d] it." Second, even if the dating service could be considered a content provider for publishing its customers' profiles, it was exempt from liability because it did not "create[ ] or develop [ ] the particular information at issue." The anonymous user entered Carafano's phone number, address and fabricated sexual proclivities, and his entries were "transmitted unaltered to profile viewers." The service was not a content provider of the offending information because it "did not play a significant role in creating, developing or 'transforming'" it.

Carafano differs from our case in at least one significant respect: The prankster in *Carafano* provided information that was not solicited by the operator of the web site. The web site sought information about the individual posting the information, not about unwitting third parties. Nothing in the questions the dating service asked suggested, encouraged or solicited posting the profile of another person, and the web site's policies prohibited altogether the posting of last names and contact information. While *Carafano* is written in broad terms, it must be read in light of its facts. *Carafano* provided CDA immunity for information posted by a third party that was not, in any sense, created or developed by the web site operator—indeed, that was provided *despite* the web site's rules and policies. We are not convinced that *Carafano* would control in a situation where defamatory, private or otherwise tortious or unlawful information was provided by users in direct response to questions and prompts from the operator of the web site.

Imagine, for example, www.harrassthem.com with the slogan "Don't Get Mad, Get Even." A visitor to this web site would be encouraged to provide private, sensitive and/or defamatory information about others—all to be posted online for a fee. To post the information, the individual would be invited to answer questions about the target's name, addresses, phone numbers, social security number, credit cards, bank accounts, mother's maiden name, sexual orientation, drinking habits and the like. In addition, the web site would encourage the poster to provide dirt on the victim, with instructions that the information need not be confirmed, but could be based on rumor, conjecture or fabrication.

* * *

While mapping the outer limits of *Carafano's* protection of web sites that solicit and post users' responses is an interesting and difficult task, we need not undertake it today because Roommate does more than merely publish information it solicits from its members. Roommate also channels the information based on members' answers to various questions, as well as the answers of other members. Thus, Roommate allows members to search only the profiles of members with compatible preferences. For example, a female room-seeker who is living with a child can only search profiles of room-providers who have indicated they are willing to live with women and children. Roommate also sends room-seekers e-mail notifications that exclude listings incompatible with their profiles. Thus, Roommate will not notify our female about room-providers who say they will not live with women or children.

While Roommate provides a useful service, its search mechanism and e-mail notifications mean that it is neither a passive pass-through of information provided by others nor merely a facilitator of expression by individuals. By categorizing, channeling and limiting the distribution of users' profiles, Roommate provides an additional layer of information that it is "responsible" at least "in part" for creating or developing. Whether these actions ultimately violate the FHA is a question the district court must decide in the first instance.

3. Finally, we consider whether the CDA exempts Roommate from liability for publishing the content its members provide in the "Additional Comments" portion of their profiles. Members provide this information by filling in a blank text box. Next to this box, Roommate advises users that "[w]e strongly recommend taking a moment to personalize your profile by writing a paragraph or two describing yourself and what you are looking for in a roommate." The responses to this query produce the most provocative and revealing information in many users' profiles. Some state that they "Pref[er] white Male roommates," while others declare that they are "NOT looking for black muslims." Some don't want to deal with annoyances such as "drugs, kids or animals" or

"smokers, kids or druggies," while others want to stay away from "psychos or anyone on mental medication." More friendly folks are just looking for someone who will get along with their significant other or their most significant Other [*sic*].

We conclude that Roommate's involvement is insufficient to make it a content provider of these comments. Roommate's open-ended question suggests no particular information that is to be provided by members; Roommate certainly does not prompt, encourage or solicit any of the inflammatory information provided by some of its members. Nor does Roommate use the information in the "Additional Comments" section to limit or channel access to listings. Roommate is therefore not "responsible, in whole or in part, for the creation or development of" its users' answers to the open-ended "Additional Comments" form, and is immune from liability for publishing these responses.

* * *

Having determined that the CDA does not immunize Roommate for all of the content on its web site and in its e-mail newsletters, we remand for a determination of whether its non-immune publication and distribution of information violates the FHA. We also vacate the dismissal of the state law claims so that the district court may reconsider whether to exercise its supplemental jurisdiction in light of our ruling on the federal claims.

Broker Liability: Fair Housing Act
MEYER v. HOLLEY
537 U.S. 280, 123 S.Ct. 824 (2003)

BREYER, Justice. The Fair Housing Act forbids racial discrimination in respect to the sale or rental of a dwelling. The question before us is whether the Act imposes personal liability without fault upon an officer or owner of a residential real estate corporation for the unlawful activity of the *corporation's* employee or agent. We conclude that the Act imposes liability without fault upon the employer in accordance with traditional agency principles, i.e., it normally imposes vicarious liability upon the corporation but not upon its officers or owners.

For purposes of this decision we simplify the background facts as follows: Respondents Emma Mary Ellen Holley and David Holley, an interracial couple, tried to buy a house in Twenty-Nine Palms, California. A real estate corporation, Triad, Inc., had listed the house for sale. Grove Crank, a Triad salesman, is alleged to have prevented the Holleys from obtaining the house—and for racially discriminatory reasons.

The Holleys brought a lawsuit in federal court against Crank and Triad. They claimed, among other things, that

both were responsible for a fair housing law violation. The Holleys later filed a separate suit against David Meyer, the petitioner here. Meyer, they said, was Triad's president, Triad's sole shareholder, and Triad's licensed "officer/broker," see Cal.Code Regs., tit. 10, §2740 (1996) (formerly Cal. Admin. Code, tit. 10, §2740) (requiring that a corporation, in order to engage in acts for which a real estate license is required, designate one of its officers to act as the licensed broker); Cal. Bus. & Prof. Code Ann. §§10158, 10159, 10211 (West 1987). They claimed that Meyer was vicariously liable in one or more of these capacities for Crank's unlawful actions.

The District Court consolidated the two lawsuits. * * * It dismissed the claims against Meyer in his capacity as officer of Triad because (1) it considered those claims as assertions of *vicarious* liability, and (2) it believed that the Fair Housing Act did not impose personal liability upon a corporate *officer*. The District Court stated that "any liability against Meyer as an officer of Triad would only attach to Triad," the corporation.

* * *

The District certified its judgment as final to permit the Holleys to appeal its vicarious liability determination. The Ninth Circuit reversed those determinations.

* * *

The Court of Appeals recognized that "under general principles of tort law corporate shareholders and officers usually are not held vicariously liable for an employee's actions," but, in its view, "the criteria for the Fair Housing Act" are different.

* * *

Meyer, in his capacity as Triad's sole owner, had "the authority to control the acts" of a Triad salesperson. Meyer, in his capacity as Triad's officer, "did direct or control, or had the right to direct or control, the conduct of a Triad salesperson." And even if Meyer neither participated in nor authorized the discrimination in question, that "control" or "authority to control" is "enough … to hold Meyer personally liable." The Ninth Circuit added that, for similar reasons, Meyer, in his capacity as Triad's license-related officer/broker, was vicariously liable for Crank's discriminatory activity.

Meyer sought certiorari. We granted his petition, to review the Ninth Circuit's holding that the Fair Housing Act imposes principles of strict liability beyond those traditionally associated with agent/principal or employee/employer relationships.

* * *

The Fair Housing Act itself focuses on prohibited acts. In relevant part the Act forbids "any person or other entity whose business includes engaging in residential real estate-related transactions to discriminate," for example, because of "race." [42 U.S.C. § 3605(a).] It adds that "[p]erson" includes, for example, individuals, corporations, partnerships, associations, labor unions, and other organizations. It says nothing about vicarious liability.

Nonetheless, it is well established that the Act provides for vicarious liability. This Court has noted that an action brought for compensation by a victim of housing discrimination is, in effect, a tort action. And the Court has assumed that, when Congress creates a tort action, it legislates against a legal background of ordinary tort-related vicarious liability rules and consequently intends its legislation to incorporate those rules. * * *

It is well established that traditional vicarious liability rules ordinarily make principals or employers vicariously liable for acts of their agents or employees in the scope of their authority or employment. * * * And in the absence of special circumstances it is the corporation, not its owner or officer, who is the principal or employer, and thus subject to vicarious liability for torts committed by its employees or agents. The Restatement §1 specifies that the relevant principal/agency relationship demands not only control (or the right

to direct or control) but also "the manifestation of consent by one person to another that the other shall act *on his behalf* (3)27, and consent by the other so to act." (Emphasis added.) A corporate employee typically acts on behalf of the corporation, not its owner or officer.

The Ninth Circuit held that the Fair Housing Act imposed more extensive vicarious liability—that the Act went well beyond traditional principles. The Court of Appeals held that the Act made corporate owners and officers liable for the unlawful acts of a corporate employee simply on the basis that the owner or officer controlled (or had the right to control) the actions of that employee. We do not agree with the Ninth Circuit that the Act extended traditional vicarious liability rules in this way.

For one thing, Congress said nothing in the statute or in the legislative history about extending vicarious liability in this manner. And Congress' silence, while permitting an inference that Congress intended to apply *ordinary* background tort principles, cannot show that it intended to apply an unusual modification of those rules.

* * *

For another thing, the Department of Housing and Urban Development (HUD), the federal agency primarily charged with the implementation and administration of the statute, has specified that ordinary vicarious liability rules apply in this area. And we ordinarily defer to an administering agency's reasonable interpretation of a statute. * * *

The Ninth Circuit further referred to an owner's or officer's "non delegable duty" not to discriminate in light of the Act's "overriding societal priority." 258 F.3d, at 1131, 1132 (citing *Chicago v. Matchmaker Real Estate Sales Center, Inc., supra*, at 1096-1097, and *Walker v. Crigler, supra*, at 904-905). And it added that "[w]hen one of two innocent people must suffer, the one whose acts permitted the wrong to occur is the one to bear the burden." 258 F.3d, at 1132.

"[A] nondelegable duty is an affirmative obligation to ensure the protection of the person to whom the duty runs." *General Building Contractors Assn., Inc. v. Pennsylvania*, 458 U.S. 375, 396, 102 S.Ct. 3141, 73 L.Ed.2d 835 (1982) (finding no nondelegable duty under 42 U.S.C. §1981). Such a duty imposed upon a principal would "go further" than the vicarious liability principles we have discussed thus far to create liability "although [the principal] has himself done everything that could reasonably be required of him," W. Prosser, Law of Torts §71, p. 470 (4th ed. 1971), and irrespective of whether the agent was acting with or without authority.

* * *

The judgment of the Court of Appeals is vacated, and the case is remanded for further proceedings consistent with this opinion.

1866 Civil Rights Act, 195
1968 Fair Housing Act, 195
Americans with Disabilities Act of 1990, 200
apparent (or ostensible) authority, 185
blockbusting, 196
buyer broker, 189
commission, 174
dual agency, 189
exclusive agency, 177
exclusive right to sell, 176
express authority, 184
Fair Housing Amendments Act of 1988, 195
fiduciary duty, 187
general agent, 184
implied authority, 184
Interstate Land Sales Full Disclosure Act, 193
listing agreement, 176

little Sherman acts, 183
mandatory agency disclosure laws, 188
multiple listing service, 182
net listing agreement, 179
open listing agreement, 177
partially disclosed principal, 185
procuring cause of sale, 178
real estate broker, 174
real estate salesperson, 174
REALTORS®, 175
secret agent, 186
Sherman Antitrust Act, 182
special agent, 184
steering, 196
subagent, 182
undisclosed principal, 185

1. Mariko hired two real estate agents to sell a large tract of land. Her contract with the agents provided that the agents would (1) pay all expenses incurred in getting the property ready to sell, (2) have the property surveyed and divided into town lots and have the streets graded, and (3) use their best efforts to sell the property and not be paid for expenses incurred except for a specified share of the sale proceeds. The contract did not specify a time limit for performance. After the agents had performed their part of the agreement and had found buyers for several of the lots, Mariko attempted to terminate the agreement for no apparent cause. May she cancel the agreement? Why or why not?

2. Green owned a house worth $150,000 that was subject to a $50,000 mortgage. In response to a newspaper advertisement, Green called Trusty Realty to make arrangements for the sale of his house. A salesperson for Trusty persuaded Green to exchange his house for a new $200,000 house owned by Trusty and to assume a mortgage on the new house in the amount of $150,000. Trusty agreed to assume the mortgage on the old house. No other payments were to be made. After Green's house was transferred, Green sued Trusty for actual and punitive damages. Should Green win? Why or why not?

3. Carlos wanted to sell his farm for $600,000; and he signed open listing agreements with two brokers, Smith and Jones. Smith found a potential purchaser, Marley, who offered $600,000 to Carlos at 10:00 a.m. on March 2. The offer was accepted by Carlos. Later in the day before details such as the amount of down payment and date of possession were settled by Carlos and Marley, Jones produced a potential purchaser, Buckley, who offered $630,000 for the farm. Carlos accepted the offer and sold the farm to Buckley. Does Carlos owe a commission to Smith? Why or why not?

4. Cleon listed his business property with Chumney, a real estate broker. The listing agreement included the following provision: "During the life of this contract if you find a buyer who is ready, able and willing to buy, lease or exchange said property, ... or if I agree to an exchange of said property, or any part thereof, or if said property or any part thereof is sold, leased or exchanged during said term by myself or any other person, firm, or corporation, I agree to pay you the 6 percent commission." Assume that the agreement covered the period from June 8, 2004, to December 8, 2004, and that on August 2, 2004, Cleon sold the property to Super Tire Mart (which had in no way dealt with Chumney) for $120,000. Before the sale, Chumney had shown the property to several prospective buyers, had placed a "For Sale" sign on the property, and had advertised in the newspaper. Chumney's expenses totaled $73. Is Cleon liable to Chumney for damages? Why or why not? If Cleon is liable, what is the amount of damages?

5. Gould and Broadway Realty entered into a written listing agreement (as required by state law) that gave Broadway the exclusive right to sell Gould's property. The agreement provided that Broadway was to receive a commission at "the going rate in the area for comparable transactions." Within the time period specified in

the agreement, Gould sold the property for $14,500,000. If the going rate for comparable transactions is 10 percent, is Broadway entitled to a commission of $1,450,000? Why or why not?

6. Paula entered into an exclusive sales agreement with Flora, a real estate agent. The agreement read: "June 16, 2004, Exclusive sale of property. #26 Prospect Street, West Bridgewater, Mass., to my agent Flora. We are asking $120,000 (will take as low as $110,000). She is to have exclusive sale of same—for 90 days. Paula." Flora advertised the property, discussed the sale with many prospective buyers, and kept a key to the house. During the listing period, however, Flora had to leave town for a week; when she returned, she discovered that Paula had sold the property to a relative for $100,000. Flora sued Paula for her commission. Will Flora win? Why or why not?

7. The Marin County Board of Realtors consists of three-fourths of the brokers actively engaged in selling residential real property in Marin County, California. The board provides a number of benefits to its members, of which the most important is the only multiple listing service for residential property operating exclusively in Marin County. Multiple listing is a system of pooling each member's listings in a central registry. This service is available only to board members, who are prohibited by the board's bylaws from disseminating published listings to nonmembers. Palsson, a licensed real estate salesperson, applied to the board for membership after obtaining employment with an active member. His application was denied because the board found that as an airline flight engineer, he did not meet the requirements of one of the board's bylaws—a member must be "primarily engaged in the real estate business." This provision was enforced through sanctions against the active members who shared offices with or employed a person who had been denied membership in the board. Thus, a salesperson denied membership also was denied employment with 75 percent of the residential brokers in Marin County. Are the board's actions legal? Why or why not?

8. The Smalleys owned a quarter section of land in Merrick County. They entered into a real estate listing contract with Laurent, a real estate broker. Laurent was instructed by the Smalleys to secure the best price she could for the property but under no circumstances to take less than $1,500 an acre. Laurent was contacted by two prospective purchasers. One purchaser was Laurent's uncle, who offered $1,500 an acre; and the other was Post, who offered $2,000 an acre. Laurent informed the Smalleys only of her uncle's offer, which they accepted; and a purchase agreement was signed. Subsequently, as joint owners, Laurent and her uncle transferred the same property for $2,000 an acre to Post. When the Smalleys learned of the sale to Post, they sued Laurent for the profits of the second sale as well as for the $12,000 commission previously paid to Laurent. Will they win? Why or why not?

9. Rossi signed a sales agreement giving Larker the exclusive right to sell his house. The agreement provided that Larker could sign a sales agreement for Rossi and could receive from the buyer a cash deposit (earnest money) to be held for Rossi. The Golds agreed to purchase the house for $210,000 and made a $5,000 cash deposit, which was delivered by Larker to Rossi. They also paid $110,500 to Larker over the next few months, although this money was never given to Rossi. Rossi now demands payment of the balance due. How much do the Golds owe Rossi? Why?

10. Mantecon, a buyer's agent, informs Jameson, his client, who is sixty-five years old and about to retire, about certain potential problems with the house Jameson is interested in buying. Mantecon warns Jameson that "even though those high ceilings may be pleasing to the eye, with our cold winters your heating bills will be out of sight." Also, because of your age, Mantecon advises Jameson, "you will likely have a tough time climbing those stairs to the master bedroom upstairs as you grow older and possibly become disabled." Recognizing these problems, Jameson offers less money because he realizes that he may have to pay more for heating and might someday have to convert a downstairs office into a bedroom. Chatfield, the broker who is representing Sullivan, the seller, advises his client not to take Jameson's offer, that Sullivan should hold out for a higher price. If Mantecon were representing both Jameson and Sullivan as a dual agent, could he ethically make these representations to his clients? Can you ethically serve two principals with adversarial interests? Explain your answers.

ENDNOTES

1. *The Proper Role of the Lawyer in Residential Real Estate Transactions* 13 (American Bar Association, 1976).

2. See Ohio Rev.Code Ann. §4735.07.

3. G. Nelson and D. Whitman, *Real Estate Transfer, Finance and Development* 11 (1981). See: http://www.mortgagenewsdaily .com/real_estate_license/ for licensing requirements for all the states (last visited March 5, 2010).

4. See Ohio Rev.Code Ann. §4735.10.

5. 997 P.2d 239 (Ct.App.Or. 2000).

6. *Frankel v. Allied Mills, Inc.,* 369 Ill. 578, 17 N.E.2d 570 (1938).

7. S. Sheridan, *Policing Cyber Ads*, Broward Daily Business Review A1 (July 21, 1997).

8. R. Aalberts and T. Townsend, *Real Estate Transactions on the Internet and Personal Jurisdiction*, 10 Journal of Real Estate Literature 27 (2001).

9. R. Powell and P. Rowan, *Powell on Real Property*, 84C.04[2] (1993).

10. *West v. Barnes*, 351 S.W.2d 615 (Tex.Civ.App. 1961).

11. 170 A.D.2d 941, 566 N.Y.S.2d 764 (1991).

12. A. Gaudio, *Real Estate Brokerage Law* (1987) citing *Banks Real Estate Corp. v. Gordon*, 353 So.2d 859 (Fla.App. 1977).

13. *Averill v. Hart and O'Farrell*, 101 W.Va. 411, 132 S.E. 870 (1926).

14. *Julius Haller Realty Co. v. Jefferson-Gravois Bank*, 161 Mo.App. 472, 144 S.W.2d 174 (1940).

15. *Flamingo Realty, Inc. v. Midwest Development, Inc.*, 110 Nev. 984, 879 P.2d 69 (Nev. 1994).

16. 33 N.J.L. 247 (1869).

17. *Mayo v. Century 21 Action Realtors*, 823 S.W.2d 466 (Ky.App. 1992).

18. 274 Wis. 40, 79 N.W.2d 354 (1956).

19. 106 Ohio App. 369, 154 N.E.2d 827, 7 O.O.2d 105 (1958).

20. *Alexander v. Smith*, 180 Ala. 541, 61 So. 68 (1912).

21. *People v. Colorado Springs Bd. of Realtors*, 692 P.2d 1055, 1059 (Colo. 1984).

22. Powell and Rohan, supra note 9, at 84C.04[2].

23. 421 U.S. 773, 95 S.Ct. 2004, 44 L.Ed.2d 572 (1975).

24. 339 U.S. 485, 70 S.Ct. 711, 94 L.Ed. 1007 (1950).

25. 444 U.S. 232, 100 S.Ct. 502, 62 L.Ed.2d 441 (1980).

26. *Brokers: Here's an Antitrust Red Flag for Real Estate Boards and Multiple Listing Exchanges*, 5 Real Estate Law Report 1 (No. 7) (1975).

27. J. Hagerty, *Real-Estate Sites Raise Commissions*, Wall Street Journal D1 (December 24, 2003).

28. N. Hawker, *An Epilogue: Reflections on United States v. National Association of Realtors®"* 37 Real Estate Law Journal 194 (Fall 2008). See http://www.justice.gov/atr/cases/f233600/233607.htm to view the settlement. (Last visited on March 5, 2010).

29. *Id.* at 195.

30. M. Rich, *Firms Try to Expand Commercial Listings Online*, Wall Street Journal B10 (May 22, 2002).

31. J. Reilly, *Agency Relationships in Real Estate* 4 (1994).

32. W. Seavey, *Law of Agency* §28 (1964).

33. 136 So.2d 257 (Fla.App. 1962).

34. M. Goldhaber, *Windows on Main Street*, Part 1, at http://www.mouseplanet.com/articles.php?art=mg030611mg, (last visited March 5, 2010).

35. 918 P.2d 1157, 1164 (Haw. App. 1996).

36. *Thompson v. Hoagland*, 100 N.J. Super. 478, 242 A.2d 642 (1968).

37. 70 Ariz. 257, 219 P.2d 339 (1950), modified 70 Ariz. 408, 222 P.2d 789 (1950).

38. 116 Ga.App. 175, 156 S.E.2d 402 (1967).

39. K. Pancak et al., *Real Estate Agency Reform: Meeting the Needs of Buyers, Sellers and Brokers*, 25 Real Estate Law Journal 345 (1997). Nevada law states the following regarding mandatory agency disclosure: Nevada Administrative Code 645.637 "In each real estate transaction involving a licensee, as agent or principal, the licensee shall clearly disclose, in writing, to his client and to any party not represented by a licensee, his relationship as the agent of his client or his status as a principal. The disclosure must be made as soon as practicable, but not later than the date and time on which any written document is signed by the client or any party not represented by a licensee, or both. The prior disclosure must then be confirmed in a separate provision incorporated in or attached to that document and must be maintained by the real estate broker in his files relating to that transaction."

40. G. McClelland et al., *Buyer Brokering—Changing Some of the Rules in Residential Real Estate Transaction*, 18 Michigan Real Property Review 113 (1991).

41. Colo. Rev. Stat. §12-61-802(6) (2001). See generally A. M. Olazabel, *Redefining Realtor Relationships and Responsibilities: The Failure of State Regulatory Responses*, 40 Harvard Journal on Legislation 65 (2003). See also A. M. Olazabel and R. Sacasas, *Real Estate Agent as "Superbroker": Defining and Bridging the Gap Between Residential Realtors' Abilities and Liabilities in the New Millennium*, 30 Real Estate Law Journal 173 (Winter 2001/2002).

42. A. Yarborough, *The Practice of Sub-Agency Is Dead. For Gosh Sakes, Let's Bury It!* 3 Real Estate Educators Association Journal 31 (2003).

43. G. McClelland et al., *supra* note 40.

44. G. Cameron, *Buyer Brokering—More Complicated Than It Sounds*, Practical Real Estate Lawyer 23 (November 1996).

45. *Lingsch v. Savage*, 29 Cal.Rptr. 201, 204 (1993).

46. 152 Cal.App.3d 90, 199 Cal.Rptr. 383 (1984). See also N. Ordway and C. Yee, *Risk Reduction: The New Frontier in Real Estate Education*, Real Estate Educators Association Journal 21 (Spring 1990).

47. 657 A.2d 420, 428 (N.J. 1995).

48. S. Strauss et al., *Agents Now Are Liable to Buyers*, Real Estate Law Journal B11 (April 10, 1995).

49. *Hopkins v. Fox & Lazo Realtors*, 132 N.J. 426, 625 A.2d 1116 (1993).

50. *Smith v. Inman Realty Co.*, 846 S.W.2d 819 (Tenn.Ct.App. 1992).

51. *Trenta v. Gay*, 191 N.J. Super. 617, 468 A.2d 737 (1983).

52. R. W. Hahn et al., *Bringing More Competition to Real Estate Brokerage*, 35 Real Estate Law Journal 86, 98 (Summer 2006). See also N. Knox, *Home Shoppers Do Their Hunting Online*, USA Today 1B (February 9, 2007).

53. J. Bain and R. Guttery, *The Coming Downsizing of Real Estate: Implications of Technology*, 3 Journal of Real Estate Portfolio Management 1 (1997).

54. S. Ham and R. Atkinson, *Modernizing Home Buying: How IT Can Empower Individuals, Slash Costs, and Transform the Real Estate Industry*, Washington, DC: Progressive Power Institute: Washington, DC 6 (2003).

55. Aalberts and Townsend, *supra* note 8.

56. A useful summary of the Act is contained can be accessed at http://www.hud.gov/offices/hsg/ramh/ils/ilshome.cfm (last visited March 5, 2010).

57. 794 F.Supp. 1327 (D.S. Car. 1992).

58. 920 F.Supp. 1345 (E.D. Mich. 1996); affirmed 127 F.3d 478 (6th Cir. 1997).

59. 15 U.S.C. 1701(6).

60. R. Cartlidge, *The Interstate Land Sales Full Disclosure Act: What Does It Mean for Developers and Condo Buyers?* Green Buildings and Environmental Trends, March 29, 2009, http://www.greenbuildingenvirotrends.com/tags/interstate-land-sales-full-dis-1/ (last visited on March 4, 2010).

61. *NAREB Code of Ethics,* Oregon History Project, http://www
.ohs.org/education/oregonhistory/historical_records/dspDocu
ment.cfm?doc_ID=C62459FE-B688-7AC7-1F037E830F143F40
(last visited March 5, 2010).

62. 392 U.S. 409, 88 S.Ct. 2186, 20 L.Ed.2d 1189 (1968).

63. See *Ragin v. The New York Times,* 923 F.2d 995 (2d. Cir.
1991).

64. See Fair Housing—It's Your Right, http://www.hud.gov/offices/
fheo/FHLaws/yourrights.cfm (last visited March 5, 2010).

65. R. Aalberts, *Strict Liability Under the Fair Housing Act: A Legal Sleight of Hand?* 24 Real Estate Law Journal 4 (Spring
1996).

66. *Walker v. Crigler,* 976 F.2d 900 (4th Cir. 1992). See also *Chicago v. Matchmaker Real Estate Sales Center,* 982 F.2d 1086
(7th Cir. 1993).

67. *John Wieland Homes and Neighborhoods Sued by EEOC for
Race Discrimination,* U.S. Equal Opportunity Commission,
http://www.eeoc.gov/press/4-30-09a.html (last visited on
March 5, 2010).

68. Fair Housing—It's Your Right, *supra* note 64.

69. See Fair Housing—It's Your Right, *Id.*

70. M. A. Wolff, *The Fair Housing Amendments Act of 1988: A
Critical Analysis of "Familial Status,"* 54 Missouri Law Review
393 (1989).

71. 42 USC §3602(k) (2002).

72. 42 USC §3607(b)(2)(C).

73. Fair Housing—It's Your Right, *supra* note 64.

74. R. Aalberts and R. Hoyt, *Appraisers and the Fair Housing Act:
Accessibility Requirements for the Disabled,* 12 Journal of Real
Estate Research 429 (1996).

75. R. Aalberts, *Suits to Void Discriminatory Evictions of Disabled
Tenants Under the Fair Housing Amendments Act: An Emerging Conflict?* 33 Real Property, Probate and Trust Journal 649
(1999).

76. 909 F.Supp. 814 (D. Colo. 1995).

77. *Jones v. Alfred H. Mayer Co.,* 392 U.S. 409, 88 S.Ct. 2186, 20
L.Ed.2d 1189 (1968).

78. *How the Disabilities Act Affects Real Estate,* 23 The Mortgage
and Real Estate Executives Report 4 (September 15, 1990); I.
Shur, *Title III of the Americans With Disabilities Act,* ACCA
Docket 24 (Summer 1992).

79. S. McDonough, *Radio Shack Settles with Wheelchair Users,*
Ledger-Enquirer.com (June 22, 2005).

80. *National Federation of the Blind v. Target,* 452 F. Supp. 946
(N.D. Cal. 2006). See also *National Association of the Blind v.
Target,* Disabilities Rights Advocates, http://www.dralegal.org/
cases/private_business/nfb_v_target.php (last visited March 5,
2010).

81. MASS. GEN. LAWS ANN. ch. 151B, §(4)(6)(a) (West 1996 &
Supp. 2003).

82. *City of Edmunds v. Oxford House, Inc.,* 514 U.S. 725, 115 S.Ct.
1776, 131 L.Ed 8011 (1995).

83. R. Aalberts, *Will the ADA Strike Out?* 30 Real Estate Law
Journal 3 (2001).

84. R. Fausset, *FEMA Rules Thwart Plans for "Katrina Cottages,"*
Las Vegas Review Journal 31 (April 2, 2006). See also *Katrina
FEMA Trailer Turmoil,* CBS News Report, http://www
.cbsnews.com/video/watch/?id=5278240n (last visited March
3, 2010).

85. A. Packer, *Judge Rejects LV Law,* Las Vegas Review Journal 1
(November 21, 2006).

86. 431 U.S. 85, 97 S.Ct. 1614, 52 L.Ed.2d 155 (1977).

87. *Id.*

© MACIEJ NOSKOWSKI/iStockphoto (RF)

The Real Estate Contract

LEARNING OBJECTIVES

After studying Chapter 7, you should:

- Learn the basic legal requirements for a real estate contract

- Recognize and know additional provisions important to a real estate contract

- Be able to differentiate and apply contractual remedies and ways to avoid contracts

contract

A promise or set of promises for the breach of which the law gives a remedy, or the performance of which the law in some way recognizes as a duty.

"My idea of an agreeable person," said Hugo Bohum, "is a person who agrees with me."

Benjamin Disraeli, Lothair

"Everyone says buying your first apartment makes you feel like an adult. What no one mentions is that selling it turns you right back into a child."

Anderson Cooper, CNN Commentator

A study of the principles of contract law as they apply to real estate transactions is especially important for several reasons. A person often signs a preprinted offer to purchase or sell without understanding that it is legally binding. In addition, an individual may sign an offer without understanding the terms included in the standard form. Even when the printed terms are understood, the buyer and seller may not understand the "implied" terms of the **contract**[1]— those obligations that are imposed by the law even when the contract document is silent. Many people do not consult an attorney before signing even when the form clearly states that it is a contract, perhaps because of the common belief that an attorney should be contacted, if at all, only to handle the closing. Once the buyer and the seller have signed the contract, however, there is little an attorney can do to extricate a client from a disadvantageous commitment or to negotiate specific terms and conditions that would serve to avoid later disputes. While preprinted forms are frequently a good place to start in preparing an offer, the offer also should reflect agreements reached between the buyer and the seller on distinctive aspects of the transaction. (For a real estate contract/purchase and sale agreement, see www.cengagebrain.com [see page xix in the Preface for instructions on how to access the free study tools for this text].)

Contract law distinguishes between how a contract is first formed and how the rights and duties contained in the contract are performed. This distinction between formation and performance is especially important in real estate transactions. Contracts are frequently formed and performed at the same time.

When you purchased this book, for example, you paid for the book and took permanent possession of it simultaneously. A typical real estate contract, however, is rarely formed and performed at the same moment. Indeed, the **installment contract** (also called an *installment land contract*), which is discussed in Chapter 9, essentially blends a real estate contract and a mortgage and normally takes years to perform. The typical real estate contract is formed when the buyer and the seller exchange in writing the buyer's promise to purchase with the seller's promise to convey the property. A gap of weeks or months between formation and performance allows the buyer to examine title to the property, inspect its condition and purchase insurance (Chapter 8), and obtain financing (Chapter 9). Final performance of the real estate contract will take place at the closing (Chapter 10) if the property's title and condition are as represented in the contract and if the buyer is able to obtain financing. Defects in the property's title or condition or the buyer's inability to close if she cannot obtain financing can result in either the seller's or the buyer's default under the contract.

This chapter first examines requirements if the real estate contract is to be binding. The chapter then covers a number of provisions that, although not necessary to a binding contract, serve to protect the buyer and seller and therefore should be included in the contract. Finally, the chapter discusses legal principles under which the contract is void or voidable. Throughout this discussion, it is important to keep in mind an underlying purpose of the law of contracts—to facilitate the exchange of property.[2]

One topic that is not discussed in this chapter is the deed. A deed, covered in detail in Chapter 10, is *not* a real estate contract, but a written instrument used to convey title or ownership of a property interest from one party to another.

Legal Requirements

Statute of Frauds

Reginald and Robin were at a party when Reginald offered to purchase Robin's farm for $400,000. They proceeded to discuss details of the purchase, and Robin accepted Reginald's offer. When they concluded their negotiations, they announced their agreement in detail to the people present at the party and they sealed their agreement with a handshake. Is the agreement binding?

Prior to 1677, Reginald and Robin would be held to their agreement, which could be proven through the testimony of the witnesses. This was accomplished in a ceremony called a "livery of seisin" in which Robin, standing on his land, would hand over to Reginald a twig, clod of dirt, or some other symbol and utter well recognized words of conveyance reflecting his ownership interest. However, allowing such oral ceremonies or "handshake" agreements led to certain types of fraud. For example, if Reginald wanted Robin's farm but Robin refused to sell, Reginald might pay witnesses to testify that Robin had orally agreed to sell the property even when no such agreement had been made. Witnesses could also be bribed to say that Robin expressed words of conveyance that transferred only a life estate when he may have actually conveyed the more valuable fee simple absolute. To prevent such fraud, the English Parliament enacted the **Statute of Frauds** in 1677 requiring certain contracts, including contracts for the sale of real estate,

installment contract

Contract for the sale of real estate in which the seller finances the sale and the buyer pays the seller the purchase price over time.

Statute of Frauds

"No action shall be brought upon any contract or sale of lands, tenements, or hereditaments, or any interest in or concerning them ... unless the agreement upon which such action shall be brought, or some memorandum or note thereof, shall be in writing, and signed by the person to be charged therewith or some other person thereunto by him lawfully authorized."

to be in writing. The Statute of Frauds continues to have profound influence, and modern versions have been adopted in every state. Moreover, the statute applies not only to contracts, but also to nearly all legal instruments that pertain to real estate, including mortgages and deeds. Following is an application of Connecticut's version of this classic law, which has lost some of its rigidity through the years.

A CASE IN POINT

In *Fruin v. Colonnade One at Old Greenwich Limited Partnership*,[3] Fruin contracted to build a condominium for Colonnade One for $255,000. Due to lengthy delays, Fruin later attempted to avoid the contract. He claimed that the price was indefinite due to a rider that stated that "if any one bedroom end unit in Old Greenwich Gables having a floor plan and comparable footage as that of this unit is sold for a lower price than the price set forth in this Agreement, then the price of the subject unit will be reduced to said lower price...." The court explained that "[t]he statute of frauds requires that the essential terms and not every term of a contract be set forth [in writing] therein. The essential provisions of a [real estate] contract are the purchase price, the parties, and the subject matter for sale. The plaintiff [Fruin] claims that the use of the word 'comparable' in the purchase agreement at issue here makes it impossible to calculate the purchase price." The court held that "[t]he price of the plaintiff's unit could, therefore, be ascertained with reasonable certainty, and there is no violation of the statute of frauds."

part performance

An exception to the Statute of Frauds rule that allows for the oral contract for a sale of land if the party seeking enforcement has partially performed the contract.

estoppel

One person cannot claim a right to the detriment of another person when the latter was entitled to rely and did in fact rely on the first person's conduct.

Although the Statute of Frauds was designed to prevent fraud, the strict application of the statute would produce an unfair result in some circumstances. For example, suppose that Robin did agree orally to sell his farm and that Reginald moved onto the farm and rebuilt the farmhouse. When Reginald finished improving the property, could Robin force him to leave because the agreement was not in writing? If the court strictly followed the Statute of Frauds, Robin could force Reginald to leave and strip him of his investment.

For reasons such as the foregoing, an exception to the statute has been developed in many states to prevent such unfairness when there has been **part performance** of the contract. One statement of the exception is as follows: "Where, acting under an oral contract for the transfer of an interest in land, the purchaser with the assent of the vendor (a) makes valuable improvements on the land, or (b) takes possession thereof or retains a possession thereof existing at the time of the bargain, and also pays a portion or all of the purchase price, the purchaser or the vendor may specifically enforce the contract."[4]

The following classic California case, based on the equitable doctrine of **estoppel**, discusses another exception created to prevent unfairness.

A CASE IN POINT

In *Monarco v. LoGreco*,[5] Christie LoGreco's mother and stepfather orally promised that he would receive the family farm if he worked on it until both of them died. The stepfather, who survived his wife, willed the estate to his grandson, Carmen Monarco, instead. LoGreco could not enforce the promise because of the Statute of Frauds. The court, however, ruled that Monarco was estopped from claiming the estate due to the oral promise made to LoGreco and his reasonable reliance and decision to stay and work on the farm for room, board, and spending money for the twenty-year period that transpired until his mother's and stepfather's deaths.

While the Statute of Frauds dictates what basic information shall be contained in writing for a real estate contract to be enforceable, the **parol evidence rule** discussed in the next case from New York prescribes rules for excluding oral representations that a party may attempt to include in a real estate contract.

A CASE IN POINT

In *Mitchill v. Lath*,[6] the Laths, in negotiating the sale of their farm to Mitchill, orally promised to remove a nearby small house that Mitchill found objectionable. Relying on their promise, Mitchill signed a written contract to purchase the farm. However, the final contract did not include the Laths' promise to remove the house; when the Laths later refused to remove it, the court held that the Laths would not be held to their promise. According to the court, the promise to remove the house did not constitute a separate contract, but was merely part of the real estate transaction. And the real estate contract represented the final agreement describing the rights and duties of the parties. In the words of the court, "an inspection of this contract shows a full and complete agreement, setting forth in detail the obligations of each party. On reading it one would conclude that the reciprocal obligations of the parties were fully detailed." The court also rejected Mitchill's argument that the oral agreement was admissible under a three part exception to the parol evidence rule because (1) it was collateral to the written agreement; (2) it did not contradict express or implied provisions of the written contract; (3) and it was not a provision ordinarily expected to be embodied in the writing.

parol evidence rule

Provides that if the parties have put their contract in writing and intend the writing to be their final agreement, evidence of prior or contemporaneous agreements reached during negotiations may not be used in court to vary or contradict the written agreement.

The practical implications of the parol evidence rule are obvious. When you put your agreement in writing, comprised of all the written and oral terms that have been the subject of negotiations, it is important to remember that any kind of side agreements that are not in the final document may not be enforced in court. This is particularly important because standard, preprinted (sometimes called boilerplate) contracts nearly always contain an "integration" or "merger" clause that further reinforces the parol evidence rule. Still, the parol evidence rule, like the Statute of Frauds, has its exceptions designed to prevent unfairness. For example, parol evidence is admissible in court for showing that a *later* agreement varies the terms of the original written contract. Thus, if Lath had orally promised Mitchill that he would remove the small house *after* the contract was signed, Mitchill could have enforced that oral promise. It is noteworthy that boilerplate contracts often contain a "written modifications" clause that also requires that such oral promises be in writing. Also, as stated in the *Mitchill* case, there is a three element exception if the promise is deemed collateral to the written agreement. Other exceptions include admitting parol evidence when clarifying confusing or conflicting terms in the agreement or when such evidence is necessary to prove that the written contract was the result of a mistake, duress, undue influence, or fraud. Despite the protections the parol evidence rule provides, it is not uncommon for a party to attempt to enforce oral promises by alleging a number of the foregoing defenses and, by doing so, forcing the other party to settle to avoid spending valuable time and money in a prolonged lawsuit. That is why parties, particularly in complex and delicate contract negotiations, must exercise great care and consider a letter of intent (LOI) (discussed below) to avoid the possibility of these kinds of legal challenges arising later.

Negotiating the Written Contract

A contract represents a mutual agreement between parties that usually takes the form of an offer by one party and an acceptance by the other party. In most real estate transactions, a seller hires a broker (refer to Chapter 6) to find a prospective purchaser who will make an offer, which is then accepted by the seller. The purchaser can generally cancel the offer anytime before it is accepted by the seller, even when the offer states that it will be held open for a specified time. The offeror's termination of the offer prior to the offeree's acceptance is called **revocation**.

revocation
The termination of an offer by the offeror prior to an acceptance by the offeree.

> A seller agreed that a potential purchaser had three days to accept his counteroffer. Before the three days had expired, the seller revoked the counteroffer and accepted another party's offer. In *Rellinger v. Bremmeyr* in Chapter 6 on page 204, the court considers the seller's liability to the original party.

END OF CHAPTER CASE

option contract
An option is an enforceable promise that limits the offeror's power to revoke the offer. The option is said to be "exercised" when the offeree accepts the offer in accordance with the terms of the option contract.

A major exception to the revocation rule is the **option contract**.[7] (For an option agreement for the purchase of real estate, see www.cengagebrain.com [see page xix in the Preface for instructions on how to access the free study tools for this text].) Assume that a buyer persuades a seller to offer real estate for sale at the specified price of $100,000. However, the buyer does not want to accept the offer immediately because of certain business considerations. For example, the buyer might want to secure other options to purchase real estate in the same area or might want to obtain municipal approval for a proposed use.

To prevent revocation of the seller's offer, the buyer should negotiate an option contract in which the buyer pays the seller a specified sum (e.g., $10,000) in return for the seller's promise to hold the offer open to the buyer for a certain time period, such as six months. Often the option contract states that if the holder of the option decides to buy the property, the $10,000 will be applied toward the purchase price. But regardless of whether the offer is accepted, the seller keeps the $10,000 in exchange for giving up the right to revoke the offer.

mailbox rule
Derived from the 1818 case of *Adams v. Lindsell*, this rule provides that once the offeree has placed its letter of acceptance in a means of transit outside of its control—for example, in the mail—it is too late for the offeror to revoke.

In most cases, where an option contract is not used, an offer is accepted when the seller signs the agreement and communicates the acceptance to the buyer. In face-to-face transactions, communication is no problem because the buyer is present and can observe the seller signing the agreement. As the following Florida case explains, a **mailbox rule**[8] has been developed to determine the moment the acceptance goes into effect if contracts are negotiated over long distances.

A CASE IN POINT

In *Morrison v. Thoelke*,[9] sellers signed and mailed an acceptance of the purchaser's offer to buy real estate. Before the contract arrived, however, the sellers called the purchaser's attorney and canceled the acceptance. The court decided that the sellers had made a binding acceptance when the contract was mailed, citing Corbin, *Contracts* §§78 and 80: "Where the parties are negotiating at a distance from each other, the most common method of making an offer is by sending it by mail; and more often than not the offeror has specified no particular mode of acceptance. In such a case, it is now the prevailing rule that the offeree has power to accept and close the contract by mailing a letter of acceptance, properly stamped and addressed, within a reasonable time. The contract is regarded as made at the time and place that the letter of acceptance is put into the possession of the post office department."

mirror image rule

A doctrine that states for a valid contract to exist, the terms of the offeree's acceptance must correspond exactly to the offer made by the offeror.

counteroffer

A statement by the offeree that has the legal effect of rejecting the offer and of proposing a new offer to the original offeror.

letter of intent

An instrument that serves to gauge each party's commitment to a future contractual relationship before the parties reach agreement on a formal contract.

In accepting the buyer's offer, the seller is bound by the **mirror image rule** of contract law: the acceptance must be on the terms stated in, or must mirror, the offer. If the seller changes one of the terms of the offer (no matter how slight) before signing, the seller has not accepted the offer; instead, the seller has made a **counteroffer** to the buyer that may or may not be accepted by the buyer. Furthermore, a counteroffer kills the original offer, so the seller cannot thereafter accept that offer. (See Figure 7.1.)

To prevent termination of the offer, a seller might adopt the strategy of accepting the offer as presented and then renegotiating the terms of the original contract, as suggested in the following example from an Arizona case:[10] "It is the law that when A offers B to enter into a contract on certain terms, and B declines to accept those terms but offers a counter proposition, the original offer loses its effect, and is thereafter only open to acceptance by B when renewed by A. On the other hand, if A makes an offer which is unconditionally accepted by B, the fact that B, after such acceptance, proposes a modification of the original contract, which is declined by A, does not affect the validity of the original contract." Of course, a strategy which counts on the other party modifying a contract presents risks as well. As pointed out in the above scenario, the offeror may *not* choose to modify the contract, thus rendering the offeree bound to the contract. If the disappointed offeree reneges on the contract he erroneously predicted he could modify, he may be subject to legal and equitable remedies, topics discussed later in the chapter.

Another strategy that some sellers and buyers employ, particularly when negotiating commercial real estate and other complex transactions, is the **letter of intent** (LOI). (For a LOI to purchase real estate, see www.cengagebrain.com [see page xix in the Preface for instructions on how to access the free study tools for this text].) A LOI is often used as a preliminary instrument for enabling the parties to focus on material terms, such as price and financing, before finalizing the agreement. A LOI can serve not only as a useful starting point for the negotiations but also as a gauge of each party's commitment before they move on to the next step. If a LOI is drafted carefully and correctly, it should not bind the parties unless they express a desire to be bound. For example, both parties may agree to be bound by a confidentiality clause but then provide that the price in the LOI does not serve as an offer, but only as a preliminary figure for negotiation. A LOI is, of course, subject to the same rules as any contract for the conveyance of real estate. Thus, if it is in writing and contains language indicating an intent to be contractually bound, a party is legally bound in the same way as he or she would be in a normal real estate contract.[11]

Required Terms in the Written Contract

The Statute of Frauds' requirement of a "writing" for the sale and purchase of real estate includes certain necessary written terms. If the four essential terms discussed shortly are

FIGURE 7.1
Effect of Counteroffer

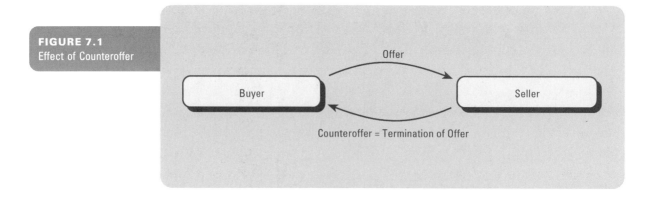

included in the written agreement, the contract will be enforceable under the Statute of Frauds, even when the terms are written informally, such as on a receipt, on the back of a napkin, or in the margin of a textbook.

As the following classic case from Virginia demonstrates, courts are unconcerned with the length of the agreement as long as the essentials are present.

A CASE IN POINT

In *Lucy v. Zehmer*,[12] the court held that the following agreement was binding on the people who signed it, A. H. and Ida Zehmer: "We hereby agree to sell to W. O. Lucy the Ferguson Farm complete for $50,000, title satisfactory to buyer." The Zehmers claimed that the agreement was signed as a joke and that Mr. Zehmer, who had been drinking, "was high as a Georgia pine." However, the court concluded that Zehmer was not too drunk to make a valid contract and that he never told the other party that he was joking.

This case brings out two additional issues: whether additional contract terms are prudent even when not required and whether the seller, Zehmer, possessed the capacity to contract despite his intoxication. Both of these issues are addressed later in this chapter.

Names of Buyer and Seller The contract must, at a minimum, contain the names of both the buyer and the seller. However, the names do not have to be included within the body of the agreement; the signatures of the parties are sufficient.

Description of the Real Estate The contract should include a description of the real estate sufficiently detailed so that a court can identify the real estate without considering evidence outside the contract. For example, if the real estate was described as "1507 South Lake Irving Drive, County of Beltrami, Minnesota," a court would have to look outside the agreement to determine which city in Beltrami County has a South Lake Irving Drive.

Consideration: The Price The law requires that if one party is to be held to a contractual promise, the other party must give something in exchange, in **consideration**, for the promise. Thus, if Tom promises to transfer his real estate to Mary, Mary must give up something in exchange, usually her promise to pay for the real estate. As long as something is promised, no matter what its economic value, the contract will be enforced. For example, real estate can be sold legally for just $1. In the early Virginia case of *Hale v. Wilkinson*,[13] Hale agreed in 1863 to sell his house and fourteen acres to Wilkinson for $10,000, payable on an installment basis in Confederate money. Wilkinson made the payments, but Hale refused to execute a deed. Hale claimed that the price was inadequate since the currency was worthless after the defeat of the Confederacy. The court, in holding for Wilkinson, cited the rule that inadequacy of consideration is no defense in the absence of fraud since the Confederate money had economic value at the time the agreement occurred.

Most jurisdictions require that for the real estate contract to be enforceable, it must include a statement of the purchase price that is the consideration.[14] It is noteworthy that a deed, which is *not* a contract but an instrument for conveying a property interest, generally does not have to cite the purchase price. Deeds are discussed in Chapter 10. The statement of the price must be in terms clear and definite enough for a court to enforce, as it was in the *Fruin v. Colonnade One at Old Greenwich Limited Partnership*

consideration
The cause, motive, price, or impelling influence that induces a contracting party to enter into a contract.

case discussed on page 221. Real estate contracts often lack such precision. If the contract merely states the price, it is assumed that a cash sale was intended and that the payment is due at closing. But errors occur even with simple cash sales. Details of the price are most likely to lack clarity and completeness in contracts that call for the buyer to make deferred payments, usually on an installment basis over a period of time. The next case from Connecticut demonstrates this issue.

A CASE IN POINT

In *Montanaro v. Pandolfini*,[15] the contract stated that the buyer was to give a "purchase money mortgage to seller in the amount of eighteen thousand dollars ($18,000) payable monthly for 15 years at 5%." The seller later refused to perform the contract and, when sued by the buyer, claimed the price terms were not specific enough. The court agreed with the seller, citing the following rule: "We have uniformly held that such an agreement must state the contract with such certainty that its essentials can be known from the memorandum itself, without the aid of parol proof, or from a reference contained therein to some other writing or thing certain; and these essentials must at least consist of the subject of the sale, the terms of it and the parties to it, so as to furnish evidence of a complete agreement."

In applying the rule, the court could not determine the amount of the monthly payment. The parties might have intended equal monthly payments, much like mortgage payments to a bank. Or the parties might have intended steady principal payments with varying total monthly payments depending on the interest due. Or the parties even might have intended the buyer to make whatever monthly payments he could. Whatever the intention, it was not specified in the contract. Furthermore, the agreement was defective in failing to state when the monthly payments would begin.

ETHICAL AND PUBLIC POLICY ISSUES

Is It Ethical to Allow Buyers and Sellers to Decide the Price of Real Estate No Matter How Disproportionate It May Be to Its Real Value?

Problem 10 at the end of the chapter includes a discussion of a policy applied in the civil law legal system that, unlike the common law, protects unwary sellers from charging too little for their real estate.

Signatures of the Parties   The written purchase agreement should be signed by both the seller and the buyer. However, the law requires only the signature of the person against whom enforcement of the contract is sought. For example, John and Mary enter into a written agreement whereby Mary agrees to purchase John's house but only Mary signs the agreement. If Mary later refuses to perform the contract, she is liable on the contract because she signed. However, if John refused to turn the house over to Mary, she could not enforce the agreement against him unless he had signed it.

Often the contract is signed by an agent of the seller or purchaser. Many states require not only that the agent sign the purchase agreement but also that the authorization given the agent by the seller or purchaser be in writing.

Can a real estate contract be signed using an electronic signature? Since the passage of the federal Electronic Signatures in Global and National Commerce Act (E-Sign) in 2000, all electronic contracts, signatures, and other records involving a transaction that affects interstate commerce, including the sale, lease, or exchange of real estate, are considered legal even if they are contrary to a state's statutory or case law, such as the Statute of

Frauds. This federal preemption of state law is meant to create uniformity among the states. An electronic signature is defined broadly under E-Sign to include "an electronic sound, symbol, or process, attached to or logically associated with a contract or other record and executed or adopted by a person with the intent to sign the record."[16] The Act permits the states some variation if they adopt the Uniform Electronic Transactions Act (UETA).[17] This exception, however, will likely have little effect since the UETA sanctions the use of electronic real estate transactions in a manner that, in many cases, parallels E-Sign. The practical implications of E-Sign are varied and complex—although quite necessary—in the age of e-commerce. As one concerned commentator sees it:

> [I]f you sent me an e-mail that said: "I'll buy your property at 450 W. Meyer in Chicago for $50,000," and I typed at the top of this message "O.K." and hit "return," it is quite likely that we would have a binding real estate contract. All you would have to show is that the typing of the word "O.K." indicated my intent to express agreement. The fact that I did not type out my name would not matter, because I "attached" an "electronic symbol" (i.e., the word "O.K.") to a contract. The contract would still have to meet standards of clarity and certainty, and perhaps an exchange this informal would not meet those standards in some jurisdictions. But the point is that a relatively simple and perhaps thoughtless act might result in the formation of a serious contractual obligation.[18]

A recent case from New York, *Stevens v. Publicis*,[19] addressed the issue of whether a person's name typed in an e-mail constitutes a signature required under that state's Statute of Frauds. The Court ruled that "e-mail transmissions [that] bore the typed name of the sender at the foot of the message" constituted "signed writings." At least one other New York state court ruled that an e-mail which simply signed off with "I'll talk to you later" was also legally sufficient under the state's statute. In general, these courts argue that as long as the source of the communication and the authority of the sender are established, the contracts are enforceable.[20]

Courts will continue to address e-mail issues relating to real estate in the future. In the meantime, those engaged in real estate transactions on the Internet must be very careful what they state in an e-mail as they maneuver in an evolving but still unclear legal environment.

Alternatives to the Conventional Real Estate Contracts: Land Exchanges and Lease-to-Own Agreements

Lease-to-Own Contracts   "Lease-to-own" contracts, also called "lease with an option to purchase" agreements, are now increasingly being used by those buyers who wish to eventually buy a home but must wait for their credit rating to be repaired to secure a mortgage. (To see a lease with an option to buy agreement, see www.cengagebrain.com [see page xix in the Preface for instructions on how to access the free study tools for this text].) The contract is essentially a lease with an option to buy property at an agreed upon price. Normally the sale is stated to occur within a specified time in the future, such as three years or less. The negotiated option is typically a percentage of the price, for example, one to five percent, and is credited, along with the rents and a rent premium, to the purchase price if the lessee buys the property. If the option to buy is not exercised, the buyer will lose the option fee and rent premium.

Land Exchanges   An alternative to the cash sale of real estate is where a piece of land is exchanged or swapped for another. There are significant tax advantages to land exchanges for commercial and real estate investors. Indeed, under Internal Revenue Code (IRC) §1031, with an exchange of "like kind" investment real estate, a seller can defer paying capital gains taxes provided that certain statutory requirements are satisfied. All investment real estate is "like kind" regardless of whether it is undeveloped or improved. According to one expert, IRC §1031 exchanges (also called *Starker Exchanges*) are "a vast multi-billion dollar-per-year industry."[21]

In general, the IRC §1031 land exchange process works in the following manner. Assume that B, a large real estate investment company, wants to sell a piece of property to A for $1 million. Since B had acquired the property that it now wants to sell (called the "relinquished property") two years ago for $800,000, it would now be subject to capital gains taxes on $200,000. B, of course, would like to defer paying the tax; so it approaches C, a company that specializes in IRC §1031 exchanges, and hires C as its *qualified intermediary* (QI). After closing the deal with A, B (the *exchangor*) instructs that the $1 million be transferred directly to C the QI, which holds the money in an escrow account. B then begins searching for a property to buy (called the "replacement property"), which it must do quickly. B has only 45 days to identify one or more properties and 180 days total from the earlier date from which B sold its land to A or the due date when B files its income taxes (including extensions) to close the deal. These deadlines are absolute and cannot be extended. Assume that B, within 30 days, identifies a property owned by D. D, the *exchangee*, is willing to sell its land to B for $1 million, which is paid by the intermediary, C. If the deal closes within the 180-day limit, B can defer the capital gains tax it would have been subject to on the $200,000. Figure 7.2 illustrates the process.

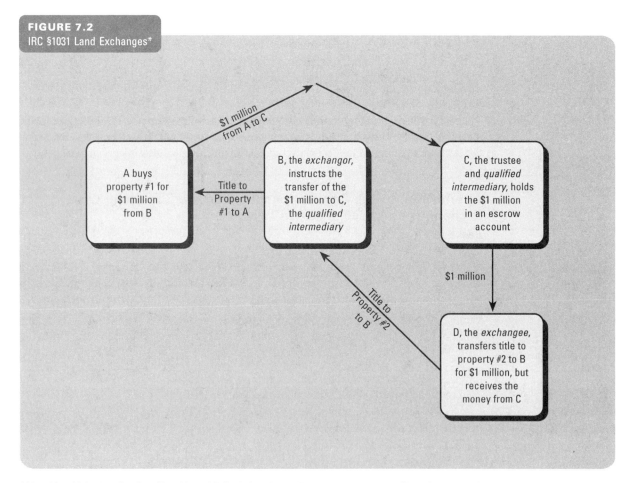

FIGURE 7.2
IRC §1031 Land Exchanges*

*Adapted from M. Bowden, *Save Your Clients Money With Tax-Deferred Property Exchanges*, Lawyers Weekly USA B14 (May 29, 2000).

The IRC §1031 exchange law does not require a QI. For example, if the previous process had occurred simultaneously, the use of the QI would not be necessary. However, because property sales, particularly commercial land transactions, are complicated, the typical delayed exchange requires an intermediary since the *exchangor* cannot have actual or constructive possession of the funds coming from the sale of the relinquished property.

Although §1031 exchanges confer significant tax benefits for many commercial parties, there has been an unfortunate downside to them as well. Most states exercise little regulatory oversight over the industry, and as a result, a number of sellers in particular have been stung by unethical QIs. For example, QIs in some instances have embezzled the money that was assumed to be safe in their escrow accounts. As a result, those who engage in these transfers must be careful to choose only those QIs which are adequately capitalized and enjoy a good business reputation.[22]

Additional Contract Provisions

The Statute of Frauds' requirements, as stated earlier in *Fruin v. Colonnade One at Old Greenwich Limited Partnership,* include only the bare bones of the real estate contract. Additional provisions, although not required by law, should be negotiated and included in the writing to avoid harsh or unfavorable results for the seller or the buyer and to provide clarity about how such matters should be resolved. Such additional provisions also can avoid later disputes. The next section begins by discussing the impact that two important real estate concepts—marketable title and equitable conversion—have on real estate transactions and the corresponding contractual provisions.

Marketable Title

marketable title
Title to real estate that is reasonably free from encumbrances, defects in the chain of title, and other problems that affect the title.

"Title," which is discussed in Chapter 8, is the formal right to the ownership of real property as reflected by a historical record. The term **marketable title** refers to title "which is free from reasonable doubt, and a title is doubtful and unmarketable if it exposes the party holding it to the hazard of litigation."[23] In the words of another court,[24] a marketable title "is one that can again be sold to a reasonable purchaser, a title that a man of reasonable prudence, familiar with the facts and apprised of the questions of law involved, would in the ordinary course of business accept."

The general rule is that if the contract is silent, the law presumes that the vendor is to convey marketable title clear of restrictions. Since the law assumes marketable title, why should the parties state otherwise in their contract? To understand the reasons for addressing marketable title issues in the contract, *four* common problems are examined. Then Marketable Record Title Acts and the merger rule are discussed.

Easements and Restrictive Covenants   Most real estate is subject to easements (refer to Chapter 4) and/or restrictive covenants (see Chapter 13),[25] and these make the title unmarketable.[26] For example, a seller who promises to convey marketable title will be unable to perform the contract if a utility company has a recorded easement running through the center of the property. To avoid this result, the agreement should state that the property is "subject to easements and restrictions of record." While this language solves the seller's problem because the buyer would have agreed to purchase the property subject to the recorded utility easement, the language might cause the buyer problems. Most buyers sign real estate contracts allowing the seller to convey "subject to easements and restrictions of record" without understanding the nature of the recorded easements. This is a dangerous practice. A buyer who does not check records or require the seller to list the easements to which the sale is subject runs the risk that there might be easements crossing the property that materially affect the use or market value of the real estate.

Zoning and Building Code Restrictions

In most cases, real estate is subject to both zoning and building code restrictions. For instance, Marc agrees in writing to sell a parcel of real estate to Jennifer, who wants to build a restaurant on the property. After the contract is signed, Jennifer learns that the property is zoned for residential use only; furthermore, Jennifer could not build the restaurant she had planned because of building code restrictions. May Jennifer back out of the contract by claiming that the title is unmarketable?

According to the general rule, the property's existing building and zoning code restrictions do not make the title unmarketable, because these are imposed in furtherance of public policy, not by private agreements. The buyer must determine the nature of such restrictions before signing the purchase agreement or make the contract contingent on the approval of the appropriate local government agency. The courts are divided on whether the seller's use of the property in violation of zoning or building ordinances makes the title unmarketable, allowing the buyer to back out of the contract.[27] As discussed later in this chapter, a building code violation may be a defect that the seller is obligated to disclose to the buyer whether or not the defect renders the title unmarketable in the particular jurisdiction.

Mortgages and Other Liens

Assume that when Marc signed the contract to sell his real estate to Jennifer, the real estate was subject to a mortgage that Marc had taken out or to another type of lien such as a tax or mechanic's lien. (See Chapter 9.) The seller typically will not have funds to satisfy an existing mortgage until the closing date, when he applies some or all of the sale's proceeds to satisfy such a mortgage. May Jennifer avoid the contract because of the lien even if Marc promises he will pay off the lien from the funds made available by Jennifer at the closing? In most states, the title will still be considered marketable if the mortgagee or lien holder is ready and willing to release the lien after receiving payment at the closing. To be safe, however, the seller, Marc, should include in the contract a provision that he will satisfy any liens at closing.

Access

The buyer should make a physical inspection of the property to ensure access, and she should verify access with a survey of the property. The courts generally hold that the title is marketable even when the owner does not have legal access, as access affects only the property's value, not its title.[28] Such a buyer, however, can still gain access by proving, often unfortunately after an expensive lawsuit, that there is an easement by prior use or necessity as discussed in Chapter 4.

Marketable Record Title Acts

Given the usual requirement that the seller must provide a marketable title, a purchaser, aided by a knowledgeable attorney, can easily claim that a title is unmarketable. You might assume that Marc is selling Jennifer property that President John Quincy Adams originally granted in a land **patent** to a pioneer family in 1825. The property had changed hands fifteen times between 1825 and 1990, when Marc acquired it. If Jennifer wanted to avoid the contract, her attorney might "flyspeck" the title. That is, the attorney would closely examine each of the fifteen conveyances to determine whether something might make the title unmarketable. He might discover, for example, that the wife of a grantor in 1899 had not signed the deed, that an agent signed the deed for a vendor but no written authorization was recorded, or that an executor of the estate of a deceased party sold the property in 1910 but that there was no proof on record that he had authority to make the sale.

patent
A grant of a privilege, property, or authority to an individual by the government.

To alleviate the problem of proving marketable title in such circumstances, especially when the alleged defect occurred so many years ago that it is difficult for the seller to correct or disprove it, many states have enacted **Marketable Record Title Acts**. These acts provide that specified types of claims are invalidated when the public records from the **root of title**[29] to the date of the title search do not reflect the claims. For example, if no one has ever pressed a claim concerning the rights of the wife of the grantor who failed to sign the deed in 1899, the title is considered marketable and would therefore not have to be cured.

The Acts also consider a title marketable when there are no defects in the title over a certain time span, usually the preceding forty-year period. Each Act contains certain exceptions, such as the rights of people who are in adverse possession (discussed in Chapter 10) of the real estate, easements that are clearly observable by examining the property, and rights of the state. Thus, the Marketable Record Title Acts function like a statute of limitations, simplifying title status by allowing purchasers to rely on the record title for the statutory period.

Even states that do not have Marketable Record Title Acts may recognize that title searches need examine title only for a sufficient length of time as is necessary to establish the property's present legal status. In *Coe v. Hays*,[30] a Maryland court held that title was marketable when the source of title to a grantee in 1896 could not be established but good title could be traced to a grantor of a deed made fifty-seven years before the present transaction. The court held that fifty-seven years was a sufficient and customary period for a title search.

Marketability and the Merger Rule   The seller must provide marketable title at the time of closing rather than on the date the contract is signed. Most contracts specify that the seller must pay for and provide evidence of title, usually in the form of an abstract of title or a title insurance policy. If the contract is silent, the buyer must secure her own evidence of title.

If at the closing, the seller cannot provide marketable title but the purchaser decides to complete the transaction anyway, the purchaser loses the right to object to the conditions that make the property unmarketable. In such a case, the contract is said to merge with the deed, with the result that the rights of the parties will be defined *after* the closing by the deed rather than by the contract. (See Figure 7.3.) As a result, it is common

---

Marketable Record Title Acts

State laws that limit the enforceability of old claims and interests.

root of title

A transaction in the seller's chain of title "being the most recent to be recorded as of a date prior to the statutory number of years before the time marketability is being determined."

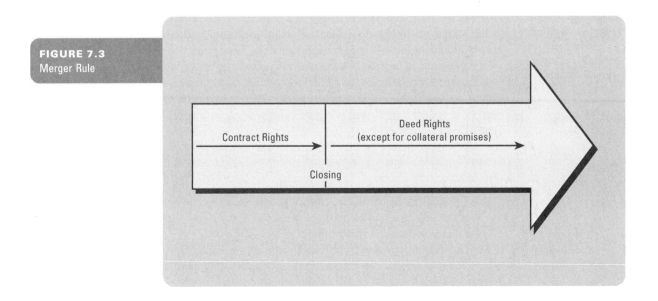

FIGURE 7.3
Merger Rule

Contract Rights → Deed Rights (except for collateral promises) →

Closing

merger rule

That the contract merges into (and is replaced by) the deed, except for collateral promises.

for buyers to require that certain warranties and promises of the seller "survive," or extend beyond, the closing.

There is an important legal exception to the **merger rule** illustrated by the following Massachusetts case.

A CASE IN POINT

In *Lipson v. Southgate Park Corp.*[31] the plaintiff entered into a contract with the defendant on October 3 under which the defendant was to transfer a parcel of land and construct a house in accordance with detailed plans and specifications. On the following January 20, after the house was built, the plaintiff paid the purchase price and the defendant delivered a deed to the land. The plaintiff later sued the defendant for damages, claiming that the building was erected in an unskillful manner, the plans and specifications were not followed, and the wrong building materials were used.

The defendant conceded that the plaintiff was correct, but claimed that the plaintiff could not collect because of the merger rule. The court cited the general rule and the exception from an earlier case: "In *Pybus v. Grasso*, we stated the rule to be that: 'The acceptance of a deed of conveyance of land from one who has previously contracted to sell it, discharges the contractual duties of the seller to the party so accepting except such as are embodied in the deed....' We went on, however, to say that: 'To the general rule as stated above there is an exception to the effect that promises in the original agreement which are additional or collateral to the main promise to convey the land and are not inconsistent with the deed as given are not necessarily merged in the deed, but may survive it and be enforced after the deed is given.'"

Applying the exception to the merger rule for collateral promises, the court decided that the promise to construct the house was collateral to the promise to convey the land and consequently survived the deed: "A provision in a contract as to title and possession will usually be merged in an accepted deed. However, the provisions imposing an obligation upon the defendant to erect a dwelling were so far collateral to the undertaking relating to title and possession, as to indicate that the omission of these provisions from the deed was without an intent to preclude their survival."

Equitable Conversion

equitable conversion

A doctrine under which a buyer who signs a real estate contract is immediately regarded as the equitable owner of the real property, while the seller has an equitable interest in the purchase price.

The doctrine of **equitable conversion** developed from a principle of equity: "Equity regards as done that which ought to be done." Once a real estate contract is signed, what "ought to be done" is that the purchaser should acquire the real estate and the seller should receive the purchase price. Thus, under the doctrine of equitable conversion, the buyer is regarded as the equitable owner of the property from the date of contract. The seller's interest is, as of the contract date, converted into personal property (the purchase price) even though the seller retains legal title to the real property, which serves as security before the purchase price is paid. In theory, the purchaser's interest is converted into real property.

Treating the seller's interest as personal property and the buyer's interest as real property during the interval between signing the contract and the closing has several consequences:

1. If the seller dies before the closing, the purchase price will pass to the representative of the seller's estate as personal property. If the buyer dies, the buyer's interest will pass to her heirs as real property.
2. The risk of decreases in the land's value and the benefits of increases go to the buyer.
3. Unless otherwise determined in the purchase agreement, the buyer bears losses that result from natural causes or the acts of third parties.

Suppose that Marc entered into a written agreement to sell his $100,000 house to Jennifer. They scheduled the closing for June 15. On June 1, the house was struck by lightning and burned to the ground. Under the equitable conversion rule, the loss would fall on Jennifer, who would have to pay $100,000 to Marc for the charred remains of the house.

This rule can be a harsh one because most buyers do not purchase property insurance until the closing. To avoid this result, a number of states, including California and Texas,[32] (see endnote 32 for complete list of states) have enacted the Uniform Vendor and Purchaser Risk Act, which provides that if the contract does not specify otherwise, the risk of loss shall remain with the vendor unless legal title or possession has been transferred to the purchaser or the purchaser causes the loss. Whether or not a state in which the property is located has enacted the Uniform Risk Act, the contract should specify who bears the risk of loss so that the specified party is certain to carry appropriate insurance coverage.

Other Contract Provisions

The parties should negotiate and include in the purchase and sale agreement a number of additional terms. While the circumstances and complexity of each transaction may suggest specific areas to be addressed, the following generic issues should be addressed in the contract.

> **earnest money**
> A portion of the purchase price given to the seller when the contract is signed as evidence of the buyer's good faith and willingness to perform the contract.

Earnest Money   The contract usually provides that the buyer's deposit, called **earnest money**, will be held by a third party until closing when it is released to the seller's account. This third party may be the broker, the buyer's attorney, the seller's attorney, or an escrow agent. If the seller defaults under the contract, the contract typically provides that the earnest money deposit will be returned to the buyer. In turn, the buyer's deposit is typically tendered to the seller in the event of the buyer's default. Earnest money deposits are *not* considered down payments, (although the amount can be applied to the purchase price if stated in the contract) but rather a liquidated damages provision, discussed below. Liquidated damages clauses are also discussed in detail in Chapter 9.

The potential for losses to both parties if there is a breach can be significant. The seller will remove the property from the market when the contract is signed, and a buyer's default will cause the seller to incur additional marketing and carrying costs. Other seller expenses incurred after the contract is signed and before closing takes place include the cost of proving title and, unless the listing agreement contains a "no deal, no commission clause" or a similar state statute (as discussed in Chapter 6), the seller must pay the broker's commission. For these reasons, the seller should ensure that the contract requires the buyer to make a down payment of earnest money that is large enough to cover expenses. A substantial deposit also motivates the buyer to close. As the following Ohio case illustrates, buyers should keep in mind that if they breach the contract, they may lose their earnest money deposits.

A CASE IN POINT

In *Ottenstein v. Western Reserve Academy,*[33] Ottenstein entered into a contract to purchase ten lots in Hudson, Ohio, from Western Reserve Academy for approximately $185,340. The plaintiff paid $5,000 in earnest money when the contract was signed, but he never paid the balance. Finally, the Academy sold the lots to another party; and the buyer brought suit to recover the earnest money. The court, in following the majority rule, declared that the earnest money was forfeited even when the contract did not mention forfeiture.

Even when the buyer defaults, courts may be reluctant to allow the seller to retain the buyer's entire deposit if the amount of the deposit is clearly disproportionate to the seller's damages. Under these circumstances, forfeiture of the deposit may be viewed as an unenforceable penalty instead of a reasonable liquidated damages provision that is intended to ensure compensation to the seller.[34] For example, a Pennsylvania court held that the seller's retention of the buyer's deposit in the amount of 60 percent of the purchase price crossed the line of permissible compensation.[35] However, this rule is not used in many states, including New York, as discussed in *Uzan v. 845 UN Limited Partnership* on page 255, where a showing of disparity of bargaining power between the parties, such as in transactions involving an unsophisticated buyer or seller, duress, fraud, illegality, or mutual mistake, is the only way to reduce or vitiate the buyer's duty to forfeit the earnest money deposit when he breaches the contract. In all likelihood, buyers have generally been providing overly high earnest money deposits to sellers because they erroneously thought their real estate agent, often a subagent, was representing their interests, an issue discussed in Chapter 6. In actuality, subagents represent the interests of sellers, who naturally want the largest earnest money deposit possible. With the increasing use of buyers' agents, this practice should become less prevalent.

Fixtures   As discussed in Chapter 2, the contract should specify which fixtures, if any, will be retained by the seller and which fixtures will be included in the sale. If the seller shows the home with, for example, a dining room chandelier that he intends to remove, the seller should clearly reserve this right in the contract. The fixture clause related to lighting might provide that "lighting fixtures, except the dining room chandelier, are included." Other standard items to consider in the contract's fixture clause include the washer and dryer, ceiling fans, kitchen appliances, and window treatments. An itemized list protects the buyer and the seller by making their intent a matter of record.

Contingencies   Performance of a real estate contract is commonly made contingent on the occurrence of a certain event, such as a change in the zoning law, the sale of the buyer's present house, or the buyer obtaining a loan at a specified interest rate. In recent years, many sellers and buyers have also made the sale contingent on having their attorneys approve the contract.[36] **Contingencies** are placed in the contract for the protection of one of the parties, but that party may choose to waive the contingency. For instance, the contract could be made subject to the buyer obtaining a loan at an interest rate below six percent; yet a buyer who cannot obtain a loan for less than six percent may waive the condition and hold the seller to the contract. The following New Hampshire court discusses the important issue of sales that are contingent on securing financing.

contingency
An event that may not occur.

When a purchase agreement is subject to a financing contingency, what are the buyer's obligations to pursue financing? In *Renovest Company v. Hodges Development Corp.* on page 251, the court resolves that question.

END OF CHAPTER CASE

Contingencies are especially important in construction contracts. When these contingencies are explicit, they will be enforced as agreed on by the parties. Thus, if an owner hires an architect to prepare plans for a new home but the plans are "subject to the owner's satisfaction," the architect will not be paid if the owner is honestly dissatisfied.

The condition has not been met. The architect, therefore, will want to attach the buyer's "satisfaction" to more objective conditions of performance.

In many construction contracts, certain conditions are implied. The most important of these conditions relates to the owner's duty to pay the contractor. It is implied that this duty is conditional on the contractor completing the structure exactly as promised. If the contractor does not complete his part of the agreement, the condition has not been met and the owner does not have to pay.

This implied condition would often lead to an unfair result if the courts strictly applied it. For example, Amber hires a contractor, Dylan, to build a $300,000 house. After Dylan completes the house, Amber discovers that the bathroom tile is the wrong color and refuses to pay Dylan anything since Dylan has not met the condition of completing the building as promised. Most courts, realizing that this result would be unfair to Dylan, apply the **substantial performance doctrine**.

substantial performance doctrine

Substantial performance occurs when a contractor has performed enough of the contract to deserve payment.

Under the substantial performance rule, if Dylan has substantially performed the contract—which is a question of fact that must be determined on a case-by-case basis—he is entitled to his payment minus deductions to compensate Amber for his failure to perform the contract exactly. In this case, assuming that Dylan's performance was considered to be substantial, Dylan would be entitled to $300,000 less the cost of replacing the tile. If Dylan's performance was not considered substantial enough—for example, if he used the wrong set of plans in building the house—Dylan would receive nothing. However, in some states, courts hold that if Amber lives in or otherwise uses a house that has not been substantially completed as promised, she will enjoy an unjust windfall unless Dylan receives payment equivalent to the value of the house.

Easements   A seller's grant of an easement to the buyer or reservation of an easement should be spelled out in the contract. Easements were discussed in Chapter 4. As noted in this chapter's discussion of marketable title, the seller should ensure that the buyer's purchase is subject to easements of record.

Time for Performance   Amanda signed a purchase agreement on May 5 offering to buy Leo's house for $400,000. She heard nothing from Leo, so on May 25, she signed a contract to purchase a house from Sam for $390,000. On May 26, she received Leo's acceptance of her offer in the mail. Is she liable on both contracts?

The answer to this surprisingly common dilemma depends on whether the court thinks that a reasonable time has passed between the time Amanda made her offer and the time Leo accepted it. If an unreasonably long time has passed, the offer would be considered canceled. To avoid this problem, a buyer signing a purchase agreement should state in the offer that the seller's acceptance must be received within a certain time period—for example, five days. This provision forces sellers such as Leo to act promptly, especially since Amanda can revoke the offer at any time—even before the stated five-day period passes. The provision also avoids claims that the seller accepted the offer under the mailbox rule in cases where the agreement did not arrive until several days later.

Several other time provisions should be inserted into the agreement to avoid unnecessary delay by one of the parties. Times should be established for the following:

1. The seller's delivery of the evidence of title
2. The buyer's review of the evidence of title
3. Correction of title defects by the seller
4. The closing date
5. Possession by the buyer

Although these times should be included in the contract, the contract is still enforceable without them, as the following Texas case points out.

A CASE IN POINT

In *Buehring v. Hudson*,[37] Hudson entered into a written contract to sell his house to Buehring. Hudson later sold the house to other people; and when sued by Buehring, he claimed that the contract was unenforceable because the date for closing was not stated. The court, in holding for Buehring, concluded, "The fact that the contract of sale fixed no time for its performance did not evidence that the minds of the parties had not met with respect to an essential element of the contract. When a contract of sale fixes no time for performance, the law allows a reasonable time. In other words, if the parties do not agree upon the time, an agreement for performance within a reasonable time will be implied."

time is of the essence

The parties must do what is required by the time specified in a contract.

The contract may also include a provision that **time is of the essence**, which has the effect of turning the contractual time periods into "drop-dead" dates with a strict requirement of performance by the contract's specific deadlines or dates. The parties also must strictly comply with times specified in contingencies.

Proration   Ordinarily, the seller in a real estate transaction has made certain advance payments for taxes, insurance, fuel oil, and other expenses of home ownership. The buyer may become obligated for expenses incurred during the period of the seller's ownership. For example, real estate taxes for the year 2010 may be due on January 1, 2011. Taxes charged for a past period are typically known as being payable **in arrears**.

in arrears

Having unpaid debts, outstanding obligations, or overdue payments.

Through a contractual agreement to **prorate**, the parties can ensure that such expenses are fairly adjusted at closing. A proration agreement provides that the buyer is to reimburse the seller for payments by the seller that cover any period of time after the buyer takes possession. The seller will be debited any unpaid obligations as of the closing date.

prorate

The act of adjusting, dividing, or prorating property taxes, interest, insurance premiums, rental income, etc., between buyer and seller proportionately to time of use or date of closing.

Rick and Candy closed on the purchase of a condominium from Tommy and Lindsay on June 15, 2010. Property taxes in the amount of $1,200 for the year 2010 are due on January 1, 2011. The condominium association assessment, payable in advance, is $120 per month. At closing, Rick and Candy will receive a credit for unpaid real estate taxes in the amount of $650 ($100 per month for six and one-half months). Tommy and Lindsay will receive a credit for their advance payment of the condominium association assessment in the amount of $60.

If the contract does not contain a proration provision, a court will not force proration, although some states have statutes that require proration of taxes in the absence of a contrary agreement. In addition, section 164(d) of the IRC provides that the real property taxes are to be treated as imposed on the buyer and seller based on their periods of ownership.

Type of Deed and Estate   In many states, unless the contract states otherwise, the seller must transfer to the buyer a fee simple estate under a general warranty deed; in other states, the seller only has to give a quitclaim deed. Consequently, for reasons to be discussed in Chapter 10, to protect his interests, the buyer should require the seller to deliver a general warranty deed.

Execution by Facsimile and Electronic Transfer   Facsimile, or fax, machines have become a commercial standard in the transmission of the offer, counteroffer, and acceptance. The parties may want to consider including a statement in the contract indicating that they intend their signatures by facsimile to serve as originals and to be binding.[38]

As discussed earlier, real estate transactions and signatures can now be sent electronically under the new federal E-Sign statute. But what about voice mail and telephone conversations? Can they be considered an electronic sound, symbol, or process like e-mail? Under E-Sign "[a]n oral communication or a recording of an oral communication shall not qualify as an electronic record…."[39]

Environmental Problems   It is increasingly common for buyers, particularly in commercial transactions, to insist on environmental site assessments to establish that they are "innocent landowners" under federal law and therefore not liable for cleaning up contaminated property. (See Chapter 14.) The buyer wants to ensure that the contract allows sufficient access to the property to perform the environmental assessment. To further establish environmental innocence, the buyer should ask the seller to represent in the contract that there are no conditions that would constitute a violation of environmental law.[40] Typical sellers are willing to make representations only for occurrences during their periods of ownership. Buyers also may want to conduct an inspection to protect themselves from potentially dangerous, even life-threatening, substances such as asbestos, toxic waste, and radon. One environmental threat is toxic molds that thrive on sheetrock, gypsum, and other standard building material in moist areas caused by leaky roofs and pipes. California, Michigan, Texas, and at least nine other states (see endnote 41 for a complete list of states that require mold disclosure) now have statutes or regulations requiring sellers, lessors, and their agents, to disclose whether they know or have reasonable cause to believe that mold exists in the property.[41] A family in Texas whose home was invaded by an especially lethal airborne form of toxic mold suffered serious neurological injuries. Eventually, a jury awarded the family $32 million in damages against its insurer, which breached its duty of good faith when it refused to compensate the family members for their losses.[42] Another environmental hazard that has recently surfaced is imported drywall from China that allegedly emits smelly, corrosive gases that may ruin air conditioning and other household systems.

Inspections   The buyer will want to ensure that professional inspectors can gain access to the property. Many "nonbuilder" home sale contracts, those for used homes, provide that the seller will credit the buyer up to a designated threshold for certain defects disclosed by a professional inspection report. An "as-is" purchaser (discussed later in this chapter) typically reserves the right to cancel the contract by a certain date if the inspection reports disclose sufficient adverse information. Even when the buyer has the seller disclosure in hand and has a third-party warranty, inspections can be of assistance in avoiding unpleasant surprises.

warranty

A promise that certain facts are truly as they are represented to be and that they will remain so, subject to any specified limitations. In certain circumstances, a warranty will be presumed, known as an "implied" warranty.

Warranties

Cicero recently purchased his first house. Within one year of moving in, sewage from the septic tank backed up three inches deep into his basement. The smell eventually became so bad that the septic tank system, which had been negligently designed, had to be rebuilt at a cost of some $30,000. Can Cicero recover this amount in a breach of **warranty** action against the vendor?

Cicero's ability to recover will differ depending on which of four possible factual variations applies to the case.

express warranty

An express promise made by the seller to the buyer as to the quality, condition, or performance of the thing being sold.

Express Warranties   First, Cicero should ask if the vendor gave an **express warranty** for the condition of the septic tank system. The express warranty may be directly from the seller, as the next case from Iowa demonstrates.

A CASE IN POINT

In *Ware v. Uhl,*[43] the seller stated in his offer to sell his house that he "warrants that the heating and air conditioning systems, plumbing system, all appliances and all mechanical equipment, included as part of the purchase price, will be *in working condition* as of either the date of possession or settlement" (emphasis added by the court). The court ruled that the words *in working condition* are clear and unambiguous and demonstrated the seller's intent to be contractually bound to provide the foregoing systems in working order.

Home Owners Warranty (HOW) plan

A warranty developed by the National Association of Home Builders in which a buyer is covered for certain defects in new homes and condominiums.

In addition, a number of warranty insurance arrangements have been developed. For instance, many purchasers of new homes and condominiums are now covered by the **Home Owners Warranty (HOW) plan** developed by the National Association of Home Builders. Under this plan, based on a British home warranty insurance program that began in 1936, a buyer is covered for defects in plumbing, cooling, heating, and electrical systems for two years and for major structural defects for ten years. The coverage, which is required by law in some states, extends to anyone who purchases the home within the ten-year period. Buyers of used homes may also acquire warranty coverage from private companies. While such third-party warranties can be a great source of comfort to the buyer, some warranty companies have had financial difficulties, causing problems for the warranted parties seeking to collect on the warranties.[44]

If the seller or a third-party plan expressly warranted the condition of the septic tank, the seller or insurer would be obligated to pay the cost of repairing Cicero's septic tank system. The remaining three examples assume that no express warranties have been given.

Contract with Builder   If Cicero had contracted with a builder who was to build the house according to certain specifications, it is implied, even when the contract is silent, that the builder gives Cicero an **implied warranty of habitability** (also called the implied covenant of workmanlike construction) that the job will be completed in a workmanlike manner and that the house will be habitable. The defective septic system represents a breach of such a warranty for which the builder would be liable.

implied warranty of habitability

An implied promise by a home builder that the premises have been completed in a workmanlike manner and are fit for habitation.

Purchase of New Home   If instead of hiring a builder to build the house, Cicero purchased a home that the contractor had just completed, should the result be different from the previous example? The traditional approach was called the doctrine of **caveat emptor,** or "let the buyer beware." Under this historical view, no implied warranties passed with the sale of an existing new home. The rationale for this approach, followed in an ever-declining number of states, is that in purchasing a completed house, the buyer has a chance to inspect the builder's work before entering into the contract.

caveat emptor

Means literally "let the buyer beware." The doctrine places the responsibility of the inspection of real or personal property on the buyer. The buyer receives no guarantees or warranties on property purchased.

Most courts have become critical of this rationale in recent years. The typical buyer is not a professional, as is the seller-builder, and is not able to spot defects. Furthermore, many defects do not become apparent until the new house settles and is used for two or three years. Therefore, the modern trend is to give the person who purchases a newly completed home from a builder an implied warranty that the house is habitable and that the builder has completed the house in a workmanlike manner. In some cases, the definition of a builder includes an owner who acts as her own general contractor.

The facts in Cicero's case are based on *Tavares v. Horstman,*[45] in which the Wyoming court adopted the modern approach in deciding that the vendor-builder breached an implied warranty in designing and constructing the septic system. The rationale for this decision, as stated by a Rhode Island court,[46] is that

> [t]he old rule of caveat emptor does not satisfy the demands of justice in such cases. The purchase of a home is not an everyday transaction for the average family, and is in many instances the most important transaction of a lifetime. To apply the rule of caveat emptor to an inexperienced buyer, and in favor of the builder who is daily engaged in the business of building and selling houses, is manifestly a denial of justice.

Despite this rationale, courts in several states have held that contractors can disclaim warranties through appropriate contract language.[47]

Purchase of Used Home   In the sale of a *used* home, the general rule is that no warranties are implied against builders; however, as discussed below, there are a growing number of states that are whittling away at the rule. Thus, if Cicero had purchased a used home, he would have had to bear the cost of rebuilding the defective septic tank system. Cicero would have been unable to recover from the builder because he did not contract directly with the builder—that is, he was not in privity with the builder.

Was the seller of a house with defective insulation liable to the purchaser based on his breach of the implied warranty of habitability or failure to disclose? In *Kaminszky v. Kukuch* on page 253, the court addresses that question.

END OF CHAPTER CASE

However, from the following Indiana case in 1976, to a recent 2008 case issued by the Iowa Supreme Court,[48] more courts are ruling that builders are subject to warranty liability to purchasers of used homes. (See endnote 48 for a list of states in which builders are subject to warranty liability for purchasers of used homes.)

A CASE IN POINT

In *Barnes v. Mac Brown & Co., Inc.,*[49] Mac Brown built and sold a house in the late 1960s to the Shipmans, who then resold the house to Barnes in 1971. Barnes later discovered that the basement walls were cracked and that the basement leaked. The Indiana Supreme Court decided that implied warranties could pass from the builder to Barnes as the purchaser of the used house. "The logic which compelled this change in the law of personal property is equally persuasive in the area of real property. Our society is an increasingly mobile one. Our technology is increasingly complex. The traditional requirement of privity between a builder-vendor and a purchaser is an outmoded one."

privity of contract
A direct contract between two parties.

As the preceding case demonstrates, a lack of **privity of contract** between Mac Brown and Company, the builder, and Barnes did not prevent Barnes from asserting a successful implied warranty of habitability claim against Brown. But could Barnes have sued the Shipmans, a private party, for breach of an implied warranty of habitability? The answer is no. Generally, this kind of warranty can be claimed only against a party who is in the

TABLE 7.1 Implied Warranty of Habitability

TYPE OF SELLER	DOES SELLER GIVE IMPLIED WARRANTY TO BUYER?
Builder who builds home	Yes
Builder who sells prebuilt home	Yes
Owner of used home	No. In some states, buyer can claim an implied warranty of habitability against the home builder without privity of contract, but not against the owner.

business of building and selling houses, not private homeowners. Moreover, the implied warranty of habitability generally does not protect a *buyer* of commercial buildings, who is presumed to be more sophisticated and therefore better able to protect himself.[50]

In addition, most states now impose a statutory duty on the seller to disclose known material facts that are *not* readily observable to the buyer, a subject discussed later in this chapter. The following was noted in a landmark Florida case:[51]

> *Modern concepts of justice and fair dealing have given our courts the opportunity and latitude to change the legal precepts in order to conform to society's needs. Thus the tendency of the more recent cases has been to restrict rather than extend the doctrine of caveat emptor. The law appears to be working toward the ultimate conclusion that full disclosure of all material facts must be made whenever fair conduct demands it.*

Table 7.1 shows, in general, the current legal environment concerning the implied warranty of habitability.

Builder's Tort Liability   In addition to being subject to warranty liability for structural defects, a contractor is liable when the purchaser or a third person is injured by a defect that was a hidden, dangerous condition known to the builder or by a defect resulting from the builder's negligence.[52]

In a few jurisdictions, including Arkansas, the District of Columbia, Michigan, New Jersey, Ohio, and Tennessee, builders have also been held liable to injured homeowners and lessees, under a **strict liability theory**, which declares that a seller in the business of selling products is liable for damages resulting from the sale of an unreasonably dangerous, defective product. This development is especially significant because a builder, particularly of mass-produced tract homes and condominiums, may be held liable even though he "has exercised all possible care in the preparation and sale of his product," according to Section 402A of the Second Restatement of Torts.[53]

Furthermore, privity of contract is not an issue under the strict liability rule; Section 402A applies the rule even when the user or consumer has not contracted with the seller. The following New Jersey case illustrates the strict liability principle.

strict liability theory
Liability without fault. A seller in the business of selling products is liable for damages in the sale of a defective product that is unreasonably dangerous.

A CASE IN POINT

In *Schipper v. Levitt & Sons, Inc.*,[54] the defendant builder was a well-known mass developer of houses, including houses in Willingboro (Levittown), New Jersey. One of the houses was sold to the Kreitzers, who were advised in a homeowner's guide that "you will find the hot water in your Levittown house much hotter than that to which you are accustomed." The Kreitzers were burned on

continues

continued

several occasions by the hot water and complained to Levitt, but nothing was done. Later the Kreitzers leased the house to Schipper, who noticed that the water was extremely hot and warned his wife and children to be careful until he could determine how to regulate it. Shortly thereafter, Schipper's sixteen-month-old son was scalded by hot water from a bathroom sink. The son was hospitalized four times, including one stay of seventy-four days, and had to undergo two skin grafting operations. The court decided that even though there was no privity of contract between Schipper and Levitt, Levitt should be liable for the injuries under the strict liability principle if the hot water system was proven to be unreasonably dangerous.

In remanding the case for further trial, the court observed: "The law should be based on current concepts of what is right and just and the judiciary should be alert to the never-ending need for keeping its common law principles abreast of the times. Ancient distinctions which make no sense in today's society and tend to discredit the law should be readily rejected as they were step by step in *Henningsen* and *Santor.* We consider that there are no meaningful distinctions between Levitt's mass production and sale of homes and the mass production and sales of automobiles and that the pertinent overriding policy considerations are the same. That being so, the warranty or strict liability principles of *Henningsen* and *Santor* should be carried over into the realty field, at least in the aspect dealt with here. Incidentally, recent reference to the sweep of Levitt's mass production approach may be found in the July 1963 issue of *American Builder*, at pages 42–45 where the president of Levitt, in response to an inquiry as to whether its policy of 'no changes' would be applied in the building of its more expensive homes at Long Island, had this to say: 'We intend to hold to our mass production approach in Long Island. People buy Cadillacs, don't they, and they're mass produced.'"

economic loss rule

A party suffering only economic loss from the breach of an express or implied contract may not assert a tort claim arising from the breach unless an independent action under tort law exists.

In some states, tort liability, such as strict liability and negligence, asserted against homebuilders, subcontractors, and others who supply component parts to a house, is barred by the **economic loss rule**. The doctrine prevents a homeowner from recovering tort damages when the defect causes damage just to the defective product. The plaintiff's recovery is limited to contractual or warranty damages, which are typically less than tort damages. For example, under the economic loss rule, if Whiteside Construction builds a home and sells it to Gustafson, and the roof is later found to be defective, causing leaks and damage to the floors and drywall, Gustafson cannot sue Whiteside Construction for negligent construction or under a theory of strict liability but could assert a claim against Whiteside under his contract or warranty. However, if the defective roof collapses and injures Gustafson, he would be able to sue Whiteside for negligence and in some states as listed above, strict liability, even though they have a contract.

Construction defect litigation has become an expensive problem for builders, particularly in fast-growing areas of the Sun Belt where some tract homes and condominiums are built quickly with little regard to quality. In an attempt to control the costs of litigation, particularly apparent nuisance suits, while at the same time helping homeowners with legitimate claims, a growing number of states have adopted so-called "Fix It" or "Right to Cure" laws. These laws require homeowners to give written notice and specify a period of time to allow the homebuilder to repair construction defects.[55] Many of these statutes also have mandatory mediation requirements in which builders and homeowners must first attempt to resolve their differences before resorting to lawsuits, a topic discussed next.

LEED Buildings and Liability

LEED Buildings and Liability A recent, but rapidly growing trend in real estate is the construction of environmentally friendly buildings. In the late 1990s, the U.S. Green Buildings Council (USGBC) initiated a voluntary program to encourage so-called "green buildings" to promote sustainability and compatibility with the environment. The program, called Leadership in Energy and Environmental Design (LEED) offers certifications at various levels of achievement—Certified, Silver, Gold, and Platinum. Each certification specifies a range of criteria from buying more local building materials to using solar and wind energy sources. The response from builders and developers, who are often given handsome tax credits and see reduced operating costs from lowered energy bills, has been significant. Companies have also discovered that a LEED certification can be beneficial for marketing their businesses as environmentally friendly.

Yet, legal problems have cropped up. Most cases deal with breaches of contract and warranty, in which buyers and tenants have felt their expectations have not been met. For example, representations made that LEED buildings are healthier and more productive are, according to some critics, misleading or unattainable. And because the cost of building in conformance to LEED specifications can be more expensive, buyers have argued that their investments were not worth the added costs. The potential exposure to litigation will likely intensify until the program matures and expectations become better known and understood.[56]

Contractual Remedies and Alternative Dispute Resolution

The buyer and the seller enter the contract with the expectation that they will proceed to the closing. Several legal remedies are available to the other party when one of the parties is unwilling or unable, despite his or her obligations under the contract, to complete the transaction.

Specific Performance

specific performance
With this remedy, courts order a breaching party to perform the contract.

Specific performance is a remedy under which the parties are compelled to proceed with the specific terms of the contract. The typical contract for the sale of goods does not need to be specifically enforced for the buyer to obtain the subject of the contract. For example, if you contract to purchase a computer and specify the processor, RAM, modem, memory, and other features, you can obtain a similarly configured computer even if the seller does not reserve a specifically designated serial number for you. The theory underlying real estate contracts differs and is based on the presumption that each parcel of property is unique. Under this view, the buyer would not obtain the benefit of her bargain if a different property was substituted or if she received monetary damages that allowed her to purchase a different property. Specific performance is an equitable remedy, an appeal to the court's conscience.

A court might not enforce a contract that it believes is unfair, is inequitable, or will result in hardship. As one Montana court said, "Factors courts consider include execution of a contract under circumstances unfavorable to the defendant because of lack of advice, and the difference in the parties' business experience and knowledge."[57] Therefore, the court did not award the remedy of specific performance when the seller was "the victim of mistaken information and inaccurate advice" and the buyer "was a well-known professional investor, and had extensive education, background and experience in business."[58]

Damages

damages
A monetary award that a losing party must pay the winning party in a lawsuit.

When the remedy of specific performance is not available or when the nonbreaching party prefers a monetary solution, **damages** are the preferred remedy for breach of contract. One noted commentator explained that

[t]he damages usually available for breach of a real estate contract can be divided into two types. One is restitution, or reliance, putting the innocent buyer or seller in at least as good a position as she was before she became entangled in a deal that fell apart. The

other is compensatory, or benefit of the bargain, or expectation damages—putting the injured party in the position she would have been in had the contract been performed. Litigants must usually choose one or the other.[59]

Real estate contracts frequently provide that the seller's remedy in the event of the buyer's breach will be retention of the buyer's deposit. As previously noted, however, the courts are reluctant to allow the seller to retain an earnest money deposit in residential home sales that is disproportionate in amount to the actual damages resulting from the buyer's breach.

Alternative Dispute Resolution

Specific performance or damages are only awarded as a result of a lawsuit. Lawsuits, however, are typically long, expensive, and divisive Thus, parties involved in disputes have, in recent years, sought to lessen these obstacles by settling their differences through **alternative dispute resolution** or ADR. The two most common methods of ADR are **arbitration** and **mediation**.

Although both methods settle disputes successfully, they differ in many ways. A third party acting as an arbitrator has the authority to decide the dispute. A third-party mediator, on the other hand, attempts to help the disputing parties negotiate a settlement and unlike the arbitrator, does not have the authority to bind the parties to a specific outcome. Parties agreeing to arbitration typically grant arbitrators broad latitude to decide issues of fact as well as what law to apply to the dispute. Few restrictions are imposed on the arbitrator since she is typically a professional, such as a lawyer or retired judge. In real estate, some are also experts in the field, such as a retired contractor arbitrating a construction defect case. Procedurally, the parties seeking an arbitration must submit information to the arbitrator. This information includes who is involved in the dispute, what the nature of the dispute is, what amount of money or other remedy is being sought, where the arbitration should take place, and whether the parties intend to be bound by the final decision or award. The arbitrator's award is generally final and not subject to review by courts. The few exceptions are when the award was the result of corruption, fraud, or wrongdoing by the arbitrator—such as bias exhibited toward one party—if the arbitrator exceeded the authority the parties conferred on her, or if the ruling violates public policy. In contrast to what arbitrators do, mediators assist parties in reaching a mutually acceptable decision in an informal atmosphere. A mediator is a facilitator who typically deliberates privately with the parties, called caucusing, and then brings them together to discuss their disagreements face-to-face. Often a mediator's most challenging tasks are to minimize hard feelings and to heal a once-productive business relationship, for example, between a contractor and one of its regular subcontractors.

Due to the cost and time efficiencies of ADR, many types of real estate contracts now routinely contain mediation and arbitration clauses. However, is mediation or arbitration always the correct procedure? According to some experts, they are not. For example, when a dispute requires quick resolution, a mediation clause that does not provide specifics on where and when the mediation will occur and how the mediator will be selected sometimes results in delays in the filing of a necessary lawsuit or arbitration. Arbitration may not always be the most effective process either. If, for instance, the better solution is to go to court to seek an equitable remedy, such as an injunction, or if large-scale discovery is necessary, such as in a complex case, mandating arbitration could actually hinder the fair and effective resolution of the case. And unlike an appellate court decision, an arbitration does not create a binding precedent, which can impede the development of important case law.

For these reasons, real estate buyers and sellers are wise not to accept so-called boiler-plate or standard ADR clauses without first thinking about their implications. The

---

alternative dispute resolution

Various methods of resolving disputes outside traditional legal and administrative forums.

arbitration

The submission of a dispute to an impartial third party as an alternative to traditional litigation in court.

mediation

The process by which a neutral third person assists and encourages parties in conflict to reach a settlement that will be satisfactory to them all.

clauses should, for example, be structured to the unique problems that can crop up in real estate.[60] The next California case discusses how plaintiffs will sometimes regret that they signed a contract compelling arbitration when instead going to court might have increased the possibility of receiving greater damages.

A CASE IN POINT

In *Gravillas v. Coldwell Banker Residential Brokerage Company*,[61] an arbitration clause contained in a purchase agreement provided that any "bodily injuries or wrongful death" that might result in the purchase of the home would be excluded from arbitration (see endnote 61 for the language of the clause). The plaintiff/homebuyers alleged that from buying and living in a defective house, they suffered from great stress, resulting in the pregnant wife incurring, among other problems, gestational diabetes. The defendant Coldwell Banker sued to compel arbitration arguing that these were *not* bodily injuries as contemplated under the arbitration contract, and so could not be heard in court. The court ruled that "… if emotional distress were considered a bodily injury, the arbitration exclusion in the Agreement could apply in virtually every dispute, rendering the arbitration provision a nullity. Few, if any, claims would ever be subject to arbitration. Because the exclusion should not 'swallow' the binding arbitration rule we decline to construe 'bodily injury' to include purely emotional distress." The court also pointed out that "The [plaintiffs] may have hoped to build their dream home and *live happily ever after*, but there is a reason that tag line belongs only in fairy tales. Building a house may turn out to be a stress-free project; it is much more likely to be the stuff of urban legends—the cause of bankruptcy, marital dissolution, hypertension and fleeting fantasies ranging from homicide to suicide …. 'No reasonable homeowner can embark on a building project with certainty that the project will be completed to perfection.'"

Avoiding the Contract

Courts may allow a person to avoid or rescind performance (also called *rescission*) of a real estate contract under certain circumstances, described as follows.

Mistake

The seller may make a mistake in an offer—for example, by offering to sell a farm for $790 per acre instead of an intended $970 per acre. That party cannot, however, use the mistake as an excuse for refusing to perform the contract. If, however, the mistake is "palpable," or obvious to the other party, the contract generally can be avoided. A court may find that the mistake is palpable if, for example, the seller offers to sell the farm for $9.70 per acre instead of $9,700 per acre. The law applies an objective standard: a party will be held to the expressed agreement regardless of what the party was thinking. However, **mutual mistake**—a mistake by both parties—will be grounds for avoiding the contract as the following Vermont case discusses.

mutual mistake
A mistake by both parties that is grounds for avoiding a contract.

A CASE IN POINT

In *Berard v. Dolan*,[62] the plaintiff entered into a written contract to purchase the defendant's store. The defendant told the plaintiff that the property was subject to a mortgage that could be assumed by the plaintiff, and the plaintiff indicated that he would have to assume the mortgage to finance the

continues

continued

purchase. After the contract was signed, the parties discovered that the mortgage actually covered other property as well as the store and that the plaintiff could not assume the mortgage by purchasing the store alone.

Because of this mutual mistake, the plaintiff was allowed to avoid the contract and recover his down payment. But the court also noted that if only the plaintiff had been mistaken, there could be no avoidance. "The defendant testified that when he talked with the plaintiff about the sale of the property and the subject of mortgages he knew that the only mortgage on it also covered other property. If the jury believed this statement there was no mutual mistake and they were required under the charge of the court to return a verdict for the defendant. Their verdict shows that they did not believe this testimony but found that the defendant was mistaken as to what property was covered by the mortgage and mistakenly believed before the payment was made that only the store property was covered."

The trend has also been to allow the contract to be avoided when both of the following conditions are present:

1. Enforcement of the contract against the mistaken party would be oppressive, or at least result in an unconscionably unequal exchange of values.
2. Rescission would impose no substantial hardship on the other.[63]

Minority and Other Forms of Incapacity

The policy in most states is to protect minors within a reasonable time after they reach the age of majority (which is eighteen unless legally emancipated) by allowing them to avoid liability under contracts to sell real estate. However, as the next case from Vermont ruled, the defense does have its limits.

A CASE IN POINT

In *Spencer v. Lyman Falls Power Co.*,[64] the plaintiff sold his real estate four months before reaching the age of majority. The property was later resold, and the new purchaser made improvements on the property totaling $93,000. Seventeen years after reaching the age of majority, the plaintiff filed suit, claiming that he wanted to avoid the contract. The court noted that other courts have disagreed about how long the minor has to disaffirm a contract after reaching the age of majority. In a few states, the minor may disaffirm the contract anytime after becoming an adult unless the individual has ratified the contract. This court, however, adopted the majority rule that the minor must disaffirm the contract within a reasonable time after reaching the age of majority. The court held that the minor here could not disaffirm the contract because seventeen years was well beyond a reasonable time. The court also noted that the minor would be held to the contract in any event because in standing by and allowing the purchaser to make large expenditures, his ratification would be implied.

The issue of minors buying property, including real estate, may become more common due to the ease of buying through the Internet. In 1999, for example, a thirteen-year-old boy made the top bids to buy real estate on eBay. One of the items he successfully bid on was a $1.2 million medical office in Florida, which was later avoided because of his age.

Minors are not the only parties that state law seeks to protect. For example, a contract can be avoided if a person is so intoxicated from alcohol or drug use that he cannot appreciate the fact that he is entering into a contractual relationship. This issue, among others, was raised in the *Lucy v. Zehmer* case discussed earlier. Courts generally allow avoidance of the contract only when the intoxicated party can restore the other party to the status quo, that is, the position they would have been in had they not entered into the contract so that the aggrieved party does not suffer a loss.

People who are adjudicated insane can automatically avoid a contract and cannot be held liable. On the other hand, a person who has not formally been declared insane but is determined by a court after the fact to actually be insane can choose to disavow the contract; but he also must give back any property he received from the other party.[65]

duress

Entering into a contract under the pressure of an unlawful act or threat.

Duress

A person who enters into a contract under **duress**—that is, as the result of wrongful force or a threat that prevents exercising of free will—may avoid the contract. To determine whether a person was placed in such fear that the person was acting against her free will, the courts apply a subjective test—that is, what the person under duress actually thought. For instance, in a Missouri case, a son-in-law threatened to make it "hotter than hell" for his deceased wife's parents until they deeded certain real estate to him. The parents were suffering from typhoid fever at the time, and they thought he was threatening to burn down their house with them in it. Applying the subjective test, a court canceled the deed.[66]

undue influence

A person in a dominant position takes advantage of the weaker party.

Undue Influence

If a person in a dominant position—for example, an attorney, a physician, or a close relative—persuades another person to sell real estate or enter into any other contract under circumstances in which it appears the other person is not acting of his own free will (**undue influence**), the contract, as discussed in the following South Carolina case, may be avoided.

representation

A statement, express or implied, made by one of two contracting parties to the other party before or at the time of making the contract in regard to some past or existing fact, circumstance, or state of facts pertinent to the contract that is influential in bringing about the agreement.

A CASE IN POINT

In *Hodge v. Shea*, a seventy-six-year-old patient who was a chronically ill alcoholic in great pain signed a contract to sell valuable real estate to his physician, who had been treating him at least once daily. Under the contract, the physician was given the right to purchase twenty acres, with a market value of $1,200 an acre, in exchange for $4,000 and an automobile. When the physician later brought suit to enforce the contract, the court denied him recovery, noting that on the basis of the inadequacy of the purchase price and the confidential relationship between the parties, there was a presumption that the physician had taken advantage of the patient.[67]

Misrepresentation

Sellers typically make **representations** about the property in the course of a sale. While a warranty looks forward to the character, title, or quality of the property as it should be after closing, the representation's focus is on facts as they exist at or prior to closing.

misrepresentation

A false statement of a material fact.

Misrepresentation, the seller's false representation, is a common claim raised by the purchaser of real estate. A seller can effectively misrepresent the property by failing to disclose hidden conditions or latent defects. In addition, either directly or through a broker,[68] the vendor often makes exaggerated claims about the property. An examination of real estate advertisements in any newspaper offers ready illustrations: "Victorian house updated for 20th-century living," "immaculate house—the best value in town," or "mechanically fit, on a quiet court."

Courts face the problem of distinguishing between mere sales talk, sometimes called **puffing**, to be regarded with skepticism by the purchaser, and misrepresentation that entitles the purchaser to avoid the contract. Misrepresentation is defined as "the false representation of a material fact that is relied on by the other party to the contract."[69] Many cases, such as the following Arkansas case, turn on whether a statement was one of fact or opinion.

puffing
A seller's expression of opinion that is not made as a representation of a fact.

A CASE IN POINT

In *Cannaday v. Cossey*,[70] the Cannadays purchased a house from Cossey, who, during negotiations, told them it was a "good house." Cossey also told the Cannadays that he had seen flying ants around the premises for about forty years. After moving in, the Cannadays discovered that the house was seriously damaged by termites. The court refused to allow rescission, finding that Cossey was unaware of the termites and his statement that the house was in "good condition" was a statement of opinion. "A general statement of this kind amounts only to an expression of opinion and cannot be relied on by the purchaser as an assurance against the various defects that are apt to be found in an older dwelling."

Even when a party misrepresents a material fact, courts in certain situations will not allow the other party to avoid the contract if the fact could have been verified. For example, if the seller tells the purchaser that the taxes on the property are $5,000 per year when in fact they are $8,000 per year, the purchaser might not be allowed to back out of the contract on the basis of misrepresentation if the actual amount of taxes could easily have been checked by calling the local taxing authority.

The same principle might hold true when the seller makes a statement of law such as "Under the zoning law covering this property, you can build a racquetball court." Every person is presumed to know the law, and the purchaser can make her own investigation to determine whether the zoning laws do in fact allow such use. However, there has been a trend to protect the innocent party by avoiding application of these rules when possible. This trend results from the "recognition of a new standard of business ethics, demanding that statements of fact be at least honestly and carefully made."[71]

Perhaps the toughest question is whether misrepresentation can be proven when the seller is *silent*. Many courts have concluded that misrepresentation exists, even in the absence of a statement, in order to prevent an unfair or harsh result. In several of these cases, however, the seller has done or said something that is very close to a false representation of fact. For instance, if the plumbing in a house is in bad condition and the seller paints over water stains caused by leakage, this concealment has been considered equal to a false representation. Also, statements by the seller that are true as stated but that require clarification have been treated as misrepresentations.

Even when a silent seller does not conceal a defect or make incomplete statements, some courts follow principles of equity in allowing buyers to rescind contracts when the property contains a serious hidden defect. Legal remedies, such as a damage award, are also possible. In the Washington state case of *Obde v. Schlemeyer*,[72] Schlemeyer sold Obde an apartment house that Schlemeyer knew was infested with termites. The court, in allowing Obde to recover damages, decided that in such cases, the seller has a duty to inform the buyer of the termites. The court indicated that such a duty exists when the vendor knows of concealed defects that are dangerous to the property, health, or life of the purchaser.

Liability for nondisclosure is not necessarily limited to cases involving physical defects in the property. In *Reed v. King*,[73] for instance, a California appellate court held that both the seller of a house and a real estate agent could be held liable when they failed to disclose to the buyer that five people had been murdered in the house ten years earlier. The court emphasized that a buyer must prove that the murders had a significant effect on the market value of the house.

Is the seller obligated to disclose to the buyer that a home is haunted? In *Stambovsky v. Ackley* on page 254, the court addresses this novel issue.

END OF CHAPTER CASE

While a "haunted" house as discussed in *Stambovsky* can create a stigma, thus lowering its price, a crime committed in a house also can create a problem for sellers. For example, the homes and apartments in which the grisly Jeffrey Dahmer and John Wayne Gacy mass murders occurred could not be sold no matter how the landlord attempted to remodel them. They were eventually demolished. The condominium where Nicole Brown Simpson and her friend Ron Goldman were brutally murdered was sold for $200,000 less than its asking price even after the address was changed and the property was remodeled. The owners of the house in which JonBenet Ramsey was murdered have likewise found it difficult to sell.[74]

Experts contend that such stigmatized homes take two to seven years longer to sell than it would normally take. One reason is that after the *Stambovsky* case, about half the states required sellers to disclose such information, although usually for only a relatively short period of time. For example, in California, the information does not have to be disclosed three years after the crime, while in South Dakota, the time period is 12 months.[75] Other disclosures that are now legally required are discussed next.

Should buyers of penthouse apartments be able to rescind the purchase agreement and recover their deposits because of fear of another 9/11 terrorist attack? In *Uzan v. 845 UN Limited Partnership* on page 255, the court discusses those issues.

END OF CHAPTER CASE

Statutory Duties to Disclose Defects

It is estimated that nondisclosure of defects is raised in two-thirds of the claims that buyers make against sellers.[76] Most state legislatures, understandably concerned about these claims, have enacted statutes that clarify the seller's duty to make disclosure. Indeed, only a few states today adhere to the principle of caveat emptor in which a seller has no common law duty to disclose latent defects to a buyer.[77] Even some of these states have carved out exceptions. In Alabama, for example, caveat emptor does not apply to the sale of new homes or to instances when the defect can harm the health and welfare of the home buyer.[78] These statutes also do not generally relieve the seller from the common law duties to disclose, as discussed earlier. Thus, plaintiffs may assert actions under both the state statute and the common law to enhance their chances for recovering damages. One commentator has noted that "the statutory and common law disclosure duties run concurrently but are not identical."[79]

The state disclosure statutes vary considerably in their content. On the one hand, legislation in many states requires sellers to disclose physical defects although some of these laws limit disclosure to specific matters (environmental hazards, for instance).[80] On the other hand, a number of states, as discussed earlier, have passed laws protecting sellers from liability for failing to disclose facts that might have a psychological impact on the buyer, such as a murder on the property.

The clear trend has been to expand the seller's disclosure requirements. As noted in Chapter 6, some courts have extended the seller's (and the seller's broker and subagent) obligations of disclosure to off-site conditions materially affecting the value of the property.[81]

Many states also require sellers to disclose a home's condition on a statutorily prescribed form, and the seller's completion of this form and the buyer's acknowledgment of receipt frequently are part of the sales contract. Ohio's statutory form, for example, is required for the seller's disclosure in all conveyances of residential units, irrespective of the number of units conveyed.[82] (For a copy of Ohio's property disclosure form, see www.cengagebrain.com [see page xix in the Preface for instructions on how to access the free study tools for this text].) However, these statutes require normal home sellers to disclose only those facts that they *actually know*, as the following Oregon case demonstrates, not what they *should have known* had they exercised reasonable care.

A CASE IN POINT

In *Cameron v. Harshberger*,[83] Harshberger sold property to Cameron in which Harshberger represented in the "real property disclosure statement" that to his knowledge he was not aware of "any boundary disputes, easements or rights of way affecting the property." Shortly after the sale, Cameron discovered that his property encroached on a public right of way. The court ruled that, like the common law, the statute creating the disclosure statement only requires the seller to disclose what he knows. "[S]ellers owe no duty to exercise reasonable care in the communication of factual information to purchasers in an arms' length business transaction...."

California has a particularly long and demanding list of information that sellers must disclose. The list includes natural hazards such as whether the area is subject to flood risks (including dams that may fail) and whether threats from wildfires exist. Earthquake and seismic zones as well as unusual ground movement experienced during earthquakes must also be disclosed. Moreover, under California's version of Megan's Law, discussed in Chapter 6, all real estate purchase agreements and leases must include written notice of a database containing the names of registered sex offenders and the way buyers and lessees can access the database.[84]

Federal laws also exist that require the disclosure of certain property defects. One important example obligates sellers or lessors (and their real estate agents) of certain residential property constructed before 1979 to disclose the presence of lead-based paint hazards and to provide an informational pamphlet prepared by HUD. (For a copy of HUD's lead-based paint disclosure form, see www.cengagebrain.com [see page xix in the Preface for instructions on how to access the free study tools for this text].) The buyer or lessee's acknowledgment of receipt is a required element of the contract or lease.[85]

Moreover, beginning in 2010, contractors, as well as carpenters, plumbers, and heating, air conditioning, and window installers, who are renovating property built before 1979, must be Environmental Protection Agency (EPA) certified to ensure that exposure to lead paint is eliminated. Critics point to a potential crisis due to the lack of certified professionals coming on the heels of a vast infusion of stimulus money from the Obama Administration aimed at creating more energy efficient retrofits in homes.[86]

> **as-is clause**
> Without warranty, as shown in its existing physical condition, with all faults and imperfections.

Sellers sometimes want to include an **as-is clause**, a type of exculpatory clause, in the real estate contract to minimize their liability for the property's condition. Under the typical as-is clause, a buyer agrees to purchase the property in as-is condition, waiving the seller's obligation to bring the condition of the property to a legally or contractually designated standard. An as-is clause is essentially a strong signal to the buyer to employ an inspector to make extensive inspections of the property's condition and ask specific questions about the quality of the real estate, particularly when the as-is clause specifies in detail areas such as the roof or the plumbing. The buyer should have the right to cancel the contract when he is not satisfied with the inspectors' reports.

Even an as-is clause in a real estate contract does not relieve the seller from her obligation to make disclosures about the property's condition.[87] For example, the clause does not typically relieve the seller of any obligations under state disclosure statutes and a state's common law to disclose latent defects known by the seller—those defects that are not readily discoverable by the buyer or her inspectors through the exercise of reasonable diligence. It has been observed that a "common misunderstanding among real estate professionals is the belief that an 'as-is' provision in a real estate sale contract completely relieves the seller of the duty to disclose to the buyer any of the property's defects—whether patent or latent—whether or not known by the seller."[88] While such a statement might protect an innocent seller from liability for a defect discovered by the buyer after the closing, it should not shield a seller who has lied to the buyer.[89] Table 7.2 summarizes the various scenarios, in general, in which as-is clauses may be enforceable against the buyer.

Although it is difficult to prove that a seller was aware of a latent defect, the following case demonstrates how one West Virginia buyer was able to do so.

A CASE IN POINT

In *Stempel v. Dobson*, Jeffrey and Judith Stempel signed a real estate contract in which they agreed to buy Lewis and Carol Dobson's house "as-is." After moving into the house, the Stempels discovered substantial structural damage due to prior termite infestation. The Stempels subsequently contacted the party who had originally sold the house to the Dobsons, who reported that there had been visible termite damage to the floor when he had purchased the house seven years ago. The Stempels sued the Dobsons for fraudulent concealment. The court ruled that "the existence of an 'as-is' clause in a contract of sale for real estate will not relieve the vendor of his obligation to disclose a condition which substantially affects the value or habitability of the property and which condition is known to the vendor, but not to the purchaser, and would not be disclosed by a reasonable and diligent inspection. Such failure to disclose constitutes fraud."[90]

TABLE 7.2 Enforceability of As-Is Clauses*

TYPE OF DEFECT	IS "AS IS" ENFORCEABLE AGAINST BUYER?	EXAMPLE
Patent defect; one that is readily discoverable by the buyer upon reasonable inspection and investigation.	Yes	Visible water spot on ceiling
Latent defect; neither seller nor buyer is aware of it, but seller adds language to the as-is clause disclaiming responsibility for specific kinds of defects.	Yes	Defective plumbing or wiring hidden in the wall, termites
Latent defect; seller is aware of the defect but does not disclose any information when the buyer inquires about it.	No	Defective plumbing or wiring hidden in the wall, termites
Latent defect; seller is aware, but buyer does not specifically inquiry about it.	No	Defective plumbing or wiring hidden in the wall, termites

*Adapted from M. Jennings, *From the Courts*, 31 Real Estate Law Journal 132 (2002).

As discussed in the following Kansas case, buyers who are defrauded may forfeit a remedy if they do not take prompt action.

A CASE IN POINT

In *Morse v. Kogle*,[91] the Morses relied on alleged misrepresentations by the vendor when they entered into a contract to purchase a residence on March 21. On March 25, the Morses told a real estate agent of the misrepresentation; but because they saw "no use having any arguments about it," they asked him to resell the property. The property was not resold; and on April 18, the Morses brought suit, claiming rescission. The court refused to allow rescission because in offering the house for resale, the Morses had acted as if they were the owners and, therefore, had ratified the contract. The court cited the following rule from an earlier case: "If, after discovery or knowledge of facts which would entitle a party to rescind, he treats the contract as a subsisting obligation and leads the other party to believe that the contract is still in effect, he will have waived his right to rescind. Prompt action is essential when one believes himself entitled to such relief."

CASES

Contingencies
RENOVEST COMPANY v. HODGES DEVELOPMENT CORP.
135 N.H. 72, 600 A.2d 448 (1991)

HORTON, Justice. * * * The plaintiff, Renovest Company (Renovest), entered into a purchase and sale agreement with the defendant, Hodges Development Corporation (Hodges), on June 30, 1986, for a two-building apartment complex in Franklin. The agreed-upon purchase price was $1,476,000 and the initial deposit paid to Hodges at the signing of the contract was $65,000. The contract specified that the deposit would serve as liquidated damages if Renovest failed to close on or before September 3, 1986.

Three conditions precedent to the buyer's obligation to perform were contained in the contract. At issue here are paragraph 3(b), relating to physical inspection of the property, and paragraph 3(d) relating to the buyer's obtaining financing at certain rates and terms. No portion of the contract stated expressly that time was of the essence. The provision relating to inspection called for the inspection to be completed within fourteen working days, and specified that if the inspection was unsatisfactory, the "Buyer shall have three (3) days from the date of completion of such inspection in which to notify Seller of his disapproval, and this Agreement shall be null and void and all deposits hereunder shall be refunded in full." The outside date on this condition was July 24. The financing provision contained a forty-five-day limit, after inspection of the seller's business records, in which the buyer was required to notify the seller of an intention to invoke the financing condition clause. Paragraph 9 of the contract required that all notices be given in writing.

Renovest first inspected the buildings on July 10, 1986, sending a partner and a building inspector. It was during this inspection that Renovest discovered a crack in the exterior of one building, and it consulted with Hodges the next day. Whether Hodges agreed to extend the deadline in order to allow further inspection by Renovest is disputed. Further investigation was performed on July 17 and 23 by another engineer, and his report on August 6 contained his opinion that the building would require "underpinning" of the foundation in order to prevent further settling of the building. Underpinning involves stabilization of the building's foundation. Based on this report, Renovest wrote to Hodges on August 7, terminating the transaction and demanding return of the $65,000 deposit. Hodges undertook its own engineering study, which commenced with borings on August 12 and culminated in an evaluation report dated August 26. This report described the cracking as cosmetic, found the problem building structurally sound, and rejected the need for underpinning. Hodges shared this report with Renovest.

Renovest did initially undertake to secure the financing by approaching four banks. Two of these, the Bank of New England and the Shawmut Bank, were favorably disposed toward the financing application, up to the time that Renovest notified them of the results of the engineer's report about the building's structural problems. Upon receipt of this information, the banks indicated they would not continue to process the loan applications until the issue of the building's structural soundness was resolved. Although time still remained in which to meet the financing deadline, Renovest never pursued the applications further. A second letter sent by Renovest to Hodges on August 12 asserted the failure to obtain financing, as well as an unsatisfactory result of the inspection of Hodges's books and records, as additional grounds for the termination of the contract. Renovest no longer asserts the books and records contingency as a ground for the termination.

At trial on its suit to obtain return of its deposit, Renovest presented three witnesses and introduced the deposition of a fourth witness. After Renovest rested, Hodges moved to dismiss, both orally and in writing, and the judge granted the motion based on the court's findings of fact.

* * *

In his order dismissing the complaint, the trial judge found that time was of the essence for the exercise of the rights under the conditions precedent. The judge based his conclusion on the strict time provisions applicable to performance of the conditions, concluding that these provisions required strict compliance with the timetables established. The court therefore determined that the late notification precluded the plaintiff's invoking its right to terminate the agreement under the physical inspection condition. The court

apparently also determined that no waiver of the deadline occurred during the relevant period.

Renovest correctly asserts that ordinarily time is not made of the essence in a contract, absent some indication that the parties intended otherwise. The mere fact that a date is stated in the contract is not sufficient, by itself, to alter this rule.

* * *

Renovest's argument is inapplicable in the present case, because the terms involved are express conditions precedent. The plaintiff's duty to perform under the contract was made "subject to" performance of these conditions. Where "the occurrence of a condition is required by the agreement of the parties, rather than as a matter of law, a rule of strict compliance traditionally applies." E. A. Farnsworth, *Contracts* §8.3, at 544 (8th ed. 1982).

* * *

Renovest asserts that it was unable to obtain financing for the project and, therefore, was excused from performing by paragraph 3(d). That paragraph, under the heading "Conditions Precedent to Buyers [sic] Obligation to Perform," reads:

> "d. This Agreement is subject to Buyer obtaining a written commitment for First Mortgage financing from a lending institution with the following terms. ... The commitment to be obtained within 45 days from the date of Buyers [sic] receipt of the books and records. Buyer shall notify Seller in writing within 45 days from review of the books and records of his intention to exercise the right to terminate this Offer under this mortgage contingency clause."

We also reject Renovest's reliance upon this provision.

Under New Hampshire law, every contract contains an implied covenant of good faith performance and fair dealing. Reasonable efforts must be undertaken to secure financing.

While initially Renovest met this duty, by initiating the loan process, its later conduct supports the trial judge's finding that performance of the agreement was not excused by Renovest's inability to obtain financing. Renovest asserts that it sought the financing required under the contract, but after making the lending institutions aware of the purported construction deficiencies, it assumed that financing would be unavailable.

The question whether any structural defects were material to financing rested solely with the banks. Having undertaken to secure financing, Renovest was committed to affirmatively seeking such financing, with activity "reasonably calculated to obtain the approval by action or expenditure not disproportionate in the circumstances." Reasonable efforts by Renovest were required to determine and communicate the accurate status of the observed building flaws. The evidence showed that the engineering report reflecting absence of structural defects was not shared with the interested banks. The record lends ample support to the trial court's finding that Renovest's attempts to secure financing were terminated prematurely.

* * *

[The trial court decision is affirmed.]

Implied Warranty
KAMINSZKY v. KUKUCH
553 N.E.2d 868 (Ind.App. 3 Dist. 1990)

STATON, Judge. Judit and Tibor Kaminszky appeal from a negative judgment in favor of Abel W. Kukuch. They had sought to have the sale of a house rescinded for breach of an implied warranty of fitness for habitation.

* * *

The evidence supporting the findings of the trial court shows that Abel Kukuch owned a house that he used as rental property. In 1978 he hired a professional to install insulation. He testified that he relied on the expertise of the contractor to use the best insulation available but that he was not informed what kind of insulation was used.

At the time the insulation was installed Deena Hardin and her family were renting the house. Hardin testified that it was obvious the house had been insulated because there were plugs visible on the outside of the house. She also testified that she and her family experienced no problems as a result of the insulation.

Prior to the Kaminszkys' purchase of the house in 1985, they inspected the house three times. During one of their inspections they observed insulation similar to what had been in their previous residence. They did not inquire about the type of insulation.

After they purchased the house they noticed an odor; Judit noticed a "different" taste in her mouth and began to experience skin irritation and dizziness. While cleaning the house the Kaminszkys discovered an access panel covered with wallpaper. On closer inspection they found a different type of insulation than they had observed previously. They took a sample of this insulation to the Lake County Health Department where it was determined to be urea-formaldehyde foam insulation. At this point Judit called the realtor and told him to "reverse the buy."

Several months later the Kaminszkys filed a complaint against Kukuch alleging breach of the implied warranty of habitability, failure to disclose, and mutual mistake. The Kaminszkys asked for rescission of the sale and damages. After a three-day bench trial the lower court ruled in favor of Kukuch. The trial court made specific and detailed findings of fact in support of the judgment.

* * *

I. Implied Warranty

Kaminszkys contend that the formaldehyde insulation is a latent defect which constitutes a breach of the implied warranty of habitability and thus requires rescission of the sale. We need not determine whether the urea-formaldehyde foam insulation constitutes a latent defect because Kukuch is not a builder-vendor and therefore cannot be held liable for the breach of an implied warranty of habitability.

The Indiana Supreme Court initially applied the warranty theory in *Theis v. Heuer* (1972), 280 N.E.2d 300, 306. In *Theis* our Supreme Court held that there is "an implied warranty of fitness for inhabitation in the sale of a new house by the builder-vendor to the immediate purchaser." The warranty was extended to subsequent purchasers by *Barnes v. Mac Brown and Company, Inc.* (1976), 342 N.E.2d 619, 620. The warranty was limited to builder-vendors by *Vetor v. Shockey* (1980), Ind.App., 414 N.E.2d 575, 577.

[The] Kaminszkys cite *Callander v. Sheridan* (1989), Ind.App., 546 N.E.2d 850, for the proposition that Kukuch is a builder-vendor liable for the implied warranty of habitability. In *Callander* the seller assumed the responsibilities of a builder-vendor by acting as a general contractor: he modified the house plan, hired subcontractors and supervised their work. Kukuch did not undertake such responsibility; he hired a professional to install the insulation and he relied on that individual's expertise. Kukuch is not liable under the theory of breach of the implied warranty of habitability.

II. Disclosure

The Kaminszkys contend that Kukuch should have disclosed the presence of formaldehyde insulation. The trial court found that:

> there is no contention that the defendant misrepresented or made any fraudulent representations to the plaintiffs in regard to the condition of the house.

Kukuch testified that he relied on the installer to use the best insulation available and that he did not know what kind of insulation had actually been used. The evidence supports the finding of the trial court.

III. Inspection Clause

The purchase agreement contained an inspection clause which stated in pertinent part:

> The property has been inspected and accepted by the buyer "as is" in its present condition and shall be delivered in such present condition to them at the time provided.... Purchaser is relying entirely for its condition upon his own examination and purchaser hereby releases the seller, brokers, REALTOR(S) and sales people herein from any and all liability relating to any defect or deficiency affecting said real estate, which release shall survive the closing of the transaction.

Kaminszkys cite *Callander v. Sheridan* at 546 N.E.2d 853, for the proposition that this clause does not release a seller from liability for latent defects. Their argument overlooks the fact that Callander, the seller in that case, was also a builder-vendor. As a builder-vendor, Callander could not escape liability by reliance on the release contained in the inspection clause.

In contrast, Kukuch is only a seller, not a builder-vendor, therefore, the inspection clause protects him from liability for latent defects.

Affirmed.

Nondisclosure
STAMBOVSKY v. ACKLEY
169 A.D.2d 254, 572 N.Y.S.2d 672 (1991)

RUBIN, Justice. Plaintiff, to his horror, discovered that the house he had recently contracted to purchase was widely reputed to be possessed by poltergeists, reportedly seen by defendant seller and members of her family on numerous occasions over the last nine years. Plaintiff promptly commenced this action seeking rescission of the contract of sale.

Supreme Court reluctantly dismissed the complaint, holding that plaintiff has no remedy at law in this jurisdiction.

The unusual facts of this case, as disclosed by the record, clearly warrant a grant of equitable relief to the buyer who, as a resident of New York City, cannot be expected to have any familiarity with the folklore of the Village of Nyack. Not being a "local," plaintiff could not readily learn that the home he had contracted to purchase is haunted. Whether the source of the spectral apparitions seen by defendant seller are parapsychic or psychogenic, having reported their presence in both a national publication (*Readers' Digest*) and the local press (in 1977 and 1982, respectively), defendant is estopped to deny their existence and, as a matter of law, the house is haunted. More to the point, however, no divination is required to conclude that it is defendant's promotional efforts in publicizing her close encounters with these spirits which fostered the home's reputation in the community. In 1989, the house was included in a five-home walking tour of Nyack and described in a November 27th newspaper article as "a riverfront Victorian (with ghost)." The impact of the reputation thus created goes to the very essence of the Bargain between the parties, greatly impairing both the value of the property and its potential for resale. The extent of this impairment may be presumed for the purpose of reviewing the disposition of this motion to dismiss the cause of action for rescission and represents merely an issue of fact for resolution at trial.

While I agree with Supreme Court that the real estate broker, as agent for the seller, is under no duty to disclose to a potential buyer the phantasmal reputation of the premises and that, in his pursuit of a legal remedy for fraudulent misrepresentation against the seller, plaintiff hasn't a ghost of a chance, I am nevertheless moved by the spirit of equity to allow the buyer to seek rescission of the contract of sale and recovery of his downpayment. New York law fails to recognize any remedy for damages incurred as a result of the seller's mere silence, applying instead the strict rule of caveat emptor. Therefore, the theoretical basis for granting relief, even under the extraordinary facts of this case, is elusive if not ephemeral.

"Pity me not but lend thy serious hearing to what I shall unfold" (William Shakespeare, Hamlet, Act I, Scene V [Ghost]).

From the perspective of a person in the position of plaintiff herein, a very practical problem arises with respect to the discovery of a paranormal phenomenon: "Who you gonna' call?" as the title song to the movie "Ghostbusters" asks. Applying the strict rule of caveat emptor to a contract involving a house possessed by poltergeists conjures up visions of a psychic or medium routinely accompanying the structural engineer and Terminix man on an inspection of every home subject to a contract of sale. It portends that the prudent attorney will establish an escrow account lest the subject of the transaction come back to haunt him and his client—or pray that his malpractice insurance coverage extends to supernatural disasters. In the interest of avoiding such untenable consequences, the notion that a haunting is a condition which can and should be ascertained upon reasonable inspection of the premises is a hobgoblin which should be exorcised from the body of legal precedent and laid quietly to rest.

* * *

With respect to transactions in real estate, New York adheres to the doctrine of caveat emptor and imposes no duty upon the vendor to disclose any information concerning the premises unless there is a confidential or fiduciary relationship between the parties or some conduct on the part of the seller which constitutes "active concealment." Normally, some affirmative misrepresentation or partial disclosure is required to impose upon the seller a duty to communicate undisclosed conditions affecting the premises.

Caveat emptor is not so all-encompassing a doctrine of common law as to render every act of non-disclosure immune from redress, whether legal or equitable. "In regard to the necessity of giving information which has not been asked, the rule differs somewhat at law and in equity, and while the law courts would permit no recovery of *damages* against a vendor, because of mere concealment of facts *under certain circumstances*, yet if the vendee refused to complete the contract because of the concealment of a material fact on the part of the other, equity would refuse to compel him so to do, because equity only compels the specific performance of a contract which is fair and open, and in regard to which all material matters known to each have been communicated to the other" (*Rothmiller v. Stein,* 38 N.E. 718 [emphasis added]).

* * *

The case law in this jurisdiction dealing with the duty of a vendor of real property to disclose information to the buyer is distinguishable from the matter under review. * * * No case has been brought to this court's attention in which the property value was impaired as the result of the reputation created by information disseminated to the public by the seller (or, for that matter, as a result of possession by poltergeists).

Where a condition which has been created by the seller materially impairs the value of the contract and is peculiarly within the knowledge of the seller or unlikely to be discovered by a prudent purchaser exercising due care with respect to the subject transaction, nondisclosure constitutes a basis for rescission as a matter of equity. Any other outcome places upon the buyer not merely the obligation to exercise care in his purchase but rather to be omniscient with respect to any fact which may affect the bargain. No practical purpose is served by imposing such a burden upon a purchaser. To the contrary, it encourages predatory business practice and offends the principle that equity will suffer no wrong to be without a remedy.

* * *

In the case at bar, defendant seller deliberately fostered the public belief that her home was possessed. Having undertaken to inform the public at large, to whom she has no legal relationship, about the supernatural occurrences on her property, she may be said to owe no less a duty to her contract vendee. It has been remarked that the occasional modern cases which permit a seller to take unfair advantage of a buyer's ignorance so long as he is not actively misled are "singularly unappetizing" (Prosser, Law of Torts §106, at 696 [4th ed. 1971]). Where, as here, the seller not only takes unfair advantage of the buyer's ignorance but has created and perpetuated a condition about which he is unlikely to even inquire, enforcement of the contract (in whole or in part) is offensive to the court's sense of equity. Application of the remedy of rescission, within the bounds of the narrow exception to the doctrine of caveat emptor set forth herein, is entirely appropriate to relieve the unwitting purchaser from the consequences of a most unnatural bargain. [The court therefore reinstated plaintiff's action for rescission of the contract.]

* * *

Rescission Due to Fear/Recovery of Earnest Money Deposit
UZAN v. 845 UN LIMITED PARTNERSHIP
10 A.D.3d 230 (N.Y.App.Div. 2004)

MAZZARELLI, Judge. This appeal presents the issue of whether plaintiffs, who defaulted on the purchase of four luxury condominium units, have forfeited their 25% down payments as a matter of law. Because the governing purchase agreements were a product of lengthy negotiation between parties of equal Bargaining power, all represented by counsel, there was no evidence of overreaching, and upon consideration of the fact that a 25% down payment is common usage in the new construction luxury condominium market in New York City, we hold that upon their default and failure to cure, plaintiffs forfeited all rights to their deposits pursuant to the rule set forth in *Maxton Builders, Inc. v. Lo Galbo.*

Facts

In October 1998, Defendant 845 UN Limited Partnership (sponsor or 845 UN) began to sell apartments at The Trump World Tower (Trump World), a luxury condominium building to be constructed at 845 United Nations Plaza. Donald Trump is the managing general partner of the sponsor. Plaintiffs Cem Uzan and Hakan Uzan, two brothers, are Turkish billionaires who sought to purchase multiple units in the building.

In April 1999, plaintiffs and an associate executed seven purchase agreements for apartments in Trump World. Only four of those units (the penthouse units) are the subject of this lawsuit and appeal. As relevant, Cem Uzan defaulted on contracts to buy two penthouse units on the 90th floor of the building, and Hakan defaulted on contracts to purchase two other penthouse units on the 89th floor.

The building had not been constructed when plaintiffs executed their purchase agreements. In paragraph 17.4 of those contracts, the sponsor projected that the first closing in the building would occur on or about April 1, 2001, nearly two years after the signing of the agreements.

The condominium offering plan included a section titled "Special Risks to be Considered by Purchasers," which stated:

> Purchasers will be required to make a down payment upon execution of a Purchase Agreement in an amount equal to 10% of the purchase price, and within 180 days after receipt of the executed Purchase Agreement from Sponsor or 15 days after Purchaser receives a written notice or amendment to the Plan declaring the Plan effective, whichever is earlier, an additional down payment equal to 15% of the purchase price …

Once construction was completed, the building's offering plan was amended to require a 15% down payment. Notably, both the original and the amended offering plans prominently disclosed the sponsor's right to retain the *entire down payment* should there be an uncured default.

Negotiations Preceding Execution of the Purchase Agreements

Plaintiffs were represented by experienced local counsel during the two-month-long negotiation for the purchase of the apartments. There were numerous telephone conversations between counsel, and at least four extensively marked-up copies of draft purchase agreements were exchanged. In consideration for plaintiffs' purchase of multiple units, the sponsor reduced the aggregate purchase price of the penthouse units by more than $7 million from the list price in the offering plan for a total cost of approximately $32 million. Plaintiffs also negotiated a number of revisions to the standard purchase agreement, including extensions of time for payment of the down payment. As amended, each purchase agreement obligated plaintiffs to make a 25% down payment: 10% at contract, an additional 7 1/2% down payment twelve months later, and a final 7 1/2% down payment 18 months after the execution of the contract. At no time did plaintiffs object to the total amount required as a non-refundable down payment.

* * *

The executed purchase agreements provide, at paragraph 12(b), that:

> [u]pon the occurrence of an Event of Default … [i]f Sponsor elects to cancel … [and i]f the default is not cured within … thirty (30) days, then this Agreement shall be deemed canceled, and Sponsor shall have the right to retain, as and for liquidated damages, the Down payment and any interest earned on the Down payment.

Plaintiffs paid the first 10% down payment installment for the penthouse units on April 26, 1999 when they signed the purchase agreements. They paid the second 7 1/2% installment in April 2000, and the third 7 1/2% installment in October 2000. The total 25% down payment of approximately $8 million was placed in an escrow account.

Default, Failure to Cure, and This Action

On September 11, 2001, terrorists attacked New York City by flying two planes into the World Trade Center, the city's two tallest buildings, murdering thousands of people. Plaintiffs, asserting concerns of future terrorist attacks, failed to appear at the October 19, 2001 closing, resulting in their default. By letter dated October 19, 2001, plaintiffs' counsel stated:

> [W]e believe that our clients are entitled to rescind their Purchase Agreements in view of the terrorist attack which occurred on September 11 and has not abated. In particular, our clients are concerned that the top

floors in a "trophy" building, described as the tallest residential building in the world, will be an attractive terrorist target. The situation is further aggravated by the fact that the building bears the name of Donald Trump, perhaps the most widely known symbol of American capitalism. Finally, the United Nations complex brings even more attention to this location.

That day 845 UN sent plaintiffs default letters, notifying them that they had 30 days to cure. On November 19, 2001, upon expiration of the cure period, the sponsor terminated the four purchase agreements.

Plaintiffs then brought this action. They alleged that Donald Trump had prior special knowledge that certain tall buildings, such as Trump World, were potential targets for terrorists. Plaintiffs also alleged that Trump World did not have adequate protection for the residents of the upper floors of the building. In their first cause of action, plaintiffs averred that the sponsor's failure to advise prospective purchasers of the specific risks of a terrorist attack on Trump World, and to amend the offering plan to describe these risks, constituted common-law fraud and deceptive sales practices pursuant to General Business Law §352. Plaintiffs' second claim is that the same acts constituted violations of General Business Law §§349 and 350. The third cause of action sought a declaratory judgment that the down payment was an "unconscionable, illegal and unenforceable penalty." The IAS court dismissed plaintiffs' first two claims in a March 2000 order not on appeal.

Motions for Summary Judgment

After exchanging discovery and conducting various depositions, plaintiffs moved for summary judgment on their third cause of action, arguing that forfeiture of the down payments was an unenforceable penalty. In support of their motion, plaintiffs submitted an attorney's affirmation to which were annexed: the pleadings, correspondence between counsel, the IAS court's order denying dismissal of the declaratory judgment cause of action, and certain news articles and promotional materials about the Trump World Tower.

Defendant opposed the motion and cross-moved for summary judgment, asserting that defaulting vendees on real estate contracts may not recover their down payments.

* * *

The Role of the 25% Down Payment

In his affidavit in support of the cross motion, Donald Trump stated that he sought 25% down payments from pre-construction purchasers at the Trump World Tower because of the substantial length of time between contract signing and closing, during which period the sponsor had to keep the units off the market, and because of the obvious associated risks. Trump also affirmed that down payments in the range of 20% to 25% are standard practice in the new construction luxury condominium submarket in New York City. He cited three projects where he was the developer, The

Trump Palace, 610 Park Avenue and Trump International Hotel and Tower, all of which had similar down payment provisions. Trump also noted that,

> [i]n new construction condominium projects, purchasers often speculate on the market by putting down initial down payments of 10% and 15% and watching how the market moves. If the market value increases, they will then make the second down payment. If the market prices drop, they may then walk away from their down payment.

* * *

Defendant also presented a compilation of sixteen recent condominium offering plans, all of which required down payments of either 20% or 25% of the purchase price for the unit. Fourteen of the sixteen offering plans required 25% down payments. Further, defendant provided proof that in July 2001, plaintiff Cem Uzan closed on the purchase of an apartment on the 80th floor of Trump World after making a 25% down payment, and that he had previously purchased another apartment at 515 Park Avenue, also with a 25% down payment provision.

The Order Appealed

After hearing oral argument on the motion, the IAS court granted defendant partial summary judgment, finding that plaintiffs forfeited the portion of their down payment amounting to 10% of the purchase price, pursuant to *Maxton Builders, Inc. v. Lo Galbo.* The court held that the remainder of the down payment was subject to a liquidated damages analysis to determine whether it bore a reasonable relation to the sponsor's actual or probable loss. Defendant appeals from that portion of the order which denied it full relief.

Discussion

More than a century ago, the Court of Appeals, in *Lawrence v. Miller,* held that a vendee who defaults on a real estate contract without lawful excuse cannot recover his or her down payment. It reaffirmed this holding in *Maxton, supra,* again in 1986. The facts of *Lawrence* are common to real estate transactions, and parallel those presented here. In that case, plaintiff made a $2000 down payment on the purchase of certain real estate, and then defaulted. The seller refused to extend plaintiff's time to perform the contract, retained the down payment, and ultimately sold the property to another purchaser. In plaintiff's subsequent action for a refund of the down payment, the Court of Appeals affirmed a judgment dismissing the complaint, stating:

> To allow a recovery of this money would be to sustain an action by a party on his own breach of his own contract, which the law does not allow. When we once declare in this case that the vendor has done all that the law asks of him, we also declare that the vendee has not so done on his part. And then to maintain this action would be to

declare that a party may violate his agreement, and make an infraction of it by himself a cause of action. That would be ill doctrine.

For over a century, courts have consistently upheld what was called the *Lawrence* rule and recognized a distinction between real estate deposits and general liquidated damages clauses. Liquidated damages clauses have traditionally been subject to judicial oversight to confirm that the stipulated damages bear a reasonable proportion to the probable loss caused by the breach. By contrast, real estate down payments have been subject to limited supervision. They have only been refunded upon a showing of disparity of bargaining power between the parties, duress, fraud, illegality or mutual mistake.

In *Maxton*, plaintiff had contracted to sell defendants a house, and accepted a check for a 10% down payment. When defendants canceled the contract and placed a stop payment on the check, plaintiff sued for the down payment, citing the *Lawrence* rule. Defendants argued that plaintiff's recovery should be limited to its actual damages. In ruling for the vendor, the Court of Appeals identified two legal principles as flowing from *Lawrence.* First, that the vendor was entitled to retain the down payment in a real estate contract, without reference to his actual damages. Second, the "parent" rule, upon which the first rule was based, that one who breaches a contract may not recover the value of his part performance.

The Court noted that the parent rule had been substantially undermined in the 100 years since *Lawrence.* Many courts had rejected the parent rule because of criticism that it produced a forfeiture "and the amount of the forfeiture increases as performance proceeds, so that the penalty grows larger as the breach grows smaller."

The Court also noted that since *Lawrence,* the rule of allowing recovery of down payments of not more than 10% in real estate contracts continues to be followed by a "majority of jurisdictions," including in New York. Thereafter, the court noted the long and widespread reliance on the *Lawrence* rule in real estate transactions, and it concluded that, based upon notions of efficiency and avoiding unnecessary litigation, the rule should remain in effect.

After acknowledging that "[R]eal estate contracts are probably the best examples of arms length transactions," the Court broadly concluded:

> Except in cases where there is a real risk of overreaching, there should be no need for the courts to relieve the parties of the consequences of their contract. **If the parties are dissatisfied with the rule of [*Lawrence*], the time to say so is at the bargaining table.**

The *Maxton/Lawrence* rule has since been followed by this Court as well as the other departments to deny a refund of a down payment when a default has occurred.

* * *

Applying the reasoning of these cases to the facts of the instant matter, it is clear that plaintiffs are not entitled to a return of any portion of their down payment. Here the 25% down payment was a specifically negotiated element of the contracts. There is no question that this was an arm's length transaction. The parties were sophisticated business people, represented by counsel, who spent two months at the bargaining table before executing the amended purchase agreements.

Further, the record evidences that it is customary in the pre-construction luxury condominium industry for parties to price the risk of default at 25% of the purchase price. The purchase agreements included a detailed non-refundable down payment clause to which plaintiffs' counsel had negotiated a specific amendment. That amendment allowed for the payment of 25% of the purchase price in three installments: 10% at contract, an additional 7 1/2% twelve months later, and a final 7 1/2% eighteen months later. Clearly, plaintiffs were fully aware of and accepted the requirement of a non-refundable 25% down payment for these luxury pre-construction condominiums. In fact, Cem Uzan has purchased two other condominiums, one in the same building, with similar down payment provisions.

Plaintiffs negotiated the payment of the 25% down payments in installments to spread their risk over time. In the event of a severe economic downturn, plaintiffs were free to cancel the deal, capping their losses at the amount paid as of the date of their default. For the sponsor, the 25% deposit served to cover its risk for keeping the apartments off the market should the purchaser default.

Finally, there was no evidence of a disparity of bargaining power, or of duress, fraud, illegality or mutual mistake by the parties in drafting the down payment clause of the purchase agreements. The detailed provision concerning the non-refundable deposit was integral to the transaction. If plaintiffs were dissatisfied with the 25% non-refundable down payment provision in the purchase agreements, the time to have voiced objection was at the bargaining table. Because they chose to accept it, they are committed to its terms. Thus, upon plaintiffs' default and failure to cure, defendant was entitled to retain the full 25% down payments.

Accordingly, the order of the Supreme Court, New York County (Alice Schlesinger, J.), entered July 21, 2003, which, to the extent appealed from, denied defendant 845 UN Limited Partnership's motion for summary judgment, should be reversed, on the law, with costs, defendant's motion granted and the complaint dismissed. The Clerk is directed to enter judgment in favor of defendant-appellant dismissing the complaint as against it.

KEY TERMS

alternative dispute resolution, 243
arbitration, 243
as-is clause, 250
caveat emptor, 238
consideration, 225
contingency, 234
contract, 219
counteroffer, 224
damages, 242
duress, 246
earnest money, 233
economic loss rule, 241
equitable conversion, 232
estoppel, 221
express warranty, 238
Home Owners Warranty (HOW) plan, 238
implied warranty of habitability, 238
in arrears, 236
installment contract, 220
letter of intent, 224
mailbox rule, 223
Marketable Record Title Acts, 231
marketable title, 229

mediation, 243
merger rule, 232
mirror image rule, 224
misrepresentation, 246
mutual mistake, 244
option contract, 223
parol evidence rule, 222
part performance, 221
patent, 230
privity of contract, 239
prorate, 236
puffing, 247
representation, 246
revocation, 223
root of title, 231
specific performance, 242
Statute of Frauds, 220
strict liability theory, 240
substantial performance doctrine, 235
time is of the essence, 236
undue influence, 246
warranty, 237

PROBLEMS

1. The Farringtons entered into a signed agreement to sell their real estate to the Tucsons. The price was stated in the agreement as follows: "Sum of fifty thousand dollars ($50,000). Approximately one-third down, the balance to be paid over a period of 10 years at 7% interest. This option to expire in 30 days. One hundred dollars ($100.00) to be paid at time of agreement with said amount to be applied on purchase price." Is this an enforceable agreement? Why or why not?

2. Nellie sold a small hotel to George. During the contract negotiations preceding the sale, Nellie told George that the hotel earned $2,000 a month. Following the sale, George learned that although this figure was accurate, most of the income resulted from the operation of the hotel as a brothel. Does Nellie's statement about hotel income constitute misrepresentation? Why or why not?

3. Bert orally promised Ernie that if Ernie quit his job to care for Bert, who was elderly and ill, Ernie would receive Bert's real estate at Bert's death. Ernie quit his job and cared for Bert until Bert died two years later. No will or deed was found. Assuming that Ernie lived on the property before Bert's death, is Ernie entitled to Bert's real estate? Why or why not?

4. The Lowerys owned a farm consisting of 365 acres. They arranged to sell the farm by public auction; bids were to be given orally. The sale was to be for cash with a 10 percent down payment due at the auction and the balance due upon transfer of the deed. Couture was the highest bidder at the auction. Since the auction was on a Saturday, Couture orally sought and was granted permission by the Lowerys to deliver the down payment on Monday after his bank opened. On Monday, Couture presented the Lowerys with the down payment; but they refused to accept it. Can Couture enforce their agreement? Why or why not?

5. Schaeffler hired Newcomb to build a house and promised to pay Newcomb the cost of materials and an agreed profit. Schaeffler was to provide Newcomb with the drawings and specifications to erect the residence. Work began in July and continued until September, when Newcomb reported to Schaeffler that cracks had developed in the foundation and walls of the structure. The damage was partially due to a soil defect and partially due to Newcomb's deviation from specifications that had been submitted to him. Schaeffler personally paid to correct the soil condition and sought recovery of his cost from Newcomb. Newcomb claims that he substantially performed the contract and that Schaeffler owes him the balance of his profit due on the job. Decide.

6. Hartley purchased a new house from Ballou, the builder. Hartley inspected and obtained possession of the house shortly after the closing. On several occasions, the basement of Hartley's new home flooded after a rainstorm. Hartley informed Ballou of the problem; and Ballou attempted to rectify the problem, but to no avail. Hartley sued Ballou for breach of the implied warranty that the house was fit and suitable for its intended purpose as a residence. What defenses should Ballou assert? Who will win? Why?

7. Bassford, who was seeking a home in the Denver area, was shown a new house owned by Cook. While inspecting the house, Bassford observed substantial cracks in the interior walls. Cook informed Bassford that an engineer had determined that the cracks were the result of the settling of the house. Cook stated that corrective action was being taken and informed Bassford that minor soil conditions required keeping water away from the foundation. Assuming that Cook is telling Bassford all of the facts (as far as he knows) about the house's condition, can Bassford still rescind the contract? Why or why not?

8. Johnson purchased a house and lot from Lina. During negotiations for the sale, Lina represented the lot width to be sixty feet when, in fact, it was only fifty feet. There were no physical boundaries that made the lot's width easily discernible by the naked eye. Johnson, upon discovery of the true width of the lot, promptly brought action for rescission of the sale on the ground of misrepresentation. Will he win? Why or why not?

9. Able decided to sell his hotel. Able told Baker, a potential purchaser, that the hotel was in "A-1 condition." In fact, unknown to Able or Baker, the walls of the hotel were structurally defective and ready to collapse. Baker relied on Able's statement and bought the hotel. When Baker learned of the defective walls, she sued to rescind the sale. Able claimed that his statement was innocently made and therefore Baker is not entitled to rescission. Who is correct? Why?

10. Goodman owned property worth $100,000. Unaware of its value, Goodman sold it for cash to Alvarez for $30,000. If Goodman's property was in Mississippi, it would be governed by the common law. The common law does not second-guess the adequacy of the consideration paid for land, so the sale would be final. However, if the property was located in neighboring Louisiana, which uses the civil law legal system, Goodman would be allowed to rescind the sale under a civil law doctrine called "lesion beyond moiety."

    Lesion beyond moiety allows the seller to rescind a sale of land (the doctrine does not apply to personal property) if the land was sold for less than one-half its value. The right must be exercised within four years of the sale. Goodman also would have to reimburse the buyer, Alvarez, for any improvements Alvarez may have made to the land. Which doctrine is more ethical? Should the onus be placed on a buyer to determine the land's value and pay more than one-half to avoid harming the seller? Goodman also could assert the right if Alvarez sold the land to another party. What effect could that action have on titles and the merchantability of land? On the other hand, should there be laws, like the doctrine of lesion beyond moiety, to protect an unsophisticated buyer from a bad deal? Should the government promote efficiency and finality to the sale of real estate, or should it protect people like Goodman from themselves? Explain your answers.

ENDNOTES

1. Restatement, Second, of Contracts §1 (1981).
2. See E. Allen Farnsworth, I *Farnsworth on Contracts* 6 (1990).
3. 38 Conn.App. 420; 662 A.2d 129 (Conn. App. 1995).
4. Restatement of Contracts §197 (1932). The Restatement, Second, of Contracts §129 (1981) provides: "A contract for the transfer of an interest in land may be specifically enforced notwithstanding failure to comply with the Statute of Frauds if it is established that the party seeking enforcement, in reasonable reliance on the contract and on the continuing assent of the party against whom enforcement is sought, has so changed his position that injustice can be avoided only by specific enforcement."
5. 35 Cal.2d 621; 220 P.2d 737 (1950).
6. 247 N.Y. 377, 160 N.E. 646 (1928).
7. E. Farnsworth, I *Farnsworth on Contracts* 286 (1990).
8. 1 B & Ald. 681, 106 Eng.Rep. 250 (K.B. 1818).
9. 155 So.2d 889 (Fla.App. 1963).
10. *Hargrave v. Heard Inv. Co.,* 56 Ariz. 77, 105 P.2d 520 (1940).
11. G. Poindexter, *Letters of Intent in Commercial Real Estate,* 28 Real Estate Law Journal 195 (2000).
12. 196 Va. 493, 84 S.E.2d 516 (1954).
13. 62 Va. (21 Grat.) 75 (1871).
14. D. Thomas, 12 *Thompson on Real Estate* 233 (1994).
15. 148 Conn. 153, 168 A.2d 550 (1961).
16. 15 U.S.C. §7006(5).
17. Uniform Electronic Transactions Act §2(7), (8).
18. P. Randolph, *Has E-Sign Murdered the Statute of Frauds?* 15 Probate and Property 23 (2001).
19. 854 N.Y.S. 2d 690 (1st Dep't 2008).
20. S. Kramarsky, *New York Law Journal,* May 22, 2008, accessed at http://www.law.com/jsp/nylj/PubArticleNY.jsp?hubtype=technologyToday&id=1202421520608 (last visited March 29, 2010).
21. M. Bowden, *Save Your Clients Money With Tax-Deferred Property Exchanges,* Lawyers Weekly USA B14 (May 29, 2000).
22. J. Sikora, *The Elephant in the Like Kind Exchange Room: Rollover Regime,* 38 Real Estate Law Journal 169 (Fall 2009). Sikora suggests the statute should be amended to employ a rollover in place of the current exchange requirement in order to eliminate the problems created by unscrupulous qualified intermediaries.
23. *Peatling v. Baird,* 168 Kan. 528, 213 P.2d 1015 (1950).
24. *Siedel v. Snider,* 241 Iowa 1227, 44 N.W.2d 687 (1950).
25. An easement gives one person the right to use another person's land for a specified purpose; see Chapter 4. A restrictive covenant is a private restriction on land use resulting from a contract; see Chapter 13.
26. However, some courts have held that title is marketable where the easement causes only minor intrusion or the purchaser was aware of the easement when the contract was signed. R. Cunningham, W. Stoebuck, and D. Whitman, *The Law of Property* 693 (1984).
27. E. Freyfogle, *Real Estate Sales and the New Implied Warranty of Lawful Use,* 71 Cornell Law Rev. 1 (1985), citing M. Friedman, *Contracts and Conveyances of Real Property* (4th ed. 1984).
28. *Sinks v. Karleskint,* 130 Ill. App. 3d 527, 474 N.E.2d 767 (1985). Some states do, however, require access as a condition of marketable title, as in *Barasky v. Huttner,* 210 A.D.2d 367, 620 N.Y.S.2d 121 (N.Y.App.Div. 1994).
29. R. Boyer, H. Hovenkamp, and S. Kurtz, *The Law of Property* 513 (4th ed. 1991).
30. 661 A.2d 220 (Md.App. 1995).
31. 345 Mass. 621, 189 N.E.2d 191 (1963).
32. The states which have adopted the Uniform Vendor and Purchaser Risk Act are California, Hawaii, Illinois, Michigan, Nevada, New Mexico, New York, North Carolina, Oklahoma, Oregon, South Dakota, Texas, and Wisconsin.
33. 54 Ohio App.2d 1, 374 N.E.2d 427, 8 O.O.3d 22 (1977).
34. *Glezos v. Frontier Investments,* 896 P.2d 1230 (Utah App. 1995) (applying Nevada law).
35. *Olmo v. Matos,* 653 A.2d 1 (Pa. Super. 1995).
36. *Moran v. Erk,* 11 N.Y.3d 452, 901 N.E.2d 187 (2008).
37. 219 S.W.2d 810 (Tex.Civ.App. 1949).
38. M. Piccoli, *Executing Real Estate Contracts by Fax,* Probate & Property (May/June 1995).
39. 15 U.S.C. §7001(c)(6) (2000).
40. T. Reid and R. Maniscalco, *A Closer Look at Seller Representations in Commercial Real Estate,* Probate and Property 12 (Nov./Dec. 1991); J. Todd, *Handling Environmental Law Concerns in Real Estate Transactions,* 19 Real Estate Review 76 (1989). States requiring that mold be disclosed in a sale or lease are Arizona, California, Georgia, Iowa, Louisiana, Michigan, Mississippi, Montana, New Jersey, Oklahoma, Rhode Island, and Texas. See http://www.realtor.org/realtororg.nsf/pages/moldchart0403 (last visited March 29, 2010).
41. R. Aalberts, *Will Toxic Mold Become the Next Asbestos?* 31 Real Estate Law Journal 103 (2002).
42. R. McCafferty, *Molds Cause Untold Damage,* USA Weekend 10 (Oct. 12–14, 2001).
43. 2002 WL 1332775 (Iowa App. 2002).

44. See K. Blumenthal, *Some Home Buyers Find Their Warranties Can Be Nearly Useless*, Wall Street Journal (November 30, 1994).

45. 542 P.2d 1275 (Wyo. 1975).

46. *Padula v. J.J. Deb-Cin Homes, Inc.*, 111 R.I. 29, 298 A.2d 529 (1973).

47. Disclaimers that do not specifically refer to warranties, such as a general sale "as-is" clause, may not be effective. See F. Powell and J. Mallor, *The Case for an Implied Warranty of Quality in Sales of Commercial Real Estate*, 68 Wash. U. L. Q. 305 (1990).

48. *Speight v. Walters Development Co.*, 774 N.W.2d 108 (Iowa 2008).

49. *Barnes v. Mac Brown & Co., Inc.*, 264 Ind. 227, 342 N.E.2d 619 (1976). The states which provide an implied warranty of habitability to buyers of used houses are Arizona, Arkansas, Idaho, Indiana, Louisiana, Maine, Mississippi, Nebraska, New Hampshire, New Jersey, North Carolina, Ohio, Oklahoma, Rhode Island, South Carolina, Texas, West Virginia, and Wyoming. Source: *Speight v. Walters, supra* note 48.

50. *Dawson Industries, Inc. v. Godley Construction Co., Inc.*, 224 S.E. 2d 266 (Ct. App. N.C. 1976). See also F. Powell and J. Mallor, *supra* note 47. The authors conclude that "some courts have refused to extend an implied warranty to the sale of commercial property...." *Id.* at 336.

51. *Johnson v. Davis*, 480 So.2d 65, 629 (Fla. 1986).

52. W. Keeton et al., *Law of Torts* §104A, at 724 (5th ed. 1984).

53. J. Allee, *Product Liability* §2.04[2] 1984.

54. 44 N.J. 70, 207 A.2d 314 (1965).

55. S. Hsieh, *'Right to Cure' Laws Could Slow Construction Defect Claims*, Lawyers Weekly USA 14 (September 29, 2003).

56. D. Dahl, *Will 'green certification' issues lead to litigation?* USA Weekly, (September. 2, 2008). See also D. Prum and S. Del Percio, *Green Building Claims: What Theories Will a Plaintiff Pursue, Who Has Exposure, and A Proposal for Risk Mitigation*, 37 Real Estate Law Journal 243 (Spring 2009).

57. *Double AA Corporation v. Newland Company*, 273 Mont. 486, 905 P.2d 138, 141 (1995).

58. *Id.*

59. G. Lefcoe, *Real Estate Transactions* 403 (2nd ed. 1997).

60. M. Donner, *Litigation Avoidance 101*, Probate and Property 19 (May/June 2003).

61. 143 Cal.4th 761, 49 Cal. Rptr.3d 531 (Cal. Ct. App. 2006). The language of the arbitration agreement stated:

"Notice: by initialing in the space below you are agreeing to have any dispute arising out of the matters included in the 'arbitration of disputes' provision decided by neutral arbitration as provided by California law and you are giving up any rights you might possess to have the dispute litigated in a court or jury trial. By initialing in the space below you are giving up your judicial rights to discovery and appeal, unless those rights are specifically included in the 'arbitration of disputes' provision. If you refuse to submit to arbitration after agreeing to this provision, you may be compelled to arbitrate under the authority of the California Code of Civil Procedure. Your agreement to this arbitration provision is voluntary.

"We have read and understand the foregoing and agree to submit disputes arising out of the matters included in the 'arbitration of disputes' provision to neutral arbitration."

62. 118 Vt. 116, 100 A.2d 581 (1953).

63. J. Calamari and J. Perillo, *Contracts* 387 (3rd ed. 1987).

64. 109 Vt. 294, 196 A. 276 (1938).

65. *Go-Mart v. Olson*, 198 W. Va. 559; 482 S.E.2d 176 (1996).

66. See M. Jennings, *Business: Its Legal, Ethical, and Global Environment* 437–438 (8th ed. 2009).

67. 252 S.C. 601, 168 S.E.2d 82 (1969).

68. In most real estate transactions, the broker is a special agent hired to find a purchaser and has no authority to make statements on behalf of the vendors. Consequently, the vendor is not liable for the statements of the agent unless the statements were specifically authorized. However, the vendee is allowed to rescind a transaction resulting from a misrepresentation because the vendor is not allowed to retain the proceeds of a fraud committed for his benefit. W. Seavey, *Law of Agency* §28 at 50, §92 at 164 (1964).

69. If the false representation is intentional, the technical name of the theory is fraud. In many states, a buyer who seeks damages (as opposed to rescission of the contract) must prove intentional misrepresentation. W. Keeton et al., *Prosser and Keeton on Torts* 734 (5th ed. 1984).

70. 228 Ark. 1119, 312 S.W.2d 442 (1958).

71. W. Keeton et al., *supra* note 52 at 751 752.

72. 56 Wash.2d 449, 353 P.2d 672 (1960).

73. 145 Cal.App.3d 261, 193 Cal.Rptr. 130 (1983).

74. C. Rampell, *For Sale: Scene of a Crime*, USA Today (August 7, 2006).

75. *Id.*

76. J. Lawlor, *Seller Beware*, ABA Journal 90 (August 1992).

77. F. Roberts, *Let the Seller Beware: Disclosures, Disclaimers and "As Is" Clauses*, 31 Real Estate Law Journal 303 (2003).

78. L. Zumpano and K. Johnson, *Real Estate Brokerage Liability and Property Disclosure*, Real Estate Law Journal 285 (2003).

79. F. Roberts, *supra* note 77 at 311.

80. Lawlor, *supra* note 76.

81. *Strawn v. Canuso*, 657 A.2d 480 (N.J. 1995).

82. K. Lahey and D. Redle, *The Ohio Experience: The Effectiveness of Mandatory Real Estate Disclosure Forms*, 25 Real Estate Law Journal 319 (1997); K. Pancak et al., *Residential Disclosure Laws: The Further Demise of Caveat Emptor*, 24 Real Estate Law Journal 291 (1996).

83. 165 Ore.App. 353; 998 P.2d 221 (Ore. 2000).

84. See http://homebuying.about.com/od/homedisclosures/Understanding_Home_Disclosures.htm (last visited March 29, 2010).

85. 24 C.F.R. §35.86, 40 C.F.R. §745.103, implementing the Residential Lead-Based Paint Hazard Act of 1992, 42 U.S.C. §4852d.

86. D. Hauck, *Most home remodeling will soon require EPA-certified workers*, USA Today, http://content.usatoday.com/communities/greenhouse/post/2010/03/lack-of-epa-certified-workers-could-stall-home-remodeling/1 (last visited March 19, 2010).

87. B. Mashian and S. Lu, *A Seller Can't Hide Behind 'As-Is' Clause*, National Law Journal (October 31, 1996).

88. *Caramante v. Barton*, 114 A.D.2d 680, 494 N.Y.S.2d 498 (1985).

89. *Loughrin v. Superior Court*, 19 Cal.Rptr. 161 (Cal.App. 1993).

90. 184 W. Va. 317, 400 S.E.2d 561 (1990).

91. 162 Kan. 558, 178 P.2d 275 (1947).

Title and Insurance

© MACIEJ NOSKOWSKI/iStockphoto (RF)

LEARNING OBJECTIVES

After studying Chapter 8, you should:

- Understand title to real estate

- Be able to explain how title, property and liability insurance function

title

The right to possess real estate as evidenced by a historical record.

"Cursed be he that removeth his neighbour's landmark."

Deuteronomy Chapter 27, Verse 17

"Insurance: An ingenious modern game of chance in which the player is permitted to enjoy the comfortable conviction that he is beating the man who keeps the table."

Ambrose Bierce

During the interval between the signing of a real estate contract and the closing, three important activities usually take place:

1. The seller must prove that she has **title** to the real estate under the contractually established standard.
2. The buyer makes arrangements for property and liability insurance.
3. The buyer borrows money to finance the purchase.

This chapter and Chapter 9 examine those transactions.

Title

A buyer can acquire such rights to real estate only as the seller has the power to convey. When you purchase a home, you do not expect to forfeit your rights one month, one year, or one decade later if your seller dies. Yet that would be the result if the seller had a life estate and conveyed the life estate to you. Similarly, you do not expect a stranger to ring your doorbell and claim the right to share your house with you. Yet that would be the result if your seller owned the property as a tenant in common. Although the rules governing recording and title are technical, they go to the heart of the real estate transaction: giving the purchaser the rights to real estate that she expects.

There are many processes existing in the American legal system that protect property owners' reasonable expectations of what they own. Indeed, recordation, title examination, and insurance, among others discussed in this chapter have been instrumental in promoting the economic vitality of the United States. This fact has not gone unnoticed in other countries, which, in recent years, have made the transition to a market economy. Russia, for example, in making its conversion recognized the necessity for creating new measures designed to protect property titles. As one commentator on Russia's new title registration law notes:

> The registration system is an important development in Russia's economic transition toward a market economy. First, registered right holders have great tenure security and will be willing to undertake long-term improvement on their property, which leads to higher production. Second, lenders feel more secure taking registered property as collateral. This not only provides right holders with capital for improvements, but also encourages the credit industry. Third, transactions involving immovables [real estate] become cheaper and safer, which increases marketability of the immovable property. Fourth, greater security of rights promotes development of the market for immovable objects. All these business opportunities will eventually attract more foreign capital to Russia, and this promotes development of the Russian market economy.[1]

As noted in Chapter 7, the seller's obligation to convey title of a certain defined quality is typically established in the real estate contract. The contract usually provides that the seller must furnish "evidence" of title to the buyer, and the buyer verifies that the title is satisfactory prior to closing. Sellers have *three* methods available to prove that they have good title: abstract and opinion, title insurance, and the Torrens system. These methods are based on the legal framework of recording and on recording statutes. Indeed, as you will learn in this chapter, if the recording process is not carried out properly, establishing marketable title and protecting property rights can be greatly compromised.

Recording Statutes

Recording Defined   **Recording** (also called *recordation*) takes place in local governmental offices, typically the county seat, where legal documents are placed in compilations known as the *public records*. The first recording system under the common law legal system was established in England in 1535. The Statute of Enrolments required freehold landowners in all the English counties to record their deeds. The system was set up to prevent fraudulent secret deed conveyances, but some historians also contend that King Henry VIII wished to know who all the freehold land owners were to maintain political control. The earliest American recordation system was created in the Massachusetts Bay colony in 1640. Today there are 3100 separate recording systems located in the counties of the U.S.[2]

Legal instruments affecting land, including real estate contracts (discussed in Chapter 7), mortgages (Chapter 9), leases (Chapter 11), and financing statements for fixtures (Chapter 2), can be recorded as long as they comply with legal form requirements. Recording gives **constructive notice** to the rest of the world that the property has been conveyed to a new owner. That is, the law presumes that a purchaser has notice of documents that have been recorded whether or not the purchaser or her agent has checked the records. Once the purchaser or agent has examined the records, the constructive notice that had been presumed by the law upon recording becomes **actual notice**. Beyond constructive notice, actual notice also can be acquired personally, such as being informed that someone besides the purported seller actually owns the property. Finally, **inquiry notice** occurs when a purchaser has possession of certain facts imposing a further duty to inquiry. For example, this would occur if, for example, the purchaser inspects the land he is considering to buy and observes a dirt road which appears to have been used recently. At that point, he would have duty to inquiry whether there is an unrecorded interest such as a prescriptive easement (discussed in Chapter 4) before he makes the purchase.

---

recording
The act of placing in the public record documents that give the world notice of the information therein.

constructive notice
Notice imputed to a person by law due to its existence in the public records whether the person has actually inspected the public records or not.

actual notice
Title information that is acquired personally by someone.

inquiry notice
Notice of facts that create a duty to inquire further whether unrecorded interests exist.

Although recordation is a critical process in real estate law, a deed that has *not* been recorded is still valid between the seller and the purchaser. Nevertheless, it is important to remember that if the deed is not recorded, third parties may acquire better rights to the property than the purchaser.

Certain requirements must be met before an instrument can be recorded. A deed, for example, must meet the usual requirements for a valid deed (discussed in Chapter 10). If a major error exists in the deed, the recording does not protect a purchaser who has recorded the deed. Major errors include defects in the legal description of the property or in the grantor's name. If, for example, the grantor's name of Aalberts was spelled as *Alberts* in a deed, this conveyance could be missed in a title search. A similar result would occur if Lot 2, Block 12 was mistranscribed as Lot 12, Block 2. In each case, the document could be outside the chain of title. The "chain of title" is discussed later in this chapter. As the following Mississippi case shows, simple mistakes in the public record can result in significant losses.

A CASE IN POINT

In *Saxon v. Saxon*[3] a deed for rural land was executed, delivered to the purchaser, and recorded. However, the court held that the deed did not give notice to later purchasers because the description in the deed did not include the section number: "The registration of an instrument is constructive notice to the world of the contents of the paper there recorded or intended to be recorded, and of its particular contents only, and it will have no operation or effect unless the original instrument correctly and sufficiently describes the premises which are to be affected." Because the deed was void, the plaintiff, who possessed the land for more than ten years, gained ownership rights under adverse possession.

In addition to the usual deed requirements, many states impose special requirements for recording purposes only. These formalities are intended to protect the integrity of the public records. One such requirement is that the grantor must acknowledge the instrument before a public official, such as a notary public. Another special requirement is that all real estate taxes must be paid before the instrument is recorded. And under the case law in some states, the deed must be in English. For example, one New York court held that a deed executed partly in Polish was not entitled to be recorded. The purpose of recording is to give notice, and this purpose would be defeated if deeds were executed and recorded in other languages.[4]

The Common Law Approach The following sequence of events illustrates how the common law approach and recording statutes operate.

1. Owen owned Whitecaps Cottage. On June 10, Owen deeded Whitecaps to Abby, who paid Owen $180,000.
2. On June 20, Owen deeded the same property to Bo, who also paid $180,000 for the property. Bo did not know that the property had already been sold to Abby.
3. On June 21, Owen left the country for Costa Rica with his $360,000 and was never seen again.

Who owns Whitecaps now, Abby or Bo?

Before **recording statutes** were enacted, the common law rule was simple and easy to apply: the first deed prevails over later deeds. This principle was often expressed under the maxim "first in time, first in right." Thus, in the previous example, Abby would own

recording statutes
State statutes that govern the manner in which documents are recorded in the public record and the effect such recording has on subsequent purchasers, creditors, mortgagees, and other parties who may have an interest in the property.

Whitecaps and Bo's only recourse would be against the fraudulent seller of the real estate, Owen. As in the example, however, the fraudulent seller of the real estate may be unavailable or insolvent. Recording statutes, described as follows, often reverse the common law priority.

Types of Statutes   Three types of recording statutes (summarized in Table 8.1) have been enacted by various states. The first two types (notice and race-notice statutes) protect the **bona fide purchaser**, a purchaser who does all of the following:

1. Pays valuable consideration for the property (or, in the case of a mortgage, lends money to the owner).
2. Buys in good faith.
3. Has no notice of the earlier sale. As discussed earlier, notice may be actual (personally acquired) or constructive (recorded in the public record).

Under recording statutes, the date on which the critical documents were placed on public record becomes important in determining who has the rights to property. To illustrate the effect of the recording acts, the date of recording will be introduced to the original facts.

1. Assume that Abby recorded her deed of June 10 on July 1.
2. Assume that Bo recorded his deed of June 20 on July 5.

The Notice Statute   The *first* type of statute, which is used in 19 states, is the **notice statute**. Thus, if Bo is a bona fide purchaser, his deed will prevail over Abby's because her deed was not recorded until July 1, eleven days after the June 20 conveyance to Bo. Bo is the legal owner because he had no personal awareness, and there was nothing in the public record on June 20 to indicate that Abby had already purchased the property.

Florida is one state that has adopted a notice statute:[5]

No conveyance, transfer or mortgage of real property, or of any interest therein, nor any lease for a term of one year or longer, shall be good and effectual in law or equity against creditors or subsequent purchasers for a valuable consideration and without notice, unless the same be recorded according to law.

See endnote 5 for a list of states that apply a notice statute.

The Race-Notice Statute   A *second* statute, which is used in 27 states and the District of Columbia, is the **race-notice statute**. Under this statute, Bo, the later purchaser, not only must record the deed in the Register of Deeds office before Abby records there but also must be a bona fide purchaser. Under this statute, Abby would have title to the property because she recorded her deed on July 1, four days before Bo recorded.

---

bona fide purchaser

A good faith purchaser who pays value and is without notice, either actual or constructive, of a prior adverse claim. In most states, the requirement that the good faith purchaser "pays value" means that a buyer who pays only "nominal consideration," a token amount disproportionately small when compared with market value, does not qualify as a bona fide purchaser.

---

notice statute

Under a "notice" recording statute, an unrecorded conveyance is not valid against later bona fide purchasers.

---

race-notice statute

Under a race-notice statute, a later purchaser not only must be bona fide but also must record the deed before other purchasers.

TABLE 8.1   Recording Statute Requirements

	REQUIREMENTS FOR LATER PURCHASER TO PREVAIL	
	BONA FIDE PURCHASER	**RECORDS FIRST**
Notice Statute	Yes	No
Race-Notice Statute	Yes	Yes
Race Statute	No	Yes

New York has adopted a race-notice statute:[6]

A conveyance of real property, within the state ... may be recorded in the office of the clerk of the county where such real property is situated.... Every such conveyance not so recorded is void as against any person who subsequently purchases or acquires by exchange or contracts to purchase or acquire by exchange, the same real property or any portion thereof ... in good faith and for a valuable consideration, from the same vendor or assignor ... whose conveyance, contract or assignment is first duly recorded.

See endnote 6 for a list of states that apply a race-notice statute.

The Race Statute The *third* type of recording statute, used only in Delaware, Louisiana, and North Carolina, is the **race statute**. Under a race statute, later purchasers do not have to be bona fide; the only question is who recorded first. Thus, the second purchaser's knowledge of the prior purchaser's claim is not material. Under the race statute, Abby would win since she recorded her deed before Bo.

> **race statute**
> Under a pure race statute, the first to record wins. The purchaser need not be bona fide or without notice.

> **ETHICAL AND PUBLIC POLICY ISSUES**
>
> ## Is It Ethical to Use Recording Statutes to Take Advantage of Someone Who Does Not Understand the Law?
>
> Problem 10 at the end of this chapter includes a discussion of policy reasons for the race statute and explains how the statute can cause problems for an unwary tenant.

The Louisiana statute reads as follows:[7]

All sales, contracts and judgments affecting immovable [real] property, which shall not be so recorded, shall be utterly null and void, except between the parties thereto. The recording may be made at any time, but shall only affect third persons from the time of the recording.

The language of recording statutes can be complex and difficult to interpret. The application of individual recording statutes often depends on the manner in which state courts have interpreted them.

Electronic Recording Chapter 7 discussed the new E-Sign statute and Uniform Electronic Transactions Act (UETA) model law. E-Sign now preempts state laws, such as the Statute of Frauds, which may inhibit the enforceability of electronic contracts, signatures, and records. UETA allows the states to adopt their own electronic laws as long as they can be harmonized with E-Sign. With the widespread prevalence of computers and electronic transactions, it is only a matter of time before real estate conveyances also will be recorded electronically. As real estate law expert Professor Dale Whitman notes:

During the past 350 years, little has changed in the way real estate conveyances are recorded in America. The system we use was developed in an agrarian society with a small population. Real estate recording has been forced to expand to serve counties with millions of residents and hundreds of thousands of land parcels. It has, unsurprisingly, failed to work effectively.... We can make recording much easier, faster and less costly. We can eliminate the very serious bottlenecks that the recording system continues to impose on real estate transfers in many parts of the nation. All this can be done with the use of digital computing technology that is virtually "on the shelf" today.[8]

Whitman proposes the following system:

1. Acceptance of real estate documents for recording in digital text form rather than as paper copies
2. Online recording of such documents via electronic mail
3. Acceptance of digital signature, rather than ink-and-paper signatures, for execution and recording of real estate conveyances
4. Online public availability of the full text of all recorded documents via the World Wide Web or other suitable gateways[9]

Although problems are inherent in such a monumental shift in recordation procedures—such as confidentiality and authentication; electronic forgeries; the use of cryptography; and, not insignificantly, opposition from county governments and title companies—modernization of this ancient but indispensable process is presently occurring in counties throughout the United States. Minnesota, a leader in the transition to electronic real estate recording, has developed a comprehensive guide and is urging lenders and others in that state's real estate industry to begin the process.[10]

Chain of Title   Title to real estate is derived from a historical record consisting of recorded deeds, not from an absolute or natural right to the property. The record of deeds links the deeds to one piece of property from early times to the present, and this is called the **chain of title**.

The chain of title creates a path through the historical records, allowing the potential buyer or lender to determine the nature of the purported owner's interest. Recorded documents may not be found in a search when they are "outside the chain of title." For example, Barbara is an owner whose deed appears in the chain of title. Barbara purchased the property from Axel. She conveys her property to Harry, who does *not* record. If Harry subsequently conveys the property to Margery, who does record, her deed is "outside" the chain of title. Margery's deed is sometimes referred to as a "wild deed" because it is both recorded and indexed but cannot be found using the grantor-grantee index, discussed below. Because of this, when Barbara then conveys the property to Danny, Danny will be the owner of the property because Margery's deed was outside the chain of title and did not provide Danny with constructive notice of her interests. Thus, when Danny performed a title search, Harry's name did not appear in the grantee index; nor did Barbara's name appear in the grantor index due to Harry's failure to record his deed. The only information Danny was able to glean from the public record was that Barbara still owned the property since her name appeared in the grantee index as the grantee of the property she bought from Axel. This made it appear to Danny that Barbara was the current owner and therefore the proper grantor. The foregoing process is summarized below.

> *An instrument which does not constitute a regular link in the chain of title or which is not identified by a recital in an instrument in such chain, is not considered properly recorded and does not give constructive notice to subsequent purchasers or incumbrancers.*[11]

It is noteworthy that even though Danny did not have constructive notice, if he had received *actual* notice of Margery's interest, Danny would not have qualified as a bona fide purchaser required under notice and race-notice statutes discussed previously in this chapter. Figure 8.1 illustrates the foregoing example.

chain of title

A record of successive conveyances (or other forms of alienation) affecting a particular parcel of land that are arranged consecutively from the government or original source of title down to the present holder.

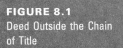

FIGURE 8.1
Deed Outside the Chain of Title

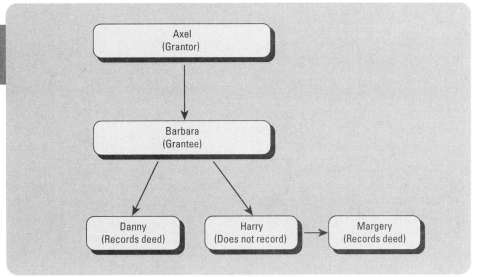

tract index

A land records system in which conveyances of interests in real property are indexed geographically by tracts.

To create a chain, a person must engage in detective work, aided by one of two indexes. The **tract index** in the county office lists each tract of land separately and includes all prior conveyances as well as all mortgages and liens placed on the parcel. The tract index makes it easy to create a chain of title because a person checking title need obtain only a correct legal description of the property and then find where that description is indexed. After locating the tract, one finds that the entire chain of title appears in one place unlike the grantor-grantee index in which it is necessary for the title examiner to hunt down every transaction in multiple volumes. For this reason, the wild deed problem, discussed earlier, is generally avoided in a tract index. Unfortunately, the tract index (sometimes with a grantor-grantee index as well) is only used in various counties in Iowa, Louisiana, Nebraska, North Dakota, Oklahoma, South Dakota, Utah, Wisconsin, and Wyoming. Some commentators contend that the tract index is little used because of added costs and because of opposition from the title insurance industry which takes information from the grantor-grantee index and recreates its own tract indexes in their title plants.[12]

grantor-grantee index

A land records system in which conveyances of interests in real property are indexed in two separate indices, first alphabetically according to the grantor's surname and then alphabetically according to the grantee's surname.

The other much more common index is called the **grantor-grantee index**. This lists the names of all grantors and all grantees (grantor-grantee index and grantee-grantor index) alphabetically in separate volumes. As noted in Chapter 7, most marketable title legislation requires a review of the index for the preceding forty years in order to create a chain of title. For instance, as shown in Table 8.2, assume that Woody wants to purchase property from Kate Acker and needs to determine whether Kate has title. His first question would be, did Kate ever purchase the property. To answer that question, Woody would review the grantee indexes until he found that Kate had purchased the real estate (that is, was a grantee) from John Jones in 1998. Then Woody might wonder whether Kate had already conveyed the property to someone else after she acquired the land in 1998. To answer the question, Woody would review the grantor indexes from 1998 to the present. Next, he would follow the same process to determine the date that John Jones acquired the real estate and whether, after John Jones' acquisition and before conveying the land to Kate, John Jones had sold it to a third party. Woody would then continue the process for John Jones' grantor and for previous owners over the forty-year period.

TABLE 8.2 Grantor and Grantee Indexes

GRANTOR-GRANTEE INDEX

DATE OF RECORDING	GRANTOR	GRANTEE	LOCATION	TYPE OF INSTRUMENT	VOLUME	PAGE
July 1, 1998	Jones, Alice	Freud, Fred	Lodi	Deed	5,200	553
May 25, 1998	Jones, John	Acker, Kate	Medina	Deed	5,199	305
March 4, 1998	Jones, Zeke	Smith, Sara	Westfield	Easement	Ease. 125	87

GRANTEE-GRANTOR INDEX

DATE OF RECORDING	GRANTEE	GRANTOR	LOCATION	TYPE OF INSTRUMENT	VOLUME	PAGE
June 9, 1998	Able, Betty	Thomas, Gary	Wadsworth	Deed	5,199	801
May 25, 1998	Acker, Kate	Jones, John	Medina	Deed	5,199	305
April 15, 1998	Adler, Bob	Riley, Ralph	Brunswick	Deed	5,197	451

Proof of Title

It is common practice to obtain a professional determination of whether the sellers have good title. The following three methods are used to make this determination.

abstract of title

A compilation of the chain of title, usually prepared by a title company or an attorney, providing copies or summaries of all recorded instruments including deeds, mortgages, mortgage discharges, and tax liens.

title opinion

A written statement from an attorney which gives an analysis of the title search regarding the current ownership rights in the property. It states whether there is any kind of lien or cloud in the title to the property.

certificate of title

A statement of opinion by an attorney that describes the state of the title to a parcel of land.

Abstract and Opinion   The first method combines the use of an **abstract of title** and a legal opinion. A complete abstract of title is reprinted at the end of this chapter. Although the abstract lists and summarizes instruments such as deeds and mortgages, it does not indicate whether they are legally valid. If an owner dies, for example, the legal question arises of who has the authority to make a conveyance from the deceased owner's estate. Consequently, the abstract should be reviewed by an attorney who will render a **title opinion**. In some areas, it is common practice for an attorney to render an opinion, sometimes called a **certificate of title**, based on a review of the recorded instruments rather than on an abstract of title. A lawyer has a duty to disclose clearly in her opinion any item existing in the public record that might constitute a claim or "cloud" on the title. If she fails and is found negligent, she is liable for damages.

The grantor-grantee index references certain volumes and pages. A title examiner can find a brief description of the property and the instrument in question (e.g., deed, easement, mortgage, or lease). A proper title examination must closely scrutinize this information to ensure that the instruments in question were properly executed (i.e., proper signatures, witnesses, and acknowledgments) and to determine what interest was conveyed (fee simple or life estate) and whether there are any restrictive covenants (discussed in Chapter 12) in the instruments. Moreover, other important information that is *not* generally found in the grantor-grantee index may appear in other indexes and offices. These instruments are important because they too may affect the quality of the title. (For a title search form, see www.cengagebrain.com [see page xix in the Preface for instructions on how to access the free study tools for this text].) When claims against the title are not paid off or otherwise disposed of, the buyer is responsible for them once the title passes. For example, a judgment lien for nonpayment of a money debt filed against the owner encumbers a landowner's real property located in the county. It is also important for the title examiner to determine whether the seller owes any federal, state, or local taxes and assessments. Nonpayment of federal or state income taxes can create a lien on all of the taxpayer's property. Delinquent local property taxes and assessments for sewer and sanitation, mechanics' liens, and even liens placed by homeowners' associations (HOA) can similarly encumber the property. Table 8.3 lists other kinds of information generally contained in the public record that a title examiner must look for to ensure the quality of the title.

Despite the best efforts of title examiners to determine whether the seller has a marketable title, using an abstract and title opinion to prove marketable title has inherent problems. One major problem is that the opinion or certificate covers only the title as it is established by instruments on record. But in many cases, an instrument that appears to be valid may contain hidden defects. For example, Tom, age seventeen, conveys a parcel of real estate to Dick. Dick records his deed from Tom and shortly thereafter signs a contract to sell the real estate to Harry. If Harry hired a title company to prepare an abstract and an attorney to review the abstract, the record would show that Dick had good title since Tom's age does not appear on the record and therefore is not in the abstract. In fact, Dick has voidable title. As noted in Chapter 7, a minor can avoid a contract and recover the real estate by disaffirming the contract before or within a reasonable time after reaching the age of majority. Similar hidden problems could arise if the recorded deed was signed by an incompetent person (such as a person who is later adjudged to be insane), if the signature on a deed was forged, or if a deed was never legally delivered to the grantee. In recent years, many counties in various states, including California, Massachusetts, Minnesota, Nevada, New Jersey, and Wisconsin, have switched to electronic recordation of deeds, mortgages, and other instruments. The conversion has, perhaps predictably, created new problems when county employees fail to use the new systems properly.

slander of title
Occurs when one publishes information which is untrue and disparaging to another's property interests in land that can result in the impairment of its marketability.

Sometimes intentional and harmful acts are perpetrated against property owners which are meant to create bogus claims against their land, harming their titles. In those cases, the property owner can sue in an action for **slander of title** since these false claims can cause the land to become unmarketable, as the next case from Vermont demonstrates.

TABLE 8.3 Title Examination Information Generally Not Found in the Grantor-Grantee Index

INFORMATION	GENERAL LOCATION IN PUBLIC RECORD*	IMPORTANCE OF INFORMATION TO TITLE EXAMINER
Judgment lien	Real property records	Places a lien on all of debtor's real property in county
Federal and state income taxes	Special index for federal and state tax liens	Places a lien on all of debtor's property
County and city taxes and assessments	Tax assessor's office	Places a lien on debtor's real property in county
Uniform Commercial Code (UCC)	UCC Financing Statement Index in county records	Gives notice of purchase money security interest (PMSI) on fixtures
Lis pendens	Real property records	Gives notice of a civil action pending against title to real property; buyer could be subject to a future successful judgment and lien
Probate court records	Probate court records	Gives information on validity of property owner's will and who inherited decedent's property

*Location of this information may vary by state and county.

A CASE IN POINT

In *Wharton v. Tri-State Drilling and Boring*[13] the defendant Tri-State Drilling admitted that it mistakenly drilled a well on plaintiff Wharton's property. When Wharton confronted Tri-State and refused to pay for the well, Tri-State offered to buy an easement from Wharton so that it could access the well for Bean, who paid for the well. Wharton refused because he felt the easement would encumber his land and impair his ability to sell it. Tri-State then billed Wharton and filed a notice of mechanic's lien against his land when he refused to pay. Wharton later failed to sell his land because he could not secure title insurance. At the trial court Wharton prevailed and was awarded compensatory and punitive damages. The appeals court upheld the judgment stating that in an action for slander of title, Wharton proved that Tri-State falsely and maliciously published a statement that caused him to suffer special damages and also upheld the award of punitive damages, stating that these damages are warranted to "punish conduct that is morally culpable … and to deter a wrongdoer … from repetitions of the same or similar actions."

In all of the preceding examples, the abstract and the attorney's opinion would show good title; however, the purchaser would receive a voidable or void title. And in each case, the purchaser would not have recourse against the title company or the attorney because abstracts and opinions are expressly limited to matters on the public record. Even if the defect appears on the public record, the attorney preparing the opinion might not be liable for failure to point out the defect. Negligence or malpractice can be difficult to prove when the title opinion involves questions of interpretation of deeds, wills, and other documents. Determining who is liable for these mistakes can also be complicated.

A government worker failed to properly index a mortgage, resulting in the mortgagee losing his security interest after the mortgagor, who did not disclose the mortgage, sold the property that appeared in the public record to be unencumbered. Can the worker's employer as well as the lawyer who failed to verify the recording be held liable? A Pennsylvania appeals court in *Antonis v. Liberati* on page 286, addresses these issues.

END OF CHAPTER CASE

title insurance

Insurance designed to indemnify a landowner for losses from defects in the title or liens against the land.

Title Insurance   **Title insurance** answers the question of how a purchaser or lender can be protected from hidden risks such as a forged signature, a minor grantor, or an undelivered instrument. A title insurance company issues title insurance after a review of the recorded instruments. This is similar to the review undertaken in preparing an abstract and opinion. If the company is satisfied that title is good, it issues a policy covering the purchaser and her heirs for as long as they own the property. Only one premium is paid at the time the policy is purchased, and the amount of the premium varies depending on the locale. Rates are often reduced significantly when the purchaser sells the insured property and when the policy is reissued to a new purchaser within a certain period. An owner also may obtain an inflation rider to increase the amount of coverage over time as the value of the real estate increases. Most types of insurance look forward in time to insure against future risks. Unlike such insurance policies, title insurance looks *backward* in time to insure against defects in the historical record, the property's chain of title. Thus, the "effective date" of a title insurance policy marks the end moment for which title insurance provides protection; transfers and encumbrances after that date are not insured.

The two most common types of policies are those issued to the owner and those issued to the mortgagee-lender. Nearly all lenders require a **mortgagee title insurance policy** to insure the validity and priority of their lien. Although purchasers are required by the lender to pay for the lender's title policy, they are not protected by it. The lender's policy provides coverage only for the lender in the amount of the mortgage loan and for risks that affect the security interest of the lender. Furthermore, if the title company is forced to pay the lender, it takes an assignment of the note and mortgage from the lender, thereby acquiring the right to collect the loan from the owner. For example, say that Aaron sold property to Jake with a forged deed. Unfortunately for Jake, the land is actually owned by Zack. Jake finances the $200,000 sale with a mortgage loan from Northern National Bank and puts a down payment of $20,000 on the purchase. But Jake does not own the land, so he could not encumber it with the mortgage. With just a mortgagee title insurance policy, only Northern National Bank would be paid for its loss, and Jake would lose his investment unless he can recover from Aaron. To avoid this problem, Jake should have acquired a separate **owner's title insurance policy** to protect his equity in the real estate. In some states, title companies are required by law to notify the purchaser of the availability of a separate policy. In addition, the new Real Estate Settlement Protection Act of 2010, discussed in Chapter 10, explains in its Good Faith Estimate section that to protect a borrower's interest, it is necessary to purchase the owner's title insurance policy. The purchaser-borrower buying both the mortgagee and owner's title insurance policies typically benefits from a **simultaneous issue discount**; that is, the title insurer makes a better rate available because, in effect, it is searching the property only once.

Most companies use title insurance forms developed by the American Land Title Association (ALTA), a title insurance industry trade association. (For an ALTA owner's policy, see www.cengagebrain.com [see page xix in the Preface for instructions on how to access the free study tools for this text].) The owner's policy insures against losses that occur when one of the following occurs:

1. The title belongs to someone else.
2. The title is subject to a lien, an encumbrance, or another defect.
3. The owner lacks a right of access to and from the land.
4. The title is unmarketable.
5. The title is defective due to errors in executing and recording legal instruments.

Thus, the policy owner is protected from problems discussed previously, such as forgery and minority; and he is covered if marketable title issues arising prior to the policy's effective date become a problem when he tries to sell the property.

Assume that Mark entered into a contract to purchase real estate from Rosy, who was supposed to produce marketable title. Before closing, it was discovered that the title was unmarketable; but because a title insurance company was willing to issue a policy, Mark decided to purchase the property anyway. If Mark tries to sell the property later but a prospective purchaser refuses to complete the transaction because of the unmarketable title, Mark might sustain a loss were it not for his title insurance coverage.

A commitment to issue title insurance precedes the issuance of a title insurance policy. The **title commitment** contains a list of requirements. If Northern Bank is making a mortgage loan to Amy and Jakob for their purchase of a new home, for example, the commitment for the mortgagee policy would list as requirements the deed from the seller and the mortgage from Amy and Jakob to Northern Bank. Since Northern Bank would expect to have a first mortgage on the property, the commitment would also require the recorded satisfaction or discharge of any existing liens. For example, if Albert and

mortgagee title insurance policy
Insurance that protects the lender against loss or damage resulting from defects in the title or the enforcement of liens against the land.

owner's title insurance policy
Insurance that protects the purchaser borrower's equity against loss or damage resulting from defects in the title or from the enforcement of liens against the land.

simultaneous issue discount
Discount in the premium price paid by the purchaser borrower for buying both a mortgagee and an owner's title insurance policy.

title commitment
A letter from a title insurance company in which it commits to issuing a title insurance policy on the insured subject to certain conditions and requirements.

Roberta, the sellers, had given a mortgage in favor of Greenwich Bank, the commitment would require the satisfaction of that mortgage before the title company was obligated to insure the first mortgage of Northern Bank.

A title company must, in good faith, assume *three* duties under a title insurance policy should the insured suffer a loss. The title company must (1) indemnify the insured for any loss he suffers; (2) cure title defects if possible; and (3) if there is litigation involving the status of title, bear the costs and attorney's fees. Curing a title defect can often be simple actions such as supplying a missing acknowledgment from a notary or paying an outstanding recording fee or transfer tax. An **action to quiet title** is, for example, a common type of title litigation. In such an action, the plaintiff seeks a judicial resolution of a claim adverse to its title. For example, say Troy claims he is the rightful heir to his deceased father's land which the estate's administrator had sold to Conner. To determine who actually owns the land, Conner's title insurer could initiate an action to quiet title. If Troy prevailed, the insurer would have to pay him for his interest in his father's property. Should the title company refuse to bear the costs and attorney's fees of litigation concerning title to the insured property, the penalties can be severe, as the following Missouri case reveals, since it is breaching its good faith duty.

action to quiet title

An action compelling someone to establish his claim of an interest in land or forever be estopped from asserting it.

A CASE IN POINT

In *Fohn v. Title Insurance Corp. of St. Louis,*[14] the plaintiffs purchased twenty-five acres of land, which were insured by the defendant title company. As the plaintiffs were constructing a shopping center on the land, they discovered a sign advertising a cave and learned that the one-half acre of property around the sign was claimed by someone else. The title insurance company refused to participate in later litigation, and the plaintiffs eventually lost the half acre. The plaintiffs then sued the title company and recovered attorney's fees and punitive damages in addition to actual damages (the difference in their property value with and without the disputed segment). The attorney's fees and punitive damages were awarded because of the company's wrongful refusal to participate in the original suit to determine title.

exclusions/exceptions

Certain potential defects or liens against a title to land that are excluded from coverage in a title insurance policy.

Title insurance contains several **exclusions** and **exceptions** that the owner should carefully review before purchasing a policy. *Four* general types of exclusions are common. *First*, policies exclude coverage for losses resulting from governmental regulation of the property, such as environmental protection laws and building and zoning ordinances. *Second*, risks relating to the government's right to take the property (that is, the right of eminent domain) are excluded. *Third*, title insurance does not provide coverage for defects, liens, claims, and other matters (1) created or agreed to by the insured, (2) known by the insured but not by the company, (3) resulting in no loss to the insured, or (4) created after the policy was issued. In the *Fohn* case just discussed, for example, the title company claimed it was not liable because the insured parties knew of the sign advertising the cave and did not disclose it to the company when the policy was issued. The court, however, concluded that the insureds' discovery of the sign did not mean that they knew that another party actually owned the surrounding property. *Fourth,* title insurers do not cover losses incurred when a mortgage lien becomes unenforceable based on state usury laws, or consumer credit protection or truth-in-lending laws.

Was Lawyers Title Insurance Company relieved of liability for payment to First Federal on a $6.5 million mortgagee policy under the policy's exclusion for matters known to the claimant and not disclosed in writing to the title company because the lender knew that its borrower had been convicted for bank fraud? In *Lawyers Title Ins. v. First Federal Savings Bank* on page 288, the court resolves that question.

END OF CHAPTER CASE

general (standard) exceptions

Certain potential defects or liens against a title to land that are not contained in the public record and are excluded from coverage in a title insurance policy.

Exceptions to coverage fall into *two* categories: general and specific. **General exceptions** (also known as **standard exceptions**) provide that there is no coverage for certain matters not on the public record (such as the rights of an adverse possessor; an unrecorded easement or mechanic's lien; and matters that would be disclosed by an accurate survey and inspection of the premises, such as an encroachment). (Easements, mechanics' liens, and adverse possession are covered in Chapters 4, 9, and 10, respectively.) Also, it is common to see general exceptions contained in owners' policies while deleted in lenders' policies. Still, the title company typically deletes standard exceptions provided from owners' policies if it receives appropriate documentation. To delete an exception for "parties in possession," for example, the title company will require an owner's affidavit that the owner knows of no other parties claiming possession. A standard exception for matters to be disclosed in a survey can be replaced by specific exceptions relating to actual matters disclosed in a current survey.

gap

The time period between the issuance of a title commitment and the recording of the documents to be insured.

One standard exception addresses the period between the issuance of the title commitment and the recording of the documents to be insured. This period is referred to as the **gap**. Amy and Jakob, for example, may be closing their purchase on February 28, and the effective date of the title policy may be February 26—the date closest to the closing date for which the title company has access to all documents of record. Assume that Amy and Jakob's closing is in the afternoon and that their closing agent will send the deed and mortgage to the courthouse by courier to be recorded the next morning. What will protect Amy and Jakob from a lien recorded during the gap, the period of time from the last search of the title records until the recording of the document (such as the deed) to be insured? This risk is often assumed by the title company, which will "insure the gap" if it has adequate documentation.

specific (special) exceptions

Certain actual or potential defects or liens against a title that are unique to a certain piece of property and are excluded from coverage in a title insurance policy.

Specific exceptions (also known as **special exceptions**) relate to problems unique to the insured property. For example, title coverage might expressly exclude public utility easements or building and use restrictions. Certain exceptions, such as unpaid taxes, will be listed in the company's commitment to insure the property, which is given to the purchaser before closing; but it will not be included in the final policy if taxes are paid before closing. A commitment and policy for a condominium unit will list the Condominium Declaration (an instrument creating a condominium) as a special exception. For example, a Condominium Declaration often contains plats and plans displaying the condominium's common areas, such as parking areas, swimming pools, and tennis courts. If title problems later emerge involving the common areas, they would not be covered under the title policy. It is wise to review the actual documents that are the subject of special exceptions. Despite the exclusions and exceptions, title insurance is the most effective method of protecting title. The number of claims paid by companies has increased in recent years, an increase based in part on the considerable number of claims relating to white-collar crime, such as fraud and forgery.[15]

Torrens system

A system for registration of land under which a court issues a certificate of title that states the status of the title.

Torrens System In a few states, Colorado, Georgia, Hawaii, Massachusetts, Minnesota, New York, North Carolina, Ohio, and Washington, the **Torrens system** (developed in Australia by Robert Torrens based on a system in use in the shipping industry) is available as a voluntary alternative to the recording system. Under the system that Torrens developed for real estate transactions, the register of titles issues a "Torrens" certificate to a purchaser whenever property is transferred, after first cancelling the seller's certificate.[16] Unlike the recording system, in which the recorded instruments are merely evidence of title and are not approved by the title office, the Torrens certificate is the title and a chain of title is not prepared before property is conveyed.

To bring real estate under the Torrens system, the title must first be registered. Registration begins when an owner applies to the appropriate local court and the court investigates the title and related matters, such as whether the land is occupied. Next, the court notifies everyone who claims an interest in the real estate and schedules a trial to determine whether the applicant is really the owner. If the applicant has good title, the court orders the title to be registered; from that point on, title passes with the issuance of a Torrens certificate, free of all encumbrances except those noted on the certificate.[17] Although used in as many as 21 states in the late nineteenth century, the Torrens system was viewed as impracticable primarily for its relatively high costs, technically burdensome, duplicative, and antiquated procedures, and opposition from courthouse bureaucrats. Yet, some reformers today tout its effectiveness for clearing difficult titles and for preventing adverse possession problems.[18]

The Future of Title Insurance Practices

Title insurance, like many other aspects of real estate practice, is changing and modernizing rapidly as a result of advances in technology. Change is necessary not only in an effort to remain competitive but also partially in response to consumer activists and Fannie Mae and Freddie Mac (discussed in more detail in Chapter 9), which are influential in real estate lending. Consumer groups believe that title insurance is too expensive and can be made cheaper by adopting more efficient methods.

One way in which the title insurance industry is modernizing and streamlining its operations is by using "title plants." These consist of libraries of legal instruments, including deeds, mortgages, and judgment, that the industry gleans from county records and then scans into computers.[19] In fact, many observers contend that private title libraries are much more efficient and accurate than the public record itself, which normally requires title examiners to go to a number of places to effectively review a title. An article in the *Wall Street Journal* describes how computers and title plants have facilitated a title search:

> *At Fidelity National's Office in Santa Ana, Calif., which deals with large national lenders, Lonnie Maxwell, a 41-year old retired U.S. Marine, selects a county from a list on his computer screen, types in an address and gets the tax record for the property. He uses his mouse to order a map of the parcel, then clicks on the names of the people on the tax record and puts up a computerized list showing a color-coded chain of ownership for the property. With another click, Mr. Maxwell locates liens and judgments pertaining to the property. He prints out copies of all the information needed to prepare a title report, then sends this information on to a title examiner for analysis. Total time: about 10 minutes.[20]*

ETHICAL AND
PUBLIC POLICY
ISSUES

Are Title Insurance Companies Serving Their Consumers Properly, or Should They Be More Regulated?

For years, title insurance companies have given "referral fees" or "rebates" to real estate and mortgage brokers and attorneys who sent the companies homebuyers to purchase title insurance policies. Some of these rebates were as high as 50 percent of the policy's price. Since most homebuyers know very little about title insurance, few objected. However consumer groups and regulators see this as a collusive relationship that drives up prices in an industry where there is little risk. While the federal government has not intervened, California and New York are attacking this practice and have levied significant fines.[21] In a market in which the consumer knows little about the product, should other states follow the lead of California and New York?

Property and Liability Insurance

While title insurance protects the purchaser's rights to property, property and liability insurance cover risks related to the condition of the property and injuries occurring on it. Because the coverage of these policies is entirely different and the risks related to ownership, hazards, and liability are significant, the prudent real estate purchaser will, in addition to title insurance, acquire property and liability insurance before closing.

The effective date of the coverage should coincide with the assumption of the risk of loss by the purchaser. As noted in Chapter 7, most states declare that the risk of loss falls on the purchaser at the time the contract is signed if the contract is silent due to the doctrine of equitable conversion. However, in practice, contracts usually state that the risk remains with the seller until closing or until the buyer takes possession. In addition, 13 states have adopted the Uniform Vendor and Purchaser Risk Act, which also provides that the seller retains the risk of loss until the closing. For these reasons, the buyer typically does not obtain insurance until the closing date and generally in most cases, purchases a new insurance policy. The seller may, if he wishes, assign his insurance coverage to the buyer. However, the insurance contract is a personal one between the seller and the company. Therefore, the insurance company must approve the assignment; otherwise, it is ineffective, leaving the assignee-buyer without coverage. This is often a trap for the unwary buyer. For instance, in many cases, the seller will give the buyer a written assignment of the policy at the closing. Although the assignment is forwarded to the insurance company at closing, the company's approval normally takes one to two weeks. During the period before approval, the buyer has no coverage and must personally bear any losses resulting from damage to the premises.

The following sections on property and liability coverage assume that the buyer is purchasing a new homeowner's insurance policy. Following the discussion of property and liability coverage, the concept of insurable interest and issues that are unique to mortgage and commercial insurance are examined.

Property Coverage

Most homeowners' insurance policies today cover two types of losses:

1. Losses resulting from damage to property
2. Losses arising when another person is injured on the property

Property damage provisions under a standard homeowner's policy cover the dwelling, appurtenant structures such as a garage or a gazebo, and personal property incidental to the occupancy of the dwelling—even when the loss of the owner's personal property occurs at another location, such as leaving a shopping bag of newly purchased clothes at the mall restaurant that are then taken by a thief. The amount of coverage on the dwelling determines the coverage on the other property. For instance, appurtenant structures might be insured for 10 percent of the coverage on the dwelling and personal property for 50 percent of that amount. A homeowner also is covered for additional living expenses—for example, 20 percent of the value of the dwelling—when the owner cannot occupy the house because of damage. Homeowners' policies also may cover certain losses that do not directly relate to the insured's property. For example, some policies now provide identity and financial fraud coverage from the unauthorized use or theft of the insured's credit cards.

A homeowner usually chooses one of *three* common forms of homeowners' policies depending on the number and type of perils against which she wants to insure the property. Under the **Basic Form** (HO-1), there is coverage for eleven perils: fire or lightning; loss of property removed from endangered premises (for example, property removed from a house that is threatened by a fire next door); windstorm or hail; explosion; riot or civil commotion; aircraft; vehicles; smoke; vandalism and malicious mischief; theft; and breakage of glass that is part of the building.

One popular form of policy—the **Broad Form** (HO-2)—adds seven additional perils: falling objects; weight of ice, snow, and sleet; collapse of building; accidental damage involving steam or hot water heating systems or appliances for heating water; accidental discharges of water or steam from a plumbing, heating, or air-conditioning system or appliance; freezing of plumbing, heating, air-conditioning systems, and appliances; and accidental injuries involving certain electrical equipment. The **Comprehensive Form** (HO-3), the most popular form of policy, is often called the **"all-risk" form** because all perils are covered, with specified exceptions for events such as flood, earthquake, landslide, tidal waves, war, terrorism, and nuclear attack as well as more prosaic problems such as mold, sewer backup, ongoing neglect (i.e. losses from termite infestation for a long period), and trampolines. Although fire is a covered peril, many insurers will also exclude it if the home is in an undeveloped area far from a fire station. Losses for various luxury and collectible items such as antiques, jewelry, furs, watches, collectibles, guns, and coin collections also are not covered although the homeowner can obtain supplemental coverage for these. Companies also offer inflation-guard endorsements that automatically raise policy coverage at periodic intervals as an added measure of protection. The next case from New York provides a judicial interpretation of a policy's exclusion for earth movement.

Basic Form

A property and liability policy that provides coverage for landowners from eleven specified perils.

Broad Form

A property and liability policy that provides coverage for landowners from eighteen specified perils.

Comprehensive ("all-risk") Form

Property and liability policy that provides coverage for landowners from all perils except enumerated exceptions.

A CASE IN POINT

In *Loretto-Utica Properties Corp. v. Douglas Company*, an insurance company argued that its exclusion for damage caused by earth movement meant that it was not liable for damages resulting from "frost heave." The court agreed[22] based on its determination that frost heave is caused when moist soil freezes and causes an upward thrust of the pavement or ground. Since the upward thrust of the ground resulted in the insured's claim for structural damage to its walls, the exclusion relieved the insurance company of liability.

Regardless of the form the homeowner selects, each policy's coverage contains a number of exclusions that should be reviewed carefully. For instance, the coverage for specified personal property losses normally excludes items such as the loss of animals, birds, fish, motorized vehicles, and aircraft.

One of the most recent "perils" to be excluded in many HO-3 policies is mold. Mold is responsible for millions of dollars in claims. However, some policies still cover mold if it is caused by an accidental discharge of water or steam. Following is a typical clause from a current HO-3 "all-risk" policy:

> *We do not insure ... for loss ... [c]aused by ... [m]old, fungus or wet rot. However, we do insure for loss caused by mold, fungus or wet rot that is hidden within the walls or ceilings or beneath the floors or above the ceilings of a structure if such loss results from the accidental discharge or overflow of water or steam within: (a) A plumbing, heating, air conditioning or automatic fire protective sprinkling system, or a household appliance, on the residence "premises;" or (b) A storm drain, or water, steam or sewer pipes, off the "residence premises."*[23]

Besides excluding specified risks, property insurance policies can, as a matter of public policy, cover only those perils that are "fortuitous," or that occur by chance. The reason is that covering predictable events could generate fraud. The following case from Washington state examines how the courts determine "fortuitous loss" in an "all-risk" property insurance policy.

In *Churchill v. Factory Mutual Insurance Company* on page 289, the court rules on the definition of "fortuitous" in a case involving mold damage to property.

END OF CHAPTER CASE

A second excluded "peril" of recent importance to owners of commercial real estate in particular is terrorism. Prior to the terrorist attacks on September 11, 2001, policies covered losses related to terrorism. After the total destruction of the World Trade Towers in New York City, however, insurers began to exclude the risk. In response, lenders refused to lend money if buildings were not insured against terrorist attacks. The impasse was eventually solved in late 2002 when the Terrorist Risk Insurance Act (TRIA) was signed into law. Under the Act, the federal government covers 90 percent of losses related to terrorist attacks that are greater than $5 million up to a cap of $90 billion.[24] In late 2007, TRIA was extended for another seven years.[25]

ETHICAL AND PUBLIC POLICY ISSUES

Should the Government Provide Federally Subsidized Flood Insurance for Those Who Live in High-Risk Areas?

In the wake of Hurricane Katrina in 2005, a vigorous debate arose over whether the federal government should continue its National Flood Insurance Program (NFIP). In one of the worst natural disasters in U.S. history, hundreds of thousands of people saw their homes totally or partially destroyed from flooding. Many of these homeowners and tenants had NFIP insurance that, at the time, cost about $438 a

continues

continued

year, with a cap of $250,000 for the home and $100,000 for contents. Even though this coverage is fairly low considering the cost of real estate, the aggregate cost for the nation's taxpayers is in the billions. Federal flood insurance exists because private insurers are not willing to underwrite the risk. About 26 percent of those who live in special flood hazard areas (SFHAs) will suffer flood damage within a mortgage's typical thirty-year term. Most of New Orleans, for example, is below sea level; therefore, most people live in a SFHA. For years, social scientists have observed that people are very poor at adequately gauging the risk of natural hazards such as floods, earthquakes, and tornadoes. Therefore, people continue to live in and move to these hazardous areas. Indeed, the Gulf Coast is one of the fastest-growing areas in the country even though it continues to be assailed by hurricanes that some climate scientists claim are growing in ferocity and numbers due to global warming.[26] Should the federal government continue its policy of subsidizing people who, many believe, are making bad choices so they can live in flood-prone areas? Americans may have a legal right to live on floodplains and in cities such as New Orleans, but do they have a moral right? Should citizens in states that have few natural hazards pay higher taxes to bail out those who live in these hazardous locations?

The next case from Louisiana discusses why many Gulf Coast citizens, due to the wording of their policies, do not have homeowners' insurance coverage for rebuilding their homes.

Are floods that were the result of levees which allegedly broke due to negligent design and construction after Hurricane Katrina, and which subsequently inundated 80 percent of New Orleans, covered by "all-risk" policies? In *In Re: Katrina Canal Breaches Litigation* on page 291, the court rules on this important decision.

END OF CHAPTER CASE

In light of this case and other factors, some observers claim that the "invisible hand" of economic forces, a concept attributed to eighteenth-century economist Adam Smith, will accomplish what politicians may be unwilling to do—force people to relocate from hazardous areas. With the cost of homeowners' policies skyrocketing in New Orleans and along the Gulf Coast, for example, many people may not be able to afford the insurance to live there although it is quite certain that the federal government will continue to provide subsidized flood insurance to those in coastal areas and floodplains, a topic of significant political controversy.[27] Many victims of Katrina's destruction may also benefit from a 2009 federal court decision in Louisiana which ruled that four individuals and a business be reimbursed for property losses caused by the U.S. Army Corps of Engineers' "gross negligence" in failing to maintain the canals and levees around the New Orleans area. This case will spur many more plaintiffs to initiate suits against the Corps with possibly billions of dollars in damages awarded to flood victims.[28]

The most recent issue relating to property loss is Chinese drywall. In 2005 a spike in new home building primarily in the southeastern states (see endnote 29 for states in which Chinese drywall was installed), arose in part from significant destruction caused by hurricanes.[29] This triggered high demand for drywall. One major source of this important building material was China, which uses fly ash, a residue of its coal burning power plants, to manufacture it. Unfortunately, fly ash in Chinese drywall contains dangerous compounds that emit a sulphur-based gas, creating a horrific "rotten egg" smell, which corrodes copper building components, such as air conditioners. Some builders have voluntarily replaced the drywall at significant costs. Moreover, the Consumer Product Safety Commission has issued guidelines to remediate the problem. Insurers have been fighting claims that homeowners' policies should cover the loss. In one of the first cases in a trial court in New Orleans, a state district judge rejected insurers' claims that the "Pollution or Contamination" (POL), "Gradual or Sudden Loss" and "Faulty, Inadequate or Defective Planning" (FIDP) exclusions exonerate them from coverage of losses caused by the drywall.[30]

Limitations: Policy Limitations and Coinsurance Clauses

The maximum amount of coverage is set forth in the policy declarations; as previously noted, the coverage for appurtenant structures, unscheduled personal property, and additional living expense is a specified percentage of the coverage for the dwelling. An owner cannot recover more than the maximum specified in the declaration; and in many cases, the owner will recover less than the maximum coverage—even when damage is greater than that amount. Why would the owner recover less than the amount of damage and the policy amount? Standard policies state, for example, that coverage is limited to the interest of the insured. Thus, if Charley and Joan purchase a $500,000 building as tenants in common with equal interests and Charley takes out a $500,000 policy in his name alone, he can recover only $250,000—the value of his interest—in the event the building is completely destroyed.

coinsurance clause

A clause in a property insurance policy in which the insurer provides indemnity for only a certain percentage of the insured's loss, reflecting the relative division of risk between insurer and insured.

Another common limitation is a form of **coinsurance clause** included in insurance policies. Although these clauses are not uniform,[31] a typical clause in a homeowner's policy provides that if the building is insured for 80 percent or more of the full replacement cost, the coverage will include the full cost of repair or replacement up to the policy limits. However, if the amount of insurance is less than 80 percent of the full replacement cost, the coverage will not exceed the larger of (1) the actual cash value of the part of the building damaged or destroyed or (2) the proportion of the replacement cost of the damaged structure that the full amount of insurance applicable to the building bears to 80 percent of the full replacement cost of the building. The following hypothetical case illustrates how coinsurance can affect how much the insured can recover.

A CASE IN POINT

Clyde purchased an old Victorian home for $120,000, which, because of its intricate and detailed construction, would cost $160,000 to replace. He wanted to save insurance premiums; and reasoning that buildings are seldom completely destroyed, he purchased only $80,000 coverage. Later a fire destroyed the roof, which had an actual value of $1,000 but would cost $4,000 to replace. Since Clyde's coverage was less than 80 percent of the full replacement cost, Clyde is not entitled to the full cost of repair or replacement up to policy limits. Instead, recovery is limited to the larger of (1) the actual cash value of the part of the building damaged or destroyed (in this case, $1,000) or (2) the proportion of the replacement cost of the damage ($4,000) that the total amount of insurance ($80,000) bears to 80 percent of the full replacement cost of the building. (Because 80 percent of $160,000 is $128,000, this proportion is $80,000/128,000 = 5/8 and 5/8 of $4,000 is $2,500.) Consequently, the company will pay only $2,500 of Clyde's $4,000 loss even though Clyde had $80,000 worth of coverage. Clyde must bear the remaining loss; that is, he becomes the coinsurer and pays $1,500.

Owners should insure for at least the percentage specified in the policy (in Clyde's case, 80 percent) to receive protection up to policy limits. Many homeowners are under-insured because home replacement costs rise even faster than the rate of inflation and insurance coverage quickly falls below the required percentage. The amount of required insurance that a homeowner needs should be assessed periodically. One study indicated that as many as 58 percent of homeowners' policies are undervalued.[32]

Inadequate coverage for losses to personal property in the house also can occur. For example, if personal computers are destroyed, homeowners' policies typically cover only what the computer is worth. Since computers depreciate quickly, the insurance typically covers only a small fraction of the purchase price.

ETHICAL AND PUBLIC POLICY ISSUES

Should the Cost of Property Insurance Be Based on a Person's Credit Rating?

The cost of insurance varies according to the risks posed to the property. For example, if a homeowner installs smoke detectors, automatic sprinklers, and a burglar alarm system, the risk of fires and burglaries is lowered. In such cases, the insurer typically discounts the premium. But should insurance companies be able to use a homeowner's credit rating for setting premium rates and renewal of policies? According to insurance sources, a person's lifestyle, including the way he manages money, can predict how that person manages other risks. This also can include how well he takes care of property. For example, a person who is chronically in debt might not be able to afford basic home repairs. If, for example, a violent storm hits the house, the lack of repairs may exacerbate the problem. Moreover, industry sources claim that there is a statistical relationship between those who are bad credit risks and the likelihood of filing a homeowner's claim and inflating the claim to make up for the deductible. Still, a growing number of state insurance commissioners do not agree with the insurance industry and have outlawed the practice. According to the Texas Insurance Commissioner: "I have a hard time believing that a hailstorm knows which house has a good credit score and which doesn't."[33] Moreover, many people, particularly the elderly and new immigrants, do not use credit cards. A person who uses credit cards and pays his bills faithfully can enhance his credit rating. Credit reports, frequently in error, also can hurt a person's rating. In light of these arguments, do you believe that using a person's credit rating to set premiums is ethical? Are similarly situated people, such as those who take good care of their property, likely to be charged different premium rates simply because of their credit rating? Insurers owe a legal, if not a moral, duty of trust to their insureds. Is this duty being breached by suspect correlations? On the other hand, if credit ratings have some predictive value, won't the use of credit ratings result in the majority of creditworthy homeowners paying lower premiums?

Liability Coverage

The liability provisions in most homeowners' policies provide coverage for damages that the insured is legally obligated to pay as the result of an accident caused by the insured's negligent (but not intentional) acts or accidents that simply occurred on the insured's property. Liability coverage also includes the costs of defending lawsuits. Policies cover accidents both on and away from the insured premises. For instance, a homeowner will usually be covered for damages if a guest slips on a tool that the owner left on the side-walk or for damages caused when the insured hit a golf ball that injured another golfer or when a visitor tripped and fell when walking down the owner's stairs.

workers' compensation
Compensation provided to employees who suffer injury or sickness arising out of and in the course of employment.

Liability coverage does not apply to damages claimed by an employee such as a full time chauffeur. For such losses, specific liability coverage is available under **workers' compensation**. In one recent case of first impression from Tennessee, *Wait v. Travelers Indemnity Co. of Illinois,*[34] the state supreme court ruled that an employee who worked in a home office could not receive workers' compensation coverage for an injury suffered as a result of an assault in her home. The court argued that, even though the injury was in the "course of employment," it did not "arise out of her employment" and so was "purely coincidental, or contemporaneous, or collateral, with the employment." It is noteworthy that in some states Waits might have prevailed because their laws only require that the injury be in the course of employment to invoke workers' compensation coverage.

Liability policies also exclude from coverage injuries intentionally inflicted on others by the insured. The definition of an intentional or willful act has been the subject of judicial interpretation, as the following case from California involving a now deceased movie star demonstrates.

A CASE IN POINT

In *Aetna v. Sheft*,[35] Aetna Insurance Company issued a homeowner's policy to the late actor Rock Hudson providing coverage "if a claim is made or a suit is brought against any insured for damages because of bodily injury or property damage to which this coverage applies...." The policy excluded property damage or injury "which is expected or intended by the insured." The court found that Rock Hudson had engaged in high-risk behavior with his companion in knowing that he had AIDS and concealing his condition. The court held that this conduct was inherently harmful and fell within the exclusion for intentional acts. The insurance company was not liable to Hudson's estate or to the companion.

As a result of the Rock Hudson case (and other cases involving lesser-known insureds), the insurance industry's standard homeowner's liability policy now includes a communicable disease exclusion. This means that insureds who have transmitted HIV, AIDS, herpes, and other sexually transmitted diseases are no longer covered by their homeowners' insurance.[36]

Insurers are now more reluctant to cover homeowners with dogs. Dog bites cost insurers hundreds of millions of dollars a year. To contain these costs, insurers either exclude dogs completely or prohibit certain dangerous breeds such as rottweilers, pit bulls, and malamutes from coverage in their policies.[37] The following Wisconsin case addresses a dog bite issue.

A CASE IN POINT

In *Pawlowski v. American Family Mutual Insurance Co.*[38] Waterman, recently unemployed, and his two dogs moved into his friend Seefeldt's apartment. Seefeldt also had three dogs and a high fence in her backyard. One day Waterman came home and opened the door, unintentionally allowing the dogs to run out the front door. One of the dogs ran across the street and bit Colleen Pawlowski three times. Pawlowski sued Seefeldt and her insurer under Wisconsin's statute creating strict liability for owners of dogs that injure persons, other animals, and property. Defendants argued that Seefeldt was not liable because she did not "own, harbor or keep the dogs." Seefeldt's argument was that she "relinquished that status" when Waterman, the true owner, let his dogs out. The trial court ruled in the defendants' favor, but the appeals court reversed it, ruling that "one who shelters or maintains a dog on his or her premises, i.e. has custody of dog at his or her home, is a 'keeper' under the strict liability dog-bite statute." However, the court did caution that the "casual presence of a dog will not suffice to transform a person into a keeper" under the statute.

There are several other noteworthy issues revealed in the *Pawlowski* case. *First*, in at least three states, Wisconsin, Louisiana, and Rhode Island, insurers can be sued directly under the state's "direct action statute." These statutes reverse the traditional common law, used in the rest of the country, which provides that the injured party cannot sue the defendant's insurance company because he does not have privity of contract. *Second*, Wisconsin employs a strict liability statute, but state laws do vary. Other states apply a "one bite" rule in which the owner is not liable until her dog first bites a person, revealing the dog's dangerous propensities. Other states have adopted a general negligence standard. (See endnote 38 for reference to dog bite laws by state.)

Injuries resulting from business pursuits also are typically excluded from coverage. For example, a policy might provide coverage for accidental injury to a visitor shopping at an owner's garage sale. The owner who regularly held such sales might lose her coverage, however, because the activity would be considered a business pursuit as this Maryland case points out.

A CASE IN POINT

In *McCloskey v. Republic Insurance Co.,* a child was fatally injured under the care of the insured in her home day care business. The homeowner's liability insurance policy did not cover this tragic occurrence, as the injury occurred in the course of a "business pursuit."[39]

Insurable Interest

insurable interest

A sufficient interest in the property to be insured so that the loss of the property would result in monetary damage to the insured.

The insured must have an **insurable interest** to collect on a policy; that is, the insured must have an interest in the property such that he will suffer a loss if the property is damaged or destroyed. In the absence of an insurable interest, the insurance contract would be nothing more than a wager; and wagering contracts are illegal in most states. And with property insurance, unlike life insurance, the insurable interest must exist not only when the policy was taken out but also at the time of the loss. Mortgagees, as mentioned, have an insurable interest in the mortgagor's property since the mortgagee would suffer a loss in the event of a title defect or physical property loss.

Does the mother and guardian of minor children have an insurable interest in their residence when the children, not the mother, hold title to the property? In *Motorists Mutual Insurance Co. v. Richmond* on page 295, the court resolves that question.

END OF CHAPTER CASE

Mortgage Insurance

Similar to the mortgagee title insurance policy, in which the buyer must purchase insurance to protect the lender's interest in having a marketable title on the home that collateralizing the loan, the buyer must typically purchase a homeowner's policy to protect the lender's interests in physically preserving the collateral. The mortgagee requires this so that, should the property be destroyed by a fire for example, the proceeds of the insurance policy will be applied for the benefit of the mortgagee who had initially loaned the money on the condition that the house would continue to serve as adequate collateral for the loan.

As Chapter 9 explains in greater detail, the mortgagee has a legal interest in the mortgaged real estate and consequently has an insurable interest up to the amount of the debt. Since the mortgagor, as owner, also has an insurable interest, the mortgagee and the mortgagor may be able to obtain separate policies covering the same property. If the property is damaged or destroyed, each party could collect on his or her policy and would have no rights to the proceeds of the other policy. Since the insurance company that pays on a mortgagee's policy may step into the mortgagee's shoes and assert the mortgagee's right to collect the balance of the debt from the mortgagor (a process called **subrogation**), it is especially important for the mortgagor to purchase separate coverage.

The situation changes if, as is nearly always the case, the mortgage requires the mortgagor to acquire insurance for the benefit of the mortgagee or to add the mortgagee as a named insured in the policy. Furthermore, if the mortgagor refuses to purchase the required coverage, the mortgagee may obtain its own coverage and charge the premiums to the mortgagor. However, this problem does not often arise because most mortgagees stipulate that the mortgagor must periodically place money in an escrow or impound account, discussed in Chapter 9, from which the insurance and taxes are paid.

If the mortgagee must collect on such a policy, the mortgagor's debt is discharged up to the amount of the proceeds. This means that if Amanda's $200,000 home is completely destroyed by a forest fire but has an outstanding mortgage debt of $100,000, the insurance proceeds will be paid out first to discharge the debt, leaving her with $100,000 to rebuild, assuming she insured it for 80 percent or more of its full replacement costs. Thus, if she chooses to rebuild, she will likely need to finance the construction of a house of similar value with a new mortgage to cover the difference.

Under the **mortgagee loss clause** now in common use (known as the **standard clause**), the mortgagee's insurance will not be invalidated by an act that would cancel the coverage of the mortgagor-owner. For example, if the mortgagor intentionally destroyed the property by arson, the company would still be liable to the mortgagee. In such cases, the insurance company would pay the claim but would then step into the shoes of the mortgagee to collect the debt from the mortgagor.

Although insurance coverage under the mortgagee loss clause is not canceled by the acts of the mortgagor, in certain cases, the mortgagee will be unable to collect because of its own carelessness. For example, the mortgagee must notify the insurance company of any change in ownership or increase of hazard of which the mortgagee is aware. And if the mortgagor fails to pay the insurance premium, the mortgagee must pay the premium after the insurance company demands payment. The mortgagee is also bound by basic coverage provisions such as the policy limits stated in the declaration and coinsurance provisions.

Other forms of **mortgage insurance** should not be confused with the foregoing. One type, discussed in Chapter 9, is issued by the Fair Housing Administration (FHA) to insure loans to relatively risky homebuyers. Moreover, private lenders typically require mortgagors to buy private mortgage insurance, or PMI. PMI pays for losses should the mortgagor default on her payments and lose the property in a foreclosure. The term mortgage insurance is also often applied to a type of life policy that pays off the balance of a mortgage upon the death or disability of the insured.

Commercial Insurance

Commercial real estate insurance raises unique concerns beyond the scope of this text. Businesses, like homeowners, must have both property and liability insurance. For

---

subrogation

Right of an insurer, upon payment of a claim, to "step into the shoes" of its insured and assert any claim that the insured may have against others.

mortgagee loss (standard) clause

A clause in a mortgage insurance policy that indemnifies the mortgagee for a loss even if the act that damages or destroys property would not otherwise provide coverage for the mortgagor.

mortgage insurance

Insurance protecting the mortgagee from losses when encumbered property is damaged or destroyed.

liability coverage, businesses typically purchase comprehensive general liability (CGL) policies. These policies are often very broad and can cover almost any risk to which the insurer agrees. Retailers, for example, should have coverage for mishaps that may occur on their premises, such as slips and falls.

Beyond liability coverage, businesses should insure their premises from losses. Moreover, they should include specific endorsements to insure against losses resulting from damage to elevators, non-owned property within the control of the business, and employees' property. The coinsurance clause in commercial insurance policies sometimes includes a formula based on replacement cost, as in the homeowner's policy example previously explained. Or the calculations might be based on actual cash value. Under the actual cash value approach, assuming an 80 percent coinsurance requirement, an owner of an office building with an actual cash value of $300,000 who insures the property for $120,000 recovers 50 percent of the actual cash value of property losses: $120,000 divided by $240,000 (0.8 × $300,000). Finally, business owners frequently insure against income losses that result from property damage. Likewise, commercial tenants can buy business interruption and rent insurance, particularly if the commercial landlord requires it in the lease.

CASES

Recording Systems
ANTONIS v. LIBERATI
821 A. 2d 666 (Pa. Commonw Ct. 2003)

PRESIDENT JUDGE COLINS. Joseph Liberati and Janice Jeschke Beall appeal from an order of the Court of Common Pleas of Beaver County that denied their post-trial motions and entered judgment against them and in favor of Michael Antonis. We affirm the order of the trial court as it applies to Liberati and we remand this matter to the trial court with instructions to enter judgment notwithstanding the verdict in favor of Beall.

Michael Antonis accepted a note and mortgage from Boghas Paul Mouradian to secure the sum of $44,450.00 that Antonis had loaned to Mouradian. The property subject to the mortgage was a 16-acre tract of unimproved land in Beaver County. The mortgage and note were prepared by attorney Joseph J. Liberati, who delivered the documents to the office of the Recorder of Deeds for Beaver County on December 19, 1997. Antonis called Liberati on several occasions to ask if the documents had been recorded. Liberati repeatedly assured Antonis that everything was in order. However, in the process of recording the documents, a clerk in the Recorder's office misspelled Mouradian's name and the mortgage was indexed incorrectly. As a result, Mouradian was later able to sell the property without disclosing the existence of the mortgage and without paying anything to Antonis. Antonis read about the sale in a newspaper and called Liberati, who a few days later told Antonis about the clerical error. Liberati recommended that Antonis file suit against the Recorder of Deeds. Antonis first sued the

purchasers of the property, who successfully defended on the grounds that they had no notice of the mortgage. Antonis then sued Liberati, who joined the Recorder of Deeds, Janice Jesche Beall, and Mouradian's Estate. The jury found in favor of Antonis and against Beall, Liberati, and the Estate. The trial court denied post-trial motions filed by Beall and Liberati, and these appeals followed.

The questions we are asked to consider are 1) whether Beall, a municipal employee, can be found liable for damages under the facts of this case pursuant to 16 P.S. § 9892; 2) whether Beall is immune from liability pursuant to the law known as the Political Subdivision Tort Claims Act ***; 3) whether Liberati had a duty to ensure that the mortgage was indexed correctly; and 4) whether Mouradian's fraud was an intervening act that relieves Liberati from liability.

Beall asks us to grant j.n.o.v. or, in the alternative, a new trial.

* * *

We grant j.n.o.v. for Beall because the trial court committed two clear errors of law in refusing to grant her post-trial motions. The first was that it found that Beall was statutorily liable for a typographical error made by a member of her staff, and the second that Beall was not immune to liability pursuant to the Tort Claims Act because it found there was no injury to persons or property in this case as defined by the Act.

The trial court found Beall liable for the clerical error of a member of her staff pursuant to 16 P.S. § 9852 which requires as soon as said indexes are prepared it shall be the duty of the recorder to index in its appropriate place and manner every deed and mortgage thereafter recorded in his office, at the time the same is recorded, and in case he neglects to do so he and his sureties shall be liable in damages to any person aggrieved by such neglect.

This statute was enacted into law in 1875, but the facts of the case before us were addressed almost 100 later by our Supreme Court in *Orris v. Roberts,* 392 Pa. 572, 141 A.2d 393 (1958). In *Orris,* the Court held that a recorder of deeds was not liable for a clerical error made by a member of the Recorder's staff in improperly indexing a judgment note. What the Court said in *Orris* speaks to such an important point of public policy that we will quote it here at length.

The fundamental reason why a public official is not liable for the negligent act of a subordinate is contained in what Chief Justice Gibson recognized over a hundred years ago in *Schroyer v. Lynch.* [8 Watts 453 (Pa.1839)]. No government could be constructed on the principle of the master and servant relation, which would make a public officer personally liable for the negligent acts of a subordinate. If the rule were otherwise, the burden which such a liability would impose on public officers (most of whom serve on fixed modest salaries) would be onerous to the point of being unbearable. If Roberts were to be held liable for the negligence of the indexing clerk in his office under the facts of this case, all public officers would be liable for the negligent acts committed, within the scope of their employment, by all employees under the control of such officers. It is unnecessary to multiply the many illustrations, that readily come to mind, of the dire consequences to which such a rule would lead. It is sufficient to observe that a recovery against a public officer for such a liability might readily consume several years' salary or even the savings of a life-time. Public service would indeed become a perilous venture which could be undertaken safely only by those who are so impecunious as to be permanently execution-proof.

* * *

In her motion for post-trial relief Beall also claimed immunity from liability pursuant to the Section 8541 of the Tort Claims Act which provides, "Except as otherwise provided in this subchapter, no local agency shall be liable for any damages on account of any injury to a person or property caused by any act of the local agency or an employee thereof or any other person." Section 8542(a) of the Act lists eight exceptions to this immunity, none of which apply to the facts of this case. The trial court did not rely on any one of those exceptions, however, but found that "This case does not involve injury to person or property. Instead, the injury involved was the loss of a contract right to receive money. Therefore, the immunity statute does not apply." In so finding, the trial court ignores the fact that a person can suffer economic injury in the loss of money just as he or she can suffer a physical injury in the form of a broken leg. A note evidencing a debt is property as surely as is real estate or any other tangible thing. The trial court committed clear error in finding that Beall was not immune from suit pursuant to the Tort Claims Act. Accordingly, we will instruct the trial court to enter j.n.o.v. in favor of Beall and against Antonis.

The trial court, relying on *Prouty v. Marshall,* 225 Pa. 570, 74 A. 550 (1909), instructed the jury that it was Liberati's obligation, as Antonis' attorney, to verify that the note and mortgage were recorded properly after he delivered them to the Recorder's Office. Here is what our Supreme Court said in *Prouty:*

It is an easy matter for a mortgagee, or a grantee in each particular instance, either in person, *or by a representative,* to look at the record, and see that the instrument has been properly entered…. There is every reason why it should be made the duty of the mortgagee to see that his instrument is properly recorded. This will not in any way interfere with the principle that, when the instrument is certified as recorded, it shall import notice of the contents from the time of filing; but that must be understood as in connection with an instrument properly recorded. As said above, the record is notice of just what it contains, no more and no less. The obligation of seeing that the record of an instrument is correct must properly rest upon its holder. If he fails to protect himself, the consequence cannot justly be shifted upon an innocent purchaser.

Liberati argues that *Prouty* does not establish a standard of care for attorneys and that it was necessary to present expert testimony to establish that standard. Expert evidence, however, is not required when the issue of negligence is clear enough to be concluded as a matter of law. *Storm v. Golden,* 371 Pa.Super. 368, 538 A.2d 61 (1998). The trial court properly relied on *Storm* in finding that *Prouty's* admonition that "It is an easy matter for a mortgagee … either in person, *or by a representative,* to look at the record, and see that the instrument has been properly entered." imposed an obligation on Liberati, by law, to ensure that the documents were properly recorded and that expert testimony was, therefore, not required.

[8] Liberati's assertion that Mouradian's fraud is a superseding cause of Antonis harm defies simple logic. The fact is that Mouradian would not have been able to defraud Antonis absent Liberati's breach of his duty to Antonis. Liberati's breach was an antecedent cause of Antonis' harm.

Accordingly, the order of the trial court is affirmed to the extent that it denied Liberati's post-trial motions.

Order

AND NOW, this 21st day of April 2003, the order of the Court of Common Pleas of Beaver County is reversed as it may apply to Janice Jeschke Beall and we remand this matter to the trial court with instructions to enter j.n.o.v. in her favor and against Michael Antonis; and It is further Ordered that the order of the Court of Common Pleas of Beaver County is affirmed as it may apply to Joseph J. Liberati.

COHN, District Judge. * * * The Court finds that the following facts are not in dispute:

1. In November, 1988, Henry L. Ewald (Ewald) contacted Joseph Michael (Michael), Senior Vice-President in charge of commercial lending at First Federal, about financing the purchase of a 426 unit apartment complex known as Westland Towers Apartments (Westland Towers). Ewald said that he could purchase the property for approximately $10,000,000 and that he would be willing to put up $3,500,000 of his personal savings if First Federal would provide the remaining $6,500,000. In support of his proposal, Ewald furnished First Federal with a personal financial statement, an independent appraisal of Westland Towers, and income and balance sheets. However Ewald did not provide First Federal with a preliminary agreement of purchase or make a formal written mortgage loan application.

2. First Federal lending policies require that all loans in excess of $1,000,000 be submitted to the Senior Loan Committee (the Committee) and approved by its board of directors. Michael, Mark Beatens (Beatens), First Vice-President in charge of commercial lending, and Joseph DiCicco (DiCicco), the loan officer in charge of the Ewald loan, were the bank officers directly responsible for processing the loan, preparing the loan package, and presenting it to the Committee for approval.

3. The loan package was presented to the Committee on January 6, 1989. Michael, Beatens, and DiCicco represented to the Committee that the proceeds of the proposed loan would be used to purchase Westland Towers, that the price would be determined by a neutral appraisal, and that the $3,500,000 down payment would come from Ewald's personal savings, which would be verified prior to closing. The Committee approved the loan on the basis of these representations.

4. Sometime after the meeting, however, Ewald informed Michael, Beatens, and DiCicco that he had already purchased Westland Towers outright from his own savings, but that he still wanted the $6,500,000 mortgage loan. Ewald said that $2,500,000 of the loan proceeds would be used to repay an unidentified third party who had financed the purchase and the remaining $4,000,000 would go to James Petcoff, a substantial customer of First Federal who wanted to form a medical malpractice insurance company. Following the meeting with the Committee, Michael, Beatens, and DiCicco prepared an addendum to the loan package report reflecting this new information.

5. In preparation for the closing, First Federal directed Ewald to obtain a policy of mortgage title insurance.

On January 17, 1989, Ewald and his attorney, Walter Sakowski (Sakowski), contacted Lawyers Title and requested $6,500,000 worth of title insurance on behalf of First Federal, representing that the titleholder to Westland Towers was Ewald's company, 426 co., inc., and that the purpose of the proposed mortgage was to "refinance" the property. First Federal never directly participated in the application for title insurance and made no representations of any kind to Lawyers Title.

6. On January 18, 1989, Ewald recorded a deed from H-G Westland Associates Limited Partnership (H-G) to 426 co., inc., with the Oakland County Register of Deeds. On that same day, Ewald also recorded discharges of two mortgages on Westland Towers held by the Riggs National Bank and Far West Savings and Loan Association (Riggs). Both the deed and mortgage discharges were forgeries.

7. The mortgage loan was closed on January 20, 1989. As part of the closing, 426 co., inc. executed a commercial form of mortgage granting First Federal a first lien on Westland Towers in the amount of $6,500,000. On the date of the closing, First Federal did not have a commitment for the issuance of mortgage title insurance from Lawyers Title because of certain problems with the discharge of the Riggs mortgages. No funds were distributed at that time.

8. On January 23, 1989, Ewald or Sakowski revised the discharges of the Riggs mortgages. Lawyers Title subsequently delivered to First Federal a commitment for mortgagee title insurance in which Lawyers Title agreed to issue a policy insuring First Federal's $6,500,000 mortgage as a first lien on Westland Towers, subject to certain stipulated conditions and encumbrances. The commitment stated that 426 co., inc. was the title holder of Westland Towers free and clear of any liens or encumbrances, except those customary to outright ownership.

9. Immediately following the closing, First Federal asked Lawyers Title to pick up and record the January 20, 1989 mortgage. Lawyers Title did not record the mortgage with the Register of Deeds until January 27, 1989.

10. On January 24, 25, and 26, following receipt of the commitment showing 426 co., inc. as the title holder, checks totalling $6,500,000 were issued by First Federal directly to Henry Ewald.

11. * * * Lawyers Title issued a mortgage title insurance policy in the amount of $6,500,000 on March 9, 1989. At no time did any employee of First Federal ever see the forged deeds or mortgage discharges.

12. On October 2, 1989, First Federal was notified by representatives of H-G that the deeds from H-G to 426 co.,

inc. and the discharges of the Riggs mortgages were forgeries and that its mortgage was invalid. H-G subsequently filed an action in the Wayne County Circuit Court seeking to cancel First Federal's mortgage and quiet title. First Federal then filed a civil action against Ewald for fraud and breach of contract and asserted a constructive trust against Petkoff's medical malpractice insurance company. A portion of the loan proceeds were part of the general funds of the Petkoff's insurance company or on deposit with the State of Michigan. Ewald was indicted in the Eastern District of Michigan for acts associated with his criminal actions. On May 1, 1990, he pled guilty to one count of bank fraud, 18 U.S.C. §1344. He is currently awaiting sentencing.

13. On October 4, 1989, First Federal filed a written claim with Lawyers Title for payment under the policy. Following an investigation, Lawyers Title disclaimed liability on the grounds that First Federal had "personal knowledge or intimation" of defects in 426 co., inc.'s title to Westland Towers. Specifically, Lawyers Title says that at the time the loan was made, First Federal was aware of the following facts which, taken together, should have been sufficient to put a reasonable person on notice of defects in its mortgagor's title to Westland Towers:

(a) In 1978, Ewald was convicted of bank fraud in two separate cases and subsequently served over a year in federal prison.

(b) Ewald did not intend to use the bulk of the proceeds of the loan to finance the purchase of Westland Towers, but rather intended to finance Petkoff's malpractice insurance venture. Petkoff was an established customer of First Federal at that time, but could not obtain additional funds from First Federal because he was already deeply in debt and overextended.

(c) Ewald's personal financial statement reflected that 80% of his personal assets consisted of a $7,500,000 undescribed note, not yet due.

[In this case, First Federal claims that payment is due on the policy and has filed a motion for summary judgment.]

* * *

The terms of the mortgage title insurance policy * * * [are as follows]:

The following matters are expressly excluded from the coverage of this policy and the Company will not pay loss or damage, costs, or attorneys' fees or expenses which arise by reason of:

(3) Defects, liens, encumbrances, adverse claims or other matters:

(b) not known by the Company, not recorded in the public records at Date of Policy, but *known to the insured claimant* and not disclosed in writing to the Company by the insured claimant prior to the date that the insured claimant became an insured under this policy;

[emphasis added]. The policy goes on to define the terms "knowledge" or "known" as "actual knowledge, not constructive knowledge or notice which may be imputed to an insured by reason of the public records as defined in this policy or any other records which impart constructive notice of matters affecting the land."

* * *

[T]he Court is reluctant to impose a duty of inquiry given the "actual knowledge" standard adopted by the language of the policy. Such a duty would seriously compromise the very purpose of mortgage title insurance. As First Federal notes, an insured would have no way of knowing how much information would be sufficient to put it on notice of an obligation to make further investigation. The guesswork that such an inquiry requires would undermine the very security that title insurance is supposed to afford. It would also provide a title insurer a ready escape clause when a title transfer goes sour. In this area, more than perhaps any other, bright line rules are required to protect both the title insurance industry and those who depend on it.

* * *

Accordingly, First Federal's motion for summary judgment is granted.

"All-Risk" Insurance Policy: "Fortuity" Requirement
CHURCHILL v. FACTORY MUTUAL INSURANCE COMPANY
234 F. 2d 1182 (W.D. Wash. 2002)

Order

ZILLY, District Judge. This matter comes before the Court on Plaintiff the Estate of James Campbell's motion for partial summary judgment. The Court GRANTS IN PART and DENIES IN PART Plaintiff's motion for partial summary judgment.

Background

This case arises out of an insurance claim made by Plaintiffs Clinton R. Churchill, David A. Heenan, Richard W. Gushman II, and Ronald J. Zlatoper, Trustees for the Estate of James Campbell against Defendant Factory Mutual Insurance Co. ("FM"), for mold and water intrusion damage at the Alderwood Plaza Shopping Center in Lynnwood, WA ("Alderwood"). Alderwood is insured for property damage by an insurance policy issued by Defendant to the Estate of James Campbell ("the Estate").

FM's insurance policy provided coverage to the Estate between September 1, 1995, to September 1, 2000. The policy states that it insures against: "ALL RISKS OF PHYSICAL LOSS OR DAMAGE, except as hereinafter excluded, to the property described hereinafter." The policy is FM's standard "Form 3000." The policy does not contain any exclusion containing the words or phrases "mold," "seepage," "water damage," "leakage," or "wet or dry rot."

FM's prior all-risk policy, the Form 2000, which was the predecessor of the Form 3000 policy sold to the Estate, contained an express exclusion for "mold, wet and dry rot." FM has reinserted a mold exclusion into its current standard all-risk policy, the Global Advantage 2002. The Estate purchased the Alderwood Plaza Shopping Center in December 1987. In August 2000, a tenant commented that her store had a moldy odor. The Estate became aware of the presence of mold in November 2000 after an investigation regarding the tenant's complaint. The Estate gave FM notice of the claim by letter on March 2, 2001. On July 17, 2001, the Estate submitted its first "Water Damage and Mold Remediation Claim," and sought payment from FM.

The Estate filed the present action on February 15, 2002. Plaintiff brings claims for Breach of Contract, Breach of the Implied Covenant of Good Faith and Fair Dealing, Tortious Breach of the Covenant of Good Faith and Fair Dealing, Declaratory Relief, and Unfair and Deceptive Business Practices. FM's Answer asserts that several policy exclusions bar coverage of the Estate's claim.

Plaintiff seeks partial summary judgment on three grounds. First, the Estate seeks dismissal of FM's affirmative defenses to coverage based on its policy exclusions. [The second two grounds for dismissal are not covered in this edited case.]

Analysis

* * *

Interpretation of Insurance Policy

* * *

The interpretation of insurance policy language is a question of law. The rules for interpreting insurance contracts are well-settled in Washington. In an all-risk insurance policy, any peril that is not specifically excluded in the policy is an insured peril.

The insurer bears the burden of proving that a claim falls within the scope of an exclusion. "Exclusionary clauses in insurance policies are strictly construed against the insurer." *Stouffer & Knight v. Cont'l Cas. Co.,* 96 Wash.App. 741, 747, 982 P.2d 105 (1999). A policy should be interpreted in a way that gives effect to each provision.

1. Requirement that losses be "fortuitous"

An insured bears the burden of showing that its loss falls within the scope of the policy's insured losses. The Court finds as a matter of law that an all-risk insurance policy only covers "fortuitous" losses. Under an all-risk policy, "recovery is allowed for fortuitous losses unless the loss is excluded by a specific policy provision." G. Couch, L. Russ, & T. Segalla, 10 *Couch on Insurance Law,* §148:50 (3d ed.1996). Despite its express terms, every all-risk policy "'contains an unnamed exclusion—the loss must be *fortuitous* in nature.'" *Intermetal Mexicana, S.A. v. Ins. Co. of N. Am.,* 866 F.2d 71, 75 (3d Cir.1989).

The fortuity requirement exists as a matter of public policy because it would encourage fraud to permit recovery on an insurance loss which is certain to occur.

* * *

This Court follows the reasoning of the Eastern District of Washington in *Underwriters,* 790 F.Supp. 1043, 1048 (E.D.Wash.1991), and believes that the Washington Supreme Court would adopt a definition of "fortuitous" that would contain the following elements:

(a) a loss which was certain to occur cannot be considered fortuitous, and may not serve as the basis for recovery under an all-risk insurance policy;

(b) in deciding whether a loss was fortuitous, a court should examine the parties' perception of risk at the time the policy was issued;

(c) ordinarily, a loss which could not reasonably be foreseen by the parties at the time the policy was issued is fortuitous.

The Court also finds as a matter of law that under an all-risks policy, the insured bears the burden of showing that it suffered a loss and that the loss is fortuitous. However, the insured need not demonstrate the precise cause of damage for the purpose of proving fortuity.

[Author's Note: In the foregoing discussion, the court ruled, as a matter of law, as to the definition of *fortuitous* but did not apply it to the facts of the case. The plaintiff would be required in a subsequent motion to prove whether the mold damage was caused by a fortuitous event.]

2. Interpretation of policy exclusions

Once the insured shows that the loss falls within the scope of the policy's insured losses, the insurer must show that a loss is specifically excluded to avoid coverage. The exclusions in the Form 3000 policy include:

- loss or damage or deterioration arising from delay;
- faulty workmanship, material, construction or design from any cause;
- deterioration, depletion, rust, corrosion or erosion, wear and tear, inherent vice or latent defect;
- settling, cracking, shrinking, bulging or expansion of foundations, floors, walls, ceilings and/or roofs;
- changes in temperature damage, changes in relative humidity damage;
- contamination, including but not limited to pollution, or hazardous materials; and
- changes in color, flavor, texture, or finish.

* * *

No policy exclusion specifically excludes mold or water intrusion damage. Thus, the Court finds that as a matter of contract interpretation, the plain language of the Form 3000 policy is not ambiguous and does not exclude mold or water intrusion damage. An ambiguity exists only when "the language on its face is fairly susceptible to two different but reasonable interpretations." *Kish v. Ins. Co. of N. Am.,* 125 Wash.2d 164, 171, 883 P.2d 308 (1994).

In the alternative, if the policy exclusions were ambiguous, the Court would still find as a matter of law that the Form 3000 does not exclude mold or water intrusion damage.

(a) The Court must construe any ambiguity against the insurer.

The Court must resolve ambiguities against the insurer. "Exclusionary clauses in insurance policies are strictly construed against the insurer." *Stouffer & Knight v. Cont'l Cas. Co.,* 96 Wash.App. 741, 747, 982 P.2d 105 (1999).

* * *

Because the Court must resolve ambiguities against the insurer, the Estate should prevail on its argument that because mold or water intrusion damage is not specifically excluded in the Form 3000 policy, it is covered by the policy.

* * *

Conclusion

For the foregoing reasons the Court GRANTS IN PART and DENIES IN PART Plaintiff's motion for partial summary judgment, docket no. 48. IT IS HEREBY ORDERED AS FOLLOWS:

[P]ursuant to FED. R. CIV. P. 56(d), the Court finds [GRANTS IN PART] as follows regarding the following questions of law:

(a) An all-risk insurance policy contains an unnamed exclusion that losses be fortuitous. This Court adopts a definition of "fortuitous" that contains the following elements:
   (i) a loss which was certain to occur cannot be considered fortuitous, and may not serve as the basis for recovery under an all-risk insurance policy;
   (ii) in deciding whether a loss was fortuitous, a court should examine the parties' perception of risk at the time the policy was issued;
   (iii) ordinarily, a loss which could not reasonably be foreseen by the parties at the time the policy was issued is fortuitous.
   Plaintiff bears the burden of showing that its loss is fortuitous in nature.

(b) As a matter of contract interpretation, the Court finds that the Form 3000 policy does not exclude mold or water intrusion damage because there is no specific exclusion. Alternatively, if the contract were ambiguous, any ambiguity must be construed against the insurer, so the Estate's interpretation that the policy does not exclude mold or water intrusion damage would prevail. Extrinsic evidence supports the Estate's interpretation.

* * *

IT IS SO ORDERED.

"All-Risk" Insurance: Contract Interpretation
IN RE: KATRINA CANAL BREACHES LITIGATION
495 F.3d 191 (5th Cir. 2007)

KING, Circuit Judge. On the morning of August 29, 2005, Hurricane Katrina struck along the coast of the Gulf of Mexico, devastating portions of Louisiana and Mississippi. In the City of New Orleans, some of the most significant damage occurred when levees along three major canals—the 17th Street Canal, the Industrial Canal, and the London Avenue Canal—ruptured, permitting water from the flooded canals to inundate the city. At one point in Katrina's aftermath, approximately eighty percent of the city was submerged in water.

Each plaintiff in this case is a policyholder with homeowners, renters, or commercial-property insurance whose property was damaged during the New Orleans flooding. Despite exclusions in their policies providing that damage caused by "flood" is not covered, the plaintiffs seek recovery of their losses from their insurers. Their primary contention is that the massive inundation of water into the city was the result of the negligent design, construction, and maintenance of the levees and that the policies' flood exclusions in this context are ambiguous because they do not clearly exclude coverage for an inundation of water induced by negligence. The plaintiffs maintain that because their policies are ambiguous, we must construe them in their favor to effect coverage for their losses.

We conclude, however, that even if the plaintiffs can prove that the levees were negligently designed, constructed, or maintained and that the breaches were due to this negligence, the flood exclusions in the plaintiffs' policies unambiguously preclude their recovery. Regardless of what caused the failure of the flood-control structures that were put in place to prevent such a catastrophe, their failure resulted in a widespread flood that damaged the plaintiffs' property. This event was excluded from coverage under the plaintiffs' insurance policies, and under Louisiana law, we are bound to enforce the unambiguous terms of their insurance contracts as written. Accordingly, we conclude that the plaintiffs are not entitled to recover under their policies.

I. Factual Background and Procedural History

The cases in this appeal are a handful of the more than forty currently pending cases related to Hurricane Katrina that have been consolidated for pretrial purposes in the Eastern District of Louisiana. In several of the consolidated cases, property owners are suing their insurers to obtain recovery under homeowners, renters, and commercial-property policies for the damage their property sustained during the inundation of water into the city that accompanied the hurricane. This appeal involves four such cases: *Richard Vanderbrook et al. v. Unitrin Preferred Insurance Company et al.* ("the *Vanderbrook* action"), *Xavier University of Louisiana v. Travelers Property Casualty Company of America* ("the *Xavier* action"), *Gladys Chehardy et al. v. State Farm Fire & Casualty Company et al.* ("the *Chehardy* action"), and *Kelly A. Humphreys v. Encompass Indemnity Company* ("the *Humphreys* action").

[Author's Note: Since all four cases have similar facts and legal outcomes, just the Vanderbrook action is being covered.]

A. The Vanderbrook Action

In the *Vanderbrook* action, eight individuals ("the *Vanderbrook* plaintiffs") filed a petition for damages in Louisiana state court against their insurers. The *Vanderbrook* plaintiffs allege that "[s]ometime between 10:00 and 11:00 A.M. on August 29, 2005, before the full force of [Hurricane Katrina] reached the City of New Orleans, a small section of the concrete outfall canal wall known as the 17th Street Canal, suddenly broke, causing water to enter the streets of the [c]ity," resulting in damage to their insured property. They assert that the water damage "was not the result of flood, surface water, waves, [tidal] water, tsunami, seiche, overflow of a body of water, seepage under or over the outfall canal wall or spray from any of the above but was water intrusion, caused simply from a broken levee wall."

The *Vanderbrook* plaintiffs allege that their insurers have refused to adjust or pay for their losses, despite "a sudden break in the concrete wall of the levee outfall canal" not being described in any of their policies as an excluded loss. They assert that their insurance policies are contracts of adhesion and are "unduly and unreasonably complex," resulting in their lack of understanding of the policies' provisions. And they allege that the policies' exclusions are so "oppressive" to them and "unreasonably favorable" to the insurers that the exclusions are unconscionable and void. The *Vanderbrook* plaintiffs seek compensatory damages, additional damages for the insurers' arbitrary and capricious conduct, interest, expert fees, and attorney's fees.

Plaintiffs-appellees James Capella and Madeline Grenier were insured through defendant-appellant Hanover Insurance Company ("Hanover"), plaintiffs-appellees Peter Ascani III

and Gregory Jackson were insured through defendant-appellant Standard Fire Insurance Company ("Standard Fire"), and plaintiff-appellee Richard Vanderbrook was insured through defendant-appellant Unitrin Preferred Insurance Company ("Unitrin"). The Hanover, Standard Fire, and Unitrin policies provide coverage for risk of direct physical loss to structures on the property as well as for certain risks of loss to personal property, as long as the loss is not an excluded peril. The policies contain the following flood exclusion:

We do not insure for loss caused directly or indirectly by any of the following. Such loss is excluded regardless of any other cause or event contributing concurrently or in any sequence to the loss.

....

... Water Damage, meaning:

... Flood, surface water, waves, tidal water, overflow of a body of water, or spray from any of these, whether or not driven by wind....

Plaintiffs-cross-appellants Mary Jane Silva and Robert G. Harvey Sr. were insured through defendant-cross-appellee State Farm Fire and Casualty Company ("State Farm"). The State Farm policies insured against loss to the dwelling and for certain losses to personal property except as excluded by the policy. The policies contained the following flood exclusion:

We do not insure under any coverage for any loss which would not have occurred in the absence of one or more of the following excluded events. We do not insure for such loss regardless of: (a) the cause of the excluded event; or (b) other causes of the loss; or (c) whether other causes acted concurrently or in any sequence with the excluded event to produce the loss; or (d) whether the event occurs suddenly or gradually, involves isolated or widespread damage, arises from natural or external forces, or occurs as a result of any combination of these:

....

... Water Damage, meaning:

(1) flood, surface water, waves, tidal water, overflow of a body of water, or spray from any of these, all whether driven by wind or not....

The *Vanderbrook* action was removed to federal court on the basis of diversity jurisdiction. Hanover, Standard Fire, Unitrin, and State Farm filed Rule 12(c) motions for judgment on the pleadings, contending that the *Vanderbrook* plaintiffs' losses were excluded under their respective policies. In a single eighty-five-page order issued on November 27, 2006, the district court addressed the availability of coverage under the policies at issue in all four cases in this appeal, first addressing the *Vanderbrook* action. With respect to Hanover, Standard Fire, and Unitrin, the district court denied their motions and ruled that the plaintiffs' policies insured them against loss from water damage resulting from levee breaches where the breaches were induced by negligence. The court determined that the policies' flood exclusions were ambiguous because the term "flood" was susceptible to two reasonable definitions: one that relates to floods resulting from natural causes only and one that relates to floods resulting from both natural causes and negligent or intentional acts.

* * *

Having concluded that the term "flood" as used in the exclusions was ambiguous, the district court construed the Hanover, Standard Fire, and Unitrin policies in the insureds' favor and concluded that the policies covered water damage caused by a ruptured levee where the rupture was due to the levee's inadequate design, construction, or maintenance. Because the plaintiffs alleged that the post-Katrina inundation of water into the City of New Orleans was caused by negligent design, construction, and maintenance of the levees alongside the city's canals, the court decided that if the plaintiffs could prove their allegations, they could prevail. Accordingly, the district court denied Hanover's, Standard Fire's, and Unitrin's motions.

With respect to State Farm's policies, however, the district court concluded that the flood exclusion's "lead-in" clause removed any ambiguity and clearly excluded coverage for all floods, whether natural or not. The "lead-in" language on which the district court relied provides in part: "We do not insure for such loss [i.e., loss resulting from flood] regardless of … the cause of the excluded event or … whether the event … arises from natural or external forces." The court granted State Farm's motions and dismissed the actions against it.

* * *

E. Appeal

* * *

All defendants except State Farm now appeal the district court's order concluding that the water damage resulting from the levee breaches was not excluded by their policies' flood exclusions. The *Chehardy* plaintiffs and the *Vanderbrook* plaintiffs cross appeal the district court's grant of State Farm's motions to dismiss. And Humphreys cross appeals the district court's denial of her motion for partial summary judgment on the issue whether her policy's hurricane-deductible endorsement provides coverage for her losses.

* * *

III. Discussion

A. Controlling Law

In diversity cases such as these, federal courts must apply state substantive law. In determining which state's substantive law controls, the court applies the choice-of-law rules of the forum state. The parties agree that in these Louisiana actions involving the interpretation of insurance policies issued in Louisiana for property located in Louisiana, Louisiana's substantive law controls.

* * *

Under Louisiana law, "[a]n insurance policy is a contract between the parties and should be construed by using the general rules of interpretation of contracts set forth in the Louisiana Civil Code." *Cadwallader v. Allstate Ins. Co.,* 848 So.2d 577, 580 (La.2003). The Louisiana Civil Code provides that "[i]nterpretation of a contract is the determination of the common intent of the parties." LA. CIV. CODE ANN. art. 2045 (1987). An insurance contract must be "construed according to the entirety of its terms and conditions as set forth in the policy, and as amplified, extended, or modified by any rider, endorsement, or application attached to or made a part of the policy." LA.REV.STAT. ANN. §22:654 (2004). Interpretation of an insurance contract generally involves a question of law.

"The words of a contract must be given their generally prevailing meaning." "When the words of a contract are clear and explicit and lead to no absurd consequences, no further interpretation may be made in search of the parties' intent." La. Civ.Code Ann. art. 2046 (1987). "If the policy wording at issue is clear and unambiguously expresses the parties' intent, the insurance contract must be enforced as written."

Where, however, an insurance policy includes ambiguous provisions, the "[a]mbiguity … must be resolved by construing the policy as a whole; one policy provision is not to be construed separately at the expense of disregarding other policy provisions." "Words susceptible of different meanings must be interpreted as having the meaning that best conforms to the object of the contract." La. Civ.Code Ann. art. 2048 (1987). "A provision susceptible of different meanings must be interpreted with a meaning that renders it effective and not with one that renders it ineffective." *Id.* art. 2049 (1987).

Ambiguity may also be resolved through the use of the reasonable-expectations doctrine—i.e., "by ascertaining how a reasonable insurance policy purchaser would construe the clause at the time the insurance contract was entered." "The court should construe the policy 'to fulfill the reasonable expectations of the parties in light of the customs and usages of the industry.'" "A doubtful provision must be interpreted in light of the nature of the contract, equity, usages, the conduct of the parties before and after the formation of the contract, and of other contracts of a like nature between the same parties." La. Civ.Code Ann. art. 2053 (1987).

"If after applying the other general rules of construction an ambiguity remains, the ambiguous contractual provision is to be construed against the drafter, or, as originating in the insurance context, in favor of the insured." The Louisiana Civil Code provides: "In case of doubt that cannot be otherwise resolved, a provision in a contract must be interpreted against the party who furnished its text. A contract executed in a standard form of one party must be interpreted, in case of doubt, in favor of the other party." La. Civ.Code Ann. art. 2056 (1987). "Under this rule of strict construction, equivocal provisions seeking to narrow an insurer's obligation are strictly construed against the insurer." "That strict construction principle applies only if the ambiguous policy provision is susceptible to two or more *reasonable* interpretations; for the rule of strict construction to apply, the insurance policy must be not only susceptible to two or more interpretations, but each of the alternative interpretations must be reasonable." *Cadwallader,* 848 So.2d at 580. The fact that a term is not defined in the policy itself does not alone make that term ambiguous.

"An insurance contract, however, should not be interpreted in an unreasonable or strained manner under the guise of contractual interpretation to enlarge or restrict its provisions beyond what is reasonably contemplated by unambiguous terms or achieve an absurd conclusion." "Courts lack the authority to alter the terms of insurance contracts under the guise of contractual interpretation when the policy's provisions are couched in unambiguous terms." *Cadwallader,* 848 So.2d at 580.

The policies in this case—which are homeowners, renters, and commercial-property policies—are all-risk policies. All-risk policies "create a special type of coverage that extends to risks not usually covered under other insurance; recovery under an all-risk policy will be allowed for all fortuitous losses not resulting from misconduct or fraud, unless the policy contains a specific provision expressly excluding the loss from coverage." *Carbon v. Allstate Ins. Co.,* 719 So.2d 437, 440 (La.1998). Insurers may, however, limit their liability under all-risk policies: "[A]bsent a conflict with statutory provisions or public policy, insurers, like other individuals, are entitled to limit their liability and to impose and to enforce reasonable conditions upon the policy obligations they contractually assume." But "[e]xclusionary provisions in insurance contracts are strictly construed against the insurer, and any ambiguity is construed in favor of the insured." *Ledbetter v. Concord Gen. Corp.,* 665 So.2d 1166, 1169 (La.2006).

B. Flood Exclusions

The plaintiffs contend that their policies' flood exclusions do not unambiguously exclude coverage for losses caused by an inundation of water resulting from a breached levee where the breach occurred in part because the levee was negligently designed, constructed, or maintained. The plaintiffs urge us to conclude that the term "flood" is ambiguous in this context and that the policies must be construed in favor of coverage. By contrast, the insurers maintain that the policies unambiguously exclude coverage for the inundation of water resulting from the breached levees.

The Louisiana Supreme Court has not interpreted a flood exclusion in the context of breached levees. We must therefore make an *Erie* guess and determine, in our best judgment, how that court would resolve the issue if presented with this case.

The plaintiffs first contend that because the term "flood" is not defined in the policies, it is ambiguous—indeed, the *Chehardy* plaintiffs say that the term's undefined status makes it per se ambiguous—requiring us to construe the term in favor of coverage. But the fact that a term used in an exclusion "is not defined in the policy itself ... alone does

not make the exclusion ambiguous; instead, [the court] will give the term its generally prevailing meaning."

* * *

The plaintiffs also maintain that because the insurers could have more explicitly excluded floods that are caused in part by negligence, their failure to do so in these policies makes the flood exclusions ambiguous.

* * *

But the fact that an exclusion could have been worded more explicitly does not necessarily make it ambiguous. Nor does the fact that other policies have more explicitly defined the scope of similar exclusions. As the Louisiana Supreme Court stated in *Cadwallader* when interpreting the term "relative":

> We therefore reject the plaintiffs' arguments that the flood exclusions in the policies before us are ambiguous in light of more specific language used in other policies.

Furthermore, even where the scope of an exclusion is not readily apparent, we do not immediately construe that exclusion in favor of coverage. Instead, we first apply the general rules of contract construction set forth in the Civil Code. Under those rules, we give the words of a contract their "generally prevailing meaning." Dictionaries, treatises, and jurisprudence are helpful resources in ascertaining a term's generally prevailing meaning. When the words of a policy provision are clear and unambiguous in the context of the facts of the case and do not lead to an absurd result, we apply the provision as written without any further interpretation. La. Civ.Code Ann. art. 2046.

To ascertain the generally prevailing meaning of the term "flood," we begin by considering dictionary definitions of the term. Each of the dictionaries we have accessed lists more than one definition of "flood," but the existence of more than one definition of a term does not itself make the term ambiguous.

The Oxford English Dictionary has two pertinent definitions of "flood": (1) "[a]n overflowing or irruption of a great body of water over land not usually submerged; an inundation, a deluge" and (2) "[a] profuse and violent outpouring of water; a swollen stream, a torrent; a violent downpour of rain, threatening an inundation." *Webster's Dictionary* defines "flood" as "a rising and overflowing of a body of water that covers land not usu[ally] under water ...[;] an outpouring of considerable extent ...[;] a great downpour." *Webster's Third New International Dictionary* 873 (2002). The sixth edition of *Black's Law Dictionary* defines "flood" as follows: "An inundation of water over land not usually covered by it. Water which inundates area of surface of earth where it ordinarily would not be expected to be." *Black's Law Dictionary* 640 (6th ed.1990). "Flood" itself is not defined in the current (eighth) edition of *Black's Law Dictionary,* but "floodwater" is defined as "[w]ater that escapes from a watercourse in large volumes and flows over adjoining property in no regular channel." *Black's Law Dictionary* 1622 (8th ed.2004). The most straightforward definition comes from the *American*

Heritage Dictionary: "An overflowing of water onto land that is normally dry." *American Heritage Dictionary* of the English Language 674 (4th ed.2000). Finally, of particular interest is the discussion of "flood" in the *Columbia Encyclopedia,* which specifically includes in the definition the inundation of water resulting from the bursting of a levee:

> [I]nundation of land by the rise and overflow of a body of water. Floods occur most commonly when water from heavy rainfall, from melting ice and snow, or from a combination of these exceeds the carrying capacity of the river system, lake, or ocean into which it runs....
>
> ... Less predictable are floods resulting from ... the bursting of a natural or man-made dam or levee.

We also consider the definitions of "flood" in treatises. Appleman's Insurance Law and Practice defines "flood waters" as "those waters above the highest line of the ordinary flow of a stream, and generally speaking they have overflowed a river, stream, or natural water course and have formed a continuous body with the water flowing in the ordinary channel." 5 John Alan Appleman & Jean Appleman, Insurance Law and Practice §3145 (1970). And *Couch on Insurance* defines "flood" as "the overflow of some body of water that inundates land not usually covered with water."

Additionally, we look to jurisprudence, both from Louisiana courts and from courts outside Louisiana. In *Riche v. State Farm Fire & Casualty Co.,* an intermediate Louisiana court interpreted a policy's exclusion for "flood, surface water, tidal water or tidal wave, overflow of streams or other bodies of water, or spray from any of the foregoing, all whether driven by wind or not."

* * *

In light of these definitions, we conclude that the flood exclusions are unambiguous in the context of this case and that what occurred here fits squarely within the generally prevailing meaning of the term "flood." When a body of water overflows its normal boundaries and inundates an area of land that is normally dry, the event is a flood. This is precisely what occurred in New Orleans in the aftermath of Hurricane Katrina. Three watercourses—the 17th Street, Industrial, and London Avenue Canals—overflowed their normal channels, and the levees built alongside the canals to hold back their floodwaters failed to do so. As a result, an enormous volume of water

inundated the city. In common parlance, this event is known as a flood.

* * *

The plaintiffs finally contend that the reasonable expectations of homeowners insurance policyholders would be that damage resulting from man-made floods would be covered. "[A]scertaining how a reasonable insurance policy purchaser would construe the clause at the time the insurance contract was entered" is one way that ambiguity in an exclusion clause may be resolved. *La. Ins. Guar. Ass'n,* 630 So.2d at 764. But "Louisiana law ... precludes use of the reasonable expectations doctrine to recast policy language when such language is clear and unambiguous." *Coleman v. Sch. Bd. of Richland Parish,* 418 F.3d 511, 522 (5th Cir.2005). As we have explained, the flood exclusions in the policies are unambiguous in the context of the specific facts of this case; thus, we need not resort to ascertaining a reasonable policyholder's expectations. For the sake of thoroughness, however, we will briefly address a few of the parties' arguments.

* * *

In sum, we conclude that the flood exclusions in the plaintiffs' policies are unambiguous in the context of the facts of this case. In the midst of a hurricane, three canals running through the City of New Orleans overflowed their normal boundaries. The flood-control measures, i.e., levees, that man had put in place to prevent the canal's floodwaters from reaching the city failed. The result was an enormous and devastating inundation of water into the city, damaging the plaintiffs' property. This event was a "flood" within that term's generally prevailing meaning as used in common parlance, and our interpretation of the exclusions ends there. The flood is unambiguously excluded from coverage under the plaintiffs' all-risk policies, and the district court's conclusion to the contrary was erroneous.

* * *

IV. Conclusion

With respect to the *Vanderbrook* action, the district court's grant of State Farm's motion for judgment on the pleadings is AFFIRMED. The denial of the motions for judgment on the pleadings filed by Hanover and Standard Fire is VACATED and REMANDED.

[Author's Note: The *Xavier, Chehardy,* and *Humphrey* cases were also vacated and remanded.]

Insurable Interest
MOTORISTS MUTUAL INSURANCE CO. v. RICHMOND
676 S.W.2d 478 (Ky.App. 1984)

CLAYTON, Judge. Motorists Mutual Insurance Company (Motorists) appeals from a judgment of the Whitley Circuit Court awarding Linda Durham Richmond, her infant children and her mortgagee, Farmers National Bank, a total

sum of $29,000.00 under the terms of a fire insurance policy issued by Motorists to Richmond on January 12, 1982. The sole question on appeal is whether the appellees had an insurable interest in the insured property at the time of issuance of the policy and the time of the loss. We believe that they did and affirm the decision of the circuit court.

In May of 1964, Richmond married Eddie Durham. During the course of their thirteen-year marriage, she bore two children, Melody, born in 1967, and James, born in 1971. Together the couple purchased a lot and home in Whitley County, Kentucky, on October 2, 1976. The two divorced in August of 1977 under a decree, the terms of which provided for the sale of their home within six months. However, the ordered sale never occurred. Instead, Richmond and Durham attempted to reconcile their differences until March 2, 1981, at which time she and the two children moved out.

Prior to her departure, however, numerous improvements were made to the residence including repaneling the interior walls, installing new ceilings, carpeting, walkways, patio and front porch. Both individuals contributed equally to the cost of the alterations and to payment of a preexisting mortgage on the home. Thereafter, on February 21, 1980, Richmond deeded over her legal interest in title to the property to her former husband. Approximately one year later he executed a second mortgage on the property to Farmers National Bank in the sum of $4,865.00. He subsequently died intestate of a chronic heart condition on June 18, 1981, leaving Melody and James his only heirs at law.

Immediately after her former husband's death, the widow returned to the home with her two minor children and set up residence. She began making payments on the 1981 mortgage indebtedness and continued to do so until the residence was totally destroyed by fire October 1, 1982.

Ten months prior to the loss, Richmond secured fire insurance with Motorists in the following manner. In early January she contacted Mosley Insurance Agency requesting coverage. Gene Mosley, agent for Motorists, went to the house to take pictures, make measurements, and generally inspect the premises. During his tour of the premises, Mosley requested Richmond to sign a receipt, apparently an insurance application, and asked if there was a lien against the property. Richmond replied that there was a lien but then erroneously added that it was in her name. Mosley then departed, filling out the remainder of the application himself, including checking a portion signifying that Richmond was sole owner of the home. Richmond never spoke with Mosley again until the date of the loss and she never received a copy of the application. The policy became effective on January 12, 1982, ten days before she was named administratrix of the estate of Eddie Durham.

Two months later, on March 9, 1982, Linda Richmond assumed the outstanding mortgage debt on Durham's 1981 mortgage note along with an additional debt Durham left outstanding with Farmers for the purchase of a boat. The total indebtedness of the newly executed consolidation note was $7,575.53. Linda's signature on that note appears both in her personal capacity and as administratrix of Durham's estate. The added indebtedness apparently was assumed by Linda under an added loan clause in the 1981 mortgage.

Had she not executed the March 9, 1982, mortgage foreclosure proceedings would have been imminent.

Following destruction of the home, Linda presented a claim with Motorists of $15,000.00 for personal property destroyed in the blaze and was paid $11,740.80. However, Motorists refused to make any payment for the destroyed residence claiming instead that Richmond possessed no insurable interest.

Seeking to avoid payment under the contract, Motorists would now cast Richmond as nothing more than a trespassing squatter who "surrepticiously" [sic] returned to the residence and thereafter fraudulently represented her true lack of ownership interest. Motorists would further tacitly imply that the fire was of mysterious origin by its statement that "[a]t the time of the fire she and her new husband had moved out." We cannot accept these base characterizations. They are not supported by the record or the law.

Linda Richmond, both before and after the death of her late former husband, made substantial monetary contribution to the maintenance and improvement of the destroyed residence. As natural guardian for her minor children, and later as administratrix of the Durham estate, she was obligated to provide for the care and custody of their offspring, including the duty to protect their home, of which the children became sole owners in fee simple by statute of descent upon the death of their father. Thus, when Richmond returned to the property following Durham's death she was not a surrepticious [sic] trespasser. Her offspring and she as their guardian were fully entitled to use and dominion over the premises. While not possessed of title, Richmond certainly possessed an insurable interest in the residence; first, by her status as natural guardian for the protection of her minor children's interest; and second, by her extensive pecuniary investment in the residence. * * * Richmond's situation is identical to that found in *McElrath v. State Capital Insurance Co.,* 184 S.E.2d 912 (1971). In *McElrath,* the insurer, State Capital Insurance Company (State Capital), issued a three year policy of fire insurance on McElrath's home in October of 1967. On January of 1970 the widow's residence was destroyed by fire. McElrath timely submitted a claim with State Capital which denied coverage, in part due to McElrath's supposed lack of an insurable interest. The Court of Appeals of North Carolina quickly dispensed with the defendant insurer's argument stating,

> Defendant contends that the court should have granted its motion for a directed verdict for the reason that plaintiff had no interest in the property capable of being insured. The deed to the property was in the name of plaintiff's husband who died intestate in 1946 leaving plaintiff and six minor children surviving. Since that date plaintiff has been in possession of and has exercised dominion over the property. She has paid all taxes, kept the property insured and made all repairs. There is no suggestion of fraud or that defendant assumed any risk it did not intend to assume when it issued the policy. "In general, it is

well-settled law that a person has an insurable interest in the subject matter insured where he has such a relation or connection with, or concern in, such subject matter that he will derive pecuniary benefit or advantage from its preservation, or will suffer pecuniary loss or damage from its destruction, termination, or injury by the happening of the event insured against."

* * * The judgment of the Whitley Circuit Court is affirmed.

Abstract of Title[40]

1. Caption

Situated in the Township of Audrain, in the County of Dore and in the State of Ohio, and Being the Northwest quarter of the Southeast quarter, and the North half of the Southeast fraction of the Southwest quarter of Section 34, Township one South, of Range five East, containing 83 acres of land, more or less.

2.

	STATE DEED
The State of Ohio	Date of Instrument? August 5, 1835
	Filed: December 16, 1842
TO	Recorded in Volume 12, Page 236 of the Record of Deeds of Dore County, Ohio
John Glander	Consideration $132.33
	Estate conveyed:
	What if any defect in instrument? None.

Description: The Southeast fraction of the West half of Section No. 34, Township one South of Range five East within the land and containing 105 acres of land, more or less.

Regularly signed, sealed, witnessed and acknowledged. (See Figure 8.2.)

3.

	WARRANTY DEED
John Glander and Elizabeth Glander, his wife	Date of Instrument? September 4, 1847
	Filed: June 4, 1848
	Recorded in Volume 2, Page 315 of the Record of Deeds of Dore County, Ohio
TO	Consideration $390.00
Henry Joseph Boehmer	Estate conveyed: Fee simple
	What if any defect in instrument? None.

Description: Situated in the County of Dore and State of Ohio and bounded and described as follows, to-wit: The Southeast fraction of the West half of Section No. 34, Township one South, Range five East, containing 105.86 acres, more or less.

Also, the Northeast fraction of Section No. 34, Township one South, Range five East, containing 71.51 acres of land, more or less.

Regularly signed, sealed, witnessed and acknowledged.

4.

	WARRANTY DEED
Henry Joseph Boehmer and Mary Boehmer, his wife	Date of Instrument? January 29, 1848
	Filed: November 28, 1848
	Recorded in Volume 2, Page 405 of the Record of Deeds of Dore County, Ohio
TO	Consideration $155.00
Mathias Hellman	Estate conveyed: Fee simple
	What if any defect in instrument? None.

Description: Situated in the County of Dore and State of Ohio and bounded and described as follows, to-wit: The Northeast fraction of the Southwest quarter of Section 34, Township one South, Range five East, containing 43.20 acres of land, more or less.

Regularly signed, sealed, witnessed and acknowledged.

FIGURE 8.2
State Deed

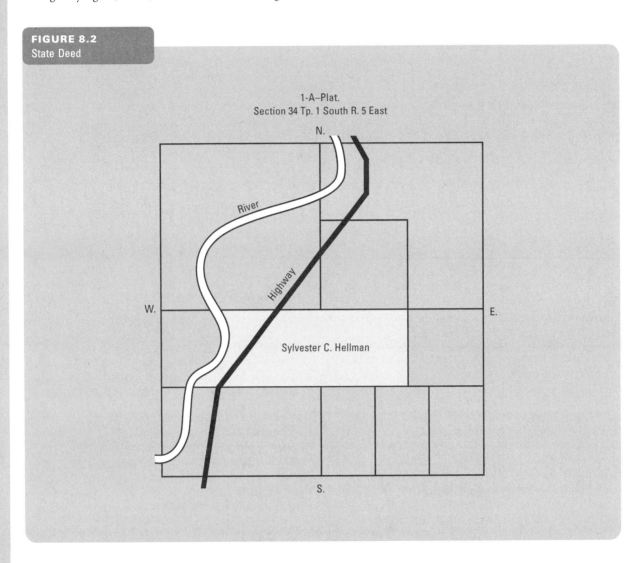

1-A–Plat.
Section 34 Tp. 1 South R. 5 East

5.

STATE DEED

The State of Ohio

TO

J. C. McCowen

Date of Instrument? September 16, 1853
Filed: January 7, 1854 at 12:30 P.M.
Recorded in Volume 87, Page 93 of the
Record of Deeds of Dore County, Ohio
Consideration $160.00
Estate conveyed:
What if any defect in instrument? None.

Description: The Southeast quarter of Section No. 34, Township one South, Range five East, containing 160 acres of land.
Regularly signed, sealed, witnessed and acknowledged.

6.

WARRANTY DEED

John McCowen and Drucilla
McCowen, his wife

TO

Mathias Hellman

Date of Instrument? August 10, 1854
Filed: November 9, 1854
Recorded in Volume 11, Page 164 of the
  Record of Deeds of Dore County, Ohio
Consideration $120.00
Estate conveyed: Fee simple
Defects: None.

Description: The West half of the Northwest quarter of the Southeast quarter of Section 34, Twp 1 S of R 5 E, in the county of Dore, Ohio, containing 20 acres of land.
  Regularly signed, sealed, witnessed and acknowledged.

7.

WARRANTY DEED

John McCowen and Drucilla
McCowen, his wife

TO

Mathias Hellman

Date of Instrument? January 14, 1860
Filed: September 12, 1860
Recorded in Volume 14, Page 221 of the
  Record of Deeds of Dore County, Ohio
Consideration $140
Estate conveyed: Fee simple
What if any defect in instrument? None.

Description: Situated in the County of Dore in the State of Ohio and in _____ and bounded and described as follows: Being the East half of the Northwest quarter of Section 34, Township one South, Range five East, containing 20 acres of land in the County of Dore, Ohio.
  Regularly signed, sealed, witnessed and acknowledged.

8.

WARRANTY DEED

Mathias Hellman

TO

Joseph Hellman

Date of Instrument? April 2, 1883
Filed: May 11, 1883
Recorded in Volume 42, Page 426 of
  the Record of Deeds of Dore County, Ohio
Consideration $3500.00
Estate conveyed: Fee simple
What if any defect in instrument? None.

Description: Situated in the Township of Audrain, in the County of Dore and State of Ohio and being the Northeast fraction of the Southwest fractional quarter, and the Northwest quarter of the Southeast quarter of Section 34, Township one South of Range five East, containing 80 acres of land, more or less.
  Regularly signed, sealed, witnessed and acknowledged.

9.

WARRANTY DEED

Joseph Hellman and Bernadina
Hellman husband and wife

TO

Sylvester C. Hellman

Date of Instrument? October 17, 1929
Filed: April 28, 1930 at 4:15 P.M.
Recorded in Volume 139, Page 398 of
  the Record of Deeds of Dore County, Ohio
Consideration $1.00
Estate conveyed: Fee simple
What if any defect in instrument? None.

Description: Situated in the Township of Audrain, County of Dore and State of Ohio, and being the Northeast fraction of the Southwest fractional quarter, and the Northwest quarter of the Southeast quarter of Section 34, Township one South, of Range five East, and containing 80 acres of land, more or less.

Regularly signed, sealed, witnessed and acknowledged.

10.
Certificate to Recorder
Real Estate Devised by Will

Probate Court, Dore County, Ohio

To the County Recorder of said County:

I the undersigned, Probate Judge of said County, do hereby certify that on the 18th day of March, A.D. 1930, the Last Will and Testament of Joseph Hellmann, late of said County, was duly admitted to probate in this Court, and the same has been duly recorded in Volume P Page 159 of the Records of Wills in this office.

That by the terms of said Will certain real estate was devised to Bernadina Hellmann and Sylvester Hellman.

That the following is a description of said real estate as is contained in the Will, to-wit:

Second: I give, devise and bequeath to my beloved wife, Bernadina, the farm on which we now reside together with all chattel property I may have at the time of my decease. She to have full possession of same during her natural life. After the death of my beloved wife, I give to my son, Sylvester, the aforementioned farm located in Section 34, Audrain Township, Dore County, Ohio, containing 83 acres of land, together with all chattels. He, however, must pay all funeral expenses and debts contracted by my said wife. Also to pay my following named children within three years after the death of my said wife as follows:

Witness my signature and the seal of said Court, this 6th day of January, 1931.

W. M. Bunge,
Probate Judge
By Mary McLeasure
Deputy Clerk

[*Seal*]

Recorded in Vol. 141, Page 191
Record of Deeds of said County

11.
Application for Probate of Will

Dore County, Ohio
Probate Court,

In the Matter of The Last Will and Testament of Joseph Hellmann, Deceased.	}	Application To Admit To Probate

To the Probate Court of said County:

Your petitioner respectfully represents that Joseph Hellmann, late a resident of the Township of Audrain in said County, died on or about the 4th day of March, A.D., 1930, leaving an instrument in writing, herewith produced, purporting to be his last Will and Testament.

That the said Joseph Hellmann died leaving Bernadina Hellmann, widow, who resides at Fort Audrain, Ohio, and the following named persons his only next of kin, to-wit:

NAME	DEGREE OF KINSHIP	P.O. ADDRESS
Mathias Hellmann	Son	Fort Audrain, Ohio
Otto Hellmann	Son	Delton, Ohio
Christina Brinkman	Daughter	Fort Audrain, Ohio
Bernadina Beining	Daughter	Fort Audrain, Ohio
Mary Hellmann	Daughter	Fort Audrain, Ohio
Sylvester Hellmann	Son	Fort Audrain, Ohio

Your petitioner offers said Will for Probate and prays that a time may be fixed for the proving of the same, and that said above named persons resident in this State may be notified according to law of the pendency of said proceedings.

Sylvester Hellmann,
Petitioner

Properly verified.

12.
Last Will and Testament

In the name of the Benevolent Father of All: Amen.

I, Joseph Hellmann, of the Township of Audrain, County of Dore and State of Ohio, being about 70 years of age and of sound and disposing mind and memory, do make, publish and declare this my last will and testament, hereby revoking and annulling any and all will or wills by me made heretofore:

First: My will is that all my just debts and funeral expenses be paid out of my estate as soon after my decease as shall be found convenient.

Second: I give, devise and bequeath to my beloved wife Bernadina the farm on which we now reside together with all chattel property I may have at the time of my decease. She to have full possession of same during her natural life. After the death of my beloved wife I give to my son Sylvester the aforementioned farm located in Section thirty-four, Audrain Township, Dore County, Ohio, containing eighty-three (83) acres of land together with all chattels. He, however, must pay all funeral expenses and debts contracted by my said wife. Also to pay my following named children within three years after the death of my said wife as follows:

Item 3. My son Mathias to get Seven Hundred ($700.00) Dollars, I having paid him Eight Hundred ($800.00) Dollars.

Item 4. My son Otto to get Fifteen Hundred ($1500.00) Dollars.

Item 5. My daughter Christina Brinkman to get Fourteen Hundred ($1400.00) Dollars. She having been paid One Hundred ($100.00) Dollars.

Item 6. My daughter Bernadina Beining to get Fourteen Hundred ($1400.00) Dollars. She having been paid One Hundred ($100.00) Dollars.

Item 7. My daughter Mary to get Eighteen Hundred ($1800.00) Dollars and the privilege of remaining and living on said farm with my son Sylvester, as long as she lives, and to occupy the East upstairs room. However in case Sylvester is forced to sell, then my daughter may so give up the aforesaid privileges.

Item 8. I desire that there be no appraisement of my property and ask that the court omit the same.

Item 9. I hereby revoke any and all wills formerly made by me.

In Testimony Whereof, I have set my hand to this my last will and testament at Fort Audrain, Ohio, this 8th day of April in the year of our Lord one thousand nine hundred and twenty-four.

Joseph Hellmann

The foregoing instrument was signed by the said Joseph Hellmann in our presence, and by him published and declared as and for his last will and testament and at his request, and in his presence, and in the presence of each other, we hereunto subscribe our names as attesting witnesses, at Fort Audrain, Ohio, this 8th day of April, A.D., 1924.

Anton J. Berelman	resides at Fort Audrain, Ohio
Rudolph Rasbe	resides at Fort Audrain, Ohio
Filed March 18, 1930	

13.

NOTE: The order for hearing, the admission to probate and record, the waiver of notice and consent to probate, the testimony of witnesses to the will, the application for letters, the issuance of letters; the order for bond; and the proof of publication of notice to creditors are all regular and complete and are not set out.

14.
Journal Entry

IN PROBATE COURT
Dore County, Ohio
May 13, 1930

In the matter of the Estate
of Joseph Hellman,
Deceased.
}
Estate Not Subject to Tax

Determination of Inheritance Tax

Sylvester C. Hellman as Administrator of the estate of Joseph Hellman, deceased, having filed an application duly verified, for a finding and order that said estate and the successions therein are exempt from any inheritance tax under the laws of Ohio, the same came on for hearing.

And the Court being fully advised in the premises, finds and determines that the gross value of said estate is $885.86; the debts and costs of administration are $585.00, and the net actual market value thereof is $300.86. Said decedent died leaving three sons and three daughters, and that as a result said estate and the successions therein are exempt from such inheritance tax.

It is ordered that the court costs on this proceeding taxed at $3.00 be certified to the County Auditor to be paid and credited in the manner provided by law.

W. M. Bunge, *Probate Judge*

Filed May 13, 1930.

15.

In the Matter of the Estate of
Joseph Hellman,
Deceased.
}
IN PROBATE COURT
Dore County, Ohio
Saturday May 2, 1931.

The first and final account of Sylvester Hellman, Administrator with will annexed of the estate of Joseph Hellman, deceased, herein filed on the 23rd day of March, A.D., 1931, came in this day for hearing and settlement, due notice thereof having been published according to law. No exceptions having been filed thereto, and no one now appearing to except or object to the same; and the Court having carefully examined said account and the vouchers therewith and all matters pertaining thereto, and being fully advised in the premises, finds the same to be in all respects just and correct and in conformity to law.

It is ordered that the same be and hereby is approved, allowed and confirmed.

The Court further finds said Administrator with will annexed chargeable with the assets of the estate of said Joseph Hellman to the amount of $929.11 and that he is entitled to the credits in the sum of $929.11 and that there is no balance due to said estate.

And the Court further finding that said estate has been duly and fully settled, it is ordered that said Administrator with will annexed be discharged and his bond released from further liability. It is ordered that said account and the proceedings herein be recorded in the records of this office, and that said Administrator with will annexed pay the costs herein taxed at $5.00.

W. M. Bunge, *Probate Judge*

Filed May 2, 1931.

16.

Sylvester Hellman

TO

The General Utilities Co.
of Deshler, Ohio

EASEMENT
Date of Instrument, April 22, 1933
Recorded May 17, 1933 in Volume 143
at Page 596
No defects in instrument

Grants the right to construct, operate and maintain its lines through and along the following described property: The Northeast 43.1 acres of the Southwest quarter of section 34, Township one South, Range five East.

17.
Tax Statement

The tax duplicates of the Treasurer's Office and the records of the Auditor's Office and Surveyor's Office of Dore County, Ohio, show the following in connection with the taxes levied against caption lands:

Amount of Special Assessments and Terms:
No specials
Description of Land as it Appears
   on the Duplicates:

Sec. 34 NW1/4, SE1/4	40A
Sec. N1/2 SE fr. SW1/4	43.10A
Assessed Value of Land	$4390.00
Buildings	$2340.00
Total	$6730.00

Current Taxes:

Paid	Taxes for the first half of the year 1937, due and payable in December 1937	$33.65
Unpaid	Taxes for the last half of the year 1937, due and payable in June 1938	$33.65

18.

State of Ohio, County of Dore

I hereby certify that the annexed abstract, which is furnished _____, as prospective mortgagee for use in passing on the title to premises covered thereby, is a correct abstract of the title to the land described in the caption thereof, to-wit:

Caption Lands

in the said county and state: that said abstract correctly shows all matters affecting or relating to the said title which are of record or on file in said county, including conveyances, deeds, trust deeds, land and other liens, attachments and foreign or domestic executions in the hands of the sheriff, certificates of authority to pay taxes, suits pending by or against owners of record within the last two years or against Sylvester Hellman, notices of Federal liens, tax sales, tax deeds, probate proceedings, special proceedings, and unsatisfied judgments and transcripts of judgments from United States and State courts against owners of record or against Sylvester Hellman, notices of liens on bail bonds or recognizances filed against said premises, or against owners of record on or since April 1, 1929, or against Sylvester Hellman, under chapter 14, section 13435-5, of laws of Ohio of 1929; that said abstract also shows all bankruptcy proceedings and certified copies of orders of adjudication and orders approving bonds of trustee in bankruptcy proceedings by or against any party who, within three years past, has been an owner of record of said land or against Sylvester Hellman on file or of record in said county; that all taxes and special assessments against said premises are paid in full to and including the first installment of the taxes for the year 1937 and that there are no outstanding installments of special assessments to become due in the future.

Dated at _____, Ohio this 2nd day of May, A.D. 19_____, at 10:00 o'clock A.M.

C. W. McLain
Abstracter

Continued to this date and recertified as above, this _____ day of _____, A.D. 19_____, at _____ o'clock _____M.

KEY TERMS

PROBLEMS

1. Siedel lived in a state that has a "notice" recording statute. On August 1, he deeded his real estate to Alpha, the deed providing that "Seidel conveys and warrants Sunnybrook Farm to Alpha." On November 1, Siedel deeded the same real estate to Beta, the deed providing that "Siedel conveys and warrants Sunnybrook Farm to Beta." Both Alpha and Beta recorded their deeds on the date of purchase. Who is the owner of Sunnybrook now? Why?

2. Jones deeded his real estate to Hamilton on April 24, although Jones continued to live on the property. Jones deeded the same real estate to Randall on June 29. Randall, who had no knowledge of the prior sale, immediately took possession of the property. Hamilton recorded his deed on August 5, and Randall recorded his deed on August 20. A state statute provides that a deed is not valid against later purchasers without notice of the deed if the later purchase was made before the deed was recorded. Who is entitled to the real estate—Jones, Hamilton, or Randall? Why?

3. Shifty sold his farm to Leroy on November 1 for $275,000. Leroy immediately recorded his deed and took possession of the farm. On December 1, Shifty sold the farm for $5 to his brother-in-law, Crafty, who recorded his deed on that date. A dispute over ownership of the farm later developed between Leroy and Crafty. Assuming that the state has a "notice" recording statute, list all arguments that Leroy should raise to prove that he is entitled to ownership.

4. Holt borrowed $80,000 from Andrew and gave him a mortgage on a lot that Holt owned in the city of Savannah. The mortgage was promptly recorded, but the recorder mistakenly listed the debt on the record as $40,000 instead of $80,000. Holt then sought to obtain a loan from Terrell. After examining the county records, which showed a mortgage of only $40,000, Terrell decided to lend Holt the funds he sought and take a junior mortgage. Later Andrew sought to

foreclose the first mortgage. Terrell claimed that his junior mortgage gave him priority to proceeds from the foreclosure sale above $40,000. Is he correct? Why or why not?

5. Review the abstract reprinted in this chapter. If you were purchasing this property, would you be satisfied that the seller has good title? Why or why not?

6. Hall deeded property to Morse in 1997, but Morse did not record the deed until 2002. In 2000, Hall deeded the same property to Clark, who immediately recorded the deed. At the time of her purchase, Clark knew about the earlier deed to Morse. In 2003, Clark deeded the property to Curtis, who did not know about the Morse deed. In a notice state, who owns the property now—Morse or Curtis? Why?

7. Jake and Dolly, husband and wife, owned certain property as joint tenants. In October, Dolly separated from Jake and went to Nevada, where she obtained a divorce on November 13. However, the couple continued to own the property as joint tenants. Jake lived on the property; and to cover improvements he had made on the land, Jake obtained fire insurance as the sole insured. Dolly had no knowledge of the improvements or the fire insurance. Fire later destroyed the improvements; and when Jake died, Dolly became sole owner of the property. Dolly claimed that she was entitled to the fire insurance proceeds that were paid into Jake's estate. Did she have a valid claim? Why or why not?

8. Pell purchased a home in St. Louis. The home was mortgaged to the Putnam Saving and Loan Association (Putnam), which obtained fire insurance from Fidelity Insurance Company. The standard mortgage clause in the policy provided that "loss or damage, if any, under this policy, shall be payable to the mortgagee ... and this ... interest ... shall not be invalidated ... by any change in the title ownership of the property.... The mortgagee ... shall notify this Company of any change of ownership or occupancy or increase of hazard which

shall come to the knowledge of said mortgagee; … otherwise this policy shall be null and void." On September 14, 1992, Pell sold the property to Miller; but Miller's deed was not recorded until July 19, 1993. Putnam had no actual knowledge of the sale but was given the impression that Pell was contemplating a sale. When the property was partially destroyed by fire, Putnam sought to recover under the fire policy. Fidelity argued that Putnam cannot recover because the policy violated the standard mortgage clause by not giving notice of the change of ownership. Decide.

9. Richard Fiess owned a State Farm homeowner's policy (HO-2) that contained the following provision: "We do not cover loss caused by:

   (1) wear and tear, deterioration, or loss caused by any quality in property that causes it to damage or destroy itself.
   (2) rust, rot, mold, or other fungi.
   (3) dampness of atmosphere, extremes of temperature.
   (4) contamination.
   (5) rats, mice, termites, moths, or other insects.

   We do cover *ensuing loss* caused by collapse of the building or any part of the building, water damage, or breakage of glass that is part of the building if the loss would otherwise be covered under the policy."

   After a hurricane caused damage to his house, Fiess tore down the sheetrock and found mold caused by water from the hurricane as well as from other water sources occurring before the hurricane. Fiess argued that the "ensuing loss" clause covers mold remediation, while State Farm countered that the previous clause, stating that mold is not covered, excludes coverage. Who is correct? Explain.

10. Yakamoto is a freshman at Loyola University in Louisiana. Louisiana is a race statute state. Yakamoto requests a written one-year lease from his landlord, Flaherty, so that he can lock in his rent at $400 a month. Yakamoto, however, does not record the lease in the public record since he is totally unaware of the law which requires recordation for a lease to be effective against third parties. Shortly before he moves into his new apartment, he finds out that another student, Thistle (a third party), has negotiated to lease the apartment for $600 a month. Yakamoto is also told that Flaherty, aware of Louisiana's race statute, had instructed Thistle to record his lease in the public record immediately, which he does. A lawyer at the student legal services at Loyola advises Yakamoto that Thistle has established a priority over Yakamoto's leasehold interest by recording his interest first. Since few apartments are available, the only one that Yakamoto can find costs him $600 a month. Yakamoto can sue Flaherty for breach of the lease, among other actions, but the cost of hiring a lawyer for Yakamoto is prohibitive. In fact, Flaherty had calculated that by leasing to Thistle, the extra $200 a month for twelve months was worth breaching the lease contract considering that, in all likelihood, a student would not be able to afford a lawyer. If Yakamoto was in a notice or race-notice state, Thistle would likely have had actual notice of Yakamoto's occupancy of the apartment since Yakamoto had already placed his name on the mailbox and had met and talked to students in adjacent apartments.

Is the race statute a fair and ethical law? Can the race-notice and notice statutes also be exploited to someone's advantage? For example, under those two statutes, a person can allege that the person with a superior claim to the property had notice even when he did not and force him into costly litigation in an effort to settle. Under a race statute, the only relevant fact is who wins the race to record the instrument. Thus, the race statute prevents this kind of litigation and creates efficiencies that the other two statutes do not. At the same time, however, a race statute may sacrifice fairness to people such as Yakamoto for the sake of efficiency. Which do you believe is the most ethical system? Why?

ENDNOTES

1. L. Batalov, *The Russian Title Registration System for Realty and Its Effect on Foreign Investors*, 73 Washington Law Review 989 (1998).
2. S. Martin, *Adverse Possession: Practical Realities and an Unjust Enrichment Standard,* 34 Real Estate Law Journal 133 (Fall 2008).
3. 242 Miss. 491, 136 So.2d 210 (1962).
4. *Moroz v. Ransom,* 158 Misc. 443, 285 N.Y.S. 846 (1936).
5. Fla. Stat. Ann. §695.01(1) (1992). States that use a notice statute are Alabama, Arizona, Connecticut, Florida, Illinois, Iowa, Kansas, Kentucky, Maine, Massachusetts, Missouri, New Hampshire, New Mexico, Oklahoma, Rhode Island, South Carolina, Tennessee, Vermont, and West Virginia. See http://www.legalmatch.com/law-library/article/recording-acts .html (last visited April 7, 2010). See also https://www.agentxtra .net/Extranet/singlesource/content/underwriting/RecordingActs .htm for citations (last visited April 7, 2010).
6. N.Y. *Real Property Law* §291 (McKinney 1989). States that use a race-notice statute are Alaska, Arkansas, California, Colorado, District of Columbia, Georgia, Hawaii, Idaho, Indiana, Maryland, Michigan, Minnesota, Mississippi, Montana, Nebraska, Nevada, New Jersey, New York, North Dakota, Ohio (regarding mortgages, OH follows the Race statute), Oregon, Pennsylvania (regarding mortgages, PA follows Race), South

Dakota, Texas, Utah, Virginia, Washington, Wisconsin, and Wyoming. See http://www.legalmatch.com/law-library/article/recording-acts.html (last visited April 7, 2010). See also https://www.agentxtra.net/Extranet/singlesource/content/underwriting/RecordingActs.htm for citations (last visited April 7, 2010).

7. La. Rev. Stat. 9:2756 (2008).

8. D. Whitman, *Digital Recording of Real Estate Conveyances*, 32 John Marshall Law Review 227 (1999).

9. *Id.* at 233.

10. See *Minnesota Electronic Real Estate Recording: Trusted Submitter Advisory Guide* at http://www.sos.state.mn.us/docs/tsa_guide-v_1_2007_06_21.pdf (last visited August 6, 2007) and http://www.sos.state.mn.us/index.aspx?page=364 (last visited June 6, 2010).

11. R. Boyer, H. Hovencamp, and S. Kurtz, *The Law of Property* 600 (4th ed. 1991).

12. L. Sher and C. Sher, *Finding and Buying Your Place in the Country* 323 (5th ed. 2000)

13. 175 Vt. 464, 824 A.2d 531 (Sup. Ct. 2003).

14. 529 S.W.2d 1 (Mo. Sup. Ct. 1975).

15. W. Donohoe, *White Collar Crime in Real Estate Causing Industry Concern*, The Guarantor 6, 7 (May/June 1986).

16. 1 American Land Title Association, *The Title Industry: White Papers*, Ch. 5, 2–5 (1976).

17. *State v. Westfall*, 85 Minn. 437, 89 N.W. 175 (1902).

18. S. Martin, *supra* note 2 at 144-145.

19. R. Simon, *Refinancing Boom Puts New Pressure on Title Industry*, Wall Street Journal A1 (December 18, 2002).

20. *Id.* at A9.

21. L. Pleven, *Deciphering Title Insurance*, Wall Street Journal B1 (December 31, 2005). See also S. Sirmans and R. Dumm, *Title Insurance: An Historical Perspective*, 14 Journal of Real Estate Literature 293 (2006).

22. 630 N.Y.S.2d 917 (Sup. Ct. 1995).

23. E. Klayman, *Toxic Mold: A Growing Problem for the Real Estate Industry*, 31 Real Estate Law Journal 225 (2002).

24. R. Aalberts, *Fear versus Risk: Have Certain Types of Real Estate Become Economically Imperiled since 9/11?* 32 Real Estate Law Journal 104 (2003).

25. See http://www.doi.ne.gov/bulletin/cb116.pdf. (last visited April 20, 2010) for the specific provisions of TRIA's extension to December 31, 2014.

26. R. Aalberts, *Hurricane Katrina: Will New Orleans Real Estate Emerge From the Devastation?* 34 Real Estate Law Journal 269 (2005).

27. R. Jervis, *Katrina case raises costly question*, USA Today, http://www.usatoday.com/news/nation/2009-11-22-levees_N.htm, November 22, 2009 (last visited April 22, 2010).

28. K. Chu, *Insurance Costs Become 3rd Storm*, USA Today, http://www.usatoday.com/money/perfi/insurance/2007-04-02-gulf-recovery-usat_N.htm, April 2, 2007 (last visited April 22, 2010).

29. Alabama, Arizona, California, Florida, Louisiana, Mississippi, Nevada, New Jersey, Ohio, Texas, Virginia, Washington, Wisconsin, and Wyoming. See J. Kilpatrick and C. Miner, *Chinese Drywall*, A Greenfield Advisors White Paper 2, (2009).

30. See http://chinesedrywallblog.com/category/insurance-coverage for discussions about ongoing court actions concerning Chinese drywall (last accessed April 22, 2010).

31. See W. Keeton, *Insurance Law* §3.7 (1971), for a discussion of the New York Standard Coinsurance Clause. See also M. McQueen, *Housing Boom's Dark Side: Underinsurance Lurks as a Nasty Surprise*, B1 (August 26, 2006).

32. M. McQueen, *Underinsured? StarTribute.com*, http://www.startribune.com/206/story/911004.html, January 2, 2007.

33. N. Neusner, *Property Insurers Deep Score*, U.S. News and World Report 41 (June 17, 2002).

34. 240 S.W.3d 220 (Tenn. Sup. Ct. 2007).

35. 989 F.2d 1105 (9th Cir. 1992).

36. D. Eidsmore and P. Edwards, *Sex, Lies, and Insurance Coverage? Carrier Coverage Defenses for Sexually Transmitted Disease Claims*, 34 Tort and Insurance Law Journal 921 (1999).

37. See P. Kolbe et al., *Bodily Injury Liability and Residential Property Values: Canine Risks*, 34 Real Estate Law Journal 43 (2005).

38. 315 Wis. 2d 799, 762 N.W. 2d 802 (Wis. Appeals 7 2008). To see a list of state dog bite laws access: http://www.edgarsnyder.com/dog-bite/dogbite-law/index.html (last visited April 22, 2010).

39. 559 A.2d 385 (Md.App. 1989), cert. denied 566 A.2d 101 (Md. 1989).

40. This short, though complete, abstract is reprinted with permission from Flick, *Abstract and Title Practice*, Vol. 1, pp. 22–40 (2d ed. 1958). Copyright, 1958, West Publishing Company.

© MACIEJ NOSKOWSKI/iStockphoto (RF)

Financing the Real Estate Purchase

9

LEARNING OBJECTIVES

After studying Chapter 9, you should:

- Be familiar with the federal regulation of residential lending, loan application, and commitment

- Know about the various mortgage documents

- Be able to differentiate between the rights and duties of sellers and buyers after the closing

- Understand how mortgage termination occurs by payment, transfer, or foreclosure

- Be aware of installment contracts and their role in real estate finance

- Be able to explain the scope and importance of statutory liens

"Suppose one of you wants to build a tower. Will he not first sit down and estimate the cost to see if he has enough money to complete it? For if he lays the foundation and is not able to finish it, everyone who sees it will ridicule him...."

Luke 14:28–29

"Neither a borrower nor a lender be, For a loan oft loses both itself and friend, And borrowing dulls the edge of husbandry."

William Shakespeare, Hamlet, Act 1, Scene 3

Most real estate purchasers do not write a personal check to complete the purchase. Instead, buyers often obtain financing from institutional lenders.

Three types of security arrangements are frequently used, either separately or concurrently. (See Figure 9.1.)

1. The creditor might ask for security in the form of personal property—for example, an automobile owned by the debtor. As discussed in Chapter 2, Article 2 of the Uniform Commercial Code (UCC) governs how a creditor acquires a security interest in personal property. If a borrower defaults on car payments, the lender might repossess and sell the car. The proceeds from the car sale would then be applied against the debt.

2. The creditor might ask the debtor to find a third party with a good credit record (called a *surety*) who will agree to become liable along with the debtor on the loan. For example, Bill and Louise want to buy their first home instead of continuing to rent. The lender is not satisfied with their credit history and agrees to make the loan only if Bill's parents **guarantee** the loan—that is, share the responsibility for payments. This type of transaction is governed by the law of suretyship.

3. The creditor might ask for security in the form of real estate, in which case the debtor will give the creditor a promissory note and a mortgage covering the real estate. This chapter focuses on the rights and duties of the lender and borrower when a real estate **mortgage**[1] is given to secure the loan.

FIGURE 9.1
Security Arrangements

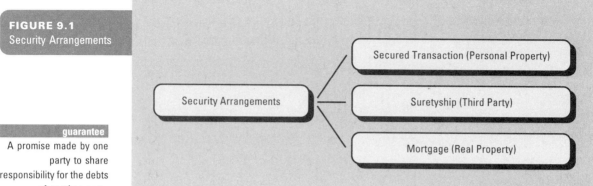

FIGURE 9.1
Security Arrangements

guarantee

A promise made by one party to share responsibility for the debts of another party.

mortgage

An interest in land created by a written instrument providing security for the performance of a duty or the payment of a debt.

promissory note

A promise or an engagement in writing to pay a specified sum at a time therein stated or on demand or at sight to a person named therein (or to his order or bearer).

debtor

One who owes a debt.

payee

The person to whom or to whose order a check, bill of exchange, or promissory note is made payable.

mortgagor

A borrower who transfers an interest in property to the mortgagee as security for the repayment of a loan.

mortgagee

A lender who receives an interest in property from the mortgagor as security for the repayment of a loan.

The law of mortgages is very complex; its origins date back to early Saxon law of medieval England, and there are many variations from state to state. To make mortgage law more manageable, this chapter defines essential note and mortgage terms, reviews federal regulation of lending, and covers a typical mortgage transaction in chronological order beginning with the loan application and concluding with repayment of the loan or foreclosure. After discussing mortgage law, the chapter examines an alternative method of financing—the installment, or land, contract—and concludes with a review of other interests, such as a mechanic's lien, that might impair the value of the mortgage. The closing of the mortgage loan is discussed in the next chapter.

Definitions

Two primary documents evidence the mortgage loan. The *first* is the debt instrument, or **promissory note**. (For a promissory note, see www.cengagebrain.com [see page xix in the Preface for instructions on how to access the free study tools for this text].) The promissory note is evidence of the indebtedness of the debtor to the lender. It is the primary "contract of obligation."[2] The person who borrows money under the note is called the **debtor**, and the person who lends money is called the **payee**.

The *second* document is the mortgage. A person who borrows money to complete a real estate purchase and gives an interest in real estate as security for the debt becomes a **mortgagor**. The party who lends money—the creditor—becomes a **mortgagee** upon taking an interest in real estate as security for the loan. Any individual may lend money and become a mortgagee, although mortgagees are usually professional lenders such as savings and loan associations, commercial banks, mortgage banks, and insurance companies. In the following discussion of a mortgage transaction, unless otherwise noted, you can assume that the purchaser is borrowing money from a savings and loan institution or from a commercial bank.

The buyer of real estate, also known as the *vendee*, becomes a debtor when she executes a promissory note promising to repay the loan amount. The same buyer-debtor is also referred to as the mortgagor when she grants the lender-mortgagee a security interest in the real estate. A mortgagor is often heard to say "I must pay my mortgage this month." Technically, this is incorrect since the mortgagor is actually paying the debt represented by the promissory note rather than the mortgage, which is simply a legal instrument used to secure the debt. The correct phrasing is "I must pay my mortgage note this month."

Under the common law, the mortgage was considered to be a transfer of title to the real estate from the mortgagor to the mortgagee. The transfer would become void if the mortgagor paid the debt as promised. A few states still consider mortgages to be title transfers, at least in regard to the form of the transaction; these states are referred to as **title theory** states. The modern view, however, is that the mortgage represents merely a lien—that is, a type of security that gives the creditor the right to have property sold and to be paid from the proceeds—rather than a transfer of title. States that view the mortgage as a security interest and not as a transfer of title are referred to as **lien theory** states. Apart from a few exceptions to be noted later, the rights and duties of the mortgagor and mortgagee are now identical under both the title and lien theories.

A **conventional first mortgage**, a mortgage given to a lender other than the seller, is a type of mortgage loan that will be featured when the typical mortgage transaction is discussed in this chapter. (For a conventional first mortgage, see www.cengagebrain.com [see page xix in the Preface for instructions on how to access the free study tools for this text].) Buyers who, among other reasons, cannot qualify for a conventional first mortgage may choose other mortgage types, such as a Department of Veterans Affairs (VA) or a Federal Housing Administration (FHA) mortgage. These important mortgages are discussed in more detail in later sections of this chapter.

In some cases, the transaction may take a different form even though the legal effect is similar to that of the conventional mortgage. One common variation is the **deed of trust**. (See www.cengagebrain.com (see page xix in the Preface for instructions on how to access the free study tools for this text)for a deed of trust form.) Under this arrangement, the trustor (debtor) deeds legal title to the property by means of a deed of trust to an independent third party (trustee) to hold for the beneficiary (creditor) as security for the loan. It is noteworthy that despite the *appearance* that legal title to the real estate is being conveyed to the trustee, in lien theory states, only a lien on the property is generally transferred to the mortgagee. When the loan is fully paid, the trustee clears the trustor's title by recording a Deed of Reconveyance. This procedure is analogous to when a car's title is conveyed to and held by a lender until the loan is paid off at which time the title instrument is re-conveyed to the owner with the lien cancelled.

With most deeds of trust, if the debtor defaults, the trustee will foreclose on the secured property and sell it on behalf of the beneficiary in a proceeding called a *power of sale*. Except at times when the real estate market is under great distress, this generally enables the creditor to recoup its investment and is typically done more quickly than a judicial foreclosure used with mortgages. This is because a nonjudicial process is used in which no court proceedings are involved.

Deeds of trust are also used to create a type of investment vehicle. A company lends money, particularly for the purchase of raw land and to finance new construction, secured by deeds of trust. The company then sells interests in the deeds of trust as real estate investments. If the debtors default, the investment is secured by the property which is then seized and sold. This offers some assurance that the investors will not lose money, unless the collateralized real estate has lost its value. This practice is sometimes referred to as "hard money lending."[3]

A *second* variation is the **purchase money mortgage**, which technically results whenever the borrowed money is used to purchase the real estate that is given as security. In many cases, however, the term is limited to transactions in which the seller deeds property to the buyer and takes a mortgage from the buyer to secure any part of the purchase price that has not yet been paid.

A *third* variation is the **reverse annuity mortgage**. Many retirees own valuable homes that they do not want to sell, but they need cash to meet daily living expenses. Because

---

title theory

A mortgage in which the mortgagor transfers title to property to the mortgagee to secure the repayment of a loan.

lien theory

The modern view of mortgage law in which the mortgagor transfers a security interest in the property to the mortgagee to secure the repayment of a loan.

conventional first mortgage

A mortgage made by a private lender that is not insured or guaranteed by a government agency.

deed of trust

An instrument serving the same function as a mortgage in which the borrower places the title to property in trust to secure the repayment of a loan owed to the beneficiary of the trust.

purchase money mortgage

A mortgage given by the buyer of real property to the seller or lender to finance the purchase price.

reverse annuity mortgage

A mortgage, generally used by elderly homeowners, in which money is borrowed in the form of monthly payments and secured by the equity in the home.

they have little income, they do not qualify for a traditional mortgage. A possible solution is a reverse annuity mortgage, where the homeowner, who must be at least sixty-two to qualify for the FHA-insured mortgage, receives a monthly payment from a bank for as long as the individual remains in the home. In this scenario, the bank receives a mortgage on the home and the homeowner receives money in the form of a loan based on her age. With the money, the homeowner can do what she wishes including paying off an existing mortgage. A 62-year-old, for instance, would qualify for a loan worth 57 percent of the home's value, while a 94-year-old could get up to 85 percent. Principal and interest are not due until the homeowner sells the property or dies. If the amount due at sale or death exceeds the value of the property, the FHA will cover the loss under a program that went into effect in 1991.[4]

As a result of abuses by some lenders, the U.S. Department of Housing and Urban Development (HUD) now has disclosure requirements for these mortgages and has aggressively pursued those individuals who have victimized elderly homeowners typically living on fixed incomes.

The reverse annuity mortgage is expected to be an important source of retirement money in coming years as the huge baby boom generation retires and taps into the equity in their homes. Still, these mortgages are not suitable for everyone. As a rule, reverse mortgages impose on the homeowner substantial transactions costs and fees, amounting to as much as 10 percent of the property's value over the life of the loan.[5]

A *fourth* variation is the creation of a mortgage that is second (or even third, fourth, etc.) to a first mortgage. In the event of default and foreclosure of the first mortgage, the first mortgage will be paid off, followed by the second mortgage, with anything remaining going to the owner. If the second mortgage alone is foreclosed, the rights of the first mortgagee are not impaired; and a purchaser at the foreclosure sale may take title subject to the first mortgage or be required to pay off the first mortgage to clear title to the property.

A *final* variation of the regular mortgage is the **equitable mortgage**. In many cases, a court in equity will treat a transaction as a mortgage even though the documents do not meet the legal requirements (to be discussed shortly); such a mortgage is called an *equitable mortgage*. Often a court will create an equitable mortgage to protect a creditor. For example, if a debtor signs a note that states that it is secured by a real estate mortgage but no real estate mortgage is formally drawn up, a court will hold that an equitable mortgage has been created because of the intention of the parties expressed in the note.[6]

In other cases, an equitable mortgage will be declared for the protection of the debtor. This happens most frequently when a debtor deeds her real estate to a creditor with no mention in the deed that the conveyance is intended only as security on the loan. If a court determines that the parties did in fact intend the deed as security, the creditor's interest will be only that of a mortgagee and not as the owner of the property, and the debtor will be allowed to recover the property by paying off the debt.

In determining the intention of the parties, courts focus on *three* factors:

1. Did the grantor owe money to the grantee at the time of conveyance and thereafter?
2. Is the land worth considerably more than the amount of the loan given in payment for the land?
3. Did the grantor continue to act as owner after the conveyance? To answer this question, courts stress the grantor's continued possession of the property and the grantor's payment of taxes and insurance premiums.[7] As the next Oregon case reveals, proving that an equitable mortgage exists enables a debtor to retain title to his property but he must still pay off the mortgage debt.

equitable mortgage
A lien that is placed on real property to secure the payment of money based on the clear intent of the parties but that lacks the essential features of a legal mortgage.

A CASE IN POINT

In *Leathers v. Peterson*[8] the grantor, who could not obtain a loan elsewhere because of his drinking and spending habits, borrowed between $10,000 and $24,000 from a friend who was also his accountant. When the grantor deeded property worth $40,000 to his friend, the court held that the deed was really a mortgage because of the disparity between the amount of the advance and the value of the property.

Federal Regulation of Residential Lending

fair lending laws
Federal legislation created to outlaw various forms of discrimination in real estate lending practices.

An expanding body of federal legislation regulates the business of mortgage lending. This legislation can be grouped into two categories. The *first*, known as **fair lending laws**, addresses lending discrimination based on the borrower's personal characteristics or the location of the collateral. A *second* set of federal legislation focuses on the disclosure to the borrower of loan terms and procedures. A *third* set of laws, discussed later in the chapter, provide other protections for borrowers, such as the outlawing of prepayment penalties. These state and federal laws are designed generally to protect borrowers who are purchasing homes—often a person's largest lifetime investment. Commercial lending is not as regulated as residential lending and is typically the end result of intense negotiations between sophisticated parties, such as banks and commercial developers who do not need the protections afforded to homebuyers. The differences between laws governing residential and commercial lending practices are noted throughout the chapter.

Fair Lending Laws

Fair Housing Act
Title VIII of the Civil Rights Act of 1968, which prohibits discrimination in housing based on race, color, religion, sex, national origin, disability, or family status.

Fair Housing Act   The **Fair Housing Act**,[9] discussed in Chapter 6, is a threshold law that prohibits discrimination in housing finance.

Equal Credit Opportunity Act
Federal law that prohibits discrimination in credit decisions based on an applicant's gender, marital status, religion, race, color, national origin, age, or receipt of welfare.

Equal Credit Opportunity Act   The **Equal Credit Opportunity Act**[10] provides that a lender may *not* refuse a loan because of a person's gender, marital status, religion, race, color, national origin, age, or receipt of welfare if the person is eligible for credit in all other respects. This means, for example, that lenders cannot question applicants about their plans to have children in the future, cannot require additional cosigners because the applicant is a single woman, and cannot refuse to put an account in the names of both husband and wife. In addition, within thirty days of the creditor's receipt of the completed application for credit, the creditor must notify loan applicants of any "adverse action" taken. The loan applicant is entitled to a timely explanation of the reasons for the creditor's adverse action.[11]

Community Reinvestment Act
Federal law that establishes certain recordkeeping, reporting, and loan requirements for financial institutions.

Community Reinvestment Act   Like the Home Mortgage Disclosure Act discussed in the next section, the **Community Reinvestment Act (CRA)** forces lenders to abandon a practice known as **redlining**. The term originates from the alleged practice by some lenders and insurance firms of mapping out risky areas with boundaries of red ink. Critics of redlining claim that this practice discriminates on the basis of race and contributes to the decline of inner cities. Many lending institutions deny that redlining is practiced. Opponents of the prohibition against redlining argue that lenders should have the right to select their customers on the basis of traditional credit standards and should not be forced to accept real estate as security that does not meet those standards.

redlining
Occurs when lenders refuse to make mortgage loans or impose stricter mortgage terms in certain neighborhoods.

The CRA[12] requires financial institutions to make loans in each community in which they take deposits. The Act

> requires each of the four federal financial agencies ... to assess an institution's record of "meeting credit needs of its community, including low- and moderate-income neighborhoods, consistent with safe and sound operations" and to consider an institution's CRA record when evaluating its application for a deposit facility or other action needing regulatory approval. These agency ratings are public and bring community groups and advocates into the political and policy process.[13]

To accomplish the Act's goal, an agency reviews an institution's lending record when an application is filed with the agency (for example, to open a new branch or to merge with another institution).[14] Activist groups and neighborhood organizations also scrutinize a bank's loan practices to ensure that they are complying with the CRA.

The CRA was targeted by some critics during the 2007–2009 recession and subprime mortgage meltdown for having exerted too much pressure on banks since the 1990s to lend to unqualified borrowers in order to avoid a confrontation with government regulators. CRA supporters have responded by displaying data that show that only a very small percentage of subprime loans were originated by banks subject to the Act.[15]

Home Mortgage Disclosure Act
Federal law requiring financial institutions to furnish the federal government with information about loan applicants and their approval rate by race, gender, and income.

Home Mortgage Disclosure Act The **Home Mortgage Disclosure Act**[16] requires mortgage lenders to disclose data on the location of their mortgage applications and loans. In addition, the race, gender, and income of applicants and borrowers are subject to disclosure. The reasoning behind the Act's creation is that analysis of this data can disclose "the statistical smoking gun that signals discriminatory practices, whether intentional or not."[17]

Home Ownership and Equity Protection Act
An amendment to the Truth in Lending Act created to prevent predatory lending practices.

Home Ownership and Equity Protection Act The **Home Ownership and Equity Protection Act** (HOEPA), enacted in 1994 as an amendment to the Truth in Lending Act (TILA), discussed in the next section, is designed to prevent various illegal and unethical practices collectively known as **predatory lending**. Many states, with North Carolina becoming the first in 1999, have also adopted similar, often stricter, laws.

Beginning in the 1990s and early 2000s, more flexible and lax mortgage lending policies, particularly in the subprime mortgage market, combined with very high employment rates due to a vibrant economy enabled many people who would previously not have qualified for a mortgage loan to finance the purchase of homes for the first time. Unfortunately, the benefits of greater home ownership spawned unscrupulous lending activities by some who preyed on people who were often ill-equipped economically and often not sufficiently sophisticated to understand the complexities of real estate finance.

predatory lending
Deceptive loan application and closing practices that take advantage of borrowers who lack sufficient sophistication, economic stability, and knowledge to protect themselves from illegal and unethical lending practices.

For example, many of these borrowers, due to less than perfect credit histories, spotty employment records, and little cash for a down payment, were eligible only for subprime mortgages. Other borrowers, who might have qualified for prime mortgages, were often persuaded to take out a subprime loan, sometimes with adjustable rates, by brokers and lenders who might benefit in some way, such as earning new and higher origination fees, a yield spread premium (YSP), discussed below, and other fees. To make matters worse, subprime loans and the risks that they may impose appear to have had a disparate impact on minorities, with blacks and Hispanics nearly 3 and 2.6 times more likely to receive these loans respectively.[18]

Generally, subprime loans carry a risk premium of several percentage points higher than prime mortgages, which are reserved for borrowers with nearly perfect credit ratings. Although subprime mortgages are not illegal (and can, if carried out honestly and properly, provide a useful financing vehicle for many who could not otherwise qualify for a home loan), HOEPA was enacted to scrutinize the more extreme practices.

HOEPA is triggered in one of the following ways:

- *When the annual percentage rate (APR) at consummation of the loan exceeds the yield for comparable Treasury securities by more than eight percentage points (ten percentage points for second mortgages).*
- *When the total points and fees paid by the consumer exceed the greater of 8 percent of the loan amount or a set dollar amount of $579 (2010). (These are the same for a second mortgage.)*[19] *The set dollar amount is adjusted every year based on the consumer price index.*

In addition to harming many individual borrowers, subprime and predatory lending practices in general also caused major worldwide economic problems in recent years when investors purchased bonds and other mortgage-backed securities composed of these risky loans. The loans, when originated, were often based on questionable lending standards as well as ratings some critics maintain were manipulated by Wall Street investment banks who exerted undue influence on ratings agencies such as Moody's and Standard and Poor's. Indeed, of AAA-rated subprime mortgage-backed securities issued in 2006, 93 percent were later downgraded to junk status (noninvestment or speculative grade bonds). This caused a liquidity crisis in the credit markets that bankrupted a large number of subprime lenders and later helped set off a worldwide credit crisis.[20]

Predatory lending practices are not limited to just subprime loan practices, however, and in fact vary greatly and evolve quickly, limited only by the perpetrators' imaginations. Predatory lenders, for example, have employed former used-car salesmen to peddle loans door-to-door with highly structured sales pitches creating the impression, particularly among the elderly and less sophisticated, that they are professionals working in the borrowers' best interests.[21]

One common form of predatory lending is financing the payment of single-payment credit life insurance over the life of the mortgage. Normally the premium is paid in full when the policy is taken out. Another practice is inducing a borrower to refinance, called "flipping" a mortgage, within a short period of time, resulting in higher points and fees and sometimes foreclosure. Other examples include steep prepayment penalties (discussed later in the chapter), exorbitant balloon payments, negative amortization, high appraisal costs, and illegal yield-spread premiums, which are sometimes kicked back to the broker who originated the loan against the borrower's interests

Possibly the most egregious form of predatory lending is known as *equity stripping*. The lender purposely creates a scenario in which the unknowing borrower is destined to default on the loan. It can arise, for example, when a lender persuades an often trusting and unsophisticated homeowner into financing a loan for the entire amount of the equity at a very high interest rate or convinces him to use a balloon note with the expectation that the homeowner will ultimately fail to make payments. The lender will then take the house in a foreclosure sale and capture the person's equity.[22]

In *Bankers Trust of California v. Payne*, a creditor loaned money to a seventy-four-year-old man to reface his home. The debt was secured by a mortgage on the man's home. If the lender violated HOEPA when it executed the loan, can the violation be used by the mortgagor as a defense for his failure to pay the loan? In the case on page 353, the court discusses the issue.

END OF CHAPTER CASE

The *Bankers Trust of California v. Payne* case exemplifies a sad but growing problem among older homeowners, exacerbated during the recent deep recession. Many of these homeowners, living on fixed incomes, were conned into refinancing their homes, some of which were not even encumbered by mortgage debt and were often the source of the owner's retirement income through reverse mortgages, a topic discussed earlier. Often these loans were "no doc" loans (no proven income was required) with adjustable rates used by mortgage brokers who were aggressively trying to originate loans to pocket commissions. When rates ratcheted up, these mortgages went into foreclosure and the elderly mortgagors were forced out. The lenders benefited from the fees generated and in some cases skimmed the equity by placing the only bid and buying the foreclosed properties.[23]

In 2010 Congress passed the Dodd-Frank Wall Street Reform and Consumer Protection Act (Dodd-Frank Act) This new law, which will be discussed throughout this chapter, directs various agencies, including the new Bureau of Consumer Financial Protection, to draft new regulations to further combat the practices, including changes in the triggers and thresholds to better protect consumers from high cost mortgages, discussed above, as well as new and more severe penalties for violations.

Disclosures of Loan Terms and Procedures

Truth in Lending Act The federal **Truth in Lending Act**[24] (TILA) requires lenders to make mandatory disclosures when advertising the terms of a consumer loan or when advising individual borrowers of loan costs. (For a Truth in Lending form, see www.cengagebrain.com [see page xix in the Preface for instructions on how to access the free study tools for this text].) It is implemented by **Regulation Z**.

The *four* major elements of mandatory disclosure are as follows:

1. The **finance charge**. This is the total dollar amount paid for credit, which includes any charge payable directly or indirectly by the consumer and imposed directly or indirectly by the creditor as an incident to or as a condition of the extension of credit. It does not include any charge of a type payable in a comparable cash transaction. Thus, in effect, any amount the borrower pays to get the loan that is required by the creditor should be included in the finance charge even if it is paid to a third party.[25]

   Although the finance charge is broadly defined, there are some exceptions. For example, in determining whether a lender should have included courier charges imposed by a title company in the lender's finance charge disclosure, a court noted that the title company was wearing "two hats"[26]—the hat of the lender's closing agent and the hat of the title insurer interested in removing prior liens. The court held that the courier fee need not be disclosed "when the title company is making its own decisions on how to carry out its responsibility as settlement agent at closing … even if the lender has a perfectly clear idea of what the title company is going to do."[27]

2. The **annual percentage rate** (APR). This rate is higher than the interest rate alone because the APR includes all fees and charges. It measures the cost of credit as a yearly rate. Special disclosure requirements for variable rate mortgages include disclosure of when the rate can be increased, what limitations exist on the amount of increase, and whether the loan includes a conversion option to a fixed-rate instrument.

3. The **amount financed**. This is defined as "the cash available from the loan to the borrower for use in the transaction."[28]

4. The **mandatory right of rescission**. When borrowers use their residence as security for a consumer loan such as a second mortgage (the right does not apply to first

---

Truth in Lending Act
Federal law regulating the disclosure of certain credit terms to enable a borrower to make the most favorable credit decision.

Regulation Z
Regulations issued by the Federal Reserve Board pursuant to the Truth in Lending Act entrusting the agency to supervise all banks in the Federal Reserve System and to ensure their compliance with the Act.

finance charge
Any charge for the extension of credit.

annual percentage rate
The cost of credit according to its yearly rate.

amount financed
Cash available to the borrower from the loan for use in the transaction.

mandatory right of rescission
A borrower's right under the Truth in Lending Act to rescind, within three days, certain kinds of loans secured by the debtor's home.

mortgages) to finance home improvements, college expenses, or lines of credit, the Act requires that they have *three* days after closing to cancel the credit transaction. The Act requires lenders to notify borrowers of this right of rescission. The typical result of the mandatory right of rescission is that refinancing transactions are held in escrow (and the documents not recorded) until after the rescission period. The major exception, as mentioned, to the three-day right of rescission is when the borrower finances his residence with a note and first mortgage. Lenders who fail to disclose the mandatory disclosures must pay civil damages up to $2,000.[29]

Does a borrower have the burden of proving reliance damages when the lender fails to disclose both the finance charge and the annual percentage rate in the loan documents? In *Smith v. Gold Country Lenders* on page 355, the court rules on the issue.

END OF CHAPTER CASE

TILA also regulates advertisements by lenders. An advertisement containing certain loan information "triggers" a legal duty to make TILA disclosures. For example, lenders commonly state the amount of the down payment ("10 percent down" or "90 percent financing"), the payment amount ("monthly payments of $600"), the number of payments ("80 monthly payments and you pay off the mortgage"), the repayment period ("15 years to pay"), or the amount of any finance charge ("financing costs less than $400"). If any of those statements appear in the advertisement, the lender must disclose (1) the amount or percentage of the down payment; (2) the terms of the repayment; and (3) the APR, which must be spelled out in full. Statements such as "Easy monthly payments" and "Low down payment accepted" are considered sales talk, or puffery; therefore, they do not trigger the disclosure requirements.[30]

It is noteworthy that the new Dodd-Frank Act adds significant amendments to TILA including borrower qualifications for loans.

Real Estate Settlement Procedures Act
Federal law that regulates the disclosure of closing costs in advance and prohibits kickbacks to professionals involved in real estate closings.

Real Estate Settlement Procedures Act The **Real Estate Settlement Procedures Act** of 1974 (RESPA) was the result of a 1972 study by HUD. The study concluded that on a national level, settlement costs for purchasing a home ranged from less than 1 percent to 10 percent of the purchase price. The study also discovered that kickbacks and undisclosed commissions were paid to professionals involved in real estate closings. On the basis of the study, Congress found, in Section 2 of the Act, "that significant reforms in the real estate settlement process are needed to insure that consumers throughout the nation are provided with greater and more timely information on the nature and costs of the settlement process and are protected from unnecessarily high settlement charges caused by certain abusive practices that have developed in some areas of the country."

RESPA applies to transactions in which all of the following take place:

1. The loan will be secured either by a first or subordinate lien on residential property.
2. The residential property contains or will contain a one- to four-family structure.
3. The lender is federally related, the lender is a creditor under the Consumer Credit Protection Act, or the loan is federally related.[31] RESPA's requirements do not apply to cash, seller-financed, private investor, or commercial transactions.

Three reforms to achieve the Act's goals were included in the original Act with significant new revisions taking effect in 2010. *First*, to provide more effective advance disclosure of settlement costs, the Act requires the lender to give the borrower a copy of a HUD guide to settlement costs no later than three days after the loan originator, generally the lender or mortgage broker, receives the borrower's loan application. This booklet provides advice on how to shop for professional services and summarizes home buyers' rights and obligations.[32] At the same time, the lender is required to provide the applicant with a good faith estimate (GFE) of settlement service charges. The applicant also has the right, upon her request, to inspect a Uniform Settlement Statement that itemizes all charges imposed on the borrower one business day preceding the settlement or closing of the loan.

Second, the Act states that people who give or accept kickbacks or referral fees are liable for civil damages and are subject to maximum criminal penalties of one year in prison and a fine of $10,000 per violation. Also, a settlement services provider that is handling the closing cannot require the buyer to purchase title insurance from a particular company, but can list companies from which a borrower might choose. The new 2010 provisions also state that the cost of title insurance cannot exceed 10 percent of the estimates provided in the Uniform Settlement Statement.

Third, most lenders require borrowers, generally those who have a down payment of less than 20 percent, to deposit funds in a reserve, impound, or escrow account to cover future insurance and tax charges the lender pays on the property. These funds are deposited monthly with the mortgage payment, with each monthly escrow payment representing approximately one-twelfth of the annual charges. Under RESPA, the amount the borrower pays into the escrow account at closing is limited to a sum sufficient to make the required payments due by the date of the first mortgage payment plus an extra cushion not to exceed two monthly escrow payments. Lenders must also perform an escrow account analysis yearly and must notify the borrower if there is a shortage and provide a refund if there is an excess. Although not required by RESPA, several states require lenders to pay interest on funds deposited in escrow accounts. RESPA's impact on closing procedures, including the significant new reforms created in 2010, is discussed further in Chapter 10.

Loan Application and Commitment

mortgage broker

A broker who, for a fee, places loans with investors but does not service the loans.

The buyer's first step in obtaining financing to complete the real estate purchase is to deliver a loan application to the creditor. The buyer can consider loan terms available from commercial banks, savings banks, mortgage bankers, and mortgage brokers. A **mortgage broker** does not lend money; instead he or she "is a specialist in compiling the financial details"[33] of the real estate loan along with information about the borrower and presenting this loan package to potential lenders. The mortgage broker is typically compensated by receiving a percentage of the lender's origination fee for the loan as well as, but not always, the YSP discussed later in this chapter. Courts have held that the broker owes a fiduciary duty to both the lender and the borrower, although in recent years, the subprime mortgage crisis revealed that brokers rarely gave or requested from loan applicants all of the information they needed to make informed decisions.[34] In fact, brokers who do hold themselves out as experts to help borrowers in evaluating the merits of various kinds of mortgages and informing them concerning the best loan, but then fail to do so, are held liable for breaching fiduciary duties.[35] Mortgage brokers have also been heavily criticized for harming investors in the secondary market who purchased mortgages they originated which were subsequently bundled up in debt instruments that were doomed for failure, a topic discussed on pages 320–321 "Ethical and Public Policy Issues."

Still, home buyers, can benefit because of their brokers' access to multiple lenders and their knowledge of different financing options from different sources as long as the broker is acting in their best interests. In all mortgage loans a **yield spread** exists which is the spread or difference between the interest rate charged to the borrower and the market rate. A yield spread premium (YSP), an amount above the yield spread, is also charged sometimes for the extra services mentioned above. All too often, however, mortgage brokers have acted in their own self interests since the YSP, along with the origination fee, is how they are compensated. One of Congress's aims in the Dodd-Frank Act, is to eliminate the financial incentives, such as a broker being paid when he originates a higher interest rate loan or YSP. The ethical and public policy issues surrounding the YSP are discussed next.

yield spread

The difference between the interest rate paid by the consumer and the market interest rate.

ETHICAL AND PUBLIC POLICY ISSUES

Is It Unethical for a Mortgage Broker to Bring His Client to a Lender Who Charges a Premium On the Yield Spread?

Many critics for years have claimed that charging a premium on top of the yield spread, or yield spread premium (YSP) can, in certain circumstances, result in illegal and unethical practices by brokers and lenders. Problem 10 at the end of the chapter includes a discussion of the practice and how the recently passed Dodd-Frank Act introduces new legal, ethical, and public policy provisions to address the issue.

The Dodd-Frank Act now requires that all mortgage originators, both brokers and those "retail" originators working within a lending institution, must be licensed and qualified and be registered in the Nationwide Mortgage Licensing System and Registry. Before the Act, licensing was regulated under state laws.

In addition to originating loans, mortgage brokers will often *service* the loans they broker on behalf of the mortgage note holder. This can occur whether the mortgage is retained in the portfolio of the mortgage banker who made the loan or the note is sold into the secondary mortgage, a topic discussed below. This normally involves collecting the monthly payments and maintaining the escrow accounts to make certain that the property is insured and that the property taxes were paid.

The Great Recession of 2007–2009 revealed a problem regarding servicers. For example, servicers are often paid extra fees both when borrowers fall behind in their payments and also for handling foreclosures. On the other hand, if a workout between the distressed borrower and lender is achieved—which often results in the lowering of the principal and interest payments—a servicer is paid less. This resulted in servicers being incentivized *not* to engage in workouts with defaulting mortgagors. Compounding the problem, servicers work for those who hold the debt instruments and notes and therefore have a fiduciary duty to advance the interests of those parties; and foreclosure can often be preferable to a workout for them.

To counter the disincentive to fashion a workout, various new federal and state laws, including the Home Affordable Modification Program (HAMP), encourage and sometimes require servicers to engage in mediation with distressed mortgagors, albeit the results have been decidedly mixed. HAMP, under its provision titled the Helping Families Save Their Homes Act of 2009, also confers a safe harbor from civil liability to residential mortgage loan servicers and loan originators who engage in loss mitigation efforts.

A **mortgage banker,** unlike the mortgage broker, actually funds the loan. "Mortgage brokers arrange mortgages; mortgage bankers actually originate them. In fact, one-third

mortgage banker

A banker who originates, sells, and services mortgage loans.

of conventional residential loans and three-fourths of government-underwritten loans in the country are originated by mortgage bankers."[36]

Life insurance companies, credit unions, and consumer credit companies also provide financing. In addition, the seller may be willing to take back a purchase money mortgage for a portion of the sales price to finance the purchase or to take a mortgage lien subordinate to the first mortgage as a down payment.

The borrower typically selects not only the type of lender but also the type of mortgage loan. Like any other consumer product, mortgage loans can vary substantially in their form and price. Rates for different lenders' loan packages are typically published in the business section of local newspapers and on the Internet. In fact, mortgage brokerage and lending over the Internet is common. Some commentators see this as a positive development for creating greater competition and efficiencies that should result in lower mortgage origination costs and lower interest rates. Mortgage brokers are able to do this in large part because mortgage loan applications can now be electronically verified, with credit checks and appraisals also being done online, although the Dodd-Frank Act now requires so-called high cost mortgages (those with higher than normal fees) to be appraised physically. The mortgage documents, which are computer-generated, can then be given to the borrower once the loan is approved. One particularly intriguing development is the borrower posting his mortgage application on the Internet. Brokers or lenders then tender an offer to loan money to the borrower that will, as two real estate experts have noted, "… result in lenders seeking borrowers, not vice versa."[37]

Mortgages, as was previously noted, can differ significantly not only in their price but also in their form and material terms that bind the mortgagor. For example, the Federal Housing Administration, operating under HUD, insures loans to qualified borrowers who may not otherwise have the means to buy a house. An **FHA mortgage loan**, like conventional mortgages, is generally obtained through mortgage bankers, not directly from the FHA. Moreover, the FHA must agree to insure the lender before the mortgage is issued since these loans are often made with small down payments and can be risky. For example, the FHA requires only a 3.5 percent down payment.

To retain its reputation in the mortgage industry, the FHA must protect itself and the borrower. To do so, the FHA has set various criteria for loans in addition to the down payment requirement, for example, the maximum dollar amounts for the loan, construction standards required of the home, and the creditworthiness of the borrower. It is noteworthy that the number of borrowers applying for FHA mortgage loans expanded greatly during the Great Recession of 2007–2009 since it was one of the few sources of capital for home loans that existed after many banks either collapsed or were reluctant to make home loans.

A **VA mortgage loan**, which is not insured but guaranteed, is only for qualified military veterans. Under a VA loan, the eligible veteran may not have to make a down payment as long as the property appraises for the entire amount of the loan.

With both VA and FHA loans, the terms of the mortgage and note, such as the interest rate and discount points, are established by government regulations. These two loans should be contrasted with a conventional mortgage loan, which is the featured mortgage throughout this chapter. A conventional mortgage is executed in favor of a private lender and therefore is not insured or guaranteed by the government. Since conventional mortgages are not as regulated (and the lender is therefore not as protected from the risk of a default), the terms are usually more beneficial to the lender, with a higher down payment, higher interest rate, and so on, although competition among private lenders has often been intense. As stated previously, until the meltdown in the subprime mortgage market starting in 2007, lenders tended to lend more to borrowers with questionable credit backgrounds. Since then, standards have been significantly toughened to prevent such a reoccurrence. The Dodd-Frank Act of 2010 also requires that lenders make a good faith

FHA mortgage loan
A mortgage loan that is insured by the Fair Housing Administration.

VA mortgage loan
A mortgage loan that is guaranteed by the Department of Veterans Affairs.

effort to determine whether borrowers can afford to pay the mortgage note, while borrowers must provide proof of their income and other sources of wealth.

Because conventional lenders do not want to depend *only* on the collateralized real estate to decrease their risks, they typically protect themselves by requiring a borrower who puts less than a 20 percent down payment on the loan to buy **private mortgage insurance** (PMI). This insurance is payable to the lender if the borrower defaults. However, for all home mortgages created on or after July 29, 1999, the PMI must be automatically terminated once mortgagors pay their mortgage balances down to at least 78 percent of their home's original purchase price. Once the mortgage balance drops to 80 percent of the original value, the homeowners also may have the insurance removed, but it must be requested. Moreover, mortgagors must be advised of their rights at the closing and once a year thereafter. Still, due to the increased risk, mortgages obtained with "high-risk" or subprime loans, homeowners who have not kept their payments current for a year prior to the time of termination, and mortgagors who have liens placed on their property must still pay PMI regardless of their mortgage balances.

A law passed in 2007 also allows certain homeowners to deduct PMI from their taxes. One of the main reasons for the tax break was to discourage borrowers from taking out so-called "piggy-back" mortgages. Under this arrangement, borrowers finance the first mortgage with 20 percent down to avoid paying the PMI, but after the closing would use the equity to finance a second mortgage or line of credit. The second mortgages, often subprime and with variable interest rates, were also seen as contributors to the recent subprime mortgage crisis.[38] With a significant tightening of lender practices since the crisis, piggy-back loans are now very rare.

Up to this point, the discussion of mortgages assumed a fixed rate of interest. Of course, different pricing assumptions are at play with **adjustable rate mortgages** (ARMs). The interest rates for this loan vehicle, which is used in conventional and FHA-insured mortgage transactions but not in VA mortgage transactions, vary over the life of the loan under terms agreed to at closing. For example, the interest rates for ARMs are indexed based on one-, three-, or five-year Treasury securities. These loans contain a margin, typically capped, that is set at an amount between the contract and index rates. There is also an adjustment period that can vary (e.g., every six months or every year) during which time the index rate can be changed. Thus, a borrower with a short-term index, a shorter adjustment period, and a higher cap can expect more volatility and greater potential risk. ARMs, especially those with short-term indices and adjustment periods, were blamed for some of the unprecedented foreclosures that occurred during the 2007–2009 subprime mortgage crisis.

Seduced by the lower initial monthly payments and with the assumption that their homes would appreciate in value, many homeowners chose a type of ARM called "Option ARMs." This instrument also created financial problems that helped trigger the mortgage crisis and meltdown in 2007. These instruments offered borrowers the choice of how they wanted to pay their monthly notes: interest only, on an adjustable rate, or with a fixed rate. Many opted for the interest only ARMs (often with low or nonexistent down payments) The downside risk, however, was that if the market did not appreciate, homeowners would never accumulate equity since only interest and therefore no principal was being paid. Unfortunately for many, interest rates later adjusted upwards. When this occurred, many homeowners could no longer afford to pay their notes. Some of the properties went into foreclosure, flooding the market with excess housing inventory, which then caused home values to depreciate further. The Dodd-Frank Act of 2010 requires that lenders who make such risky loans and then sell the loan into the secondary market must now own no less than five percent of the loan to assure that they too share some risk, that is, have some "skin in the game."[39]

private mortgage insurance

Default insurance on conventional loans provided by private insurers.

adjustable rate mortgage

A mortgage loan that allows the interest rate to change at specific intervals over the maturity of the loan.

Table 9.1 on page 322 describes the traditional fixed-rate mortgage, the adjustable rate mortgage, and other loan structures including balloon mortgages, wraparounds, and loan assumptions.[40]

Once the borrower has evaluated different loan options, she will typically file loan applications for her preferred loan program. Although not always the case in recent years, lenders since the residential mortgage meltdown evaluate much more closely the borrower's personal financial information, such as the borrower's earning capacity and credit rating, to ensure that the borrower has sufficient financial strength to make the payments that would be due under the promissory note. As mentioned earlier, the new Dodd-Frank Act of 2010 also makes this legally mandatory.

The borrower who is tempted to exaggerate her earnings or present a rosy picture of her financial status on the loan application should think twice. It is a federal offense to provide false statements on a bank's loan documents, an offense that was commonplace until the recent residential mortgage meltdown.[41]

The lender also evaluates the proposed collateral for the loan through an appraisal to determine whether the security for the loan is adequate. If the bank is satisfied with the applicant's credit rating and is convinced that the real estate offers sufficient security, the bank will send the applicant a **commitment** that sets forth the terms of the loan and the conditions that must be met before closing. If the loan application is legally considered an offer, the commitment is regarded as the bank's acceptance. As a result, the applicant immediately becomes liable for a commitment fee, which the bank charges for holding the mortgage funds for a specific time—three months, for instance. If, on the other hand, the loan application is drafted as an invitation to make an offer, both the applicant and the bank view the commitment as an offer that the applicant must accept within a certain time period—for example, ten days.

The lender's commitment to make the mortgage loan is typically subject to conditions. These conditions may include, for example, an appraisal of the property for a minimum designated amount or copies of the borrower's tax return.

A commitment fee is also due whether or not a loan is eventually made. For instance, in the Massachusetts case of *Weiner v. Salem Five Cents Savings Bank*, the defendant banks committed themselves to lend a developer a specified sum in exchange for a commitment fee of $54,000. When, through no fault of the banks, the loan was never made, the banks were allowed to retain the developer's fee.[42]

Borrowers have increasingly asserted that lenders should be held liable for the borrower's losses resulting from mortgage transactions. Lender liability is a special concern in the loan application process because borrowers may incur large losses on the basis of oral promises allegedly made by lenders. As a result many states have laws, often as part of their statute of frauds, which require that real estate loans must be in writing to be enforceable.[43]

commitment
A bank's acceptance of a loan application.

ETHICAL AND PUBLIC POLICY ISSUES

Is It Unethical to Loan Money to Risky Borrowers?

In the late 1990s, lenders began to originate subprime mortgages to borrowers with imperfect credit and low down payments. The attitude among mortgage bankers and the secondary market was that subprime lending was good business as long as borrowers paid a higher interest rate to reflect their higher risk of default. Homeownership began to increase during this time. However, mortgage brokers who originated these loans not only overlooked obvious credit problems but also did not require certain documents to prove income; and they usually did not explain to often unsophisticated borrowers the

continues

continued

consequences of some key terms of these mortgages, many of which would later affect the borrowers' ability to repay. For example, many of these mortgages were adjustable rate in which monthly payments were based on a low-interest "teaser" rate but adjusted higher if interest rates increased. These brokers, who often did not owe the borrowers fiduciary duties, were more concerned about closing the deals to receive their commissions than they were with the rights of the borrowers. Once the mortgages were originated, they were typically sold in the secondary mortgage market and securitized. Investors gladly bought these riskier securities that had high yields and were secured by real estate. By 2007, interest rates did increase and borrowers had to pay more each month. Those individuals who were unable to pay defaulted on the loans and lost their homes through foreclosure. With added housing inventory, house prices plummeted across the United States. As the value of the mortgage-backed securities decreased, investors sold them, causing the American and world securities exchanges to experience uncertainty and volatility. Moreover, capital dried up for home loans, causing a liquidity crisis. Many economists claim that the mortgage meltdown was the catalyst for the Great Recession of 2007–2009.

What should have been done differently to avoid these serious problems? Should brokers disclose more and be required to act as fiduciaries to borrowers? In 2010, Congress passed the Dodd-Frank Act which outlaws lenders and brokers from steering potential buyers to loans with predatory characteristics. Should the federal government have left it more to the market to make these changes? Will these significant new laws unduly burden the lending industry resulting in higher priced mortgages? Is it unethical that these new, more stringent standards may deprive people who at one time had the chance to buy a home from buying now?[44]

Environmental Law

Environmental law has a major impact on lenders. Environmental problems can jeopardize the value of the lender's collateral. Environmental law also can impose risks to the lender in taking title to the collateral through foreclosure. Environmental law is discussed in more detail in Chapter 14.

The Comprehensive Environmental Response, Compensation and Liability Act (also known as Superfund and CERCLA) created an exclusion from liability in a 1996 amendment—the secured lender exclusion—designed to protect lenders who do not participate in the management of mortgaged property. Despite the exclusion, lenders continue to be guarded in the loan application process and now require the borrower to complete an environmental risk assessment at both the application and foreclosure stages as well as buying environmental liability insurance before they approve the loan.[45]

The Mortgage Documents

The closing of the mortgage transaction usually is accomplished concurrently with the closing of the real estate transaction. Although the number of documents executed at the closing (also called the closing of escrow) has proliferated, the mortgagor signs two primary documents at closing: a note and a mortgage (described in further detail later in the chapter). The mortgagee then disburses the loan, less mortgage closing costs, and the loan is used by the borrower to complete the purchase. The closing process and associated costs, including mortgage closing costs, are the subject of Chapter 10.

The Note

In signing a note at the closing, the mortgagor promises to pay a specified principal amount plus interest on or before a certain date. In most cases, a mortgage without a note is worthless because it secures nothing. However, a note that is not secured by a

TABLE 9.1 Alternative Financing Techniques

TYPE	DESCRIPTION	CONSIDERATIONS
Fixed-Rate Mortgage	Fixed interest rate, usually long-term; equal monthly payments of principal and interest until debt is paid in full.	Offers stability and long-term tax advantages. Interest rates may be higher than other types of financing. New fixed rates are rarely assumable.
Fifteen-Year Mortgage	Fixed interest rate. Requires down payment or monthly payments higher than thirty-year loan. Loan is fully repaid over fifteen-year term.	Frequently offered at slightly reduced interest rate. Offers faster accumulation of equity than traditional fixed-rate mortgage but has higher monthly payments. Involves paying less interest, but this may result in fewer tax deductions.
Adjustable Rate Mortgage	Interest rate changes over the life of the loan, resulting in possible changes in monthly payment, loan term, and/or principal. Some plans have rate or payment caps.	Starting interest rate is slightly below market, but payments can increase sharply and frequently if index increases. Payment caps prevent wide fluctuations in payments but may cause negative amortization. Rate caps limit amount total debt can expand.
Renegotiable Rate Mortgage (Rollover)	Interest rate and monthly payments are constant for several years; changes possible thereafter. Long-term mortgage.	Less frequent changes in interest rate offer some stability.
Balloon Mortgage	Monthly payments based on fixed interest rate, usually short-term; payments may cover interest only with principal due in full at end of term.	Offers low monthly payments but possibly no equity until loan is fully paid. When due, loan must be paid off or refinanced. Refinancing poses high risk if rates climb.
Graduated Payment Mortgage	Lower monthly payments rise gradually (usually over five to ten years), then level off for duration of term. With adjustable interest rate, additional payment changes are possible if the index changes.	Easier to qualify. Buyer's income must be able to keep pace with scheduled payment increases. With an adjustable rate, payment increases beyond the graduated payments can result in additional negative amortization.
Shared Appreciation Mortgage	Below-market interest rate and lower monthly payments in exchange for a share of profits when property is sold or on a specified date. Many variations.	If home appreciates greatly, total cost of loan jumps. If home fails to appreciate, projected increase in value may still be due, requiring refinancing at possibly higher rates.
Assumable Mortgage	Buyer takes over seller's original below-market-rate mortgage.	Lowers monthly payments. May be prohibited if due on sale clause is in original mortgage. Not permitted on most new fixed-rate mortgages.
Seller Take-Back	Seller provides all or part of financing with a first or second mortgage.	May offer a below-market interest rate; may have a balloon payment requiring full payment in a few years or refinancing at market rates, which could sharply increase debt.
Wraparound	Seller keeps original low-rate mortgage. Buyer makes payments to seller who forwards a portion to lender holding original mortgage. Offers lower effective interest rate on total transaction.	Lender may call in old mortgage and require higher rate. If buyer defaults, seller must take legal action to collect debt.
Growing Equity Mortgage (Rapid Payoff Mortgage)	Fixed interest rate but monthly payments may vary according to agreed-upon schedule or index.	Permits rapid payoff of debt because payment increases reduce principal. Buyer's income must be able to keep up with payment increases.
Land Contract	Seller retains original mortgage. No transfer of title until loan is fully paid. Equal monthly payments based on below-market interest rate with unpaid principal due at end of loan.	May offer no equity until loan is fully paid. Buyer has few protections if conflict arises during loan.
Buy-Down	Developer (or another party) provides an interest subsidy that lowers monthly payments during the first few years of the loan. Can have fixed or adjustable interest rate.	Offers a break from higher payments during early years. Enables buyer with lower income to qualify. With adjustable rate mortgage, payments may jump substantially at end of subsidy. Developer may increase selling price.
Rent with Option	Renter pays "option fee" for right to purchase property at specified time and agreed-upon price. Rent may or may not be applied to sales price.	Enables renter to buy time to obtain down payment and decide whether to purchase. Locks in price during inflationary times. Failure to take option means loss of option fee and rental payments.

TABLE 9.1	Alternative Financing Techniques (continued)	
Reverse Annuity Mortgage (Equity Conversion)	Borrower owns mortgage-free property and needs income. Lender makes monthly payments to borrower, using property as collateral.	Can provide homeowners with needed cash. At end of term, borrower must have money available to avoid selling property or refinancing.
Subprime Mortgage	Borrower with impaired credit record pays higher interest on mortgage, often with variable rate, due to higher risk.	Allows borrowers with impaired credit to qualify for a mortgage. If variable interest rates increase, borrowers may default on payments.

recourse note
A loan in which the borrower is personally liable for payment in the event of a default.

nonrecourse note
A loan in which the lender's recourse to satisfy the loan is against the collateral, not against the borrower's personal assets.

negotiable note
Any writing to be a negotiable instrument within this Article must (a) be signed by the maker or drawer; (b) contain an unconditional promise or order to pay a sum certain in money and no other promise, order, obligation, or power given by the maker or drawer except as authorized by this Article; (c) be payable on demand or at a definite time; and (d) be payable to order or to bearer.

mortgage is still an enforceable debt, although it is unsecured and therefore typically harder to collect. The promissory note may be a recourse note, or the lender may agree that the note is "without recourse."

Under a **recourse note**, the borrower is personally liable for the amount of the debt. When the security for the debt is foreclosed and sold and the proceeds of the foreclosure sale are insufficient to repay the lender the amount due under the note, the borrower is personally liable for the deficiency. The typical note executed by a borrower in a residential real estate transaction is a recourse note, although in some states the recourse provisions in these notes are unenforceable under "antideficiency judgment laws" discussed later in this chapter.

With a **nonrecourse note**, the borrower is not personally liable; and if the note is not repaid, the lender's only recourse is foreclosure.[46] If the foreclosure proceeds are insufficient to satisfy the amount due under the note, the lender has no recourse against the borrower's other assets. Nonrecourse notes are often sought by sophisticated commercial developers who possess a strong enough bargaining position with the lender to receive this advantageous term. However, due to the added risk, lenders typically charge a higher interest rate for these notes.

The Negotiable Note   Notes may be divided into *two* broad categories: negotiable and nonnegotiable. A **negotiable note** is one that meets the requirements of Section 3-104 (1) of the UCC. (For a negotiable promissory note, see www.cengagebrain.com [see page xix in the Preface for instructions on how to access the free study tools for this text].) The following Florida case demonstrates the importance of the note's wording for proving that it is negotiable.

A CASE IN POINT

In *Holly Hill Acres, Ltd. v. Charter Bank of Gainesville*,[47] the maker of a note was sued by a bank that had purchased the note from the payees, Rogers and Blythe. The main legal issue in the case was whether the note was negotiable, since it included the following language: "This note with interest is secured by a mortgage on real estate, of even date herewith, made by the maker hereof in favor of the said payee, and shall be construed and enforced according to the laws of the State of Florida. The terms of said mortgage are by this reference made a part hereof."

The court concluded that the note was not negotiable because it did not contain an unconditional promise to pay, but was conditioned on the terms of the mortgage. The court distinguished another case, holding that a note was negotiable when it read "this note secured by mortgage," on the grounds that the language merely referred to the mortgage but was not conditioned on the mortgage.

The introduction of adjustable rate notes led to litigation over whether their variable interest component caused the adjustable notes to be nonnegotiable. In response, "almost all states have enacted statutes making them negotiable. Most of these statutes are based on a revised UCC provision deleting the 'sum certain' language, and substituting a 'fixed amount of money' standard which applies only to the loan principal."[48]

secondary market

A market in which money market instruments are traded among investors.

The lender's ability to sell a loan in the **secondary market** is facilitated when the note is negotiable since it affords the buyer of the note certain important legal advantages. A nonnegotiable note also can be sold or assigned by the lender. However, such notes are more difficult to sell because the purchaser's rights are limited since the purchaser cannot qualify as a holder in due course, a topic discussed later in the chapter. Consequently, from the lender's viewpoint, it is essential that all notes meet the UCC requirements for negotiability.

> *Mortgagors may not realize that their loan payments probably don't wind up in their lender's hands; more than half of all home mortgages are sold into the "secondary mortgage" market by the lenders who originated them. Federal law does require that lenders alert their borrowers that their loans might be sold, but the significance of this disclosure is probably lost on most borrowers.*
>
> *On the other side of the secondary mortgage market are mortgage investors. They buy and sell mortgages and other loans. Mortgages are often pooled so that cross-country or even international investors may wind up owning a piece of the same mortgage pool. The process is called "**securitization**" because the ultimate investor ends up owning a security—an undivided interest in a large number of mortgages, called mortgage-backed securities (MBS)—rather than owning individual mortgages.[49]*

securitization

A process in which an asset is converted into a pool of securities that are offered to investors.

Mortgage-backed securities, although in existence for many years, have become notorious as one of the principal culprits for causing the mortgage crisis and Great Recession of 2007–2009. In particular, those securities containing subprime mortgages, discussed earlier, had a significant impact on the economic downfall. Although it is noteworthy that securities composed of prime mortgages with very high loan-to-value ratios—such as those in which homeowners borrowed up to and even exceeding 90 percent, "Option ARMs," and other mortgage instruments—were also instrumental in the mortgage meltdown. Further magnifying the problem, many of the subprime mortgage bonds, often rated AAA by rating agencies, were divided and distributed among many debt pools and sold to investors around the world. As the *Wall Street Journal* explained in one glaring example: "In one case, a $38 million subprime-mortgage bond created in June 2006 ended up in more than 30 debt pools and ultimately caused roughly $280 million in losses to investors by the time the bond's principal was wiped out in 2008…"[50] Yet, it is somewhat ironic, as the foregoing article further points out: "Even at its peak, subprime lending accounted for a relatively small portion of the overall mortgage lending." Indeed, the destruction caused by subprime mortgages was greatly out of proportion to their actual numbers.

Fannie Mae

A private shareholder-owned corporation regulated by the federal government that provides a secondary market for the buying and selling of both government-backed and conventional mortgages.

Two of the largest buyers of mortgage-backed loans in the secondary market are the Federal National Mortgage Association, better known as **Fannie Mae**, and the Federal Home Loan Mortgage Corporation, or **Freddie Mac**. Both of these corporations were, prior to September 2008, private and shareholder-owned but occupied a unique niche in finance referred to as government-sponsored enterprises (GSEs), so-called because they were closely regulated by the federal government. After that date, both were placed under the conservatorship of the Federal Housing Finance Agency.[51]

Freddie Mac

A private shareholder-owned corporation regulated by the federal government that provides a secondary market for the buying and selling of both government-backed and conventional first mortgages.

For many years, Fannie Mae and Freddie Mac demanded high standards from those lenders whose mortgages they purchased. However, when the subprime mortgage markets began to chip away at some of Fannie and Freddie's market share, they began to buy so-called Alt-A loans. These loans were riskier and often did not require full documentation of borrowers' income or assets.

Fortunately, after the federal takeover, the two organizations continued to buy large blocks of much safer FHA, VA, and conventional loans. This furnished the primary mortgage market, composed of mortgage bankers, with a desperately needed buyer for the mortgages the bankers originated. In fact, after the collapse of many lending institutions in 2008, Fannie and Freddie bought 9 out of every 10 newly originated mortgages, as well as leading in the modification of loans, making them critical in propping up a very fragile, residential lending sector in critical need of liquidity.

Fannie and Freddie's ongoing troubles came on the heels, and may have even contributed to, one of the greatest declines in housing values in American history. Still, in the end, the bailout of the two secondary market giants and their survival, albeit in a different form, and the indispensable capital they infuse into the housing market possibly may have saved the U.S. and even the world economy from suffering even greater upheavals.[52]

A third organization, the Government National Mortgage Association, or **Ginnie Mae, is a government agency within HUD.** It does not actually buy loans or issue mortgage-backed securities. Instead, Ginnie Mae guarantees the payment of interest and principal on bonds issued by private thrifts and mortgage bankers. Ginnie Mae's bonds are backed by VA and FHA mortgages.

Despite Fannie and Freddie's problems, the three organizations will continue to infuse capital into the primary market, enabling mortgage bankers to lend money to prospective home buyers. Unfortunately for taxpayers in general, Fannie and Freddie, by mid-2010, owed over $160 billion to the federal government under a bailout plan, with potentially billions more that may have to be drawn in the future from the unlimited fund set up by Congress.[53]

Key Note Terms   The use of notes in real estate financing raises issues relating to due on sale clauses and usury laws as well as acceleration clauses.

Acceleration Clause   Under an **acceleration clause,** if the debtor defaults on any one payment, the entire debt becomes due immediately at the lender's option. Without an acceleration clause, the lender cannot foreclose the entire mortgage until the end of the term of the note; instead, the only recourse is to foreclose on each individual overdue payment.[54] An acceleration clause is not enforced unless the mortgagee acts in an equitable and fair manner, as illustrated by the following Arkansas case.

Ginnie Mae

An agency within the Department of Housing and Urban Development that guarantees the payment of interest and principal on bonds issued by private thrifts and mortgage bankers. The bonds are backed by VA and FHA mortgages.

acceleration clause

An acceleration provision is a term in a mortgage (or in the obligation it secures) that empowers the mortgagee upon default by the mortgagor to declare the full amount of the mortgage obligation immediately due and payable. An acceleration becomes effective on the date specified in a written notice by the mortgagor delivered after default.

A CASE IN POINT

In *Harrell v. Perkins,*[55] the note and mortgage contained the following acceleration clause: "If default be made at any time in payment of any of said installments for a period of 60 days, all of the remaining installments not then due shall at the option of the holder at once become due and payable, for the purpose of foreclosure." The mortgagee, who lived next door to the mortgaged property, persuaded the mortgagor to obtain an FHA loan to pay off the mortgage at a discount. While the FHA loan was in process and after the mortgagor had made over $11,000 in improvements to meet FHA requirements, the mortgagee told the mortgagor that she need not make further monthly payments until she received the FHA loan. However, the mortgagee later changed his mind, refused to accept the defaulted monthly payments, and brought foreclosure proceedings. The court denied foreclosure on the grounds that "equity will relieve against acceleration when the creditor's conduct has been responsible for the debtor's default."

due on sale clause

A special type of acceleration clause that causes the entire debt to become due upon the sale of the property.

Due on Sale Clause   A **due on sale clause** requires the entire debt to be due immediately at the lender's option upon the *sale* of the property. The purchaser must obtain a new mortgage or renegotiate the existing mortgage with the lender, often at a higher interest rate.

Before 1982, many state courts refused to honor these due on sale clauses because, among other reasons, courts held that the clauses unreasonably prevented borrowers from selling their property. Such a restriction, discussed in Chapter 5, can be illegal since it places an illegal restraint on a person's ability to alienate property. In 1982, the Supreme Court decided that pursuant to federal regulations, federally chartered savings and loan associations could enforce due on sale clauses.[56] More importantly, also in 1982, Congress enacted the Garn–St. Germain Depository Institutions Act, which provides that all lenders may enforce due on sale clauses. Due on sale clauses, although detrimental to buyers who want to assume low-interest notes, can, if they are not honored by mortgagors, cause great financial problems for lenders who can ill afford to carry in their portfolio low-interest-bearing debt once rates go up. Moreover, without a due on sale clause, the lender is unable to appraise the credit risk of the buyer who is assuming the loan. Federal regulatory agencies must protect the interests of those who deposit their money in these lending institutions, as well as the federal government, which insures many of these deposits.

> Can a lender who has agreed that it will not unreasonably withhold consent to a transfer condition its waiver of the due on sale clause on an increase in interest rates? In *Rubin v. Centerbanc Federal Savings & Loan Association* on page 355, the court discusses this issue.

END OF CHAPTER CASE

Despite the preemption of state law by the Garn–St. Germain Act, a real estate purchaser can still assume at a low interest rate an existing mortgage that does not contain a due on sale clause, although today virtually all conventional, FHA, and VA loans contain the clause. Even when a mortgage contains a due on sale clause, some borrowers, particularly those with poor credit ratings, attempt, perhaps illegally, to avoid due on sale clauses by not disclosing the sale to the lender as well as not recording the transaction in the public record.[57] Due on sale clauses and their impact on sales subject to mortgages, wraparound mortgages, and mortgage assumptions are discussed later in this chapter.

usury law

Laws that forbid the lending of money in excess of rates prescribed by law.

Interest Rate—Usury Limitations   **Usury law** is especially complex because of variations among states and because, within each state, the law is subject to a number of exceptions. In some states, for example, certain lenders, such as building and loan associations, may be exempt from the law. In addition, loans to certain borrowers, often businesses, may be exempt. In many states, certain transactions, including real estate loans and credit arrangements made by the seller as part of a sale, may be exempt. Finally, certain payments to the lenders, such as appraisal fees and credit reports, are exempt because they represent fees for services rendered rather than compensation paid for the use of money. Charges collected by the lender and paid to third parties are clearly exempt. In addition, federal law preempts state usury laws for loans made by federally related and state-chartered lenders and secured by residential mortgages. The federal law allowed the states to opt out of the federal preemption if they made a timely reinstatement of their own usury law.

The penalties imposed for charging a usurious rate of interest are also subject to much variation. In some states, the creditor forfeits both principal and interest; while in other states, only part or all of the interest is forfeited. In a few states, the creditor forfeits a multiple of the interest. For instance, in the South Carolina case of *Davenport v. Unicapital Corp.,*[58] the borrowers agreed to pay a 14 percent interest rate, while the maximum lawful rate was 7 percent. The court decided that a mortgage that secured the debt should be canceled, and the plaintiffs were entitled to recover twice the amount of usurious interest.

Prepayment and Exit Fees   While the lender is concerned primarily with negotiability, the acceleration clause, and the impact of usury laws, the borrower should insist that the note contain an "on or before" clause that allows the borrower to pay off the mortgage in full on or before the due date. This clause allows the borrower to obtain refinancing if interest rates drop significantly. Commercial loans, on the other hand, often have elaborate prepayment clauses that can be the subject of forceful negotiation.

Lenders, of course, are wary of early payments because of the interest they will lose; so the lenders charge a **prepayment fee** (also called a *prepayment penalty* or *premium*) if the mortgage is paid off in the early years of the loan. The risk is greatest when the prepayment is made when interest rates are declining, which means that the lender not only loses a higher-yielding debt instrument but also must search for a new outlet to reinvest the money.

By law, FHA and VA loans as well as federally chartered credit union loans cannot contain prepayment fee clauses. Moreover, many states have laws that forbid prepayment fees on residential mortgages. Prepayment fees are routinely included in commercial real estate loans and are enforceable. Subprime residential mortgages require prepayment fees and typically operate for the first three to five years of the loan, although in most cases they are being eliminated under the new Dodd-Frank Act. Mortgagors with subprime loans have been penalized by having to pay up to 3 percent of the loan amount if they sell, consolidate debts, or refinance their homes during that time. Consumer groups contend that charging prepayment fees is a form of predatory lending since these borrowers are not properly informed of the penalty clauses. Lenders argue that they must use them to cover the risk and costs of issuing subprime loans.[59] It is noteworthy that disclosure of prepayment fees is required in the new 2010 HUD-1 form required under RESPA.

Courts further scrutinize prepayment fees, particularly with home loans, to ensure that the fees represent the lender's anticipated loss when there is an early loan payoff. If the fees do not represent the anticipated loss, courts construe them as additional interest payments that constitute an unreasonable penalty. A prepayment fee that fails a liquidated damages analysis—the amount of loss the lender would incur due to an early payoff—is deemed by many courts to be unenforceable.[60]

Still, prepayment fees are almost never set aside by courts in commercial mortgages, regardless of the fee's amount, since they are seen as the result of negotiations between presumptively sophisticated business parties. As such, commercial lenders require borrowers to agree to a "yield maintenance" or a "defeasance" agreement as a condition of the loan. Under a yield maintenance agreement, the borrower must structure payments to the creditor so it can continue to receive its expected yield. In a defeasance agreement, the expected payments continue to come to the lender but are derived from revenue from securities, usually Treasury notes, purchased by the borrower. These payments are a substitution for the payments that the lender would have received had the borrower continued to pay the mortgage note as agreed upon.[61]

Occasionally, a lender will attempt to accelerate the mortgage loan and at the same time recover a prepayment fee. A number of courts have held that the lender is not

prepayment fee
A fee that is imposed when a promissory note is paid before it is due.

entitled to prepayment fees following acceleration. However, the fee may be allowed when the loan documents clearly allow recovery after acceleration or when the borrower has intentionally defaulted on the mortgage payments.[62] In construction loans, for example, a loan can be called in and accelerated when the mortgagor fails to meet deadlines for attaining building permits or scheduled deadlines for finishing certain stages in a project. The following Ohio case illustrates what happens when the most common reason for acceleration, a default in payments, occurs.

A CASE IN POINT

In *In re Hidden Lake Limited Partnership*[63] the mortgagor defaulted on the mortgage loan, which contained a clause stating that any acceleration of the debt would trigger the prepayment premium. The court ruled that the clause was enforceable as a form of liquidated damages.

Instead of paying off the full amount early, some borrowers make extra monthly payments early in the loan period, thus reducing the total amount of interest paid on the loan. If the borrower in these cases is unable to make monthly payments at a later date because of financial hardships or other reasons, the additional early payments cannot generally be used to cover the defaulted payments.

exit fee
A fee that is imposed when a promissory note is paid before it is due or when it matures.

A prepayment fee is distinguishable from an **exit fee**. Exit fees are payable to the lender when the loan is paid early and are payable *even* at the loan's maturity date. Exit fees are not used in residential mortgages, but they are common in commercial and construction loans.[64] Since it is crucial to distinguish between an exit fee and a prepayment fee, the wording of the loan document, as the following Louisiana case discusses, must be closely scrutinized to determine the nature of the fee.

In *Delta Rault Energy 110 Veterans, L.L.C. v. GMAC Commercial Mortgage Corp.* on page 356, the court decides whether an exit fee is, in reality, an illegal prepayment penalty.

END OF CHAPTER CASE

Security for the Note: The Mortgage

The mortgage, the instrument that grants the lender security for the note, can have different legal effects. In lien theory states, the mortgage provides the lender security for the debt in the form of a lien on the borrower's real property. In title theory states, the mortgage acts as the conveyance of a "defeasible fee." That is, title to the property is conveyed to the lender, subject to "defeasance"—transfer of title to the borrower upon repayment of the loan. In addition, intermediate theory states hold that "prior to default, mortgagees hold mere liens or, 'at best, a superficial title,' but that after default they acquire a legal interest."[65] (See endnote 65 for a list of states that apply the lien, title, or intermediate theories to mortgages).

The primary difference between title and intermediate theory states is that in the absence of a contrary agreement, the mortgagee in an intermediate theory state is not entitled to possession until default, while in a title theory state, the mortgagee is entitled to possession upon the giving of the mortgage. However, even in a title theory state, the mortgage instrument typically grants the borrower the right of possession until default; and some states by statute grant the mortgagors the right to possession until default.

Form Because the mortgage is a grant of either a security interest in real property (in lien theory states) or a defeasible fee (in title theory states), the form of mortgage includes many of the elements found in a deed (discussed in the following chapter). For instance, the mortgage must be in writing and should name the parties, describe the property subject to the mortgage, and include any warranties given by the mortgagor. Like the deed, the mortgage should include words granting the mortgagee an interest in the property. In title states, these words are *convey and warrant,* while in lien states, the term *mortgage and warrant* is used. Finally, like a deed, the mortgage should be in the form required for recording—that is, it should be acknowledged in front of a notary and witnessed where required by state law. The form of residential mortgages, like the notes they secure, has become increasingly uniform largely because of the requirements of the secondary market and federal standards.

In most states, an unrecorded mortgage, like an unrecorded deed, will be subject to the rights of a later bona-fide purchaser or mortgagee, such as one who had no actual notice. In one situation, however, the usual priority rules under the recording statutes are not followed. When the purchaser of real estate gives a mortgage at the same time that title to the property is acquired and uses the entire loan to pay for the real estate (called a *purchase money mortgage*), the mortgage is given priority over earlier legal claims and liens (such as a judgment lien, discussed later in this chapter) made against the mortgagor/buyer even though the claims may have been recorded. The reason for this rule is that before the purchase, the mortgagor has no interest against which the earlier claims can be applied and at the time of purchase, the mortgagor receives property title that is instantaneously subject to the mortgage. The following Michigan case illustrates the application of this rule.

A CASE IN POINT

In *Fecteau v. Fries,*[66] Fries decided to purchase several lots; and on August 6, he borrowed money from Patterson to make the purchase. He executed a note and mortgage to Patterson. On August 11, the seller, Fecteau, delivered a deed to Fries, and Fries gave Fecteau a purchase money mortgage on the same property covered by the Patterson mortgage. In a later foreclosure proceeding, the court was asked to decide which mortgage had priority—Patterson's mortgage, which was recorded first, or Fecteau's mortgage. The court decided that Fecteau's mortgage had priority, citing earlier authority to the effect that the deed and the Fecteau mortgage "executed at the same time are to be construed together as one instrument. They constitute an indivisible act." The court further noted that there was never a moment between Fries' taking title and giving Fecteau the mortgage on August 11 in which Fries could have encumbered the title. This is in contrast to when Fries borrowed money from Patterson on August 6. At that time Fries executed only a note and a mortgage, but did not actually take title to the property.

In addition to the usual requirements for executing and recording a deed, certain provisions are included in the mortgage but not the deed.[67] For example, the mortgage often includes the terms of the debt and the mortgagor's duties with regard to taxes, insurance, and repairs (discussed in greater detail in following sections). However, as a general rule, the mortgage does not have to state information about the debt that it secures. As a result, anyone interested in the property has a duty to inquire about the current status of the debt—even when the obligation is described in the mortgage.[68] However, some states do require that particular information be included in the mortgage. Illinois, for example, requires inclusion of the amount secured and maturity date.[69]

Future Advance Clause   The statement of consideration and its effect on later purchasers becomes more complicated when the mortgage is given to secure a **future advance**. A future advance is a sum to be disbursed by the lender after the mortgage is given. For example, a bank that is loaning money to fund construction will advance additional sums after the loan closing to pay for construction as it proceeds. Thus, the lender's advances increase with the value of its security. Residential homeowners, on the other hand, may use their equity to secure a home equity line of credit.

> **future advance**
> Money that is loaned after a mortgage has attached and that is secured by the mortgage.

To understand future advance financing, assume that Conner mortgaged his property to First Bank on June 10. The mortgage was to secure a loan of $450,000 that was to be paid to Conner in installments of $150,000 on September 1, October 1, and November 1. First Bank made the three payments; but on September 15, before the last two payments were made, Second Bank loaned Conner $300,000 and took a mortgage on the same property. Each mortgage was recorded on the day it was executed. Now Conner is in default on both mortgages, the two banks foreclose, and the property is worth a total of $600,000. How should the $600,000 be divided?

Common Law Approach   The critical legal issue in answering that question under the common law is whether First Bank was obligated to make the future advances on the promised dates. If the advances were obligatory, the common law rule is simple and easy to apply: the mortgagee who is obligated to make future advances has priority over later mortgagees and purchasers. This is fair to First Bank, of course, because of its binding obligation; and it is fair to Second Bank, which could ascertain from the mortgage on record and from related documents that First Bank's loan was obligatory. Obligatory future advance loans are especially common in the construction industry. In this case, if its payments were obligatory, First Bank would be paid in full, while Second Bank would receive the remaining $150,000.

If the advances of First Bank were not obligatory but were made at the bank's option after Conner had requested the advance, the rule followed in most states would be that the optional advance under the prior mortgage has priority unless the prior mortgagee, First Bank, had received actual notice of the intervening claim. In this case, if First Bank had no actual notice, the results would be the same as just discussed. However, if Second Bank had given notice of its loan on September 15, First Bank would have priority for its loan of September 1 ($150,000), Second Bank would have priority for its loan of September 15 ($300,000), and First Bank would then receive the remaining $150,000. This is fair because First Bank, after receiving notice, has the option of refusing to make additional loans. In some states, the recording of Second Bank's intervening mortgage constitutes constructive notice to First Bank and has the same effect as actual notice. In these states, a lender such as First Bank must search the records for intervening claims before making the optional advance.

Statutory Approach   Statutes in many states simplify the common law approach by providing that the first mortgagee has priority regardless of whether the future advances are obligatory or optional.[70] Under these statutes, First Bank would be paid in full and Second Bank would recover $150,000. Chapter 2 of the *Restatement of Mortgages* adopts this approach, rejecting the distinction between optional and future advances.[71]

Rights and Duties After Closing

The mortgage instrument may (and usually does) spell out the duties of the mortgagor and mortgagee with regard to the mortgaged premises. The courts have developed a number of rules, although often the contractual agreements between lender and borrower control the rights and duties of the parties.

Possession

In theory, the right to possession should pass with the title to the real estate. As a result, in title states, the mortgagee would be entitled to possession. In lien states, the possession would remain with the mortgagor until foreclosure. In practice, however, possession remains with the mortgagor in virtually every transaction, even in title states, pursuant to state statutes providing that the mortgagor is entitled to possession until default or under provisions in the mortgage instrument. The law favors possession by the mortgagor so strongly that in some lien states, it is against public policy for the mortgagor to give up possession even though a provision in the mortgage allows it.[72]

A mortgagee who does take possession (for example, after default) must manage the property with the same care a prudent owner would provide and is liable for the reasonable rental value of the property he occupies or rents to another, which is deducted from the mortgagor's debt. In most states, the **mortgagee-in-possession** is not entitled to payment for services in managing the property unless the mortgage stipulates a fee.

The mortgagee often requests that the court appoint a **receiver** to take possession of the property and manage it in the interim between default and foreclosure. The court's appointment of the receiver protects the lender from the liabilities and responsibilities otherwise placed on it as a mortgagee-in-possession.

mortgagee-in-possession
A lender who takes possession of the real property, securing the debt prior to foreclosure.

receiver
A person appointed by the court to manage property in litigation or the affairs of a bankrupt party.

Rents and Profits

Real estate, especially commercial and industrial real estate, can produce valuable rents and profits. Rentals may come from a lease executed before the mortgage. Unless the lessee had subordinated its lease to the mortgagee, foreclosure of the mortgage would not terminate the lease. A lease made *after* the mortgage is taken out, however, is subject to the mortgage and terminated by foreclosure. This scenario created problems for some residential tenants during the 2007–2009 mortgage crisis when the lessors' mortgagees forced these tenants to vacate their homes after they took title to the properties after the foreclosure. In many instances, the tenants were not even aware that their lessors had defaulted on their mortgages. The legal dimensions of the problem will be further explored in Chapter 11.

The right to rents and profits generated by real estate belongs to the person in possession—in most cases, the mortgagor. Allowing the mortgagor to retain rents and profits is in accord with the intention of the parties, for mortgages usually state that only the land is to be security, not the profits from the land. However, many mortgages, especially for nonresidential properties, include an assignment of rents and profits in the mortgage.

Yet in *two* instances, a court in equity will order the rents and profits to be collected for the benefit of the mortgagee, who must deduct them from the amount of the debt. In the *first* situation, the mortgagee must prove that the mortgagor is insolvent or that the debt is otherwise uncollectible and that the mortgagee's security in the property is insufficient to cover the debt. One court in Florida made the following statement:

> The right to appropriate the rent and profits which equity gives the mortgagee, where a receiver is appointed at his instance, does not result from any specific pledge of such rents contained in the mortgage. Equity makes the mortgage, as between mortgagor and mortgagee, a charge upon the rents and profits whenever the mortgagor is insolvent and the security is inadequate.[73]

In the *second* situation, the mortgagor assigns the rents and profits to the mortgagee as additional security. Courts have interpreted such assignments to be valid, but only after the mortgagee has taken possession of the real estate.

Some assignment of rent agreements provide that they serve as absolute assignments to the mortgagee and are not conditioned upon the borrower's default. Despite their absolute language, such assignments rarely transfer rent payments to the lender immediately. Interpretation and enforcement of these agreements differ widely among the states.

Repairs and Improvements

As a general rule, a mortgagor has no duty to repair the mortgaged property if the property has been damaged through no fault of his own. As a corollary, when the mortgagor does make repairs or improvements, the cost cannot be deducted from the debt even though such changes benefit the mortgagee by increasing the value of the security.

waste

A destructive use of real property by one in rightful possession.

The mortgagor in possession is not allowed to commit **waste**. Waste occurs when the value of the secured real estate decreases through the action or inaction of the mortgagor. Waste is committed, for example, when the mortgagor mortgages the property and then begins to run a strip mining operation that impairs the value of the land. Waste, committed by a life tenant to the detriment of a future estate holder, was discussed in detail in Chapter 5.

The duty to prevent waste applies to both the mortgagor and the mortgagee-in-possession. A mortgagee-in-possession has the duty to make reasonable and necessary repairs and can add his or her cost to the mortgagor's debt as the following Indiana case illustrates.

A CASE IN POINT

In *Wise v. Layman,*[74] where the mortgagee was allowed to recover the cost of wallpaper, plumbing, window shades, screens, and the sodding of a yard, the court observed that "what are reasonable and necessary repairs depends upon the particular circumstances of each case. The said expenditures made by appellee, in our opinion, were for reasonable and necessary repairs to keep the property from deterioration...."

If the expenditure is considered an improvement rather than a repair, the mortgagee is not entitled to reimbursement. Not only is this consistent with the rule that mortgagors cannot deduct the cost of improvements from the mortgage debt, but it also prevents an injustice to the mortgagor as an Oregon court asserts.

A contrary holding under such circumstances would mean that at his discretion a mortgagee can put improvements upon real estate to such an extent as to render it impossible for the mortgagor to redeem. His additions might vastly enlarge the value of the land, but prevent redemption by the mortgagor for the want of funds to meet the increase though he might be able to pay the original debt. It would practically destroy the debtor's right of redemption but leave intact the creditor's right to foreclose.[75]

Taxes

The mortgagor, as the owner of the land, has the duty to pay taxes. The borrower's payment of taxes is critical to the lender, as the taxing authority's tax lien has priority over the mortgage debt. The mortgage typically provides that the mortgagor has the duty to pay taxes, and that failure to pay is one of the material acts of default that will trigger the acceleration clause.

Because of the critical importance of tax payments, mortgage documents often require the mortgagor to make monthly payments, together with its payments of principal and interest, in the amount of one-twelfth the annual tax bill. The lender holds these tax payments in an escrow account, also known as a *reserve* or *impound* account. The requirement to escrow (or impound) taxes is prevalent in high-loan-to-value mortgages, but is often waived if the mortgagor pays over 20 percent of the purchase price.

Insurance

The typical mortgage also requires the borrower to maintain hazard insurance on the property. Without insurance, the lender risks the total or partial loss of its collateral in the event of fire, flood, and other insurable hazards. In high-loan-to-value mortgages, the lender frequently requires that the borrower place insurance payments in an escrow (or impound) account, as is done for taxes. As discussed in previous sections of this chapter, RESPA limits the amount a residential borrower pays into escrow accounts at closing. One issue to be resolved through reference to the mortgage and applicable law is whether the insurance proceeds must be used to restore the property or whether the lender can instead apply the insurance proceeds against the sums due under the note. In one recent Connecticut case, a mortgagee, who was not named as the loss payee on the policy, was able to claim an equitable lien and recover insurance proceeds to apply to sums due on the note after a fire destroyed the defaulting mortgagor's home.[76]

Mortgage Terminations

The relationship between the mortgagor and mortgagee may terminate under one of three scenarios:

- *when the mortgage is paid in full by the mortgagor*
- *when the mortgagor transfers the mortgage to a buyer*
- *when the mortgagee forecloses on the mortgage and the property is sold at a public or private sale*

Terminating the Mortgage by Payment in Full

A mortgagor may discharge the mortgage through periodic payments over the life of the mortgage. The mortgagor may prefer to make a lump sum payment before the due date, although this may subject the mortgagor to a prepayment fee if the mortgage so provides. Without language in the note and mortgage allowing prepayment and unless local or federal law grants the borrower the right of early payment, most courts hold that the borrower does not have the right of prepayment and must make a **perfect tender in time**.[77,78] This rule has been tempered, however, by the general elimination of prepayment fees for residential properties, but is still very applicable with commercial loans which often require, as discussed earlier, prepayment fees or other arrangements such as yield maintenance or defeasance agreements.

In most cases, payment is made when the mortgaged property is sold; the purchaser usually obtains her own mortgage that will cover the seller's equity and pay off the seller's mortgage. If the mortgagor makes an offer to pay the mortgage in full—a tender of payment—on the due date (or earlier if allowed by the mortgage) and the mortgagee refuses to accept payment, the mortgage is canceled and no additional interest is due on the loan. The tender, of course, must be at a proper time and place as indicated in this classic Michigan case.

perfect tender in time
Absent statutory or express contractual language to the contrary, a borrower has no right to prepay his mortgage or deed of trust obligation prior to the maturity date specified on the underlying promissory note and the agreed upon payment schedule is to be enforced.

A CASE IN POINT

In *Waldron v. Murphy,*[79] the mortgagors tendered payment to the president of the mortgagee bank in the middle of a street when the bank president was going to visit a neighbor. When the bank president told the mortgagors to make payment at the bank on the following morning, they refused to do so; later they argued that their tender discharged the mortgage. The court disagreed, deciding that the time and place of tender were not reasonable.

As discussed previously, when the mortgagor sells the mortgaged property to a purchaser, the purchaser pays the full purchase price (either in cash or from a new loan he secures) from which the mortgagor pays off (and thus terminates) the mortgage at closing. For example, assume that Mary owns a house worth $200,000 subject to a mortgage in favor of First Bank. Mary still owes $150,000 to First Bank. She now wants to sell her house to Nick, who agrees to pay $200,000. Nick also agrees to a down payment of $10,000 and secures the remaining $190,000 with a mortgage loan from Second Bank. At the closing, Second Bank will tender the $190,000 to Mary. She will then pay off the remaining $150,000 she owes First Bank, which has agreed to accept the payment in full. Mary also receives a mortgage discharge, or **satisfaction** of her mortgage from First Bank. In the end (disregarding her closing costs), Mary will pocket the difference between what Nick pays her ($190,000) from his loan from Second Bank and what she owes her mortgagee ($150,000), or $40,000, plus the $10,000 she receives from Nick as his downpayment.

> **satisfaction**
> The discharge of a mortgage.

When payment in full is accepted by the mortgagee, such as First Bank, it is important that Mary, the mortgagor, demand the note and a mortgage discharge, or satisfaction, in return. The discharge should be recorded immediately; in the absence of a discharge, the mortgage will continue to cloud the title, thus making it unmarketable. Most states provide statutes that require the mortgagee to issue a recordable satisfaction of mortgage soon after the mortgagor's proper payment of the loan. Still, some states, such as Louisiana, Massachusetts, Montana, Nebraska, and Oregon, do not.[80] Thus, if the mortgagor in those states fails to record the discharge, anyone viewing the public record may still assume that the property is encumbered by the mortgage. A property owner who seeks to refinance or sell would be required at that time to file the discharge of the mortgage note.

Mortgage Transfer by Seller/Mortgagor to Buyer

Although not as common as it once was, mainly because of due on sale clauses, a seller/mortgagor may choose to transfer the mortgage to the buyer as discussed below.

> **sale subject to a mortgage**
> A sale in which the buyer agrees to purchase property subject to the mortgage lien.

Sale Subject to Mortgage   One means of transferring a mortgage is a **sale subject to a mortgage**. Another alternative, also discussed below, is a mortgage assumption. Both a mortgage assumption and a sale subject to a mortgage are attractive marketing features when interest rates are rising. To illustrate these two alternatives, assume that Mary owns a house worth $200,000 that she has mortgaged to First Bank for $150,000 at a 6 percent interest rate. She now sells her house to Nick. Nick pays $50,000 in cash at the closing. (See Figure 9.2.) Under the terms of their agreement, Mary, instead of discharging the mortgage at the closing when she is paid by Nick, executes a private agreement (sometimes called a *counter letter*) with Nick in which he agrees to make monthly payments to her, which she will then make to the bank. Nick likes this arrangement because a new loan would require him to pay 8 percent. The deed to Nick in this situation would state that the conveyance is subject to the mortgage to First Bank.

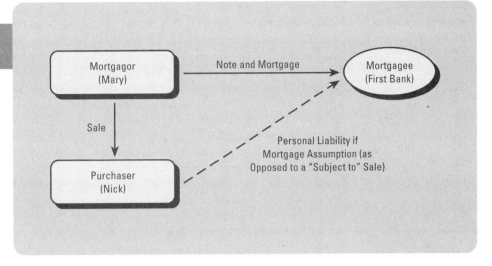

FIGURE 9.2
Transfer by Mortgagor

It is quite likely that Nick will not record his deed since he and Mary are probably violating the mortgage's due on sale clause, a topic discussed in "Ethics and Public Policy Issues" later in this chapter.

A sale subject to a mortgage has the following legal consequences:

1. The mortgagor, Mary, remains personally liable for the mortgage loan.
2. The purchaser, Nick, is not personally liable to First Bank.
3. The house is still subject to the mortgage, which may be foreclosed by First Bank on Mary's default.
4. If Nick loses the property on foreclosure, he may recover damages from Mary on the basis of their agreement.[81]

Wraparound Mortgage   One variation on a sale subject to a mortgage is a financing device known as a *wraparound mortgage*. The **wraparound mortgage**[82] (also called an *all-inclusive trust deed*) is used when the seller finances part of the purchase in addition to leaving the existing loan in place. For example, Mary sells her $200,000 house to Nick, who pays $20,000 in cash. Nick signs a promissory note to Mary for $180,000, representing the $30,000 loaned by Mary and the $150,000 owed to First Bank. Mary is not released from the loan to First Bank; instead, she agrees to continue to pay the loan to First Bank using Nick's payments to her as the source of funds.

As in a sale subject to a mortgage, wraparounds violate the due on sale clause contained in most residential mortgages. However, commercial loans often do not contain these clauses or are successfully negotiated for, allowing wraparounds, as well as a sale subject to a mortgage, to be used to finance the purchase of businesses and other commercial properties.

wraparound mortgage
A junior mortgage that secures a promissory note, the face amount of which is the total of the unpaid balance of the first note secured by the senior mortgage, and those funds advanced or to be advanced by the wraparound lender.

> When the holder of a deed of trust foreclosed on property, the foreclosure proceeds were insufficient to satisfy its loan. In *Adams v. George* on page 357, the court resolves whether Carol George, who had purchased the property under a wraparound mortgage, is liable for the deficiency.

END OF CHAPTER CASE

mortgage assumption
An agreement between the seller-mortgagor and a buyer in which the buyer agrees to assume the obligation for the seller's mortgage debt.

Mortgage Assumption   Instead of a "subject to" sale, a **mortgage assumption** might be arranged. Nick pays Mary $50,000 at closing and assumes and agrees to pay the $150,000 mortgage to First Bank. Such an arrangement may have advantages for Nick because, as noted shortly, the interest rates on older mortgages such as Mary's might be lower than the rate for new loans and the mortgage closing costs for an assumption are minimal. The major distinction between the "subject to" sale and the assumption is that when the purchaser, Nick, assumes personal liability to First Bank, he must make up the deficit (that is, pay a deficiency judgment) if a foreclosure sale does not cover the amount of debt on the mortgage.

Although assumptions are rare today because of due on sale clauses, some lenders are in recent years allowing so-called "friendly transfers" or assumptions due to a high number of distressed properties threatened by foreclosure. Under this kind of workout, a borrower, with the permission of the lender, transfers the property to a "trusted party," often a relative or a friend who pays part or all of the principal and interest owed by the seller. The trusted party then makes the payments until the former owner is stable and secure financially. Once that occurs, the former owner reassumes the mortgage or refinances the mortgage.

surety
One who promises to pay the debt of another.

Novation   Many mortgagors mistakenly believe that because the purchaser has assumed and agreed to pay the mortgage, the mortgagors are no longer liable. Mary, as the seller-mortgagor, does, in fact, remain liable as a **surety**, a person equally liable with the principal debtor, Nick. If Nick defaults, First Bank, the mortgagee, can still collect from Mary, although Nick, if he is able, must indemnify Mary if she pays the deficiency judgment.

novation
The substitution by mutual agreement of one debtor for another whereby the original debtor's obligation is extinguished.

To eliminate this liability, Mary should obtain a release from First Bank when the property is sold. This arrangement, under which all three parties agree that the purchaser is substituted for the mortgagor-seller, is called a **novation**. Mortgagees, however, are often reluctant to release a seller-mortgagor such as Mary. Still, if Nick makes timely payments to First Bank for a reasonable period of time, First Bank might feel secure enough in Nick's ability to pay the mortgage to allow the novation. Mary also can pay First Bank to release her from the note.

ETHICAL AND PUBLIC POLICY ISSUES

Is It Ethical to Violate a Due on Sale Clause?

In the previous scenarios in which the mortgagor sells the property but does not discharge the seller's mortgage, a potentially serious legal and ethical issue can arise: the violation of a due on sale clause. A due on sale clause, discussed earlier in this chapter, exists in virtually every residential mortgage instrument. It requires that in the event of a sale, the entire loan becomes due and payable. Yet in some cases, a seller may privately convey title to the property to the purchaser without informing the lender. On its face, it may appear advantageous to both sellers and buyers to ignore the clause and not inform the lender; however, there are potential repercussions for violating a due on sale clause which can impact other parties, such as lenders, investors, and bank depositors. Do you feel that due on sale clauses violate landowners' rights to freely sell their property? If so, does that create a moral justification to ignore these clauses? Is it fair, for example, to other borrowers who may have to pay higher rates on their mortgage loans because their lenders hold low-interest loans in their portfolio?

Table 9.2 summarizes what parties may incur liability in the foregoing scenarios if a default and a foreclosure occur and the mortgagee enforces a deficiency judgment.

TABLE 9.2 Mortgage Termination by Sale or Transfer—Personal Liability of Parties

TRANSACTION	PRIMARILY LIABLE PARTY	SECONDARILY LIABLE PARTY (SURETY)	LIABILITY TO WHICH MORTGAGEE?
Termination by sale—discharge of seller's mortgage	Buyer	None	Buyer's mortgagee
Sale subject to the mortgage*	Seller	None	Seller's mortgagee
Mortgage assumption**	Buyer	Seller	Seller's mortgagee
Mortgage assumption and release of seller by novation	Buyer	None	Seller's mortgagee

*Buyer may be liable for damages to seller based on a private agreement.

**Buyer must legally indemnify seller if seller pays mortgagee for a deficiency

Transfer by Mortgagee

Method and Effect of Transfer Mortgagees commonly sell mortgages in the secondary market to financial institutions, government agencies, and private parties. Often these sales take place without the knowledge of mortgagors, who continue to make payments to the original mortgagee. While the borrower's right to assign the obligation to repay the loan is restricted by the due on sale clause, the lender suffers no such impediment in assigning its right to receive the borrower's money.

For example, assume that Darcy has mortgaged her property to First Bank and First Bank now wants to sell the mortgage to Second Bank. (See Figure 9.3.) To accomplish this, First Bank will negotiate Darcy's note to Second Bank—by delivery alone if the note is a bearer instrument or by proper endorsement of the note if it is payable to the order of First Bank—and will give Second Bank an assignment of the mortgage, which should be recorded. However, even if the mortgage is not assigned, it passes automatically to Second Bank as security for the note. An assignment of the mortgage alone, however, gives Second Bank nothing since the mortgage serves only as security for the note. The mortgage follows the note; the note does not follow the mortgage.

The legal effect of the note transfer is determined by the nature of the note. If the note is nonnegotiable—that is, if it does not meet the requirements discussed below in

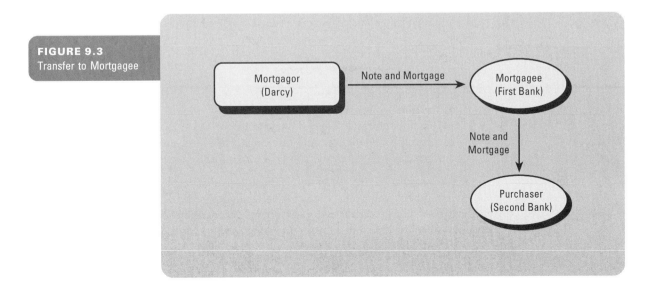

FIGURE 9.3
Transfer to Mortgagee

the chapter—the purchaser, Second Bank, acquires only the interest of First Bank subject to any defenses, both personal and real, that Darcy has against First Bank. For instance, if Darcy had been defrauded by First Bank when the loan was made, she could raise fraud as a defense against Second Bank.

holder in due course
A person who has purchased the note in good faith, for value, and without notice of defenses.

On the other hand, if the note is negotiable and is sold to a **holder in due course**, the holder in due course takes the note free of personal defenses of the borrower. An example of a personal defense is the payment by the borrower to First Bank after First Bank's assignment of the loan or an allegation of fraud against First Bank. If Second Bank qualifies as a holder in due course, it does not have to worry about such personal defenses, although Darcy can still press her legal rights against First Bank since the lender who originates the note can only be a holder but cannot be a holder in due course since it is not purchasing the note.

The borrower still retains "real" defenses, as defined by the UCC, even after negotiation of the note to a holder in due course. The same result might occur with a nonnegotiable note if the mortgagor signed a waiver of defense agreement, giving up the right to assert defenses. In mortgage transactions, this agreement usually takes the form of an **estoppel certificate** under which the mortgagor in the earlier example, Darcy, would state to the purchaser, Second Bank, that she has no defenses. Second Bank might require an estoppel certificate as a result of the risk of Darcy raising these defenses should she later attempt to rescind the debt.

estoppel certificate
A written statement in which a mortgagor asserts that she has no defenses to a note.

Real and Personal Defenses

Even when a negotiable note is transferred or a waiver of defense clause is used, certain defenses—most of which are called **real defenses**—could be raised by the mortgagor when sued on the debt by a holder in due course.

real defenses
Defenses that are valid against all holders of negotiable notes, including holders in due course.

Real defenses include:

1. Minority age of the mortgagor (less than 18)
2. Void transactions, such as a note and mortgage given to pay an illegal gambling debt
3. Fraud in the execution, where the mortgagor was tricked into executing documents that she had no reason to believe were a note and mortgage
4. Bankruptcy of the mortgagor
5. Forgery of the mortgagor's name on the note
6. An unauthorized alteration of the note
7. Mortgagor adjudicated insane by a court

In addition to these defenses, the Federal Trade Commission (FTC) has ruled that consumer purchasers and borrowers (goods and services for personal, family, or household use) can raise any available defenses, including **personal defenses**, against a holder in due course. Personal defenses include:

personal defenses
Defenses valid against holders of negotiable notes but not against holders in due course.

1. Breach of contract and warranty
2. Lack or failure of consideration
3. Fraud in the inducement, where the mortgagor signs documents as a result of lies about the terms, conditions, and other material aspects of the note and mortgage
4. Incapacity due to age, mental condition, or infirmity unless adjudicated as such

The mortgage crisis of 2007–2009 has sparked lively debate over the role of the holder in due course rule claiming that it may have facilitated some of the illegal and unethical practices that helped contribute to a worldwide economic recession. One commentator has even called for the elimination of this long established rule:

By making one adjustment in current law—eliminating the transferee/principal's status as a holder-in-due-course—the existing residential mortgage market can be reformed to provide appropriate incentives to the agent, the originator of the mortgage note, so that the originator will only induce the putative mortgagor to contract those mortgages that have a significant probability of being performed per all of their terms. I posit that the correct way to align incentives is to eliminate the transferee's status as a holder-in-due-course in residential real estate transactions by federally preempting state laws that provide that status.[83]

Under the Dodd-Frank Act, a mortgagor in default will have a so-called "Consumer Foreclosure Defense" in which he can allege against the note's holder. Among these defenses are that the broker or lender who originated the loan violated the Act's reasonable repayment requirements. For example, under the Act the loan originator must have been reasonable in evaluating whether the borrower could repay the loan at the time is was originated. The Act also contains antisteering provisions which are designed to prevent lenders from encouraging borrowers to take high cost, predatory mortgages. In essence, this becomes a new defense against a holder in due course.

Notice of Transfer   The sale of Darcy's note and mortgage to Second Bank might cause Darcy to pay the wrong creditor if she has not been notified, a problem that unfortunately does occur. Many of the problems relating to failures to notify mortgagors of an assignment of their note and mortgage have been hopefully resolved by amendments to RESPA. Any lender making a federally related mortgage loan, which includes those regulated by a federal agency (such as FHA or VA mortgage loans) or intended to be sold to a government-chartered corporation (such as Freddie Mac or Fannie Mae—now government owned) is required to make certain disclosures relating to assignments and transfers between those who service the mortgage. For instance, at the time of application, the lender must disclose information about whether loan servicing or the loan might be assigned. The lender also is required to provide designated statistical information relating to the likelihood of such assignment.[84] Further, within fifteen days of the transfer, both the transferor (called the "Goodbye Letter") and transferee (called the "Hello Letter") of the servicing rights must, under RESPA, notify the borrower in writing of designated information relating to the assignment.[85] In 2009, President Obama signed into law the Helping Families Save Their Homes Act, expanding the RESPA provisions and conferring residential borrowers more rights for when there is an assignment of their mortgage to a new holder. The impetus for the Act was the wave of foreclosures that hit the housing market in 2007–2009. Many of the mortgagors wished to notify their creditors to negotiate a workout but could not find who owned their mortgage notes. Many mortgage servicing companies were also little help partly due to the sheer volume of requests for workouts, a topic discussed earlier in this chapter. Under the new Act, incorporated as an amendment to TILA, a new creditor must notify the mortgagor within 30 days of the transfer of a residential mortgage. The notification must contain the following:

1. The identity, address, and telephone number of the new creditor
2. The date of transfer
3. How to reach the new creditor or its agent
4. The place where the transfer of ownership is recorded
5. Any other relevant information regarding the creditor

The new Act also provides the mortgagor with the right to sue for up to $4,000 in damages if the creditor violates the disclosure requirements.[86]

Electronic Transfer of Mortgages

Prior chapters discussed the current and future effects of the Internet on the real estate industry. These changes, some likely to be momentous in scope, range from

brokerage to real estate contracts and recordation. The all-important process of negotiating and transferring mortgage loans is also undergoing change due to several legal
and technological developments. One is the Mortgage Electronic Registration System
(MERS), created in 1993. MERS maintains a computer system for electronically
tracking servicing rights of those with various ownership interests in loans negotiated
from the primary to the secondary market. Since loans are often traded, typically
many times during their lifetimes, MERS alleviates the cumbersome system of hand-
recording in the public record of each county every time there is a mortgage assignment. This is accomplished by having MERS listed in the public record as the holder
of the mortgage. When a mortgage is transferred from one MERS subscriber to another, the assignment is noted electronically, but not on paper, in the public record.
All of the major parties in the mortgage industry (such as mortgage bankers and brokers) who lend and service the loans, key organizations in the secondary market
(such as Fannie Mae and Freddie Mac) who buy the loans, and the title and mortgage
insurance companies, subscribe to and pay fees to maintain MERS, which is itself a
corporation owned by major investment banks.[87] MERS came under close scrutiny by
the courts in the mortgage crisis of 2007–2009 when many borrowers claimed that it
was not a proper party for bringing foreclosure proceedings as discussed in the next
Kansas case.

A CASE IN POINT

In the case of *Landmark National Bank v. Kesler*,[88] the purchaser of a second mortgage, Sovereign
Bank, as well as MERS, filed a motion to set aside a default judgment in Kesler's bankruptcy case
on property secured by a first mortgage held by Landmark Bank. The holder of the second mortgage,
Millennia Mortgage Co., was given notice of the sale; however, neither Sovereign, who purchased
Millennia's note, nor MERS, who was Sovereign's nominee filed in the public record, was given notice. The Kansas Supreme Court ruled that MERS was just a "strawman" and not an agent and thus
lacked the power to foreclose. Sovereign also could not set aside the judgment because it was not
actually registered in the county's public record, but in MERS' name. The court also rejected both
parties' argument that they were denied their due process rights, asserting that "[t]he Due Process
Clause does not protect entitlements where the identity of the alleged entitlement is vague."

Due to the court cases as well as the new Helping Families Save Their Homes Act,
MERS has vowed to reform its system. It is introducing the MERS® InvestorID program,
which gives notice to the primary borrowers when a note is transferred to a new
investor.[89]

Another development is the electronic negotiable instrument provision in the Electronic Commerce in Global and National Commerce Act, or E-Sign, a federal statute discussed in Chapters 7 and 8. This provision, which applies only to notes secured by real
property, allows the holder of an electronic promissory note to be a holder in due course
just as if he were the holder of an actual paper note. However, E-Sign does require that
substantial security measures exist in the creation, transfer, and storage of the note.[90]
Moreover, the Uniform Real Property Recording Act was approved in 2004 by the
National Conference of Commissioners on Uniform State Laws (NCCUSL) and enacted
in seven states and the District of Columbia. This Act, designed to harmonize with
E-Sign, allows holders to be protected as holders in due course.[91]

Mortgage Termination by Foreclosure

foreclosure

Process initiated by the mortgagee to sell the collateralized real estate to satisfy the mortgagor's debt.

The final method of terminating the relationship between the mortgagor and mortgagee is **foreclosure**. Foreclosure involves a chronological sequence of *four* events that are best understood by referring to the history of mortgage law, which represents centuries of struggle between lenders and borrowers.[92] Historically, the mortgage was regarded as a conveyance of title to the mortgagee, subject to the condition that if the entire mortgage were paid on the due date, the conveyance of title to the mortgagee would be void. Thus, the mortgagor had a legal right of redemption on the date the mortgage was due and paid in full; but if the mortgagor failed to exercise this right (for example, if his carriage broke down on the way to the bank and the payment was one day late), the right to redeem the title was lost and the property belonged to the mortgagee.

default

Failure by a debtor to pay the note or carry out other obligations.

Today the failure to pay on the due date—the **default**—is the *first* event leading to foreclosure; however, today most lenders exercise **forbearance**—giving borrowers more and varying degrees of time to pay before calling them into default. The absolute right of redemption on the due date was often unjust, especially in cases such as the one in which the mortgagor failed to pay because of circumstances beyond his control. To provide relief, courts in equity began to allow mortgagors additional time for redemption in cases of hardship. (Courts of equity are described in Chapter 1.) By the seventeenth century, this right—known as the **equity of redemption**[93]—was given to all mortgagors.

forbearance

When a creditor allows the debtor to delay payment of a debt after it becomes due.

Today the *second* event in a foreclosure is the running of the time period in which a mortgagor may exercise the equity of redemption. This right is considered so important that courts will not allow a mortgagor to waive the right, which has become synonymous with the mortgagor's interest—the owner's "equity"—in the value of the property above the mortgage debt.

equity of redemption

A term used in the law of mortgages to describe either (1) the right in equity of the mortgagor to redeem after default in the performance of the conditions in the mortgage or (2) the estate which remains in the mortgagor after the execution of the mortgage.

The lenders' response to the creation of the equity of redemption was to file suit to cut off or foreclose the equity. Foreclosure, the *third* event in the foreclosure process, generally results in a lender's taking title or in sale of the property, discussed next.

Finally, many states believe that mortgagors should have an additional time period after a foreclosure sale to redeem the property; and statutes have been enacted to give the mortgagor a redemption period, usually running six months or a year. Thus, the running of the **statutory redemption** period is the *fourth* and (depending on state law) last event in the foreclosure process. Many of these statutes, generally exercised today in just a few states, such as Alabama, Colorado, Indiana, Iowa, Kansas, Michigan, Minnesota, New Jersey, North Dakota, and Wyoming, were passed during the Great Depression of the 1930s to enable those who lost their property in foreclosure (particularly farmers) additional time to reacquire their land should their economic fortunes, such as the harvest of a crop, change for the better. One negative aspect of the right of redemption is that it places a cloud on the title. For example, if a house is purchased before the redemption period ends, the original mortgagor, if he can pay the debt, still has a right to buy back his property. Moreover, during the period the mortgagor is generally permitted to occupy the property. Figure 9.4 illustrates the four steps involved in foreclosure.

statutory redemption

A time period provided by statute during which the mortgaged property can be redeemed.

In the states in which the statutory right of redemption exists, but where lenders are legally able, lenders will only offer to secure loans with deeds of trust instead of mortgages. This is due to the fact that after the power of sale is exercised—in contrast to a mortgagor's right of statutory redemption—all of the trustor-debtor's rights to the land generally terminate.

right of reinstatement

A legal right under a deed of trust in which the borrower in default can cure the debt prior to the trustee's acceleration of the note.

Although loans secured by deeds of trust are often not subject to a statutory right of redemption, these instruments do provide the trustor-debtor with the legal right to cure the debt for a period of time *prior* to the foreclosure sale under the trustor's **right of reinstatement**. Moreover, the borrower, by law, cannot waive the right just as he or she

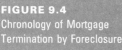

FIGURE 9.4
Chronology of Mortgage
Termination by Foreclosure

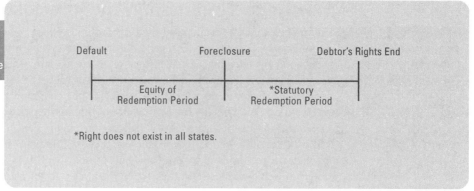

strict foreclosure

A process by which the
lender takes title to the
property after obtaining a
court order foreclosing
the equity of redemption.

cannot waive the equity of redemption. Generally, the period of time in which the right of reinstatement can be exercised is equivalent to the period of time in which the equity of redemption runs in a mortgage.

Lenders in only Vermont and Connecticut employ a procedure called **strict foreclosure**.[94] Lenders foreclose by taking full title to the property or by holding a public sale. Those lenders who take full title to the property do so by obtaining a court order foreclosing the equity of redemption. The laws surrounding equity and statutory rights of redemption are complex and can vary significantly among the states. In endnote 95, there is a reference to information for the laws of each particular state.[95]

Most foreclosures involve one of two types of public sale.[96] *First, foreclosure by sale* may be accomplished by a court-ordered sale that takes place after notice has been given to all parties with an interest in the property and after a hearing. This method, called a **judicial sale**, is available by statute in every state, but required by law in at least 13 states to safeguard the interests of the mortgagor.[97] To avoid the time and expense of a judicial sale, lenders in those states which allow both foreclosure methods prefer a *second* approach: a sale pursuant to a **power of sale clause** in the mortgage, whereby the mortgagor authorizes the trustee or court to sell the property after default at a public sale advertised and open to all bidders, but without court proceedings. This is called a **nonjudicial sale**. Deeds of trust, as stated earlier, typically allow the power of sale method of foreclosure that enables the trustee to sell the property privately on behalf of the lender-beneficiary instead of generally having an officer of the court, such as a civil sheriff, oversee it. (See endnote 97 for a list of states that use the judicial and nonjudicial approach to foreclosure.)

judicial sale

A decree of a court
directing the sale of
mortgaged property.

power of sale clause

A clause contained in
mortgages and deeds of
trust granting the lender
or trustee the right to sell
the property upon default.

nonjudicial sale

A foreclosure conducted
without a court
proceeding pursuant to
the rights granted under
the power of sale.

With both the judicial sale and, in some states, the exercise of a power of sale, statutes and custom dictate that notice of the sale be published in a local newspaper, generally in the legal notices sections, and posted on the property and that the sale be conducted by a public official such as a sheriff. However, in most of those states that allow deeds of trust, the trustee or his agent, generally a company or an attorney, personally conducts the sale on behalf of the beneficiary/lender.

With both kinds of foreclosure sales, the lender is often the only bidder at the sale, particularly when property values have become depressed. The mortgagee can bid up to the amount of the debt without paying cash, although the mortgagee's right to bid should be specified in a mortgage containing a power of sale clause. Any other party that outbids the mortgagee will receive title to the property. At the conclusion of the sale, a deed is executed by the person conducting the sale, although in a number of states, the mortgagor still holds the right to redeem the property by paying the purchase price within the statutory redemption period.

Although there are several similarities between judicial foreclosure and the exercise of a power of sale, one difference in particular has often been litigated in recent years. With a judicial foreclosure, the property is sold only after the debtor has had an opportunity to be heard in court; but this right is waived under a power of sale clause. Under the due process requirements of the Constitution, an owner is entitled to notice and to an opportunity for a hearing before property is taken. However, these requirements apply only to **state action**. Thus, the legal issue becomes this: Does the exercise of a power of sale clause involve sufficient state action to require a court hearing? There is a split of opinion on this question, although most courts have decided there is insufficient state involvement to require a hearing.[98] Because of these and other legal and policy objections to their use, power of sale clauses in mortgages or deeds of trust are not allowed in many states.

Statutes of limitation in each state bar suits on mortgage notes after a specified time period. Thus, a lender that neglects to enforce its rights on the note, such as failing to demand payment of a loan in default for a certain period of time, will lose its rights to collect the debt. Furthermore, many states have special statutes declaring that a mortgage will operate as a lien on the real estate only for a certain time after the note is due and payable. As a result of the latter statutes, a creditor who still might be able to collect on the note on which the statute of limitations has not run would be unable to foreclose the mortgage and sell the collateral. Thus, the note would become an unsecured debt.

On the other hand, if the property has lost much of its value and the mortgagor has other assets, can a mortgagee choose to treat the debt as unsecured? Generally, it can sue the mortgagor personally for the entire amount owed on the note and bypass the collateral.

During the 2007–2009 recession and mortgage meltdown, the ability of the holders of mortgage-backed securities (MBS) to force mortgagors into foreclosure was called into question. As discussed earlier, MBSs are made up of thousands of bundled mortgages; thus, ownership is disparate and their structure highly complex. This makes it very difficult to identify and prove who actually owns the mortgage notes secured by the foreclosed properties. If the holders of the securities can't prove their ownership interests in the specific collateral they are seeking to foreclose, some courts have argued that they have no standing to sue. One 2007 study revealed that out of 1,722 foreclosures,[99] 40 percent could not prove ownership by producing the mortgage note. In a 2007 ruling, a federal judge in Cleveland ruled that several large financial institutions had failed to produce the necessary documents and so could not proceed to foreclosure.[100] More suits have followed in a number of other states. It is noteworthy that the earlier discussion on MERS is also related to the *Landmark National Bank v. Kesler* case discussed in this chapter. That case, although with distinguishable facts to the "Cleveland cases", resulted in a mortgagee failing to produce the necessary documentation as well and therefore its standing to seize property in a foreclosure.

Deficiency Judgments After the Foreclosure Sale

If the sale proceeds exceed the first mortgage debt, first the junior mortgagees and then the mortgagor are entitled to the excess. If the proceeds of the sale of the collateral are less than the amount of the debt that remains on the note, the mortgagee is entitled to recover the deficiency from the mortgagor after the court awards the mortgagee a **deficiency judgment**. This commonly occurs when property values become depressed since the present value of the property can sink to levels lower than the amount of the debt still owed on the note.

Assume that Darcy borrows $100,000 from First Bank to finance a house that cost $105,000, but she later defaults and loses her house in a foreclosure sale. After paying

state action
A close involvement between a state or another government entity and the challenged action.

deficiency judgment
A court order stating that the borrower still owes money when the security for the loan does not entirely satisfy a defaulted debt.

down the principal, she still owes $95,000; but the foreclosure sale yields only one bid from First Bank for the house's current fair market value of $80,000. Darcy would still personally owe First Bank the debt that remains to be paid on the note, or $15,000.

Some states, by law, have modified the operation of deficiency judgments to protect mortgagors. For example, when the mortgagee purchases the property at the sale at a price below the market value and the market value exceeds the debt, courts do not hold the mortgagor liable for a deficiency. The fair market value provision is put into place to protect mortgagors when the mortgagee, usually the only bidder, tries to lowball its bid price to create a greater deficiency. This has been very beneficial for mortgagors during deep economic downturns when real estate values can plummet below the mortgage debt, such as what occurred in the Great Recession of 2007–2009.

In a few states, deficiency judgments have been abolished or limited by statute, particularly when the collateralized property is the mortgagor's home or farm. These laws, called *antideficiency judgment* statutes, are generally Depression Era laws created at the time to help struggling homeowners and farmers. Some states, including Alaska, Arizona, California, Hawaii, Montana, Nevada, North Dakota, Oklahoma, Oregon, and Washington, have, in effect, also abolished deficiency judgments by requiring all mortgage notes to be nonrecourse when used to finance a person's primary residence. Recourse and nonrecourse notes were discussed earlier in this chapter. Other states, such as Minnesota, protect homeowners from a deficiency judgment if a nonjudicial power of sale foreclosure is used.

Deficiency judgments can still be pursued against the homeowner who defaults on a second mortgage or a home equity loan. In some states, like California, the protection only applies to purchase money mortgages, which is the mortgage that initially financed the purchase of the home. If the homeowner subsequently refinances and the real estate is foreclosed upon, the lender may pursue the borrower for a deficiency judgment. (See endnote 101 for state-by-state laws regarding deficiency judgments.[101])

Exposure to deficiency judgments has always been a distinct risk for borrowers. Although for years many investors and buyers assumed that real estate only goes up in value, numerous historical examples clearly refute this assumption. For example, in Los Angeles, from 1989 to 1996, the average home lost 20 percent of its value after experiencing a 77 percent increase in prior years. Due to the oil bust of the 1980s, Houston witnessed a fall in the average home value from $78,600 to $61,800. Rather than wait until a foreclosure, many homeowners would "drive to the bank and drop off their keys to their homes and just leave."[102] Similarly, when the insurance industry left Hartford, Connecticut, in the late 1980s, home values plummeted by 67 percent. In the Great Recession of 2007–2009, some cities and states, particularly states that had experienced housing booms, like California, Florida, and Nevada, suffered decreases in fair market values that exceeded 40 and even up to 60 percent, causing mortgagors added financial stress, including possible bankruptcy in order to discharge their deficiency judgments. During this time, many borrowers engaged in a practice referred to as "strategic defaulting." They simply walked away from their homes and investments even though they could still pay their notes since the prospects of recovering their former values appeared to be virtually unattainable. This caused an even greater inventory of homes flooding the market, causing prices to drop further and equity to continue to evaporate. The ethical dimensions of strategic defaulting are discussed below.

These examples illustrate the obvious point. Real estate, like any investment, is subject to economic influences; but with real estate, unlike many other investments, it is not uncommon for a property's value to fall below the note's principal, resulting in a deficiency judgment.[103]

ETHICAL AND
PUBLIC POLICY
ISSUES

Is It Ethical for Borrowers to Strategically Default on Their Mortgage Notes?

During the recent Great Recession of 2007–2009, many borrowers simply gave up on paying their mortgage notes because the value of their properties had dropped well below the amount of the debts. Many, however, could still afford to pay their notes but chose to default anyway since the prospects of regaining their properties' value appeared to be unattainable for many years. Of course, if borrowers default, they lose their properties, often their homes. Moreover, in some states they can still be pursued for a deficiency judgment if the notes' holders feel there is a chance to collect on the remaining debt. The borrowers' credit ratings also suffer. Some borrowers also may feel shame for breaching their obligations. On the other hand, businesses routinely breach contracts if it appears to be a prudent business decision and often go into Chapter 11 bankruptcy to force a restructuring of their debts. This enables companies to continue in business which may save jobs. Is it ethical for private homeowners to strategically default?

Single Family Mortgage Foreclosure Act of 1994

Federal law regulating high-risk residential loans held by the Department of Housing and Urban Development.

Soldiers and Sailors Civil Relief Act of 1940

Federal law providing time limitations on foreclosures of homes owned by those in active military service.

deed in lieu of foreclosure

The mortgagor deeds the property to the lender in exchange for the lender's agreement to release the mortgagor from liability under the promissory note.

The widely disparate foreclosure procedures among the states, discussed earlier, have long contrasted with the relative standardization of mortgage origination for residential property. Congress responded to the increased costs of collection incurred by these various foreclosure procedures by enacting the **Single Family Mortgage Foreclosure Act of 1994**.[104] This Act imposes a uniform nonjudicial power of sale procedure for single family foreclosures on certain (often high-risk) mortgage loans assigned to and held by HUD. This law preempts state laws that mandate judicial sales. Congress's reason for enacting this law was that the power of sale procedure is necessary to reduce the extra time and costs of judicial sales so that foreclosed properties can be resold more quickly to families who need homes.

Lenders must also comply with the **Soldiers and Sailors Civil Relief Act of 1940**.[105] Under this Act, the enforcement of certain obligations, including mortgages and installment contracts, entered into by active members of the military service prior to their entry into the military service is temporarily suspended while they serve in the military.[106] For instance, this Act was invoked by reservists during the Persian Gulf crisis in 1991 as well as more recently during the conflicts in Iraq and Afghanistan.

Deed in Lieu of Foreclosure, Workouts, Short Sales, and Mediation

On occasion, the mortgagor will agree to convey title to the lender voluntarily. This negotiated transfer of title from the borrower to the lender, known as a **deed in lieu of foreclosure**, is typically in exchange for the lender's agreement to release the borrower from liability under the note. This means of private settlement is more commonly used by lenders who do not want to be involved in a long foreclosure process (often found in states mandating judicial sales and statutory redemption rights), during which time property can deteriorate and be vandalized before the lender is able to take title. Only the borrower's note with the lender who settled is discharged, and other liens may still attach to the property. Moreover, the settlement represents the forgiveness of a debt for which the debtor may still incur income tax liability, although Congress exempted residential properties (but not investment properties) from this tax liability from 2008 to 2012 to discourage foreclosures and encourage workouts.

Mortgagees generally seek "workout" agreements to prevent defaulting mortgagors from slipping into foreclosure proceedings. Mortgagors who have been otherwise diligent in paying their notes, but may have fallen into hard times due to unemployment, divorce, illness, or other catastrophic events, are given particular deference. Moreover, the FHA and VA, as well as Fannie Mae and Freddie Mac, require or highly encourage the lenders with which they deal to perform workouts with defaulting parties. Lenders prefer not to take back properties since legal and other fees associated with foreclosures are often expensive and the time and cost to manage and resell the properties can be considerable. In addition, foreclosures often occur when economic conditions have deteriorated, further impairing the lenders' ability to reduce their housing inventory.

workout

A mutual effort by a property owner and lender to avoid foreclosure or bankruptcy following a default.

Workouts between lenders and borrowers after a default can take many forms. Sometimes lenders renegotiate a repayment plan that will stretch out arrearages over an extended period of time, modify the original debt with a lower interest rate, or convert a variable rate into an affordable fixed rate. Lenders may also waive the due on sale clause and permit a qualified buyer to assume the defaulting party's property to avoid foreclosure.

short sale

A sale agreed to by the seller, buyer, and lender in which the proceeds fall short of what is owed to the lender.

If these approaches do not work, mortgagees will sometimes consent to a **short sale** in which the lender agrees to accept the proceeds from the sale of the home even when it does not cover the note. This works well for mortgagors when real estate prices plummet due to a recession; it also generally avoids a deficiency judgment and a hit on their credit scores. Mortgagees, on the other hand, avoid the costs of foreclosure and the addition of more housing inventory to manage and sell. And, unlike foreclosed homes which are sometimes damaged and vandalized, short sale properties are typically in good condition since the sellers continue to live in them and have incentives to sell them. Parties in short sales, however, do have competing interests which are often difficult to resolve. The mortgagor is very eager to discharge his mortgage debt and so seeks to sell the real estate quickly, while the mortgagee must be convinced the mortgagor is really insolvent and is thus really unable to continue paying the note. Moreover, since the market price is always less than the note (or the mortgagee wouldn't have agreed to it), the mortgagee will not sell it for less than what it would be expected to bring at the foreclosure sale. Lastly, the buyer is often seeking a deal on a distressed property and expects a deeply discounted price. Eventually, however, if a short sale or other kinds of loss mitigation efforts fail, lenders must foreclose to recoup their losses.[107]

Short sales as a workout alternative were aided in 2010 by new rules under the Home Affordable Foreclosure Alternatives (HAFA) program, a program for distressed homeowners who participate in the federal Home Affordable Modification Program (HAMP). HAFA, which runs through 2012, streamlines short sales. It requires that homeowners must first try to modify their loans, but if they do not qualify or cannot afford to, they and participating servicers will attempt to work out a short sale. The main requirements are that homeowners must demonstrates hardship, their home payment must exceed 31 percent of their gross income, and their unpaid principal must not exceed $730,000. If the short sale is completed, the mortgagor will not be exposed to a deficiency judgment. Some commentators are hopeful since over 100 mortgage servicers covering over 89 percent of mortgage debt outstanding in the United States are involved with the program.[108] Similarly, the Helping Families Save Their Homes Act of 2009 provides a "safe harbor" from civil liability for residential mortgage loan servicers and loan originators who engage in loss mitigation efforts such as those who participate in HAMP.

There have been other federal efforts to help distressed homeowners created recently as well. The HOPE for Homeowners program was set up to help those whose real estate value is much less than what they owe (sometimes called being "underwater") to reduce their monthly payments by converting to fixed 30-year FHA-insured loans. Similarly, the Home Affordability Refinance Program was created to help underwater homeowners subject to Fannie Mae or Freddie Mac mortgages to refinance into more stable, fixed mortgages. The Dodd-Frank Act also has infused billions of dollars to stabilize neighborhoods subject to mass foreclosures and to assist mortgagors in default. Lastly, many states have comparable programs to help distressed homeowners.

Mandatory or voluntary mediation, a topic covered in Chapter 7, has also been employed in recent years to facilitate workouts between lenders and troubled borrowers. State laws differ greatly, but some of the statutes mandatorily require the lender to show their calculations of how much they would lose by foreclosing as compared to modifying the loan. Once this information is available, both parties are better able to form some kind of workout to prevent foreclosure.[109]

Effect of Bankruptcy on Foreclosure

Federal bankruptcy law exists to protect debtors and to give them a fresh start. Bankruptcy can be important in foreclosures because once a debtor files a bankruptcy petition, an automatic stay on a foreclosure sale is created. This can cause serious problems for a mortgagee seeking to sell the mortgaged land quickly since the stay cannot be lifted during typically lengthy bankruptcy proceedings. However, there are *three* ways that a mortgagee can lift the automatic stay:

1. The mortgagee can prove that it is not being "adequately protected" during the bankruptcy period—generally because the property is declining in value. A mortgagee can request that the debtor maintain and insure the property or make payments as a means of protecting the property or can request foreclosure.
2. The mortgagee can prove that the debtor has no equity in the property—for instance, if the property has a value less than the note.
3. The mortgagee can prove that the property is not necessary for the reorganization or liquidation of the debtor's estate. For instance, assume that the debtor has five commercial properties. Four are productive, but one is vacant. The vacant property may be deemed an economic liability and therefore not important in reorganizing the debtor's estate and regaining a fresh start.[110]

One important issue related to bankruptcy is whether mortgagors automatically lose their homes to their mortgagees when they file for foreclosure. Mortgagors filing for bankruptcy must list all of their debts, including their mortgage debts, but may request a "reaffirmation" of certain debts which often includes the mortgage debt. Under a reaffirmation, a party agrees not to discharge the debt in bankruptcy and to continue paying the mortgage note according to its original terms. If the mortgagor defaults on the note after bankruptcy, the mortgage securing the loan allows the holder to seize the property.

Is a homeowner filing for bankruptcy vulnerable to creditors other than her mortgagee if she has excess equity over the amount owed on the mortgage note? A home's equity (the amount over the mortgage debt) is often a target of general creditors. The answer to that depends on the homestead exemption law of the state where the homeowner resides since some states protect all of a home's equity while others protect very little. This topic will be discussed in more detail in Chapter 10.

Installment Contracts

installment contract

Contract for the sale of real estate in which the seller finances the sale and the buyer pays the seller the purchase price over time.

An alternative to mortgage financing is the **installment contract** (also called a *land contract* or *contract for deed*). Under this arrangement, the purchaser takes possession of the real estate and makes installment payments to the seller until the purchase price is paid in full, at which time the purchaser receives a deed. With the cash sales contract, which has been the focus of our attention up to this point, there is a gap of several weeks or months between the signing of the contract and the closing, at which time the purchaser obtains financing and checks the title. With an installment contract, the gap will last for years because the contract is the method of financing. Installment contracts are especially popular when loans are unavailable from commercial mortgage lenders since installment contract sellers are often willing to accept a lower down payment and a lower interest rate.

The installment contract is, in many respects, a blend of a cash sales contract or real estate contract, covered in Chapter 7, and a mortgage. (For an installment land contract, see www.cengagebrain.com [see page xix in the Preface for instructions on how to access the free study tools for this text].) Like the cash sales contract, the installment sales contract should contain provisions covering matters such as the type of title, the method of proving title, the times for performance, and the type of deed to be delivered at closing. Like the mortgage, the installment sales contract will include provisions covering the terms of payment, the purchaser's duty to pay taxes and insure the premises, the seller's right to accelerate payment of future installments on the purchaser's default, and the purchaser's duty not to commit waste. Refer to the previous review of mortgage law and to the sales contract in Chapter 7 for discussion of the legal effect of these provisions. In addition, the following unique concerns may arise when installment contracts are used.

Interest of Parties

Bob and Barb, husband and wife, have decided to purchase a house as tenants by the entirety. In signing a cash sales contract, buyers such as Bob and Barb often neglect to specify the form of ownership in the contract, although the deed will state the nature of the buyers' interests. With an installment contract, however, it is especially important for buyers to state their ownership interests and survivorship rights because, with the installment contract in effect over several years, it is likely that one of the parties will die before the contract is completely performed.

Proof of Title

The purchaser in a land contract should require an abstract of title, title insurance policy, or other proof of title when the contract is signed. But even this proof of title does not fully protect the buyer, who does not receive a deed until the last installment payment has been made. Thus, the buyer might discover after making payments for fifteen years that the seller had conveyed the property to an innocent third party during the long time period after the contract was signed and before receipt of a deed. To prevent such a possibility, the purchaser should live on the premises or record the installment contract. Either action would be constructive notice to third parties of the purchaser's interest; however, in race states, recordation would be imperative to protect the purchaser's interest.

Remedies on Default

When the purchaser defaults on an installment contract, the seller has available, in addition to a full range of contract remedies, the remedy of foreclosure previously discussed. Most installment contracts also stipulate that if the purchaser defaults, the property, improvements on the property, and all payments that have been made are forfeited to the seller, sometimes called "strict forfeiture." In some cases, this is a harsh penalty—for instance, if a purchaser has made payments over several years and then is late on one payment. To alleviate this problem, statutes in several states grant the purchaser a certain period, such as six months, to make the overdue payments. Furthermore, according to judicial interpretation, sellers who elect to exercise their rights under the forfeiture clause may not recover under other remedies for breach of contract. In the absence of these statutes, some courts, such as the following one in South Carolina, have created an equitable period of redemption when purchasers default on their installment land contracts.

A CASE IN POINT

In *Lewis v. Premium Investment Corp.*,[111] William Lewis entered into an installment contract to purchase a lot. The contract contained the following default provision: "In the event the Purchaser should fail to make any due installment, and such default shall continue for a period of thirty (30) days, the Seller shall have the right to declare this contract terminated and all amounts previously paid by the Purchaser will be retained by the Seller as rent." Lewis defaulted after more than eleven years of payments. Later Lewis tried to pay the arrears, but the seller refused. On appeal, the court ruled that an equitable right of redemption exists in spite of the strict forfeiture provision in the installment land contract.

The South Carolina Supreme Court explained that an "installment land contract is frequently called a 'poor man's mortgage' because the vendor, as with a mortgage, finances the purchaser's acquisition of the property by accepting installment payments on the purchase price over a period of years, but the purchaser does not receive the benefit of those remedial statutes protecting the rights of mortgagors." Moreover, courts have the power to "deny or delay forfeiture when fairness demands."

Statutory Liens

A lien is the right of a creditor to have the debtor's property sold and to be paid from the proceeds. A creditor may obtain a lien as a result of a contract with the debtor; for example, the debtor may give the creditor a mortgage on real estate or a security interest in personal property. A creditor also may obtain a lien without the debtor's contractual agreement by following certain statutory requirements. **Statutory liens are especially important to mortgagees because, in many cases, they are given priority over a contractual (or consensual) lien, like a mortgage or deed of trust, thus lessening the value of the mortgagee's security.

> **statutory lien**
> A lien created by state statute that is placed on land to ensure payment of certain debts.

Mechanics' Liens

> **mechanic's lien**
> A type of statutory lien placed on real property to ensure payment to those who supply labor, services, or materials for improvement of the real property.

Mechanics' liens are given to people who furnish labor, services, or materials in connection with the improvement of real estate. Since the first statute in 1791, enacted by the Maryland legislature to encourage the construction of Washington, D.C., mechanics' liens have been designed to facilitate construction by giving security for payment to participants in the construction process. Although mechanic's lien statutes vary widely from state to state and can be extremely complex, they have certain common objectives.

> *For example, these [mechanics'] liens attach only to privately owned property and are designed to protect those persons involved in the construction process, including, in some cases, those parties not in contractual privity with the owner, such as subcontractors, by giving a lien for work performed and materials furnished in improving and enhancing the value of real property. In addition, the constitutionality and validity of these statutes have been upheld despite claims that they abridge freedom of contract and that they amount to a taking of property without due process of law.[112]*

While mechanic's lien statutes apply only to improvements on nongovernmental properties, payment bonds are typically required as a substitute to mechanics' liens on public projects. For example, the Miller Act's bonding requirements provide "payment security to subcontractors and others providing labor and materials on federal construction projects, and therefore encourages broader participation in these projects, and it enables the government to meet its equitable obligation to see that those whose work has gone into construction of a public project are paid."[113]

While the general policy objectives of mechanic's lien law are clear, specific issues can be complicated. The key issues are as follows:

1. When does the owner of real estate subject her interest to a possible mechanic's lien?
2. Who is entitled to a lien?
3. What type of work is covered?
4. What is the procedure for claiming a lien?
5. What are the priorities among lien holders?

The following sections consider these issues in order.

Owner's Contract or Consent   The states are not in agreement as to what the owner must do to subject her interest to a possible mechanic's lien. Obviously, it would be unfair to allow a contractor to construct a building secretly on the owner's property and then claim a lien for the value of the building. Just as obvious, if an owner has contracted for the construction of a building, the contractor should be entitled to a lien to secure the owner's payment.

Problems arise when a case falls between these extremes. For example, what if the owner did not contract directly with the builder but did consent to the construction under a contract between the builder and an installment contract purchaser or a tenant? Or what if the owner did not consent but knew of the construction? In general terms, for a mechanic's lien to attach to the owner's interest, some states require a contract by the owner, other states require only the consent of the owner, and still other states hold that the owner's knowledge alone is enough unless the owner makes it known immediately that he will not be responsible for the work. In addition, specific rules sometimes allow a lien when a tenant makes improvements required by the lease.

An electrical contractor filed a mechanic's lien on a tavern after the lessee authorized the contractor to repair code violations. In ***Christensen v. Idaho Land Developers, Inc.*** on page 358, the court considers whether the contractor who makes repairs under agreement with the tenant is entitled to a mechanic's lien.

END OF CHAPTER CASE

Once the legal rule for the particular state is determined, consent or knowledge becomes a question of fact whether or not there was a contract, as the following Illinois case demonstrates.

A CASE IN POINT

In *Fettes, Love and Sieben, Inc. v. Simon,*[114] a tenant hired a plumbing firm to install nine bathrooms in the leased building. While the bathrooms were being installed, the husband of the owner of the building visited the tenant and observed the work in progress. Later, when the tenant failed to pay, the plumbing firm filed a mechanic's lien. The court refused to enforce the lien: "The foundation of a mechanic's lien is the contract with the owner of the land for the improvement thereof and the furnishing of material and labor according to the contract, in connection with the statute giving the lien.... The contract for the improvements must either have been made with the owner or with one

continues

continued

whom the owner has authorized or knowingly permitted to have done the work for him. The defendant in the present case did not enter into any contract, either express or implied, with the plaintiffs nor did she perform any acts that would indicate that she gave her husband authority to act for her as her agent. She cannot be said to have knowingly permitted the alterations to be made on the premises since there was no evidence that she knew the work was being undertaken nor did she acquiesce in accepting the alleged benefits."

Persons Entitled to Lien   Statutes in each state determine the persons entitled to a lien, and the statutes usually include anyone—whether a general contractor or a subcontractor—who furnishes labor or materials for the improvement of the real estate. In many instances, the statutory language requires interpretation by a court. For instance, may a company that leases earth-moving equipment to a subcontractor claim a mechanic's lien for the rental payments? It might be argued that the equipment constitutes materials or that it constitutes labor since it is a modern substitute for manual labor. However, some courts, such as in New Mexico, have interpreted the lien law more narrowly and refuse to allow such liens.[115]

> **New York Rule**
> Owners who pay a general contractor when they have no notice of other liens are discharged up to the amount of payment.

> **Pennsylvania Rule**
> Owners who pay a general contractor before the time for filing subcontractor claims has expired might be liable to the subcontractors if the general contractor defaults.

Additional problems are created by allowing liens to subcontractors, who contract with a general contractor rather than with the owner. (See Figure 9.5.) If the owner pays the general contractor the full contract price and the general contractor fails to pay subcontractors, must the owner pay the subcontractors to avoid a lien? Different approaches have been developed to resolve this problem. For example, in some states using the **New York Rule**, owners who pay the general contractor when they have no notice of other claims will be discharged up to the amount of the payments. In those states that apply the **Pennsylvania Rule** (see Figure 5), subcontractors must notify owners within a specified time period of their intention to claim a lien; owners who pay the general contractor before the time period expires risk having to pay subcontractors as well if the general contractor defaults, disappears, or goes bankrupt. In such cases, the owner must pay

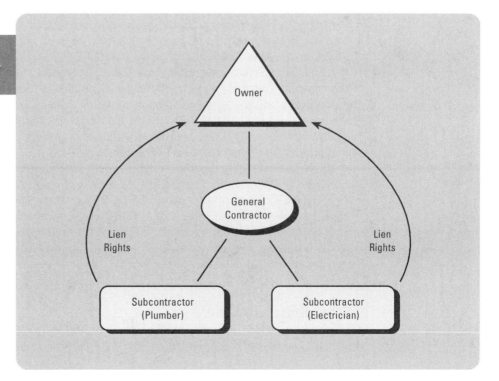

FIGURE 9.5
Subcontractors' Liens—
Pennsylvania Rule

more than what he originally contracted for. To protect themselves, owners in states using the Pennsylvania Rule, should obtain from the general contractor a sworn statement listing the subcontractors and, from each subcontractor on the list, a waiver of lien rights as the claims are paid.

Work Covered   Mechanics' liens are available only when the work results in a permanent improvement of the real estate, as the following Louisiana case illustrates.

A CASE IN POINT

In *Broadmoor Lumber Co. v. Liberto*,[116] with the consent of his landlord, a tenant who leased a store entered into a contract for the installation of shelving. To prevent the shelves from falling, the tenant had them attached to a plywood strip on the wall; but the shelves could be removed without seriously damaging the building. When the lumber company that supplied the lumber for the shelves filed a lien on the property, the court refused enforcement because the removable shelving was not a permanent improvement. The court also decided that the landlord was not liable for the materials since the only recourse against him in this case was under the lien statute.

Procedure for Claiming a Lien   In addition to any notices required of subcontractors, every lien claimant must record a lien statement specifying the amount due and the nature of the improvement within a certain period (for example, ninety days) after the work is completed. After recording the lien, the claimant must commence an action to enforce the lien within a limited time period—for instance, one year. If the court decides that the lien is valid, the property will be sold to satisfy the debt.

Priority   The priority given a lien claimant varies considerably from state to state. To illustrate, on April 15, the owner of a vacant lot hires a contractor to build a house. Work begins on May 15, and the house is completed on August 15. On September 15, the owner sells the house to a young couple; and they finance the purchase with a mortgage to Last Bank, which records the mortgage on that date. However, the seller does not pay the contractor.

Assume, in this state, contractors have ninety days to file a lien after completing work. The contractor records a lien on November 2. Mechanics' liens in most states are not given priority on the basis of the time of recording. Instead, priority usually dates from another event. In many states, the event is the date work commences—in this case, May 15. In other states, the event is the date of the contract: April 15. In only a few states does priority date from recording: November 2.

Under the first two approaches, the lien would have priority over the interests of the mortgagee and purchasers. Thus, unless the bank or the purchasers paid the contractor, the property could be sold to satisfy the contractor's lien. The bank or the purchaser would have recourse against the seller—if the seller could be found and was not bankrupt. To avoid losses from mechanics' liens that have not yet been recorded, purchasers should investigate the property for signs of recent improvements and, if there have been improvements, hold back part of the purchase price or place the purchase price in escrow until the period for recording liens has expired.

Other Statutory Liens

Other statutory liens might be filed against real estate and other property. These liens include environmental liens (discussed in Chapter 14), attachment liens, and judgment

attachment lien

A lien placed on real and personal property in which the court seizes the defendant's property on behalf of the plaintiff to ensure satisfaction of a judgment that might be awarded.

liens. An **attachment lien** is often used to prevent a defendant from hiding or selling property (especially personal property such as cars) before the conclusion of a lawsuit. In most cases, if the court decides that there is cause to believe that the defendant will secrete the property, the plaintiff will post a bond and a writ (that is, an order) of attachment will be issued directing the sheriff to seize the property in question.[117] If the property is real estate, the attachment is recorded to give notice to prospective purchasers. After attachment is ordered (and if the plaintiff ultimately wins the case), a writ of execution will be issued authorizing the sheriff to sell the attached property to satisfy the judgment.

judgment lien

A lien that attaches to a defendant's property when the plaintiff wins a judgment in the jurisdiction in which the property is located.

If an attachment lien is not used, the plaintiff may enforce a judgment through a **judgment lien**. A judgment lien is given upon the judgment being rendered, upon the judgment being recorded, or after a court order. A judgment lien allows the creditor to attach any number of assets, including bank accounts, wages, and inventory, as well as real estate. Once the creditor records the judgment lien the lien acts as a cloud on the title that prevents the debtor from selling the real estate since a buyer would still be subject to the lien. The judgment lien enforcement procedure is similar to the attachment lien procedure.

CASES

Home Ownership and Equity Protection Act
BANKERS TRUST OF CALIFORNIA v. PAYNE
188 Misc.2d 726; 730 N.Y.S.2d 200 (N.Y. 2001)

VAUGHAN, Judge. [Plaintiff, Bankers Trust of California acting as a trustee for Delta Funding Company, sought a summary judgment against the borrower and defendant Errol Payne, who defaulted on a home loan. Payne countered by raising, among other arguments, a defense pursuant to the Home Ownership and Equity Protection Act of 1994 (HOEPA). After the court held for Payne, the plaintiff moved to reargue and renew its request for a summary judgment.]

Defendant is a 74-year-old native of Trinidad and is the owner of the subject property, which is located at 463 Rutland Road in Brooklyn, New York, where he has resided for over 20 years. Defendant asserts that in early 1996, he was approached by a representative of Delta Funding Corporation (Delta), the servicing agent for plaintiff which is engaged in the business of issuing mortgage loans, and that such representative repeatedly solicited him to take out a $90,000 loan to reface his property. Defendant claims that due to the fact that certain documents appeared altered between the time that he reviewed them and the time that he executed them, he timely canceled that loan. Defendant states that he was then solicited by and secured a loan for $50,000 from FHB Lending Corporation (FHB). He claims that he only received $16,443.16 of this FHB loan, and that after he complained about this, he was contacted by a person who told him that he could retrieve the rest of the $50,000 loan, but only if he agreed to take out an additional $25,000 loan. Defendant asserts that he was then driven to an office where he met with a

representative of Delta and was told that he was signing an application for a $25,000 loan. Defendant, in fact, signed a mortgage loan for $75,000.

Defendant asserts that he did not receive funds from this $75,000 mortgage loan, and that he was shocked when he received a notice from Delta demanding that he make monthly payments of over $700 towards a $75,000 mortgage. He claims that he did not believe that he had signed mortgage closing documents and would never have knowingly taken such a large loan because he could not afford it. He states that out of fear that he would lose his home, he made the monthly payments against the loan in a timely manner through December 1999.

The subject note and mortgage are dated November 6, 1997. They reflect a loan in the principal amount of $75,000, secured by defendant's home, payable in monthly installments of $713.68 at the interest rate of 10.99% and at the default interest rate of 24%. Plaintiff brought this action on December 28, 1999, alleging that defendant has defaulted on the mortgage by failing to make monthly payments due on June 1999 through December 1999, and seeking foreclosure of the mortgage.

* * *

In addition to the issues raised by defendant's defenses of fraud and the issues raised regarding the disbursement of the loan proceeds, defendant has raised a defense pursuant to the Home Ownership and Equity Protection Act of 1994

(15 USC @ 1639) ("the HOEPA") which precludes the granting of summary judgment in favor of plaintiff. The HOEPA is an amendment to the Truth in Lending Act (15 USC @ 1601 et seq.) ("the TILA") which added consumer protections to that Act. Congress enacted the HOEPA as an amendment to the TILA "to provide borrowers some protection from predatory loans."

Where a mortgage loan is a "mortgage" under the definition set forth in 15 USC @ 1602(aa)(1), it is subject to the requirements and restrictions of the HOEPA (15 USC @ 1639). To qualify as a "mortgage" within the definition of 15 USC @ 1602 (aa)(1), a mortgage loan must be a "consumer credit transaction" with a "creditor," secured by the "consumer's principal dwelling," and must be a second or subordinate residential mortgage as opposed to a "residential mortgage transaction," a "reverse mortgage transaction," or a transaction under an "open end credit plan." Additionally, either the annual percentage rate of interest at consummation for the loan transaction must exceed certain levels or "the total points and fees" payable by the borrower at or before closing must exceed the greater of 8 percent of the total loan amount or $400.

Where a mortgage loan meets this definition and violates the provisions of the HOEPA, the mortgagor has a right to rescind the mortgage loan transaction pursuant to 15 USC @ 1635 and to receive the TILA statutory penalties pursuant to 15 USC @ 1640(a)(4).

Such violation also constitutes a defense in a mortgagee's foreclosure action against the mortgagor.

Pursuant to 15 USC @ 1639(d), a mortgage loan may not provide for an increased rate of interest upon default, and, pursuant to 15 USC @ 1639(c), a mortgage loan may not contain a prepayment penalty, unless it falls within the limited exception in 15 USC @ 1639(c)(2). Additionally, a creditor violates the HOEPA if it "engage[s] in a pattern or practice of extending credit to consumers under mortgages referred to in section 1602 (aa) ... based on the consumers' collateral without regard to the consumers' repayment ability, including the consumers' current and expected income, current obligations, and employment."

The mortgage note at issue specifies that after default, the interest rate rises to 24%. It thus includes a provision for an increased rate of interest upon default in violation of 15 USC @ 1639(d). It also contains a "prepayment rider" which authorizes a prepayment penalty of 5% of the loan principal, which constitutes a provision for a prepayment penalty in violation of 15 USC @ 1639(c)(1)(A). Furthermore, defendant claims that Delta did not ask him for verification of his income or otherwise certify the loan's affordability, and, therefore, extended credit to him without regard to his repayment ability in violation of 15 USC @ 1639(h).

Thus, the mortgage loan at issue, on its face, contains violations of the HOEPA. In opposition to defendant's argument regarding his defense under the HOEPA, plaintiff contends that such violations of the HOEPA are irrelevant because the mortgage loan does not meet the definition of a mortgage set forth in 15 USC @ 1602(aa)(1) and is, therefore, not subject to the requirements of the HOEPA. In addressing this contention, the court notes that it is undisputed that plaintiff is a "creditor" within the meaning of 15 USC @ 1602(f).

Additionally, the mortgage loan was taken to pay off an existing loan from another lender and for refacing work on defendant's home. It thus constituted a second or subordinate mortgage loan and involved a "consumer credit transaction." In addition, since the mortgage broker, Allstate Consultants, was paid a fee of $6,375 or 8.5% of the loan principal, the total points and fees defendant paid at or before closing exceeded eight percent of the total loan amount.

Plaintiff argues, however, that the loan was not secured by defendant's principal dwelling because the term "dwelling" is defined in 15 USC @ 1602(v) as a "residential structure ... which contains one to four family housing units." It asserts that at the time defendant applied for the loan, the premises contained five units. In support of this assertion, plaintiff has submitted the Small Residential Income Appraisal Report of C.P. Appraisals, Inc., which reflects that in addition to the four family housing units, the premises contained a restaurant/club on the first level. This report, however, states that the restaurant/club was "non-functioning." Defendant has submitted a printout from the New York City Department of Housing Preservation and Development, reflecting that his home is, in fact, legally registered as a four-family building. Thus, there is no evidence that the building at issue was ever registered as other than a four-family dwelling and the appraiser's report does not establish that at the time of the loan, the building was being used for commercial purposes or that there was an illegal commercial fifth unit in operation at such premises.

Moreover, as noted above, the definition of "dwelling" under 15 USC @ 1602(v) only requires that the dwelling be a residential structure "contain[ing] one to four family housing units." There is no further requirement or exemption specified therein. The building at issue did contain four family housing units, and the loan was not taken for a business or commercial purpose. Additionally, the subject mortgage itself states on page 3 thereof that it "covers real property principally improved by a one to four family dwelling" and the assignment of the mortgage from Delta to Bankers Trust Company of California, N.A. expressly states that "this is a mortgage subject to special rules under the Federal Truth in Lending Act."

* * *

Consequently, inasmuch as plaintiff has failed to show that the court overlooked or misapprehended the law or facts and since it is merely attempting to rehash questions already decided by the court, it has failed to set forth a valid basis for reargument. Plaintiff also has not presented any additional material facts which establish a valid basis for renewal.

Accordingly, plaintiff's motion for reargument and renewal is hereby denied.

Truth in Lending Act
SMITH v. GOLD COUNTRY LENDERS
289 F.3d 1155 (9th Cir. 2002)

FLETCHER, O'SCANNLAIN, and BERZON, Circuit Judges. Debtor Geraldine Smith cross-appeals a decision by the Bankruptcy Appellate Panel ("BAP") denying her claim for actual damages as a result of Gold Country Lender's [sic] violation of the Truth in Lending Act ("TILA"), 15 U.S.C. §1601. We have jurisdiction pursuant to and review the decision of the BAP *de novo*. For the reasons assigned, we affirm. In June 1994, Smith borrowed $28,000 through Gold Country and executed a $28,000 note and deed of trust on a California property. That same day Smith also executed a cross-collateral installment note to Gold Country for $43,000 at 12% interest and a cross-collateral deed of trust recorded against real property Smith owned in Oregon as additional security. The bankruptcy court found that Gold Country violated 15 U.S.C. §1638(a)(3) & (4), when, acting as a creditor, it failed to conspicuously disclose and define the "finance charge" and "annual percentage rate" (designated as such) in any of the documents executed in the June 1994 transaction. The court found that these violations subjected Gold Country to civil liability. However, the court also found that while Smith was entitled to $1000 in statutory damages, the maximum allowed by statute at that time, she failed to show, and was therefore not entitled to, any actual damages under 15 U.S.C. §1640(a)(1). [Author's note: The maximum as of 2004 is $2,000.]

"Except as otherwise provided in this section, any creditor who fails to comply with any requirement imposed under this part … with respect to any person is liable to such person in an amount equal to … (1) any actual damage sustained by such person as a result of the failure;…."

The BAP agreed, holding that where "a debtor cannot establish that he or she would have either gotten a better interest rate or foregone the loan completely, then no actual loss is suffered." Because Smith failed to prove detrimental reliance on the financing terms offered by the creditor, the BAP affirmed the bankruptcy court's denial of her claim for actual damages. The bankruptcy court and the BAP relied on cases from other circuits holding that such detrimental reliance must be shown in order to receive an award for actual damages. Circuit courts that have decided the issue have held that detrimental reliance is an element of a TILA claim for actual damages.

We join with other circuits and hold that in order to receive actual damages for a TILA violation, *i.e.*, "an amount awarded to a complainant to compensate for a *proven* injury or loss," Black's Law Dictionary 394 (7th ed. 1999), a borrower must establish detrimental reliance. Without any evidence in the record to show that Smith would either have secured a better interest rate elsewhere, or foregone the loan completely, her argument must fail—she presents no proof of any detrimental reliance, *i.e.*, any actual damage. Accordingly, we affirm the judgment of the BAP denying Smith's claim for actual damages.

AFFIRMED.

Due on Sale Clauses
RUBIN v. CENTERBANC FEDERAL SAVINGS & LOAN ASSOCIATION
487 So.2d 1193 (Fla. App.2 Dist. 1986)

SCHOONOVER, Judge. Appellant, Leslie A. Rubin, general partner of Leslie A. Rubin Limited, by and for Leslie A. Rubin, Limited, a Florida limited partnership, seeks review of a final judgment entered in favor of appellee, Centerbanc Federal Savings & Loan Association, in an action on a mortgage contract. We affirm.

In 1977, the mortgagor, Leslie A. Rubin, borrowed $450,000 from Centerbanc to finance the purchase of a building. A promissory note and mortgage were executed to secure repayment of the borrowed funds. The mortgage contained * * * [the following due on sale clause]:

16. The whole of said principal sum and interest shall become due at the option of the mortgagee in the event of any sale, or any other change of ownership of the mortgaged property or any sale or other transfer of the interest of the mortgagor, whether occurring by voluntary act or involuntarily or by operation of law or otherwise without the prior written consent of the mortgagee, consent will not be unreasonably withheld.

At the closing of the transaction, the phrase, "consent will not be unreasonably withheld," was added to paragraph 16 at the mortgagor's request.

In 1983, the mortgagor entered into a contract for the sale of a one-half interest in the building. The bank would not consent to the sale unless the purchaser agreed to increase the interest rate specified in the note and mortgage to the prevailing market rate. The purchasers refused to buy the property unless the interest rate remained the same.

When an agreement between all concerned could not be reached, the mortgagor filed an action seeking specific performance of the mortgage contract, damages for breach of contract, and damages for tortious interference with an advantageous relationship with a bona fide prospective purchaser. At the conclusion of a trial on the merits, the court found for the bank. The court specifically found that * * * the bank did not unreasonably withhold its consent to an assumption of the mortgage by requiring an increase in the interest rate. This appeal timely followed.

The mortgagor contends that the trial court erred in allowing the bank to demand, as a condition to giving its consent to assumption of the mortgage, that the interest rate in the note and mortgage be increased. We disagree.

It is now settled that a lender may enter into or enforce a contract containing a due-on-sale clause with respect to a real estate loan. Any limitation of this right must be clearly set forth in the contract involved. The lender, whether private or institutional, may enforce such a clause without showing an impairment of security.

We, therefore, must look to the contract to determine the rights and limitations of the parties.

* * *

In this case, paragraph 16 * * * allows the lender to accelerate the loan where the lender's written consent has not been obtained prior to a change in ownership, and limits the withholding of this consent only to that which is reasonable. Because due-on-sale provisions may be enforced, not only to prevent impairment of security, but to protect the financial stability of mortgage lenders by enabling them to receive current interest rates on the money they lend, it is reasonable for a lender to withhold consent to an assumption unless the parties agree to increase the interest rate to the prevailing market rate.

* * * We hold, therefore, that the bank did not unreasonably withhold its consent to assumption of the mortgage by requiring an increase in the interest rate to the prevailing market rate. The trial court, accordingly, did not err in entering a judgment for the bank, and we affirm.

Exit Fees and Prepayment Clauses

DELTA RAULT ENERGY 110 VETERANS, L.L.C. v. GMAC COMMERCIAL MORTGAGE CORP.

2004 WL 1752859 (E.D. La. 2004)

BARBIER, Judge. Before the Court is defendant's Motion to Dismiss for failure to state a claim upon which relief may be granted and, alternatively for Partial Summary Judgment. Plaintiffs oppose the motion. Upon consideration of the briefs, arguments of counsel, the record, and applicable law, the Court finds that defendant's motion should be GRANTED.

Background

On July 10, 2000, plaintiffs, Delta Rault Energy 110 Veterans ("Delta Rault") and Clements Realty ("Clements"), executed a promissory note for $8,200,000.00 to obtain short-term financing from defendant, GMAC Commercial Mortgage Corporation ("GMAC"), for the purchase of the Stewart Enterprise Building. In Section 2.06 of the promissory note there is a provision that establishes an "Exit Fee." The terms of this provision state that on the date a prepayment of principal is made, or on the date of maturity of the loan, or when the loan becomes immediately due, defendant must pay a fee equal to 1% percent of the original principal amount of the promissory note. However, the same provision allows for a waiver of the Exit Fee if defendant provides the permanent financing. During the term of the promissory note, plaintiffs obtained permanent financing from a source other than defendant.

In order to close the loan for permanent financing with the lender, plaintiffs had to pay the mortgage with defendant. In order to completely satisfy the mortgage, plaintiffs paid

the Exit Fee of $82,000. On September 30, 2003, plaintiffs filed suit against defendant, seeking to recover the Exit Fee payment and seeking damages for defendant's alleged delayed repayment of certain reserve account deposits.

* * *

I Classification of the Exit Fee

Plaintiffs contend that the Exit Fee is more like a prepayment penalty and is merely an invalid stipulated damages clause because it does not reasonably approximate the damages that defendant would sustain due to plaintiffs' early repayment. Instead, plaintiffs argue that the amount is arbitrary, and the parties must make a reasonable attempt to approximate the damages. Plaintiffs state that no effort was made to "truly estimate" the damages. However, according to John Murray, Enforceability of Prepayment-Premium Provisions in Commercial Loan Documents, Real Estate Law and Practising Course Handbook Series (1999), exit fees are charged in connection with short-term financing, and it is unclear whether the fees are additional interest, a prepayment penalty, or some other fee.

Therefore, exit fees are not automatically considered prepayment penalties or stipulated damages. In fact, in the present case, it is clear that the Exit Fee is not a prepayment penalty or stipulated damages, but is either an additional fee connected to the loan or deferred interest. First, the note explicitly states that the Exit fee is "consideration for

Lender's making of the loan to Borrower," and that defendant would not otherwise have been willing to make the loan but for plaintiffs' covenant to pay the Exit Fee. Further, the contract stated that the Exit Fee would be owed to defendant even if the loan went to maturity. Thus, plaintiffs' argument that the Exit Fee is simply a prepayment penalty or stipulated damages must fail. Instead, this Court finds that the Exit Fee was an additional fee or deferred interest added as consideration for defendant making the loan.

* * *

Conclusion

This Court finds that the Exit Fee was negotiated as an additional fee or deferred interest added as consideration for the loan. Further, the Exit Fee provision of the Note is clear and unambiguous, and parol evidence is inadmissible to determine the parties' intent. Accordingly,

IT IS ORDERED that defendant's Motion to Dismiss for failure to state a claim upon which relief may be granted and, alternatively for Partial Summary Judgment is GRANTED.

Mortgage Assumption
ADAMS v. GEORGE
119 Idaho 973, 812 P.2d 280 (1991)

BISTLINE, Justice. The Adams' complaint alleged that Carol J. George had purchased [from Unruh/Friesen] real property which was encumbered by a deed of trust granted by a preceding owner. The Adams alleged that this trust deed had been assigned to them; they claimed that appellant had assumed and agreed to pay the obligation it secured. They further alleged that the deed of trust had been foreclosed but that a deficiency remained with respect to the underlying obligation for which the trust deed had been given as security. They sought to recover from George the amount of the deficiency together with attorney fees and costs incurred in litigation.

Both parties moved for summary judgment. In ruling for the Adams, the district court determined that George had assumed personal liability for the indebtedness which remained after foreclosure of the trust deed. The court heard evidence on the issue of the claimed deficiency and entered judgment for the Adams for $15,763, which included interest, attorney fees and costs. George's appeal assigns error in so being held liable.

* * *

George asserts that the transaction between George and Unruh/Friesen was a "wraparound mortgage" (WAM) transaction. The principal defining characteristic of a WAM is the "wrapping" of the existing debt owed by the seller to a prior seller or lending institution. The new buyer obligates herself or himself to the seller, who in turn remains obligated to pay the existing mortgage debt. While buyers and sellers frequently choose to handle preexisting mortgage obligations by requiring that the new buyer assume them, the use of the WAM is a mutually exclusive alternative to the more conventional "straight assumption."

The Idaho appellate courts have not had occasion to discuss WAMs. A Texas appellate court recently described the wraparound mortgage:

The wraparound mortgage is a relatively new financing device which is used instead of a conventional junior lien mortgage. The wraparound mortgage is a subsequent and subordinate mortgage secured by real property upon which there exists a first mortgage that is outstanding and unsatisfied. The purchase money wraparound mortgage differs from a conventional second mortgage in that the *wraparound seller in the transaction remains personally liable under any prior obligation, but the purchaser never becomes personally obligated for such. A distinctive feature of such a transaction is the agreement by the wraparound seller that upon receipt of the debt service on the wraparound mortgage a deduction will be made therefrom and remitted directly to the first mortgagee to credit the required debt service on the first mortgage.*

Greenland Vistas, Inc. v. Plantation Place Assoc., Ltd., 746 S.W.2d 923, 925 (Tex. 1988) [emphasis added].

* * *

There is a critical distinction between one who purchases property and agrees to assume an existing debt and one who merely purchases property "subject to" an existing encumbrance.

The mere conveyance of mortgaged property "subject to" an existing encumbrance granted to secure an existing mortgage does not constitute an assumption of personal liability by the purchaser. This distinction is well recognized in Idaho. The purchaser is not personally liable to pay an obligation secured by an existing encumbrance unless the assumption is proved by clear and convincing evidence.

There is evidence that George's purchase of the property was "subject to" the existing encumbrances. The warranty deed contains the "subject to" language. * * * The closing statements denote that the property was "conveyed subject to" the two existing obligations.

* * *

The district court's grant of summary judgment to the Adams is vacated, and the cause is remanded to the district court for a jury trial on the issue of whether George assumed the obligation created by the Adams note. * * *

Mechanic's Lien
CHRISTENSEN v. IDAHO LAND DEVELOPERS, INC.
104 Idaho 458, 660 P.2d 70 (App. 1983)

BURNETT, Judge. We are asked to decide whether a contractor who makes repairs and improvements to real property, under agreement with a tenant, is entitled to impose a laborer's and materialman's lien against the landlord's interest in the property. Upon the facts presented in this case, the district court entered summary judgment holding that the contractor was entitled to such a lien. We affirm.

The facts essential to our opinion are undisputed. The landlord, Idaho Land Developers, Inc., leased a tavern and restaurant to the tenants, William P. Kelly and Kelly Enterprises, Inc., for a period of fifteen years. The lease instrument required the tenants to "maintain the plumbing, heating, air conditioning equipment, and electrical outlets ... and all other maintenance."

The lease further provided that the tenants "shall not do or permit to be done in said premises anything that would be dangerous, illegal or unlawful under the ordinances of the City of Idaho Falls...."

After approximately four months had elapsed under the lease, the landlord received a letter from the chief electrical inspector of the City of Idaho Falls. The letter, addressed to the landlord with copies to the tenants and to the city fire department, listed thirty-one "electrical violations and deficiencies" found during an inspection of the subject property. The violations and deficiencies included numerous instances of improper wiring, inadequate receptacles, missing outlet covers, and loose or open wiring. The inspector's letter advised that the corrections "must be made within fifteen days from receipt" of the letter. The landlord forwarded the letter to the tenants, who then engaged a contractor, Loc Electric, to remedy all the violations and deficiencies. The contractor performed the work as requested, but the tenants failed to pay. A claim of lien for labor and materials was filed of record against the property. When the landlord similarly failed to pay, the contractor successfully sued to foreclose the lien.

* * *

The contractor's claim of lien was grounded in I.C. §45-501, which provides, in pertinent part, as follows:

> Every person performing labor upon, or furnishing materials to be used in the ... alteration or repair of ... any structure has a lien ... for the work or labor done or materials furnished, whether done ... or furnished at the instance of the owner of the building ... or his agent.

As a general principle, a tenant is not the "agent" of the landlord, for the purpose of §45-501, merely by virtue of a lessor-lessee relationship. * * * However, this principle has two closely related corollaries in Idaho. First, a landlord's interest in real property may be subjected to a lien, for work performed by agreement with the tenant, if the lease specifically requires the tenant to see that the work is done. Second, the landlord's interest may be subjected to a lien if he requests the work to be done. The latter corollary applies to any case where the landlord has done "some act in ratification of, or consent to [,] the work done and the furnishing of material and labor."

In the present case, the district court did not distinguish between these two corollaries. However, the court held that the general requirements imposed by the lease— that the tenants "maintain" the premises, and that they refrain from any unlawful use of the premises—were rendered "specific" in their application when the landlord forwarded to the tenants the city's letter enumerating thirty-one corrections needed in the electrical system on the premises. This view of the case invokes the first corollary, that a landlord's interest is lienable if the lease specifically requires the work in question. The court also held that the landlord's act of forwarding the city's letter to the tenants represented "a ratification or a consent for the work to be done." This view would bring the case within the second corollary.

* * *

[The district court judgment is affirmed.]

KEY TERMS

PROBLEMS

1. Thelma held a mortgage on property owned by Louise. The mortgage contained an acceleration clause. Because of an error in her arithmetic, Louise made one monthly payment for less than the amount due. After discovering her mistake, Louise paid the correct amount one day late. Can Thelma foreclose the mortgage? Why or why not?

2. Floyd deeded his farm to Little Mercy Hospital at a time when he was a patient and in debt to the hospital. After signing the deed, he retained possession of the farm without paying rent until his death. Should the farm be included in his estate? Why or why not?

3. First Bank has agreed to finance Henry's purchase of a house. The mortgage closing has been scheduled for April 30, and Henry's first mortgage payment is due on June 1. Under their agreement, First Bank is to collect $600 each month to be placed in an escrow account for the payment of real estate taxes. The annual taxes of $7,200 are due on December 1 each year. What is the maximum amount that the bank can collect from Henry at the closing to place in the escrow account? Why?

4. In Problem 3, assume that Henry agreed to pay First Bank 10 percent interest annually on the loan, which was the maximum interest allowed by law. The bank also charged Henry for a credit report, a survey, a lender's title insurance policy, attorney's fees payable to the bank's attorney, an appraisal fee, and a fee for preparation of legal documents used in the mortgage closing. These charges and a bank commission of $10,000 were deducted from the amount of the loan, with the remainder distributed to Henry. Is the loan usurious? Why or why not?

5. Elmo decided to sell his house, which was mortgaged to Last Bank. After Elmo found a buyer who was willing to pay cash, Last Bank advised him that he could not pay off the balance due on the mortgage but, instead, had to continue his monthly payments. Is Elmo entitled to pay off the mortgage? Why or why not?

6. In Problem 5, assume that Elmo's mortgage contained a due on sale clause. Would Elmo's sale of the house trigger the due on sale clause, thus entitling Elmo to pay off the mortgage in full? Why or why not?

7. Edith obtained a mortgage on her house from Pioneer Corporation. Unknown to Edith, the president of Pioneer sold her mortgage and note to a bank. Edith continued to make her mortgage payments to Pioneer, and the president used the payments for his personal expenses. Later, when the president's scheme was discovered, the bank demanded that Edith make these payments again. What arguments should Edith raise in defense? Explain.

8. Agnes borrowed money from National Savings Bank and signed a mortgage agreement whereby she agreed to pay the maximum rate of interest allowed by law. The mortgage agreement did not allow Agnes to prepay the mortgage in full. Agnes later decided to prepay the mortgage, and she offered to pay the bank a prepayment fee of three percent of the original amount of the mortgage debt. If you work for National as a loan officer, what legal question would you want to resolve before accepting Agnes's offer? Why?

9. On February 4, Stewart gave Hughes a mortgage to secure a debt of $100,000. Hughes was obligated to advance $55,000 of this amount in the future. The mortgage was recorded on February 7; and the $55,000 was advanced in April, May, July, and August. However, on November 6, Ashdown Hardware acquired a mechanic's lien for materials furnished to improve the mortgaged property. The lien was effective from the date materials were originally furnished—February 21. Does the Hughes mortgage or the Ashdown lien have priority if the property is sold? Why?

10. For years, legal and ethical controversies surrounded the Real Estate Settlement Procedures Act. They involved possible kickbacks or referral fees given to mortgage brokers by lenders bringing in clients who are being charged above-market interest rates. Consumer advocates argued that borrowers were paying more than they should for these loans. For example, the difference between what a borrower pays in interest and the market interest rate is called the *yield spread*. However, if a borrower pays extra (or a premium) because of the deal struck between the broker and the lender, he is paying a *yield-spread premium*. For example, say a mortgage broker secures for the borrower an interest rate of 5.60% versus the par rate of 5.25%. For this, the broker gained a higher fee based on the higher interest rate. Under the Real Estate Settlement Procedures Act, paying a premium on the yield spread was not a violation if the broker performs services reasonably equivalent to the premium amount. Lenders argued that mortgage brokers were, in fact, performing important services. For example, they put their clients together with lenders who would defer closing and other upfront costs so that a borrower could afford the loan. However, critics have long asserted that this assumes that the client cannot afford the upfront costs and that the broker is providing a service of placing him with the right loan at a reasonable fee. Moreover, some clients, opponents argued, could afford the lower mortgage interest rates; instead, they are steered to lenders and brokers who take advantage of naive borrowers. For years, the Department of Housing and Urban Development did not require lenders to make specific disclosures about how much yield spread is being charged, although some lenders voluntarily disclosed this information.[118]

In 2010, Congress directly addressed the issue in the Dodd-Frank Act. Under the Act, lenders and brokers cannot be compensated based on the terms of the loan. This means that even if a broker originates a higher interest loan, he cannot gain additional money for it. The fees also have to paid directly from the borrower so they he is aware of them. Predictably many in the lending industry argue that this will take away much of the incentive for brokers to tailor a loan to the client's resources and interests. Proponents counter that they should never have been compensated anyway if a higher interest rate was warranted for the borrower because this was in the borrower's best interest, but that more often than not, the broker was only acting to advance his own financial interest. Is the Dodd-Frank Act a more ethical approach? Or are there less intrusive ways to protect borrowers without a law that may create disincentives to brokers and possibly cause other problems in the industry. After all, the borrower has always been free to shop around for the best rates and does not have to take out a loan from someone pushing a YSP on him. Explain your answer.

ENDNOTES

1. R. Boyer et al., *The Law of Property* 638 (4th ed. 1991).
2. *McCook National Bank v. Myers,* 243 Neb. 853, 859, 503 N.W.2d 200, 204 (1993).
3. M. Shustek and D. Jacobs, *Trust Deed Investments* (2001).
4. M. Pacelle, *Reverse Mortgages for Elderly Slated to Be Expanded*, Wall Street Journal 6 (May 21, 1991).
5. N. Timiraos, *Seniors Drawn To Mortgages That Give Back,* Wall Street Journal 1, 6A (June 10, 2009).

6. *Trustees of Zion Methodist Church v. Smith,* 335 Ill.App. 233, 81 N.E.2d 649 (1948).

7. *Alber v. Bradley,* 321 Mich. 255, 32 N.W.2d 454 (1948).

8. 195 Or. 62, 244 P.2d 619 (1952).

9. 42 U.S.C. §§3601 *et seq.* (1992).

10. 15 U.S.C. §§1691 *et seq.*

11. See W. Naeher, *Recent Developments Under the Equal Credit Opportunity Act,* Probate & Property 44 (January/February 1996).

12. 12 U.S.C. §§2901–2907.

13. P. Mahoney, *The Community Reinvestment Act: Storm Clouds Clearing,* Probate & Property 53 (January/February 1996).

14. G. Nelson and D. Whitman, *Real Estate Finance Law* 809 (1985).

15. R. Neiman, *Don't Blame the CRA for Causing the Housing Bubble,* Wall Street Journal A20 (December 5-6, 2009).

16. 12 U.S.C. §2801 *et. seq.*

17. S. Roberts, *If You Don't Weed Out Bias, Janet Reno Will,* American Banker 19 (April 18, 1994).

18. V. Been et al., *The High Cost of Segregation: Exploring Racial Disparities in High Cost Lending,* 36 Fordham Urban Law Journal 361 (2009).

19. To see how the HOEPA triggers are calculated, visit http://www.stls.frb.org/hmdaregcamendments/pages/hoepa_status.html (last accessed June 28, 2010).

20. P. Krugman, *Berating the Raters,* New York Times A23 (April 25, 2010).

21. C. Hammond, *Predatory Lending—A Legal Definition and Update,* 34 Real Estate Law Journal 176 (2005).

22. P. Obara, *Predatory Lending,* Banking Law Journal 541 (June 2001).

23. E. Schultz, *Older Borrowers, Out in the Cold,* Wall Street Journal D1 (April 14, 2009).

24. 15 U.S.C. §1601 *et seq.*

25. P. Barron, *Federal Regulation of Real Estate* 10–10 (1992).

26. *Cowen v. Bank United of Texas, FSB,* 70 F.3d 937, 942 (7th Cir. 1995).

27. *Id.,* at 943.

28. P. Barron, *Federal Regulation of Real Estate* 10–8 (1992).

29. 15 U.S.C. §1640(a)(2)(A) (2001).

30. http://www.kaarmls.com/truthinlendinglongversion1.htm (last visited June 28, 2010).

31. P. Barron and M. Berenson, *Federal Regulation of Real Estate and Mortgage Lending,* 1996 Cumulative Supp. S2–7 (1996).

32. To access the new HUD Settlement Book go to: http://www.hud.gov/offices/hsg/ramh/res/Settlement-Booklet-January-6-REVISED.pdf (last visited June 28, 2010).

33. M. Madison et al., *The Law of Real Estate Financing* 3–85 (1997).

34. *Id.,* at 3–85 to 3–88. See also R. Aalberts, *Exploding Arms and Subprime Loans: Must Every Decade Have a Real Estate Crisis?* 36 Real Estate Law Journal 3 (2007).

35. See e.g., *Armstrong v. Republic Realty Mortgage Corp.,* 631 F.2d 1344 (8th Cir. 1980).

36. G. Lefcoe, *Real Estate Transactions* 442 (2nd ed. 1997).

37. J. Bain and R. Guttery, *The Coming Downsizing of Real Estate: Implications of Technology,* 3 Journal of Real Estate Portfolio Management 1 (1997).

38. A. Hoak, *Mortgage Insurance Gaining Steam: PMI Is Tax Deductible in 2007, But That Isn't the Only Reason It's Popular,* MarketWatch (April 17, 2007).

39. N. Timiraos and J. Haggerty, *Mortgage Impact Is Mixed,* Wall Street Journal A4 (June 28, 2010).

40. Table 9.1 is adapted from *The Mortgage Money Guide* (1994), courtesy of the Federal Trade Commission with recent additions.

41. See 18 U.S.C. §1014.

42. 371 Mass. 897, 360 N.E.2d 306 (1977).

43. See, e.g., Texas Business and Commerce Code, §26.02 (2010).

44. See R. Aalberts, *supra* note 34.

45. R. Suskind, *Fleet Financial to Broaden Requirement of Environmental Liability Insurance,* Wall Street Journal A2 (June 24, 1992); J. Kotvis, *Lender Liability Issues,* Environmental Aspects of Real Estate Transactions (1995).

46. *Restatement of Property-Security (Mortgages)* §1.1 and comment (Tent. Draft No. 1, 1991).

47. 314 So.2d 209 (Fla.App. 1975).

48. G. Lefcoe, *The Promissory Note in Real Estate Transactions,* in 13 *Thompson on Property* 521, 629, 14 (1981, 1995 Supp.).

49. G. Lefcoe, *Real Estate Transactions* 522 (2nd ed. 1997).

50. C. Mollenkamp and S. Ng, *How a Little Lending Had a Big Impact,* Wall Street Journal C1 (May 3, 2010).

51. J. Hagerty et al., *U.S. Seizes Mortgage Giants,* Wall Street Journal A1, A14 (September 8, 2008).

52. R. Samuelson, *Fixing Fannie and Freddie,* Newsweek 41 (September 8, 2003).

53. L. Woellert and J. Gittelsohn, *Fannie and Freddie Fix at $160 billion with $1 trillion Worse Case,* Bloomberg News (June 13, 2010).

54. *Restatement of Property (Mortgages)* §8.1(a) (Tent. Draft No. 5, 1996).

55. 216 Ark. 579, 226 S.W.2d 803 (1950).

56. *Fidelity Federal Savings & Loan Association v. de la Cuesta,* 458 U.S. 141, 102 S.Ct. 3014, 73 L.Ed.2d 664 (1982).

57. L. Guenther, *Lenders Go After "Silent Sales" That Pass on Old Low Rates,* Wall Street Journal 27 (April 28, 1982). See also R. Aalberts, *Creative Financing Scores a Comeback in Nevada Real Estate Market: But Are All Inclusive Trust Deeds Legal?* 5 Nevada Bar Journal 24 (1997).

58. 267 S.C. 691, 230 S.E.2d 905 (1976).

59. J. Hechinger, *Nasty Surprise Haunts Some Folks' Mortgage: A Prepayment Penalty,* Wall Street Journal A1 (August 6, 2001).

60. J. Murray, *Default Interest Rates, Late Charges, and Exit Fees: Are They Enforceable?* Modern Real Estate Transactions, American Law Institute-American Bar Association Course of Study, ALI/ABA, July 27-30, 2005.

61. R. Hoyt, R. Aalberts and P. Poon, *Commercial Mortgage Prepayment: Prepayment Fee, Yield Maintenance, or Defeasance,* 12 Journal of Real Estate Practice and Education 17 (2009).

62. D. Stark, *New Developments in Enforcing Prepayment Charges After an Acceleration of a Mortgage Loan,* 26 Real Property, Probate and Trust Journal 213 (1991).

63. 247 B.R. 722 (Bankr. S.E. Ohio 2000).

64. J. Murray, *supra* note 60.

65. J. Curtis, *Mortgages, Deeds of Trust and Related Liens,* 12 Thompson on Real Property 333 (1994).

Lien Theory states are: Alaska, Arizona, California, Colorado, Florida, Hawaii, Idaho, Indiana, Iowa, Kansas, Kentucky, Louisiana, Michigan, Minnesota, Missouri, Montana, Nebraska, Nevada, New Hampshire, New Mexico, New York, North Dakota, Ohio, Oklahoma, Oregon, South Carolina, South Dakota, Texas, Utah, Washington, West Virginia, Wisconsin, and Wyoming.

Title Theory states are: Alabama, Georgia, Maine, Maryland, Mississippi, Pennsylvania, Rhode Island, Tennessee, and Vermont.

Intermediate Theory states are: Arkansas, Connecticut, Delaware,

District of Columbia, Illinois, Massachusetts, New Jersey, North Carolina, and Virginia.

66. 253 Mich. 51, 234 N.W. 113 (1931).

67. In some transactions, these provisions might appear in the note instead of the mortgage while the note provisions discussed earlier might appear in the mortgage. For example, the mortgagor's promise to keep the property in good repair might appear in the note, in the mortgage, or in both. Probably the more conservative approach would be to include essential provisions in the mortgage itself to make those terms part of the public record or at least to incorporate by reference the note into the mortgage.

68. *Restatement of Property-Security (Mortgages)* §1.5 (c) and comment (Tent. Draft No. 1, 1991).

69. *Northridge Bank v. Lakeshore Commercial Fin. Corp.,* 365 N.E.2d 382 (Ill.App. 1977).

70. *Restatement of Property-Security (Mortgages)* §2.1, *Statutory Note on Future Advances* (Tent. Draft No. 1, 1991).

71. *Restatement of the Law Third, Property (Mortgages)* (1997).

72. R. Kratovil, *Modern Mortgage Law and Practice* §294 (1972).

73. *Carolina Portland Cement Co. v. Baumgartner,* 99 Fla. 987, 128 So. 241 (1930).

74. 197 Ind. 393, 150 N.E. 368 (1926).

75. *Caro v. Wollenberg,* 83 Or. 311, 163 P. 94 (1917).

76. *Webster Bank v. Encompass Insurance Co. of America,* 2007 Conn. Super. LEXIS 558 (2007).

77. See, e.g., *Young v. Sodaro,* 456 S.E.2d 31 (W.Va. 1995).

78. *Id.*

79. 40 Mich. 668 (1879).

80. R. W. Freyermuth, *Why Mortgagors Can't Get No Satisfaction,* 72 Missouri Law Review 1159 (Fall 2007).

81. If the deed had not contained the "subject to" clause, Nick also could have recovered on the theory that a warranty against encumbrances was breached.

82. M. Madison et al., *The Law of Real Estate Financing* 8–18 (1997).

83. A. Johnson, *Preventing a Return Engagement: Eliminating the Mortgage Purchasers' Status as a Holder-in-Due-Course: Properly Aligning Incentives Among the Parties,* 37 Pepperdine Law Review 529 (2010).

84. P. Barron, *Federal Regulation of Real Estate* 2–53 (1992).

85. *Id.,* at §2.07(2).

86. Truth in Lending Act, § 131 (2009).

87. R. Arnold, *Yes, There Is Life on MERS,* Probate & Property 33 (July/August 1997).

88. 289 Kan. 528, 216 P.3d 158 (Kan. Sup. Ct. 2009).

89. R. Aalberts, *Is There Life in MERS?* 38 Real Estate Law Journal 417 (Spring 2010).

90. J. Winn and R. Witte, *E-Sign of the Times,* E-Commerce Law Report (July 2000).

91. P. Brumfield et al., *Coming to a Screen Near You—"eMortgages"—Starring Good Law and Prudent Standards—Rated "XML,"* 62 Business Lawyer 295 (2006).

92. R. Kratovil, *Modern Mortgage Law and Practice* §§2–7 (1972).

93. *Reitman v. Whitaker,* 74 N.D. 504, 23 N.W.2d 393 (1946).

94. *Restatement of Property-Security (Mortgages)* §3.1 comment (Tent. Draft No. 1, 1991).

95. See http://loanforensicauditors.com/client-toolbox/state-foreclosure-statutes for a list of states' statutory right of redemption laws (last visited on June 29, 2010).

96. *Restatement of Property-Security (Mortgages)* §3.1, *supra* note 94.

97. *Id.,* at §3.2 comment. For a list of states and what foreclosure procedure they apply, see http://www.all-foreclosure.com/procedures.htm (last visited on June 29, 2010).

98. See, for example, *Northrip v. Federal Nat. Mtg. Ass'n.,* 527 F.2d 23 (6th Cir. 1975).

99. G. Mortenson, *Foreclosures Hit a Snag for Lenders,* New York Times 15 (November 15, 2007).

100. *Id.*

101. For state-by-state information on deficiency judgment laws see http://www.all-foreclosure.com/procedures.htm (last accessed on June 29, 2010).

102. *Land Fever,* Las Vegas Weekly 18–20 (November 13-19, 2003).

103. R. Aalberts, *Does the American Public Need a Crash Course in Deficiency Judgments Laws?* 34 Real Estate Law Journal 1 (2006).

104. 12 U.S.C. §§3751–67.

105. 50 U.S.C. §§501 *et seq.*

106. C. Yzenbaard, *Residential Real Estate Transactions* 159–60 (1991).

107. L. Sichelman, *Lenders Willing to Assist Borrowers Through Difficulties,* Las Vegas Review Journal 6E (September 17, 2005).

108. M. Lerner, *Real Estate: HAFA short sale rules may help sellers,* http://www.bankrate.com/finance/real-estate/hafa-short-sale-rules-may-help-sellers-1.aspx (last accessed March 15, 2010).

109. J. Schweers, *More homeowners turn to mediation after foreclosure,* USA Today, http://www.usatoday.com/money/economy/housing/2010-05-28-foreclosure28_CV_N.htm (last accessed June 3, 2010). See also G. Walsh, *Foreclosure Mediations: Can They Make a Difference?* 43 Clearinghouse Review 355 (November/December 2009).

110. D. Hinkel, *Practical Real Estate Law* 284–85 (2000).

111. 351 S.C. 167, 568 S.E. 2d 361 (Sup. Ct. 2002).

112. S. Siegfried, *Introduction to Construction Law* 62 (1987).

113. R. Cushman, *Fifty State Construction Lien Law* 4 (1992).

114. 46 Ill.App.2d 232, 196 N.E.2d 700 (1964).

115. *Lembke Constr. Co. v. J.D. Coggins Co.,* 72 N.M. 259, 382 P.2d 983 (1963).

116. *Broadmoor Lumber Co. v. Liberto,* 162 So.2d 800 (La.App. 1964).

117. Under a 1991 Supreme Court ruling, the defendant is entitled to notice and a hearing before the writ is issued. *Connecticut v. Doehr,* 111 S.Ct. 2105, 115 L.Ed.2d 1 (1991).

118. E. Klayman, *Yield Spread Premiums, Illegal Referrals, and the Real Estate Settlement Procedures Act: Blurred Vision,* 32 Real Estate Law Journal 222 (2003).

CHAPTER 10

Closings and Taxation; Other Methods of Acquisition

LEARNING OBJECTIVES

After studying Chapter 10, you should:

- Learn about deeds

- Understand the closing process

- Be familiar with the taxation of real estate

- Be able to identify other methods of real estate acquisition

"[T]he basic system of real estate titles and transfers—and the related matters concerning financing and purchase of homes—cries out for re-examination and simplification. In a country that transfers not only expensive automobiles but multimillion dollar airplanes with a few relatively simple papers, I believe that if American lawyers will put their ingenuity and inventiveness to work on this subject they will be able to devise simpler methods than we have now."

Former Chief Justice Warren E. Burger

"The difference between death and taxes is death doesn't get worse every time Congress meets."

Will Rogers

real estate closing
The event at which the real estate contract is finally performed.

The purchaser takes many steps to acquire real estate, from working with a broker and selecting the property to obtaining a commitment for financing and conducting inspections. These steps culminate with the **real estate closing**, when the buyer pays for the property and the seller conveys title.

At closing, the buyer settles the mortgage transaction to gain access to the loan proceeds. The buyer then pays the seller, who delivers a deed to the buyer. Because of title requirements and the mechanics of the settlement process, however, a third party typically receives and records the deed on the buyer's behalf and reconciles receipts and disbursements.

The deed is the key to a successful closing; it is the legal instrument that transfers title from the seller to the buyer. This chapter emphasizes the form of the deed and its delivery. Other aspects of the closing process also are summarized, including the law of taxation as it affects the acquisition of real estate.

Chapters 6 through 9 dealt with acquiring real estate by purchase (as does this chapter), in which event the real estate is transferred by deed. *Two* other methods of acquiring real property are discussed at the end of this chapter:

1. Transfer of real estate at the death of the owner by will or by intestate succession in the absence of a will
2. Adverse possession

© MACIEJ NOSKOWSKI/iStockphoto (RF)

avulsion

The sudden removal of soil from a property owner's land that is deposited upon another's land, by the action of water. The soil in such cases belongs to the owner from whose land it is removed.

accretion

The slow addition to land by deposition of water-borne sediment. The land so formed belongs to the owner upon whose property the deposit is made.

Although not discussed in this chapter, real estate can also be transferred by court order or by an act of the legislature. Moreover, the physical ownership of land can be literally gained and lost through the following erosive processes involving the interaction between land and water: **avulsion**, **accretion**, and **reliction**.

Deeds

While the contract is a promise to convey the real estate, the **deed** is the actual instrument of conveyance. A practical consequence of the deed's transfer of title is that the deed, unlike an executory contract, is valid even in the absence of consideration. Although the deed transfers title from the seller to the grantee, it does not provide evidence of the seller's title. The buyer relies on his own title examination for that assurance.

Under the historical **merger rule**, discussed in Chapter 7, the contract is merged into the deed; terms of the contract also not contained in the deed can no longer be enforced unless the contract states that they survive the closing or unless they are collateral to the deed. The buyer should also determine that the deed contains restrictive covenants or similar arrangements critical to the transaction or he may suffer a fate similar to the buyer in the following Rhode Island case.

A CASE IN POINT

In *Haronian v. Quattrocchi*[1] a buyer entered into an option agreement to purchase property that was part of a larger parcel owned by the seller. The option limited the commercial development of the parent tract by the seller and granted a right-of-way to the buyer. Neither the deed nor the right-of-way conveyance delivered at closing restricted the seller's commercial development. The buyer sued the seller to prevent his erection of a miniature golf course and batting cages, which would have violated the option's restriction. The court applied the doctrine of merger, holding that a deed that contained no restriction on development nullified the terms of the option contract.

reliction

The gradual and imperceptible withdrawal of water from land. In a permanent withdrawal the owner of the contiguous property acquires ownership of the dry land created.

deed

A written instrument used to convey real estate from one party to another.

merger rule

When the real estate contract merges into and is replaced by the deed.

general warranty deed

A deed that conveys grantor's title and contains warranties of title.

It is noteworthy that a restrictive covenant limiting commercial development in the deed from the seller would have protected the buyers.

Types of Deeds

Two types of deeds are commonly used in real estate transactions: the warranty deed and the quitclaim deed. Real estate contracts usually specify that a type of warranty deed is to be delivered by the seller. If the real estate contract fails to specify a warranty deed, the seller generally may give a quitclaim deed.

Warranty Deed   There are *two* classes of warranty deeds. Under a **general warranty deed** (see www.cengagebrain.com [see page xix in the Preface for instructions on how to access the free study tools for this text] for an example of a general warranty deed), usually required by a real estate contract and presumed by law in some states, the seller gives three warranties:

1.   The covenant of seisin, a warranty that the seller has good title to the real estate and that he has the legal right to convey the interest he purports to own
2.   The covenant against encumbrances, a warranty that the title is not encumbered by interests such as a lien, a lease, or an easement unless the deed states otherwise
3.   The covenant of quiet enjoyment, a warranty that the property will not be taken by someone with a better title

While, if these warranties are breached, the seller will be liable for damages, the buyer may be unable to find the seller or the seller may be insolvent. Therefore, a buyer should not rely solely on these warranties as assurance of good title. Instead, buyers should use abstracts of title, title opinions, and title insurance (all discussed in Chapter 8) as a more reliable way to protect their titles.

On occasion, the real estate contract allows the seller to give a **special warranty deed**, under which the seller gives warranties only for claims that arise "under, by or through" the seller but does not give warranties for title defects created before she acquired title. To illustrate, Louise deeded a parcel of land to Tom. The land was subject to a mortgage given to Last Bank by Santiago, who sold Louise the property. The deed did not state that title was subject to the mortgage, and Last Bank later foreclosed. If Louise had given a general warranty deed, she would be liable for damages resulting from the foreclosure even though the encumbrance—the mortgage—was placed on the land by Santiago before she acquired the real estate. However, if she had given a special warranty deed, she would not be liable for preexisting mortgages, such as the mortgage Santiago gave to the Last Bank, but only for mortgages and other defects that she created.

It should be noted that "Warranty deeds don't mean that the seller has good title. Anyone can sign a deed to any property. The general warranty deed just gives the grantee a cause of action against sellers who don't own what they purported to sell." For example, if Harry conveyed the Brooklyn Bridge to Sally by general warranty deed, Sally would have a legal claim against Harry.[2]

Quitclaim Deed   If Harry conveyed the Brooklyn Bridge to Sally under a quitclaim deed, Sally would *not* have a claim against him. However, the owner of the bridge certainly would have a claim against Harry for slander of title, discussed in Chapter 8, if Harry had recorded the deed. Under a **quitclaim deed** (see www.cengagebrain.com [see page xix in the Preface for instructions on how to access the free study tools for this text] for an example of a quitclaim deed), the seller makes no warranties; he only transfers whatever title or interest he has to the buyer. The quitclaim deed entails a greater risk for the buyer because if the seller has no right, title, or interest in the land, the buyer, as mentioned, has no recourse against the seller. Quitclaim deeds are often used to remove a **cloud on the title**, such as settling a boundary dispute, and are seen simply as a release of the seller's rights.

In some states, **bargain and sale deeds** are used instead of quitclaim deeds, having the same legal effect except that the buyer under a bargain and sale deed will not be considered an innocent purchaser for value.[3] As is more fully explained in Chapter 8, the failure to be considered an innocent purchaser for value, in states with notice and race-notice recording statutes, can result in the buyer losing title to a prior purchaser who did not record her deed.

Formal Requirements

A deed—whether written in longhand in everyday language, preprinted as a form, or produced with a word processor—must be in writing. Most states have passed statutes establishing "short form" deeds. These statutes simplify deed forms since they designate language for warranty, quitclaim, and other forms of deeds. Even in a short form, deeds must typically meet the minimal requirements described as follows.

Grantor   The first critical element of the deed is the name of the **grantor**. Although it is sound practice to name the grantor, other designations that identify the grantor are sufficient. For example, if the deed states that the conveyance is by "We the heirs of Whitmill Stephens" and is signed by the heirs, the designation is sufficient for identification. Furthermore, the name may suffice even if the grantor's name is misspelled, a

---

special warranty deed
A deed that conveys grantor's title but contains warranties protecting only those title defects created by the grantor.

quitclaim deed
A deed conveying the grantor's interests.

cloud on the title
An outstanding claim or encumbrance that, if valid, would affect or impair the title of the owner of a particular estate and has that effect on its face, but can be shown to be invalid or inapplicable.

bargain and sale deed
In some states, a deed in which the grantee receives title but is not considered an innocent purchaser for value. The grantee receives title but no warranties.

grantor
A transferor of property.

middle initial is not used, the name in the body of the deed (Henry S. Woodworth) is different from the signature (Harry S. Woodworth), or a fictitious name is used—as long as the grantor can be easily identified. The best practice, however, is to use the grantor's name in the same form that it appears in the original conveyance.[4,5]

capacity

The mental ability to understand the nature and effect of one's acts.

The deed will be voidable if the grantor lacks **capacity**, even if the form of the deed is correct. For individuals, capacity means that the grantor must be of full age, which is eighteen. The grantor also must be of sound mind: the grantor must be capable of reasonable understanding of the nature and effect of the conveyance. Old age, sickness, or extreme physical disability are irrelevant as long as mental capacity is present.

> John Thomas's children alleged that their late father lacked the mental capacity to convey five lots to their stepmother. In *Thomas v. A.L. Neal* on page 397, the court discusses the requirements for capacity and resolves whether the frail and elderly Mr. Thomas had the requisite mental capacity.

END OF CHAPTER CASE

If the property is owned by more than one party, all joint owners should sign the deed as grantors. If the property is conveyed by a married person, the spouse should be named as a grantor and should sign the deed, even though the spouse is not an owner, to remove dower, curtesy, and homestead claims. (Dower, curtesy, and homestead are discussed later in this chapter.) If property is deeded by a single person, the name of the grantor should be followed by the words *a single person* to avoid possible concern about the need for a spouse's signature when title is later examined.

A corporation must be in existence to have legal capacity to convey real property by deed and to authorize the conveyance. To illustrate, a sale of substantially all of a corporation's assets must, under a traditional rule of corporate law, be approved by both the corporation's board of directors and a majority of its shareholders. Consequently, a person purchasing substantially all of the real estate from a corporation should find answers to the following questions before closing:

1. Does the corporation legally exist under state law?
2. Was the sale approved by the board of directors and a majority of shareholders?
3. Does the corporate officer who signs the deed on behalf of the corporation have the authority to do so under the bylaws or pursuant to a corporate resolution?

grantee

The party to whom the deed conveys title.

Grantee   A deed must name the **grantee** clearly enough to identify him. For example, the grantee's name may be sufficient even though it is misspelled ("David Kessler" when his name was "David Kesler"), part of the name is omitted, the grantee is not identified by name ("William Farley and wife" or "Hannah Simshauser and her children"), or a fictitious name is used.[6,7,8] As discussed in Chapter 8, mistakes or omissions in the grantee's name can create chain of title problems.

A deed naming a grantee not legally in existence (for example, a deceased person or a corporation that has not been formed under state law) does not operate as a conveyance because it is impossible to deliver the deed. However, as a Maryland court ruled, if the corporation were to come into existence later and delivery were then made, the conveyance would be valid.[9] Also, a deed to a corporation that had not paid franchise taxes and whose charter had been forfeited was held by a Texas court to be a valid deed.[10] The corporation was deemed to be able to receive title and to be in existence because it had a statutory right to reinstatement.

The same general approach is used with deeds that omit the name of the grantee: the deeds are invalid while blank; but once the grantee's name is added by someone with authority to do so, the deed becomes valid. However, in some states, such as the following case from California points out, this authority to act as an agent must be written.

A CASE IN POINT

In *Green v. MacAdam,*[11] MacAdam served as Green's attorney and advised his client to sign several deeds to her property in blank. MacAdam later filled in one of the deeds, naming his secretary as grantee; sold part of the property to a third party; and kept the proceeds. A court held that the deed to the secretary was void: "Though the decisions of other jurisdictions are not in entire harmony upon the question, it has been definitely decided in this state that under our statute of frauds the name of the grantor or the grantee or the description of the property cannot be inserted by an agent of the grantor, in the absence of the latter, unless the agent's authority be in writing. If the authority of the agent be not in writing, his insertion of the name of the grantor or grantee or description of the property does not pass title."

Historically, the words *and his heirs* following the grantee's name were required to grant a fee simple absolute estate. Today these words of inheritance (also called words of limitation) are not required. It is still important, however, that the deed clearly specify the interests of the parties and the manner in which they are taking title. For instance, if property is deeded to "Francis Lucas, a single man, and Joseph Lucas and Matilda Lucas, his wife," what are the interests of the parties? Does each party have a one-third interest as a tenant in common? Or does Francis have a one-half interest as a tenant in common with Joseph and Matilda, who hold their one-half interest as tenants by the entirety? Or does Francis have a one-third interest as tenant in common, with Joseph and Matilda holding the remaining two-thirds interest as tenants by the entirety? Although a Pennsylvania court eventually adopted the second construction in this case,[12] a great deal of time, expense, and uncertainty could have been avoided by clearly stating the intention in the deed.

Addresses It is common practice to include the addresses of the parties in the deed. Although a deed without addresses is valid, in some states it is not eligible for recording.

Words of Conveyance A deed must show a present intention on the part of the grantor to transfer her interest to the grantee. A warranty deed uses the words *convey and warrant* to transfer title. Although older deed forms often list the warranties that are given by the grantor, modern statutes provide that the warranties are given, listed or not, when the words *convey and warrant* are used. A quitclaim deed uses the words *convey and quitclaim* to transfer the grantor's interest.

habendum clause
The portion of a deed describing the ownership rights transferred.

Habendum Clause Deeds may contain a **habendum clause** that states what type of land interest (fee simple, life estate, etc.) is being conveyed to the grantee. Often this clause simply repeats language provided in the granting clause.

Government Survey

A standard rectangular system of describing land existing in the majority of American states.

When interpreting a deed where there is an apparent conflict in language in both the granting clause and the habendum clause, how do the courts determine the grantor's intent? The court resolves this issue in *In re Tazian v. Cline* on page 398.

END OF CHAPTER CASE

township

A square tract of land approximately six miles on each side used in the Government Survey system.

metes and bounds

A way of describing land by listing the compass directions and distances of the boundaries.

principal meridian

North and south survey line of reference intersecting with an east-west base line to form a starting point in the Government Survey system.

base lines

East-west survey reference lines intersecting with a north-south principal meridian to form a starting point in the Government Survey system.

range lines

North-south running survey lines spaced approximately six miles apart used in the Government Survey system.

township lines

East-west running survey lines spaced six miles apart used in the Government Survey system.

section

Parcel of land in the Government Survey system comprising one square mile, or 640 acres. There are 36 sections in a township.

Description   One of the most important—and complex—requisites for a valid real estate contract or deed is an accurate description of the land being conveyed. As a general rule, the description must be clear enough that the land can be identified without the aid of outside evidence. Most deeds contain one of *four* types of descriptions. The owner and mortgagee should examine a survey of the property, which verifies the legal description and depicts its application in graphic form. A surveyor is the professional authorized by state law to prepare property descriptions.

Government Survey   The *first* type is the U.S. **Government Survey**, developed after the Revolutionary War to survey the Northwest Territory (Illinois, Indiana, Ohio, Michigan, and Wisconsin) so that the land could be sold to pay war debts. The Government Survey is also used in Alabama, Florida, and Mississippi and west of the Mississippi River with the exception of Texas.[13] Where available, it offers the simplest method of survey. The key to the Government Survey is the **township**, which, in theory, is a square tract six miles to a side. In actuality, of course, townships cannot be perfectly square because square townships cannot fit into a circle (in this case, the earth) because township lines converge as they approach the Poles. To compensate for this convergence, there are odd lots (called *fractional forties* or *eighties* or *government lots*) along the north and west sides of each township. Once the pattern of development diverges from the geometrical grid, the surveyor often employs a **metes and bounds** description (see "Metes and Bounds," which follows) to accurately describe the boundaries of the subdivided parcel.

To illustrate the Government Survey, the following description from a deed will be used: "The East 1/2 of the West 1/2 of the Southwest 1/4 of the Southeast 1/4, Section 22, T1S-R2E." With a Government Survey description, the property is located by reading the description from back to front. You begin by locating the township, T1S-R2E. Government surveying begins with two reference lines: a principal meridian line running north and south and a base line running east and west. There are also survey lines running between the **principal meridian** and the **base line**. North-south running lines called **range lines** exist about every six miles on both sides of the principal meridian. **Township lines** are east-west lines spaced about every six miles extending from the base line. Township and range lines delineate townships; thus, once the intersection of these two lines is found, it is easy to locate the township. In this case, T1S means that the township is in the first row of townships—that is, in the first township line—running in an east-west direction south of the base line. R2E means that the township is situated in the second row of townships—that is, the second range—running in a north-south direction east of the principal meridian. This township, like all others, is divided into thirty-six **sections**, each of which is 640 acres. The sections are numbered as indicated in Figure 10.1. After Section 22 is located, the southeast quarter of the section is found, then the southwest quarter of that quarter, then the west half of that quarter, and finally the east half of that half. (See Figure 10.2.)

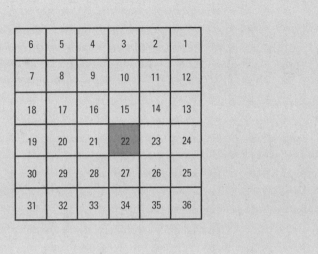

FIGURE 10.1
A Township

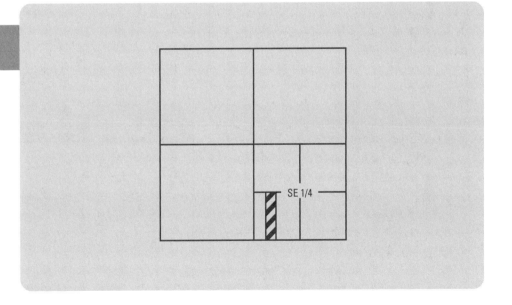

FIGURE 10.2
Section 22

Metes and Bounds The *second,* and oldest, method of description is by metes and bounds, under which property is described "in terms of distance (metes) and direction (bounds) based on the location of permanent man-made monuments or corners of parcels using the rectangular survey system or the recorded plat system."[14] The survey begins at a designated point called a monument, which might be a tree or a rock, and then proceeds to define the boundary in terms of angles and distances until returning to the monument. The selected monument should be capable of identification by future surveyors; it should not be a temporary object or improvement. The property is located by reading the description from beginning to end.

Commencing at the iron pipe marking the south west corner of the east half of the south west quarter of section twenty seven; thence north on the west line of said east half of the south west quarter of section twenty seven, 521.76 feet to the center line of Geddes Road; thence deflecting 118 degrees eighteen minutes to the right 126.03 feet along the center line of Geddes Road to an iron pipe; thence south deflecting sixty one degrees forty eight minutes thirty seconds to the right 324.82 feet to an iron pipe and brick monument, thence southerly deflecting five degrees and three minutes to the right 136.16 feet to an iron pipe; thence west deflecting 83 degrees fifty five minutes to the right 98.13 feet to the place of beginning.

plat

A recorded map of a parcel of real estate that has been subdivided.

Plats   Many **plats**, the *third* type of description, subdivide the property into lots, each of which is numbered. Once a plat has been recorded, a description is sufficient when it refers to the plat and lot number—for instance, "Lot 9, Vinewood Subdivision, recorded in Liber 6 of Plats, page 30, Washtenaw County Records."

Informal Description   One of the preceding methods should be used whenever property is conveyed. Occasionally, however, an informal description, the *fourth* type, is sufficient to pass title if the property can be identified with certainty. For instance, references to property by its popular name ("Commencement Plantation, consisting of 1330 acres") or by street numbers ("my property at 91 and 95 East Webster Avenue, Muskegon, Michigan") have been judged sufficient to identify the property.[15,16]

Even when the description is uncertain on its face, courts have developed rules that may be applied to interpret and clarify the language, as illustrated by the following classic, but still relevant, case from Pennsylvania.

A CASE IN POINT

In January 1784, the owners of Pennsylvania, John Penn and John Penn, Jr., contracted to sell a parcel of land in the "manor of Pittsburgh, lying and being in a point formed by the junction of the two rivers Monongahela and Allegheny; bounded on two sides by the rivers aforesaid, on a third side by the top or ditch of Fort Pitt." The deed given pursuant to the contract stated that the two rivers were the boundaries of the real estate, but the deed also referred to a plat of the real estate that showed open spaces for Water Street and Duquesne Way between the real estate and the river. In interpreting this deed a century later, a court noted the obvious ambiguity between the general description and the plat description and, citing rules of interpretation from earlier cases, decided that the precise and accurate description in the plat governed the more general language in the deed.

In the words of the court: "The precise and accurate description and location of the lots, furnished by the plan given in evidence by plaintiff herself, cannot be controlled by the general language of the deed calling for the rivers as boundaries of the respective blocks of lots. The plan, which was incorporated with the deed for the very purpose of definitely fixing the location of lots, clearly shows that they did not extend to the water line on either river, nor include any of the land in controversy. The parties to the deed never intended that they should; nor is there any evidence that would justify a jury in finding that they did. Those who were concerned in laying out the town, that was destined soon to become a great city, never dreamed that the lots, accurately described on the plan, embraced any portion of the narrow, open space on each river, evidently intended as a means of public access to and along the rivers."[17]

In cases involving boundary line disputes, courts also look beyond the description in a deed. For example, Derek and Dylan are neighboring farmers. The monuments used to identify the boundary line between the farms have been removed, and Derek and Dylan do not know where the boundary should be. Consequently, they orally agree to establish a new boundary and mark it with a fence or another permanent monument. A court will enforce an oral agreement in this situation (even though it violates the Statute of Frauds) because the parties' acts may be used to interpret the description of the land in each owner's deed. Although courts, such as the following Arkansas court, attempt to clarify language whenever possible, in some cases, the description of the real estate is so indefinite that the deed must fail.

A CASE IN POINT

In *Miller v. Best*,[18] the court was asked to interpret three deeds that contained descriptions such as "Thirty acres in the northern part of Spanish Grant No. 2425 and West and adjoining the ten acre tract known as the Will Lemon's Tract." The court concluded: "It is settled that 'part' descriptions such as these are void for indefiniteness.... Although a surveyor testified that he was able to locate the tracts from the descriptions we have quoted, he must have relied upon physical evidence such as fences, for the language of the deed supplies no clue that could lead to an identification of the property. The rule is that the conveyance itself must furnish that clue."

deed reservation

The creation by deed of a new right out of an estate that has been transferred to a buyer.

deed exception

Excepting from a transfer a part of an estate that has already been created.

consideration

The payment received by the grantor in exchange for the real estate.

Exceptions and Reservations The description of the real estate is often followed by clauses under which the grantor creates and reserves a *new* right out of the estate granted, termed a **deed reservation**, or excepts a part of the estate that is *already in existence*, called a **deed exception**. For example, a grantor who sells part of a farm that has an access drive running through it would incorporate a reservation of an easement for himself; but if he had already sold the remainder of the farm and the easement to a third party, he would make an exception for the easement to the new owner in the deed. Although the terms are theoretically distinct, there is a tendency to use the words *exception* and *reservation* synonymously in deeds.

Statement of Consideration While **consideration** is necessary to enforce an executory real estate contract (a contract not yet performed or executed), discussed in Chapter 7, it is *not* required that a grantor receive consideration for a deed. In other words, it is the grantor's prerogative to give away the property. However, several states require by statute that some consideration be stated in the deed whether the conveyance is a gift or another type of transaction.

Even in the absence of a statute, it is customary to state the consideration. In the words of one Missouri court:

> It is true that a deed without any consideration is good as between the parties or their heirs. However, it is a simpler, and a usual and sound conveyancing practice to recite at least a nominal consideration, so that a stated consideration will appear on the face of the deed. We have held that any ... stated sum of money in excess of one cent, one dime, or one dollar which are the technical words used to express nominal considerations, is a valuable consideration within the meaning of the law of conveyancing.[19]

While it is not required that the true consideration be stated on the deed, transfer taxes are based on the actual consideration paid to the grantor.

In cases where the grantor is to receive payment, courts are not concerned whether the consideration is adequate payment for the land; as long as some consideration is given, it is considered legally sufficient. However, this rule does not apply if the inadequacy is so great as to be unconscionable or to amount to fraud as demonstrated in the following Missouri case.

A CASE IN POINT

In *Frey v. Onstott*, a seventy-year-old woman deeded valuable property to a close friend, a young woman, for $1 (which was never paid) with the promise that if the elderly woman wanted the property back, her close friend would cancel the deed. Later the younger woman refused to cancel the deed, arguing the transaction was valid and binding. The elderly woman sued to recover her property. In its ruling in favor of the grantor, the court stated that "[t]he general rule is that mere inadequacy of price or consideration is no ground for claiming the rescission of a contract in equity.... Equity does not undertake to act as the guardian of mankind. It does not aid people who make foolish bargains. But there are exceptions to the rule, which apply with peculiar force, where the parties do not stand in equal positions, do not possess equal knowledge, and where there are circumstances of fraud and oppression, on the one part, and of distress and submission, on the other."[20] In this case, the court concluded that the younger woman committed fraud when she made the promise and then did not cancel the deed.

Date　Although most deeds are dated as a matter of custom, a deed without a date is still valid.

Execution　A deed concludes with the signatures of the grantor and witnesses and an **acknowledgment** of the signatures by a notary public.

> *An acknowledgment is a written statement made by a notary public or other designated public officer and attached to the document. It proclaims that the person who executed the document has appeared before the officer and acknowledged that he or she is the person who executed the document and that he or she has done so of his or her free will.[21]*

An acknowledgment is not a *guarantee* that the person signing the instrument is actually that person, but it does give *reasonable assurance* because notaries request identification and, as a normal practice, memorialize the information in their notary logs. The grantor must sign the deed; but on occasion, the grantor will specifically authorize another person to execute the deed through a document known as a power of attorney. The **power of attorney** should be recorded with the deed. The witnesses and acknowledgment are not generally required to make a deed valid; however, they are required in some states to make the deed eligible for recording.

acknowledgment
Verifying a signature by declaration in front of a notary public.

power of attorney
An instrument appointing an agent to conduct business on behalf of a principal.

A man in ill health signed a durable power of attorney in favor of his wife. A durable power of attorney gives an agent the broad authority to make decisions regarding a principal's legal affairs even after the principal becomes incapacitated. The document in this case was witnessed and acknowledged by a notary public/lawyer. The notary public failed to read the document out loud and to ask him if his act was free and voluntary. In *Poole v. Hyatt* on page 400, the Maryland court decides, in this case of first impression, whether to adopt the positions in most states, which do not require the notary to read the document aloud for the acknowledgment to be legally valid.

END OF CHAPTER CASE

Delivery

There is a popular misconception that a conveyance of real estate will be effective if there is a deed that meets the preceding requirements. The misconception is illustrated by the all-too-common "safe-deposit box" case. In a Nevada case, *Allenbach v. Ridenour,*[22] Ridenour deeded property to his son but did not tell his son of the deed. Ridenour continued to pay taxes on the real estate and even leased it to others. Shortly after Ridenour's death, the deed was found in Ridenour's safe-deposit box along with a will, executed the same day as the deed, that referred to the deed and noted that the deed would be placed in escrow with a bank. The court held that the deed was invalid because there had been no legal delivery. **Delivery** usually requires all of the *three* following elements:

> **delivery**
> A grantor's transfer and relinquishment of a deed to the grantee.

1. A physical delivery by the grantor to the grantee
2. An intention on the part of the grantor to convey title
3. Acceptance of title by the grantee (See Figure 10.3.)

Delivery must take place during the lifetime of the grantor; after death, the transfer is made by means of a will.

> **acceptance**
> Acts, conduct, or words that indicate an intent to take title to property described in a deed.

The third requirement, **acceptance** by the grantee, is rarely litigated. Acceptance is presumed even when the grantee dies before being advised of the deed unless the facts clearly indicate otherwise. The first two requirements have been subject to a great deal of litigation, and most cases fall into one of four categories.

Delivery to Grantee without Conditions   In a typical case where the grantee takes physical possession of the deed at the closing, there is a presumption that legal delivery has been made, although this presumption can be rebutted by other evidence as shown in the following Georgia case.

A CASE IN POINT

In *Keesee v. Collum,*[23] a father called his four children to his bedside three days before his death; opened a tin box; and removed $2,630, which he divided into four shares. He also removed a deed that named one daughter as grantee and laid the deed beside his cot. The daughter picked up the deed, looked at it, and placed it with the other papers. The father kept the deed and the money, stating, "I will fix the rest tomorrow, I have got to lay down"; but he died before taking further action. The court held that there was no delivery on these facts: "Even though the evidence authorized a finding that at the time the grantor was preparing a division of his property, and Mrs. Keesee at one time had physical possession of the deed to her for a few minutes, the jury, under the facts and circumstances appearing, were authorized to find that the maker did not intend to surrender dominion over the deed. Apparently all the children felt that the grantor had not completed delivery of the money or the deeds, because when he instructed his son to put the papers up, all the money and the deeds were returned to the grantor's trunk. The delivery of a deed is complete as against the maker only when it is in the hands of or in the power of the grantee or someone authorized to act for him, with the consent of the grantor, and with intention that the grantee hold it as a muniment of title. But a mere manual delivery to the grantee is not sufficient, where the intention of the grantor to surrender the dominion is not present."

> **FIGURE 10.3**
> Delivery Requirements

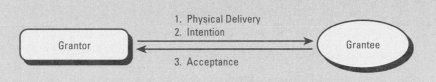

Similarly, if the grantor retains physical possession of the deed, a presumption exists that delivery was not intended.

Did Alice Ramsey's deed to Allen Walters effectively convey the property when she deeded the property to him during the course of an illness but maintained occupancy and paid taxes after her recovery? In *Johnson v. Ramsey* on page 402, the court resolves this and other issues regarding Ramsey's conveyance.

END OF CHAPTER CASE

The presumption that delivery was not intended due to the grantor's retention of the deed may also be rebutted. For example, a Michigan court ruled that a valid delivery may occur when the grantor retains the deed but signs and records it.[24] The presumption was also rebutted in the following California case.

A CASE IN POINT

In *Shaver v. Canfield,*[25] Willis, a widower, delivered three deeds to his daughter, Nettie. After reading them and thanking her father, Nettie gave them back to him for safekeeping in his little tin box. Willis continued to collect and keep rent from the property, and he later mortgaged the property. He also remarried; and after his death, his second wife claimed that the deeds to Nettie were invalid.

The court disagreed with the widow: "Where a deed has been delivered the fact that the grantee allows it to remain in the custody of the grantor will not invalidate it. A deed may be returned after delivery to the grantor, so as to insure that it would not be placed on the record without affecting the delivery. The fact that Mr. Canfield collected the rents or a greater portion of them, and used them for himself and mortgaged the property without the knowledge of the grantee, did not affect the delivery.... The fact that after the delivery of the deeds they were placed in a tin box in the grantor's room would not affect the legality of the delivery."

Delivery to Grantee on Oral Condition   Sven attended Bemidji State University. One winter he decided to travel across the state to watch the annual hockey game between his university and its archrival St. Cloud State University. Because Sven considered this a dangerous mission (hockey rivalries often stir up the fans' emotions), he signed the deed to all of his real estate to his roommate Ole and then handed the deed to him, saying, "I want you to have this property if I do not return alive." When Sven returned, he discovered that Ole had recorded the deed and refused to deed the property back to Sven. Should the deed be canceled? Although all decisions are not in agreement, most courts would decide that Ole now owns the property because the intention of the grantor should be evidenced only by the writing in the deed, not by oral statements that may or may not have been made.

Delivery to a Third-Party Agent   When a deed is delivered to a third party instead of to the grantee, the major legal issue is whether the third party was acting as the agent of the grantor or the grantee. A delivery to the grantor's agent is not legally valid because the deed could be revoked at the grantor's discretion since the agent, by definition, is controlled by the grantor. Delivery occurs once the grantor's agent delivers the deed to the grantee. A delivery to the grantee's agent, however, is legally valid.

Delivery to an Independent Third Party with Conditions A grantor often delivers a deed to an independent third party who is to hold the deed until certain conditions have been met. This is a valid method of delivery unless the conditions are within the control of the grantor.

escrow

A system of document transfer in which a deed, a bond, or funds are delivered to a third person to hold until all conditions of the escrow are fulfilled.

The most common instance of delivery to a third party is the commercial **escrow**. As an example of this method, assume that Cedric has contracted to purchase a new house from Rowena for $200,000. Cedric does not want to pay Rowena $200,000 at the closing in return for the deed because he is fearful that he would have to pay any mechanics' liens that might be filed after the closing if Rowena was judgment proof. Rowena, however, refuses to deliver the deed until she receives her money. This impasse could be resolved if Rowena delivered the deed to a third-party escrowee, such as a title company or bank, which would, in turn, deliver the deed to Cedric when the condition—payment—was met. Cedric would deliver the $200,000 to the escrowee at the closing on the condition that the money would be paid if no liens were filed within the time period allowed by law. (See Figure 10.4.)

If an escrow arrangement is used, the legal delivery date will be the date when the conditions are met. However, to avoid injustice in certain cases, a court might relate the title back to the date the grantor delivered the deed to the escrowee. In the preceding case, for example, if Rowena died between the time she delivered the deed to the escrowee and the date the conditions were met, most courts would consider the first date as the delivery date to avoid claims to the property made by Rowena's heirs.

The Closing Process

closing

The consummation of the sale of real estate.

Closing a real estate transaction involves completing both the mortgage transaction and the real estate transfer. A large number of documents and checks change hands in a very short time. Closings are generally organized in *one of two* ways. In the *first* closing, sometimes referred to as the "California Closing" or "Western Style Closing," the parties deliver executed documents and required funds to an escrow agent. The escrow agent

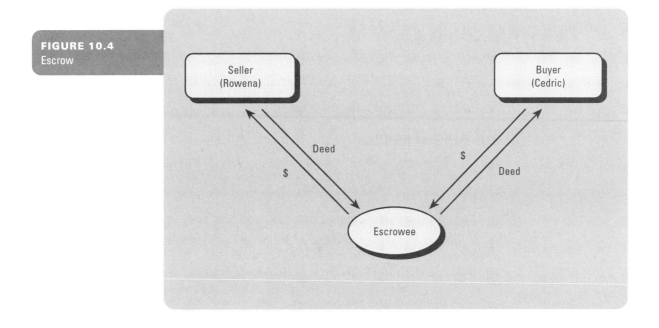

FIGURE 10.4
Escrow

"holds the buyer's funds until the title insurer notifies her that the seller's deed was recorded and there were no prior adverse interests of record."[26] Under this arrangement, the seller and buyer usually do not even meet each other. The historical genesis of the California Closing was the 1840s California Gold Rush. Because claimants could not leave their mining claims or "stakes" to record their interests, for fear of claims jumpers, they relied on third party agents who would gather the necessary legal instruments and make and record the transactions in their absence.

In the *second* type, sometimes called the "New York Style Closing,"[27] the participants actually meet across the table. Visualize, for example, the seller and her "seconds"—an attorney, the mortgagee, and the real estate broker—on one side of the table and the buyer and his "seconds"—the mortgagee and an attorney—seated on the other side of the table.

The form of closing statement for one- to four-family residential closings of federally-related mortgage loans is referred to as a **HUD-1**.[28] The Real Estate Settlement and Procedures Act (RESPA), discussed in Chapter 9, designates the person handling the closing on behalf of the lender as the **settlement agent** (also called a *closing agent or a settlement service provider*); this person usually conducts the closing.[29] Although states differ in their approaches, closing agents are not required by law to be licensed attorneys when they preside over closings, as the next Kentucky case demonstrates.

HUD-1

The Department of Housing and Urban Development's (HUD's) closing statement form for residential property financed with federally related mortgage loans.

settlement agent

A third party who handles the closing of a real estate transaction.

A CASE IN POINT

In *Countrywide Home Loans, Inc. v. Kentucky Bar Association*,[30] a lender argued that closing agents did not need to be attorneys to supervise a "New York Style" closing. The Kentucky Supreme Court ruled in the lender's favor, stating that using nonlawyer closing agents is legal as long as the agent does not provide legal advice. The court further noted that "[b]ecause most of the closing documents are prepared by the lender and legal issues are almost always resolved prior to the closing, the closing agent's role at the closing table is to present the documents to the parties, to instruct the parties where to sign, and to disburse funds."

Flow of Money

Whether a HUD-1 closing statement or a privately designed form is used (for a cash, seller financed, or commercial real estate closing), the flow of money is reflected in debits and credits on the closing statement. A new HUD-1 closing statement went into effect on January 1, 2010 and is discussed below.

The Revised RESPA

RESPA was created in 1974 to regulate the real estate settlement servicing industry which had been plagued by years of corrupt practices. Title companies and other services misled consumers and were rarely punished. Kickbacks to mortgage brokers and others for steering business in another's direction were commonplace. Unfortunately, since RESPA's inception, settlement practices are still plagued by ethical and legal problems. In the decade of 2000 and leading up to the real estate mortgage crisis of 2007–2009, some observers felt that the industry hit its nadir. Many blamed the U.S. Department of Housing and Urban Development (HUD) which lacked the staffing or political will to attack the problems. Under the Bush Administration, changes to RESPA were proposed in 2008 and went into effect in 2010.[31]

Good Faith Estimate form

A closing form required by HUD regulation that accompanies the HUD-1 form designed to better inform consumers about the terms of the loan and estimated settlement charges.

The most important feature in the new RESPA law is a consumer-friendly, easy-to-read **Good Faith Estimate form** (GFE).[32] Among the important information now required in the new GFE are:

1. The term (15, 30 year etc.) of the mortgage loan
2. Disclosure about whether the interest rate is fixed or variable
3. Whether there is a prepayment penalty if the borrower refinances later
4. Whether there is a balloon note
5. The total closing costs

The GFE encourages consumers to use the foregoing information and compare it to other loan offers in a section titled "Using the shopping chart."

The GFE as well as the new HUD-1 form, discussed below, are integrated and referenced to each other as well. For example, HUD-1, line 1103 titled "Owner's title insurance" references GFE #5, which states: "You may purchase an owner's title insurance policy to protect your interest in the property."

The new GFE also discloses to buyers the financial implications of paying settlement costs upfront. This issue also involves the controversial yield-spread premium (YSP) discussed in Chapter 9. Some mortgage brokers and retailers encourage borrowers to finance some of their settlement costs, such as points and origination fees, rather than pay upfront even though the borrower may be able to afford them. For this, the agent often receives extra compensation since the interest rate will generally be higher. For the borrowers, however, this can often mean a higher monthly payment for the term of the mortgage note, typically 30 years. To inform and help consumers understand better the issue, the new GFE instructions plainly state, with certain important information in bold print, the following:

- *If you want to choose this same loan with **lower settlement charges**, then you will have a **higher interest rate**.*
- *If you want to choose this same loan with a **lower interest rate**, then you will have **higher settlement charges**.*

Below this statement, the GFE also contains a section titled "Using the Tradeoff Table." This table specifically discloses to the borrower the actual dollar difference in the monthly payment by comparing the above two scenarios. The aim is to make this crucial decision more transparent. A prudent borrower, for example, may now choose to pay the upfront settlement costs since he will have a lower interest rate.

Borrowers will now also receive important information regarding their pending loan more quickly. The new RESPA now requires loan originators to provide borrowers the following: the GFE, a HUD-prepared Settlement Cost Booklet[33], which gives in-depth information on the settlement process, and the Mortgage Servicing Disclosure Statement,[34] which informs borrowers whether their lenders intend to service the loan or transfer it to another holder. All three materials must be given to borrowers within three business days after they submit all the necessary information to their loan originators.[35]

The "estimates" contained in the GFE, moreover, can now be better characterized as a binding forecast since lenders are responsible for overages. Still, lenders can be excused for overages by certain events beyond their control, such as Acts of God, disasters, emergencies, and inaccurate information and also have 30 days to cure any overages. There are also fee tolerances allowed on some charges, such as both the lender's and buyer's title insurance, of up to 10 percent, but only if the buyer selects a title insurer on a list provided by the settlement agent. However, there is zero tolerance on the estimates of such important fees as the origination fee, loan points, and transfer taxes. Some critics are concerned about the lists that settlement agents will provide, arguing that large and powerful title insurers will make sure that their smaller competitors are purged and potential borrowers will lack the time or sophistication to hunt for other such providers.

The Mortgage Closing

The flow of funds is initiated as the buyer closes his mortgage loan. The buyer signs the note and mortgage and receives a credit for the amount of the loan less itemized closing costs, prepayment of interest, and funds to be placed in escrow with the lender. (See Figure 10.5.) The prudent buyer will have reviewed the closing statement the day before the closing, at which time the Uniform Settlement Statement (HUD-1) must be furnished under RESPA.

In order to better understand and follow the placement of the information presented below see Figure 10.5. The new HUD-1 form can also be accessed at http://www.hud.gov/offices/hsg/ramh/res/hud1.pdf as well as the new GFE which is accessed at http://www.hud.gov/content/releases/goodfaithestimate.pdf. In addition, the new HUD Settlement Cost Booklet can be viewed in a cite provided in endnote 33. This booklet lists and explains in greater detail the *following* mortgage closing costs.

1. Loan origination charge, often a percentage of the loan charged to cover administrative costs in processing the loan (line 801 of the HUD-1, GFE #1).
2. Loan discount, or points, used to offset restrictions on yield imposed by government regulation, each point being equal to one percent of the mortgage amount (line 802 of the HUD-1, GFE #2). Many buyers prefer to pay loan points by separate check to safeguard the tax deductibility of this charge as interest. As noted in the YSP discussion above, points can be financed over the life of the loan, but can result in a higher interest rate. GFE #2 specifically provides this information derived from calculations made in the "Using the Tradeoff Table" on GFE page 3.
3. Fee for an appraisal that the lender uses to determine the value of the security (line 804 of the HUD-1, GFE #3). Sometimes a seller pays for the appraisal when she applies for the loan. The amount, which would be marked on line 804 as "POC" (paid outside of closing), would be shown but not included in the total fees brought to the settlement.[36]
4. Credit report fee to cover the cost of a report on the borrower's credit history (line 805 of the HUD-1, GFE #3).
5. Fee for a tax service provider for information on the real estate property taxes (line 806, GFE #3).
6. Fee to a service for gathering information on whether the property is in a flood zone (line 807 of HUD-1, GFE #3). It is noteworthy that the lender selects all the servicers for the buyer that are listed on the foregoing lines 3–6 as well as determining their costs. Those persons or companies performing the services are listed on GFE #3.
7. Other fees, which are deemed necessary for the closing, can be written in on line 808 of the HUD-1. One such fee can be for a lender-required inspection of a building that has recently been constructed.
8. Premium for private mortgage insurance (PMI), which is required on certain high-loan-to-value loans, (normally those with less than a 20 percent down payment) to protect the lender against loss if the borrower defaults (lines 902 and 1003 of the HUD-1). Line 902 lists any upfront premium payments, while line 1003 provides monthly payments of premiums that will be made to an escrow or impound account. GFE #9 provides the initial charge for PMI, as well as property insurance and taxes.

FIGURE 10.5
HUD-1 Closing Statement

A. Settlement Statement (HUD-1)

U.S. DEPARTMENT OF HOUSING AND URBAN DEVELOPMENT

B. Type of Loan

| 1. ☐ FHA   2. ☐ RHS   3. ☐ Conv. Unins. | 6. File Number: | 7. Loan Number: | 8. Mortgage Insurance Case Number: |
| 4. ☐ VA   5. ☐ Conv. Ins. | | | |

C. Note: This form is furnished to give you a statement of actual settlement costs. Amounts paid to and by the settlement agent are shown. Items marked "(p.o.c.)" were paid outside the closing; they are shown here for informational purposes and are not included in the totals.

D. Name & Address of Borrower:	E. Name & Address of Seller:	F. Name & Address of Lender:
G. Property Location:	H. Settlement Agent:	I. Settlement Date:
	Place of Settlement:	

J. Summary of Borrower's Transaction

100. Gross Amount Due from Borrower

101. Contract sales price	
102. Personal property	
103. Settlement charges to borrower (line 1400)	
104.	
105.	

Adjustment for items paid by seller in advance

106. City/town taxes to	
107. County taxes to	
108. Assessments to	
109.	
110.	
111.	
112.	

120. Gross Amount Due from Borrower

200. Amounts Paid by or in Behalf of Borrower

201. Deposit or earnest money	
202. Principal amount of new loan(s)	
203. Existing loan(s) taken subject to	
204.	
205.	
206.	
207.	
208.	
209.	

Adjustments for items unpaid by seller

210. City/town taxes to	
211. County taxes to	
212. Assessments to	
213.	
214.	
215.	
216.	
217.	
218.	
219.	

220. Total Paid by/for Borrower

300. Cash at Settlement from/to Borrower

301. Gross amount due from borrower (line 120)	
302. Less amounts paid by/for borrower (line 220)	( )
303. Cash ☐ From ☐ To Borrower	

K. Summary of Seller's Transaction

400. Gross Amount Due to Seller

401. Contract sales price	
402. Personal property	
403.	
404.	
405.	

Adjustments for items paid by seller in advance

406. City/town taxes to	
407. County taxes to	
408. Assessments to	
409.	
410.	
411.	
412.	

420. Gross Amount Due to Seller

500. Reductions In Amount Due to Seller

501. Excess deposit (see instructions)	
502. Settlement charges to seller (line 1400)	
503. Existing loan(s) taken subject to	
504. Payoff of first mortgage loan	
505. Payoff of second mortgage loan	
506.	
507.	
508.	
509.	

Adjustments for items unpaid by seller

510. City/town taxes to	
511. County taxes to	
512. Assessments to	
513.	
514.	
515.	
516.	
517.	
518.	
519.	

520. Total Reduction Amount Due Seller

600. Cash at Settlement to/from Seller

601. Gross amount due to seller (line 420)	
602. Less reductions in amount due seller (line 520)	( )
603. Cash ☐ To ☐ From Seller	

The Public Reporting Burden for this collection of information is estimated at 35 minutes per response for collecting, reviewing, and reporting the data. This agency may not collect this information, and you are not required to complete this form, unless it displays a currently valid OMB control number. No confidentiality is assured; this disclosure is mandatory. This is designed to provide the parties to a RESPA covered transaction with information during the settlement process.

9. Fee for the services of a title agent (line 1102 of the HUD-1, GFE #4).
10. Premium for the lender title insurance (line 1104 of the HUD-1, GFE #4).
11. Costs for government recording and transfer charges (lines 1200–1206, GFE #7 and #8).

FIGURE 10.5
HUD-1 Closing Statement
(Continued)

L. Settlement Charges

	Paid From Borrower's Funds at Settlement	Paid From Seller's Funds at Settlement
700. Total Real Estate Broker Fees		
Division of commission (line 700) as follows:		
701. $ to		
702. $ to		
703. Commission paid at settlement		
704.		
800. Items Payable in Connection with Loan		
801. Our origination charge $ (from GFE #1)		
802. Your credit or charge (points) for the specific interest rate chosen $ (from GFE #2)		
803. Your adjusted origination charges (from GFE A)		
804. Appraisal fee to (from GFE #3)		
805. Credit report to (from GFE #3)		
806. Tax service to (from GFE #3)		
807. Flood certification (from GFE #3)		
808.		
900. Items Required by Lender to Be Paid in Advance		
901. Daily interest charges from to @ $ /day (from GFE #10)		
902. Mortgage insurance premium for months to (from GFE #3)		
903. Homeowner's insurance for years to (from GFE #11)		
904.		
1000. Reserves Deposited with Lender		
1001. Initial deposit for your escrow account (from GFE #9)		
1002. Homeowner's insurance months @ $ per month $		
1003. Mortgage insurance months @ $ per month $		
1004. Property taxes months @ $ per month $		
1005. months @ $ per month $		
1006. months @ $ per month $		
1007. Aggregate Adjustment –$		
1100. Title Charges		
1101. Title services and lender's title insurance (from GFE #4)		
1102. Settlement or closing fee $		
1103. Owner's title insurance (from GFE #5)		
1104. Lender's title insurance $		
1105. Lender's title policy limit $		
1106. Owner's title policy limit $		
1107. Agent's portion of the total title insurance premium $		
1108. Underwriter's portion of the total title insurance premium $		
1200. Government Recording and Transfer Charges		
1201. Government recording charges (from GFE #7)		
1202. Deed $ Mortgage $ Releases $		
1203. Transfer taxes (from GFE #8)		
1204. City/County tax/stamps Deed $ Mortgage $		
1205. State tax/stamps Deed $ Mortgage $		
1206.		
1300. Additional Settlement Charges		
1301. Required services that you can shop for (from GFE #6)		
1302. $		
1303. $		
1304.		
1305.		
1400. Total Settlement Charges (enter on lines 103, Section J and 502, Section K)		

12. Charges for additional required services. A typical charge would be a survey, which a lender may require to determine the location of a building, easements, and lot lines. These services must be enumerated in the HUD-1 form lines 1301–1305 and GFE #6).

It is noteworthy that title insurance premiums, which are normally paid by the borrower, are deducted from the amount of the loan, even though they are incurred to protect the lender (see Chapter 8). The buyer should hire an attorney for guidance throughout the closing process as well as purchase owner's title insurance to safeguard her own interests because the Lender Title Insurance Policy only protects the loan amount, not the purchase price. Thus, a buyer who does not obtain an Owner's Policy is not protected from title defects that impair the buyer's equity in the property. The new HUD-1 line 1103 and GFE #5, discussed above, also explain this information to buyers in a better way now.

Title insurance is discussed in more detail in Chapter 8.

Appraisals and Appraiser Liability

All lenders require that mortgaged property be appraised before the closing, An appraisal is crucial since no lender obviously wants to secure its loan with collateral worth less than the amount of the loan. Because appraisals are not scientifically precise, appraisers are sometimes sued for alleged mistakes. Property buyers must pay for appraisals, reflected on HUD-1 line 804, GFE #3, which are made primarily for the benefit of the lender.

Since the contract to perform the appraisal is between the lender and the appraiser, the lender can sue for damages. Can the buyer also sue the appraiser for a negligent appraisal? There is a split in the courts on this issue. Some courts have held that since it is foreseeable that an appraisal will be relied on by the purchaser to determine value, a purchaser can sue the appraiser for damages for a negligent appraisal.[37] On the other hand, purchasers cannot sue appraisers who are working for lenders making Federal Housing Administration (FHA) and Department of Veterans Affairs (VA) loans. These laws are created, according to the courts, to protect the government and lenders rather than the purchaser. Likewise, some courts have ruled that appraisals for conventional loans are also designed to protect lenders, not purchasers.[38]

Appraisers, like other real estate professionals, must adhere to prescribed standards of competency. These standards, promulgated by the Appraisal Foundation, appear in the *Uniform Standards of Professional Appraisal Practice* (USPAP). All members of the Appraisal Foundation must adhere to these standards, as do licensees in most states. In general, USPAP requires appraisers to (1) have the knowledge and experience necessary to complete a specific appraisal assignment or (2) disclose the appraiser's lack of knowledge or experience to the client.[39]

The importance of proper and ethical appraisal methods in the closing process cannot be understated. Significant problems occur when unethical appraisers bow to pressure from lenders, mortgage brokers, and others to appraise property in excess of its objective value. Many of these parties rationalize higher appraisals by assuming that home prices will continue to rise. In the 1980s, inflated appraisals made before the precipitous fall in oil prices contributed to the collapse of savings and loans and banks, first in Texas, Louisiana, and other oil- and gas-producing states, and then across the country. In reaction, Congress passed the Financial Institutions Reform, Recovery and Enforcement Act of 1989 (FIRREA), in which all appraisers who work for federally chartered or insured lending institutions must be licensed or certified by their states.

Unfortunately, in recent years, many appraisers have forgotten the lessons learned in the 1980s. When property values began to soar across the United States in the early 2000s, appraisers again were pressured by mortgage brokers and lenders to make inflated appraisals to justify larger mortgages. The inflated equity also was used to finance subordinate mortgages and home equity lines of credit, many being subprime loans with adjustable interest rates. Later, when interest rates increased and mortgagors defaulted, the subprime mortgage crises followed, a topic discussed in Chapter 9.[40]

Due to overinflated appraisals and other fraud caused by lender/appraiser collusion during the housing and mortgage crisis of 2007–2009, Fannie Mae and Freddie Mac adopted in 2009 the Home Valuation Code of Conduct (HVCC). Since the two are the primary sources of mortgage capital in the secondary market in the United States, the HVCC has become the standard for most lenders. Under its provisions, loan officers, mortgage brokers, or real estate brokers are *not* allowed to select appraisers directly. Instead, most appraisal requests must now be passed first through an appraisal management company (AMC) which then selects the appraiser. An AMC can take as much as 40 percent of the appraisal fee, prompting many appraisers to complain that the new provisions are squeezing them economically.[41] The new financial reform law, the Dodd-Frank Act passed in 2010, also requires that appraisals of property which are collateralized by certain "high cost" loans (those with exceptionally high fees and other closing costs) must be done on-site instead of just using computer accessed data.

The Property Closing

While page 2 of the HUD-1 Settlement Statement reflects primarily lender and settlement costs, page 1 focuses on the buyer-seller transaction. The settlement charges computed on page 2 are included on line 103 of page 1 (for the borrower-buyer's charges) and line 502 (for the seller's settlement charges). The major cost item on page 1 of the settlement statement is the charge to the buyer for the contract sales price, which appears as a debit on line 101.

In most transactions, various adjustments must be made to the purchase price. Certain items should be added to the price. If, for example, the buyer closes on April 2 and the seller paid a homeowner's assessment (such as for new sidewalks and curbs) for the month of April on April 1, the seller deserves a credit from the buyer for the twenty-nine days of homeowner's assessments prepaid by the seller and benefiting the buyer's term of ownership. (See HUD-1 lines 212 and 512). Taxes and insurance premiums that have been prepaid by the seller also should be prorated and charged to the buyer, as illustrated on lines 211 and 511 of the HUD-1 statement. The buyer-seller proration of taxes, which differs from tax reserves that may be required by the lender, appears on lines 1004–1006. (Figure 10.6 contains Attorneys' Title Insurance Fund, Inc.'s standards for prorations.)

Items charged to the seller must be subtracted from this new figure. These include the amount of the buyer's earnest money deposit if it becomes part of the down payment (HUD-1 line 201), any unpaid utility bills, and state transfer taxes. After these adjustments have been made, the buyer writes a check to the settlement agent for the amount of cash to close—that is, the purchase price net of buyer-seller debits and credits less the amount of the loan plus mortgage closing costs and settlement costs.

On the seller's side of the transaction, the seller must satisfy any outstanding mortgages or liens against the property unless, of course, the buyer is assuming the existing mortgage. For example, the seller must be debited for the amount of the existing loan (HUD-1 line 503). The seller is debited for the real estate commission due the real estate broker (HUD-1 line 703), which is computed on the gross sales price, not on the amount the seller actually receives. The seller also is debited for other required prorations or payments, such as county real estate taxes for the year of the closing (HUD-1 line 511).

FIGURE 10.6
Standards for Prorations

October 16 is the date of the closing. What is the charge for an item payable in arrears having a cost of $215 for October?

Incorrect method:

$$\frac{\$215/\text{month}}{31\ \text{days}} = \$6.9354838/\text{diem. Round to }\$6.94.\ \text{Multiply by 16 days}$$
$$= \$111.04$$

The proper procedure is to do this in one continuous equation.

Correct method:

$$\frac{\$215/\text{month}}{31\ \text{days}} \times 16\ \text{days} = \$110.96774\ \text{or, after rounding, }\$110.97$$

The difference is that you did not strike the = key in the first example until the end of the chain of calculations. Instead, you continued straight through without a pause, striking the = key only at the end.

If your calculator has a switch to select the number of decimal places in the display and calculations, set it for *F* (Floating decimals). If there is no *F*, choose the largest number of decimals; or if there is no switch, begin the calculations.

If you want to see any interim figures, such as the per diem, do not use the = key; instead, strike the next operator key, such as the × key in the correct example above. This prevents interference with the calculation by rounding off prematurely.

When you are multiplying or dividing by numbers as large as 365, premature rounding off often causes inaccurate results. Since everyone at the closing is striving for accuracy, even small errors or two "right" answers will result in additional discussion, wasting everybody's time.

Flow of Documents

The seller and the buyer execute and should receive copies of the itemized settlement or closing statement listing the charges already discussed. In addition, the buyer should receive the following:

1. From the seller, a deed, a receipt for payment, a copy of the seller's mortgage discharge, a bill of sale if personal property is being sold, the seller's property insurance policy if it has been assigned, receipts for payment of the most recent utility bills and taxes, and the title insurance policy. Many contracts provide that the seller must provide "evidence" of title but that the cost of the Owner's Title Policy is the buyer's responsibility. In fact, the buyer typically receives a *copy* of the deed from the seller or the escrow agent. The original deed is typically recorded immediately following the closing and a copy is sent to the buyer following recording.
2. From the mortgagee, copies of the note, mortgage, and other mortgage closing documents. The seller should receive the mortgage note and the mortgage discharge from the mortgagee.

Amid the bustle and confusion of the closing, *three* important matters deserve emphasis:

1. The abstract of title or title insurance policy is often certified for a date two or three weeks prior to closing and should be brought up to date to ensure that there have

been no last-minute liens or transfers. Many states require that the title insurer "insure the gap." This insurance protects the buyer from title defects that may arise between the time of the last title search and the recording of the deed. Even if gap insurance is not required under state law, the buyer should request this coverage. (The gap was discussed in Chapter 8.)

2. The legal documents (deed, buyer's mortgage, and seller's mortgage discharge) should be recorded (a topic covered extensively in Chapter 8) immediately after the closing to avoid later transfers to good faith buyers in states which apply race and race-notice statutes or for a buyer to "win" the race to record first in race-statute states.

3. The buyer should ask for the keys to the house to avoid being locked out of the newly purchased home.

Taxation of Real Estate

The acquisition and sale of real estate receive favorable treatment under the tax law, even after significant tax reform in recent years. Chapter 5 discussed the impact of tax law on investment forms of real estate ownership such as the limited partnership, S corporation, and real estate investment trusts (REIT). Although detailed coverage of tax law is beyond the scope of this book, the tax benefits connected with the ownership and sale of real estate are summarized as follows.

Taxation of Seller

The tax law favors real estate sellers in *three* respects. *First,* it is often advantageous from a tax standpoint for a seller to receive the purchase price in installments—for instance, under a land contract or by taking a purchase money mortgage from the buyer. By spreading the gain over several years, the seller can avoid a higher tax rate that might result if the entire gain were taxed in one year. The seller also may be able to defer part of the tax until the installment payments are received. However, the benefits of installment sales are generally unavailable to a "dealer." A dealer, so designated by the Internal Revenue Service (IRS), is a real estate professional who holds real estate for sale to customers, but whose profits are typically taxed as ordinary income instead of as capital gains. Capital gains are typically taxed at a much lower rate. An "investor," on the other hand, often enjoys the benefits of capital gains treatment.

Second, it is possible for a seller who is selling a principal residence to avoid tax completely. A principal residence may be a cooperative apartment, a condominium, or even a houseboat. Under the Taxpayer Relief Act of 1997,[42] a single taxpayer enjoys a $250,000 exclusion on the sale of a principal residence while taxpayers enjoy an exclusion of $500,000 if married and filing jointly. These exclusions are generally available once every two years. Special rules apply to widows, widowers, and divorced spouses.

These exclusions replace the "rollover" provisions of prior law, under which a taxpayer could defer payment of capital gains taxes by purchasing a more expensive principal residence within two years of the sale. The taxpayer's ability to take advantage of the recurring $500,000 or $250,000 exclusion replaces the prior "one-time only" capital gains exclusion for taxpayers over the age of fifty-five.

Thus, under the new law, a principal residence sold for more than its acquisition and improvement costs promises to provide the taxpayer an unusual form of profit: gains in which the federal government does not share.

The *third* tax benefit attaches to the transfer of real estate, called a §1031 land exchange, results when the seller trades property held for business or investment purposes for like-kind property—that is, other real estate. In such cases, tax payment, as discussed in Chapter 7, is deferred until the property received in the trade is sold.

Taxation of Buyer

The acquisition of real estate brings both tax burdens and tax benefits to the buyer. The major tax burden is the real property tax that is levied by local governments. Most of the tax revenue used to support local governments, including school systems, is derived from the property tax. Property taxes can vary greatly. The variation is caused by *two* factors. *First*, property taxes are based on the assessed value of a house, but the methods of assessment vary from state to state. In some states, homes are assessed at 100 percent of market value; in other states, the assessment might be based on only 25 or 30 percent of market value.[43] *Second*, the tax rate is subject to a great deal of variation. As an illustration of one method of taxing property, assume that Chen just purchased a used home for $120,000. State law where Chen lives provides that all property must be assessed at 50 percent of market value—in this case, $60,000. The annual tax rate in Chen's city is approximately 70 mills. One mill is equal to 1/1000 of a dollar; or stated another way each mill is the equivalent of $1 per thousand dollars of the property's assessed value. In Chen's case, the tax bill would be $70 for each $1,000 of assessed valuation, or $4,200.

With the burdens of real property ownership come a number of tax benefits for the buyer. Most notably, property taxes and mortgage interest payments may be deducted for federal income tax purposes. The amount of mortgage interest that can be deducted depends on the type of debt. When a loan is obtained to purchase, build, or improve a residence, for instance, mortgage interest on the portion of the loan that exceeds $1 million cannot be deducted. Moreover, deductions cannot be made on interest on home equity loans that exceed $100,000.

A buyer who decides to convert her home into a rental property might enjoy greater tax benefits. *First*, she can depreciate the property (a topic discussed in Chapter 5), which allows the owner an annual deduction on a residential property over a 27.5-year period (39 years for commercial) using straight-line depreciation. Thus, a $300,000 house (after subtracting the land's value) provides a tax deduction of $10,909 a year. The amount depreciated will be used to reduce the "cost basis" or original purchase price, resulting in a higher capital gain when the property is sold. Still, for property investors, long-term (assets held for over one year) capital gains are taxed at 15 percent (although the tax rate is 25 percent for those gains related to depreciation), which is significantly lower than the ordinary income tax rate. Still, it is important to note that capital gains rates are a highly political issue that have historically gone both up and down depending on, among other factors, what political party is in power.

Second, owners can deduct the cost of normal repairs to maintain the property and can depreciate long-term improvements such as a new roof, which add to property value. *Third*, unless paid by the tenant, property taxes, insurance, property management fees, utilities, property association dues, landscaping, and garbage disposal are deductible. *Finally*, travel expenses, whether within a city or over a long distance, can be deducted if they are necessary and proper in overseeing the investment. It is noteworthy that depreciation and other losses in real estate in which the rental property owner is actively involved can offset the owner's salaried income and gains from others investments, such as stocks and bonds, but begin to phase out if she has an adjusted gross income exceeding $100,000 and are generally gone once her income exceeds $150,000. Still, those losses that cannot be deducted become suspended until such time as they can be deducted in the future.[44]

ETHICAL AND
PUBLIC POLICY
ISSUES

Is It Ethical and Sound Public Policy to Allow Homeowners to Deduct the Interest Paid on Their Mortgage Notes from Their Federal Income?

The right to deduct interest on mortgage loans has long been considered to be one of the "sacred cows" that government cannot touch. Changing this tax benefit, which has been available since income taxes were created in 1913, would undoubtedly cause a huge political backlash as well as economic repercussions. In the short run, many homeowners would have to reassess what they could afford since the deduction makes owning a home more affordable, particularly in states with higher real estate prices.

Still, many policymakers argue that the deduction should be eliminated or at least reduced due to other more pressing problems and to create fairer overall tax policy. For example, as discussed previously, homeowners already have a significant tax benefit when they sell their homes due to the $250,000 (single) and $500,000 (married, joint filers) limit, excluding them from having to pay capital gains taxes on those amounts. Moreover, some argue that the interest deduction robs the treasury of billions of dollars while the country faces sizeable budget deficits. It is also the government's largest subsidy to housing.

Interest deductions also create incentives to borrow as much as possible, particularly for speculators who use highly leveraged loans to buy and sell property while enjoying a tax break. Speculators can cause housing markets to reach unrealistic highs, often resulting in painful price corrections that can harm the overall economy.

For homeowners it may cause a buyer to purchase a larger house in order to maximize the deduction. As the recent mortgage and housing crisis has demonstrated, when people buy more than they can afford it can result in severe economic consequences. Interest deductions also favor wealthier homeowners. For example, lower- and middle-class homeowners seldom itemize since their interest payments are less than the standard deduction. Therefore, according to tax experts, 80 percent of the benefits go to the top earning 20 percent of taxpayers while the bottom 60 percent receives three and one-half percent of the benefits because many do not itemize. Moreover, renters, also typically poorer than homeowners, cannot deduct their rent.[45] The benefit also creates an enhanced subsidy to citizens in states with the most expensive real estate, such as California and New York.

Americans have always considered owning a home to be part of the American dream. Homeowners also may contribute to the stability and enrichment of neighborhoods and communities. Ending the deduction would mean that some people could no longer afford a home, at least until the market adjusts to the change. Should the mortgage interest deduction be changed or eliminated? Do the same arguments apply to second homes and vacation homes or to investment properties?

Tax Reform Act of 1986
A tax statute that simplified the income tax code, broadened the tax base, eliminated many tax shelters (including for real estate), and created new reporting requirements.

Foreign Investment in Real Property Tax Act
A tax statute that imposes a withholding requirement on nonresident aliens and foreign business entities that acquire real estate in the United States.

Real Estate Reporting Requirements

The **Tax Reform Act of 1986** requires that the contract sales price be reported to the IRS. The person conducting the closing (for example, an attorney or a title company) is responsible for reporting the price; if there is no closing agent, the burden falls on (in the following order) the lender, the seller's broker, the buyer's broker, or the buyer.

The **Foreign Investment in Real Property Tax Act** (FIRPTA) imposes a withholding requirement on buyers who acquire real property from nonresident aliens and foreign business entities. According to the income tax regulations, "Transferees of U.S. real property interests are required to deduct and withhold a tax equal to 10 percent of the amount realized by the transferor, if the transferor is a foreign person and the disposition takes place on or after January 1, 1995."[46] Section 1461 of the Internal Code provides that a withholding agent or transferee who fails to withhold becomes personally liable for the amount to be paid.

These tough withholding requirements are subject to certain exemptions. One exemption to the withholding requirement provides that the transferee or agent can obtain a **Non-Foreign Affidavit** on a form designated by the Treasury Regulations[47] in which the transferor certifies that she is a domestic person. The transferee can rely on this affidavit unless he knows it is false. Another exemption states that withholding is not required if the purchase price is $300,000 or less and one of the transferees acquires the property for use as a residence.[48] The FIRPTA, which was created in 1980 to protect American farmland from foreign buyers, has been criticized by those who complain that it imposes barriers upon foreigners wishing to invest in U.S. real estate. Critics argue that the U.S. economy would benefit more from a free and open market, particularly during periods when land prices are severely depressed, as the United States has witnessed in the late 2000s.

> **Non-Foreign Affidavit**
>
> A sworn statement by the buyer or his agent that states that the seller is not a foreign person under the Foreign Investment in Real Property Tax Act.

Other Methods of Real Estate Acquisition
Death

On the death of the owner, title or interests in real estate may pass to persons designated in the decedent's will. In the absence of a will, state statutes determine ownership.

> **will**
>
> A legal instrument disposing of a person's property at death.

Wills   Transfer of property by **will** differs from transfer by deed. While a deed is effective upon delivery, a will is effective only upon the moment of death. While a person conveying property by deed is called the *grantor*, a person conveying property by will is referred to as the **testator**. Since the will is not effective until the testator's death it can be revoked during his lifetime. Unlike a deed, a will may pass title to personal property.

> **testator**
>
> A person who dies leaving a valid will.

In some states, oral wills (also called a **noncupative or nuncupative will**) are valid, at least to transfer personal property, if made shortly before death and verified by a specified number of witnesses. In most cases, however, the will must be in writing and must meet certain requirements determined by the law of the state where the decedent's real estate is located or, if personal property is in question, the state of the decedent's residence. In most states, the formal requirements are simple and easy to meet: the will must be signed by the testator and witnessed by two or, in some states, three witnesses who also sign the will.

> **noncupative (or nuncupative) will**
>
> An oral will.

A **holographic** (or handwritten) **will** is recognized in many states when certain requirements are met. Generally, the language must indicate the testator's intent that this is his last will and testament, and it must be written totally in the testator's handwriting, dated, and signed. Unlike noncupative wills, holographic wills do not usually require witnesses.

> **holographic will**
>
> A will written and signed entirely in the testator's handwriting.

Holographic wills are easy to draft and are typically executed without an attorney's assistance. Thus, they are inviting targets for those who may want to contest them at probate. Holographic wills are also relatively easy to forge, presenting another problem. Probably the most famous contesting of a holographic will occurred when the late billionaire Howard Hughes died. In a holographic will purportedly written by Hughes, Melvin Dummar—a stranger who claimed he was picked up by Hughes in the middle of the Nevada desert—was left one-sixteenth of his estate worth $156 million. The Hughes estate fiercely contested the will's validity and in a subsequent trial a jury found it to be a forgery.

The following case illustrates the problems that may arise when ambiguous words written by a legally unsophisticated testator appear in a holographic will—a problem that could have easily been avoided with a lawyer's counsel.

What did the testator mean when he wrote the word *money* in his holographic will? In the case of *In re Estate of Goyette* on page 403, the court rules on the testator's intentions.

END OF CHAPTER CASE

All states have statutes for creating a valid will, sometimes referred to as a "statutory will." Often these statutes include forms and specify requirements such as the number of witnesses required. Lawyers who assist their clients in estate planning typically use this will. (For an example of a statutory will, see www.cengagebrain.com [see page xix in the Preface for instructions on how to access the free study tools for this text].)

Some states also allow "electronic wills." These wills are written and stored in an electronic record and generally must contain at least one "authentication characteristic" of the testator. Examples of an authentication characteristic include a fingerprint, a retinal scan, and a digitized signature.[49]

In addition, every state imposes certain mental requirements on the testator, no matter what form of will he uses, as a condition of the will's validity:

1. The testator must have the intention to make a will, which is usually determined by the language in the will.
2. The testator must have the capacity to make a will, which means that the testator must have reached the age of majority, eighteen, and must be of sound mind.
3. Finally, the will is invalid if it was executed as the result of fraud, undue influence, or mistake.

The following Arizona case illustrates the nature of the mental requirements as well as how a lucid interval may influence how a court views a testator with alleged mental disabilities.

A CASE IN POINT

In the case of *In re Stitt's Estate,*[50] a sixty-five-year-old woman, shortly before her death, executed a will under which her property was to pass to certain relatives, the Mormon Church, and the American Cancer Society. When the will was challenged, there was testimony that at the time she wrote the will, the woman screamed at all hours; cursed the brother who helped her with household tasks; rarely bathed or groomed herself; and often wore little clothing, thus indecently exposing herself. The court, in considering these idiosyncrasies, concluded that the will was still valid: "The rule is that even though a testator does suffer from delusions or hallucinations, unless the will itself was a creature or product of such delusions or hallucinations, it is not invalid. While in the instant case the contestants have put on much testimony of what they might consider delusions or hallucinations, they have not put on any testimony that the will was a creature or a product of the supposed delusions or hallucinations." Moreover, the court stated that disinterested witnesses had observed that at the time Mrs. Stitt dictated the will, had it read back to her, and then signed, she appeared to be "normal in all respects."

Although state laws generally do not require the following provisions, most wills follow a standard format which do:

1. Publication clause, which is a statement of the testator's name, capacity ("being of sound mind"), and intention to make a will

2. Revocation clause, stating that all earlier wills are revoked
3. Burial instructions
4. Payment of debts, specifying which property is to be used to pay the decedent's debts
5. Specific bequests, or gifts of personal property by will
6. Devises, which are gifts of real property by will
7. Residuary clause, governing disposition of all property not covered by a specific bequest or devise
8. Penalty clause, which penalizes a party named in the will who contests the will
9. Name of guardian of minor children
10. Name of personal representative

The required signatures of the testator and witnesses (if required by law) follow the preceding provisions.

executor

A person designated by the testator to carry out the directions of the testator's will.

administrator

A person appointed by the court to administer the estate of a decedent who died without a valid will.

The personal representative of a decedent's estate is also known as the **executor** or, when there is no will, **administrator**. The personal representatives should be responsible people because they are charged with performing the dictates set forth in the will and the law that governs administering the estate.

The first step in the probate process is to file the will in a probate court. There it is reviewed to determine whether formal requirements have been met. The personal representative, now under probate supervision, assembles and manages the decedent's assets, pays taxes and other claims, distributes the assets according to the directions in the will, and renders a final accounting to the probate court. If there is no will, the probate court will name the administrator, usually one of the decedent's closest relatives or someone who will, by law, inherit a portion of the estate.

codicil

An addendum to a will.

Because a testator can revoke her will at any time and so by its very nature the will is effective only at death, the will should be revised occasionally to reflect the changing circumstances of the testator. The revision can be accomplished by means of a supplement to the will, known as a **codicil**, or through a completely new will. (Henry Ford's will, Appendix C, includes a codicil.) The importance of updating a will was well illustrated in 2008, when 28-year-old actor Heath Ledger died from an accidental drug overdose. Ledger left nothing to his girlfriend and 2-year-old daughter because his Australian will, written in 2003, had not been updated; thus all of his property went to those named in his will—his parents and siblings.

The following questions are important in determining whether a revision is necessary: Has one of the beneficiaries died? Has the testator purchased real estate in another state? Have assets declined in value or been sold? Has the personal representative or guardian died or moved away? Has property been purchased jointly? Has there been a change in the law, especially the law relating to taxation of estates? Have special provisions for children, such as naming guardians, bequests to new children and grandchildren, as well as even to those not yet born, been made?

intestate

A person who dies without a will.

When a testator writes a holographic will that is recognized in his state and then moves to a state where it is not recognized, is that will still valid? Generally, wills are valid as long as they comply with either the laws where they are executed or where the person dies.

descent and distribution statute

A state statute that provides for the distribution of property when a person dies without a valid will.

Intestacy   It is estimated that two out of three American adults die **intestate**, without leaving a will. Each state has adopted a **descent and distribution statute** describing who receives the decedent's property. The statutes might also govern distribution of a part of the estate in cases where the will is incomplete. Title to *real* property descends to heirs designated by the intestacy law of the state in which the property is located even if the decedent had not been a resident of the state. The law of the state in which the decedent had her permanent home or residency governs distribution of the estate's *personal* property.

Below are *five* examples which illustrate the operation of state descent and distribution statutes. Although state intestacy laws vary considerably, the following are based on the Uniform Probate Code (UPC) presently adopted in nineteen states (see endnote 51 for information regarding what states have adopted the UPC). *First*, assume that Harry was unmarried, did not have children, and died intestate. Both his real and personal property pass to his parents or, if his parents are not living, to his brothers and sisters. If the brothers and sisters are not living, the property passes to their children; but if there are no nieces and nephews, the property goes to the next of kin beginning with the grandparents.[51]

Second, if Harry was married but died intestate leaving no children or parents, his wife receives his entire estate. If both parents survive, his widow receives the first $200,000 of his estate (which might be all of it) plus 75 percent of the balance with the remainder going to his parent or parents.[52]

Third, Harry was married and left a widow, his only three children are from that marriage, and his widow has no other children. She will receive 100 percent of his estate.[53]

Fourth, Harry was married and left a widow and two children by the marriage in addition to one child from his prior marriage. The first $100,000 plus 50 percent of any balance will go to his widow, with his children receiving the rest of the estate.[54]

Finally, Harry was married and left a widow and three children by the marriage and his widow has one child from a prior marriage. The first $150,000 plus 50 percent of any balance goes to his widow, with Harry's children receiving the rest of the estate.[55]

As stated, while the results can vary considerably from these examples depending on state law, the pattern of distribution is likely to be similar—even in non-UPC states. For example, in community property states, discussed in Chapter 5, if the decedent dies without a will, the surviving spouse is entitled to one-half of the community property since her one-half interest in the community already vested when the property was acquired during the marriage. However, the decedent's separate property is likely to be distributed in a manner similar to what was described in the second and third examples. In fact, the UPC provides an adaptation of the provisions discussed above for states using the community property system.

dower

Under the common law, a widow's right to receive at her husband's death a life estate in one-third of the inheritable lands that he owned during their marriage.

Dower and Homestead   The idea of a **dower** right originated in Medieval Europe based on Germanic law and became recognized in the courts of England by the 14th century. Dower rights were originally designed to operate as a constraint on the ability of a husband to disinherit his wife when, because the legal existence of a woman ended at marriage, a widow might be left with no property upon the death of her husband. However, the prevailing attitude of that period was that the widow should receive a better fate.[56] In the words of Sir Joseph Jeckyl, an 18th century English judge:

> *The relation of husband and wife, as it is the nearest, so it is the earliest, and therefore the wife is the proper object of the care and kindness of the husband; the husband is bound by the law of God and man, to provide for her during his life, and after his death, the moral obligation is not at an end, but he ought to take care of her provision during her own life.*[57]

The solution at common law was to give the widow a dower right in the decedent's real estate. The dower right gave the widow a life estate in one-third of the inheritable land owned by the husband during the marriage. A woman who was divorced when the decedent died would not have a dower right since she was no longer married and so therefore could not be her late husband's widow. Property held in joint tenancy or tenancy by the entireties is not subject to dower; this property is not inheritable since the surviving joint owner rather than the decedent's estate will immediately own the property no longer subject to the decedent spouse's interest. If the husband held property as a tenant in common, his share would be inheritable and therefore subject to the widow's dower interest in that share. A dower right should not be confused with a dowry, which in some cultures is the property brought to the marriage by the bride.

In states that allow widows a dower right, some give widowers a similar right called **curtesy**, while others give both spouses a dower right. The practical effect of dower today is that *both* spouses must sign a deed even if one of their names does not appear on it; otherwise, the title is not marketable. Most states, however, have eliminated both dower and curtesy. These states, by statute, give the surviving spouse the right to an **elective share** of a portion of the decedent's entire estate (for example, one-third or one-half of both real and personal property) in cases where the provisions made for the spouse in a will do not meet the statutory threshold. For example, if Jorge died with an estate worth $600,000 but left his wife, Elena, only $100,000, Elena could elect to take a one-third share, or $200,000.

A **homestead** is the family home and the land surrounding it. In some states, the homestead is limited in terms of acres; for instance, in Kansas, a rural homestead is limited to 160 acres; an urban homestead, to 1 acre. In other states, the homestead is limited to a dollar amount (for example, $50,000). The homestead laws are designed to protect the family from eviction by most creditors, such as unsecured creditors, and from the whims of an improvident spouse. As one method of protection, a surviving spouse is given or may elect the right to retain the homestead upon a spouse's death even if the will does not provide for this. A notable exception is the mortgagee of the homestead, who is allowed to seize the property when the owner defaults on the loan if the mortgagor waives his homestead rights. All conventional, FHA, and VA loans require the homestead waiver; if not, the mortgagee would also be subject to the homestead exemption and would, in essence, be a general, unsecured creditor with little chance of recouping its losses.

Even before death, the homestead may be exempt from sale by most creditors of only one spouse. Moreover, the homestead cannot be sold by only one spouse unless the other spouse agrees to the sale as the next case from Wyoming demonstrates.

curtesy

Under the common law, a surviving husband's rights in land owned by his wife.

elective share

A state statute that allows a surviving spouse to take a designated share of the decedent spouse's estate instead of the share provided for in the decedent spouse's will.

homestead

A person's residence and the land surrounding it.

A CASE IN POINT

In *Stolldorf v. Stolldorf*,[58] Howard and Otie Stolldorf were married in 1918 and lived together in Nebraska until separating in 1930, when Howard moved to Wyoming. In 1942, Howard purchased a house in Cheyenne; and shortly before his death in 1960, he deeded the home to a third party. After Howard's death, Otie claimed that the deed was invalid under Article 19, Section 9, of the Wyoming Constitution: "A homestead as provided by law shall be exempt from forced sale under any process of law, and shall not be alienated without the joint consent of husband and wife, when that relation exists." The Wyoming statutes further provided that the homestead might consist of a house and lot of any size but that the value of the right could not exceed $4,000. The court decided that Otie could claim a homestead right because the parties had never been divorced, and it gave the person who purchased the property from Howard three options: (1) pay Otie $4,000; (2) sell the house and give Otie $4,000 of the proceeds; or (3) if the house could not be sold for over $4,000, give Otie full title to the property.

Title agents sometimes require a "continuous marriage affidavit" from both spouses at the closing of the sale of their home. This affidavit is designed to provide assurance that the property is a homestead and therefore that liens or judgments naming only one spouse do not impair the buyer's title.

The laws of the state in which the property is located govern the rights to homestead.[59] The states differ, for example, on whether homestead protection shields a property owner from forfeiture actions tied to the use and possession of controlled substances. In *State v. Ten (10) Acres of Land,*[60] the Oklahoma court held that property used to cultivate marijuana and subject to forfeiture under a state dangerous substances act was protected from forfeiture by the state's homestead laws. In contrast, a Washington court[61] held that Washington's homestead exemption did not protect the property owner using the land to cultivate marijuana from forfeiture.

In recent years, controversy has arisen in some states that have unlimited homestead protections. Most states do not protect a homestead's equity excessively with at least two states, New Jersey and Pennsylvania, providing no protection. Still, in those states, if mortgagors go into bankruptcy, they are afforded $20,200 in protection under federal bankruptcy law if they choose the federal instead of the state exemptions. In at least seven states, however—Arkansas, Florida, Iowa, Kansas, Oklahoma, South Dakota, and Texas—most creditors cannot place a lien on the homestead property and force a sale to satisfy debts, no matter what the owner's equity is.[62] (See endnote 62 for accessing information on all the states' homestead exemptions.) For example, Burt Reynolds declared bankruptcy in Florida in 1996 with a homestead worth $2.5 million; but his creditors could not touch his equity. Other celebrities, including O. J. Simpson, who has a $33.5 million civil judgment still in effect against him for the assault and battery (resulting in wrongful death) of his ex-wife and her friend, are reputed to have moved to Florida to protect their assets under the state's unlimited homestead exemption. Still, Simpson's homestead protection may be jeopardized since he is now a resident of Nevada (and "guest" of its prison system) and the Florida homestead law requires that the claimant must own and *occupy* the premises.[63]

If a party petitions for bankruptcy and then sells his homestead, can he keep the amount that falls within the homestead exemption? In *Pasquina v. Cunningham,*[64] a federal appeals court ruled that Massachusetts' homestead exemption law also protected the post-petition proceeds of the sale up to its limit, which was $300,000 at that time. Thus, the bankrupt party was able to keep from creditors a $250,000 gain he made in the sale.

In reaction to the foregoing abuses, Congress added a provision in the Bankruptcy Reform Act of 2005 that limits homestead exemptions for those people attempting to evade creditors. Now a person must be a resident of the state for 1,215 days (3.3 years) before she can claim a homestead exemption in that state. Moreover, even a person who qualifies as a resident cannot claim more than a $125,000 exemption if she owes civil judgments for intentional torts, as in the Simpson case, or if she violates federal and state securities laws, like those committed by various officers at Enron, WorldCom, and other companies in the early 2000s.[65]

A homestead property, as mentioned earlier, is normally not protected from all creditors including, as mentioned, the property's mortgagee. Homeowners are also not normally protected from tax and mechanic's lienholders as discussed in Chapter 9.

ETHICAL AND PUBLIC POLICY ISSUES

Should Those Who Commit Various Criminal Acts Lose Their Homes to Their Creditors?

The corporate scandals early in the 21st century that involved high-ranking executives in companies such as Enron and WorldCom resulted in huge civil judgments. Many of these executives bought or maintained mansions in Texas and Florida to protect their assets. In the future, due to the Bankruptcy Reform Act of 2005, certain people will not be able to protect their homesteads and will lose their homes. Problem 10 at the end of the chapter discusses whether this change in public policy is moral.

Adverse Possession

adverse possession

A means of acquiring the title to another's land by openly taking possession of it for a prescribed period of time.

prescription

A means of acquiring an easement through adverse use over a prescribed period of time.

claim of right

An adverse possessor's claim of land as his own.

It is possible for a person to obtain ownership of real estate or an easement at no cost by means of **adverse possession** if certain requirements are met. Adverse possession is a method of acquiring ownership in the land of another. As discussed in Chapter 4, **prescription** is a method of acquiring an easement. There are several sound policy reasons for adverse possession. It encourages landowners to make full use of their land. For example, if they do not protect their property rights in a timely way, someone else may occupy, use, and eventually gain ownership of their property and make more productive uses of the land. Moreover, adverse possession facilitates the transfer of land by removing old claims, which are often difficult to prove due to a lack of witnesses and other evidence. As one commentator once observed about adverse possession: "If we had no doctrine of adverse possession, we should have to invent something very much like it."[66]

Five tests must be met if a person is to acquire ownership by adverse possession; these requirements are in many respects similar to the requirements for an easement by prescription. As summarized by a New York court,[67] "the essential elements of adverse possession are as follows: (1) possession must be hostile and under **claim of right**, (2) it must be actual, (3) it must be open and notorious, (4) it must be continuous, and (5) it must be exclusive."

Hostile Possession   A person claiming real estate by adverse possession must take possession of the land in a manner that is hostile to the interests of the owner. Hostility does not mean that the person must be actually and personally hostile or offensive to the owner, as discussed by the court in the Minnesota case of *Meyers v. Meyers*. It does, however, require that the possessor occupy the land without the owner's permission and with the intention of claiming ownership.

A CASE IN POINT

In *Meyers v. Meyers*, Robert Meyer's parents deeded a house to him individually. Robert also was married and lived in the house with his wife Bernadine. Robert and Bernadine divorced in 1954 after a violent argument in which the police forcibly removed him from the house. Robert left the state and did not return until 1979. Upon his return, his children asked him to deed the house to Bernadine; but he replied that he would "burn it down first." In response, Bernadine sued to gain title by adverse possession, arguing that she had been in "actual, open, hostile, continuous, and exclusive possession for 15 years" as required under state law. Robert argued that the possession was permissive and not hostile. The court stated that "[t]he general rule of law is that the existence of a family relationship between the claimant of land and the record owner ... creates the inference, if not the presumption, that the original possession by the claimant of the other's land was permissive and not adverse...." The court dismissed Bernadine's argument that Robert's forcible removal after a domestic dispute was a declaration of Bernadine's adverse holding of the property.[68]

In discussing the hostile requirement, courts sometimes state that the possession must be under a "claim of right," simply another way of saying that the possessor intends to claim ownership and does so without the permission of the owner or co-owner, as the following California case discusses.

A CASE IN POINT

In *Dimmick v. Dimmick*,[69] two brothers owned a ranch, which they farmed together until one of the brothers told the other that he was not going to continue in the farming operations. The other brother continued to farm, paid off the mortgage, paid the taxes, and made a number of improvements on the ranch without any financial assistance from his brother. After several years, the brother in possession brought suit claiming that he had acquired title by adverse possession. The court held that there was no adverse possession because the possession was permissive rather than hostile. Citing earlier cases, the court noted that "the exclusive occupancy of a cotenant is deemed permissive; it does not become adverse until the tenant out of possession has had either actual or constructive notice that the possession of the cotenant is hostile to him."

A common adverse possession case is the boundary line dispute, and often the outcome turns on the hostile requirement. For example, Michael and Alex own adjoining farms that are separated by a fence that Alex built thirty years ago. Alex now discovers that he built the fence on Michael's property fifty feet beyond the true boundary line. When Michael orders Alex to remove the fence, Alex refuses on the ground that he owns the property by adverse possession. Michael claims that Alex cannot prove that the possession was hostile since Alex admittedly built the fence and used the strip as the result of an innocent mistake.

In *Ebenhoh v. Hodgman* on page 405, a landowner claims ownership over his neighbor's strip of land by adverse possession.

END OF CHAPTER CASE

In most states, courts have decided that Alex's actual possession of the strip meets the hostile test even though Alex never intended to take his neighbor's property. Under this view, Alex would win even if he testified, "I do not want anything not belonging to me" and "I did not do it deliberately."[70] In other states, following the more traditional view, Alex's intention will determine the outcome. Thus, if Alex testifies that he actually intended to claim all land within the fence, he will win. But if he testifies that he intended to claim only to the true boundary line, his actions will not be considered hostile and he will lose the case.

Actual Possession   To claim ownership by adverse possession, the possessor must enter the land and make actual use of it in a manner appropriate to the nature of the land and the locality. In some states, the type of possession required is defined by statute. Under the California statute, for instance, possession occurs only if the property is protected by a substantial enclosure or if it has been cultivated or improved.[71] In most states, however, the courts must determine what constitutes actual possession on a case-by-case basis. For example, in one Oregon case, the court decided that a party had acquired title by adverse possession through use of the land for grazing from April to November each year for over twenty years. The court cited the rule in the American Law of Property that "possession may exist in a person who uses the land in the way in which an average owner of the particular type of property would use it though he does not reside on it and his use involves considerable intervals in which the land is not actually used at all."[72]

There is one situation generally where only constructive, not actual, possession of the real estate is required: when the person entering the land has a deed that appears to give her title to the land, but for some reason the deed is invalid. It is said that the person has **color of title** through the defective deed, as opposed to gaining title through the already discussed claim of right. The deed might be invalid for any number of reasons—for example, because the grantor had no title or because the grantor, unknown to the grantee, was insane. If the grantee has color of title under such a deed, the amount of land claimed by adverse possession is measured by the description in the deed rather than by the land actually possessed by the grantee. For example, if Shustek, the grantee, was deeded 40 acres of rural land, but only actually occupied 10 acres of it, such as a cabin he lived in and a fenced enclosure, he could still lay claim to the additional 30 acres. Furthermore, the period of time necessary to establish adverse possession is often reduced substantially.

Open and Notorious Possession   The actual use of the land by the adverse possessor must be open enough that the owner, when visiting the land, knows that his land is being claimed; and the use must be notorious enough that it would be generally known by people living in the vicinity. In the words of a Pennsylvania court, citing earlier authority, the adverse possessor "must unfurl his flag on the land, and keep it flying so that the owner may see, if he will, that an enemy has invaded his domains, and planted the standard of conquest."[73] In the following Indiana case, the court tackles the issue of whether a person can claim property by adverse possession when detection would be very difficult indeed.

color of title
An adverse possessor's claim to land derived from an invalid legal document.

A CASE IN POINT

In *Marengo Cave Co. v. Ross,*[74] a cave company used a cave, which extended beneath the adjoining owner's property, for a number of years. The court concluded that adverse possession had not been established: "Here the possession of appellant was not visible. No one could see below the earth's surface and determine that appellant was trespassing upon appellee's land.... We cannot assent to the doctrine that would enable one to trespass upon another's property through a subterranean passage and under such circumstances that the owner does not know, or by the exercise of reasonable care could not know, of such secret occupancy, for 20 years or more and by so doing obtained a fee simple title as against the holder of the legal title."

Continuous Possession   An adverse possessor must use the land for a specified period in a manner that is appropriate to the nature of the land. For example, in the Alabama case of *Turnipseed v. Moseley,*[75] Turnipseed claimed by adverse possession thirty-nine acres of wooded swampland on the basis of his occasional cutting and selling of timber from the land over a twenty-year period. The court held that his use was not continuous: "Such intermittent acts evidencing possession are regarded as merely transitory trespass without legal right."

Although the time varies, in many states the continuous possession must last a period of twenty years. When the adverse possessor sells her interest before the required time or when the property passes to the possessor's heirs at death, the periods of successive possession may be "tacked" (added on) together. Thus, in a North Carolina case, when property passed from Eli to his son-in-law Bill, then to Bill's heirs, and then to

D. J. Jacobs, the possession of all parties could be tacked together to meet the twenty-year requirement.[76] (See endnote 76 for information regarding the number of years necessary for adverse possession by state.)

The sale of the property by the owner of record will not interrupt the accumulation of the time needed to prove continuous possession. However, if the owner of record is under a disability such as insanity or minority, the owner will have an additional period after the disability has been removed to evict the possessor. A Pennsylvania court has held that a buyer could not tack the grantor's period of ownership to claim a parcel when the grantor's deed made no reference to the parcel. The court stated "that the only method by which an adverse possessor may convey title asserted by adverse possession is to describe in the instrument of conveyance by means minimally acceptable for conveyancing of realty that which is intended to be conveyed."[77]

Exclusive Possession   The possessor must have exclusive possession. This means that the possessor cannot share possession and use of the land with the owner or with other parties. For example, in a California case, a person claimed adverse possession of a lot overlooking the ocean on the basis of her weekly visits to picnic and enjoy the view. The court held that this was not actual possession and, furthermore, "there was nothing … to indicate exclusive ownership or possession. It was no more than other persons residing in the city might have done and probably did."[78] Exclusive possession is also evidence that the record holder of title has been ousted from his property. Some courts incorporate the "exclusive" requirement within the "actual" requirement.

Government Land   If the five tests are met, a claimant will become the owner of the real estate even though her interest is not written in a deed or recorded in the public record. A buyer from the prior and displaced owner—the record owner—will acquire no rights. However, even when the requirements have been met, a person cannot claim government property by adverse possession unless the government is using the land for a proprietary activity, one designed to make a profit. Although at one time government land could be acquired by homesteading, the Homestead Act (passed in 1862 to encourage settlement of the frontier) was repealed in 1976.

ETHICAL AND PUBLIC POLICY ISSUES

Should There Be a "Good Faith" Requirement for a Person to Claim Adverse Possession?

The issue of whether an adverse possessor of another's property should do so in good faith has been debated for years. In a highly publicized case in Boulder, Colorado, in 2007 the McLeans, a retired judge and his lawyer wife, knowingly used 1,400 square feet of their neighbors', the Kirlins', property for 25 years for a garden, to store wood, and to entertain as well as a walkway to their patio. When the Kirlins realized this they put up a fence. The McLeans responded by initiating an adverse possession suit in which they succeeded in gaining, for free, one-third of the Kirlins' property.[79] Is it ethical and good public policy that adverse possession laws contain a good faith requirement? Presently only a few states, including Colorado as a result of this case, as well as Louisiana, which subscribes to the civil law, have such a requirement. Should the importance of possession and the most efficient use of land overrule the need to be fair to those who may lose their land like the Kirlins?

Capacity

THOMAS v. A.L. NEAL

600 So.2d 1000 (Ala. 1992)

ALMON, Justice. This appeal arises from an action filed by A.L. Neal that sought to quiet title to certain real property located in Houston County, Alabama. The trial court * * * held that Neal owned the entire and undivided fee simple interest in the property, with no restrictions.

John Thomas, by virtue of a deed dated October 3, 1966, was the owner of real property that consisted of five lots located in a Houston County subdivision. On January 31, 1984, by warranty deed, he conveyed this property to his wife, Adeline Thomas. John Thomas died intestate on August 3, 1985, survived by his wife and the defendants/appellants, his four children from a previous marriage ("the children"). The children filed an "Amended Affidavit of Title" on January 2, 1986, stating that they were the sole heirs of Thomas and that, because he had died intestate, they were the owners of the five lots located in Houston County.

On July 11, 1990, Adeline Thomas conveyed, by quitclaim deed, the five lots to her brother, A.L. Neal. All of these conveyances were recorded in the probate records of Houston County.

The only issue is whether the trial court erred in finding that John Thomas was competent when he conveyed the property to his wife. The children argue that there was insufficient evidence to support the trial court's conclusion that John Thomas possessed the requisite mental capacity to convey the property, that the deed to Adeline Thomas should therefore be set aside and the property declared vested in John Thomas at his death, and that they, as the sole heirs of John Thomas, are both the legal and equitable owners of the five lots.

* * *

The presumption is that every person is sane, until the contrary is proven. Therefore, the children had the burden of proving to the reasonable satisfaction of the trial court that Thomas was incompetent and thus unable to understand in a reasonable manner the nature and effect of his act at the very time he conveyed the property to his wife.

To void a conveyance of land because of mental incapacity, one must show that the conveyor was unable to understand and comprehend what he was doing. Mere sickness, weakness of intellect, advanced age, or mental enfeeblement are insufficient reasons to invalidate a conveyance. The conveyor's mind must have been so impaired at the time of the conveyance that he was incapable of acting intelligently and voluntarily during the transaction.

The record shows that John Thomas was an elderly man, although the record does not reveal his exact age. He could not read or write and signed only his mark to the deed. He had one of his legs amputated and was bedridden. He also suffered from cancerous sores in his mouth that made it difficult for him to speak and to be understood when speaking. Thomas also had heart trouble and had suffered a stroke. The record does not reveal the date that each of these illnesses occurred, but it can be said that Thomas was a very ill man.

A witness to the signing of the deed testified that John Thomas was able to understand things that were said to him and that when he signed the deed he was sitting on the side of the bed in street clothes. This testimony somewhat conflicted with the testimony of the other witness to the signing of the deed, who testified that Thomas signed it while propped up in bed in his bed clothing; however, we find that this is an insignificant contradiction and in no way determinative of Thomas's mental state.

One of the witnesses to the signing of the deed also testified that he explained the deed to Thomas, that to the best of his knowledge Thomas was competent to sign it, and that, when he asked Thomas if he knew it was a deed, Thomas replied "yes." He further testified that he spoke with Thomas for about 45 minutes before he signed the deed.

One of the children testified that he questioned his father's competency, but that the last time he had seen or spoken to his father was in August 1984, while his father was in a hospital. This was about seven months after Thomas had signed the deed conveying the property to his wife.

A neighbor of the Thomases' testified that Thomas could not feed himself and that he was unable to make sense out of what Thomas was saying. Thomas's niece, who also provided some sort of nursing services for Thomas, testified that Thomas was a very ill man and that he could not communicate what he wanted; however, the niece was unable to testify as to what time period she was referring to, except to say that he was incoherent during the last three months of his life.

Furthermore, no medical testimony or hospital records were submitted at trial, and there is no documentation in the record of any mental incompetency or mental disorder. The majority of the testimony from the children consisted only of accounts of how sick and ill Thomas was, and there was no evidence presented to indicate that Thomas was mentally incompetent. As previously stated, old age, mere sickness, and infirmity are not sufficient reasons to set aside a deed for lack of mental competency.

The trial court did not err in holding that the children had failed to carry their burden of proving that Thomas was incompetent and unable to understand the nature and effect of his act of signing the deed. Furthermore, there was evidence to support the trial court's finding that Thomas was competent when he signed the deed, and we can in no way say that the trial court's finding that Thomas was competent is plainly and palpably wrong. The judgment is due to be, and it is hereby, affirmed.

Deed Construction
IN RE TAZIAN v. CLINE
686 N.E.2d 95 (Ind. Sup. Ct. 1997)

SULLIVAN, Justice. Neither party disputes the following facts. Alice Cline purchased a 4.24 acre strip of land in Allen County from United Railroad Corporation/Penn Central Corporation by quitclaim deed on May 15, 1985, and duly recorded the deed. This strip of land abutted the property of Zohrab and Naomi Tazian. United Railroad Corporation/Penn Central Corporation was the successor railroad in interest to the Fort Wayne Jackson & Saginaw Railroad Company ("Fort Wayne Railroad"). The Fort Wayne Railroad acquired its interest in the strip of land from S. Cary Evans and his wife through a handwritten deed dated February 10, 1873. The interpretation of this deed is the single issue on appeal. The handwritten deed from Evans to the Fort Wayne Railroad reads as follows:

This indenture made this 10th day of February AD 1873 between Cary Evans & wife of the first part and the Fort Wayne, Jackson & Saginaw Railroad Company of the second part. Witnesseth that the said parties of the first part in consideration of five hundred dollars to them in hand paid by the party of the second part the receipt whereof is hereby acknowledged and in further consideration of the benefits anticipated from said railroad when constructed do grant and convey and warrant to the party of the second part and their successors and assigns a strip of land fifty feet in width on West side of railroad over, across, and through the following described tract of land situated in the County of Allen and State of Indiana, viz:

The South West Quarter of Section Two (2), Township Thirty-one (31) North, Range Twelve (12) East, formerly owned by William … Hawley deceased deeded by Wm. E. Hawley to S.C. Evans recorded record 55, page 438 said strip of ground to be on and along the central line of said railroad as the same shall be finally located on such tract of land and of such width on each side of said central line as the final location of said railroad by said company shall determine. With the right also for the safety of said railroad to cut down standing timber on the outside of either outer line of said strip of ground which by falling would endanger said railroad or any of its structures to have and to hold all and singular the said premises in and by these presents released and conveyed unto the said Fort Wayne, Jackson & Saginaw Railroad Company and their successors and assigns forever for the uses and purposes therein expressed.

In witness whereof, the said parties of the first part have hereunto set their hands and seals this day and year first above written.

Discussion

I.

Indiana courts frequently face issues related to the ownership and use of parcels of land formerly used as railroad rights-of-way. Some such cases require the construction of nineteenth and early twentieth century deeds conveying interests to railroads. Therefore, as we interpret the nineteenth century deed at issue in this case, we do so with the aid of nearly a century's worth of common law decisions dealing with conveyances to railroads.

Here we must determine whether the Fort Wayne Railroad held fee simple to the strip of land or whether the Fort Wayne Railroad held a mere easement. If the Fort Wayne Railroad held a mere easement, then summary judgment in favor of Cline would have been improper as that easement would have been extinguished upon abandonment by the United Railroad Corporation/Penn Central Corporation and United Railroad Corporation would have had no interest to convey to Cline. However, if the Fort Wayne Railroad held fee simple title to the parcel of land, Cline owns the strip of land and summary judgment in favor of Cline was proper.

* * *

One of the most important rules in the construction of deeds is so to construe them that no part shall be rejected. The object of all construction is to ascertain the intent of the parties and it must have been their intent to have some meaning in every part. It never could be a man's intent to contradict himself; therefore we should lean to such a construction as reconciles the different parts, and reject a construction which leads to a contradiction….

Accordingly, in construing a deed, a court should regard the deed in its entirety, considering the parts of the deed together so that no part is rejected.

"The tendency of modern decisions is to disregard technicalities and to treat all uncertainties in a conveyance as ambiguities subject to be cleared up by resort to the intention of the parties as gathered from the instrument itself, the circumstances attending the leading up to its execution, and the subject matter and the situation of the parties as of that time ...." (citations omitted).

We begin by looking at the granting clause of the deed. The deed states "in consideration of five hundred dollars to them in hand paid ... and in further consideration of the benefits anticipated from said railroad when constructed do grant and convey and warrant ... a strip of land ... over, across, and through the following described tract of land."

We agree with the trial court and the Court of Appeals that the language "do grant and convey and warrant" is consistent with the controlling property statute in effect at the time of conveyance (and still in place today) which provides that any conveyance worded as: "'A.B. conveys and warrants to C.D.' [here describe the premises] 'for the sum of' [here insert the consideration] shall be deemed and held to be a conveyance in fee simple to the grantee...."

However, as pointed out by Judge Staton in his dissent, that same statute also provides that "if it be the intention of the grantor to convey any lesser estate, it shall be so expressed in the deed." Although the use of this language "grant and convey and warrant" favors the construction of the deed as conveying a fee simple absolute to the railroad company, such language is just a factor in determining whether the parties intended to grant a fee or an easement. We will look to other parts of the deed to see if the grantor expressed an intention to convey a lesser estate than fee simple.

* * *

The granting clause conveys a "strip of land fifty feet in width on West side of railroad ... over, across, and through" the described tract of land.

A deed that conveys a right generally conveys only an easement. The general rule is that a conveyance to a railroad of a strip, piece, or parcel of land, without additional language as to the use or purpose to which the land is to be put or in other ways limiting the estate conveyed, is to be construed as passing an estate in fee, but reference to a right of way in such conveyance generally leads to its construction as conveying only an easement.

The granting clause in the present deed does not appear to be limited to conveying only a right, nor does the deed describe the interest conveyed as a right of way. Rather, the particular language provides that the Evanses "do grant and convey and warrant ... a strip of land." Applying the settled general rule of this state, this language supports construction of the deed as conveying fee simple to the railroad.

The only mention of a right is the right granted to the railroad in the habendum clause to "to cut down standing timber on the outside of either outer line of said strip of ground which by falling would endanger said railroad or any of its structures...." We will address this part of the deed in Part II, infra.

* * *

II.

As no part of the deed is to be rejected, we now look to the language following the description of the land (including that part of the deed customarily referred to as the "habendum" clause).

> With the right also for the safety of said railroad to cut down standing timber on the outside of either outer line of said strip of ground which by falling would endanger said railroad or any of its structures to have and to hold all and singular the said premises in and by these presents released and conveyed unto the said Fort Wayne, Jackson & Saginaw Railroad Company and their successors and assigns forever for the uses and purposes therein expressed.

The Court of Appeals majority concluded that this clause "does not specifically limit the granting clause's conveyance of a fee simple" and the language of the deed "conveyed a fee simple estate ... without any limitation on the uses or purposes of the land." The dissent and the Tazians argue that the phrase "refers to the previous discussion of railroad operations within the deed, thus limiting the grant."

Particular debate centers around the concluding language of the habendum clause, "for the uses and purposes therein expressed." In that the habendum clause serves to explain the granting clause in a deed, we read the concluding language to be a cross-reference to the granting clause—"for the uses and purpose therein expressed," i.e., the uses and purposes expressed in the granting clause. As earlier discussed, the granting clause does not limit the uses and purposes of the strip of land. As such, we view this language as merely restating that the grantee's uses and purposes are not limited.

Black's Law Dictionary 710 (6th ed. 1990) defines the habendum clause as follows:

> Portion of deed beginning with the words "To have and to hold." The clause usually following the granting part of the premises of a deed, which defines the extent of the ownership in the thing granted to be held and enjoyed by the grantee. The office of the "habendum" is properly to determine what estate or interest is granted by the deed, though office may be performed by the premises, in which case the habendum may lessen, enlarge, explain, or qualify, but not totally contradict or be repugnant to, estate granted in the premises.

Black's Law Dictionary 700 (6th ed. 1990) defines granting clause as follows:

> That portion of a deed or instrument of conveyance which contains the words of transfer of a present interest. "The object of the habendum clause is said to be 'to set

down again the name of the grantee, the estate that is to be made and limited, or the time that the grantee shall have in the thing granted or demised, and to what use.' It may explain, enlarge, or qualify but cannot contradict or defeat, the estate granted by the premises, and where the grant is uncertain, or indefinite concerning the estate intended to be vested in the grantee, the habendum performs the office of defining, qualifying or controlling it."

Finally, without being dispositive, we note the habendum to the grant being "forever," a temporal descriptor more consistent with the conveyance of a fee than of an easement here.

III.

The appellate courts of this state have frequently construed eighteenth and early nineteenth century deeds conveying interests in strips of land to railroads as conveying mere easements.

However, the deed we examine today is different.

This deed is not a preprinted form prepared by the railroad.

More importantly, this deed does not describe the interest conveyed as a railroad right of way nor does the language limit the conveyance as for railroad purposes or railroad uses.

Conclusion

We grant transfer, summarily affirm the opinion of the Court of Appeals and affirm the trial court's grant of summary judgment in favor of Cline.

Notary Public Acknowledgment
POOLE v. HYATT
344 Md. 619; 689 A.2d 82 (1997)

WILNER, Judge. The question presented here is whether, for there to be a valid acknowledgment of a deed or of a power of attorney authorizing the conveyance of real estate, the person signing the instrument must make an affirmative oral declaration in the presence of the notary public confirming the signatory's understanding of the instrument and his or her intent in executing it. The answer is "no."

I. Background

This appeal arises from a dispute over property in Montgomery County, Maryland acquired more than 60 years ago by Ethel J. Poole (Ethel) and her husband, N. Purdum Poole.

* * *

N. Purdum Poole died in 1958. In 1976, Ethel, then 76 years of age, conveyed the entire tract to herself and Bernard, as "joint tenants with the right of survivorship." She claimed that the purpose of the conveyance was to save estate taxes upon her death. Bernard neither requested nor received any income from the property, and he made no contribution to its upkeep.

Bernard's health began to fail in 1985. He was, at the time, living with petitioner, Glenda Donivan, now Glenda Poole, whom he married in 1990. * * *

In December, 1991, Glenda hired a Pennsylvania attorney, Robert Clofine, to prepare a durable power of attorney and will for Bernard in favor of herself. Mr. Clofine brought the documents to Bernard's home where, on December 17, 1991, Bernard signed them. We are informed that, in his will, Bernard left his entire estate to Glenda. In the power of attorney, Bernard appointed Glenda as his attorney-in-fact, with broad power to manage his real and personal property.

The document mentioned the Montgomery County property and gave Glenda the power to sell it "for such consideration and upon such terms as [Glenda] shall think fit" and to execute, acknowledge, and deliver deeds for its conveyance. The power of attorney also purported to give Glenda an unrestricted right "to make gifts."

Bernard's signature on the power of attorney was notarized by Mr. Clofine. In his certificate, Clofine attested that Bernard, "known to me (or satisfactorily proven) to be the person whose name is subscribed to the within instrument" had personally appeared "and acknowledged that he executed the same for the purposes therein contained."

Two months later, at Glenda's request, Mr. Clofine prepared a deed under which Glenda, acting as Bernard's "duly constituted attorney-in-fact," conveyed Bernard's undivided interest in the Montgomery County property, which he then held as joint tenant with Ethel, to Bernard and Glenda, as tenants by the entireties. Glenda signed that deed, for which there was no consideration, on February 22, 1992. Clofine notarized the document, attesting that Glenda had personally appeared, that she was known or satisfactorily proven to be the person whose name was subscribed to the instrument as attorney-in-fact for Bernard, and that she acknowledged that she executed the deed as the act of her principal for the purposes therein contained.

Bernard died three days later. The deed was recorded in Montgomery County on March 2, 1992, although Ethel did not learn of it until she received her tax bill in July, 1992. Ethel died in October, 1992. On December 16, her estate filed this action in the Circuit Court for Montgomery County.

* * *

After taking Mr. Clofine's deposition, Ethel filed a motion for partial summary judgment on Counts I and II on a new theory, not pled in the complaint. She claimed, based on Clofine's deposition testimony, that neither Bernard nor Glenda had made any oral statement in the presence of Clofine acknowledging that they were signing the respective documents for the purposes contained therein. On that basis, she argued that there was no acknowledgment of either the power of attorney or the deed and, for that reason, both were ineffective.

In June, 1994, the court granted that motion, holding that both the power of attorney and the deed were void because of defective acknowledgments.

* * *

We granted Glenda's petition for certiorari to consider the two questions presented therein:

1. Is an acknowledgment on a deed and power of attorney defective if the notary public, having watched the person sign the documents, does not read the language of the acknowledgment certificate aloud to the signatory and ask if the act was free and voluntary—or utilize other such words to further confirm the voluntariness, etc. of the act?
2. If such failure does render the acknowledgment defective, is the defect such to render the deed or other instrument void?

II. Discussion

* * *

The Function Of An Acknowledgment

* * *

Although the formality required in the early statutes has abated, as any notary public can now take an acknowledgment wherever the grantor may be, the fundamental purpose seems to be the same, of preventing fraud by providing some evidence of identity and volition—that the person stated in the deed as the grantor has, in fact, signed the deed and understands that what he or she has signed is a deed conveying property.

* * *

What Is Required?

The cases involving the adequacy of acknowledgments fall into two broad categories—those involving the sufficiency of the notary's certificate, i.e., whether facially it complies with the requirements of the applicable statute, and those involving the accuracy of the certificate, i.e., whether the fact or event attested to actually occurred.

The cases in the first category are more numerous and involve such things as a blank where the name of the grantor should be. We are not concerned here with deficiencies of that kind. Mr. Clofine's certificates are facially sufficient.

The issue, then, is whether a certificate that the person appearing "acknowledged the foregoing deed to be his [or her] act," as prescribed in or that he or she "acknowledged that [he or she] executed the same for the purposes contained therein," can rest on the notary's observations and general impressions or whether it requires some sort of affirmative declaration by the grantor. There are only a few cases on this point.

* * *

Some of these cases, in terms of both pronouncements and outcome, are controlled by the specific language of a governing statute. If a statute requires a verbal declaration for a valid acknowledgment, the absence of such a declaration may well be fatal. Where, as in Maryland, there is no such statutory mandate, however, we think that the Massachusetts approach is unnecessarily rigid and formalistic. We follow instead the lead of the Iowa Court and hold that an acknowledgment does not require an oral declaration but may arise from circumstances and conduct. Specifically, we hold that, although a clear oral expression is preferable because it provides direct evidence of the signatory's knowledge and intent, when a signatory (1) appears personally before a notary for the purpose of having the notary witness and attest to his or her signature, (2) the signatory appears to be alert and is under no apparent duress or undue emotional or intoxicating influence, (3) it is clear from the overall circumstances that the signatory understands the nature of the instrument he or she is about to sign, and (4) he or she signs the instrument in the presence of the notary with the apparent intent of making the instrument effective, the signatory is effectively acknowledging to the notary that the instrument is being signed voluntarily and for the purpose contained therein.

* * *

Requiring some sort of oral declaration would, at best, be of only marginal assistance in preventing fraud. An imposter willing to forge someone's signature to a deed would not likely be deterred by having to make a brief, innocuous statement before a notary public; nor would a signatory actually subject to real duress or undue influence likely balk at making such a statement. If such fraud, duress, or undue influence can be proven, the instrument would be set aside for that reason; the lack of an oral declaration is unnecessary for that purpose. What such a requirement might do, however, is encourage lawsuits to upset instruments simply because of noncompliance with that requirement, even when the transaction was otherwise perfectly valid, and thus put at substantial risk the trust and confidence necessarily reposed in the land records.

For these reasons, we hold that the Court of Special Appeals erred in affirming the summary judgment. The case will be remanded for further proceedings on all counts of Ethel's complaint and on Glenda's counterclaim.

Consideration, Delivery, and Description
JOHNSON v. RAMSEY
307 Ark. 4, 817 S.W.2d 200 (1991)

HAYS, Justice. This is an appeal from a declaratory judgment entered in the Mississippi Chancery Court. The facts are not in dispute. On July 15, 1970, the appellee, Alice Ramsey, purchased from D.S. and Elizabeth Laney a lot in Osceola, Arkansas, on Poplar Street.

Ramsey executed a note and deed of trust to the Laneys for the purchase price in the sum of $4,500.00 payable at $40.00 per month.

On August 10, 1970, Alice Ramsey executed a warranty deed to Allen Walters for the Poplar Street property. The warranty deed omitted one of the calls so that the property was incorrectly described. [Author's Note: A "call" is a visible natural object or landmark included in a metes and bounds legal description as a boundary point; the legal description in Mrs. Ramsey's deed was incorrect because a call was omitted.]

The deed from Ramsey to Walters provided for $10.00 consideration paid by Walters "and other good and valuable consideration, including, but not limited to, the payment of all sums due D.S. Laney on a Promissory Note dated July 15, 1970.…"

On April 2, 1990, the appellant, Robert Johnson, obtained a default judgment against Allen Walters arising from a motor vehicle collision. Thereafter, the Mississippi Circuit Court issued a writ of execution commanding the sheriff to recover from Allen Walters the amount of the judgment granted in favor of Johnson. The sheriff returned the writ *nulla bona*, however, when it was discovered that Allen Walters had record title to the Poplar Street property; a second writ of execution was issued.

On June 22, 1990, Walters executed a quitclaim deed to Alice Ramsey for the Poplar Street property. The deed recited that Allen Walters was reconveying the property that was "held in trust" by Walters on behalf of Alice Ramsey. Because of the reconveyance to Alice Ramsey the sheriff declined to execute the second writ of execution.

In August of 1990 Alice Ramsey filed a suit for declaratory judgment, naming Robert Johnson and the sheriff as defendants. Ramsey asked that she be declared the owner in fee simple of the Poplar Street property and for an injunction to prevent a sale of the property. The sheriff was subsequently released from the suit.

* * *

After a hearing the court found that * * * Alice Ramsey was the owner in fee simple of the Poplar Street property. Robert Johnson appeals the finding regarding the ownership of the Poplar Street property.

In a letter opinion, the chancellor made the following findings: Allen Walters had no interest in the Poplar Street property because the property description in the deed from Ramsey to Walters is faulty; Walters does not seek reformation of the deed and Robert Johnson lacks standing to seek

that relief; if the litigation was between Ramsey, the grantor, and Walters, the grantee, the court would find that the erroneous description in the deed should be reformed, and Walters had no interest in the Poplar Street property because there has been a total lack of consideration.

Johnson challenges the chancellor's findings, arguing that consideration was not relevant to the deed's validity and reformation was not necessary because the August 10th deed made specific reference to the deed of trust executed to Laney which contained a correct legal description of the property. Johnson insists that all essential elements of a deed were proven and the court should have found that Allen Walters owned the Poplar Street property.

We agree with Johnson that consideration and reformation are not necessary for the validity of this deed, however, the requirement of delivery of the deed is lacking, thus, the chancellor did not err in finding that the Poplar Street property did not belong to Allen Walters.

First, turning to the issues of consideration and reformation, we have said that inadequacy of consideration is not a ground for setting aside a voluntary conveyance. We have also held that a deed will not be invalid for uncertainty of description if a proper description is furnished by reference to another instrument.

The chancellor's findings on reformation and consideration do not warrant reversal because there was no delivery of the deed. A deed is inoperative unless there has been delivery to the grantee and an essential element of a valid delivery is the grantor's intention to pass title immediately, thus giving up dominion and control of the property. Even though a presumption of delivery of a deed attaches when the deed is recorded, as occurred here, that presumption may be rebutted by other factors pertaining to the deed.

Alice Ramsey testified that in August of 1970 she became ill and did not think she was going to live. At that time she had several children living at home and decided Allen Walters would be the person who would maintain her property for her children. Speaking about the execution of the warranty deed to Walters, Ramsey stated, "… I didn't mean to give it to him then, I just meant for him to see after it so my kids could have somewhere to stay because there wasn't nobody … I didn't have no relatives around and the kids was small." Ramsey further testified that she paid all payments on the property as well as the property taxes. At trial the following exchange took place between Ramsey's attorney and Allen Walters:

Q.: Well, did you claim that you owned the property?

A.: Well, I didn't own it because I didn't pay nothing on it. All I know is that she just put it over into my name on account of she was sick, she was having this problem.

Q.: And you never have claimed to own the property?

A.: No, sir. Never have claimed to own it. I haven't paid nothing on it.

The testimony of Alice Ramsey corroborated by Allen Walters showed that Ramsey did not intend to give up dominion of her property. This testimony sufficiently rebuts the presumption of delivery of the deed. Consequently, Allen Walters did not receive any interest in the Poplar Street property.

* * *

[The lower court judgment is affirmed.]

Wills-Interpretation
IN RE ESTATE OF GOYETTE
123 Cal. App. 4th 67 (2004)

ROBIE, Judge. What does the phrase "my money" mean in a holographic will? Here, we conclude the trial court correctly concluded this term included bank accounts and certificates of deposit, a money market account, a Fidelity U.S. Government Reserves Fund, United States treasury bills and United States savings bonds. We shall affirm.

Factual and Procedural Background

Joseph Goyette died in 2001. He had no spouse nor children when he died. He was survived by his cousins, sisters Joanne Ramos, Eleanor Harkey, and Kathryn Ramey. Over the years, Harkey and her sisters lived next door to Goyette. Harkey lived there until the date of Goyette's death.

Goyette's holographic will states:
"I wish to leave to James Hayward Fifty percent of my money and Fifty percent of my money to my neighbor and friend Vi York.
"I wish to leave James Hayward the lot across the street from my home.
"I wish to leave Vi York my home and the lots around it."

At the time of his death, Goyette's estate (appraised at $742,196.85) was comprised of the following assets:

- Retirement savings accounts, $231,480.20
  checking and savings accounts,
  and certificates of deposit
- Money market account $ 81,878.64
- Fidelity U.S. Government $ 9,576.14
  Reserves Fund
- United States treasury bills $304,183.55
- United States savings bonds $ 25,627.60
- Real property $ 78,500.00
- Miscellaneous personal property $ 10,950.00

The court appointed Goyette's cousin, Joanne Ramos, as the administrator of his estate. In her "First & Final Report of Administration; Petition for Final Distribution; Allowance of Statutory Attorney's and Administrator's Compensation," Ramos sought permission to distribute all of the above assets and the miscellaneous personal property located on the real property to James Hayward and Vivian York.

Subsequently, Ramos filed a petition for instructions from the court as to what assets constituted "'money' ... distributable to Vivian York and James Hayward and what assets, if any, are 'residue' distributable to the heirs" under the law of intestacy. Ramos eventually withdrew that initial petition for instructions but later filed a second petition for instructions requesting that the court determine which of Goyette's assets constituted "my money."

York and Hayward argued "my money" meant all of Goyette's wealth. In response, Harkey argued "my money" referred only to "funds (or medium of exchange, i.e. cash or cash equivalents)."

On October 29, 2003, the trial court concluded that the following assets constituted "my money" and were distributable to York and Hayward: (a) the retirement savings accounts; (b) checking and savings accounts; (c) certificates of deposit; (c) the money market account; (d) the Fidelity U.S. Government Reserves Fund; (e) the United States treasury bills; and (f) the United States savings bonds.

Discussion

I Standard Of Review

"A will must be construed according to the intention of the testator as expressed therein, and this intention must be given effect if possible. Each case depends on its own particular facts and precedents are of small value." Stated another way, "'The paramount rule in the construction of wills, to which all other rules must yield, is that a will is to be construed according to the intention of the testator as expressed therein, and this intention must be given effect as far as possible.'"

Probate Code section 21122 guides the interpretation of wills: "The words of an instrument are to be given their ordinary and grammatical meaning unless the intention to use them in another sense is clear and their intended meaning can be ascertained. Technical words are not necessary to give effect to a disposition in an instrument. Technical words are to be considered as having been used in their technical sense unless (a) the context clearly indicates a contrary intention or (b) it satisfactorily appears that the instrument was drawn solely by the transferor and that the transferor was unacquainted with the technical sense."

"In reviewing a trial court's construction of a will, we are free to independently interpret the instrument as a matter of law unless the trial court's interpretation turned upon the credibility of extrinsic evidence or required resolution of a conflict in the evidence. 'The possibility that conflicting inferences can be drawn from uncontroverted evidence does not relieve the appellate court of its duty independently to interpret the instrument; it is only when the issue turns upon the credibility of extrinsic evidence, or requires resolution of a conflict in that evidence, that the trial court['s] determination is binding.'"

II "My Money" Meant Goyette's Financial Assets

Harkey argues the trial court erred in its ruling because "the term 'money' as used in Goyette's will includes only cash and bank accounts; it does not include investments." We reject this argument.

A. Case Law Concerning "Money" Shows That Term, Standing Alone, Is Ambiguous

Several California cases have addressed the issue of what a testator means when he or she uses the term "money" in a will.

In Estate of Stadler, the testatrix left specific bequests to several beneficiaries and concluded her will with the phrase, "Divide the rest between Hoerners & Chas Fischer (money left over when Settled.[)]" The question was whether the phrase "money left over when Settled" included the testatrix's real property which was otherwise not mentioned in the will. The court stated, "The word 'money' used in wills is essentially ambiguous. In a bequest it means money and money only, unless there is in the context of the will something to indicate that the testator intended a more extended meaning. When used in a will it has no fixed or technical meaning, but is a term of flexible scope having either a restricted or a wide meaning according to the signification which the testator intended to give the word, and may be used to mean cash only, personal property, or even wealth—that is, property of any kind that may be converted into cash. Where the context of a will discloses the intent of the testator to attribute to the word 'money' a specific meaning which is more comprehensive than the meaning ordinarily given to it, that meaning will be adopted and may comprehend any class of property defined by the context." The court concluded the testatrix used the term "money" in its most flexible sense. The court concluded that it was doubtful the testator understood the distinction between different types of property and that because she made a will it evidenced her intention not to die intestate. Further, the fact that the will was silent about bonds and a promissory note she owned was an indication she did not distinguish between "money" and other types of property.

Similarly, in Estate of Whitney the court attempted to determine the testator's intent in the will that directed the executor to "see that money from the estate be tythed to the amount of twenty-five per cent and given" to three named charities. The cash in the testatrix's estate at the time was $138.98, while the entire estate was worth $21,014.98. The court concluded "money" meant the sum total value of the estate, and not merely the cash in the testatrix's bank accounts at the time of her death. The court concluded the will reflected that the testatrix knew what her assets were based on her description of those items in her other bequests. Further, the use of the terms "money from [the] estate" and "tythed," and the use of a residuary clause that left the residue to her grandson, evidenced her desire to include the total value of the estate in determining the amount to provide to the three charities.

* * *

B. Other Relevant Canons Of Construction Of Wills Support The Trial Court's Ruling

Given the inherent ambiguity of the term "money," we must turn to other rules of construction to assist us in determining what Goyette meant in his will. The fact that he made a will raises the presumption that he intended to dispose of all of his property. Further, as stated in Estate of O'Connell, "Once the testamentary scheme or general intention [of a will] is discovered, the meaning of particular words and phrases is to be subordinated to this scheme, plan or dominant purpose."

Here, we ascertain from the will's face a general scheme to benefit York and Hayward. The will names these two beneficiaries only and singles them out to receive all of Goyette's real property, and his "money." In line with this general scheme, it makes sense that his use of the term "my money" includes all of Goyette's financial assets.

Goyette's will also shows Goyette's lack of legal sophistication. His bequests of his real property do not identify that real property in any technical or legal sense. He bequeathed "the lot across the street from [his] home" and "[his] home and the lots around it." Like the court in Estate of Stadler lack of legal sophistication supports the conclusion that Goyette used the term "my money" in its most flexible sense to include all of his financial assets.

This interpretation is also consistent with the rule that prefers a construction of a term of a will that avoids complete or partial intestacy. It is the strongly favored policy of the law that wills be construed in a manner that avoids intestacy. To this end, Probate Code section 21120 provides, "The words of an instrument are to receive an interpretation that will give every expression some effect, rather than one that will render any of the expressions inoperative. Preference is to be given to an interpretation of an instrument that will prevent intestacy or failure of a transfer, rather than one that will result in an intestacy or failure of a transfer."

Here, if we were to construe "my money" to mean only Goyette's bank accounts and not the other financial assets, the treasury bills, money market account, and savings bonds, then almost 50 percent of his estate would pass to the cousins through the law of intestacy. Under the construction placed on the term "my money" by the trial court, less than 1 percent of the estate's assets will pass in that manner. Given the preference for an interpretation that avoids intestacy, we find no error in the court's construction.

Harkey argues the presumption against intestacy does not apply where the testator clearly intended that partial intestacy result. As explained by Estate of Beldon "A court's inquiry in construing a will is limited to ascertaining what the testator meant by the language which was used. If he used language which results in intestacy, and there can be no doubt about the meaning of the language which was used, the court must hold that intestacy was intended. A testator has the right to make a will which does not dispose of all of his property but leaves a residue to pass to his heirs under the law of succession. Such a will is not the usual one but when the language

which leads to that result is clear the will must be given effect accordingly." Here, we find nothing in his will that constitutes a clear expression of Goyette's intent that his financial assets pass by intestate succession.

Given the ambiguity in the term "my money," the readily apparent scheme in the will to benefit Hayward and York, and the preference against the estate passing through intestacy whenever possible, we conclude the trial court correctly concluded the term "my money" included all of Goyette's financial assets.

Disposition

The judgment is affirmed. York and Hayward shall recover their costs on appeal.

Adverse Possession
EBENHOH v. HODGMAN
642 N.W.2d 104 (Minn. Ct. App. 2002)

ANDERSON, Judge. Appellants James and Carma Ebenhoh brought a district court action against respondents claiming ownership of a disputed tract of property through adverse possession and boundary by practical location. The district court concluded that appellants failed to show exclusive, continuous, and hostile use of the disputed tract and therefore did not satisfy the elements of adverse possession. Likewise, the district court concluded that respondents did not sufficiently acquiesce to a fence line and therefore appellants failed to establish a boundary by practical location. We reverse and remand.

Facts

In 1942, Richard and Alma Tincher owned an 80-acre parcel of farmland in Dodge County. On the same day in 1942, the Tinchers deeded the north 40 acres (Hodgman parcel) to LeRoyal Sanders (Sanders), and the south 40 acres (Ebenhoh parcel) to Edward Ebenhoh, father of appellant James Ebenhoh (Ebenhoh). That same year, Ebenhoh's father constructed an east-west fence, made of steel and wood posts and barbed wire, dividing the two parcels. It is unclear why Ebenhoh's father constructed the fence.

Ebenhoh testified that between 1942 and 1955 his father repaired the fence every year to ensure that the cattle that grazed on the Ebenhoh parcel, after the crops were harvested, would not stray. In 1956, the cattle operation ceased. After 1956, however, Ebenhoh and his father continued to farm the Ebenhoh parcel. Ebenhoh testified that they would plant crops close to the fence, probably within a foot of the fence line where possible.

On February 6, 1968, Ebenhoh purchased the Ebenhoh parcel from his father. Between 1969 and 1984, Ebenhoh continued to farm the Ebenhoh parcel in the same manner by planting crops close to the fence line. In 1985, Ebenhoh experienced financial difficulties and leased the Ebenhoh parcel to

respondent Frank Hodgman and another individual. Between 1986 and 1996, Ebenhoh leased the Ebenhoh parcel to a canning company, which cultivated asparagus. Since 1996, Ebenhoh's son-in-law has leased the Ebenhoh parcel, and continues to farm the property.

Respondent Frank Hodgman testified that he purchased the Hodgman parcel from his parents in 1976, who had purchased the property from Sanders in 1955. He also testified that he sold the Hodgman parcel to his brother, respondent Donald Hodgman, in 1993.

A surveyor testified that respondent Donald Hodgman retained him in 1993 to survey the Hodgman parcel (1993 survey). The surveyor testified that the 1942 fence line was located approximately 11 feet north of the "true" boundary line dividing the two parcels. Appellants concede that the 1993 survey correctly locates the true boundary line between the two parcels.

In August 2000, appellants brought a district court action to establish the boundary between the two parcels. Ebenhoh alleged that the 1942 fence line constituted the boundary between the two parcels and that he, his father, and his lessees, have adversely possessed the disputed tract for the 15-year statutory period. Ebenhoh also alleged that the fence line constituted a boundary by practical location.

The district court concluded that although Ebenhoh showed that he openly and actually used the disputed tract for 15 years, he failed to show that his use was exclusive, continuous, or hostile. The court also concluded that Ebenhoh failed to show that the fence line constituted a boundary by practical location. This appeal followed.

Issue

Are appellants entitled to the disputed tract through adverse possession?

Analysis

* * *

Before title through adverse possession can be established, there must be clear and convincing evidence of actual, open, hostile, continuous, and exclusive possession by the alleged disseizor for the statutory 15-year period. Evidence tending to establish adverse possession must be strictly construed, "without resort to any inference or presumption in favor of the disseizor, but with the indulgence of every presumption against him."

* * *

Appellants argue the district court erred as a matter of law when it concluded that Ebenhoh's use of the disputed tract was not exclusive, continuous, or hostile. Respondents do not challenge the district court's conclusions that Ebenhoh's use of the disputed tract was both actual and open; therefore, our review is limited to whether Ebenhoh's use of the disputed tract constituted, as a matter of law, exclusive, continuous, and hostile use of the disputed tract for the statutory 15-year period.

We conclude the district court erred as a matter of law when it concluded that Ebenhoh did not establish, by clear and convincing evidence, exclusive, continuous, and hostile use of the disputed tract for 15 years.

A. Exclusivity

The exclusivity requirement is met if the disseizor takes "possession of the land as if it were his own with the intention of using it to the exclusion of others."

The district court found that respondents and other parties "continued to use the disputed area for hunting and fishing purposes throughout the years." Consequently, the district court concluded that Ebenhoh did not exclusively use the disputed tract for the statutory period.

The district court's factual finding that respondents and other third parties used the disputed tract for hunting and fishing is clearly erroneous. There is nothing in the record that suggests the disputed tract was ever used for hunting and fishing. Respondents agree. Respondents, however, argue that there is other evidence in the record that suggests Ebenhoh's use of the disputed tract was not exclusive: (1) respondents' father, Ralph Hodgman, briefly entered the area in 1964 to straighten a creek that meandered near the fence line; and (2) the parties assisted each other with their respective farm operations.

The record, however, is clear that Ebenhoh, his father, and his lessees were the only individuals to use the disputed tract, save for the brief and insubstantial entries onto the property referenced by respondents. Ebenhoh testified that between 1942 and 1956 the fence prevented cattle from leaving the Ebenhoh parcel. It is also undisputed that for 30 years, between 1956 and 1986, Ebenhoh, his father, or his lessees planted crops as close as possible to the fence line. Respondent Frank Hodgman testified that during his ownership of the Hodgman parcel between 1976 and 1993 he never used

the property abutting the fence line. It is also undisputed that it was not until 1998, 56 years after the fence was constructed, that respondent Donald Hodgman placed white flags in Ebenhoh's soybean field marking the 1993 survey line.

* * *

There is simply no evidence in the record that the disputed tract was used, save for a few intermittent entries, by anybody but Ebenhoh, his father, and his lessees. Therefore, the district court's finding of fact that the tract was used for hunting and fishing is clearly erroneous. Moreover, the court's conclusion of law that Ebenhoh did not exclusively use the disputed tract for the statutory period was also erroneous and appellants have established, as a matter of law, that they exclusively used the disputed tract for the statutory period.

B. Continuity

Adverse possession for any consecutive 15-year period is sufficient to establish continuity of use, and the statutory period must only be completed before bringing an adverse-possession action. "The possession of successive occupants, if there is privity between them, may be tacked to make adverse possession for the requisite period." "The possession of a tenant is, as to third parties, the possession of the landlord."

The district court found that the canning company used most of the Ebenhoh parcel to cultivate asparagus between 1986 and 1996; the court also found that the canning company did not cultivate asparagus on the disputed tract, but rather used the disputed tract to move its machinery in and out of the field. The district court therefore concluded that the canning company's use of the disputed tract between 1986 and 1996 constituted occasional, not continuous, use.

The district court's findings of fact are not clearly erroneous. But the district court erred in its conclusion of law. Even if we were to accept the district court's highly questionable conclusion that the canning company's use of the disputed tract to move its machinery in and out of the Ebenhoh parcel did not constitute sufficient continuous use of the disputed tract between 1986 and 1996, the canning company's use of the disputed tract during that period is irrelevant. Ebenhoh's father cultivated crops and grazed cattle on the disputed tract between 1942 and 1956. Ebenhoh, his father, and his lessees cultivated crops, up to the fence line, between 1956 and 1986. By the time the canning company leased the Ebenhoh parcel in 1986, Ebenhoh, his father, and his lessees, had used the disputed tract continuously for 44 years.

Therefore, the district court erred as a matter of law when it concluded that appellants failed to establish continuous use of the disputed tract for the statutory period.

C. Hostility

While it is true that assertion of adverse title need not be always expressly or affirmatively declared, but may be shown by circumstances, proof of inception of hostility must in all cases be clear and unequivocal. The hostility requirement "does not refer to personal animosity or physical overt acts against the record owner of the property." *Ehle v. Prosser,* 197 N.W.2d 458, 462 (1972). To establish hostility of use, the disseizor must "enter and take possession of the lands as if they were his own * * * with the intention of holding for himself to the exclusion of all others." *Thomas,* 78 N.W.2d at 388. Hostility is flexibly determined by examining "the character of the possession and the acts of ownership of the occupant." *Carpenter v. Coles,* 77 N.W. 424, 424 (1898).

Nevertheless, this general rule is tempered when a close family relationship exists between the record owner of the property and the alleged disseizor:

> [T]he existence of a close family relationship between the claimant of land and the record owner * * * create[s] the inference, if not the presumption, that the original possession by the claimant of the other's land was permissive and not adverse and that when such original use was thus permissive it would be presumed to continue as permissive, rather than hostile, until the contrary was affirmatively shown. *Norgong v. Whitehead,* 31 N.W.2d 267, 269 (1948).

The district court recognized that it is unclear why Ebenhoh's father constructed the 1942 fence; therefore, according to the court, any speculation about the purpose of the fence did not constitute clear and convincing evidence that Ebenhoh's father made a hostile claim to the disputed tract in 1942. The district court found that the Hodgmans and Ebenhohs were part of a close family that regularly socialized together; indeed, it is undisputed that the parties are first cousins who periodically assisted each other with their respective farming operations. Ebenhoh's father lent his brother-in-law, respondents' father, money without demanding security. Because of this familial relationship, the district court concluded that the relationship created a presumption that Ebenhoh's possession of the disputed tract from 1955 until the present was permissive, and not hostile.

The district court's findings of fact are not clearly erroneous. The district court, however, erred as a matter of law when it concluded that Ebenhoh's possession of the disputed tract was not hostile.

Even though Sanders and Ebenhoh's father are deceased, and thus cannot explain why the fence was constructed or whether the use of the disputed tract was originally permissive, that does not mean that Ebenhoh's father's undisputed use of the tract to cultivate crops and graze cattle between 1942 and 1956 is not relevant in determining hostility of use. Such logic could lead to an absurd legal rule where undisputed actual, open, continuous, and exclusive use of property for multiple decades could not result in adverse possession of that property because the original use of the property *may* have been permissive. It is also undisputed that after 1956 Ebenhoh, his father, and his lessees, continued to farm the disputed tract, as close as possible to the fence line, until at least 1998 when Ebenhoh's son-in-law began to honor the 1993 survey line.

Therefore, Ebenhoh's use of the disputed tract was hostile, in the sense that Ebenhoh and his father entered the disputed tract and took possession as if the tract was their own since 1942, with the intention of holding the tract to the exclusion of all others. The district court implied this conclusion when it concluded that Ebenhoh's use of the disputed tract was "open": "Th[e] fence gave the Hodgmans notice that the Ebenhohs were *claiming [the] land as theirs* and were using it in an actual and open manner for farming purposes." Moreover, because this hostility commenced when Sanders, who was unrelated to Ebenhoh's father, owned the Hodgman parcel, it should not be presumed that Ebenhoh's father's original use of the disputed tract was permissive.

We also note that respondents advance no authority for the hypothetical proposition that a transfer of property to a close family member of an adjoining property owner renders permissive that adjoining property owner's otherwise hostile use of property. Respondents' father, their predecessor-in-interest, should have been on notice that Ebenhoh's father used the disputed tract to cultivate crops and graze his cattle when he purchased the Hodgman parcel from Sanders in 1955. The mere fact that respondents' father purchased property near a relative neither converted well-established hostile use of the disputed property to non-hostile use, nor does such a purchase toll the statutory period.

Finally, because we conclude that appellants have established, as a matter of law, that they adversely possessed the disputed tract for the 15-year statutory period, we decline to decide whether the fence line constituted a boundary by practical location.

We therefore reverse and remand this case to the district court. We direct the district court to enter judgment in favor of appellants and to enter an order establishing the boundary between the two parcels as the 1942 fence line identified by the 1993 survey.

KEY TERMS

acceptance, 373
accretion, 364
acknowledgment, 372
administrator, 389

adverse possession, 393
avulsion, 364
bargain and sale deed, 365
base lines, 368

PROBLEMS

1. Parks agreed to deed a tract of real estate to Hamilton; and shortly after Hamilton's death, Parks executed a deed to Hamilton. Hamilton's widow and ten children now claim title to the property under the deed. Do they have title? Why or why not?

2. Julius went to his banker, Armstrong, and asked him to prepare deeds conveying two eight-acre tracts of land. Armstrong prepared the deeds, but the names of the grantees were not included because Julius could not remember the names of his grandchildren who were to receive the land. After Julius died, Armstrong discovered the names of the grandchildren, added their names to the deeds, and delivered the deeds to them. Are these valid deeds? Why or why not?

3. Fenwick, a Roman Catholic bishop, acquired certain land from a fellow bishop. Bishop Fenwick later attempted to convey the property to Eliza Ann Scanlon. Eliza Ann, a minor, was married to Thomas Scanlon. The marriage was unknown to Fenwick; and in the deed, Fenwick used Eliza Ann's maiden name, Eliza Ann Castin. Does Eliza Ann have title to the property? Why or why not?

4. Charlie lived on a 110-acre farm with his daughter Maggie. Charlie had a deed prepared that conveyed sixty-five acres of the farm to Maggie and handed the deed to her. Maggie and Charlie then placed the deed in a dresser drawer where they kept their personal papers. When Charlie died several years later, Maggie recorded the deed. Maggie's sister now claims that the conveyance was invalid because there was no effective delivery. Is the sister correct? Why or why not?

5. Mahala inherited a small tract of land from her father. She divided the land between her two sons, Emzy and Benton, and executed and delivered to them separate deeds of conveyance. Afterwards, when Mahala's two daughters voiced their displeasure over the conveyances, the two sons voluntarily surrendered the deeds (which were not recorded) and the deeds were destroyed. New deeds were then executed and delivered to the sons, requiring them to pay each daughter for the property. Sometime later Mahala, dissatisfied with the new deeds, entered her sons' home during their absence and destroyed the deeds. When the sons threatened to prosecute Mahala for housebreaking, Mahala executed and delivered replacement deeds to them under duress. She then claimed that the replacement deeds were invalid. If she is correct, does she still own the real estate? Why or why not?

6. Jones owned two adjoining lots. One lot was conveyed to Miller, who operated a business on the property. The second lot was conveyed to the East Fork Baptist Church. Later, because of poor business conditions,

Miller removed his machinery from the lot. The members of the congregation cleaned up Miller's lot and occasionally trimmed the small shade trees growing there. On occasion, when the weather permitted, Sunday school services were held on the lot, dinners were served under the shade trees during all-day meetings, and the lot served as a parking area for churchgoers. After these activities had taken place for about forty years, the church leased both lots to an oil company. Miller claims that the company cannot drill for oil on his lot. Is he correct? Why or why not?

7. Isabel recently acquired title to land that was wild, undeveloped, and not suitable for farming; but it was suitable for hunting, fishing, and recreational purposes. Prior to Isabel's acquisition, Edwin had made use of the land for over twenty years. He had built a hunting cabin on the land; cleared portions of the land; and used the land every year for hunting, fishing, and vacations. He also paid taxes on the property for a period of twenty-five years. Isabel now seeks to evict Edwin, who claims title by adverse possession. Isabel claims that Edwin cannot establish adverse possession because he never fenced, posted, or lived continuously on the property. Is she correct? Why or why not?

8. James owned real estate in the city of New Haven. James executed a quitclaim deed purporting to give his son James Jr. an undivided two-thirds interest and his brother John an undivided one-third interest in the property. His attorney prepared and kept the deed with the understanding that it was to go to John and James Jr. when James died. James continued in possession of the property until his death. After James's death, the attorney showed the deed to James Jr. and John, who had it recorded. Now James's widow, Elizabeth, claims that the quitclaim deed is null and void because delivery was not made during her husband's life. Is she correct? Why or why not?

9. Tilley acquired property fronting on Conesus Lake. In constructing a cement wall to serve as a breakwater, Tilley mistakenly enclosed a parcel of land belonging to West. Tilley later built a shuffleboard court and planted shrubs and grass on West's property. When West sought to evict him, Tilley claimed title to the land by adverse possession. West argued that Tilley could not establish adverse possession because Tilley's use of the land resulted from a mistake rather than an intention to claim ownership. Is West correct? Why or why not?

10. The corporate scandals in the early 2000s involving Enron, WorldCom, Global Crossing, and other companies resulted in civil lawsuits against some of their top executives. These suits have resulted in huge multi-million dollar judgments in cases brought by disgruntled shareholders and former employees who lost their pensions. To protect their personal resources, some of these executives purchased or built multi-million dollar mansions in order to qualify for their state homestead exemption. For example, former WorldCom CFO Scott Sullivan built a $15 million mansion in Boca Raton, Florida. Andrew Fastow, ex-CFO of Enron, built an 11,400-square-foot $1 million home in one of Houston's most exclusive neighborhoods.[80] Not surprisingly, Florida and Texas are two of five states in which, before the Bankruptcy Reform Act of 2005, all of a homestead's equity was exempted from civil judgments. Often potential judgment debtors liquidate non-exempt assets, such as stocks and bonds, and invest in homestead property.

   Proponents of homestead exemptions argue that there are compelling economic and historical reasons to justify them. For instance, Arkansas, Florida, Iowa, Kansas, Oklahoma, South Dakota, and Texas—all important agricultural states—have homestead laws, in part, to protect farmers who fall on bad times. And in the case of Texas, the law encourages businesspeople to take risks in highly speculative businesses such as oil and gas exploration. Moreover, Florida wants to protect its large retirement community from creditors and to attract wealthy people to the state, as well as its farmers. Despite the argument that homestead exemptions help the state's economy, creditors who are unable to collect these judgments raise the cost of credit that everyone must pay to compensate for these losses. Do homestead laws such as those in Texas and Florida give the greatest good to the greatest number? Is the unlimited homestead exemption a right worth protecting, or are there other more compelling rights to protect? Does the Bankruptcy Reform Act of 2005 go far enough in discouraging the evasion of creditors by hiding behind the exemption? Does the new law discourage risk taking by businesspeople?

ENDNOTES

1. 653 A.2d 729 (R.I. 1995).
2. G. Lefcoe, *Real Estate Transactions* (2nd ed. 1997).
3. M. Friedman, *Contracts and Conveyances of Real Property* 872–73 (1991).
4. *Stephens v. Perkins,* 209 Ky. 651, 273 S.W. 545 (1925).
5. *Woodward v. McCollum,* 16 N.D. 42, 111 N.W. 623 (1907).
6. *Langley v. Kesler,* 57 Or. 281, 110 P. 401 (1910).
7. *Ballard v. Farley,* 143 Tenn. 161, 226 S.W. 544 (1920).
8. *Faloon v. Simshauser,* 130 Ill. 649, 22 N.E. 835 (1889).
9. *Zulver Realty Co. v. Snyder,* 191 Md. 374, 62 A.2d 276 (1948).
10. *Lighthouse Church v. Texas Bank,* 889 S.W.2d 595 (Tex.App. 1994).

11. 175 Cal.App.2d 481, 346 P.2d 474 (1959). In some states, even an authorized agent cannot fill in a description of the property. *Barth v. Barth,* 19 Wash.2d 543, 143 P.2d 542 (1943).

12. *Heatter v. Lucas,* 367 Pa. 296, 80 A.2d 749 (1951).

13. R. Kratovil, *Real Estate Law* §49 (6th ed. 1974).

14. B. Miller, *Working with Legal Descriptions,* The Practical Real Estate Lawyer 46 (March 1997).

15. *Vaughn v. Swayzie,* 56 Miss. 704 (1879).

16. *Stamp v. Steele,* 209 Mich. 205, 176 N.W. 464 (1920).

17. *Schenley v. City of Pittsburgh,* 104 Pa. 472 (1883).

18. 235 Ark. 737, 361 S.W.2d 737 (1962).

19. *Brown v. Weare,* 348 Mo. 135, 152 S.W.2d 649 (1941).

20. 357 Mo. 721, 210 S.W.2d 87 (1948).

21. A. Gaudio, *Transfers by Deed,* in R. Powell and P. Rohan, 14 *Powell on Real Property* 81A–63 (1997).

22. 51 Nev. 437, 279 P. 32 (1929). Apparently the result would be the same if the grantor had told the grantee or third parties of the deed. *Orris v. Whipple,* 224 Iowa 1157, 280 N.W. 617 (1938).

23. 208 Ga. 382, 67 S.E.2d 120 (1951).

24. *Tackaberry v. Monteith,* 295 Mich. 487, 295 N.W. 236 (1940).

25. 21 Cal.App.2d 734, 70 P.2d 507 (1937).

26. G. Lefcoe, *Conveyancing Procedures,* in David Thomas, ed., 11 *Thompson on Real Property* 336, 35 (1994, 1995 supp.).

27. *Id.* This is one term for this closing style.

28. Section 2601 of RESPA authorizes HUD's promulgation of this form. To view RESPA's new HUD-1 form see http://www .hud.gov/offices/hsg/ramh/res/hud1.pdf (last accessed July 3, 2010).

29. See generally, O. Beasley, *Real Estate Settlement Procedures Act,* 407 PLI/Real 645 (1994).

30. 113 S.W. 3d 105 (Ky. 2003).

31. R. Aalberts, *Seeking a New Balance: Will RESPA's Latest Reforms Cure What Ails the Real Estate Settlement Servicing Industry?* 39 Real Estate Law Journal 1 (Summer 2010).

32. For a copy of RESPA's new Good Faith Estimate form, see http://www.hud.gov/content/releases/goodfaithestimate.pdf (last accessed July 3, 2010).

33. To view a copy of the required booklet titled "Buying Your Home, Settlement Costs and Information" visit http://www .hud.gov/offices/hsg/ramh/res/Settlement-Booklet-January-6 -REVISED.pdf (last accessed July 3, 2010).

34. For a copy of a loan servicing disclosure statement, see http:// usmortgagecenter.com/wp-content/uploads/2010/05/14-Servic ing-Disclosure-Statement.pdf (last accessed July 3, 2010).

35. See "Buying Your Home, Settlement Costs and Information," *supra* note 33 at 3.

36. J. Wickell, *Your Guide to Home Buying/Selling,* http://home buying.about.com/cs/titleescrow/a/hud1_settlement.htm (last accessed September 3, 2007).

37. See, e.g., *Larsen v. United Federal Savings & Loan Association,* 300 NW 2d 281 (Iowa 1981).

38. *Liability to Real-Property Purchaser for Negligent Appraisal of Property's Value,* 21 ALR 4th 870-71 (1983).

39. R. Hoyt and R. Aalberts, *Appraisers and the Fair Housing Law: Accessibility Requirements for the Disabled,* 12 Journal of Real Estate Research 429 (1996).

40. R. Aalberts, *"Exploding Arms" and Subprime Loans: Why Must Every Decade Have a Real Estate Crisis?* 36 Real Estate Law Journal 3 (2007).

41. J. Hagerty, *Appraisers Under Fire—Again,* Wall Street Journal D1 (August 18, 2009).

42. 111 Stat 788, 836.

43. The assessment might also depend on the date of acquisition. Under Proposition 13—an amendment to the California Constitution approved by voters in 1978—property assessments were set at 1975 levels until property is sold, when it is reassessed at current market value. Thus, a person who has owned a house for a long time might pay only a fraction of the tax his neighbor pays on an identical house that was recently purchased. P. Barrett, *Justices Uphold Proposition 13 of California,* Wall Street Journal A3 (June 13, 1992). The Supreme Court has ruled that Proposition 13 does not violate the Equal Protection Clause of the U.S. Constitution. *Nordlinger v. Hahn,* 505 U.S. 1, 112 S.Ct. 2326, 120 L.Ed.2d 1 (1992).

44. V. Marino, *Reaping the Tax Benefits From Rental Property,* New York Times 22 (February 22, 2007).

45. N. Timiraos, *Mortgage Deduction Looks Less Sacred,* Wall Street Journal A8 (February 27, 2009).

46. Treas. Reg. §1.1445-1 (2009).

47. Treas. Reg. §1.1445-2(b)(2) (2009).

48. Treas. Reg. §1.1445-2(d)(1) (2009).

49. See, e.g., Nevada Revised Statute §133.085 (2006).

50. 93 Ariz. 302, 380 P.2d 601 (1963).

51. UPC §§2-103(2)-2-103(4). For a link specifying which states use the UPC, access: http://www.nccusl.org/nccusl/uniformact _factsheets/uniformacts-fs-upc.asp (last accessed on July 5, 2010).

52. UPC §§2-102(1)(i)-(2).

53. UPC §2-102(1)(ii).

54. UPC §2-102(4).

55. UPC §2-102(3).

56. R. Petzke, *A Short Essay on Dower's Eroding Foundation,* 4 Michigan Real Property Review 2 (1977).

57. *Banks v. Sutton,* 2 P. Williams 700 (1732).

58. 384 P.2d 969 (Wyo. 1963).

59. *Rider v. Rider,* 887 S.W.2d 255 (Tex.App. 1994).

60. 877 P.2d 597 (Ok. 1994).

61. *Tellevik v. Real Property Known as 6717 100th Street S.W., Located in Pierce County,* 921 P.2d 1088 (Washington Ct.App. 1996).

62. For specific information on all the states' homestead exemptions, see http://www.legalconsumer.com/bankruptcy/laws.

63. Florida's homestead statute provides as follows: "**Fla. Stat. §222.05** Any person *owning and occupying* any dwelling house, including a mobile home used as a residence, or modular home, on land not his or her own which he or she may lawfully possess, by lease or otherwise, and claiming such house, mobile home, or modular home as his or her homestead, shall be entitled to the exemption of such house, mobile home, or modular home from levy and sale as aforesaid." (Emphasis provided).

64. *Pasquina v, Cunningham,* 513 F.3d 318 (1st Cir. 2008).

65. R. Aalberts, *Bankruptcy Reform and Homestead Protection: Is the Castle Crumbling?* 34 Real Estate Law Journal 3 (2005).

66. R. Cunningham et al., *The Law of Property,* 2nd ed. 815 (1993).

67. *Evans v. Francis,* 101 N.Y.S.2d 716 (1951).

68. 368 N.W.2d 391 (Minn.App. 1985).

69. 58 Cal.2d 417, 24 Cal.Rptr. 856, 374 P.2d 824 (1962).

70. *Flynn v. Korsack,* 343 Mass. 15, 175 N.E.2d 397 (1961).

71. *Hayes v. Mitchell,* 184 Cal.App.2d 301, 7 Cal.Rptr. 364 (1960).

72. *Springer v. Durette,* 217 Or. 196, 342 P.2d 132 (1959).

73. *Robin v. Brown,* 308 Pa. 123, 162 A. 161 (1932).

74. 212 Ind. 624, 10 N.E.2d 917 (1937).

75. 248 Ala. 340, 27 So.2d 483 (1946).

76. *International Paper Co. v. Jacobs,* 258 N.C. 439, 128 S.E.2d 818 (1963). The following link lists the states and how many years it takes for adverse possession: http://www.lawchek.com/resources/forms/que/advposs.htm (last accessed July 5, 2010).

77. *Baylor v. Soska,* 658 A.2d 743 (Pa. 1995).

78. *Hart v. All Persons,* 26 Cal.App. 664, 148 P. 236 (1915).

79. *McLean and Stevens v. DK Trust and Kirlin,* Boulder District Court Case No. 06 CV 982 (filed Oct. 4, 2006). See also, S. Martin, *Adverse Possession: Practical Realities and an Unjust Enrichment Standard,* 37 Real Estate Law Journal 133, 138 (Fall 2008) for an excellent discussion of good faith in adverse possession law.

80. J. Swartz, *Homes of the Rich and Famous,* USA Today (July 15, 2002). See also, L. Ponoroff and S. Knippenberg, *Debtors Who Convert Their Assets on the Eve of Bankruptcy: Villains or Victims of the Fresh Start?* 70 New York University Law Review 235 (1995).

Landlord and Tenant

© MACIEJ NOSKOWSKI/iStockphoto (RF)

LEARNING OBJECTIVES

After studying Chapter 11, you should:

- Learn about leasehold estates and licenses

- Understand laws regarding a landlord's choice of tenant

- Recognize required lease provisions

- Be acquainted with suggested lease provisions

- Be aware of both landlord and tenant remedies

- Be familiar with the scope of a landlord's tort liability

freehold estate
An indefinite estate in life or in fee.

leasehold estate
An estate in real property that lasts for a definite period of time.

"A house she hath, 'tis made of such good fashion,
The tenant ne'er shall pay for reparation,
Nor will the landlord ever raise her rent
Or turn her out of doors for non-payment:
From chimney tax this cell is free
To such a house who would not tenant be?"

Seventeenth-Century English Tombstone

"Dear Landlord, Please don't put a price on my soul. My burden is heavy;
My dreams are beyond control."

Bob Dylan, from song "Dear Landlord"

As noted in Chapter 5, an estate is one's interest in real or personal property. Interests in real property may be divided into two broad categories:

1. Freehold estates, characterized by their indefinite duration since no one knows when the estate will end
2. Leasehold estates, which usually last for a definite period of time

A **freehold estate** is considered to be an interest in real property, and the owner of the estate has both title and the right to take possession of the land. A **leasehold estate** (sometimes called a *nonfreehold estate*), while an interest in real property, is traditionally classified as a "chattel real," a personal property interest in real estate. This classification has significance in several contexts. For example, the leasehold estate "at common law was a chattel real and personal property; upon the death of the owner of this estate intestate, it passes as any other personalty to the deceased tenant's personal representative. While it is an estate in real property, it is not real property."[1] Real property, on the other hand, passed directly and immediately to the decedent's heir. Although the tenant does not have title to the real property, she has the right to take possession of the property for a stated period. When the lease ends, the right to possession reverts back to the landlord. The landlord's interest during the period of the lease is a future estate called a "reversionary interest."

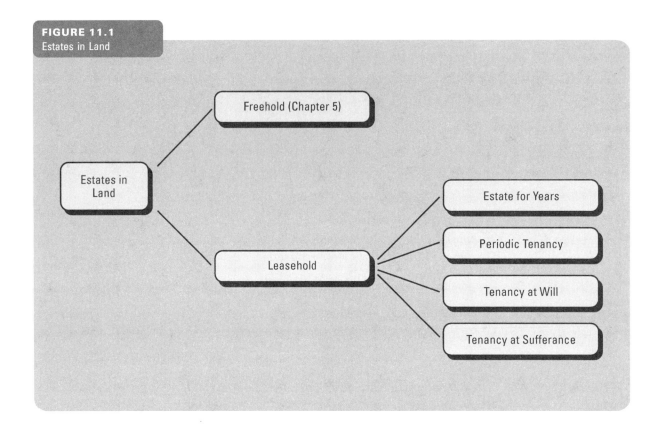

FIGURE 11.1
Estates in Land

The *four* types of leasehold estates are as follows:

1. The estate for years
2. The periodic tenancy
3. The tenancy at will
4. The tenancy at sufferance (See Figure 11.1.)

This chapter covers the following:

▬ *The leasehold estates (along with licenses and cooperatives)*
▬ *The contract used to create a leasehold estate—the lease*
▬ *The remedies available to the landlord or tenant when the landlord has breached a duty established by the lease or by law*
▬ *The landlord's tort liability to the tenant or to visitors on the premises.*

Leasehold Estates and Licenses

Estate for Years

estate for years

An estate of fixed duration—a year or a multiple or fraction of a year. The essential characteristic of this estate is its duration.

An **estate for years**,[2] an estate that has a definite beginning and a definite end, is the most common type of leasehold estate. The length of time between the beginning and end may be one day, or it may be ten thousand years. In some states, however, a lease for a definite term exceeding a certain period (for example, more than 100 years in Massachusetts) is considered to be a fee simple absolute estate by statute.

The parties may select the lease's duration as long as the state does not limit its length. In one Delaware case, for example, the court decided that an estate for years was created when one person leased property to another person in the year 1800 for a term of two thousand years at an annual rent of $10.07.[3]

Most leases provide that they will terminate under specified conditions, including the lessee's nonpayment of rent. Unless the estate for years is terminated under a specified condition of the lease, it will terminate at the end of the period. The rights of the tenant cease automatically at midnight on the last day of the term. Under the common law, the landlord is not required to send the tenant a notice to leave since the lease itself serves as the notice. However, the landlord must give notice, as is often the case, if required under state statute.

Periodic Tenancy

A **periodic tenancy**[4] lasts for a period of time that is automatically renewed until the landlord or tenant gives notice that it will end. Thus it is sometimes referred to, depending on the periods in question, as an estate "from year to year," "month to month," or even "week to week." The periodic tenancy can be created by the express agreement of the landlord and tenant, or its creation may be implied. For example, if the landlord and tenant sign a lease that states everything except the term of the lease, it is implied that they intended a periodic tenancy. An implied periodic tenancy also is created when the tenant takes possession of the property under a defective lease as the following classic case from New York discusses.

> **periodic tenancy**
>
> A tenancy that endures for a certain period of time and for successive periods of equal length unless terminated at the end of any one period by notice of either party. The chief characteristics that distinguish periodic tenancies from other nonfreehold estates are the continuity of the term and the requirement of notice to terminate the tenancy.

A CASE IN POINT

In *Laughran v. Smith,*[5] the tenants took possession of the rental property on May 1 under a five-year lease that was void because the landlord never signed it. The court decided that by "the entry, occupation, and payment of rent they became tenants from year to year, with the right to terminate the lease on the 30th day of April of any year on giving due notice."

Periodic tenancies are commonly created when a tenant remains on the premises at the conclusion of an estate for years. The tenant's remaining in possession (or "holding over") is considered to be an offer to rent the premises under a periodic tenancy. If the landlord accepts the offer by treating the tenant as a periodic tenant, the rent and the length of the renewable periods are determined by the original lease. Today, often there is a provision in the commonly used one-year residential leases where the landlord and tenant agree that it will become month-to-month periodic tenancies if the tenant remains past the one-year term. Still, under the common law when the original lease was for a term of more than one year, the periodic tenancy is considered to be from year to year.

The rule making the tenant liable for another lease term is sometimes harsh. For instance, if a tenant remains in her apartment for three days after the end of a one-year lease, she will be liable for another full year's rent. For this reason, some states have modified this rule by statute. Yet the objective of the rule, particularly when the U.S. was primarily agrarian, is to protect tenants as a class. As one Maryland court noted:

> *The rule imposes a penalty upon the individual tenant wrongfully holding over, but ultimately operates for the benefit of tenants as a class by its tendency to secure the agreed surrender of terms to incoming tenants who have severally yielded possession of other premises in anticipation of promptly entering into the possession of the new.... [A]s the value of any piece of property is largely dependent upon its actual or potential continuing yield in periodic rent, the social and economic importance of the landlord*

being able certainly to deliver, and the prospective tenant so to obtain possession on the stipulated day, is obvious.[6]

holdover tenant
A tenant who retains possession after the expiration of a leasehold interest.

In some situations, the **holdover tenant** remains on the property involuntarily because of circumstances beyond her control. When this happens, the tenant is not liable for a new term as the following classic New York case points out.

A CASE IN POINT

In *Regan v. Fosdick,*[7] the tenant was unable to leave an apartment until 19 days after the term ended because the tenant's child had scarlet fever and was quarantined on the premises under a board of health order. When the landlord later brought suit on the theory that the tenancy had been renewed, the court decided in favor of the tenant because the tenant was forced to remain on the premises by circumstances beyond his control.

Regardless of the method used to create a periodic tenancy, the usual method of termination is by notice to quit, given by either the landlord or the tenant. At common law, a six-month notice was required to terminate a year-to-year tenancy, while the notice for tenancies with shorter periods was determined by the length of the period. For instance, a one-month notice was required to terminate a month-to-month tenancy. Today the time period for giving notice in most states is determined by statute, with year-to-year tenancies requiring less than six months notice. To compute the time period, days are counted beginning with the day after the notice was served and ending with the last day of the rental period.

Although the notice does not have to use legal terminology, it must be clear and unambiguous as this Massachusetts case demonstrates.

A CASE IN POINT

In *Torrey v. Adams,* a tenant leased property under a year-to-year lease ending May 1 each year.[8] The tenant wrote to his landlord, "I want to tell you that I will have to give up the apartment when the lease expires, June 1, 1921, as I shall break up housekeeping. I expect to return East early in May to see about things and trust this will be satisfactory to you." The tenant moved from the apartment in May but was held liable for rent for the rest of the year because the notice "must be so certain that it cannot reasonably be misunderstood, and if a particular day is named therein for the termination of the tenancy that day must be the one corresponding to the conclusion of the tenancy, or the notice will be treated as a nullity. The notice would have been sufficient if in any form of words it had provided for the termination of the lease on May 1, 1921."

tenancy at will
A landlord-tenant relationship that endures only so long as both parties agree to its continuance is an estate at will. The chief characteristic of the tenancy is its durational insecurity since either party may terminate the tenancy at any time.

Tenancy at Will

A **tenancy at will**[9] is characterized by its indefinite duration; it may be terminated at any time after the landlord or the tenant gives proper notice. In most states, the tenant has a statutory right to remain on the premises for a specified period (for example, thirty days) after notice is given.

A tenancy at will may be created expressly by contract between the parties, or it may be implied. For example, a landlord owns an apartment building that she wants to sell. If potential buyers would prefer to purchase the building free of long-term leases, the landlord might lease each apartment under a tenancy at will that expressly provides that "the lease shall last until the landlord sells the property." Even if this clause is omitted from the lease, a tenancy at will might be implied if the landlord and tenant made no agreement specifying the term of the lease.

Tenancy at Sufferance

tenancy at sufferance

A tenancy in which the tenant's possession of the leased property continues even though the tenant's rights have terminated.

A **tenancy at sufferance** results when a person in possession of real estate refuses to leave after his rights to occupy the property have ceased. This technically is not an estate because the tenant has no right or permission to remain on the real estate; however, neither is the occupancy a trespass because the tenant's original entry onto the property was lawful. For example, Lanny leased an apartment to Bennett for one year; the lease is to end September 1, 2012. If Bennett does not leave the apartment by September 1, he will become a tenant at sufferance and will become liable for damages based on the reasonable rental value of the property. To discourage both residential and commercial tenants from remaining in possession past the expiration of their leases, some states, such as Florida, require the tenants to pay double rent until they leave.[10] The landlord also could decide to treat Bennett's holding over as an offer to create a periodic tenancy, as discussed previously.

Licenses

license

A privilege to enter the premises for a certain purpose, which does not give the licensee any title, interest, or estate in such property.

In many business transactions, it is important to determine whether a leasehold estate or a **license** has been created. A lease gives the tenant an estate in the form of an exclusive right to possession of the property. As noted in Chapter 4, a license—which is a privilege and therefore only confers permission to enter the premises for a specified purpose—gives the licensee no legal right, title, or interest in the property.

In *Nextel of New York, Inc. v. Time Management Corporation* on page 451, the court rules on whether the plaintiff possessed a nonexclusive license or a commercial lease for its cell phone antennae and equipment.

END OF CHAPTER CASE

Landlord's Choice of Tenant
Initial Selection of Tenant

The landlord is prohibited from deciding whether to rent to a prospective tenant based on the prospect's membership in a protected group. As discussed in Chapter 6, the Civil Rights Act of 1866 prohibits a landlord's discrimination on the basis of race in selecting tenants. Title VIII of the Civil Rights Act of 1968, as amended in 1988 (also called the Fair Housing Act, or FHA), provides that the landlord may not discriminate on the basis of race, color, religion, national origin, sex, handicap, or family status (that is, families with children) in leasing a dwelling. State and local fair housing legislation often adds additional categories of prohibited discrimination. For example, some state and local governments have laws prohibiting housing discrimination based on sexual orientation,[11] illegitimate children in the household, or criminal record.[12] (See endnote 11 for states and information on antidiscrimination laws in housing based on sexual orientation).

testers

People working for government agencies or public interest groups who pose as tenants to detect whether landlords are violating antidiscrimination laws.

The enforcement of the FHA has been greatly enhanced by the ability of public interest groups to employ **testers** to see if protected groups are accorded the same treatment as others. For example, the Metropolitan Milwaukee Fair Housing Council sent black and white shoppers to the Shorecrest Apartments.[13] Shorecrest gave the shoppers different information about unit availability and rental rates based on their race. The court held that the testers had uncovered sufficient incidents of discrimination to prove a "pattern of discrimination," and the court upheld a jury's award to the testers of damages for their emotional distress.

Despite federal and state legislation, landlords, as the following New York court points out, sometimes have considerable leeway in selecting tenants.

A CASE IN POINT

In *Kramarsky v. Stahl Management,*[14] a landlord refused to rent an apartment to an African-American divorcee who was general counsel to the New York Commission on Human Rights, because the landlord believed she might cause trouble as a tenant. When the prospective tenant brought suit, the landlord proved that he was not discriminating on the basis of race or marital status: 60 percent of his apartments were rented to unmarried people and 30 percent to African Americans. The court decided that discrimination on the basis of intelligence is legal. According to the court, a landlord "may decide not to rent to singers because they are too noisy, or not to rent to baldheaded men because he had been told they give wild parties. He can bar his premises to the lowest strata of society, should he choose, or to the highest, if that be his personal desire."

Disabled Tenants   Illegal discrimination can also come about due to physical structures and obstacles that create a discriminatory *effect* on disabled tenants. For example, the FHA's protections for the disabled, also discussed in Chapter 6, require that new multifamily dwellings, defined as "buildings with four or more units in which first occupancy is on or after March 13, 1991," must be made accessible to the disabled. This Act is aimed at helping tenants who are wheelchair users. These dwellings, which include most apartments and condominiums, must include the following:

- *An accessible building entrance on accessible routes*
- *Accessible and usable public and common use areas, such as swimming pools and laundry rooms*
- *Usable doors within the entire premises, with clear passage of 32 inches opening to 90 degrees*
- *Routes into and through the dwelling unit, including only a one-half- to three-quarter-inch threshold*
- *Light switches, electrical outlets, thermostats, and other environmental controls in accessible locations*
- *Reinforced walls for grab bars*
- *Usable kitchens and bathrooms for wheelchair maneuverability*

A landlord also cannot refuse a disabled tenant who wants to modify her dwelling at her own expense, although the landlord can require the tenant to pay to restore the apartment to the condition prior to modification when she leaves.

Commercial landlords also must comply with Title III of the Americans with Disabilities Act (ADA), which prohibits hotels, shopping centers, bars, restaurants, movie theaters, athletic clubs, and many other places of public accommodation from discriminating against disabled individuals. The Act requires the removal of existing architectural barriers by installing ramps and curb cuts, widening doors, and adding accessible parking if these and other measures are "readily achievable" (accomplished with little difficulty or expense). The Act also provides that places of public accommodation and commercial facilities built after 1993, as well as buildings and areas that are undergoing alterations in older existing buildings, be made "readily accessible" to the disabled.[15] The readily accessible requirement may even apply to accessing "virtual" commercial facilities. Recently, blind consumers were certified in a class action suit against Target, claiming that Target.com discriminates against them under the ADA. The plaintiffs contend that the Target.com web site must be made accessible to them by providing alterations such as screen-reader software that vocalizes the web site's text and contents.[16]

Discrimination Based on Marriage Status   Can a landlord refuse to rent to a cohabiting unmarried couple on the basis that their relationship violates the landlord's religious values? A number of states now have statutes and court rulings forbidding this discriminatory practice. In *Smith v. Fair Employment and Housing Commission,*[17] a California court ruled that enforcement of a state statute banning inquiries about marital status or associated discrimination did not conflict with the landlord's First Amendment rights or state constitutional rights to the free exercise of her religion. Consequently, the landlord was required to rent to the unmarried couple.

On the other hand, the Massachusetts court in *Attorney General v. Paul Desilets*[18] used a balancing test to consider whether the landlord could refuse to rent to the unmarried couple. On one side of the scale is Massachusetts's interest in enforcing the right of cohabiting unmarried couples to freely lease. On the other side is the landlord's right to free religious exercise based on the Massachusetts Declaration of Rights and the federal constitution. Because the strength of the state's interest in allowing the couple to rent had not been sufficiently demonstrated, the court determined that resolution by summary judgment was inappropriate. A trial was needed to determine the strength of the state's interest. The foregoing discusses the status of antidiscrimination laws in renting to unmarried couples. What happens, however, when a single person rents an apartment *after* which her partner moves in, thereby violating lease provisions restricting cohabitation? This issue is discussed on page 433 on the law governing a tenant's use of the property.

Tenant Screening   Although landlords cannot legally exclude tenants protected under fair housing legislation, they may legally screen out potentially troublesome tenants not protected by law. Some landlords have enlisted the help of tenant-screening services. Using advanced computer technology, these businesses, many associated with large credit-reporting agencies, conduct background checks of prospective tenants, looking in particular for those who may have a record of rent defaults and apartment abuse. However, like credit-reporting agencies, these businesses can make mistakes. In reaction, some states, such as New York and Minnesota, have statutes that require landlords to inform those who are rejected of the service's name and address so they can challenge any inaccuracies.[19]

In some cases, landlords may be compelled by law to discriminate in the selection and eviction of certain dangerous and undesirable tenants to protect their law-abiding tenants and their property. Chief among these are tenants and guests involved in drug-related activities. For example, landlords have been held liable for damages and have been required to pay fines and even forfeit their properties for illegal drug-related activity by tenants. This can include the manufacture, sale, or use of drugs that occurred on or near their premises.[20] Moreover, under the amended federal Anti-Drug Abuse Act of 1988, all federal public housing agencies must provide in the lease (which every tenant must sign) a provision that any tenant or anyone under the tenant's control will be evicted for any drug-related activity on or near the premises as the next California case explains.

In *Department of Housing and Urban Development v. Rucker* on page 451, the U.S. Supreme Court rules on whether public housing authorities can evict tenants for their guest's drug use on their premises.

END OF CHAPTER CASE

One of the biggest problems for landlords whose property may involve drug activity centers on the manufacturing of methamphetamines, or "meth." Meth is a highly addictive drug often produced in makeshift labs in residential housing. Its use has created serious social and economic problems for individuals and society, as well as the potential for explosions, chemical fires, and the release of toxic chemicals into the environment. In response, some states are shifting the responsibility to landlords to combat the effects of these labs. For example, many states require the landlord to remediate the premises by removing the toxic chemicals that meth production creates. Other states, such as Missouri and Nevada, generally oblige the owner, when selling the property, to disclose to prospective buyers that there was once a meth lab on the premises.[21]

Some public- and private-sector landlords now test prospective tenants for drugs. They also test existing tenants on an annual basis or those tenants for whom there is a reasonable suspicion of illegal drug use. Although there have been no reported lawsuits in the private sector yet, drug testing of tenants might violate certain federal and state laws. For example, if a large company with apartments in different areas of a city tests its tenants in poorer, predominately minority neighborhoods but not in wealthier, nonminority neighborhoods, it could be in violation of the FHA since it would have a disparate impact on a protected group. Also, depending on how the testing is conducted, it may violate common law privacy rights, among other state laws. The activities of public housing agencies, moreover, raise constitutional issues. Despite these legal and ethical issues, commentators have noted that most tenants are in favor of drug testing to reduce or eliminate drug activity where they live.[22]

As the foregoing discussion demonstrates, landlords may try to protect their tenants from other tenants who threaten their person and their property. The next California case discusses whether a landlord has a legal duty to exclude dangerous tenants from renting.

A CASE IN POINT

In *Castaneda v. Olsher*,[23] the plaintiff, Ernest Castaneda, resided in a mobile home park owned by George Olsher. Castaneda was shot accidentally as the result of a gang battle across the street from his residence. Castaneda sued Olsher for, among other actions, "breaching a duty not to rent to known gang members." The court ruled in Olsher's favor, stating "[g]ang members do not … announce their gang affiliations on housing applications. If landlords regularly face liability for injuries gang members cause on the premises, they will tend to deny rental to anyone who might be a gang member or, even more broadly, to any family one of whose members might be in a gang. The result in many cases would be arbitrary discrimination on the basis of race, ethnicity, family composition, dress and appearance, or reputation. All of these are, in at least some circumstances, illegal and against public policy and could themselves subject the landlord to liability."

ETHICAL AND
PUBLIC POLICY
ISSUES

Is It Ethical Public Policy for Local Governments to Require Prospective Tenants to Show Landlords Proof of Citizenship or Legal Residency Status Before They Can Rent?

A growing number of U.S. cities are attempting to pass ordinances that would have the effect of denying a person a place to live unless that person can prove she is in the country legally. To enforce these ordinances, landlords would be fined and would have their business licenses revoked if they rented to illegal aliens. Many argue that since the federal government has not been able to stem the flow of illegal aliens—some of whom may be terrorists—local governments must take on the task. Opponents maintain that this is solely the job of the federal government and that many of these laws are simply a disguised form of racism and xenophobia. California, for example, passed a law in 2007 that forbids local governments from requiring landlords to inquire or report the immigration status of tenants. Opponents further argue that even if illegal aliens are not here legally, they still have a human right to dignity, including the right to shelter that trumps written laws. Are these ordinances going too far, or are they necessary for fighting the illegal alien problem?

Retaliatory Eviction

After the landlord has selected a tenant and leased an apartment, does the landlord have complete freedom to refuse to *renew* the lease as long as she does not violate fair housing legislation? As the following Hawaii case demonstrates, the traditional answer has been yes.

A CASE IN POINT

In *Aluli v. Trusdell,*[24] the landlord brought suit to evict a tenant who was leasing an apartment under a month-to-month periodic tenancy. The tenant claimed that the reason for his eviction was due to his activities as an organizer and member of a tenants' union. Although the tenant alleged that the eviction would deprive him of his First Amendment rights to freedom of speech and association, the court decided in favor of the landlord: "If it is true that he is seeking possession of the rented premises for the sole reason that he disagrees or dislikes the tenant's communicative or associative activities, is not the landlord also protected by the First Amendment in expressing these disagreements or dislikes? ... [T]he landlord-tenant relationship is a contractual one in our jurisdiction. If we accept the tenant's contention, it would mean that we would be substantially altering this relationship and impairing the traditional right of a landlord to recover possession of the demised premises under the terms of a lease." The *Aluli* case also illustrates the vulnerability of tenants with a periodic tenancy who can lose their leasehold quickly.

retaliatory eviction
An eviction of a tenant for complaining about the condition of the leased premises or violations of the law.

However, if the lease is *not* up for renewal, landlords who evict their tenants in retaliation for asserting their rights against their landlords, called **retaliatory eviction**, may be liable for damages. For example, in a majority of states, a landlord cannot retaliate against a tenant by raising rent, decreasing services, or terminating a lease because of any one of the following:

1. The tenant attempted to enforce rights under the lease or state law
2. The tenant reported health or building code violations to a government authority
3. The tenant joined a tenants' union

Is it illegal for a landlord to retaliate against a tenant for refusing to engage in sexual relations with the landlord? Although it is unlikely that Congress contemplated this when it passed the 1968 FHA, the next Ohio case of first impression established the rule of law on the issue.

A CASE IN POINT

In *Shellhammer v. Lewallen*,[25] Norman Lewallen, the landlord, approached his tenant, Tammy Shellhammer, and asked her to pose nude for him. She refused. Later he offered to pay her to have sex with him. Several months later Shellhammer was evicted—ostensibly for withholding her rent while waiting for Lewallen to provide her with a working refrigerator. The federal circuit upheld the magistrate's finding that Lewallen was liable under the Fair Housing Act for evicting Shellhammer in retaliation for her refusal to have sex with him.

According to commentators, sexual harassment of tenants has become a significant problem, particularly for lower-income, single women with few housing alternatives.[26] In 2004, in the largest tenant sexual harassment case ever, a federal judge in Kansas City, Missouri, ordered a landlord to pay $1.1 million in damages to eleven women who were threatened with retaliatory evictions if they did not have sex with the landlord. The women also were subjected to unwanted verbal sexual advances and sexual touching.[27] In 2008, an owner of more than 50 rental units in the Cincinnati, Ohio, area settled a lawsuit by paying $1 million to 12 of his former female tenants. These women were also lower-income tenants renting apartments who received federally subsidized rent on the Department of Housing and Urban Development's Section 8 program.[28]

Even where there is no statute, courts in some states have developed a **retaliatory eviction** defense that can be raised by tenants after landlord retaliation.[29] The tenant's protection against retaliatory action is often broadened by a rebuttable presumption in favor of the tenant that a landlord's action is retaliatory if it occurred, within, for example, 90 days of the tenant's actions. For example, in an Illinois case, *Reed v. Burns,* the landlord failed to rebut the presumption that a letter giving the tenant thirty days' notice was in retaliation for three tenant letters complaining about rodents and electrical and plumbing problems. The court ruled that the tenant was entitled to damages.[30] The following Iowa case discusses how the issue of retaliatory eviction is resolved in that state.

A CASE IN POINT

In *Hillview Associates v. Bloomquist*,[31] mobile home park tenants formed a tenant association to improve the cleanliness and safety of the park. Some tenants were involved in altercations with the landlord's representative, and the tenants later received notices of eviction from their landlord. The court stated that to determine whether a landlord's primary motivation is not retaliatory, the following must be considered: (a) the landlord's decision was a reasonable exercise of business judgment; (b) the landlord in good faith desires to dispose of the entire leased property free of all tenants; (c) the landlord in good faith desires to make a different use of the leased property; (d) the landlord lacks the financial ability to repair the leased property and therefore, in good faith, wants to have it free of any tenant; (e) the landlord was unaware of the tenant's activities that were protected by statute; (f) the landlord acted at the first opportunity after he learned of the tenant's conduct; and (g) the landlord's act was not discriminatory. The court ruled that while some of the tenants could be evicted for assaulting the landlord's representative, three tenants were evicted for their participation in the tenant association. The court emphasized that "[U]nder Iowa law, tenants may organize and join a tenant's [sic] association free from fear of retaliation."

Required Lease Provisions

Introduction: Residential versus Commercial Leases

lease

A contract conveying a property interest (leasehold estate) to a tenant.

The **lease** is a unique legal hybrid: it not only is a contract between the landlord and tenant but also is an instrument that conveys a property interest—a leasehold estate—to the tenant. The reasons for the lease's dual nature are historical. In early English law, the lease was regarded merely as a contract. But in the 15th and 16th centuries, when England was dependent on an agrarian economy, the need to stabilize the lease of agricultural land became important. The lease then came to be regarded solely as a conveyance of the landlord's entire interest, for the term of the lease, much like how a deed conveys a freehold interest. With the coming of the Industrial Revolution, residential and commercial leases in heavily populated urban areas became predominant; these leases are more similar to contracts than to conveyances. The net result is that courts today use both property and contract law concepts in fashioning the rights and duties of the landlord and tenant.[32]

Courts sometimes distinguish between residential and commercial leases. The general principles of landlord-tenant law covered in the sections that follow normally apply to both types of leases (except where noted). However, courts are sometimes more willing to modernize the law governing residential leases in recognition of the importance of shelter, moving the law of residential leasing closer to the law of contracts. In the words of a California court: "The typical city dweller, who frequently leases an apartment several stories above the actual plot of land on which an apartment building rests, cannot realistically be viewed as acquiring an interest in land; rather he has contracted for a place to live."[33] About 15 states have enacted statutes based on a model law—the Uniform Residential Landlord and Tenant Act (URLTA)—that apply only to residential leases emphasizing this policy (see endnote 34 for the states that apply the Act).[34]

Commercial leases can involve the rental of space within an existing building and the rental of land, called the ground lease. Under a commercial ground lease, the tenant leases property and agrees to construct a building on the leased land. Thus, these leases tend to be for a term of many years. Courts are less willing to reform the law of commercial leases; as a result, these leases are "still by and large governed by a body of [property] law that crystallized in medieval times."[35] For example, the implied warranty of habitability, considered to be the major development in landlord-tenant law in recent years, generally applies only to residential leases. However, as discussed in *Gym-N-I Playgrounds, Inc. v. Snider* on page 453, a few states now recognize an implied warranty of suitability for commercial properties.[36] Similarly, various rent-related remedies, such as rent withholding, are often limited to residential leases.

Nevertheless, developments in the law governing residential leases are important to commercial landlords and tenants—at least when space, as opposed to ground, is leased. A person who rents an office in an office tower acquires more than an interest in land. Like the residential tenant, a commercial tenant contracts for "a package which includes not merely walls and ceilings, but also adequate heat, light and ventilation, serviceable plumbing facilities, secure windows and doors, proper sanitation, and proper maintenance."[37] Moreover, many commercial tenants now demand that their landlords provide a "wired" infrastructure with broadband and software applications. Therefore, it is logical that in the years to come, the traditional property law concepts governing commercial leases will gravitate toward the modern contract law concepts governing residential leases. (For a residential and commercial lease and a checklist for a commercial lease, see www.cengagebrain.com [see page xix in the Preface for instructions on how to access the free study tools for this text].)

Writing Requirements

Every lease, whether residential or commercial, should be in writing to avoid later controversies about the terms of the agreement. Most states include leases within their Statute of Frauds' writing requirement but (discussed in Chapter 7) only when the lease term is for more than one year. The required writing must include *four* essential provisions:

1. Names and signatures of the parties
2. A description of the property
3. The term of the lease
4. The amount of rent

A lease containing the four required provisions is valid between the landlord and the tenant. However, in many states two additional requirements must be met if the lease is to be recorded:

1. The lease must be witnessed.
2. The signatures must be acknowledged by the landlord and tenant before a notary public.

Almost all states have established provisions for recording leases. As one example, in Wisconsin, all leases may be recorded; but only leases for more than one year must be recorded to be valid against later purchasers.[38] In states with race statutes governing their recording processes, it is more critical to record residential leases. As discussed in Chapter 8, in a dispute between two lessees, the first lessee to record prevails even when there is notice of an unrecorded leasehold interest.

When the lease for a period of longer than one year is not written or any of the essential terms is missing, the lease is usually invalid. But when the tenant takes possession of the property under an invalid lease, a tenancy at will is created; when the tenant takes possession and pays rent, there is a periodic tenancy. When the tenant takes possession, pays rent, and makes improvements on the property, the lease is enforced under the **substantial performance doctrine**. In one case, an Oregon court held that there was substantial performance when the tenant took possession, paid rent, planted rosebushes, installed expensive carpet, and painted the house.[39]

> **substantial performance doctrine**
> Substantial performance occurs when a contractor has performed enough of the contract to deserve payment.

Names and Signatures

The lease must name both the landlord and the tenant. When the landlord is an individual (and not a partnership or corporation), it may also be wise to name the spouse of the landlord to avoid problems arising under dower and curtesy laws (see Chapter 10) as well as community property law (see Chapter 5). Like a contract for the sale of real estate, the lease must be signed by the party to be charged, although in some states, a lessee who has not signed will be bound by the lease if he has taken possession of the property.

Description of Property

Because the lease is a conveyance of property as well as a contract, the lease must describe the property with the same certainty required in a deed or a mortgage. Furthermore, the landlord should specifically reserve any rights that will not pass to the tenant. For example, the lease conveys to the tenant the exclusive right to possess the real estate, and even the landlord cannot enter the premises without the tenant's permission. Consequently, if the landlord wants to enter the property to show an apartment to prospective tenants, the right should be specifically reserved in the lease. Many states, by statute, also allow landlords to enter in emergencies or if they give notice of at least 24 hours before entering.

In addition to the described property, the tenant receives a number of incidental rights necessary for the use and enjoyment of the premises unless the lease states otherwise. For instance, a tenant who leases an apartment in a building is entitled to use the building's halls and stairways to reach the apartment even though the right is not specified in the lease. If the whole building is leased, the tenant has the right to use the outside walls and roof for advertising purposes as the next Connecticut case points out.

A CASE IN POINT

In *Monarch Accounting Supplies, Inc. v. Prezioso*,[40] the landlord leased a building to a tenant for a five-year term and then leased the roof to another party for advertising. The court decided that the lease gave the tenant the right to the roof even though it was not specifically mentioned in the lease and that rents the landlord received for leasing the roof should go to the tenant.

In some cases, a tenant who leases a building has the implied right to use the landlord's adjoining land and buildings. In *McDaniel v. Willer*,[41] a Missouri case, the landlord operated a general store and used a building on a nearby lot to store fertilizer. When he leased the store, the tenant was given the right to use the storage building even though that right was not mentioned in the lease.

The Lease Term

The date the lease begins and the duration of the tenancy should be clearly stated in the lease. If they are not and if a court cannot ascertain the intended term, the lease will be considered a tenancy at will or a periodic tenancy.

Rent

rent
Consideration paid for the use of property.

The lease must state the consideration (**rent**) that the landlord is receiving in exchange for possession of the property. If no rent is stated in the lease, either the leasehold will be considered a gift from the landlord or the tenant will be liable for the reasonable value of her possession of the property. The lease also should state the time and place for the rent payment. If no time is stated, payment is due on the last day of the period. For instance, if rent is paid monthly, the rent would be due on the last day of the month. If no place is stated, payment is due at the rented premises.

Any method may be used to calculate rent as long as a specific amount can be determined by the use of the method. Each of the following methods is permissible:

1. A specific dollar amount
2. A graduated rental calling for predetermined periodic increases in the rent
3. A cost-of-living index method by which the rent is adjusted on the basis of the index
4. A percentage method by which the rent is based on the volume of the tenant's business on the leased property
5. An appraisal method that calculates rent as a percentage of the appraised value of the rental property[42]

Although not all courts agree, the traditional rule is that an option to extend a lease is unenforceable when the lease provides that rent will be determined by mutual agreement of the landlord and the tenant at the end of the original lease.[43]

Rent control laws, which exist in many U.S. cities and a few states, are also a factor many landlords must consider when setting the amount of rent they charge. Although these laws take away a landlord's ability to set the amount of rent she charges based on competitive market forces, they are constitutional, as the next U.S. Supreme Court case points.

A CASE IN POINT

In California, virtually every large city except San Diego has adopted rent controls, which cover half the state's population. The San Jose rent control ordinance provides that landlords are entitled to automatic eight percent annual increases; increases higher than eight percent may be challenged by tenants on the basis of personal hardship. Landlords attacked this provision on the grounds that it was unconstitutional because it forced them to subsidize the poor. In the 1988 decision *Pennell v. San Jose*, the U.S. Supreme Court disagreed, stressing that the law provides landlords with a fair return on their investments while at the same time protecting tenants from unfair rent increases.[44]

Although rent control laws are legal if crafted properly and in harmony with a state's constitution and statutes, they continue to be vigorously debated as to whether they advance a wise public policy.

ETHICAL AND PUBLIC POLICY ISSUES

Are Rent Control Laws a Fair and Ethical Public Policy?

Proponents of rent control laws argue that even though tenants may pay a fair market rent when they begin their leasehold the fairness is short-lived. With no rent control laws to prevent subsequent rent increases, they contend that they would have to incur unacceptably high transaction costs to move to another location. They also point out that many laws, such as tax deductions on mortgage interest, are a kind of subsidy provided only to homeowners. Since these subsidies are unavailable to renters, who are often poorer, renters should be helped by laws such as rent control. Tenants also argue that, if they are allowed to remain in their homes at reasonable rents, the landlord gains through tenants' sweat equity when they maintain and improve their residences. Rent control advocates further point out that these laws are now tailored to be fairer to landlords, including exemptions for developers of new housing, as well as "hardship relief" provisions which allow certain landlords the right to increase rents even if they exceed the law's stated reasonable rate of return. Lastly, some argue that shelter is a basic human right that trumps a landlord's right to charge high rents even if the market allows it.

Opponents claim that rent control laws are a very poor means of allocating housing space. For example, they reduce housing quality since landlords are loath to put more money into these properties when their return on investment is so low. Moreover, these laws discourage the quantity of new housing since developers will not be able to charge what is necessary to make a profit. Opponents further argue that, although rent control laws might help some renters, many more are not covered, such as those who move into previously rent-controlled properties and who now must pay market rents. Ironically, the rent charged in these situations is also higher due to the economic distortions caused by rent control laws. Thus, it is not fair to all renters. Finally, opponents assert that the local agencies which oversee rent control laws are inept, inefficient, and often manipulated by opportunistic politicians. Are rent control laws an ethical public policy? What are your views?

The residential landlord typically collects monthly rent from her tenants; and she pays ad valorem real estate taxes, property and liability insurance, and maintenance from the rent. This is called a "gross lease." The commercial landlord's practices vary significantly, but the commercial leases used most often are "complete net," "triple net," and "bond leases." A commercial tenant would typically pay its share of ad valorem real property taxes, common area maintenance, and insurance in addition to rent. Leases for retail space often require that the store pay "percentage rent," a percentage of sales above a certain floor, or "breakpoint." Percentage rent allows the landlord to share in the tenant's success in its mall or shopping center and allows the tenant to pay a lower rental fee until its sales reach a predetermined level.

Many brick-and-mortar retail tenants, due in part to competition by Amazon.com and other online businesses, are developing web sites to sell online to complement their in-store sales. But this new development sometimes interferes with the landlord's ability to collect what he is owed under a percentage rent approach. For example, assume that Amy visits a store and sees a dress that she likes, but it is not the right color. Amy can access the store's web site while she is at the store to find the color she wants. However, since Amy technically bought the dress in cyberspace instead of in physical space, the store is not credited for the sale and the landlord loses money if rent is based on a percentage basis. In response, some commercial landlords, using the percentage-rent method, are now using so-called "wired leases" with tenants to capture some of the rent they would otherwise lose. Other landlords, such as the Saint Louis Galleria Mall in Missouri, prohibit their tenants from exhibiting "signs, insignias, decals or other advertising or display devices which promote and encourage the purchases of merchandise via e-commerce."[45]

Security Deposit

security deposit
Money deposited by a tenant with a landlord as security for the performance of the lease.

The landlord commonly requires a tenant to make an additional advance payment—called a **security deposit**—to cover the tenant's liability for unpaid rent, unpaid utility bills, or damage to the premises. Many state statutes, several of which cover residential leases only, regulate security deposits. Although the statutes are not identical, they have several features in common. *First*, statutes define the security deposit (for instance, as any amount that must be paid in advance apart from the actual rent) and limit the amount of the deposit, often to one month's rent. *Second*, statutes limit the landlord's use of the security deposit. In some states, the deposit cannot be used to reimburse the landlord for ordinary wear and tear that may be reasonably expected in the normal course of apartment living.

Third, legislation limits the landlord in his interim use of the deposit; the landlord may have to post bond to cover the deposit or place the deposit in a special bank account and pay interest on the deposit to the tenant. *Finally*, statutes prescribe the procedure for returning a security deposit. In some states, a landlord must mail a claim for damages to the tenant within a specified period or else waive the right to damages. Also, in many states, the landlord has the burden of bringing suit to justify retention of the security deposit. Often these statutes impose strict procedural duties on landlords. The next Indiana case discusses whether a tenant's procedural requirements under security deposit statutes should also be strictly construed.

A CASE IN POINT

In *Lae v. Householder*,[46] the tenants vacated the premises but waited 47 days to mail a written request for the return of their security deposit. Under Indiana's security deposit statute, the tenant must make the request within 45 days, after which the landlord has a legal duty to submit an itemized list of damages and a check for the net balance. The appeals court ruled in favor of the

continues

continued landlord, holding that the tenants failed to comply with the statute's explicit requirement. The Indiana Supreme Court overruled the appeals court, arguing that the primary purpose of the statute is to equalize a bargaining position between tenants and landlords that is often unbalanced in the landlord's favor. Therefore, even though the tenants were two days late in making their request, the landlord still owed the duty to submit a list of damages and a check for the balance. The court emphasized that the notice requirement is primarily to inform the tenant of his responsibilities so that the landlord does not wrongfully withhold the deposit.

The *Lae* case demonstrates how courts sometimes look at the overall purpose of a statute instead of strictly adhering to the statute's plain meaning and text. Other courts in this situation might be inclined to adhere strictly to the statutory requirement even if it does create a hardship on tenants. The different ways that courts interpret statutes are discussed in Chapter 1.

Suggested Lease Provisions

A number of provisions, even if not required by law, should be included in the lease to avoid expensive, time-consuming litigation. The issues most likely to cause a dispute are discussed next and may be grouped into *three* categories:

- *The condition of the premises*
- *The tenant's use of the property*
- *The transfer of lease interests*

unconscionable contract
A contract so one-sided as to be oppressive and unfair.

contract of adhesion
A contract in which one party is in a superior bargaining position and the other party has no realistic opportunity to bargain over the terms.

In most cases, the three provisions listed above can be changed by the lease terms. However, the ability to alter legal rights and duties by contract is sometimes restricted by the doctrine of unconscionability. An **unconscionable contract** or provision is unfair to one of the parties who is in a weak bargaining position. A contract between a party in a strong position (who can dictate the contract terms on a take-it-or-leave-it basis) and a weaker party (who needs the subject matter of the contract) is termed a **contract of adhesion**. These doctrines are generally used successfully only by residential tenants, since commercial tenants are presumed to be more sophisticated in such matters and have a better bargaining position as the next case from New York reveals.

A CASE IN POINT

In *Weidman v. Tomaselli*,[47] a clause in an apartment lease provided that if the tenant breached the lease agreement, he would pay additional rent of $100 to cover the attorney's fees and court costs incurred by the landlord. When the tenant later breached the agreement and the landlord brought suit for the $100, the court listed the requirements of an adhesion contract: "A contract of adhesion is a contract in relation to a necessity of life, drafted by or for the benefit of a party for that party's excessive benefit, which party uses its economic or other advantage to offer the contract in its entirety solely for acceptance or rejection by the offeree. Thus, the elements of a contract of adhesion are (1) a necessity of life; (2) a contract for the excessive benefit of the offeror; (3) an economic or other advantage of the offeror; and (4) the offer of the proposed contract on a take-it-or-leave-it basis."

The court decided that this lease was an adhesion contract with an unconscionable clause and refused to enforce the clause. According to the court: "Given the overwhelming need for housing, the respondents must do exactly as the petitioner demands, or shelter will be denied. Had the petitioner demanded that the respondents fall to their knees and grovel before him, the respondents perforce

continues

continued would have swallowed their pride and done so, or be condemned to remain outside, never to come in from the cold. Here, the petitioner demanded that the respondents grovel not physically, but legally. The petitioner's unbargainable price is that the respondents agree to clause after clause of terms to the excessive benefit of the petitioner."

Condition of Premises

Beginning on September 1, Derek leased a building to Amy for one year. After Amy took possession of the property, she discovered that she could not use the building because the plumbing needed repair. Who has the duty to repair the plumbing, Derek or Amy? The answer to this question often depends on whether the plumbing was defective when the lease was made on September 1 or became defective after Amy took possession.

Conditions Existing When Lease Was Made The traditional rule applied to the sale of property generally and to leases in particular is **caveat emptor**, or "let the buyer beware." In lease cases, the rule was based on the assumption that the tenant could inspect the premises and discover any problems, such as defective plumbing, before signing the lease. If the tenant refused to make the inspection or decided to rent the property despite the defect, the tenant could not later force the landlord to correct the defect unless the lease specifically imposed that duty on the landlord.

A major exception to the traditional rule has developed in recent years as a result of state statutes and cases involving primarily the lease of residential property, called the **implied warranty of habitability**, also discussed in more detail below. Under this exception to the rule of caveat emptor, the landlord must provide premises that are suitable for residential use even when the lease does not impose the duty on the landlord.[48] In particular, the landlord must fix latent (hidden) defects (see Chapter 7), although the courts are currently split on whether the tenant becomes responsible for patent (obvious) defects since tenants have the right to inspect the premises before signing the lease. As observed by a Washington D.C. court, the typical tenant lacks the skill to make repairs and enters into the lease expecting "a well-known package of goods and services."[49] In the following Hawaii case, the court discusses why the implied covenant of habitability is necessary for protecting tenants.

---

caveat emptor

"Let the buyer beware." Requires tenants to examine and judge the quality of the premises on their own.

implied warranty of habitability

An implied promise by a landlord that the premises are fit for habitation.

A CASE IN POINT

In *Lemle v. Breeden*,[50] Lemle rented a home in Honolulu from Breeden. Shortly after moving into the apartment, Lemle realized that there were rats in the home. Before vacating the premises, Lemle and his family spent three nights camped in the living room, unable to sleep because they were worried about the rats. They could hear the rats scurrying across the roof, and the rats could enter the house through various openings.

The court held that Lemle was entitled to recover an advance payment of rent and his security deposit because the landlord had breached an implied warranty of habitability: "The application of an implied warranty of habitability in leases gives recognition to the changes in leasing transactions today. It affirms the fact that a lease is, in essence, a sale as well as a transfer of an estate in land and is, more importantly, a contractual relationship. From that contractual relationship an implied warranty of habitability and fitness for the purposes intended is a just and necessary implication. It is a doctrine which has its counterparts in the law of sales and torts and one which when candidly countenanced is impelled by the nature of the transaction and contemporary housing realities. Legal fictions and artificial exceptions to wooden rules of property law aside, we hold that in the lease of a dwelling house, such as in this case, there is an implied warranty of habitability and fitness for the use intended."

One issue that arises with the implied warranty of habitability is whether a residential tenant can waive it. The states are split on this issue. Many states have deemed the waivers unenforceable as a violation of public policy. This is also the position taken by the URLTA used in about 15 states (see endnote 34 for a list of states that apply the URLTA). A number of states take a more ad hoc approach. For example, they generally do not allow the waiver if it is contained in a standard form (boilerplate) lease agreement frequently used in residential leasing practices. If it is not in a boilerplate lease, courts look at such factors as the parties' bargaining positions, the nature of the negotiations, and whether a lawyer represented the tenant to determine whether the waiver is unconscionable or part of a contract of adhesion, discussed earlier.

Conditions Arising after Tenant Takes Possession   At common law, the tenant assumed any risks that arose after she took possession on the theory that these risks should fall on the party in possession of the property. Thus, if a tornado destroyed the building that Amy leased from Derek, Amy would still be liable for rent for the remainder of the lease term since the tenancy was considered primarily a lease of the land rather than of the building.[51]

The common law duty to pay rent no longer applies in many states when the premises are destroyed by a natural force.[52] More importantly, the landlord bears the risk of changed conditions if he has a duty to keep the premises in repair, a duty that has increasingly been imposed on the landlord. The nature of that duty is examined next.

The Duty to Repair   At common law, the landlord, who had no right to enter the leased premises, had no duty to make repairs on the property. The tenant also had no duty to make major repairs but was required to make "tenantable repairs" to prevent waste. These were described in the New York case of *Suydam v. Jackson*:[53]

> *At common law the lessor was, without express covenant to that effect, under no obligation to repair, and if the demised premises became, during the term, wholly untenantable by destruction thereof by fire, flood, tempest or otherwise, the lessee still remained liable for the rent unless exempted from such liability by some express covenant in his lease. But the lessee was under an implied covenant, from his relation to his landlord, to make what are called "tenantable repairs." ... The lessee was not bound to make substantial, lasting or general repairs, but only such ordinary repairs as were necessary to prevent waste and decay of the premises. If a window in a dwelling should blow in, the tenant could not permit it to remain out and the storms to beat in and greatly injure the premises without liability for permissive waste; and if a shingle or board on the roof should blow off or become out of repair, the tenant could not permit the water, in time of rain, to flood the premises, and thus injure them, without a similar liability. He being present, a slight effort and expense on his part could save a great loss; and hence the law justly casts the burden upon him.*

The common law rule has been altered in recent years by statutes and case law involving residential leases. Under the modern approach, the landlord is responsible for keeping the property in the condition required by housing codes. Many states go further and require the landlord to repair defects that make the apartment uncomfortable, even when there is no building code violation. The underlying theory is that a landlord gives an implied warranty of habitability, discussed earlier; that is, the landlord promises that the apartment will be fit for residential use. This implied warranty is the logical consequence of modern living patterns since tenants generally lack the skills to inspect the property effectively or to make repairs and must rely on the landlord's assurances that the premises are habitable.[54] Some variation of this doctrine has been adopted in all the states. In the next Utah case, the court ruled on whether the tenant must still pay rent when the implied warranty of habitability is breached.

A CASE IN POINT

In *Wade v. Jobe,* Lynda Jobe discovered numerous defects in the home she rented from Clyde Wade, including accumulated sewage and a foul odor. After the city inspector declared the premises unsafe for human occupancy, Jobe vacated the home and refused to pay the rent owed. When Wade sued, Jobe counterclaimed, arguing she did not owe the rent because Wade breached the implied warranty of habitability. The court remanded the case to the trial court stating that "[I]f the trial court determines that he [Wade] was not in breach, the landlord will be entitled to payment for all the past due rent. If the trial court determines that his breach of the warranty of habitability totally excused the tenant's rent obligation (i.e., rendered the premises virtually uninhabitable), the landlord's action to recover rent due will fail."[55]

There may be limitations to the landlord's implied duty to keep the premises repaired, such as when a tenant, a third party, or a natural force has caused the condition. The landlord also has no duty to make minor repairs to conditions that do not make the apartment unlivable or do not constitute a substantial violation of the housing code.[56] Furthermore, the tenant must notify the landlord of the changed conditions and give the landlord a reasonable time to make corrections.[57] Although a breach of building code requirements can be an easily ascertained violation of the implied warranty of habitability, other conditions may require a careful assessment of the facts. As stated earlier, the tenant cannot easily waive the implied warranty of habitability unless a defect is clearly disclosed to the tenant.[58]

A few states, such as Texas and New Jersey, also recognize an **implied warranty of suitability**, an extension to commercial property of what the implied warranty of habitability is to residential property. The landlord impliedly warrants that facilities essential to the use of the commercial premises are free from latent defects and will remain in suitable condition. This implied warranty can typically be waived by commercial tenants, unlike its residential equivalent. In the next Texas case, the court discusses this implied warranty.

> **implied warranty of suitability**
> An implied promise by a commercial landlord that facilities essential to the use of the commercial premises are free from latent defects and will remain in suitable condition.

Can the implied warranty of suitability be waived when the commercial tenant signs a lease that contains an as-is clause? In *Gym-N-I Playgrounds, Inc. v. Snider* on page 453, the court ruled on this issue.

END OF CHAPTER CASE

Lease Provisions The preceding rules governing conditions in existence when the lease was made and arising after the tenant takes possession apply only in the absence of a lease term that specifically addresses the issue. In other words, the landlord and tenant may rewrite these rules and establish their own list of rights and duties. However, a residential lease provision that is unconscionable or that violates public policy is not enforced. Thus, if a tenant lives in a city where there are very few residential apartments available and a landlord offers a lease to the tenant containing a waiver of the implied warranty of habitability on a take-it-or-leave-it basis, it is unlikely that a court would enforce the waiver even in a state that may allow waivers in general, as discussed above.[59] One common lease provision is a "no pets" clause created to protect the landlord's carpeting, furniture, and other property. However, in certain instances, even these can violate public policy as the next Wisconsin case reveals.

A CASE IN POINT

In *Bronk v. Ineichen*,[60] two deaf tenants vacated their apartment after a contentious confrontation with their landlord in which the landlord refused to let them keep their dog. The tenants claimed that the dog was a "hearing dog" trained to alert his masters to the ringing of doorbells, telephone, and smoke alarms and to carry notes. The court ruled that the landlord's refusal to reasonably accommodate the disabled tenants in his "rules, policies, practices, or services when such accommodations may be necessary to afford such person equal opportunity to use and enjoy a dwelling" violates the Fair Housing Act.

Lease provisions altering the duties imposed by law should be drafted with great care. For example, a tenant might make a general promise in the lease to keep the property repaired or to leave it in the condition it was in when she took possession. If the property is destroyed by a trespasser or by a natural cause such as a hurricane, a court applying the traditional view of landlord-tenant relationships might hold the tenant responsible for rebuilding or repairing the property.[61]

Tenant's Use of Property

No Lease Provision   In the absence of a lease provision restricting use, the tenant may use the property for any legal purpose consistent with the nature of the property or the intentions of the parties. One contentious issue is whether a landlord can prevent his unmarried tenant from coinhabiting, as the next case from New York discusses.

A CASE IN POINT

In *Edwards v. Roe*,[62] a landlord tried to evict an unmarried female tenant on the grounds that she was using the apartment to engage in sexual intercourse with a male friend. The court held that the tenant was not acting illegally because, since this was not a commercial activity, she was not engaged in prostitution and because New York law does not proscribe normal sexual intercourse between unmarried consenting adults. The court also held that the tenant could not be evicted under a statute allowing eviction when the apartment is used for immoral purposes: "If the test be personal to me, I hold that, without a showing—and there is none—that she has harmed anyone, respondent has done nothing immoral. And if the test be the response of the 'ordinary' or 'average' man or woman, assuming that it makes sense to posit the existence of such a person, I hold that, given the ethical standards of the day, respondent has done nothing immoral."

For the reasons stated in *Edwards*, only a handful of states now have laws prohibiting opposite-sex couples from living together, and those that do seldom enforce the laws.[63] Moreover, as discussed earlier, landlords also cannot initially refuse to lease to unmarried couples under most state laws. The following section discusses the ethical issues of whether gay and lesbian couples also have rights to live together.

ETHICAL AND PUBLIC POLICY ISSUES

Is It an Unethical Issue and a Violation of Public Policy for Landlords to Evict Gay and Lesbian Tenants for Behavior That Violates the Landlord's Personal and Religious Views?

In Problem 10 at the end of the chapter, the issue is discussed.

The tenant's right to make physical changes is typically addressed in the lease. When a lease contemplated "erections and additions," for example, the tenant's alterations that enlarged a gas station and probably increased its value were not waste and did not breach the lease.[64] If the lease is silent, the tenant can generally make physical changes to enhance the use of the property but may not make structural alterations, even when the alterations increase the value of the real estate. For example, if a tenant has leased a building for use as a coffee shop, she could install a counter and stoves but could not tear down or build partitions on the property. The rule against alterations has been criticized in recent years; and it is likely that in the future, more courts will allow alterations that are necessary for the tenant to make reasonable use of the property.[65] Moreover, as discussed earlier, as well as in Chapter 6, under the FHA, disabled tenants must be allowed to build wheelchair ramps, although the tenant can be required to pay for the restoration of the property to its former condition when he leaves.

The FHA policy reflects a more broadly recognized legal principle. A tenant who has made physical changes in the property must restore the property to its original condition when possible. (Domestic fixtures were discussed at greater length in Chapter 2.) However, the tenant is not responsible for changes due to normal wear and tear that result from reasonable use of the property. Consequently, the tenant would not be responsible for refinishing wooden floors that had become scuffed through the tenant's normal use but would have to repair damage caused by using skateboards on the floors.[66]

Lease Provisions   The parties to a lease can, and usually should, insert a clause in the lease specifying the proposed use of the property as the following New York case explains.

A CASE IN POINT

In *Lyon v. Bethlehem Engineering Corp.*,[67] the lease limited the use of the building to "the following purposes, and those only: Restaurant, stores, store-rooms and offices ... and sales-rooms." The tenant allowed Roxy Theatres Corporation to attach an electric sign forty feet tall and sixty feet long on the roof of the building. The court, in holding that this use violated the lease, observed that a tenant "in the absence of restrictions contained in a lease, may use a leased building in any lawful way not materially different from that to which it is adapted, and for which it was constructed. The right to exclusive occupation granted by a lease entitles a tenant to use the premises in the same manner that the owner might have used them.... The landlord may, however, by express provisions in a lease, limit and restrict the use of a building to specific purposes. He has a legal right to control the uses to which his building may be put and may do so by appropriate provisions in a lease."

In lease provisions restricting use, often the key word is *only*. If the lease provision states that the property is to be used for a billiards hall but omits the word *only*, the tenant is free to make other uses of the property. If the landlord decides to restrict the use of the property "for a billiards hall only," the tenant may use the property only for billiards and related purposes. For instance, the tenant could not use the premises as a pancake shop. The tenant could sell and rent cue sticks because this would be related to the permitted use. As discussed shortly, if the lease provision limits the tenant to only one use and the use becomes illegal, the lease is invalid.

Frequently, a lease clause provides that a commercial tenant may not use the premises in a manner that competes with the landlord's business. Alternatively, the lease might provide that the landlord will not compete with the tenant in using or leasing property. For example, if a tenant rented space in a shopping mall for a natural food store under a long-term lease, the tenant might insist on such a clause to prevent the landlord from renting space to competing natural food stores. Are promises by the landlord or tenant not to compete with the other's business legal? There are *two* views. In many states, the promises are valid, although they must be limited in scope to protection of the other party's interests.[68] In other states, the promises are unenforceable, often because of state antitrust statutes.

In residential leases, it is common to insert a lease provision in which tenants are banned from "any nuisance, any offensive noise, odor or fumes; or any hazard to health." In a recent and potentially far-reaching case in Boston, a couple who were heavy smokers was successfully evicted because other tenants complained that the secondhand smoke infiltrated the apartment's ventilation system, causing health threats.[69]

Interference with Use   Once the tenant's use has been established by law or by the lease, the tenant has the right to use the property without interference. Interference with use might come from three sources:

- *Interference from the landlord*
- *Interference from outsiders*
- *Interference from the government*

Interference by Landlord   Interference by the landlord may be *passive* or *active*. Passive interference occurs when, as previously discussed, the landlord fails to meet her duty to keep the property in good condition, thus making it unusable. Active interference occurs when the landlord or someone under her control interferes with the tenant's use of the property. For example, in an apartment complex with a swimming pool, since the landlord retains control of common areas such as the pool, the landlord might interfere with the tenant's use of the apartment by throwing wild poolside parties late at night or by failing to prevent other tenants from hosting late-night poolside parties.

The landlord is liable whether the interference is passive or active and whether it is caused by the landlord directly or by individuals under the landlord's control. The courts usually reason that the landlord gives the tenant an implied **covenant of quiet enjoyment**; this promise is breached when there is landlord-related interference with the tenant's quiet enjoyment of the property. As discussed shortly, a tenant who is forced to leave the premises as a result of the landlord's breach—a constructive eviction—is no longer liable for rent.

Interference by Outsiders   Two types of outsiders can interfere with the tenant's use of the property. The *first* type is an outsider with a legal interest superior to that of the tenant. For example, a landlord mortgaged a home to First Bank to finance its purchase. After the mortgage was recorded, the landlord leased the house to a tenant for a term of

covenant of quiet enjoyment

An assurance by the landlord that she will not interfere with the tenant's use of the property.

three years. In this case, First Bank's prior recorded interest is superior to the tenant's leasehold interest; if First Bank foreclosed on the mortgage, it could evict the tenant. The landlord would be liable if the tenant was evicted—that is, when a third party (here First Bank) interfered with the tenant's use (that is, quiet enjoyment) of the property.[70] But if the landlord gave the mortgage to the bank *after* the lease was signed and recorded, the bank's interest would be inferior to that of the tenant and the bank could not evict the tenant on foreclosure.

Interference of a tenant's rights by a landlord's mortgagee emerged as a particularly important issue during the Great Recession of 2007–2009. When large numbers of landlords defaulted on their mortgage notes, tenants were quickly evicted by their landlords' mortgagees after the foreclosure sale. Many of these tenants were not even aware that their landlords had defaulted and continued paying their rents while the landlords, who had stopped paying their mortgagees, sometimes for months, pocketed the rents. In response, the federal government and some states passed statutes giving such tenants new rights. Under the federal law, a part of the Helping Families Save Their Homes Act of 2009, mortgagees holding a federally-related mortgage loan must allow tenants to continue occupying their residential properties for the term left on the lease, even if it extends after the foreclosure sale, and it further states that tenants can only be evicted for good cause. Tenants must also be given a 90-day notice if the mortgagee intends not to renew the lease once the tenancy ends. This law expires at the end of 2012.

Commercial tenants frequently enter into **Subordination, Nondisturbance and Attornment Agreements** with the lender. In these agreements, the tenant agrees to subordinate the lease to the lien of the lender's security instrument and to "attorn to," or acknowledge, a lender who assumes the role of landlord through foreclosure; in turn, the lender agrees not to disturb the tenant's quiet enjoyment under the lease.

The *other* type of outsider is one with no legal interest in the property or with an interest inferior to that of the tenant. If this type of outsider interferes with the tenant's use, the tenant, as "owner" for the term of the lease, must take action directly against the outsider and cannot hold the landlord liable. Many courts hold that this rule applies even when the tenant initially attempts to take possession of the property. For instance, generally if the tenant is to take possession under a one-year lease beginning September 1 and the previous tenant wrongfully refuses to leave the apartment, these courts will require the tenant to commence proceedings to remove the wrongdoer.[71] However, other courts have adopted the "English rule," which places the duty to remove holdover tenants on the landlord.[72]

Interference by Government   A tenant is not liable when a lease restricts her to a particular purpose and that purpose becomes illegal as the result of government action. Thus, a tenant would not be liable when a lease provides that property is to be used "as a retail liquor store only" if the state or federal government later enacts legislation (for example, the Volstead Act) making it illegal to sell liquor.

A more difficult question arises when government action causes the tenant's business to become unprofitable even though the tenant can continue its use. Under the contract law doctrine of **frustration of purpose**, if an unforeseeable event defeats the purpose of the contract even though performance is still physically and legally possible, the parties will be excused from performance.

This rule originated in the "Coronation Cases." Several people rented rooms to watch a procession scheduled in connection with the coronation of Edward VII. When the king became ill, the procession was canceled and the renters claimed they were no longer liable on their contracts. In the resulting litigation, the court held that performance of the contracts was excused because the reason for making them had been destroyed.

Subordination, Nondisturbance and Attornment Agreement

An acknowledgment by a tenant that the leasehold interest is lower in priority than the lien placed by the landlord's mortgagee in exchange for the mortgagee agreeing not to disturb the tenant's occupancy under the lease.

---

frustration of purpose

A defense to the performance of a contract when the objectives of the contract have been defeated by unforeseen circumstances arising after the formation of the agreement.

In the United States, although there is some authority to the contrary, courts have been reluctant to apply the frustration of purpose doctrine to leases. Moreover, in many commercial leases, it is not uncommon to see a "Hell or High Water" clause which states that the tenant must pay no matter what happens. These clauses neutralize the contractual and lease defenses of frustration of purpose and impossibility of performance and are, between commercial parties, generally enforceable.

Transfer of Leasehold Interests

assignment

The lessee's transfer of the entire unexpired remainder of the lease term to the sublessee.

Assignee's Rights and Duties   Either the landlord or the tenant may assign his entire interest in the leasehold to a third party—the assignee. The effect of an **assignment** is that the assignee steps into the shoes of the party who has made the assignment and takes over the rights and duties of the assignor. (See Figure 11.2.) For the tenant's assignee, this includes paying the rent directly to the landlord as the following Tennessee case reveals.

A CASE IN POINT

In *Ernst v. Conditt,*[73] Ernst leased a tract of land to Rogers, who used the property to operate a go-cart track. Rogers, the lessee, later assigned the lease to Conditt. Conditt took possession of the property but refused to pay rent to Ernst claiming that it was a sublease transaction, not an assignment. When Ernst brought suit, the court decided that Conditt, as an assignee, took over both the rights and the duties of Rogers.

It is noteworthy that the court in *Ersnt* would have reached the same conclusion if the landlord, Ernst, had sold his reversionary interest to a third party who then would have sued Conditt; the third party would take over the rights of Ernst (for example, the right to collect rent) but would also be liable for the duties imposed by the lease agreement or by law (for example, a duty in the lease to keep the go-cart track repaired).

In stepping into the assignor's shoes, the assignee acquires no greater rights than the assignor possessed and takes the rights subject to any defense that could be raised by the other party to the contract. Thus, in *Ernst,* Conditt, the assignee, would have the

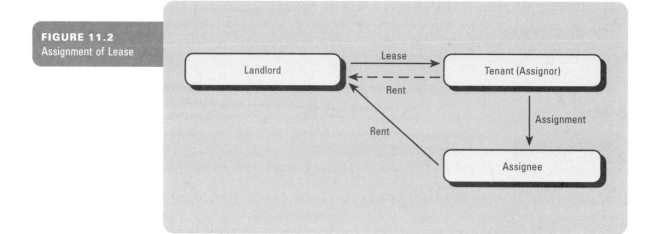

FIGURE 11.2
Assignment of Lease

same rights conferred to Rogers, his assignor, under the lease agreement, as well as any legal defenses that Rogers had.

In the next case, a New Jersey court addresses the issue of the rights an assignee has in the assignment of a lease.

A CASE IN POINT

In *Martinique Realty Corp. v. Hull,*[74] the landlord owned a fifty-five-unit apartment building in Passaic, New Jersey. One of the tenants leased an apartment for a five-year term and prepaid over $8,400 of the agreed rent. The landlord later sold the property to a third party, who was unaware that the tenant had prepaid the rent. When the new owner sued the tenant for failing to make monthly rental payments, the court held that the tenant was not liable: "This is but an illustration of the general rule that the assignee of a contract right takes subject to all defenses valid against his assignor.... It is long settled that the purchaser of a lessor's interest in property has a duty to make inquiry as to the extent of the rights of any person in open, notorious and exclusive possession of the premises; if the duty is not discharged, then notice is imputed to the purchaser of all facts which a reasonably prudent inquiry would have revealed."

Assignor's Rights and Duties   A landlord or tenant who assigns leasehold rights to a third party remains obligated to perform the lease duties if the third party defaults. Thus, in the *Ernst* case previously discussed, if the landlord could not collect the rent from the assignee, Conditt, he could collect from the original tenant, Rogers.

There are *two* exceptions to the rule that the assignor remains liable on the lease obligations. *First*, the assignor is not liable when the other party to the lease agrees to release the assignor from liability and to accept the assignee in her place. This is called a **novation.** For instance, say Tom, a tenant, assigns his lease interest to Andy, the assignee. If the landlord, Linda, plus Tom and Andy all agree to a novation releasing Tom, he would no longer be liable for the lease obligations. *Second*, once an assignment has been made, the assignor remains liable only for promises made in the lease but is *not* liable for obligations imposed by law. Thus, in the above example, even without a novation, Tom would no longer be bound to adhere to any legal obligations, only contractual duties. Similarly, in many cases, even when a landlord, such as Linda, does not expressly promise to keep the property in good repair, the obligation to do so under the implied warranty of habitability is imposed by law. Thus, if Linda, the landlord, sells or assigns her interest to a third party, George, the general rule is that the Linda's legal duty as the landlord to keep the property repaired ceases *unless* she had already breached her obligation to repair at the time of sale. In either case, however, George, the assignee, would now be legally obligated to make the repairs.[75]

Sublease   An assignment should be distinguished from a sublease. With an assignment, the tenant transfers the entire interest to a third party. With a **sublease**, the tenant transfers *only a part* of the leasehold estate. For example, the tenant might transfer only a part of the remaining lease term (one year of the remaining two years) or only a part of the property (two rooms out of five), although some courts consider an assignment of a portion of the premises a partial assignment rather than a sublease. In subleasing the property, the tenant has carved a new leasehold estate out of the original leasehold. The rights and duties of the subtenant are governed by the agreement between the tenant and subtenant; the subtenant does not step into the shoes of the tenant under the original lease because, unlike in an assignment, he is not taking the leasehold estate created by

novation

The substitution by mutual agreement of one debtor for another whereby the original debtor's obligation is extinguished.

sublease

A grant by a tenant of an interest in leased property less than she possesses.

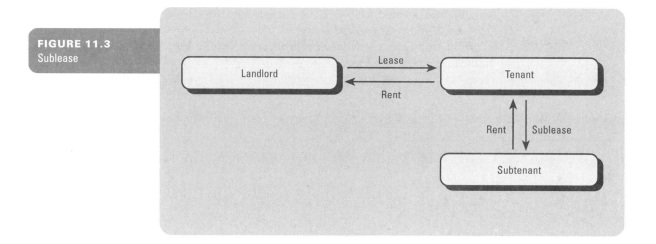

FIGURE 11.3
Sublease

that lease. The original tenant remains liable to the landlord under the original lease but would receive the rent from the subtenant. (See Figure 11.3.)

For example, college students commonly sublease their apartments without fully understanding the legal consequences. Assume that Sam, a student at Midwest U, leases an apartment close to campus. Later Tom moves in and occupies Sam's apartment for the duration of a summer session. If Tom fails to pay Sam his portion of the rent, Sam must still pay the full rent to the landlord. Sam's only recourse is to pursue Tom, the subtenant, for the rent he owes Sam.

Consider the *Ernst* case again on page 436, for an illustration of the practical ramifications of the distinction between an assignment and a sublease.

A CASE IN POINT

Ernst, the landlord, sued the third party, Conditt, for unpaid rent. When the original tenant transferred his interest to Conditt, he used the language "I hereby sublet" to Conditt. In the lawsuit, Conditt's defense was that as a subtenant rather than an assignee, he did not take over the duties of the original tenant under the lease and therefore was not liable to the landlord for rent. The court held that regardless of what the parties called the transfer, this was in reality an assignment and that Conditt was liable. In reaching this decision, the court cited earlier authority to the effect that if "the instrument purports to transfer the lessee's estate for the entire remainder of his term it is an assignment, regardless of its form or of the parties' intention. Conversely, if the instrument purports to transfer the lessee's estate for less than the entire term—even for a day less—it is a sublease, regardless of its form or of the parties' intention."

The distinction between an assignment and a sublease also is important when the tenant holds the property under a tenancy at will. Generally, a tenancy at will exists only as long as the landlord and tenant want it to continue; most courts hold that by transferring his interest, whether by assignment or sublease, the tenant has shown that he no longer wants the estate to continue and thereby terminates the lease.

Lease Clauses Prohibiting Assignments and Subleases A landlord commonly inserts a clause in the lease prohibiting assignments or subleases. While such clauses are generally valid, courts try whenever possible to interpret them narrowly because the law favors the ability to transfer property freely. For example, if a lease states only that the tenant may not sublease an apartment, the clause would not prevent the tenant from assigning the lease because an assignment is different from a sublease. In addition, a tenant could allow a *licensee* to use the property even though the lease prohibits assignment and subleasing.

Leases also commonly provide that the tenant may not assign or sublease her interest without the landlord's consent. Most courts hold that under such clauses, landlords may refuse consent even when the refusal is unreasonable and even seek damages and injunctive relief against the tenant. But several courts have decided that the landlord may not withhold consent unless she has a "fair, solid and substantial cause or reason."[76] For example, when a clause provided that the landlord could not unreasonably withhold consent, a Missouri court held that the landlord was being unreasonable when refusing consent without seeing the sublease.[77] In the following Louisiana case, a court ruled on a similar issue.

Was a commercial landlord unreasonable in withholding consent from its tenant to sublet to another commercial tenant? In *Tenet HealthSystem Surgical, L.L.C. v. Jefferson Parish Hospital Service District No. 1* on page 455, the court addresses the issue.

END OF CHAPTER CASE

As a result of increasing acceptance of the minority view, it is likely that approval clauses will more frequently be worded to give landlords an absolute right to withhold consent, although tenants, particularly commercial tenants with a good bargaining position, will attempt to temper these clauses in their favor.[78] One reason commercial landlords bargain for the right to withhold consent is to prevent an undesirable tenant mix. For example, a lessee assigning or subletting to a busy government agency, such as the office of social welfare, in a building of professionals can cause friction and problems among the tenants, as well as take up valuable parking spots.[79]

Remedies

Tenant's Remedies

remedy
The means by which a right is enforced or the violation of a right is prevented, redressed, or compensated.

A tenant has several **remedies** available when there has been interference with his leasehold rights. The remedies vary considerably depending on the nature of the interference, yet most of them fall into *three* broad categories:

- *Termination of the Lease*
- *Damages*
- *Rent-related remedies*

The first two categories—the tenant's termination of the lease and damages from the landlord—represent the tenant's traditional remedies. Rent-related remedies, such as rent withholding, rent application, and rent abatement, found in the third category, have become popular in recent years.

Termination of Lease When there has been interference with the tenant's leasehold rights, the tenant typically may terminate the lease by vacating the premises; after

constructive eviction

A substantial and injurious interference of the tenant's possession by the landlord or someone acting under his authority that renders the premises unfit for the purposes for which they were demised or that deprives the tenant of the beneficial enjoyment of the premises, causing him to abandon them, provided that the tenant abandons the premises within a reasonable time.

termination, the tenant is no longer obligated to pay rent. The tenant may terminate the lease in some cases even when the landlord is not at fault—for example, when a natural force such as a hurricane destroys the property or a governmental act makes the tenant's use of the property illegal.

In most cases, the termination results because the landlord breached duties arising under the lease or by law. This commonly occurs when the landlord's breach interferes with the tenant's use and enjoyment of the property to such an extent that the tenant is forced to leave the property and terminate the lease. The courts describe the landlord's breach as a **constructive eviction**[80] of the tenant; and as in the case of an actual eviction, the evicted tenant is relieved of the obligation to pay rent. Tenants, however, must vacate the premises quickly; otherwise, their continued presence is seen as a waiver of their rights. This can create hardships, particularly on residential tenants, who must find a new place to live quickly. The next Washington state case illustrates the doctrine for a commercial tenant.

A CASE IN POINT

In *Washington Chocolate Co. v. Kent*,[81] Washington Chocolate Company leased half a basement in a warehouse from Kent and used the property to store cocoa beans in burlap sacks. Kent retained control of the rest of the building. Government authorities later discovered that the beans stored in the basement were infested with rats. The company immediately notified Kent, who attempted to eliminate the rats but was unsuccessful. As a result, the government seized and destroyed 6,382 pounds of beans and the company abandoned the premises.

When the company sued Kent for the value of the beans and related expenses, such as expenses the government charged, Kent countersued for rental payments allegedly due. The court held that because Kent retained control of the building and the rats constituted a nuisance, Kent had breached the implied covenant of quiet enjoyment and was liable to the company for damages. Furthermore, because the company had been constructively evicted from the premises by the presence of rats, it was not liable for rent arising after it abandoned the property.

Damages   The *second* traditional remedy—damages—is available when the landlord has breached a duty imposed by the lease or by law. A tenant terminating a lease can also seek damages, as illustrated by the *Washington Chocolate Co.* decision discussed above. Alternatively, the tenant, as shown in the following New York case, may decide to sue for damages while continuing the lease.

A CASE IN POINT

In *Garcia v. Freeland Realty, Inc.*,[82] the tenant, Garcia, discovered that his children were eating paint and plaster that was flaking off the walls of his apartment. When the landlord refused to plaster and paint the walls, Garcia did the job himself and sued the landlord for the cost of supplies and labor. The court awarded damages after noting that "lead poisoning is limited mainly to the children of the poor in New York City; and that the eating of such plaster and paint flakes by children leads to lead poisoning with the consequences of mental retardation and death."

Rent-Related Remedies   The traditional remedies of lease termination and damages are often unsuitable, especially in cases involving a residential lease. Termination requires the tenant to move her family and belongings out of the home and to search for a new residence, which is a difficult task in areas where the occupancy rates are high. To collect damages, the tenant has the burden of commencing what might be a time-consuming and expensive legal proceeding.

Rent-related remedies, the *third* category, allow the tenant to use her only real leverage—rental payments—to correct a defect in the apartment or to force the landlord to fulfill his duties. In some states, rent-related remedies are not allowed; these states follow the historical view that a lease is a conveyance of an interest in real estate. Under the **independent covenants** approach, the promise to pay rent for that real estate is independent of other promises that might be given in the lease. Other states have rejected this historical approach, holding that in residential leases, the tenant's promise to pay rent is dependent on the landlord's meeting the lease obligations. As the court noted in the influential opinion from Washington D.C. of *Javins v. First National Realty Corp.*,[83] the traditional view

> *may have been reasonable in the rural, agrarian society; it may be continue to be reasonable in some leases involving farming or commercial land. In these cases, the value of the lease to the tenant is the land itself. But in the case of the modern apartment dweller, the value of the lease is that it gives him a place to live.... When American city dwellers, both rich and poor seek "shelter" today, they seek a well known package of goods and services—a package which includes not merely walls and ceilings, but also adequate heat, light and ventilation, serviceable plumbing facilities, secure windows and doors, proper sanitation, and proper maintenance.... In our judgment the trend toward treating leases as contracts is wise and well considered.... Since a lease contract specifies a particular period of time during which the tenant has a right to use his apartment for shelter, he may reasonably expect that the apartment will be fit for habitation for the time period for which it is rented.*

The modern dependent covenants approach, originally applied to residential tenants, has been extended in some states, such as in Massachusetts as demonstrated in the following case, to commercial leaseholds as well.

independent covenant
A promise that is not dependent on a reciprocal promise.

A CASE IN POINT

In *Wesson v. Leone Enterprises, Inc.*,[84] Leone Enterprises complained to Wesson, the landlord, that roof leaks were interfering with its business operations. When Wesson failed to repair the leaks, Leone notified the landlord that it was vacating the premises before the end of a five-year lease; Wesson then sued for back rent. Leone countersued for constructive eviction. On appeal, the Massachusetts Supreme Court ruled that a leaking roof was not severe enough or "untenantable" to constitute a constructive eviction. However, the court adopted the doctrine of "mutually dependent covenants" for commercial leaseholds, explaining that "[t]he rule ... is based on a logical extension of the position taken by a significant number of judicial decisions which have applied the [dependence of obligations] doctrine in connection with the failure of the landlord to fulfill his obligations in regard to the condition of the leased property.... It also reflects our view of the better reasoned path to follow in modernizing the law of commercial leases." Accordingly, the court ruled that Leone did not owe Wesson rent for the remainder of the lease term due to Leone's breach of its covenant to repair.

dependent covenant
A promise made in return for a reciprocal promise.

Three types of rent-related remedies have been developed in states following the modern **dependent covenants** approach: rent withholding, rent application, and rent abatement.[85]

Rent Withholding   Under several state statutes and court decisions, the tenant may withhold rent until the landlord fulfills her obligations. State laws are not uniform on the procedure that the tenant must follow. In some states, the tenant may retain the rent, while in other states, the tenant must deposit the rent in court or in an escrow account.

Rent Application   Under several state statutes, the tenant may use the rent to remedy the landlord's breach of duty. For example, a California statute provides that a tenant may, after notice to the landlord of a defect in the premises, repair the defect and apply up to one month's rent toward the repair.[86] The same result has been reached under a few city ordinances that require landlords to set aside a security deposit that could be used to keep the premises repaired.

Rent Abatement   Several state statutes allow a tenant to reduce her rent in certain situations. Massachusetts legislation, for instance, provides that if an apartment violates housing laws, the tenant has to pay only fair value for use of the property rather than the agreed rent.

A more drastic form of rent abatement has been reached in states using traditional remedies under the theory of **partial actual eviction**. This theory provides that if the landlord evicts the tenant from a part of the premises, the tenant owes no rent even if the tenant uses the rest of the property. Thus, if the tenant rents a house and lot and the landlord later refuses to allow the tenant to use the basement, the tenant can continue to use the house without paying rent.

partial actual eviction
Physically depriving a tenant of possession of a portion of the premises.

Landlord's Remedies

General Remedies   In addition to the landlord's rights against a holdover tenant (discussed previously with periodic tenancies), the landlord may, upon the tenant's default, use the traditional remedies of obtaining damages from the tenant and terminating the lease. A landlord, as well as other kinds of creditors seeking to collect debts, is often tempted to use **self-help** in enforcing these remedies; that is, the landlord might try to evict the tenant personally or seize and sell the tenant's property (which is called the **right of distress**). However, the landlord's ability to use self-help is limited by most states. A landlord who enters the property to evict a tenant will be held criminally liable under statutes prohibiting forcible entry that most states have adopted. The landlord who evicts a tenant also might be liable for damages if he commits an intentional tort, such as assault and battery. Some states, like New Hampshire, also have statutes which protect tenants who owe back rent from such self-help methods as cutting off a tenant's water and utilities, including even cable television.[87]

self-help
Acting independently of the courts.

right of distress
A right under the common law allowing the landlord to seize a tenant's goods to satisfy a debt for past rent.

What constitutes force under the forcible entry statutes varies from state to state, although it is clear, as declared in a classic case from North Carolina, that force has been used when a person, threatening and cursing the occupant, "kicked down the door, entered the house, and fell over something, by which his leg was unfortunately broken, instead of his neck."[88] Probably one of the most publicized incidents of self-help to regain property, although not in a landlord-tenant scenario, occurred in 2007, when O. J. Simpson attempted to recover sports memorabilia, soon to be displayed in a Las Vegas casino, that he claimed he owned. Simpson's threats that no one could leave the room, accompanied by armed accomplices, were caught on audio and video recordings. He was subsequently convicted of armed robbery and kidnapping and sentenced to 15 years in prison, with possible parole in nine years.

While obviously risky, self-help can generally be used more safely to oust a licensee since he has only a privilege and therefore not the rights of a tenant, although, as the next Washington D.C. case demonstrates, the difference between a tenant and a licensee is not always readily apparent.

A CASE IN POINT

In *Harkins v. Win Corporation*,[89] Harkins occupied a room in a hotel. He signed a hotel registration card and paid a weekly occupancy charge of $85. After Harkins fell into arrears and was warned that he would be removed from his room, management changed his locks and effectively dispossessed him of his room. Harkins filed a complaint stating that he was a tenant and not a roomer and so should have been evicted as a tenant under the law. The court stated that the "common law remedy of self-help to evict a roomer was still permissible, though no longer available to evict a tenant." The court explained that the following factors must be examined when distinguishing between a roomer and a tenant: "(1) whether the owner provided furnishings, linens, towels, and daily maid service to the occupant; (2) the owner's right to access the room; (3) the number of rooms provided; (4) the scheduled interval for payment (e.g., daily, weekly, monthly); (5) the substance of the contract between the owner and the occupant; and (6) any other conditions of occupancy." In this case, Harkins paid by the week, he was provided linens and maid service, and all of the furniture in his room was owned by management. Therefore, the court ruled that he was in fact a roomer and could be evicted by self-help methods.

Distress is often allowed under state statutes that authorize the landlord to seize and sell the tenant's property for unpaid rent. But such statutes have been declared unconstitutional when they allow seizure of the tenant's property without notice and an opportunity for a hearing.[90]

Although the landlord is limited in using self-help, most states allow her to bring an action to evict the tenant under a statute entitled (depending on the state) "Summary Proceedings," "Forcible Entry and Detainer," or "Action for Dispossession." Shortly after the landlord files a complaint pursuant to these statutes, the matter will be heard by the court; if the landlord prevails, the court will issue a writ ordering a local official to remove the tenant on a specified date, usually a few days after the hearing.

As discussed throughout this chapter, tenants are considered in breach of their leases for failing to pay rent, not maintaining the premises, and breaking the rules and obligations set out in the lease provisions. However, these grounds for eviction may be tempered by public policy under both state and federal laws. For instance, landlords in dwellings covered under the FHA have a duty to accommodate their disabled tenants in the tenants' ability to lease and use the dwelling. This has been construed by some courts as requiring a landlord to accommodate disabled tenants with pets (such as hearing or seeing eye dogs even if the lease has a "no pets clause") or mentally disabled and dangerous tenants.[91] The next case from Illinois discusses whether a landlord must accommodate a disabled tenant who was late in paying her rent.

A CASE IN POINT

In *Anast v. Commonwealth Apartments*,[92] Anast, the tenant, suffered from mental illness. After she fell several months behind in her rent due to hospitalization, the landlord evicted her, depositing her belongings on the street. After she was discharged from the hospital, she sued to regain

continues

continued

her apartment, arguing that her landlord must reasonably accommodate her disability by waiting for her to recover before demanding the rent. The court denied the landlord's motion to dismiss and ruled that although a landlord does not have to do everything that is "humanly possible to accommodate a disabled person," the Fair Housing Act requires a weighing of the costs to the landlord against the benefits to the disabled tenant.

Tenants who owe rent are sometimes pursued by collection agencies. However, tenants are protected under the Fair Debt Collection Practices Act (FDCPA). This means if a collection agency—which includes attorneys who regularly engage in debt collection—is as a New Jersey Court pointed out, "abusive, deceptive or unfair," the tenant may have a remedy, including damages and a cease-and-desist order.[93]

Abandonment A tenant's abandonment of the premises before the end of the lease term gives the landlord a choice of *three* options. Assume, for example, that Terri has leased an apartment from Sam for one year. After two months, Terri leaves the apartment and mails the keys to Sam. Terri's actions constitute an offer to surrender the premises to Sam and terminate the lease. Sam's *first* option is to accept the offer, thus relieving Terri from further liability for rent.

Sam's *second* option would be to do nothing, in which case Terri remains liable for the rent. However, in states in which the lease is considered to be more of a contract than a conveyance of an interest in real estate, the contract rule of **mitigation of damages** applies. Under this rule, the nonbreaching party to the contract—the landlord—must attempt to reduce damages by re-letting the premises to a new tenant. The reasons for adopting the mitigation rule were reviewed by a Nebraska court:

> *The traditional view is that a lease creates an interest or estate in land and, therefore, the lessor need not concern himself with a lessee's abandonment of his own property. A modern lease of a business building ordinarily involves multiple and mutual running covenants between lessor and lessee. It is difficult to find logical reasons sufficient to justify placing such leases in a category separate and distinct from other fields of the law that have forbidden a recovery for damages which the plaintiff by reasonable efforts could have avoided. The perpetuation of the distinction between such a lease and a contract, in the application of the principle of mitigation of damages, is no longer supportable. We, therefore, hold that a landlord may not unreasonably refuse to accept a qualified and suitable substitute tenant for the purpose of mitigating the damages recoverable from a tenant who has abandoned the leased premises prior to the expiration of the term.*[94]

Sam's *third* approach as a non-breaching landlord is to retake possession of the premises and attempt to mitigate damages voluntarily, even when the state does not require mitigation. This can be a risky practice for the landlord because, if the landlord fails to notify the tenant that he is taking possession and attempting to re-let the premises on the tenant's behalf, a court, such as the following California court, may treat the landlord's actions as an acceptance of the tenant's offer to surrender the property.

> *The landlord, upon an abandonment by the tenant, may retake possession of the premises on behalf of the tenant, re-let the premises for the tenant's account, and hold the tenant for the difference. If the landlord simply takes possession of the premises and re-lets them at a lower rent, such act is inconsistent with the absolute dominion of the tenant, and constitutes an acceptance of the implied offer to surrender, and terminates the lease. But if the landlord notifies the tenant that the retaking is on behalf of the*

mitigation of damages
A duty imposed on injured parties that requires them to attempt to minimize their damages.

tenant, and that he intends to sublet to another on behalf of the tenant to mitigate da-mages, the re-letting does not operate as an acceptance of the abandonment, and no surrender by operation of law results.... Normally, the notice must be given before the re-letting to allow the tenant to object or to make other arrangements if he so desires.[95]

When Crown Industries vacated its retail space before the end of the lease term, the landlord allowed a museum of natural history to occupy the space rent-free. In *Mesilla Valley Mall v. Crown Industries* on page 457, the court determined the effect of the museum's occupancy on Crown's liability for unpaid rent.

END OF CHAPTER CASE

Landlord's Tort Liability

Chapter 12 discusses the property owners' duties to people on or outside their property. In the case of leased property, these duties can be allocated to either the landlord or tenant. This section discusses the landlord's and tenant's tort liabilities. Liability in tort results when the law imposes a duty of care on the landlord or tenant, and the breach of that duty causes injury. (Tort law is explained in greater detail in Chapter 12.)

When someone is wrongfully injured as the result of activities or defective conditions on leased property, the tenant generally is liable as possessor of the property and the landlord is not liable. If a dangerous condition was in existence when the property was leased, the landlord would escape liability under the principle of caveat emptor. If the condition arose during the lease, the tenant, who is in exclusive possession and control of the property, must correct it. Courts have increasingly developed *exceptions* to these general principles, discussed as follows. When the exceptions apply, the landlord becomes liable to the tenant or to a third party injured on the premises.

Hidden Dangers Known to Landlord

A landlord who knows or should have known of hidden dangers on the premises, as the next case from Indiana reveals, is under a duty to disclose these dangers to the tenant.

A CASE IN POINT

C. Jeffrey Dickison was on the upstairs balcony of an apartment rented by his friend, Susan Moody. "Feeling romantically inclined, he took a step toward Moody to kiss her, but slipped on some twigs or branches littering the balcony floor. As he slipped, he clutched the balcony's twenty-seven-inch-high wooden railing. The rail failed. Both he and Moody, who had grabbed him to prevent his fall, tumbled to the ground below. Dickison suffered a fractured skull and scapula, a concussion, a broken nose, and lost his sense of smell and impaired his sense of taste."[96] In *Dickison v. Hargitt,* the court held that if the landlord has actual knowledge of hidden defects not known to the tenant, such as a rotted handrail, the landlord has a duty to warn the tenant. The landlord's duty to warn the tenant of known hidden defects also extended to guests of the tenant.

However, as a Michigan court states in the next case, if the landlord does not know of the risk or if the tenant is also aware of the risk, no duty to warn arises.

A CASE IN POINT

In *Rhoades v. Seidel*,[97] August Seidel rented a house to Rhoades. After taking possession, Rhoades contracted typhoid fever which, he alleged, was caused by a noxious gas coming from an open sewer in the cellar. When Rhoades brought suit, the court held that Seidel was not liable. According to the court, both parties knew of the existence of the open sewer when the lease was made and at that time, Seidel did not know and had no reason to know that a noxious gas would emanate from the sewer.

In a modern case applying this principle, an Alabama court held that the landlord was not liable for injuries to the tenant resulting from an open gas line since the landlord had no duty to inspect the line and it was not a known latent defect.[98]

Injury Outside the Premises

A landlord, according to the next Iowa case, may be liable to individuals injured outside the premises as the result of a defect that existed when the lease was made.

A CASE IN POINT

In *Barrett v. Stoneburg*, a landlord leased a two-story brick building to a tenant who agreed to keep the building repaired. When the lease was made, the building was old and in a dangerous condition, with cracked walls and sagging windows. Shortly thereafter, the building collapsed, damaging a car parked in front of the building. The tenant was held liable for his negligence in maintaining the building, but "the landlord also is liable where the injury resulted from the permanent condition of the building (not the use thereof by the tenant) and such condition existed at the time of the lease."[99]

Premises Leased for Public Admission

A landlord who leases property that is to be used for public admission and who knew that a dangerous condition existed when the lease was made faces, as a Connecticut court discusses next, liability for resulting injuries.

A CASE IN POINT

In *Webel v. Yale University*,[100] a woman in a beauty shop visited the ladies' room, the floor of which was seven inches higher than the floor of the shop. The raised floor caused the woman to fall, and the woman sued the landlord—Yale University—for her injuries. The court decided that if the woman could prove the alleged facts, she could recover damages from Yale on the ground that the landlord leased "premises on which he knows or should know that there are conditions likely to cause injury to persons entering upon them, that the purpose for which the premises are leased involves the fact that people will be invited upon the premises as patrons of the tenant, and that the landowner knows or should know that the tenant cannot reasonably be expected to remedy or guard against injury from the defect."

Landlord Reserves Control

A landlord often retains control over parts of the premises, such as hallways and stairways, that are for the common use of all tenants. The landlord, as an Illinois court ruled, is liable for injuries that result when the common area is not properly maintained.

A CASE IN POINT

In *Mangun v. F.C. Pilgrim Co.*, an eighty-three-year-old tenant opened her oven and a mouse jumped out. Frightened by the mouse, the woman fell and fractured her hip. She claimed that the landlord was liable for her injuries on the ground that he negligently maintained the areas under his control by permitting those areas to become infested with mice. In affirming a decision in favor of the tenant, the court stated the rule that "where a portion of the premises is reserved for common use and is under the landlord's control, a duty is imposed upon him to use ordinary care to keep such portion in a safe condition. The fact that the actual injury occurred on the demised premises should make no difference if the cause of the injury was the landlord's negligent maintenance of a common area."[101]

Landlord's Repair of Premises

A landlord is liable for injuries that result when he has a duty to repair the premises but fails to do so. For example, a landlord with a statutory duty under New York law to repair an apartment will be liable if the ceiling falls and injures a tenant.[102] A landlord also is liable when she voluntarily makes repairs in a negligent manner, even when she had no duty to keep the premises repaired. Thus, a Missouri landlord who voluntarily repaired a second-floor porch banister was held liable when the banister gave way, causing the tenant's young daughter to fall eighteen feet onto a hard surface.[103]

For years, landlords who included promises in leases to make repairs would be liable only for contractual damages if their nonperformance resulted in a tenant suffering a personal or property loss. Most states now will hold landlords liable in tort if they breach their promises to repair and the breach results in an injury or property damage.[104]

Liability for Tenant's Activities

In certain circumstances, a landlord is liable for the acts of her tenants. In *Uccello v. Laudenslayer*,[105] a California court held that a landlord could be held liable to a third party who was injured by a vicious dog that the tenant kept on the premises. However, the court limited such liability to cases in which the landlord has actual knowledge of the dog's vicious nature and has the right to terminate the tenancy. In a case involving a tenant who kept a tiger, a Washington state court held that the landlord has an independent duty of care to foreseeable victims because the lease involved special risks.[106]

Landlord's Liability for Criminal Acts

In a Michigan case, *Samson v. Saginaw Professional Bldg., Inc.*,[107] the landlord leased the fourth floor of a professional building to a mental health clinic. One morning a secretary who worked for an attorney with offices on the fifth floor entered the elevator on her way to a local coffee shop. A patient receiving treatment at the clinic was the only other person in the elevator; and as the elevator started down, he pushed the emergency stop button, robbed the secretary, and began stabbing her with a knife. He then restarted the elevator and ran away when it reached the ground floor, although he was later apprehended. Should the landlord be held liable in tort for the criminal act of the mental patient?

In resolving cases such as this, *two questions have been especially troublesome. First,* does the landlord have a duty to the tenant to use reasonable care in preventing criminal conduct? In answering that question, courts generally examine closely those situations in which a landlord may be held liable for defective conditions. The reasons usually cited for imposing a duty on the landlord are that the landlord has a duty to keep the property repaired (for example, door locks and security systems) or has control of common areas. In *Samson,* the court concluded that

> *... the landlord has retained his responsibility for the common areas of the building which are not leased to his tenants. The common areas such as the halls, lobby, stairs, elevators, etc., are leased to no individual tenant and remain the responsibility of the landlord. It is his responsibility to insure that these areas are kept in good repair and reasonably safe for the use of his tenants and invitees. The existence of this relationship between the defendant and its tenants and invitees placed a duty upon the landlord to protect them from unreasonable risk of physical harm.*

Even when a landlord has a duty to a tenant and has breached the duty (for example, by not installing an adequate security system), a *second* question must be answered: Was the injury caused by the landlord's negligence or, instead, by the intervening act of an independent third party, the criminal? If a person is to be held liable for his wrongful act, the act must be not only the cause in fact of the injury but also the proximate (or legal) cause of the injury. **Proximate cause** is one that in a natural sequence of events unbroken by an intervening event results in an injury. Without limiting liability to proximate causes, the chain of liability would be endless—the "fatal trespass done by Eve was cause of all our woe."[108] As a general rule, when a person's negligent act provides the opportunity for another person to commit a criminal act, the criminal act is an intervening event that relieves the negligent party from liability.

An important exception has developed, however, in cases where the negligent party should have *foreseen* the likelihood that the crime would be committed. Relying on this exception, many courts have decided that landlords should be held liable. In *Samson,* the court held that the

> *fact that such an event might occur in the future was foreseeable to this defendant. It had even been brought to its attention by other tenants in the building. The magnitude of the risk, that of a criminally insane person running amok within an office building filled with tenants and invitees, was substantial to say the least.*

In other cases, courts have held that the criminal act was foreseeable because the leased property was located in a high-crime area or because of prior criminal activity on the property (the "prior similar incidents" rule).

Following the 9/11 attacks on the World Trade Center, there has been speculation as to whether landlords should be liable to tenants and others for terrorist activity, arguably foreseeable criminal behavior. Commentators contend that terrorist attacks, while foreseeable in general, are very unforeseeable as to specific places. Commercial landlords today, especially in so-called iconic buildings such as the Empire State Building in New York City and the Willis Tower (formerly the Sears Tower) in Chicago, often negotiate a waiver from liability from terrorist activity. An exception to the view that terrorist

proximate cause

The cause that in natural and continuous sequence unbroken by an intervening cause produces an injury.

attacks are unforeseeable in specific places might be illustrated by the 1993 attack on the same World Trade Center destroyed on 9/11. Eight years prior to the 1993 attack, a report commissioned by the Port Authority of New York and New Jersey warned that the underground garage was a likely target. However, no appropriate security measures were undertaken.[109]

A related issue, as a Georgia court discusses, is whether landlords should be liable for the foreseeable criminal acts committed by their employees.

A CASE IN POINT

In *TGM Ashley Lakes, Inc. v. Jennings*,[110] Danielle Jennings was strangled to death in her apartment by Calvin Oliver, the apartment complex maintenance man. Oliver was a convicted felon and recidivist who had full access to all residents' keys. When Oliver applied for the job, the leasing manager failed to check Oliver's criminal history even though Oliver revealed that he had been in trouble with the law and served time. In fact, Oliver had felony convictions for rape, armed robbery, larceny, and residential burglaries. The court ruled that TGM was not liable under the principle of *respondeat superior* since he was acting outside the course of his employment. However, the court ruled that TGM was liable for negligent hiring, which requires "a showing that, given the employee's dangerous propensities, the victim's injuries should have been foreseen as the natural and probable consequence of hiring the employee." In this case, TGM did not even follow its own hiring policies by failing to investigate Oliver's criminal background. TGM also violated its key control policies and knew about a recent series of unforced entries and robberies. It failed to warn residents about those crimes.

Modern Trend in Landlord Liability

Beginning with the 1973 *Sargent v. Ross* decision by the New Hampshire Supreme Court,[111] many more courts have questioned the need to "squeeze the facts [of a particular case] into one of the common law exceptions."[112] Indeed, the court pointed out that landlords "are immune from these simple rules of reasonable conduct which govern other persons in their daily activities" and in fact possess a kind of "quasi-sovereignty," Furthermore, states for years have (and many still do) applied the common law rules in which the rights and duties imposed on those who enter residential and commercial properties are to be determined by whether they are classified as trespassers, licensees, or invitees, a topic explored in depth in Chapter 12. In order to simplify these confusing approaches, some courts, instead, have adopted general negligence principles under which "landlords are simply under a duty to exercise reasonable care under the circumstances."[113]

In 1985, the California Supreme Court moved the law one step beyond this trend in holding that a landlord could be subject to strict liability in *Becker v. IRM Corp.*[114] This decision was short-lived, however, when the California Supreme Court overruled its own decision imposing strict liability 10 years later in *Peterson v. Superior Court.*[115] The court concluded that imposing strict liability on the landlord would not lead to safer construction when the landlord was not also the builder. The court also drew an analogy between the seller of used equipment and the landlord, noting that imposing strict liability on either would not necessarily reduce risks. In ruling that a landlord and a hotel operator were not strictly liable, the court confirmed their liability "under general tort principles for injuries resulting from defects in their premises if they have breached the applicable standard of care."[116] A tenant or a guest also can bring strict liability causes of action against manufacturers of defective products. For example, the injured hotel guest in the *Peterson* case reached a $600,000 settlement with the manufacturer of the bathtub in which she slipped and was injured. A landlord also may owe general duties of care toward victims of crimes as the next Idaho case reveals.

> Patricia was assaulted and raped when working in her insurance agency office one Sunday morning. In *Sharp v. W.H. Moore, Inc.* on page 458, the court discusses whether the landlord had a duty of care to the tenant even if no prior similar incidents had occurred at the building.

END OF CHAPTER CASE

Exculpatory Clauses

exculpatory clause
A contract clause that releases one of the parties from liability for his wrongful acts.

A landlord faced with increasing liability for injuries on the leased premises may be tempted to include an **exculpatory clause** in the lease. The general rule regarding the validity of exculpatory clauses and a major exception are noted in the following Texas case.

A CASE IN POINT

In *Crowell v. Housing Authority of City of Dallas,*[117] a tenant was killed by carbon monoxide from a defective gas heater in his apartment. When his son sued the landlord, the Dallas Housing Authority, the agency raised in defense an exculpatory clause in the lease that provided "... nor shall the Landlord nor any of his representatives or employees be liable for any damage to person or property of the Tenant, his family, or his visitors, which might result from the condition of these or other premises of the Landlord, from theft or from any cause whatsoever."

The court stated as a general rule that agreements "exempting a party from future liability for negligence are generally recognized as valid and effective except where, because of the relationship of the parties, the exculpatory provision is contrary to public policy or the public interest. If the contract is between private persons who bargain from positions of substantially equal strength, the agreement is ordinarily enforced by the courts. The exculpatory agreement will be declared void, however, where one party is at such disadvantage in bargaining power that he is practically compelled to submit to the stipulation."

In applying the rule in this case, the court decided that the exculpatory clause was contrary to public policy and void because the landlord dictated the terms of the lease and the tenant had no choice but to accept the terms because decent housing was not otherwise available.

It is noteworthy that the *Crowell* court also stated in dictum that the public policy considerations for not honoring an exculpatory clause in a residential lease would differ from those of a commercial lease, since in the latter case the parties are more sophisticated and therefore have more equalized bargaining positions.

CASES

Leasehold Interest or License?
NEXTEL OF NEW YORK, INC. v. TIME MANAGEMENT CORPORATION
297 A.D. 2d 282, 746 N.Y.S.2d 169 (2002)

FRED T. SANTUCCI, J.P., MYRIAM J. ALTMAN, SONDRA MILLER and LEO F. McGINITY, Judges.

[The trial (Supreme) court granted the plaintiff, Nextel, a Yellowstone injunction (a preliminary injunction that prevents an eviction of a commercial tenant until the dispute is resolved), from which the landlord, Time Management, seeks an appeal.]

* * *

The defendant contends that the Supreme Court erred in granting [an] … injunction to the plaintiff Nextel of New York, Inc. (hereinafter Nextel), because the parties' agreement merely granted Nextel a non-exclusive license to utilize a portion of the premises for its cellular telephone antennae and equipment. "The central distinguishing characteristic of a lease is the surrender of absolute possession and control of property to another party for an agreed-upon rental." A license gives no interest in land. It confers only the non-exclusive, revocable right to enter the land of the licensor to perform an act. Whether a given agreement is a lease or a license depends upon the parties' intentions.

We agree with the Supreme Court's determination that the parties' agreement herein was a lease. The agreement provided for Nextel to install its antennae on the roof of the defendant's building and to occupy 200 square feet of interior space as described in the plans expressly annexed to the lease. While several other cellular telephone carriers also occupied the roof and other portions of the building, pursuant to the equipment room plan, Nextel was to partition off an existing room by building a wall and by adding a new door to access its portion of the newly-created room. Nextel was to install a new "HVAC" unit to maintain the environment in its room, and radio equipment to handle the telephone signals. Nextel's sophisticated electronic equipment would occupy the entire new room, and thus its access thereto was to be exclusive.

The term of the lease was for five years, with five automatic renewal terms of five years each. Nextel retained title to its equipment; the equipment would not become fixtures. Nextel's employees were to have unlimited access to the premises. Nextel had the expressly-granted right to quiet enjoyment. In short, the parties' agreement "contain[ed] many provisions typical of a lease and conferring rights well beyond those of a licensee or holder of a mere temporary privilege." Accordingly, the Supreme Court properly determined that the agreement was a lease and not a license.

The defendant's remaining contentions are without merit.

Retaliatory Eviction for Drug Use
DEPARTMENT OF HOUSING AND URBAN DEVELOPMENT v. RUCKER
535 U.S. 125, 122 S.Ct. 1230 (2002)

REHNQUIST, Chief Justice. With drug dealers "increasingly imposing a reign of terror on public and other federally assisted low-income housing tenants," Congress passed the Anti-Drug Abuse Act of 1988. The Act, as later amended, provides that each "public housing agency shall utilize leases which … provide that any criminal activity that threatens the health, safety, or right to peaceful enjoyment of the premises by other tenants or any drug-related criminal activity on or off such premises, engaged in by a public housing tenant, any member of the tenant's household, or any guest or other person under the tenant's control, shall be cause for termination of tenancy." 42 U.S.C. §1437d(l)(6) (1994 ed., Supp. V). Petitioners say that this statute requires lease terms that allow a local public housing authority to evict a tenant when a member of the tenant's household or a guest engages in drug-related criminal activity, regardless of whether the tenant knew, or had reason to know, of that activity. Respondents say it does not. We agree with petitioners.

Respondents are four public housing tenants of the Oakland Housing Authority (OHA). Paragraph 9(m) of respondents' leases, tracking the language of §1437d(l)(6), obligates the tenants to "assure that the tenant, any member of the household, a guest, or another person under the tenant's control, shall not engage in … [a]ny drug-related criminal activity on or near the premise[s]." Respondents also signed an agreement stating that the tenant "understand[s] that if I or any member of my household or guests should violate this lease provision, my tenancy may be terminated and I may be evicted."

In late 1997 and early 1998, OHA instituted eviction proceedings in state court against respondents, alleging violations of this lease provision. The complaint alleged: (1) that the respective grandsons of respondents William Lee and Barbara Hill, both of whom were listed as residents on the leases, were caught in the apartment complex parking lot smoking marijuana; (2) that the daughter of respondent

Pearlie Rucker, who resides with her and is listed on the lease as a resident, was found with cocaine and a crack cocaine pipe three blocks from Rucker's apartment; and (3) that on three instances within a 2-month period, respondent Herman Walker's caregiver and two others were found with cocaine in Walker's apartment. OHA had issued Walker notices of a lease violation on the first two occasions, before initiating the eviction action after the third violation.

United States Department of Housing and Urban Development (HUD) regulations administering §1437d(l)(6) require lease terms authorizing evictions in these circumstances. The HUD regulations closely track the statutory language, and provide that "[i]n deciding to evict for criminal activity, the [public housing authority] shall have discretion to consider all of the circumstances of the case...." The agency made clear that local public housing authorities' discretion to evict for drug-related activity includes those situations in which "[the] tenant did not know, could not foresee, or could not control behavior by other occupants of the unit." 56 Fed.Reg. 51560, 51567 (1991).

After OHA initiated the eviction proceedings in state court, respondents commenced actions against HUD, OHA, and OHA's director in United States District Court. They challenged HUD's interpretation of the statute under the Administrative Procedure Act, arguing that 42 U.S.C. §1437d(l)(6) does not require lease terms authorizing the eviction of so-called "innocent" tenants, and, in the alternative, that if it does, then the statute is unconstitutional. The District Court issued a preliminary injunction, enjoining OHA from "terminating the leases of tenants pursuant to paragraph 9(m) of the 'Tenant Lease' for drug-related criminal activity that does not occur within the tenant's apartment unit when the tenant did not know of and had no reason to know of, the drug-related criminal activity."

A panel of the Court of Appeals reversed, holding that §1437d(l)(6) unambiguously permits the eviction of tenants who violate the lease provision, regardless of whether the tenant was personally aware of the drug activity, and that the statute is constitutional. An en banc panel of the Court of Appeals reversed and affirmed the District Court's grant of the preliminary injunction. That court held that HUD's interpretation permitting the eviction of so-called "innocent" tenants "is inconsistent with Congressional intent and must be rejected." We granted certiorari, and now reverse, holding that 42 U.S.C. §1437d(l)(6) unambiguously requires lease terms that vest local public housing authorities with the discretion to evict tenants for the drug-related activity of household members and guests whether or not the tenant knew, or should have known, about the activity.

That this is so seems evident from the plain language of the statute. It provides that "[e]ach public housing agency shall utilize leases which ... provide that ... any drug-related criminal activity on or off such premises, engaged in by a public housing tenant, any member of the tenant's household, or any guest or other person under the tenant's control, shall be cause for termination of tenancy." 42 U.S.C. §1437d(l)(6) (1994 ed., Supp. V). The en banc Court of Appeals thought the statute did not address "the level of personal knowledge or fault that is required for eviction." Yet Congress' decision not to impose any qualification in the statute, combined with its use of the term "any" to modify "drug-related criminal activity," precludes any knowledge requirement. As we have explained, "the word 'any' has an expansive meaning, that is, 'one or some indiscriminately of whatever kind.'" Thus, any drug-related activity engaged in by the specified persons is grounds for termination, not just drug-related activity that the tenant knew, or should have known, about.

The en banc Court of Appeals also thought it possible that "under the tenant's control" modifies not just "other person," but also "member of the tenant's household" and "guest." The court ultimately adopted this reading, concluding that the statute prohibits eviction where the tenant, "for a lack of knowledge or other reason, could not realistically exercise control over the conduct of a household member or guest." But this interpretation runs counter to basic rules of grammar. The disjunctive "or" means that the qualification applies only to "other person." Indeed, the view that "under the tenant's control" modifies everything coming before it in the sentence would result in the nonsensical reading that the statute applies to "a public housing tenant ... under the tenant's control." HUD offers a convincing explanation for the grammatical imperative that "under the tenant's control" modifies only "other person": "by 'control,' the statute means control in the sense that the tenant has permitted access to the premises."

Implicit in the terms "household member" or "guest" is that access to the premises has been granted by the tenant. Thus, the plain language of ... requires leases that grant public housing authorities the discretion to terminate tenancy without regard to the tenant's knowledge of the drug-related criminal activity.

* * *

There is an obvious reason why Congress would have permitted local public housing authorities to conduct no-fault evictions: Regardless of knowledge, a tenant who "cannot control drug crime, or other criminal activities by a household member which threaten health or safety of other residents, is a threat to other residents and the project." With drugs leading to "murders, muggings, and other forms of violence against tenants," and to the "deterioration of the physical environment that requires substantial government expenditures 42 U.S.C. §11901(4) (1994 ed., Supp. V), it was reasonable for Congress to permit no-fault evictions in order to "provide public and other federally assisted low-income housing that is decent, safe, and free from illegal drugs." §11901(1) (1994 ed.).

* * *

The en banc Court of Appeals held that HUD's interpretation "raise[s] serious questions under the Due Process

Clause of the Fourteenth Amendment," because it permits "tenants to be deprived of their property interest without any relationship to individual wrongdoing." But both of these cases deal with the acts of government as sovereign. In *Scales*, the United States criminally charged the defendant with knowing membership in an organization that advocated the overthrow of the United States Government. In *Danaher*, an Arkansas statute forbade discrimination among customers of a telephone company. The situation in the present cases is entirely different. The government is not attempting to criminally punish or civilly regulate respondents as members of the general populace. It is instead acting as a landlord of property that it owns, invoking a clause in a lease to which respondents have agreed and which Congress has expressly required. *Scales* and *Danaher* cast no constitutional doubt on such actions.

The Court of Appeals sought to bolster its discussion of constitutional doubt by pointing to the fact that respondents have a property interest in their leasehold interest. This is undoubtedly true, and Greene held that an effort to deprive a tenant of such a right without proper notice violated the Due Process Clause of the Fourteenth Amendment. But, in the present cases, such deprivation will occur in the state court where OHA brought the unlawful detainer action against respondents. There is no indication that notice has not been given by OHA in the past, or that it will not be given in the future. Any individual factual disputes about whether the lease provision was actually violated can, of course, be resolved in these proceedings.

We hold that "Congress has directly spoken to the precise question at issue." Section 1437d(l)(6) requires lease terms that give local public housing authorities the discretion to terminate the lease of a tenant when a member of the household or a guest engages in drug-related activity, regardless of whether the tenant knew, or should have known, of the drug-related activity.

Accordingly, the judgment of the Court of Appeals is reversed, and the cases are remanded for further proceedings consistent with this opinion.

It is so ordered.

Implied Warranty of Suitability—Commercial Tenants

GYM-N-I PLAYGROUNDS, INC. v. SNIDER
158 S.W.3d 78 (Tex. App. Ct. 2005)

PEMBERTON, Justice. This case centers on the applicability and effect of an "as is" clause in a commercial lease. Gym-N-I Playgrounds, Inc., leased a building from Ron Snider. Under the terms of the lease, Gym-N-I agreed to accept the building "as is" and disclaimed reliance on warranties and representations. After the building was destroyed by fire, Gym-N-I sued Snider, asserting various claims relating to the condition of the building. Relying in part on the "as is" clause, Snider moved for summary judgment, which the district court granted. On appeal, Gym-N-I argues that summary judgment was improper because the lease containing the "as is" provision had expired and that the provision was otherwise unenforceable. For the reasons stated below, we affirm the district court's grant of summary judgment.

Background

The following facts are not in dispute. Snider originally owned both Gym-N-I, a playground equipment manufacturing company, and the building in which Gym-N-I was located. Patrick Finn and Bonnie Caddell had both worked in the building for several years as Gym-N-I employees. Starting in 1987, Finn performed numerous tasks for Gym-N-I, including installing playground equipment, purchasing materials, maintaining mechanical equipment, looking after human resources concerns, and performing other odd jobs. Caddell performed bookkeeping services for the company, first as an independent contractor from 1984 to 1987, then continuing as a Gym-N-I employee for another six years.

Snider's approximately 20,075-square-foot building was slightly over the threshold triggering the fire sprinkler requirement under the City of New Braunfels Code of Ordinance. The New Braunfels fire marshal, Elroy Friesenhahn, communicated this fact to Snider. Although Friesenhahn recommended that Snider install a fire sprinkler system, he did not require it because the building was only 75 square feet over the square-footage threshold and because he was uncertain whether hazardous materials were stored in the building. Snider considered installing a sprinkler system but ultimately chose not to do so.

Finn and Caddell bought the Gym-N-I business from Snider on September 30, 1993, and entered into a commercial lease of the building with Snider. The lease contained the following provision:

Tenant [Gym-N-I] accepts the Premises "as is." Landlord [Snider] has not made and does not make any representations as to the commercial suitability, physical condition, layout, footage, expenses, operation or any other matter affecting or relating to the premises and this agreement, except as herein specifically set forth or referred to and Tenant hereby expressly acknowledges that no such representations have been made. Landlord makes no other warranties, express or implied, of merchantability, marketability, fitness or suitability for a [document not legible]. Any implied warranties are expressly disclaimed and excluded.

On January 31, 1995, Gym-N-I and Snider executed an amendment to the lease. The amendment provided that, upon 90-day advance written notice, Gym-N-I would have the option of renewing the lease for three two-year terms. The amendment further provided that the terms and conditions of the original lease would apply to the renewal term, except that rent during this period would be determined by mutual agreement of the parties.

The term of the original lease expired on September 30, 1996, without Gym-N-I having exercised the renewal option. However, for nearly four years thereafter Gym-N-I continued to pay, and Snider continued to accept, rent each month. Other than the unexercised renewal option, the sole written instrument in the record contemplating a continuation of the original lease was a holdover clause.

On August 10, 2000, a fire completely destroyed the building and its contents. Gym-N-I sued Snider, asserting claims of negligence, fraud under the Deceptive Trade Practices Act ("DTPA"), and breach of the implied warranty of suitability. Specifically, Gym-N-I argued that Snider's failure to install a sprinkler system as required by the City of New Braunfels Code of Ordinances constituted gross negligence and negligence per se and that leasing the premises in such a condition violated the DTPA and breached the implied warranty of suitability. Gym-N-I also argued that Snider negligently failed to inform it of an overloaded electrical system and other wiring problems in the building.

Snider filed a traditional motion for summary judgment asserting that all of Gym-N-I's claims were barred by the "as is" clause and by a valid waiver-of-subrogation clause. Snider further argued that the lease contained other valid waivers of express and implied warranties that barred certain claims and that Gym-N-I had admitted that no misrepresentations had been made by Snider. The district court granted partial summary judgment in favor of Snider, which was later merged into a final judgment. This appeal followed.

Discussion

* * *

Implied warranty of suitability

* * * The supreme court first adopted the implied warranty of suitability in [*Davidow v. Inwood N. Prof'l Group-Phase I, 747 S.W.2d 373, 377 (Tex.1988).*] The implied warranty of suitability is an extension to commercial leases of the implied warranty of habitability, which only applies to residential property. The supreme court held that, unless the warranty is waived, a landlord in a commercial lease impliedly warrants that facilities vital to the use of the premises for their intended commercial purpose are free from latent defects and will remain in suitable condition.

* * * While the supreme court in *Davidow* approved one means of waiving the implied warranty of suitability— if "the parties to a lease expressly agree that the tenant will repair certain defects, then the provisions of the lease will control"—it did not state that this is the *only* method by which the implied warranty of suitability can be waived. Rather, the

supreme court explicitly stated that determination of whether there has been an actionable breach of the implied warranty of suitability depends on the particular circumstances of the case. One of the factors to be considered in that analysis is "whether the tenant waived the defects." Among other factors a court may consider are: (1) the nature of the defect; (2) its effect on the tenant's use of the premises; (3) the length of time the defect persisted; (4) the age of the structure; (5) the amount of the rent; (6) the area in which the premises are located; and (7) whether the defect resulted from any unusual or abnormal use by the tenant. In short, *Davidow* indicates that there is more than one way to override or waive the implied warranty of suitability.

We find this interpretation of *Davidow* to be consistent with other areas of our law of implied warranties. For example, the legislature has adopted the Uniform Commercial Code ("U.C.C."), including the U.C.C.'s implied warranties of "merchantability" and "fitness for a particular purpose" provisions. The implied warranty of good workmanship may also be waived contractually.

We are mindful that the implied warranty of habitability generally cannot be waived. Although the implied warranty of suitability has its legal roots in the implied warranty of habitability, they are not identical legal concepts. In 2002, the supreme court outlined the policy concerns associated with the sale of a residential home that support the implied warranty of habitability. The court noted that "purchase of a [new] home is … in many instances the most important transaction of a lifetime." The court also noted that the implied warranty of habitability protects "the average home-buyer who lacks the ability and expertise to discover defects in a new house." Such considerations, although not wholly without application, are less persuasive in the context of commercial leases and the implied warranty of suitability. In any event, as we have already noted, the supreme court has squarely ruled that the implied warranty of suitability may be contractually waived. Thus, it is clear that the two warranties are not identical.

In this case, we must decide whether this particular "as is" clause was sufficient to waive the implied warranty of suitability. The lease in this case explicitly mentions that Snider made no warranties, including the implied warranty of suitability. The "as is" provision was even underlined and set in all-capitals for emphasis. In addition, both Finn and Caddell testified in depositions that they realized the "as is" provision was in the lease, were told by counsel that it highly favored Snider, and understood the provision's intent and scope. Finally, as noted above, it is undisputed that Finn and Caddell knew of the building's condition, including the absence of a sprinkler system and the fact that the fire code issues had been a concern. Consequently, we find that the implied warranty of suitability was waived in this case by the "as is" clause and that the district court acted appropriately in granting summary judgment for Snider on Gym-N-I's breach of the implied warranty of suitability claim.

Having rejected all of Gym-N-I's arguments concerning the "as is" clause as a bar to its claims, we overrule Gym-N-I's second issue.

Conclusion

Having found that waiver provisions of the original lease were incorporated into the holdover lease, that the "as is" waiver provision of the lease was valid, that the "as is" provision waived the implied warranty of suitability, and that there were no genuine issues of material fact preventing application of the "as is" clause, we have determined that the district court could have appropriately relied on that clause to grant summary judgment in favor of Snider. We affirm the judgment of the district court.

Transfer of Leasehold Interest
TENET HEALTHSYSTEM SURGICAL, L.L.C. v. JEFFERSON PARISH HOSPITAL SERVICE DISTRICT NO. 1
426 F.3d 738 (5th Cir. 2005)

DAVIS, Circuit Judge. Tenet HealthSystem Surgical, L.L.C. appeals the judgment of the district court dismissing its claims for breach of lease and other claims against the defendant Jefferson Parish Hospital Service District No. 1, operator of West Jefferson Medical Center. Based on our conclusion that West Jefferson's denial of consent to Tenet's proposed assignment of the lease was unreasonable, we reverse.

I.

In April 2001, Tenet HealthSystem Surgical, L.L.C. ("Tenet") contracted to lease space in a building owned by Marrero Shopping Center, Inc. ("MSC") in Marrero, Louisiana. The lease provided for an initial term of five years and granted Tenet the right to renew for additional five-year terms through April 2021. Under terms of the agreement, Tenet was permitted to use the premises "for out patient surgical procedures and general medical and physicians offices, including related uses and for other purposes reasonably acceptable to Landlord." The lease allowed the lessee to assign the lease with the consent of the lessor and provided that such consent "shall not be unreasonably withheld." Tenet occupied the premises and began operating an outpatient surgical center.

In June 2003, West Jefferson Medical Center ("West Jefferson") purchased the property from MSC subject to the Tenet lease and other leases affecting the shopping center. The leased premises are located adjacent to the West Jefferson hospital campus and were a strategic purchase by West Jefferson to allow for future expansion of its facilities.

Tenet ceased doing business as a surgery center in August 2003. It sought to assign the lease to Pelican Medical-West, L.L.C. ("Pelican"). Pelican intended to use the premises for an occupational medicine clinic. Occupational medicine clinics primarily provide medical services to industry, treating mainly workmen's compensation cases, although walk-in business from the general public is also accepted. The services offered include urgent care, primary care, physical examinations, x-rays, phlebotomy, drug and alcohol testing, laboratory services, and minor surgical procedures.

On August 29, 2003, Tenet dispatched a letter to West Jefferson requesting consent to assign the lease to Pelican for use permitted under the lease and to alter the leased premises according to a plan that had been attached. West Jefferson responded that it would not approve the assignment, and, after a request by Tenet, explained that one of the reasons it had denied the requested assignment was that Pelican intended to use the premises in a manner that competed with West Jefferson. The other stated reasons were later mooted by settlement or withdrawn.

Tenet filed suit in the 24th Judicial District Court in Jefferson Parish in September 2003, asserting claims for breach of the lease, violation of the Louisiana Unfair Trade Practices Act and Consumer Protection Laws, and unconstitutional deprivation of Tenet's property rights. The suit was subsequently removed to federal court on federal question grounds. West Jefferson asserted a counterclaim seeking a declaratory judgment that its refusal to consent to the sublease was reasonable and that its refusal did not constitute an unconstitutional deprivation of Tenet's property rights. In its argument in favor of summary judgment on the reasonableness of its consent, West Jefferson added the argument that it was reasonable in refusing consent to the assignment because the proposed use of the facility was not a permitted use under the terms of the lease.

On June 18, 2004, the district court granted summary judgment in favor of West Jefferson on its counterclaim. The district court held that the reasonableness of West Jefferson's actions must be considered from the perspective of West Jefferson. It also held that "West Jefferson did not unreasonably withhold consent to the proposed assignment to a third party who intended to open an urgent care, occupational medicine, and primary care facility whose operations were outside the scope of the activities of the assignor lessee, and intended to broaden the operations on the leased premises to include new areas of competition with the lessor." Because it found that West Jefferson's actions did not breach the lease, Tenet's other claims failed as well.

After the court granted summary judgment, the parties agreed to settle their claims related to proposed alterations to the premises; however, they expressly preserved Tenet's right to appeal the district court's holding that West Jefferson acted reasonably in denying the sublease because Pelican would provide more competition with West Jefferson. Tenet now appeals.

II.

Under Louisiana law, "[t]he lease contract is the law between the parties in defining their respective rights and obligations." In interpreting a lease, like other contracts, courts are bound to give legal effect to written contracts in accordance with the true intent of the parties. This intent is to be determined by the words of the contract when they are clear, explicit and do not lead to absurd consequences.

Article 2725 of the Louisiana Civil Code governs a lessee's right to sublease or assign the lease.

The lessee has a right to underlease, or even to cede his lease to another person, unless this power has been expressly interdicted. The interdiction may be for the whole, or for a part; and this clause is always strictly construed.

When a lease contains the requirement that lessor's consent is required to sublease with no limitation, the lessor's right to refuse will be protected unless the lessor has abused that right. When a lease provides that the lessor's consent to assign the lease may not be unreasonably withheld, as is the case in the MSC/Tenet Lease, "the lessor's right to refuse will be judicially protected unless the lessor's refusal was unreasonable." "[W]ithholding consent is 'unreasonable' where there are no 'sufficient grounds for a reasonably prudent business person to deny consent.'"

These rules have been applied in few Louisiana cases, but the following applications emerge. A lessor may reasonably refuse his consent to a proposed sublease or assignment if the proposed sublessee or assignee is financially inferior to the present lessee, if the sublessee's activities don't fall within the permitted uses in the lease or if the sublessee's use would inhibit the lessor's ability to lease other spaces in the leased property, if the sublessee won't delineate his proposed activities or if the sublease causes the lessor to lose a tenant on the same property. A lessor's refusal to consent to a sublease or assignment will be found to be unreasonable if the reasons given for the refusal are pretextual or if the proposed sublessee is identical to the lessee in financial status and proposed use of the property.

West Jefferson argues that its refusal to consent to Tenet's proposed assignment to Pelican was reasonable on two grounds. First, West Jefferson asserts that Pelican's contemplated uses of the facility exceed those permitted under the lease. Second, West Jefferson asserts that its refusal was reasonable because the proposed use of the facility poses more competition to its adjacent hospital. We will address each in turn.

A.

The use provision of the lease states:

Tenant shall use and occupy the Leased Premises for out patient surgical procedures and general medical and physician's offices, including related uses and for other purposes reasonably acceptable to Landlord.

Tenet used the facility for an outpatient surgery center. Pelican planned to use the facility for an occupational medical clinic. As described by Dr. Kotler, the owner of Pelican, occupational medicine describes the type of customer the clinic solicits, primarily members of the workforce. The services offered by an occupational medicine practice are quite comprehensive, from physical examinations and drug screening to low acuity emergencies, depending on the demands of the employer and the walk-in patient. The clinic can treat patients presenting with depression, lacerations, broken bones, abdominal pain, or pneumonia, and provides related lab and x-ray services. In our view, nothing in this description takes the proposed practice outside the limits of a "general medical and physician's offices, including related uses," a permitted use under the lease.

* * *

B.

West Jefferson also opposes the lease assignment from Tenet to Pelican on the basis that Pelican's broadened scope of operations would include new areas of competition with its hospital. Whether this objection is reasonable depends on from whose perspective reasonableness should be judged. The Louisiana Supreme Court has stated that withholding consent is unreasonable where there are no "sufficient grounds for a reasonably prudent business person to deny consent." West Jefferson argues that a reasonable business person in its position would deny consent to assign a lease that would bring new competition into the immediate area where it does business. Tenet argues that reasonableness must include consideration for the parties' expectations as of the inception of the lease, at which time Tenet's lessor was not a competitor to its operations. The resolution of this issue depends on two factors: (1) whether reasonableness is judged on objective factors or whether it can be judged on factors personal to the lessor, and (2) whether reasonableness is judged based on the alignment of the lessor and lessee as of the inception of the lease or at the time of the proposed assignment.

No Louisiana cases deal with a situation in which the identity of the lessor changed and the consent to assign was refused for reasons personal to the new lessor. We look for guidance then to treatises and case law from other jurisdictions. Those sources indicate that when determining the reasonableness of a landlord's refusal to consent to an assignment of a lease, the standard is that of a reasonable prudent man and, in applying that standard, the personal taste and convenience of the landlord should ordinarily not be considered.

In determining whether a landlord's refusal to consent was reasonable in a commercial context, only factors that relate to the landlord's interest in preserving the leased property or in having the terms of prime lease performed should be considered. Among factors a landlord can consider are the financial responsibility of the proposed subtenant, the legality and suitability of proposed use and nature of the occupancy.

A landlord's personal taste or convenience are factors not properly considered. Rather the landlord's objection "must relate to ownership and operation of leased property, not lessor's general economic interest." Under this standard, West Jefferson's refusal to consent to the assignment of the Tenet lease because Pelican would be a new competitor relates not to the ownership and operation of the leased property, but to West Jefferson's general economic interest as the operator of an adjacent business.

We have found only one case dealing with a situation, like that in this case, in which the landlord at the time of the request for consent was not the original landlord. In [a New York case] *American Book Co. v. Yeshiva University Development Foundation, Inc.,* American Book Company leased three floors and basement space in a commercial building for executive and general offices, stockroom and storage. As in today's case, the lease could be assigned with the written consent of the landlord, which consent could not unreasonably be withheld. Some years after the inception of the lease, the building was acquired by Yeshiva University Development Foundation, Inc. When American Book sought consent to assign its lease to Planned Parenthood-World Population, the new landlord denied its consent on the basis that it considered the activities of the proposed subtenant to be inconsistent with the present use of the premises and with the educational activities of the university.

The New York Supreme Court concluded that the denial of consent was unreasonable. It noted that considering objective factors only, the proposed subtenant was "financially responsible, engaged in a respectable and legal activity, and intends to use the entire space of the prime tenant for identical purposes—as executive offices and a stockroom for its publications." The court held that a religious institution operating a commercial enterprise should be held to established standards of commercial responsibility. "Arbitrary considerations of personal taste, sensibility, or convenience do not constitute the criteria of the landlord's duty under an agreement such as this." The objection of the new landlord was based on who the landlord was, not on any attributes of the proposed tenant. The court also noted that when the plaintiff entered into the lease originally, it had the right to assign the lease to anyone who was financially, morally and legally acceptable by objective standards, and who would use the space in accordance with the provision of the lease. The university, as successor in interest to the prior owners, stepped into the previous owner's shoes and did not increase their rights under the lease. Instead, the court concluded that the lessee had a fixed contractual right which could not be varied because the successor landlord happened to have different attributes, likes, dislikes and activities.

The rationale applied in *American Book* is compelling and not inconsistent with the law of the state of Louisiana. This rule respects the expectations of the parties as of the inception of the lease while protecting the landlord's right to reject a proposed sublessee who places at risk the landlord's interest in the leasehold or in having terms of prime lease performed. As applied to the facts of this case, West Jefferson's reason for denying consent to the assignment to Pelican based on increased competition is wholly personal to West Jefferson and does not relate in any way to an objective evaluation of Pelican as a tenant. Further, allowing West Jefferson to deny consent on a basis personal to it, a successor owner who took subject to the existing lease, would expand West Jefferson's rights under the lease to the detriment of the lessee in a manner not bargained for in the lease itself. Accordingly, we conclude that West Jefferson's refusal of consent to the assignment of the lease on the basis of increased competition was unreasonable.

III.

For the reasons stated above, we concluded that the district court erred in concluding that West Jefferson reasonably refused to consent to the assignment of the Tenet lease to Pelican. The judgment of the district court in favor of West Jefferson is reversed and the case remanded to the district court for further proceedings consistent with this opinion.

REVERSED AND REMANDED.

Landlord's Remedies

MESILLA VALLEY MALL v. CROWN INDUSTRIES
111 N.M. 663, 808 P.2d 633 (1991)

RANSOM, Justice. * * * The essential facts of this case are few and uncontested. Crown Industries, doing business as Lemon Tree, Inc., occupied retail premises at the Mesilla Valley Mall in Las Cruces under a long-term lease with the Mesilla Valley Mall Company. Lemon Tree had attempted to renegotiate the terms of the lease, but the Mall Company refused to make adjustments. Lemon Tree advised the Mall Company that it simply would vacate the premises, and it did so on January 20, 1989. Rent was paid only to February 1, and the unpaid rent under the unexpired portion of the lease totaled $35,056.58.

The Mall Company repossessed the premises and, beginning on February 1, 1989, allowed the Las Cruces Museum of Natural History to occupy the space rent free in the interest of promoting good community relations. The Museum remodeled the premises for its own use and has occupied the premises continuously since it first took possession. The Mall

Company describes the Museum as a tenant at sufferance. In the past, the Museum has occupied several locations in the Mall. The Museum occupied these locations, and the space at issue in this case, with the understanding that it would immediately vacate the premises at the request of the Mall Company should another rent-paying tenant become available.

In April 1989 the Mall Company brought suit to collect all amounts due under the lease. At trial Lemon Tree raised the affirmative defense of surrender and acceptance. The trial court determined that after the lessee had abandoned the property the Museum's rent-free tenancy was for the benefit of the lessor and not the lessee, and that this use was inconsistent with the rights of the lessee. Specifically, the court found "nothing in the lease agreement allowed the Mall to re-enter the property for any other purpose [than to relet for the benefit of the tenant], and, in particular to re-lease the property for no rent and for its own benefit." The court concluded that under the doctrine of surrender and acceptance the lease agreement terminated on February 1, 1989.

In the absence of legal justification, a tenant who abandons occupancy before the expiration of a lease remains liable for rent for the remainder of the term; and, under traditional common-law property rules, the landlord is under no obligation to relet the premises to mitigate the tenant's liability under the lease. The landlord, however, may elect to retake possession on behalf of the tenant and to relet the premises for the tenant's account. Or, the landlord may choose to accept what is in effect the tenant's offer to surrender the leasehold, thereby terminating the lease and leaving the tenant liable only for rent that accrued before the acceptance.

A surrender and acceptance of the lease may arise either from the express agreement of the parties or by operation of law. Here, there is no contention that there was a surrender and acceptance by express agreement of the parties. A surrender by operation of law only can occur when the conduct of the landlord is inconsistent with the continuing rights of the tenant under the lease. Thus, where the landlord has re-appropriated the property for his own use and benefit and not for the benefit of the original tenant as well, surrender and the acceptance results by operation of law. Cancellation of the lease occurs under principles of estoppel because it would be inequitable for either landlord or tenant to assert the continued existence of the lease.

In this case Lemon Tree claims the Mall Company relet the premises solely for its own benefit. The Mall Company admits the presence of the Museum attracts large numbers of potential customers to the Mall and so benefits the Mall Company and its tenants, but the Mall Company claims its actions were permissible under the lease and the lease is controlling. In this case it is true that the lease provides the lessor may relet the premises without terminating the lease. When a clause in a lease permits the landlord to relet the premises, the clause creates a presumption that the re-entry and reletting of the premises was not the acceptance of a surrender or a termination of the lease. However, the reletting still must be for the benefit of the original tenant as well as for the justifiable ends of the landlord. If not, the landlord's actions would be inconsistent with a continued landlord-tenant relationship to which the landlord seeks to hold the tenant.* * *

The lease provisions in this case regarding reletting are consistent with these principles; that is, the lease itself suggests that any reletting will benefit the original tenant. The lease states that if the landlord elects to relet in the event of abandonment of the leased premises, then rentals received by the landlord shall be applied against the debts of the tenant who shall remain liable for any deficiency, and any residue shall be held by the landlord and applied in payment of future rent as it becomes due. The lease clearly anticipates some payment of rent and in no way suggests that the Mall Company can simply donate the occupancy of the premises to a third party or use the property for any purpose whatsoever.

* * *

[The trial court decision is affirmed.]

Landlord's Liability for Criminal Acts
SHARP v. W.H. MOORE, INC.
118 Idaho 297, 796 P.2d 506 (1990)

BISTLINE, Justice. * * * On May 12, 1985, Patricia Sharp was an employee of the Jess Swan Insurance Agency, whose offices were located in a building leased by Swan Insurance from W.H. Moore, Inc. W.H. Moore had contracted with Security Investment to act as property manager for the building. Security Investment, in turn, contracted with Security Police to provide the protective patrols for the building.

On the Sunday morning in question, Sharp was working alone in her office at 1199 Shoreline Drive, Boise, Idaho. While there, she was assaulted and raped by an unknown assailant who may have gained access to the building through an unlocked third floor fire escape door.

Sharp filed her complaint and demand for a jury trial on January 24, 1986. W.H. Moore, Inc. and Security Investments filed a motion for summary judgment on May 28, 1986. Security Police filed its motion for summary judgment on June 26, 1986. The district court granted both motions on the basis that, under the circumstances of this case, the defendants owed no duty of care to Sharp.

* * *

The question of whether a landlord owes a duty of reasonable care to the tenants of the property was settled by our recent decision in *Stephens v. Stearns*, 678 P.2d 41 (1984). There, Justice Donaldson, with three judges agreeing, wrote [emphasis added]:

> [W]e today decide to leave the common-law rule and its exceptions behind, and we adopt the rule that a landlord is under a duty to exercise reasonable care in light of all the circumstances.
>
> We stress that adoption of this rule is not tantamount to making the landlord an insurer for all injury occurring on the premises, but merely constitutes our removal of the landlord's common-law cloak of immunity.... *We hold that defendant Stearns did owe a duty to plaintiff Stephens to exercise reasonable care in light of all the circumstances, and that it is for a jury to decide whether that duty was breached.*

In addition to the clear rule of *Stephens*, other legal principles favor the recognition of a requirement of due care in the circumstances present here. One is the familiar proposition that one who voluntarily assumes a duty also assumes the obligation of due care in performance of that duty. A landlord, having voluntarily provided a security system, is potentially subject to liability if the security system fails as a result of the landlord's negligence. * * * While the landlord/tenant relationship does not in and of itself establish a duty to keep doors locked, once Moore and Security Investments had initiated a locked door policy and had employed a security service with the intent of keeping the doors locked, they undertook such a duty and are subject to liability if they failed to perform that duty with a reasonable standard of care.

Another reason for finding a duty of care to exist in this case is the general rule that each person has a duty of care to prevent unreasonable, foreseeable risks of harm to others. * * * Foreseeability is a flexible concept which varies with the circumstances of each case. Where the degree of result or harm is great, but preventing it is not difficult, a relatively low degree of foreseeability is required. Conversely, where the threatened injury is minor but the burden of preventing such injury is high, a higher degree of foreseeability may be required. Thus, foreseeability is not to be measured by just what is more probable than not, but also includes whatever result is likely enough in the setting of modern life that a reasonably prudent person would take such into account in guiding reasonable conduct.

Defendants argue that they are entitled to summary judgment on the issue of foreseeability because the plaintiff failed to come forward with any evidence that prior similar incidents of criminal activity had occurred in the building or in its vicinity. * * *

The solid and growing national trend has been toward the rejection of the "prior similar incidents" rule. See, e.g., *Rowe v. State Bank of Lombard*, 531 N.E.2d 1358 (1988) (simply because no violent crimes had been committed at the office parking area does not render criminal actions unforeseeable as a matter of law); *Samson v. Saginaw Professional Bldg. Inc.*, 224 N.W.2d 843 (1975). * * *

Reduced to its essence, the "prior similar incidents" requirement translates into the familiar but fallacious saying in negligence law that every dog gets one free bite before its owner can be held to be negligent for failing to control the dog. That license which is refused to a dog's owner should be withheld from a building's owner and the owner's agents as well. There is no "one free rape" rule in Idaho.

* * *

Thus, in addition to the rule of *Stephens v. Stearns*, imposing a duty of reasonable care, under the circumstances, running from landlords or owners to their tenants as a matter of law, there are ample additional reasons for imposing such a duty on the landlord in this case. It remains for a jury to determine whether there was any breach of that duty. Therefore the summary judgment as to Moore is reversed and remanded. [The court also reversed the summary judgments for Security Investments and Security Police.] * * *

KEY TERMS

assignment, 436
caveat emptor, 429
constructive eviction, 440
contract of adhesion, 428
covenant of quiet enjoyment, 434
dependent covenant, 441
estate for years, 414
exculpatory clause, 450
freehold estate, 413
frustration of purpose, 435
holdover tenant, 416
implied warranty of habitability, 429

implied warranty of suitability, 431
independent covenant, 441
lease, 423
leasehold estate, 413
license, 417
mitigation of damages, 444
novation, 437
partial actual eviction, 442
periodic tenancy, 415
proximate cause, 448
remedy, 439
rent, 425

PROBLEMS

1. Shakespeare leased property to Sinclair Refining Company for a term of five years at a rental of $5,000 per month. Thirty-three days before the end of the term, Sinclair notified Shakespeare that it would be vacating the premises; but Sinclair did not actually move until four months after the end of the term. Sinclair claims that it is liable only for four months' rent since the original lease called for a monthly rental. Shakespeare claims that Sinclair is liable for an additional five years' rent as a holdover tenant. Who is correct? Why?

2. Larry owns a house that he leased to Tom for one year. Six months after Tom took possession, the bathroom floor began to sink as the result of termite infestation and Tom could no longer use the bathroom. Tom claims that Larry, as landlord, has the duty to repair the termite damage. Larry claims that tenants such as Tom must continue to pay rent even if the whole house crumbles as the result of termite damage. Who is correct? Why?

3. An intruder raped a state university student in her dormitory early one morning. The dormitory doors, although equipped with locks, were always kept unlocked. Prior to the rape, campus security had received reports of men being seen in the women's bathroom and the student had personally complained twice to a dorm manager about strangers loitering in lounges and hallways. Stories about numerous crimes in dormitories had also been published in the student newspaper. Is the state liable to the student for damages? Why or why not?

4. In 1939, Lena leased a building to Mary that was to be used "solely as a filling station and not for restaurant or lunch counter purposes" for a five-year period at a rental of $100 per month. After three years, Mary offered to restore possession of the property to Lena. Mary claimed that World War II government regulations that froze the sale of automobiles and rationed the sale of gasoline made it impossible for her to use the leased property as a filling station. Lena refused to terminate the lease and claimed that Mary must pay rent for a full five-year term. Is Lena correct? Why or why not?

5. Clarence owned a large apartment complex. Approximately 20 percent of his apartments were leased to African Americans. Clarence required all prospective tenants to prove that their weekly income, after taxes and debts had been subtracted, was at least 90 percent of the monthly rent. Several African-American welfare recipients were refused apartments because they did not meet this test. They sued Clarence, claiming that the test violated the 1866 Civil Rights Act and the 1968 Fair Housing Act, both of which prohibit racial discrimination. Is Clarence liable? Why or why not?

6. On August 25, 1992, Chauncey, a university student, leased an apartment near the university from Snidely on a month-to-month basis. The state statute provided that a landlord must give a one-month notice to quit in order to terminate a month-to-month tenancy. Snidely served Chauncey with a notice to quit on February 25, 1993, ordering him to leave the apartment on March 25, 1993. Is this a valid notice? Why or why not?

7. In January, Pilgrim Properties hired Sam as custodian and furnished him with an apartment in the building where he worked. Two months later Sam was fired for failing to perform his janitorial duties, but he refused to give up the apartment. Pilgrim brought suit to recover possession. What type of property interest does Sam have? Will Pilgrim win? Why or why not?

8. Dickey leased a vacant piece of real estate to Minit-Man Corporation (MM) for 10 years. The lease provided that the property was to be used for "the business of washing and cleaning automobiles … and for no other purpose." MM was to pay rent equal to 12½ percent of its annual gross sales with a minimum payment of $1,800 per year. MM installed a car wash on the property but discontinued the business after five years. Although MM continued to pay the minimum rental, Dickey brought suit to evict MM on the grounds that MM had defaulted by discontinuing the business. Is Dickey correct? Why or why not?

9. Joe owned a two-story building. The first floor was leased to a shoe store, and the second floor was leased to Kate for a club. Kate hired John, a professional window washer, to wash the outside of the second-floor

windows. After washing the windows at least once a month for over two years, John was injured in a fall from the second-story window. The fall resulted when decayed wood in the window frame failed to hold John's safety belt. Are Joe and Kate liable for John's injuries? Why or why not?

10. While investigating a reported weapons disturbance in a private home, police entered the apartment of two gay partners, Tyron Garner and John Lawrence, who were engaged in a consensual sex act. Both were arrested for violating Texas's criminal sodomy laws. The law prohibited anal and oral intercourse between homosexuals while not prohibiting the same conduct for straight couples. In *Lawrence v. Texas*,[118] the U.S. Supreme Court ruled that the law violates constitutional rights to privacy. Critics of Texas's law argue that the law not only was discriminatory but also was used as a way to target gay tenants for eviction. Moreover, in states that outlaw sodomy by both heterosexual and homosexual couples, enforcement of the law was aimed mostly at gays and lesbians. Opponents also maintain that the government should not regulate sodomy at all. Those who support the law, such as the Pro-Family Law Center, contend that the law reflects "a need to protect the natural family from any influence that would harm it." Opponents counter that the pro-family argument is just a cover-up for deep-seated prejudices against homosexuals.

Although Garner and Lawrence were not involved in an eviction, do you think their landlord should have a right to evict them if their actions violate his personal and religious views? Do landlords have rights superior to those of tenants in deciding moral conduct within their premises? Do people have legal and ethical rights to privacy in their bedrooms that supersede the rights of both landlords and the government? Explain your answer.

ENDNOTES

1. R. Boyer, et al., *The Law of Property* 246 (4th ed. 1991).
2. R. Schoshinski, *American Law of Landlord and Tenant* 33 (1980, Feb. 1997 Supp.).
3. *Monbar, Inc. v. Monaghan*, 18 Del.Ch. 395, 162 A. 50 (1932).
4. R. Schoshinski, *American Law of Landlord and Tenant* 46–47 (1980, Feb. 1997 Supp.).
5. 75 N.Y. 205 (1878).
6. *A. H. Fetting Mfg. Jewelry Co. v. Waltz*, 160 Md. 50, 152 A. 434 (1930).
7. 19 Misc. 489, 43 N.Y.S. 1102 (1897).
8. 254 Mass. 22, 149 N.E. 618 (1925).
9. R. Schoshinski, *American Law of Landlord and Tenant* 60 (1980, Feb. 1997 Supp.).
10. See *Keeton v. RJ & RK, Inc.*, 858 So. 2d 349 (Fla. Ct. App. 2003).
11. Miami Beach, Florida, Ordinance No. 92-2824. At least 12 states and Washington D.C., as well as many cities, have antidiscrimination statutes prohibiting such discrimination. See http://public.findlaw.com/civil-rights/housing-discrimination/tenant-fair-housing-orientation.html (last accessed July 14, 2010).
12. Conn. Gen. Stat. Ann. §8-45, 45a (1971).
13. *U.S. v. Balistrieri*, 981 F.2d 916 (7th Cir. 1993).
14. 92 Misc.2d 1030, 401 N.Y.S.2d 943 (1977).
15. R. Aalberts and R. Hoyt, *Appraisers and the Fair Housing Act: Accessibility Requirements for the Disabled*, 12 Journal of Real Estate Research 429 (1996).
16. *National Federation of the Blind v. Target, Corp.*, 2007 WL 2846402 (N.D. Cal. October 2, 2007).
17. 913 P.2d 909 (1996).
18. 418 Mass. 316, 636 N.E.2d 233 (Mass. 1994).
19. D. D'Urso, *Tenant Screening Agencies: Implications for Landlords and Tenants*, 26 Real Estate Law Journal 44 (Summer 1997).
20. D. Lang, *Get Clean or Get Out: Landlords Drug-Testing Tenants*, 2 Washington University Journal of Law and Policy 459 (2000); R. Aalberts, *Can Tenants in Privately Owned Apartments Be Drug Tested?* Journal of Real Estate Research 201 (2002); R. Aalberts, *Drug Testing: Does it Violate Rights of Privacy?* 38 Real Property, Probate and Trust Journal 479 (2003).
21. N. Allen, *Digest of Selected Articles—Effects of Meth Labs on Real Estate*, 35 Real Estate Law Journal 338 (2006).
22. D. Babwin, *For Renters, A Drug Test Before Signing Lease*, Washington Post, November 4, 2000.
23. 41 Cal.4th 1205, 162 P.3d 610 (2007).
24. 54 Hawaii 417, 508 P.2d 1217 (1973). However, the holding in *Aluli* was limited in *Windward Partners v. Delos Santos*, 59 Hawaii 104, 577 P.2d 326 (1978), where the court concluded that retaliatory eviction is available as a defense when a commercial or residential tenant has been evicted as a result of asserting a statutory (as opposed to a constitutional) right.
25. 770 F.2d 167 (6th Cir. 1985).
26. R. Cahan, *Comment, Home is No Haven: An Analysis of Sexual Harassment in Housing*, 1987 Wisconsin Law Review 1061 (1987).
27. *Justice Department Announces Largest Harassment Verdict*, http://www.usdoj.gov/opa/pr/2004/May/04_crt_324.htm (last accessed July 15, 2010).
28. See http://www.justice.gov/opa/pr/2008/September/08-crt-776.html (last accessed July 15, 2010).
29. *Toms Point Apartments v. Goudzward*, 72 Misc.2d 629, 339 N.Y.S.2d 281 (1972). Courts in some states limit the defense to residential leases.
30. 238 Ill.App.3d 148, 606 N.E.2d 152 (1992).
31. 440 N.W.2d 867 (1989).
32. *Restatement, Second, Property, Landlord and Tenant*, Introduction, 4, 5 (1977).

33. *Green v. Superior Court,* 10 Cal.3d 616, 111 Cal.Rptr. 704, 517 P.2d 1168 (1974).

34. The following states have adopted, with some modifications, the Uniform Residential Landlord Tenant Act: Alaska, Arizona, Florida, Hawaii, Iowa, Kansas, Kentucky, Montana, Nebraska, New Mexico, Oregon, Rhode Island, South Carolina, Tennessee, and Virginia. To access the model act see: http://www.law .upenn.edu/bll/archives/ulc/fnact99/1970s/urlta72.htm (last accessed July 23, 2010).

35. G. Greenfield and M. Margolies, *Implied Warranty of Fitness in Nonresidential Leases,* 45 Albany Law Review 855 (1981).

36. *Id.* In *Davidow v. Inwood North Professional Group,* 747 S.W.2d 373 (Tex. 1988); however, the court decided that the implied warranty of habitability is also implied in commercial leases as an implied warranty of suitability.

37. *Javins v. First National Realty Corp.,* 428 F.2d 1071 (D.C. Cir. 1970).

38. Wis. Stat. Ann. §706.01.

39. *Wallace v. Scoggin,* 18 Or. 502, 21 P. 558 (1889).

40. 170 Conn. 659, 368 A.2d 6 (1976).

41. 216 S.W.2d 144 (Mo.App. 1948).

42. *Restatement, Second, Property, Landlord and Tenant* §12.1, Comment a (1977).

43. *ETCO Corporation v. Hauer,* 161 Cal.App.3d 1154, 208 Cal.Rptr. 118 (1984).

44. 108 S.Ct. 849, 99 L.Ed.2d 1 (1988).

45. R. Aalberts, *Retail Real Estate and Online Sales: Will Excess Space Be the Real Y2K Problem?* 28 Real Estate Law Journal 285 (2000).

46. 789 N.E. 2d 481 (Ind. Ct. App. 2003).

47. 81 Misc.2d 328, 365 N.Y.S.2d 681 (1975).

48. *Restatement, Second, Property, Landlord and Tenant* §5.1 (1977).

49. *Javins v. First National Realty Corp.,* 428 F.2d 1071, 1074 (D.C. Cir. 1970).

50. 51 Hawaii 426, 462 P.2d 470 (1969).

51. However, if Amy rented only one apartment in a large apartment complex, she would not be liable for rent after the destruction of the apartment building because, in this case, she would not be renting the land.

52. *Restatement, Second, Property, Landlord and Tenant* §5.4 (1977).

53. 54 N.Y. 450 (1873).

54. See *Javins v. First National Realty Corp., supra* note 49. See also *Jobe v. Wade,* 818 P.2d 1006 (Utah 1991). See M. Stewart et al. *Every Landlord's Legal Guide* 176 (9th ed. 2008).

55. *Jobe v. Wade, id.*

56. *Restatement, Second, Property, Landlord and Tenant* §5.5 (1977).

57. *Garner v. LaMarr,* 88 Ga.App. 364, 76 S.E.2d 721 (1953).

58. *Gym-N-I Playgrounds, Inc. v. Snider,* 158 SW 3d 78 (Tex. App. Ct. 2005).

59. *Restatement, Second, Property, Landlord and Tenant* §5.6 (1977).

60. 54 F.3d 425 (7th Cir. 1995).

61. *Bradley v. Holliman,* 134 Ark. 588, 202 S.W. 469 (1918).

62. 68 Misc.2d 278, 327 N.Y.S.2d 307 (1971).

63. *N.D. Legislator Wants to Scrap Law Against Unmarried Couples Living Together,* USA Today (January 18, 2007). The other states that still have laws against cohabitation are Florida, Michigan, Mississippi, North Carolina, Virginia, and West Virginia.

64. *Snow v. Winn,* 607 P.2d 678 (Ok. 1980).

65. *Restatement, Second, Property, Landlord and Tenant* §12.2 (1977). The Fair Housing Act requires that landlords allow handicapped tenants to make reasonable alterations in their apartments.

66. *Id.*

67. 253 N.Y. 111, 170 N.E. 512 (1930).

68. *Goldberg v. Tri-States Theatre Corp.,* 126 F.2d 26 (8th Cir. 1942).

69. R. Ranalli and J. Saltzman, *Jury Finds Heavy Smoking to Be Grounds for Eviction,* Boston Globe (June 16, 2005).

70. R. Cunningham, W. Stoebuck, and D. Whitman, *The Law of Property* §6.31 (1984).

71. *Teitelbaum v. Direct Realty Co.,* 172 Misc. 48, 13 N.Y.S.2d 886 (1939).

72. *Dieffenbach v. McIntyre,* 208 Okl. 163, 254 P.2d 346 (1952).

73. 54 Tenn.App. 328, 390 S.W.2d 703 (1964).

74. 64 N.J.Super. 599, 166 A.2d 803 (1960).

75. *Restatement, Second, Property, Landlord and Tenant* §16.3 (1977).

76. *Mitchell's, Inc. v. Nelms,* 454 S.W.2d 809 (Tex.Civ.App. 1970). See also *Restatement, Second, Property, Landlord and Tenant* §15.2 (1977), which adopts the minority view, and *Kendall v. Ernest Pestana, Inc.,* 40 Cal.3d 488, 220 Cal.Rptr. 818, 709 P.2d 837 (1985).

77. *D. L. Development, Inc. v. Nance,* 894 S.W.2d 258 (Mo.Ct. App. 1995).

78. M. Levin, *Withholding Consent to Assignment: The Changing Rights of the Commercial Landlord,* 30 DePaul Law Review 109, 142 (1980).

79. V. Marino, *10 Ways to Stumble in Commercial Real Estate,* New York Times 24 (November 12, 2006).

80. S. Smith, Annotation, *Failure of Landlord to Make, or Permit Tenant to Make, Repairs or Alterations Required by Public Authority as Constructive Eviction,* 86 American Law Reports 3d 352 (1978).

81. 28 Wash.2d 448, 183 P.2d 514 (1947).

82. 63 Misc.2d 937, 314 N.Y.S.2d 215 (1970).

83. 428 F.2d 1071, 1074, 1075, 1078 (D.C. Cir. 1970), *cert. denied* 400 U.S. 925.

84. 437 Mass. 708, 774 N.E.2d 611 (2002).

85. *Restatement, Second, Property, Landlord and Tenant* §§4 11.1–11.3 (1977).

86. Cal.Civ.Code §1942.

87. See New Hampshire Statute RSA 540-A:3,I. See also *Lally v. Flieder,* 159 N.H. 350, 986 A.2d 652 (Sup. Ct. 2009).

88. *State v. Jacobs,* 94 N.C. 950 (1886). See W. Prosser, *Law of Torts* §23 (4th ed. 1971).

89. 771 A.2d 1025 (D.C.App. 2001).

90. See, e.g., *Ragin v. Schwartz,* 393 F.Supp. 152 (W.D.Pa. 1975).

91. R. Aalberts, *Suits to Void Discriminatory Evictions of Disabled Tenants Under the Fair Housing Amendments Act: An Emerging Conflict?* 33 Real Property, Probate and Trust Journal 649 (1999).

92. 956 F.Supp. 792 (N.D. Ill. 1997).

93. *Hodges v. Feinstein, Raiss, Kelin & Booker, LLC,* 893 A.2d 21 (N.J. Super. 2006).

94. *Bernstein v. Seglin,* 184 Neb. 673, 171 N.W.2d 247 (1969).

95. *Dorcich v. Time Oil Co.,* 103 Cal.App.2d 677, 230 P.2d 10 (1951).

96. 611 N.E.2d 691, 693 (Ind.Ct. App. 1993).

97. 139 Mich. 608, 102 N.W. 1025 (1905).

98. *Casey v. Estes,* 657 So.2d 845 (Ala. 1995).

99. 238 Iowa 1068, 29 N.W.2d 420 (1947).

100. 125 Conn. 515, 7 A.2d 215 (1939).

101. 32 Ill.App.3d 563, 336 N.E.2d 374 (1975).

102. *Altz v. Leiberson,* 233 N.Y. 16, 134 N.E. 703 (1922).

103. *Henderson v. Dolas,* 217 S.W.2d 554 (Mo. 1949).

104. W. Keeton et al., *Prosser & Keeton on Torts* 443 (5th ed. 1984).

105. 44 Cal.App.3d 504, 118 Cal.Rptr. 741 (1975). See also *Restatement, Second, Property, Landlord and Tenant* §18.4 (1977).

106. *Frobig v. Gordon,* 849 P.2d 676 (Wash.App. 1993).

107. 393 Mich. 393, 224 N.W.2d 843 (1975).

108. W. Prosser, *Law of Torts* 236 (4th ed. 1971).

109. C. Mustafa, Comment, *The Implied Covenant of Warranty of Habitability, Foreseeability, and Landlord Liability for Third-Party Criminal Acts,* 54 UCLA L. Rev. 971 (2007).

110. 590 S.E.2d 807, 264 Ga. App. 456 (2003).

111. *Sargent v. Ross,* 113 N.H. 388, 308 A.2d 528 (1973).

112. *Stephens v. Stearns,* 106 Idaho 249, 678 P.2d 41 (1984).

113. *Id.* Among the states that have adopted the reasonable care standard are Arizona, California, Massachusetts, New York, Utah, and Wisconsin.

114. 38 Cal.3d 454, 213 Cal.Rptr. 213, 698 P.2d 116 (1985).

115. 43 Cal.Rptr.2d 836, 899 P.2d 905 (Cal. 1995) (en banc).

116. *Id.* at 851, 920.

117. 495 S.W.2d 887 (Tex. 1973).

118. *Lawrence v. Texas,* 539 U.S. 558, 123 S.Ct. 2472 (2003).

Land Use and Regulation

© MACIEJ NOSKOWSKI/iStockphoto (RF)

Rights and Duties of Landowners and Occupants

© MACIEJ NOSKOWSKI/iStockphoto (RF)

LEARNING OBJECTIVES

After studying Chapter 12, you should:

- Learn about tort law in general

- Recognize and distinguish trespass to land, nuisance, and invasion of privacy

- Understand the law of lost, misplaced, and abandoned property

- Be aware of the duties owed to persons outside real estate as well as the duties to persons entering the land

"The house of everyone is to him as his castle and fortress, as well for his defence against injury and violence as for his repose."

Sir Edward Coke

"LAND: A part of the earth's surface, considered as property. The theory that land is property subject to private ownership and control is the foundation of modern society, and is eminently worthy of the superstructure. Carried to its logical conclusion, it means that some have the right to prevent others from living; for the right to own implies the right exclusively to occupy, and in fact laws of trespass are enacted wherever property in land is recognised. It follows that if the whole area of terra firma is owned by A, B and C, there will be no place for D, E, F and G to be born, or, born as trespassers, to exist."

Ambrose Bierce, Devil's Dictionary

Acquiring real estate through purchase, lease, death, or adverse possession brings the owner a bundle of rights and duties that affect a person's ability to develop and use the property. This chapter considers the rights and duties arising under tort law. Although this chapter includes numerous examples involving real estate owners, the rules also apply to tenants or other occupants of real estate. Later chapters (Chapters 13 and 14) discuss the private and public control of land use by contract, planning and zoning, and environmental legislation.

After a brief summary of tort law, this chapter examines the following rights of an owner or occupant of real estate:

1. The right to damages or injunctive relief when someone trespasses or creates a nuisance
2. The right to privacy
3. The right to personal property discovered on the real estate

Owning or occupying real estate also results in certain duties to persons outside the real estate and to persons entering the real estate. These duties are covered after a discussion of landowner rights.

Tort Law

tort

A civil wrong that causes harm to person, property, or reputation.

negligence

The failure to do what a reasonable person would have done under the same circumstances.

duty

A legal obligation.

contributory negligence

Conduct by a plaintiff that is below the standard to which he is legally required to conform for his own protection. Along with the negligence of the defendant, it is a contributing cause of the plaintiff's harm.

A **tort** is a wrongful act that injures another person's body, property, or reputation. Torts commonly fall within one of *three* categories: negligence, intentional tort, and strict liability. (See Figure 12.1.) The key to a **negligence** action, the *first* tort category, is a **duty** owed by the person committing the tort to the injured party. Once the duty has been established—for example, the duty of an automobile driver to operate the automobile in a reasonable manner—the victim must prove that the duty was breached and that the breach caused injury to the victim.

Even if negligence has been established, the victim might not be allowed to recover damages if his own negligence contributed to the loss; such a situation comes under the doctrine of **contributory negligence**. The defendant's proof of the plaintiff's contributory negligence serves as a defense to the plaintiff's action. That is, the plaintiff's action is barred by the defendant's proof that the plaintiff also was negligent.

In recent years, most courts have shifted from the contributory negligence approach to the **comparative negligence** theory. In most states, if the plaintiff's contributory negligence equals or exceeds (depending on state law) half the fault incurred by both parties, the plaintiff will not receive damages.[1] (See endnote 1 to access information on what contributory and comparative negligence approaches the states follow). For example, assume that Messer injured Miller in a car accident and Miller's damages were assessed at $10,000. If Miller's fault or contributory negligence was determined to be 40 percent, he would receive only 60 percent of the damages, or $6,000; however, if his fault was 50 percent or more, Miller would receive no damages. A few states, such as Washington state as discussed in the case below, employ a pure comparative negligence approach in which the plaintiff can be awarded damages as long as she is not 100 percent contributorily negligent.

A CASE IN POINT

In *Seal v. Naches Seal Irrigation District*,[2] Seal, the owner of a cherry orchard, sued the Irrigation District for negligence. Seal alleged that the District's carelessness allowed water to seep from its irrigation canal into his cherry orchard. The water then caused the growth of a harmful fungus that damaged his trees. The trial court found the plaintiff to be 95 percent contributorily negligent for the injury to his trees for failing to adequately prune, fertilize, and irrigate. The appellate court upheld the ruling and awarded Seal $46,200 for gross damages, which was reduced by 95 percent to $2,310.

FIGURE 12.1
Tort Categories

comparative negligence

Under comparative negligence statutes or doctrines, negligence is measured in terms of percentage and any damages allowed shall be diminished in proportion to the amount of negligence attributable to the person for whose injury, damage,

(continued)

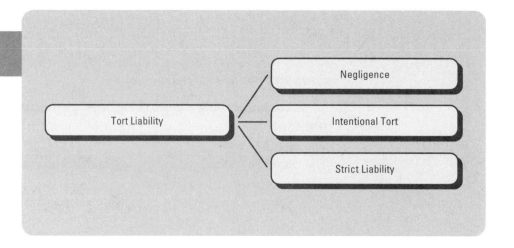

comparative negligence
(continued)

or death recovery is sought.
In most states, the person
seeking the recovery
receives no damages when
her proportion of fault
exceeds 50 percent or more.

A plaintiff may also be denied recovery under the defense of **assumption of risk**. The defense applies when the victim possesses actual awareness of a risk and then chooses voluntarily to incur it.[3] As the next Ohio case points out, the extent of the risk does not have to be known precisely, but must be one associated with the activity.

A CASE IN POINT

In *Rees v. Cleveland Indians Baseball Company*,[4] Donna Rees was hit in the face by a broken baseball bat during a game between the Cleveland Indians and the New York Yankees. The court stated that to prove assumption of risk, "the plaintiff need only consciously expose himself to the known risk, not directly to the exact episode which causes the injury." In this case, the court noted that Rees "watched the Indians games on television and attended non-professional games on a weekly basis" and "[s]he admitted that while watching games on television, she saw the bat fly from a batter's hands and saw a player swing and break a bat." The court ruled that the assumption of risk defense was appropriate "because of her [Rees's] familiarity with the stadium, the game of baseball, and the specific location of her seat." Therefore, the court stated that "she knew that she was unprotected from objects that might enter the stands."

assumption of risk

A defense to a negligence
action that occurs when
the plaintiff knows and
appreciates the risks and
voluntarily chooses to be
exposed to the risks.

The *second* tort category—**intentional tort**—requires proof that the wrongful act was intentional and that the act caused an injury. For instance, if an automobile driver intentionally hits a pedestrian, the driver will be liable for the intentional tort of battery. Intentional torts include all of the following:

1. **Battery**, the harmful or offensive touching of another person without consent
2. **Assault**, an attempted or threatened battery
3. **False imprisonment**, the unlawful detention of another person
4. **Conversion**, the unjustified taking or detention of another person's property

intentional tort

An intentional wrongful
act that causes injury.

In many cases, the commission of an intentional tort also constitutes a criminal act.

The *third* type of tort—**strict liability**—imposes liability even though the party has not been negligent and has not intentionally caused injury. Strict liability often results when a person is engaged in dangerous or abnormal activities, such as blasting operations. In recent years, the most common example of strict liability is the liability imposed on a business that sells a defective product. Section 402A of the *Restatement (Second) of Torts* imposes strict liability on the seller even though "the seller has exercised all possible care in the preparation and sale of his product." For example, in the *Embs v. Pepsi Cola Bottling Co.* case discussed at the end of the chapter, a customer was injured in a grocery store by an exploding 7-UP bottle. The bottler was not negligent since it had exercised the same care as a reasonable bottler similarly situated, but was still found liable under strict liability.

strict liability

Responsibility for personal
or property damage
regardless of whether it
was caused by a negligent
or intentional act.

Trespass to Land

Elements

trespass

Any unauthorized
intrusion or invasion of
private premises or land
of another.

A **trespass** occurs when a person physically enters another person's land. At one time, a person who entered another person's land was strictly liable even though the entry was not intentional and not negligent. However, the modern view is that a person will not be held liable for trespass unless it is proven that she intentionally or negligently entered the land of another.[5] According to Section 166 of the *Restatement (Second) of Torts*, "except where the actor is engaged in an abnormally dangerous activity, an unintentional and non-negligent entry on land" does not result in liability. For example, in the classic U.S. Supreme Court case, *Parrot v. Wells, Fargo & Co.*,[6] the employees of a freight carrier, Wells Fargo, used a hammer to open a box containing nitroglycerine, causing an explosion that damaged the plaintiff's property. The Court decided that the carrier should not be held liable for causing a trespass since it was not proven that the employees were negligent. In the Texas case of *Malouf v. Dallas Athletic Country Club*,[7] the court held that golfers who hit balls from an adjacent country club into neighboring homes and cars were not liable for trespass. Although the golfers intended to hit the golf balls, they did not intend to hook or slice their balls to reach the plaintiff's property; they were merely trying to reach the sixth hole.

Once the required negligent or intentional entry is shown, courts require proof of a physical invasion of the land. For example, a blasting operation that is carried on at all hours of the night and causes extreme discomfort to residents of the neighborhood will not result in liability because noise alone does not constitute a physical invasion. However, the deposit of heavy objects or even dust and particles too small to be observed by the human eye on the neighboring premises would result in liability for trespass. As discussed in Chapter 3, the trespass might be below the surface or, as the following New York case discusses, above the surface.

A CASE IN POINT

In *Butler v. Frontier Telephone Co.*,[8] the plaintiff brought an ejectment action against a telephone company that had run a telephone wire over his property 30 feet above the land. The court decided that there had been a physical invasion of the plaintiff's interest in the land. "According to the fundamental principles …, space above land is real estate the same as the land itself. The law regards the empty space as if it were a solid, inseparable from the soil, and protects it from hostile occupation accordingly…. [A]n owner is entitled to the absolute and undisturbed possession of every part of his premises, including the space above as much as a mine beneath."

Plaintiffs in a trespass action must prove that they have the right to possession of the real estate. The landowner who leases property and grants the exclusive right of possession to a tenant would not be allowed to recover in trespass if a trespasser intruded on the property. Similarly, if the trespasser damages the property that is subject to the landlord's reversionary interest, the trespasser may be liable to the landlord such as for loss of rent, but not on the basis of trespass.[9]

One modern issue, decided by a California court, is whether trespass can occur through cyberspace.

A CASE IN POINT

In *Intel Corp. v. Hamidi*, a disgruntled ex-Intel employee sent a barrage of e-mails to Intel employees, harshly criticizing management. Intel sued, claiming that the e-mails placed on Intel's network and equipment constituted a trespass. The California Supreme Court ruled that the real issue in this case was one of free speech, not trespass. The court stated that: "[H]e [Hamidi] no more invaded Intel's property than does a protester holding a sign or shouting through a bullhorn outside corporate headquarters, posting a letter through the mail, or telephoning to complain of a corporate practice."[10] Still, the court made it clear that other kinds of speech, such as commercial speech, including spam, are not afforded the same protection under the First Amendment.

In a later case distinguishable from *Hamidi*, the federal Second Circuit Court of Appeals ruled in a case from New York that a cybertrespass did occur when a company used an automated computer program to scour the databases of a competitor.[11]

The *Hamidi* and other "cybertrespass" cases are not prosecuted under the theory of trespass to land; rather, they are prosecuted under the theory of trespass to chattels (personal property) since the offensive e-mails enter the landowner's computer hardware and network. However, the distinction between the two theories appears to be more academic than practical.

Because trespass (as well as nuisance, discussed later in this chapter) is often committed by the adjacent landowner's intentional acts, property loss is not covered by the offending party's homeowner's insurance. As discussed in Chapter 8, insurance, as a matter of public policy, does not provide coverage for intentional acts of the insured as the next case from Georgia points out.

A CASE IN POINT

In *Georgia Farm Bureau Mutual Insurance Co. v. Vanhuss*,[12] Vanhuss, a chicken farmer, was sued by adjacent landowners in a residential neighborhood for trespass and nuisance for diverting the natural flow of a stream onto their properties and for nuisance from activities on his chicken farm. In both cases, Vanhuss was requested to desist, but he ignored the entreaties. His insurance company sought a declaratory judgment claiming that the policy did not cover intentional trespass and nuisance. The court ruled there was no coverage since Vanhuss intentionally allowed both activities to happen in an ongoing manner.

One unique, albeit inflammatory, application of trespass occurred in 2010, when Arizona passed a statute in which all illegal aliens could be prosecuted as trespassers. The pertinent provision in the statute states: "In addition to any violation of federal law, a person is guilty of trespassing if the person is both: 1. present on any public or private land in the state. 2. in violation of 8 United State Code 1304(e) or 1306(a)." As the foregoing discussion of trespass indicates, trespass has for centuries been used primarily by private landowners to exclude others from their lands. The use of it to exclude a whole class of people from an entire state indeed raises very thorny constitutional issues as well as a political issue by serving notice to the federal government that state law will be applied if the federal government cannot protect the state from illegal incursions into the country.[13]

Damages

A trespasser faces liability for *four* possible types of damages. *First*, in any case, the trespasser will be liable for at least **nominal damages** because, as a North Carolina court stated:

> it is an elementary principle that every unauthorized, and therefore unlawful entry, into the close of another, is a trespass. From every such entry against the will of the possessor, the law infers some damage; if nothing more, the treading down the grass or the herbage, or as here, the shrubbery.[14]

For example, when the defendant's employee removed "about forty canoe loads of sand" from the plaintiff's beach, no actual damages were proven and a New Hampshire court awarded nominal damages of one dollar.[15] However, the *Restatement (Second) of Torts* does call for the elimination of nominal damages if the trespass is not intentional.[16]

nominal damages

A trifling sum awarded to a plaintiff in an action where there is no substantial loss or injury to be compensated, but still the law recognizes a technical invasion of his rights or a breach of the defendant's duty, or in cases where, although there has been a real injury, the plaintiff's evidence entirely fails to show its amount.

compensatory damages

Damages that compensate the injured party for the injury sustained and nothing more, such as will simply make good or replace the loss caused by the wrong or injury.

Second, **compensatory damages** will be awarded in cases where harm is proven. In many cases, the plaintiff may recover the lesser of one of the following:

1. The depreciation in the value of the land as a result of the trespass
2. The cost of restoring the land[17]

Third, if the trespasser has acted willfully, entering the land knowing that she is wrong, as the following court from Maine ruled, her actions could result in a court awarding **punitive damages**.

A CASE IN POINT

In *Elliott v. Sherman*,[18] the plaintiffs owned two summer estates between a summer hotel and the sea. The defendant ordered employees of the hotel to cut down trees on the summer estates, which had beautified and sheltered the estates from onlookers, so that there would be a direct view from the hotel to the sea. The court, in awarding $16,000 in damages to the plaintiffs, noted that "there was credible evidence from which the jury could find that the trespasses were committed at the direction of the defendant, that his action in this respect was willful, and knowingly taken in total disregard of the plaintiffs' property rights.... The attitude of the defendant is well shown by the un-contradicted testimony of a witness who testified that the defendant stated, prior to the cutting of the trees on the Collins property and upon being told they would make trouble: 'To hell with them. Let them sue me. All they can get is the cost of the trees.'"

punitive damages

Damages other than compensatory damages that may be awarded against a person to punish her for outrageous conduct.

statutory compensation measures

Damages prescribed by statute.

Finally, double or triple damages may be allowed the owner under **statutory compensation measures** in cases of willful trespass. For example, a Michigan statute provides that

any person who (a) cuts down or carries off any wood, underwood, trees, or timber or despoils or injures any trees on another's lands, or (b) digs up or carries away stone, ore, gravel, clay, sand, turf, or mold or any root, fruit, or plant from another's lands, or (c) cuts down or carries away any grass, hay, or any kind of grain from another's lands without permission of the owner of the lands, or on the lands or commons of any city, township, village, or other public corporation without license to do so, is liable to the owner of the land or the public corporation for 3 times the amount of actual damages.[19]

Privileged Trespass

In many cases, a property owner will be unable to recover damages from a trespasser because the trespass is privileged. As a general rule, privileges are based on the social value of the act in question; as the social purpose of the act becomes greater, the trespasser achieves broader protection. Several privileges are especially relevant to trespass;[20] they are discussed next.

Consent   An owner who has consented to another person's entry on his land cannot recover on a trespass theory. Although consent is often referred to as a privilege, as Justice Holmes noted in discussing assault, "the absence of lawful consent is part of the definition."[21] In the next case from South Carolina, a property owner attempted to show he had not lawfully consented to an entry of land by the phone company at a time when phone companies owned everyone's phones.

A CASE IN POINT

In *Plate v. Southern Bell Telephone & Telegraph Co.*,[22] the plaintiff sued the defendant telephone company for willful trespass when the company entered his apartment to remove his telephone, which the telephone company owned. The removal took place after the plaintiff had failed to pay his telephone bill for three months. The company employee who removed the telephone gained entrance to the apartment with the assistance of a person who had a master key to all of the apartments in the building.

In deciding that the company had not committed a trespass, the court noted that the plaintiff had agreed to the telephone company's regulations when he applied for telephone service. One of the regulations provided that "the Company's employees and agents may enter said premises at any reasonable hour, … upon termination or cancellation of the service, to remove such instruments and lines." This agreement gave the company the privilege to enter the property, subject only to the condition that the company not commit a breach of peace, an exception not applicable to this case.

consent

A voluntary agreement by a person with sufficient legal capacity to do something proposed by another.

A person who exceeds the scope of the owner's **consent** can become a trespasser. In the Minnesota case of *Copeland v. Hubbard Broadcasting, Inc.*,[23] homeowners allowed a student to accompany their veterinarian on a home visit. However, the "student" was a television reporter who secretly videotaped and later broadcast the home's interior as part of an investigative report. The court held that the property owner stated a trespass claim. However, when an ophthalmic clinic consented to having *Primetime Live* do a "fair and balanced" broadcast segment, an Illinois court did not recognize the clinic's trespass claim when the actual broadcast was more of an exposé, claiming that the surgeon performed unnecessary procedures for money.[24]

Reclamation of Personal Property   A person commonly attempts to reclaim her personal property by entering the land of another in *three* situations. *First*, the personal property may be on the land as a result of the latter owner's wrongful act such as a theft or conversion. In such cases, the owner of the personal property is entitled to enter the land to remove the property, although she must act reasonably and must first request that the real estate owner return the goods.

Second, if the personal property is on another person's land because of an act of God, the owner of the personal property may enter the land to remove the property, although she will be liable for damage caused during the removal. For instance, the owner of a gazebo blown onto a neighbor's property during a tornado may retrieve it; but she must pay for the shrubbery she ruins in the process of removal.

Finally, if the personal property is on someone else's land through the personal property owner's fault, there is no right of entry. For example, an animal owner who allows the animal to run onto a neighbor's land does not have the right to enter the land to retrieve the animal. Furthermore, the owner of a trespassing animal is liable for damages that the animal caused, even when the animal's owner is unaware of the trespass. However, an exception, as a New York court noted, has been created for dogs and cats.

A CASE IN POINT

In *Bishop v. Plescia,*[25] the plaintiff left his registered schnauzer, Fifi, who was in heat, in his fenced-in backyard while he answered the telephone. When he returned, he discovered Fifi in a misalliance with a nonpedigreed mongrel by the name of Sneaker. After separating the dogs, Fifi's owner asked a veterinarian to administer shots to avoid conception; but as a result of the shots, Fifi developed an infection and could no longer be bred. When the plaintiff sued Sneaker's owner for damages, the court decided for the defendant on the grounds that Sneaker did not exhibit vicious propensities but was merely following his natural instincts.

public necessity

A legal privilege to enter or destroy another's property in the public interest.

private necessity

The entering or destruction of another's property to protect a person's property, health, or safety.

Necessity   When it is necessary to save life or property, a person is privileged to enter the land of another in certain instances. Some cases involve **public necessity**, as when one person enters another's land to dynamite a building to stop a fire that threatens a town. In such cases, the owner of the real estate is not entitled to compensation from the trespasser because "the 'champion of the public' is not required to pay out of his own pocket for the general salvation."[26,27]

In cases of **private necessity**, which results when people act to protect themselves or their property, trespassers are liable for actual damages. For example, a man who ties his boat to someone else's dock during a storm must pay for any resulting damages to the dock.[28]

Operation of Law   A public officer is privileged to enter the land of another to execute legal process—for example, to seize property under a writ of execution or to arrest a person under a warrant. The privilege extends to cases in which an arrest may be made without a warrant. In one case, a California ranch owner sued agents of the U.S. Immigration Service, alleging a trespass on his land when agents entered without a warrant to arrest laborers who were in the United States illegally. In deciding in favor of the agents, the court observed that the agents had the right to make an arrest without a warrant when they reasonably believed that a felony was being committed.[29] Some states, by statute, have characterized public officers, such as firefighters and police officers, as licensees. Sometimes called the "firefighters rule," the law not only allows the officer to enter the premises in the course of his duties but also imposes a duty of care on the landowner. The duties owed a police officer/licensee are discussed in the *Flodquist v. Palmieri* case on page 497 in this chapter.[30]

Forcible Entry   Owners are privileged to enter their land to remove people who are living there without permission. For instance, if a tenant remains in an apartment after the period of the lease, the landlord is technically not committing a trespass when he physically removes the tenant. However, because of the potential for harm when a person uses force, most states have made forcible entry by the owner a criminal offense and have allowed the person evicted to recover damages for assault and battery. Instead, the dispossessed landowner should commence a civil action in the courts, where possession can often be recovered within a matter of days.[31]

ETHICAL AND PUBLIC POLICY ISSUES

Should Landowners Always Be Allowed to Forcibly Oust Squatters?

Squatters, due to lack of affordable, adequate housing, often have few housing alternatives and sometimes inhabit empty, dilapidated buildings. Should landowners, some of whom have virtually ignored the property for years, be able to forcibly evict these squatters, many of whom have lived there for years and have even improved the property and surrounding neighborhoods? Or should squatters, in certain situations, be afforded property rights? This issue is discussed in Problem 10 at the end of the chapter.

Private Property and Free Speech Whether a private property owner—such as the owner of a mall or shopping center—can restrict free speech activities is one of the more difficult trespass-related questions to reach the Supreme Court in recent years. In 1972, the Court held that individuals have no right under federal law to distribute literature protesting the draft and the Vietnam War in a privately owned shopping center.[32] However, in 1980, in the case of *Pruneyard Shopping Center v. Robins,*[33] the U.S. Supreme Court held that such rights might exist under state law, clearing the way for states to form their own rules. In *Pruneyard,* the California Supreme Court, previous to the appeal to the high court, had determined that commercial property owners could establish the "time, place, and manner" for making speeches and petitioning and allowed smaller retail establishments to exclude these activities.

Courts that have considered the issue since 1980 are divided over whether to allow free speech activities at shopping centers and malls.[34] One New Jersey case ruled that citizens opposed to military intervention in the Persian Gulf should be allowed to distribute leaflets in a shopping center, reasoning that the center is the modern equivalent of a downtown.[35] Concern has been expressed that such decisions elevate free speech rights over property rights, thus increasing the common area maintenance costs of the mall's merchants.[36] Free speech advocates and petitioners, on the other hand, are upset that some malls limit their activities to just a few days a week and have established "blackout days" on the busiest shopping days of the year. The tension between property and speech-related activities has also been evident in conflicting decisions about whether union members, such as in the following Connecticut case, can distribute handbills in front of stores.[37]

Was it legal for a mall owner to exclude from the mall's common areas labor union members who wanted to hand out information on employees' rights? In *United Food and Commercial Workers Union, Local 919, AFL-CIO v. Crystal Mall Associates, L.P.* on page 506, the Connecticut Supreme Court addressed the issue.

END OF CHAPTER CASE

Trespass to Abate a Nuisance A person injured by nuisance is privileged to enter the land of another person to abate the nuisance. However, the injured party must act within a reasonable time after discovering the nuisance; if a reasonable time has already passed, most courts will decide that the party should have commenced an action in court rather than use self-help. In most states, the injured party also must notify the owner, when possible, that he intends to enter the property to abate the nuisance. If these requirements are met, the injured person may use reasonable force to terminate the nuisance and may even go so far as to destroy property, such as a dam, a telephone pole, a barge, or a dog, when it is a nuisance.[38]

Nuisance

The law of nuisance has confused lawyers and property owners for centuries. In the words of the eminent authority on tort law, Professor William Prosser,

> there is perhaps no more impenetrable jungle in the entire law than that which surrounds the word 'nuisance.' It has meant all things to all men, and has been applied indiscriminately to everything from an alarming advertisement to a cockroach baked in a pie. There is general agreement that it is incapable of any exact or comprehensible definition.[39]

Nuisance Defined

Private Nuisance   Although the term *nuisance* cannot be precisely defined, the general character of private and public nuisances can be distinguished. A **private nuisance** "is an unreasonable interference with the use or enjoyment of land without there being a trespass or physical invasion."[40] As a New York court noted,

> *every person is bound to make a reasonable use of his property so as to occasion no unnecessary damage or annoyance to his neighbor. If he makes an unreasonable, unwarrantable or unlawful use of it, so as to produce a material annoyance, inconvenience, discomfort, or hurt to his neighbor, he will be guilty of a nuisance to his neighbor.*[41]

This chapter focuses primarily on the law of private nuisance because of its impact on the rights of a landowner.

Public Nuisance   A **public nuisance** is one that damages the rights of the public in general. Creating a public nuisance is a criminal act, and public nuisances are often defined by specific statutes such as the following from Michigan:

> *Any building, vehicle, boat, aircraft or place used for the purpose of lewdness, assignation or prostitution or gambling, or used by, or kept for the use of prostitutes or other disorderly persons, or used for the unlawful manufacture, storing, possessing, transporting, sale, keeping for sale, giving away, bartering, furnishing or otherwise disposing of any narcotic and/or hypnotic drug as defined by law or of any vinous, malt, brewed, fermented, spirituous or intoxicating liquors or any mixed liquors or beverages, any part of which is intoxicating, is hereby declared a nuisance.*[42]

Under this statute, the attorney general, a prosecuting attorney, or any citizen may bring an action for an injunction to stop the nuisance. If the court issues an injunction and the injunction is violated, the offender may be fined up to $1,000 and imprisoned for as long as six months.

As discussed in Chapter 11, meth labs can incur civil and criminal liability for landlords. In some states they are considered to be a public nuisance as well.

It is possible that even a lawful business, as a South Carolina court ruled, will be considered a public nuisance because of the manner it operates.

private nuisance
The unreasonable interference with the use or enjoyment of land without there being a trespass or physical invasion.

public nuisance
An unreasonable interference with a right that is common to the general public.

A CASE IN POINT

In *State v. Turner,* the court held that a dance hall was a public nuisance: "Although the defendants may have a license for the sale of wine and beer, and the drinking of it on the premises violates no statutory law, they have no right to habitually allow the assembling in and around the Circle Bar of noisy, drunken, boisterous crowds, whose noise and profanity disturb the peace and quiet of the public coming within the range of its influence. One who knowingly suffers or permits such conduct commits a public nuisance."[43]

Because of its broad scope, the concept of public nuisance is being advanced by some plaintiffs in novel situations. Manufacturers of lead paint, for instance, have been sued for creating a public nuisance in a number of states, including Rhode Island, Wisconsin, and Missouri, as well as a number of counties and municipalities. Nearly all of these cases, however, were eventually dismissed on appeal. Some commentators are also concerned that public nuisance laws will be wielded as a legal "sword" in the future against firearm manufacturers and sellers, smokers (for emitting passive smoke), and even restaurants that serve fatty foods.[44]

A public nuisance might also be a *private* nuisance in some instances. However, individuals are allowed to recover damages only when their individual injury differs in kind from the injury to the public. For example, a house of prostitution might be considered a public nuisance because of its effect on public morals; the house might also be a private nuisance if the late-night activities disturb neighboring landowners' sleep. Massive Christmas lights and displays on the defendant's home and land that resulted in extreme traffic congestion and motor vehicle accidents were held in an Arkansas case to form the basis of both a public and private nuisance.[45] Neighborhood residents suffered a public nuisance, and two homeowners who lost access to and from their homes suffered a private nuisance not shared by the public.

Elements of Private Nuisance Act A private nuisance is an act interfering with property rights causing substantial and unreasonable harm. (See Figure 12.2.) The act may be intentional, which is usually the case, or negligent. In a few cases, a defendant will be held strictly liable under nuisance theory, especially when the defendant has engaged in a dangerous activity, such as running a blasting operation. In discussing the type of act that may result in nuisance liability, a North Carolina court observed:

> *Much confusion exists in respect to the legal basis of liability in the law of private nuisance because of the deplorable tendency of the courts to call everything a nuisance, and let it go at that.... The confusion on this score vanishes in large part, however, when proper heed is paid to the sound propositions that private nuisance is a field of tort liability rather than a single type of tortious conduct; that the feature which gives unity to this field of tort liability is the interest invaded, namely, the interest in the use and enjoyment of land; that any substantial nontrespassory invasion of another's interest in the private use and enjoyment of land by any type of liability forming conduct is a private nuisance; that the invasion which subjects a person to liability for private nuisance may be either intentional or unintentional; that a person is subject to liability for an intentional invasion when his conduct is unreasonable under the circumstances of the particular case; and that a person is subject to liability for an unintentional invasion when his conduct is negligent, reckless or ultrahazardous.[46]*

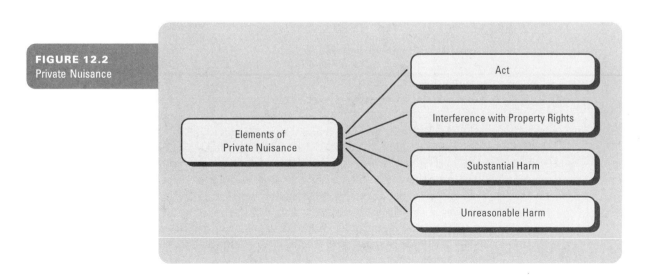

FIGURE 12.2
Private Nuisance

Elements of Private Nuisance — Act — Interference with Property Rights — Substantial Harm — Unreasonable Harm

Interference with Property Rights   Because, by definition, a private nuisance is an interference with the use of one's land, plaintiffs in a nuisance action must prove that they have a property interest in the affected land and that there was interference with this interest. The interference normally does not involve a physical invasion of the land—which would be grounds for a trespass action—although it is possible for one activity to create both trespass and nuisance liability. For instance, a blasting operation might cause a trespass by throwing debris on neighboring land and might also create a nuisance because of the resulting noise.

Substantial Harm   The plaintiff in a nuisance action must prove that the harm is substantial. Courts often state that substantial harm must be of a permanent rather than temporary nature. While permanency might be a requirement if the plaintiff were seeking an injunction to prevent harm in the future, there have been many cases where courts have found that a nuisance resulted from a single activity by the defendant. The burial of a dead cow or a factory's release of gases into the air after a fan malfunction[47] are examples of such cases. With the advent of new "green" energy sources, new issues over private nuisance have emerged, such as in the following West Virginia case.

Can windmills constructed to generate electricity be considered a private nuisance? In *Burch v. NedPower Mount Storm, LLC* on page 508, the West Virginia Supreme Court considered this important issue.

END OF CHAPTER CASE

More important than permanency is the question of whether a reasonable person would object to the harm as the next Massachusetts case discusses.

A CASE IN POINT

In *Rogers v. Elliott*,[48] the plaintiff had suffered a sunstroke and, as a result, was subject to convulsions when he heard loud noises. The plaintiff's father asked Father Elliott, the priest in charge of a Catholic church across the street from the plaintiff's house, not to ring the church bell one Sunday because of the plaintiff's illness. The priest ignored the request and rang the bell as usual, with the result that the plaintiff suffered convulsions. The court decided that the bell ringing was not a nuisance because it did not affect ordinary people.

Other activities determined by the courts *not* to be nuisances have ranged from playing croquet[49] (Washington, D.C.) to digging worms (Louisiana).[50] Residents' fear of contracting cancer from uranium mill emissions (Colorado)[51] or of the future health effects of oil contamination (Virginia)[52] have also been held insufficient to state a nuisance claim.

Nuisances have been found, however, in cases where the defendant's factory produced odors and soot that caused the plaintiffs to experience nausea, vomiting, and headaches (Michigan);[53] where the defendants manufactured jewelry by using a 500-pound drop hammer, causing the plaintiff's house to tremble and his newspaper to shake as he was reading it (Rhode Island);[54] and where the operation of a factory interfered with a plaintiff's sleep (New York).[55]

One common nuisance problem, discussed in the following Kansas case, stems from trees that can cause substantial harm to another's property.

A CASE IN POINT

In *Pierce v. Casady*, the defendant's tree contained a split on one limb that leaned precariously toward plaintiff's property. If it fell, it would likely damage the plaintiff's garage, home, and automobile. The plaintiff petitioned the court for a declaratory judgment to have the tree removed as a nuisance. The court explained that there are three theories for finding a tree a nuisance: "First, a tree is a nuisance when it constantly drops branches and requires constant maintenance. Second, a tree is a nuisance when there is a statute so defining it. Finally, a tree becomes a nuisance when it does substantial harm or creates an immediate danger of causing harm." The court, in this case of first impression in Kansas, adopted the third approach as law and ruled that the tree could cause substantial harm due to "the split in the fork of the tree located above plaintiff's property, the squeaking sound when the wind blows … and the angle at which the tree leans toward plaintiff's property…." Therefore, the court ordered the defendant to abate it as a nuisance by either removing the entire tree or cutting it off at the property line.[56]

Unreasonable Harm   The *last* element necessary to prove the existence of a nuisance—unreasonable harm—is more complex than the other elements because courts examine all pertinent factors in the case to determine reasonableness. Courts, such as the Ohio court quoted below, have traditionally attempted to balance the interests of both parties in nuisance cases because of the two competing principles present in every case:

> *The principle that every person is entitled to use his property for any purpose that he sees fit, and the opposing principle that everyone is bound to use his property in such a manner as not to injure the property or rights of his neighbor. For generations courts, in their task of judging, have ruled on these extremes according to the wisdom of the day, and many have recognized that the contemporary view of public policy shifts from generation to generation.*[57]

Determining an appropriate remedy is closely related to the question of reasonableness. The court in most cases must decide whether to use injunctive relief to abate the nuisance or to award damages. An award of damages is always the preferred remedy because injunctive relief often puts the defendant out of business. Courts have historically refused to grant equitable relief, such as an injunction, when the legal remedy—damages—was adequate.

Courts commonly consider *six factors* in determining whether an activity is unreasonable and whether the plaintiff should be awarded damages or injunctive relief. It should be emphasized that the plaintiff must prove all *elements* to win his case, but not necessarily all *factors*. The reason is that the court considers only those factors it considers applicable to the case. Moreover, some factors may carry less weight than others in determining unreasonable harm.

The Activity's Value to Society   The *first* factor courts often consider, such as the Washington state court did in the following case, is the social and economic value to society of the activity in question.

A CASE IN POINT

In *Bartel v. Ridgefield Lumber Co.*,[58] smoke, sawdust, and burned lumber blew from the defendant's sawmill onto the plaintiff's land and damaged vegetables, fruits, and clothing hung in the yard. While the court held the defendant liable for damages, it refused to enjoin the activity: "Here the plaintiff's property is of comparatively small value and importance. That of the respondent is of great value. If we held that defendant must not, under any circumstances, cast sawdust, smoke and cinders on plaintiff's property, then we, in effect, forever close the mill. This, under the circumstances, we will not do. The manufacture of lumber is the most important business of western Washington, and no unnecessary interference therein will be permitted.... Apparently defendant is solvent and capable of responding to such damages as the plaintiffs may suffer. It is infinitely more equitable, under all the circumstances, to require them to enforce payment of their damages than to force the closing of this manufacturing plant."

The court in *Bartel* echoed the philosophy of Lord Justice James in an earlier English case:

> *If some picturesque haven opens its arms to invite the commerce of the world, it is not for this court to forbid the embrace, although the fruit of it should be the sights, the sounds, and smells of a common seaport and shipbuilding town, which would drive the Dryads and their masters from their ancient solitudes.*[59]

Coming to the Nuisance   The *Bartel* case also raised a *second* factor—whether the plaintiff moved near an existing nuisance. The *Bartel* court followed the majority approach in awarding the plaintiff damages even though the sawmill was in operation when the plaintiff purchased the neighboring farm. Another example is the New Mexico case of *Mahone v. Autry*,[60] in which the court held that the defendant's operation of riding stables was a nuisance, even though there were no residences near the stable when it was established and the area became residential only after a number of years.

To protect farmers from nuisance actions caused by urban sprawl, some states have passed "Right to Farm" laws. For example, in Vermont, farmers are protected from lawsuits for agricultural activities "established prior to surrounding non-agricultural activities."[61]

In the next case, a Missouri court was asked to decide whether those who build close to fraternity houses should prevail in a nuisance action.

A CASE IN POINT

In *Edmonds v. Sigma Chapter of Alpha Kappa Lambda Fraternity*,[62] Edmonds sued a fraternity at Central Missouri State for nuisance due to noise, litter, and shooting of firearms during parties attended by hundreds of people. The fraternity house was located in a rural area, but Edmonds later built his home close to it. The appeals court ruled that even though plaintiff had "come to the nuisance," the frat house's activities were sufficient enough to constitute a private nuisance. The appeals court also upheld the lower court's injunction that included four limitations to the fraternity's activities. The fraternity must (1) fence its property with a closed gate during late-night hours, (2) not have gatherings of over 200 people, (3) not allow the shooting of firearms, and (4) furnish a list of people to whom Edmonds could report further disturbances.

Just as the plaintiff who "comes to the nuisance" is usually allowed to prevail, the plaintiff who does nothing to prevent the establishment of a nuisance may later be allowed relief. For instance, when the plaintiff knew that his neighbor was constructing a baseball diamond but did not object until a year later, an Iowa court noted that

> *... if plaintiff had attempted to prevent construction of the diamond or playing of games before they were so conducted as to be a nuisance in fact he would have been met with the rule that a threatened or anticipated nuisance will not be enjoined unless it clearly appears a nuisance will necessarily result from the act it is sought to enjoin. Relief will usually be denied until a nuisance has been committed where the thing sought to be enjoined may or may not become such, depending on its use or other circumstances.... Knowledge or acquiescence in the erection of a structure will not estop one from suing to abate it as a nuisance because of the manner of its operation. Plaintiff was not required to anticipate that the diamond would be so used as to become a nuisance.*[63]

Hardship   A *third* factor important to the courts is the hardship to the plaintiff suffering the nuisance compared to the hardship to the defendant if the nuisance were abated. In the following case, the U.S. Supreme Court addressed this problem when it arose in Missouri.

A CASE IN POINT

In *Harrisonville v. W.S. Dickey Clay Co.*,[64] the small town of Harrisonville, Missouri, built a sewage disposal plant at a substantial cost. The operation of the plant polluted a small stream that ran through the plaintiff's stock farm, and the plaintiff asked the court to close the plant. The court decided that since the plaintiff's injuries amounted to only $500, an award of damages would be more appropriate than injunctive relief: "Where substantial redress can be afforded by the payment of money and the issuance of an injunction would subject the defendant to grossly disproportionate hardship, equitable relief may be denied although the nuisance is indisputable."

The Activity's Location   *Fourth,* courts often consider the location of the activity that has created the alleged nuisance. In one Ohio case, for example, the defendant raised ducks, sometimes as many as a thousand, on his farm in a rural farming area. The plaintiff, who lived across the road from the defendant, complained that the ducks created a nuisance because their quacking kept her awake all night. The court disagreed, noting that raising ducks was a proper pursuit in this location and that a person must suffer discomfort resulting from the "circumstances of the place and the usual business carried on in the vicinity."[65] In many cases, the question of whether an activity is proper for a given area is determined by a zoning ordinance. Even where an activity is allowed by a zoning ordinance, however, the activity must be conducted in a reasonable manner.

Prevention of Damage   A *fifth* factor that courts consider, as in the Michigan case below, is whether the damage can be prevented, especially when the courts are faced with the question of closing a business.

A CASE IN POINT

In *Mitchell v. Hines*,[66] the defendant raised 400 pigs in his piggery and fed them by dumping garbage in open fields. He plowed under any uneaten garbage. The piggery created a revolting odor, especially during warm weather; and the plaintiffs asked the court to close it. The court reluctantly did so, noting that the odor could not otherwise be avoided. "To so conduct a piggery on a large scale is difficult, if not impossible, even when great care is taken and the most advanced methods are used in disposing of the remainder of the garbage.... We have a case where for some years the piggery was conducted on a small scale and was not objectionable. Then, either the increased size of the piggery or the condition of the fields through the continued dumping of garbage thereon, or both, created such odors that this suit resulted.... The court of equity is reluctant to bar the operation of a lawful business and will not do so if a remedy may be applied to the nuisance incidental thereto. However, tests do not show any satisfactory means of carrying on a large-scale garbage-feeding piggery. No method of feeding garbage to pigs on a commercial scale, as is here the case, in a manner that will not constitute a nuisance has been disclosed by the proof."

The Defendant's Motive   *Finally*, courts consider the defendant's motive. The general rule is that if the defendant is motivated only by malice or spite, the activity will be enjoined as the following Michigan court points out.

A CASE IN POINT

In *Burke v. Smith*,[67] two neighbors started to quarrel; and one of them, the defendant, erected wooden screens on his own property that shut out the light and view from the plaintiff's windows. At trial, it was shown that the screens had no necessary, useful, or ornamental purpose. The court ordered the defendant to remove the screens. "It must be remembered that no man has a legal right to make a malicious use of his property, not for any benefit or advantage to himself, but for the avowed purpose of damaging his neighbor. To hold otherwise would make the law a convenient engine, in cases like the present, to injure and destroy the peace and comfort, and to damage the property of one's neighbor for no other than a wicked purpose, which in itself is, or ought to be unlawful. ... What right has the defendant, in the light of the just and beneficent principles of equity, to shut out God's free air and sunlight from the windows of his neighbor, not for any benefit or advantage to himself, or profit to his land, but simply to gratify his own wicked malice against his neighbor? None whatever."

Several states have enacted statutes dealing with the erection of "spite fences." These statutes typically prohibit the malicious erection of a fence at a specified height (for example, six feet) for the purpose of annoying neighbors.

Table 12.1 summarizes the discussion on the foregoing six factors.

Nuisance actions as well as actions in trespass, negligence, and strict liability were used long before present-day environmental statutes and regulations (discussed in Chapter 14) when legal actions were first used to remedy environmental concerns. They still have a role in environmental law today. These actions have been applied in cases ranging from low-level radiation from a nearby plant, to airborne pollutants from both a paper mill and a landfill, to the discharge of contaminated water into a stream.[68]

TABLE 12.1 Factors Considered to Prove the Element of Unreasonable Harm in a Private Nuisance

FACTORS	ISSUE	EXAMPLE IN BOOK
Activity's Value to Society	Is the plaintiff's harm greater than the economic and social value to society?	Harm to plaintiff's land was less than the economic and social value of continuing the defendant's sawmill.
Coming to the Nuisance	Should the plaintiff prevail even if he came to the existing nuisance?	Plaintiff building home close to a fraternity house was awarded injunction limiting fraternity's nuisance activities.
Hardship	Is plaintiff's hardship greater than defendant's hardship?	Defendant's pollution caused by sewage plant justified damages to plaintiff but not injunction due to greater hardship on town.
Activity's Location	Is the location normal for the activity causing the nuisance?	Defendant's ducks on rural farm was normal to location and therefore not a nuisance.
Prevention of Damage	Can the damage caused by the nuisance be prevented?	Smells from defendant's piggery could not be prevented and the piggery was closed.
Defendant's Motive	What was the defendant's motive that resulted in the nuisance?	Defendant's screens erected to block sun and view after quarrel with neighboring plaintiff were removed.

Invasion of Privacy

Tort Right to Privacy

The complexity of modern society, coupled with an increasing population and an aggressive press, has resulted in greater judicial respect for a "right to be let alone," or a right to privacy. The impetus for the recognition of this right was an article entitled "The Right to Privacy," published in 1890 in the *Harvard Law Review* by Samuel D. Warren and Louis D. Brandeis. In the article, the authors observed:

> *The press is overstepping in every direction the obvious bounds of propriety and of decency. Gossip is no longer the resource of the idle and of the vicious, but has become a trade, which is pursued with industry as well as effrontery. To satisfy a prurient taste the details of sexual relations are spread broadcast in the columns of the daily papers. To occupy the indolent, column upon column is filled with idle gossip, which can only be procured by intrusion upon the domestic circle. The intensity and complexity of life, attendant upon advancing civilization, have rendered necessary some retreat from the world, and man, under the refining influence of culture, has become more sensitive to publicity, so that solitude and privacy have become more essential to the individual; but modern enterprise and invention have, through invasions upon his privacy, subjected him to mental pain and distress, far greater than could be inflicted by mere bodily injury.*[69]

There are *four* types of **invasion of privacy** actions:

1. In many states, a person may recover damages when her name or picture is used to advertise a product without her permission. This is sometimes referred to as the "right of publicity."
2. A person may recover damages when there is objectionable publicity of private information, as when a commercial motion picture dealt with a famous murder trial and disclosed the present identity of the defendant in the trial, a reformed prostitute.[70]

invasion of privacy
Four separate torts: (a) appropriation—the unauthorized use of a person's name, likeness, or personality for the benefit of another; (b) public disclosure of a private fact—unreasonably offensive publicity concerning the private life of a person; (c) false light—unreasonably offensive publicity placing the victim in a false light; (d) intrusion—an unreasonably offensive intrusion into someone's private affairs or concerns.

3. It is wrong to put a person in a false light in the public eye. Under this principle, Lord Byron was able to prevent the circulation of a poem that had been falsely attributed to him.[71]

4. Another type of invasion of privacy is one directly related to the rights of a property owner: the wrongful intrusion into the plaintiff's physical privacy. Examples include a person making an illegal search of a home, someone using electronic eavesdropping equipment, someone making unwanted telephone calls, and a physician allowing a friend to observe a home birth.

> Can a hotel be held liable for invasion of privacy for the Peeping-Tom activities of its employees spying on guests in their rooms through a hole in the wall? In *Carter* v. *Innisfree Hotel, Inc.* on page 510, the court addresses the issue.

END OF CHAPTER CASE

constitutional right to privacy

A privacy right based on the due process clause of the Fifth and Fourteenth Amendments and implied in the First, Third, Fourth, Fifth, and Ninth Amendments to the U.S. Constitution.

Constitutional Right to Privacy

Beginning with the case of *Griswold v. Connecticut*[72] in 1965, the Supreme Court has articulated a **constitutional right to privacy** that also affects the rights of landowners. This right is based on the due process clauses in the Fifth and Fourteenth Amendments. However, other amendments, such as the Fourth Amendment's prohibition of unreasonable searches and seizures, also create an expectation of privacy as this U.S. Supreme Court case that arose in Georgia demonstrates.

A CASE IN POINT

In a decision following *Griswold*, in *Stanley v. Georgia*,[73] the Supreme Court decided that a person has the right to engage in certain otherwise criminal activities in the privacy of his own home. The police investigated the defendant in that case for alleged bookmaking activities. During the course of the investigation, state and federal agents entered Stanley's home with a search warrant and found little evidence of bookmaking activity, although they did discover three reels of film. Using a projector they found in the home, they viewed the film, concluded it was obscene, and arrested Stanley on charges of possession of obscene matter. Stanley was convicted by a jury.

The Supreme Court reversed the conviction on appeal. According to the Court: "This right to receive information and ideas, regardless of their social worth, is fundamental to our free society. Moreover, in the context of this case—a prosecution for mere possession of printed or filmed matter in the privacy of a person's home—that right takes on an added dimension. For also fundamental is the right to be free, except in very limited circumstances, from unwanted governmental intrusions into one's privacy.... [W]hatever may be the justifications for other statutes regulating obscenity, we do not think they reach into the privacy of one's own home. If the First Amendment means anything, it means that a State has no business telling a man, sitting alone in his own house, what books he may read or what films he may watch. Our whole constitutional heritage rebels at the thought of giving government the power to control men's minds."

Given the *Stanley* decision, courts now face the question of whether other types of activities also should be privileged within the home. A far-reaching opinion in this regard was *Ravin v. State*,[74] in which the Alaska Supreme Court ruled unanimously that possession of marijuana by adults at home for personal use is constitutionally protected. The *Ravin* decision stood until 1990, when voters in Alaska passed a law making possession of small amounts of marijuana—even in the home—a crime. In 2003, however, an Alaskan appeals court decriminalized marijuana, returning it to its pre-1990 status.

ETHICAL AND PUBLIC POLICY ISSUES

Are Patdowns to Gain Entrance to Sporting and Other Events an Invasion of Privacy?

Since the events of 9/11 and the ongoing threat of terrorist activity, security measures in public places have soared. In 2005, the San Francisco 49ers, as part of a National Football League policy, implemented a patdown search of all those who entered the stadium. The policy was challenged as an illegal invasion of privacy under California's constitution. Although the plaintiff ticketholders lost at the trial and first appeals level, the state supreme court overruled them and remanded the case for further deliberation.[75] The high court instructed the lower court that the reasonableness of requiring ticketholders to submit to a patdown must be looked at from both subjective and objective standards in light of "customs, practices and physical settings surrounding particular activities." These must be balanced against competing social interests: in this case, the security and protection of the fans. Are patdowns an ethical policy? Are there less restrictive and intrusive ways to accomplish the same goal without physically touching the fans? Should cost be a factor? For example, electronic devices might be less intrusive but might result in higher ticket prices. Would you personally find this practice an invasion of your privacy?

Lost, Mislaid, and Abandoned Property

When a person misplaces or loses personal property, the finder of the property usually may keep it against all but the rightful owner. In the leading case from England of *Armory v. Delamirie*,[76] the plaintiff, a chimney sweep, found a piece of jewelry and took it to the defendant, a goldsmith, for appraisal. An employee of the goldsmith removed the jewels, and the goldsmith refused to return them. The court decided that the finder, the chimney sweep, was entitled to the jewels subject only to the rights of the original owner, who was not a party to the case.

locus in quo
"The place in which" lost personal property is found.

The rights of the finder, however, are often subordinate to those of the owner of the *locus in quo,* that is, the owner of the "place in which" the personal property is found. Although the issue of who owns lost and mislaid property is complicated and can differ among the states, the following are general legal approaches applied in deciding who has the superior right to possession and, if the owner of the personal property never appears, the right to keep the goods.

lost property
Property with which the owner has involuntarily parted and he does not know where to find.

Public v. Private Premises   Many courts will decide for the owner of the *locus* if the personal property has been discovered in a private rather than a semipublic place; according to an Illinois court, "if the premises on which the property is discovered are private it is deemed that the property discovered thereon is and always has been in the constructive possession of the owner of said premises and in a legal sense the property can be neither mislaid nor lost."[77] Thus, if property, such as a necklace, is discovered in a bank lobby—a semipublic area—the finder would be entitled to possession; but if the necklace is discovered in a safe-deposit room—a private area—the bank may keep the property.

mislaid property
Property that has been deliberately placed somewhere but forgotten.

Lost v. Mislaid   Courts may also make a distinction between lost and mislaid property. **Lost property** is property with which a person has parted through carelessness; for example, a glove might fall out of someone's pocket. Property that a person has intentionally laid down and then forgotten where it was laid is **mislaid property**; for instance, a person might place gloves on a hat rack in a restaurant and leave without them.[78] The finder is entitled to possession of lost property, whereas the owner of the *locus* can keep mislaid property since the personal property owner is likely to return; if he does, the owner of the *locus* will be holding the property for him.

Some courts have held that if an employee discovers the goods, the employee has the duty to turn the goods over to the employer. In one case, a chambermaid in the defendant's hotel discovered eight $100 bills in the dresser drawer of a room she was cleaning. The Oregon court decided that the hotel owner was entitled to the money: "The decisive feature of the present case is the fact that plaintiff was an employee or servant of the owner or occupant of the premises, and that, in discovering the bills and turning them over to her employer, she was simply performing the duties of her employment."[79]

Embedded in Soil   When the property is found buried or affixed in the ground, the owner of the *locus* is entitled to possession. Thus, in the case of the finders' discovery of a prehistoric Indian canoe embedded in the soil, the court decided that the owner of the *locus* was entitled to possession.[80]

Treasure Trove   Most American courts will hold for the finder if the buried property is considered treasure trove: gold, silver, money, or coins. A few states, however, adopt the approach that treasure trove, such as money, is mislaid property and so belongs to the landowner.[81] (See endnote 81 for the treasure trove laws of the states). Still, to qualify as a treasure trove, the owner must have intended to recover the property later, even though the burial may have occurred centuries ago. Thus, ancient artifacts that were part of a ritual burial have been deemed *not* to be treasure trove under the common law.

Despite the general rule favoring the finder in many cases, the owner of the *locus in quo* will generally prevail if the finder of lost property, mislaid property, or treasure trove was a trespasser on the property. In the Illinois case of *Bishop v. Ellsworth*,[82] the defendants, three small boys, discovered a bottle containing $12,590 in the plaintiff's salvage yard. When the plaintiff sued the boys to determine ownership of the money, the trial court dismissed the complaint on the grounds that the plaintiff had not stated a cause of action. The appellate court reversed the trial court and remanded the case for trial, noting that "if the discoverer is a trespasser such trespasser can have no claim to possession of such property even if it might otherwise be considered lost."

Many states have created legislative solutions, particularly to resolve the sometimes troublesome public/private issue discussed above, by passing **estray statutes**. Under these laws, a finder of lost (but generally not mislaid) property files a report, typically with a county clerk who then advertises the information. After a period of time passes, if no one successfully claims ownership, the finder gains legal title.

Abandoned Property   When property is **abandoned**, that is, property the owner deliberately deposits in a place with no intention of later reclaiming it, the former owner has surrendered those property rights. Still, additional legal issues do arise, such as whether the police can legally search a person's trash that has been left for pickup, an issue discussed in the following Oregon case.

estray statutes
Statutes defining what rights finders have in property when the true owners are unknown.

abandoned property
Property that has been permanently surrendered by the owner.

A CASE IN POINT

In the *State of Oregon v. Howard*,[83] the police learned from a source that the defendant Howard purchased iodine-e used to manufacture methamphetamines. The police asked the sanitation department to turn over Howard's garbage gathered after regular pickups. After two collections, the police were able to glean the necessary evidence to make an arrest. The Oregon Supreme Court

continues

continued ruled that Howard had no "ownership or possessory interest in the garbage once the sanitation department had collected it." The court further stated that a person retains "no constitutionally protected privacy interest in abandoned property" and that "when a person gives up all rights to control the disposition of property, that person also gives up his or her privacy interest in the property in the same way that he or she would if the property had been abandoned."

At what point is property abandoned? In another Oregon case, *State v. Purvis,* a hotel guest was arrested after drugs were found in the guest's wastebasket. The court ruled the "objects which the defendant deposited in the ash trays and waste baskets can be regarded as abandoned property in which he [the guest] retained no protected privacy [or property] interest."[84]

ETHICAL AND PUBLIC POLICY ISSUES

Should There Be Limitations to How Abandoned DNA Is Collected by the Police?

In a widely publicized crime story from California, Adolph Lautenberg was found guilty and sentenced to life in prison in 2003 for murdering a woman in the early 1970s. He was also suspected of killing at least five other women around that time. In 2003, he confessed the murders to his daughter-in-law, who informed the police. Once the investigation began, police needed forensic evidence to tie Lautenberg to semen found on one of the murder and rape victims. The police didn't have probable cause to arrest Lautenberg and didn't want to ask him for a DNA sample for fear he would disappear. To retrieve the DNA, the police set up a ruse. Lautenberg had a sidewalk business selling homemade canes. An undercover policeman told him he'd like to buy him a cup of coffee to learn more about his hobby. Lautenberg drank the coffee and another undercover policeman grabbed it. It tested positive to the perpatrator's DNA found in the semen on the murder victim. Although the seizure was challenged on the grounds that Lautenberg had not yet abandoned the coffee cup since he had not thrown it in the trash, the appeals court rejected the argument.[85]

The foregoing and other cases are beginning to be criticized as overly invasive and potentially dangerous to civil liberties. For example, in one case, a suspected criminal was sent a letter and asked to return some information about joining a fake class action lawsuit. The saliva left from licking the envelope resulted in a conviction. Unlike garbage, which can be withheld and controlled until abandoned, a person's DNA is abandoned constantly, from spitting on the sidewalk to shedding finger cells on a soda bottle. Should there be legal protections from the way this kind of evidence is seized? Should other evidence be required first before pursuing abandoned DNA? Does this create too much power for police and the government? For instance, would it be possible for police to gather DNA and put it on a database and then run it through a computer every time a new crime is committed? Could other parties steal the DNA, which could then be later used by employers and health insurers to discriminate? Or is this just advanced and effective detective work necessary for arresting dangerous criminals?

As discussed previously in this chapter, property owners have a right of privacy that enables them to exclude other private parties from wrongfully intruding into their homes and other protected physical space. Does this right also extend to abandoned property? In the Washington, D.C., case of *Danai v. Canal Square Associates,* a landlord found a letter in the trash retrieved from the offices of his commercial tenant. The letter was later used to impeach the tenant's testimony in a trial over a lease renewal. The court ruled that "she [plaintiff] had no reasonable expectation of privacy in trash she discarded in her wastepaper basket that ended up in a locked community trash room under the control of the [landlord's] property managers."[86]

TABLE 12.2 Ownership of Lost, Mislaid, and Abandoned Property

LEGAL APPROACH APPLIED	TYPE OF PROPERTY OR PLACE IT IS FOUND	WHO OWNS IT?	EXAMPLES IN BOOK
Private v. Public Approach	In private place	Owner of property (*locus in quo*)	Necklace in bank's safe-deposit room
Private v. Public Approach	Semipublic place	Finder of property	Necklace in bank's lobby; gloves left in a restaurant
Lost v. Mislaid Approach	Lost property	Finder of property	Glove falling out of owner's pocket
Lost v. Mislaid Approach	Mislaid property	Owner of property (*locus in quo*)	Gloves left in restaurant hat rack
Buried or Embedded Property	Private property	Owner of property (*locus in quo*)	Prehistoric Indian canoe
Treasure Trove	Private property	Varies by state law: finder or owner (*locus in quo*)	Gold, silver, money, and coins
Abandoned Property	Private, semipublic, or public place	Finder	Drugs in wastebasket; letter and drug paraphernalia in trash

Finally, some forms of abandoned property, such as cars left on the sides of roads, cannot in some states be claimed by a finder, but must "escheat" to the state. Escheat is discussed in Chapter 13.

Table 12.2 provides a review for how the law treats ownership of lost, mislaid, and abandoned property.

Duties to Persons Outside the Real Estate

The trespass, nuisance, privacy, and lost or mislaid property theories provide rights to landowners and occupiers. This section discusses the following:

- The duties a landowner or occupier owes to persons outside the real estate
- The duties owned to persons entering the real estate

Injuries Caused by Conditions

Greta owned a house on Easy Street that had an old oak tree in the front yard. One day a limb from the tree fell on Henry, who was driving his motorcycle past Greta's house. Must Greta pay for Henry's injuries?

The answer may turn on whether the injury was caused by a *condition* or by an *activity* on the land. In this case, the injury was caused by a condition—the state of the tree. The owner would not be liable under the traditional rule for injuries caused by conditions. The rule was fair in England and frontier America, where owners often owned huge tracts of undeveloped land and could not constantly examine and eliminate potential dangers from their land holdings.

In modern urbanized America, however, it is much easier for an owner or occupier to examine and maintain real estate. As a result, courts have determined that the owner will be held liable for injuries resulting from conditions on the property to passersby in *two* types of cases. *First*, an owner will be held liable if he *knew or should have known* about the condition that caused the injury if the real estate is located in an urban area. *Second*, even when the real estate is located in a rural area, owners will be liable if they *actually know* that the condition is dangerous or if they have created the condition. Thus, even if Greta lived on a large farm, if she knew the limb was dangerous or if she had planted and cultivated the tree, she would be liable to Henry.

The modern tendency to hold the owner liable is qualified when the condition threatens an adjoining owner rather than a passerby. Although several courts allow an adjoining owner to recover damages for a noxious (that is, poisonous or otherwise dangerous) plant or tree, other courts have decided that the best remedy for an adjoining landowner is **self-help**. Under the self-help approach, when a rotten limb extends from a neighbor's property onto your land, your only remedy is to cut off the limb. Still, as the court in *Pierce v. Casady* noted (see page 479), if cutting off the branch that extends over the property will kill the tree, the landowner must compel the neighbor to abate the nuisance or sue for damages if an injury occurs.[87]

> **self-help**
> Acting independently of the courts.

Still, the duties owed to neighbors are indeed limited as the next case from New Hampshire discusses.

A CASE IN POINT

In *Belhumeur v. Zilm*[88] the plaintiff was injured on his own property when wild bees nesting in his neighbor's tree attacked him. Plaintiff contended that the defendants had "allowed" the bees to nest on their premises. The trial court ruled in a summary judgment that the defendants had no common law duty to abate the wild bees by removing the tree and the bees. On appeal the state supreme court upheld the trial court ruling that "to require a landowner to abate all harm potentially posed to his neighbors by indigenous animals, plants or insects naturally located upon his property would impose an enormous and unwarranted burden." The court further stated that "While we do not lightly dismiss 'the social importance of protecting the plaintiffs[s'] interest' in avoiding injury caused by wild bees, we find that interest outweighed by the 'importance of immunizing the defendant[s] from extended liability." The court also ruled that the defendant was not liable for nuisance since he had not "contributed to [the] existence" of the bees or their nest on the property."

Injuries Caused by Activities

Returning to the case of Henry and Greta, instead of being hurt by a falling limb, suppose Henry was injured by a Frisbee™ that Greta threw while she was standing on her lot. Under the general principles of tort law discussed earlier in this chapter, Greta is held liable whenever she intentionally injures a passerby (an intentional tort) or when she fails to exercise reasonable care (negligence).

What should be the result if Henry is injured by Greta's activities on her land that do not fall within intentional tort or negligence theory? For example, Greta decides to fumigate her house with cyanide; and because of an unprecedented wind that no reasonable person would expect, the cyanide blows onto neighboring property and injures Henry. May Henry collect damages from Greta? The answer is to be found within a third area of tort liability—strict liability, discussed earlier in this chapter. This area was originally developed and applied to real estate owners in an 1868 English decision, *Rylands v. Fletcher.*

A CASE IN POINT

In *Rylands v. Fletcher,*[89] after the defendants constructed a reservoir on their land, water from the reservoir entered an abandoned coal mine and eventually flooded the plaintiff's neighboring mine. Under the law in existence at that time, the plaintiff could not recover on either trespass or nuisance theory; and it was determined that the defendants were not negligent. The court, however, decided that the defendants should still be held liable because they were making abnormal use of their land.

Most courts have adopted the special strict liability theory embodied in the *Rylands* decision, although such cases could often be resolved in the United States today by using a trespass or nuisance approach, at least where the injured party is a landowner. The major question in applying the theory of strict liability is the largely factual determination of what constitutes an abnormal or nonnatural use of the land. In deciding whether an activity is abnormal or not natural, most courts assess the nature of the community, the character of the real estate, and the dangers in the particular activity.[90] Thus, the *Rylands* approach is very close to U.S. Supreme Court Justice Sutherland's description of nuisances as "the right thing in the wrong place—like a pig in the parlor instead of the barnyard."[91] For instance, an owner who allows water to collect in a dangerous place, such as a cellar that is close to neighboring land, is strictly liable for damage caused by the water, while there is no strict liability for water collected in household pipes because this is a normal use of the land.

In recent years, some courts have focused more on the "abnormally dangerous" character of the defendant's activities than on the abnormal use of the land. In *State Department of Environmental Protection v. Ventron,*[92] for example, the Supreme Court of New Jersey held the defendant chemical companies liable on the basis that their disposal of toxic waste was abnormally dangerous. The same court also decided that a defendant can be liable not only to adjoining landowners but also to purchasers of contaminated property. While this approach expands the environmental liability of real estate sellers by permitting purchasers to recover damages (such as medical monitoring costs) that are not allowed under federal legislation,[93] other courts, such as in Massachusetts, have held that the seller's liability is limited when the contract provides that the purchaser will conduct an environmental assessment.[94] The following Washington state case discusses the factors that courts use in determining whether activities are abnormally dangerous.[95]

A CASE IN POINT

In *Klein v. Pyrodyne Corp.,*[96] a five-inch mortar was knocked into a horizontal position during a fireworks display conducted by Pyrodyne. The rocket exploded near a crowd of onlookers and injured Danny and Marion Klein. When the Kleins sued Pyrodyne in strict liability for their injuries, the court applied the following factors:

1. Existence of a high degree of risk of some harm to the person, land, or chattels of others
2. Likelihood that the harm that results from it will be great
3. Inability to eliminate the risk by the exercise of reasonable care
4. Extent to which the activity is not a matter of common usage
5. Inappropriateness of the activity to the place where it is carried on
6. Extent to which its value to the community is outweighed by its dangerous attributes

The court found that Factors 1, 2, and 3 were present in the fireworks display as well as Factor 4, "The court explained that it is an activity that is not 'of common usage' and that presents an ineliminably high risk of serious bodily injury and of property damage. We therefore hold that conducting public fireworks displays is an abnormally dangerous activity justifying the imposition of strict liability."

Duties to Persons Entering the Land

Returning to the original example, would Greta be liable for Henry's injuries if he was injured on her property, not as a passerby? Although at first glance it might appear logical to apply the same rules to injuries on and outside the land, courts are concerned that the owner's accountability for injuries on her land will limit her use and enjoyment of the property. Because the law traditionally favored free use of one's land, the owner's liability is often limited depending on the legal status of the person who enters the land. As "the social policy pendulum has swung from the nineteenth century objective of promoting the free and unfettered use of land, to the twentieth century concern for public safety,"[97] however, these categories have been subject to exceptions and, in some cases, they have been merged.

In most cases, the person entering the real estate falls into one of the *four* categories discussed next: as a trespasser, child trespasser, licensee, or invitee. That is, there are four possible "hats" that the person might be wearing, each of which alters the owner's duties as well as the rights the person entering the real estate has. (See Figure 12.3.)

Trespassers

trespasser

One who enters land without permission of the owner.

The person entering the land might be a **trespasser**—someone on the land without the permission of the owner. The principle favoring the owner's free use of the land has the greatest appeal in cases of trespass. The general rule is that the owner is not liable for injuries to the trespasser when the owner is unaware of the trespasser on the land. An owner who knows that the trespasser is on the property must not intentionally injure the trespasser. Most states also require an owner who is engaged in activities on the property to exercise reasonable care not to injure known trespassers and to warn them of hidden dangers of which the landowner is aware. As one Pennsylvania court observed:

> It is true that, unless and until the property owner, or the operator of the instrumentality involved, becomes apprised of his presence no duty in regard to the trespasser's safety arises, but when the owner or operator is put on guard as to the presence of the trespasser, the latter immediately acquires the right to proper protection under the circumstances.[98]

The major difficulty is determining whether the owner knew the trespasser was on the land. Although the owner's knowledge of the trespasser's presence is usually a question of fact, the law presumes that the owner knows of the trespasser—even when the owner is unaware of the individual trespasser's presence—when the owner knows that

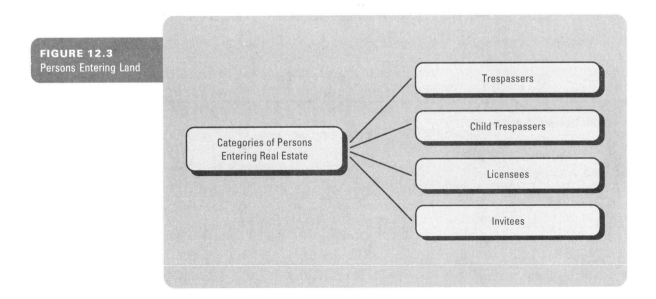

FIGURE 12.3
Persons Entering Land

Categories of Persons Entering Real Estate

- Trespassers
- Child Trespassers
- Licensees
- Invitees

trespassers frequently enter the property. For example, a homeowner who knows that students from a nearby college continually cross his backyard on the way to and from classes must exercise reasonable care in his activities and in warning the students of known concealed dangers such as a high-tension wire. The Supreme Court of Missouri recently ruled on a case involving a landowner who maintained a three-eighths-inch wire cable across his road meant to "dissuade" four-wheelers from intruding on his property. The court concluded that the landowner should be found liable to two trespassers who sustained serious injuries if, upon remand to the trial court, it was discovered that he did not adequately warn people about the cables.[99]

A special type of trespasser—a person who enters the property to commit a criminal act —has caused legal controversy in recent years. Concerned by the increase in crime, some owners have developed special security devices—such as shotgun traps, explosive devices, and dangerous animals—to deter criminal trespassers. In one well-publicized example, owners of a jewelry store in San Francisco, victimized by five break-ins, placed two 4-inch tarantulas in their window display. While often effective, such devices raise a difficult legal issue: May a criminal injured by the security device recover damages from the owner?

As a general rule, owners may use dangerous security devices to protect their property only if they could legally have used the same measure of deterrence had they *personally* confronted the criminal. Owners may not use deadly force to defend their property in person or through remote security devices because the law values human life more than property rights. Thus, an owner who is not present cannot use deadly force in the form of a security device to deter petty thieves.[100]

> Should Edward Briney be held liable to a trespasser who was seriously injured by a gun rigged by Briney to fire at trespassers when the door to a room in his unoccupied farmhouse was opened? In *Katko v. Briney* on page 511, the court discusses the question.

END OF CHAPTER CASE

An exception to the rule enunciated in the famous case of *Katko v. Briney* is when deadly force is used to protect a homeowner's life and that of his family.

ETHICAL AND PUBLIC POLICY ISSUES

When Is It Legal and Moral to Use Killing Force to Protect Yourself from Personal Injury When an Intruder Enters Your Home?

A number of states have passed statutes based on the "Castle Doctrine." In Texas and about 15 other states, a person imminently threatened in his house, workplace, or vehicle has no duty to retreat and can use deadly force to repel the intruder. The property owner who uses deadly force also is generally protected from civil liability. In other states, a person threatened in his home must attempt a reasonable flight from the attacker before using deadly force. However, if he has no remaining means of escape and is seriously threatened, he may then use killing force against the intruder.[101] Which of these two laws is the most ethical? Can killing another person be morally justified? If so, under what circumstances can it be? Would requiring a person to retreat from the intruder only put the homeowner in greater danger of harm? Do intruders surrender their rights under the law, including their right to life, when they engage in certain criminal activities?

Do landowners also have a duty to trespassers to prevent harm to the trespassers caused by parties other than the landowers? The next Minnesota case addresses this issue.

A CASE IN POINT

In *Doe v. Brainerd International Raceway*,[102] "Doe," a 16-year-old runaway, illegally entered the Brainerd International Raceway. Doe voluntarily entered the wet T-shirt contest; and within fifteen minutes, contestants began stripping. "At that point, most of the contestants left the stage, but the four or five women remaining on stage [including Doe] continued a sexual performance which included complete nudity and oral sex." The crowd, mostly men, remained for about one hour and watched. Doe claimed that she was encouraged to continue with her sexual display so that she could win the contest. She also admitted that "she was drunk and high on cocaine...."

She later filed a lawsuit claiming that management and the raceway should have protected her from the sexual encounters. The Minnesota Supreme Court stated that "[T]he outcome of the case turns on the extent of the duty owed by a landowner and operator of a place of amusement to a trespasser in a civil cause of action for injuries resulting from the criminal activity of third parties. We reverse the court of appeals and hold that a landowner does not have a duty of care to a trespasser when the trespasser knows or should be aware of the risks involved and helped create the risks."

Child Trespassers

After graduating from college, William purchased a ten-acre parcel of land in a rural area and excavated a small pond on the land, which he used for swimming and boating. Two years later a nine-year-old boy, who entered the property without William's permission, drowned after diving from a dock that William had built at one end of the pond. If William is sued for damages by the drowned boy's parents, he might argue that under the trespasser rules just discussed, an owner is not liable for injuries to an unknown trespasser, or even to a known trespasser, unless the injury is caused by a hidden dangerous condition.

But should the usual trespasser rules apply to children? The Supreme Court originally provided an answer in 1873,[103] in a case that allowed recovery by a child injured while playing with a railroad turntable. While the **attractive nuisance doctrine** originally required that the child trespasser be attracted to the danger, most courts have now dropped this requirement. For the recovery of damages under the attractive nuisance theory, courts now require the injured party to prove *five* elements when young children trespassing on land are injured by a structure or other artificial condition.[104] In William's case, the child was young and was injured while using an artificial condition—the dock that William had built at the edge of the custom-made pond. Thus, parents in most states will be allowed to recover damages if they can prove the following elements.

First, the possessor must know or should know that young children are likely to trespass on the land where the artificial condition is located. If William's pond is located in a remote area far from dwellings, it is unlikely that this element could be proven. But if the pond is adjacent to a playground used by young children, the owner should know that young children are likely to trespass.

Second, the owner must know or should know that the artificial condition exists and must realize or should realize that it involves an unreasonable risk of serious harm or death to young children. Almost any artificial condition can be dangerous in the hands of young children. For example, if William left a beach towel on the dock, a young child might use the towel to "snap" another child and, in so doing, blind the child. Although

> **attractive nuisance doctrine**
>
> A duty of reasonable care owed to a trespassing child unable to appreciate the danger from an artificial condition or activity on land to which the child can be expected to be attracted.

William should know of this potential danger, it is not considered an unreasonable risk. In other words, William is not expected to childproof his property because doing so would be impractical and virtually impossible.

The question in William's case is whether water—like the towel—should be regarded as an ordinary or unreasonable risk. The risk of drowning in water is always a risk, but is generally not considered an unreasonable risk because children are taught from a very early age the danger of water. However, if other factors were involved, William might be liable. For instance, if the dock was located in extremely shallow water and the young child drowned after striking his head on the bottom of the pond, a court would probably determine this to be an unreasonable risk.

Even where the condition obviously involves an unreasonable risk, the landowner will not be liable if she has no reason to know of its existence as the next case from Pennsylvania demonstrates.

A CASE IN POINT

In *Norton v. City of Easton*,[105] the defendant operated a service station and stored wrecked cars, which he towed for the city to an adjacent lot. A group of boys went to the station to obtain a map, visited the lot, and began looking through the cars. In one wrecked automobile, the boys discovered a box of .22 bullets in the glove compartment. They took the bullets and later put them in a matchbox and lit it. The box exploded, and one of the boys—the plaintiff—was blinded. The court decided that the service station owner should not be held liable because the owner did not know that the bullets were in the glove compartment and had no reason to know of their existence.

Third, it must be proven that the young child, because of his age, did not realize the risk created by the artificial condition. Thus, even a landowner who knows that the artificial condition is unreasonably dangerous will not be liable if the child who was injured was old enough to appreciate the danger. In the Louisiana case of *Richards v. Marlow*, a thirteen-year-old girl slipped and injured her mouth while walking on a wet pipe that had been part of a pier on the defendant's property. The court denied recovery on the grounds that a thirteen-year-old should realize the risk of balancing on the pipe in such conditions.[106]

In William's case, the issue is whether a nine-year-old should realize the risk of diving off the dock. As previously discussed, water itself is such an obvious danger that it is not generally considered an unreasonable risk even to a very young child. However, the risk of diving into shallow water is one that a nine-year-old might not appreciate. That is a question for the jury; but if the injured child has reached a certain age, which usually varies from thirteen to sixteen depending on state law, the judge will not allow a jury verdict for the child.[107]

Fourth, the risk to young children must be great compared to the utility of the artificial condition to the owner and the burden of removing the danger. In William's case, the utility of the pond would possibly outweigh the risk to young children. As a California court noted,

> where ponds do not exist naturally [they] must be created, in order to store water for stock and domestic purposes, irrigation, etc. Are we to hold that every owner of a pond or reservoir is liable in damage for any child that comes uninvited upon his premises and happens to fall in the water and drown? If so, then upon the same principle must the owner of a fruit tree be held liable for the death or injury of a child who, attracted by the fruit, climbs into the branches, and falls out? But this, we imagine, is an absurdity, for which no one would contend.[108]

However, a different conclusion might be reached regarding the dock. The utility of the dock could easily be questioned and the danger more easily removed.

Finally, the owner must fail to exercise reasonable care. For instance, an owner who does not protect children by fencing in a swimming pool faces potential liability. In William's case, it could be argued that the duty of reasonable care would require that the dock be removed, at least if the other elements were present.

The Gregorys' two-year-old child drowned in the Johnsons' unfenced side yard pool when the father was visiting friends who were neighbors of the Johnsons. In *Gregory v. Johnson* on page 513, the court discusses the application of the attractive nuisance doctrine to these facts.

END OF CHAPTER CASE

In most states, owners such as William will be liable for injuries to young children if those five elements can be proven. In a few states, however, the attractive nuisance doctrine has been rejected for reasons stated by a Maine court in *Lewis v. Mains:*[109]

Sympathy is quickly aroused by the injuries of a child, and that emotion is both natural and proper. In such a mood, courts have sometimes substituted moral or sentimental obligations for legal obligations. In so doing they tend to curtail unreasonably the proper use of property by an owner in order to confer protection upon a person wrongfully thereon. We have never imposed upon a property owner the obligation of due care to protect a trespasser even though the trespasser was a child of tender years.... Upon whom then does the duty devolve to protect small children from dangers which they may encounter while trespassing? Surely upon their most natural custodians and protectors, the parents.

Licensees

licensee

A person permitted to enter another's property for the licensee's own purposes and not for the benefit of the possessor.

A **licensee** is a person who enters the land of another without invitation or for some purpose not connected with a business conducted on the land. The person is distinguished from a trespasser because the entry is with the permission or at the toleration of the owner.

Michael Swanson was injured diving into shallow water during a visit to Eileen McKain's house. In *Swanson v. McKain* on page 514, the court determined whether McKain had a duty to warn Swanson of the conditions in Puget Sound by resolving whether Swanson was an invitee or a licensee.

END OF CHAPTER CASE

The owner's duties to a licensee are similar to those owed a *known* trespasser. In most states, an owner who is engaged in activities on the property must exercise reasonable care not to injure licensees and, furthermore, must warn licensees of any hidden dangers of which the owner is aware.

recreational use statutes

State statutes that limit a landowner's liability when a member of the public is injured while using the land for recreational purposes.

In a few states, the only duty of the owner is to avoid intentional injury to the licensee: "Generally speaking, the owner of land in Maryland owes no duty with respect to the condition of his land to a trespasser, or even to a licensee, whose presence upon the land is known to him, except to abstain from willful or wanton misconduct."[110] A similar rule exists in many states under **recreational use statutes**, which apply when the injured person uses the owner's land for a recreational use (such as hunting, fishing, camping, or snowmobiling) without paying a fee. One issue is whether recreational use statutes protect landowners who open their land to invited guests only, as discussed in an Illinois case.

A CASE IN POINT

In *Hall v. Henn*,[111] the Henn family built and maintained a sled run in their backyard. The sled run was not open to the general public; it was open only to certain invited friends and neighbors who would then have to be supervised. Ellen Hall, a friend of one of Henn's neighbors, began to use the sled run after obtaining permission from Mrs. Henn. On the third try, she fell on the icy stairs, breaking her right arm and tearing an anterior cruciate ligament in her knee. In its ruling for the plaintiff, the Illinois Supreme Court stated that "[t]he Recreational Use of Land and Water Act exists to encourage owners of land to make land and water available to the public for recreational or conservation purposes by limiting their liability toward persons entering thereon for such purposes." In interpreting the Illinois statute, the court ruled that "the Act's protections are *not* available to landowners who restrict the use of their property to invited guests only." The court added that "were we to ignore [the statute's] express caveat that the property in question be made available for such purposes *to the public*, we would largely eliminate premises liability in the state."

Recreational use statutes may, however, protect owners of public recreational facilities in urban areas. In *City of Bellmead v. Torres*,[112] the Texas Supreme Court ruled that a player injured during a softball tournament could not sue the City of Bellmead for injuries on the city's premises.

An Oregon court in *Reynolds v. Nichols*[113] considered the owner's duty, under the majority rule, to use reasonable care when the plaintiff, a guest in his neighbors' home, was stabbed by another guest. The plaintiff sued his neighbors, claiming that the defendants did not exercise reasonable care because they served the other guest alcoholic beverages and failed to restrain him when he attacked the plaintiff. The court held that the plaintiff failed to prove the host's knowledge that the guest had violent propensities; such knowledge was a necessary element to find the host liable for serving alcoholic beverages. The court also concluded that the defendants had no duty to aid a guest endangered by another guest.

The owner's duty to warn licensees of hidden dangers was at issue in the following Illinois case.

A CASE IN POINT

In *Smith v. Goldman*,[114] the plaintiff was injured when riding his bicycle on a bicycle path located on the defendant's property. He fell from his bike into a pool and was injured by debris that had collected in the pool. The court acknowledged that a landowner has a duty to warn licensees and known trespassers of hidden dangers on the bicycle path. However, the duty does not extend to warning of all hidden debris located near the path that might increase a fallen bicyclist's injuries. A reasonable person riding a bicycle should know that such debris normally exists along bicycle paths. Consequently, the court held for the defendant.

Perhaps the most difficult question facing courts is how to determine whether the person entering the land has the status of a licensee. As an illustration of the application of the licensee test, cases involving two common types of licensees are examined. *First*, as discussed by an Arizona court, it is widely recognized that social guests and relatives are licensees.

A CASE IN POINT

In *Bisnett v. Mowder*,[115] a woman was injured while visiting the defendants' home. After sitting at the edge of the defendants' swimming pool with her feet dangling in the water, the woman walked across the patio to pick up her cigarettes. On the way, she slipped and was injured. The court noted the general rule that a social guest is a licensee, and the owner therefore must warn the guest of hidden dangers. While a licensee should be aware of the danger of slipping on a wet spot near a swimming pool, in this case, there were additional factors. The defendants had recently repainted the patio, thus making the patio more slippery than usual. In fact, other guests had slipped on the patio and the owners had given warnings to others to be careful. Because of these factors, the appellate court concluded that the case should be tried by a jury, and it remanded the case for trial.

The *second* common type of licensee is the person who visits the property in an attempt to sell something to the owner. Under the original definition, such a person, according to a New York ruling, enters the premises without an express or implied invitation and therefore is a licensee.

A CASE IN POINT

In *Stacy v. Shapiro*,[116] the court decided that a woman hired by a manufacturer to visit homemakers, demonstrate the company's products, and leave coupons with the homemakers was a licensee: "Clearly the plaintiff had not been invited by anyone. She went upon the premises in her own interest and that of her employers. Consequently, the housewives upon whom she intended calling did not know that she was coming. The plaintiff … was only a bare licensee upon the premises."

Finally, as noted earlier, firefighters and police officers, as shown in a Connecticut case, can be characterized as licensees when they are performing their duties.

A CASE IN POINT

In *Flodquist v. Palmieri*,[117] Flodquist, a policeman, was summoned to a Fourth of July beer party after it had "erupted into a melee." Upon arriving, he claimed he was injured when one of the party members threw a beer keg at him, which caused serious injuries. He subsequently sued the two owners of the property, Palmieri and Lucia, for breaching their duties owed to him as a licensee. The court explained that "because the plaintiff was a law enforcement officer in the course of performing his official duties, he is subject to the firefighter rule, which gives a law enforcement officer the status of a licensee in a personal injury action against a landowner for harm sustained during the course of duty." In this case, the court ruled there was no evidence that the landowners knew or had reason to know that the party would turn violent, nor would the landowners be expected to know that the police would not be able to realize this danger once they arrived. The court granted a summary judgment in favor of the landowners.

As the *Flodquist* case points out, the landowner owes a lower duty of care to a police officer since he is a licensee. However, in a later Connecticut case, a police officer was accidentally injured while chasing the defendant after breaking up a party where there were illegal drugs. This time, however, the defendant was *not* the landowner, and so therefore was not shielded by the licensee standard. Instead, the court ruled that a negligence standard should be applied.[118]

Invitees

invitee

Someone who is present on another's land with the express or implied invitation of the occupier of the land.

In most cases, an **invitee** is a business visitor. A few courts limit invitee status to only those persons whose presence brings potential economic benefit to the landowner. Most courts, however, have adopted a much broader definition that extends invitee status to anyone who has been invited to the premises and who has an implied assurance that the owner has exercised reasonable care to make the premises safe.[119]

The use of this broader definition has resulted in judicial decisions that may appear illogical. For instance, social guests are clearly invited to the premises by the landowner, but they are considered to be licensees rather than invitees. The reason given by the courts is that the social host makes no implied assurance that reasonable care has been taken to make the premises safe. Instead, the guest is treated as one of the family and cannot recover if injured by a hidden danger unknown to the owner. However, when members of the public are invited to the premises, even if there is no economic benefit to the owners, such people are considered to be invitees because, by making the invitation, the owners implicitly assure the public that reasonable care has been exercised to make the premises safe. Thus, persons attending free lectures or a college reunion are considered invitees.[120]

The owner owes a full duty of reasonable care to a visitor who can be classified as an invitee. In other words, the policy that favors the owner's free use of the land, which resulted in limiting the owner's duty to trespassers and licensees, bows to the policy of protecting the invitee from injury. Thus, the owner must exercise reasonable care in conducting activities on the land so as not to injure invitees. In some cases, like the following one from Georgia, this requires the owner to take affirmative action.

A CASE IN POINT

In *Sneider v. Hyatt Corp.,*[121] a woman who had checked into the Hyatt Hotel in Atlanta committed suicide by jumping from the twenty-first floor. When her husband and daughter sued the hotel, the hotel moved for a summary judgment on the grounds that it owed no legal duty to the woman to prevent the suicide. The court refused to grant summary judgment, noting that the hotel may owe a legal duty in such circumstances and that duty would require the hotel to take affirmative action to prevent suicides. The plaintiffs stressed that the hotel knew other similar suicides had occurred, the woman had been inebriated when she arrived at the hotel, the woman arrived with no luggage, and the hotel employees observed her wandering around the twenty-first floor in a confused state.

In addition to conducting activities in a reasonable manner, the owner must warn invitees of hidden dangerous conditions. This duty extends—and this is the major distinction between the duty owed the licensee and that owed the invitee—even to those conditions of which the owner has no actual knowledge if the court decides that the owner should have known of the danger. The question of whether the owner should have known of hidden dangers is frequently litigated. In *Wamser v. City of St. Petersburg,*[122] a boy was severely injured when a shark attacked him at a beach operated by the city of St. Petersburg, Florida.

The court concluded that the city had no duty to warn swimmers of the danger since this was the first recorded shark attack in the history of the beach and the city had no reason to foresee the danger. Still, since the city now has notice of this risk, it may incur liability should a shark attack occur again.

In the common situation where a customer slips and falls on an object in a store, the major legal question is whether the store had reason to know of the danger as a Nebraska court discusses next.

A CASE IN POINT

In *Williams v. Bedford Market, Inc.,*[123] a customer claimed that she slipped in a small puddle of water, about two inches wide, on the floor of the store. The court noted that the store would be liable for injuries caused by foreign substances on the floor if (1) the storekeeper or employees created the dangerous condition or (2) if the owner did not remove the substance within a reasonable time after learning of its existence. These duties do not make the owner an insurer against all injuries to customers. In this case, the court, in concluding that the store was not liable, relied on evidence that the store was mopped and swept every night and that spills were usually cleaned up within five minutes.

Even when the owner is aware of the danger, there is no liability to invitees who know or should know of the danger. In *House v. European Health Spa,*[124] an invitee at the defendant's health spa slipped on a foreign substance as she entered the shower. During the trial, she admitted that on previous visits to the spa, the showers were slippery and dirty and that she had slipped before. The South Carolina court held that she could not recover because of her knowledge of the danger.

In recent years, some states, like the following court in Connecticut, have created a new rule for premises liability relating to self-serve businesses such as salad bars.

A CASE IN POINT

In *Kelly v. Stop and Shop, Inc.,* the plaintiff, Kelly, slipped at a self-service salad bar. At trial, Kelly, as a business invitee, had to prove under existing Connecticut law that "the defendant had actual or constructive notice of the piece of lettuce that allegedly had caused the plaintiff's fall." However, on appeal, the state supreme court overruled the trial court and adopted the "mode of operation" rule. Under the rule, "a plaintiff establishes a prima facie case of negligence upon presentation of evidence ... [that] a foreseeable risk of injury to customers [exists] and that the plaintiff's injury was proximately caused by an accident within the zone of risk. The defendant may rebut the plaintiff's evidence by producing evidence that it exercised reasonable care under the circumstances." In this case, "the defendant knew of the dangers associated with maintaining a self-service salad bar, the defendant had a policy of stationing an attendant at the salad bar for the purpose of keeping the area clean and safe. Moreover, the plaintiff testified that she fell when she slipped on a 'wet, slimy piece of ... lettuce' while she was making a salad at the salad bar. This evidence was adequate to permit a finding that the salad bar created a foreseeable risk of danger to customers. A mode-of-operation charge is appropriate when loose items that are reasonably likely to fall to the ground during customer or employee handling would create a dangerous condition." The case was reversed and remanded to the trial court to apply the new rule to the case.[125]

Some legal commentators consider the "mode of operation" rule, now applied in about half the states, as being too strict. However, courts adopting it counter that the older "actual and constructive notice" rule was formed before the advent of self-serve businesses and the unique hazards those operations can produce, sometimes by the patrons themselves.

Because of the higher duty of care owed the invitee, many cases hinge on the question of whether the plaintiff is considered an invitee or a licensee. This question is complicated by the fact that the status of a person may change; that is, a person may switch hats while on the premises. A California court in *Sheridan v. Ravn*[126] gave the following example:

> *A restaurant or a lunch room has a place for the public to come in, has a counter at which they may sit, a place where they may give their order, or pay their bills as the case may be, or any other part of the premises to which the public is invited, either directly or by implication, or because of the position or character of the place, but if a person went behind the counter, for instance, he would cease being an invitee. That is not where he belongs; he would then be a licensee, even though the proprietor said, "You may come back of the counter and see how I slice the bacon," or whatever is going on. It would be a matter in which the proprietor wouldn't have any interest, merely for the accommodation of the customer.*

The following Washington state case demonstrates why a person's status as a licensee or invitee can be decisive in recovering damages.

A CASE IN POINT

In *Pagarigan v. Phillips Petroleum Co.*,[127] the plaintiff took his car to a service station to have the car radio repaired. When he returned later, he found the defendant station mechanic working in the lubrication room. The mechanic said he would talk about the radio as soon as he finished with the car on which he was working. While the plaintiff was waiting in the lubrication room, a car fell from a hoist and injured him. The defendant argued that the plaintiff could not recover because he was a licensee. The court rejected this argument and ruled for the plaintiff, noting that he retained his invitee status because he entered the lubrication room for a business purpose.

In another Washington state case, a spectator who entered a racetrack through an unattended main gate without paying an admission fee was held to be a licensee, not an invitee, and the track owners were not held to be liable for the spectator's injuries from an out-of-control race car.[128]

The landowner's liability for the acts of criminals has been litigated frequently in recent years, as illustrated by the following Florida case.

A CASE IN POINT

In *Rosier v. Gainesville Inns Associates*,[129] the plaintiffs, who were attending homecoming at the University of Florida, stayed at the Holiday Inn in Gainesville with their children. When they returned to their room at night, they locked their door but did not lock the chain latch. During the night, the wife awoke when an intruder entered the room. The husband, in attacking the intruder, was stabbed;

continues

continued and the wife also suffered a minor injury. Before fleeing, the intruder grabbed a key on the floor that he apparently had used to enter the room. When the plaintiffs sued the hotel, the trial court dismissed the complaint and the plaintiffs appealed. The appellate court reversed the trial court decision, noting that a jury could find the hotel liable on the facts. Guests in a hotel are invitees, and there was evidence the hotel knew burglaries had occurred in the past. Consequently, the case was remanded for trial.

In a similar case from Pennsylvania,[130] a woman was assaulted in a shopping center parking lot at 9:30 p.m. after leaving work. The court refused to overturn a jury verdict against the mall. The court noted that the defendant mall owner should have known of the danger since the defendant was aware of 77 car thefts in the past year. Once it has been determined that the owner should have known of the danger, the jury must decide whether the owner took adequate measures to prevent further criminal activity and to warn customers and employees of the danger. Likewise, in a Louisiana case, after a customer was shot by an armed robber in a restaurant's parking lot, the restaurant was liable because an earlier armed robbery inside the restaurant should have placed a reasonable person on notice that its exterior was even more dangerous.[131]

When an invitee is criminally attacked *outside* the defendant's premises, some courts, such as the following one from Washington, D.C., also determine whether the defendant exercised "exclusive control" over the area, while other courts employ a so-called "substantial special use" rule.

A CASE IN POINT

In *Novak v. Capital Management and Development Corp.,*[132] "twelve to fifteen thugs" attacked and permanently injured the plaintiffs, Novak and Validvia, as they left the Zei Club, a bar and dance club. The trial court ruled in the defendant's favor, stating that the club did not exercise "exclusive control" over the alley and that two similar assaults per month did not make it sufficiently foreseeable. The appeals court reversed and remanded, stating that the trial court should look instead at whether the club put the alley to a "substantial special use" since, as the court noted, it "was immediately outside the only exit from the club and was the most common path for departing patrons." The court also stated that two attacks per month did create foreseeability that future criminal attacks would occur.

After shopping, Dorothy McClung was abducted, raped, and stuffed in a trunk, where she suffocated. Were the store and shopping center liable for failing to provide security measures in the parking lot? In *McClung v. Delta Square Limited Partnership* on page 515, the court discusses the owner's and occupant's liability for criminal occurrences on their premises.

END OF CHAPTER CASE

In contrast to the decisions just mentioned, there are cases in which owners have not been held liable for injuries resulting from criminal activity. For instance, some courts have cited a public policy rationale, as pointed out in the following quote from a

Michigan case, for refusing to require the owner of a business to provide armed security guards to protect customers.

> *The inability of government and law enforcement officials to prevent criminal attacks does not justify transferring this responsibility to a business owner.... To shift the duty of police protection from the government to the private sector would amount to advocating that members of the public resort to self-help. Such a proposition contravenes public policy.*[133]

Courts also may decide in favor of an owner who had no reason to know of the criminal activity. In the South Carolina case of *Shipes v. Piggly Wiggly St. Andrews, Inc.,*[134] a customer who had been assaulted in a supermarket parking lot was denied recovery on the grounds that the store had no reason to expect criminal acts. The store was located in a quiet neighborhood, and the only previous criminal activity in the parking lot was the theft of a tape deck from a car. The next California case discusses whether a business is liable to a patron for its actions during a holdup.

A CASE IN POINT

In *Kentucky Fried Chicken of California v. Brown,* Kathy Brown was held up at gunpoint in a Kentucky Fried Chicken store. She surrendered her cash and wallet to the robber promptly, but she alleged that the restaurant employee's failure to promptly comply with the robber's demands for money in the cash register resulted in further injury to her. The California Supreme Court recognized a business proprietor's duty of reasonable care to its invitees, including the duty to take reasonable action to protect its patrons when criminal conduct is ongoing. The court ruled, however, that Kentucky Fried Chicken was not liable for failure to immediately comply with the robber's demands, under the rationale that the "public as a whole is much better served if would-be robbers are deterred by knowledge that their victims have no legal duty to comply with the robber's demands and are under no duty to surrender their property in order to protect third persons from possible injury."[135]

The tragic terrorist attacks on the World Trade Center on September 11, 2001, may magnify this issue: What duty does a commercial entity owe to its business invitees who are the victims of mass murder and mayhem? A possible analogy may be provided by *Lopez v. McDonald's.*[136] In that 1984 case, a heavily armed man entered a McDonald's in Chula Vista, California, and began shooting. He killed 21 individuals and wounded 11 others before the police killed him. The McDonald's was located in a high-crime area characterized by less dangerous crimes than murder, such as robberies, thefts, assaults, and batteries.

The appeals court in *Lopez* ruled that liability should be determined by the foreseeability of the kind of event that had occurred. In this situation, the business owner should be liable only for foreseeable criminal activities, and so might be held liable to an invitee who was robbed or assaulted, but should not be liable for extraordinary occurrences such as mass murder.

Although acts of terrorism, especially after 9/11, concern most Americans, these acts are still extremely rare and therefore not reasonably foreseeable in specific places. In light of heightened awareness and security in the country, the likelihood of these acts is reduced even further.

Another recent American tragedy, the killing of more than 30 students and faculty, and the wounding of 24 more at Virginia Tech University by a fellow student in 2007, raises the issue of whether universities, as landowners, owe duties to protect their students. Students are generally classified as invitees. However, many states follow the *Restatement (Second) of Torts* that provides for a "special relationship" between a university and its students requiring that the university protect them. Thus, once a university's administration is put on notice that students may be harmed, it must act reasonably to protect its students. Virginia Tech was aware that the killer suffered from mental illness, including extensive delusions and threats he had made to kill others in papers he had written that faculty and staff had read. Moreover, once he had killed several students, the university warned the students through e-mails that may not have conveyed the necessary urgency so that students could have taken measures to protect themselves.[137] Given these facts, it appears that the university may not have sufficiently protected its students from a foreseeable threat of harm. In 2008, however, the opportunity to litigate and answers these important issues largely disappeared when, in exchange for waiving their rights to a lawsuit, the victims accepted a $11 million settlement from the state.

Merging the Categories

The traditional approach—determining the owner's liability according to which of the four hats the visitor wears (whether a trespasser, child trespasser, licensee, or invitee)—has offered the landowner a certain measure of immunity from suit, but it has also resulted in a complex body of law full of subtle distinctions. In the words of Lord Denning in an English case:

> A canvasser who comes on your premises without your consent is a trespasser. Once he has your consent he is a licensee. Not until you do business with him is he an invitee. Even when you have done business with him, it seems rather strange that your duty towards him should be different when he comes up to your door from what it is when he goes away. Does he change his colour in the middle of the conversation? What is the position when you discuss business with him and it comes to nothing? No confident answer can be given to these questions. Such is the morass into which the law has floundered in trying to distinguish between licensees and invitees.[138]

Because of such frustrations, a statute was enacted in England in 1957 that requires an owner to exercise the same duty of care to both licensees and invitees. In the United States, some states have followed the English approach. Courts in a slight majority of the states today,[139] beginning with the 1968 California case of *Rowland v.* Christian,[140] have abolished the distinction between invitees, licensees, and even trespassers. In the following case the Alaska Supreme Court abolished the three classifications or trichotomy in that state.

A CASE IN POINT

In *Webb v. City and Borough of Sitka,*[141] the plaintiff fell and broke her hip after stubbing her toe on the sidewalk in Sitka, Alaska. When she sued the city, the trial court, in dismissing the complaint, stated the traditional rule that her status as a licensee or an invitee had a bearing on the city's liability. On appeal, the Alaska Supreme Court overruled the trial court, stating that the rigid common law classifications were outdated.

The court decided that the better rule is that "a landowner or owner of other property must act as a reasonable person in maintaining his property in a reasonably safe condition in view of all the circumstances, including the likelihood of injury to others, the seriousness of the injury, and the burden on the respective parties of avoiding the risk."

In this case, the court determined that a jury should consider whether the sidewalk was reasonably safe in view of the likelihood of injury to others, the burden of avoiding injury, and the seriousness of potential injury. The court also concluded that the jury should consider whether the plaintiff's negligence had contributed to the injury. The case was remanded for a jury trial.

Is the owner of a bar liable for the injuries of a patron who, in a highly intoxicated condition, leaves the premises to urinate behind the bushes rather than use the establishment's indoor facilities? In *Hendricks v. Lee's Family, Inc.* on page 517, the court discusses the issue of foreseeability in determining the duty of reasonable care under the circumstances.

END OF CHAPTER CASE

In the Nebraska case of *Heins v. Webster County,*[142] a father fell after visiting his daughter in the hospital where she worked. His daughter was the hospital's director of nursing. The father claimed that the intention of his visit was to plan his appearance as Santa Claus in the hospital play, a purpose sufficient to change his status from licensee (a social visitor to his daughter) to invitee (a participant in a hospital function). The court overturned the traditional distinction between licensees and invitees, holding that owners and occupiers are required to exercise reasonable care for lawful visitors. Thus, the father's recovery was not dependent upon his plans to be Santa Claus.

Similarly, the Iowa Supreme Court in 2009 rejected the licensee/invitee distinction and adopted a general negligence standard in a slip and fall case. The court declared that the historical rationale for the trichotomy was outdated, stating: "The distinctions which the common law draws between licensee and invitee were inherited from a culture deeply rooted to the land, a culture which traced many of its standards to a heritage of feudalism."[143]

Some states, such as Michigan discussed next, have also adopted a so-called "limited duty" standard that defines the duties owed to persons in particular places, such as spectators at sporting events.

A CASE IN POINT

In *Benejam v. Detroit Tigers, Inc.,*[144] Alyssia Benejam, a young girl, was attending a Detroit Tigers baseball game. She was seated along the third base line close to the field with a protective net in front of her. A player's bat broke; and a fragment curved around the net, crushing her fingers. There was no evidence that the bat fragment went through the net or that the net was defective. The court, in this case of first impression in Michigan, remanded the case to the trial court, ruling that the usual invitee rule should no longer govern, but instead that a "limited duty" rule should now be applied to sporting events. The court stated that "we hold that a baseball stadium owner that provides screening behind home plate sufficient to meet ordinary demand for protected seating has fulfilled its duty with respect to screening and cannot be subjected to liability for injuries resulting to a spectator by an object leaving the playing field." The court justified its ruling by explaining that "the limited duty rule leaves the baseball stadium owner free, without fear of liability, to accommodate the majority of fans who prefer unobstructed and uninsulated contact with the game. Under usual invitor-invitee principles of liability, fear of litigation would likely require screening far in excess of that required to meet the desires of baseball fans."

Owners of sporting facilities often use the assumption of risk defense when someone is injured on their premises, as in the *Rees v. Cleveland Indians Baseball Company* case on page 469. These facilities also use signs to notify patrons of risks and place disclaimers on the backs of tickets. For example, in *Rees*, the back of the plaintiff's ticket read as follows: "The holder assumes all risk and danger incidental to the game of baseball occurring prior to, during or subsequent to the actual playing of the game, including specifically (but not exclusively) the danger of being injured by thrown bats, or fragments thereof, and thrown or batted balls." In referring to this language, as well as other warnings, the court concluded that it "is not inclined to impute liability to the Baseball Defendants after they provided multiple warnings that the Reeses could have reasonably perceived but did not."[145]

Patrons who participate in a potentially dangerous sporting activity such as snowtubing, skiing, and horseback riding often must sign a Waiver, Defense, Indemnity and Hold Harmless Agreement and a Release of Liability. These exculpatory forms, although effective in thwarting a lawsuit in some states, have been successfully challenged in others for failing to warn the participant adequately about the nature of the risks and for violating public policy that discourages premises owners from waiving their own negligence.[146] Table 12.3 summarizes the various duties owed to persons entering another's land.

> **workers' compensation statutes**
> A state system that provides fixed awards to employees and their dependents for employment-related accidents or diseases.

No-fault laws also may affect the liability of a landowner. For example, under **workers' compensation statutes**, an employer must pay for an employee's injury incurred on the job even if the employer is not at fault for the injury. In return for automatic compensation, the employee gives up the right to sue the employer under traditional tort theories. In recent years, many statutes have been broadened to include part-time workers hired by a homeowner. In some states, household employees such as babysitters and gardeners are subject to workers' compensation laws. For example, if a babysitter in one of these states accidentally burned himself on the kitchen stove, the homeowner would be liable for medical expenses and disability wages regardless of fault. However, if a landowner exercises little control over the worker, such as a carpenter hired to remodel a bathroom, the worker would likely be classified as an independent contractor and could not recover workers' compensation. Still, he would have the right to sue the landowner for negligence if the landowner knew or should have known about a hazard and failed to warn the worker about it. The distinction between an employee and an independent contractor employs an in-depth factual analysis of each case that is beyond the scope of this book.

> **product liability**
> The liability of a manufacturer, a supplier, a wholesaler, an assembler, a retailer, or a lessor of a defective product that causes damage or injury to a consumer or user.

Another type of no-fault law is **product liability**, whereby the seller of a defective product will be liable even if she has exercised all possible care. This liability has been extended even to cover a customer in a store who is injured by a product before it is sold as shown in Kentucky case on the following page.

TABLE 12.3 Summary of Landowner's Duties to Persons Entering the Land

CATEGORY OF PERSON	DUTY OWED
Trespasser	Duty not to intentionally injure and to use reasonable care to warn known trespassers of hidden dangers of which the owner is aware
Child trespasser	Duty of reasonable care to prevent injury to a child unable to appreciate dangers associated with an artificial condition or activity that he is attracted to and to which the owner is or should be aware
Licensee	Duty of reasonable care not to injure licensee as well as warn licensee of known dangers
Invitee	Duty not to intentionally injure and to warn invitee of hidden dangers of which the owner is or should be aware
General duties of care*	Duty to maintain property in a reasonably safe condition in light of all circumstances

*Adopted in those states that have abolished distinctions between licensees, invitees, and trespassers.

A CASE IN POINT

In *Embs v. Pepsi-Cola Bottling Co. of Lexington, Kentucky, Inc.*,[147] the plaintiff was walking down an aisle in a store when she heard a noise that sounded "like a shotgun." When she looked down, she saw a gash in her leg and green pieces of a 7-UP bottle on the floor. The store manager, who immediately took the plaintiff to the hospital, advised her that several 7-UP bottles had exploded that week. The court held all parties in the distributive chain liable even though no 7-UP was sold to the plaintiff.

In explaining this decision, the court noted that "[o]ur expressed public policy will be furthered if we minimize the risk of personal injury and property damage by charging the costs of injuries against the manufacturer who can procure liability insurance and distribute its expense among the public as a cost of doing business; and since the risk of harm from defective products exists for mere bystanders and passersby as well as for the purchaser or user, there is no substantial reason for protecting one class of persons and not the other. The same policy requires us to maximize protection for the injured third party and promote the public interest in discouraging the marketing of products having defects that are a menace to the public by imposing strict liability upon retailers and wholesalers in the distributive chain responsible for marketing the defective product which injures the bystander. The imposition of strict liability places no unreasonable burden upon sellers because they can adjust the cost of insurance protection among themselves in the course of their continuing business relationship."

CASES

Trespass and Free Speech

UNITED FOOD AND COMMERCIAL WORKERS UNION, LOCAL 919, AFL-CIO v. CRYSTAL MALL ASSOCIATES, L.P.

270 Conn. 261, 852 A.2d 658 (2004)

KATZ, Judge. The plaintiff, United Food and Commercial Workers Union, Local 919, AFL-CIO, appeals from the judgment of the trial court denying its request for injunctive relief. The plaintiff sought to enjoin the defendants, Crystal Mall Associates, L.P., and its management company (defendant), from prohibiting its entry into the common areas of the Crystal Mall (mall), a privately owned shopping mall located in the town of Waterford, for the purpose of distributing literature and speaking to patrons concerning the issue of employees' rights. The plaintiff claims that the defendant violated its right to freedom of speech under article first, and 5, of the constitution of Connecticut and its right to freedom of assembly under article first, §14, of the constitution of Connecticut.

* * *

The record and a joint stipulation the parties submitted to the trial court reveal the following facts and procedural history. The dispute between the parties began on July 7, 1997, when the plaintiff filed a complaint arising from the defendant's request that the plaintiff leave the Crystal Mall Hometown Fair (Hometown Fair), an event held on March 1, 1997. After a complaint by Filene's, one of the mall's tenant stores, mall staff

had asked the members of the plaintiff union to leave the fair, and they had done so in a peaceful manner. Thereafter, the plaintiff sought a temporary injunction prohibiting the defendant from denying it access to and participation in any future fairs or similar events and from creating and enforcing any policy that would have the effect of denying the plaintiff access to such events. The plaintiff also sought an award of damages and costs, including attorney's fees, based on the defendant's violation of the plaintiff's state constitutional rights to free speech and assembly. On October 8, 1997, after a hearing on the matter, the trial court, *Stengel, J.,* denied the application for temporary injunctive relief, stating that, on the basis of this court's decision in *Cologne v. Westfarms Associates,* the plaintiff was not likely to succeed on the constitutional issues raised, that the plaintiff had not sustained its burden of proof that there was irreparable harm and that the plaintiff had not presented evidence that the defendant had planned to hold future fairs.

Thereafter, on December 28, 2001, the plaintiff wrote to the defendant that some of its members intended to enter the mall on January 9, 2002, "'to distribute literature and talk with people in the mall concerning employee rights under the state and federal laws.'" In this letter, the plaintiff represented that its members would "'be peaceful and limit their activity to the common areas of the mall and not the tenant stores.'" Additionally, the plaintiff asserted that the distribution of information was "'not an organizational effort.'" By letter dated January 2, 2002, the defendant denied the plaintiff permission to enter the mall for the plaintiff's stated purposes.

Thereafter, in an amended complaint filed on March 28, 2002, the plaintiff sought this permanent injunction to enjoin the defendant from denying access to the mall, in violation of the plaintiff's state constitutional rights to freedom of speech and assembly, as well as from creating or enforcing any policy that would have such an effect. In addition, the plaintiff sought costs, attorney's fees and such other relief as the "court may deem necessary and proper." On August 15, 2002, the trial court, *Quinn, J.,* relying on this court's decision in *Cologne,* denied the injunction. Specifically, the trial court concluded that the state constitutional rights to freedom of speech and assembly may not be exercised against a private property owner's wishes when that property consists of a large regional shopping center. In addition, the court disagreed with the plaintiff's contention that this matter is factually distinguishable from *Cologne* because, in the present case, both the state and the town of Waterford had been involved directly in the construction of the mall. This appeal followed. Additional facts will be set forth as necessary.

* * *

Our analysis begins with a brief review of this court's decision in *Cologne v. Westfarms Associates.* In *Cologne,* the plaintiffs, the Connecticut National Organization for Women and one of its members, sought permission to solicit shoppers at the Westfarms Mall, which is located partly in the town of Farmington and partly in the town of West Hartford, to sign petitions in support of the proposed equal rights amendment to the federal constitution. As in the present case, the Westfarms Mall permitted various activities on its premises, including informational programs and various exhibitions and other events.

* * *

After reviewing the language and history of our state constitutional provisions guaranteeing freedom of expression from governmental regulation, this court concluded that those provisions were "designed as a safeguard against acts of the state and do not limit the private conduct of individuals or persons." The court further concluded that the public use of a private shopping mall did not transform the mall owners' refusal to allow political speech within the mall into state action.

It is well settled that there is no right under the first amendment to the United States constitution for a person to use a privately owned shopping center as a forum to communicate without the permission of the property owner. A state, however, may adopt greater protection for free expression on private property, so long as such protection does not

conflict with any federally protected property right of the owners of private shopping centers.

* * *

Since the decision in *Cologne,* courts in other jurisdictions that have considered this issue overwhelmingly have chosen *not* to interpret their state constitutions as requiring private property owners, such as those who own large shopping malls, to permit certain types of speech, even political speech, on their premises.

In contrast, only five states—California, Colorado, Massachusetts, New Jersey and Washington—currently hold that a state may require private shopping mall owners to permit some form of political activity in common areas of the mall. As we noted in *Cologne,* "[b]oth the California and Washington decisions rely in part upon the highly significant role which initiative, referendum and recall sponsored directly by the citizenry have played in the constitutional schemes of those states, and the practical importance of access to large congregations of voters in order to obtain signatures on petitions used to implement those rights. The Massachusetts decision was expressly limited to the solicitation of signatures needed by political candidates for access to the ballot and relied, not upon its freedom of speech provision, but upon a state constitutional guarant[ee] of an equal right to elect officers and to be elected, for public employments.

In *Bock v. Westminster Mall Co.,* the Colorado Supreme Court held that its state constitution protected political leafletting in a large shopping mall. In so concluding, the court viewed the mall, which enjoyed a "prominent location in the City [of Westminster (city)] across the street from the City Hall" as being so entangled with the government that there was sufficient state action to trigger the protection of Colorado's constitutional free speech provision.

* * *

In *New Jersey Coalition Against War in the Middle East v. J.M.B. Realty Corp.,* the New Jersey Supreme Court held that regional and community shopping centers must permit leafletting on "societal issues" because, "[a]lthough the ultimate purpose of these shopping centers is commercial, their normal use is all-embracing, almost without limit, projecting a community image, serving as their own communities, encompassing practically all aspects of a downtown business district, including expressive uses and community events." Applying a multifactored approach that it first had enunciated in *State v. Schmid* the court found that several elements supported its conclusion that the malls in question, although privately owned property, were nonetheless subject to the state's constitutional free speech guarantee.... [T]he court took extensive note of the open and inviting nature of malls, noting that, although the primary purpose of the shopping centers may be profit, the "all-inclusiveness" of the property invites the public to do more than just shop.

* * *

To conclude that the minimal state involvement present in this case was sufficient to constitute state action, we would have to disregard much of the reasoning in *Cologne* that differentiated between state and private action, essentially eviscerate *Cologne*'s conclusion that the public use of a private shopping mall did not transform the mall owners' refusal to allow political speech within the mall into state action, and depart drastically from the case law, relying in part on *Cologne*, in the overwhelming majority of other jurisdictions. We do not, however, foreclose the possibility that a proper interpretation of the Connecticut constitution *could* lead to the conclusion that our state action requirement is more expansive than its federal counterpart. After all, "[w]e have …

determined in some instances that the protections afforded to the citizens of this state by our own constitution go beyond those provided by the federal constitution, as that document has been interpreted by the United States Supreme Court. Thus, should an appropriate case present itself, we may reconsider the issue. We therefore leave for another day the determination of the exact contours of our state action doctrine, and thus, whether to deviate from the federal model.

The judgment is affirmed.

In this opinion the other justices concurred.

Private Nuisance

BURCH v. NEDPOWER MOUNT STORM, LLC

647 S.E.2d 879 (W.Va. 2007)

MAYNARD, Justice. The appellants appeal the April 7, 2006, order of the Circuit Court of Grant County that dismissed their nuisance claim in which they sought an injunction against the appellees, NedPower Mount Storm, LLC and Shell WindEnergy, Inc., to enjoin the appellees from constructing a wind power electric generating facility in close proximity to the appellants' property. For the reasons that follow, we reverse the circuit court and remand for proceedings consistent with this opinion.

Facts

By final order dated April 2, 2003, the Public Service Commission ("the PSC") granted NedPower Mount Storm LLC, an appellee herein, a certificate of convenience and necessity to construct and operate a wind power electric generating facility along the Allegheny Front in Grant County. NedPower has entered into a contract with appellee Shell WindEnergy, Inc., to sell the entire facility to Shell upon its completion. It is contemplated that the wind power facility will be located on a site approximately 14 miles long with an average width of one-half mile. The facility is to include up to 200 wind turbines. Each turbine is to be mounted on a steel tower approximately 15 feet in diameter and 210 to 450 feet in height, and have three blades of approximately 115 feet.

The appellants are seven homeowners who live from about one-half mile to two miles from the projected wind turbines. On November 23, 2005, the appellants filed a complaint in the Circuit Court of Grant County seeking to permanently enjoin NedPower and Shell WindEnergy, Inc., from constructing and operating the wind power facility on the basis that it would create a private nuisance. Specifically, the appellants asserted that they will be negatively impacted by noise from the wind turbines; the turbines will create a "flicker" or "strobe" effect when the sun is near the horizon; the turbines will pose a significant danger from broken blades, ice throws, and collapsing towers; and the wind power

facility will cause a reduction in the appellants' property values.

* * *

By order of April 7, 2006, the circuit court granted the appellees' motion for judgment on the pleadings and dismissed the appellants' action with prejudice.

* * *

The appellants now appeal the circuit court's order.

* * *

Discussion

* * *

Our reading of the appellants' complaint indicates that the appellants allege, as private nuisances, that the wind turbines will cause constant noise when the wind is blowing and an increase in noise as the wind velocity increases; the turbines will create an eyesore as a result of the turbines' "flicker" or "strobe" effect when the sun is near the horizon; and proximity of the appellants' property to the turbines will result in a diminution in the appellants' property values. We will now determine the legal effect of each of these allegations under our settled law of nuisance.

First, the appellants allege that the noise from the turbines will constitute a nuisance. This Court has held that "[n]oise alone may create a nuisance, depending on time, locality and degree." We have further held that "[w]here an unusual and recurring noise is introduced in a residential district, and the noise prevents sleep or otherwise disturbs materially the rest and comfort of the residents, the noise may be inhibited by a court of equity." These holdings are grounded on a principle that is essential to a civil society which is that "every person … has the right not to be disturbed in his house; he has the right to rest and quiet and not to be materially disturbed in his rest and enjoyment of home by loud noises." Thus, we find that the appellants' allegation of noise is cognizable under our law as an abatable nuisance.

Second, the appellants allege that a "flicker" or "strobe" effect from the turbines will create an eyesore. Traditionally "courts of equity have hesitated to exercise authority in the abatement of nuisances where the subject matter is objected to by the complainants merely because it is offensive to the sight." This Court has explained in further detail that [e]quity should act only where there is presented a situation which is offensive to the view of average persons of the community. And, even where there is a situation which the average person would deem offensive to the sight, such fact alone will not justify interference by a court of equity. The surroundings must be considered. Unsightly things are not to be banned solely on that account. Many of them are necessary in carrying on the proper activities of organized society. But such things should be properly placed, and not so located as to be unduly offensive to neighbors or to the public.

When an unsightly activity is not properly placed, when it is unduly offensive to its neighbors, and when it is accompanied by other interferences to the use and enjoyment of another's property, this Court has shown a willingness to abate the activity as a nuisance. *Mahoney v. Walter,* it was held: The establishment of an automobile salvage yard with its incident noise, unsightliness, hazards from the presence of flammable materials, open vehicles, rodents and insects, and resultant depreciation of adjoining residential property values in an area which, though unrestricted and containing some commercial businesses, is primarily residential, together with the interference with the use, comfort and enjoyment of the surrounding properties caused by its operation, may be a nuisance and may be abated by a court of competent jurisdiction.

We hold, therefore, that while unsightliness alone rarely justifies interference by a circuit court applying equitable principles, an unsightly activity may be abated when it occurs in a residential area and is accompanied by other nuisances.

Third, the appellants allege that construction of the wind turbines will cause a reduction in their property values. With regard to the legal effect of mere diminution in the value of property, this Court has explained:

Upon the question of reduction in value of the plaintiffs' properties, as the result of the establishment of the used car lot nearby, we find this statement in Wood on Nuisances, 3rd Edition, §640: "Mere diminution of the value of the property, in consequence of the use to which adjoining premises are devoted, unaccompanied with other ill-results, is *damnum absque injuria.*" Also in 66 C.J.S., Nuisances, §19, P. 771, it is stated that: "However, a use of property which does not create a nuisance cannot be enjoined or a lawful structure abated merely because it renders neighboring property less valuable."

* * *

The establishment of what is commonly known as a "used car lot" with its incident noise, light, unsightliness and resultant depreciation of adjoining residential property values in an area which, though unrestricted and without the corporate limits of a town or city, was across a highway from zoned residential property lying within the corporate limits, and which area had previously been exclusively residential on both sides of the highway for a distance of approximately one-fourth of a mile, and which "used car lot" greatly interferes with the use, comfort and enjoyment of such surrounding residential properties, constitutes a nuisance in fact, and may be abated by a court of equity.

* * *

We hold, therefore, that an activity that diminishes the value of nearby property and also creates interferences to the use and enjoyment of the nearby property may be abated by a circuit court applying equitable principles. In addition, the landowners may seek compensation for any diminution in the value of their property caused by the nuisance.

* * *

Therefore, when we apply these holdings to the instant facts, we must conclude that, as a lawful business which has been granted a siting certificate by the PSC, the appellees' wind power facility cannot be considered a nuisance *per se.*

However, the fact that the appellees' electric generating facility does not constitute a nuisance *per se* a does not mean that it cannot be abated as a nuisance. It is also true that a business that is not a nuisance *per se* may still constitute a nuisance in light of the surrounding circumstances.

Applying the above law to the allegations in the appellants' complaint, and taking these allegations as true, we conclude that the allegations are legally sufficient to state a claim to prospectively enjoin a nuisance. Stated differently, it does not definitively appear to us that the appellants can prove no set of facts in support of their claim. The appellants have alleged certain injury to the use and enjoyment of their properties as a result of constant loud noise from the wind turbines, the turbines' unsightliness, and reduction in the appellants' property values. If the appellants are able to adduce sufficient evidence to prove these allegations beyond all ground of fair questioning, abatement would be appropriate. Therefore, we find that the circuit court erred in ruling that the appellants failed to assert any facts of a private nuisance that would support a prospective injunction.

* * *

Conclusion

In conclusion, having found no basis in law for the circuit court's ruling that dismissed on the pleadings the appellants' nuisance claim for an injunction, we reverse the April 7, 2006, order of the Circuit Court of Grant County, and we remand this case to the circuit court for proceedings consistent with this opinion.

Reversed and remanded.

INGRAM, Justice. Paul Carter and Wendy Carter sued Innisfree Hotel, Inc. ("Innisfree"); Birmingham Civic Center Hotel, d/b/a Travelodge; Travelodge Motels and Motor Hotels; Forte Hotels, Inc.; and Eagle Security, Inc., alleging various claims arising out of an alleged "peeping Tom" incident during their stay at the Birmingham Civic Center Travelodge hotel. The trial court entered a summary judgment in favor of all defendants. The Carters appeal from the summary judgment as it relates to Innisfree.

* * *

On February 25, 1993, the Carters traveled from their home in Huntsville to attend a concert that evening at the Birmingham Civic Center. They planned to spend the night in Birmingham after the concert. Because they were unfamiliar with the Birmingham area, they drove around the area near the Civic Center to locate a hotel convenient to that location. Being familiar with the "Travelodge" name, the Carters decided to rent a room for the night at the Birmingham Civic Center Travelodge. They checked into Room 221 that afternoon, and, after purchasing fast food, went back to their room to eat and relax. While in the room, they heard knocking and scratching sounds, which appeared to emanate from behind a wall near the bathroom; the wall was covered by a mirror. However, they assumed that the sounds were from a neighboring room. The Carters conducted their private marital activities that afternoon, including sexual intercourse, without regard to the strange noises. Wendy was undressed in front of the mirror for nearly two hours that afternoon, while applying her makeup and fixing her hair in preparation for the concert. Before the concert, while Paul was brushing his teeth in front of the mirror, he noticed two scratches in the mirror at eye level. He did nothing about the scratches at that time. The Carters went to the concert as they had planned.

After the concert, Paul again looked into the mirror and saw the scratches. He then removed the mirror and found two round, dime-sized scratches on the back of the mirror. Wendy later described the view through the mirror as "like looking through regular glass with the back gone." Upon closer inspection, Paul found a large hole in the wall behind where the scratches were placed on the mirror. There was a hollow space approximately 1.5 feet wide between the Carters' wall and the wall of the adjoining room, which allows for maintenance workers to repair wiring and plumbing pipes. After looking at the hole closely, the Carters noticed a hole in the wall of the adjoining room that was covered by the mirror in that room. There was black electrical tape stuck onto the mirror of the other room; when Wendy pulled the tape off, the Carters discovered scratches on that mirror as well.

Believing that someone had spied on them through the mirror, Paul walked down to the registration desk to complain and to request a refund. Paul asked the person behind the desk whether he could use her telephone to call the police; she allegedly told him, "[T]here's a pay phone around the corner," and refused to allow him to use the office telephone. Paul said a hotel security guard at the desk told him, "[O]kay, boss man, just go back up to your room. Don't worry about it." The guard then accompanied Paul back to the room. According to Paul, after seeing the holes, "[the guard] said it was nothing. That's all he kept saying. He was the one that was acting the strangest out of all of them." Paul then telephoned the police and asked them to investigate; they were not able to identify the alleged "peeping Tom." After the police and several maintenance workers left, the Carters checked out of the hotel and drove back to Huntsville. Paul testified that he has suffered chronic nervousness and sleeplessness since the incident. Wendy testified that she and Paul have had strains in their marriage resulting from nervousness and paranoia she has suffered due to the incident.

Innisfree, a management corporation, manages the Travelodge hotel pursuant to a contract with Merchants Bank of Kansas City, the owner of the hotel. Innisfree contracts with a security personnel company to provide security for the premises. Nora Ward, a manager employed by Innisfree, later found scratches on the mirrors of 13 other rooms at the hotel; 6 other rooms had holes cut into the wall behind the mirror, similar to the hole in Room 221. She testified that her investigation revealed that the holes had been cut to facilitate the servicing of cable wiring.

Ward also testified that access into the maintenance space between the rooms may be gained only by cutting a hole into the wall; this is not disputed by the Carters. However, Ward admitted that the mirrors in the Carters' room and the adjoining room could be removed for viewing from one room into the other through the holes and scratches. * * *

* * *

The Carters contend that the trial court erred in entering a summary judgment in favor of Innisfree on their claims of invasion of privacy, breach of contract, negligence, outrage, and fraud.

This Court defines the tort of invasion of privacy as the intentional wrongful intrusion into one's private activities in such a manner as to outrage or cause mental suffering, shame, or humiliation to a person of ordinary sensibilities. One may invade another's privacy through either an intrusion upon a physical space, such as a trespass, or by an invasion of one's "emotional sanctum"; the law prohibits a wrongful intrusion into either of these areas of privacy. In defining the invasion of privacy tort, the Phillips Court quoted comment b to Restatement (Second) of Torts §652B (1977):

The invasion may be physical intrusion into a place in which the plaintiff has secluded himself, as when the defendant forces his way into the plaintiff's room in a hotel or insists over the plaintiff's objection in entering his home. It may also be use of the defendant's senses, with or without mechanical aids, to oversee or overhear the plaintiff's private affairs, as by looking into his upstairs window with binoculars or tapping his telephone wires. It may be by some other form of investigation or examination into his private concerns....

After reviewing the evidence, we conclude that a jury could reasonably find that the Carters' privacy had been intruded upon by Innisfree; therefore, the summary judgment was inappropriate on the Carters' invasion of privacy claim.

* * *

We ... note that Innisfree maintains that "[p]roof that someone had invaded the Carters' privacy is a prerequisite for recovery." It contends that, because the Carters did not actually see someone behind the wall and had only a suspicion that someone was watching them, there was no such proof. We disagree. Because the scratched mirror and the hole in the wall of Room 221 gave a secret viewing access into Room 221 from the adjoining room, a jury could find a wrongful intrusion into the Carters' right to privacy, and

a jury could reasonably infer that the intrusion arose through the actions of Innisfree's agents, who have control over the hotel. The Carters need not prove the actual identity of the "peeping Tom," nor need they demonstrate actual use of the spying device, although, as we have already stated, a jury could reasonably infer from the evidence that the mirror and hole had been used to spy on them. There is no need for the Carters to establish that they saw another's eyes peering back at them through their mirror. Although the absence of proof that anyone used the scratches for spying may be relevant to the question of the amount of damages to which the Carters would be entitled, it is not fatal to their case. There can be no doubt that the possible intrusion of foreign eyes into the private seclusion of a customer's hotel room is an invasion of that customer's privacy, as such an invasion is defined in Phillips, supra.

Even if it is proven that a third party, someone other than an agent of Innisfree, caused the holes and scratches, Innisfree may be held liable for the invasion of the Carters' privacy. It had "an affirmative duty, stemming from a guest's rights of privacy and peaceful possession, not to allow unregistered and unauthorized third parties to gain access to the rooms of its guests."

* * *

The judgment in favor of Innisfree is affirmed as to the Carters' claims of fraud and outrage. However, that judgment is reversed as to the Carters' claims of invasion of privacy, breach of contract, and negligence.

AFFIRMED IN PART; REVERSED IN PART; AND REMANDED.

Criminal Trespassers
KATKO v. BRINEY
183 N.W.2d 657 (Iowa 1971)

MOORE, Chief Justice. The primary issue presented here is whether an owner may protect personal property in an unoccupied boarded-up farm house against trespassers and thieves by a spring gun capable of inflicting death or serious injury.

We are not here concerned with a man's right to protect his home and members of his family. Defendants' home was several miles from the scene of the incident to which we refer infra.

* * *

At defendants' request plaintiff's action was tried to a jury consisting of residents of the community where defendants' property was located. The jury returned a verdict for plaintiff

and against defendants for $20,000 actual and $10,000 punitive damages.

* * *

Most of the facts are not disputed. In 1957 defendant Bertha L. Briney inherited her parents' farm land in Mahaska and Monroe Counties. Included was an 80-acre tract in southwest Mahaska County where her grandparents and parents had lived. No one occupied the house thereafter.

Her husband, Edward, attempted to care for the land. He kept no farm machinery thereon. The outbuildings became dilapidated.

For about 10 years, 1957 to 1967, there occurred a series of trespassing and housebreaking events with loss of some household items, the breaking of windows and "messing up of the property in general." The latest occurred June 8, 1967, prior to the event on July 16, 1967 herein involved.

Defendants through the years boarded up the windows and doors in an attempt to stop the intrusions. They had posted "no trespass" signs on the land several years before 1967. The nearest one was 35 feet from the house. On June 11, 1967 defendants set "a shotgun trap" in the north bedroom. After Mr. Briney cleaned and oiled his 20-gauge shotgun, the power of which he was well aware, defendants took it to the old house where they secured it to an iron bed with the barrel pointed at the bedroom door. It was rigged with wire from the doorknob to the gun's trigger so it would fire when the door was opened. Briney first pointed the gun so an intruder would be hit in the stomach but at Mrs. Briney's suggestion it was lowered to hit the legs. He admitted he did so "because I was mad and tired of being tormented" but "he did not intend to injure anyone." He gave no explanation of why he used a loaded shell and set it to hit a person already in the house. Tin was nailed over the bedroom window. The spring gun could not be seen from the outside.

No warning of its presence was posted.

Plaintiff lived with his wife and worked regularly as a gasoline station attendant in Eddyville, seven miles from the old house. He had observed it for several years while hunting in the area and considered it as being abandoned. He knew it had long been uninhabited. In 1967 the area around the house was covered with high weeds. Prior to July 16, 1967 plaintiff and McDonough had been to the premises and found several old bottles and fruit jars which they took and added to their collection of antiques. On the latter date about 9:30 P.M. they made a second trip to the Briney property. They entered the old house by removing a board from a porch window which was without glass. While McDonough was looking around the kitchen area plaintiff went to another part of the house. As he started to open the north bedroom door the shotgun went off striking him in the right leg above the ankle bone. Much of his leg, including part of the tibia, was blown away. Only by McDonough's assistance was plaintiff able to get out of the house and after crawling some distance was put in his vehicle and rushed to a doctor and then to the hospital. He remained in the hospital 40 days.

Plaintiff's doctor testified he seriously considered amputation but eventually the healing process was successful. Some weeks after his release from the hospital plaintiff returned to work on crutches. He was required to keep the injured leg in a cast for approximately a year and wear a special brace for another year. He continued to suffer pain during this period.

There was undenied medical testimony plaintiff had a permanent deformity, a loss of tissue, and a shortening of the leg.

* * *

Plaintiff testified he knew he had no right to break and enter the house with intent to steal bottles and fruit jars therefrom. He further testified he had entered a plea of guilty to larceny in the nighttime of property of less than \$20 value from a private building. He stated he had been fined \$50 and costs and paroled during good behavior from a 60-day jail sentence. Other than minor traffic charges this was plaintiff's first brush with the law. On this civil case appeal it is not our prerogative to review the disposition made of the criminal charge against him.

The main thrust of defendants' defense in trial court and on this appeal is that "the law permits use of a spring gun in a dwelling or warehouse for the purpose of preventing the unlawful entry of a burglar or thief." * * *

In the statement of issues the trial court stated plaintiff and his companion committed a felony when they broke and entered defendants' house. The court referred to the early case history of the use of spring guns and stated under the law their use was prohibited except to prevent the commission of felonies of violence and where human life is in danger. The instruction included a statement breaking and entering is not a felony of violence.

* * *

The overwhelming weight of authority, both textbook and case law, supports the trial court's statement of the applicable principles of law.

* * *

Restatement of Torts, section 85, states: "The value of human life and limb, not only to the individual concerned but also to society, so outweighs the interest of a possessor of land in excluding from it those whom he is not willing to admit thereto that a possessor of land has, as is stated in §79, no privilege to use force intended or likely to cause death or serious harm against another whom the possessor sees about to enter his premises or meddle with his chattel, unless the intrusion threatens death or serious bodily harm to the occupiers or users of the premises. * * * A possessor of land cannot do indirectly and by a mechanical device that which, were he present, he could not do immediately and in person. Therefore, he cannot gain a privilege to install, for the purpose of protecting his land from intrusions harmless to the lives and limbs of the occupiers or users of it, a mechanical device whose only purpose is to inflict death or serious harm upon such as may intrude, by giving notice of his intention to inflict, by mechanical means and indirectly, harm which he could not, even after request, inflict directly were he present."

* * *

In addition to civil liability many jurisdictions hold a land owner criminally liable for serious injuries or homicide caused by spring guns or other set devices.

In Wisconsin, Oregon and England the use of spring guns and similar devices is specifically made unlawful by statute.

* * *

Affirmed.

Attractive Nuisance
GREGORY v. JOHNSON
249 Ga. 151, 289 S.E.2d 232 (1982)

CLARKE, Justice. We granted certiorari to determine if the facts of this case present a jury issue on the liability of a landowner under the doctrine referred to as attractive nuisance. In a five to four decision, the Court of Appeals held the defendants were entitled to judgment as a matter of law. We reverse.

The Gregorys brought a wrongful death action to recover for the death by drowning of their two year old child in a swimming pool owned by the Johnsons. The Johnsons' home is on a corner lot in a residential area. The pool is situated in their side yard and is equipped with a diving board and a slide which emptied into the pool. Neither the yard nor the pool was fenced in or barricaded in any way. Mr. Gregory had taken his son to visit friends who were neighbors of the Johnsons. At some point during the visit it was noticed that the child was missing. He was found fully clothed and drowned in the pool.

The Gregorys sued the Johnsons on the grounds of negligence and the maintenance of an attractive nuisance. The Johnsons' home is three blocks from an elementary school. The Gregorys contended that young children were known to be in the vicinity of the pool and that the Johnsons had been warned about the presence of children and had refused to erect a fence to protect them. They further contend that the presence of a playground-type slide on an open lot is likely to attract children to play and that a young child could not appreciate the dangers of a slide over water. The complaint alleges that the failure of the Johnsons to take any precautions to guard against injury to children under these circumstances is a breach of duty which gives rise to recovery under theories of negligence and attractive nuisance.

The Johnsons answered denying negligence, and asserting that the Gregorys were contributorily negligent in failing to attend to the child. The Johnsons then moved for summary judgment which was supported by affidavits setting forth the following: (1) They were not at home at the time of the death of the child; (2) the child was not invited upon the premises; and (3) they had no knowledge of the presence of the child on the premises prior to the discovery of the body. Based upon the evidence submitted by these affidavits the trial court granted summary judgment.

* * *

The Restatement Second sets forth five conditions which must be met to sustain a cause of action for trespassing children.

§339. Artificial Conditions Highly Dangerous to Trespassing Children

A possessor of land is subject to liability for physical harm to children trespassing thereon caused by an artificial condition upon the land if

(a) the place where the condition exists is one upon which the possessor knows or has reason to know that children are likely to trespass, and

(b) the condition is one of which the possessor knows or has reason to know and which he realizes or should realize will involve an unreasonable risk of death or serious bodily harm to such children, and

(c) the children because of their youth do not discover the condition or realize the risk involved in intermeddling with it or in coming within the area made dangerous by it, and

(d) the utility to the possessor of maintaining the condition and the burden of eliminating the danger are slight as compared with the risk to children involved, and

(e) the possessor fails to exercise reasonable care to eliminate the danger or otherwise to protect the children.

Comment (b) to this section notes that the rule as stated is followed in the majority of states in this country. In comment (j) it is stated that the rule generally does not apply to dangers of fire, falling from heights, and water. These are said to be normally understood by children absent other factors creating additional risks of harm or foreseeable dangers to children who cannot appreciate the nature of the harm. A swimming pool in a residential setting is often found to be a condition which could present issues of negligence and foreseeable risk of injury.

The application of the Restatement rule leads to different results when dealing with a natural pond and water hazards associated with industry as opposed to recreational swimming pools located in areas where children are known to play.

We find the approach of the Restatement on this issue is sound and not in conflict with the laws of this state. A landowner is not an insurer of the safety of children, even if he chooses to build a swimming pool. "While it is actionable negligence for one to leave unguarded on a part of his own premises, which he knows is frequented by children of tender years for the purpose of play, a dangerous thing or condition which may injure such children, he is not required to provide against remote or improbable injuries to children playing upon his land." *McCall v. McCallie,* 171 S.E. 843 (1933). The duty imposed is to exercise reasonable care to prevent foreseeable injury, not to protect against any injury.

If all of the first four conditions of the Restatement are found to exist, it must also be proved that "the possessor fails to exercise reasonable care to eliminate the danger or otherwise protect the children." Restatement §339(e).

* * *

Under the facts of the present case the Johnsons have established that the child was not invited and that they had no knowledge of the presence of that particular child. These facts do not establish an absence of negligence as a matter of law in the face of the allegations and evidence of the Gregorys. Issues exist as to the Johnsons' knowledge of the presence of children who cannot appreciate the danger, and if they had reason to know of the dangers whether the failure to erect a fence, under all of the circumstances amounts to a failure to exercise reasonable care.

The Court of Appeals' affirmance of summary judgment in this case is also based upon the premise that it is the duty of the child's parents to provide for his safety. In their answer the Johnsons contend that if they were in fact negligent that the deceased's parents were contributorily negligent in attending to the child so as to bar or proportionately reduce any recovery. The issue of the Gregory's negligence, like the issue of the Johnsons' negligence, is a question for the jury in this case.

Judgment reversed.

Duty to Licensee
SWANSON v. MCKAIN
59 Wash.App. 303, 796 P.2d 1291 (1990)

ALEXANDER, Chief Judge. Michael Swanson appeals a summary judgment order of the Pierce County Superior Court dismissing his personal injury action against Jerry and Mary Ellen McKain. We affirm.

Viewing the facts in a light most favorably to Swanson, it is apparent that on the morning of March 15, 1986 Michael Swanson suffered injuries after diving into shallow water off Camano Island. At that time Swanson and four other individuals were guests at a nearby beachfront home owned by Jerry and Mary Ellen McKain. They had all arrived at the home approximately two days before at the invitation of the McKains' daughter, Eileen. On the evening before the accident, the group had gathered at the McKain cabin and discussed getting up at 4 o'clock to watch Halley's Comet which was to appear in the sky the following morning. Eileen McKain proposed that they should all go swimming at that time.

At approximately 4:00 a.m. the following morning, Eileen McKain, Michael Swanson and two other persons left the McKain house and went down to the beach. Swanson waded out into the water approximately 50 to 75 yards, at which point the water was knee-deep. Swanson then dove into the water and immediately sustained an injury to his head which rendered him a quadriplegic.

Swanson filed a complaint against Jerry and Mary Ellen McKain and Eileen McKain seeking damages for the injuries he sustained. He alleged in his complaint that they breached a duty to warn him of the dangers and characteristics of the tidal waters into which he dove. Specifically, Swanson contended that he struck his head on hidden, floating, transient debris in the water (i.e., "a log or stump"), the existence of which, he alleged, Eileen McKain knew or should have known about and of which she failed to warn.

* * *

In determining whether the McKains had a duty to warn Swanson of natural conditions pertaining to Puget Sound, the common law classification of persons entering upon real property (i.e. invitee, licensee or trespasser) are determinative of the duty of care owed by the owner or occupier of the property. Where, as here, the facts surrounding the complaining party's entry upon the property in question are not contested, the determination of the legal status of that entrant as either an invitee, licensee or trespasser is a question of law.

Swanson contends that he was an "invitee" of the McKains. The classification of "invitee" has been defined as including both public invitees and business visitors. Swanson asserts that he was a "business visitor" because his presence economically benefited the McKains due to the fact that he: (1) brought some firewood with him at the request of Eileen McKain, (2) repaired a dripping faucet in the McKains' cabin while there, (3) contributed funds toward the purchase of groceries, and (4) contributed to Eileen McKain's contacts in the legal community as a law student in that Swanson was an attorney.

The term "business visitor" has been defined as:

… a person who is invited to enter or remain on land for a purpose directly or indirectly connected with business dealings with the possessor of the land.

Restatement (Second) of Torts §332 (3) (1965).

* * *

We conclude that the significant factor which establishes an entrant upon real property as a business visitor, for purposes of qualifying that person as an invitee, is whether the entrant was invited to enter or remain on the property for a purpose directly or indirectly *connected with business dealings of the owner or occupant*. Of the four factors cited by Swanson as support for his argument that he was an invitee, only his allegation that his presence indirectly benefited Eileen McKain's contacts in the legal community is relevant to any "business purpose" of the McKains. Even viewing that fact in the light most favorable to Swanson, as we must, we conclude as a matter of law that the conduct was merely incidental to his status as a guest of the McKains and was insufficient to qualify him as an invitee.

We conclude, therefore, that Swanson was merely a guest of the McKains and, therefore, a licensee. A licensee is defined as a person who is privileged to enter or remain on land only by virtue of the possessor's consent. A licensee includes a "social guest," which is defined as a person who has been invited but does not meet the legal definition of invitee.

We now address whether the duty owed to licensees includes a duty to warn of natural conditions associated with bodies of water. Washington has adopted the Restatement (Second) of Torts §342 (1965), as the standard of care owed to licensees.

* * *

Under the Restatement standards, there exists a duty to exercise reasonable care toward licensees where there is a known dangerous condition on the property which the possessor can reasonably anticipate the licensee will not discover or will fail to realize the risks involved.[148]

The McKains assert that the duty owed to licensees does not encompass the duty to warn of natural conditions associated with bodies of water. In support of this contention, they cite *Ochampaugh v. Seattle,* 588 P.2d 1351 (1979). In

Ochampaugh, the plaintiff brought a wrongful death action against the City of Seattle for the death of his two sons who drowned in a pond situated on the City's property, alleging that the pond constituted an attractive nuisance. The Washington state Supreme Court affirmed the trial court's dismissal of the action on summary judgment, holding that natural bodies of water do not constitute dangers which come within the doctrine of "attractive nuisance" because their dangers are open and apparent.

Swanson seeks to distinguish *Ochampaugh,* because it dealt solely with the doctrine of attractive nuisance. We disagree and find *Ochampaugh* to be authoritative. Although the court addressed the doctrine of attractive nuisance, the basis for its holding was its conclusion that the risks associated with natural bodies of water are obvious and apparent. The duty owed to licensees, similarly excludes the duty to warn or protect a licensee from those conditions which the licensee knows or has reason to know. Accordingly, we find the holding of *Ochampaugh,* that risks associated with natural bodies of water are open and apparent, to be conclusive on the issue of whether or not a licensee should be deemed to know, or have reason to know of such risks.

* * *

For the reasons stated above, we conclude, as a matter of law, that the McKains did not breach any duty they owed to Swanson by failing to warn him of the potential for floating debris in the water. Consequently, the trial court did not err in granting summary judgment.

Owner Liability for Criminal Activity
MCCLUNG v. DELTA SQUARE LIMITED PARTNERSHIP
937 S.W.2d 891 (Tenn. 1996)

WHITE, Justice. On September 7, 1990, thirty-seven-year-old Dorothy McClung, plaintiff's wife, went shopping at Wal-Mart in the Delta Square Shopping Center in Memphis. As she was returning to her parked car around noon, Mrs. McClung was abducted at gunpoint and forced into her car by Joseph Harper, a fugitive from Chattanooga. Later, Harper raped Mrs. McClung and forced her into the trunk of her car where she suffocated. Her body was found by hunters in a field in Arkansas the day after the abduction. Harper confessed, and was convicted of kidnapping, rape, and murder. He committed suicide after being sentenced to life in prison.

Plaintiff filed suit against defendants on his own behalf and on behalf of his and Mrs. McClung's three minor children. In his suit, he alleged that defendant Wal-Mart, the anchor tenant at the Delta Square Shopping Center, and defendant Delta Square, the owner and operator of the center, were negligent in failing to provide security measures for the parking lot and that their negligence was the proximate cause of Mrs. McClung's death.

* * *

To establish negligence, one must prove: (1) a duty of care owed by defendant to plaintiff; (2) conduct falling below the applicable standard of care that amounts to a breach of that duty; (3) an injury or loss; (4) cause in fact; and (5) proximate, or legal, cause. Our focus here is primarily on the first element: the duty of care. That question—the duty which the defendant owed plaintiff—is a question of law to be determined by the court.

* * *

The trial court and the Court of Appeals based the award of summary judgment in this case on *Cornpropst v. Sloan,* 528 S.W.2d 188 (Tenn 1975), in which this Court held that shop owners do not owe to customers a duty to protect them against criminal acts of third parties unless the owner knew or should have known the acts were occurring or about to occur. In that case, decided more than two decades ago, a female shopper, while walking to her car in a shopping center's parking lot, was assaulted and narrowly escaped being kidnapped. * * * ... *Cornpropst* established the principle in Tennessee that businesses not attracting or providing a favorable environment for crime have no duty to protect customers, unless (1) the business knows or has reason to know that criminal acts are occurring or about to occur on the premises, which (2) pose an imminent probability of harm to a customer. In determining whether the business had reason to know, the Court concluded that "[c]onditions in the area [of the defendant business] are irrelevant."

* * *

After careful consideration of the jurisprudence of other jurisdictions and our own, we adopt the following principles to be used in determining the duty of care owed by the owners and occupiers of business premises to customers to protect them against the criminal acts of third parties: A business ordinarily has no duty to protect customers from the criminal acts of third parties which occur on its premises. The business is not to be regarded as the insurer of the safety of its customers, and it has no absolute duty to implement security measures for the protection of its customers. However, a duty to take reasonable steps to protect customers arises if the business knows, or has reason to know, either from what has been or should have been observed or from past experience, that criminal acts against its customers on its premises are reasonably foreseeable, either generally or at some particular time.

In determining the duty that exists, the foreseeability of harm and the gravity of harm must be balanced against the commensurate burden imposed on the business to protect against that harm. In cases in which there is a high degree of foreseeability of harm and the probable harm is great, the burden imposed upon defendant may be substantial. Alternatively, in cases in which a lesser degree of foreseeability is present or the potential harm is slight, less onerous burdens may be imposed. By way of illustration, using surveillance cameras, posting signs, installing improved lighting or fencing, or removing or trimming shrubbery might, in some instances, be cost effective and yet greatly reduce the risk to customers. In short, "the degree of foreseeability needed to establish a duty decreases in proportion to the magnitude of the foreseeable harm" and the burden upon defendant to engage in alternative conduct. "As the gravity of the possible harm increases, the apparent likelihood of its occurrence need be correspondingly less to generate a duty of precaution." Prosser & Keeton on the Law of Torts at 171. The degree of foreseeability needed to establish a duty of reasonable care is, therefore, determined by considering both the magnitude of the burden to defendant in complying with the duty and magnitude of the foreseeable harm.

As a practical matter, the requisite degree of foreseeability essential to establish a duty to protect against criminal acts will almost always require that prior instances of crime have occurred on or in the immediate vicinity of defendant's premises. Courts must consider the location, nature, and extent of previous criminal activities and their similarity, proximity, or other relationship to the crime giving rise to the cause of action. To hold otherwise would impose an undue burden upon merchants.

The balancing approach we adopt appropriately addresses both the economic concerns of businesses and the safety concerns of customers who are harmed due to the negligence of one seeking their business. * * * The criminal who intends to strike in defendant's parking lot will not enter defendant's store to announce his intentions and thereby provide defendant actual notice of the impending attack. In short, this new rule provides the fairest and most equitable results. It creates a duty in limited circumstances, giving merchants neither absolute immunity nor imposing absolute liability. It recognizes the national trend that businesses must justifiably expect to share in the cost of crime attracted to the business. It encourages a reasonable response to the crime phenomenon without making unreasonable demands.

* * *

We reject defendants' argument that it owed plaintiff's wife no duty because the attack was not reasonably foreseeable. In the seventeen months prior to the abduction, the numerous reports of crime to police on or near defendants' premises included a bomb threat, fourteen burglaries, twelve reports of malicious mischief, ten robberies, thirty-six auto thefts, ninety larcenies, and one attempted kidnapping on a parking lot adjacent to defendants' parking lot. * * *

Considering the number, frequency, and nature of the crimes reported to police, management's acknowledgement of security problems, and other evidence in the record, we conclude that the proof would support a finding that the risk of injury to plaintiff's wife was reasonably foreseeable.

Of course, foreseeability alone does not establish the existence of a duty. On remand, the magnitude of the potential harm and the burden imposed upon defendants must also be weighed to determine the existence of a duty. While we know little from this record about the extent of injury to customers as a result of criminal acts on or near defendants' premises, we are persuaded that whatever the extent of the injuries, the magnitude of the potential harm was substantial given the nature of the crimes reported to police.

* * *

In weighing the magnitude of harm and the burden imposed upon defendant, the court must consider whether imposing a duty to take reasonable measures to protect patrons from the consequences of criminal acts of third persons would place an onerous burden—economic or otherwise—upon defendants. If it does not, then the court must consider whether the burden outweighs the foreseeability and gravity of the possible harm, so as to preclude the finding of a duty to take reasonable steps to protect patrons. We hasten to point out, however, that the question of duty and of whether defendants have breached that duty by taking or not taking certain actions is one for the jury to determine based upon proof presented at trial. Additionally, if properly raised as a defense, under our doctrine of comparative fault, a plaintiff's duty to exercise reasonable care for her own safety would be weighed in the balance.

* * *

In conclusion, this record, viewed in light of the principles set forth in this opinion, precludes an award of summary judgment. Assuming for purposes of this analysis that defendants were negligent, we are unable to conclude that all reasonable persons must agree, as a matter of law, that defendants' negligence in failing to provide any security measures did not create a favorable environment for criminal activity. Considering the number, nature, and frequency of crimes committed on or near defendants' premises, it is not beyond the realm of reasonable anticipation that a jury could conclude that defendants' negligence created a foreseeable risk of harm to plaintiff's wife, and that defendants' negligence was a substantial factor in bringing about that harm.

For the reasons stated above, the judgments of the lower courts are reversed. The case is remanded to the trial court for further proceedings consistent with this opinion. The principles set forth today apply to all cases tried or retried after the date of this opinion and all cases on appeal in which the issue in this case has been raised. Costs shall be taxed to defendants.

Premises Liability—Modern Approach
HENDRICKS v. LEE'S FAMILY, INC.
301 A.D.2d 1013, 754 N.Y.S.2d 454 (2003)

CARPINELLO, Judge. Appeal from an order of the Supreme Court (Nolan Jr., J.), entered May 14, 2002 in Albany County, which granted defendants' motions for summary judgment dismissing the complaint.

On September 15, 1999, plaintiff sustained serious physical injuries after falling from a retaining wall near the loading dock at the rear of Ziggy's Sports Bar & Barbecue. The loading dock area is separated from the bar's parking lot by a grassy slope containing several bushes and trees. On the night in question, plaintiff was leaving Ziggy's when she decided to urinate behind the bushes. After plaintiff proceeded through the vegetation, one of her companions heard a loud crash and thereafter found plaintiff at the bottom of the loading dock. Seeking damages for her injuries, plaintiff commenced this action against the lessee of the building and the owner of the premises, alleging, *inter alia*, negligence based on premises liability. Upon defendants' motions for summary judgment, Supreme Court found, *inter alia*, that plaintiff's presence in the area was not reasonably foreseeable and, therefore, dismissed plaintiff's first and second causes of action alleging premises liability. As plaintiff did not contest the dismissal of the third cause of action and she failed to offer evidentiary proof in opposition to the fourth cause of action, the court dismissed those claims as well. Plaintiff appeals.

It is well settled that property owners and occupiers owe a duty of reasonable care under the circumstances to keep their premises safe. The scope of that duty is defined by "the foreseeability of the possible harm" an issue which can be resolved by the court "when but a single inference can be drawn from undisputed facts." Here, Supreme Court correctly granted defendants' motions for summary judgment. It simply was not foreseeable that plaintiff, in a highly intoxicated state, would leave the parking area to urinate behind the bushes rather than use the establishment's indoor facilities. Plaintiff does not set forth evidence that she was precluded from using the bar's restrooms.

Furthermore, it has been held that "the likelihood of the injured party's presence in light of the frequency of the use of the area determines the question of foreseeability." Testimony by representatives of defendants establishes that the grassy area was meant to be decorative and not intended to be used by the bar's patrons as a thoroughfare. In addition, the owner testified that no similar accidents had occurred on this property in over 25 years.

ORDERED that the order is affirmed, with one bill of costs.

KEY TERMS

abandoned property, 486
assumption of risk, 469
attractive nuisance doctrine, 493
comparative negligence, 468–469
compensatory damages, 472
consent, 473
constitutional right to privacy, 484
contributory negligence, 468
duty, 468
estray statutes, 486
intentional tort, 469

invasion of privacy, 483
invitee, 498
licensee, 495
locus in quo, 485
lost property, 485
mislaid property, 485
negligence, 468
nominal damages, 471
private necessity, 474
private nuisance, 476
product liability, 505

PROBLEMS

1. Sears, Roebuck, and Co. was constructing a 110-story building in Chicago. After the construction had progressed to a height of 50 stories, various plaintiffs filed suit to enjoin any further construction of the building. The plaintiffs alleged that the building, if completed, would interfere with television reception in certain areas because the broadcasting antennas of Chicago television stations were lower than the contemplated structure. Does the building constitute a nuisance? Why or why not?

2. A real estate developer bought inexpensive land adjoining a cattle feedlot and built a new city for senior citizens. The developer then filed suit in an attempt to force the feedlot company to move because people were reluctant to purchase homes in the city as a result of odor and flies from the feedlot. If the odor and flies are causing substantial harm, should the judge order the company to move the feedlot elsewhere? Why or why not?

3. Wilbur, an attorney, lived in a residential area in Tulsa, Oklahoma. The area was zoned for family dwellings, although the zoning ordinance allowed residents to rent rooms and apartments in dwellings they occupied. However, the ordinance prohibited residents from advertising that rooms and apartments were available for rent. Adda rented rooms in a house she owned across the street from Wilbur. She displayed a sign in the front of her home that read "Rooms, Meals."

   Wilbur, without notice to Adda, entered her property and destroyed the sign. When he was subsequently charged with malicious mischief, he argued that he had the right to abate the nuisance. Assuming the sign was a nuisance, is Wilbur correct? Why or why not?

4. Thaw owns and occupies a residence valued at $300,000 in Brookside Place in West Hartford. The home has an elaborate air-conditioning system that cost $46,000. The ordinary, average-sized single house in West Hartford uses an air-conditioning unit having approximately a 60,000-BTU capacity; the air-conditioning system installed for Thaw's residence has a 300,000-BTU capacity. Nair, a neighbor, claims that the operation of Thaw's air-conditioning unit causes excessive noise that has affected her health. Is the unit a nuisance? Why or why not? Would the result be the same if the unit was of the type that emitted the sounds typically made by home air-conditioning units? Explain.

5. Friendship Farms Camps, Inc., leased a farm for use as a campground. Youth day camps were initially held on the property; but in later years, a number of weekly high-school marching-band camps were held. The Parsons and the Combs, who lived across the road from Friendship, brought an action against Friendship to abate an alleged nuisance and to make a claim for damages. They claim that during the summer months, loud band music and electronically amplified voices could be heard from 7:00 or 8:00 a.m. until 9:00 or 10:00 p.m. They claimed that the noise interfered with their sleep and use of their property during the evening hours. Decide the case.

6. While watching a Chicago Cubs baseball game at Wrigley Field, a ten-year-old boy who was sitting in the area behind home plate was hit in the eye by a foul ball. The injury resulted in hospitalization and surgery. Should the baseball team be held liable for the boy's injury? Why or why not?

7. A six-year-old boy was severely burned and permanently deformed when he trespassed on hospital property and fell into a pile of smoldering ashes. Hospital employees knew that children played in the area where the accident occurred but did not install a protective screen or store the ashes in nearby metal drums. Children could not tell by looking at the surface of the ash pile that live ashes were underneath. Should the hospital be held liable for the boy's injuries? Why or why not?

8. Cities Service Company operates a phosphate rock mine in Polk County, Florida. On December 3, 1971, a break in a dam occurred in one of Cities Service's settling ponds. As a result, approximately one billion gallons of phosphate slime escaped from the pond into Whidden Creek, which flows into Peace River, thereby killing countless numbers of fish and inflicting other damage. The State of Florida filed a suit against Cities Service for damages, claiming Cities Service is strictly liable for all damages because of its hazardous use of the land. Decide the case, giving reasons for your decision.

9. The North Carolina State Highway Commission leased land from Harry for the purpose of excavating and removing land and gravel. Harry and his family lived on a small portion of the land. As a result of the excavation by the Commission, a large pit was created that ultimately filled with water. The pit reached a depth of twelve feet and was used by neighboring children for swimming. While walking on a sandbar, Harry's thirteen-year-old daughter slipped into deep water and drowned in the pit. Is the State Highway Commission liable for damages? Why or why not?

10. In many large cities, there is often a lack of adequate, affordable housing for the poor. Sometimes the only place they can live is in buildings in abandoned, deteriorating inner-city neighborhoods. It is a common practice for landowners and local government officials to work together to forcibly evict the squatters. Their reasons vary. Often "slumlords" retain their property for investment reasons. In fact, many buildings become dilapidated because landowners are speculating that the neighborhoods will eventually change, enabling them to sell their land for a large profit when the neighborhood is "gentrified," a term used when slum neighborhoods are renovated. Until this happens, however, the landowners rarely maintain the property since the buildings will almost certainly be demolished or totally remodeled when the gentrification begins. Ironically, this lack of attention gives them and the local government ammunition to evict squatters since the buildings are often in a dangerous condition. Moreover, local governments not only want safer structures to protect the public but also want the property improved to increase their tax base.

Squatters, on the other hand, contend that they improve the neighborhoods by making the buildings habitable and thwart illegal activities such as drug dealing and prostitution. Squatters also argue that they have rights under adverse possession, discussed in Chapter 10, or should be treated as having leasehold interests, which affords them some protection under eviction statutes. Both of these rights can give landowners pause to forcibly evict squatters. Homeless advocates also argue that all humans have moral rights to live in dignity, including a place to live. If they are evicted, they may have to live on the street or in their cars. Whose legal and moral rights are greater—those of the landlord or the squatters? Does the gentrification of an old, dangerous neighborhood in which the poor are displaced give the greatest good to the greatest number? Explain.

ENDNOTES

1. To view the states' laws regarding contributory and comparative negligence, see http://www.mwl-law.com/CM/Resources/CONTRIB-NEG-CHART-1.28.10.pdf (last accessed July 27, 2010).
2. 51 Wash.App. 1, 751 P.2d 873 (1988).
3. W. Keeton et al., *Prosser and Keeton on Torts* 486–487 (5th ed. 1984).
4. 2004 WL 2610531 (Ohio App. 8 Dist. 2004).
5. Keeton et al., *supra* note 3 at 67–68.
6. 82 U.S. (15 Wall.) 524, 21 L.Ed. 206 (1872).
7. 837 S.W.2d 674 (Tex.Civ.App. 1992).
8. 186 N.Y. 486, 79 N.E. 716 (1906).
9. *Walden v. Conn,* 84 Ky. 312, 1 S.W. 537 (1886).
10. 30 Cal.4th 1342, 71 P.3d 296, 1 Cal. Rptr.3d 32 (2003).
11. *Register.com v. Verio, Inc.,* 356 F.3d 393 (2nd Cir. 2004).
12. 243 Ga.App. 26, 532 S.E.2d 135 (Ga.App. 2000).
13. To see Arizona's new law, Senate Bill 1070, go to http://www.azleg.gov/legtext/49leg/2r/bills/sb1070s.pdf (last accessed July 27, 2010).
14. *Dougherty v. Stepp,* 18 N.C. 371 (1835).
15. *Hahn v. Hemenway,* 96 N.H. 214, 72 A.2d 463 (1950).
16. *Restatement (Second) of Torts* §163 (1965).
17. *Welker v. Pankey,* 225 S.W.2d 505 (Mo.App. 1949).
18. 147 Me. 317, 87 A.2d 504 (1952).
19. Mich. Comp. Laws Ann. §600.2919.
20. W. Keeton et al., *supra* note 3 at 112.
21. *Ford v. Ford,* 143 Mass. 577, 10 N.E. 474 (1887).
22. 98 F.Supp. 355 (E.D. S.C. 1951).
23. 526 N.W.2d 402 (Minn.Ct.App. 1995).
24. *Desnick v. American Broadcasting Companies, Inc.,* 44 F.3d 1345 (7th Cir. 1995).
25. Civil Court of the City of New York (December 2, 1975), reported in 62 American Bar Association Journal 370 (1976).
26. *Surocco v. Geary,* 3 Cal. 69 (1853).
27. W. Keeton et al., *supra* note 3 at 147.
28. *Vincent v. Lake Erie Transportation Co.,* 109 Minn. 456, 124 N.W. 221 (1910).
29. *Taylor v. Fine,* 115 F.Supp. 68 (S.D. Cal. 1953).
30. *Flodquist v. Palmieri,* No. 38940, 2000 WL 1207273 (Conn. Super. Aug. 1, 2000).
31. W. Keeton et al., *supra* note 3 at 145.
32. *Lloyd Corp., Ltd. v. Tanner,* 407 U.S. 551, 92 S.Ct. 2219, 33 L.Ed.2d 131 (1972).
33. 447 U.S. 74, 100 S.Ct. 2035, 64 L.Ed.2d 741 (1980).
34. E. Richards, *Raising the Banner of States Rights to Prevent Private Abridgment of Speech,* 23 American Business Law Journal 155, 198 (1985). See *Hurley v. Gay Group of Boston,* 515 U.S. 557 (1995), which reviewed the Massachusetts law permitting free speech on commercial properties.
35. *New Jersey Coalition v. J.M.B. Realty Corp.,* 650 A.2d 757 (N.J. 1994).
36. J. Smith et al., *Demonstrating at the Mall,* National Law Journal B11, B20 (April 20, 1995).
37. See J. Gibeaut, *Labor Intensive,* ABA Journal 42 (February 1997), and cases cited therein.
38. W. Keeton et al., *supra* note 3 at 642-643.
39. *Id.* at 616.

40. R. Wright, *Land Use* 17 (1994).

41. *Canfield v. Quayle,* 170 Misc. 621, 10 N.Y.S.2d 781 (1939).

42. *Michigan Compiled Laws Annotated* §600.3801 *et. seq.*

43. 198 S.C. 487, 18 S.E.2d 372 (1942).

44. R. Aalberts, *The Old Common Law Collides with the 21st Century as "Little Rhody Paints Sherwin-Williams in a Corner,"* 35 Real Estate Law Journal 5 (2006).

45. *Osborne v. Power,* 890 S.W.2d 570 (Ark. 1994).

46. *Morgan v. High Penn Oil Co.,* 238 N.C. 185, 77 S.E.2d 682 (1953).

47. *E. Rauh & Sons Fertilizer Co. v. Shreffler,* 139 F.2d 38 (6th Cir. 1943).

48. 146 Mass. 349, 15 N.E. 768 (1888).

49. *Akers v. Marsh,* 19 App.D.C. 28 (1834).

50. *Hobson v. Walker,* 41 So.2d 789 (La.App. 1949).

51. *Boughton v. Cotter Corp.,* 65 F.3d 823 (10th Cir. 1995).

52. *Adams v. Star Enterprise,* 51 F.3d 417 (4th Cir. 1995).

53. *People v. Detroit White Lead Works,* 82 Mich. 471, 46 N.W. 735 (1890).

54. *Blomen v. N. Barstow Co.,* 35 R.I. 198, 85 A. 924 (1913).

55. *Frank v. Cossitt Cement Products,* 197 Misc. 670, 97 N.Y.S.2d 337 (1950).

56. 11 Kan.App.2d 23, 711 P.2d 766 (Kan.Sup.Ct. 1985).

57. *Antonik v. Chamberlain,* 81 Ohio App. 465, 78 N.E.2d 752, 37 O.O. 305 (1947).

58. 131 Wash. 183, 229 P. 306 (1924).

59. *Salvin v. North Brancepeth Coal Co.,* 9 Ch.App. 705 (1874).

60. 55 N.M. 111, 227 P.2d 623 (1951).

61. 12 Vt. Stat. §5753 (2004). See also *Trickett v. Ochs,* 838 A.2d 66 (Vt. 2003).

62. 87 S.W.3d 21 (Mo. Ct. App. 2002).

63. *Amdor v. Cooney,* 241 Iowa 777, 43 N.W.2d 136 (1950).

64. 289 U.S. 334, 53 S.Ct. 602, 77 L.Ed. 1208 (1933).

65. *De Albert v. Novak,* 78 Ohio App. 80, 69 N.E.2d 73, 33 O.O. 425 (1946).

66. 305 Mich. 296, 9 N.W.2d 547 (1943).

67. 69 Mich. 830, 37 N.W. 838 (1888).

68. F. Powell, *Trespass, Nuisance, and the Evolution of Common Law in Modern Pollution Cases,* 21 Real Estate Law Journal 182 (1992).

69. W. Keeton et al., *supra* note 3 at 849.

70. *Melvin v. Reid,* 112 Cal.App. 285, 297 P. 91 (1931).

71. *Lord Byron v. Johnston,* 2 Mer. 29, 35 Eng.Rep. 851 (1816).

72. 381 U.S. 479, 85 S.Ct. 1678, 14 L.Ed.2d 510 (1965).

73. 394 U.S. 557, 89 S.Ct. 1243, 22 L.Ed.2d 542 (1969).

74. 537 P.2d 494 (Sup. Ct. Alaska 1975).

75. *Sheehan v. San Francisco 49ers,* 45 Cal.4th 992, 201 P.3d 472, 89 Cal.Rptr.3d 594 (Sup. Ct. 2009).

76. 1 Strange 505, 93 Eng.Rep. 664 (1722).

77. *Bishop v. Ellsworth,* 91 Ill.App.2d 386, 234 N.E.2d 49 (1968).

78. *Jackson v. Steinberg,* 186 Or. 129, 200 P.2d 376 (1948).

79. *Id.*

80. *Allred v. Biegel,* 240 Mo.App. 818, 219 S.W.2d 665 (1949).

81. States which have specifically recognized that finders own the treasure trove are Arkansas, Connecticut, Delaware, Georgia, Indiana, Iowa, Louisiana, Maine, Maryland, New York, Ohio, Oregon, and Wisconsin. Tennessee, Idaho, and New Jersey have adopted the rule that the landowner owns the treasure trove. See John Kleberg, "Treasure Trove in the United States" at http://www.muenzgeschichte.ch/downloads/laws-usa.pdf (last visited August 4, 2010).

82. 91 Ill.App.2d 386, 234 N.E.2d 49 (1968).

83. 342 Or. 635 (2007).

84. 438 P.2d 1002 (1968).

85. *People v. Adolph Lautenberg,* 2008 WL 2814480 (Cal. App. 2 Dist.) (Unpublished Decision).

86. 2004 WL 2735451 (D.C. App. 2004).

87. 11 Kan.App.2d 23, 711 P.2d 766 (Kan.Sup.Ct. 1985).

88. 157 N.H. 233, 949 A.2d 162 (2008).

89. L.R. 3 H.L. 330 (1868).

90. W. Keeton et al., *supra* note 3 at 549.

91. *Village of Euclid v. Ambler Realty Co.,* 272 U.S. 365, 47 S.Ct. 114, 71 L.Ed. 303 (1926).

92. 94 N.J. 473, 468 A.2d 150 (1983). See J. Benedetto, *Generator Liability Under the Common Law and Federal and State Statutes,* 39 Business Lawyer 620 (1984).

93. *T&E Industries, Inc. v. Safety Light Corps.,* 123 N.J. 371, 587 A.2d 1249 (1991). See J. Chen and K. McSlarrow, *Application of the Abnormally Dangerous Activities Doctrine to Environmental Cleanups,* 47 Business Lawyer 1031 (1992).

94. *Wellesley Hills Realty Trust v. Mobil Oil Corp.,* 747 F.Supp. 93 (D.C. Mass. 1990).

95. See generally W. Johnson, *Common-Law Strict Liability in Tort of Prior Landowner or Lessee to Subsequent Owner for Contamination of Land with Hazardous Waste Resulting from Prior Owner's or Lessee's Abnormally Dangerous or Ultrahazardous Activity,* 13 American Law Review 5th 600 (1994, 1996).

96. 117 Wash.2d 1, 810 P.2d 917 (1991).

97. J. Ketchum, *Missouri Declines an Invitation to Join the Twentieth Century: Preservation of the Licensee-Invitee Distinction in Carter v. Kinney,* 64 University of Missouri-Kansas City Law Review 393 (1995).

98. *Frederick v. Philadelphia Rapid Transit Co.,* 337 Pa. 136, 10 A.2d 576 (1940).

99. *Humphrey v. Glenn,* 167 S.W.3d 680 (Mo. 2005).

100. See W. Keeton et al., *Prosser and Keeton on Torts* 134–36 (5th ed. 1984).

101. K. Shannon, *Governor Signs Bill Expanding Deadly Force Rights,* Houston Chronicle (March 27, 2007).

102. 512 N.W.2d 617 (Minn. 1995).

103. *Sioux City & Pacific R. Co. v. Stout,* 84 U.S. (17 Wall.) 657, 21 L.Ed. 745 (1873).

104. *Restatement (Second) of Torts* §339 (1965). The attractive nuisance doctrine also covers children who are licensees or invitees.

105. 249 Pa.Super. 520, 378 A.2d 417 (1977).

106. 347 So.2d 281 (La.App. 1977).

107. W. Keeton et al., *supra* note 3 at 408-409.

108. *Peters v. Bowman,* 115 Cal. 345, 47 P. 113 (1897).

109. 150 Me. 75, 104 A.2d 432 (1954).

110. *Duff v. United States,* 171 F.2d 846 (4th Cir. 1949).

111. 802 N.E.2d 797 (Ill. 2003).

112. 89 S.W.3d 611 (Tex. 2002).

113. 276 Or. 597, 556 P.2d 102 (1976).

114. 53 Ill.App.3d 632, 11 Ill.Dec. 444, 368 N.E.2d 1052 (1977).

115. 114 Ariz. 213, 560 P.2d 68 (1977).

116. 212 App.Div. 723, 209 N.Y.S. 305 (1925).

117. No. 389490, 2000 WL 1207273 (Conn.Super. August 1, 2000).

118. *Levandoski v. Cone,* 841 A.2d 208 (Conn. 2004).

119. W. Keeton et al., *supra* note 3 at 419.

120. *Id.* at 422-423.

121. 390 F.Supp. 976 (N.D. Ga. 1975).

122. 339 So.2d 244 (Fla.App. 1976).

123. 199 Neb. 577, 260 N.W.2d 316 (1977).

124. 269 S.C. 644, 239 S.E.2d 653 (1977).

125. 281 Conn. 786, 918 A.2d 249 (2007).

126. 91 Cal.App.2d 112, 204 P.2d 644 (1949).

127. 16 Wash.App. 34, 552 P.2d 1065 (1976).

128. *Barrett v. Faltico,* 117 F.Supp. 95 (E.D. Wash. 1953).

129. 347 So.2d 1100 (Fla.App. 1977).

130. *Morgan v. Bucks Associates,* 428 F.Supp. 546 (E.D. Pa. 1977).

131. *Romaguarea v. Piccadilly Cafeterias, Inc.,* 648 So.2d 1000 (La.Ct. App. 1994).

132. 452 F.2d 902 (D.C. Cir. 2006).

133. *Williams v. Cunningham Drug Stores,* 429 Mich. 495, 418 N.W.2d 381 (1988).

134. 269 S.C. 479, 238 S.E.2d 167 (1977).

135. *Kentucky Fried Chicken of California, Inc. v. Brown,* 14 Cal. 4th 814, 829, 927 P.2d 1260, 1270, 59 Cal.Rptr.2d 756, 766 (Cal. 1997).

136. 193 Cal.App.3d 495, 238 Cal.Rptr. 436 (Cal.App. 1987).

137. A. Sebok, *Could Virginia Tech Be Held Liable for Che Seung Hui's Shootings?* Findlaw (April 24, 2007).

138. *Dunster v. Abbott,* 2 All Eng.Rep. 1572 (1953).

139. See *Koenig v. Koenig,* 766 N.W. 2d 635 (Sup. Ct. Iowa 2009), which discusses the trend toward abolishing the trichotomy of licensee, invitee, and trespasser.

140. *Rowland v. Christian,* 69 Cal.2d 108, 70 Cal.Rptr. 97, 433 P.2d 561 (1969).

141. 561 P.2d 731 (Alaska 1977).

142. 250 Neb. 750, 552 N.W.2d 51 (Neb. 1996).

143. *Koenig, supra* note 140.

144. 246 Mich. App. 635 N.W.2d 219, 246 Mich. App. 645 (2001).

145. See *Rees v. Cleveland Indians Baseball Company, supra* note 4.

146. *Hanks v. Powder Ridge Restaurant Corp.,* 276 Conn. 314, 886 A.2d 734 (2005).

147. 528 S.W.2d 703 (Ky. 1975).

148. In contrast, a possessor of land owes invitees an affirmative duty to discover dangerous conditions. As stated in comment b to section 343, a possessor of land owes an invitee:

> *… the additional duty to exercise reasonable affirmative care to see that the premises are made safe for the reception of the visitor, or at least to ascertain the condition of the land, and to give such warning that the visitor may decide intelligently whether or not to accept the invitation, or may protect himself against the danger if he does accept it.*

© MACIEJ NOSKOWSKI/iStockphoto (RF)

Legal Planning and Regulation of Land Use

13

LEARNING
OBJECTIVES

After studying Chapter 13, you should:

- Learn about private control of land use

- Be familiar with the governmental ownership and regulation of land

- Explain how land use planning works

- Understand and distinguish planned unit developments, condominiums, time-sharing, and cooperatives

"Every man holds his property subject to the general right of the community to regulate its use to whatever degree the public welfare may require it."

Theodore Roosevelt

"The problem with planning is that it has been overtaken by mathematical models—traffic, density, impact assessment, public costs etc. discarding common sense and empirical observation."

Andres Duany, Urban Planner

In pioneer America, the person who acquired fee simple ownership of real estate had almost complete freedom to use the land for any purpose. The owner was free to build a house or factory or store, clear the land and farm it, erect a gaudy structure and tasteless signs, or develop the property into a place of natural beauty.

As the population increased, the United States became more settled and urbanized, resulting in a number of restrictions on individual freedom to use and develop real estate. Sometimes the restrictions were created through the common law of torts, sometimes through private agreements. In most cases, though, the restrictions came about through government regulation of real estate. (See Figure 13.1.) This chapter covers both private and public control of land use and land use planning. In addition, the chapter discusses the interplay between the Fifth Amendment's prohibition against taking private property for public use without just compensation and land use regulation. Development and ownership vehicles allowing common use of facilities and infrastructure such as planned unit developments, condominiums, time-sharing, and cooperatives are discussed; these have become popular planning tools to maximize use of increasingly scarce land. Environmental laws are discussed in Chapter 14.

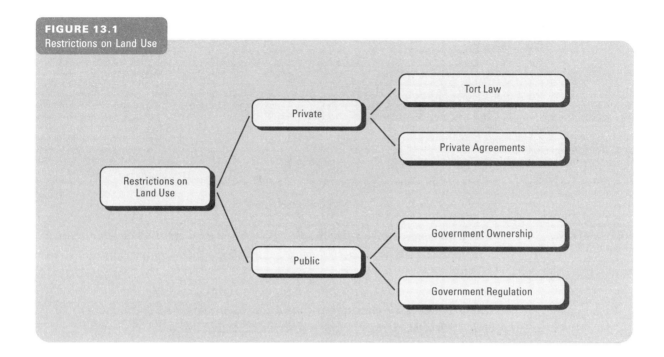

FIGURE 13.1
Restrictions on Land Use

Private Control of Land Use
Common Law Tort Remedies

Chapter 12 examined tort remedies that affect the ownership and use of real estate. Four of these torts—nuisance, trespass, strict liability, and negligence—have often been used to limit the use of land.[1] **Nuisance** is the tort theory most effectively applied to limiting objectionable land uses, but a private nuisance action is not an unqualified and universal remedy for all abuses. (The private nuisance action was defined and contrasted with public nuisance cases in Chapter 12.) Courts deciding a **private nuisance** claim balance the economic harm to the plaintiff with the economic loss that will result if the defendant is enjoined from using the land for its present purpose. Courts in a private nuisance suit can consider only the limited interests that are represented by the parties. As a New York court noted in *Boomer v. Atlantic Cement Co.*:[2]

> … *it seems manifest that the judicial establishment is neither equipped in the limited nature of any judgment it can pronounce nor prepared to lay down and implement an effective policy for the elimination of air pollution. This is an area beyond the circumference of one private lawsuit. It is direct responsibility for government and should not thus be undertaken as an incident to solving a dispute between property owners and a single cement plant—one of many—in the Hudson River Valley.*

Despite these problems, the private nuisance action remains more popular than the **public nuisance** action because public officials often are reluctant to prosecute nuisance cases and because governmental acquiescence in the nuisance will prevent the government from succeeding in its action. Furthermore, private litigants who want to bring a private nuisance action can do so only when they can prove that their injury is different in kind from the public injury.[3] For instance, in the classic Wisconsin case of *Kuehn v. City of Milwaukee*,[4] a professional fisherman on Lake Michigan was denied injunctive

nuisance
The unreasonable interference with the use or enjoyment of land without a physical invasion.

private nuisance
The unreasonable interference with a private person's use or enjoyment of land without a physical invasion.

public nuisance
An unreasonable interference with a right that is common to the general public.

relief against city authorities who were dumping garbage into the lake. He could not prove that his injury was unique because other members of the public used the waters of Lake Michigan for fishing. Owners of an outdoor movie theater, an outdoor restaurant, and a large motel, however, were allowed to bring a private nuisance action against the City of Fond du Lac, Wisconsin, because of "obnoxious and offensive odors" from the city's sewage disposal plant.[5] The court held that the plaintiffs' injuries were sufficiently different in kind and degree from the general public to support the private nuisance claim.

trespass

An unlawful interference with a person's property or rights.

A second tort theory—**trespass**—is available when a physical invasion of a person's land by visible or even invisible matter results from the use of another's land. An Oregon court held that the intrusion of fluoride particulates from a Reynolds Metals Company plant was a trespass:

> In this atomic age even the uneducated know the great and awful force contained in the atom and what it can do to a man's property if it is released. In fact, the now famous equation $E = mc^2$ has taught us that mass and energy are equivalents and that our concept of "things" must be reframed. If these observations on science in relation to the law of trespass should appear theoretical and unreal in the abstract, they become very practical and real to the possessor of land when the unseen force cracks the foundation of his house. The force is just as real if it is chemical in nature and must be awakened by the intervention of another agency before it does harm.[6]

Likewise, in the following Texas case a federal court ruled on whether particulates constitute trespass.

A CASE IN POINT

In *Stevenson v. E.I. DuPont De Nemours and Co.*,[7] plaintiffs alleged that heavy metal particulates emitted from DuPont's petrochemical plant were damaging their health and diminishing the value of their property. Tests indicated that the airborne particulates from the plant had settled in plaintiff's soil and on his roof. The court, the Fifth Circuit Court of Appeals, upheld the district court's ruling that trespass had occurred but remanded the case on the issue of damages.

strict liability

Responsibility for personal or property damage regardless of whether it was caused by a negligent or intentional act.

negligence

The failure to do what a reasonable person would have done under the same circumstances.

Another tort theory is **strict liability**. It requires proof that the landowner was engaged in abnormally dangerous activities or that she was making a nonnatural use of the land, while a **negligence** action requires the plaintiff first to prove the existence of an objective standard of care and then to prove that the defendant did not meet that standard.

Obtaining relief and compensation under the common law theories is frequently slow and expensive. Proving the elements of a tort is difficult, and courts are reluctant to act before harm occurs. A prime example is found in the best-selling book *A Civil Action*, which was made into a movie starring John Travolta. It illustrates vividly the real-life difficulties of proving negligence in a toxic tort environmental case set in Woburn, Massachusetts, in the 1980s. The plaintiffs, most of whom were parents of children who died of leukemia, alleged, among other theories, that the deaths were caused by harmful chemicals that had been negligently poured into the ground by employees of corporate giants Beatrice Foods and W. R. Grace and Company. To prove their case, the plaintiffs had to prove by a preponderance of the evidence that the employees had dumped the chemicals and that the chemicals entered the groundwater, migrated into the city's water supply, and then caused the children's cancer. In the end, the plaintiffs settled for much less money than they and many other observers had expected, due in large part to the tremendous time, complexity, and expense of the litigation, all of which overwhelmed plaintiffs' counsel.[8]

Yet common law actions are still important because, in the words of one commentator, they "will continue to be the major tool in individual rights oriented land use disputes."[9] Some commentators even favor the common law remedies and private covenants over governmental regulation, including zoning. Professor Richard Epstein, an outspoken libertarian, asks: "Can zoning provide an improvement to the common-law system in proportion to its increase in costs and delay? I suspect that the answer to this question is negative, and that we should here, as in other areas, seek to find ways to clip the wings of zoning authorities."[10] Still, many other legal experts find Epstein's views unworkable and favor the ongoing efforts of government to regulate land use, a topic extensively covered later in this chapter. Voluntary land restrictions, discussed in the next section, together with the common law remedies, remain vital land use planning and control devices.

Voluntary Restrictions on Land Use

There are *three* private negotiated and voluntary ways to terminate land use:

- *Negative easements (discussed in Chapter 4)*
- *Defeasible fees (discussed in Chapter 5)*
- *A restrictive* **covenant running with the land** *(discussed next)*

covenant running with the land
A contractual promise that passes with the land.

The restrictive covenant running with the land is unique because it binds not only the parties but also later owners of the land. The covenant is distinguished from an easement in that the easement is an interest in land, while the covenant is merely a contractual promise that passes or runs with the land.[11] While an easement gives its owner certain rights in the land of another, a restrictive covenant limits the land's permissible uses. The covenant may also be distinguished from the defeasible fee in that a defeasible fee terminates when the promise is not kept, while a breach of covenant results in an action for damages or injunctive relief. Thus, distinguishing between the two can have important remedial consequences, as the following classic Massachusetts case demonstrates.

A CASE IN POINT

In *Gray v. Blanchard*, a person deeded land to a buyer with the restriction that "this conveyance is upon the condition that no windows shall be placed in the north wall of the house." When the buyer later placed windows in the north wall, the seller commenced an action charging that the buyer must forfeit his estate. The court held for the seller on the grounds that the promise constituted a condition, not a covenant. The court noted that "we cannot help the folly of parties who consent to take estates upon onerous conditions, by converting conditions into covenants.... [I]t was a voluntary bargain, and if they did not choose to take the estate they should have rejected it altogether."[12]

Creation of Covenants   Covenants are created by signing a document, often a deed that typically spells out restrictions on land use or refers to a recorded plat containing details of the restrictions. Covenants also can be recorded in a separate detailed document, such as a Declaration of Covenants, Conditions, & Restrictions (CC&Rs), which is then referred to in both the plat and the deed. The written covenant must comply with the Statute of Frauds (discussed in Chapter 7) since it pertains to land and include *three* characteristics:

1. The writing should state an intention that the covenant runs with the land—for example, by stating that it binds the assignees or successors of the grantee.
2. The covenant should "touch and concern" the land—that is, the promise must relate to the land in such a way as to affect the land's value.[13]
3. There should be privity of estate, which, although subject to many interpretations, generally means that if a party is to be bound by a covenant, the party must hold the same estate as the person who originally made the promise.[14]

Some jurisdictions have relaxed the third requirement and would allow, for example, the covenants to be enforced even if an owner of a fee simple absolute carved out a lesser estate and conveyed a life tenancy or an estate for years.[15]

If any one of the three requirements is not met, the covenant operates as a binding contract only against the original parties to the contract and will not bind later purchasers of the real estate—that is, the covenant will *not* run with the land. For instance, assume that Derek enters into a written contract to provide transportation to his neighboring landowner, Conner. If Conner later sells his land to Chad without assigning this right, Chad is not entitled to the transportation because this type of right is personal to Conner and does not "touch and concern" the land as required under the second element.[16] Once the requirements are met, the "running of the covenant with the land means that the burdens or benefits of the covenant pass to those who succeed to the estate of the original contracting parties."[17]

Interpretation of Covenants   Covenants are strictly interpreted, as a Connecticut court noted: "Restrictive covenants, being in derogation of the common law right to use land for all lawful purposes, are to be narrowly construed and are not to be extended by implication. If their language is of doubtful meaning, it will be construed against rather than in favor of the covenant."[18] In the following Alabama case, the defendants found out how important it is to be clear when wording a covenant.

A CASE IN POINT

In *Bear v. Bernstein*,[19] the courts faced the legal issue of whether a duplex or four-unit apartment house could be built when a restrictive covenant in a deed provided that the land was to be "used only for residential purposes … and that only one residence shall be erected on … the lot." The court noted that a number of other courts interpret this language to mean there shall not be a plurality of occupancy, while still other courts maintain it prohibits only plurality of houses or buildings.

The court interpreted the covenant to restrict the number of buildings: "Though it is the duty of the courts to give full force and effect to any restraint placed on the use of property intended by the parties, the rule is that restrictions against its free use and enjoyment are not favored in law and being in derogation of such right, are to be strictly construed against the enforcement thereof. Where the language of the restriction is clear and unambiguous it will, of course, be given its manifest meaning, but its construction will not be extended by implication or include anything not plainly prohibited and all doubts and ambiguities must be resolved against the party seeking enforcement."

Similarly, a Colorado court in *Double D. Manor, Inc. v. Evergreen Meadows Homeowners' Association*[20] held that a restrictive covenant permitting only one "single-family dwelling" on each site restricted the structures that could be placed on the site, not the use; the court ruled that the site's use of the property as a residential care facility for seven developmentally disabled children was consistent with the covenant.

With the increasing use of group homes in residential neighborhoods to house the disabled, courts, such as in the following New Mexico case, are not only strictly interpreting the wording in the restrictive covenants that attempt to exclude these homes but also examining them for possible violations of public policy.

Can a neighborhood group enjoin a group home for AIDS victims from locating in its community? In *Hill v. Community of Damien of Molokai* on page 566, the court ruled on the validity of a covenant that restricted property to single-family residences only.

END OF CHAPTER CASE

Even if a covenant has been stated in clear and unambiguous language, courts consider the following issues in deciding whether to enforce a covenant.

Change in the Neighborhood   *Two* types of change in the neighborhood might result in a decision that land use restrictions are no longer enforceable. The *first* type of change, discussed in the Illinois case below, occurs within the restricted area when certain owners violate the restrictions with the apparent acquiescence of other owners.

A CASE IN POINT

In *Watts v. Fritz*,[21] a covenant restriction stated that no more than one house could be built on each lot in a subdivision. When Fritz attempted to subdivide his lot to build two houses, Watts claimed that Fritz was acting in violation of the restrictions. The court held for Fritz because there had been other violations within the subdivision: "[T]he evidence showed that there had been several subdividings of lots in the subdivision with the building of more than one dwelling on a lot as originally platted. Plaintiff, himself, acknowledged that one such subdividing and building took place across the street from him after he purchased his property.... There is no showing that plaintiff took any action to prevent the subdividing of the lot across the street from him or the building of a dwelling on it other than to talk to the developer and possibly an attorney. No positive preventative action was taken. Minor violations of a restriction will not prohibit the subsequent enforcement of it. However, where there has been acquiescence of prior violations of the very substance of a general plan or particular restriction, the plaintiff will be held to have waived any right he may have had to enforce it."

The *second* type of change occurs outside the area restricted by a covenant. Courts will refuse to enforce the restrictions if the change in the surrounding area is so great as to make enforcement of the covenant oppressive and inequitable. A Maryland court discusses this point next.

A CASE IN POINT

In *Norris v. Williams,*[22] a one-acre parcel of land was restricted to use for residential purposes only. In the years following the creation of the restriction, the parcel was surrounded by businesses, including a bowling alley, restaurant, paint shop, bakery, liquor store, filling station, food store, hardware store, tobacco shop, men's clothing store, poolroom, laundry, barbershop, and sewage disposal plant.

  The court determined that the restriction should no longer be enforced: "Under the circumstances now existing, the covenant made by Grace and his wife in 1917 is no longer effective for the purpose for which it was imposed. It is evident that the purpose of the restriction was to make the locality a suitable one for residences; but, owing to the general growth of the town, and the development of the neighborhood west of the avenue as a business district, this purpose can no longer be accomplished. It is conceded that there is no one who could enforce the restriction. But even if it could be enforced, it would not restore to the locality its residential character. It would, therefore, be oppressive and inequitable to give effect to the covenant. As the changed condition of the locality has resulted from causes other than breach of the covenant, it is clear that to enforce the restriction could have no effect other than to injure and harass the owners without effecting the purpose for which it was intended."

Expiration Time   Another problem the *Norris* court faced was that the restriction provided that the parcel be used for residential purposes for a period of 50 years. Although the court held that the covenant would not be enforced because of changed conditions, courts would have enforced the covenant for the time stated had there been no change in neighborhood conditions. And if no time is stated, according to the Norris court, "it will be implied that some reasonable limitation adapted to the nature of the case was intended, and the restriction will be construed as extending for no longer period of time than the nature of the circumstances and the purposes of the imposition indicate as reasonable." Several states, such as Minnesota, have enacted statutes stipulating that all CC&Rs are valid for only a limited period of time—for example, 30 years.[23]

Zoning Ordinances   In the *Norris* case, the land in question had been zoned for commercial use. This factor alone would not invalidate the restriction, for a covenant may establish a more limited use of the land, as a Colorado court points out below, than that allowed by a zoning ordinance.

A CASE IN POINT

In *Lidke v. Martin,*[24] the defendants hoped to erect apartment buildings on a lot that was restricted by a covenant to single-family dwellings. The covenant also provided that it was not to be "construed as conflicting with any terms or regulations of the present or future Jefferson County zoning ordinance." The zoning regulations allowed apartment buildings on the property. The court held that the apartments could not be built because the incorporation of the zoning ordinance into the covenant was intended only to incorporate sections of the zoning ordinance that provided more restrictive standards than the covenant.

  On the other hand, in cases where the zoning ordinance requires a more limited use than the restrictive covenant, whether or not the covenant has a "no conflict clause," the zoning ordinance prevails.

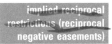

implied reciprocal restrictions (reciprocal negative easements)

Restrictions that form part of a general plan of development that prevent landowners from making certain uses of their land even when their deeds do not mention the restrictions. Also called reciprocal negative easements.

Implied Reciprocal Restrictions   Occasionally, the owner of a subdivision will place restrictions on some lots when the owner sells them but will fail to mention restrictions in the deeds to the other lots. Are the owners of the lots without restrictions legally bound by the covenants? As a general rule, they will be bound if the restrictions are part of a general plan of development and if the purchasers had notice of the restrictions. Such restrictions, as discussed in the next case from Michigan, are called **implied reciprocal restrictions** or **reciprocal negative easements**.

A CASE IN POINT

In *Allen v. City of Detroit*,[25] an owner of 11 lots sold 10 of the lots with restrictions limiting their use to residential purposes. The 11th lot was sold to the city of Detroit without restrictions, and Detroit planned to build a firehouse on the property. However, the court held that the restrictions were binding on Detroit: "The law is well settled that building restrictions of the character shown are in the nature of reciprocal negative easements and may be created upon a division and conveyance in severalty to different grantees of an entire tract. That a portion of the conveyances do not contain the restriction will not defeat the same. Although some of the lots may have written restrictions imposed upon them and others not, if the general plan has been maintained from its inception, if it has been understood, accepted, relied on, and acted upon by all in interest, it is binding and enforceable on all inter se. It goes with the land and is equally binding upon all purchasers with notice."

Unenforceability of Racially Discriminatory Covenants   The Fourteenth Amendment prohibits the states from interfering with an individual's rights by engaging in discriminatory conduct. Among the civil rights protected are the rights to acquire, enjoy, own, and dispose of property. This raises the following legal issue: If individuals create discriminatory restrictions, may the states enforce the restrictions? The Supreme Court addressed this issue in the following pivotal case.

A CASE IN POINT

In *Shelley v. Kraemer*,[26] a deed restriction provided that the real estate was not to be "occupied by any person not of the Caucasian race, it being intended hereby to restrict the use of said property … against the occupancy as owners or tenants of any portion of said property for resident or other purpose by people of the Negro or Mongolian Race."

The Supreme Court held that such restrictions alone do not violate the Fourteenth Amendment as long as no **state action** is involved. However, the Court concluded that state courts could not enforce this type of restriction because the judicial proceedings would constitute state action. "We hold that in granting judicial enforcement of the restrictive agreements in these cases, the States have denied petitioners the equal protection of the laws and that, therefore, the action of the state courts cannot stand. We have noted that freedom from discrimination by the States in the enjoyment of property rights was among the basic objectives sought to be effectuated by the framers of the Fourteenth Amendment. That such discrimination has occurred in these cases is clear. Because of the race or color of these petitioners they have been denied rights of ownership or occupancy enjoyed as a matter of course by other citizens of different race or color." The Fourteenth Amendment declares "that all persons whether colored or white, shall stand equal before the law of the States, and, in regard to the colored race, for whose protection the amendment was primarily designed, that no discrimination shall be made against them by law because of their color."

state action

Governmental, as opposed to private, action.

State courts are also prohibited from awarding damages for breach of discriminatory restrictions. In *Barrows v. Jackson*,[27] the U.S. Supreme Court declared that if a state sanctioned the use of restrictive covenants by awarding damages for their breach, the result "would be to encourage the use of restrictive covenants ... [which] would constitute state action as surely as it was state action to enforce such covenants in equity."

Beyond race, restrictive covenants that discriminate against other protected groups are also unenforceable. One important example involves the disabled, who are not afforded the broad constitutional protections of race, but are protected under the federal Fair Housing Act (FHA) as well as by many state housing acts. Many of the cases dealing with this issue involve restrictive covenants that prohibit all but single-family residences in a planned unit development. Thus, when a group home for the disabled—such as for AIDS victims, recovering drug or alcohol users, or the mentally retarded—is proposed, neighbors sometimes seek to enjoin their operations, arguing, among other things, that these are nonresidential land uses and that the inhabitants are not real families. For example, in *Hill v. Community of Damien of Molokai*[28] (see page 566 for an edited version of the case) a New Mexico court ruled that a restrictive covenant was unenforceable *not* because the neighbors actually *intended* to use the covenants to discriminate, but because they produced a discriminatory *effect* on AIDS victims. Likewise, in *Deep East Texas Regional Mental Health and Mental Retardation Services v. Kinnear*,[29] a Texas court ruled that the FHA renders these restrictive covenants unenforceable, stating that the "strong public policy supporting group homes overcomes the public policy which favors the right of property owners to create restrictive covenants." In that case, neighbors had sought an injunction to stop the construction of a proposed community house for the mentally challenged that allegedly violated the neighborhood's architectural requirements.

Covenants as Private Planning   Developers of planned unit developments (discussed later in this chapter), through their successor homeowners' associations (HOAs), often impose restrictive covenants to maintain architectural controls, restrict incompatible uses, and assess fees for the maintenance of common areas. The developer will record CC&Rs to assure prospective purchasers of the continuity of certain desirable features. In discussing covenants running with the land, a California court noted:

> *Although the relevant doctrines go back centuries, they are more vital than ever today as California becomes increasingly crowded and people live in closer proximity to one another. Planned communities have developed to regulate the relationships between neighbors so all may enjoy the reasonable use of their property. Mutual restrictions on the use of property that are binding upon, and enforceable by, all units in a development are becoming ever more common and desirable.*[30]

In this spirit, an Iowa court[31] ruled that Kenneth Norple's erection of a 35-foot-tall pipe on his roof, whether for the display of an American flag or for his ham radio antennae, was prohibited by a subdivision restrictive covenant that banned the erection of exterior structures without the community association's approval. However, in 2006, the "Freedom to Display the American Flag Act" was signed into law. The Act states that:

> *A condominium association, cooperative association or residential real estate management association may not adopt or enforce any policy, or enter into any agreement, that would restrict or prevent a member of the association from displaying the flag of the United States on residential property within the association....*[32]

A related issue is whether these kinds of restrictions stifle First Amendment rights of free speech and expression. The threshold question is whether an HOA's activities encompass a "state action," since First Amendment rights exist to protect citizens from the actions of federal, state, or local governments, not from private parties. Although there are exceptions to the state actor requirement, such as judicial enforcement of private laws as articulated in the *Shelley v. Kraemer* case, discussed above in this chapter, there are no cases on point. Moreover, disposition of any case would depend a great deal on how the challenged HOA operates.[33]

Although CC&Rs may appeal to those who find their neighbors' property uses objectionable, they also take away many freedoms. Many find the sacrifice worth it, however, since homeowners' and neighborhood associations often protect land values and maintain amenities such as common areas. Indeed, according to the Community Associations Institute,[34] around 6.1 million Americans in 2009 lived in 305,000 association-governed communities. However, in some cases, the elected neighborhood associations, which are in charge of policing the rules, may be overly zealous, especially in cases in which picky, inconsequential rules, such as the size, color, and placement of garbage cans or the kinds of flowers that can be planted.

Associations are also in charge of collecting dues to finance the upkeep of common areas such as swimming pools and parking lots and can levy fines for failure to comply with common area rules. When fees or dues are not paid, the association can place a lien on the property and foreclose to satisfy the unpaid assessments. Indeed, in some states, like Colorado, HOAs benefit from a "super lien" law in which these associations have priority over a first mortgage for up to a certain amount of time—typically six months—of delinquent assessments. Since the recession of 2007–2009 and the subsequent high foreclosure rates, other states including Alabama, Alaska, Connecticut, Minnesota, and Nevada have passed similar laws to help economically distressed HOAs.

In response to association abuses, many association members are lobbying state legislatures for protective laws, called the "homeowners' bill of rights." Among the protections that some states provide are open meeting rules and the prohibition of rules that ban pets.[35] One issue of importance is whether CC&Rs can exclude cellular towers that provide telephone service to the area, as discussed in the following New York case.

A CASE IN POINT

In *Chambers v. Old Stone Hill Road*,[36] a large tract of land was platted in 1957 with restrictive covenants limiting development to single-family homes. In 1998, plaintiffs objected when the defendant homeowners' association leased 2,000 square feet to Verizon Wireless to construct a 120-foot cellular telephone antenna and equipment shed to provide service. The defendant claimed that it could lease the property because of the federal Telecommunications Act (TCA) of 1996, which reduced the extent of regulation on telecommunication technologies. The Act provides that state or local governments cannot exclude wireless services without substantial reasons. The New York Court of Appeals, affirming the lower appellate division, ruled that the TCA "does not expressly or impliedly preempt the power of private citizens to enforce restrictive covenants or otherwise limit the judicial enforcement of those private agreements."

Commercial Covenants, Conditions, and Restrictions   Developers, and sometimes anchor tenants of large shopping malls, are increasingly requiring commercial tenants to abide by CC&Rs. Much like those restrictions used in residential developments, the aim of the restrictions is to control the physical aspects and use of the tenants' businesses. For example, the CC&Rs dictate a store's size, color, design, signage, and set-back requirements within the mall, as well as any obnoxious or undesirable uses that other tenants and the landlord may find objectionable. Unlike commercial leases, which are negotiated with each new tenant, CC&Rs can be especially important since they run with the land and are binding on all future tenants. Yet like all covenants restricting another's land use, they are strictly construed, even when used by local merchants trying to keep out a highly competitive retail giant, as the next North Dakota case discusses.[37]

A CASE IN POINT

In *Dan's Super Market, Inc. v. Wal-Mart*,[38] the owner of two adjacent parcels designated for retail development sold one parcel to Dan's to operate a supermarket. As part of the sale, Dan's negotiated a covenant restricting food store competition on the adjacent site. In 1989, Wal-Mart purchased the adjacent parcel and opened a discount store and soon began selling food and grocery items. Dan's sought to enjoin Wal-Mart from selling food and grocery items, arguing that it violated the restrictive covenant. The covenant in question broadly prohibited the sale of virtually all food items, but contained the following exception: "... provided, however, that this restriction shall not apply to ... any sale of those items of miscellaneous small food snack items, prepared sandwiches, or other items which are intended to be consumed upon the premises, which are sold by discount store operators such as Shopko, K-Mart, Woolworth's, Target, or similar discount store operators, including but not limited to the sale of nuts, candy, similar snack items, prepared sandwiches, or other items which are intended to be consumed upon the premises."

The court explained that the covenant was highly ambiguous since it could not be determined what the exceptions included. Accordingly, the court ruled against Dan's, noting that the law requires that a covenant's language must be strictly construed against the party seeking to restrict another's use of real property.

Governmental Ownership and Regulation of Land

Government controls land use in *two* ways:

1. The government itself owns and controls a vast amount of the nation's total acreage.
2. The government regulates privately owned real estate through zoning regulations, through state and federal land use plans (discussed shortly), and through environmental legislation (the subject of the next chapter).

Governmental Ownership of Real Estate

The federal government owns over 650 million acres (2.63 million square kilometers), or approximately 29 percent, of the nation's land.[39] (See reference in endnote 39 for a map of the federal public domain.) The national park system encompasses over 80 million acres;[40] the U.S. Forest Service manages over 193 million acres;[41] and the Fish and Wildlife Service, over 97 million acres.[42] The Bureau of Land Management (BLM) manages 253 million acres; in addition, the Bureau manages mineral estates underlying 700 million acres.[43] Various other agencies own the balance. One-third of public lands are in Alaska, where the U.S. ownership comprises 66 percent of the state. Most of the remaining federal lands are in eleven western states: the government owns 82.9 percent of Nevada, 64.2 percent of Utah, 62.2 percent of Idaho, 59.9 percent of Oregon, 49.7 percent of Wyoming, 46.8 percent of California, 44.7 percent of Arizona, 36.3 percent of Colorado, 34.1 percent of New Mexico, 27.8 percent of Montana, and 26.8 percent of Washington.

While some federal land was part of the original public domain, the remaining acreage has been acquired from private owners.[44] Federal or state governments use *three* methods to acquire privately owned land:

- *Escheat*
- *Condemnation*
- *Dedication* (See Figure 13.2.)

Escheat   In feudal law, if a tenant in possession of land died leaving no heirs or if the tenant committed a felony, the land would revert to the lord of the manor or to the Crown. Under today's application of the **escheat** doctrine, when a person dies with no known and discoverable heirs, her property escheats to the state. Although historically only real property would escheat to the state, today personal property goes to the state as well. Most states have statutes that allow one of its state agencies to retain unclaimed personal property, such as money found in mattresses, dormant money accounts, and contents of safe-deposit boxes, and then to publicize in the newspaper and in other legal notices for a period of time during which potential heirs can make a claim before the property escheats to the state. These laws operate much like the estray statutes for lost property discussed in Chapter 12.

To what degree can a relative inherit before a deceased's property escheats to the state? Although it varies by state law, the Uniform Probate Act, used in some states, includes only those relatives who are direct descendants of the deceased's paternal and maternal grandparents. Thus, if someone died with no spouse, children, parents, or siblings, only her grandparents, aunts and uncles, and first cousins could inherit. However, nearly half the states still allow unlimited collateral relatives, such as second cousins, to inherit. The distant relatives are sometimes called "laughing heirs" to indicate their reaction to inheriting property from a relative they likely never knew.[45]

Condemnation   The state has the right to condemn—that is, to take—private property for public purposes. This right—called **eminent domain**—has been described as "an inseparable attribute of sovereignty—an inherent power founded on the primary duty of government to serve the common need and advance the general welfare."[46] According to the *Annals of Tacitus*, this right goes back at least to Roman times. The

escheat

A reversion of property to the state when no individual is available who legally qualifies to inherit it.

eminent domain

The power of government to take private property for public use upon the payment of just compensation.

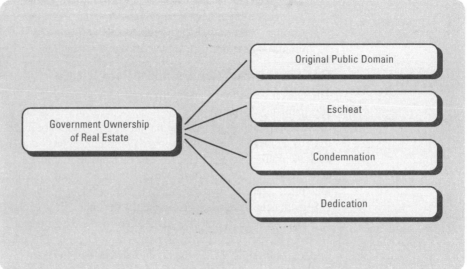

FIGURE 13.2
Government Ownership of Real Estate

Government Ownership of Real Estate

- Original Public Domain
- Escheat
- Condemnation
- Dedication

term *eminent domain* possibly originated with Hugo Grotius, an early 17th century Dutch philosopher and jurist, who declared that the state may take or destroy property for the public good but noted that "when this is done the state is bound to make good the loss to those who lose their property."[47]

In the United States, the power of the federal government to take private property is recognized in the Fifth Amendment to the Constitution, which provides "nor shall private property be taken for public use, without just compensation." The Fourteenth Amendment states that "no state shall ... deprive any person of life, liberty, or property, without due process of law." The Fourteenth Amendment's due process clause has been interpreted to require states to comply with the Fifth Amendment when they take private property, although in most cases, the same result would be reached under state constitutions. Thus, for both state and federal **condemnation**, the key questions are these:

1. Is there a public use?
2. Was there just compensation?

Public Use   Courts are reluctant to define the term **public use** absolutely because, as noted by one Connecticut court, public use "changes with varying conceptions of the scope and function of the government, and other differing circumstances brought about by an increase in population and new modes of communication and transportation."[48] The question of whether the use is public is a judicial question that is measured by constitutional standards,[49] and an absolute definition is precluded by the fact-specific nature of the question. In deciding whether private property is being taken for a public use, courts do not consider whether the public use was necessary or whether other property would be better suited; those are questions for the governmental authority exercising the power of eminent domain, not the courts. As Justice Douglas observed in the precedent-setting 1954 case of *Berman v. Parker*,

> *Subject to specific constitutional limitations, when the legislature has spoken, the public interest has been declared in terms well nigh conclusive. In such cases the legislature, not the judiciary, is the main guardian of the public needs to be served by social legislation.... This principle admits of no exception merely because the power of eminent domain is involved. The role of the judiciary in determining whether that power is being exercised for a public purpose is an extremely narrow one.... The concept of the public welfare is broad and inclusive.*[50]

The public use question often arises when the extent of the government's condemnation is an issue. For example, there may be a question whether condemnation proceedings resulted in the government's taking an easement, a fee simple defeasible, or a fee simple absolute. In such cases, a court, as noted in a New Jersey case, must determine the nature of the public use, for the general rule is that "in condemnation proceedings an estate of such quality may be taken as is reasonably necessary for the accomplishment of the purpose in aid of which the proceedings are brought."[51]

The public use issue also is raised when the government initially condemns private property and then sells or leases the property to private individuals. This has often happened when local governmental agencies engaged in slum clearance projects acquired the slum area by eminent domain, and then sold the land to private individuals or companies for redevelopment. This is what occurred in the *Berman v. Parker* case, discussed previously. The public *use* requirement is then generally met because the *purpose* of the condemnation is to eliminate the slum area. According to a West Virginia court:

> *Slum areas, because of the congestion, filth and unsanitary conditions which are their ever-lasting qualities, are the breeding places of crime, immorality and disease. These*

condemnation

The process of taking private property for public use through the power of eminent domain.

public use

A use that confers some benefit or advantage to the public.

evils necessarily and inevitably strike at the heart of the happiness and well being of all the people of a community. They cannot run rampant in any part of a community without stretching their tentacles menacingly throughout its entire length and breadth.... Any purpose leading toward [slum clearance] ... is a public purpose.[52]

Government attempts to acquire property through condemnation and resell it to private parties are not limited to slum clearance. In *Hawaii Housing Authority v. Midkiff*,[53] the U.S. Supreme Court upheld a Hawaiian law that allowed the government to take land from private estates, subdivide it, and resell the lots to homeowners. The law, according to the Court, served a public purpose because a concentration of land ownership in Hawaii (seventy-two owners controlled 94 percent of nongovernment land in Hawaii) had caused a critical shortage of residential property.[54]

In 2005, the U.S. Supreme Court ruled definitively in the following landmark case on whether governments could condemn land for private development.

> Can the government claim private property for a public use if the property is used for the benefit of private economic development? In *Kelo v. City of New London* on page 567, the U.S. Supreme Court decides the issue.

END OF CHAPTER CASE

The reaction to the *Kelo* case across the country was strong but mixed. Indeed, few property law cases have stirred up the passions of the American public as much as this case did. On the one hand, many private developers as well as local governments were relieved that they could proceed with long-planned developments without concern about legal challenges.[55] However, in many states, there was a clear political backlash led by property rights proponents. Relying on Justice Stevens' language that the Kelo case does not "preclude[s] any State from placing further restrictions on its exercise of the takings power ...," states quickly passed statutes and courts issued opinions that placed serious obstacles on governments seeking to condemn private land for private development. By 2007, 37 states passed statutes or constitutional amendments limiting *Kelo*. Although these post-*Kelo* laws vary, they have at least *two common themes*: (1) the protection of private landowners from state and local governments taking private property for a so-called "highest and best use" for the benefit of other private landowners, and (2) an exception allowing private developers to improve blighted land.[56] The state of Georgia's "Landowner's Bill of Rights and Private Property Protection Act," for example, allows condemnation for public use in the following four instances: "(A) Transfer of the land to public ownership; (B) Transfer of the property to a private entity that is a public utility; (C) Lease of the property to private entities that occupy an incidental area within a public project, or (D) The remedy of blight."[57]

Since blight is difficult to characterize and could be used as a surreptitious means for condemning property for private development, many states have attempted to develop more precise definitions. For example, under Georgia's new law, blight encompasses land that is unsafe due to natural disasters, abandoned and uninhabitable land, Environmental Protection Agency (EPA) Superfund sites, sites of repeated illegal activity, or unsanitary and unhealthy places. The statute also specifically states that aesthetic conditions do not constitute blight.[58]

Just Compensation   When the government takes fee simple ownership of real estate, the Fifth Amendment's requirement of **just compensation** means that the owner is entitled to the fair market value of the interest he held in the land. While the determination of public use is largely determined by state statute, it is a judicial function to determine the amount of just compensation. The property's value is determined by considering the most profitable use of the land even though the land was being used for other purposes at the time of the taking as the following New York case points out.

just compensation

Compensation that is fair to both the owner and the public when property is taken for public use through eminent domain.

A CASE IN POINT

In *Huie v. Campbell*,[59] a city condemned land that was used as a dairy farm and a boarding house for summer guests. After the condemnation but before a hearing to determine compensation, bluestone and flagstone were discovered on the property; the owners claimed that the value of these deposits should have been considered in the compensation award. The court agreed, noting that "the owners are entitled to compensation for the value of the premises for any purpose, irrespective of its previous use."

Additional problems arise when the condemnation of property results in lost profits or, in the reverse situation, when condemnation results in special benefits. Courts generally disallow evidence of lost profits because such evidence is often too speculative and the business usually can be moved to another location.[60] However, most courts will allow evidence of lost profits if the profits come from the intrinsic nature of the condemned property, such as real estate used as a stone quarry, as a turnpike, or for agricultural purposes. On the other hand, if the owner of the condemned property receives benefits as a result of the condemnation, such as the increased access to land he still owns adjacent to what was taken, should the value of the benefit be deducted from the award? Although a number of approaches have been developed by the courts, the trend is to deduct all benefits, even those that the owner shares with the general public, from the condemnation award.

If the government condemns only a part of the property, just compensation is measured by the value of the portion taken plus the decrease in fair market value to the balance of the property caused by the condemnation, as stated by a New Mexico court:

The general rule for arriving at just compensation for property not taken but adversely affected is the so-called 'before and after' rule; and this poses the question: What was the value before the taking, and what is now the market value after the taking? The owner of property, ordinarily, is entitled to receive the difference between these sums.[61]

Regulatory Takings: The "Inverse Condemnation" Problem   Determining whether governmental activities, regulations, or requirements amount to a taking of private property that triggers the just compensation requirement is a difficult matter for the courts. The issue of whether a taking has occurred is easily resolved when the government consciously decides to take title to an individual's property and begins condemnation proceedings. The issue becomes more complicated when the government *does not actually take ownership* of the property through condemnation proceedings, but instead *regulates property* in a manner that restricts the owner's use and enjoyment of his property. A landowner seeking relief typically reverses the normal condemnation procedure—where the government initiates the action—and sues the government using an **inverse condemnation**[62] action.

inverse condemnation

Actions brought by landowners alleging that a taking of their property has resulted from activities of public agencies or private bodies vested with the authority to condemn.

In the landmark 1922 U.S. Supreme Court opinion in *Pennsylvania Coal Co. v. Mahon*,[63] a coal company asserted that a state statute was a taking of the company's coal rights when it forbade coal mining that would cause the subsidence of a residential home. In holding that a taking had occurred, the Court said:

> *Government hardly could go on if to some extent values incident to property could not be diminished without paying for every such change in the general law. As long recognized some values are enjoyed under an implied limitation and ... must yield to the police power. But obviously the implied limitation must have its limits or the contract and due process clauses are gone. One fact for consideration in determining such limits is the extent of the diminution. When it reaches a certain magnitude, in most if not all cases there must be an exercise of eminent domain and compensation to sustain the Act.*

The Court's conclusion remains a useful test: "The general rule, at least, is that while property may be regulated to a certain extent, if the regulation goes too far it will be recognized as a taking."[64]

There are *four scenarios*, detailed in the discussion that follows, in which a regulatory action is considered to be a taking:

1. When there is an actual physical invasion of someone's private property, no matter how slight
2. When a regulation does not cause a landowner to lose all economically beneficial use of her property but (a) the regulation impacts her investment-backed expectations, (b) does not advance a legitimate governmental interest, and (c) has an economic impact on the landowner
3. When a regulation results in the landowner essentially losing all economically beneficial use of his property
4. When a government's actions, such as a dedication, an exaction, or an impact fee, do not have a sufficient connection, or nexus, to the landowner's development plans (See Table 13.1.)

Referring to *Scenario 1*, a taking may occur when there is a physical invasion on private land. In *Loretto v. Teleprompter Manhattan CATV Corp.*,[65] the U. S. Supreme Court ruled that a New York state law that required landlords to allow television cable companies to install cable facilities in their apartment buildings without compensation constituted a taking. The Court further stated that even though the cable facilities' intrusion was very slight—they occupied at most only one-and-one-half cubic feet of the landlords' property—*any* physical intrusion by the government (or by its agents) is a taking.

Referring to *Scenario 2,* a taking may occur when a regulation does not cause a landowner to lose all economically beneficial use of her property, but the regulation (a) impacts her investment-backed expectations, (b) does not advance a legitimate governmental interest, and (c) has an economic impact on the landowner.

In the years following the *Pennsylvania Coal* decision, the Supreme Court has attempted to strike a more balanced approach between private property rights and government regulation. In *Penn Central Transportation Co. v. City of New York*,[66] the Court decided that there was no "'set formula' for determining when 'justice and fairness' require that economic injuries caused by public action be compensated.... [The decision] depends largely 'upon the particular circumstances....'" In *Penn Central*, the Court held that the application of New York's landmark preservation law to the Grand Central terminal did not constitute a taking. New York allowed the railroad to transfer development rights for the airspace over the terminal even though it denied the railroad's application to develop a tower directly over the terminal. The Court in *Penn*

TABLE 13.1   Actions That Trigger a Regulatory Taking

STATE ACTION	TEST	CASE EXAMPLE
Physical taking or appropriation of private property	Is there any physical invasion of private property, no matter how slight?	Apartment owner must be compensated for TV cable placed on building. *Loretto v. Teleprompter Manhattan CATV Corp.*

Regulatory taking (inverse condemnation)	Two tests:
	a. Does the land use regulation deprive the owner of essentially all economically beneficial use of his property?
	
	OR
	
	b. Regulation does *not* deprive owner of all economically beneficial use of property. Court must consider three factors:
	  1. Does regulation impact owner's investment-backed expectations?
	  2. What is the character of the government's actions? Do they advance a legitimate governmental interest?
	  3. What is the economic impact of the regulation on the landowner's property?
		a. Owner could not develop his beachfront property after state initiated building moritorium. *Lucas v. South Carolina Coastal Commission*
		
		b. Air rights were taken from train terminal, depriving it of opportunity to build office tower. Owner could still operate terminal consistent with its investment-backed expectations, receive TDRs, and continue business operations; therefore, there was no taking. *Penn Central Transportation Co. v. City of New York*

Dedication of land, exactions, and impact fees imposed on property development.	Is there a sufficient nexus or "rough proportionality" between the dedication, exaction, or impact fee and the proposed development?	Owner must dedicate land for an easement for storm water drainage and pedestrian and bike pathway to receive building permit to expand store and parking lot. Court found that no reasonable relationship existed between dedication of land and the permit for store expansion. *Dolan v. City of Tigard*

Central also advanced *three* factors that must be examined on a case-by-case, or *ad hoc*, basis to determine whether a regulatory taking exists. In considering the *first* factor, the owner's investment-backed expectations, the Court ruled that the railroad's existing operation of the terminal was consistent with its distinct, investment-backed expectations. *Second*, the nature of the government's actions should be scrutinized. Does the regulation, for example, advance a legitimate state objective? In this case, the law helped to preserve the city's historical landmark. *Third*, the Court stated that the economic impact of the regulation must be analyzed. Here the court observed that the railroad was able to earn a reasonable return on its investment in the terminal, even with the restrictions placed on the air rights. (See Table 13.1.)

In a more recent takings case, the issue arose as to whether a landowner can claim a *temporary* regulatory taking of his property as a result of an ordinance passed by a regional planning commission. In *Tahoe-Sierra Preservation Council, Inc. v. Tahoe Regional Planning*,[67] an ordinance was passed temporarily prohibiting all development in an environmentally sensitive area near Lake Tahoe. The moratorium, which lasted for 32 months, was devised so that a regional planning commission would have time to create a new development plan. The U.S. Supreme Court, which backed the planning commission, declined again (as it did in *Penn Central*) to apply a *per se* (meaning "taken alone" or "by itself") rule. The Court stated that "[i]n our view the answer to the abstract question whether a temporary moratorium effects a taking is neither 'yes, always' nor 'no, never'; the answer depends on the circumstances of the case." The Court explained that the *Penn Central* factors, discussed previously, must be applied to the unique facts of the case. Here the Court decided that "[a] rule that required compensation for every delay in the use of property would render routine government processes prohibitively expensive or encourage hasty decision-making." The Court also downplayed the economic impact since it was temporary.

Because it is sometimes difficult to know when an inverse condemnation arises, as opposed to a government-initiated condemnation, the **ripeness requirement** becomes an important threshold issue. This was discussed in *Williamson County Regional Planning Commission v. Hamilton Bank*,[68] in which the Supreme Court held that the owner's claim was not ripe until he sought a variance from zoning requirements.[69] In contrast, in the next case, the Supreme Court determined that the landowner had satisfied the ripeness requirement.

ripeness requirement
The constitutional requirement that before a case can be heard in court, it must have ripened, or matured, into a controversy worthy of adjudication.

A CASE IN POINT

In *Suitam v. Tahoe Regional Planning Agency*,[70] in 1972, Bernadine Suitam purchased an undeveloped lot with her husband, who later died. In 1987, the Tahoe Regional Planning Agency, the regional land use regulatory agency, determined that Suitam could not construct a home on her lot because it was located in an environment zone in which permanent construction was not allowed. Her lot had utilities available at the lot line and was surrounded on three sides by residential development. Although Suitam could not build on her lot, Tahoe Regional Planning Agency's plan provided her with transferable development rights (TDRs) that could be sold to another property owner to increase their permissible development.

Mrs. Suitam sued the Tahoe Regional Planning Agency, arguing that she was entitled to compensation because the land use regulations effected a taking of her property. The lower courts held that Mrs. Suitam's takings claim was not ripe because she had not attempted to sell her TDRs.

However, the Supreme Court held that Mrs. Suitam's takings claim was ripe. The Court noted that there is no question about how the regulations apply to Mrs. Suitam's land, nor is there any further discretionary decision by the agency relating to her land. "Mrs. Suitam seeks not to be free of the regulations but to be paid for their consequences.... The only discretionary step left to an agency ... is enforcement, not determining applicability."

In a subsequent Supreme Court case, *Palazzolo v. Rhode Island*,[71] the issue of ripeness arose again. In that case, the landowner, Anthony Palazzolo, had been seeking permission for years from the Rhode Island Coastal Resources Management Council to develop his land into a private beach club. He was consistently denied a permit since he was requesting permission to fill in land consisting of protected, environmentally sensitive wetlands. He eventually sued for damages, alleging that the regulations constituted a taking. The Council argued that Palazzolo must continue to petition that body to determine whether there may be other permissible ways to use the land, such as uses that might involve less filling and would therefore be legal. The Court, however, saved Palazzolo from what appeared to be the Council's attempt to create a never-ending regulatory petitioning requirement, stating that "once it becomes clear that the agency lacks the discretion to permit any development, or the permissible uses of the property are known to a reasonable degree of certainty, a taking claim is likely to have ripened."[72]

The issue of how to fashion a *remedy* for those who suffer a loss from an inverse condemnation has also drawn the attention of the High Court. In *United States v. Causby*,[73] discussed in Chapter 3, the Causbys claimed that repeated trespasses by military aircraft over their land at low altitudes constituted a taking and an implied contractual duty to pay for the use of the land. The Supreme Court determined that the United States was liable for damages because it had taken an easement of flight across the claimants' land.

The Court has also determined that the remedy of the resolution of an inverse condemnation action after a successful challenge is not adequate. Instead, the government must pay damages for the period of time when the regulation was in effect. For example, when Los Angeles County adopted an interim ordinance prohibiting structures within a flood protection area, First English Evangelical Lutheran Church alleged that a taking had occurred when it could not operate its church camp. In a 1987 decision, the Supreme Court held that damages would be the appropriate remedy if the church was denied all use of its property for the multiyear period.[74] According to the Court,[75] "inverse condemnation is predicated on the proposition that a taking may occur without … formal proceedings.… [W]here the government's activities have already worked a taking of all use of property, no subsequent action by the government can relieve it of the duty to provide compensation for the period during which the taking was effective."

Referring to *Scenario 3* on page 538, a taking may occur when a regulation results in the landowner essentially losing all economically beneficial use of his property. In the next precedent-setting case, the U.S. Supreme Court addresses this issue.

Did the State of South Carolina's passage of the Beachfront Management Act result in a taking when a property owner essentially lost all economically beneficial use of his land when he could no longer erect permanent structures on his property? In *Lucas v. South Carolina Coastal Council* on page 570, the Court addresses the question.

END OF CHAPTER CASE

The per se test issued in the *Lucas* case stands in contrast to the ad hoc approach provided in *Penn Central* and later in *Tahoe-Sierra Preservation Council, Inc.* However, because the facts in *Lucas* are quite rare, the *Lucas* per se test is applied less often than the *Penn Central* ad hoc rule. (See Table 13.1.)

In a recent 2010 application of the Lucas per se test, the U.S. Supreme Court in *Stop the Beach Renourishment Inc. v. Florida*[76] addressed an issue unique to regulatory takings. The case revolves around Florida's program of renourishing beaches depleted by erosion caused by hurricanes. When this occurs, the state establishes an "erosion control line" that supersedes the traditional mean high water mark which, under the common law, establishes the boundary for determining littoral (land abutting seas and lakes) property boundaries and ownership (see Chapter 3). The property owners argued that this was a taking since they no longer possessed the traditional rights under the common law to gain ownership of more beach property over time through accretions and relictions (see Chapter 10). The Court in upholding a Florida Supreme Court decision rebutted plaintiffs' arguments asserting that the renourishment was like an avulsion, which is a sudden gain or loss of land in which boundaries do not change, a long held rule under the common law. The Court also argued that the littoral owners had no rights to land once underwater but that is now dry land.

Speculation was also raised that since the Florida court's ruling, as opposed to one produced in reaction to a statute or ordinance, spawned this inverse condemnation action, a new kind of taking, called a "judicial taking," should be created. Four justices, Scalia, Roberts, Alito, and Thomas, called for the establishment of this new doctrine in their concurring opinion, but were opposed by Justices Ginsburg and Breyer, who stated that such a doctrine could not be formed in the case since there was no actual taking.

However, the two justices did not outright disagree with the idea, possibly setting the stage for the doctrine's creation when the right case is heard in the future.

In *Palazzola v. Rhode Island*,[77] discussed earlier regarding the issue of ripeness, a takings problem existed similar to the one enunciated in *Lucas*. As articulated in *Lucas*, and discussed in Chapter 12, all property owners are by operation of law subject to common law limitations, such as nuisance. However, in *Palazzola*, there was a *preexisting regulation* outlawing the development of wetlands when the owner bought his property in 1978. The Rhode Island Supreme Court ruled that since Palazzola was aware of the wetland regulations, he could not have reasonably expected to develop his property. Thus, the state government's actions did not constitute a taking for which Palazzola should be compensated even though he lost essentially all economically beneficial use of his land. However, the U. S. Supreme Court reversed Rhode Island's decision and ruled that:

> *Were we to accept the State's [Rhode Island] rule, the post-enactment transfer of title would absolve the State of its obligation to defend any action restricting land use, no matter how extreme or unreasonable. A State would be allowed, in effect, to put an expiration date on the Takings Clause. This ought not to be the rule. Future generations, too, have a right to challenge unreasonable limitations on the use and value of land.[78]*

dedication

A private landowner's conferral of an interest in land to the government for the public interest.

common law dedication

A dedication expressed or implied under the common law. An express dedication is one expressly manifested by deed, recorded plats, or explicit written or oral manifestations but not executed pursuant to a statute. An implied dedication is created by a landowner's act or course of conduct in which a reasonable inference can be drawn that he intended to dedicate the property interest to the public.

statutory dedication

A dedication created pursuant to a statute.

subdivision map acts

Statutes that control the subdivision of land by establishing conditions for approval of a plat or subdivision map.

plat

A recorded map of a parcel of real estate that has been subdivided.

Dedication   **Dedication** takes place when a private landowner gives the public the ownership of or the right to use her real estate. A dedication is also sometimes challenged as a government taking, an issue presented in *Scenario 4* below. Under the common law, dedication occurs when both of the following takes place:

1. The landowner shows an intention that the real estate be used for a public purpose.
2. There is an acceptance in the form of actual public use.[79]

Following a **common law dedication**, which may be express or implied, the public has not acquired ownership of the land but merely the right to use the land for a particular purpose, which might be for a park, a wharf, a highway, or a school.[80]

The major problem arising from common law dedication is proving the owner's intention that his property be used for a public purpose. For example, Smith owns 100 acres of land, which she plans to sell. She decides that she will get more money for the property if she creates a park in the center and tells her neighbors that she is dedicating a defined area for public use as a park. A common law dedication occurs when the people in the area actually use the land as a park. On the other hand, if Jones owns a store and paves a strip of land between the store and the street so that the public will walk by the store windows, there is no dedication because there is no intention to dedicate to the public.[81]

The much more common form of dedication is **statutory dedication**. The process of statutory dedication is often defined by **subdivision map acts** that control the subdivision of land. The local municipality will establish conditions for approving a plat or subdivision map within the authority of a statewide act.[82] Many state statutes provide that a person who records a **plat**—a map that subdivides a piece of real estate into lots, streets, parks, and common areas—is offering to dedicate the streets, parks, and common areas to the public. (For an example of a plat map, see www.cengagebrain.com [see page xix in the Preface for instructions on how to access the free study tools for this text].) After the offer has been made, acceptance takes the form of official action or public use.[83] Statutory dedication, if the statute and the plat so provide, may result in public acquisition of title to the real estate. (For a Platting Ordinance for creating public streets and other common areas, see www.cengagebrain.com [see page xix in the Preface for instructions on how to access the free study tools for this text].) The creation of a plat raises *three* common legal problems, the first two relating to dedication. *First,* the language of the plat that dedicates land to the public is often ambiguous. Thus, courts may have to decide whether all of the following occurred:

1. The owner intended to dedicate the land to the public or merely to the subdivision lot owners.
2. The person making the dedication has retained title to the dedicated area.
3. The dedication restricts the land to certain uses.

For instance, a developer who creates a subdivision that includes a park should specifically state on the plat that the park is not dedicated to the public but is only for the use of the lot owners, if that is the intent. Without such specific language, a court might determine that the public has the right to use the park.

A *second* problem arises when a municipality attempts to force dedication on real estate developers. Subdivision controls and related dedication requirements assist municipalities in covering costs associated with development; such costs include schools, roads, sewer and water, police and fire protection, libraries, and parks. For example, in Clark County, Nevada, where Las Vegas is located, developers must donate 2.5 acres for every 1,000 homes they build and pay $200 to $300 per home for traffic signals.[84]

The legality of such controls, fees, and dedication requirements (that is, whether these impositions on private property owners constitute a government taking) is tested by their relationship to the burdens imposed by the associated development.

Referring to *Scenario 4* on page 538, a taking may occur when a government's action, such as a dedication, exaction, or impact fee, does not have a sufficient connection or nexus to the landowner's development plans. The Supreme Court considered this problem in the next case.

A CASE IN POINT

In *Nollan v. California Coastal Commission,*[85] the Nollans owned a beachfront lot in Ventura, California. When they applied for a permit to replace a bungalow on their lot, the California Coastal Commission granted the permit—subject to the condition that they dedicate to the public an easement to cross their property, which was situated between two public beaches.

The Nollans challenged the condition on the grounds that it represented an unconstitutional taking of their property. The Supreme Court decided that a forced dedication of property rights must serve the same purpose as the ban on development that would have occurred had the Nollans not been forced to dedicate the easement. Where there is not a sufficient connection between the dedication and the development ban, just compensation is required. In this case, in the words of Justice Scalia, "It is quite impossible to understand how a requirement that people already on the public beaches be able to walk across the Nollans' property reduces any obstacles to viewing the beach created by the new house." The test of the required dedication is whether it enjoys a "rational nexus" with the permit condition.

Another case that tested dedication requirements, *Dolan v. City of Tigard,*[86] strengthened the "rational nexus" requirement. In *Dolan,* the city required Mrs. Dolan to dedicate a greenway for storm water drainage and a pedestrian and bike path as a permit condition for an expansion of her electrical and plumbing supply store, which was located within a 100-year floodplain. The Supreme Court observed that the city had not explained why a public greenway, not a private one, was required for flood control. It also held that the city failed to show a "reasonable relationship" between the trips to be generated by Mrs. Dolan's expansion and the pedestrian and bicycle path requirement. While noting that land use planning is commendable, the Court found that the city's requirements were a compensable taking: "No precise mathematical calculation is required, but the city must make some sort of individualized determination that the required dedication is related both in nature and extent to the impact of the proposed development." (See Table 13.1.)

The *third* problem raised by creation of a plat is that states have placed stringent platting and development restrictions on developers, largely as a result of unregulated real estate developments in the 1920s that led to severe losses by individual investors. For example, in creating a subdivision, a developer might be required to prepare a preliminary plat and submit it to a number of governmental agencies—such as the local municipality, the road commission, the drain commission, and the health department—for approval. Upon approval by the agencies, a final plat—which includes certificates from a surveyor, the applicant, the plat board, the state treasurer, and other governmental agencies—is prepared and recorded. A developer who fails to comply with subdivision requirements may face both civil and criminal penalties.

public trust doctrine
A theory that the government holds its lands in trust for the public.

Public Trust Doctrine   Once the government has acquired title to real estate through escheat, eminent domain, or dedication, what is the government's duty with respect to public lands, beyond specific statutory duties? A theory that has been popular with environmentalists in recent years—the **public trust doctrine**—views the government as the holder of lands in public trust as this classic U.S. Supreme Court case explains.

A CASE IN POINT

The leading case of *Illinois Central Railroad v. Illinois*[87] involved an 1869 grant of submerged lands by the Illinois legislature to the Illinois Central Railroad. The lands extended for one mile along the central business district in Chicago and one mile out from the shoreline—thus covering virtually the entire commercial waterfront of Chicago. After a few years, the legislature brought an action to have the original grant declared invalid.

The U.S. Supreme Court invalidated the grant on the basis that the title to the navigable waters of Lake Michigan is "different in character from that which the state holds in lands intended for sale.... It is a title held in trust for the people of the state that they may enjoy the navigation of the waters, carry on commerce over them, and have liberty of fishing therein freed from the obstruction or interferences of private parties."

The principle emerging from this opinion has been summarized by a commentator as follows:

When a state holds a resource which is available for the free use of the general public, a court will look with considerable skepticism upon any governmental conduct which is calculated either to reallocate that resource to more restricted uses or subject public uses to the self-interest of private parties.[88]

While the public trust doctrine has been applied mainly in cases involving submerged lands or parklands, the doctrine may be used whenever governmental regulation is questioned.[89]

Zoning

The traditional method of governmental regulation of private real estate has been through municipal zoning ordinances. (For an example of a zoning map, see www.cengagebrain.com

[see page xix in the Preface for instructions on how to access the free study tools for this text].) Zoning ordinances originally divided towns and cities into *three* areas: residential, commercial, and industrial. In recent years, zoning ordinances have become more complex. A typical ordinance for a midsize city, for instance, might include the following zones:

1. Residential, often with a large number of subclassifications for various types of single-family or multiple-family dwellings
2. Agricultural
3. Office
4. Public lands
5. Commercial, often with many subclassifications
6. Industrial

exclusive zoning

Method of zoning in which land use is limited to the zoned use.

cumulative zoning

Zoning classification that allows more restrictive land uses in lesser-restricted areas.

Modern zones may be either **exclusive zoning** (also called *noncumulative*) or cumulative zoning. When an area has exclusive zoning, the property cannot be utilized for more restrictive uses. For example, an area zoned for heavy industrial use cannot be used for light industrial, commercial, or residential purposes. On the other hand, if the ordinance calls for **cumulative zoning**, more restrictive uses are allowed. Under a cumulative zoning ordinance, a single-family dwelling would be allowed in an area zoned for townhouses and apartments. However, the opposite is not permitted. Townhouses and apartments would not be permitted in the area zoned for single-family housing. Even if an area is zoned exclusively for one use, the ordinance commonly allows certain "accessory" uses. For instance, when a lot is zoned for single-family dwellings, the owner typically is allowed to construct a private garage, swimming pool, garden house, toolshed, private greenhouse, or playhouse.

Zoning ordinances include area, height, and placement regulations in addition to specification of permitted uses. These regulations may include minimum lot sizes; minimum usable floor area; minimum usable open space; minimum parking; maximum height; and required setbacks from the front, rear, and sides of the lot. Zoning regulations are complemented by building codes that specify construction requirements in greater detail. Thus, to obtain a building permit from a municipality, an owner must comply with both the building code and the zoning ordinance.

In zoning cases, legal problems tend to cluster around *three* basic issues:

1. Is the ordinance valid?
2. Should an exception be made to the ordinance?
3. Is the ordinance exclusionary?

police power

The power of a state to exercise control to protect the health, safety, morals, and welfare of the public.

Validity of Zoning Ordinance   **Police power** tests the validity of zoning ordinances, which are presumed to be valid unless they are "clearly arbitrary and unreasonable, having no substantial relation to the public health, safety, morals or general welfare."[90] Comprehensive zoning was first upheld in the important and precedent-setting U.S. Supreme Court case from Ohio discussed next.

A CASE IN POINT

In *Village of Euclid v. Ambler Realty Co.*,[91] Ambler Realty challenged the Euclid zoning ordinance enacted in 1922, on the grounds that it deprived the company of property without due process of law. Ambler owned 68 acres of land that, it argued, was worth $10,000 per acre for industrial uses but only $2,500 per acre for the purely residential uses allowed under the zoning ordinance.

continues

continued The Supreme Court upheld the ordinance, noting that the exclusion of buildings devoted to business, trade, etc., from residential districts bears a rational relation to the health and safety of the community. Some of the grounds for this conclusion are promotion of the health and security from injury of children and others by separate dwelling houses from territory devoted to trade and industry; suppression and prevention of disorder; facilitating the extinguishment of fires, and the enforcement of street traffic regulations and other general welfare ordinances; aiding the health and safety of the community by excluding from residential areas the confusion and danger of fire, contagion, and disorder which in greater or less degree attach to the location of stores, shops, and factories.

The police power also extends aesthetic goals; for instance, a zoning ordinance that prohibited outdoor advertising signs unrelated to the business conducted on the premises has been upheld.[92] In the words of the Supreme Court, "It is within the power of the legislature to determine that the community should be beautiful as well as healthy, spacious as well as clean." The Court noted:

Miserable and disreputable housing conditions may do more than spread disease and crime and immorality. They may also suffocate the spirit by reducing the people who live there to the status of cattle. They may indeed make living an almost insufferable burden. They may also be an ugly sore, a blight on the community which robs it of charm, which makes it a place from which men turn. The misery of housing may despoil a community as an open sewer may ruin a river. We do not sit to determine whether a particular housing project is or is not desirable. The concept of the public welfare is broad and inclusive.... The values it represents are spiritual as well as physical, aesthetic as well as monetary. It is within the power of the legislature to determine that the community should be beautiful as well as healthy, spacious as well as clean, well-balanced as well as carefully patrolled.[93]

The next California case illustrates what a number of cities and towns are attempting to do under their police powers and zoning ordinances: keep out big-box retail stores.

A CASE IN POINT

In *Wal-Mart Stores, Inc. v. City of Turlock*,[94] Turlock adopted a zoning ordinance prohibiting big-box retail stores that contain a full-service grocery department. The city justified the ordinance on the grounds that the big-box stores cause existing grocery stores, which often anchor neighborhood commercial centers, to go out of business, resulting in the deterioration of the centers and surrounding residential areas. When the ordinance was challenged by Wal-Mart, the appeals court ruled as follows: "(1) a city may exercise its police power to control and organize development within its boundaries as a means of serving the general welfare, (2) the City [of Turlock] made a legitimate policy choice when it decided to organize development using neighborhood shopping centers dispersed throughout the city, (3) the ordinance was reasonably related to protecting that development choice, and (4) no showing was made that the restrictions significantly affected residents of surrounding communities. Accordingly, the restrictions in the ordinance bear a reasonable relationship to the general welfare and, thus, the City constitutionally exercised its police power."

The proliferation of adult bookstores, theaters, and massage parlors has been troublesome to city officials in recent years, especially because officials have generally been unsuccessful in prosecuting pornography cases. Many cities now use zoning ordinances to limit the sale of pornographic materials and services to certain areas. Although these ordinances have resulted in a direct confrontation between the rights of cities to restrict land use and the rights of individuals to exercise their First Amendment right to free speech and expression, the Supreme Court upheld such ordinances in 1976.[95] This issue, however, remains contentious, as discussed in the following Wisconsin case.

A CASE IN POINT

In *Blue Canary Corp. v. City of Milwaukee*,[96] the owner of a burlesque theater that featured nude and erotic dancing appealed the city's denial of a permit. The denial was issued because the theater violated city zoning laws that allowed adult entertainment only in certain areas of Milwaukee. The court ruled that "[T]he City has not prohibited the plaintiff from operating a burlesque theater, with or without nudity. It has merely prohibited the operation of such a theater in proximity to a residential neighborhood. Milwaukee is a large city and the plaintiff does not deny that there are abundant convenient locations in which the operation of such a theater would not violate the City's zoning law. In these circumstances, … the impairment of First Amendment values is slight to the point of being invisible, since the expressive activity involved in the kind of striptease entertainment provided in a bar has at best a modest social value and is anyway not suppressed but merely shoved off to another part of town, where it remains easily accessible to anyone who wants to patronize that kind of establishment."

In addition to police power concerns, the constitutional rights to both *substantive and procedural due process* impact the validity of zoning ordinances. A Washington state court applied a *three-part* test to determine whether a zoning ordinance violates the property owner's substantive due process rights: *first*, whether the ordinance is aimed at achieving a legitimate public purpose; *second*, whether the ordinance uses reasonably necessary means to accomplish that purpose; and *third*, whether the ordinance is unduly oppressive to the owner.[97] Procedural due process concerns were evident in a New York case, *Anthony v. Town of Brookhaven*,[98] when the court considered whether a property owner had received sufficient notice of the proposed rezoning of his property.

nonconforming use

In zoned areas, a use that does not conform with the area's zoning, but that existed before the zoning requirement became effective.

Exceptions to Zoning Ordinances: Nonconforming Uses and Variances Owners of real estate may be allowed to use their land in a manner that conflicts with a zoning ordinance when the land qualifies as a nonconforming use or when they obtain a variance. Some land may already be in use for a purpose when a zoning ordinance is adopted that makes the use illegal. To be fair to the owner and to avoid claims that there was a taking, a zoning ordinance may provide that the **nonconforming use** may continue (or be "grandfathered" in) after the effective date of the ordinance. In the next South Dakota case, the court rules in a nonconforming use case.

amortization provision

Zoning ordinance provision that allows a nonconforming use to continue only for a specified number of years.

For a certain use of land to be grandfathered in as a nonconforming use, how much of it must have existed to qualify as a permissible exception to a new zoning law? In *City of Platte v. Overweg* on page 571, the Supreme Court of South Dakota addresses the issue.

END OF CHAPTER CASE

Some ordinances contain **amortization provisions** that allow a nonconforming use to continue only for a specified number of years; such provisions have been upheld by most courts. For instance, when a challenge was made to a Los Angeles ordinance requiring that nonconforming uses cease within five years, the court concluded that the ordinance was valid:

> The distinction between an ordinance restricting future uses and one requiring the termination of present uses within a reasonable period of time is merely one of degree, and constitutionality depends on the relative importance to be given to the public gain and to the private loss. Zoning as it affects every piece of property is to some extent retroactive in that it applies to property already owned at the time of the effective date of the ordinance. The elimination of existing uses within a reasonable time does not amount to a taking of property nor does it necessarily restrict the use of property so that it cannot be used for any reasonable purpose. Use of a reasonable amortization scheme provides an equitable means of reconciliation of the conflicting interests in satisfaction of due process requirements.[99]

Even if the nonconforming use is permitted to continue, the owner may not be able to increase or alter the use. Whether the nonconforming use has been increased or altered is a question of fact for the court as pointed out in the following Kentucky case.

A CASE IN POINT

In *Franklin Planning & Zoning Commission v. Simpson County Lumber Co.*,[100] the city contended that a landowner [Potts], who was allowed nonconforming use of his residential property to store building materials, could not use the property to store saw logs. The court held that this was not an increase in the use: "Regardless of our sadness at seeing the elimination of the 'spreading chestnut tree,' and the village smith, it must be admitted that in the interest of progress the law favors the gradual elimination of 'nonconforming' uses of property in our cities. It naturally follows that such nonconforming uses as are tolerated under the law cannot be enlarged.... Admitting the saw logs were stacked higher than the brick and not so symmetrically, unless they obstruct the view or impede the natural flow of air we cannot see wherein their storage back of the barn is materially different from the storage of the stacks of brick. Accordingly, ... the 'nonconforming use' by Potts of his property has not been enlarged by the storage of saw logs on the property. There is no contention that Potts plans a sawmill. It goes without saying that a sawmill in such a residential community would be such an enlargement as appellants oppose."

An owner who abandons a nonconforming use must thereafter use the property in accordance with the zoning ordinance. For instance, when the owner of a slaughterhouse in Maryland that was a nonconforming use removed the smokestack and discontinued the use, the property lost its exemption from the zoning laws.[101]

When an owner wants to use his land in a manner that conflicts with a zoning ordinance that has already been enacted, the owner can apply to the zoning board for an authorization (called a **variance**) to use the land in a manner not allowed by the ordinance.

To secure a variance, an owner generally must meet *three* tests:

1. The owner must prove that the land will not yield a reasonable rate of return if used as zoned.
2. There must be proof that the hardship is unique to the property and does not affect other property in the area.
3. It must be shown that the variance will not change the essential character of the neighborhood.[102]

variance
Permission given by the zoning board to a landowner that allows deviation from the land use dictated in the zoning ordinances.

However, as the next Connecticut case demonstrates, granting variances can be controversial with the public, so courts will often scrutinize them closely.

A CASE IN POINT

In *Bloom v. Zoning Board of Appeals of the City of Norwalk*,[103] Kevin and William Conroy and Steven Cook owned and operated a restaurant in Norwalk, Connecticut. The restaurant was a permitted use under the zoning code's business use for the area, but the restaurant was a nonconforming use because the building violated the zoning code's front setback requirements. The owners were granted a building permit to construct a dormer above the nonconforming portion of the structure, and the owners had completed substantial construction of the renovations when neighbors complained that the building permit had been improperly issued and an associated variance improperly granted. The city zoning ordinance strictly limited the alteration of nonconforming structures when the enlargement increased the extent of nonconformity. The Connecticut Supreme Court noted that the restaurant had been a viable business before the construction of the improvements, and the only basis for the hardship claimed in the variance application was "the owner's reliance on the improperly granted building permit." The court held that the variance had been improperly issued. As a result, the owners had to restore the restaurant to its condition prior to undertaking the expansion.

If the variance is not granted, perhaps because the owner's plight is not unique to the area, other remedies might be available. One solution would be to seek an amendment of the zoning ordinance to change the regulations for the entire neighborhood. For instance, rezoning was ordered in a Florida case in which an area zoned for single-family residences was located on a six-lane highway and near gas stations, a Super Burger restaurant, several automobile dealers, and a fish market.[104] However, **spot zoning**—where the city reclassifies a single piece of property for a use inconsistent with the neighborhood—is *not* allowed since it is, in effect, a form of unplanned zoning or zoning after the fact. For example, a Missouri court refused to amend a zoning ordinance to allow the building of a mortuary in a residential area.[105]

A landowner who seeks to change zoning can also be subjected to voter approval through a referendum as the following U.S. Supreme Court points out.

spot zoning
Rezoning for a use inconsistent with the neighborhood.

A CASE IN POINT

In *City of Eastlake v. Forest Lake Enterprises, Inc.*,[106] a developer could not build a high-rise apartment on his property because a zoning change was not approved at a referendum. The U.S. Supreme Court held that the referendum requirement is valid. Although the Court noted that a referendum unrelated to the police power would not be upheld, use of the referendum does not in itself constitute an unconstitutional delegation of power: "Under our constitutional assumptions, all power derives from the people, who can delegate it to representative instruments which they create. In establishing legislative bodies, the people can reserve to themselves power to deal directly with matters which might otherwise be assigned to the legislature."

special exceptions
Zoning ordinances that prescribe special land use exceptions.

Many zoning ordinances contain built-in provisions for variation without the need for amendment each time. For example, it is common for ordinances to provide for **special exceptions** that would allow churches, schools, and parks to be established in residential areas. If the ordinance includes such exceptions, the three tests for a variance do not apply and the special use must be permitted. It is also common for zoning ordinances to

floating zones
Where a zoning ordinance provides for land uses but does not allocate land to those uses.

provide for **floating zones** where, for example, the ordinance provides for a light indus-trial zone but does not allocate land to this zone until a landowner makes a request.[107] **Cluster zoning** allows the density of residential areas to be increased in exchange for substantial associated open space, such as parks, playgrounds, and woodlands. The over-all project density is not increased in an area approved for cluster zoning; the density is merely "clustered" to create associated open space. Planned unit developments, discussed later in the chapter, are frequently developed under such zoning.

cluster zoning
Zoning that allows a developer to depart from site development and density standards as long as part of the development is left as open space.

Exclusionary Zoning   Exclusionary zoning ordinances are created to exclude classes of people and structures from certain areas or districts of a municipality. Although these laws vary greatly in their language they generally fall within *three* types: (1) define what structures are permissible, (2) require single-family homes to be occupied by "single-housekeeping units" only, and (3) require that the household be comprised of related persons only. The third factor, discussed later, is often unenforceable. The first two factors are generally legal although not without controversy, as the following discussion demonstrates.[108]

ETHICAL AND PUBLIC POLICY ISSUES

exclusionary zoning
Zoning ordinances that exclude specific classes of persons, structures, and businesses from designated areas or districts.

Should Exclusionary Zoning Laws Contain Exceptions for Structures and Equipment to Encourage Alternative Energy Sources?

Former Vice President Al Gore, a highly influential advocate against global warming and climate change, sought to build solar panels to lessen his personal dependence on electricity generated by fossil fuels. Gore lives in a multimillion-dollar home in the upscale Nashville suburb of Belle Meade. Belle Meade's zoning laws prohibit power-generating equipment from being placed on rooftops where it makes a great deal of noise. Gore was able to persuade the zoning commission to make an exception to the zoning ordinance since solar panels make no noise. Still, the city's law continue to require that solar panels not be visible from the street or from an adjoining property. Although not true in Gore's case, some possible locations for solar are not always optimal for receiving sunlight and so might be easily seen. Do citizens and the government owe a moral duty to advance environmental concerns, such as lessening dependence on fossil fuels and climate change, as well as dependence on foreign oil from countries hostile to the United States? If so, should these duties have priority over other obligations, such as promoting neighborhood aesthetics and preventing nuisances?[109]

As stated previously, exclusionary zoning ordinances that require a household to be comprised only of related people often run afoul of the law. For example, some cities attempt to use zoning laws to exclude group homes for the disabled from locating in residential neighborhoods, similar to the restrictive covenants that were discussed previously. These zoning laws are being challenged under the FHA, as illustrated by the following U.S. Supreme Court case that involved a group home for recovering alcoholics.

Was a zoning provision that defined "family" as "persons [without regard to number] related by genetics, adoption, or marriage, or a group of five or fewer [unrelated] persons" exempt from the Fair Housing Act's coverage, which seeks to protect the disabled? In *City of Edmonds v. Oxford House, Inc.* on page 572, the U.S. Supreme Court created an important precedent.

END OF CHAPTER CASE

Exclusionary zoning laws also have been ruled illegal under other federal laws, including Title II of the Americans with Disabilities Act and the Vocational Rehabilitation Act of 1973. In *Innovative Health Services v. City of White Plains*,[110] a federal court in New York ruled that the city's zoning laws, which excluded a drug and alcohol treatment center from the downtown area, were illegal. The city claimed that the center did not qualify as a "business or professional office." The court, however, ruled that both of these Acts prohibit state and local governments from discriminating against the disabled in their governmental activities, including their "policies, practices and procedures."

In *Village of Belle Terre v. Boraas*,[111] the U.S. Supreme Court in the following case determined whether a zoning ordinance adopted by Belle Terre, New York, was constitutional. In effect, the ordinance prevented more than two unrelated people from living together in a single-family dwelling. Six students from the nearby campus at SUNY in Stony Brook rented a house in Belle Terre, a village of only one square mile and containing just 220 houses. When notified that their house-sharing violated the zoning ordinance, they sued the village in federal court, asking that the ordinance be declared unconstitutional because it deprived them of equal protection under the law.

A CASE IN POINT

In *Village of Belle Terre v. Boraas*,[112] the Supreme Court applied a traditional two-tier test to determine whether the zoning ordinance was an equal protection violation, and the Court decided for the village. If legislation violates a fundamental interest such as the right to free speech or is based on a suspect classification such as race, it will be declared unconstitutional unless it advances a compelling governmental interest. Since there was no fundamental constitutional right or interest in the case, the Supreme Court stated that the legislation is only required to bear a reasonable relationship to a permissible governmental objective when it does not violate a fundamental interest or contain a suspect classification; that is, there must be a rational basis for the legislation.

The Supreme Court applied the rational basis test in upholding the statute:

"It involves no procedural disparity inflicted on some but not on others. It involves no 'fundamental' right guaranteed by the Constitution, such as voting, the right of association, the right of access to the courts, or any rights of privacy. We deal with economic and social legislation where legislatures have historically drawn lines which we respect against the charge of violation of the Equal Protection Clause if the law be 'reasonable, not arbitrary' and bears 'a rational relationship to a [permissible] state objective.' It is said, however, that if two unmarried people can constitute a 'family,' there is no reason why three or four may not. But every line drawn by a legislature leaves some out that might well have been included. That exercise of discretion, however, is a legislative, not a judicial, function."

While the *Belle Terre* and *City of Edmonds* cases are somewhat similar in their facts, there are important distinctions between the two. The zoning provision in *Belle Terre* was legal because it established laws for single-housekeeping units of two people, even when unrelated. Additional inhabitants such as children had to be related to the first two family members. Thus, two, but not six, unrelated students could have lived in the house. The law reflected the norm in the small, homogeneous village of Belle Terre, which was made up predominately of nuclear families. The zoning law in *City of Edmonds* required *all* those in the household to be related, which, in effect, excluded group homes that are commonly found in larger, more diverse cities such as Edmonds. The *City of Edmonds* case also involved a protected class (the disabled) which invokes stronger protections than afforded students who are not in a protected class.

After the devastating 2007–2009 recession, many homeowners lost their homes to foreclosures. With few qualified buyers, many empty homes were soon occupied by the homeless or large groups of unrelated people trying to survive by pooling their money to pay rent. In some of the worst-hit cities, like Las Vegas, local governments reacted by passing new laws prohibiting unrelated people over a certain number to live in one home. Since the poor and homeless are not generally included within protected legal classifications, these laws will likely survive a constitutional challenge.[113]

Given the constitutional background, courts that have considered exclusionary zoning cases have often reached conflicting results. One approach is illustrated by the next case, where the court considered the "Petaluma Plan," a land use plan adopted by Petaluma, a city 40 miles north of San Francisco.

A CASE IN POINT

In *Construction Industry Ass'n, Sonoma City v. City of Petaluma*,[114] the court reviewed the Petaluma Plan that resulted from the city's concern over a rapid growth rate, which totaled 25 percent in a two-year period. Under the plan, which was limited to the 1972–1977 period, the housing development growth rate in the city was not to exceed 500 dwelling units per year and development permits were awarded to builders who adapted their plans to other city land use plans. The plan further established a greenbelt around the city that served as a boundary for urban expansion.

Dispute arose over the purpose of the Petaluma Plan. According to the city, the plan was designed to ensure that "development in the next five years will take place in a reasonable, orderly, attractive manner, rather than in a completely haphazard and unattractive manner." The construction industry and two landowners brought suit against the city, claiming that the plan was enacted "to limit Petaluma's demographic and market growth rate in housing and the immigration of new residents." The trial court decided that the plan was unconstitutional because, since the plan involved a fundamental right—the right to travel—Petaluma would have to show a compelling interest if the plan was to be sustained.

On appeal, the appellate court declined to consider whether the right to travel was violated because the plaintiffs were asserting the right on behalf of third parties and therefore lacked standing (a concept to be considered in the following chapter). The appellate court also concluded that the Petaluma Plan was not arbitrary and unreasonable since it did bear a rational relationship to a legitimate state interest: "We conclude therefore that under *Belle Terre* ... the concept of the public welfare is sufficiently broad to uphold Petaluma's desire to preserve its small town character, its open spaces and low density of population and to grow at an orderly and deliberate pace."

Petaluma and a number of other cases add a third dimension to the regulatory power of zoning: time. While zoning limits the use and density of construction, *Petaluma* also allows municipalities to control the timing of development based on the availability of municipal services outlined in a comprehensive plan.

Inclusionary Zoning

inclusionary zoning
Zoning regulations that create incentives or requirements for affordable housing development.

Inclusionary Zoning   Exclusionary zoning can often have a discriminatory effect on the poor, many of whom are comprised of racial and ethnic minorities. In reaction to these laws, some jurisdictions, starting in the 1960s, have created **inclusionary zoning** laws to encourage affordable housing in areas that were once beyond the reach of those who lacked the means to live there. The next New Jersey case endorses the application of inclusionary zoning.

In *Southern Burlington County N.A.A.C.P. v. Township of Mount Laurel*,[115] the township of Mount Laurel, New Jersey, enacted a zoning ordinance that, by allowing only single-family detached dwellings, excluded low- and moderate-income housing such as apartments, townhouses, and mobile homes from the city. Even single-family residences in Mount Laurel were beyond the means of moderate-income families because the zoning ordinance required large lots and large buildings. The New Jersey Supreme Court concluded that "Mount Laurel permits only such middle and upper income housing as it believes will have sufficient taxable value to come close to paying its own governmental way."

The plaintiffs who challenged the ordinance represented poor minority groups, although the court noted that other groups barred by restrictive land use regulations would include young couples, elderly couples, single people, and large and growing families in the middle-income range. The issue, according to the court, was "... whether a developing municipality like Mount Laurel may validly, by a system of land use regulation, make it physically and economically impossible to provide low and moderate income housing in the municipality for the various categories of persons who need and want it and thereby, as Mount Laurel has, exclude such people from living within its confines because of the limited extent of their income and resources. "The court also noted that the "implications of the issue presented are indeed broad and far-reaching, extending much beyond these particular plaintiffs and the boundaries of this particular municipality."

The court decided that, under state law, a municipality's exercise of its zoning power to allow uses beneficial to the local tax rate was an insufficient basis to support the exclusionary character of the ordinance. The court also decided that, because the township was amenable to the installation of sewage disposal and water supply facilities, ecological or environmental concerns were not sufficient reasons for the restrictive zoning. The court concluded: "By way of summary, what we have said comes down to this. As a developing municipality, Mount Laurel must, by its land use regulations, make realistically possible the opportunity for an appropriate variety and choice of housing for all categories of people who may desire to live there, of course including those of low and moderate income. It must permit multi-family housing, without bedroom or similar restrictions, as well as small dwellings on very small lots, low cost housing of other types and, in general, high density zoning, without artificial and unjustifiable minimum requirements as to lot size, building size and the like to meet the full panoply of these needs."

The *Township of Mt. Laurel* decision was, not surprisingly, highly controversial and derided by critics as a form of social engineering. The case triggered a series of cases in New Jersey and other states, as well as the beginning of an important public policy debate that still resonates today.

Still, most states other than New Jersey have *not* accepted the Mount Laurel model of inclusionary zoning. For example, in *Christian Activities Council v. Town Council of Glastonbury*,[116] the Connecticut Supreme Court upheld a town council's denial of a new zoning plan. The rejected plan called for changing a zoning classification that established a one-acre minimum lot to more dense half-acre lots. The smaller lots would have allowed the construction of more affordable housing.

As one commentator has observed regarding developments since Mount Laurel:

Although mandatory planning obligations in a few states carry an inclusionary effect, there have been but modest extensions of the antisnob zoning principles condemning exclusionary zoning through substantive due process type Mount Laurel doctrine. The majority of states have remained silent or have enacted modest initiatives such as density bonuses to encourage affordable housing development. Most states have accepted excessive regulation and have let the provision of adequate housing to the vicissitudes of the private market and the dwindling supply of government subsidized housing.[117]

Despite setbacks, inclusionary zoning, as well as other approaches to solving housing shortages and affordability, is still being advanced in some states—in certain cases with notable success. For example, California, a state with some of the most expensive housing in the nation, requires local governments to consider providing affordable housing. One noticeable trend emerging in California is that inclusionary *zoning* is morphing into a less controversial version that can best be characterized as inclusionary *housing*. This narrower but more politically palatable approach ranges from mandating or encouraging builders to provide a minimum percentage of low- to moderate-income housing to imposing fees on developers to finance more affordable housing. California currently is a leader in providing inclusionary housing, with 107 cities and counties adopting some form of fee structure. For example, the City of Napa, which survived a legal challenge from home builders to its plan, mandates that 10 percent of all new homes built there must be affordable.[118] Likewise, the imposition of a mandatory fee on builders was upheld in *San Remo Hotel v. City and County of San Francisco*.[119] In that case, developers were forced to pay a fee for converting the San Remo Hotel from long-term residential use to tourist use in order to finance affordable housing elsewhere. Other states, such as Texas and Florida, also impose special taxes and fees to generate revenue for more affordable housing.[120] Some urban specialists are advocating inclusionary housing as a means of rebuilding post-Katrina New Orleans by requiring builders to set aside a percentage of houses for low-income families who would become eligible to buy them under a special voucher program.[121]

Some governments, instead of imposing fees, are experimenting with various incentives as a means of promoting the same goals of affordable housing that inclusionary zoning and housing seek. This has been particularly true in fast-growing areas where supply does not always keep up with demand. For example, some governments award bonuses to companies that build higher-density housing, while other governments create housing trust funds to aid developers who build low- and moderate-income housing. Financial aid for low- and moderate-income earners, particularly teachers and public safety officers, also is used. It is noteworthy, however, that since the 2007–2009 recession, home prices have plummeted to more affordable levels, which may alleviate the need for some of these programs, at least for awhile. In any case, all of these post–*Mt. Laurel* approaches have spawned public policy debates which will likely continue for years.[122]

ETHICAL AND PUBLIC POLICY ISSUES

Are Inclusionary Zoning Ordinances Not Only a Legal Means but Also an Ethical Means of Creating Sufficient Housing and Diversity in Neighborhoods?

In Problem 10 at the end of the chapter, this issue is discussed.

---

land use planning

The process of establishing the character, quality, and pattern of the physical environment for the activities of people and organizations in the planning area.

Land Use Planning

Will Rogers once said, "Buy land. They ain' makin' any more of it." But the limited supply of land, coupled with environmental concerns, has resulted in the dilution of Rogers' recommendation—which views land purely as a commodity to be bought, developed, and sold—and the emergence of **land use planning**. This orientation toward land use planning represents, in the words of James Rouse, a major developer of shopping centers, "… the most radical change in our concept of private property rights we have ever seen in the history of this country."[123]

In the past, a land developer was concerned primarily with local zoning ordinances and building codes, many of which would differ whenever real estate development moved beyond the boundaries of one local government unit. Modern land use planning places more control of the planning process at the state and, possibly, federal levels. This approach, which is directed toward larger areas of land (thus eliminating inconsistent uses of neighboring lands that happen to be in different counties, townships, or cities), requires developers to clear future developments with regional or state agencies as well as with local governmental units.

State Land Use Planning

State land use planning assumes "the proposition that it is better to grow 'smart' than 'dumb.'"[124] It relies on *four* principal methods.[125] (See Figure 13.3.) The *first* is direct state regulation of land use. In Hawaii, for example, the State Land Use Commission is authorized to classify land in the state's four counties as "urban," "agricultural," or "conservation." Counties make land use decisions within the "urban" district, while state agencies regulate the other two districts.[126] A land use plan in Maine is similar to the Hawaiian scheme, although the Maine land use commission only has power to regulate the unincorporated areas of the state; the law is designed primarily to regulate corporate developers of housing projects.

A *second* method of land use planning—involving areas of critical concern—is characterized by state regulation of a limited geographic area affected by a land use crisis.[127] Examples include the San Francisco Bay Conservation and Development Commission, the Tahoe Regional Planning Agency, the Adirondack Park Agency, the California Coastal Zone Act, and the Delaware Coastal Zone Act.[128] The Delaware Coastal Zone Act, for example, was a response to the development of new oil tanker facilities in coastal areas. The legislation prohibits additional oil refineries within a one- to six-mile zone along the Delaware Bay Coast and the Atlantic Coast and strictly regulates all other new industrial development within the same area.[129]

The land use legislation enacted in Florida blends the first two methods of state land use planning. Florida legislation, motivated by surging population and development and environmental pressures, has served as a model for other states. The Florida land use

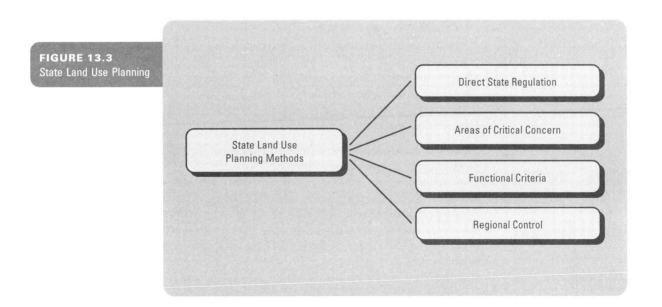

FIGURE 13.3
State Land Use Planning

State Land Use Planning Methods

- Direct State Regulation
- Areas of Critical Concern
- Functional Criteria
- Regional Control

area of critical state concern

In state land use planning, an area that has a significant impact on environmental, historical, natural, or archeological resources of regional or statewide importance.

legislation is modeled after an American Law Institute Model Act[130] and is directed toward "areas of critical state concern" and "developments of regional impact." **An area of critical state concern** is one that has a significant impact on environmental, historical, natural, or archeological resources of regional or statewide importance. These include the city of Apalachicola, Key West and the Florida Keys, and the Green and Big Cypress Swamps.

A Florida commission composed of the governor and the cabinet designates the boundaries of the areas of critical concern; all development within those boundaries must comply with state land use guidelines. A **development of regional impact**, under Florida law, is a development that is of such character, magnitude, or location as to have a substantial effect on the health, safety, and welfare of citizens of more than one county. These developments, including such major projects as airports, large subdivisions, shopping centers, and power plants, must be approved at the local level. The state land use planning agency may challenge the local decision, forcing a review of the decision by a state commission that has the power to deny permission for the development.[131]

development of regional impact

Under Florida law, a development that has such character, magnitude, or location that it has a substantial effect on the health, safety, and welfare of citizens of more than one county.

State regulation on the basis of functional criteria, such as providing housing, represents a *third* method of state land use planning. Under the Massachusetts Low and Moderate Income Housing Act,[132] a public agency or nonprofit corporation that has been denied the right to build low-income housing by a local authority may appeal the denial to a state committee that is more likely to consider what is best for the entire region.[133]

The *last* method, regional land use planning and control, was adopted by Oregon in the Portland Metropolitan District, which acts as "the only elected regional government in the nation."[134] Although other states have adopted regional development reviews, the Oregon model has been recognized for its unusually strong and successful regional plan.

In addition to the four major methods of state land use planning, the concept of **transferable development rights** (TDRs) (also discussed in Chapter 3) has gained popularity at state and local levels. Traditional methods of controlling land use—such as eminent domain and zoning—often are either too expensive or subject to variations in the form of spot zoning, variances, and zone changes. As a result, a number of governmental units have adopted the approach that the ownership of real estate consists of a bundle of individual rights, including the right to develop the real estate, and that any of these rights may be sold to someone else.

transferable development rights

A market-based system designed to preserve land. Property owners are given financial incentives to grant their rights to develop land to others.

Several municipalities have adopted a system based on TDRs in which all of the following are present:

1. A master plan is established that designates which sections of the municipality may be developed.
2. Every property owner is given "shares" or "certificates" of development rights as determined by the size or value of her land holdings.
3. Developers must present the municipality with an appropriate number of TDRs before they may develop real estate.

TDRs also are used to preserve ecological resources and landmarks and to encourage the construction of low-income housing.[135] In addition, TDRs may protect state and local governments from expensive takings lawsuits as discussed in the *Suitam* case on page 540.

Although the Supreme Court has not definitively resolved the constitutionality of TDRs, the following example demonstrates how landowners' complaints about regulatory takings may be allayed. Assume that Shustek's farm, consisting of 20 acres, is located in an area that is zoned for one dwelling for every 2 acres. He plans, at some time, to build 10 houses on his land. Later Shustek's farm is rezoned by the county to one dwelling unit for every 20 acres to create a greenbelt around the city. Now he can build only 1 house on his land when before he could build 10. However, Shustek's land, since its development potential has lessened, is in a "sending area," which means that he can sell nine TDR certificates for every house he cannot build.

Levine owns a five-acre undeveloped parcel in an urban growth area that permits 4 units per acre. He currently owns 20 units. Levine's land is deemed a "receiving area" because the county plans to redevelop this area, much of which is blighted, with more housing. As an incentive to create dense multifamily units, the planning commission now allows Levine to build up to 8 units per acre. Still, to build 8 units on the five acres, Levine needs 20 TDR certificates. He can buy Shustek's 9 TDR certificates and purchase an additional 11 certificates to fully develop his land. Shustek can sell his 9 TDR certificates for the market price. By selling his 9 TDRs to Levine, Shustek may be able to recoup much of the loss he incurred after he was allowed to build only 1 of the 10 units he had originally planned.

State land use planning terminology and goals have evolved since the first legislation more than two decades ago.[136] Land use planning is often referred to as "growth management," and state efforts have several key objectives. *First*, they strive to achieve consistency between the state, regional, and local plans. They often seek to assure that infrastructure such as roads, sewers, parks, libraries, police, and hospitals is available to serve new development concurrent with its completion. *Second*, increasing focus is being placed on avoiding urban sprawl, which consumes agricultural land and increases infrastructure costs. *Third*, municipalities recognize the importance of creating incentives for affordable housing, such as inclusionary zoning, addressed earlier in the chapter. *Finally*, the need to protect natural resources and the promotion of economic development are critical goals.

The most recent concept of state land use planning is sometimes referred to as "smart growth," an extension to growth management, a concept championed by former Vice President Al Gore. Smart growth calls for preservation of open space, urban growth boundaries, concentration of development, and more mass transit. It also calls for the use of public infrastructure funds to be used as a "carrot" to encourage these goals rather than using traditional zoning and other laws as a "stick."[137] Smart growth and growth management are not without their detractors. Some argue that laws preserving more open space limit construction and therefore create higher prices for homes, as well as force people to live in smaller and more cramped accommodations.[138]

With the election of President Barack Obama, there has been more public policy attention given to limiting the outward growth of cities. This is not only to lessen urban sprawl, but to reduce driving and therefore the polluting effects of carbon gases, which most scientists claim cause global warming. However, demographic changes, including an aging population of baby boomers that have been in place for over a decade, plus the increasing price of gasoline, have also contributed to reducing sprawl. For example, in Denver and Chicago, 25 and 40 percent of all new homes in 2007 were built in the central part of those cities, up noticeably from the 1990s.[139]

Federal Land Use Planning

Federal land use legislation includes over 100 federal land-oriented programs that may be grouped under *two* main headings: natural resources and physical development.[140] The following are examples of natural resources agencies and programs:

- *Services of the Department of Agriculture—including the Agricultural Stabilization and Conservation Service, Soil Conservation Service, and the Forest Service—administer programs relating to land use.*
- *The BLM manages approximately 253 million acres of federal public land as well as an additional 700 million acres of mineral estates.*

- *A number of agencies are responsible for water programs.*
- *Several agencies are involved in land use in particular areas such as the Alaska Power Administration and the Bonneville Power Administration.*

The following agencies and programs deal with physical development:

- *The Farmers Home Administration is involved in the development of rural housing.*
- *The Department of Housing and Urban Development (HUD) administers most federal housing programs, including the Interstate Land Sales Full Disclosure Act (see Chapter 6), housing rehabilitation, and construction of low- and moderate-income housing.*
- *The Economic Development Administration oversees a number of programs to assist economically distressed areas, including ongoing efforts in Appalachia, as well as helping to rebuilt ports and roads in post-Katrina Louisiana.[141]*
- *The Department of Commerce administers regional development programs.*
- *Several federal agencies sponsor programs to assist the development of sanitation facilities.*
- *The Department of Transportation administers most transportation programs and conducts transportation research and planning.*

Other federal programs, individually or in combination, often affect land use. It is claimed, for example, that urban sprawl has been assisted by federal policies encouraging the purchase of single-family homes. These policies include what has been termed the "familiar litany" of the effect of FHA mortgage insurance for homeowners, the interstate highway system, and the allowance of a tax deduction for home mortgage interest.[142]

The federal government also can *limit* local planning initiatives. *Two* notable examples are the Religious Land Use and Institutionalized Persons Act of 2000 (RLUIPA) and the Telecommunications Act (TCA) of 1996. The *first* law, RLUIPA, was passed after religious groups complained that local planning and zoning boards were restricting their religious activities. Many religious groups want to build or use churches and temples in residential areas close to their membership, but they are not allowed to build under strict zoning laws. For example, an Orthodox rabbi in Miami was threatened with arrest for conducting prayer meetings in a converted garage in a residential area. The rabbi argued that since the members of the synagogue cannot drive motorized vehicles on the Sabbath, the synagogue must locate near them. The zoning board also required the synagogue to have as many parking spaces as seats in the house of worship even though no members drove! Opponents of RLUIPA argue that houses of worship, particularly the new Christian megachurches, create traffic and congestion problems. The opponents also maintain that RLUIPA violates the First Amendment and Equal Protection Clause of the Fourteenth Amendment by favoring religious landowners over other users.[143]

RLUIPA can create difficulties for local governments when religious groups oppose their zoning ordinances. For example, if a local government imposes a land use provision that imposes a "substantial burden on the religious exercise of a person, including a religious assembly or institution," the local government's ordinance must pass a "strict scrutiny" test. This means that government must show that it is advancing a compelling governmental interest with an ordinance that creates the least restrictive means of accomplishing it. If the strict scrutiny test is not satisfied, the zoning ordinance cannot be enforced against the religious organization.[144]

There are many lingering questions concerning RLUIPA, such as its constitutionality and whether congestion, traffic, and aesthetics are compelling governmental interests. RLUIPA became especially contentious after 9/11, when questions arose concerning the construction of mosques in residential neighborhoods.[145] A recent and heated debate surrounding the issue of land use and religion concerns the decision in 2010 to allow a

Muslim community center and mosque to be built near "Ground Zero" in lower Manhattan, the site of World Trade Center Towers destroyed by Muslim terrorists on 9/11. Proponents argue that it will help foster a better understanding of Islam, while opponents see it as an ironic slap in the face against the victims and their families. As some commentators have pointed out, if its construction should be blocked, RLUIPA would provide a strong defense for allowing the mosque.[146]

It is noteworthy that some states have similar statutes to protect religious organizations from discriminatory zoning and city ordinances. As the next case from Texas demonstrates, some of the laws are applied to regulate some unexpected religious practices.

A CASE IN POINT

In *Merced v. Kasson*,[147] Merced, a member of the Santeria religion, originated in Cuba and based on a fusion of West African and Roman Catholic elements, was blocked by a City of Euless ordinance which prohibited, for health reasons, the slaughter of animals within the city limits. Merced argued that animal sacrifice, mainly lambs, goats, and chickens, was an integral part of the religion in which animal blood is used to engage and honor spirits called *orishas*. Merced also claimed that no Santeria temples existed in Texas, so home sacrifice was necessary. Merced also proved that there was no material threat to sanitation. The federal appeals court first ruled that RLUIPA did not apply since that law only covers discriminatory zoning. The court did state, however, that the Texas Religious Freedom and Restoration Act protects religions, like Santeria, from discriminatory city ordinances. Thus, the city must prove there is a compelling governmental interest for the ordinance and that the ordinance offers the less restrictive means of advancing the interest. In applying the tests, the court ruled that the court failed on both accounts, arguing first that Merced's practices did not pose a problem to sanitation and that others, like hunters, were able to slaughter animals in the city. The court further ruled that alternative means, other than a complete ban on the Santeria's religious practices, could also be created to advance the goal of sanitation.

The *second* federal law is the federal TCA of 1996. Although the placement of cellular towers can be regulated to an extent by state and local zoning law, local governments must articulate sound reasons for their regulations as a Michigan court explains.

A CASE IN POINT

In *New Par v. City of Saginaw*,[148] New Par, a provider of cell phone service, sought a building permit from the City of Saginaw to erect a 150-foot cell tower. The request did not comply with Saginaw's minimum-size zoning requirement for "light industrial" use, so New Par requested a variance. The zoning board denied the request. The federal district court overruled the City of Saginaw; and on appeal, the circuit court affirmed the district court ruling. The court stated that the three reasons submitted by the board—(1) aesthetics, (2) health and safety issues relating to electromagnetic emissions, and (3) whether New Par could locate on other property—were not supported by substantial evidence in the written record. The court stated that "[a]t the Board meetings in this case aesthetic concerns were mentioned only a few times, and they were never discussed. In regard to the second concern, the Act explicitly prohibits local board decision-making 'on the basis of the environmental effects of radio frequency emissions to the extent that such facilities comply with the Commission's regulations concerning such emissions.' And the third concern simply does not go to any of the criteria set out in the Zoning Code regarding when the Board can grant a zoning variance."

Planned Unit Developments, Condominiums, Time-Sharing, and Cooperatives

A number of real estate arrangements have been developed that utilize shared facilities to make better use of the limited supply of real estate. Such arrangements include many planning and regulatory tools within the privately created community regime. Four of the most popular of these developments are planned unit developments, condominiums, time-sharing, and cooperatives.

Planned Unit Developments

planned unit development

Land developed as a single unit according to a plan, with a specified minimum contiguous acreage. The planned unit development contains one or more residential clusters or planned unit residential developments and one or more public, quasipublic, commercial, or industrial areas. The ratio of nonresidential uses to residential uses is specified in the zoning ordinance.

Typically, a **planned unit development** consists of a concentrated area of homes or townhouses. In addition, common areas are designated for recreational and community uses. A buyer acquires a home or a townhouse in a planned unit development by means of traditional forms of ownership. For example, Sam and Sally can purchase their townhouse as tenants by the entirety. The documents of record establishing the planned unit development require Sam and Sally also to be members of a homeowners' association, a nonprofit corporation. This association owns the common areas. Each homeowner has the right to use the common areas subject to the restrictions set forth in the association agreement, and each homeowner must pay a reasonable share of the association's expense for maintaining the common areas.[149] A typical planned unit development is organized with the extensive use of easements to establish access to utilities, rights to maintain party walls, and use of parking areas and walkways. Are all property owners and association members liable when a member is negligently injured in common areas? The next case from California addresses the issue.

A CASE IN POINT

In *Cody F. v. Falletti*,[150] a minor who lived in Rancho Tehama Subdivision, a planned unit development, was mauled by dogs owned by one of the residents on an easement (street) owned by the association. The plaintiff alleged that all the residents of Rancho Tehama were liable for failing to enforce restrictions that state that nonhousehold dogs (in this case, guard dogs) should not have been allowed in the subdivision and for failing to prevent the dogs from escaping from the property. The court ruled in favor of the association, explaining: "[T]he right of control that attends ownership of an easement has a narrower scope than the right of control that accompanies fee ownership of real property. Therefore, the corresponding duty to third parties in managing the property interest must also be narrower in scope and tied to the reason that the easement is granted."

Condominiums

condominium

A system that combines separate ownership of individual units with joint ownership of common areas.

The word **condominium** is derived from the Latin word meaning "joint ownership or control." Condominiums have been used throughout history whenever land was costly and limited in supply. For example, condominiums were common in ancient Rome, especially near the Forum, where real estate was scarce and expensive; they also were common in the walled cities of medieval Europe.[151] Although condominiums first appeared in the United States in the late 1940s, condominium ownership of housing became popular in the 1960s and 1970s. Today purchasers can acquire condominiums in office buildings, parking structures, grain elevators, marinas, and campgrounds. Every state has a condominium statute regulating this form of ownership.

The purchase of a condominium involves *two* forms of ownership:

1. The buyer owns the condominium unit—the living space, for example—in any of the traditional forms of ownership. In essence, the condominium owner owns the *air* within the condominium and that with which the air has contact (the interior walls, floor, and ceiling, typically in fee simple absolute).

2. The condominium purchaser's acquisition of her unit also includes an undivided interest, as a tenant in common, in the common areas of the condominium, such as the swimming pool, tennis courts, space between units, roof, and land under the structure.

The condominium owner cannot sell her interest in the common area separately from her unit. A Florida decision stated:

> *that the undivided share in the common elements appurtenant to each unit shall not be separated from the unit; that a share in the common elements cannot be conveyed or encumbered except together with the unit; and that the shares in the common elements appurtenant to units shall remain undivided and not subject to action for partition.... [O]ne must reach the inescapable conclusion that all condominium units have an undivided share of the common elements and neither can exist separately from the other.*[152]

The Recession of 2007–2009 created a significant economic problem for condominium owners when many of them went into foreclosure and abandoned their properties. Those owners who remained were forced to continue paying the fixed costs, such as insurance and maintenance, necessary for the common areas. In some cases, this created a domino effect when those who were left in the development were unable to pay the higher costs causing additional condominium owners to default on their mortgages and thus a new cycle of foreclosures.

Two documents are especially important to the condominium buyer. The *first* and most important document is the **master deed** (also known as the **enabling declaration**, the **declaration of conditions**, or the **condominium document**). In most cases, the master deed:

1. Authorizes a board of directors to administer the condominium affairs in line with the bylaws and to assess the owners for adequate maintenance of the condominium
2. Describes the condominium units and the common areas and any restrictions on their use
3. Establishes the undivided interest percentage, which is the ratio of one unit to the total number of units as determined by original value, living area, or market price

In some cases, all units are given an equal share. The undivided interest percentage is used to determine the owner's interest in the common area, the owner's number of votes in meetings of the owners' association, and the owner's share of maintenance and operating expenses. To change the provisions of the master deed, the consent of 75 to 100 percent of the owners is usually required.[153]

The *second* important document contains the **bylaws**, which generally govern the internal affairs of the condominium in the same manner that bylaws govern the internal operations of a corporation. Condominium bylaws usually establish the responsibilities of the owners' association; the voting procedures to be used at association meetings; the qualifications, powers, and duties of the board of directors; the powers and duties of the officers; and the obligations of the owners with regard to assessments,

---

master deed (enabling declaration, declaration of conditions, condominium document)

The recorded document that authorizes the election of a condominium's board of directors, describes the condominium units and the common areas, and establishes the owner's undivided interest percentage. Also referred to as the enabling declaration, the declaration of conditions, and the condominium document.

bylaws

A document governing the operation details of a condominium.

maintenance, and use of the units and common areas.[154] One important difference between the bylaws and the master deed is that amendment of the bylaws usually requires only a majority vote.

In examining condominium documents, the buyer should be aware of a number of at least *four* potential legal problems. *First,* the monthly assessment fee should be closely analyzed. Disreputable developers have been known to initially establish a low monthly assessment to encourage buyers. Later the assessment is dramatically increased to cover actual costs. The buyer should determine whether the initial maintenance costs are realistic. In addition, if the condominium has been in existence for several years or is a converted rental property such as an apartment house, the purchaser must consider the cost of repairing common elements such as the roof, wiring, and plumbing. While state statutes often require that certain reserves be established for such capital repairs, the buyer should know whether funds are on hand to cover such major expenditures.

Second, the buyer should review the insurance provisions. The need for liability insurance is especially critical because some courts have held that even a member of the owners' association may sue the association for negligence in maintaining common areas. In such cases, most state laws provide that condominium owners are liable only for their proportionate share of the damages, although a Mississippi statute declares that individual owners have no personal liability for damages resulting from use of the common area.[155] In any event, the association should purchase sufficient insurance to cover potential liability. In addition to having liability insurance, the association should purchase errors and omissions (E&O) coverage for the association officers and directors, workers' compensation insurance to cover employees, and fire insurance for the common areas. The owners, of course, must maintain their own insurance coverage for the individual units as the following California case points out.

Is a condominium association liable to a condominium owner who is a crime victim? In *Frances T. v. Village Green Owners Association* on page 574, the court considers whether the association and individual directors should be held liable for an owner's injuries.

END OF CHAPTER CASE

Third, purchasers should recognize that a condominium represents a unique form of private government that involves certain restrictions on the owners' freedom as well as tolerance of others. In the words of a California court:

> *Inherent in the condominium concept is the principle that to promote the health, happiness, and peace of mind of the majority of the unit owners since they are living in such close proximity and using facilities in common, each unit owner must give up a certain degree of freedom of choice which he might otherwise enjoy in separate, privately owned property. Condominium unit owners comprise a little democratic subsociety of necessity more restrictive as it pertains to use of condominium property than may exist outside of the condominium organization.*[156]

For example, a purchaser should consider the impact of restrictions on the right to rent or resell the condominium unit. Many condominium statutes permit restraints upon alienation—such as a requirement that the association approve a prospective purchaser—as long as the restraints are not used to discriminate illegally.[157] Restrictions can also involve, as in the *Frances T.* case, referenced above, the right to change the exterior of the unit or the right, as the next Massachusetts cases discusses, to have pets in the condominium.

A CASE IN POINT

In *Granby Heights Association, Inc., v. Dean*,[158] the Massachusetts court determined that a restriction on pets in the common areas was, in practical effect, a restriction on pets in the individual condominium units. Such restrictions are valid if disclosed in the condominium documents. Since the applicable restrictions were not appropriately disclosed, the court held that they were invalid.

Finally, prospective purchasers of condominium units should determine who owns the land and common areas. It was common practice for some condominium developers to retain ownership of the land and common areas, lease them to the association for 99 years, and then proceed to charge exorbitant rent to the association. Moreover, some developers, particularly with cooperatives, discussed below, would lease back to themselves the income producing areas, such as garages, health club facilities, and laundry rooms, at below market prices and then enjoy a significant cash flow.[159]

In response, there have been state and federal laws passed to counteract the contracts made by developers that are unfair to owners. Some states have enacted statutes that allow owners to cancel contracts made when the developer controlled the newly created condominium or cooperative. The federal Condominium and Cooperative Conversion Protection and Relief Act of 1980 allows subsequent owners in a condominium conversion project to terminate maintenance and management contracts with the original developer or sponsor if the contracts were made while the latter controlled the condominium association or cooperative.

The conversion of apartments into condominiums is subject to other forms of regulation when the rights of tenants are involved. To protect tenants, several municipalities have enacted laws that prevent or greatly restrict eviction. A law enacted in Brookline, Massachusetts, represents one of the strongest forms of protection in that purchasers of condominium units are prohibited from evicting preconversion tenants. Although attacked on constitutional grounds, this law has been upheld because owners are allowed a fair return on their investment and there is a public need for rental units.[160]

Time-Sharing

time-sharing
Joint lease or ownership of property that is used individually for designated periods of time.

As the name implies, **time-sharing** involves a form of shared ownership that allows each owner the right to use property at a specified time each year. A purchaser of a time-share interest in a Colorado condominium, for example, might be given the right to use the property every year during the first week in February. The sharing of the condominium purchase price and maintenance fees among many owners has been intended to make time-sharing an economical form of ownership. Some owners, however, have discovered that there is a poor market for time-share resales and that sales' costs and commissions are high.

The owner's interest in a time-share may be characterized legally as a fee simple, a lease, or a license.[161] Fee simple ownership is commonly in *one of two* forms:

1. A time-span estate, which, in effect, is a tenancy in common
2. An interval estate, which allows the purchaser to use the property during a specified time period for a set number of years, after which time title reverts to the purchasers as tenants in common

The time-share lease, sometimes called the *vacation lease*, is similar to interval ownership except that when the lease ends after a certain number of years, ownership reverts to the lessor rather than to the time-share owners. The time-share license, also known as the *club membership*, differs from the other forms of ownership in that a specific unit within the development often is not designated in advance and thus may change from year to year.

As a result of aggressive marketing techniques by time-share developers, many states have enacted laws to protect purchasers. These laws, for instance, require that sales proceeds be held in escrow until construction is complete and give buyers a specified time in which to cancel their contracts.[162] Time-share companies that violate these laws may have to pay substantial penalties as this Florida case shows.

A CASE IN POINT

In *Resort Timeshare Resales v. Florida*,[163] the defendant timeshare company, Resort Timeshare Resales (RTR), was charged with failing to give consumers notice of their right to cancel within three days, as required under Florida law. Civil penalties of $50,000 were assessed against the company, as well as $25,000 each against three individuals who worked for the company. The penalties were challenged as being unconstitutionally excessive. The court ruled in favor of the consumers, stating: "[T]here is evidence in this case that as many as 38,000 customers had been victimized. RTR charged consumers $395 for its services. During the relevant time period RTR took in over $13 million in income and, for example, Lawrence Cohen [one of the employees penalized] was paid in excess of $300,000 annually. We do not, accordingly, find that the penalties were excessive."

Cooperatives

cooperative

A multiunit complex in which the owners have an interest in the entire complex and a lease of their own apartments.

The **cooperative** is a unique arrangement in which the tenants own the landlord. The tenants acquire shares of stock in an entity, usually a corporation, which owns the building. The shares of stock carry rights to occupancy of the unit. Capital from the sale of stock in the corporation is used as a down payment in purchasing an apartment building to be used as a cooperative. Apartments in the building are then leased to the shareholders, who pay enough rent to cover the corporation's mortgage, operating costs, taxes, and other expenses. As in the case of other leaseholds, each tenant's interest in the cooperative, represented by the lease and stock certificate, is regarded as personal property as the following New York court explains.

A CASE IN POINT

In *State Tax Commissioner v. Shor*,[164] restaurateur Toots Shor purchased stock in a New York cooperative and received a proprietary lease, but he was later evicted for nonpayment of monthly charges. In a subsequent dispute among Shor's creditors over his interest in the cooperative, a creditor with a lien on his real estate claimed that the lien had priority. The court disagreed on the grounds that under the law of New York and other states, an interest in a cooperative is personal property.

While many principles of landlord and tenant law govern the cooperative arrangement, *four* special legal issues relate specifically to the cooperative:

1. Under a normal leasehold, the rights and duties of the parties are spelled out in the lease. In the cooperative, many of the rights and duties also are included in the lease (called a *proprietary lease*); but since the cooperative is usually incorporated, the shareholder-tenant also should closely examine the articles of incorporation and the bylaws. The bylaws, for example, cover matters such as the right to sell the certificates, the sale price, and the grounds for terminating the shareholder's rights. A court in New York City, where cooperatives are common, held, for example, that a board of directors acted in excess of its authority in establishing a minimum, or "floor price," for the sale of units to third parties.[165] The court viewed the minimum price as an unreasonable restraint on alienation and held that the floor price was beyond the board's authority as established by the cooperative's documents.

2. The person investing in a cooperative should recognize that, as the name implies, the housing arrangement is a group enterprise with a philosophy of "all for one and one for all." For example, if certain tenants neglect or refuse to pay their monthly charges, the other members must make up the difference to avoid a mortgage foreclosure or a sale to pay delinquent taxes.

3. Interests in a cooperative may be difficult to transfer after an increase in the corporation's equity in the property. For example, assume that 10 investors each purchase $20,000 worth of stock in a cooperative corporation; and they use the money as a down payment to purchase a 10-unit apartment building for $2 million. The corporation borrows the remaining $1.8 million and gives the lender a mortgage. As the years pass, the value of the building increases to $2.5 million, while the mortgage is reduced to $1 million. The corporation's equity is now worth $1.5 million, or $150,000 per shareholder. If one of the shareholders decides to sell her interest, she might have to find a purchaser who is able to pay cash because her individual interest is personal property that cannot be used to secure a mortgage. To avoid this result, the shareholder-tenants might decide to refinance the mortgage and thus reduce the equity to make the interests more saleable.

4. The last important legal issue in a cooperative arrangement is whether laws regulating the sale of securities apply to the sale of shares in a cooperative. This question was considered by the Supreme Court in the following case.

A CASE IN POINT

In *United Housing Foundation, Inc. v. Forman*,[166] fifty-seven residents of Co-op City, the largest cooperative in the United States, sued the corporations that built, promoted, and operated the cooperative, claiming violations of the antifraud provisions of the Securities Act of 1933 and the Securities Exchange Act of 1934. To lease an apartment in Co-op City, prospective tenants had to purchase 18 shares of stock at $25 per share for each room in the apartment. The shares could not be sold to a nontenant; and when leaving Co-op City, a tenant could not sell his shares for more than $25 per share plus a fraction of the mortgage principal he paid during the tenancy.

The Supreme Court decided that there was no sale of securities under federal securities law because of the nonprofit nature of the arrangement. "What distinguishes a security transaction—what is absent here—is an investment where one parts with his money in the hope of receiving profits from the efforts of others, and not where he purchases a commodity for personal consumption or living quarters for personal use." In its decision, the Supreme Court left open the question of whether securities law would apply had the shareholders been allowed to sell their shares for a profit.

FROST, Justice. Defendant-Appellant Community of Damien of Molokai (Community) appeals from the district court's ruling in favor of Plaintiffs-Appellees, enjoining the further use of the property at 716 Rio Arriba, S.E., Albuquerque, as a group home for individuals with AIDS. Plaintiffs-Appellees argue that the group home violates a restrictive covenant. The Community contends that the group home is a permitted use under the covenant and, alternatively, that enforcing the restrictive covenant against the group home would violate the Federal Fair Housing Act.

The underlying facts of this case are not in dispute. The Community is a private, nonprofit corporation which provides homes to people with AIDS as well as other terminal illnesses.

In December 1992 the Community leased the residence at 716 Rio Arriba, S.E., Albuquerque, located in a planned subdivision called Four Hills Village, for use as a group home for four individuals with AIDS. The four residents who subsequently moved into the Community's group home were unrelated, and each required some degree of in-home nursing care.

Plaintiffs-Appellees, William Hill, III, Derek Head, Charlene Leamons, and Bernard Dueto (hereinafter Neighbors) live in Four Hills Village on the same dead-end street as the group home. Shortly after the group home opened, the Neighbors noticed an increase in traffic on Rio Arriba street, going to and from the group home. The Neighbors believed that the Community's use of its house as a group home for people with AIDS violated one of the restrictive covenants applicable to all the homes in the sixteenth installment of Four Hills Village. Installment sixteen encompasses the Community's group home and the Neighbors' houses. The applicable covenant provides in relevant part:

No lot shall ever be used for any purpose other than *single family residence purposes.* No dwelling house located thereon shall ever be used for other than *single family residence purposes,* nor shall any outbuildings or structure located thereon be used in a manner other than incidental to such *family residence* purposes. The erection or maintenance or use of any building, or the use of any lot for other purposes, including, but not restricted to such examples as stores, shops, flats, duplex houses, apartment houses, rooming houses, tourist courts, schools, churches, hospitals, and filling stations is hereby expressly prohibited.

Reservations, Covenants and Restrictions, Four Hills Village (Sixteenth Installment) (filed in the Bernalillo County Clerk's Office, Apr. 5, 1973) (emphasis added). The Neighbors specifically argue that the term "single family residence" does not include group homes in which unrelated people live together.

On August 12, 1993, the Neighbors filed for an injunction to enforce the covenant and to prevent further use of the Community's house as a group home. The Community defended on the grounds that the covenant did not prohibit the group home and, in the alternative, that enforcement of the covenant would violate the FHA.

* * *

The first issue before us is the applicability of the Four Hills restrictive covenant to the Community's group home. As this Court noted in *Cain v. Powers,* in determining whether to enforce a restrictive covenant, we are guided by certain general rules of construction. First, if the language is unclear or ambiguous, we will resolve the restrictive covenant in favor of the free enjoyment of the property and against restrictions. Second, we will not read restrictions on the use and enjoyment of the land into the covenant by implication. Third, we must interpret the covenant reasonably, but strictly, so as not to create an illogical, unnatural, or strained construction. Fourth, we must give words in the restrictive covenant their ordinary and intended meaning.

At issue here is the proper interpretation of the restriction, "No lot shall ever be used for any purpose other than single family residence purposes." The trial court held that the Community's use of property as a group home for four, unrelated individuals with AIDS violated this restriction.

In reaching its conclusion that the group home violated the residential use restriction, the trial court made two specific findings regarding the nature of the current use of the home. The court found that the "Community uses the house … as a non profit hostel for providing services to handicapped individuals" and that the "Community uses of the residence are much closer to the uses commonly associated with health care facilities, apartment houses, and rooming houses than uses which are commonly associated with single family residences." Thus the trial court apparently concluded that the property was being used for commercial purposes rather than residential purposes. However, we find that the trial court's conclusions are incorrect as a matter of law.

It is undisputed that the group home is designed to provide the four individuals who live in the house with a traditional family structure, setting, and atmosphere, and that the individuals who reside there use the home much as would any family with a disabled family member. The four residents share communal meals. They provide support for each other socially, emotionally, and financially. They also receive spiritual guidance together from religious leaders who visit them on Tuesday evenings.

* * *

The Neighbors also argue on appeal that the four, unrelated residents of the group home do not constitute a "single family" as required by the restrictive covenant. The Neighbors contend that the restrictive covenant should be interpreted such that the term "family" encompasses only individuals related by blood or by law. We disagree.

The word "family" is not defined in the restrictive covenant and nothing in the covenant suggests that it was the intent of the framers to limit the term to a discrete family unit comprised only of individuals related by blood or by law. Accordingly, the use of the term "family" in the covenant is ambiguous. As we noted above, we must resolve any ambiguity in the restrictive covenant in favor of the free enjoyment of the property. Construction therefore militates in favor of a conclusion that the term "family" encompasses a broader group than just related individuals and against restricting the use of the property solely to a traditional nuclear family.

* * *

Second, there is a strong public policy in favor of including small group homes within the definition of the term "family." The federal government has expressed a clear policy in favor of removing barriers preventing individuals with physical and mental disabilities from living in group homes in residential settings and against restrictive definitions of "families" that serve to exclude congregate living arrangements for the disabled. The FHA squarely sets out this important public policy. * * *

* * *

Both the federal and state governments have expressed a strong policy encouraging locating group homes in single-family residential areas and treating them as if they constituted traditional families. This overwhelming public policy is extremely persuasive in directing us toward an expansive interpretation of the term "family."

* * *

We conclude that the Community is entitled to continue operating its group home for individuals with AIDS both under the Four Hills restrictive covenants and under the Fair Housing Act. Accordingly, for the reasons discussed above, the trial court's ruling is reversed and the injunction is vacated. IT IS SO ORDERED.

Eminent Domain—Public Purpose
KELO v. CITY OF NEW LONDON
545 U.S. 469, 125 S.Ct. 2655 (2005)

Justice, STEVENS. In 2000, the city of New London approved a development plan that, in the words of the Supreme Court of Connecticut, was "projected to create in excess of 1,000 jobs, to increase tax and other revenues, and to revitalize an economically distressed city, including its downtown and waterfront areas." In assembling the land needed for this project, the city's development agent has purchased property from willing sellers and proposes to use the power of eminent domain to acquire the remainder of the property from unwilling owners in exchange for just compensation. The question presented is whether the city's proposed disposition of this property qualifies as a "public use" within the meaning of the Takings Clause of the Fifth Amendment to the Constitution.

I

The city of New London (hereinafter City) sits at the junction of the Thames River and the Long Island Sound in southeastern Connecticut. Decades of economic decline led a state agency in 1990 to designate the City a "distressed municipality." In 1996, the Federal Government closed the Naval Undersea Warfare Center, which had been located in the Fort Trumbull area of the City and had employed over 1,500 people. In 1998, the City's unemployment rate was nearly double that of the State, and its population of just under 24,000 residents was at its lowest since 1920.

These conditions prompted state and local officials to target New London, and particularly its Fort Trumbull area, for economic revitalization. To this end, respondent New London Development Corporation (NLDC), a private nonprofit entity established some years earlier to assist the City in planning economic development, was reactivated. In January 1998, the State authorized a $5.35 million bond issue to support the NLDC's planning activities and a $10 million bond issue toward the creation of a Fort Trumbull State Park. In February, the pharmaceutical company Pfizer Inc. announced that it would build a $300 million research facility on a site immediately adjacent to Fort Trumbull; local planners hoped that Pfizer would draw new business to the area, thereby serving as a catalyst to the area's rejuvenation. After receiving initial approval from the city council, the NLDC continued its planning activities and held a series of neighborhood meetings to educate the public about the process. In May, the city council authorized the NLDC to formally submit its plans to the relevant state agencies for review. Upon obtaining state-level approval, the NLDC finalized an integrated development plan focused on 90 acres of the Fort Trumbull area.

The Fort Trumbull area is situated on a peninsula that juts into the Thames River. The area comprises approximately 115 privately owned properties, as well as the 32 acres of land formerly occupied by the naval facility. The development plan encompasses seven parcels. Parcel 1 is designated for a waterfront conference hotel at the center of a "small urban village" that will include restaurants and shopping. This parcel will also have marinas for both recreational and commercial uses. A pedestrian "riverwalk" will originate here and continue down the coast, connecting the waterfront areas of the development. Parcel 2 will be the site of approximately 80 new residences organized into an urban neighborhood and linked by public walkway to the remainder of the development, including the state park. This parcel also includes space reserved for a new U.S. Coast Guard Museum. Parcel 3, which is located immediately north of the Pfizer facility, will contain at least 90,000 square feet of research and development office space. Parcel 4A is a 2.4-acre site that will be used either to support the adjacent state park, by providing parking or retail services for visitors, or to support the nearby marina. Parcel 4B will include a renovated marina, as well as the final stretch of the riverwalk. Parcels 5, 6, and 7 will provide land for office and retail space, parking, and water-dependent commercial uses.

The NLDC intended the development plan to capitalize on the arrival of the Pfizer facility and the new commerce it was expected to attract. In addition to creating jobs, generating tax revenue, and helping to "build momentum for the revitalization of downtown New London," the plan was also designed to make the City more attractive and to create leisure and recreational opportunities on the waterfront and in the park.

The city council approved the plan in January 2000, and designated the NLDC as its development agent in charge of implementation. The city council also authorized the NLDC to purchase property or to acquire property by exercising eminent domain in the City's name. The NLDC successfully negotiated the purchase of most of the real estate in the 90-acre area, but its negotiations with petitioners failed. As a consequence, in November 2000, the NLDC initiated the condemnation proceedings that gave rise to this case.

II

Petitioner Susette Kelo has lived in the Fort Trumbull area since 1997. She has made extensive improvements to her house, which she prizes for its water view. Petitioner Wilhelmina Dery was born in her Fort Trumbull house in 1918 and has lived there her entire life. Her husband Chad (also a petitioner) has lived in the house since they married some 60 years ago. In all, the nine petitioners own 15 properties in Fort Trumbull—4 in parcel 3 of the development plan and 11 in parcel 4A. Ten of the parcels are occupied by the owner or a family member; the other five are held as investment properties. There is no allegation that any of these properties is blighted or otherwise in poor condition; rather, they were condemned only because they happen to be located in the development area.

In December 2000, petitioners brought this action in the New London Superior Court. They claimed, among other things, that the taking of their properties would violate the "public use" restriction in the Fifth Amendment. After a 7-day bench trial, the Superior Court granted a permanent restraining order prohibiting the taking of the properties located in parcel 4A (park or marina support).

After the Superior Court ruled, both sides took appeals to the Supreme Court of Connecticut. That court held, over a dissent, that all of the City's proposed takings were valid. It began by upholding the lower court's determination that the takings were authorized by chapter 132, the State's municipal development statute. That statute expresses a legislative determination that the taking of land, even developed land, as part of an economic development project is a "public use" and in the "public interest." Next, relying on cases such as *Hawaii Housing Authority v. Midkiff*, and *Berman v. Parker*, the court held that such economic development qualified as a valid public use under both the Federal and State Constitutions.

Finally, adhering to its precedents, the court went on to determine, first, whether the takings of the particular properties at issue were "reasonably necessary" to achieving the City's intended public use, and, second, whether the takings were for "reasonably foreseeable needs," The court upheld the trial court's factual findings as to parcel 3, but reversed the trial court as to parcel 4A, agreeing with the City that the intended use of this land was sufficiently definite and had been given "reasonable attention" during the planning process.

We granted certiorari to determine whether a city's decision to take property for the purpose of economic development satisfies the "public use" requirement of the Fifth Amendment.

III

Two polar propositions are perfectly clear. On the one hand, it has long been accepted that the sovereign may not take the property of *A* for the sole purpose of transferring it to another private party *B*, even though *A* is paid just compensation. On the other hand, it is equally clear that a State may transfer property from one private party to another if future "use by the public" is the purpose of the taking; the condemnation of land for a railroad with common-carrier duties is a familiar example. Neither of these propositions, however, determines the disposition of this case.

As for the first proposition, the City would no doubt be forbidden from taking petitioners' land for the purpose of conferring a private benefit on a particular private party. Nor would the City be allowed to take property under the mere pretext of a public purpose, when its actual purpose was to bestow a private benefit. The takings before us, however, would be executed pursuant to a "carefully considered" development plan. The trial judge and all the members of the Supreme Court of Connecticut agreed that there was no evidence of an illegitimate purpose in this case. Therefore, as was true of the statute challenged in *Midkiff*, the City's development plan was not adopted "to benefit a particular class of identifiable individuals."

On the other hand, this is not a case in which the City is planning to open the condemned land—at least not in its entirety—to use by the general public. Nor will the private lessees of the land in any sense be required to operate like common carriers, making their services available to all comers. But although such a projected use would be sufficient to satisfy the public use requirement, this "Court long ago rejected any literal requirement that condemned property be put into use for the general public." Indeed, while many state courts in the mid-19th century endorsed "use by the public" as the proper definition of public use, that narrow view steadily eroded over time. Not only was the "use by the public" test difficult to administer (*e.g.,* what proportion of the public need have access to the property? at what price?), but it proved to be impractical given the diverse and always evolving needs of society. Accordingly, when this Court began applying the Fifth Amendment to the States at the close of the 19th century, it embraced the broader and more natural interpretation of public use as "public purpose."

* * *

The disposition of this case therefore turns on the question whether the City's development plan serves a "public purpose." Without exception, our cases have defined that concept broadly, reflecting our longstanding policy of deference to legislative judgments in this field.

In *Berman v. Parker*, this Court upheld a redevelopment plan targeting a blighted area of Washington, D.C., in which most of the housing for the area's 5,000 inhabitants was beyond repair. Under the plan, the area would be condemned and part of it utilized for the construction of streets, schools, and other public facilities. The remainder of the land would be leased or sold to private parties for the purpose of redevelopment, including the construction of low-cost housing.

The owner of a department store located in the area challenged the condemnation, pointing out that his store was not itself blighted and arguing that the creation of a "better balanced, more attractive community" was not a valid public use. Writing for a unanimous Court, Justice Douglas refused to evaluate this claim in isolation, deferring instead to the legislative and agency judgment that the area "must be planned as a whole" for the plan to be successful. The Court explained that "community redevelopment programs need not, by force of the Constitution, be on a piecemeal basis— lot by lot, building by building." The public use underlying the taking was unequivocally affirmed.

* * *

In *Hawaii Housing Authority v. Midkiff*, the Court considered a Hawaii statute whereby fee title was taken from lessors and transferred to lessees (for just compensation) in order to reduce the concentration of land ownership. We unanimously upheld the statute and rejected the Ninth Circuit's view that it was "a naked attempt on the part of the state of Hawaii to take the property of A and transfer it to B solely for B's private use and benefit."

* * *

Viewed as a whole, our jurisprudence has recognized that the needs of society have varied between different parts of the Nation, just as they have evolved over time in response to changed circumstances. Our earliest cases in particular embodied a strong theme of federalism, emphasizing the "great respect" that we owe to state legislatures and state courts in discerning local public needs. For more than a century, our public use jurisprudence has wisely eschewed rigid formulas and intrusive scrutiny in favor of affording legislatures broad latitude in determining what public needs justify the use of the takings power.

IV

Those who govern the City were not confronted with the need to remove blight in the Fort Trumbull area, but their determination that the area was sufficiently distressed to justify a program of economic rejuvenation is entitled to our deference. The City has carefully formulated an economic development plan that it believes will provide appreciable benefits to the community, including—but by no means limited to—new jobs and increased tax revenue. As with other exercises in urban planning and development, the City is endeavoring to coordinate a variety of commercial, residential, and recreational uses of land, with the hope that they will form a whole greater than the sum of its parts. To effectuate this plan, the City has invoked a state statute that specifically authorizes the use of eminent domain to promote economic development. Given the comprehensive character of the plan, the thorough deliberation that preceded its adoption, and the limited scope of our review, it is appropriate for us, as it was in *Berman*, to resolve the challenges of the individual owners, not on a piecemeal basis, but rather in light of the entire plan. Because that plan unquestionably serves a public purpose, the takings challenged here satisfy the public use requirement of the Fifth Amendment.

* * *

Just as we decline to second-guess the City's considered judgments about the efficacy of its development plan, we also decline to second-guess the City's determinations as to what lands it needs to acquire in order to effectuate the project. "It is not for the courts to oversee the choice of the boundary line nor to sit in review on the size of a particular project area. Once the question of the public purpose has been decided, the amount and character of land to be taken for the project and the need for a particular tract to complete the integrated plan rests in the discretion of the legislative branch."

In affirming the City's authority to take petitioners' properties, we do not minimize the hardship that condemnations may entail, notwithstanding the payment of just compensation. We emphasize that nothing in our opinion precludes any State from placing further restrictions on its exercise of the takings power. Indeed, many States already impose "public use" requirements that are stricter than the federal baseline. Some of these requirements have been established as a matter of state constitutional law, while others are expressed in state eminent domain statutes that carefully limit the grounds upon which takings may be exercised. As the submissions of the parties and their *amici* make clear, the necessity and wisdom of using eminent domain to promote economic development are certainly matters of legitimate public debate. This Court's authority, however, extends only to determining whether the City's proposed condemnations are for a "public use" within the meaning of the Fifth Amendment to the Federal Constitution. Because over a century of our case law interpreting that provision dictates an affirmative answer to that question, we may not grant petitioners the relief that they seek.

The judgment of the Supreme Court of Connecticut is affirmed.

It is so ordered.

Taking

LUCAS v. SOUTH CAROLINA COASTAL COUNCIL
505 U.S. 1003, 112 S. Ct. 2886, 120 L.Ed.2d 798 (1992)

Justice SCALIA delivered the opinion of the Court.

In 1986, petitioner David H. Lucas paid $975,000 for two residential lots on the Isle of Palms in Chadton County, South Carolina, on which he intended to build single-family homes. In 1988, however, the South Carolina Legislature enacted the Beachfront Management Act, which had the direct effect of barring petitioner from erecting any permanent habitable structures on his two parcels. A state trial court found that this prohibition rendered Lucas's parcels "valueless." [The South Carolina Supreme Court reversed.] This case requires us to decide whether the Act's dramatic effect on the economic value of Lucas's lots accomplished a taking of private property under the Fifth and Fourteenth Amendments requiring the payment of "just compensation."

* * *

Prior to Justice Holmes' exposition in *Pennsylvania Coal Co. v. Mahon*, 260 U.S. 393 (1922), it was generally thought that the Takings Clause reached only a "direct appropriation" of property, or the functional equivalent of a "practical ouster of [the owner's] possession." *Transportation Co. v. Chicago*, 99 U.S. 635 (1879). Justice Holmes recognized in *Mahon*, however, that if the protection against physical appropriations of private property was to be meaningfully enforced, the government's power to redefine the range of interests included in the ownership of property was necessarily constrained by constitutional limits. If, instead, the uses of private property were subject to unbridled, uncompensated qualification under the police power, "the natural tendency of human nature [would be] to extend the qualification more and more until at last private property disappear[ed]." These considerations gave birth in that case to the oft-cited maxim that, "while property may be regulated to a certain extent, if regulation goes too far it will be recognized as a taking."

Nevertheless, our decision in *Mahon* offered little insight into when, and under what circumstances, a given regulation would be seen as going "too far" for purposes of the Fifth Amendment. In 70-odd years of succeeding "regulatory takings" jurisprudence, we have generally eschewed any "set formula" for determining how far is too far, preferring to "engag[e] in … essentially ad hoc, factual inquiries," *Penn Central Transportation Co. v. New York City*, 438 U.S. 104, 124 (1978). We have, however, described at least two discrete categories of regulatory action as compensable without case-specific inquiry into the public interest advanced in support of the restraint. The first encompasses regulations that compel the property owner to suffer a physical "invasion" of his property. In general (at least with regard to permanent invasions), no matter how minute the intrusion, and no matter how weighty the public purpose behind it, we have required compensation. For example, in *Loretto v. Teleprompter Manhattan CATV Corp.*, 458 U.S. 419 (1982), we determined that New York's law requiring landlords to allow television cable companies to emplace cable facilities in their apartment buildings constituted a taking, even though the facilities occupied at most only 1½ cubic feet of the landlords' property.

The second situation in which we have found categorical treatment appropriate is where regulation denies all economically beneficial or productive use of land. As we have said on numerous occasions, the Fifth Amendment is violated when land-use regulation "does not substantially advance legitimate state interests or *denies an owner economically viable use of his land.*"

We have never set forth the justification for this rule. Perhaps it is simply, as Justice Brennan suggested, that total deprivation of beneficial use is, from the landowner's point of view, the equivalent of a physical appropriation. * * *

Where "permanent physical occupation" of land is concerned, we have refused to allow the government to decree it anew (without compensation), no matter how weighty the asserted "public interests" involved, *Loretto v. Teleprompter Manhattan CATV Corp.*—though we assuredly would permit the government to assert a permanent easement that was a preexisting limitation upon the land owner's title. We believe similar treatment must be accorded confiscatory regulations, i.e., regulations that prohibit all economically beneficial use of land: Any limitation so severe cannot be newly legislated or decreed (without compensation), but must inhere in the title itself, in the restrictions that background principles of the State's law of property and nuisance already place upon land ownership. A law or decree with such an effect must, in other words, do no more than duplicate the result that could have been achieved in the courts—by adjacent landowners (or other uniquely affected persons) under the State's law of private nuisance, or by the State under its complementary power to abate nuisances that affect the public generally, or otherwise.

On this analysis, the owner of a lake bed, for example, would not be entitled to compensation when he is denied the requisite permit to engage in a landfilling operation that would have the effect of flooding others' land. Nor the corporate owner of a nuclear generating plant, when it is directed to remove all improvements from its land upon discovery that the plant sits astride an earthquake fault. Such regulatory action may well have the effect of eliminating the land's only economically productive use, but it does not proscribe a productive use that was previously permissible under relevant property and nuisance principles. The use of these properties for what are now expressly prohibited purposes was always unlawful, and (subject to other constitutional limitations) it was open to the State at any point to make the implication of those background principles of nuisance and property law explicit. In light of our traditional resort to "existing rules or understandings that stem from

an independent source such as state law" to define the range of interests that qualify for protection as "property" under the Fifth (and Fourteenth) amendments, this recognition that the Takings Clause does not require compensation when an owner is barred from putting land to a use that is proscribed by those "existing rules or understandings" is surely unexceptional.

* * *

It seems unlikely that common-law principles would have prevented the erection of any habitable or productive improvements on petitioner's land; they rarely support prohibition of the "essential use" of land. The question, however, is one of state law to be dealt with on remand. * * *

The judgment is reversed and the cause remanded for proceedings not inconsistent with this opinion.

[Author's Note: The Supreme Court of South Carolina, in *Lucas v. South Carolina Coastal Council*, 424 S.E.2d 484 (1992), responded to the Supreme Court's opinion by ruling that there was no basis under the common law to preclude Lucas from building on his lot, ruled that Lucas was entitled to damages for the temporary taking, and noted Lucas's right to apply for a special permit. According to G. Lefcoe, *Real Estate Transactions* 1042 (2nd ed. 1997), "the state eventually compensated Lucas nearly $1,000,000 and took title to the two lots. The owners of the houses adjacent to the lots sought to purchase them as permanent open space, but the state turned down their offer and sold instead to the highest bidder for development."]

Zoning Changes and Non-Conforming Uses
CITY OF PLATTE v. OVERWEG
738 N.W.2d 911 (Sup. Ct. So. Dak. 2007)

ERICKSON, CIRCUIT JUDGE. Overweg is a resident of Platte, South Dakota. Jerry Overweg was employed at the local Ford dealership and garage on a full-time basis. In 1994, he obtained a sales tax license and began moonlighting doing minor starter and alternator repairs from his garage on property not subject to this action.

In 1997, the City began requiring residents to secure a building permit before engaging in any construction activity. Prior to 1997, the City had a zoning ordinance. This zoning ordinance was neither valid nor enforceable because it was enacted without a comprehensive plan being in place. On July 7, 1997, the City adopted a comprehensive plan. Pursuant to this plan, the City enacted a zoning ordinance on November 1, 1999. The zoning ordinance permits certain non-conforming uses that were in effect on the date the zoning ordinance was enacted; however, the non-conforming uses were not to be enlarged upon, expanded or extended.

On June 23, 1997, Jerry Overweg received a building permit for a 36' x 50' x 14' metal garage on the property subject

to this action. Overweg told the City Council that the permit was for residential purposes. He then constructed the metal garage and, later, their home.

The location of the Overweg home and the metal garage are in an R-1 District according to the 1999 zoning ordinance. The R-1 District is for residential use only. The R-1 District does not permit any structure to be used for commercial garages or automobile repair shops.

Prior to July 31, 2001, Jerry Overweg filed sales and use tax reports with the South Dakota Department of Revenue every six months for work he did out of his prior garage and his new metal garage. During 1998 through 1999 the gross revenues from Overweg's repair business were less than $800. In 2000, the sales tax reports show an increase in gross revenues.

On or about April 1, 2001, Overweg terminated his employment with the local Ford garage. He then engaged in the automotive and repair business full-time under the name of Overweg Glass and Auto Repair. The business was located in his metal garage.

Overweg agrees that the business violates the current zoning ordinance; however, Overweg contends that the business is grandfathered in under the non-conforming use provisions of the ordinance.

The circuit court held that Overweg's prior use of the property for automobile repair was sporadic, limited and occasional. It further held that the use of the property as an automotive repair business cannot be grandfathered in under the City's current zoning ordinance because "the use from and after 2001 to the present is a different use and a significant expansion of the prior use, and not merely an intensification of a prior use." The circuit court also found that the current use as a glass repair and automotive repair business is illegal and in violation of the current zoning ordinance.

* * *

Issues

Whether Overweg's use of the property prior to the enactment of the zoning ordinance was sufficient to establish it as a non-conforming use.

Whether Overweg's use of the property after the City enacted its zoning ordinance constituted either a different, enlarged, and/or expanded use of their property.

Whether Overweg's current use of the property is a violation of the City's Zoning Ordinance.

Decision Issue

Whether Overweg's use of the property prior to the enactment of the zoning ordinance was sufficient to establish it as a non-conforming use.

In *Brown County v. Meidinger*, 271 N.W.2d 15, 18 (S.D. 1978) this Court addressed the issue of the grandfathering of non-conforming uses. This Court found that the appellant has the burden of proving that any prior non-conforming use was, in fact, used for such non-conforming use and was not "a very minimal and sporadic use, incapable of sufficiently exact determination to accord it any grandfather rights." *Id.* Further, this Court found that an ordinance "is to be, and should be, strictly construed and any provisions limiting nonconforming uses should be liberally construed." *Id.*

Overweg's moonlighting business was originally started at a previous residence as a part-time business doing minor starter and alternator repairs. In 1997 Overweg applied for and received a building permit for a metal garage for residential purposes on the current property. Initially, the metal garage was used for storage of vehicles, recreational equipment and building supplies while the Overweg's new home was constructed. The zoning ordinance went into effect November 1, 1999. On or about April 1, 2001, Overweg terminated his primary employment at the Ford garage and began operating Overweg Glass and Auto Repair from his new home and the metal storage garage.

Based on *Meidinger, supra,* the trial court was not clearly erroneous when it concluded that prior to the enactment of the zoning ordinance Overweg's use of the metal garage for a repair business was minimal and sporadic. At the time Overweg started using the metal garage to conduct his glass and auto repair business he was employed full time for the Ford Garage. The family moved to the new home near the metal garage in January 1999. During the first six months of 1999 Overweg had $114 in income from the repairs being done in the metal garage. During the second six months of 1999 that amount increased to $163.85. In late 2000 or early 2001 Overweg quit moonlighting in vehicle repair at the request of his employer for at least two months. During the first part of 2001 Overweg did very little repair work while his new residence was being constructed at this site. It was not until May 2001, well after the November 1, 1999 enactment date of the ordinance, that Overweg quit his job with Ford and began working full-time at the metal garage repairing vehicles.

Overweg has the burden "to clearly establish the prior use to avail himself of the 'grandfather rights.'" *Meidinger,* 271 N.W.2d at 18. This Overweg failed to do. Prior to enactment of the zoning ordinance, the use of this metal garage for glass and auto repair was very minimal and sporadic and, incapable of sufficiently exact determination to accord it any grandfather rights.

As a result of this decision, we need not address the two remaining issues.

Exclusionary Zoning
CITY OF EDMONDS v. OXFORD HOUSE, INC.
514 U.S. 725, 115 S.Ct. 1776 (1994)

GINSBURG, J. The Fair Housing Act (FHA or Act) prohibits discrimination in housing against, *inter alios,* persons with handicaps. Section 807(b)(1) of the Act entirely exempts from the FHA's compass "any reasonable local, State, or Federal restrictions regarding the maximum number of occupants permitted to occupy a dwelling." This case presents the question whether a provision in petitioner City of Edmonds' zoning code qualifies for §3607(b)(1)'s complete exemption from FHA scrutiny. The provision, governing areas zoned for single-family dwelling units, defines "family" as "persons [without regard to number] related by genetics, adoption, or marriage, or a group of five or fewer [unrelated] persons."

The defining provision at issue describes who may compose a family unit; it does not prescribe "*the* maximum number of occupants" a dwelling unit may house. We hold that §3607(b)(1) does not exempt prescriptions of the family-defining kind, *i.e.*, provisions designed to foster the family character of a neighborhood. Instead, §3607(b)(1)'s absolute exemption removes from the FHA's scope only total occupancy limits, *i.e.*, numerical ceilings that serve to prevent overcrowding in living quarters.

I

In the summer of 1990, respondent Oxford House opened a group home in the City of Edmonds, Washington (City), for 10 to 12 adults recovering from alcoholism and drug addiction. The group home, called Oxford House-Edmonds, is located in a neighborhood zoned for single-family residences. Upon learning that Oxford House had leased and was operating a home in Edmonds, the City issued criminal citations to the owner and a resident of the house. The citations charged violation of the zoning code rule that defines who may live in single-family dwelling units. The occupants of such units must compose a "family," and family, under the City's defining rule, "means an individual or two or more persons related by genetics, adoption, or marriage, or a group of five or fewer persons who are not related by genetics, adoption, or marriage."

Oxford House asserted reliance on the Fair Housing Act, which declares it unlawful "[t]o discriminate in the sale or rental, or to otherwise make unavailable or deny, a dwelling to any buyer or renter because of a handicap of … that buyer or renter." The parties have stipulated, for purposes of this litigation, that the residents of Oxford House-Edmonds "are recovering alcoholics and drug addicts and are handicapped persons within the meaning" of the Act.

Discrimination covered by the FHA includes "a refusal to make reasonable accommodations in rules, policies, practices, or services, when such accommodations may be necessary to afford [handicapped] person[s] equal opportunity to use and enjoy a dwelling." Oxford House asked Edmonds to make a "reasonable accommodation" by allowing it to remain in the single-family dwelling it had leased. Group homes for recovering substance abusers, Oxford urged, need 8 to 12 residents to be financially and therapeutically viable. Edmonds declined to permit Oxford House to stay in a single-family residential zone, but passed an ordinance listing group homes as permitted uses in multifamily and general commercial zones.

Edmonds sued Oxford House in the United States District Court for the Western District of Washington, seeking a declaration that the FHA does not constrain the City's zoning code family definition rule. Oxford House counterclaimed under the FHA, charging the City with failure to make a "reasonable accommodation" permitting maintenance of the group home in a single-family zone. The United States filed a separate action on the same FHA "reasonable accommodation" ground, and the two cases were consolidated. Edmonds

suspended its criminal enforcement actions pending resolution of the federal litigation.

* * *

II

The sole question before the Court is whether Edmonds' family composition rule qualifies as a "restrictio[n] regarding the maximum number of occupants permitted to occupy a dwelling" within the meaning of the FHA's absolute exemption. In answering this question, we are mindful of the Act's stated policy "to provide, within constitutional limitations, for fair housing throughout the United States." We also note precedent recognizing the FHA's "broad and inclusive" compass, and therefore according a "generous construction" to the Act's complaint-filing provision. Accordingly, we regard this case as an instance in which an exception to "a general statement of policy" is sensibly read "narrowly in order to preserve the primary operation of the [policy]."

A

Congress enacted §3607(b)(1) against the backdrop of an evident distinction between municipal land-use restrictions and maximum occupancy restrictions.

Land-use restrictions designate "districts in which only compatible uses are allowed and incompatible uses are excluded." These restrictions typically categorize uses as single-family residential, multiple-family residential, commercial, or industrial.

Land use restrictions aim to prevent problems caused by the "pig in the parlor instead of the barnyard." In particular, reserving land for single-family residences preserves the character of neighborhoods, securing "zones where family values, youth values, and the blessings of quiet seclusion and clean air make the area a sanctuary for people." To limit land use to single-family residences, a municipality must define the term "family"; thus family composition rules are an essential component of single-family residential use restrictions.

Section 3607(b)(1)'s language—"restrictions regarding the maximum number of occupants permitted to occupy a dwelling"—surely encompasses maximum occupancy restrictions. But the formulation does not fit family composition rules typically tied to land-use restrictions. In sum, rules that cap the total number of occupants in order to prevent overcrowding of a dwelling "plainly and unmistakably," fall within §3607(b)(1)'s absolute exemption from the FHA's governance; rules designed to preserve the family character of a neighborhood, fastening on the composition of households rather than on the total number of occupants living quarters can contain, do not.

B

Turning specifically to the City's Community Development Code, we note that the provisions Edmonds invoked against Oxford House, ECDC §§16.20.010 and 21.30.010, are classic examples of a use restriction and complementing family composition rule. These provisions do not cap the number of people who may live in a dwelling. In plain terms, they direct that dwellings be used only to house families.

A separate provision caps the number of occupants a dwelling may house, based on floor area:

"Floor Area. Every dwelling unit shall have at least one room which shall have not less than 120 square feet of floor area. Other habitable rooms, except kitchens, shall have an area of not less than 70 square feet. Where more than two persons occupy a room used for sleeping purposes, the required floor area shall be increased at the rate of 50 square feet for each occupant in excess of two."

This space and occupancy standard is a prototypical maximum occupancy restriction.

Edmonds nevertheless argues that its family composition rule, ECDC §21.30.010, falls within §3607(b)(1), the FHA exemption for maximum occupancy restrictions, because the rule caps at five the number of unrelated persons allowed to occupy a single-family dwelling. But Edmonds' family composition rule surely does not answer the question: "What is the maximum number of occupants permitted to occupy a house?" So long as they are related "by genetics, adoption, or marriage," any number of people can live in a house. Ten siblings, their parents and grandparents, for example, could dwell in a house in Edmonds' single-family residential zone without offending Edmonds' family composition rule.

Family living, not living space per occupant, is what ECDC §21.30.010 describes. Defining family primarily by biological and legal relationships, the provision also accommodates another group association: Five or fewer unrelated people are allowed to live together as though they were family. This accommodation is the peg on which Edmonds rests its plea for §3607(b)(1) exemption. Had the City defined a family solely by biological and legal links, §3607(b)(1) would not have been the ground on which Edmonds staked its case. It is curious reasoning indeed that converts a family values preserver into a maximum occupancy restriction once a town adds to a related persons prescription "and also two unrelated persons."

* * *

The parties have presented, and we have decided, only a threshold question: Edmonds' zoning code provision describing who may compose a "family" is not a maximum occupancy restriction exempt from the FHA under §3607(b)(1). It remains for the lower courts to decide whether Edmonds' actions against Oxford House violate the FHA's prohibitions against discrimination set out in §§3604(f)(1)(A) and (f)(3)(B). For the reasons stated, the judgment of the United States Court of Appeals for the Ninth Circuit is

Affirmed.

Liability of Condominium Directors
FRANCES T. v. VILLAGE GREEN OWNERS ASSOCIATION
42 Cal.3d 490, 229 Cal.Rptr. 456, 723 P.2d 573 (1986)

BROUSSARD, Justice. The question presented is whether a condominium owners association and the individual members of its board of directors may be held liable for injuries to a unit owner caused by third-party criminal conduct. Plaintiff Frances T., brought suit against the Village Green Owners Association (the Association) and individual members of its board of directors for injuries sustained when she was attacked in her condominium unit, a part of the Village Green Condominium Project (Project). * * * [The trial court dismissed plaintiff's complaint, and plaintiff appealed.]

On the night of October 8, 1980, an unidentified person entered plaintiff's condominium unit under cover of darkness and molested, raped and robbed her. At the time of the incident, plaintiff's unit had no exterior lighting. The manner in which her unit came to be without exterior lighting on this particular evening forms the basis of her lawsuit against the defendants.

The Association, of which plaintiff was a member, is a nonprofit corporation composed of owners of individual condominium units. The Association was formed and exists for the purposes set forth in the Project's declaration of covenants, conditions and restrictions (CC&Rs). The board

of directors (board) exercises the powers of the Association and conducts, manages and controls the affairs of the Project and the Association. Among other things the Association, through its board, is authorized to enforce the regulations set forth in the CC&Rs. The Association, through the board, is also responsible for the management of the Project and for the maintenance of the Project's common areas.

At the time of the incident, the Project consisted of 92 buildings, each containing several individual condominium units, situated in grassy golf course and park-like areas known as "courts." Plaintiff's unit faced the largest court. She alleges that "the lighting in [the] park-like area was exceedingly poor, and after sunset, aside from the minuscule park light of plaintiff's, the area was in virtual … darkness. Of all the condominium units in [plaintiff's court] … plaintiff's unit was in the darkest place."

* * *

[After her unit was burglarized and in the midst of what she termed an "exceptional crime wave" in the Project, in] May 1980 plaintiff and other residents of her court had a meeting. As court representative plaintiff transmitted a formal request to the Project's manager with a copy to the board that more lighting be installed in their court as soon as possible.

Plaintiff submitted another memorandum in August 1980 because the board had taken no action on the previous requests. The memorandum stated that none of the lighting requests from plaintiff's court had been responded to. Plaintiff also requested that a copy of the memorandum be placed in the board's correspondence file.

By late August, the board had still taken no action. Plaintiff then installed additional exterior lighting at her unit, believing that this would protect her from crime. In a letter dated August 29, 1980, however, the site manager told plaintiff that she would have to remove the lighting because it violated the CC&Rs. Plaintiff refused to comply with this request. After appearing at a board meeting, where she requested permission to maintain her lighting until the board improved the general lighting that she believed to be a hazard, she received a communication from the board stating in part: "The Board has indicated their appreciation for your appearance on October 1, and for the information you presented to them. After deliberation, however, the Board resolved as follows:

You are requested to remove the exterior lighting you added to your front door and in your patio and to restore the Association Property to its original condition on or before October 6. If this is not done on or before that date, the Association will have the work done and bill you for the costs incurred."

The site manager subsequently instructed plaintiff that pending their removal, she could not use the additional exterior lighting. The security lights had been installed using the same circuitry used for the original exterior lighting and were operated by the same switches. In order not to use her additional lighting, the plaintiff was required to forego the use of all of her exterior lights. In spite of this, however, plaintiff complied with the board's order and cut off the electric power on the circuitry controlling the exterior lighting during the daylight hours of October 8, 1980. As a result, her unit was in total darkness on October 8, 1980, the night she was raped and robbed.

* * *

The fundamental issue here is whether petitioners, the condominium Association and its individual directors, owed plaintiff the same duty of care as would a landlord in the traditional landlord-tenant relationship. We conclude that plaintiff has pleaded facts sufficient to state a cause of action for negligence against both the Association and the individual directors.

* * *

The Association contends that under its own CC&Rs, it cannot permit residents to improve the security of the common areas without prior written permission, nor can it substantially increase its limited budget for common-area improvements without the approval of a majority of the members.

But regardless of these self-imposed constraints, the Association is, for all practical purposes, the Project's "landlord." And traditional tort principles impose on landlords, no less than on homeowner associations that function as a landlord in maintaining the common areas of a large condominium complex, a duty to exercise due care for the residents' safety in those areas under their control.

* * *

Under the facts as alleged by plaintiff, the [individual] directors named as defendants had specific knowledge of a hazardous condition threatening physical injury to the residents, yet they failed to take any action to avoid the harm; moreover, the action they did take may have exacerbated the risk by causing plaintiff's unit to be without any lighting on the night she was attacked.

* * *

In this case plaintiff's amended complaint alleges that each of the directors participated in the tortious activity. Under our analysis, this allegation is sufficient to withstand a demurrer. However, since only "a director who actually votes for the commission of a tort is personally liable, even though the wrongful act is performed in the name of the corporation" (*Tillman v. Wheaton-Haven Recreation Ass'n, Inc.*, 517 F.2d 1141, 1144), plaintiff will have to prove that each director acted negligently as an individual. Of course, the individual directors may then present evidence showing they opposed or did not participate in the alleged tortious conduct.

* * *

We conclude that the trial court erred in sustaining the Association's and directors' demurrer to the negligence cause of action. * * * The judgment is therefore reversed and remanded to the trial court for further proceedings consistent with this opinion.

KEY TERMS

amortization provision, 547
area of critical state concern, 556
bylaws, 561
cluster zoning, 550
common law dedication, 542
condemnation, 535

condominium, 560
cooperative, 564
covenant running with the land, 526
cumulative zoning, 545
dedication, 542
development of regional impact, 556

PROBLEMS

1. Inez lived in an East Cleveland home with her son, Dale; his son Dale, Jr.; and another grandson, John. The two boys were first cousins: John, who was 10 years old, came to live with his grandmother after his mother's death. An East Cleveland housing ordinance limited the occupancy of a dwelling unit to members of a single family. Inez was informed that John was an "illegal occupant" and that he would have to leave the home. Inez refused to comply with the ordinance, and the city filed a criminal charge against her. Is the ordinance constitutional? Why or why not?

2. Mayme owned six lots in Block #2 of an addition to the city of Harrodsburg. All of the lots contained a covenant restricting the use of the land to residential purposes. Mayme sold the six lots to various purchasers. Each deed contained the restrictive covenant and a statement that it ran with the land. Thereafter, Kentucky Highway No. 35 was rerouted around the city of Harrodsburg and small portions of the lots were obtained by condemnation proceedings. As a result of the rerouting of the highway, traffic in the area of the lots increased greatly; approximately 500 motor vehicles passed the lots on the highway each hour. The Longs purchased one of the six lots with the intention of operating it as a used-car lot. They thought that the lot was best suited for business purposes after the rerouting of the highway. All of the other lots had been developed for residential purposes and contained residential dwellings. However, a number of commercial enterprises had been built near Block #2. Is the restrictive covenant enforceable against the Longs? Why or why not?

3. To erect a power plant, the Union Electric Co. sought to acquire by condemnation land owned by Saale. The land was zoned for agricultural uses, with authorization also for residential purposes. Saale argues that the value of the land should be determined by the land's potential for industrial use, which would result in a higher valuation. He reasons that since the land will be used for a power plant—an industrial use—it should have the value of industrial property. Is Saale correct? Why or why not?

4. Marie Ida owns land in Mount Ayr, Iowa. Her land is not located in a slum area. The Low-Rent Housing Agency of Mount Ayr, through its power of eminent domain, claims the land of Marie Ida for low-income housing purposes. Marie Ida objects to the condemnation, arguing that the use of her land for low-income housing is not a public use and that only slum areas can be taken. Is she correct? Why or why not?

5. State University has been given the right to acquire real estate through condemnation proceedings. State decides to acquire 10-and-one-half acres of Joe's land, which it wants to use to build an 18-hole golf course. Joe objects, claiming that the university has not proven the necessity of taking his land. Is Joe correct? Why or why not?

6. The City of Lansing commenced a condemnation action to take an easement through an apartment complex. The easement was to be used by Continental Cablevision, a private cable television company, to provide cable television service to tenants living in the apartments. Should the condemnation be allowed? Why or why not?

7. Venerose owned a parcel of land in the village of Larchmont. He entered into a lease with Burger King, which intended to construct and operate a restaurant on the premises in which it would offer its patrons a limited

menu, fast service, and minimal prices. Burger King applied for a building permit to construct the proposed restaurant. At the time of the application, the zoning ordinance permitted all types of restaurants. However, the village board amended the zoning ordinance after the Burger King application to outlaw all fast-food restaurants. The Burger King building permit was denied under the amended zoning ordinance, and Burger King brought suit to obtain a building permit. Will Burger King win? Why or why not?

8. The Castlewood Terrace subdivision was subdivided and platted in 1896. The deeds to the Castlewood Terrace lots contained covenants restricting the use of the lots to single-family residences. Paschen acquired several lots in Castlewood Terrace with full knowledge of a restriction on the types of residences that could be built in the subdivision. Fifty years later, Castlewood Terrace was surrounded by high-rise multiple-family residences. The value of Paschen's property, when used for single-family residences, is $110,000, yet the value of the same property is roughly $256,000 if used for high-rise multiple-family residences. Paschen brings suit to have the restrictive covenants removed so that a high-rise multiple-family residence can be built on his property. Pashkow, a neighbor, objects to the removal of the restriction. Who should prevail—Paschen or Pashkow? Why?

9. Garramone leased property that extended over two different zoning areas in the village of Lynbrook, Nassau County, New York. One portion of the property was zoned for commercial use, while the other portion was zoned for residential use. Garramone planned to build a roller skating rink on the leased property. To facilitate off-street parking, Garramone sought a variance on the portion of the property zoned for residential use. The village board of appeals granted Garramone a variance on the grounds that a denial would cause him unnecessary hardship. The board noted that if the skating rink was built on only the commercial portion of the leased property, access to the rear portion would be obstructed and patrons would be required to park on the streets, thus causing traffic problems. Adjoining landowners object to the granting of the variance and file suit against the zoning board of appeals. Is the variance legal? Why or why not?

10. The concept of inclusionary zoning has been advocated as a means of creating diversity and a more vibrant streetscape. For example, the mayor of Las Vegas wants zoning ordinances that will create neighborhoods in which "blue and white collar workers and their children mingle."[167] To accomplish this, the mayor would require developers who are planning to build expensive condominiums and housing close to the downtown area to sell a share of their homes at 10 to 20 percent below market prices to qualified buyers. These buyers would include police officers, teachers, nurses, and young professionals. The mayor, who grew up in a diverse neighborhood in Philadelphia, claims that his early life experiences gave him a certain worldview that "contributed to my thirst for knowledge and made me want to be part of a heterogeneous society."

Opponents contend that inclusionary zoning is unnecessary government interference with the free market and that, to create neighborhood diversity, the government should relax its laws and allow, among other things, more land to be available to create a greater supply. Inclusionary zoning proponents contend that even with more land, the wealthy would seize it first and destroy any chances for a diverse neighborhood. Is there a moral duty to supply affordable housing to those at all socioeconomic levels? Is diversity a worthy enough goal to justify government interference with the free market? Do diverse neighborhoods create the greatest good to the greatest number in a community? Explain your answers.

ENDNOTES

1. Comment, *Environmental Land-Use Control: Common Law and Statutory Approaches*, 28 University of Miami Law Review 135 (1973).

2. 26 N.Y.2d 219, 309 N.Y.S.2d 312, 257 N.E.2d 870 (1970).

3. Note, *Private Remedies for Water Pollution*, 70 Columbia Law Review 734 (1970).

4. 83 Wis. 583, 53 N.W. 912 (1892).

5. *Costas v. City of Fond du Lac*, 24 Wis.2d 409, 129 N.W.2d 217 (Wis. 1964).

6. *Martin v. Reynolds Metals Co.*, 221 Or. 86, 342 P.2d 790 (1959).

7. 327 F.3d 400 (5th Cir. 2003).

8. J. Harr, *A Civil Action* (1996).

9. Comment, *Environmental Land-Use Control: Common Law and Statutory Approaches*, 28 University of Miami Law Review 135, 152 (1973). See also F. Powell, *Trespass, Nuisance, and the Evolution of Common Law in Modern Pollution Cases*, 21 Real Estate Law Journal 182 (1992).

10. R. Epstein, *A Conceptual Approach to Zoning: What's Wrong with Euclid*, 5 New York University Environmental Law Journal 277, 291 (1996).

11. R. Boyer et al., *The Law of Property* 320 (4th ed. 1991).

12. 25 Mass. (8 Pick.) 284 (1829).

13. The *Restatement (Third) of Property*, section 3.2, dispensed with the "touch and concern" requirement on the basis that the effect of the "touch and concern" requirement was

"whether the servitude arrangement violates public policy. Servitudes that formerly were held invalid for failure to touch or concern land remain invalid … if they impose unreasonable restraints on alienation, undue restraints on trade, or if they are unconscionable or lack a rational justification." *Restatement (Third) of Property*, Servitudes section 3.2 comment a (T.D. No. 2, 1991).

14. R. Boyer et al., *The Law of Property* 321 (4th ed. 1991).

15. R. Cunningham et al., *The Law of Property* 476 (2nd ed. 1993).

16. *The Wiggins Ferry Co. v. The Ohio and Mississippi Rwy. Co.*, 94 Ill. 83 (1879).

17. R. Boyer et al., *The Law of Property* 321 (4th ed. 1991).

18. *Rossini v. Freeman*, 136 Conn. 321, 71 A.2d 98 (1949).

19. 251 Ala. 230, 36 So.2d 483 (1948).

20. 773 P.2d 1046 (Col. 1989) (en banc).

21. 29 Ill.2d 517, 194 N.E.2d 276 (1963).

22. 189 Md. 73, 54 A.2d 331 (1947).

23. Minn.Stat.Ann. §500.20.

24. 31 Colo.App. 40, 500 P.2d 1184 (1972).

25. 167 Mich. 464, 133 N.W. 317 (1911).

26. 334 U.S. 1, 68 S.Ct. 836, 92 L.Ed. 1161 (1948).

27. 346 U.S. 249, 73 S.Ct. 1031, 97 L.Ed. 1586 (1953).

28. 911 P.2d 861 (N.M. Sup.Ct. 1996).

29. 877 S.W.2d 500 (Tex.App. 1994).

30. *Citizens for Covenant Compliance v. Anderson*, 12 Cal. 4th 345, 906 P.2d 1314 (Cal. 1995).

31. *Stone Hill Community Association v. Norple*, 492 N.W.2d 409 (Iowa 1992).

32. Pub. Law 109-243, 120 Stat. 572 (enacted July 24, 2006). See also B. Craig, *Construction and Constitutionality of the Freedom to Display the American Flag Act*, 36 Real Estate Law Journal 7 (Summer 2007).

33. See L. Chadderdon, *No Political Speech Allowed: Common Interest Developments, Homeowners Associations, and Restrictions on Free Speech*, Journal of Land Use and Environmental Law 233 (Spring 2006) which discusses in detail the four exceptions to the state actor requirement and how they may apply to HOAs.

34. For statistics on HOAs see http://www.caionline.org/info/research/Pages/default.aspx (last accessed July 28, 2010).

35. M. Benjamin, *Hi, Neighbor, Want to Get Together? Let's Meet in Court!* U.S. News & World Report 20 (October 30, 2000).

36. 1 N.Y.3d 424, 806 N.E.2d 979 (2004).

37. M. Rosendorf and J. Seidman, *Restrictive Covenants—The Life Cycle of a Shopping Center*, Probate and Property 33 (September–October 1998).

38. 38 F.3d 1003 (8th Cir. 1994).

39. This figure represents a decline of 100 million acres since the seminal study, *One Third of the Nation's Land*, published by the Public Land Law Review Commission in 1970. To access more information on public lands see *Public Land Statistics* (2009) at http://www.blm.gov/public_land_statistics/pls09/Cover.pdf. To see a map of the public domain access http://www.blm.gov/public_land_statistics/pls09/minerals_l48_plss.pdf (last accessed July 30, 2010).

40. See National Park System: http://www.nps.gov/index.htm (last accessed July 30, 2010).

41. See U.S. Forest Service: http://www.fs.fed.us/documents/USFS_An_Overview_0106MJS.pdf (last accessed July 30, 2010).

42. Fish and Wildlife Service: http://www.fws.gov/ (last accessed July 30, 2010).

43. Bureau of Land Management: http://www.blm.gov/wo/st/en.html (last visited July 30, 2010).

44. *Id.* The federal government also frequently leases and sells its real estate to private parties. For example, in fast-growing western states in cities such as Las Vegas and Phoenix, surrounding BLM land is in great demand.

45. D. DeRosa, *Intestate Succession and the Laughing Heir: Who Do We Want to Get the Last Laugh?* 12 Quinnipiac Probate Journal 153 (1997).

46. *Bergen County Sewer Authority v. Borough of Little Ferry*, 5 N.J. 548, 76 A.2d 680 (1950).

47. *Valentine v. Lamont*, 25 N.J.Super. 342, 96 A.2d 417 (1953).

48. *Barnes v. City of New Haven*, 140 Conn. 8, 98 A.2d 523 (1953).

49. *Perellis v. Mayor & City Council of Baltimore*, 190 Md. 86, 57 A.2d 341 (1948).

50. *Berman v. Parker*, 348 U.S. 26 (1954).

51. *Valentine v. Lamont*, 25 N.J.Super. 342, 96 A.2d 417 (1953).

52. *Chapman v. Huntington Housing Auth.*, 121 W.Va. 319, 3 S.E.2d 502 (1939).

53. 467 U.S. 229, 104 S.Ct. 2321, 81 L.Ed.2d 186 (1984).

54. See M. Bixby, *The "Public Use" Requirement After Midkiff*, 24 American Business Law Journal 621 (1986).

55. D. Sander and P. Pattison, *The Aftermath of Kelo*, 34 Real Estate Law Journal 157 (2005); R. Aalberts, *Property Rights Take a Hit After Kelo*, 34 Real Estate Law Journal 133 (2005).

56. L. Blais, *Urban Revitalization in the Post-Kelo Era*, 34 Fordham Urban Land Journal 657 (2007). See also E. Lopez et al., *Pass a Law, Any Law, Fast! State Legislative Responses to the Kelo Backlash*, 5 Review of Law and Economics (2009), available at http://www.bepress.com/rle/vol5/iss1/art5 (last accessed August 2, 2010).

57. Ga. Code Ann. §22-1-1 (4) (2005).

58. *Id.* at §22-1-1 (1)(A)(B).

59. 281 App.Div. 275, 121 N.Y.S.2d 86 (1953).

60. See L. Oswald, *Goodwill and Going-Concern Value: Emerging Factors in the Just Compensation Equation*, 32 Boston College Law Review 283 (1991).

61. *Board of County Commissioners of Santa Fe County v. Slaughter*, 49 N. M. 141, 158 P.2d 859 (1945).

62. R. Wright, *Land Use* 160 (3rd ed. 1994).

63. 260 U.S. 393, 43 S.Ct. 158, 67 L.Ed. 322 (1922).

64. 260 U.S. at 415, 43 S.Ct. at 160.

65. 458 U.S. 419 (1982).

66. 438 U.S. 104, 98 S.Ct. 2646, 57 L.Ed.2d 631 (1978). For discussion of the issues left unresolved by *Penn Central*, see G. Siedel, *Landmarks Preservation After Penn Central*, Real Property, Probate and Trust Journal 340 (1982).

67. 535 U.S. 302, 122 S. Ct. 1465, 152 L.Ed.2d 517 (2002).

68. *Williamson County Reg. Planning Comm'n v. Hamilton Bank*, 473 U. S. 172 (1985).

69. The requirement of ripeness has been soundly criticized by commentators, who observe that it is difficult for the landowner to determine when it has made a sufficient number of use or variance applications to confirm that it will be denied reasonable use. See, e.g., M. Berger, *Regulatory Takings Under the Fifth Amendment: A Constitutional Primer* (1994). Mr. Berger has represented the property owners in a number of the cases cited in this section. Others, however, view such decisions as *Lucas* and *Dolan* as "part of a significant shift away from the deference traditionally accorded land-use

regulators in the past and to presage even further assaults upon government attempts to balance private property rights and the public welfare." M. Wolf, *Fruits of the "Impenetrable Jungle": Navigating the Boundary Between Land-Use Planning and Environmental Law*, 50 Washington University Journal of Urban & Contemporary Law 5, 8 (1996).

70. 520 U.S. 725, 117 S.Ct. 1659, 137 L.Ed.2d 980 (1997).

71. 533 U.S. 606, 121 S.Ct. 2448, 150 L.Ed.2d 592 (2001).

72. *Id.* at 2459.

73. 328 U.S. 256, 66 S.Ct. 1062, 90 L.Ed. 1206 (1946).

74. *First English Evangelical Lutheran Church of Glendale v. County of Los Angeles*, 482 U.S. 304, 107 S.Ct. 2378, 96 L.Ed 250 (1987).

75. *Id.* On remand; however, a California appellate court denied compensation to the church on the grounds that there never had been a taking. 210 Cal.App.3d 1353, 258 Cal.Rptr. 893 (1989). However, the rule enunciated in the case still stands as precedent.

76. 130 S. Ct. 2592 (2010).

77. 121 S.Ct. 2448, 150 L.Ed.2d 592 (2001).

78. *Id.* at. 2462–63.

79. W. Burby, *Real Property* 284 (3rd ed. 1965).

80. H. Tiffany, *Real Property*, §538, 542 (abr. 3rd ed. 1970).

81. *Nickel v. University City*, 239 S.W.2d 519 (Mo.App. 1951).

82. G. Lefcoe, *Real Estate Transactions* 1054–1055 (2d ed. 1997).

83. W. Burby, *Real Property* 284 (3rd ed. 1965).

84. B. Wargo, *County Drops Plan to Boost Impact Fees*, Business Las Vegas 1 (September 7, 2007).

85. 483 U.S. 825, 107 S.Ct. 3141, 97 L.Ed.2d 677 (1987).

86. 512 U.S. 374, 114 S.Ct. 2309, 129 L.Ed.2d 304 (1994).

87. 146 U.S. 387, 13 S.Ct. 110, 36 L.Ed. 1018 (1892).

88. J. Sax, *The Public Trust Doctrine in Natural Resources Law: Effective Judicial Intervention*, 68 Michigan Law Review 471 (1970).

89. *Id.* See also F. Powell, *The Public Trust Doctrine: Implications for Property Owners and the Environment*, 25 Real Estate Law Journal 255 (1997).

90. *Village of Euclid v. Ambler Realty Co.*, 272 U.S. 365, 47 S.Ct. 114, 71 L.Ed. 303 (1926).

91. *Id.*

92. *United Advertising Corp. v. Borough of Metuchen*, 42 N.J. 1, 198 A.2d 447 (1964).

93. *Berman v. Parker*, 348 U.S. 26, 75 S.Ct. 98, 99 L.Ed. 27 (1954).

94. 138 Cal.App.4th 273, 41 Cal.Rptr.3d 420 (2006). See generally F. Powell, *Economic regulation and the Power to Zone*, 38 Real Estate Law Journal 421 (Spring 2010).

95. *Young v. American Mini Theatres, Inc.*, 427 U.S. 50, 96 S.Ct. 2440, 49 L.Ed.2d 310 (1976). See generally T. Triehy, *Zoning Out Adult-Oriented Businesses: An Analysis of the Recent Ninth Circuit Decision in Dream Palace v. County of Maricopa*, 33 Real Estate Law Journal 422 (Spring 2005).

96. 270 F.3d 1156 (7th Cir. 2001).

97. *Brutsche v. City of Kent*, 898 P.2d 319 (Wash.App.Div. 1995).

98. 596 N.Y.S.2d 459 (App.Div. 1993).

99. *City of Los Angeles v. Gage*, 127 Cal.App.2d 442, 274 P.2d 34 (1954).

100. 394 S.W.2d 593 (Ky. 1965).

101. *Beyer v. Mayor of Baltimore*, 182 Md. 444, 34 A.2d 765 (1943).

102. R. Boyer et al., *The Law of Property* 454 (4th ed. 1991).

103. 233 Conn. 198, 658 A.2d 559 (Conn. 1995).

104. *Stokes v. Jacksonville*, 276 So.2d 200 (Fla.App.1973).

105. *Mueller v. C. Hoffmeister Undertaking Co.*, 343 Mo. 430, 121 S.W.2d 775 (1938).

106. 426 U.S. 668, 96 S.Ct. 2358, 49 L.Ed.2d 132 (1976).

107. R. Boyer et al., *The Law of Property* 456–57 (4th ed. 1991).

108. F. Alexander, *The Housing of America's Families: Control, Exclusion and Privilege*, 54 Emory Law Journal 1231 (2005).

109. *Gore's Solar Plans Thwarted by Upscale Neighborhood's Rules*, USA Today (March 3, 2007).

110. 117 F.3d 37 (2nd Cir. 1997).

111. 416 U.S. 1, 94 S.Ct. 1536, 39 L.Ed.2d 797 (1974).

112. *Id.* Courts also have developed two approaches that lie between the "compelling interest" and the "rational basis" tests. Under one approach, adopted by the Court of Appeals in *Belle Terre*, the state must show that the legislation does in fact advance a permissible state objective. The second approach utilizes a "sliding scale" analysis whereby the legislation will be scrutinized more closely when it affects interests of greater constitutional significance. See Note, *Zoning Ordinances Limiting the Number of Unrelated Individuals in a Dwelling Unit*, 88 Harvard Law Review 119 (1974); F. Gibson, *Zoning and the Equal Protection Clause—Village of Belle Terre v. Boraas*, 14 American Business Law Journal 370 (1977); S. White and E. Paster, *Creating Effective Land Use Regulations Through Concurrency*, 43 National Resources Journal 753 (2003).

113. J. Twitchell, *Homeless in Serene Country Estates prompt action from city*, Las Vegas Sun (February 13, 2009) http://www .lasvegassun.com/news/2009/feb/13/henderson-limit-residents -single-family-homes (last accessed on September 12, 2009).

114. 522 F.2d 897 (9th Cir. 1975).

115. 67 N.J. 151, 336 A.2d 713 (1975).

116. 735 A.2d 231 (Conn. 1999).

117. J. Kushner, *Smart Growth: Urban Growth Management and Land-Use Regulation Law in America*, 32 Urban Lawyer 211, 227 (Spring 2000).

118. See *Home Builders Association of Northern California v. Napa*, 90 Cal. App. 4th 188 (2001).

119. 27 Cal.4th 643 (2002).

120. C. Talbert et al., *Recent Developments in Inclusionary Zoning*, 38 Urban Lawyer 701 (2006).

121. *Bruce Katz Discusses a New Vision of New Orleans*, Interview on National Public Radio (September 14, 2005).

122. N. Knox, *Buyers in More Markets Find Housing Out of Reach*, USA Today 1A (June 27, 2006).

123. *Stop Signs for Developers Going Up All Over U.S.*, 76 U.S. News & World Report 40 (1974).

124. J. DeGrove, *State Growth Management Programs: A Brief Overview*, 1 ALI-ABA Land Use Institute 14 (1996).

125. This classification system comes from R. Tager, *Innovations in State Legislation: Land Use Management* 5–7 (1973).

126. The descriptions of direct state regulation systems are paraphrased from J. Low, *State Land Use Control: Why Pending Federal Legislation Will Help*, 25 Hastings Law Journal 1165 (1974).

127. *Id.* at 1175.

128. *Id.*

129. R. Tager, *supra* note 125 at 5.

130. J. Low, *supra* note 126, 1187.

131. *Id.* at 1181–1183. To access information on Florida's Areas of Critical State Concern see http://www.dca.state.fl.us/fdcp/

DCP/acsc/index.cfm (last accessed August 1, 2010). To access information on Florida's Developments of Regional Impact see http://www.dca.state.fl.us/fdcp/DCP/DRIFQD/index.cfm (last accessed August 1, 2010).

132. Mass Gen. Laws Ann. Ch. 40B, §§20–23 (West 1996).

133. R. Tager, *supra* note 125 at 6.

134. J. DeGrove, *Coping with Regional Problems in the Age of the "Devolution Revolution,"* 1 ALI-ABA Land Use Institute 107 (1996).

135. J. Rose, *The Transfer of Development Rights: A Preview of an Evolving Concept,* 3 Real Estate Law Journal 330 (1975).

136. This conclusion is summarized from J. DeGrove, *supra*. at note 124.

137. J. Kushner, *Smart Growth: Urban Growth Management and Land-Use Regulation in America,* 32 Urban Lawyer 211 (2000).

138. S. Greenhut, *Suburban Life Isn't Sinful,* Las Vegas Review-Journal D1 (December 24, 2005). To read more about Smart Growth see http://www.smartgrowth.org (last visited August 1, 2010).

139. R. Gold and A. Campoy, *Oil Industry Braces for Drop in U.S. Thirst for Gasoline,* Wall Street Journal A1, A12 (April 13, 2009).

140. *National Land Use Policy Legislation: An Analysis of Legislative Proposals and State Laws,* Senate Comm. on Interior and Insular Affairs, 93rd Congress, 1st Session, at 99. The descriptions of existing federal programs are paraphrased from this analysis. See also pp. 23–39 for a chronological summary of major enactments, statements, and actions related to land use policy.

141. For more information on the U.S. Economic Development Administration see http://www.eda.gov (last accessed August 1, 2010).

142. R. Holland, *National Growth Policy: Notes on the Federal Role,* 1973 Urban Law Annual 59.

143. R. Aalberts, *The Religious Land Use and Institutionalized Persons Act: Devil or Angel?* 31 Real Estate Law Journal 281 (2003). See also S. Green, *Zoning In and Out Churches: Limits on Municipal Zoning Powers by the Religious Land Use and Institutionalized Persons Act,* 37 Real Estate Law Journal 163 (Fall 2008).

144. *Guru Nank Sikh Society of Yuba City v. County of Sutter,* 456 F.3d 978 (2006).

145. See generally Aalberts, *supra* note 143.

146. See http://www.religiousliberty.tv/tag/ground-zero-mosque (last accessed August 1, 2010).

147. 577 F.3d 578 (5th Cir. 2009).

148. 301 F.3d 390 (6th Cir. 2002).

149. See A. Grezzo, *Condominiums: Their Development and Management* 17 (1972).

150. 92 Cal.App. 4th 1232, 112 Cal.Rptr.2d 593 (2001).

151. Grezzo, *supra* note 149 at 1–3.

152. *Daytona Development Corp. v. Bergquist,* 308 So.2d 548 (Fla. App. 1975).

153. See *Questions About Condominiums* 27–31 (HUD, 1974).

154. *Id.* at 31–33.

155. Miss. Code Annot. §89-9-29 (1972).

156. *Hidden Harbour Estates, Inc. v. Norman,* 309 So.2d 180 (Fla. App. 1975).

157. *Powell on Real Property* §633.36(5)(b) (1969).

158. 647 N.E.2d 75 (Mass.App.Ct. 1995).

159. See http://cooperator.com/articles/557/1/Terminating-Sponsor -Leases/Page1.html (last accessed August 1, 2010).

160. *Loeterman v. Town of Brookline,* 524 F.Supp. 1325 (D.Mass. 1981).

161. These forms of ownership are discussed in detail in M. Burck, *Timesharing: The Pie in the Sky,* Lawyer's Supplement to the Guarantor 1 (July, August 1979).

162. H. Work, *Before You Buy Your Week at That Condo,* U.S. News & World Report 45 (July 19, 1982). See generally El Cameron and S. Maxwell, *Protecting Consumers: The Contractual and Real Estate Issues Involving Timeshares, Quartershares, and Fractional Ownership,* 37 Real Estate Law Journal 278 (Spring 2009).

163. 766 So.2d 382 (Fla.App. 2000).

164. *State Tax Comm. v. Shor,* 43 N.Y.2d 151, 400 N.Y.S.2d 805, 371 N.E.2d 523 (1977).

165. *Oakley v. Longview Owners, Inc.,* 628 N.Y.S.2d 468 (S.Ct. 1995).

166. 421 U.S. 837, 95 S.Ct. 2051, 44 L.Ed.2d 621 (1975).

167. M. Squires, *Inclusionary Zoning Pitched as a Means to Achieve Diversity,* Las Vegas Review-Journal 18 (February 1, 2004).

Environmental Law and Regulation

© MACIEJ NOSKOWSKI/iStockphoto (RF)

LEARNING OBJECTIVES

After studying Chapter 14, you should:

- Learn about environmental legislation

- Be familiar with judicial review of administrative decisions

"We are the only species able to change the natural world, so we must be stewards of the world."

Jane Goodall, Primatologist

"If you've seen one redwood tree, you've seen them all."

Ronald Reagan

Concerns about protecting the environment and the search for remedies for past contamination have a pervasive effect on real estate transactions and on business operations. The common law of nuisance, once the law's primary remedy for environmental contamination, has been supplemented by a complex scheme of federal, state, and local environmental law and regulation. This chapter provides an overview of the environmental laws that have the greatest impact on real estate transactions and ownership.

Prior to the federalizing of environmental laws and policy, discussed next, state and local environmental laws and agencies generally created and enforced environmental policy in their respective jurisdictions while the federal government primarily focused on conservation and preservation of public lands. This highly fragmented approach proved to be ineffective as grave threats to the environment began to emerge.

Many Americans first gained awareness of environmental problems after the 1962 publication of biologist Rachel Carson's bestselling book, *A Silent Spring*. Carson warned about the dangers of commonly used pesticides like DDT and the destruction these chemicals were inflicting on the country's natural environment. Many environmental historians maintain that the sorry state of America's environmental health came to a head in 1969 as a result of two highly visible events. One occurred in Cleveland, Ohio, when sparks from a passing train ignited oil slicks and debris on the Cuyahoga River setting off a raging fire. In the other, 100,000 barrels of oil were released into the Pacific Ocean off the coast of Santa Barbara, California, after a blowout from an offshore rig. The resulting oil slick

National Environment Policy Act (NEPA)

A federal statute that requires federal agencies to prepare environmental impact statements when proposed federal action significantly affects the quality of the human environment.

killed thousands of birds and ruined beaches. The national press closely reported the two events with vivid images of the vast damage to both land and animals. The outcry from the American citizenry helped set the political winds in motion with President Richard Nixon signing the landmark **National Environment Policy Act (NEPA)** on January 1, 1970. Nixon, viewed by many as an unlikely champion of the environment, subsequently signed the Clean Air and Clean Water Acts as well.

Environmental Legislation
National Environmental Policy Act

NEPA directed that U.S. regulations and laws are to be interpreted according to the following national environmental policy:

> *The Congress, recognizing the profound impact of man's activity on the interrelations of all components of the natural environment, particularly the profound influences of population growth, high-density urbanization, industrial expansion, resource exploitation, and new and expanding technological advances and recognizing further the critical importance of restoring and maintaining environmental quality to the overall welfare and development of man, declares that it is the continuing policy of the Federal Government, in cooperation with State and local governments and other concerned public and private organizations, to use all practicable means and measures, including financial and technical assistance, in a manner calculated to foster and promote the general welfare, to create and maintain conditions under which man and nature can exist in productive harmony, and fulfill the social, economic, and other requirements of present and future generations of Americans.... The Congress recognizes that each person should enjoy a healthful environment and that each person has a responsibility to contribute to the preservation and enhancement of the environment.*

NEPA established the Council on Environmental Quality (CEQ), the federal government's "watchdog" of environmental policy, and requires all federal agencies to factor environmental consequences into their decisions.[1] Most importantly, the Act instructs federal agencies to include an **environmental impact statement** (EIS) "in every recommendation or report on proposals for legislation and other major federal actions significantly affecting the quality of the human environment." Neither Congress (when considering legislation) nor the courts (before they issue a decision) are required to prepare an EIS. The statement must cover all of the following:

environmental impact statement

A document that analyzes the environmental impact of a proposed federal action.

1. The environmental impact of the proposed action
2. Any adverse environmental effects that cannot be avoided should the proposal be implemented
3. Alternatives to the proposed action
4. The relationship between local short-term uses of man's environment and the maintenance and enhancement of long-term productivity
5. Any irreversible and irretrievable commitments of resources that would be involved in the proposed action should it be implemented

Most NEPA litigation to date has focused on the procedural issues of whether a statement is necessary and—if a statement has been prepared—whether it is legally adequate, as the next U.S. Supreme Court case explains.

Was the U.S. Forest Service required to prepare an environmental impact statement for nine timber sales in the Sequoia National Forest? In *Sierra Club v. U.S. Forest Service* on page 603, the court considered the Sierra Club's challenge based on the Forest Service's failure to prepare an EIS of the timber sales.

END OF CHAPTER CASE

After the EIS is issued, NEPA does *not* require agencies to elevate environmental concerns over all others. Still, agencies must include environmental considerations when making decisions by taking a hard and objective look at the environmental impact and examining alternatives. The agency may ultimately decide, for example, that economic and military issues outweigh the environmental concerns raised in the EIS.

The Supreme Court in *Robertson v. Methow Valley Citizens Council*[2] made it clear that NEPA is a procedural, not a substantive, law. Thus, NEPA does not confer upon agencies the authority to create regulations containing environmental rights and duties but instead "merely prohibits uninformed—rather than unwise—agency action." Still, an agency that ignores the serious environmental concerns raised in the EIS will likely find itself in the crosshairs of an environmental group such as the Sierra Club.

NEPA's passage has resulted in few permanent injunctions, although the Act has caused long delays, modifications, and abandonment of some federal projects. Debate continues on whether NEPA has helped the environment. Detractors have observed that the Supreme Court has sometimes shown little support for it, rendering it relatively ineffective, while supporters claim that the Act has elevated environmental law to what has become an integral part of federal agency decision making. Moreover, supporters point to the fact that over 80 countries around the world have also adopted laws based on NEPA.[3]

State Laws Modeled after NEPA

Due to the influence of NEPA, many states have enacted similar laws. These laws require states and municipalities to consider the environmental impact of proposed projects. In addition, a growing number of jurisdictions including California, Hawaii, Minnesota, New York, Puerto Rico, and Washington State "include within the broad sweep of their environmental assessment procedures all local government land use decisions, such as rezonings, subdivision map act approvals, or general plan amendments, even when those decisions are taken primarily to facilitate private development projects."[4]

Environmental Protection Agency

Environmental Protection Agency (EPA)

The federal agency that establishes environmental standards and enforces environmental laws.

The **Environmental Protection Agency (EPA)** was established in 1970 to coordinate the government's environmental activities. Its functions include establishing and enforcing environmental protection standards; conducting research on the adverse effects of pollution and on methods and equipment for controlling it; gathering information to strengthen environmental protection programs and recommending policy changes; assisting others through grants, technical assistance, and other means in arresting pollution of the environment; and developing and recommending to the president new policies for the protection of the environment.

The EPA is an independent agency with a mandate from Congress to regulate the environment. Unlike most independent agencies, however, its head can be removed at the whim of the president. This makes the EPA more vulnerable to political fighting, particularly between environmental groups and groups representing the interests of business and industry. Moreover, the EPA does not enjoy cabinet-level status, although some presidents, including President Obama, have included the head of the agency in cabinet meetings. Periodically there has been a push to upgrade the EPA to cabinet-level status but it has often met robust opposition, most recently by Congress. This issue, among many others, reflects the fact that environmental policies can be divisive and highly politicized, with material changes in environmental policies often reflecting the policies of the political party that is currently occupying the White House and controlling Congress.[5]

Specific Federal Environmental Protection Legislation

CERCLA   The inappropriate deposit of hazardous waste has contaminated entire communities. Congress responded to widespread publicity and concern about land contamination with the **Comprehensive Environmental Response, Compensation, and Liability Act (CERCLA**, also known as Superfund), enacted in 1980, and the Resource Conservation and Recovery Act (RCRA), passed in 1976, which is discussed in a later section. These two laws resulted, in part, from public concern about Love Canal, near Niagara Falls, New York, a residential housing development containing over 100 homes and a school built over a ditch used as a municipal and industrial chemical dumpsite for more than 30 years. Inhabitants of Love Canal suffered lesions and burns from puddles of toxic water in their backyards as well as chronic diseases such as leukemia and birth defects.[6]

> **Comprehensive Environmental Response, Compensation, and Liability Act (CERCLA)**
>
> The federal statute that provides for the cleanup of hazardous waste sites.

According to the CEQ, CERCLA has four primary elements:[7]

First, it establishes an information-gathering and analysis system that will enable federal and state governments to characterize chemical dump site problems more accurately and to develop priorities for their investigation and response.

Second, the Act establishes federal authority to respond to hazardous substance emergencies and to clean up leaking chemical dump sites.

Third, the Act creates a hazardous substance response trust fund [known as Superfund] to pay for the removal, remedy, and cleanup of released hazardous substances and hazardous waste sites.

Fourth, the Act makes those persons responsible for hazardous substance release liable for cleanup and restitution costs.

Section 104 of CERCLA defines broadly the "responsible parties" (also called *potentially responsible parties*, or PRPs) liable for cleanup costs for contaminated properties. The four categories of responsible parties are as follows:

1. A current owner or operator of a hazardous waste facility
2. One who owned or operated a facility in the past when hazardous waste was disposed
3. A generator of hazardous waste
4. A transporter of hazardous waste[8]

Unfortunately, for many PRPs, environmental liabilities attached to a site can sometimes exceed the site's land value. Moreover, PRPs are held *strictly liable* as well as *jointly and severally liable*. This means, in a worst case scenario, that a party can be liable to the EPA for an expensive environmental cleanup even if it wasn't negligent and can be responsible for paying the entire judgment unless other PRPs contribute. Due to the potentially severe liability imposed by CERCLA, it can greatly impact real estate transactions and mortgage lending. To lower the costs of expensive cleanups, defendants who pay can sue other PRPs for "contribution," in which the latter must contribute a fair share of the judgment. In the next case from Texas, a federal court addresses the issue of contribution.

A CASE IN POINT

In *Elementis Chromium v. Coastal States Petroleum Co.*,[9] Elementis Chromium sued El Paso Energy for contribution for cleanup costs incurred on its property. El Paso subsequently sued Magellan Terminals and Amerada Hess for contribution. The district court ruled that "El Paso was 89.95% responsible for the contamination at the Elementis property, and that Magellan and Hess were 10.05% responsible." However, the district court treated Magellan and Hess "as a collective entity for the purposes of allocating responsibility" and "imposed joint and several liability upon the two companies for their share of the cleanup costs." On appeal, the Fifth Circuit ruled that a liable party is entitled to recover only "proportional shares of judgment from other tort-feasors whose negligence contributed to the injury and who were also liable to the plaintiff." Thus, Magellan and Hess's contribution must be severed, making them liable to El Paso only for their proportional share of the cleanup costs.

What happens if a party *voluntarily* cleans up a contaminated property and then seeks contribution from another responsible party? In *Cooper Industries v. Aviall Services, Inc.*,[10] the U.S. Supreme Court ruled that a private party that has *not* been sued by the EPA for a CERCLA violation may not seek contribution from another responsible party. The reaction to the *Cooper Industries* case by both environmental and business interests was swift and critical. Environmentalists believed the ruling would create disincentives for voluntary cleanups, while businesses thought that other polluters also should bear cleanup costs. In a 2007 case, *United States v. Atlantic Research Corp.*, the Supreme Court ruled that CERCLA does allow a party that voluntarily remediates a polluted site "cost recovery" from the other parties, which is the actual cost of cleanup.[11]

In its early years, CERCLA was criticized because of the lack of progress in remediating contaminated sites. In response, in 1986, Congress created a schedule to quicken the pace. The sites that needed particular attention were listed on the National Priorities List (NPL). The list now appears on a database called the Comprehensive Environmental Response, Compensation, and Liability Information System (CERCLIS). This system has generally succeeded in expediting cleanup operations.[12] From 1980, when the Superfund was created, to 2010, 1,277 sites have been designated for cleanup. Of these sites, 343 have been cleaned up and deleted from the NPL. The 934 sites left are still technically active sites, with 61 sites proposed for possible Superfund remediation in the future.[13] (To access the CERCLIS list of cleanup sites by state, see endnote 13).

A recent analysis of cleanup operations concluded that over 70 percent of the responsible parties have performed the necessary remediation.[14] For the remaining parties that do not voluntarily perform the cleanup, the EPA (or a state equivalent agency) arranges for the cleanup. In these situations, owners may be forced to pay cleanup costs.[15] The federal government is entitled to place a lien on the property until the cleanup costs have been paid. Similar liens are allowed under state laws.

Amendments to CERCLA contained in the **Small Business Liability Relief and Brownfields Revitalization Act** (Brownfields Act) potentially ease some of the economic burdens on certain businesses. The Act was created in 2002 to provide owners with additional defenses under CERCLA, as well as to give investors incentives to develop brownfields, addressed later in this chapter. For instance, under the Act, the EPA can

Small Business Liability Relief and Brownfields Revitalization Act

A federal statute establishing defenses to CERCLA and creating incentives to develop brownfields.

TABLE 14.1   Defenses under CERCLA

POTENTIALLY RESPONSIBLE PARTIES (PRPs)	DEFENSES AVAILABLE	PUBLIC POLICY UNDERLYING DEFENSE
Current owner or operator of hazardous waste facility	De minimus defense	To protect those who contribute little waste to the contaminated site
Past owner or operator of facility when the waste was disposed	De minimus defense	To protect those who contribute little waste to the contaminated site
Generator of the waste	De minimus and de micromis defenses	To protect those who generate or contribute little waste to the contaminated site
Transporter of the waste	De minimus and de micromis defenses	To protect those who contribute little waste to the contaminated site
Landowner-Seller	De minimus defense*	To protect those who contribute little waste to the contaminated site
Landowner-Buyer	Innocent landowner defense, acts of God, de minimus defense, contiguous property owner defense, bona fide prospective purchaser defense*	To protect landowners who practice environmental due diligence or contribute little waste to the contaminated site or to encourage landowners to develop brownfields
Landowner-Buyer's lender	Security interest exemption	To protect lenders who foreclose and take title to contaminated properties and then attempt to sell property promptly

*Landowner-seller also may be afforded protection in a private contract in which the buyer purchases the property "as is" as provided in a Hold Harmless Clause.

reduce the amount of a responsible party's cleanup settlement if the party can prove that payment would impose great difficulty. Among the considerations is whether the party can afford its portion of the cleanup and still stay in business. Other payment alternatives also can be considered if the party cannot pay at the time of settlement.[16] Additional defenses provided under the Brownfields Act are discussed throughout this chapter and appear in Table 14.1.

Will a property owner or purchaser who buys a contaminated property that is not on the EPA list still be liable later for its cleanup? A federal court in the next New York case addresses the issue.

A CASE IN POINT

In *State of New York v. Shore Realty Corp.*,[17] Donald LeoGrande incorporated Shore Realty Corp. to purchase a 3.2-acre site, which was surrounded by water on three sides, to develop a condominium. He was aware at the time of purchase that the site had been used as a hazardous waste storage site, but the site was not on an EPA list. Hazardous chemicals were added to the tanks after Shore Realty took ownership, including when the site was leased to a third party. Moreover, leaking and corroded tanks were observed during a state inspection within the lease period. LeoGrande, as operator, and his company were later sued for the cost of cleanup. The court held that CERCLA "unequivocally imposes strict liability on the current owner of a facility from which there is a release or threat of release, without regard to causation." The fact that the site was not listed did not absolve the owner of liability.

Superfund Amendments and Reauthorization Act (SARA)

A federal statute amending CERCLA and establishing cleanup funding and new defenses for purchasers of land.

Liability for cleanup can be especially onerous when imposed on innocent purchasers of contaminated property. As a result, Congress amended CERCLA in 1986 (the **Superfund Amendments and Reauthorization Act,** or **SARA**) to provide a defense for purchasers (sometimes called the "innocent landowner defense") who had no reason to know of the hazardous substance.[18] To avoid liability, however, purchasers must demonstrate that at the time they acquired the property, they undertook an "appropriate inquiry," also called a "due diligence environmental review," into the previous ownership and uses of the property.[19] A due diligence review can involve as many as *three phases* of evaluation, depending on the likelihood of contaminants present, and can cost thousands of dollars.

Generally, prospective buyers conduct at least a *Phase I* evaluation, which often is the only step needed to successfully assert the innocent landowner defense. This typically includes a review of public records, interviews and questionnaires with those who may be familiar with the area, a visit to the site, and an analysis of any environmental records retained by the seller. If the Phase I evaluation reveals the possibility of contaminants, a *Phase II* assessment will follow with a scientific inquiry normally involving the testing of soil and water samples for all possible contaminants. Finally, if Phase II reveals the presence of contaminants, a *Phase III* evaluation will detail the extent of the contamination and the cost of remediation. At this point, since it is almost certain that the sale was made contingent on whether contaminants are discovered, the buyer may back out of the deal or try to negotiate a discount in price or persuade the seller to share in the cost of cleanup. In a 1991 policy statement, the EPA indicated that enforcement actions will not be brought against residential property owners unless certain exceptions apply, such as the owner's involvement in releasing hazardous waste.[20]

The requirement of an "appropriate inquiry" has made environmental assessments "a routine component of any real estate transaction. The environmental facts have become as important to an overall evaluation of a property as traditional information, such as location, tax assessment, market value, and resale potential."[21] Landowners who fail in their duty to investigate the environmental condition of their land—not only before ownership but also as an ongoing obligation—may have to pay a significant amount for the cleanup.

In 2006, the EPA promulgated new regulations as a result of concerns about the unprofessional manner in which environmental due diligence was being conducted. Appropriate environmental inquiries must now be conducted by an "environmental professional" who must meet specific education, training, and experience criteria. The professional, especially in Phase 1, must conduct more comprehensive interviews that go back further in time to evaluate prior land uses and must conduct visual inspections of the property as well as adjoining land.[22]

The Brownfields Act also clarifies and expands CERCLA's innocent landowner defense. *First,* buyers of easements, as well as those who lease from property owners, are protected when they exercise due diligence. *Second,* purchasers will be protected only if they take reasonable steps to prevent future releases. *Finally,* the amendment specifically spells out what constitutes an "appropriate inquiry," thus providing landowners with clearer guidance.[23]

Sellers will often require buyers of property suspected of having environmental problems to purchase the property "as is" (see Chapter 7) and buyers will sometimes plead ignorance if any contaminants are subsequently discovered. Still, as the next New York case demonstrates, these provisions afford little protection from expensive cleanup costs.

A CASE IN POINT

In *New York v. DelMonte,*[24] Samuel DelMonte acquired a piece of land in 1992 for no money and accepted it "as is." The property was adjacent to other land that DelMonte owned, and he expected to use this "free" property as his parking lot. A year earlier the New York Department of Environmental Conservation (DEC) found that there was lead in the area, although it was not specifically known to be on DelMonte's site. DelMonte acknowledged that fact but claimed he was not aware that lead was on his site. Moreover, he did not conduct an appropriate inquiry to uncover the presence of contaminants before or after he acquired the land. In 1993, the DEC found lead on his site and classified it as a significant threat to public health. DelMonte still did not clean up the site voluntarily, nor did he take precautions to keep off trespassers. Two years later the DEC found that an excavation had occurred on the land and that children and vagrants were active on it. In reaction, it ordered an emergency cleanup that cost $161,773 and sued DelMonte for reimbursement. He refused to pay, claiming he was unaware of the lead when he bought the property. The court, in a summary judgment, ruled in favor of the DEC, stating that DelMonte had failed to conduct a reasonable inquiry as to whether the land contained contaminants. The fact that there was lead in the general area and that the former owner, a construction business, had given the land to him free should have caused him to make the inquiry.

If a landowner such as DelMonte is insolvent, can an agency such as the DEC or the EPA recover from the previous owner? The seller in this case gave away the land and required DelMonte to take the land "as is" apparently because it suspected that the property might contain contaminants. Unfortunately for the prior owner, the "as is" provision, sometimes called a "hold harmless clause," is binding only on the parties who sign the agreement. Under the concept of joint and several liability, discussed earlier, allowed under CERCLA and state equivalent laws, the agency can choose to pursue either or both parties for the entire cost. Thus, the prior owner will be required to bear the entire cost if the buyer is insolvent, despite the as-is clause. A seller of contaminated land cannot simply transfer his contamination problems away. In the *DelMonte* case, however, the seller was insolvent; so the DEC pursued only DelMonte for the cleanup.

While CERCLA can result in substantial liability for property owners, there are several other defenses in addition to the innocent landowner defense. For example, PRPs are not liable for contamination caused by acts of God or war. Another defense, at least for diminishing the cost of cleanup, is the "de minimus" party defense. A typical de minimus party is one who has *disposed* of relatively small and nontoxic amounts of contaminants at the site. However, a landowner who *finds* that he has contaminants on his land also can use the defense if he did not release them or did not allow them to exist on the land. Under this defense, parties are required to pay a small portion of the entire cleanup costs. In return, they receive closure since the EPA promises not to sue again for any future remediation costs. This process typically takes place relatively quickly.

A similar CERCLA defense was created by the Brownfields Act in 2002. Under Title I of the Act, both transporters and generators are exempt from liability if they contributed a very small amount of hazardous waste material (defined as 110 gallons of liquid waste or 200 pounds of solid waste) to an NPL site. Called the "de micromis" exemption or defense, a PRP can still be held liable if the EPA determines that the hazardous waste "contributed significantly, either individually or in the aggregate, to the costs of the response action or natural resource restoration with respect to the facility."[25] Moreover, the PRP has the burden of proving it qualifies under the de micromis defense.

CERCLA's strict "chain of title" liability has caused procedural changes in mortgage lending, as lenders are concerned about their potential liabilities if they foreclose on the real estate taken as security for the loan. Lender concern was aggravated by a ruling in the 1990 case of *U.S. v. Fleet Factors*[26] that lender liability may attach if the lender attempts to influence the borrower's hazardous waste disposal. Other courts held that a lender taking title at a foreclosure sale, a very typical occurrence, is the same as any other purchaser at such a sale.[27] The EPA later promulgated a rule limiting lender liability, but in 1995, the court in *Kelly v. EPA*[28] held that the rule exceeded the EPA's authority. Congress reinstated the EPA's limited lender safe harbor rule, sometimes called the "security interest exemption," in 1996,[29] although many lenders and their legal counsel still view environmental laws as "treacherous waters" and the safe harbor as a way merely to "chart a safer course."[30] The security interest exemption to CERCLA's liability provisions clarifies those lender activities that can result in the loss of the exemption and requires lenders to attempt to sell the property promptly after foreclosure.

One of the unintended, as well as negative, consequences of CERCLA and state superfund laws has been the emergence of **brownfields**. Brownfields are sites or property close to sites that no one will buy and develop at any price because of the actual or perceived existence of hazardous substances. Few buyers will risk potentially large cleanup costs. The inability of buyers to limit their liability due to CERCLA's application of the doctrines of strict and joint and several liability, discussed earlier, also inhibits sales. Thus, as a result of CERCLA, many urban and rural brownfields, often in poor neighborhoods, are in a state of economic and social decline and decay.

The Brownfields Act of 2002 amends CERCLA to provide some legal protection to developers who own land in the vicinity of brownfields and to certain purchasers of brownfields. The "contiguous property owner defense" provides protection to those who purchase land "that is or may be contaminated by a release or a threatened release of a hazardous substance from real property that is not owned by that person...."[31] Still, landowners are immune only when they comply with a number of conditions, including not contributing to the waste and taking reasonable steps to monitor and prevent the waste from being released in the future.

The Brownfields Act further amends CERCLA to provide a "bona fide prospective purchaser defense." The defense protects those who buy a contaminated site after all hazardous substances have been released. In return, the new owner must cooperate fully with any governmental cleanup operation by investigating and releasing information about the hazardous substances at the facility and cooperate to prevent any further releases. The new owner also cannot reap a windfall from the purchase; instead, she must pay back the amount of the increase in market value caused by the cleanup. Those who do not will have a lien placed on the property.[32]

In recent years, investments in brownfield developments have increased, due in part to the Brownfields Act. Observers have noted that remediated brownfields are now some of the legally and environmentally safest places to build because of the exhaustive testing done on them. Even upstate New York's Love Canal, the catalyst for passage of CERCLA, has been developed into a residential neighborhood called Black Creek Village.[33]

Brownfields are now becoming attractive investments for a variety of other reasons as well. For instance, demographic changes have made once decaying areas of cities attractive to more affluent people. This trend, called "gentrification," occurs when the new residents, often older retired individuals as well as younger single professionals, invest in new condominiums, lofts, etc. People may decide to invest and live in these once-maligned areas rather than in the suburbs to avoid long commutes. Growth controls that trigger more costly and concentrated suburban developments also have caused inner-city locations to become more desirable.[34] The European solution to brownfields

brownfields

Real estate for which redevelopment or reuse may be complicated by the presence or potential presence of a hazardous substance.

has generally been to forbid any development in greenfields in order to preserve forests and agricultural lands and to prevent urban sprawl. This has contributed to a primarily private-sector eradication of brownfields, since they are often the only lands left for businesses to develop.[35]

Table 14.1 displays the various defenses available under CERCLA as well as its amendments—SARA and the Brownfields Act.

State Superfund Laws   Most of the states have enacted laws, paralleling CERCLA, that grant state environmental agencies, such as the New York DEC, the power to respond and remediate hazardous waste discharges.[36] The state laws establish funds to respond to hazardous waste discharges; and they sometimes provide funds for monitoring, investigation, and education. Many laws allow the state agency to "impose an involuntary lien on property for repayment of hazardous substance response or cleanup costs."[37] Some state liens are accorded the status of "superliens" and can take priority over previously recorded liens. Such superpriority provisions can wipe out the value of a secured lender's collateral. While the "safe harbor" for lenders eases lender concern about direct liability, environmental liens create concern about the lender's security for loans.

The Brownfields Act also plays a role in state-sponsored brownfield cleanups. In effect, the Act provides that state law governs when a landowner fully complies with a state cleanup order. Thus, the landowner will not be subject to a later EPA order or cost recovery action. There are a number of exceptions, however, including sites already on the NPL site, sites subject to an existing order or consent decree under federal environmental laws, and land contaminated by PCBs and petroleum products.[38]

Emergency Planning and Community Right-to-Know Act (EPCRA)

Federal statute that provides information to the public about hazardous chemicals in their communities and encourages planning for emergencies.

EPCRA   The **Emergency Planning and Community Right-to-Know Act (EPCRA)** also was included in the 1986 CERCLA amendment known as SARA. Prompted in part by a 1984 disaster in Bhopal, India, where more than 2,000 people lost their lives when chemicals escaped from tanks at a Union Carbide factory, the Act is designed to provide information to the public about hazardous chemicals in their communities and to encourage planning for emergencies. For instance, industries must file information at both the state and local levels about chemicals they use. Other laws dealing with dangerous chemicals include the Federal Insecticide, Fungicide, and Rodenticide Act, which regulates pesticides, and the Toxic Substances Control Act, which places controls on chemicals that represent unreasonable health or environmental risks.

Resource Conservation and Recovery Act (RCRA)

Federal statute that regulates the treatment, storage, and disposal of hazardous wastes.

RCRA   The **Resource Conservation and Recovery Act (RCRA)** regulates the treatment, storage, and disposal of hazardous wastes. Under RCRA, the EPA has developed "cradle-to-grave" regulations that cover everything from the generation to the disposal of hazardous wastes. For example, generators are required to report on-site activities; when wastes are shipped, detailed records are required in a "manifest" identifying the kind of waste as well as the generator, transporter, and receiving facility; and facilities that treat, store, or dispose of hazardous wastes are not allowed to operate without a permit. RCRA also encourages states to lessen their use of municipal landfills by developing solid waste management and recycling programs. Criminal liability for violating RCRA applies to individual employees as well as to businesses.

Underground storage tanks (USTs), also regulated under RCRA, pose a special problem. Early estimates revealed that USTs are located at 1.5 to 2 million regulated facilities throughout the United States and that 10 to 30 percent of them were leaking petroleum products, predominately gasoline and chemicals.[39] Under authority provided by RCRA, the EPA has developed extensive regulations governing installation of new USTs and upgrading of existing tanks.[40] In addition, RCRA requires UST owners to report the existence and designated characteristics of USTs and requires the reporting of releases from such tanks.

RCRA imposes standards on the land disposal of hazardous wastes, largely geared to prevent the contamination of groundwater. The Act bans disposal of certain substances at landfills, requiring that such substances be treated with the best-demonstrated available technology. RCRA also gives the EPA authority to deal with "imminent hazards" to prevent public harm.

Like CERCLA, RCRA has substantial enforcement mechanisms in place. The EPA, the states, and the U.S. Department of Transportation are responsible for enforcing the Act and can use compliance orders, consent decrees, and civil penalties. RCRA, as well as most other environmental statutes, can also be enforced through citizen suits. These suits empower a private person to bring a civil action against a violator of RCRA—and even against the EPA—for not performing a nondiscretionary duty. Under RCRA, a private cause of action can be filed against any person "who has contributed or who is contributing to the past or present handling, storage, treatment, transportation, or disposal of any solid or hazardous waste which may present an imminent and substantial endangerment to health or the environment...."[41] One issue, discussed by the Supreme Court next, is whether citizen suits under RCRA permit a person who has paid for a cleanup the right to recover its cost against a former owner.

A CASE IN POINT

In *Meghrig v. KFC Western, Inc.*,[42] KFC Western purchased property to build a Kentucky Fried Chicken restaurant in Los Angeles. During construction, petroleum was discovered on the property. The county ordered KFC to remove and dispose of the oil-tainted soil, which cost the company $211,000. Three years later KFC brought a citizen suit under RCRA to recover the cost from Alan Meghrig, the former owner, claiming he had "contributed to the handling, storage, treatment, transportation, or disposal" of the waste. The U.S. Supreme Court ruled in Meghrig's favor, stating: "Section 6972(a) [of RCRA] does not contemplate the award of past cleanup costs, and ... permits a private party to bring suit only upon an allegation that the contaminated site presently poses an 'imminent and substantial endangerment to health or the environment,' and not upon an allegation that it posed such an endangerment at some time in the past."

Clean Air Act
A federal statute designed to improve the quality of the nation's air.

Why didn't KFC pursue Meghrig under CERCLA for indemnification of its cleanup costs? Unfortunately for KFC, CERCLA expressly excludes petroleum from its definition of hazardous wastes.

Clean Air Act   Control of air and water pollution depends to a great degree on land control. For example, clean air regulations control the placement of shopping centers and other public attractions if the consequential increase in traffic would cause a violation of the air quality standards.[43]

primary air standards
Clean air standards designed to protect the public health.

The **Clean Air Act** of 1970, as amended in 1975, 1977, and 1990, creates air quality goals. Pursuant to the Act, the EPA establishes national primary and secondary ambient air standards. **Primary air standards** are designed for the protection of public health. **Secondary air standards** are those required to protect animals, plants, and property from the adverse effects of air pollution. After promulgation of the standards, states are required to adopt State Implementation Plans (SIPs), which must be approved by the EPA.

secondary air standards
Clean air standards created to protect animals, plants, and property from the adverse effects of air pollution.

A plant can be located within either an "attainment" area or a "nonattainment" area. Attainment areas have met statutory standards, while nonattainment areas have not.

While attainment areas are managed to prevent significant deterioration, nonattainment areas are targeted under state implementation plans to achieve compliance with specific pollutant standards.

In addition to approving SIPs, the EPA sets performance standards that control emissions from new (or modified) industrial plants. Special standards govern the emission of toxic substances such as asbestos and vinyl chloride. Industrial plants are viewed as major "stationary sources" of air pollution. The EPA promulgates "standards of performance" for new stationary sources, including industrial facilities that have been constructed or modified after publication of applicable regulations. The Act specifies that SIPs require permits for new stationary sources in nonattainment areas.

bubble concept

A concept that allows measuring the total discharge of pollutants from a factory rather than measuring pollutants from each separate source within the factory.

The EPA also encourages innovative approaches to pollution control, such as the **bubble concept**. Under this approach, the EPA treats a plant as if it were covered by a bubble, with all pollutants discharged through one opening, rather than a collection of separate stacks and sources. As long as the pollutants passing through the opening are below acceptable levels, individual sources within the plant are not subject to emissions limits.[44] In addition, agencies and companies keeping their emissions below established limits are issued **pollution credits**, which are sold and purchased on the open market. The use of these pollution credits can be controversial. For example, the state of New York has

pollution credits

Credits that can be earned and then sold by companies that emit pollutants below established standards.

chosen a novel approach that has prompted an intense debate: offering the credits free to companies willing to set up shop in New York. Without the credits, the companies might find it hard to do business … and either have to buy credits on the open market, or find ways to reduce pollution.[45]

Thus, the pollution credits are used as a tool to assist economic development.

Few policy debates over the environment have generated as much passion and contentiousness as global warming and climate change. A study based on a 2003 survey showed that 83 percent of 530 climate scientists "at laboratories, universities, and offices around the world nearly all agree that global warming is already underway." And although there is still not unanimity over whether it exists and what is causing it (for example, 53 percent of the climate scientists agreed that climate change is man-made), many believe that carbon dioxide (CO_2), methane, chlorofluorocarbons (CFCs), nitrous oxide, and other substances emitted into the air are the cause.[46] These gases trap heat in the earth's atmosphere, thereby creating a so-called "greenhouse" effect that heats some areas on the earth but may also produce cooling and severe weather in other areas.

Because many believe that man-made activities worldwide likely create climate change,[47] effective solutions must be international in scope to be successful. At the 1997 United Nations Conference on Climate Change in Kyoto, discussions resulted in an agreement, later called the Kyoto Protocol (KP), in which a goal was set to reduce greenhouse gases by an average of 5.2 percent below 1990 levels by 2012. The U.S. Senate responded with a resolution opposing entry into the KP, thus prompting former President Clinton not to submit it to the Senate for ratification. The KP suffered another major setback in 2001, when the Bush administration bowed out of the negotiations, calling for voluntary rather than imposed standards for reducing greenhouse gases. The administration was criticized worldwide for its actions, especially since the United States accounted for nearly 35 percent of the world's carbon dioxide emissions. Despite the lack of American cooperation, by 2010, 187 countries had ratified the KP, with the United States being the only economically significant country left in the world that had not yet done so[48] (To access a list of countries that have signed the KP, see reference in endnote 48).

When the Obama administration assumed power in early 2009, optimism grew among KP proponents that an American ratification would be imminent. In December 2009, another international conference convened in Copenhagen, Denmark, designed to further the goals set by the KP. Environmentalists and many European countries, which have already set binding limits on greenhouse gas emissions, were disappointed that the conference did not result in a global agreement and that no firm goals were established. However it is noteworthy that a system to monitor and report on progress was launched. Critics were also frustrated that only the United States and four other countries—China, India, Brazil, and South Africa—negotiated the agreement. Still, supporters of the conference contend that an important positive step was taken in combating global warming.[49] Despite the strong U.S. presence in Copenhagen, many observers feel that the Obama administration, which has been unsuccessfully pressing for a national energy policy, will not be able to muster the necessary political strength to ratify the KP in the near future.

Much like the bubble concept used under the Clean Air Act, the KP provides that countries can buy the right to emit more gases from those countries that take steps to emit less, thus injecting economic principles as an efficient way to clean the air. A good example of this was presented in an article in the *Wall Street Journal* concerning the Netherlands and Brazil.

> *The Netherlands agreed under Kyoto to cut its greenhouse gas emission 6% below 1990 levels by 2012. Cutting a ton of emission in the Netherlands is expensive: about $25 to $50, Dutch officials estimate. So for half their planned cuts, the Dutch shopped around mostly in developing countries for cheaper deals. Here in Nova Iguacu [Brazil], they've [the Dutch] agreed to buy as much methane as this landfill is expected to snag—for $15 per ton.*[50]

In the United States, the Chicago Climate Exchange (CCX) set up a similar system. Under the system, discussed in Chapter 3, companies that emit greenhouse gases and other pollutants voluntarily agree to cap emissions. If unable to do so, they must buy credits from those companies in the Exchange that earned credits by emitting less pollutants. Major companies such as Ford, DuPont, and Motorola have entered into this program to help alleviate climate change.[51]

While the CCX is private and voluntary, the Obama administration is proposing a nationwide cap-and-trade mechanism. While facing ongoing and often fierce political opposition in Congress, certain states have already entered into regional cap-and-trade agreements. Ten northeastern states, including populous Massachusetts, New York, and New Jersey, created the Regional Greenhouse Gas Initiative (or RGGI) in 2008. Under the RGGI, all fossil-fuel-burning power plants must buy credits corresponding to the amount of carbon they emit. The money goes to cash-strapped state governments. Two other state regional groups, in the Midwest and West, are also being planned based on the RGGI model. Moreover, California is developing a cap-and-trade system, which is scheduled to go into effect in 2012, although subsequent economic stress in that state may delay its implementation. Under its plan, polluters would have a cap imposed on them on how much greenhouse gases they emit every year; a company which continues to emit more than its limit would have to purchase an additional amount of credits at an auction, with the proceeds going to California state coffers.

ETHICAL AND
PUBLIC POLICY
ISSUES

Is It Ethical to Allow More Pollution to Occur in One Area to Help Lower Overall Pollution Levels Nationwide or Worldwide?

The bubble concept, the Chicago Climate Exchange, and the Kyoto Protocol allow, in some form, a mechanism for lowering overall pollution levels by buying and selling pollution credits. The result is that some areas will be more polluted than other areas. People who live in the "dirtier" areas may be subjected to more harmful pollution that can have detrimental effects on their health and safety, while those in cleaner areas will benefit. Is this ethical? Do humans have an inherently moral right to a healthy life? Is it fair and just to treat people in a different manner because of where they live? On the other hand, is it feasible to expect that pollution can be lessened without economic incentives? Should wealthier countries be required to pay a carbon tax if they continue to pollute so that the proceeds could be applied to remediate harm occurring in poorer areas? Since individuals must pay others to take away and dump their garbage and waste, and are criminally prosecuted for unloading it into forests, deserts and other prohibited areas, shouldn't governments be required to do so too if their industries "dump" their harmful pollution into the earth's atmosphere which we all must breathe? Does the world as a whole benefit from less pollution even when some people may be harmed more than others?

Under the Bush administration, the EPA was reluctant to address climate change, prompting a number of states and environmental groups to challenge the agency in court, with the Supreme Court ultimately settling the issue.

Does the EPA have authority to regulate greenhouse gases and, if so, to what extent? In *Massachusetts v. Environmental Protection Agency* on page 606, the U.S. Supreme Court addresses these issues.

END OF CHAPTER CASE

On December 7, 2009, the EPA administrator, after a public comment period in which thousands responded, signed two distinct findings regarding greenhouse gases under section 202(a) of the Clean Air Act:

- *Endangerment Finding: The Administrator finds that the current and projected concentrations of the six key well-mixed greenhouse gases—carbon dioxide (CO_2), methane (CH_4), nitrous oxide (N_2O), hydrofluorocarbons (HFCs), perfluorocarbons (PFCs), and sulfur hexafluoride (SF_6)—in the atmosphere threaten the public health and welfare of current and future generations.*
- *Cause or Contribute Finding: The Administrator finds that the combined emissions of these well-mixed greenhouse gases from new motor vehicles and new motor vehicle engines contribute to the greenhouse gas pollution which threatens public health and welfare.*

The reaction by business to the *Massachusetts v. EPA* case and the EPA's findings has been palpable. For many businesses, such as automobile manufacturers and coal-burning power plants, it is no longer a question of what to do, but how to do it, before federal and state regulators impose sanctions and new requirements. In addition to creating caps on pollution and trading credits, another policy that may emerge is a carbon tax imposed on those companies that emit CO_2. Still, a carbon tax has so far been met by intense opposition in Congress, especially in the wake of the Great Recession of 2007–2009, in which more constraints on business are seen as inhibiting the economic recovery.

Still, if some or all of these proposals become law, they will lead to an added expense for these industries. Once this occurs it is more likely that alternative energy sources, discussed in Chapter 3, as well as cleaner-burning natural gas and nuclear power, which emits little or no CO_2, will take on a greater role as prices begin to converge. Cars that emit little or no CO_2, such as those powered by electricity, also will become more commonplace, with new models such as the Nissan Leaf and the Chevy Volt being introduced in 2010.[52] Fossil fuel opponents are also waiting to see whether a public and political backlash to oil and gas exploration will emerge in the wake of the massive Gulf of Mexico oil spill caused by the explosion of BP's Deepwater Horizon oil rig in 2010.

Clean Water Act   The effects of land use on water quality are obvious. Erosion, fertilizer and animal excretion runoff, sewage disposal, and destruction of the aquifer are some examples of how land use can cause water pollution.[53] Over the years, Congress has enacted legislation directed toward control of water pollution. Control efforts today are based largely on the Federal Water Pollution Control Act of 1972—the **Clean Water Act** (CWA)—which is designed to restore the "chemical, physical, and biological integrity of the Nation's waters." To achieve this goal, pollution from point and nonpoint sources is regulated.

A **point source** is pollution that comes from a specific discharge point, such as a pipe from an industrial plant, while **nonpoint sources** include runoff from city streets, construction sites, and farms. The EPA establishes technology-based standards for industries, municipal governments, and agricultural sources under its National Pollutant Discharge Elimination System (NPDES). Under NPDES, these entities must first secure permits from the EPA or an approved state agency, which then settles on what discharge levels for certain pollutants are legally acceptable. In addition, state and local governments are required to develop plans for improving water quality, including controls on nonpoint sources. Under a separate statute—the Safe Drinking Water Act—states also must administer national standards for drinking water.[54]

The CWA establishes a system under which the EPA (or a state authorized by the EPA) issues permits authorizing discharges. This permit system has a profound effect on projects undertaken in **wetlands**, which have been increasingly recognized for their environmental significance: those "swamps, mires, bogs, and other watery land masses maintain water quality, provide wildlife habitat and breeding grounds, and assist flood control."[55]

The U.S. Army Corps of Engineers issues permits to regulate dredge and fill activities. Until recently, the Corps exercised broad and rigorous control over their issuance. In the 2001 case of *Solid Waste Agency of Northern Cook County v. U.S. Army Corps of Engineers*[56] (SWANCC), the Corps' jurisdiction was reduced when the court ruled that the Corps could no longer regulate "isolated" wetlands, that is, nonnavigable, intrastate waters. Now beyond the control of the Corps, these areas are governed by states, some of which have weaker environmental laws and enforcement. South Carolina, for example, in the year-and-a-half period after the SWANCC decision, declared 237 wetlands as isolated and therefore unprotected under federal law. Some of those wetlands were subsequently destroyed by encroaching development.[57]

The destruction of America's wetlands is alarming. In 22 states, 50 percent of the original wetlands have been lost, while in 7 states (California, Indiana, Illinois, Iowa,

Clean Water Act
A federal statute designed to improve the quality of the nation's water.

point source
Pollution that comes from a specific point.

nonpoint source
Pollution, such as runoff, that does not come from a specific point.

wetlands
"Swamps, mires, bogs, and other watery land masses [that] maintain water quality, provide wildlife habitat and breeding grounds, and assist flood control."

Kentucky, Missouri, and Ohio, all major agricultural states), 80 percent have vanished. Since the 1970s, the most extensive losses have occurred in 6 Sunbelt states: Arkansas, Florida, Louisiana, Mississippi, and North and South Carolina.[58]

The significance of wetland destruction can especially be seen in the wake of Hurricane Katrina. Some observers believe that New Orleans would have been protected if Louisiana's dwindling coastal wetlands had been better preserved over the years. Much of the state's wetlands have been destroyed by oil and gas operations, as well as the Corps' maintenance of an extensive levee system that inhibits the flow of the Mississippi River from its natural path to the Gulf, which has deprived the wetlands of replenishing soils.

In the next case, the U.S. Supreme Court further defines navigable waters and wetlands in a case decided five years after SWANCC.

Do "navigable waters," as defined under the Clean Water Act, include relatively permanent standing or flowing bodies of water as well as intermittent or ephemeral flows of water? In *Rapanos v. United States* on page 611, the Court answers that question.

END OF CHAPTER CASE

The *Rapanos* case[59] is likely to have a profound effect on how wetlands will be regulated for many years. Due to a voting split among the justices, Justice Kennedy's centrist-concurring opinion will, in the view of some experts, be the direction that courts are likely to follow. Kennedy's opinion offers a more expansive definition of navigable waters as bodies of water that include "relatively permanent, standing or continuously flowing bodies of water" *as well as* water that has a functional tie-in, or nexus, to these water bodies. While it is likely that water with the necessary nexus will mean that more areas are characterized as wetlands than they were under the majority's narrower definition in Justice Scalia's opinion, developers, planners, and others affected by the decision are concerned about the current lack of definitive guidance on the issue. In the end, it is likely to take years of lower court decisions to clarify what constitutes navigable waters under the CWA.[60]

Endangered Species Act
Federal law that protects habitats of plant and animal species designated as endangered.

Endangered Species Act   The **Endangered Species Act** (ESA) protects endangered species from the actions of federal agencies and prohibits any person from taking or harming an endangered species. The secretary of the interior, under the ESA, has the authority to list plants and animals that receive protection under the Act. Development activities can be sharply curtailed by the Act's protection of the endangered species and their habitat, which is why some critics refer to it as the "roadblock" statute.[61] One commentator notes:

a developer may secure all local land use approvals and be ready to bulldoze a site when a federal marshal orders work to stop because a species newly listed by the Secretary of the Interior as endangered or threatened with extinction has been found to live there. The chance of development being halted this way is greatest in rapidly growing states like California, Florida, Texas, and Hawaii where native plants and animals are losing ground fast.[62]

© MACIEJ NOSKOWSKI/iStockphoto (HF)

ETHICAL AND
PUBLIC POLICY
ISSUES

Should Land Developers under Some Circumstances Be Allowed to Kill or Damage Plants and Animals Protected under the Endangered Species Act?

Mishaps to endangered species can halt or even stop development activities, resulting in great financial losses. To create clearer investment-backed expectations, since 1998, the U.S. Fish and Wildlife Service has issued "No Surprises" guarantees so that developers will be protected and allowed to finish their project. In Problem 10 at the end of the chapter, the ethics and public policy reason for this guarantee is discussed.

One of the most important and ongoing controversies under the ESA is what constitutes a "taking" or harming of an endangered species. Under the ESA definition, a taking includes actions that "harass, harm, pursue, hunt, shoot, wound, kill, trap, capture, or collect, or attempt to engage in any such conduct."[63] In one particularly contentious case in 1978, the Supreme Court upheld a permanent injunction blocking the building of a dam by the Tennessee Valley Authority because of a small endangered fish called a snail darter. The suit claimed that the dam would destroy the snail darter's natural habitat.[64] The ESA also has been used to halt logging in old-growth forests of the Pacific Northwest in the habitat of another endangered species, the spotted owl. And the ESA has been controversial for triggering lawsuits by landowners who claim that enforcing its provisions constitutes a regulatory taking, discussed in Chapter 13, since it deprives them of essentially all economically beneficial uses of their land as the landowner in the next case from the Florida Keys argued.

A CASE IN POINT

In *Good v. United States,*[65] a developer was denied a permit from the U.S. Corps of Engineers to dredge and fill wetlands to gain access to navigable waters from his property. The Corps denied the permit because the property in question provides habitat for several endangered species, including the Lower Keys marsh rabbit, the mud turtle, and the silver rice rat, all of which are protected under the Endangered Species Act. In response, the developer sued the federal government, alleging, among other theories, that enforcement of the ESA constituted a regulatory taking and so deprived him of all economic value under the rule of *Lucas v. South Carolina Coastal Commission.* (See Chapter 13.) The court ruled that there was sufficient evidence that the property retained economic value even after the U.S. Fish and Wildlife Service placed restrictions on its use, particularly since the developer could still sell the transferable development rights or TDRs (see Chapter 13) to the land.

ETHICAL AND
PUBLIC POLICY
ISSUES

Are Conservation Banks an Effective Policy for Preserving Endangered Species?

While government has generally taken the lead in fashioning environmental policy, some private-sector initiatives have also gained acceptance. Often these efforts represent a compromise between the interests of real estate developers and environmentalists. One such venture is the establishment of conservation banks in which a developer, wishing to build in an area populated by endangered species, will

continues

continued

buy land in the development area. After developing the acreage and receiving approval from biologists and government agencies, the developer pays a development bank, which it typically also sets up, to maintain the land in perpetuity. Volunteers, such as scouting groups, will often clean and tend the acreage. Moreover, neighbors enjoy the area for walking and bird and animal watching, often becoming more aware and appreciative of the species being protected. While not perfect—some conservation banks have gone bankrupt and unwelcome species such as rattlesnakes have taken up residence—most say they generally are a success.[66] Of course, the purchase and maintenance of these preserves can be expensive, which drives up the cost of housing. This sometimes causes debates over whether animal and plant species, even endangered ones, are important enough that we should bear extra costs for such basic human needs as shelter. Is this an effective and ethical policy?

Environmental Justice   A number of studies have concluded that hazardous-waste landfills are disproportionately located in poor minority communities.[67] Other studies have concluded that the EPA's levy of penalties for the violation of environmental regulations varies based on whether minority residents are impacted.[68] In 1992, the National Law Journal conducted a particularly revealing and in-depth investigative study of environmental justice. Among its findings:

> *Penalties for disposing hazardous waste were 500 percent higher in white than in minority communities. In white areas, the average penalty was $355,566, while the minority average was $55,318.*
>
> *Abandoned waste sites in minority communities take 20 percent longer to be placed on the national priority list under the Superfund cleanup program.*
>
> *Action to clean up Superfund sites begins later for minority sites than in white areas.*
>
> *The EPA's cleanup method, known as containment (the capping or walling off of a hazardous site), was used in minority areas 7 percent more often than the preferable method of permanently eliminating the waste or its toxins. In white areas, the EPA permanently treats the waste 22 percent more often than it uses containment.*[69]

Former President Clinton signed Executive Order 12898 in 1994, requiring that each federal agency make environmental justice part of its mission and directing the EPA administrator to convene an interagency working group to facilitate the development of environmental justice strategies.

Environmental justice is often asserted in cases contesting the placement of a polluting plant or facility in a minority neighborhood. Plaintiffs generally do not allege that the plants were placed there intentionally to injure minorities, but that the pollution will disparately impact minorities protected under federal civil rights laws. For example, in *South Camden Citizens in Action v. New Jersey Department of Environmental Protection*,[70] a community organization was granted a preliminary injunction against the New Jersey state environmental protection agency for granting a pollution permit to a cement processing facility in a predominately minority neighborhood. However, in another case, *Lucero v. Detroit Public Schools*,[71] the plaintiffs failed to show unreasonable risks of exposure to contaminants and the likelihood of irreparable harm necessary for granting a preliminary injunction to prevent the opening of a new elementary school for predominately minority students on an allegedly contaminated site.

Environmental justice issues also emerged in post-Katrina New Orleans. Many people in New Orleans still remember the 1965 Hurricane Betsy when the city's white mayor was accused of intentionally allowing the predominately African-American Lower 9th Ward and New Orleans East to flood in order to save wealthier white areas. The perception, never proven, fueled the argument that the same neighborhoods, destroyed in 2005 by

Hurricane Katrina, would not be rebuilt, unlike white areas. Initially many planners, including those with the Urban Land Institute (ULI), called for creation of parkland in the most flood-prone areas of the Lower 9th Ward, a proposal that many city planners and social scientists considered quite reasonable. Distrust and accusations of racism caused politicians to abandon the ULI's proposals, and the rebuilding of New Orleans was plagued in subsequent years by uncoordinated, contentious, and unproductive planning,[72] although by 2010, there was palpable progress made and many of those who left have returned.

State Environmental Protection Legislation

Over the years, individual states have enacted legislation designed to control contamination of the environment. This legislation delegates considerable authority to state agencies to establish statewide environmental protection regulations. However, these agencies have been criticized for their lack of diligence in protecting the environment and for not providing enough opportunity for individual participation. As a result, a number of states allow individual citizens to file suit to protect natural resources from pollution and destruction.[73]

State environmental legislation generally can establish more rigorous standards than can corresponding federal law. In addition, as noted previously, federal environmental legislation can delegate responsibilities to the individual state for implementation and monitoring.

Judicial Review of Administrative Decisions

State and federal administrative agencies have been given a leading role in protecting the environment. The work of administrative agencies in general has been strongly criticized in recent years because agencies often lack personnel and funding or have close ties to the industry being regulated. One critic, for example, has observed:

> As the oldest independent federal regulatory agency, the Interstate Commerce Commission has set longevity records in its systematic failure to protect or further the public interest in surface transportation. Long ago, the ICC found itself surrounded by a special interest constituency that viewed the agency as an opportunity for protection from competition and for insulation from consumer demands.[74]

Agency decisions are subject to judicial review. In conducting their review, courts not only determine whether an agency followed the procedures mandated by the relevant statute but also review the actual decision of the agency. Under Section 10 of the Administrative Procedure Act, a reviewing court may set aside an agency action that is found to be any one of the following:

> (A) arbitrary, capricious, an abuse of discretion, or otherwise not in accordance with law; (B) contrary to constitutional right, power, privilege, or immunity; (C) in excess of statutory jurisdiction, authority, or limitations, or short of statutory right; (D) without observance of procedure required by law; (E) unsupported by substantial evidence [in specified circumstances]; (F) unwarranted by the facts to the extent that the facts are subject to trial de novo by the reviewing court.

In deciding whether an administrative decision is arbitrary, capricious, or an abuse of discretion, the U.S. Supreme Court has stated that a court

> must consider whether the decision was based on a consideration of the relevant factors and whether there has been an error of judgment.... Although this inquiry into the facts is to be searching and careful, the ultimate standard of review is a narrow one. The court is not empowered to substitute its judgment for that of the agency.[75]

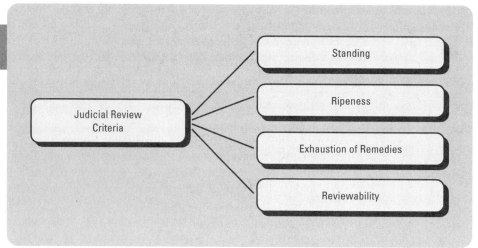

FIGURE 14.1
Judicial Review Criteria

Standing

Ripeness

Judicial Review
Criteria

Exhaustion of Remedies

Reviewability

In many cases, a court will refuse to review an agency case because any one of four criteria has not been met. (See Figure 14.1.) These criteria represent a major hurdle for private citizens who want to file environmental lawsuits. Citizen suits "are marked by lengthy, technical battles over standing, ripeness and mootness, lawyers say. Put simply, the fights are over how far the courthouse doors should be opened to citizen environmental enforcers in the first place."[76]

standing
The requirement that parties to a lawsuit have been sufficiently hurt and personally affected so as to allow them to bring a legal action.

Standing

To challenge an administrative decision, plaintiffs must first prove that they have **standing** to bring the action—that is, they have been hurt and therefore have a personal interest in the agency's action as this important U.S. Supreme Court case explains.

A CASE IN POINT

In *Association of Data Processing Service Organizations, Inc. v. Camp,*[77] the petitioners, who sold data-processing services to businesses, challenged a ruling of the comptroller of the currency to the effect that national banks may make data-processing services available to bank customers and other businesses. In a Supreme Court decision holding that the petitioners had standing, Justice Douglas applied the following tests: "Generalizations about standing to sue are largely worthless as such. One generalization is, however, necessary and that is that the question of standing in the federal courts is to be considered in the framework of Article III, which restricts judicial power to 'cases' and 'controversies.'... The first question is whether the plaintiff alleges that the challenged action has caused him injury in fact, economic or otherwise.... The question of standing ... concerns, apart from the 'case' or 'controversy' test, the question whether the interest sought to be protected by the complainant is arguably within the zone of interests to be protected or regulated by the statute or constitutional guarantee in question."

In *Sierra Club v. Morton,*[78] the Supreme Court decided that the Sierra Club did not have standing to maintain an action. The court noted that while the interest of the person bringing the action may reflect aesthetic, conservationist, and recreational values, the party seeking review must still allege that she individually suffered an injury. The Morton case (and others that followed) tended to block some environmental groups seeking standing to sue. Indeed, Supreme Court Justice Harry Blackmun, in *Lujan v. Defenders of Wildlife,* a standing case loudly condemned by environmentalists, accused the majority of taking a "slash and burn expedition through the law of environmental standing."[79] However, in an apparent reversal of the trend, the Supreme Court in *Laidlaw v. Friends of the Earth*[80] allowed an environmental group standing to bring a citizen suit under the CWA. Since the creation of the more relaxed standard announced in *Laidlaw,* lower federal courts have allowed more environmental groups standing, particularly for permit violations and challenges to government agencies attempting to avoid EISs.[81] More recently, the U.S. Supreme Court ruled on whether a state has standing to force the EPA to respond to an important environmental issue.

Does the state of Massachusetts have standing to sue the EPA to address the issue of auto greenhouse gas emissions? In *Massachusetts v. Environmental Protection Agency,* in Section IV of the opinion beginning on page 606, the U.S. Supreme Court addresses this issue.

END OF CHAPTER CASE

Do animals, whose lives are often directly affected by human interference in their natural environment, have standing to challenge environmental threats? The next case from Florida addresses the issue.

A CASE IN POINT

In *Loggerhead Turtle and Green Turtle v. The County Council of Volusia County, Florida,*[82] loggerhead and green sea turtles protected under the Endangered Species Act, with the assistance of human plaintiffs, sought an injunction to force Volusia County to ban beach driving as well as artificial light sources on the beach during the sea turtle nesting season. The turtles "alleged" that the lights disoriented them, causing them to be drawn to the light on the horizon that detrimentally affects their nesting activities. The court stated that "[t]o satisfy the 'case' or 'controversy' requirement of Article III, which is the 'irreducible constitutional minimum' of standing, a plaintiff must ... demonstrate that he has suffered 'injury in fact,' that the injury is 'fairly traceable' to the actions of the defendant, and that the injury will likely be redressed by a favorable decision." In its ruling, the court held that since the lighting was adverse to the turtles' nesting, "the Turtles have standing to sue Volusia County under the ESA's 'tak[ing]' prohibition for its regulatory actions affecting light users in Ormond Beach and New Smyrna Beach...."

ripeness
The constitutional requirement that before a case can be heard in court, it must have ripened (or matured) into a controversy worthy of adjudication.

Ripeness

Judges are reluctant to render advisory opinions on matters that are not actually in controversy because it is thought that the adjudicatory process should be reserved for actual, rather than hypothetical, problems. This policy—called the **ripeness** doctrine—stems from Article III of the U.S. Constitution, which limits judicial power to "cases" and "controversies."[83] The ripeness doctrine was also discussed in Chapter 13 as a requirement for the landowner to satisfy before bringing a "takings" claim.

A leading administrative law decision related to ripeness is *Abbott Laboratories v. Gardner,*[84] in which the U.S. Supreme Court decided that a regulation of the commissioner of food and drugs could be judicially reviewed even before it was enforced. According to the Court:

The ripeness doctrine is intricate. Nonetheless, its basic rationale is to prevent the courts, through avoidance of premature adjudication, from entangling themselves in abstract disagreements over administrative policies. The ripeness doctrine also protects the agencies from judicial interference until an administrative decision has been formalized and its effects felt in a concrete way by challenging parties. The problem is best seen in a two-fold aspect, requiring us to evaluate both the fitness of the issue for judicial decision and the hardship to the parties of withholding court consideration.

Ripeness has been applied in a number of environmental and Clean Water Act cases to deny plaintiffs their day in court. For example, in *New Hanover Township v. U.S. Corps. of Engineers,*[85] a township challenged the Corps' initial decision to allow a landowner to build a landfill. The court ruled the challenge was not ripe for judicial review since several more permits needed to be issued first before the Corps' decision was final. Ripeness is also an important issue in inverse condemnation cases (see Chapter 13) which commonly involve environmental issues.

Exhaustion of Remedies

> **exhaustion of remedies**
>
> The requirement that parties must first seek relief by availing themselves of all administrative remedies before going to court to ask for judicial action.

As a general rule, the courts will not review an administrative decision until the party has tried—and completely exhausted—all administrative remedies. However, **exhaustion of remedies** will not be mandated if the requirement would result in irreparable injury, if the administrative agency does not have jurisdiction over the matter, or if it is improbable that the party will obtain adequate relief through administrative remedies.[86]

Exhaustion of remedies arose as a material issue in the case of *Ackels v. EPA.*[87] In *Ackels* the plaintiff challenged in court an EPA decision issued under the CWA's NPDES. Ackels argued that the permit requirements imposed on his Alaska gold mine's point source emission of arsenic, among other issues, were incorrect and unreasonable. The court dismissed the case, ruling that Ackels would first have to make a request for an administrative hearing with the EPA Environmental Appeal Board and then appeal to the administrator *before* he could pursue the case in federal court.

Reviewability

> **reviewability**
>
> Under administrative law, a determination of whether a final agency action is subject to judicial review.

The last criterion a court must face—**reviewability**—raises the question of whether the issue is subject to review by the courts. The Administrative Procedure Act, section 701, states that issues are not reviewable when "(a) statutes preclude judicial review; or (b) agency action is committed to agency discretion by law." One of the major reasons judges decide that a matter is "committed to agency discretion" is that the administrative decision involves expertise beyond the ability or capacity of the court.[88]

In the U.S. Supreme Court case of *Massachusetts v. EPA* discussed earlier and presented on page 606, the issue of reviewability arose. The Bush administration argued that the EPA's decision *not* to issue regulations regarding CO_2 emissions was not reviewable by the courts. The Court repudiated the administration's position, stating that "[R]efusals to promulgate rules are [thus] susceptible to judicial review, though such review is "extremely limited" and "highly deferential." Moreover, despite the expressed rarity of a court reviewing the inaction of an administrative agency, the Court upheld the lower court ruling that a court has the authority to "reverse any such action [regarding reviewability] found to be … arbitrary, capricious, an abuse of discretion, or otherwise not in accordance with law."[89]

CASES

Environmental Impact Statement
SIERRA CLUB v. U.S. FOREST SERVICE
843 F.2d 1190 (9th Cir. 1988)

LEAVY, Circuit Judge. The Sierra Club brought this action pursuant to section 102(2)(C) of the National Environmental Policy Act (NEPA), challenging the Forest Service's decision not to prepare an environmental impact statement (EIS) for nine timber sales in the Sequoia National Forest (the Forest). The district court denied the Sierra Club's motion for a preliminary injunction to halt logging, which had already begun. * * *

This action arose in May of 1987 when the Sierra Club challenged the actual or anticipated awarding of nine timber sale contracts in the Forest: the Lion and Camp sales in the Hot Springs Ranger District, the Eye, Peyrone and Solo sales in the Tule River Ranger District, and the Bow Tie and Cabin sales in the Hume Lake Ranger District. At that time, there was no final EIS for the Forest. The Forest Service prepared environmental assessments (EAs) for eight of the nine sales, concluding that no EIS was necessary for them because logging would not significantly affect the quality of the human environment. The Forest Service categorically excluded the ninth timber sale from the need for either an EIS or an EA.

Five of the nine challenged sales contained groves of giant sequoia redwoods, which are renowned worldwide for their size and longevity. The Forest Service required a modified clearcutting method to be used in these groves whereby all vegetation except the giant sequoias is removed. The Forest Service claimed this method would enhance regeneration of the giant sequoia by exposing the bare mineral soil which they need to germinate.

* * *

NEPA requires the Forest Service to prepare an EIS for all "major federal actions significantly affecting the quality of the human environment." The Sierra Club argued that [selling the timber] was a major federal action. It argued there was a possibility of irreparable injury from clearcutting, because the Forest's aesthetic and recreational qualities would be altered forever. It also argued it would suffer irreparable procedural injury without the environmental analysis that NEPA requires. Moreover, the Sierra Club maintained that the public interest strongly favored issuing an injunction since the Forest is a major destination for travelers and visitors worldwide because of its famous giant sequoias.

* * *

Section 102(2)(C) of NEPA requires that all federal agencies include a detailed statement of environmental consequences—known as an EIS—"in every recommendation or report on … major Federal actions significantly affecting the quality of the human environment." The Council on Environmental Quality (CEQ) has promulgated regulations which bind federal agencies in implementing this requirement. Under the CEQ regulations an agency generally must prepare an EA to decide whether an EIS must be prepared.

CEQ regulations outline factors that an agency must consider in determining whether an action "significantly" affects the environment within the meaning of section 102(2)(C). These factors include, inter alia, (1) the "degree to which the effects on the quality of the human environment are likely to be highly controversial;" (2) the "degree to which the possible effects on the human environment are highly uncertain or involve unique or unknown risks;" (3) "[w]hether the action is related to other actions with individually insignificant but cumulatively significant impacts. Significance exists if it is reasonable to anticipate a cumulatively significant impact on the environment. Significance cannot be avoided by … breaking [the action] down into small component parts;" (4) "[w]hether the action threatens a violation of Federal, State, or local law or requirements imposed for the protection of the environment."

The standard to determine if an action will significantly affect the quality of the human environment is whether "the plaintiff has alleged facts which, if true, show that the proposed project may significantly degrade some human environmental factor." *Foundation*, 681 F.2d at 1177–78 (quoting *Columbia Basin Land Protection Ass'n v. Schlesinger*, 643 F.2d 585, 597 [9th Cir. 1981]). "A determination that significant effects on the human environment will in fact occur is not essential." "If substantial questions are raised whether a project may have a significant effect upon the human environment, an EIS must be prepared."

The record demonstrates the Sierra Club has presented facts which show the nine timber sales may significantly degrade some human environmental factor under each of the four [factors] listed above. The EAs either do not discuss, or do not discuss adequately, these [factors]. Consequently, the Forest Service's decision not to prepare an EIS was unreasonable.

* * *

Because substantial questions have been raised concerning the potential adverse effects of harvesting these timber sales, an EIS should have been prepared. The Forest Service's decision not to do so was unreasonable. [It] failed to account for factors necessary to determine whether significant impacts would occur. Therefore, its decision was not "fully informed and well-considered." *Endangered Species*, 760 F.2d at 986 (quoting *Vermont Yankee*, 435 U.S. at 558, 98 S.Ct. at 1219).

NEPA is primarily a procedural statute, *Oregon Envtl. Council v. Kunzman,* 817 F.2d 484, 492 (9th Cir. 1987), in that a substantial goal of NEPA's policy is the procedural process required before a major federal action affecting the environment is initiated. In *Save Our Ecosystems v. Clark,* 747 F.2d 1240, 1250 (9th Cir. 1984), this court held that "[i]rreparable damage is presumed when an agency fails to evaluate thoroughly the environmental impact of a proposed action.... [T]he policies underlying NEPA weight the scales in favor of those seeking the suspension of all action until the Act's requirements are met."

* * *

We reverse the district court's decision and order it to enter a preliminary injunction immediately halting further logging within the entirety of the nine challenged timber sales, as the Sierra Club requested in its May 8, 1987 motion. * * *

CERCLA Liability: Parent Corporation
UNITED STATES v. BESTFOODS
524 U.S. 51, 118 S.Ct. 1876, 141 L.Ed.2d 43 (1998)

SOUTER, JUSTICE. The United States brought this action for the costs of cleaning up industrial waste generated by a chemical plant. The issue before us, under the Comprehensive Environmental Response, Compensation, and Liability Act of 1980 (CERCLA), is whether a parent corporation that actively participated in, and exercised control over, the operations of a subsidiary may, without more, be held liable as an operator of a polluting facility owned or operated by the subsidiary. We answer no, unless the corporate veil may be pierced. But a corporate parent that actively participated in, and exercised control over, the operations of the facility itself may be held directly liable in its own right as an operator of the facility.

I

In 1980, CERCLA was enacted in response to the serious environmental and health risks posed by industrial pollution. "As its name implies, CERCLA is a comprehensive statute that grants the President broad power to command government agencies and private parties to clean up hazardous waste sites." *Key Tronic Corp. v. United States,* 511 U.S. 809 (1994). If it satisfies certain statutory conditions, the United States may, for instance, use the "Hazardous Substance Superfund" to finance cleanup efforts, see 42 U.S.C. §§9601(11), 9604; 26 U.S.C. §9507, which it may then replenish by suits brought under §107 of the Act against, among others, "any person who at the time of disposal of any hazardous substance owned or operated any facility." 42 U.S.C. §9607(a)(2). So, those actually "responsible for any damage, environmental harm, or injury from chemical poisons may be tagged with the cost of their actions. The term "person" is defined in CERCLA to include corporations and other business organizations, see 42 U.S.C. §9601 (9) and the term "facility" enjoys a broad and detailed definition as well. The phrase "owner or operator" is defined only by tautology, however, as "any person owning or operating" a facility, §9601(20)(a)(ii) and it is this bit of circularity that prompts our review.

II

In 1957, Ott Chemical Co. (Ott I) began manufacturing chemicals at a plant near Muskegon, Michigan, and its intentional and unintentional dumping of hazardous substances significantly polluted the soil and ground water at the site. In 1965, respondent CPC International Inc. incorporated a wholly owned subsidiary to buy Ott I's assets in exchange for CPC stock.

The new company, also dubbed Ott Chemical Co. (Ott II), continued chemical manufacturing at the site, and continued to pollute its surroundings. * * *

In 1972, CPC sold Ott II to Story Chemical Company, which operated the Muskegon plant until its bankruptcy in 1977. Shortly thereafter, when respondent Michigan Department of Natural Resources (MDNR) examined the site for environmental damage, it found the land littered with thousands of leaking and even exploding drums of waste, and the soil and water saturated with noxious chemicals. MDNR sought a buyer for the property who would be willing to contribute toward its cleanup, and after extensive negotiations, respondent Aerojet-General Corp. arranged for transfer of the site from the Story bankruptcy trustee in 1977. Aerojet created a wholly owned California subsidiary, Cordova Chemical Company (Cordova/California), to purchase the property, and Cordova/California in turn created a wholly owned Michigan subsidiary, Cordova Chemical Company of Michigan (Cordova/Michigan), which manufactured chemicals at the site until 1986.

By 1981, the federal Environmental Protection Agency had undertaken to see the site cleaned up, and its long-term remedial plan called for expenditures well into the tens of millions of dollars. To recover some of that money, the United States filed this action under §107 in 1989, naming five defendants as responsible parties: CPC, Aerojet, Cordova/California, Cordova/Michigan, and Arnold Ott. (By that time, Ott I and Ott II were defunct.) * * *

The District Court said that operator liability may attach to a parent corporation both directly, when the parent itself operates the facility, and indirectly, when the corporate veil can be pierced under state law. See *CPC Int'l, Inc. v. Aerojet-General Corp.*, 777 F.Supp. 549, 572 (W.D. Mich. 1991). * * *

* * *

Applying Michigan veil-piercing law, the Court of Appeals decided that neither CPC nor Aerojet was liable for controlling the actions of its subsidiaries, since the parent and subsidiary corporations maintained separate personalities and the parents did not utilize the subsidiary corporate form to perpetrate fraud or subvert justice.

* * *

We granted certiorari, to resolve a conflict among the Circuits over the extent to which parent corporations may be held liable under CERCLA for operating facilities ostensibly under the control of their subsidiaries. We now vacate and remand.

III

It is a general principle of corporate law deeply "ingrained in our economic and legal systems" that a parent corporation (so-called because of control through ownership of another corporation's stock) is not liable for the acts of its subsidiaries. Douglas & Shanks, *Insulation from Liability Through Subsidiary Corporations*, 39 Yale L.J. 193 (1929).

* * *

The Government has indeed made no claim that a corporate parent is liable as an owner or an operator under §107 simply because its subsidiary is subject to liability for owning or operating a polluting facility.

But there is an equally fundamental principle of corporate law, applicable to the parent-subsidiary relationship as well as generally, that the corporate veil may be pierced and the shareholder held liable for the corporation's conduct when, *inter alia*, the corporate form would otherwise be misused to accomplish certain wrongful purposes, most notably fraud, on the shareholder's behalf.

The Court of Appeals was accordingly correct in holding that when (but only when) the corporate veil may be pierced, may a parent corporation be charged with derivative CERCLA liability for its subsidiary's actions.

IV

A

If the Act rested liability entirely on ownership of a polluting facility, this opinion might end here; but CERCLA liability may turn on operation as well as ownership, and nothing in the statute's terms bars a parent corporation from direct liability for its own actions in operating a facility owned by its subsidiary. As Justice (then-Professor) Douglas noted almost 70 years ago, derivative liability cases are to be distinguished from those in which "the alleged wrong can seemingly be traced to the parent through the conduit of its own personnel and management" and "the parent is directly a participant in the wrong complained of." In such instances, the parent is directly liable for its own actions.

* * *

Under the plain language of the statute, any person who operates a polluting facility is directly liable for the costs of cleaning up the pollution. This is so regardless of whether that person is the facility's owner, the owner's parent corporation or business partner, or even a saboteur who sneaks into the facility at night to discharge its poisons out of malice. If any such act of operating a corporate subsidiary's facility is done on behalf of a parent corporation, the existence of the parent-subsidiary relationship under state corporate law is simply irrelevant to the issue of direct liability.

This much is easy to say: the difficulty comes in defining actions sufficient to constitute direct parental "operation." Here of course we may again rue the uselessness of CERCLA's definition of a facility's "operator" as "any person ... operating" the facility, which leaves us to do the best we can to give the term its "ordinary or natural meaning." And in the organizational sense more obviously intended by CERCLA, the word ordinarily means "[t]o conduct the affairs of; manage: *operate a business*." So, under CERCLA, an operator is simply someone who directs the workings of, manages, or conducts the affairs of a facility. To sharpen the definition for purposes of CERCLA's concern with environmental contamination, an operator must manage, direct, or conduct operations specifically related to pollution, that is, operations having to do with the leakage or disposal of hazardous waste, or decisions about compliance with environmental regulations.

B

With this understanding, we are satisfied that the Court of Appeals correctly rejected the District Court's analysis of direct liability. But we also think that the appeals court erred in limiting direct liability under the statute to a parent's sole or joint venture operation, so as to eliminate any possible finding that CPC is liable as an operator on the facts of this case.

1

By emphasizing that "CPC is directly liable under section 107 (a)(2) as an operator because CPC actively participated in and exerted significant control over Ott II's business and decision-making," the District Court applied the "actual control" test of whether the parent "actually operated the business of its subsidiary," as several Circuits have employed it.

The well-taken objection to the actual control test, however, is its fusion of direct and indirect liability; the test is administered by asking a question about the relationship between the two corporations (an issue going to indirect liability) instead of a question about the parent's interaction with the subsidiary's facility (the source of any direct liability). If, however, direct liability for the parent's operation of the facility is to be kept distinct from derivative liability for the subsidiary's own operation, the focus of the enquiry must necessarily be different under the two tests. "The question is not whether the parent operates the subsidiary, but rather whether it operates the facility, and that operation is evidenced by participation in the activities of the facility, not the subsidiary. Control of the subsidiary, if extensive enough, gives rise to indirect liability under piercing doctrine, not direct liability under the statutory language." See Oswald, *Bifurcation of the Owner and Operator Analysis under CERCLA*, 72 Wash.U.L.Q. 223, 257 (1994). * * *

* * * In sum, the District Court's focus on the relationship between parent and subsidiary (rather than parent and facility), combined with its automatic attribution of the actions of dual officers and directors to the corporate parent, erroneously, even if unintentionally, treated CERCLA as though it displaced or fundamentally altered common-law standards of limited liability. Indeed, if the evidence of common corporate personnel acting at management and directorial levels were enough to support a finding of a parent corporation's direct operator liability under CERCLA, then the possibility of resort to veil piercing to establish indirect, derivative liability for the subsidiary's violations would be academic. There would in essence be a relaxed, CERCLA-specific rule of derivative liability that would banish traditional standards and expectations from the law of CERCLA liability. But, as we have said, such a rule does not arise from congressional silence, and CERCLA's silence is dispositive.

2

We accordingly agree with the Court of Appeals that a participation-and-control test looking to the parent's supervision over the subsidiary, especially one that assumes that dual officers always act on behalf of the parent, cannot be used to identify operation of a facility resulting in direct parental liability. Nonetheless, a return to the ordinary meaning of the word "operate" in the organizational sense will indicate why

we think that the Sixth Circuit stopped short when it confined its examples of direct parental operation to exclusive or joint ventures, and declined to find at least the possibility of direct operation by CPC in this case.

In our enquiry into the meaning Congress presumably had in mind when it used the verb "to operate," we recognized that the statute obviously meant something more than mere mechanical activation of pumps and valves, and must be read to contemplate "operation" as including the exercise of direction over the facility's activities. * * *

Identifying such an occurrence calls for line-drawing yet again, since the acts of direct operation that give rise to parental liability must necessarily be distinguished from the interference that stems from the normal relationship between parent and subsidiary. Again norms of corporate behavior (undisturbed by any CERCLA provision) are crucial reference points. Just as we may look to such norms in identifying the limits of the presumption that a dual officeholder acts in his ostensible capacity, so here we may refer to them in distinguishing a parental officer's oversight of a subsidiary from such an officer's control over the operation of the subsidiary's facility. * * * There is, in fact, some evidence that CPC engaged in just this type and degree of activity at the Muskegon plant.

* * *

V

The judgment of the Court of Appeals for the Sixth Circuit is vacated, and the case is remanded with instructions to return it to the District Court for further proceedings consistent with this opinion.

It is so ordered.

Clean Air Act—Greenhouse Gases, Judicial Review of Administrative Actions
MASSACHUSETTS v. ENVIRONMENTAL PROTECTION AGENCY
127 S.Ct. 1438 (2007)

Justice STEVENS. A well-documented rise in global temperatures has coincided with a significant increase in the concentration of carbon dioxide in the atmosphere. Respected scientists believe the two trends are related. For when carbon dioxide is released into the atmosphere, it acts like the ceiling of a greenhouse, trapping solar energy and retarding the escape of reflected heat. It is therefore a species—the most important species—of a "greenhouse gas."

Calling global warming "the most pressing environmental challenge of our time," a group of States, local governments, and private organizations, alleged in a petition for certiorari that the Environmental Protection Agency (EPA) has abdicated its responsibility under the Clean Air Act to regulate the emissions of four greenhouse gases, including carbon dioxide. Specifically, petitioners asked us to answer two questions concerning the meaning of §202(a)(1) of the Act: whether EPA has the statutory authority to regulate green-

house gas emissions from new motor vehicles; and if so, whether its stated reasons for refusing to do so are consistent with the statute.

In response, EPA, supported by 10 intervening States and six trade associations, correctly argued that we may not address those two questions unless at least one petitioner has standing to invoke our jurisdiction under Article III of the Constitution. Notwithstanding the serious character of that jurisdictional argument and the absence of any conflicting decisions construing §202(a)(1), the unusual importance of the underlying issue persuaded us to grant the writ.

I

Section 202(a)(1) of the Clean Air Act provides:

"The [EPA] Administrator shall by regulation prescribe (and from time to time revise) in accordance with the provisions of this section, standards applicable to the emission of any air pollutant from any class or classes of new motor vehicles or new motor vehicle engines, which in his judgment cause, or contribute to, air pollution which may reasonably be anticipated to endanger public health or welfare...."

The Act defines "air pollutant" to include "any air pollution agent or combination of such agents, including any physical, chemical, biological, radioactive ... substance or matter which is emitted into or otherwise enters the ambient air." "Welfare" is also defined broadly: among other things, it includes "effects on ... weather ... and climate."

When Congress enacted these provisions, the study of climate change was in its infancy. In 1959, shortly after the U.S. Weather Bureau began monitoring atmospheric carbon dioxide levels, an observatory in Mauna Loa, Hawaii, recorded a mean level of 316 parts per million. This was well above the highest carbon dioxide concentration—no more than 300 parts per million-revealed in the 420,000-year-old ice-core record. By the time Congress drafted §202(a)(1) in 1970, carbon dioxide levels had reached 325 parts per million.

In the late 1970's, the Federal Government began devoting serious attention to the possibility that carbon dioxide emissions associated with human activity could provoke climate change. In 1978, Congress enacted the National Climate Program Act, 92 Stat. 601, which required the President to establish a program to "assist the Nation and the world to understand and respond to natural and man-induced climate processes and their implications." President Carter, in turn, asked the National Research Council, the working arm of the National Academy of Sciences, to investigate the subject. The Council's response was unequivocal: "If carbon dioxide continues to increase, the study group finds no reason to doubt that climate changes will result and no reason to believe that these changes will be negligible.... A wait-and-see policy may mean waiting until it is too late."

Congress next addressed the issue in 1987, when it enacted the Global Climate Protection Act. Finding that "manmade pollution—the release of carbon dioxide, chlorofluorocarbons, methane, and other trace gases into the atmosphere—may be producing a long-term and substantial increase in the average temperature on Earth," Congress directed EPA to propose to Congress a "coordinated national policy on global climate change," and ordered the Secretary of State to work "through the channels of multilateral diplomacy" and coordinate diplomatic efforts to combat global warming. Congress emphasized that "ongoing pollution and deforestation may be contributing now to an irreversible process" and that "[n]ecessary actions must be identified and implemented in time to protect the climate."

Meanwhile, the scientific understanding of climate change progressed. In 1990, the Intergovernmental Panel on Climate Change (IPCC), a multinational scientific body organized under the auspices of the United Nations, published its first comprehensive report on the topic. Drawing on expert opinions from across the globe, the IPCC concluded that "emissions resulting from human activities are substantially increasing the atmospheric concentrations of ... greenhouse gases [which] will enhance the greenhouse effect, resulting on average in an additional warming of the Earth's surface."

Responding to the IPCC report, the United Nations convened the "Earth Summit" in 1992 in Rio de Janeiro. The first President Bush attended and signed the United Nations Framework Convention on Climate Change (UNFCCC), a nonbinding agreement among 154 nations to reduce atmospheric concentrations of carbon dioxide and other greenhouse gases for the purpose of "prevent[ing] dangerous anthropogenic [i.e., human-induced] interference with the [Earth's] climate system." The Senate unanimously ratified the treaty.

Some five years later—after the IPCC issued a second comprehensive report in 1995 concluding that "[t]he balance of evidence suggests there is a discernible human influence on global climate" the UNFCCC signatories met in Kyoto, Japan, and adopted a protocol that assigned mandatory targets for industrialized nations to reduce greenhouse gas emissions. Because those targets did not apply to developing and heavily polluting nations such as China and India, the Senate unanimously passed a resolution expressing its sense that the United States should not enter into the Kyoto Protocol. President Clinton did not submit the protocol to the Senate for ratification.

II

On October 20, 1999, a group of 19 private organizations filed a rulemaking petition asking EPA to regulate "greenhouse gas emissions from new motor vehicles under §202 of the Clean Air Act."

* * *

On September 8, 2003, EPA entered an order denying the rulemaking petition. The agency gave two reasons for its decision: (1) that contrary to the opinions of its former general counsels, the Clean Air Act does not authorize EPA to issue mandatory regulations to address global climate change, and (2) that even if the agency had the authority to set greenhouse gas emission standards, it would be unwise to do so at this time.

* * *

III

Petitioners, now joined by intervenor States and local governments, sought review of EPA's order in the United States Court of Appeals for the District of Columbia Circuit. Although each of the three judges on the panel wrote a separate opinion, two judges agreed "that the EPA Administrator properly exercised his discretion under §202(a)(1) in denying the petition for rule making." The court therefore denied the petition for review.

* * *

[Author's Note: In the next section, the Court decides whether Massachusetts has standing to sue under the Clean Air Act.]

IV

Article III of the Constitution limits federal-court jurisdiction to "Cases" and "Controversies." Those two words confine "the business of federal courts to questions presented in an adversary context and in a form historically viewed as capable of resolution through the judicial process." *Flast v. Cohen,* 392 U.S. 83, 95 (1968). It is therefore familiar learning that no justiciable "controversy" exists when parties seek adjudication of a political question, when they ask for an advisory opinion, or when the question sought to be adjudicated has been mooted by subsequent developments. This case suffers from none of these defects.

The parties' dispute turns on the proper construction of a congressional statute, a question eminently suitable to resolution in federal court. Congress has moreover authorized this type of challenge to EPA action. That authorization is of critical importance to the standing inquiry: "Congress has the power to define injuries and articulate chains of causation that will give rise to a case or controversy where none existed before." *Lujan v. Defenders of Wildlife,* 504 U.S. 555, 562 (1992). "In exercising this power, however, Congress must at the very least identify the injury it seeks to vindicate and relate the injury to the class of persons entitled to bring suit." We will not, therefore, "entertain citizen suits to vindicate the public's nonconcrete interest in the proper administration of the law. *Lujan,* at 504 U.S. 581."

EPA maintains that because greenhouse gas emissions inflict widespread harm, the doctrine of standing presents an insuperable jurisdictional obstacle. We do not agree. At bottom, "the gist of the question of standing" is whether petitioners have "such a personal stake in the outcome of the controversy as to assure that concrete adverseness which sharpens the presentation of issues upon which the court so largely depends for illumination." "While it does not matter how many persons have been injured by the challenged action, the party bringing suit must show that the action injures him in a concrete and personal way. This requirement is not just an empty formality. It preserves the vitality of the adversarial process by assuring both that the parties before the court have an actual, as opposed to professed, stake in the outcome, and that the legal questions presented … will be resolved, not in the rarified atmosphere of a debating society, but in a concrete factual context conducive to a realistic appreciation of the consequences of judicial action." *Lujan,* 504 U.S., at 581.

To ensure the proper adversarial presentation, *Lujan* holds that a litigant must demonstrate that it has suffered a concrete and particularized injury that is either actual or imminent, that the injury is fairly traceable to the defendant, and that it is likely that a favorable decision will redress that injury. However, a litigant to whom Congress has "accorded a procedural right to protect his concrete interests," here, the right to challenge agency action unlawfully withheld—"can assert that right without meeting all the normal standards for redressability and immediacy." When a litigant is vested with a procedural right, that litigant has standing if there is some possibility that the requested relief will prompt the injury-causing party to reconsider the decision that allegedly harmed them.

Only one of the petitioners needs to have standing to permit us to consider the petition for review. It is of considerable relevance that the party seeking review here is a sovereign State and not, as it was in *Lujan,* a private individual.

* * *

These sovereign prerogatives are now lodged in the Federal Government, and Congress has ordered EPA to protect Massachusetts (among others) by prescribing standards applicable to the "emission of any air pollutant from any class or classes of new motor vehicle engines, which in [the Administrator's] judgment cause, or contribute to, air pollution which may reasonably be anticipated to endanger public health or welfare." (42 U.S.C. §7607(b)(1).) Congress has moreover recognized a concomitant procedural right to challenge the rejection of its rulemaking petition as arbitrary and capricious. Given that procedural right and Massachusetts' stake in protecting its quasi-sovereign interests, the Commonwealth is entitled to special solicitude in our standing analysis.

With that in mind, it is clear that petitioners' submissions as they pertain to Massachusetts have satisfied the most demanding standards of the adversarial process. EPA's steadfast refusal to regulate greenhouse gas emissions presents a risk of harm to Massachusetts that is both "actual" and "imminent." There is, moreover, a "substantial likelihood that the judicial relief requested" will prompt EPA to take steps to reduce that risk.

The Injury

The harms associated with climate change are serious and well recognized. Indeed, the NRC Report itself—which EPA regards as an "objective and independent assessment of the relevant science"—identifies a number of environmental changes that have already inflicted significant harms, including "the global retreat of mountain glaciers, reduction in snow-cover extent, the earlier spring melting of rivers and lakes, [and] the accelerated rate of rise of sea levels during the 20th century relative to the past few thousand years.…"

Petitioners allege that this only hints at the environmental damage yet to come. According to the climate scientist Michael MacCracken, "qualified scientific experts involved in climate change research" have reached a "strong consensus" that global warming threatens (among other things) a precipitate rise in sea levels by the end of the century, "severe and irreversible changes to natural ecosystems," a "significant reduction in water storage in winter snowpack in mountainous regions with direct and important economic consequences," and an increase in the spread of disease. He also observes that rising ocean temperatures may contribute to the ferocity of hurricanes.

That these climate-change risks are "widely shared" does not minimize Massachusetts' interest in the outcome of this litigation. According to petitioners' unchallenged affidavits, global sea levels rose somewhere between 10 and 20 centimeters over the 20th century as a result of global warming. These rising seas have already begun to swallow Massachusetts' coastal land. Because the Commonwealth "owns a substantial portion of the state's coastal property," it has alleged a particularized injury in its capacity as a landowner. The severity of that injury will only increase over the course of the next century: If sea levels continue to rise as predicted, one Massachusetts official believes that a significant fraction of coastal property will be "either permanently lost through inundation or temporarily lost through periodic storm surge and flooding events." Remediation costs alone, petitioners allege, could run well into the hundreds of millions of dollars.

Causation

EPA does not dispute the existence of a causal connection between man-made greenhouse gas emissions and global warming. At a minimum, therefore, EPA's refusal to regulate such emissions "contributes" to Massachusetts' injuries.

EPA nevertheless maintains that its decision not to regulate greenhouse gas emissions from new motor vehicles contributes so insignificantly to petitioners' injuries that the agency cannot be hauled into federal court to answer for them. For the same reason, EPA does not believe that any realistic possibility exists that the relief petitioners seek would mitigate global climate change and remedy their injuries. That is especially so because predicted increases in greenhouse gas emissions from developing nations, particularly China and India, are likely to offset any marginal domestic decrease.

But EPA overstates its case. Its argument rests on the erroneous assumption that a small incremental step, because it is incremental, can never be attacked in a federal judicial forum. Yet accepting that premise would doom most challenges to regulatory action. Agencies, like legislatures, do not generally resolve massive problems in one fell regulatory swoop. That a first step might be tentative does not by itself support the notion that federal courts lack jurisdiction to determine whether that step conforms to law.

And reducing domestic automobile emissions is hardly a tentative step. Even leaving aside the other greenhouse gases, the United States transportation sector emits an enormous quantity of carbon dioxide into the atmosphere—according to the MacCracken affidavit, more than 1.7 billion metric tons in 1999 alone. That accounts for more than 6% of worldwide carbon dioxide emissions. To put this in perspective: Considering just emissions from the transportation sector, which represent less than one-third of this country's total carbon dioxide emissions, the United States would still rank as the third-largest emitter of carbon dioxide in the world, outpaced only by the European Union and China. Judged by any standard, U.S. motor-vehicle emissions make a meaningful contribution to greenhouse gas concentrations and hence, according to petitioners, to global warming.

The Remedy

While it may be true that regulating motor-vehicle emissions will not by itself *reverse* global warming, it by no means follows that we lack jurisdiction to decide whether EPA has a duty to take steps to *slow* or *reduce* it. Because of the enormity of the potential consequences associated with man-made climate change, the fact that the effectiveness of a remedy might be delayed during the (relatively short) time it takes for a new motor-vehicle fleet to replace an older one is essentially irrelevant. Nor is it dispositive that developing countries such as China and India are poised to increase greenhouse gas emissions substantially over the next century: A reduction in domestic emissions would slow the pace of global emissions increases, no matter what happens elsewhere.

* * *

In sum—at least according to petitioners' uncontested affidavits—the rise in sea levels associated with global warming has already harmed and will continue to harm Massachusetts. The risk of catastrophic harm, though remote, is nevertheless real. That risk would be reduced to some extent if petitioners received the relief they seek. We therefore hold that petitioners have standing to challenge the EPA's denial of their rulemaking petition.

* * *

[Author's Note: *Part V deals with the Court's authority to review an agency's refusal to engage in rulemaking. The Court ruled that "[R]efusals to promulgate rules are [thus] susceptible to judicial review, though such review is "extremely limited" and "highly deferential."* National Customs Brokers & Forwarders Assn. of America, Inc. v. United States, *883 F.2d 93, 96 (C.A.D.C.1989). In this case, it ruled that the Court "may reverse any such action found to be ... arbitrary, capricious, an abuse of discretion, or otherwise not in accordance with law." 42 U.S.C. §7607(d)(9). Reviewability is also discussed on page 602 in this chapter.*

In the next section, the Court decides whether the EPA has the statutory authority to regulate greenhouse gas emissions from new motor vehicles.]

* * *

VI

On the merits, the first question is whether 202(a)(1) of the Clean Air Act authorizes EPA to regulate greenhouse gas emissions from new motor vehicles in the event that it forms a "judgment" that such emissions contribute to climate change. We have little trouble concluding that it does. In relevant part, §202(a)(1) provides that EPA "shall by regulation prescribe ... standards applicable to the emission of any air pollutant from any class or classes of new motor vehicles or new motor vehicle engines, which in [the Administrator's] judgment cause, or contribute to, air pollution which may reasonably be anticipated to endanger public health or welfare." Because EPA believes that Congress did not intend it to regulate substances that contribute to climate change, the agency maintains that carbon dioxide is not an "air pollutant" within the meaning of the provision.

The statutory text forecloses EPA's reading. The Clean Air Act's sweeping definition of "air pollutant" includes "*any* air pollution agent or combination of such agents, including *any* physical, chemical … substance or matter which is emitted into or otherwise enters the ambient air.…" §7602(g) (emphasis added). On its face, the definition embraces all airborne compounds of whatever stripe, and underscores that intent through the repeated use of the word "any." Carbon dioxide, methane, nitrous oxide, and hydrofluorocarbons are without a doubt "physical [and] chemical … substance [s] which [are] emitted into … the ambient air." The statute is unambiguous.

* * *

[Author's Note: *The Court now decides whether the EPA's stated reasons for refusing to regulate greenhouse gas emission from new motor vehicles are consistent with the statute.*]

EPA finally argues that it cannot regulate carbon dioxide emissions from motor vehicles because doing so would require it to tighten mileage standards, a job (according to EPA) that Congress has assigned to DOT. But that DOT sets mileage standards in no way licenses EPA to shirk its environmental responsibilities. EPA has been charged with protecting the public's "health" and "welfare," a statutory obligation wholly independent of DOT's mandate to promote energy efficiency. The two obligations may overlap, but there is no reason to think the two agencies cannot both administer their obligations and yet avoid inconsistency.

While the Congresses that drafted §202(a)(1) might not have appreciated the possibility that burning fossil fuels could lead to global warming, they did understand that without regulatory flexibility, changing circumstances and scientific developments would soon render the Clean Air Act obsolete. The broad language of §202(a)(1) reflects an intentional effort to confer the flexibility necessary to forestall such obsolescence. Because greenhouse gases fit well within the Clean Air Act's capacious definition of "air pollutant," we hold that EPA has the statutory authority to regulate the emission of such gases from new motor vehicles.

VII

The alternative basis for EPA's decision—that even if it does have statutory authority to regulate greenhouse gases, it would be unwise to do so at this time—rests on reasoning divorced from the statutory text. While the statute does condition the exercise of EPA's authority on its formation of a "judgment," that judgment must relate to whether an air pollutant "cause[s], or contribute[s] to, air pollution which may reasonably be anticipated to endanger public health or welfare." Put another way, the use of the word "judgment" is not a roving license to ignore the statutory text. It is but a

direction to exercise discretion within defined statutory limits.

If EPA makes a finding of endangerment, the Clean Air Act requires the agency to regulate emissions of the deleterious pollutant from new motor vehicles (stating that "[EPA] shall by regulation prescribe … standards applicable to the emission of any air pollutant from any class of new motor vehicles"). EPA no doubt has significant latitude as to the manner, timing, content, and coordination of its regulations with those of other agencies. But once EPA has responded to a petition for rulemaking, its reasons for action or inaction must conform to the authorizing statute. Under the clear terms of the Clean Air Act, EPA can avoid taking further action only if it determines that greenhouse gases do not contribute to climate change or if it provides some reasonable explanation as to why it cannot or will not exercise its discretion to determine whether they do. To the extent that this constrains agency discretion to pursue other priorities of the Administrator or the President, this is the congressional design.

EPA has refused to comply with this clear statutory command. Instead, it has offered a laundry list of reasons not to regulate. For example, EPA said that a number of voluntary executive branch programs already provide an effective response to the threat of global warming, that regulating greenhouse gases might impair the President's ability to negotiate with "key developing nations" to reduce emissions, and that curtailing motor-vehicle emissions would reflect "an inefficient, piecemeal approach to address the climate change issue."

Although we have neither the expertise nor the authority to evaluate these policy judgments, it is evident they have nothing to do with whether greenhouse gas emissions contribute to climate change. Still less do they amount to a reasoned justification for declining to form a scientific judgment. In particular, while the President has broad authority in foreign affairs, that authority does not extend to the refusal to execute domestic laws. In the Global Climate Protection Act of 1987, Congress authorized the State Department—not EPA—to formulate United States foreign policy with reference to environmental matters relating to climate. EPA has made no showing that it issued the ruling in question here after consultation with the State Department. Congress did direct EPA to consult with other agencies in the formulation of its policies and rules, but the State Department is absent from that list.

Nor can EPA avoid its statutory obligation by noting the uncertainty surrounding various features of climate change and concluding that it would therefore be better not to regulate at this time. If the scientific uncertainty is so profound that it precludes EPA from making a reasoned judgment as to whether greenhouse gases contribute to global warming, EPA must say so. That EPA would prefer not to regulate greenhouse gases because of some residual uncertainty—which, contrary to Justice Scalia's apparent belief, is in fact all that it said. The statutory question is whether sufficient information exists to make an endangerment finding.

In short, EPA has offered no reasoned explanation for its refusal to decide whether greenhouse gases cause or contribute to climate change. Its action was therefore "arbitrary, capricious, ... or otherwise not in accordance with law." We need not and do not reach the question whether on remand EPA must make an endangerment finding, or whether policy concerns can inform EPA's actions in the event that it makes

such a finding. We hold only that EPA must ground its reasons for action or inaction in the statute.

VIII

The judgment of the Court of Appeals is reversed, and the case is remanded for further proceedings consistent with this opinion.

It is so ordered.

Clean Water Act—Jurisdiction Over Wetlands
RAPANOS v. UNITED STATES
126 S.Ct. 2208 (2006)

SCALIA, Justice. In April 1989, petitioner John A. Rapanos backfilled wetlands on a parcel of land in Michigan that he owned and sought to develop. This parcel included 54 acres of land with sometimes-saturated soil conditions. The nearest body of navigable water was 11 to 20 miles away. Regulators had informed Mr. Rapanos that his saturated fields were "waters of the United States," that could not be filled without a permit. Twelve years of criminal and civil litigation ensued.

The burden of federal regulation on those who would deposit fill material in locations denominated "waters of the United States" is not trivial. In deciding whether to grant or deny a permit, the U.S. Army Corps of Engineers (Corps) exercises the discretion of an enlightened despot, relying on such factors as "economics," "aesthetics," "recreation," and "in general, the needs and welfare of the people." The average applicant for an individual permit spends 788 days and $271,596 in completing the process, and the average applicant for a nationwide permit spends 313 days and $28,915 —not counting costs of mitigation or design changes. In this litigation, for example, for backfilling his own wet fields, Mr. Rapanos faced 63 months in prison and hundreds of thousands of dollars in criminal and civil fines.

The enforcement proceedings against Mr. Rapanos are a small part of the immense expansion of federal regulation of land use that has occurred under the Clean Water Act—without any change in the governing statute—during the past five Presidential administrations. In the last three decades, the Corps and the Environmental Protection Agency (EPA) have interpreted their jurisdiction over "the waters of the United States" to cover 270-to-300 million acres of swampy lands in the United States—including half of Alaska and an area the size of California in the lower 48 States. And that was just the beginning. The Corps has also asserted jurisdiction over virtually any parcel of land containing a channel or conduit—whether man-made or natural, broad or narrow, permanent or ephemeral—through which rainwater or drainage may occasionally or intermittently flow. On this view, the federally regulated "waters of the United States" include storm drains, roadside ditches, ripples of sand in the desert

that may contain water once a year, and lands that are covered by floodwaters once every 100 years. Because they include the land containing storm sewers and desert washes, the statutory "waters of the United States" engulf entire cities and immense arid wastelands. In fact, the entire land area of the United States lies in some drainage basin, and an endless network of visible channels furrows the entire surface, containing water ephemerally wherever the rain falls. Any plot of land containing such a channel may potentially be regulated as a "water of the United States."

I

Congress passed the Clean Water Act (CWA or Act) in 1972. The Act's stated objective is "to restore and maintain the chemical, physical, and biological integrity of the Nation's waters." The Act also states that "[i]t is the policy of Congress to recognize, preserve, and protect the primary responsibilities and rights of States to prevent, reduce, and eliminate pollution, to plan the development and use (including restoration, preservation, and enhancement) of land and water resources, and to consult with the Administrator in the exercise of his authority under this chapter."

One of the statute's principal provisions is 33 U.S.C. §1311(a), which provides that "the discharge of any pollutant by any person shall be unlawful." "The discharge of a pollutant" is defined broadly to include "any addition of any pollutant to navigable waters from any point source," and "pollutant" is defined broadly to include not only traditional contaminants but also solids such as "dredged spoil, ... rock, sand, [and] cellar dirt," And, most relevant here, the CWA defines "navigable waters" as "the waters of the United States, including the territorial seas."

The Act also provides certain exceptions to its prohibition of "the discharge of any pollutant by any person." Section 1342(a) authorizes the Administrator of the EPA to "issue a permit for the discharge of any pollutant, ... notwithstanding section 1311(a) of this title." Section 1344 authorizes the Secretary of the Army, acting through the Corps, to "issue permits ... for the discharge of dredged or fill material into the navigable waters at specified disposal sites." It is the discharge of "dredged or fill material"—which, unlike traditional water pollutants, are solids that do not readily wash downstream—that we consider today.

For a century prior to the CWA, we had interpreted the phrase "navigable waters of the United States" in the Act's predecessor statutes to refer to interstate waters that are "navigable in fact" or readily susceptible of being rendered so.

After passage of the CWA, the Corps initially adopted this traditional judicial definition for the Act's term "navigable waters." *Solid Waste Agency of Northern Cook Cty. v. Army Corps of Engineers,* 531 U.S. 159, 168 (2001) *(SWANCC).* After a District Court enjoined these regulations as too narrow, the Corps adopted a far broader definition. The Corps' new regulations deliberately sought to extend the definition of "the waters of the United States" to the outer limits of Congress's commerce power.

The Corps' current regulations interpret "the waters of the United States" to include, in addition to traditional interstate navigable waters, [a]ll interstate waters including interstate wetlands," "[a]ll other waters such as intrastate lakes, rivers, streams (including intermittent streams), mudflats, sandflats, wetlands, sloughs, prairie potholes, wet meadows, playa lakes, or natural ponds, the use, degradation or destruction of which could affect interstate or foreign commerce," "[t]ributaries of [such] waters," and "[w]etlands adjacent to [such] waters [and tributaries] (other than waters that are themselves wetlands." The regulation defines "adjacent" wetlands as those "bordering, contiguous [to], or neighboring" waters of the United States. It specifically provides that "[w]etlands separated from other waters of the United States by manmade dikes or barriers, natural river berms, beach dunes and the like are 'adjacent wetlands.'"

We first addressed the proper interpretation of 33 U.S.C. §1362(7)'s phrase "the waters of the United States" in *United States v. Riverside Bayview Homes, Inc.* That case concerned a wetland that "was adjacent to a body of navigable water," because "the area characterized by saturated soil conditions and wetland vegetation extended beyond the boundary of respondent's property to ... a navigable waterway." Noting that "the transition from water to solid ground is not necessarily or even typically an abrupt one," and that "the Corps must necessarily choose some point at which water ends and land begins," we upheld the Corps' interpretation of "the waters of the United States" to include wetlands that "actually abut[ted] on" traditional navigable waters.

Following our decision in *Riverside Bayview,* the Corps adopted increasingly broad interpretations of its own regulations under the Act. For example, in 1986, to "clarify" the reach of its jurisdiction, the Corps announced the so-called "Migratory Bird Rule," which purported to extend its jurisdiction to any intrastate waters "[w]hich are or would be used as habitat" by migratory birds. See also *SWANCC,* 531 U.S. at

163-164 (2001). In addition, the Corps interpreted its own regulations to include "ephemeral streams" and "drainage ditches" as "tributaries" that are part of the "waters of the United States," provided that they have a perceptible "ordinary high water mark". This interpretation extended "the waters of the United States" to virtually any land feature over which rainwater or drainage passes and leaves a visible mark—even if only "the presence of litter and debris." Prior to our decision in *SWANCC,* lower courts upheld the application of this expansive definition of "tributaries" to such entities as storm sewers that contained flow to covered waters during heavy rainfall, and dry arroyos connected to remote waters through the flow of groundwater over "centuries."

In *SWANCC,* we considered the application of the Corps' "Migratory Bird Rule" to "an abandoned sand and gravel pit in northern Illinois." Observing that "[i]t was the *significant nexus* between the wetlands and 'navigable waters' that informed our reading of the CWA in *Riverside Bayview,*" we held that *Riverside Bayview* did not establish "that the jurisdiction of the Corps extends to ponds that are not adjacent to open water." On the contrary, we held that "nonnavigable, isolated, intrastate waters"—which, unlike the wetlands at issue in *Riverside Bayview,* did not "actually abu[t] on a navigable waterway"—were not included as "waters of the United States."

In one of the cases before us today, the Sixth Circuit held, in agreement with "[t]he majority of courts," that "while a hydrological connection between the non-navigable and navigable waters is required, there is no 'direct abutment' requirement" under *SWANCC* for "'adjacency.'" And even the most insubstantial hydrologic connection may be held to constitute a "significant nexus." One court distinguished *SWANCC* on the ground that "a molecule of water residing in one of these pits or ponds [in *SWANCC*] could not mix with molecules from other bodies of water"—whereas, in the case before it, "water molecules currently present in the wetlands will inevitably flow towards and mix with water from connecting bodies," and "[a] drop of rainwater landing in the Site is certain to intermingle with water from the [nearby river]."

II

In these consolidated cases, we consider whether four Michigan wetlands, which lie near ditches or man made drains that eventually empty into traditional navigable waters, constitute "waters of the United States" within the meaning of the Act. Petitioners, the Rapanos and their affiliated businesses, deposited fill material without a permit into wetlands on three sites near Midland, Michigan: the "Salzburg site," the "Hines Road site," and the "Pine River site." The wetlands at the Salzburg site are connected to a man-made drain, which drains into Hoppler Creek, which flows into the Kawkawlin River, which empties into Saginaw Bay and Lake Huron. The wetlands at the Hines Road site are connected to something called the "Rose Drain," which has a surface connection to the Tittabawassee River. And the wetlands at the Pine River site have a surface connection to the Pine River, which flows into Lake Huron. It is not clear whether the connections between these wetlands and the nearby drains and ditches are continuous or intermittent, or whether the nearby drains and ditches contain continuous or merely occasional flows of water.

The United States brought civil enforcement proceedings against the Rapanos petitioners. The District Court found that the three described wetlands were "within federal jurisdiction" because they were "adjacent to other waters of the United States," and held petitioners liable for violations of the CWA at those sites. On appeal, the United States Court of Appeals for the Sixth Circuit affirmed, holding that there was federal jurisdiction over the wetlands at all three sites because "there were hydrological connections between all three sites and corresponding adjacent tributaries of navigable waters."

Petitioners in No. 04-1384, the Carabells, were denied a permit to deposit fill material in a wetland located on a triangular parcel of land about one mile from Lake St. Clair. A man-made drainage ditch runs along one side of the wetland, separated from it by a 4-foot-wide man-made berm. The berm is largely or entirely impermeable to water and blocks drainage from the wetland, though it may permit occasional overflow to the ditch. The ditch empties into another ditch or a drain, which connects to Auvase Creek, which empties into Lake St. Clair.

* * *

We granted certiorari and consolidated the cases to decide whether these wetlands constitute "waters of the United States" under the Act, and if so, whether the Act is constitutional.

III

The Rapanos petitioners contend that the terms "navigable waters" and "waters of the United States" in the Act must be limited to the traditional definition of *The Daniel Ball*, which required that the "waters" be navigable in fact, or susceptible of being rendered so. But this definition cannot be applied wholesale to the CWA. The Act uses the phrase "navigable waters" as a *defined* term, and the definition is simply "the waters of the United States." Moreover, the Act provides, in certain circumstances, for the substitution of state for federal jurisdiction over "navigable waters ... *other than* those waters which are presently used, or are susceptible to use in their natural condition or by reasonable improvement as a means to transport interstate or foreign commerce ... including wetlands adjacent thereto. This provision shows that the Act's term "navigable waters" includes something more than traditional navigable waters. We have twice stated that the meaning of "navigable waters" in the Act is broader than the traditional understanding of that term. We have also emphasized, however, that the qualifier "navigable" is not devoid of significance.

We need not decide the precise extent to which the qualifiers "navigable" and "of the United States" restrict the coverage of the Act. Whatever the scope of these qualifiers, the CWA authorizes federal jurisdiction only over "waters." The only natural definition of the term "waters," our prior and subsequent judicial constructions of it, clear evidence from other provisions of the statute, and this Court's canons of construction all confirm that "the waters of the United States" in §1362(7) cannot bear the expansive meaning that the Corps would give it.

The Corps' expansive approach might be arguable if the CWA defined "navigable waters" as "water of the United States." But "the waters of the United States" is something else. The use of the definite article ("the") and the plural number ("waters") show plainly that §1362(7) does not refer to water in general. In this form, "the waters" refers more narrowly to water "[a]s found in streams and bodies forming geographical features such as oceans, rivers, [and] lakes," or "the flowing or moving masses, as of waves or floods, making up such streams or bodies." The definition refers to water as found in "streams," "oceans," "rivers," "lakes," and "bodies" of water "forming geographical features." All of these terms connote continuously present, fixed bodies of water, as opposed to ordinarily dry channels through which water occasionally or intermittently flows. Even the least substantial of the definition's terms, namely "streams," connotes a continuous flow of water in a permanent channel—especially when used in company with other terms such as "rivers," "lakes," and "oceans." None of these terms encompasses transitory puddles or ephemeral flows of water.

* * *

In addition, the Act's use of the traditional phrase "navigable waters" (the defined term) further confirms that it confers jurisdiction only over relatively *permanent* bodies of water. The Act adopted that traditional term from its predecessor statutes. On the traditional understanding, "navigable waters" included only discrete *bodies* of water. For example, in *The Daniel Ball*, we used the terms "waters" and "rivers" interchangeably. And in *Appalachian Electric*, we consistently referred to the "navigable waters" as "waterways." *The Daniel Ball*, 10 Wall. 557, 563, 19 L. Ed. 999 (1871); see also *United States v. Appalachian Elec. Power Co.*, 311 U.S. 377 (1940). Plainly, because such "waters" had to be navigable in fact or susceptible of being rendered so, the term did not include ephemeral flows. As we noted in *SWANCC*, the traditional term "navigable waters"—even though defined as "the waters of the United States"—carries *some* of its original substance: "[I]t is one thing to give a word limited effect and quite another to give it no effect whatever." That limited effect includes, at bare minimum, the ordinary presence of water.

* * *

Most significant of all, the CWA itself categorizes the channels and conduits that typically carry intermittent flows of water separately from "navigable waters," by including them in the definition of "point source." The Act defines "point source" as "any discernible, confined and discrete conveyance, including but not limited to any pipe, ditch, channel, tunnel, conduit, well, discrete fissure, container, rolling stock, concentrated animal feeding operation, or vessel or other floating craft, from which pollutants are or may be discharged." It also defines "'discharge of a pollutant'" as "any addition of any pollutant *to* navigable waters *from* any point source." The definitions thus conceive of "point sources" and "navigable waters" as separate and distinct categories. The definition of "discharge" would make little sense if the two categories were significantly overlapping. The separate classification of "ditch[es], channel[s], and conduit[s]"—which are terms ordinarily used to describe the watercourses through which *intermittent* waters typically flow—shows that these are, by and large, *not* "waters of the United States."

　　　　　　　　　★ ★ ★

Even if the phrase "the waters of the United States" were ambiguous as applied to intermittent flows, our own canons of construction would establish that the Corps' interpretation of the statute is impermissible. As we noted in *SWANCC*, the Government's expansive interpretation would "result in a significant impingement of the States' traditional and primary power over land and water use." Regulation of land use, as through the issuance of the development permits sought by petitioners in both of these cases, is a quintessential state and local power. The extensive federal jurisdiction urged by the Government would authorize the Corps to function as a *de facto* regulator of immense stretches of intrastate land—an authority the agency has shown its willingness to exercise with the scope of discretion that would befit a local zoning board.

　　　　　　　　　★ ★ ★

In sum, on its only plausible interpretation, the phrase "the waters of the United States" includes only those

relatively permanent, standing or continuously flowing bodies of water "forming geographic features" that are described in ordinary parlance as "streams[,] … oceans, rivers, [and] lakes." The phrase does not include channels through which water flows intermittently or ephemerally, or channels that periodically provide drainage for rainfall. The Corps' expansive interpretation of the "the waters of the United States" is thus not "based on a permissible construction of the statute."

IV

　　　　　　　　　★ ★ ★

Therefore, *only* those wetlands with a continuous surface connection to bodies that are "waters of the United States" in their own right, so that there is no clear demarcation between "waters" and wetlands, are "adjacent to" such waters and covered by the Act. Wetlands with only an intermittent, physically remote hydrologic connection to "waters of the United States" do not implicate the boundary-drawing problem of *Riverside Bayview*, and thus lack the necessary connection to covered waters that we described as a "significant nexus" in *SWANCC*. Thus, establishing that wetlands such as those at the Rapanos and Carabell sites are covered by the Act requires two findings: First, that the adjacent channel contains a "wate[r] of the United States," (*i.e.*, a relatively permanent body of water connected to traditional interstate navigable waters); and second, that the wetland has a continuous surface connection with that water, making it difficult to determine where the "water" ends and the "wetland" begins.

　　　　　　　　　★ ★ ★

We vacate the judgments of the Sixth Circuit in both No. 04-1034 and No. 04-1384, and remand both cases for further proceedings.

It is so ordered.

PROBLEMS

1. Oscar and Harvey leased rural land to lessees who accepted 7,000 drums of chemical waste generated by third parties for disposal on the land. The government entered into settlement agreements under which twelve of the waste generators agreed to pay 75 percent of the site cleanup costs. Oscar and Harvey, the site owners, asserted the "innocent landowner" defense when the government attempted to impose liability on them based on their status as landowners. Should this defense prevail? Why or why not?

2. Environmental legislation enacted in recent years often contains provisions that allow private citizens to sue polluters. Examples of such legislation include state environmental laws and the Federal Water Pollution Act. What is the purpose of these provisions? Without these provisions, what problems would a private citizen face in seeking court action to stop pollution? Why?

3. Leroy lives near a factory owned and operated by Smog, Unlimited. As a result of factory operations, the air in Leroy's neighborhood and the water in a local river have become polluted. Assuming that there are no environmental protection statutes relating to the company's activities, what legal theories could Leroy raise if he sued the company to stop the pollution? What problems would he encounter with each theory? Why?

4. The U.S. Secretary of the Interior announced a sale of oil and gas leases in eastern Louisiana. A 67-page environmental impact statement was filed that discussed in great detail the environmental impact of the oil-drilling operations that would result from the sale. An environmental group claims that the statement is inadequate because it does not discuss the environmental effect of alternative courses of action outside the authority of the Secretary of the Interior—such as the possible elimination of oil import quotas. Is the environmental group correct? Why or why not?

5. Students Challenging Regulatory Agency Procedures (SCRAP), a student environmental group, sued the Interstate Commerce Commission (ICC), challenging an ICC price increase in the cost of shipping goods that boosted the cost of shipping recyclable materials. SCRAP contended that the price increase had the effect of discouraging the use of recyclable goods and that it should not become effective until an environmental impact statement is filed. What defenses should the ICC raise? Are these good defenses? Explain.

6. The Scenic Hudson Preservation Conference, an association of nonprofit organizations, and the towns of Putnam Valley and Yorktown, New York, sued the Federal Power Commission (FPC) and the Consolidated Edison Company of New York, asking the court to set aside FPC orders authorizing Consolidated Edison to build Storm King, a hydroelectric project on the Hudson River. The Storm King project was to be located in an area of extreme beauty and major historical significance. The Federal Power Act provides that any party aggrieved by FPC orders may obtain court review. Do the plaintiffs have standing? Why or why not?

7. A company distributed a fungicide product, Panogen, which was registered under a federal statute as an "economic poison." After an accident involving Panogen, the Department of Agriculture suspended the registration on the grounds that Panogen was dangerous to the public. The company immediately requested an administrative hearing; but before the hearing, the company filed suit asking a court to set aside the suspension. How should the court decide the case? Why?

8. The Nuclear Regulatory Commission established a procedure for considering environmental protection in its decision-making process. Under the procedure, hearing boards that reviewed staff recommendations were not required to consider environmental issues unless they were raised by the parties involved in the hearing. Furthermore, hearing boards were prohibited from conducting independent evaluations of environmental factors when other agencies had certified that their own standards were satisfied. Does this procedure violate the National Environmental Policy Act? Why or why not?

9. Andrews owned a marsh in Maine that was considered important in the conservation and development of aquatic and marine life, game birds, and other waterfowl. Andrews wanted to deposit fill dirt in the marsh because, unless filled, the marsh had no commercial value. His application to the State Wetlands Control Board for a permit to fill the marsh was denied, and now Andrews brings suit to force the board to issue the permit. Should the permit be issued? Why or why not?

10. Bradford owns 500 acres of desert land near Las Vegas that he wants to develop. Land development in the area is potentially hampered by the Endangered Species Act, which protects threatened plant and animal species. Included in the list is the indigenous desert tortoise. Although environmentalists and others have attempted to remove the tortoise from areas of development and move them to safer places, a number are still killed in normal construction activities. Bradford plans to build a large planned unit development consisting of homes, condominiums, apartments, and businesses on his 500 acres. The cost will be in the millions; and when it is finished, the development will provide homes and jobs for many people. Housing prices in the Las Vegas

valley are also spiraling because of a large in-migration of new job seekers and retirees and less land available to develop. Bradford's planned unit development will help contain price increases and preserve affordable housing in Las Vegas.

To protect his investment, Bradford requests and receives a "No Surprises" guarantee from the U.S. Fish and Wildlife Service, which allows the "incidental taking" of species such as the desert tortoise. Do endangered species have rights to life, or can some be sacrificed so humans will benefit? In determining what gives the greatest good to the greatest number, should endangered plant and animal species be factored in? Why or why not? Consider the fact that once these species are destroyed, vital links in an interrelated and fragile ecosystem can be destroyed. This may adversely impact not only the natural environment but also humans.

ENDNOTES

1. N. Kubasek and G. Silverman, *Environmental Law* 149 (6th ed. 2008).
2. 490 U.S. 332 (1989).
3. F. Powell, *Law and the Environment* 229 (1998). See also Kubasek and Silverman, *supra* note 1 at 160.
4. G. Lefcoe, *Real Estate Transactions* 1040–41 (2nd ed. 1997).
5. N. Kubasek and G. Silverman, *supra* note 1 at 136–144.
6. E. Beck, *The Love Canal Tragedy*, EPA Journal at http://www.epa.gov/history/topics/lovecanal/01.htm (last accessed September 25, 2007).
7. Council on Environmental Quality, *Environmental Quality 1981*: 12th Annual Report 99–101 (1981).
8. S. Romaine and A. Carington, *Superfund: With Control Comes Responsibility*, Probate & Property 54 (July/August 1997).
9. 450 F.3d 607 (5th Cir. 2006).
10. 543 U.S. 157, 125 S.Ct. 577 (2004).
11. 127 S.Ct. 2331 (2007). See also N. Kubasek, *From the Environment*, 36 Real Estate Law Journal 202 (2007).
12. N. Kubasek, *Environmental Law* 214 (1994).
13. See http://www.epa.gov/superfund/sites/npl/index.htm (last accessed August 5, 2007).
14. See http://www.epa.gov/superfund/sites/npl/index.htm (last accessed August 6, 2010). The National Priorities List "means the list compiled by EPA pursuant to CERCLA section 105 of uncontrolled hazardous substance releases in the United States that are priorities for long-term remedial evaluation and response." 40 C.F.R. §300.5.
15. Environmental Protection Agency, *Your Guide to the Environmental Protection Agency* 13 (1984). For an analysis of the impact of federal environmental legislation on officer and shareholder liability, see L. Oswald and C. Schipani, *CERCLA and the "Erosion" of Corporate Law Doctrine*, 86 Northwestern Law Review 259 (1992).
16. R. Fox, *Summary of the Small Business Liability and Brownfields Revitalization Act*, SJ 059 American Law Institute—American Bar Association 69 (2004).
17. 759 F.2d 1032 (2nd Cir. 1985).
18. F. Cross, *Establishing Environmental Innocence*, 23 Real Estate Law Journal 332 (Spring 1995).
19. J. Shumate, *Real Estate Transactions in the Age of SARA*, 14 Mich. Real Property Rev. 70 (1987).
20. Environmental Protection Agency, *Policy Towards Owners of Residential Property at Superfund Sites* (1991). See also P. Grashoff et al., *Environmental Checklist for Developers and Lenders* 30 (1991).
21. M. Halloran, *Environmental Site Assessments*, 41 Practical Lawyer 61 (1995).
22. O. Marr and R. Montevideo, *Are You Making "All Appropriate Inquiries?" New U.S. EPA Final Rule Strengthens Environmental Due Diligence Standards*, 48 Orange County Lawyer 34 (2006).
23. R. Fox, *supra* note 16 at 69.
24. No. 98-CV06449E, 432838 WL 2000 (W.D. N.Y. March 21, 2000).
25. R. Fox, *supra* note 16 at 69.
26. 901 F.2d 1550 (11th Cir. 1990).
27. *Guidice v. BFG Electroplating & Manufacturing Co.*, 732 F.Supp. 556 (W.D. PA. 1989).
28. 15 F.3d 1100 (D.C. Cir. 1994), *cert. denied* 115 S.Ct. 900 (1995).
29. Public Law No. 104–208 (1996); 42 USC §101(20) (1996).
30. S. Humphreys, *Environmental Policy Alert: Congress Reinstates EPA's Lender Liability Rule*, 44 Federal Lawyer 34 (1997).
31. R. Fox, *supra* note 16 at 69.
32. *Id.*
33. R. Smith, *Developers See Green in 'Brownfield' Sites*, Wall Street Journal B1, B6 (June 1, 2005).
34. H. El Nasser, *New Growth Sprouts on USA's Brownfields*, USA Today (October 6, 2005).
35. J. Kushner, *Brownfield Redevelopment Strategies in the United States*, 22 Georgia State University Law Review 857 (2006).
36. This discussion is drawn largely from D. Nanney, *Environmental Risks in Real Estate Transactions* (2nd ed. 1993).
37. *Id.* at 57.
38. R. Fox, *supra* note 16 at 69.
39. N. Kubasek and G. Silverman, *supra* note 1 at 327–330.
40. W. Dunn and J. Shumate, *What the Borrower's Attorney Should Know About Environmental Law* 8, 49 (1989).
41. 42 U.S.C. §6972.
42. 516 U.S. 479, 116 S.Ct. 1251, 134 L.Ed.2d 121 (1996).
43. Comment, *Environmental Land Use Control: Common Law and Statutory Approaches*, 28 University of Miami Law Review 135 (1973).
44. The discussion of federal air, water, and waste legislation is drawn in part from Environmental Protection Agency, *Your Guide to the United States Environmental Protection Agency* (1984).
45. R. Hernandez, *New York Offers Pollution Permits to Lure Companies*, New York Times A1 (May 19, 1997).

46. J. Bast and J. Taylor, *Results of an International Survey of Climate Scientists* (2007).

47. Intergovernmental Panel on Climate Change (IPCC), Climate Change 2007: The Physical Science Basis: Contribution of Working Group I to the Fourth Assessment Report of the Intergovernmental Panel on Climate Change (2007) online at http://www.ipcc.ch/pdf/assessment-report/ar4/syr/ar4_syr_spm .pdf (last visited August 6, 2010). The IPCC and former Vice President Gore were both named recipients of the Nobel Peace Prize in October 2007, for their work on preventing global warming and climate change.

48. To access the countries which have signed the Kyoto Protocol, visit http://unfccc.int/files/kyoto_protocol/status_of_ratifica tion/application/pdf/kp_ratification.pdf (last accessed August 3, 2010).

49. J. Broder, *Many Goals Remain Unmet in 5 Nations Climate Deal*, New York Times at http://www.nytimes.com/2009/12/ 19/science/earth/19climate.html?pagewanted=1&_r=1 (last accessed August 3, 2010).

50. J. Ball, *To Cut Pollution, Dutch Pay a Dump in Brazil to Clean Up*, Wall Street Journal A1 (August 11, 2005).

51. See *Trading in Carbon Futures*, Public Policy Institute, http:// www.ppionline.org/ppi_ci.cfm?knlgAreaID=116&subsecID= 900039&contentID=252027 (last accessed August 6, 2010).

52. J. Carey, *Climate Wars: Episode Two*, Business Week 90 (April 23, 2007).

53. Comment, *supra* note 43 at 135.

54. Environmental Protection Agency, *supra* note 44 at 5–7. See generally Kubasek and Silverman, *supra* note 1 at 248-253.

55. M. Strand, *What is a Wetland and Why Are We Still Asking?* The Practical Real Estate Lawyer 59, 60 (March 1997). See generally Kubasek and Silverman, *supra* note 1 at 395-409.

56. 121 S.Ct. 675, 148 L.Ed.2d 576 (2001).

57. T. Watson, *Developers Rush to Build in Wetland After Ruling*, USA Today 15A (December 6, 2002).

58. Kubasek and Silverman, *supra* note 1 at 398.

59. 126 S.Ct. 2208 (2006).

60. R. Aalberts, *The Fate of Wetlands After Rapanos/Carabell: Fortuitous or Folly?* 35 Real Estate Law Journal 1 (2006).

61. F. Powell, *Environmental Law* 230 (1998).

62. G. Lefcoe, *Real Estate Transactions* 1040 (2nd ed. 1997).

63. F. Powell, *supra* note 61 at 234–35.

64. *Tennessee Valley Authority v. Hill*, 437 U.S. 153 (1978).

65. 37 Fed. Ct. Claims 81 (1997).

66. J. Fialka, *Conservation Banks Catch On, Aiding Wildlife and Builders*, Wall Street Journal B1 (February 22, 2006).

67. O. Saleem, *Overcoming Environmental Discrimination: The Need for a Disparate Impact Test and Improved Notice Requirements in Facility Siting Decisions*, 19 Columbia Journal of Environmental Law 211 (1994); R. Lazarus, *Pursuing "Environmental Justice": The Distributional Effects of Environmental Protection*, 87 Northwestern University Law Review 787 (1993).

68. M. Lavelle and M. Loyle, *Unequal Protection—The Racial Divide in Environmental Law*, National Law Journal (Sept. 21, 1992).

69. R. Aalberts, *Decentralized Enforcement and Environmental Justice: Top Priorities of the 90s?* 23 Real Estate Law Journal 3 (1994).

70. 145 F.Supp.2d 505 (D. New Jersey 2001).

71. 160 F.Supp.2d 767 (E.D. Mich. 2001).

72. A. Westfeldt, *Opportunity Lost in New Orleans*, Las Vegas Review-Journal 17A (September 9, 2007).

73. *Ray v. Mason County Drain Com'r*, 393 Mich. 294, 224 N.W.2d 883 (1975).

74. R. Fellmuth, *The Interstate Commerce Commission: The Public Interest and the I.C.C.* vii–viii (1970).

75. *Citizens to Preserve Overton Park, Inc. v. Volpe*, 401 U.S. 402, 91 S.Ct. 814, 28 L.Ed.2d 136 (1971).

76. M. Lavelle, *Limits on Lawsuits Over Private Polluters, Too*, National Law Journal 32 (December 9, 1991).

77. 397 U.S. 150, 90 S.Ct. 827, 25 L.Ed.2d 184 (1970).

78. 405 U.S. 727, 92 S.Ct. 1361, 31 L.Ed.2d 636 (1972).

79. *Lujan v. Defenders of Wildlife*, 504 U.S. 555, 605 (1992).

80. 528 U.S. 167, 120 S.Ct. 693, 145 L.Ed.2d 610 (2000). See J. Adler, *Stand or Deliver: Citizen Suits, Standing, and Environmental Protection*, 12 Duke Environmental Law and Policy Forum 39 (Fall 2001).

81. J. Bryant, *The Effect of Friends of the Earth v. Laidlaw on Standing in Environmental Law Cases*, 30 Real Estate Law Journal 97 (2001).

82. 148 F.3d 1231 (11th Cir. 1998).

83. K. Davis, *Administrative Law and Government* 81 (1975).

84. 387 U.S. 136, 87 S.Ct. 1507, 18 L.Ed.2d 681 (1967).

85. 992 F.2d 470 (3rd Cir. 1993).

86. K. Davis, *supra* note 83 at 46, 84.

87. 7 F.3d 862 (9th Cir. 1993).

88. K. Davis, *supra* note 83 at 57.

89. 127 S.Ct 1438, 1459 (2007).

GLOSSARY

1866 Civil Rights Act A post–Civil War federal statute prohibiting race discrimination in connection with real and personal property transactions.

1968 Fair Housing Act Title VIII of the Civil Rights Act of 1968 that prohibits discrimination in housing based on race, color, religion, sex, and national origin.

A

abandoned Property that has been permanently surrendered by the owner.

abstract of title A compilation of the chain of title, usually prepared by a title company or an attorney, providing copies or summaries of all recorded instruments including deeds, mortgages, mortgage discharges, and tax liens.

acceleration clause An acceleration provision is a term in a mortgage (or in the obligation it secures) that empowers the mortgagee upon default by the mortgagor to declare the full amount of the mortgage obligation immediately due and payable. An acceleration becomes effective on the date specified in a written notice by the mortgagor delivered after default.

acceptance Acts, conduct, or words that indicate an intent to take title to property described in a deed.

accretion The slow addition to land by deposition of water-borne sediment. The land so formed belongs to the owner upon whose property the deposit is made.

acknowledgment Verifying a signature by declaration in front of a notary public.

action A proceeding in a court of law in which one seeks a remedy for an alleged wrong.

action to quiet title An action compelling someone to establish his claim of an interest in land or forever be estopped from asserting it.

actual notice Title information that is acquired personally by someone.

ad coelum A person owns the space above her real estate to the extent that no one may acquire a right to such airspace that will limit the owner's enjoyment of it. This doctrine has been rejected by most courts.

adaptation test A test for determining whether personal property has become united with real property by its adaptation to the use and purpose of the real property.

adjustable rate mortgage A mortgage loan that allows the interest rate to change at specific intervals over the maturity of the loan.

administrative agency A governmental body charged with administering and implementing particular legislation.

administrative law The body of law created by administrative agencies in the form of rules, regulations, orders, and decisions to carry out regulatory powers and duties of such agencies.

administrator A person appointed by the court to administer the estate of a decedent who died without a valid will.

adverse possession A means of acquiring the title to another's land by openly taking possession of it for a prescribed period of time.

affirmative easement An easement that confers rights to use land burdened by the easement when the use would otherwise be illegal.

agricultural fixtures Articles placed in or attached to farm buildings and land for purposes of farming.

air rights The legal interest in the vertical dimension of property.

alienated An easement is "alienated" when it is transferred from one person to another.

alternative dispute resolution Various methods of resolving disputes outside traditional legal and administrative forums.

Americans with Disabilities Act of 1990 A federal statute that prohibits discrimination based on disability and requires reasonable accommodation by employers and landowners.

amortization provision Zoning ordinance provision that allows a nonconforming use to continue only for a specified number of years.

amount financed Cash available to the borrower from the loan for use in the transaction.

annexation test A key fixture test that is met when personal property is in fact annexed, fixed, or fastened onto the real property.

annual percentage rate The cost of credit according to its yearly rate.

answer A pleading responding to the plaintiff's claim set forth in the complaint.

apparent (or ostensible) authority Authority that a person appears to have to act as an agent of another if the other party's actions led a third party to reasonably believe the agency relationship existed, when, in fact, it did not.

apportioned An easement is "apportioned" when its use is divided or distributed consistent with the subdivision of the dominant tenement.

arbitration The submission of a dispute to an impartial third party; both parties generally agree in advance to abide by the arbitrator's decision.

area of critical state concern In state land use planning, an area that has a significant impact on environmental, historical, natural, or archeological resources of regional or statewide importance.

as-is clause Without warranty, as shown in its existing physical condition, with all faults and imperfections.

assembled industrial plant doctrine A doctrine that provides that plant machinery, even though not actually annexed, is constructively annexed onto real property.

assignment The lessee's transfer of the entire unexpired remainder of the lease term to the sublessee.

assumption of risk A defense to a negligence action that occurs when the plaintiff knows and appreciates the risks and voluntarily chooses to be exposed to the risks.

attachment lien A lien placed on real and personal property in which the court seizes the defendant's property on behalf of the plaintiff to ensure satisfaction of a judgment that might be awarded.

attachment of the security interest The process by which a secured party acquires a security interest in personal property or a fixture.

attractive nuisance doctrine A duty of reasonable care owed to a trespassing child unable to appreciate the danger from an artificial condition or activity on land to which the child can be expected to be attracted.

avulsion The sudden removal of soil from a property owner's land that is deposited upon another's land, by the action of water. The soil in such cases belongs to the owner from whose land it is removed.

B

bargain and sale deed In some states, a deed in which the grantee receives title but is not considered an innocent purchaser for value. The grantee receives title but no warranties.

base lines East-west survey reference lines intersecting with a north-south principal meridian to form a starting point in the Government Survey system.

Basic Form A property and liability policy that provides coverage for landowners from eleven specified perils.

bill of sale A written agreement in which one person transfers his interest in personal property to another.

blockbusting The attempt to promote sales in a racially transitional neighborhood by encouraging the idea that the transition is harmful.

Blue Sky Laws State laws that regulate the offer and sale of securities.

bona fide purchaser A good faith purchaser who pays value and is without notice, either actual or constructive, of a prior adverse claim. In most states, the requirement that the good faith purchaser "pays value" means that a buyer who pays only "nominal consideration," a token amount disproportionately small when compared with market value, does not qualify as a bona fide purchaser.

bonus money Cash paid to the lessor as consideration for the execution of an oil and gas lease.

Broad Form A property and liability policy that provides coverage for landowners from eighteen specified perils.

brownfields Real estate for which redevelopment or reuse may be complicated by the presence or potential presence of a hazardous substance.

bubble concept A concept that allows measuring the total discharge of pollutants from a factory rather than measuring pollutants from each separate source within the factory.

buyer broker A real estate agent who acts on behalf of the buyer.

bylaws A document governing the operation details of a condominium.

C

capacity The mental ability to understand the nature and effect of one's acts.

capture doctrine A doctrine that states that property owners have the right to appropriate all oil and gas from their land, including oil and gas that has migrated from neighboring properties.

caveat emptor Means literally "let the buyer beware." The doctrine places the responsibility of the inspection of real or personal property on the buyer. The buyer receives no guarantees or warranties on property purchased.

certificate of title A statement of opinion by an attorney that describes the state of the title to a parcel of land.

chain of title A record of successive conveyances (or other forms of alienation) affecting a particular parcel of land that are arranged consecutively from the government or original source of title down to the present holder.

citation Information that enables researchers to find the volume and pages where cases are published.

civil law rule A water law rule prohibiting landowners from altering or diverting the natural flow of diffused surface water.

claim of right An adverse possessor's claim of land as his own.

Clean Air Act A federal statute designed to improve the quality of the nation's air.

Clean Water Act A federal statute designed to improve the quality of the nation's water.

closing The consummation of the sale of real estate.

cloud on the title An outstanding claim or encumbrance that, if valid, would affect or impair the title of the owner of a particular estate and has that effect on its face, but can be shown to be invalid or inapplicable.

cluster zoning Zoning that allows a developer to depart from site development and density standards as long as part of the development is left as open space.

codicil An addendum to a will.

coinsurance clause A clause in a property insurance policy in which the insurer provides indemnity for only a certain percentage of the insured's loss, reflecting the relative division of risk between insurer and insured.

collateral Property that is pledged as security for the satisfaction of a debt. Collateral is additional security for performance of the principal obligation.

color of title An adverse possessor's claim to land derived from an invalid legal document.

Commerce Clause A provision in Article I, Section 8 of the U.S. Constitution giving Congress the power to regulate interstate commerce.

commission Payment by a seller of real estate to a real estate broker for finding a buyer.

commitment A bank's acceptance of a loan application.

common enemy rule Rule from the common law allowing landowners the right to take whatever measures necessary to protect and divert diffused surface water from their property.

common law The legal system originating in England after 1066. Judge-made law created when there is no controlling constitutional, statutory, or other law.

common law dedication A dedication expressed or implied under the common law. An express dedication is one expressly manifested by deed, recorded plats, or explicit written or oral manifestations but not executed pursuant to a statute. An implied dedication is created by a landowner's act or course of conduct in which a reasonable inference can be drawn that he intended to dedicate the property interest to the public.

community property Property acquired during a marriage through the efforts of either the husband or wife or both, with each having an undivided one-half interest in the property.

community property with the right of survivorship A hybrid form of concurrent ownership in which property is owned by the spouses as community property but that also provides a right of survivorship.

Community Reinvestment Act Federal law that establishes certain recordkeeping, reporting, and loan requirements for financial institutions.

comparative negligence Under comparative negligence statutes or doctrines, negligence is measured in terms of percentage and any damages allowed shall be diminished in proportion to the amount of negligence attributable to the person for whose injury, damage, or death recovery is sought. In most states, the person seeking the recovery receives no damages when her proportion of fault exceeds 50 percent or more.

compensatory damages Damages that compensate the injured party for the injury sustained and nothing more, such as will simply make good or replace the loss caused by the wrong or injury.

complaint The original or initial pleading setting forth a plaintiff's claim for relief against the defendant.

Comprehensive Environmental Response, Compensation, and Liability Act (CERCLA) The federal statute that provides for the cleanup of hazardous waste sites.

Comprehensive "all-risk" Form Property and liability policy that provides coverage for landowners from all perils except enumerated exceptions.

concurrent estate Ownership or possession of property by two or more people at the same time.

condemnation The process of taking private property for public use through the power of eminent domain.

condominium A system that combines separate ownership of individual units with joint ownership of common areas.

consent A voluntary agreement by a person with sufficient legal capacity to do something proposed by another.

conservation easement A negative easement that limits potential development or other property uses in order to preserve open space, natural resources, wildlife, and similar land uses.

consideration The cause, motive, price, or impelling influence that induces a contracting party to enter into a contract.

constitutional right to privacy A privacy right based on the due process clause of the Fifth and Fourteenth Amendments and implied in the First, Third, Fourth, Fifth, and Ninth Amendments to the U.S. Constitution.

construction mortgage A mortgage used to finance the construction or improvement of real property.

constructive annexation Personal property that is so closely related to real property that it is considered to be annexed even though it has not actually been annexed, fixed, or fastened to the real property.

constructive eviction A substantial and injurious interference of the tenant's possession by the landlord or someone acting under his authority that renders the premises unfit for the purposes for which they were demised or that deprives the tenant of the beneficial enjoyment of the premises, causing him to abandon them, provided that the tenant abandons the premises within a reasonable time.

constructive notice Notice imputed to a person by law due to its existence in the public records whether the person has actually inspected the public records or not.

contingency An event that may not occur.

contingent remainder A future interest that depends on the occurrence of an uncertain event.

contract A promise or set of promises for the breach of which the law gives a remedy, or the performance of which the law in some way recognizes as a duty.

contract of adhesion A contract in which one party is in a superior bargaining position and the other party has no realistic opportunity to bargain over the terms.

contributory negligence Conduct by a plaintiff that is below the standard to which he is legally required to conform for his own protection. Along with the negligence of the defendant, it is a contributing cause of the plaintiff's harm.

conventional first mortgage A mortgage made by a private lender that is not insured or guaranteed by a government agency.

conversion The intentional and unauthorized possession and control over another's personal property.

cooperative A multiunit complex in which the owners have an interest in the entire complex and a lease of their own apartments.

corporation A type of business organization that is owned by shareholders but managed by a board of directors who elect the executive officers.

counteroffer A statement by the offeree that has the legal effect of rejecting the offer and of proposing a new offer to the original offeror.

covenant of quiet enjoyment An assurance by the landlord that she will not interfere with the tenant's use of the property.

covenant running with the land A contractual promise that passes with the land.

cumulative zoning Zoning classification that allows more restrictive land uses in lesser-restricted areas.

curtesy Under the common law, a surviving husband's rights in land owned by his wife.

D

damages A monetary award that a losing party must pay the winning party in a lawsuit.

debtor One who owes a debt.

dedication A private landowner's conferral of an interest in land to the government for the public interest.

deed A written instrument used to convey real estate from one party to another.

deed exception Excepting from a transfer a part of an estate that has already been created.

deed in lieu of foreclosure The mortgagor deeds the property to the lender in exchange for the lender's agreement to release the mortgagor from liability under the promissory note.

deed of trust An instrument serving the same function as a mortgage in which the borrower places the title to property in trust to secure the repayment of a loan owed to the beneficiary of the trust.

deed reservation The creation by deed of a new right out of an estate that has been transferred to a buyer.

default Failure by a debtor to pay the note or carry out other obligations.

deficiency judgment A court order stating that the borrower still owes money when the security for the loan does not entirely satisfy a defaulted debt.

delay rentals Consideration paid to the lessor for the privilege of deferring commencement of drilling activities during the primary term of the lease. In the absence of drilling activity or production, failure to pay delay rentals results in termination of the lease.

delivery A grantor's transfer and relinquishment of a deed to the grantee.

dependent covenant A promise made in return for a reciprocal promise.

deposition A pretrial device in which one party orally questions the other party or a witness for the other party.

descent and distribution statute A state statute that provides for the distribution of property when a person dies without a valid will.

development of regional impact Under Florida law, a development that has such character, magnitude, or location that it has a substantial effect on the health, safety, and welfare of citizens of more than one county.

diffused surface water Water on the earth's surface that does not flow in a defined channel or stream. Water fed generally by rainfall or melting snow.

directed verdict The entry of a verdict by a trial judge, prior to allowing the jury to decide the case, when the party with the burden of proof fails to present a prima facie case.

discovery The pretrial devices that can be used by one party to obtain facts and information about the case from the other party.

diversity of citizenship A phrase used with reference to the jurisdiction of the federal courts, which, under U.S. Constitution Article III, section 2, extends to cases between citizens of different states, when the party on one side of the lawsuit is a citizen of one state and the party on the other side is a citizen of another state or between a citizen of a state and an alien (a citizen of another country).

domestic fixtures Articles that tenants attach to a dwelling to render their occupation of the premises more comfortable or convenient.

dominant estate (or dominant tenement) The land that benefits from the easement on another property. The possessor of the dominant estate is entitled to the benefits of uses authorized by the easement.

dower Under the common law, a widow's right to receive at her husband's death a life estate in one-third of the inheritable lands that he owned during their marriage.

dual agency A relationship created when an agent simultaneously represents opposite sides in a transaction.

due on sale clause A special type of acceleration clause that causes the entire debt to become due upon the sale of the property.

duress Entering into a contract under the pressure of an unlawful act or threat.

duty A legal obligation.

E

earnest money A portion of the purchase price given to the seller when the contract is signed as evidence of the buyer's good faith and willingness to perform the contract.

easement An interest in land that gives the owner the right to use real estate owned by another for a specified purpose.

easement appurtenant An easement that benefits a particular tract of land. It is incapable of existence separate and apart from the particular land to which it is annexed.

easement in gross An easement that grants a personal right to use the property of another.

economic loss rule A party suffering only economic loss from the breach of an express or implied contract may not assert a tort claim arising from the breach unless an independent action under tort law exists.

elective share A state statute that allows a surviving spouse to take a designated share of the decedent spouse's estate instead of the share provided for in the decedent spouse's will.

emblements Crops produced by a tenant's labor to which the tenant is entitled. These crops are grown annually, not spontaneously, by labor and industry.

Emergency Planning and Community Right-to-Know Act (EPCRA) Federal statute that provides information to the public about hazardous chemicals in their communities and encourages planning for emergencies.

eminent domain The power of government to take private property for public use upon the payment of just compensation.

Endangered Species Act Federal law that protects habitats of plant and animal species designated as endangered.

environmental impact statement A document that analyzes the environmental impact of a proposed federal action.

Environmental Protection Agency (EPA) The federal agency that establishes environmental standards and enforces environmental laws.

Equal Credit Opportunity Act Federal law that prohibits discrimination in credit decisions based on an applicant's gender, marital status, religion, race, color, national origin, age, or receipt of welfare.

equitable conversion A doctrine under which a buyer who signs a real estate contract is immediately regarded as the equitable owner of the real property, while the seller has an equitable interest in the purchase price.

equitable mortgage A lien that is placed on real property to secure the payment of money based on the clear intent of the parties but that lacks the essential features of a legal mortgage.

equity Justice administered according to fairness created in order to temper the strictly formulated rules of the English common law.

equity of redemption A term used in the law of mortgages to describe either (1) the right in equity of the mortgagor to redeem after default in the performance of the conditions in the mortgage or (2) the estate which remains in the mortgagor after the execution of the mortgage.

escheat A reversion of property to the state when no individual is available who legally qualifies to inherit it.

escrow A system of document transfer in which a deed, a bond, or funds are delivered to a third person to hold until all conditions of the escrow are fulfilled.

estate for years An estate of fixed duration—a year or a multiple or fraction of a year. The essential characteristic of this estate is its duration.

estoppel One person cannot claim a right to the detriment of another person when the latter was entitled to rely and did in fact rely on the first person's conduct.

estoppel certificate A written statement in which a mortgagor asserts that she has no defenses to a note.

estray statutes Statutes defining what rights finders have in property when the true owners are unknown.

exclusionary zoning Zoning ordinances that exclude specific classes of persons, structures, and businesses from designated areas or districts.

exclusions and exceptions Certain potential defects or liens against a title to land that are excluded from coverage in a title insurance policy.

exclusive agency A listing agreement between the seller of real estate and a real estate broker that gives the broker the exclusive right to sell the property and a commission on the sale, but the seller may, without owing a commission, use her own efforts to sell the property.

exclusive easement in gross A transferable easement in gross in which the grantor conveys personal rights exclusively to the grantee.

exclusive right A personal property right to enter, explore for, and extract oil and gas from another's property.

exclusive right to sell A listing agreement between a seller of real estate and a real estate broker that gives the broker the sole right to sell the property and to receive a commission on the sale regardless of whether the broker is responsible for the sale.

exclusive zoning Method of zoning in which land use is limited to the zoned use.

exculpatory clause A contract clause that releases one of the parties from liability for his wrongful acts.

executor A person designated by the testator to carry out the directions of the testator's will.

executory interest A future interest associated with the fee simple subject to an executory condition wherein the interest may return to a party other than the grantor when there is a breach of a condition to which it was granted.

exhaustion of remedies The requirement that parties must first seek relief by availing themselves of all administrative remedies before going to court to ask for judicial action.

exit fee A fee that is imposed when a promissory note is paid before it is due or when it matures.

express authority The authority a principal specifically grants an agent.

express conveyance A written instrument in which the grantor transfers an interest in land.

express reservation A right created and retained by the grantor.

express warranty An express promise made by the seller to the buyer as to the quality, condition, or performance of the thing being sold.

F

Fair Housing Act Title VIII of the Civil Rights Act of 1968, which prohibits discrimination in housing based on race, color, religion, sex, national origin, disability, or family status.

Fair Housing Amendments Act of 1988 The Act incorporated into the Fair Housing Act of 1968 that added familial status and handicap as protected classifications and strengthened enforcement procedures.

fair lending laws Federal legislation created to outlaw various forms of discrimination in real estate lending practices.

Fannie Mae A private shareholder-owned corporation regulated by the federal government that provides a secondary market for the buying and selling of both government-backed and conventional mortgages.

fee simple absolute An estate limited absolutely to its owners and their heirs that assigns forever without limitation or condition.

fee simple defeasible A fee estate that may end upon the happening of a specified event.

fee simple determinable A type of defeasible fee that ends automatically when land is used in a manner forbidden in the grant of ownership.

fee simple subject to a condition subsequent A type of defeasible fee that entitles the grantor to end the interest by exercising the right of entry after the grantee breaches a condition under which it was granted.

fee simple subject to an executory limitation or interest A type of defeasible fee that ends automatically when land is used in a manner forbidden in the grant of ownership, but vests in someone other than the grantor.

fee tail An estate in fee that descends to the grantee's direct lineal heirs and through

them to the direct lineal heirs of the next generation.

FHA mortgage loan A mortgage loan that is insured by the Fair Housing Administration.

fiduciary duty A duty to act for someone else's benefit while subordinating one's personal interests to that of another person. It is the highest standard of duty imposed by law.

finance charge Any charge for the extension of credit.

financing statement A document filed in the public record to give notice to third parties of the secured party's security interest.

fixture A legal hybrid; a piece of personal property that has become affixed to real property in such a way that it becomes part of the real property. The UCC's definition of a fixture is also instructive: [G]oods are "fixtures" when they become so related to particular real estate that an interest in them arises under real estate law.

fixture filing The filing of a financing statement in the real estate public record to perfect the security interest in a fixture.

floating zones Where a zoning ordinance provides for land uses but does not allocate land to those uses.

forbearance When a creditor allows the debtor to delay payment of a debt after it becomes due.

foreclosure Process initiated by the mortgagee to sell the collateralized real estate to satisfy the mortgagor's debt.

Foreign Investment in Real Property Tax Act A tax statute that imposes a withholding requirement on nonresident aliens and foreign business entities that acquire real estate in the United States.

four unities The four characteristics of an interest held in joint tenancy: unity of time, unity of title, unity of interest, and unity of possession.

Freddie Mac A private shareholder-owned corporation regulated by the federal government that provides a secondary market for the buying and selling of both government-backed and conventional first mortgages.

freehold estate An indefinite estate in life or in fee.

fructus industriales Vegetation, such as crops, that grows on property by the efforts of humans.

fructus naturales Vegetation that grows naturally on property and not by the efforts of humans.

frustration of purpose A defense to the performance of a contract when the objectives of the contract have been defeated by unforeseen circumstances arising after the formation of the agreement.

future advance Money that is loaned after a mortgage has attached and that is secured by the mortgage.

G

gap The time period between the issuance of a title commitment and the recording of the documents to be insured.

garnishment The satisfaction of a debt out of a losing party's property possessed by or owed by another.

general agents An agent with broad authority to act on behalf of the principal.

general exceptions (also known as standard exceptions) Certain potential defects or liens against a title to land that are not contained in the public record and are excluded from coverage in a title insurance policy.

general warranty deed A deed that conveys the grantor's title and contains warranties of title.

Ginnie Mae An agency within the Department of Housing and Urban Development that guarantees the payment of interest and principal on bonds issued by private thrifts and mortgage bankers. The bonds are backed by VA and FHA mortgages.

Good Faith Estimate form A closing form required by HUD regulation that accompanies the HUD-1 form designed to better inform consumers about the terms of the loan and estimated settlement charges.

Government Survey A standard rectangular system of describing land existing in the majority of American states.

grantee The party to whom the deed conveys title.

grantor A transferor of property.

grantor-grantee index A land records system in which conveyances of interests in real property are indexed in two separate indices, first alphabetically according to the grantor's surname and then alphabetically according to the grantee's surname.

groundwater Water beneath the earth's surface fed by rainfall or surface streams. Water that is not part of a defined underground stream.

guarantee A promise made by one party to share responsibility for the debts of another party.

H

habendum clause The portion of a deed describing the ownership rights transferred.

holder in due course A person who has purchased the note in good faith, for value, and without notice of defenses.

holdover tenant A tenant who retains possession after the expiration of a leasehold interest.

holographic (or handwritten) will A will written and signed entirely in the testator's handwriting.

Home Mortgage Disclosure Act Federal law requiring financial institutions to furnish the federal government with information about loan applicants and their approval rate by race, gender, and income.

Home Owners Warranty (HOW) plan A warranty developed by the National Association of Home Builders in which a buyer is covered for certain defects in new homes and condominiums.

Home Ownership and Equity Protection Act An amendment to the Truth in Lending Act created to prevent predatory lending practices.

homestead A person's residence and the land surrounding it.

hostile use The user must not recognize that the owner of the land has authority to prevent her use.

HUD-1 The Department of Housing and Urban Development's (HUD's) closing statement form for residential property financed with federally related mortgage loans.

I

implied authority Implementation authority; that authority necessary to carry out the express authority that the principal grants the agent.

implied easement An easement arising impliedly by reference to a plat or map, from prior use, or from necessity of use.

implied easement from prior use An easement that was apparent at the time an estate was divided and that is reasonably necessary for the use of the quasi-dominant estate.

implied easement of necessity An easement that arises by operation of law after land is divided if one of the parcels is inaccessible.

implied reciprocal restrictions or **reciprocal negative easements** Restrictions that form part of a general plan of development that prevent landowners from making certain uses of their land even when their deeds do not mention the restrictions.

implied warranty of habitability An implied promise by a home builder or landlord that the premises have been completed in a workmanlike manner and are fit for habitation.

implied warranty of suitability An implied promise by a commercial landlord that facilities essential to the use of the commercial premises are free from latent defects and will remain in suitable condition.

in arrears Having unpaid debts, outstanding obligations, or overdue payments.

inclusionary zoning Zoning regulations that create incentives or requirements for affordable housing development.

independent covenant A promise that is not dependent on a reciprocal promise.

injunction A court order prohibiting someone from doing some specified act or commanding someone to undo some wrong or injury.

inquiry notice Notice of facts that create a duty to inquire further whether unrecorded interests exist.

installment contract Contract for the sale of real estate in which the seller finances the sale and the buyer pays the seller the purchase price over time.

insurable interest A sufficient interest in the property to be insured so that the loss of the property would result in monetary damage to the insured.

intention To plan for, design, or expect a certain result.

intention test A test for determining whether personal property has become united with real property by examining the intent of the annexor.

intentional tort An intentional wrongful act that causes injury.

interrogatories A discovery device consisting of written questions generally submitted to one side of the lawsuit from the other.

Interstate Land Sales Full Disclosure Act A 1968 federal statute that regulates the sale of property across state lines by requiring certain advance filings and disclosures to prospective buyers.

intestate A person who dies without a will.

invasion of privacy Four separate torts: (a) appropriation—the unauthorized use of a person's name, likeness, or personality for the benefit of another; (b) public disclosure of a private fact—unreasonably offensive publicity concerning the private life of a person; (c) false light—unreasonably offensive publicity placing the victim in a false light; (d) intrusion—an unreasonably offensive intrusion into someone's private affairs or concerns.

inverse condemnation Actions brought by landowners alleging that a taking of their property has resulted from activities of public agencies or private bodies vested with the authority to condemn.

invitee Someone who is present on another's land with the express or implied invitation of the occupier of the land.

J

joint and several liability A liability is joint and several when the creditor may demand payment or sue one or more of the parties to such liability separately or all of them together at the creditor's option.

joint tenancy Ownership of real or personal property by two or more people in which each owns an undivided interest in the whole and each has the right of survivorship.

judgment lien A lien that attaches to a defendant's property when the plaintiff wins a judgment in the jurisdiction in which the property is located.

judicial sale A decree of a court directing the sale of mortgaged property.

jurisdiction Defines the powers of courts to inquire into the facts, apply the law, make decisions, and declare judgment. It is the legal right by which judges exercise their authority.

just compensation Compensation that is fair to both the owner and the public when property is taken for public use through eminent domain.

L

land use planning The process of establishing the character, quality, and pattern of the physical environment for the activities of people and organizations in the planning area.

lateral support The right of lateral and subjacent support is the right to have land supported by the adjoining land or the soil beneath.

law A body of rules of action or conduct prescribed by controlling authority and having binding legal force. That which must be obeyed and followed by citizens subject to sanctions is a law.

lease A contract conveying a property interest (leasehold estate) to a tenant.

leasehold estate An estate in real property that lasts for a definite period of time.

letter of intent An instrument that serves to gauge each party's commitment to a future contractual relationship before the parties reach agreement on a formal contract.

license A privilege to enter the premises for a certain purpose, which does not give the licensee any title, interest, or estate in such property.

license coupled with an interest An irrevocable license granted to a licensee to enter the licensor's property and exercise the legal rights he possesses in the licensor's property.

licensee A person permitted to enter another's property for the licensee's own purposes and not for the benefit of the possessor.

lien theory The modern view of mortgage law in which the mortgagor transfers a security interest in the property to the mortgagee to secure the repayment of a loan.

life estate An estate in which duration is measured by the life of a person.

limited liability company A hybrid form of business organization that provides the limited liability of a corporation and the tax advantages of a partnership.

limited partnership A type of partnership comprised of one or more general partners who manage the business and who are personally liable for partnership debts and one or more limited partners who contribute capital and share in profits but take no part in running the business and incur no liability with respect to partnership obligations beyond their contribution.

listing agreement A contract between a seller of real estate and a real estate broker in which the broker is authorized to serve as the seller's agent.

little Sherman acts State antitrust laws designed to regulate anticompetitive behavior within the state.

littoral Concerning or belonging to the shore (littoral rights) of coasts and waterfronts.

locus in quo "The place in which" lost personal property is found.

lost property Property with which the owner has involuntarily parted and he does not know where to find.

M

mailbox rule Derived from the 1818 case of *Adams v. Lindsell*, this rule provides that once the offeree has placed its letter of acceptance in a means of transit outside of its control—for example, in the mail—it is too late for the offeror to revoke.

mandatory agency disclosure laws State laws requiring agents to disclose to consumers the type of agents they are and the rights and duties that exist in their relationships with the consumers.

mandatory right of rescission A borrower's right under the Truth in Lending Act to rescind, within three days, certain kinds of loans secured by the debtor's home.

Marketable Record Title Acts State laws that limit the enforceability of old claims and interests.

marketable title Title to real estate that is reasonably free from encumbrances, defects in the chain of title, and other problems that affect the title.

master deed (also known as the **enabling declaration**, the **declaration of conditions**, or the **condominium document**) The recorded document that authorizes the election of a condominium's board of directors, describes the condominium units and the common areas, and establishes the owner's undivided interest percentage.

mechanic's lien A type of statutory lien placed on real property to ensure payment to those who supply labor, services, or materials for improvement of the real property.

mediation The process whereby a neutral third party aids and encourages parties to a dispute to reach a mutually satisfactory outcome.

merger rule When the real estate contract merges into and is replaced by the deed.

metes and bounds A way of describing land by listing the compass directions and distances of the boundaries.

mineral lease A lease that grants to a lessee the exclusive right to enter the lessor's premises to explore, drill, produce, store, and remove minerals specified in the lease.

mirror image rule A doctrine that states for a valid contract to exist, the terms of the offeree's acceptance must correspond exactly to the offer made by the offeror.

mislaid property Property that has been deliberately placed somewhere but forgotten.

misrepresentation A false statement of a material fact.

mistaken annexation The mistaken attachment of personal property to real property owned by someone else.

mitigation of damages A duty imposed on injured parties that requires them to attempt to minimize their damages.

mortgage An interest in land created by a written instrument providing security for the performance of a duty or the payment of a debt.

mortgage assumption An agreement between the seller-mortgagor and a buyer in which the buyer agrees to assume the obligation for the seller's mortgage debt.

mortgage banker A banker who originates, sells, and services mortgage loans.

mortgage broker A broker who, for a fee, places loans with investors but does not service the loans.

mortgage insurance Insurance protecting the mortgagee from losses when encumbered property is damaged or destroyed.

mortgagee A lender who receives an interest in property from the mortgagor as security for the repayment of a loan.

mortgagee loss clause now in common use (known as the standard clause) A clause in a mortgage insurance policy that indemnifies the mortgagee for a loss even if the act that damages or destroys property would not otherwise provide coverage for the mortgagor.

mortgagee title insurance policy Insurance that protects the lender against loss or damage resulting from defects in the title or the enforcement of liens against the land.

mortgagee-in-possession A lender who takes possession of the real property, securing the debt prior to foreclosure.

mortgagor A borrower who transfers an interest in property to the mortgagee as security for the repayment of a loan.

multiple listing service A service that provides a listing of real estate for sale by competing brokers.

mutual mistake A mistake by both parties that is grounds for avoiding a contract.

N

National Environment Policy Act (NEPA) A federal statute that requires federal agencies to prepare environmental impact statements when proposed federal action significantly affects the quality of the human environment.

natural flow theory A riparian rights doctrine, originated in England, that confers to riparian owners the right to the ordinary flow of water along their land, but undiminished in quantity and quality.

navigable water Any body of water that, by itself or by uniting with other waters, forms a continuous highway over which commerce can be carried on with other states or countries.

negative easement An easement that prevents landowners from making certain uses of their land that would otherwise be legal.

negligence The failure to do what a reasonable person would have done under the same circumstances.

negotiable note Any writing to be a negotiable instrument within this Article must (a) be signed by the maker or drawer; (b) contain an unconditional promise or order to pay a sum certain in money and no other promise, order, obligation, or power given by the maker or drawer except as authorized by this Article; (c) be payable on demand or at a definite time; and (d) be payable to order or to bearer.

net listing agreement A contract between a seller of real estate and a real estate broker in which the broker is paid as a commission the amount the sale price exceeds the price set by the seller.

New York Rule Owners who pay a general contractor when they have no notice of other liens are discharged up to the amount of payment.

nominal damages A trifling sum awarded to a plaintiff in an action where there is no substantial loss or injury to be compensated, but still the law recognizes a technical invasion of his rights or a breach of the defendant's duty, or in cases where, although there has been a real injury, the plaintiff's evidence entirely fails to show its amount.

Non-Foreign Affidavit A sworn statement by the buyer or his agent that states that the seller is not a foreign person under the Foreign Investment in Real Property Tax Act.

nonconforming use In zoned areas, a use that does not conform with the area's zoning, but that existed before the zoning requirement became effective.

noncupative or nuncupative will An oral will.

nonexclusive easement in gross A transferable easement in gross in which the grantor does not convey personal rights exclusively to the grantee, but instead retains rights to the easement in gross.

nonfreehold or leasehold estates An ownership interest in land generally of a fixed or determinable duration.

nonjudicial sale A foreclosure conducted without a court proceeding pursuant to the rights granted under the power of sale.

nonpoint sources Pollution, such as runoff, that does not come from a specific point.

nonrecourse note A loan in which the lender's recourse to satisfy the loan is against the collateral, not against the borrower's personal assets.

notice statute Under a "notice" recording statute, an unrecorded conveyance is not valid against later bona fide purchasers.

novation The substitution by mutual agreement of one debtor for another whereby the original debtor's obligation is extinguished.

nuisance The unreasonable interference with the use or enjoyment of land without a physical invasion.

O

open listing agreement A contract between a seller of real estate and a real estate broker in which the broker has a nonexclusive right to sell the property.

option contract An option is an enforceable promise that limits the offeror's power to revoke the offer. The option is said to be "exercised" when the offeree accepts the offer in accordance with the terms of the option contract.

owner's title insurance policy Insurance that protects the purchaser borrower's equity against loss or damage resulting from defects in the title or from the enforcement of liens against the land.

ownership principle A theory under which oil and gas are owned in place and can be severed and sold the same as a solid mineral.

P

parol evidence rule Provides that if the parties have put their contract in writing and intend the writing to be their final agreement, evidence of prior or contemporaneous agreements reached during negotiations may not be used in court to vary or contradict the written agreement.

part performance An exception to the Statute of Frauds rule that allows for the oral contract for a sale of land if the party seeking enforcement has partially performed the contract.

partial actual eviction Physically depriving a tenant of possession of a portion of the premises.

partially disclosed principal A principal whose existence is known but whose identity to the third party with whom its agent is dealing is not known.

partnership Section 6 of the Uniform Partnership Act defines a partnership as "an association of two or more persons to carry on as co-owners of a business for profit."

patent A grant of a privilege, property, or authority to an individual by the government.

payee The person to whom or to whose order a check, bill of exchange, or promissory note is made payable.

Pennsylvania Rule Owners who pay a general contractor before the time for filing subcontractor claims has expired might be liable to the subcontractors if the general contractor defaults.

perfect tender in time Absent statutory or express contractual language to the contrary, a borrower has no right to prepay his mortgage or deed of trust obligation prior to the maturity date specified on the underlying promissory note and the agreed upon payment schedule is to be enforced.

perfection of the security interest In secured transactions law, the process whereby a security interest is protected, as far as the law permits, against competing claims to the collateral, which usually requires the secured party to give public notice of the interest as by filing in a government office (for example, in the secretary of state's office). Perfection of a security interest deals with those steps legally required to give a secured party a superior interest in the subject property against debtor's creditors.

periodic tenancy A tenancy that endures for a certain period of time and for successive periods of equal length unless terminated at the end of any one period by notice of either party. The chief characteristics that distinguish periodic tenancies from other nonfreehold estates are the continuity of the term and the requirement of notice to terminate the tenancy.

personal defenses Defenses valid against holders of negotiable notes but not against holders in due course.

personal property All property, with the exception of real property, that can be owned.

planned unit development Land developed as a single unit according to a plan, with a specified minimum contiguous acreage. The planned unit development contains one or more residential clusters or planned unit residential developments and one or more public, quasipublic, commercial, or industrial areas. The ratio of nonresidential uses to residential uses is specified in the zoning ordinance.

plat A recorded map of a parcel of real estate that has been subdivided.

point source Pollution that comes from a specific point.

police power The power of a state to exercise control to protect the health, safety, morals, and welfare of the public.

pollution credits Credits that can be earned and then sold by companies that emit pollutants below established standards.

possibility of reverter Future interest associated with the fee simple determinable estate wherein the interest may return to the grantor when there is a breach of a condition to which it was granted.

power of attorney An instrument appointing an agent to conduct business on behalf of a principal.

power of sale clause A clause contained in mortgages and deeds of trust granting the lender or trustee the right to sell the property upon default.

predatory lending Deceptive loan application and closing practices that take advantage of borrowers who lack sufficient sophistication, economic stability, and knowledge to protect themselves from illegal and unethical lending practices.

prepayment fee A fee that is imposed when a promissory note is paid before it is due.

prescription A means of acquiring an easement through adverse use over a prescribed period of time.

prescriptive easement A right to use another's property that is inconsistent with the owner's rights and that is acquired by a use—open and notorious, adverse and continuous—for the statutory period. To a certain extent, it resembles title by adverse possession but differs to the extent that the adverse user acquires only an easement and not title.

primary air standards Clean air standards designed to protect the public health.

principal meridian North and south survey line of reference intersecting with an east-west base line to form a starting point in the Government Survey system.

prior appropriation theory A water rights doctrine that confers the primary rights to the first users of water.

private law The law governing relations between private individuals.

private mortgage insurance Default insurance on conventional loans provided by private insurers.

private necessity The entering or destruction of another's property to protect a person's property, health, or safety.

private nuisance The unreasonable interference with a private person's use or enjoyment of land without a physical invasion.

privity of contract A direct contract between two parties.

probate The court procedure by which a will is proved to be valid or invalid. In current usage, this term has been expanded to refer generally to the legal procedure wherein the estate of the decedent is administered.

procedural law Law that prescribes processes for enforcing rights or gaining redress for those who have their rights violated.

procuring cause of sale The actions of a real estate broker that are the direct and primary cause of a real estate sale.

product liability The liability of a manufacturer, a supplier, a wholesaler, an assembler, a retailer, or a lessor of a defective product that causes damage or injury to a consumer or user.

profit *a prendre* An interest in the land of another that confers rights of use and removal of the profits of the soil.

promissory note A promise or an engagement in writing to pay a specified sum at a time therein stated or on demand or at sight to a person named therein (or to his order or bearer).

prorate The act of adjusting, dividing, or prorating property taxes, interest, insurance premiums, rental income, etc., between buyer and seller proportionately to time of use or date of closing.

proximate cause The cause that in natural and continuous sequence unbroken by an intervening cause produces an injury.

public law A law that applies generally to the people of a nation or of a state; the law concerned with the organization of the state, the relations between the state and the people, the responsibilities of public officers, and the relationship between states.

public necessity A legal privilege to enter or destroy another's property in the public interest.

public nuisance An unreasonable interference with a right that is common to the general public.

public trust doctrine A theory that the government holds its lands in trust for the public.

public use A use that confers some benefit or advantage to the public.

puffing A seller's expression of opinion that is not made as a representation of a fact.

punitive damages Damages other than compensatory damages that may be awarded against a person to punish her for outrageous conduct.

purchase money mortgage A mortgage given by the buyer of real property to the seller or lender to finance the purchase price.

purchase money security interest A security interest taken by a lender or retained by a seller to secure all or part of the price of goods purchased by the borrower.

purchase of development rights A type of conservation easement conveyed to a local governmental entity in which landowners agree to restrict the use of their land in exchange for a reduction in taxes.

Q

quitclaim deed A deed conveying the grantor's interests.

R

race statute Under a pure race statute, the first to record wins. The purchaser need not be bona fide or without notice.

race-notice statute Under a race-notice statute, a later purchaser not only must be bona fide but also must record the deed before other purchasers.

range lines North-south running survey lines spaced approximately six miles apart used in the Government Survey system.

real defenses Defenses that are valid against all holders of negotiable notes, including holders in due course.

real estate broker An agent authorized under state real estate licensing laws to operate independently in a real estate brokerage business.

real estate closing The event at which the real estate contract is finally performed.

Real Estate Investment Trusts (REITs) An entity that invests in real estate ventures and must distribute at least 90 percent of its net income to investors.

real estate salesperson An agent authorized under state real estate licensing laws to act in real estate brokerage transactions only under the control and direction of a licensed real estate broker.

Real Estate Settlement Procedures Act Federal law that regulates the disclosure of closing costs in advance and prohibits kickbacks to professionals involved in real estate closings.

real property Land and anything permanently attached to it.

REALTORS® Licensed real estate brokers and salespersons who are members of the National Association of Realtors.

reasonable conduct doctrine Doctrine in water law allowing landowners to divert diffused surface water if their efforts do not unreasonably harm other landowners.

reasonable use theory A riparian rights doctrine that confers to riparian owners the reasonable use of the water that flows along their land.

receiver A person appointed by the court to manage property in litigation or the affairs of a bankrupt party.

recording statutes State statutes that govern the manner in which documents are recorded in the public record and the effect such recording has on subsequent purchasers, creditors, mortgagees, and other parties who may have an interest in the property.

recording The act of placing in the public record documents that give the world notice of the information therein.

recourse note A loan in which the borrower is personally liable for payment in the event of a default.

recreational use statutes State statutes that limit a landowner's liability when a member of the public is injured while using the land for recreational purposes.

redlining Occurs when lenders refuse to make mortgage loans or impose stricter mortgage terms in certain neighborhoods.

Regulation Z Regulations issued by the Federal Reserve Board pursuant to the Truth in Lending Act entrusting the agency to supervise all banks in the Federal Reserve System and to ensure their compliance with the Act.

reliction The gradual and imperceptible withdrawal of water from land. In a permanent withdrawal the owner of the contiguous property acquires ownership of the dry land created.

remainder A future interest created in favor of a party other than the grantor that generally follows a life estate. A remainder interest can be vested or contingent.

remainderman The holder of a remainder interest.

remedy The means by which a right is enforced or the violation of a right is prevented, redressed, or compensated.

rent Consideration paid for the use of property.

representation A statement, express or implied, made by one of two contracting parties to the other party before or at the time of making the contract in regard to some past or existing fact, circumstance, or state of facts pertinent to the contract that is influential in bringing about the agreement.

res judicata A rule that a final judgment rendered by a court of competent jurisdiction on the merits is conclusive as to the rights of the parties and their privies and as to them constitutes an absolute bar to a subsequent action involving the same claim, demand, or cause of action.

Resource Conservation and Recovery Act (RCRA) Federal statute that regulates the treatment, storage, and disposal of hazardous wastes.

Restatement of the Law of Property A series of volumes published by the American Law Institute (ALI) on various areas of the law, such as property, torts, and contracts. The Restatements state the law; note emerging trends; and, at times, suggest changes in the law. Courts and legislatures may follow the Restatements in making or interpreting law.

restraint on alienation A provision in an instrument of conveyance that prohibits the grantee from transferring the property that is the subject of the restraint.

retaliatory eviction An eviction of a tenant for complaining about the condition of the leased premises or violations of the law.

reverse annuity mortgage A mortgage, generally used by elderly homeowners, in which money is borrowed in the form of monthly payments and secured by the equity in the home.

reversion A future interest left in the grantor after the grantor conveys an estate smaller than her own. "It arises merely as a matter of simple subtraction."

reviewability Under administrative law, a determination of whether a final agency action is subject to judicial review.

revocation The termination of an offer by the offeror prior to an acceptance by the offeree.

right of distress A right under the common law allowing the landlord to seize a tenant's goods to satisfy a debt for past rent.

right of entry A future interest associated with the fee simple subject to a condition subsequent in which the grantor may elect to end the interest after the grantee breaches a condition under which it was granted.

right of reinstatement A legal right under a deed of trust in which the borrower in default can cure the debt prior to the trustee's acceleration of the note.

riparian owner The owner of land contiguous to flowing navigable water such as streams and rivers.

riparian rights The rights of an owner of land that touches a watercourse to use the water.

ripeness requirement The constitutional requirement that before a case can be heard in court, it must have ripened, or matured, into a controversy worthy of adjudication.

root of title A transaction in the seller's chain of title "being the most recent to be recorded as of a date prior to the statutory number of years before the time marketability is being determined."

royalty interest A lessor's right to share in the oil, gas, or other minerals produced under the lease, generally free of production costs.

S

S corporation A closely held corporation with no more than one hundred shareholders who elect to be taxed like partners.

sale subject to a mortgage A sale in which the buyer agrees to purchase property subject to the mortgage lien.

satisfaction The discharge of a mortgage.

secondary air standards Clean air standards created to protect animals, plants, and property from the adverse effects of air pollution.

secondary market A market in which money market instruments are traded among investors.

secret agent An agent who represents a principal whose existence and identity are unknown to the third party with whom the agent is dealing.

section Parcel of land in the Government Survey system comprising one square mile, or 640 acres. There are 36 sections in a township.

security The securities law definition of a security is extremely broad. The term *security* means "any note, stock, treasury stock, bond, debenture, evidence of indebtedness, certificate of interest or participation in any profit-sharing agreement, collateral trust certificate, preorganization certificate or subscription, transferable share, investment contract, voting-trust certificate, certificate of deposit for a security, fractional undivided interest in oil, gas, or other mineral rights, any put, call, straddle, option, or privilege entered into on a national securities exchange relating to a foreign currency, or, in general, any interest or instrument commonly known as a 'security,' or any certificate of interest or participation in, temporary or interim certificate for, receipt for, guarantee of, or warrant or right to subscribe to or purchase, any of the foregoing."

securitization A process in which an asset is converted into a pool of securities that are offered to investors.

security agreement An agreement that creates a security interest.

security deposit Money deposited by a tenant with a landlord as security for the performance of the lease.

security interest An interest in personal property or fixtures that secures payment or performance of an obligation.

self-help Acting independently of the courts.

separate property Property acquired before the marriage or acquired by the husband or wife through gift or inheritance during the marriage that is owned by a married person in his or her own right.

servient estate (or servient tenement) Land that is burdened by an easement appurtenant or an easement in gross.

settlement An agreement to terminate all or part of a lawsuit as a result of the parties' voluntary resolution of the dispute.

settlement agent A third party who handles the closing of a real estate transaction.

severance A joint tenant's transfer of her interest that terminates the joint tenancy and converts it into a tenancy in common.

severance The legal principle that defines the mechanical processes required to convert an item of real property into personal property.

Sherman Antitrust Act An 1890 federal statute that regulates anticompetitive behavior in interstate commerce.

short sale A sale agreed to by the seller, buyer, and lender in which the proceeds fall short of what is owed to the lender.

simultaneous issue discount Discount in the premium price paid by the purchaser borrower for buying both a mortgagee and an owner's title insurance policy.

Single Family Mortgage Foreclosure Act of 1994 Federal law regulating high-risk residential loans held by the Department of Housing and Urban Development.

slander of title Occurs when one publishes information which is untrue and disparaging to another's property interests in land that can result in the impairment of its marketability.

Small Business Liability Relief and Brownfields Revitalization Act A federal statute establishing defenses to CERCLA and creating incentives to develop brownfields.

Soldiers and Sailors Civil Relief Act of 1940 Federal law providing time limitations on foreclosures of homes owned by those in active military service.

special agent An agent with authority to conduct a single transaction or a limited series of transactions.

special exceptions Zoning ordinances that prescribe special land use exceptions.

special warranty deed A deed that conveys grantor's title but contains warranties protecting only those title defects created by the grantor.

specific exceptions (also known as special exceptions) Certain actual or potential defects or liens against a title that are unique to a certain piece of property and are excluded from coverage in a title insurance policy.

specific performance A type of injunction ordering the defendant to perform a specific act.

spot zoning Rezoning for a use inconsistent with the neighborhood.

standing The requirement that parties to a lawsuit have been sufficiently hurt and personally affected so as to allow them to bring a legal action.

stare decisis To abide by or adhere to decided cases. Doctrine holding that when a court has once laid down a principle of law as applicable to a certain state of facts, the court will adhere to that principle and apply it to all future cases where facts are substantially the same, regardless of whether the parties and property are the same.

state action Governmental, as opposed to private, action.

Statute of Frauds A law that disallows any suit or action involving certain classes of contracts, such as those concerning interests in land, unless the agreement is evidenced by a note or memorandum in writing signed by the party to be charged or his authorized agent.

statutory compensation measures Damages prescribed by statute.

statutory dedication A dedication created pursuant to a statute.

statutory law An act of a legislative body declaring, commanding, or prohibiting something.

statutory lien A lien created by state statute that is placed on land to ensure payment of certain debts.

statutory redemption A time period provided by statute during which the mortgaged property can be redeemed.

steering The practice of showing different properties to people of different races or ethnic backgrounds in an attempt to "steer" them to neighborhoods of like composition.

strict foreclosure A process by which the lender takes title to the property after obtaining a court order foreclosing the equity of redemption.

strict liability Responsibility for personal or property damage regardless of whether it was caused by a negligent or intentional act.

strict liability theory Liability without fault. A seller in the business of selling products is liable for damages in the sale of a defective product that is unreasonably dangerous.

subagent An agent who represents the interests of another agent. In real estate brokerage law, a broker who assists the listing broker and acts as an agent on behalf of the seller to find a buyer.

subdivision map acts Statutes that control the subdivision of land by establishing conditions for approval of a plat or subdivision map.

sublease A grant by a tenant of an interest in leased property less than she possesses.

subordinate The process by which one creditor gives up rights to another creditor.

Subordination, Nondisturbance and Attornment Agreement An acknowledgment by a tenant that the leasehold interest is lower in priority than the lien placed by the landlord's mortgagee in exchange for the mortgagee agreeing not to disturb the tenant's occupancy under the lease.

subpoena *duces tecum* A discovery device in which the court commands the production of specified documents or goods or allows the inspection of real property.

subrogation Right of an insurer, upon payment of a claim, to "step into the shoes" of its insured and assert any claim that the insured may have against others.

substantial performance doctrine Substantial performance occurs when a contractor has performed enough of the contract to deserve payment.

substantive law That part of the law that creates, defines, and regulates rights and duties of parties, as opposed to procedural law, which prescribes the method of enforcing the rights or obtaining redress for their invasion.

summary judgment A procedural device available for the prompt disposition of an action without a trial when there is no dispute as to material facts or inferences to be drawn from material facts or when only a question of law is involved.

Superfund Amendments and Reauthorization Act, or SARA A federal statute amending CERCLA and establishing cleanup funding and new defenses for purchasers of land.

surety One who promises to pay the debt of another.

syndication A group of investors who combine their funds and managerial resources to acquire real estate and other assets.

T

tacking The process of gaining a prescriptive easement by adding the user's period of possession to that of a prior adverse user in order to establish a continuous period of use for the statutory period.

Tax Reform Act of 1986 A tax statute that simplified the income tax code, broadened the tax base, eliminated many tax shelters (including for real estate), and created new reporting requirements.

tenancy at sufferance A tenancy in which the tenant's possession of the leased property continues even though the tenant's rights have terminated.

tenancy at will A landlord-tenant relationship that endures only so long as both parties agree to its continuance is an estate at will. The chief characteristic of the tenancy is its durational insecurity since either party may terminate the tenancy at any time.

tenancy by the entirety A tenancy created between a husband and wife under which they hold title to the whole property with the right of survivorship.

tenancy in common Concurrent tenancy in which there is a unity of possession but unities of time, title, and interest are not required.

tenancy in partnership The manner in which partners co-own partnership property.

testator A person who dies leaving a valid will.

testers People working for government agencies or public interest groups who pose as tenants to detect whether landlords are violating antidiscrimination laws.

third-party defendant A party the original defendant claims is liable for all or part of the damages that the plaintiff may win from the original defendant.

time is of the essence The parties must do what is required by the time specified in a contract.

time-sharing Joint lease or ownership of property that is used individually for designated periods of time.

title The right to possess real estate as evidenced by a historical record.

title commitment A letter from a title insurance company in which it commits to issuing a title insurance policy on the insured subject to certain conditions and requirements.

title insurance Insurance designed to indemnify a landowner for losses from defects in the title or liens against the land.

title opinion A written statement from an attorney which gives an analysis of the title search regarding the current ownership rights in the property. It states whether there is any kind of lien or cloud in the title to the property.

title theory A mortgage in which the mortgagor transfers title to property to the mortgagee to secure the repayment of a loan.

Torrens system A system for registration of land under which a court issues a certificate of title that states the status of the title.

tort A civil wrong that causes harm to person, property, or reputation.

township A square tract of land approximately six miles on each side used in the Government Survey system.

township lines East-west running survey lines spaced six miles apart used in the Government Survey system.

tract index A land records system in which conveyances of interests in real property are indexed geographically by tracts.

trade fixtures Articles placed in or attached to rented buildings by tenants to carry on the trade or business for which the tenants occupy the premises.

transferable development rights A market-based system designed to preserve land. Property owners are given financial incentives to grant their rights to develop land to others.

trespass Any unauthorized intrusion or invasion of private premises or land of another.

trespasser One who enters land without permission of the owner.

trust An arrangement in which one party, the trustee, holds and manages property for the benefit of another, the beneficiary.

Truth in Lending Act Federal law regulating the disclosure of certain credit terms to enable a borrower to make the most favorable credit decision.

U

Umbrella Partnership Real Estate Investment Trust (UPREIT) A type of real estate investment trust in which an umbrella partnership rather than the REIT owns a direct interest in the properties.

unconscionable contract A contract so one-sided as to be oppressive and unfair.

undisclosed principal A principal whose existence and identity are unknown to the third party with whom its agent is dealing.

undivided interest The interest of a concurrent owner entitling her to a share of the whole property but not to a specific part of it.

undue influence A person in a dominant position takes advantage of the weaker party.

Uniform Commercial Code A code of law (adopted in its entirety by all states except Louisiana) that governs commercial transactions.

unity of interest The requirement that joint owners must have equal interests in the land. One of four unities needed to create a joint tenancy.

unity of possession The requirement that joint tenants must have equal, undivided interests in the possession of the land. One of four unities needed to create a joint tenancy.

unity of time The requirement that the interests of joint tenants must vest at the same time. One of four unities needed to create a joint tenancy.

unity of title The requirement that joint tenants must acquire their interests in the same conveyance. One of four unities needed to create a joint tenancy.

usury laws Laws that forbid the lending of money in excess of rates prescribed by law.

V

VA mortgage loan A mortgage loan that is guaranteed by the Department of Veterans Affairs.

variance Permission given by the zoning board to a landowner that allows deviation from the land use dictated in the zoning ordinances.

vested remainder A future interest in which the remainderman has an absolute right to a possessory interest at the end of a prior interest.

W

warranty A promise that certain facts are truly as they are represented to be and that they will remain so, subject to any specified limitations. In certain circumstances, a warranty will be presumed, known as an "implied" warranty.

waste A destructive use of real property by one in rightful possession.

wetlands "Swamps, mires, bogs, and other watery land masses [that] maintain water quality, provide wildlife habitat and breeding grounds, and assist flood control."

will A legal instrument disposing of a person's property at death.

workers' compensation statutes A state system that provides fixed awards to employees and their dependents for employment-related accidents or diseases.

workout A mutual effort by a property owner and lender to avoid foreclosure or bankruptcy following a default.

wraparound mortgage A junior mortgage that secures a promissory note, the face amount of which is the total of the unpaid balance of the first note secured by the senior mortgage, and those funds advanced or to be advanced by the wraparound lender.

writ of execution The process of carrying out a judgment of the court. An officer of the court is ordered to take the losing party's property to satisfy the judgment debt.

wrongful annexation The illegal attaching or merging of one thing to another.

Y

yield spread The difference between the interest rate paid by the consumer and the market interest rate.

INDEX